Joint Ventures

Fourth Edition

AUSTRALIA
Law Book Co.
Sydney

CANADA and USA
Carswell
Toronto

NEW ZEALAND
Brookers
Wellington

SINGAPORE and MALAYSIA
Sweet & Maxwell Asia
Singapore and Kuala Lumpur

Joint Ventures

Fourth Edition

Ian Hewitt
Consultant, Freshfields Bruckhaus Deringer LLP

Published in 2008 by Sweet & Maxwell Limited
100 Avenue Road, Swiss Cottage
London, NW3 3PF
(http://www.sweetandmaxwell.co.uk)

Typeset by LBJ Typesetting of Kingsclere
Printed in the UK by CPI William Clowes Beccles NR34 7TL

First edition 1997 (Pearson Professional Ltd)
Second edition 2001
Third edition 2005
Fourth edition 2008

No natural forests were destroyed to make this product; only farmed timber was used and replanted.

A CIP catalogue record for this book is available from the British Library

ISBN 978 1 847 03332 1

All rights reserved. Crown copyright material is reproduced with the permission of the Controller of HMSO and the Queen's Printer for Scotland.

No part of this publication may be reproduced or transmitted in any form or by any means, or stored in any retrieval system of any nature without prior written permission, except for permitted fair dealing under the Copyright, Designs and Patents Act 1988, or in accordance with the terms of a licence issued by the Copyright Licensing Agency in respect of photocopying and/or reprographic reproduction. Application for permission for other use of copyright material including permission to reproduce extracts in other published works shall be made to the publishers. Full acknowledgment of author, publisher and source must he given. Material is contained in this publication for which publishing permission has been sought. and for which copyright is acknowledged. Permission to reproduce such material cannot be granted by the publishers and application must be made to the copyright holder. Precedents in this publication may be used as a guide for the drafting of legal documents specifically for particular clients but not for republication. Such legal documents may be provided to clients in print or electronic form, but distribution to third parties otherwise is prohibited. Precedents are provided 'as is' without warranty of any kind, express or implied, including but not limited to fitness for a particular purpose. The publishers and the author cannot accept any responsibility for any loss of whatsoever kind including loss of revenue business, anticipated savings or profits, loss of goodwill or data or for any direct or consequential loss whatsoever to any person using the precedents, or acting or refraining from actions as a result of the material in this publication.

Sweet & Maxwell Limited 2008

Contents

Preface	xv
Acknowledgements	xix
Table of Cases	xxi
Table of Statutes	xxix
Table of Statutory Instruments	xxxi
Table of European Legislation	xxxiii
Table of European Commission Decisions	xxxvii

PART A   PLANNING A JOINT VENTURE

1 Why go into a joint venture?

Growing trend towards joint ventures and alliances	1–01
Reasons for particular joint ventures	1–08
Range of joint ventures and alliances	1–11
"Equity" and "non-equity" alliances	1–13
Problems with joint ventures and alliances	1–14
Criteria for successful ventures	1–24

2 Planning the joint venture transaction

Role of the lawyers	2–01
"Big picture" issues	2–03
Transaction "road map"	2–04
Confidentiality agreement	2–06
Memorandum of understanding	2–10
Due diligence	2–18
Understanding the local regime	2–22
Third party consents and clearances	2–24
Choosing the legal form of the venture	2–27
Valuation of contributions	2–30
Joint venture documentation	2–36
Importance of contract negotiations and documentation	2–44

3 Choosing the legal form

Basic legal categories	3–01

Key issues in deciding the legal form	3–02
Advantages/disadvantages of a contractual alliance	3–06
Advantages/disadvantages of a partnership	3–11
Advantages/disadvantages of a corporate structure	3–16
Location of the JVC	3–19
Limited liability partnerships (LLP)	3–22
US limited liability company (LLC)	3–27
European Economic Interest Grouping (EEIG)	3–28
Dual-headed structures	3–31

4 Contractual alliances: an overview

Range of non-equity alliances	4–01
Key basic issues	4–06
Alliance charter	4–08
R&D/technology collaborations	4–10
Specialisation agreements	4–13
Works project joint ventures	4–15
Joint operating agreements	4–20
Risk and revenue sharing	4–22
Property development joint ventures	4–25
Supplier/procurement "partnering"	4–28

5 Equity joint ventures: the framework

Equity joint ventures as a business form	5–01
Full-function or merger-type joint ventures	5–03
Limited-function or co-operative ventures	5–06
Minority equity investment	5–13
When does a partnership exist?	5–18
General partnerships	5–21
Limited partnerships	5–27
UK limited liability partnerships	5–33
Limited company	5–35
European companies	5–38
"Hybrid" structures	5–46
Shareholders' agreement for a JVC: outline issues	5–47
Constitutional documents	5–57

6 Importance of ancillary contracts

Importance of ancillary contracts	6–01
Examples of overall JVC structures	6–03
Common issues in joint venture context	6–12

Sale and purchase/asset transfer agreements — 6–24
Funding agreements — 6–25
Intellectual property/technology Licence agreements — 6–30
Property agreements — 6–31
Employee secondment agreements — 6–32
Management agreements — 6–33
Supply agreements — 6–35
Offtake/purchase contracts — 6–37
Distributorship/marketing contracts — 6–38
Services contracts — 6–39

PART B SPECIFIC ISSUES AFFECTING THE JOINT VENTURE RELATIONSHIP

7 Capital and funding

Importance of initial capital contributions — 7–01
Contractual alliances — 7–03
Partnerships — 7–07
Corporate joint ventures — 7–09
Share capital — 7–10
Preference shares — 7–12
Non-cash contributions — 7–17
Shareholder loans — 7–19
Outside finance — 7–21
Guarantees — 7–24
Charges — 7–25
Venture capital finance — 7–27
Tax issues — 7–29
Future financing commitments — 7–34
Default — 7–44

8 Governance and management

Key governance issues — 8–02
Role of joint venture or alliance governing body — 8–04
Control — 8–12
Composition of board of directors — 8–16
Supervision by joint venture parents — 8–25
Decision-making authority of the JVC board — 8–26
Reporting relationship between JVC and parents — 8–30
Operational management — 8–31
Minority protection — 8–40
Management deadlock — 8–41

General duties of directors to JVC 8–42
Indemnity to directors of JVC 8–60
Shadow directors 8–64

9 Minority investment and protection

Background factors 9–01
Contractual protection: key aims 9–05
Board representation 9–06
Consent rights 9–09
Dilution 9–15
Dividend policy 9–19
Right to information 9–21
Other protective undertakings 9–22
Claims against majority party 9–24
Exit 9–25
Shareholders' agreement or articles of association? 9–32
Strategic equity investment 9–38

10 Deadlock and breakdown

To deal with deadlock or not? 10–01
Management structures to avoid deadlock 10–04
Boycott of meetings 10–06
Additional vote 10–09
Independent director's swing vote 10–11
Reference to mediation/expert/arbitration 10–12
Dispute review panel 10–13
Reference to parties' chairmen or chief executives 10–14
Voluntary winding-up 10–17
Sale of the JVC 10–19
Put/call options 10–20
Shoot-out procedures 10–22
"Multi-choice" approach 10–30

11 Duties between joint venture parties

Risk of self-interest and opportunistic behaviour 11–01
Contractual responsibilities and incentives 11–04
Misuse of confidential information 11–06
Non-compete 11–07
Contractual remedies 11–10
Alliance charter 11–14
Any underlying implied duties of good faith? 11–15

Express good faith obligations	11–26
Duties of directors to JVC	11–28
Statutory derivative action	11–31
Common law: fraud on a minority	11–35
Unfairly prejudicial conduct: s.994	11–36
Just and equitable winding-up	11–42

12 Transfers of shares

Effect of legal form on transferability	12–01
Range of potential transfer restrictions	12–02
Agreed sales between the parties	12–04
Pre-emption rights	12–05
Types of pre-emption right	12–06
Price	12–13
Types of "transfer" to be covered	12–22
Charges	12–24
Entire holding	12–25
Multi-party joint ventures	12–27
Revocation	12–30
Consent of continuing party still required?	12–31
Tag-along	12–33
Drag-along	12–35
Loans and guarantees	12–36
Intra-group transfers	12–38
Shareholder/regulatory approvals	12–40
Directors' discretion to refuse registration?	12–43
Deed of adherence or replacement agreement	12–45
Change of control	12–46
Shareholders' agreement or articles of association, or both?	12–47
Consequences of "wrongful" transfer	12–49

13 Exit, termination and change

Importance of exit provisions	13–01
Key issues in designing exit provisions	13–03
Fixed term/joint renewal	13–06
Termination for convenience	13–09
Liquidation/winding-up of JVC	13–12
Buy/sell options on termination	13–13
Buy-back of shares by JVC	13–15
Sale or public offering of JVC	13–17
"Multi-choice" approach	13–18
Termination for cause: general	13–20
Default	13–22

Persistent use of veto rights	13–25
Insolvency	13–26
Change of control	13–28
End of purpose	13–32
Put and call options	13–33
Sale or public offering	13–39
Third party offer	13–41
Transfer of interest to third party	13–43
Deadlock	13–44
Transformation or change	13–45
Consequences of exit/termination: general	13–46
Voluntary winding-up	13–48
Compulsory winding-up	13–49

14 Disputes: mediation, litigation and arbitration

Why are dispute resolution provisions important?	14–01
Executive level dispute resolution	14–02
Alternative dispute resolution (ADR)	14–05
Application of ADR to joint ventures and alliances	14–08
Litigation in national courts	14–15
Litigation or arbitration?	14–19
Enforcement of arbitral awards: New York Convention	14–22
Types of arbitration and leading arbitral institutions	14–24
Establishing the arbitral tribunal	14–28
Interim measures	14–32
Drafting the arbitration clause	14–34

PART C SPECIALIST ISSUES AFFECTING JOINT VENTURES

15 Tax planning

Key tax issues	15–01
Legal form of venture: corporate or "transparent"?	15–03
Location of an international JVC	15–08
UK as a location	15–09
Use of a third-country jurisdiction for location of JVC	15–10
Tax costs of contributions to the joint venture	15–12
Capital gains	15–13
Income tax consequences	15–21
Recapture of allowances	15–22
Transfer of trading losses	15–24
Transfer taxes	15–25
Financing	15–28

Tax costs of distributions	15–29
Ongoing tax issues: general	15–33
Group relief	15–34
Consortium relief	15–35
Transfer pricing	15–39
Termination: general tax issues	15–40
Termination of a JVC: CGT	15–41
Termination of a partnership	15–44
Termination of a contractual alliance	15–45

16 Competition and regulatory controls

Range of regulatory controls	16–01
EC Merger Regulation: when does it apply?	16–05
One-stop-shop principle	16–10
EC Merger Regulation: what is the test for clearance?	16–12
Ancillary restrictions	16–16
Procedure and Commission powers	16–18
Article 81: non full-function joint ventures	16–20
Agreements falling outside article 81	16–21
Material factors in assessing whether article 81 applies	16–22
Exemptions/exceptions under article 81(3)	16–23
Self-assessment and enforcement	16–27
UK Enterprise Act 2002	16–32
What are the jurisdictional thresholds?	16–36
Mergers: substantive test for clearance	16–37
Filing, procedure and timetable	16–38
UK Competition Act 1998: Chapter 1 prohibition	16–40
Industry-specific regulation	16–44
Trade remedy laws	16–46
Export/import controls	16–49
Behavioural laws	16–52
Trade-related intellectual property controls	16–53

17 Intellectual property and technology

Importance of IPR in joint ventures	17–01
What IPR exists in technology?	17–03
Key issues in different phases	17–07
Competition law	17–08
Research and development collaborations	17–09
Technology-based JVC	17–18
International technology venture with a "local" party	17–22
Trade mark licences	17–27

18 Employment

Key employment issues	18–01
EU Information and Consultation Directive	18–04
European works councils	18–06
Transfer of existing business to JVC	18–08
Harmonisation of terms and conditions	18–13
Restrictive covenants	18–17
Secondments	18–21
Work permits	18–24
Pensions for joint venture employees	18–25
Joint venture party liability for JVC pensions	18–35
Employee share schemes	18–36

19 Accounting

Overview of accounting issues	19–01
Joint venture's own accounts	19–02
Accounting treatment for the joint venture parents	19–04
Distinctions drawn by UK GAAP	19–07
What is a subsidiary undertaking?	19–08
Subsidiaries excluded from consolidation	19–09
What is an associate?	19–12
Joint venture entities under FRS 9	19–14
What is a JANE?	19–20
International Accounting Standards (IAS)	19–22
IAS 27: Subsidiaries	19–23
IAS 28: Associates	19–24
IAS 31: Joint ventures	19–26
Other European countries	19–30
US GAAP	19–31

PART D INTERNATIONAL JOINT VENTURES AND SELECTED JURISDICTIONS

20 International joint ventures

Growth in international joint ventures	20–01
Convergence of approach—or national differences?	20–08
Preparation and commercial due diligence	20–11
Understanding the local law regime	20–13
Differences in civil law systems	20–14
Joint ventures in "emerging markets"	20–16
Importance of process	20–19

	Governing law		20–22
	Arbitration		20–25
(1)	Brazil		D(1)
(2)	China		D(2)
(3)	Czech Republic		D(3)
(4)	France		D(4)
(5)	Germany		D(5)
(6)	India		D(6)
(7)	Italy		D(7)
(8)	Japan		D(8)
(9)	The Netherlands		D(9)
(10)	Poland		D(10)
(11)	Russia		D(11)
(12)	South Africa		D(12)
(13)	Spain		D(13)
(14)	United States		D(14)

PART E   PRECEDENTS

1	Information Exchange Agreement	E(l)
2	Memorandum of Understanding	E(2)
3	Legal Due Diligence Questionnaire	E(3)
4	Strategic Alliance Agreement	E(4)
5	R&D Collaboration Agreement	E(5)
6	General Partnership Agreement	E(6)
7	EEIG Formation Agreement	E(7)
8	Limited Liability Partnership Agreement	E(8)
9	50:50 Shareholders Agreement (short form)	E(9)
10	Multi-Party Shareholders' Agreement (long form)	E(10)
11	Articles of Association (UK Company)	E(ll)
12	Preference Share Rights	E(12)
13	ITC Model Corporate Joint Venture Agreement (Two-Party)	E(13)
14	Deed of Adherence	E(14)
15	Put and Call Option Agreement	E(15)
16	Shareholder Funding Agreement	E(16)
17	JVC Share Sale Agreement	E(17)
18	Support Services Agreement	E(16)
19	Technology Licence Agreement	E(17)
20	Trade Mark Licence Agreement	E(18)
21	Deadlock Resolution Clauses	E(19)
22	Arbitration and Mediation Clauses	E(20)

PART F JOINT VENTURE AND ALLIANCE CHECKLISTS

1 **Preparing for the joint venture: initial issues** F(1)
2 **Drafting the joint venture agreement** F(2)

Index

CD-ROM

Preface

"If you think you can go it alone in today's global economy, you are highly mistaken"

Jack Welch

Jack Welch summed up the position succinctly in this way during an interview whilst CEO of General Electric of the US. Joint ventures and alliances have become vital to modern business.

A "joint venture" is not a legal term of art. Our focus here is on collaborative arrangements by which two or more companies jointly and directly participate in an integrated business venture but without going so far as full merger or acquisition. This book attempts to address a range of collaborative relationships (whether they are described as joint ventures, partnerships, consortia, teaming arrangements, strategic alliances or some other term) whilst recognising that a corporate joint venture is still probably the most common, and complex, form of business collaboration to cross the desk of the transactional lawyer.

Aims of this book

This book is intended for the practitioner (whether a businessman, lawyer or other adviser). Whilst it addresses underlying legal principles, it aims principally to assist the practising lawyer in developing basic tools and skills required for these transactions including (i) a good feel for the commercial background, (ii) a knowledge of the available legal structures, (iii) awareness of the key issues likely to arise and range of solutions available, (iv) an outline understanding (if not necessarily detailed knowledge) of a range of "specialist" legal disciplines such as tax, competition law, intellectual property and employment law and (v) access to a sound base of initial forms and precedents.

There are frequent checklists which aim to assist this approach. There is rarely a simple "right" or "wrong" solution; the constructive lawyer engaged in joint venture transactions must be prepared to consider, with the client, a range of possible solutions for the particular venture.

International context

Very many joint ventures and alliances have an international dimension. Most issues and solutions are relevant whatever the nationality of the parties and wherever the joint venture or alliance is based. Insofar as this is a textbook, it is based on English law—but I have tried to address the subject throughout in an international context. Most references to particular English law cases and legislation appear in the footnotes, or in distinct sections, so that the text can be read easily by an "international" reader free of undue specific English law references. Part D brings together a discussion of issues which commonly affect international joint ventures with "local" partners, particularly in developing market countries, and includes introductory summaries of laws affecting joint ventures in a number of important jurisdictions worldwide.

Joint ventures are receiving wider attention amongst international lawyers, aided by such initiatives as the International Bar Association's distance-learning International Practice Diploma course on "International Joint Ventures" with which I have been pleased to assist. If this book in some small way assists lawyers who are engaged internationally on these interesting (and often challenging) transactions, I shall be particularly pleased.

Changes in this edition

Changes in this edition, if not so radical as in the last edition, have cumulatively been many:

- The UK Companies Act 2006, including the codification of the general duties of directors and a new statutory derivative action, has required an updating of many principles, details and references.

- Generally, increased attention has been given to the possible legal options available if a joint venture fails due to the "opportunistic" behaviour of a partner.

- There have been important developments affecting joint ventures in specialist, but vital, areas such as tax, employment, accounting and European competition law.

- Internationally, the discussion on joint ventures in "developing markets" has expanded. The summaries of laws and practice relating to joint ventures in China, India and Russia have been updated, as well as the other jurisdictions covered, and a contribution from South Africa has been added to the specific countries addressed.

- The collection of precedents has increased by the addition of a Shareholder Funding Agreement and a JVC Share Sale Agreement.

- The opportunity has been taken to improve the text in a number of places and generally to try and keep it "fresh".

Aided as ever by a team of able co-contributors, I hope that the book will continue to assist the practitioner engaged on these important, and often challenging, transactions.

Ian Hewitt
May 1, 2008

Acknowledgements

Personal thanks are, as with previous editions, due to very many people for their assistance with this book. I am grateful to many colleagues at Freshfields Bruckhaus Deringer for their contributions in specific areas despite busy client practices. In particular:

Arbitration/litigation	Nigel Rawding, Daniel Kalderimis and Devika Khanna
Competition/regulatory	Andrew Renshaw, Jan Blockx, Alison Jones and Victoria Harris
Employment	David Pollard and Kathleen Healy
Intellectual property/IT	Chris Forsyth, Hannah McCann and Lawrence Kalman
Property	Margaret Rhodes
Tax	Jonathan Cooklin and Arun Birla

and in relation to colleagues in offices contributing to the country-sections in Part D:

China	Carl Cheng, Tianfu Liu and Andrew Gardner
France	Jean Claude Cotoni and Thomas Rabain
Germany	Hildegard Bison and Johanna Schrammen
India	Pratap Amin and Bharat Anand
Italy	Mario Ortu, Ida Bassano and Giovanna Rossi
Japan	Junzabaro Kiuchi and Tatsuhiro Kubo
The Netherlands	Dirk-Jan Smit and Michael Lambooij
Russia	Michael Schwartz and Maxim Pogrebnoy
Spain	Toni Valverde and Carlos Bas
United States	Charles Peet

Additionally, within the firm, I am thankful to Geraldine Watson (professional support lawyer) for her advice and contribution—and to Yetunde Adeyemi (librarian) and Toni Partridge, Carole Hart and Donna Bridgland (secretarial) for their vital assistance.

There have again been a number of "outside" contributors who have added significantly to this book. I am particularly grateful to them:

Accounting	Janet Milligan (*PricewaterhouseCoopers*)
Brazil	Syllas Tozzini and Renato Berger (*Tozzini, Freire, Teixeira and Silva Advogados*)
Czech Republic	Marketa Zachova (*Vejmelka and Wuensch*)
Poland	Prof. Grzegory Domanski and Markek Swiatkowski (*Domanski Zakrzewski Palink sp.k*)
South Africa	Charles Douglas (*Bowmans Gillifran*)

The experience of many clients with whom my colleagues and I have worked over the years has continued to provide an important, if implicit, contribution. I also acknowledge the influence of the growing professional literature in this area and am particularly grateful to those responsible for the specific excerpts which I have included.

I am thankful as ever to my wife, Jenifer, for her continued support of this project. As with the first edition, I record my gratitude to my parents for their past encouragement when I set off on a legal career.

Ian Hewitt
May 1, 2008

TABLE OF CASES

A v B [2006] EWHC 2006 (Comm); [2007] 1 All E.R. (Comm) 591; [2007] 1
  Lloyd's Rep. 237; [2007] 2 C.L.C. 157, QBD (Comm) 14–27
A v B (Costs) [2007] EWHC 54 (Comm); [2007] 1 All E.R. (Comm) 633;
  [2007] 1 Lloyd's Rep. 358; [2007] Bus. L.R. D59; [2007] 2 C.L.C. 203,
  QBD (Comm) 14–27
Abbey Leisure Ltd, Re; sub nom. Virdi v Abbey Leisure [1990] B.C.C. 60;
  [1990] B.C.L.C. 342, CA (Civ Div) 11–42
Alvona Developments Ltd v Manhattan Loft Corp (AC) Ltd [2005] EWHC
  1567; [2006] B.C.C. 119, Ch D 10–06
Aparau v Iceland Frozen Foods Plc (No.1) [1996] I.R.L.R. 119, EAT 18–15
Arenson v Casson Beckman Rutley & Co; sub nom. Arenson v Arenson
  [1977] A.C. 405; [1975] 3 W.L.R. 815; [1975] 3 All E.R. 901; [1976] 1
  Lloyd's Rep. 179; (1975) 119 S.J. 810, HL 12–21
Astec (BSR) Plc, Re [1999] B.C.C. 59; [1998] 2 B.C.L.C. 556, Ch D
  (Companies Ct) 11–38
BICC Plc v Burndy Corp [1985] Ch. 232; [1985] 2 W.L.R. 132; [1985] 1 All
  E.R. 417; [1985] R.P.C. 273; (1984) 81 L.S.G. 3011; (1984) 128 S.J.
  750, CA (Civ Div) 7–45, 7–48
BSB Holdings Ltd, Re [1996] 1 B.C.L.C. 155, Ch D 11–39
Baumler (UK) Ltd, Re. *See* Gerrard v Koby
Belfield Furnishings Ltd, Re. *See* Isaacs v Belfield Furnishings Ltd
Berriman v Delabole Slate Ltd; sub nom. Delabole Slate Ltd v Berriman
  [1985] I.C.R. 546; [1985] I.R.L.R. 305, CA (Civ Div) 18–15
Betts v Brintel Helicopters Ltd (t/a British International Helicopters); Betts
  v KLM ERA Helicopters (UK) Ltd [1997] 2 All E.R. 840; [1998] 2
  C.M.L.R. 22; [1997] I.C.R. 792; [1997] I.R.L.R. 361; (1997) 147 N.L.J.
  561, CA (Civ Div) 18–10
Bhullar v Bhullar; sub nom. Bhullar Bros Ltd, Re [2003] EWCA Civ 424;
  [2003] B.C.C. 711; [2003] 2 B.C.L.C. 241; [2003] W.T.L.R. 1397;
  (2003) 147 S.J.L.B. 421; [2003] N.P.C. 45, CA (Civ Div) 11–29, 11–32
Bird Precision Bellows Ltd, Re [1984] B.C.L.C. 19 11–41
Bond Corporation Holdings v Granada Group, unreported, May 17, 1991.. 11–24
Borland's Trustees v Borland; sub nom. Borland's Trustees v Borland's
  Executrix, 1917 S.C. 704; 1917 2 S.L.T. 94, IH (1 Div) 13–27
Bratton Seymour Service Co Ltd v Oxborough [1992] B.C.C. 471; [1992]
  B.C.L.C. 693; [1992] E.G. 28 (C.S.), CA (Civ Div) 7–35
Brenfield Squash Racquets Club Ltd, Re [1996] 2 B.C.L.C. 184, Ch D 11–39
British Aerospace Plc v Dee Howard Co [1993] 1 Lloyd's Rep. 368, QBD
  (Comm) 14–17
Broadcasting Station 2 GB Ltd, Re [1964–1965] N.S.W.R. 1662 8–52
Bushell v Faith [1970] A.C. 1099; [1970] 2 W.L.R. 272; [1970] 1 All E.R. 53;
  (1970) 114 S.J. 54, HL 8–16, 9–37
Button v Phelps [2006] EWHC 53 (Ch), Ch D 11–24
CMS Dolphin Ltd v Simonet [2002] B.C.C. 600; [2001] 2 B.C.L.C. 704;
  [2001] Emp. L.R. 895, Ch D 11–29
CRA Ltd v New Zealand Goldfields Investments [1989] V.R. 873 7–48
Campbell v Conoco (UK) Ltd [2002] EWCA Civ 704; [2003] 1 All E.R.
  (Comm) 35, CA (Civ Div) 18–23
Canatti Holding Co Pty Ltd v Zampatti (1978) 52 A.L.J.R. 732 5–50

Cane v Jones [1980] 1 W.L.R. 1451; [1981] 1 All E.R. 533; (1980) 124 S.J. 542, Ch D 5–55
Castleburn Ltd, Re (1989) 5 B.C.C. 652; [1991] B.C.L.C. 89; [1989] P.C.C. 386, Ch D (Companies Ct) 12–21
Chez Nico (Restaurants) Ltd, Re [1991] B.C.C. 736; [1992] B.C.L.C. 192, Ch D 8–45
City Branch Group Ltd, Re. *See* Gross v Rackind
Clemens v Clemens Bros Ltd [1976] 2 All E.R. 268, Ch D 11–23
Coco v AN Clark (Engineers) Ltd [1968] F.S.R. 415; [1969] R.P.C. 41, Ch D 2–07
Company (No.002567 of 1982), Re [1983] B.C.C. 98 11–42
Company (No.007623 of 1984), Re (1986) 2 B.C.C. 99191; [1986] B.C.L.C. 362, Ch D (Companies Ct) 11–39
Company (No.003843 of 1986), Re (1987) 3 B.C.C. 624; [1987] B.C.L.C. 562, Ch D (Companies Ct) 11–42
Company (No.00370 of 1987), Ex p. Glossop, Re; sub nom. Company (No.00370 of 1987), Re, Ex p. Glossop [1988] 1 W.L.R. 1068; (1988) 4 B.C.C. 506; [1988] B.C.L.C. 570; [1988] P.C.C. 351; (1988) 85(41) L.S.G. 43; (1988) 132 S.J. 1388, Ch D (Companies Ct) 11–42
Company (No.002015 of 1996), Re [1997] 2 B.C.L.C. 1, Ch D 11–39
Continental Bank NA v Aeakos Compania Naviera SA [1994] 1 W.L.R. 588; [1994] 2 All E.R. 540; [1994] 1 Lloyd's Rep. 505; [1994] I.L.Pr. 413, CA (Civ Div) 14–17
Conway v Petronius Clothing Co Ltd [1978] 1 W.L.R. 72; [1978] 1 All E.R. 185; (1978) 122 S.J. 15, Ch D 9–21
Cook v Deeks [1916] 1 A.C. 554, PC (Can) 11–08, 11–35
Cottrell v King; sub nom. TA King (Services) Ltd, Re [2004] EWHC 397; [2004] B.C.C. 307; [2004] 2 B.C.L.C. 413; [2005] W.T.L.R. 63, Ch D   12–49
Cox v Hickman (1860) 8 H.L. Cas. 268 5–19
Credit Suisse Asset Management Ltd v Armstrong [1996] I.C.R. 882; [1996] I.R.L.R. 450; (1996) 93(23) L.S.G. 35; (1996) 140 S.J.L.B. 141, CA (Civ Div) 18–15
Cumana Ltd, Re [1986] B.C.L.C. 430 11–39
Cumbrian Newspapers Group Ltd v Cumberland & Westmorland Herald Newspaper & Printing Co Ltd [1987] Ch. 1; [1986] 3 W.L.R. 26; [1986] 2 All E.R. 816; (1986) 2 B.C.C. 99227; [1987] P.C.C. 12; (1986) 83 L.S.G. 1719; (1986) 130 S.J. 446, Ch D 9–36
Daniels v Daniels [1978] Ch. 406; [1978] 2 W.L.R. 73; [1978] 2 All E.R. 89; (1977) 121 S.J. 605, Ch D 11–35
Dawnay Day & Co Ltd v de Braconier d'Alphen [1998] I.C.R. 1068; [1997] I.R.L.R. 442; (1997) 94(26) L.S.G. 30; (1997) 141 S.J.L.B. 129, CA (Civ Div) 18–19
Dremco, Inc v South Chapel Hill Gardens, Inc 654 N.E. 2d 501, 504 (Ill. App. 1995) 11–19
Dunnett v Railtrack [2002] EWCA Civ 302 14–06
Duomatic Ltd, Re [1969] 2 Ch. 365; [1969] 2 W.L.R. 114; [1969] 1 All E.R. 161; (1968) 112 S.J. 922, Ch D 5–55
EE Caledonia Ltd (formerly Occidental Petroleum (Caledonia) Ltd) v Orbit Valve Co Europe Plc; sub nom. Elf Enterprise Caledonia Ltd (formerly Occidental Petroleum (Caledonia)) v Orbit Valve Co Europe Plc [1994] 1 W.L.R. 1515; [1995] 1 All E.R. 174; [1994] 2 Lloyd's Rep. 239; [1994] C.L.C. 647, CA (Civ Div) 18–23
EWE International Limited v Philip Jones [2004] B.C.L.C. 406 12–14
Ebrahimi v Westbourne Galleries Ltd; sub nom. Westbourne Galleries, Re [1973] A.C. 360; [1972] 2 W.L.R. 1289; [1972] 2 All E.R. 492; (1972) 116 S.J. 412, HL 11–23, 11–42

Elliot v Wheeldon [1992] B.C.C. 489; [1993] B.C.L.C. 53, CA (Civ Div).... 11–23
Erich Gasser GmbH v MISAT Srl (C116/02) [2005] Q.B. 1; [2004] 3 W.L.R. 1070; [2005] All E.R. (EC) 517; [2005] 1 All E.R. (Comm) 538; [2004] 1 Lloyd's Rep. 222; [2003] E.C.R. I-14693; [2004] I.L.Pr. 7, ECJ..... 14–17
Euro Brokers Holdings Ltd v Monecor (London) Ltd; sub nom.: Eurobrokers Holdings Ltd v Monecor (London) Ltd; Monecor (London) Ltd v Euro Brokers Holdings Ltd [2003] EWCA Civ 105; [2003] B.C.C. 573; [2003] 1 B.C.L.C. 506; (2003) 147 S.J.L.B. 540, CA (Civ Div) 7–35, 7–48
Exeter City AFC Ltd v Football Conference Ltd [2004] EWHC 831; [2004] 1 W.L.R. 2910; [2004] 4 All E.R. 1179; [2004] B.C.C. 498; [2005] 1 B.C.L.C. 238; (2004) 101(9) L.S.G. 31, Ch D 11–39
Fenston v Johnstone (HM Inspector of Taxes) [1940] 23 T.C. 29........... 5–19
Fiona Trust & Holding Corp v Privalov; sub nom. Premium Nafta Products Ltd v Fili Shipping Co Ltd [2007] UKHL 40; [2007] Bus. L.R. 1719; [2007] 4 All E.R. 951; [2007] 2 All E.R. (Comm) 1053; [2007] 2 C.L.C. 553; 114 Con. L.R. 69; (2007) 104(42) L.S.G. 34; (2007) 151 S.J.L.B. 1364, HL 14–27
Foss v Harbottle, 67 E.R. 189; (1843) 2 Hare 461, Ct of Chancery........ 11–35
Foster Bryant Surveying Ltd v Bryant [2007] EWCA Civ 200............. 11–29
French v MITIE Management Services Ltd; sub nom. MITIE Management Services Ltd v French; MITIE Managed Services Ltd v French [2002] I.C.R. 1395; [2002] I.R.L.R. 521; [2002] Emp. L.R. 888, EAT....... 18–10
Fulham Football Club Ltd v Cabra Estates Plc [1992] B.C.C. 863; [1994] 1 B.C.L.C. 363; (1993) 65 P. & C.R. 284; [1993] 1 P.L.R. 29; (1992) 136 S.J.L.B. 267, CA (Civ Div) 5–55
Gamlestaden Fastigheter AB v Baltic Partners Ltd [2007] UKPC 26; [2007] Bus. L.R. 1521; [2007] 4 All E.R. 164; [2007] B.C.C. 272, PC (Jer) .. 11–39
Gardner v Parker [2004] EWCA Civ 781; [2005] B.C.C. 46; [2004] 2 B.C.L.C. 554; (2004) 148 S.J.L.B. 792, CA (Civ Div).............. 11–30
Garry Rogers (Aust) Pty Ltd v Subaru (Aust) Pty Ltd (1999) ATPR 41—703 11–27
Gerrard v Koby; sub nom. Baumler (UK) Ltd, Re [2004] EWHC 1763; [2005] B.C.C. 181; [2005] 1 B.C.L.C. 92, Ch D (Companies Ct) 11–39
Giles v Rhind [2002] EWCA Civ 1428; [2003] Ch. 618; [2003] 2 W.L.R. 237; [2002] 4 All E.R. 977; [2003] B.C.C. 79; [2003] 1 B.C.L.C. 1; (2002) 99(44) L.S.G. 32, CA (Civ Div) 11–30
Global Container Lines Ltd v Black Sea Shipping Co, unreported, July 14, 1997, Ch D 2–16
Grace v Biagioli [2005] EWCA Civ 1222; [2006] B.C.C. 85; [2006] 2 B.C.L.C. 70; (2005) 102(48) L.S.G. 18, CA (Civ Div).............. 11–41
Greenwall v Porter; sub nom. Greenwell v Porter [1902] 1 Ch. 530, Ch D .. 5–50
Gross v Rackind; sub nom. Citybranch Group Ltd, Re; City Branch Group Ltd, Re; Rackind v Gross [2004] EWCA Civ 815; [2005] 1 W.L.R. 3505; [2004] 4 All E.R. 735; [2005] B.C.C. 11; (2004) 148 S.J.L.B. 661, CA (Civ Div) 11–39
Growth Management Ltd v Mutafchiev [2006] EWHC 2774 (Comm); [2007] 1 B.C.L.C. 645, QBD (Comm) 5–50
Guidezone Ltd, Re; sub nom. Kaneria v Patel [2001] B.C.C. 692; [2000] 2 B.C.L.C. 321, Ch D (Companies Ct) 11–42
Harman v BML Group Ltd; sub nom. BML Group Ltd v Harman [1994] 1 W.L.R. 893; [1994] B.C.C. 502; [1994] 2 B.C.L.C. 674; (1994) 91(21) L.S.G. 40; (1994) 138 S.J.L.B. 91, CA (Civ Div).................... 10–06
Hawks v McArthur [1951] 1 All E.R. 22, Ch D......................... 12–49
Helstan Securities Ltd v Hertfordshire CC [1978] 3 All E.R. 262; 76 L.G.R. 735, QBD 12–49

Hickman v Kent or Romney Marsh Sheepbreeders Association [1915] 1 Ch.
  881, Ch D 5–59
Hurst v Crampton Bros (Coopers) Ltd [2002] EWHC 1375; [2003] B.C.C.
  190; [2003] 1 B.C.L.C. 304; [2003] W.T.L.R. 659; [2002] 2 P. & C.R.
  DG21, Ch D 12–49
Inland Revenue Commissioners v Reed International Plc; sub nom. Reed
  International Plc v Inland Revenue Commissioners [1995] S.T.C. 889;
  67 T.C. 552, CA (Civ Div) 18–37
Inland Revenue Commissioners v Williamson (1928) 14 T.C. 335 5–20
Interfoto Picture Library Ltd v Stiletto Visual Programmes Ltd [1989] Q.B.
  433; [1988] 2 W.L.R. 615; [1988] 1 All E.R. 348; (1988) 7 Tr. L.R. 187;
  (1988) 85(9) L.S.G. 45; (1987) 137 N.L.J. 1159; (1988) 132 S.J. 460,
  CA (Civ Div) 11–18
Isaacs v Belfield Furnishings Ltd; sub nom. Belfield Furnishings Ltd, Re
  [2006] EWHC 183; [2006] 2 B.C.L.C. 705, Ch D (Companies Ct) ... 11–39,
                                                                  11–41
J Leo Johnson, Inc., 156 A. 2d 501, 504 (Ill. App. 1959) 11–19
Jarvis Motors (Harrow) Ltd v Carabott [1964] 1 W.L.R. 1101; [1964] 3 All
  E.R. 89; (1964) 108 S.J. 542, Ch D 13–28
Jobson v Johnson [1989] 1 W.L.R. 1026; [1989] 1 All E.R. 621; (1988) 4
  B.C.C. 488, CA (Civ Div) 7–48
Johnson v Gore Wood & Co (No.1); sub nom. Johnson v Gore Woods & Co
  [2002] 2 A.C. 1; [2001] 2 W.L.R. 72; [2001] 1 All E.R. 481; [2001]
  C.P.L.R. 49; [2001] B.C.C. 820; [2001] 1 B.C.L.C. 313; [2001] P.N.L.R.
  18; (2001) 98(1) L.S.G. 24; (2001) 98(8) L.S.G. 46; (2000) 150 N.L.J.
  1889; (2001) 145 S.J.L.B. 29, HL 11–30
Kingsley IT Consulting Ltd v McIntosh [2006] All E.R. (D) 237 11–29
Kuwait Asia Bank EC v National Mutual Life Nominees Ltd [1991] 1 A.C.
  187; [1990] 3 W.L.R. 297; [1990] 3 All E.R. 404; [1990] 2 Lloyd's Rep.
  95; [1990] B.C.C. 567; [1990] B.C.L.C. 868, PC (NZ) 8–48
Larvin v Phoenix Office Supplies Ltd; sub nom. Phoenix Office Supplies Ltd
  v Larvin; Phoenix Office Supplies Ltd, Re [2002] EWCA Civ 1740;
  [2003] B.C.C. 11; [2003] 1 B.C.L.C. 76; (2003) 100(5) L.S.G. 29, CA
  (Civ Div) 11–39
Lesotho Highlands Development Authority v Impregilo SpA [2005] UKHL
  43; [2006] 1 A.C. 221; [2005] 3 W.L.R. 129; [2005] 3 All E.R. 789;
  [2005] 2 All E.R. (Comm) 265; [2005] 2 Lloyd's Rep. 310; [2005] 2
  C.L.C. 1; [2005] B.L.R. 351; 101 Con. L.R. 1; [2005] 27 E.G. 220
  (C.S.); (2005) 155 N.L.J. 1046, HL 14–27
Libyan Arab Foreign Bank v Bankers Trust Co [1989] Q.B. 728; [1989] 3
  W.L.R. 314; [1989] 3 All E.R. 252; [1988] 1 Lloyd's Rep. 259; [1987] 2
  F.T.L.R. 509; (1989) 133 S.J. 568, QBD (Comm) 20–24
London Metropolitan University v Sackur, UKEAT/0286/06/ZT, EAT 18–15
Lyle & Scott Ltd v Scott's Trustees; Lyle & Scott v British Investment Trust
  [1959] A.C. 763; [1959] 3 W.L.R. 133; [1959] 2 All E.R. 661; 1959 S.C.
  (H.L.) 64; 1959 S.L.T. 198; (1959) 103 S.J. 661; (1959) 103 S.J. 507,
  HL 12–23
Mackay v Dick (1880–81) L.R. 6 App. Cas. 251, HL 11–26
MacPherson v European Strategic Bureau Ltd [2002] B.C.C. 39; [2000] 2
  B.C.L.C. 683; (2000) 97(35) L.S.G. 36, CA (Civ Div) 8–59
Macro (Ipswich) Ltd, Re; sub nom. Earliba Finance Co Ltd, Re; Macro v
  Thompson (No.1) [1994] 2 B.C.L.C. 354, Ch D 12–23
Martin v South Bank University (C4/01) [2003] E.C.R. I-12859; [2004] 1
  C.M.L.R. 15; [2004] C.E.C. 90; [2004] I.C.R. 1234; [2004] I.R.L.R. 74;
  [2003] O.P.L.R. 317; [2003] Pens. L.R. 329, ECJ (6th Chamber) 18–15

Medforth v Blake [2000] Ch. 86; [1999] 3 W.L.R. 922; [1999] 3 All E.R. 97; [1999] B.C.C. 771; [1999] 2 B.C.L.C. 221; [1999] B.P.I.R. 712; [1999] Lloyd's Rep. P.N. 844; [1999] P.N.L.R. 920; [1999] 2 E.G.L.R. 75; [1999] 29 E.G. 119; [1999] E.G. 81 (C.S.); (1999) 96(24) L.S.G. 39; (1999) 149 N.L.J. 929, CA (Civ Div) 11–26
Meyer v Scottish Cooperative Wholesale Society Ltd; sub nom. Scottish Cooperative Wholesale Society v Meyer; Meyer v Scottish Textile & Manufacturing Co Ltd [1959] A.C. 324; [1958] 3 W.L.R. 404; [1958] 3 All E.R. 66; 1958 S.C. (H.L.) 40; 1958 S.L.T. 241; (1958) 102 S.J. 617, HL 8–49
Mona Oil Equipment & Supply Co Ltd v Rhodesia Railways Ltd [1949] 2 All E.R. 1014; (1949–50) 83 Ll. L. Rep. 178; [1950] W.N. 10, KBD.. 11–26
Monnington v Easier Plc [2005] EWHC 2578; [2006] 2 B.C.L.C. 283, Ch D (Companies Ct) 10–06
Murad v Al-Saraj; Murad v Westwood Business Inc [2005] EWCA Civ 959; [2005] W.T.L.R. 1573; (2005) 102(32) L.S.G. 31, CA (Civ Div)...... 11–23
Nafta Products Ltd v Fili Shipping Co Ltd. *See* Fiona Trust & Holding Corp v Privalov
Nathan v Smilovitch (No.2) [2002] EWHC 1629, Ch D 11–23, 11–26
Noble A & Son (Clothing) Ltd, Re [1983] B.C.L.C. 273 .... 11–38, 11–42
Northern Counties Securities, Ltd v Jackson & Steeple, Ltd [1974] 1 W.L.R. 1133; [1974] 2 All E.R. 625; (1974) 118 S.J. 498, Ch D 11–22
O'Neill v Phillips; sub nom. Company (No.000709 of 1992), Re; Pectel Ltd, Re [1999] 1 W.L.R. 1092; [1999] 2 All E.R. 961; [1999] B.C.C. 600; [1999] 2 B.C.L.C. 1; (1999) 96(23) L.S.G. 33; (1999) 149 N.L.J. 805, HL 11–39, 11–41
Opera Photographic Ltd, Re [1989] 1 W.L.R. 634; (1989) 5 B.C.C. 601; [1989] B.C.L.C. 763; [1989] P.C.C. 337; (1989) 133 S.J. 848, Ch D (Companies Ct) 10–06
P&O Trans European Ltd v Initial Transport Services Ltd; sub nom. Initial Transport Services Ltd v P&O Trans European Ltd [2003] I.R.L.R. 128, EAT 18–09
Pavlides v Jensen [1956] Ch. 565; [1956] 3 W.L.R. 224; [1956] 2 All E.R. 518; (1956) 100 S.J. 452, Ch D 11–32, 11–35
Payne v Secretary of State for Employment [1989] I.R.L.R. 352, CA (Civ Div) 18–12
Pena v Dale [2003] EWHC 1065; [2004] 2 B.C.L.C. 508, Ch D 5–50
Percival v Wright [1902] 2 Ch. 421, Ch D 8–45, 11–22, 11–30
Peskin v Anderson [2001] B.C.C. 874; [2001] 1 B.C.L.C. 372, CA (Civ Div) 8–45, 11–30
Phillips Petroleum Co (UK) Ltd v Enron (Europe) Ltd [1997] C.L.C. 329, CA (Civ Div) 11–26
Power v Regent Security Services Ltd; sub nom. Regent Security Services Ltd v Power [2007] EWCA Civ 1188; [2008] I.R.L.R. 66; (2007) 104(47) L.S.G. 26, CA (Civ Div) 18–15
Profinance Trust SA v Gladstone [2001] EWCA Civ 1031; [2002] 1 W.L.R. 1024; [2002] B.C.C. 356; [2002] 1 B.C.L.C. 141; (2001) 98(30) L.S.G. 37, CA (Civ Div) 11–41
Puddephat v Leith (No.1); sub nom. Puddephatt v Leith [1916] 1 Ch. 200, Ch D 5–50
Quarter Master UK Ltd (In Liquidation) v Pyke [2004] EWHC 1815; [2005] 1 B.C.L.C. 245, Ch D 11–29, 11–32
Quin & Axtens Ltd v Salmon; sub nom. Salmon v Quin & Axtens Ltd [1909] A.C. 442, HL 5–59, 9–32
Quinlan v Essex Hinge Co Ltd [1997] B.C.C. 53; [1996] 2 B.C.L.C. 417, Ch D 11–39

Ringtower Holdings, Re; sub nom. Company (No.005685 of 1988) (No.2), Re (1989) 5 B.C.C. 82, Ch D (Companies Ct) 11–42
Ringuet v Bergeron (1960) 24 DLR (2d) 449, Supreme Court (Can.) 7–48
Rose v Lynx Express Ltd [2004] EWCA Civ 447; [2004] B.C.C. 714; [2004] 1 B.C.L.C. 455; (2004) 101(17) L.S.G. 31; (2004) 148 S.J.L.B. 477, CA (Civ Div) 12–22
Ross v Telford [1997] B.C.C. 945; [1998] 1 B.C.L.C. 82; (1997) 94(28) L.S.G. 26, CA (Civ Div) 10–06
Russell v Northern Bank Development Corp Ltd [1992] 1 W.L.R. 588; [1992] 3 All E.R. 161; [1992] B.C.C. 578; [1992] B.C.L.C. 1016; (1992) 89(27) L.S.G. 33; (1992) 136 S.J.L.B. 182, HL (NI) 5–50, 5–55
Safeguard Industrial Investments Ltd v National Westminster Bank Ltd [1982] 1 W.L.R. 589; [1982] 1 All E.R. 449; (1982) 126 S.J. 205, CA (Civ Div) 12–22
Saul D Harrison & Sons Plc, Re [1994] B.C.C. 475; [1995] 1 B.C.L.C. 14, CA (Civ Div) 11–39
Scottish Coal Company Ltd v McCormack [2005] CSI 11 68 18–09
Scotto v Petch; Scotto v Clarke; sub nom. Sedgefield Steeplechase Co (1927) Ltd, Re [2001] B.C.C. 889, CA (Civ Div) 12–22
Seager v Copydex Ltd (No.1) [1967] 1 W.L.R. 923; [1967] 2 All E.R. 415; 2 K.I.R. 828; [1967] F.S.R. 211; [1967] R.P.C. 349; (1967) 111 S.J. 335, CA (Civ Div) 2–07
Secretary of State for Trade and Industry v Deverell [2001] Ch. 340; [2000] 2 W.L.R. 907; [2000] 2 All E.R. 365; [2000] B.C.C. 1057; [2000] 2 B.C.L.C. 133; (2000) 97(3) L.S.G. 35; (2000) 144 S.J.L.B. 49, CA (Civ Div) 8–64
Selangor United Rubber Estates Ltd v Cradock (No.3) [1968] 1 W.L.R. 1555; [1968] 2 All E.R. 1073; [1968] 2 Lloyd's Rep. 289; (1968) 112 S.J. 744, Ch D 8–48
Shepherds Investments Ltd v Walters [2006] EWHC 836 (Ch); [2007] 2 B.C.L.C. 202; [2007] I.R.L.R. 110; [2007] F.S.R. 15; (2006) 150 S.J.L.B. 536, Ch D 11–29
South Sydney District Rugby League Football Club Ltd v News Ltd (2000) 177 A.L.R. 611 11–27
South West Launderettes v Laidler [1986] I.C.R. 455; [1986] I.R.L.R. 305, CA (Civ Div) 18–12
Specialist Ceiling Services Northern Ltd v ZVI Construction (UK) Ltd [2004] B.L.R. 403, QBD (TCC) 11–19
Spicer (Keith) v Mansell [1970] 1 W.L.R. 333; [1970] 1 All E.R. 462; (1969) 114 S.J. 30, CA (Civ Div) 5–20
Stein v Blake (No.2) [1998] 1 All E.R. 724; [1998] B.C.C. 316; [1998] 1 B.C.L.C. 573, CA (Civ Div) 11–30
Strahan v Wilcock [2006] EWCA Civ 13; [2006] B.C.C. 320; [2006] 2 B.C.L.C. 555; (2006) 103(6) L.S.G. 30, CA (Civ Div) 11–41
Suzen v Zehnacker Gebaudereinigung GmbH Krankenhausservice (C13/95) [1997] All E.R. (EC) 289; [1997] E.C.R. I-1259; [1997] 1 C.M.L.R. 768; [1997] I.C.R. 662; [1997] I.R.L.R. 255; (1997) 16 Tr. L.R. 365, ECJ 18–09
T-Mobile (UK) v Bluebottle Investments SA [2003] EWHC 379; [2003] Info. T.L.R. 264, QBD (Comm) 10–25
TSC Europe (UK) Ltd v Massey [1999] I.R.L.R. 22, Ch D 18–19
Tett v Phoenix Property & Investment Co Ltd (1986) 2 B.C.C. 99140; [1986] P.C.C. 210; (1986) 83 L.S.G. 116; (1985) 129 S.J. 869, CA (Civ Div) 12–49

Towcester Racecourse Co Ltd v Racecourse Association Ltd [2002] EWHC 2141 (Ch); [2003] 1 B.C.L.C. 260; (2002) 99(45) L.S.G. 34, Ch D.... 8–45, 11–30

Turner v Grovit (C159/02); sub nom. Turner, Re (C159/02) [2005] 1 A.C. 101; [2004] 3 W.L.R. 1193; [2004] All E.R. (EC) 485; [2004] 2 All E.R. (Comm) 381; [2004] 2 Lloyd's Rep. 169; [2004] E.C.R. I-3565; [2004] 1 C.L.C. 864; [2004] I.L.Pr. 25; [2005] I.C.R. 23; [2004] I.R.L.R. 899, ECJ 14–17

Ultraframe (UK) Ltd v Fielding; Burnden Group Plc v Northstar Systems Ltd (In Liquidation); Northstar Systems Ltd (In Liquidation) v Fielding [2005] EWHC 1638 (Ch); [2006] F.S.R. 17; [2007] W.T.L.R. 835; (2005) 28(9) I.P.D. 28069, Ch D 8–64

Union Music Ltd v Watson; Arias Ltd v Blacknight Ltd [2003] EWCA Civ 180; [2004] B.C.C. 37; [2003] 1 B.C.L.C. 453, CA (Civ Div) 10–06

Unisoft Group Ltd (No.3), Re; sub nom. Unisoft Group Ltd (No.2), Re [1994] B.C.C. 766; [1994] 1 B.C.L.C. 609, Ch D (Companies Ct) 8–64

Veba Oil Supply & Trading GmbH v Petrotrade Inc (The Robin); sub nom. Veba Oil Supply & Trading Ltd v Petrotrade Inc (The Robin) [2001] EWCA Civ 1832; [2002] 1 All E.R. 703; [2002] 1 All E.R. (Comm) 306; [2002] 1 Lloyd's Rep. 295; [2002] C.L.C. 405; [2002] B.L.R. 54, CA (Civ Div) 12–21

Vocam Europe Ltd, Re [1998] B.C.C. 396, Ch D (Companies Ct)......... 11–38

Wake-Walker v AKG Group Ltd; sub nom. Martyn Rose Ltd v AKG Group Ltd [2003] EWCA Civ 375; [2003] 2 B.C.L.C. 102, CA (Civ Div).... 13–27

Walford v Miles [1992] 2 A.C. 128; [1992] 2 W.L.R. 174; [1992] 1 All E.R. 453; (1992) 64 P. & C.R. 166; [1992] 1 E.G.L.R. 207; [1992] 11 E.G. 115; [1992] N.P.C. 4, HL 2–16, 11–26

White v Bristol Aeroplane Co; sub nom. British Aeroplane Co, Re [1953] Ch. 65; [1953] 2 W.L.R. 144; [1953] 1 All E.R. 40; (1953) 97 S.J. 64, CA 9–36

Wilkinson v West Coast Capital [2005] EWHC 3009, Ch D (Companies Ct) 11–29

Yenidje Tobacco Co Ltd, Re [1916] 2 Ch. 426, CA 10–34, 11–23, 11–41

TABLE OF STATUTES

1890	Partnership Act (53 & 54 Vict. c.39)	5–19, 5–20, 5–24
	s.1(1)	5–19
	s.2	5–19
	(1)	5–19
	(2)	5–19
	(3)	5–19
	(d)	5–19
	(e)	5–19
	s.20	6–31
	s.24	5–24
	(3)	7–07
	(4)	7–07
	s.26	13–11
	s.28	5–24
	s.29	5–24
	s.30	5–24
1907	Limited Partnerships Act (7 Edw.7 c.24)	5–28, 5–30
1930	Finance Act (20 & 21 Geo.5 c.28)	
	s.42	15–26
	(4)	15–26
1954	Landlord and Tenant Act (2 & 3 Eliz.2 c.56)	6–31
1974	Consumer Credit Act (c.39)	16–44
1977	Restrictive Trade Practices Act (c.19)	16–43
	Patents Act (c.37)	
	s.36	17–13
1978	Civil Liability (Contribution) Act (c.47)	7–24
1979	Sale of Goods Act (c.54)	6–35
1985	Companies Act (c.6)	19–07, 19–13
	s.260(1)	19–12
	Sch.4A para.20	19–12
	Sch.5	19–18
1986	Gas Act (c.44)	16–44
	Insolvency Act (c.45)	7–19
	s.88	13–26
	s.122(1)(g)	10–34, 11–42, 11–43, 13–49
	s.127	13–26
	s.213	8–59
	s.214	8–59
	s.232	8–60
	s.240(1)(a)	7–19
1988	Income and Corporation Taxes Act (c.1)	15–02
	s.28AA	15–39
	s.343(4)	15–24
	s.402(3)	15–35
	s.403C	15–36
	s.768	15–24
	s.840	13–29
	Copyright, Designs and Patents Act (c.48)	
	s.10(1)	17–13
1989	Electricity Act (c.29)	16–44
1991	Water Industry Act (c.56)	16–44
1992	Taxation of Chargeable Gains Act (c.12)	15–02
	s.7AC	15–16
	ss.29–34	15–43
	s.135	15–16
	s.138	15–18
	s.152	15–14
	s.171A	15–14
	s.179	15–17, 15–24
	s.181	15–18
	Sch.D Case I	15–04
1994	Trade Marks Act (c.26)	
	s.23	17–13
	s.30	17–29
1995	Pensions Act (c.26)	
	s.75	18–31
1996	Finance Act (c.8)	
	Sch.9 para.6	7–31
	Employment Rights Act (c.18)	
	s.141(1)	18–12
	s.146(1)	18–12
	s.218(6)	18–12
	Arbitration Act (c.23)	12–21, 14–27, 20–22
	s.46	20–22
	ss.67–68	14–13
	s.68	14–27
	s.69	14–27
1998	Competition Act (c.41)	2–25, 16–04, 16–31, 16–39, 16–40, 16–41, 16–43
	Ch.1	16–41, 16–42
	s.9	16–41

	s.39(1)	16–42
	s.60	16–39
	Sch.1 para.1(1)	16–41
1999	Contracts (Rights of Third Parties) Act (c.31)	5–55
2000	Financial Services and Markets Act (c.8)	16–44, 18–23
	Limited Liability Partnerships Act (c.12)	3–22, 3–23
	s.4(3)	3–23
	Utilities Act (c.27)	16–44
2002	Export Control Act (c.28)	2–25, 6–35, 16–49, 17–24
	Enterprise Act (c.40) ...	16–04, 16–31, 16–32, 16–34, 16–35, 16–36, 16–41, 16–43
	s.23(1)(a)	16–37
	(b)	16–36
	s.26	16–34
	s.71	16–38
	s.72	16–38
	s.76	16–38
	s.77	16–38
2003	Income Tax (Earnings and Pensions) Act (c.1)	
	s.498	18–37
	Sch.3 para.48	18–40
	Sch.4 para.35	18–37
	para.36	18–40
	Sch.5 para.11	18–39
2004	Pensions Act (c.35)	18–10, 18–27, 18–35
	s.38	18–35
	s.43	18–35
	s.257	18–10, 18–27
	s.258	18–10, 18–27
2005	Finance (No.2) Act (c.22)	15–39
2006	Companies Act (c.46)	8–47, 8–51, 8–54, 8–56, 8–62, 8–65, 9–36, 10–10, 11–31, 11–35, 11–39, 19–09, 19–10
	s.22	5–55, 5–61, 9–04, 12–47

s.25	7–35
s.29	5–62, 9–32
s.30	5–62, 9–32
s.33	5–59
s.40	5–61
s.122(1)(g)	9–04
s.168	8–16, 9–37
s.170(1)	8–45, 11–30
s.172	8–49
(2)(b)	8–51
s.173	8–49
s.174	8–47
s.175	8–56, 11–29
s.177	8–54
s.180(4)(b)	8–51
s.190	8–57
s.251	8–64
(3)	8–65
s.260	8–46, 9–04
ss.260–263	11–32
s.282(4)	8–20, 10–10
s.306	10–06
s.371	10–06
s.386(1)	9–21
s.405(3)(a)	19–10
s.448	5–35
s.459 ...	11–38, 11–39, 11–41, 11–42
ss.459–461	11–36
s.561	7–40, 9–16
s.570	7–40
s.571	7–40
s.580	2–33, 7–17
s.593	2–33, 7–17
s.630(2)	9–36
ss.684–686	9–28
s.690	13–15
s.994	3–23, 8–46, 9–04, 11–30, 11–36, 11–39, 11–41, 11–43, 12–21
ss.994–996	11–36
s.996	11–40
s.1159	13–29
s.1162	19–08
s.1166	18–37
Sch.7	19–08
Table A reg.70 ...	5–55, E(11)

TABLE OF STATUTORY INSTRUMENTS

1981 Transfer of Undertakings (Protection of Employment) Regulations (SI 1981/1794) 18–09
1989 European Economic Interest Grouping Regulations (SI 1989/638) 3–28
1995 Value Added Tax (Special Provisions) Order (SI 1995/1268) art.5 15–27
1999 Transnational Information and Consultation of Employees Regulations (SI 1999/3323) 18–06
2000 Competition Act 1998 (Concurrency) Regulations (SI 2000/260) 16–44
Competition Act 1998 (Small Agreements and Conduct of Minor Significance) Regulations (SI 2000/262) 16–42
2001 Limited Liability Partnerships Regulations (SI 2001/90) 3–23
reg.7 . . . . 3–23, 11–25
reg.8 . . . . 3–23, 11–25
Competition Act 1998 (Public Transport Ticketing Schemes Block Exemption) Order (SI 2001/319) . . 16–41
2003 Export of Goods, Transfer of Technology and Provision of Technical Assistance (Control) Order (SI 2003/2764) . . 2–25, 16–49, 17–24
Trade in Goods (Control) Order (SI 2003/2765) . . 2–25
2004 Trade in Controlled Goods (Embargoed Destinations) Order (SI 2004/318)
European Public Limited-Liability Company Regulations (SI 2004/2326) 5–39
Information and Consultation of Employees Regulations (SI 2004/3426) . . . 2–25, 6–24, 18–05, 18–10
2005 Trade in Goods (Control) (Amendment) Order (SI 2005/443) 16–49
Trade in Controlled Goods (Embargoed Destinations) (Amendment) Order (SI 2005/445) 16–49
Export of Goods, Transfer of Technology and Provision of Technical Assistance (Control) (Amendment) Order (SI 2005/468) 16–49
Occupational Pension Schemes (Employer Debt) Regulations (SI 2005/678) 18–31
2006 Transfer of Undertakings (Protection of Employment) Regulations (SI 2006/246) 2–25, 18–09, 18–10, 18–12, 18–15, 18–20, 18–21, 18–22, 18–27, 18–30, 18–37
reg.4(9) 18–10
reg.7(6) 18–15
Co-operative Society Regulations (SI 2006/2078) 3–28
2007 Civil Procedure (Amendment) Rules (SI 2007/2204)
Companies Act 2006 (Commencement No. 5, Transitional Provisions and Savings) Order (SI 2007/3495) 10–10

TABLE OF EUROPEAN LEGISLATION

Treaties and Conventions

1957 Treaty establishing the
European Economic
Community
Art.81 . . . . 16–04, 16–14,
16–15, 16–17, 16–20,
16–21, 16–22, 16–39,
16–40, 16–41, 17–15
(1) 16–17, 16–20,
16–21, 16–22, 16–23,
16–25, 16–27, 16–29,
16–30, 17–16
(3) 16–17, 16–20,
16–21, 16–22, 16–23,
16–24, 16–25, 16–26,
16–27, 16–41, 17–17,
17–26
Art.82 16–40
1968 Brussels Convention on
Jurisdiction and
Enforcement of
Judgments in Civil and
Commercial Matters . . . 14–16
1980 Convention on the Law
applicable to
Contractual Obligations
(Rome Convention)
Art.3(1) 20–24
1988 Lugano Convention on
Jurisdiction and
Enforcement of
Judgments in Civil and
Commercial Matters . . . 14–16
1994 WTO Agreement on
Trade-Related Aspects
of Intellectual Property
Rights (TRIPS) 16–53
General Agreement on
Tariffs and Trade 1994
(GATT)
Art.VI 16–47

Regulations

1985 Reg. 2137/85 on the
European Economic
Interest Grouping
(EEIG) [1985] O.J.
L124/52 . . . . 3–28, 3–29, 3–30

1999 Reg.2790/99 on the
application of Article
81(3) of the Treaty to
categories of vertical
agreements and
concerted practices
[1999] O.J. L336/21 . . . 16–24
2000 Reg.1334/2000 setting up a
Community regime for
the control of exports of
dual–use items and
technology [2000] O.J.
L159/1 (Dual–Use
Regulation) 2–25, 16–49
Reg.2658/2000 on the
application of Article
81(3) of the Treaty to
categories of
specialisation
agreements
(Specialisation Block
Exemption) [2000] O.J.
L304/3 . . . . 4–24, 16–24
Reg.2659/2000 on the
application of Article
81(3) of the Treaty to
categories of research
and development
agreements [2000] O.J.
L304/7 16–24
2001 Reg.2157/2001 on the
Statute for a European
company (SE) [2001]
O.J. L294/1 . . . . . 5–39, 5–40,
5–41, 5–42, 5–43, 5–44,
5–45
2002 Reg.1606/2002 on the
application of
international accounting
standards [2002] O.J.
L243/1 19–30
2003 Reg.1/2003 on the
implementation of the
rules on competition
laid down in Articles 81
and 82 of the Treaty
[2003] O.J. L1/1 16–25

Reg.1435/2003 on the
Statute for a European
Cooperative Society
(SCE) [2003] O.J.
L49/35 3–28
2004 Reg.139/2004 on the
control of
concentrations between
undertakings (the EC
Merger Regulation)
[2004] O.J. L24/1 2–25,
3–02, 16–04, 16–05,
16–06, 16–07, 16–10,
16–11, 16–12, 16–13,
16–14, 16–17, 16–18,
16–20, 16–31, 16–34,
16–35, 16–37, 16–41
Art.2(2) 16–12
Art.3(4) 16–08
2004 Reg.772/2004 on the
application of Article
81(3) of the Treaty to
categories of technology
transfer agreements
(Technology Transfer
Block Exemption) 17–26

Directives

1977 Dir.77/187/EC on the
approximation of the
laws of the Member
States relating to the
safeguarding of
employees' rights in the
event of transfers of
undertakings, businesses
or parts of businesses
(Acquired Rights
Directive) [1977] O.J.
L61/26 .... 18–08, 18–09
1983 Dir.83/349/EEC Seventh
Council Directive on
the Article 54(3)(g) of
the Treaty on
consolidated accounts
[1983] O.J. L211/31 ... 19–06,
19–08, 19–30
1990 Dir.90/434/EEC on the
common system of
taxation applicable to
mergers, divisions,
transfers of assets and
exchanges of shares
concerning companies of
different Member States
[1990] O.J. L225/1 15–14

Dir.90/435/EEC on the
common system of
taxation applicable in
the case of parent
companies and
subsidiaries of different
Member States
(Parent/Subsiduary
Directive) [1990] O.J.
L16/98 15–09
1994 Dir.94/45/EC on the
establishment of a
European Works
Council or a procedure
in Community–scale
undertakings and
Community–scale
groups of undertakings
for the purposes of
informing and
consulting employees
[1994] O.J. L254/64 .. 18–02,
18–06
Art.2.1 18–06
Art.3 18–06
2001 Dir.2001/23/EC on the
approximation of the
laws of the Member
States relating to the
safeguarding of
employees' rights in the
event of transfers of
undertakings, businesses
or parts of undertakings
or businesses [2001]
O.J. L82/16 18–08
Dir.2001/86/EC
supplementing the
Statute for a European
company with regard to
the involvement of
employees [2001] O.J.
L294/22 5–39
2002 Dir.2002/14/EC
establishing a general
framework for
informing and
consulting employees in
the European
Community—Joint
declaration of the
European Parliament,
the Council and the
Commission on
employee
representation [2002]
O.J. L80/29 18–04

2003 Dir.2003/41/EC on the
activities and
supervision of
institutions for
occupational retirement
provision (Pensions
Directive) [2003] O.J.
L235/10 18–26

Dir.2003/49/EC on a
common system of
taxation applicable to
interest and royalty
payments made
between associated
companies of different
Member States [2003]
O.J. L157/49 15–09

TABLE OF EUROPEAN COMMISSION DECISIONS

APW/APSA/Nordic Capical/Capio (2007) M.4367 16–13
Adecco/Manpower/Vediorbis/JV (2004) M.3419 16–09
Air France/Alitalia (2004) COMP/38.284/D2 4–04
Alfa Acciai/Cronimet/Remondis/TSR Group (2007) M.4495 16–07
Arcelor/Oyak/Erdemir (2006) M.4085 16–07
Asahi/Saint-Gobain [1994] O.J. L354/87 4–11
BP Chemicals/ICI [1984] O.J. L112/1 4–14
BP/Kellogg [1985] O.J. L369/6 16–22
BT/MCI [1994] O.J. L223/36 16–22
BP/Mobil (1996) IV/M.727 5–23
Banque Nationale de Paris/Dresdner Bank [1996] O.J. L188/37 4–04
Bertelsmann/Springer/JV (2005) M.3178 16–13
Continental/Michelin [1988] O.J. L305/33 4–11
Corning/BICC [1986] O.J. L236/30 5–23
Covisint: General Motors/Ford/Daimler-Chrysler [2001] IP/01/1155 5–10
De Beers/LVMH (2001) COMP/M.2333 5–04
EDS/Lufthansa (1995) IV/M.560 5–08
Elopak/Metal Box-Odin [1990] L209/15 16–22
Eurotunnel [1988] O.J. L311/36 16–22
Exxon/Shell [1994] O.J. L144/20 5–08
Fortis/Banco Comercial (2005) COMP/M.3556 5–04
Fortis/BCP (2005) M.3556 16–09
Fujitsu AMD Semiconductor [1994] O.J. L341/66 5–08
GEAE/P&W [2000] O.J. L58/16 16–22
GEC Siemens/Plessey [1990] O.J. C152/3 5–12
General Electric/Pratt & Whitney [1999] O.J. C206/19 5–08
General Motors/Fiat (2000) IP/00/931 5–13
Hydro Texaco/Preem (1997) COMP.REP 1997/108 5–08
IBM/Fiat (2001) COMP/M.2478 5–08
Indentrus [2001] O.J. L2249/12 5–10
Kali & Salz/Solvay (2002) COMP/M.2176 5–04
Olivetti/Canon [1988] O.J. L52/51 16–22
Olivetti/Digital [1994] O.J. L309/24 5–13
Opodo COMP/D-2/38.006 5–10
Optical Fibres [1986] O.J. L236/30 16–22
Post Office/TPG/SPPL (2002) COMP/M.1915 5–04
SES Astra/Eutelsat/JV (2007) M.4477 16–15
Solvay/Sisecam [1999] O.J. C272/14 5–08
Sonae Industria/Tarkett/JV (2006) M.4048 16–09
Sony/BMG (2004) COMP/M.3333 5–04
Telexis/EDS (1999) IP/99/715 5–08
Thales/Finmeccaica/AAS/Telespazio (2007) M.4403 16–13
VW/MAN [1983] O.J. L376/11 4–14
Vacuum Interrupters [1977] O.J. L48/32 16–22
Volbroker (2000) IP/00/896 5–10
Wegener/PCM/JV (2005) M.3817 16–15

PART A

PLANNING A JOINT VENTURE

    1   Why go into a joint venture?

    2   Planning the joint venture transaction

    3   Choosing the legal form

    4   Contractual alliances: an overview

    5   Equity joint ventures: the framework

    6   Importance of ancillary contracts

Part A of this book addresses the initial issues when a joint venture or alliance is proposed. Why enter into a joint venture? What are the "big picture" issues when planning the transaction? What is the likely role of the lawyer? What legal form should the joint venture or alliance take? What contracts or other legal documentation will be required? What are the principal commercial and legal issues to be addressed in developing the framework for the venture?

Chapter 1

Why go into a joint venture?

Joint ventures and alliances are vital to business. They have become an important strategic option for many companies, particularly those operating internationally. This chapter considers the business landscape and the growing trend towards joint ventures and alliances. It also recognises the problems which commonly arise and the often short "life cycle" of a joint venture. Are there criteria for establishing a successful joint venture or alliance? It is important for the lawyers to understand the commercial background when shaping the legal framework.

Growing trend towards joint ventures and alliances

1–01 Traditionally, the two principal models for corporate growth have been internal growth ("build") or acquisition ("buy"). Joint ventures and alliances represent an increasingly important third way ("bond" or "ally"). General business trends have contributed to this growth in joint ventures and alliances—particularly with international partners:

(1) There is a strong competitive trend towards globalisation in many industries and sectors. Greater access is now available to the emerging markets of the world's developing countries. Revenues from international markets have increased substantially for Western companies. A large number of alliances over the past decade or so have involved "cross-border" relationships.

(2) While companies have been globalising, many have also been retrenching into their core business products and services. Companies wishing to explore growth opportunities outside their core business lines are increasingly utilising equity alliances with third parties for that purpose.

(3) As companies have been refocusing on their core business lines, there has been a substantial explosion of technology innovation. New technologies, aided by the internet, have been creating new business challenges and opportunities. A substantial number of all alliances contain a technology element. Joint ventures and alliances enable companies to access innovative technology without making outright acquisitions or incurring excessive expenditure before the technology is fully proven.

1–02 Recent studies illustrate this trend. A wide-ranging survey[1] of senior executives in the UK in 2006 found that 78 per cent of the companies surveyed expected the number of their collaborative relationships with third parties to increase over the next three years. Another report of the Economist Intelligence Unit, *Foresight 2020*, identified increased collaboration with suppliers, customers and other partners as a defining feature of the company of 2020. A survey by PricewaterhouseCoopers and CFO Research Services[2] of over 200 senior US finance executives in 2004 similarly found that two-thirds of respondent companies regarded alliances as "essential or very important" to their companies' strategic goals compared with only one-quarter three years previously. As another recent report[3] summed up: "Instead of competition, the discussion in the executive offices is increasingly of collaboration".

1–03 There is evidence that joint ventures and alliances may be more successful than acquisitions in certain situations. A McKinsey study[4] found that alliances are more attractive than acquisitions when trying to launch a new business—or to enter or expand into a new geographical market:

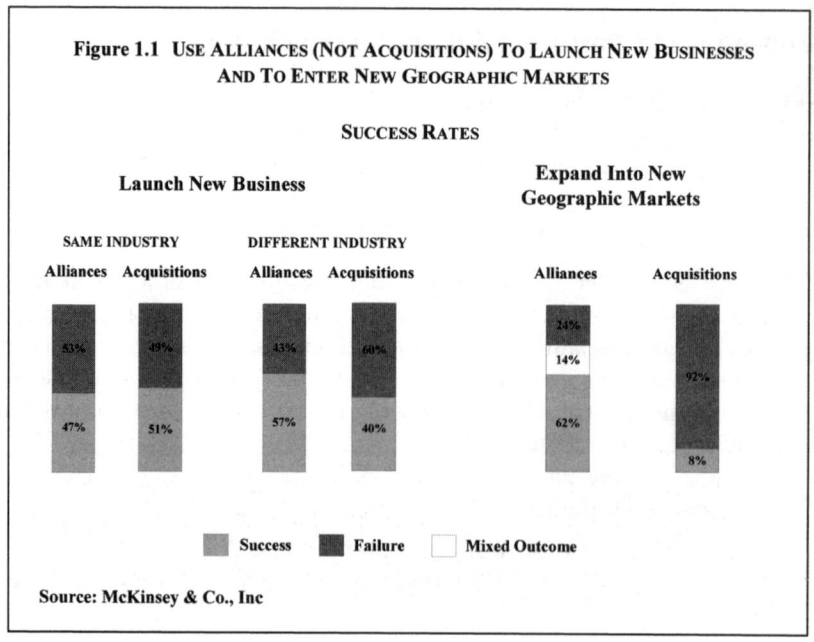

Figure 1.1 USE ALLIANCES (NOT ACQUISITIONS) TO LAUNCH NEW BUSINESSES AND TO ENTER NEW GEOGRAPHIC MARKETS

Source: McKinsey & Co., Inc

---

[1] Economist Intelligence Unit survey, October 2006.
[2] PricewaterhouseCoopers and CFO Research Services, *The CFO's Perspective on Alliances* (CFO Publishing Corp 2004).
[3] *FT Report—Understanding the Culture of Collaboration* (June 2007) at p.2.
[4] J. Bleeke and D. Ernst (eds), *Collaborating to Compete: Using Strategic Alliances and Acquisitions in the Global Marketplace* (McKinsey & Co., Inc. 1993) and further developed in J. Bleeke and D. Ernst, *The Way to Win in Cross-Border Alliances* (Harvard Business Review on Strategic Alliances, 2002).

1–04 Whilst M&A can be attractive in conferring total control, there are potential negative factors. The purchaser will usually acquire all parts of the acquired entity—both its strengths and weaknesses. Many acquisitions take place in an auction environment with the purchaser winning the bid at the highest price, often too high. The acquisition may not be able to deliver (for that price) on promised synergies, cost reductions, profit increases or accelerated development. Whilst M&A remains an important model for corporate growth (and indeed many joint ventures and alliances lead to subsequent 100 per cent acquisition or integration), there is evidence that the success rate of M&A may be low:

(1) A McKinsey study[5] of 160 acquisitions, by 157 public companies across 11 industry sectors, found that 42 per cent of acquirers suffered lower growth rates than their industry peers after the acquisitions. Indeed, 60 per cent of the companies studied failed to earn returns greater than the annual cost of capital required to fund the acquisition.

(2) A KPMG study[6] of 118 mergers and acquisitions found that 70 per cent of the transactions did not create shareholder value for the combined companies. KPMG also found no correlation between acquisition experience and success.

1–05 The trend towards joint ventures and alliances is not solely led by major companies. Alliances between small and medium enterprises ("SMEs") and larger companies—or "corporate venturing" as sometimes called in the UK—may offer business opportunities for achieving growth. The larger company can provide resources needed by the SME (e.g. management expertise, distribution channels, equity finance or R&D facilities). The smaller company retains its independence while the larger company benefits by gaining access to a new technology or product area.

1–06 Alliances are now accepted as a sound business strategy. Indeed, they can also have a positive effect on a public company's share price. Another McKinsey study[7] examined the effect of alliance announcements on the share prices of more than 2000 companies worldwide. For large alliances at least, the announcement in the case of over one-half of such alliances caused the share price of the parent to rise or fall (more than by a normal movement) and, of these, 70 per cent of the price reactions were increases—a "win rate" substantially higher than the percentage for acquirers in M&A transactions.

1–07 As two leading commentators in this field, Peter Pekar Jr and Marc S. Margulis, sum up:[8]

---

[5] Matthias M. Bekier, Anne J. Bogardus, Tim Oldham, "Why mergers fail" (*McKinsey Quarterly* 2001, Number 4).
[6] KPMG Transaction Services, *World Class Transactions: Insight Into Creating Shareholder Value Through Mergers and Acquisitions* (2001).
[7] D. Ernst, "When to think alliances" (*McKinsey Quarterly* 2000, No.4).
[8] Peter Pekar Jr and Marc S. Margulis, "Equity Alliances Take Centre Stage" (*Business Strategy Review*, London Business School, 2003, Vol.14, Issue 2).

"Management is asked to act faster, invigorate growth and capture even greater profits, while using fewer resources and less capital. Under these circumstances, it is no surprise that alliances, predicated on shared risk and on the prudent use of capital and resources, are becoming an increasingly important approach for increasing shareholder wealth and competitive strength".

Reasons for particular joint ventures

1–08 These are trends at a macro business level. At the micro level of individual joint ventures and alliances, commercial reasons or "drivers" behind a particular venture will, of course, vary depending on the circumstances of that venture. They include:

(1) *Cost savings.* A common rationale is the objective of saving costs by achieving synergy benefits through rationalisation of employment or other fixed costs or by sharing with a joint venture partner or partners the costs of research and development (R&D) or capital investment programmes (a particular feature given the magnitude of investment costs involved in many industries such as electronics, defence, pharmaceuticals, telecommunications and aero-engines).

(2) *Risk sharing.* A similar rationale behind many ventures is the wish to share with another party or parties the significant financial risks which may be involved in undertaking a speculative or capital intensive project. Projects of considerable size, such as power stations and other natural resource or infrastructure projects, are frequently undertaken as joint venture projects.

(3) *Access to technology.* Joint ventures may provide a route for a party to gain access to, and learn from, a co-venturer's technology and skills and thus accelerate entry into a particular technology or market. Joint ventures are common in industries where technology plays a key role and where that technology is rapidly changing. Technical skills and experience often comprise "organizationally embedded knowledge" where the resource is inherently tied to the organisation and cannot be easily extricated. In these cases, integration of the two organisational structures through a joint venture is necessary for the parties to gain effective access to their respective technical experience.

(4) *Expansion of customer base.* International joint ventures can provide the most effective route for a party to expand the scope of its customer base by utilising a co-venturer's strength in different geographic markets or by buying into a co-venturer's distribution or sales network.

(5) *Entry into emerging economies.* Joint ventures may also provide the best, and sometimes only realistic, route for gaining entry to new emerging markets in areas such as eastern Europe or Asia where

access to local knowledge, contacts or sponsorship is often a practical necessity.

(6) *Entry into new technical markets.* The rapid pace of technological change is itself producing new markets. Effective entry into those markets can often be accelerated by participation with another company which already has a technical start in that field or provides complementary skills; a "go-it-alone" strategy may simply take too long or cost too much.

(7) *Pressures of global competition.* On an international scale, the merger of similar businesses between two or more participants may be desirable in order to establish the economies of scale, global customer reach, purchasing power or capital investment resources necessary to meet the strength of international competition.

(8) *Leveraged joint venture.* Joining forces with a financial partner can be a method of financing an acquisition which would not otherwise be affordable—or, sometimes, structuring an acquisition in a way which can avoid consolidation of the acquired business as a subsidiary for balance sheet purposes.

(9) *Creeping sale or acquisition.* A joint venture may be a first step in an eventual full disposal or acquisition of a business—with a further tranche of the disposal or acquisition being contemplated, but perhaps not specified, for a later time.

(10) *Catalyst for change.* Sometimes there is a less obvious reason—perhaps simply a wish, by bringing in a partner, to create a catalyst for change or to stimulate more entrepreneurial activity in a particular area of a party's business.

1–09 The Economist Intelligence Unit survey in 2006 of senior executives in UK companies summarised the important drivers in moving their companies toward increased collaboration as follows:

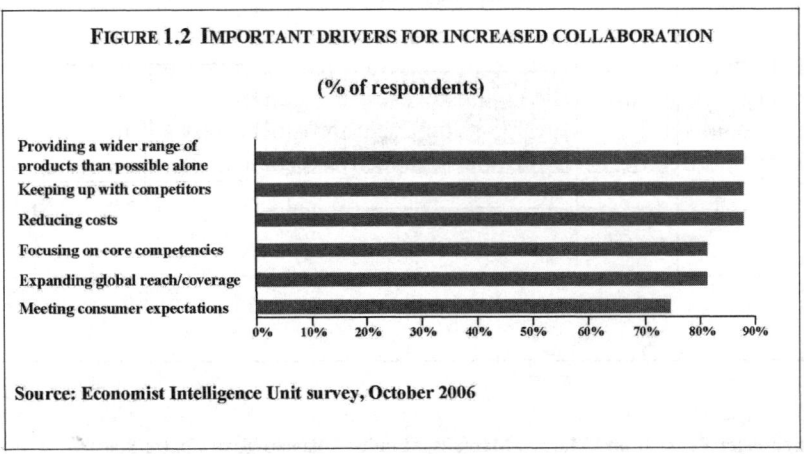

1–10 Many ventures will be based on more than one objective. The objectives may also not be the same for all parties to the joint venture. An added complexity in analysing commercial objectives in any particular case is that a joint venture or alliance may not be an "end-game" in itself. It may be an interim stage in a party's long-term business strategy or, intentionally, a short-term strategy which will be subject to review at a later stage. Joint ventures and alliances frequently change in scope and nature over time.

Range of joint ventures and alliances

1–11 We have referred generally so far to "joint ventures" and "alliances". These are not legal terms of art. They represent a wide (and sometimes confusing) range of collaborative business arrangements. A fundamental feature of a joint venture or alliance is collaboration between the participants involving a significant degree of integration between them but without going so far as full merger or acquisition. Figure 1.3 below[9] reflects a spectrum of commercial transaction types by reference to the level of commitment and degree of integration between the parties. At the far left is outsourcing; at the opposite extreme is M&A. Joint ventures and alliances lie in between. The key element for our purposes is the degree of collaboration. While many parties may refer to their suppliers, licensees or customers as their "partners", there will often not be a sufficient element of collaboration to justify the term "alliance" or "joint venture" for our purpose.

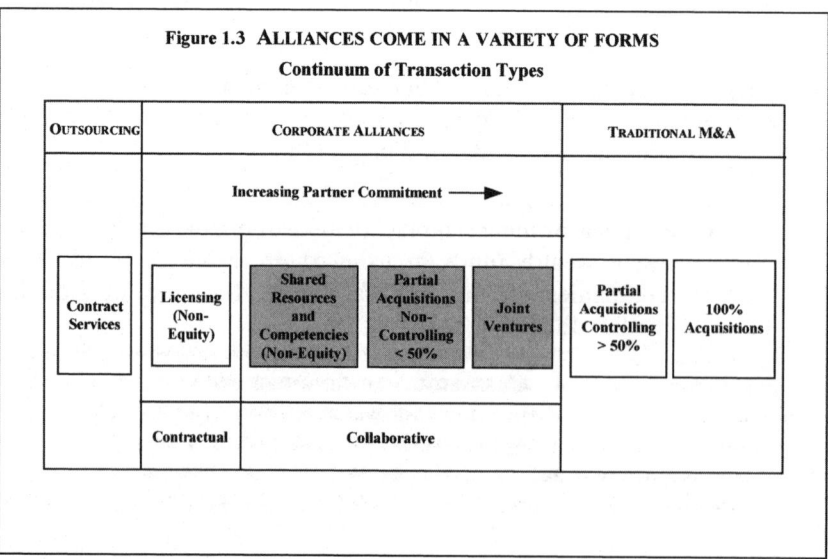

[9] See Peter Pekar Jr and Marc S. Margulis, "Equity Alliances Take Centre Stage".

1–12 A sample of deals appearing in the press over the last year or so illustrates the nature of this collaborative activity, particularly internationally, and the wide range of business transactions falling within the broad category of "joint ventures" and "alliances":

- *Sony/Sharp.* Sony is poised to invest nearly $1bn in rival Sharp's newest liquid crystal display factory in an attempt to meet growing demand for flat-panel televisions and diversify its supply chain. Sony will take a one-third stake in Sharp's LCD panel plant in western Japan, which is to be the biggest in the world. Sharp will own 66 per cent of the venture. Analysts expect the alliance to create further economies of scale and improve margins. [*FT:* 27.2.08]

- *Air France/KLM/Delta Air Lines.* Air France-KLM is aiming to use the planned merger of Delta and North West Airlines to build a long-term joint venture with the enlarged US carrier that would become the biggest player in the North Atlantic air travel market. The joint venture, in which the parties would share profits and revenues and jointly plan sales, networks and capacity, would have a turnover of $12bn and account for 30 per cent of the North Atlantic market. The merger and joint venture would have to overcome serious regulatory hurdles. [*FT:* 19.2.08]

- *Boeing/Lockheed.* Boeing and Lockheed Martin announced that they would collaborate on developing a next-generation bomber for the US Air Force. There had been speculation within the industry that the two defence giants would compete for a contract. [*FT:* 2.1.08]

- *Dow/Kuwait Petroleum Corporation.* Dow Chemical is to inject its low-growth plastics into an $11bn joint venture with Kuwait Petroleum Corporation, Kuwait's state oil company. The latter will $9.5bn for a 50 per cent stake in the venture. The joint venture underlines the growing role played by Middle Eastern companies and sovereign wealth funds in using their resources to invest in western companies looking for capital or the sale of troubled businesses. [*FT:* 13.12.07]

- *Carphone/Best Buy.* Carphone Warehouse, Europe's largest mobile phone retailer, said that it was expanding a joint venture with Best Buy, the largest US consumer electronics retailer, under which the two are setting up hundreds of in-store units selling mobile phones and technology across its US network. Carphone will supply technology and expertise and send staff to work alongside Best Buy. It is pursuing a piggyback strategy in the US and avoiding the expense and risk of establishing its own US free standing store nationwide. [*FT:* 10.11.07]

- *Sainsbury/Land Securities.* J Sainsbury have announced a property joint venture with developers Land Securities. The link-up will run for seven years and will own the freeholds of three properties with a value of £113.4m. Analysts described the joint venture as symbolic; a "toe in the water" for Sainsbury to enter in joint ventures in relation to its property asset base. [*FT:* 14.11.07]

- *Daimler/Ford.* Daimler and Ford Motor have set up a joint venture to pursue development of emission free fuel cells for cars and trucks as an alternative to petrol engines. Daimler will own 50.1 per cent of the venture and Ford 30 per cent. Ballard will hold the remaining shares. Each of the three partners will contribute $60m to the venture. [*FT:* 8.11.07]

- *Sony/Qimonda.* Sony, the Japanese electronics group, has launched a joint venture with Qimonda, a German chip maker, to design high-end memory chips for consumer gadgets. The joint venture would be called Qrentic Design. The companies said that specialists at its Tokyo-based venture would pool the German group's expertise in making D-Ram chips with Sony's skill in finding a use in products such as mobile phones and cameras. [*FT:* 3.10.07]

- *Unilever/Pepsico.* Pepsico and Unilever announced that they have agreed to expand their international partnership, Pepsi Lipton International (PLI), for the marketing and distribution of ready-to-drink tea products under the Lipton brand. The new agreement adds 11 countries to the partnership's business. Each company will continue to own 50% of the joint venture, with Pepsico paying Unilever an undisclosed sum for its share of the businesses in the new markets being transferred. The agreement is subject to approvals from a number of regulating authorities. [*FT:* 14.9.07]

- *Ralph Lauren/Richemont.* Ralph Lauren, the American clothing designer, is teaming up with Richemont, the Geneva-based owner of Cartier. They have signed a 50:50 joint venture to design, make and sell jewellery and watches. [*FT:* 6.3.07]

"Equity" and "non-equity" alliances

1–13 Joint ventures and alliances come in all shapes and sizes. Can they be defined or categorised into specific types? A practical, rather than legal, distinction for the purposes of this book is between (i) "equity" joint ventures or alliances and (ii) "non-equity" collaborative arrangements.

(1) *Equity joint ventures.* An "equity" joint venture is where each of the parties contributes capital to a jointly-owned business which is conducted as an identifiably separate business with some degree of

independent management and in which the parties share (directly or indirectly) in the profits or losses. Strategic equity joint ventures are being formed in virtually every industry. Where business objectives call for a high degree of integration and commitment, an equity joint venture is generally the appropriate structure.

(2) *Non-equity alliances*. "Non-equity" alliances do not involve direct profit or equity sharing or the creation of a separate "entity". They include collaborative arrangements such as shared resource agreements, pilot projects, R&D collaborations, joint production arrangements and network alliances. They will invariably be purely "contractual" arrangements.

This categorisation does not have any formal legal consequences. However, it is useful as a basis for discussion of the different legal forms of joint venture and alliances: see chapters 3, 4 and 5. It is the category of equity joint ventures, in particular, which leads to a wide range of legal and commercial issues discussed more fully in this book.

Problems with joint ventures and alliances

1–14 Joint ventures and alliances are sometimes perceived as a soft or easy transactional option. This is not so. There are many potential problems—both in the initial design and establishment of the joint venture and also, particularly, in its subsequent management. Compared to acquisitions, equity joint ventures are frequently more complex and time-consuming to negotiate. In M&A, the principal concerns are generally price, structure, warranties and indemnities. In equity joint ventures, these same issues usually exist together with many additional and potentially difficult issues such as: scope of the alliance (including limitations); capitalisation and relative ownership resulting from initial capitalisation; responsibility for future capital requirements; governance—both policy direction and operational management; allocation of profits and losses; technology issues (such as the rights of access and use for the parties in respect of new jointly-developed technology); restrictions on transfers of shares; dispute resolution mechanisms; exit strategies; and rights and restrictions upon termination of the alliance.

1–15 Finding an appropriate partner for a joint venture or alliance is, in itself, not straightforward. Many companies are, properly, cautious of the risks involved. The results of the Economist Intelligence Unit survey in 2006 reflect the principal risks and impediments perceived in establishing collaborations:

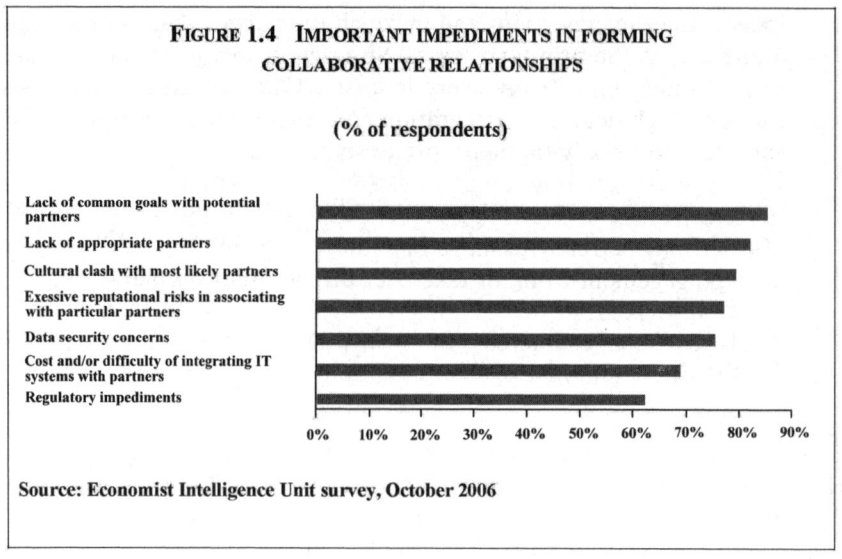

A joint venture life cycle?

1–16 Once established, many joint ventures and alliances encounter problems. There has been a growth in professional literature and management studies analysing joint ventures. Many bear out the need for a cautious approach:

(1) A McKinsey study[10] published in the early 1990s examined cross-border alliances, joint ventures and acquisitions involving 150 large companies in the US, Europe and Japan. The study found that only half of these linkages succeeded and that the average life expectancy for most alliances was approximately seven years.

(2) A study by KPMG[11] in 1997 sought the views of senior executives in 155 leading UK based manufacturing firms with experience of joint ventures. The survey revealed that, whilst joint ventures are not viewed as short-term activities, their predicted lifespans vary considerably. Half of the companies cited an average of 10 years or more as the lifespan of a joint venture, while 28 per cent mentioned an average of less than 10 years.

1–17 Alliances rarely stand still. One commentator[12] remarks:

---

[10] J. Bleeke and D. Ernst (eds), *Collaborating to Compete: Using Strategic Alliances and Acquisitions in the Global Marketplace*.

[11] KPMG Transaction Services, *Joint ventures: the triumph of hope over reality?* (1998).

[12] J. Child, D. Faulkner and S. Tallman, *Cooperative Strategy: Managing Alliances, Networks and Joint Ventures* (Oxford: Oxford University Press, 2005, p.399). Some commentators positively advocate change, e.g. *Your Alliances Are Too Stable* by D. Ernst and J. Bamford (Harvard Business Review, June 2005).

"For most alliances . . . the choice appears to be to evolve or to fail . . . The evolution of alliances can proceed along different paths and lead to quite different outcomes . . . Experience of joint ventures . . . suggests that there are two critical periods in their existence. The first comes at about two or three years of life, by which time an unsatisfactory relationship should have become evident. The second comes after about five or six years of alliance life, by which time one partner may be ready to move onto another arrangement. This could be disengagement from, or take over of, the other partner".

Indeed, it has been estimated that nearly 80 per cent of equity joint ventures ultimately end in a sale by one of the partners.[13]

1–18 Another study[14] has, indeed, attempted—somewhat starkly—to condense a typical joint venture life-cycle into the chart form shown below in Figure 1.5:

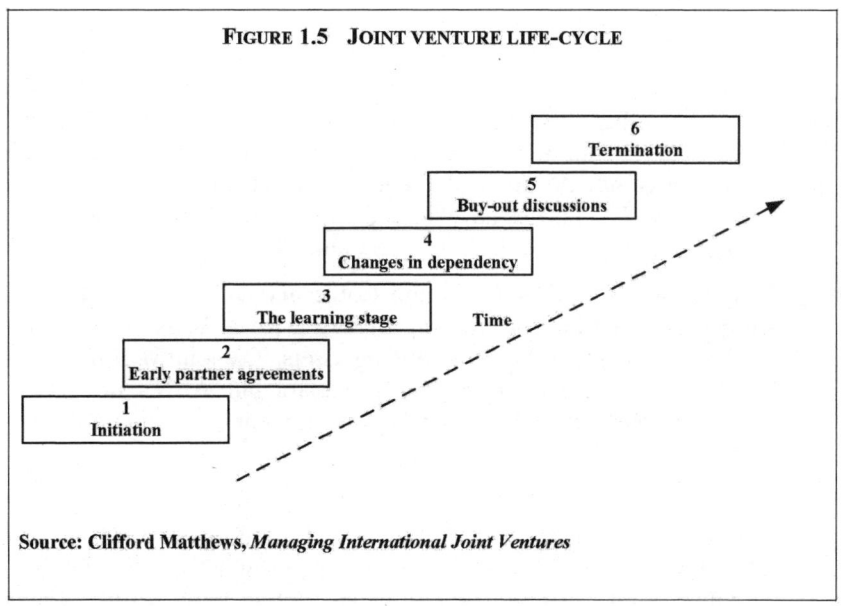

1–19 These are inevitably over-simplifications and generalisations. The circumstances of each venture will differ. The important point for the lawyers (and indeed the principals) is to recognise that most joint ventures and alliances go through a period of evaluation and change—and often termination—after a relatively short time. Some recent announcements of

---

[13] J. Bleeke and D. Ernst, *Is Your Strategic Alliance Really a Sale?* (Harvard Business Review on Strategic Alliances, 2002).
[14] Clifford Matthews, *Managing International Joint Ventures* (London: Kogan Page, 1999).

joint ventures and alliances terminating or changing in scope or direction include the following:

- *Mahindra/Renault*. Mahindra, the Indian car maker has pulled out of a $1bn joint venture with Renault and Nissan to set up a factory near Chennai. There had been media reports that Mahindra was unhappy with Renault's tie-up with Indian motorbike maker Bajaj forged last summer. Mahindra denied that this was the reason. [*FT:* 9.1.08]

- *Pearson/FT Deutschland.* Pearson is understood to be close to selling its half-share in FT Deutschland, the FT's German sister paper, to joint venture partner Gruner + Jahr, ending the UK media group's foray into foreign language newspapers. [*FT:* 16.1.08]

- *Danone/Wahaha*. Danone, the French group, is involved in a bitter dispute with its Chinese partner, Wahaha, over its joint venture. The two companies first signed a partnership in 1996 and since then the joint venture, in which Danone has a 51 per cent share, has turned Wahaha mineral water into a market leader in China. A feud has erupted with Danone accusing Wahaha of setting-up a parallel operation to make and sell the same products as the JV. Wahaha claims that it has the rights to use the Wahaha brand name. Danone claims that it should have been transferred to the JV. Wahaha's position was upheld in a decision by the Hangzhou Arbitration Commission. The parties have agreed a temporary "legal ceasefire" in the high-profile dispute. [*FT:* 11.12.07 and 24.12.07]

- *ABN Rothschild*. ABN Amro and Rothschild will end their 11–year equity capital markets partnership following Royal Bank of Scotland's deal to buy ABN's investment banking assets. The joint venture, ABN Amro Rothschild, has been very successful but ABN's investment banking merger with RBS was a logical moment to revaluate the co-operation. [*FT:* 12.12.07]

- *Scottish & Newcastle/Carlsberg*. Scottish & Newcastle has started commercial arbitration proceedings with the Arbitration Institute of the Stockholm Chamber of Commerce to examine its shareholders' agreement with Carlsberg regarding its Russian joint venture, Baltic Beverages Holdings. S&N claims that Carlsberg has triggered an option clause in the agreement by making a takeover offer for S&N and that it now has a right to buy Carlsberg's 50 per cent stake in BBH at fair value. The move is seen as a key strategy in S&N's bid defence. [*FT:* 3.11.07]

- *Smiths Group/GE*. Smiths Group and General Electric have called off their deal to put their respective detection businesses into a joint venture after a disagreement over strategy. Smiths said the decision was mutual and that it would not need to pay the £35m break-fee payable if it alone had called off the deal. [*FT:* 20.9.07]

- *MTV Russia*. MTV Networks, part of Viacom, has sold its majority stake in a Russian joint venture, MTV Russia, for $360m to Prof-Media, a local company with interests in film production, theatres and radio. The decision was part of restructuring at the cable group aimed at improving international profitability. [*FT:* 5.6.07]
- *Daimler/Chrysler*. The "marriage in heaven" between Daimler-Benz and Chrysler, as the companies called it, was celebrated in May 1998. Nine years later, the collaboration was ended in a quiet room off the main factory site of Mercedes in Stuttgart in what one observer called "the divorce on earth". "We overestimated the potential for synergies" said Daimler's chief executive. [*FT:* 15.5.07]

What are the problems?

1–20 What are the problems? Experience indicates the following as some of the principal difficulties encountered in equity joint ventures:

(1) *Sharing management.* Joint ventures invariably involve the need for the co-venturers to share management of the joint enterprise. This can lead to slower and more cautious decision-making than is the practice or culture in most companies acting alone.

(2) *Differences in culture.* Joint ventures involve two or more parties working together. This can expose differences of culture which can seriously affect the speed and harmony of that working relationship. "Culture" can include not only different cultures of nationality but also, more importantly, of corporate style and approach.

(3) *Usurping of technology.* A more basic fear, which in some cases can affect the willingness of a party to work fully together with a co-venturer, is the fear that the other party will be trying through the joint venture to be in a position to usurp its proprietary technology or market access, and then compete afterwards independently.

(4) *Different commercial objectives.* The commercial goals of joint venture parties may not always be the same, or may not remain the same; after the initial attraction, partners may end up "sharing the same bed but dreaming different dreams". Parties may not engage early enough in frank disclosure on objectives and strategy.

(5) *Who's in charge?* Frequently, joint ventures can lead to an uncertainty as to who is really in charge. Is it the parent co-venturers, or the management team of the joint venture? A wish for autonomy among the management team can create tensions with parent co-venturers who seek to maintain safeguards or tight controls over their "child".

(6) *Disagreements to resolve.* A joint venture relationship will inevitably give rise, at some stage or other, to differences and disagreements. These will need to be resolved. This will require considerable time

and ongoing communication on the part of senior management if resolution is to be achieved constructively and effectively.

(7) *Extra management time.* Similarly, if they are to be successful, joint ventures will involve significant time—and important management resources—in continuing consultation and communication between the joint venture parties throughout the life of the venture. There will be increased co-ordination and governance costs.

(8) *Financing.* A particular source of difficulty is where the parties do not have a mutually agreed plan on how to fund the growth of the joint venture—or if financing calls are greater than originally anticipated and one party is unable or unwilling to continue financing. Joint venture parties may have different profiles for financial return from the venture. Each may have to make judgments as to its own priorities in the light of other business opportunities and financing demands.

(9) *Lengthy and costly negotiations.* The negotiations to establish the joint venture can themselves be lengthy as each party prepares its position and takes time to build up its trust of the other party; they are not speedy transactions to put together. They can also be costly relationships to establish—not only in terms of management time but also in the scale of setting-up costs generally.

(10) *Managerial commitment and communications.* Parties may not include the ultimate managers of the alliance in the early due diligence process or the decision to proceed. They may generally fail to establish effective and collaborative communications among "the rank and file" of the workforce, leading to lack of real commitment.

(11) *Poorly drafted contracts.* The parties may create too loose, or poorly thought through, legal agreements—leading to subsequent ambiguities, disputes and diversion of management time.

(12) *Exit.* Joint ventures invariably come to an end at some stage (as the statistics indicate) and this termination process can itself be time-consuming and difficult. A party going into a joint venture will therefore continually need to keep an eye on "what's next?" and the potential "exit" routes and their implications.

1–21 One study,[15] based on the views of senior US finance directors, involved research into the causes of failure of joint ventures and alliances. Figure 1.5 summarises the principal factors:

---

[15] PricewaterhouseCoopers and CFO Research Services, *The CFO's Perspective on Alliances*.

PROBLEMS WITH JOINT VENTURES AND ALLIANCES   17

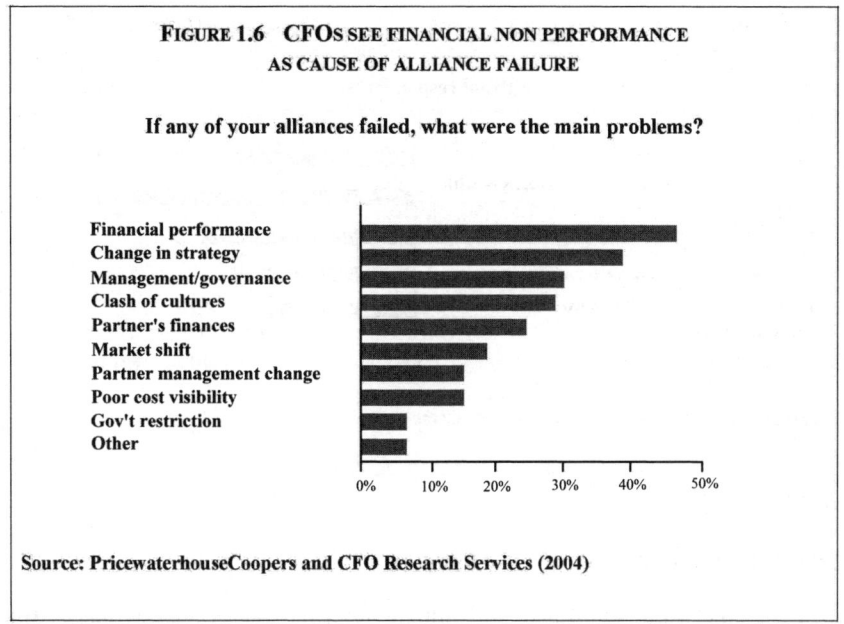

FIGURE 1.6 CFOS SEE FINANCIAL NON PERFORMANCE AS CAUSE OF ALLIANCE FAILURE

Source: PricewaterhouseCoopers and CFO Research Services (2004)

1–22 Joint ventures create, in particular, a set of management and leadership challenges. Studies are now recognising that joint venture management deserves particular attention and that techniques must be adapted to take account of the challenges and issues raised by joint ventures (compared with wholly owned operations). Different working practices of the joint venture parties provide scope for inter-partner conflict. Staff may hold more allegiance to the parent by whom they are or were employed than to the joint venture itself. Management issues also arise in relation to the extent and methods of co-ordination with the joint venture parents. One commentator[16] writes:

> "Managing collaborative ventures is rarely easy. Poor communications, clashes of culture and temperament between partners, differences of opinion as to how the venture should be run; all these and other factors combine to create a centrifugal force which can tear a collaboration apart."

1–23 Joint ventures and alliances carry business risks. The Economist Intelligence Unit survey of senior executives of UK companies studied the greatest risks posed by collaborative relationships. The principal risks identified are set out in Figure 1.7:

---

[16] *FT Report—Understanding the Culture of Collaboration* (June 2007) at p.4. See also generally J. Bamford, B. Gomes-Casseres and M. Robinson, *Mastering Alliance Strategy* (New York, John Wiley & Sons, 2003).

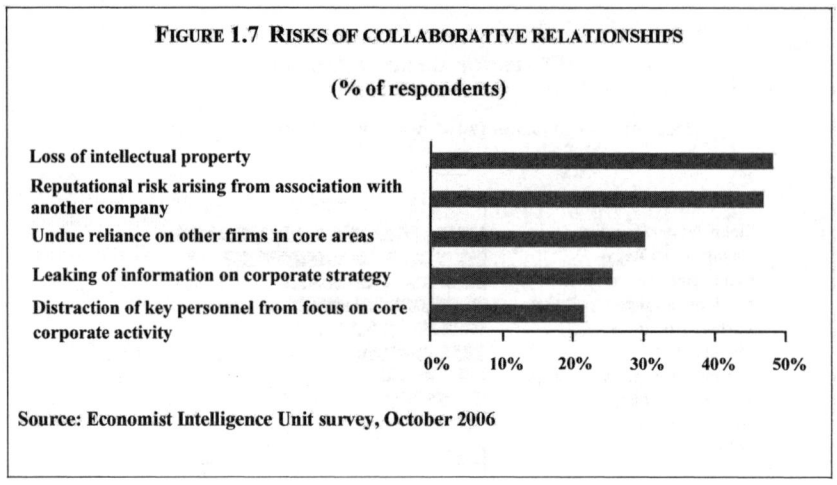

Criteria for successful ventures

1–24 Many joint ventures and alliances are, nevertheless, successful. Indeed, the growth in joint ventures and alliances over recent years appears to have been accompanied by a greater success rate—particularly by those companies which have learned to use alliances well, to adopt "best practices" and to develop dedicated alliance training programmes for their managers. Research by Booz-Allen & Hamilton[17] has concluded that "best practice" driven alliance companies are nearly three times more likely to succeed in their alliances than the average.

1–25 There is obviously no single recipe for success. What is the right formula for one company, or set of joint venture circumstances, may not be for another. One study undertaken by McKinsey[18] led to the following views:

> "Arguments over whether cross-border alliances or cross-border acquisitions are superior are beside the point; both have roughly a 50 per cent rate of success. But acquisitions work well for core businesses and existing geographic areas, while alliances are more effective for edging into related businesses or new geographic markets.
>
> Alliances between strong and weak companies rarely work. They do not provide the missing skills needed for growth, and they lead to mediocre performance.
>
> The hallmark of successful alliances that endure is their ability to evolve beyond initial expectations and objectives. This requires autonomy for the venture and flexibility on the part of the parents.

---

[17] J.R. Harbison and Peter Pekar Jr, *Smart Alliances: A Practical Guide to Repeatable Success* (New York: Jossey-Bass, 1998).
[18] J. Bleeke and D. Ernst (eds), *Collaborating to Compete*, p.18; see also para.1–03 earlier.

Alliances with an even split of financial ownership are more likely to succeed than those in which one partner holds a majority interest. What matters is clear management control, not financial ownership."

1-26 A KPMG study[19] with many leading UK-based manufacturing firms identified a variety of factors which, in the view of the respondents, would improve the setting-up of a joint venture—see Figure 1.8 below:

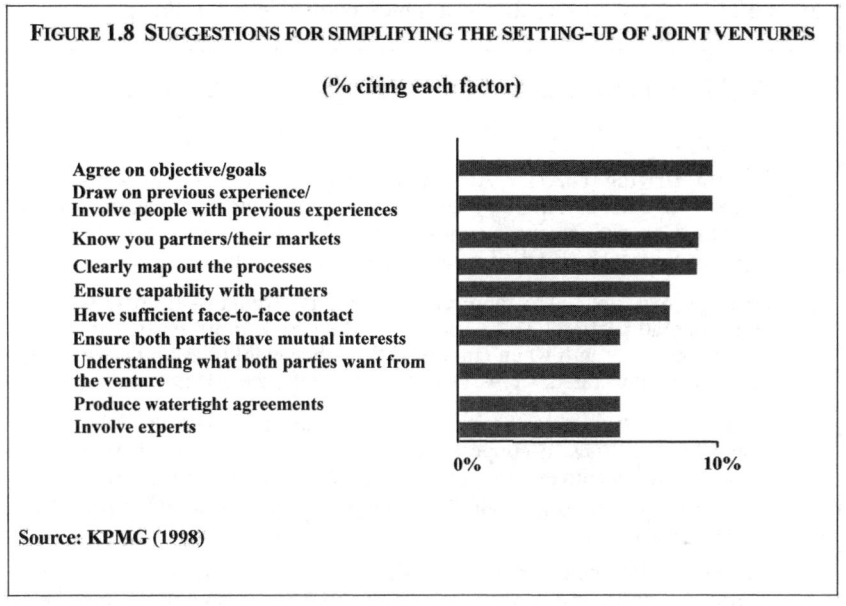

FIGURE 1.8 SUGGESTIONS FOR SIMPLIFYING THE SETTING-UP OF JOINT VENTURES (% citing each factor)

Source: KPMG (1998)

1-27 These various criteria and suggestions are not a blueprint for success, and the weighting to be given to each factor will change with the circumstances of each particular joint venture. Above all, it is the choice of joint venture partner which is of course crucial. There must be the right "fit" for the particular joint venture. For this "fit", the parties should have complementary strengths being brought to the venture, compatible cultures and clear commercial objectives and performance goals for the venture.

1-28 Management studies (some of which are mentioned in this chapter) are contributing to knowledge, training and "best practice" alliance learning. Many companies are recognising the importance of capturing and institutionalising their alliance capabilities. For those many companies with networks of diverse joint ventures and alliances critical to their business, an important challenge is to develop the skills and ways of managing effectively these external relationships as part of an overall and cohesive "extended enterprise".[20]

---

[19] KPMG Transaction Services, *Joint ventures: the triumph of hope over reality?*.
[20] Economist Intelligence Unit, *Extending the enterprise: A new model for growth* (2002).

1–29 Organisations are being formed which encourage the sharing of ideas and the recognition and sharing between participants of "best practice". For instance, the Association of Strategic Alliance Professionals (ASAP)[21] comprises member firms worldwide willing to share experiences and develop ideas of best practices and best processes. ASAP has, with The Warren Company, produced a "Strategic Alliance Best Process Workbook" which provides a practitioners' guide to the formation, management and evolution of key alliance relationships. ASAP has concluded that key characteristics of a well-structured alliance comprise the following:

ASAP: CHARACTERISTICS OF A WELL-STRUCTURED ALLIANCE

1. **Critical Driving Forces**: Are there compelling forces which push the alliance together? Without these forces, there is no true reason for the alliance. Can we achieve our goals only with an alliance? Are there any negative forces which might split the alliance over time?

2. **Strategic Synergy**: Are there complementary strengths-strategic synergy-in a potential partner? To be successful, the two or more participants must have greater strength when combined than they would have independently. Mathematically stated: "$1 + 1 \sim 3$" must be the rule; if not, walk away.

3. **Great Chemistry**: Are there cooperative efficiencies with the other company? Do they have a cooperative spirit? There must be a high level of trust so that executives can work through difficulties that will arise. Don't "sell" your company's "beauty," it must be desired by the prospective partner, not sold.

4. **Win-Win**: All members of the Alliance must see that the structure, operations, risks, and rewards are fairly apportioned among the members. Fair apportionment prevents internal dissension that can corrode, and eventually destroy the venture.

5. **Operational Integration**: Beyond a good strategic fit, there must be careful coordination at the operational level where actual implementation of plans and projects occurs.

6. **Growth Opportunity**: Is there an excellent opportunity to place our company in a leadership position-to sell a new product or service, to secure access to technology or raw material? Is one partner uniquely positioned with the "know-how" and reputation to take advantage of that opportunity.

7. **Sharp Focus**: There is a strong correlation between success of a venture and clear overall purpose-specific, concrete objectives, goals, timetables, lines of responsibility, and measurable results.

8. **Commitment & Support**: Unless top and middle management are highly committed to the success of the venture, there is little chance of success.

Source: ASAP (Strategic Alliance Best Process Workbook)

---

[21] ASAP, based in the US, has a European section: see *www.strategic-alliances.org*.

1–30 ASAP, in developing its best practice guidelines, concentrates on six different phases in the process of forming alliances:

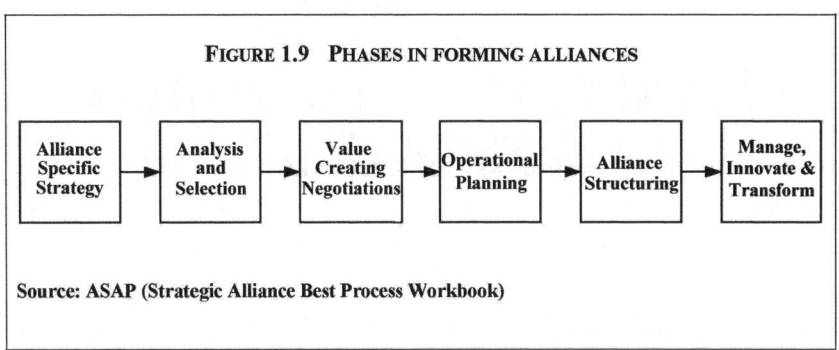

FIGURE 1.9 PHASES IN FORMING ALLIANCES

Source: ASAP (Strategic Alliance Best Process Workbook)

Within this overall framework for the formation of alliances, lawyers can play a particularly important role in Phase 3: Value Creating Negotiations and Phase 5: Alliance Structuring. Much of the remainder of this book deals with the issues which affect lawyers in carrying out this role.

1–31 This chapter has addressed the business landscape. It is for the parties themselves to design the essential commercial relationship for the particular venture. It is nevertheless important for the lawyers to recognise the commercial "drivers" behind each collaboration. This will assist them in their role of shaping the legal framework for the venture and drawing up, and negotiating, the detailed content of the joint venture or alliance arrangements.

Chapter 2

Planning the joint venture transaction

The business strategy to form a joint venture or alliance will be decided by the client. This strategy must be turned into legal form. For the lawyers, the formation of a joint venture or alliance is a transaction which requires planning, process management, third party consents and settlement of a range of different issues. The lawyers are important members of the project team. The aim of this chapter is to outline the issues likely to affect the overall legal planning of the transaction.

Role of the lawyers

2–01 The lawyers play an important part at the planning stage of many ventures. The role of the lawyers will normally be to support and advise the business client with principal responsibilities being:

(a) to alert the business negotiators to important legal issues to be addressed in establishing the venture and the options available to deal with these issues;

(b) to help structure the joint venture in the light of the business objectives and the interests of the client;

(c) to carry out any necessary "due diligence" and other legal investigations;

(d) to help in identifying, and obtaining, necessary third party clearances and consents;

(e) to ensure that the joint venture arrangements are properly and clearly documented and that the interests of the client are appropriately safeguarded;

(f) to manage the legal and other completion steps necessary to establish the joint venture; and

(g) generally, to advise constructively in helping to establish the joint venture or alliance in accordance with the client's wishes and interests.

2–02 Each joint venture and alliance is different. Some are relatively straightforward; others take a considerable time to crystallise and involve a wide range of issues. These transactions involve not only corporate, partnership and contract laws but also the application of other relevant branches of law such as competition, regulatory, intellectual property and employment laws. Qualities of patience, good organisation and a willingness to appreciate differing viewpoints and cultures in reaching consensus will frequently be as relevant as pure legal skills.

"Big picture" issues

2–03 A first step should be to identify the key legal and transaction issues which are likely to affect the formation of the particular venture. They are likely to be issues affecting both the content of the joint venture or alliance agreement and also the process of its formation. An outline "road map" can then be established. Key questions to be addressed at this initial "big picture" stage include:

(1) *Commercial objectives.* What are the primary commercial objectives of the client?

(2) *Profit sharing.* Is it or should it be an "equity" joint venture in which profits and losses will be shared—or a non-equity collaboration?

(3) *Contributions.* What initial contributions are being made by the parties into the venture?

(4) *Territory/scope.* Is the venture confined to a particular territory or technical field?

(5) *Key client interests.* What are the key interests of the client to protect such as control, exit routes, intellectual property rights, dividend return or entitlement to product output?

(6) *Commercial return.* How does the client expect to make a commercial return from the venture—dividends, payments under ancillary contracts, non-cash benefits or capital gain on exit?

(7) *Governance/control.* What rights of management control or participation does the client expect?

(8) *Non-compete.* Will there be non-compete or exclusivity restrictions on the parties?

(9) *Exit strategy.* Does the client have an exit strategy or need protections in the event of termination?

(10) *Third party consents.* What material consents, regulatory approvals, licences must be obtained or other conditions precedent satisfied before the joint venture or alliance can commence?

> More detailed Joint Venture Checklists of issues to be considered in planning a joint venture are set out in Part F of this book.

TRANSACTION "ROAD MAP"

Transaction "road map"

2–04 The course of each joint venture or alliance will be different. The lawyers should plan at an early stage a broad "road map" setting out the key legal steps, including the principal issues requiring resolution or action for the particular venture and a target timetable. Tasks likely to affect the timetable include particularly:

(a) undertaking any due diligence exercise;

(b) legal and tax structuring of the joint venture;

(c) negotiation of key commercial issues;

(d) valuation of each party's contribution;

(e) applying for relevant third party consents and, in particular, regulatory approvals.

Identification of tasks which may involve a lengthy lead time before the agreements can be concluded is an important part of the transaction-planning process. Establishing who does what, and a realistic timetable for obtaining these consents or undertaking these tasks, should be an early exercise. Some of these tasks are discussed in more detail in this chapter.

2–05 In complex joint ventures, it is often useful to maintain an action list, or status report, as a continuing document in order to keep all parties informed and to ensure that an overall perspective of progress is maintained. For instance, in the case of an equity joint venture designed to combine the existing businesses of two or more parties into a UK joint venture company (JVC), such an action list or transaction "road map" could comprise the following:

Project X: Legal "Road Map"

Action [Add columns for: Primary Responsibility; Target Date; Status]

1. **Initial documents**

- Confidentiality agreement/information exchange agreement
- Memorandum of understanding (MoU)

2. **Structure/commercial issues**

- Identify activities and companies to be contributed by each party. Decide basis for valuation
- Decide proposed proportions of equity shares in JVC for each party
- Decide (if necessary) method of "equalising" any initial difference in valuation (if 50:50 equity shares)
- Agree form of any financial audit/review to be undertaken post-Completion
- Decide legal form of joint venture (e.g. joint venture company (JVC))
- Decide location of JVC and any supporting tax structure (e.g. "income access" shares)
- Decide legal method of merger (e.g. transfer of subsidiaries or assets to JVC)
- Decide principal features of management structure, including:
    — role of board
    — representation/quorum/casting vote
    — matters to be reserved to shareholders
    — authority to be given to management
- Establish likely accounting treatment of JVC in accounts of parents
- Decide capital structure and debt/equity ratio for JVC
- Decide amount of authorised/issued share capital of JVC
- Decide amount and form of any loan capital to be issued by JVC (and any ongoing funding commitments of parents)
- Establish whether common accounting principles for JVC need to be agreed

- Decide name of JVC
- Identify entities to participate in JVC as shareholders. Need for parent company guarantees?
- Identify matters which are conditions precedent to establishment of JVC and likely timetable for approvals (see also section 5 below)
- Agree preliminary announcement/press release

3. Due diligence

- Financial/commercial/tax due diligence to be undertaken
- Technical/engineering due diligence to be undertaken
- Legal due diligence to be undertaken
- Property surveys/environmental review or audit

4. Reorganisations/preparation

- Establish steps required for any preliminary reorganisation by each party of business or subsidiaries to be contributed to JVC
- Contracts and other assets: identify any third party consents required for transfers of material assets or contracts (including change of control provisions); review effect on any borrowing covenants
- Properties: identify and establish arrangements for transfer or lease of properties to relevant subsidiaries
- Intellectual property/IT: identify and establish any need for formal transfers or licences of IPR (including use of trade marks and names) or IT systems
- Associated undertakings: identify subsidiaries and interests in other companies or joint ventures to be contributed to JVC
- Employees: identify and arrange transfers of employees to JVC or relevant subsidiaries to be contributed to JVC
- Pensions: establish pension position and proposals for ongoing arrangements
- Share options: establish effect on any existing parent company share options for relevant employees
- Guarantees/indemnities: identify any guarantees or indemnities given by parents which are to be replaced
- Support arrangements: identify any need for, and terms of, any ongoing support agreements between each parent and JVC or relevant subsidiaries, covering e.g.:
    — site support facilities
    — shared computer or telecommunications systems
    — administrative services

"BIG PICTURE" ISSUES

- Agree intra-group transfer documents to effect preliminary reorganisation(s)

5. **Regulatory approvals and other third party consents**

- Identify all required notifications to, or clearances required under, competition or other regulatory authorities including where relevant:
    — European Commission under EC Merger Regulation
    — Office of Fair Trading (UK) under Enterprise Act 2002
    — regulatory authorities in other relevant countries
- Any consents required from any relevant industry licensing authority?
- Identify consents required (commercially or legally) from major customers and/or suppliers
- Identify material tax clearances required
- Establish need for any consents under debenture trust deeds or from lenders under any other financing instruments
- Identify need to consult with, or obtain any consents from, employees or works councils
- Establish whether any consents or notification requirements apply in relation to shareholders or any relevant stock exchange (e.g. shareholder consent for Class 1 transactions under the Listing Rules of the UK Listing Authority)

6. **Settle principal legal documentation (in draft)**

- Intra-Group Transfer Agreements and ancillary agreements relating to preliminary reorganisations
- Framework or Contribution Agreement covering inter alia:
    — contribution of relevant companies and/or appropriate businesses to JVC
    — warranties and indemnities
    — valuation/audit procedures
    — conditions precedent
    — conduct prior to Completion
- Shareholders' Agreement covering inter alia:
    — board representation
    — reserved matters for parent shareholders
    — future funding
    — dividend policy
    — non-compete
    — transfer restrictions
    — dispute resolution
    — termination/break-up
- Memorandum and articles of association of JVC

- Administrative services agreements between parties and JVC
- Technology licence agreements/trade mark agreements between parties and JVC
- Business plan

7. Signing

- Board approvals and authorisations confirmed
- Signing of framework/contribution agreement (and exchange of disclosure letters, if applicable, in relation to warranties)
- Approval of agreed drafts:
  — shareholders' agreement
  — JVC's articles of association
  — administrative services agreements
  — technology licence agreements/ trade mark agreements business plan
- Announcement/press release

8. Pre-Completion

- Notification to European Commission if required under EC Merger Regulation
- Formation of JVC and adoption of memorandum and articles of association
- Confirm all fundamental consents and clearances obtained
- Confirm no regulatory action outstanding
- Confirm all other conditions precedent satisfied
- Confirm all necessary board authorisations obtained

9. Completion

- Meeting/resolution of JVC to re-organise capital and adopt new articles of association (unless previously done)
- Transfers of shares by each co-venturer to JVC in specified subsidiaries (or execution of business transfer documentation if relevant)
- Issues of shares by JVC to each co-venturer in specified numbers
- Signature of:
  — shareholders' agreement
  — administrative services agreements
  — licence agreements/trade mark agreements
  — any other ancillary contracts
- Appointment of members of board of JVC by the co-venturers

- Board meeting of JVC, inter alia, to adopt business plan
- Announcement/press release

10. Post-Completion actions

- Filings with UK Registrar of Companies
- Appointment of new directors of relevant subsidiaries
- Post-Completion financial audit/review:
  — prepare completion balance sheets
  — agree any equalisation or post-completion adjustments.

It will generally also be useful to maintain a list of documents required for the legal steps of the transaction. This should include a clear identification of which party (or adviser) is responsible for drafting or producing each particular document. The content will, of course, vary with each transaction. These steps are basically examples of sensible transaction management. Joint ventures and alliances can be complex projects and the lawyers are an important part of the project management team.

Confidentiality agreement

2–06 Exchange of information will be a key feature of most joint ventures and alliances. Parties should put in place appropriate confidentiality agreements at an early stage before initial technical information, financial data and other details are exchanged in preliminary negotiations. The agreement should cover information which is disclosed either orally or in writing.

2–07 Under English law, there are principles whereby a party can claim remedies to assert unauthorised use or disclosure of information imparted "in confidence".[1] Similar principles will apply in many other jurisdictions. However, it is preferable to have the certainty of a contractual obligation of

---

[1] A key English law case is *Seager v Copydex* Ltd [1967] 1 W.L.R. 923 where the plaintiff disclosed features of an invention to the defendant in the course of negotiations regarding its possible development. Negotiations were aborted. The defendant subsequently produced a product using, albeit unconsciously, part of the information given to it by the plaintiff. The defendant was held to have used confidential information to gain a springboard. The court awarded compensation to the plaintiff. Similarly, in *Coco v AN Clark (Engineers) Ltd* [1969] R.P.C. 41 the court indicated that this principle of confidentiality would apply to information disclosed in joint venture negotiations: "in particular, where information of commercial or industrial value is given on a business like basis, and with some avowed common object in mind, such as a joint venture . . . I would regard the recipient as carrying a heavy burden if he seeks to repel a contention that he is bound by an obligation of confidence".

confidentiality in the event that negotiations do break down. Such an agreement also serves the practical purpose of emphasising to each party the confidentiality of the information being handed over. In many cases, particularly where technical information is being disclosed, it will be wise to keep a specific list of what is disclosed and the persons to whom the information is disclosed.

2–08 Typical undertakings which will be sought, generally on a reciprocal basis from each party, include the following:

(a) not to use the information for any purpose other than in connection with the joint venture or alliance;

(b) not to disclose the information to any person except on a "need to know basis" in connection with the venture;

(c) to require each individual to whom the information is disclosed to undertake to keep such information confidential;

(d) if the negotiations break down, to return all original documents and to return or destroy all copies, secondary notes or information derived from those original documents or copies; and

(e) possibly, to keep the fact of the negotiations themselves confidential until the parties agree on an announcement.

> **An example of a two party Information Exchange Agreement is set out as Precedent 1 in Part E.**

2–09 Even with a confidentiality agreement in place, certain information may be so sensitive that a party requires special protection against potential misuse. Protective measures could include:

(a) restricting access during the due diligence process on a "need to know" basis to a small number of identified senior employees of the other party (preferably after execution of individual confidentiality undertakings);

(b) placing restrictions on copying of sensitive information or removing documents from the due diligence site;

(c) "staggering" the release of information (particularly if the proposed joint venture is with a competitor or potential competitor) so that disclosure of highly sensitive information is not made until the disclosing party is reasonably certain that the venture will proceed;

(d) possibly, making certain confidential information available only to a third party intermediary (such as accountants, solicitors, financial advisers or other specialists) who may be permitted to examine and provide a summary confirmation or report to the other party without copying or recording details of the confidential information itself.

In some jurisdictions, it is becoming more common to impose a substantial financial payment in the event of a breach of confidentiality terms. This is intended to act, *in terrorem*, as an additional discipline to ensure compliance and also to provide full and specific financial recompense for the often incalculable damages in the event of breach. Under English law, though, a clearly excessive sum is likely to be struck down as an unenforceable "penalty".

Memorandum of understanding

2–10 There is a considerable merit, in many joint ventures, in setting out the basic commercial principles which have been agreed between the parties in a letter of intent, memorandum of understanding (MoU), heads of terms or similar document. These expressions are all variants, in greater or lesser detail, of the same kind of document. An MoU is particularly useful in the case of an international joint venture or other complex transaction. For the lawyers, the MoU is often "where the job starts"; it usually represents a first step in the formal transaction process. It is an important milestone which, after the initial discussions between the principals, aims to crystallise key points and sets the foundation for finalisation of the arrangements.

Purpose of an MoU

2–11 There is sometimes a view that an MoU is not necessary and that the time spent on that document can best be spent settling the detail of the definitive agreements. Experience suggests that MoUs do, though, serve a valuable purpose in the case of most joint ventures or alliances. An MoU can:

(a) enable the senior negotiators to concentrate on establishing the basic principles of the venture;

(b) help to "seal" the fundamental undertaking and seriousness of the parties (whether or not legally binding);

(c) form a basis for any public announcements;

(d) provide a basis for approaches to regulatory authorities to initiate clearances;

(e) help to keep the transaction moving, often at an important and sensitive stage in the negotiations; and

(f) also provide a solid basis for the lawyers to proceed with the drafting of definitive agreements.

2–12 Ideally, the MoU or comparable document should be prepared by the business clients and reviewed by the lawyers. It should not be too long—rarely itself more than five or six pages. It should be an outline, setting the direction of the venture. It should be "owned" by the client. The content of the MoU will, of course, vary considerably depending on the particular venture or alliance. The Association of Strategic Alliance Professionals (ASAP) has identified the following as critical commercial points which should be addressed at this stage in most alliances:

MEMORANDUM OF UNDERSTANDING AND PRINCIPLES

1. **Purpose of the Agreement:** Outline why the alliance is being formed and what is its perceived mission. Describe the "VALUE ADDED PROPOSITION."

2. **Spirit of the Venture:** What is the commitment to the future both companies are seeking? What valued and future vision will engender communications and trust?

3. **Key Objectives and Responsibilities:** Address what products, services, or other specific projects will be included and excluded from the venture. Identify target markets (i.e. regions, user groups, etc.), and any markets excluded that will remain the domain of the partners. If the venture has purchase and supply provisions, state who will purchase or supply specific products, services, or resources from or to the owners. Clarify and specify objectives and target goals to be achieved by the alliance, when to expect achieving these objectives and goals, any major obstacles anticipated, and the point at which the alliance will be terminated (if any). Each participant should designate an Alliance Manager who will be responsible for their company's day-to-day involvement in the alliance.

4. **Method for Decision-Making:** Describe who is expected to have the authority to make what types of decisions, in what circumstances, and who reports to whom, etc.

5. **Resource Commitments:** What specific financial resources, such as cash, equity, stage payments, loan guarantees, etc., are needed for the achievement of the ultimate goals. Other "soft" resources may be in the form of licenses, knowledge, R&D, a sales force contact, production facilities, inventory, raw materials, engineering drawings, management staff, access to capital, the devotion of specific personnel for a certain percentage of their time, etc.

6. **Financial Philosophy:** "Soft" resources should be quantified with a financial figure so that a monetary value can be affixed and valued along with the cash commitments to this venture. The manner of handling cost over-runs should be agreed upon. Pricing, costing and transfer pricing procedures should be explained if applicable.

7. **Assumption of Risks and Division of Rewards:** What are the expected rewards (new product, new market, cash flow, technology, etc.?) How will the profits be divided?

> 8. **Project Specific Issues:** Who has the right to products and inventions? Who has the rights to distribute the products, services, technologies, etc.? Who gets licensing rights? If the Confidentiality and Non-Competition Agreements have not yet been drafted in final form at this point, they should be addressed in basic form here. How will agents and distributors be handled?
>
> 9. **Anticipated Structure:** This section should describe the intended structure (written contract, corporation, partnership, or equity investment, etc.)
>
> 10. **Transformation:** What do the partners foresee as the future of the alliance? How will it evolve, or unwind? Any termination provisions should be identified.
>
> **Source: ASAP,** *Strategic Alliance Best Process Workbook*

2–13 An MoU along these lines represents very much a "business" document or charter—appropriate for many collaborative alliances and ventures. In the case of a significant equity joint venture, where assets are to be contributed and more complex legal issues arise, it will generally assist subsequent contract negotiations if the parties are able to address at this initial stage the principles of other important points relating to their prospective relationship. In this scenario, the document becomes essentially a "heads of terms". The challenge is to have a serious negotiation and to outline the agreed principles but without getting unduly involved in detail more appropriate to the subsequent definitive agreements. For this purpose, the MoU or heads of terms should address, at least in principle and in a reasonably clear fashion, a number of material points relating to the proposed equity joint venture—recognising that it will often be difficult to re-negotiate, at the later stage of definitive agreements, points of principle apparently settled in the MoU or heads of terms.

2–14 Material issues to be addressed in heads of terms for an equity joint venture could include:

(1) *Parties*. Who will be the parties to the venture?

(2) *Purpose*. What is the overall purpose and scope of the venture?

(3) *Structure*. What is the likely formal structure of the venture (e.g. a jointly-owned company) subject to review in the light of further tax and financial analysis?

(4) *Equity*. What will be the equity or ownership interests of the parties in the venture?

(5) *Capital*. What will be the initial capital (including the scope of any initial asset or finance contributions)?

(6) *Future finance*. Will the parties undertake commitments (if any) to provide future financing?

(7) *Board*. What is the proposed board and management structure?

(8) *Reserved matters*. What are the principal decisions that will require the approval of the joint venture parents?

(9) *Technology*. What are the principles of any commitments to provide technology?

(10) *Non-compete*. What are the principles of any non-compete undertakings?

(11) *Warranties*. Has the broad scope (rather than detail) of any basic warranties and indemnities been agreed?

(12) *Exit provisions*. What are the principles of any particular "exit" provisions (e.g. pre-emption rights on transfer; any put or call options; any options on change of control; and/or specific termination rights)?

(13) *Deadlock*. Are there agreed mechanisms for deadlock or dispute resolution (although these will often be left for the definitive agreements)?

(14) *Confidentiality*. Will the parties give confidentiality undertakings including a requirement for mutual consent before any public announcements?

(15) *Exclusivity*. Will there be any exclusivity commitment on the parties not to negotiate, for a certain period, a similar transaction with any third party?

(16) *"Subject to contract"*. Should the MoU include a statement that (except for any confidentiality, exclusivity or non-solicitation undertakings) it is not legally binding but purely a basis for taking the venture forward and negotiating the definitive agreements?

(17) *Law*. What will be governing law of the final definitive agreements?

(18) *Conditions precedent*. Are there any major conditions precedent to be satisfied (e.g. regulatory clearances or, possibly, further due diligence) prior to commencement of the venture?

(19) *Target timetable*. Is there an agreed target for establishment of the venture and announcement of operations?

> An example of a Memorandum of Understanding for an equity joint venture is set out as Precedent 2 in Part E.

Should an MoU be legally binding?

2–15 Lawyers will generally advise against an MoU or heads of terms being legally binding-subject to the important exceptions discussed below. An MoU will rarely address points in sufficient detail, or cover all material points sufficiently comprehensively, to satisfy the standards which are necessary before a party can feel properly protected. Indeed, under English law, many terms may be void for uncertainty in any event. If an MoU is expressed to be legally binding, a party will not have the benefit of protections (such as restrictive undertakings or warranties) which may not be included at this stage. It is generally preferable for an MoU to be relatively short and expressly non-binding (except for confidentiality and any exclusivity provisions) and for detailed discussions and drafting to take place on the definitive agreements.

2–16 An important legal issue at this stage is whether or not to include an exclusivity undertaking. The English courts[2] have confirmed that exclusivity agreements, if entered into for consideration and for a defined period,[3] can create legally binding obligations which will support an injunction to prevent breach of a negative obligation not to undertake competing negotiations with a third party. This principle is limited, though. An English court will not enforce a positive obligation on a party to negotiate if it does not wish to do so.[4]

2–17 On the other hand, in international joint ventures it is important to recognise that many continental European laws (e.g. under the civil law doctrine of *culpa in contrahendo*[5]) impose a stronger test than English law and such MoUs can still give rise to liability for compensation—generally an obligation to reimburse costs—if a party does not proceed in good faith with genuine negotiations.

Due diligence

2–18 "Due diligence" and other pre-contract investigations are perhaps even more important in the case of a substantial equity joint venture than in the case of an outright corporate acquisition. Joint ventures entail ongoing relationships. It will prove extremely difficult as a commercial matter, in all but the most serious cases, to pursue warranty or other claims against a co-venturer after the commencement of the joint venture relationship; far better to be thorough in due diligence investigations prior to concluding the joint venture.

2–19 The extent and focus of "due diligence" will depend upon the nature of the contribution being made by the other party. The exercise should

---

[2] *Walford v Miles* [1992] 2 A.C. 128
[3] Or possibly a period terminable on reasonable notice—see *Global Container Limes Ltd v Black Sea Shipping Co* (1997) (unreported, 14 July 1997)
[4] The court in *Walford v Miles* referred to ". . . a duty to negotiate in good faith. Such a duty. . . cannot be imposed. . . An obligation to negotiate in good faith is. . . unworkable in practice. . ."
[5] See para.20–13 et seq.

concentrate on the key assets of the other party which are required to achieve the business objectives of the client; e.g.: technology/IPR; client/customer base; suppliers; brand names; land/buildings/facilities; major existing contracts; personnel; regulatory licences. Where it is a whole business which is being contributed by the other party to an equity joint venture, then the "due diligence" exercise will be comparable to that for a corporate acquisition. A wide range of issues may need to be investigated by the client or its professional team. Separate (but co-ordinated) investigations may include:

(a) *commercial*: investigating all relevant commercial aspects of the business being contributed: products, markets, distribution, suppliers, risk management, IT etc.;

(b) *financial*: including a review of current management accounts relating to the business to be contributed; profitability of any major contracts being brought into the venture; identifying all relevant intra-group management and similar charges or cost allocations; assessing any material differences in accounting policies between the parties;

(c) *legal*: including investigation of:
 — title to key assets and properties (including identifying any material encumbrances);
 — material contracts (including identifying contracts where any third party consent is required to transfer the benefit of the contract into the venture or the third party is entitled to trigger a right of termination upon a "change of control");
 — litigation or claims involving the assets or business being contributed (including infringement actions or any product liability claims);
 — regulatory licences held (including actual or potential claims of regulatory non-compliance or any regulatory investigations);
 — identifying any other liabilities, claims, commitments or laws which reduce the value or use of key assets being contributed;

(d) *technology*: evaluation of the technology assets; material IP/IT licences "in" and "out"; registration or protection policy for new know-how, patents and brand names; research and development facilities; infringement claims (past and current);

(e) *land/buildings/facilities*: examining the physical condition of the site and key production equipment and facilities; development plans; planning conditions and constraints;

(f) *environmental/health and safety*: investigating compliance with environmental and health and safety legislation (including potential liabilities or compliance costs faced by the business);

(g) *employees/personnel benefits*: reviewing key personnel contracts; remuneration and benefits packages; funding of pension schemes; labour agreements; comparison of the parties' respective arrangements with employees generally;

(h) *tax*: reviewing tax status; tax returns; any disputes with tax authorities; potential tax charges within the joint venture.

The approach to "legal" due diligence should be developed with the client—and with the other party where each is contributing substantial assets. Care should be taken to dovetail with, and not duplicate, other investigations being undertaken by the client and/or other specialists.

> **An example of an outline Legal Due Diligence Questionnaire for an equity joint venture is included as Precedent 3 in Part E.**

2–20 The "due diligence" exercise will need to be adapted to the circumstances of the venture—and the relationship which may already exist between the parties. A full exercise of this kind, for instance, will often not be appropriate for a start-up joint venture or a short-term collaboration to undertake a works project. The way due diligence is handled may also be less aggressive in style than a corresponding exercise prior to an acquisition. Whilst warranties and indemnities may be negotiated in the agreements, prior awareness and knowledge is nevertheless by far the preferable objective before entering into a substantial joint venture. "Due diligence" is an important stage in the preparation for a venture.

2–21 It is more satisfactory and usual, at least in the UK, for due diligence to be undertaken prior to signing a binding joint venture agreement. In some situations, where it is impracticable to obtain all necessary information prior to commitment, it may be agreed that due diligence—perhaps in defined areas—can be undertaken between signing of the initial contract and completion with a satisfactory outcome of due diligence by the relevant part(ies) being a condition precedent of completion. This leaves significant uncertainty but may be the only practical route in some circumstances.

Understanding the local regime

2–22 If the activities of a joint venture are to be based principally in a foreign jurisdiction, or if the jointly-owned vehicle is to be established in a foreign jurisdiction, it is clearly important to be aware of the basic legal framework which will affect that joint venture. Issues to be addressed in these circumstances are discussed further in chapter 20.

2–23 In the case of an equity venture based in one of the developing market countries for instance, it will generally be important to understand, at least in broad terms, the current laws and regulations which apply in the following areas:

(a) any limits on foreign participation;

(b) regulatory approvals/foreign investment controls;

(c) repatriation of profits and capital;

(d) any currency or foreign exchange controls;

(e) taxation of the venture's operations;

(f) any maximum debt/equity ratio;

(g) corporate governance and management structure (including any restriction on nationality of directors);

(h) investment incentives (including any tax exemptions, free trade zones, availability of government loans or guarantees);

(i) any restrictions affecting the terms of technology transfer;

(j) rights to acquire land and the regime for ownership of real estate;

(k) intellectual property protection;

(l) labour laws.

Early investigation of the basic legal framework in the "local" jurisdiction, and appointment of reliable legal advisers in that jurisdiction, will almost certainly be a necessary early step in any international joint venture.

Third party consents and clearances

2–24 It is vital to identify at an early stage the specific consents and clearances which will be required from third parties in order to establish the joint venture or alliance. These should include consents required for carrying out any business reorganisation or other preparatory step prior to establishing the venture. Equally important, the principal negotiators will need a realistic timetable for obtaining these consents and clearances and an assessment of any potential difficulties. This timetable will have a real impact on the timing and progress of the venture negotiations.

2–25 The following is a checklist of possible consents which may be required:

(1) *Regulatory/competition*. Joint ventures and alliances frequently require regulatory approval and it is important to review at an early stage the likely regulatory impact on any venture. Chapter 16 discusses these in greater detail. Regulatory approvals may include particularly:

(a) *Merger control*. Notification or approval requirements may apply under regulations (both national and/or European) for the control of mergers especially where the venture involves the combination of existing activities carried on by the co-venturers. Substantial equity joint ventures can fall within the EC Merger Regulation and must not be implemented until approval is obtained.

(b) *Restrictive or anti-competitive agreements.* Many countries (e.g. the UK under the Competition Act 1998) regulate agreements which contain excessive restrictions on independent competitive action by the parties. Joint ventures and alliances (taken with ancillary arrangements such as licensing or supply arrangements) frequently need to be reviewed in this context.

(c) *Foreign investment controls.* In many countries, particularly in developing markets, participation by a foreign company in a venture will require prior approval under foreign investment laws of the "local" jurisdiction in which the venture is to be based.

(2) *Industry-specific approvals.* Many countries regulate (often through a licensing procedure) the admission or conduct of participants engaged in those industries. Examples of industry-specific regulation in the UK include: banking; insurance; financial services; electricity/water/gas/telecoms; oil exploration; broadcasting; and consumer credit business. Approvals will generally be required in the UK (and many other countries) for joint ventures in these industries—whether it is a case of a start-up venture, a new entity acquiring the business carried on by one or more of the participants or an existing entity which incurs a "change of control" upon the formation of the joint venture. These situations will usually entail either a need for approval to an assignment of a licence (or the issue of a new licence) or confirmation that any right to revoke an existing licence will not be exercised.

(3) *Export controls.* Many countries impose strict controls on the transfer of specific technologies or equipment—either generally or to particular countries. A joint venture involving such a transfer of technology will invariably fall within this regime. In the UK, a system of export licensing applies under the Export Control Act 2002 and regulations made thereunder.[6]

(4) *Stock exchange/shareholders.* A company (particularly a company whose securities are listed on a public stock exchange) will need to consider whether the establishment of the particular venture requires prior approval from its shareholders and/or stock exchange,[7] or involves mandatory notification requirements.

---

[6] See, in particular, the Export of Goods, Transfer of Technology and Provision of Technical Assistance (Control) Order 2003 (SI 2003/2764) and the Trade in Goods (Control) Order 2003 (SI 2003/2765). An EU general export authorisation for dual-use items (i.e. those which can be used for both civil and military purposes) may also be applicable pursuant to Council Regulation (EC) 1334/2000.

[7] The treatment of joint ventures for this purpose is sometimes complex—being potentially a transaction comprising an "acquisition" or a "disposal" or both, depending on the particular circumstances. There is no formal guidance from the UK Listing Authority but generally:

(5) *Financing/borrowings*. A company will need to consider whether the venture involves a transaction (e.g. a disposal of the whole or part of its assets to a third party, namely the joint venture company) which requires the prior consent of lenders or trustees under the terms of any existing loan agreements, debenture stocks or trust deeds.

(6) *Contracts/customers*. A party entering a joint venture will, as a commercial matter, wish to consider the impact of the venture on existing customer or supply arrangements. If existing contracts need to be assigned, the consent of counterparties to relevant contracts will usually be required. Similarly, even if there is no change in legal identity of the contracting party itself, the setting up of a joint venture may involve a change of control of that party such as to give rise to a right of termination by the counterparty under the terms of the relevant contract. It will generally be important to obtain reassurance from that counterparty that any such right of termination will not be exercised. The issues raised by the need in a joint venture for counterparty consents in relation to commercial contracts are similar to those raised on a sale and purchase of a business. In practice, it can often be appropriate to separate the contracts into different groupings:

(a) major contracts where the consent of the counterparty is of such importance that obtaining that party's consent (or confirmation that it will be forthcoming) should be a condition precedent of the joint venture going ahead;

(b) contracts where it is advisable in due course "to get the paperwork right" and to obtain the counterparty's consent and/or to effect a formal assignment or novation in order to vest the legal rights and obligations fully in the new joint venture entity;

(c) contracts which technically require counterparty consent but where it is not considered practicable or necessary to seek those consents and where it is judged that implementing the contract in the new circumstances after the joint venture is established is extremely unlikely to give rise to any problem. In many cases, once the contract is being implemented by the parties in knowledge of the new circumstances, an effective waiver by "course of conduct" will under English law estop the counter-

---

(a) in a two party venture where A (the UK listed company) and B each contribute assets and obtain 60:40 respective equity shares in the JVC, A is usually regarded as having made an acquisition of B's contribution to the joint venture (but not a disposal of A's contribution); and (b) in the same situation but where A and B's equity shares are 50:50 and it is a deadlocked JVC, A is regarded as having made an acquisition of one-half of B's contribution to the JVC and as having made a disposal of one-half of its own contribution. The Class 1 test is satisfied if the assets disposed of (or acquired) on the establishment of the joint venture represent at least 25 per cent of the listed company's gross assets or 25 per cent of its profits or turnover if the consideration for the interest disposed of (or acquired) represents at least 25 per cent of its market capitalisation. However, the application of these tests is not straightforward (or indeed always consistent as to when the whole or part of the JVC's assets or turnover is taken into account) and the UK Listing Authority should be consulted in cases of doubt.

party from asserting any breach; this is not a pure legal solution but a practical approach. In some cases, it may be appropriate to establish provisions in the joint venture agreement for payment of compensation if the benefit of a particular contract cannot be "contributed to" or vested in the joint venture.

(7) *Taxation.* The structuring of the joint venture will often involve significant tax planning. This may well entail the need to obtain specific clearances or rulings from tax authorities. These issues are addressed more specifically in chapter 15.

(8) *Employees.* The parties will also need to review any requirement for consultation with employees or trade union representatives under any employment legislation[8] or under any agreements with unions or arrangements establishing works councils—see chapter 18.

2–26 It is important to establish a clear timetable and responsibility for making applications for consents, together with an anticipated timetable for receiving them and a contingency plan if those consents are not obtained. Material third party consents will form part of the critical path for any major joint venture.

Choosing the legal form of the venture

2–27 A crucial aspect of the planning stage will be the choice of legal form for the joint venture or alliance structure. What type of joint venture vehicle is appropriate and where should it be located or registered? The answers to these questions will be influenced by a variety of commercial, legal, tax, regulatory and accounting considerations. Key factors are likely to include:

(a) tax costs;
(b) regulatory requirements;
(c) ease of setting up;
(d) ease of termination or unwind;
(e) nature of the board or management structure;
(f) administration cost;
(g) reporting and publicity requirements; and
(h) accounting treatment.

2–28 At the structuring stage, tax planning is likely to be needed—both as to choice of joint venture vehicle and jurisdiction and other structuring

---

[8] See, in the UK, the Information and Consultation of Employees Regulations 2004 (SI 2004/3426) and the Transfer of Undertakings (Protection of Employment) Regulations 2006 (SI 2006/246). Similar laws apply in other European countries.

arrangements. Early involvement of tax advisers will be essential. Tax planning may entail the need to obtain specific clearances or rulings from tax authorities. Chapter 15 addresses tax issues in more detail.

2–29 In choosing the legal form, much may depend on whether it is an "equity" joint venture or not. If it is, the legal form is likely to be some form of corporate entity or, possibly, a partnership. If it is a "non-equity" alliance, a purely contractual arrangement is likely to be sufficient. However, variations exist within each of these basic legal forms. Chapter 3 discusses these issues in greater detail. In many cases, the nature of the joint venture structure will be clear. In other cases, it will entail detailed planning, and particularly tax planning, over a range of jurisdictions. In these cases, the challenge for the lawyers will be to provide options which are cost efficient and yet provide a workable and credible vehicle to meet the commercial objectives.

Valuation of contributions

Valuation methodology

2–30 Where business assets or technology are being contributed by one or both parties to an equity joint venture, an important part of the commercial negotiations will be agreeing the valuation, or method of valuation, of that contribution. There is no universally accepted method. The valuation methodology will be essentially a commercial matter:

(a) in some cases, it will be appropriate for valuation to concentrate solely on the net asset value of the tangible assets being contributed by each party;

(b) in others, a business-based methodology relating to the contributed assets will be appropriate such as a valuation based on an appropriate multiple of profitability (price/earnings (PE) ratio) or on earnings before interest and tax (EBIT or EBITDA) or by reference to a discounted cash flow (DCF) analysis;

(c) strategic or synergy benefits (e.g. cost savings) may also need to be taken into account;

(d) more intangible factors relating to the value of each party's overall contribution to the venture may also be relevant (such as party's contact network or particular expertise).

In some cases, inclusion of a "control premium" may be an appropriate factor in the valuation to recognise the commercial reality of the transaction if one party is effectively acquiring control of the venture. In other cases (particularly a 50:50 joint venture), the avoidance of paying any "control premium" may be one of the attractions of going the route of an equity joint venture compared with an outright acquisition.

2–31 Valuation negotiations are not an exact science. They depend heavily on the attitudes of each party to the venture. Some will attempt to negotiate a hard bargain to protect their company's financial interests; others may take a broader view of the benefits to be anticipated from a successful alliance and the interests of future goodwill and co-operation. In most cases, valuation will ultimately be a matter for commercial negotiation between the parties; in others, it may be agreed that valuation of each party's contribution should be undertaken by an independent expert. In some transactions, it will be appropriate to involve outside financial advisers to assist in the complex and sensitive valuation negotiations. This will usually be necessary where a publicly-listed company is entering into a major joint venture in order to ensure that the transaction is fair in terms of value for its shareholders.

2–32 Where the valuation of a party's contribution is made by reference to the value of the net assets being contributed, questions the parties may consider include the following:

(1) Should the valuation simply be based on past expenditure by the contributing party in acquiring and developing those assets (which may be an appropriate method in the case of valuing technology) on the basis that this is what a third party would have to spend if starting from scratch?

(2) Is it advisable to have an audit exercise undertaken at the commencement of the joint venture in order to have a precise valuation (according to agreed accounting principles) of tangible assets as at that date?

(3) Is it sufficient or appropriate, perhaps, to have a commitment that the net asset value of the business being contributed will be "not less than £X", with an undertaking of the contributing party to inject further cash funds into the joint venture if, following a completion audit, this minimum net asset test is not met?

2–33 Legal rules which can apply on a valuation of asset contributions to a joint venture include the following:

(1) English law (and many other jurisdictions) require that shares should not be issued at a discount—see s.580 Companies Act 2006. It is therefore necessary for the directors of a JVC to be satisfied that any non-cash assets being contributed to the company (including the benefit of any undertakings or rights relating to the future provision of technology) are worth at least the nominal value of the shares in the JVC being issued in exchange.

(2) There will often be a legal requirement for independent valuation where shares of a company are issued in exchange for non-cash consideration. If the JVC is a public company, under English law

there will be a requirement for an independent valuation and report by virtue of s.593 of the Companies Act 2006. However, more stringent substantive and procedural requirements applicable to non-cash contributions are required in many civil law countries, such as France and Germany.

(3) In many jurisdictions, particularly in many developing market countries, there are regulations (e.g. requirements of local banking or regulatory authorities) which apply where an interest in a joint venture is being "paid for" by non-cash contributions from a foreign party. In these cases, the non-cash contribution will often need to be independently valued and supported; e.g. the requirement for valuation by state-licensed valuers in countries such as China or Russia.

2–34 In many equity joint venture situations, it will not be the absolute value of a party's contribution which is important but the difference in value between the relative contributions of each of the different parties. The task will then be to value the gap between the different contributions and decide the consequences for equity ownership. One obvious possibility is simply to adjust the equity shares of the parties in proportion to the value of their respective contributions. In many cases, though, the parties may decide to proceed with a 50:50 ownership structure in the belief that this will create a stronger venture relationship; the task will then be to agree mechanisms to "equalise" the valuation gap.

Equalisation measures

2–35 A number of different mechanisms are potentially available to effect equalisation. Much will depend, of course, on the individual circumstances but measures can include the following:

(1) *Equalisation payment.* The most direct method of equalisation is an agreed payment between the co-venturers; e.g. if A's contribution to a 50:50 owned JVC is agreed to be worth £10 million more than B's contribution, then B would make a direct payment of £5 million to A. Tax considerations may affect this route; also, of course, the issue of whether or not cash is available to B to make such a payment.

(2) *Cash contribution.* Alternatively, in the above example, B could inject in cash a further £10 million into the assets of the JVC in order to equalise the values of the respective contributions of the parties to the JVC.

(3) *Debt rather than equity.* Even if equity in the joint venture is held 50:50, there is no reason why party A should not have a greater debt owing from the JVC (in exchange for its asset contribution) than party B. Issues which need to be resolved in relation to any such debt will include rate of interest, subordination and repayment terms. A

similar method is the use of a separate class of non-voting preference shares to be held by the party making the greater value contribution in respect of its "excess"—see also chapter 7 below.

(4) *Borrowing by the JVC.* Where the capital structure and financing capacity of the JVC permits, one route is for an amount equal to the "excess" to be borrowed by the JVC from outside banking sources and to be paid to the relevant contributing party by way of purchase price for the "excess" assets. This may, of course, reduce the borrowing capacity of the JVC for other purposes and be commercially undesirable.

(5) *Management/service charges.* It may be possible for A to extract sums from the JVC in the form of extra charges for management or other administrative services or royalties for technology licensed to the JVC. Difficulties are likely to be tax considerations and the need to justify the charges as being genuine and not equivalent to dividend distributions; also it does not enable A to receive value immediately.

(6) *Leasing of assets/adjustment of assets.* It may be possible to adjust the respective asset contributions of the parties in order to achieve greater equalisation of value. This will usually be an imperfect mechanism. Adjustments could include:

— leasing by A to the JVC of assets which would otherwise have been fully transferred (e.g. land or intellectual property rights); contribution by B to the JVC of additional assets (e.g. additional operating assets which would otherwise have remained outside the joint venture);

— retention by A outside the JVC of assets which are not essential to the JVC.

(7) *Disproportionate distribution of dividends.* One possibility for eliminating the valuation gap over time is to establish different entitlements as between the joint venture parties to dividends from the profits of the JVC, particularly during an initial period. The way in which this is structured will depend on the corporate laws of the JVC; for instance, it may be desirable to create a separate class of shares for party A with special dividend rights.

Principal Legal Documents

Joint venture documentation

2–36 An important part of the lawyer's role in joint venture transactions will include the drafting and preparation of the legal agreements required to establish the venture. They provide the legal infrastructure for the joint venture. These transactions require clear, well-drafted documentation. There may be sufficient difficulties in communication, language and negotiations between the parties without these difficulties being compounded by badly drafted documentation which can delay or hinder negotiations. It is important, as part of the transaction planning, to have a clear understanding of the principal documentation likely to be involved.

Joint venture agreement

2–37 The nature of the principal documentation for each legal form of joint venture or alliance is addressed in more detail in chapters 3, 4 and 5. It will basically comprise the following:

(1) Contractual alliance. This legal form will simply be based on the contract between the parties.

(2) Partnership. A partnership structure will centre on a partnership agreement.

(3) Corporate joint venture. In the case of a corporate joint venture, the basic documents will be a joint venture agreement or shareholders' agreement together with the relevant constitutional documents establishing the joint venture company (JVC).

In the UK the terms "joint venture agreement" and "shareholders' agreement" are often used interchangeably. The term "joint venture agreement" may in practice be more frequently used if it contains wider provisions relating to the initial establishment of the JVC, conditions precedent and the business contributions of the parties—with a "shareholders' agreement" describing an agreement focusing on the ongoing relationship between the parties as shareholders in the JVC. In some jurisdictions, the term "joint venture agreement" connotes an initial outline or formation agreement entered into before the definitive shareholders' or other agreements at the time of formal establishment of the venture. For practical purposes, the terms are used interchangeably in this book in relation to a corporate joint venture.

Framework agreement

2–38 In many complex joint ventures it can be a useful technique to have a framework agreement (or similarly named document) to set out the overall basis for the establishment of the venture. In these cases, it can often be useful, both for drafting and for commercial negotiation, to distinguish between:

(a) the arrangements for setting up the joint venture vehicle itself—to be contained in a framework agreement or, in some jurisdictions, a separate contribution agreement; and

(b) matters relating to the ongoing relationship of the parties after formation of the venture—to be contained, in the case of a JVC, in the shareholders' agreement.

2–39 If two businesses are being brought together in a jointly-owned company (JVC), the overall framework agreement for establishing the JVC may for instance deal with such issues as:

(a) transfer of the relevant businesses (or companies containing those businesses) by each party to the new JVC;

(b) the issue of shares on completion by the JVC to the joint venture parties;

(c) any principles for valuing each party's contribution and terms for equalising any shortfall;

(d) warranties and indemnities;

(e) conditions precedent, such as regulatory clearances;

(f) undertakings regarding conduct of the business of each party prior to completion; and

(g) procedures for completion and execution in agreed form of supporting legal documents (including the shareholders' agreement and any ancillary agreements or corporate resolutions required on completion).

These items could equally be included in an overall joint venture or shareholders' agreement but it often makes sense to split them into separate documents since they deal with different phases of the transaction. In many cases, though, it will simply be a matter of drafting style and preference.

Sale and purchase agreement

2–40 The establishment of the joint venture may take the form of converting an existing company with existing assets and operations into a JVC rather than creating a new company. The transaction will then involve either:

(a) the new party (B) acquiring a proportion (say 50 per cent) of the issued share capital held by the existing owner (A) of that company; and/or

(b) the new party (B) directly subscribing for and acquiring new shares in the capital of the company (the JVC) such that, after its subscription for shares, B will hold the agreed percentage of the overall share capital of the JVC.

2–41 A transaction with this structure will require:

(a) a "sale and purchase agreement" for the sale of the shares by A to B—which is likely to be an agreement in a traditional form for such transactions with warranties, indemnities, conditions precedent, pre-completion undertakings, pricing provisions and other terms appropriate for a share sale and purchase agreement; and/or

(b) a "subscription agreement" between B and the JVC for the allotment and issue of the new shares—to which the existing owner (A) is likely also to be a party giving appropriate warranties and indemnities directly to B in relation to the existing affairs of the JVC.

In each case, on completion of the acquisition and/or subscription of shares, a shareholders' agreement between A and B relating to their relationship in the JVC will come into effect in the same way as if the JVC had been newly formed. The constitutional documents of the JVC will be appropriately altered and the board of directors restructured to reflect the joint venture arrangements.

Business plan

2–42 The business plan is not, in itself, a legal document, and failure to achieve future objectives will rarely give rise to a legal claim between the parties. However, it can be an important document to ensure that the joint venture parties are "singing from the same hymn-sheet" and share common and clear objectives for the venture. It is therefore often specifically referred to and identified in the joint venture agreement. There is no established practice in relation to matters to be included in a joint venture business plan. One outline suggestion[9] follows.

BUSINESS PLAN: SUMMARY

1. **General Overview**
   - Statement of JVC objectives.
   - Summary of shareholding structure, organisation and management of JVC.
   - Description of intended manufacturing and sales activities. Products and market analyses. Competitor analysis. Estimates of turnover in years 1 to 5.

---

[9] Simon Berger, *International Joint Ventures* (London: Financial Times/Prentice Hall, 1999)

- Corporate development plan—five-year period. Strategies for growth and acquisition. Factory, premises and asset analyses. Employee and manpower requirements. SWOT analysis—strengths, weaknesses, opportunities, threats.

2. **Specific financial projections**

    - Opening balance sheet. Parties' asset contributions—any deferred contributions. Shareholder loans at commencement.

    - Sales turnover projection—years 1 and 2.
      Capital expenditure projections—years 1 and 2
      Projected expenses of business—years 1 and 2.

    - Projected profit and loss account—year 1.
      Closing balance sheet—end of year 1.
      Funds flow statement—year 1.

    - Working capital projections—years 1 and 2.
      Liquidity analysis for years 1 and 2.
      Required shareholders' loans—years 1 and 2.

3. **Appendices**

    - Site description.

    - Plant and equipment.

Source: Simon Berger, *International Joint Ventures*

A well-developed and forward-looking business plan "owned" by both parties can reduce significantly the risk of subsequent disputes and deadlock—particularly if the plan addresses issues such as policy for new business opportunities, anticipated funding needs and plans, dividend policy and application of any surplus cash.

Ancillary contracts

2–43 The discussion so far has concentrated on the principal documents relating to the joint venture vehicle itself. Equally important will often be the ancillary contracts to be concluded at the same time. These will substantially affect the legal relationship between the joint venture parties and the joint venture vehicle. For instance, agreements of the following kind may well be an integral part of the overall joint venture relationship:

(a) asset transfer agreement, or contribution agreement, relating to the transfer of assets to the JVC;

(b) supply agreements relating to raw materials, components or services for JVC;

(c) purchase agreements relating to "off-take" of products or services from the JVC;

(d) technology licence for the provision of technology and know-how to the JVC;

(e) licence of trade marks;

(f) agreement for provision of management and/or administrative services (sometimes on a transitional basis);

(g) lease or transfer of land; and

(h) secondment agreements relating to staff.

The issues relating to such agreements are covered in greater detail in legal textbooks appropriate to these specific types of transaction. Chapter 6 discusses some of the particular issues which have to be considered in a joint venture context. They can be crucial to the overall commercial arrangements relating to the joint venture or alliance.

Importance of contract negotiations and documentation

2–44 Joint venture or alliance agreements establish the legal framework for the ongoing collaboration between the parties. They are therefore important and require serious management attention. "What if ..." questions, if sensible and not too remote in the context of the particular venture, can be constructive. Contract plays a vital part in formation of joint ventures and alliances. Its role is not only to establish the legal framework—the actual process of negotiating and agreeing the contract documentation can itself generate value:

(a) the negotiations can be an important part of the process whereby the parties build a firm basis for their future business relationship; and

(b) the contract terms or principles will, at the least, create an expectation for each party that they will be followed and provide a guidance for their future behaviour in relation to the venture—irrespective of any question of legal enforcement.

Each of these roles can be of value—and particularly so in a joint venture or alliance relationship.

2–45 Therefore, rather than simply leaving the joint venture contract as something for "the lawyers to sort out", the most constructive approach is for the parties to use the contract to help build the alliance. It is suggested that this approach requires the following ingredients:

(1) *Treat the contract seriously*. Recognise that the contract must deal with many issues which are core to the success of the alliance arrangements including: purpose and scope of the alliance; contributions and funding commitments; governance and management structure; alloca-

tion of risks and rewards; rights to technology; and contingency protections for termination.

(2) *Establish an appropriate negotiating team.* Don't just leave contract negotiations to the lawyers. Most ventures and alliances call for a co-ordinated and multi-disciplinary team including: a senior management representative of the joint venture "parent"; alliance operational executives who will "own" their creation; and lawyers (and other professionals) as support advisers but as part of the team. In most cases, the lawyer should not be the key negotiator.

(3) *Keep a consistent negotiating team.* Joint ventures can take a long time to negotiate and establish. Consistency at the core of the negotiating team helps build trust and "relationship capital" with the other party.

(4) *Negotiate with a constructive mindset.* Avoid an excessive deal-making approach. Joint ventures and alliances are different from acquisitions in the vitally important respect that the contract is the beginning, not the end, of the relationship. The approach should be co-operative and not adversarial. Whilst a party should be firm, it is vital to listen—and be fair. Recognise that the client has an interest in the ongoing success of the joint venture or alliance. As one commentator[10] graphically observes:

> "This is very hard fare for lawyers, who view their role as gladiators, charged with extracting every ounce of profit and advantage for a client. In discharging their professional responsibilities, many lawyers unintentionally foster a spirit of distrust and paranoia, which is quite the opposite of what the prospective allies need."

Putting it a different way: "It is far more important to determine if 1 + 1 = 3 than to 'squeeze the last concessions' out of an opponent."[11]

(5) *Keep the contract language clear and commercial.* Sometimes easier said than done—but for most ventures greater value will be obtained by keeping the language of the contract relatively simple and commercial and (as far as practical) positive. Stress what the parties aim to achieve, what each will do, how they will communicate and promote the venture. Language is particularly important in a cross-border international alliance. Avoid the danger of over-lawyering the agreement. It is important that the contract is expressed in language which the parties can understand—and therefore "own" the principles set out in the contract. A balance has to be achieved between being "too loose" and "too detailed."

(6) *Use the contract as a building block.* The process of contract negotiating can itself create value. Contract negotiations can help the parties get used to working together. Problem-solving together is a key

---

[10] Julian Gesser, *Strategic Alliance Mediation* (Association of Strategic Alliance Professionals).
[11] Association of Strategic Alliance Professionals, *Strategic Alliance Best Process Workbook*.

alliance skill. Constructive negotiations help build communication between the parties and a mutual sense of commitment and trust. Successful negotiations can help build momentum, confidence and create "relationship capital".

Conversely, careful contract negotiations can help flush out problems which could later endanger the relationship if left undiscovered. They can assist the parties to counter many of the potential problems which lead to failure for many joint ventures and alliances such as: (i) poor preparation and not enough upfront effort; (ii) unequal expectations or lack of clarity of objectives; (iii) uncertainty as to future financing requirements or expectations; (iv) lack of communication; or (v) lack of commitment.

2–46 Contract negotiations, and the way in which they are approached, therefore have an important role in building the alliance. It is no doubt true that a joint venture or alliance will not succeed or fail because of the quality of the legal agreements—but constructive contract negotiations can create a firmer foundation for the venture and improve the chances of success. The lawyer can be an important member of that contract negotiating team.

Chapter 3

Choosing the legal form

A "joint venture" is not a legal term of art. There are few jurisdictions in which it is a defined form of legal relationship. Businessmen use the terms "joint ventures", "alliances" and "partnerships" in a loose sense. These terms reflect a business strategy of collaboration. This business strategy can be pursued in a number of different legal forms. A broad range of potential vehicles exist worldwide for structuring joint ventures and alliances. This chapter examines some of the key issues in deciding the legal form for a particular venture.

Basic legal categories

3–01 The legal forms for joint ventures and alliances can most easily be classified into the following basic formal categories:

(a) contractual alliances;

(b) partnerships;

(c) corporate joint ventures.

In some jurisdictions, the lines between these various categories may be difficult to draw in relation to particular legal forms—but this categorisation is an appropriate starting point. There also exist a number of "hybrid" structures or arrangements which it is convenient to bring together separately later in this chapter.

KEY ISSUES

Key issues in deciding the legal form

3–02 In many cases, the legal form of the joint venture or alliance "vehicle" and the location of any joint venture entity will be clear from the circumstances of the venture. In others, it will require careful and imaginative planning. In these more complex cases, decisions will be influenced by a variety of commercial, legal, tax, regulatory and accounting considerations. Key issues, particularly in relation to an international joint venture involving assets and/or parties in different jurisdictions, include the following:

(1) *Liability exposure.* Is it important for the parties to have the benefit of limited liability which a corporate entity for the venture will generally provide—or is this, in practice, not a material concern?

(2) *Tax cost.* Tax will frequently influence the choice of structure, particularly in the case of an international venture. What will be the tax costs in relation to: establishment of the joint venture? ongoing operations of the joint venture? repatriation of profits? financing and interest payments? These and other related issues are addressed in more detail in chapter 15.

(3) *Nationality considerations.* In the case of a joint venture or alliance with operations in different jurisdictions, are there national considerations—e.g. arising from political profile, tax costs or identity of the participants—which lead to a preferred structure of direct participation by the "national" companies and structuring the venture through a contractual linking of the joint operations? Possibly, an overall structure of parallel joint venture vehicles in different jurisdictions, or in different fields, may be appropriate rather than a single joint venture company with subsidiaries.

(4) *Competition law factors.* The regulatory treatment of the joint venture may vary depending on the structure. There may be advantage, for instance, in structuring the venture as a "full-function" joint venture in order to fall within the one-stop clearance regime of the EC Merger Regulation—or structuring the terms of the alliance (e.g. a research and development collaboration) so as to fall within one of the accepted exemptions. Chapter 16 addresses these issues.

(5) *"Local" jurisdiction requirements.* Do regulations or customs in the "local" jurisdiction applicable to foreign investment effectively require a certain type of entity—either to conduct business or to hold a requisite form of licence? If a jointly-owned venture requires a relevant regulatory licence, a distinct corporate entity may be required.

(6) *Management structure.* Is it desirable to have a legal form (e.g. a company) which has an entity with which senior management can clearly identify and which can have its own separate employment structure? Or is it preferable to have flexibility and for each party to have greater control over the management of its own resources which a contractual alliance generally offers?

(7) *Funding cost.* Will a particular structure reduce the cost of financing the venture? Is it better for a separate joint venture entity to be located in a jurisdiction where it can itself raise finance cost-efficiently—or is financing more efficiently raised by the parties in

their own or other jurisdictions? Should the venture be structured through a limited liability entity which may enable operations to be independently funded on a non-recourse basis? Chapter 7 addresses some of these issues.

(8) *Accounting treatment*. How will the assets and liabilities, and profits and losses, of the venture be reflected in the accounts of the joint venture parties (or their parents)? For instance, in the case of a UK parent, is it desirable—or acceptable—for the results to be consolidated as a "subsidiary undertaking" or is it preferred to achieve a form of "equity accounting"? Is it preferable to avoid debt of the joint venture entity being consolidated on the parent group's balance sheet? The nature of the joint venture vehicle and the parties' percentage interests therein may affect this accounting treatment. Chapter 19 addresses these accounting issues.

(9) *Transferability*. Is it preferable to have a structure (usually involving a separate corporate entity) which could in due course enable one party to transfer its interest, or new participants to be introduced, without legally disrupting the ownership and running of the underlying business?

(10) *Ease of termination and unwind*. Is it desirable to adopt a legal form such as a contractual alliance—which enables the venture easily to be terminated if a party becomes dissatisfied or wishes to "exit" or which enables the venture to be wound-up easily if it fails or completes its purpose?

(11) *Reporting and publicity requirements*. Is it important or desirable to use a legal form which does not involve any material financial reporting or public filing requirements (e.g. avoiding the requirement to file annual accounts applicable to a UK limited company)?

(12) *Administrative cost*. Is it unduly burdensome to adopt a legal form which will involve ongoing administrative requirements imposed by statute (e.g. the preparation and filing of annual accounts, annual return, keeping of statutory records and other statutory requirements normally applicable to a limited company)?

(13) *Formalities of formation*. Is it desirable to have a structure which can be set up quickly without undue formality or costs of registration (which a corporate venture may involve)?

The weighting to be given to each factor will vary from venture to venture. It is important to adopt a legal structure appropriate for the commercial requirements of the particular venture. In many cases a corporate joint venture will provide the identity, permanence and integration commercially required; in other cases, a corporate joint venture may be unduly cumbersome to govern and operate (or unravel) for the kind of flexible alliance contemplated by the parties.

3–03 One importance of the chosen "legal" vehicle is that this choice affects the level of customised drafting necessary to establish the desired "business" relationship. The particular legal form will have its own framework and involve a number of background rules which will apply in default of any customised drafting.

(1) A corporate entity invariably comes with a statutory code of corporate laws governing, with varying degrees of flexibility, the structure of the company. Formal constitutional documents will be required to establish the entity.

(2) A partnership usually brings into play a background statutory code (although more limited than for a corporate entity) which will apply in default of any customised rules. A partnership will involve certain general partnership law principles.

(3) A contractual alliance is formed purely by the contractual agreement between the parties. The specific contract terms adopted by the parties operate against a background of the general law of contract.

3–04 These background rules can—subject to any customised drafting—affect the legal principles in a number of areas crucial to the business relationship, for instance:

(a) the governance and management structure and division of powers between the "owners" and the "managers" of the business;

(b) rights of the individual parties (or their representatives) to bind the joint entity or alliance in respect of debts and obligations incurred during transactions with third parties;

(c) any fiduciary duties owed between the respective participants in the venture (or to the joint venture entity);

(d) the ability of a party to transfer its shares or interest in the joint venture to a third party;

(e) rights to terminate or wind-up the venture; and

(f) ease or ability to introduce new participants into the venture.

The legal form chosen for the venture will, similarly, dictate the basic form of documentation required to establish the relationship—particularly if a corporate entity is selected, with its statutory requirements for incorporation and articles of association (or by-laws). Choosing a vehicle which involves an inappropriate legal framework or set of default rules can increase the cost and time associated with joint venture formation.

CONTRACTUAL ALLIANCE

3–05 An unincorporated alliance, based on a simple contract between the parties detailing their co-operation, will suffice for many collaborative ventures and projects. (In this book, we tend to use the term "alliance" rather than "joint venture" for this legal form.) This form does not involve the creation of an independent legal entity. Such an arrangement usually involves the sharing of costs and resources, and sometimes income, on terms which do not give rise to a legal "partnership". However, beware if the arrangements do include the sharing of net profit or loss—this will commonly give rise to a partnership in law in many jurisdictions.

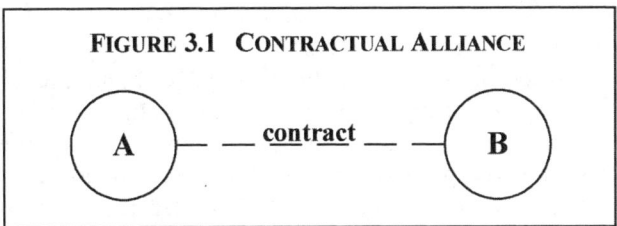

Advantages/disadvantages of a contractual alliance

3–06 A contractual alliance has a number of potential advantages and disadvantages. It will rarely, though, be an appropriate medium for the parties if they wish to establish a full "equity" joint venture. The advantages of a contractual alliance can include:

(1) *Lack of formality*. The lack of formality in forming, administering, revising and/or ending the venture.

(2) *Tax efficiency*. In many cases, greater tax efficiency can be achieved through such a structure by reason of its tax "transparency". Expenditure will be incurred directly by the alliance parties (and capable of being set off against their own profits) rather than through a separate limited company. This "transparency" may be particularly valuable if losses are expected in the early years of the venture and the parties wish to have the benefit of those losses or other tax allowances in their own tax jurisdictions—see para.15–06.

(3) *Easier to manage resources*. A party will generally retain management control over its own resources and personnel. A contractual alliance can be less cumbersome to manage than a corporate entity which will require a formal and distinct management structure.

(4) *Ease of termination and unwind*. A contractual alliance will generally be easier to terminate and unwind if a party wishes to end the venture or if the venture completes its purpose.

(5) *Flexibility*. Generally, the relative ease of amending terms and adapting the relationship, without the formality involved in a corporate structure, can be an advantage—particularly in a fast-changing industry sector.

3–07 A contractual alliance can, though, involve factors which may be disadvantages in many circumstances:

(1) *Lack of identity*. Such a structure can lack substance or identity (compared with a corporate entity) for marketing purposes or for ease of dealings with third parties.

(2) *Lack of firm organisational structure*. A contractual alliance is sometimes regarded as lacking a sufficiently firm organisational structure for employing senior management attached to the venture (compared with the position of a joint venture company where they can be directors of a company or belong to a clear employment structure within a corporate entity). The looser structure may mean that monitoring of the other party's activities or contribution is not as close as it would be in a more hierarchical corporate structure—a concern if there is a danger of "opportunistic" behaviour by the other party.

(3) *Risk of partnership*. Such an unincorporated venture can cause potential problems in many jurisdictions, including unwanted tax consequences, if the arrangements constitute a partnership in law.

(4) *Transfer*. An unincorporated venture, although generally easy to terminate and unwind, is less suitable where one party may wish at a later stage to transfer its interest in the joint venture activity to a third party.

(5) *Competition law*. Some collaborative arrangements, particularly alliances between independent competitors, can give rise to more difficult issues and analysis under anti-trust laws relating to co-operative agreements than a "merger" through a separate entity.

(6) *Need for "bespoke" drafting*. A contractual alliance depends solely on contract without the background of established corporate procedures and laws. This can sometimes be an advantage (especially in terms of flexibility) but also leads to the need for carefully drafted rules when establishing the venture. A complex contractual alliance can involve a need for detailed and "bespoke" drafting.

3–08 Some co-operative arrangements which commonly take the form of purely contractual alliances include: project bidding agreements; research and development collaborations; specialisation or joint production agreements; resource sharing arrangements; supplier/customer "partnerships"; and other strategic or multi-national services alliances. Some of these particular arrangements are examined more fully in chapter 4.

PARTNERSHIPS

3–09 A "partnership" as a legal form is simply an unincorporated undertaking, founded in a contractual relationship between the parties, which has the requisite hallmarks for partnership applicable in the relevant country. What constitutes a "partnership" will, therefore, vary from jurisdiction to jurisdiction. In some countries, the relationship will have its own legal personality—similar to a corporate entity—but a common factor running through all partnership models is that some or all of the partners will have joint and unlimited liability for the debts and liabilities of the partnership business.

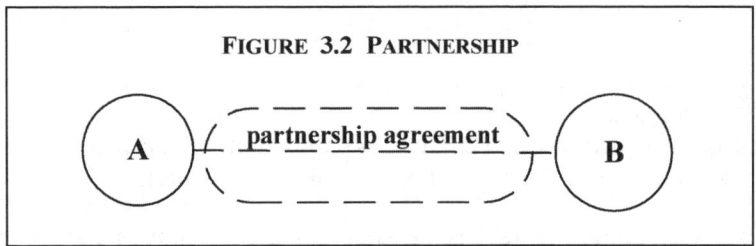

FIGURE 3.2 PARTNERSHIP

3–10 Since a partnership involves sharing of profits and losses, it is a potential legal form for an equity joint venture. The use of the partnership model is, in practice, relatively rare for a commercial joint venture business in the UK—although some contractual alliances may (unintentionally) cross the line into a "partnership" at law. However, many variants exist in civil law systems and their use is quite common in many continental European countries as a joint venture structure.

Advantages/disadvantages of a partnership

3–11 There may be good reasons, particularly in view of the tax transparency of most forms of partnership, to use this type of joint venture vehicle for structuring international equity joint ventures. A partnership—at least in the UK—may have several advantages, including:

(1) *Flexibility and simplicity*. A partnership offers flexibility and simplicity of formation (e.g. with no registration or other formalities required for formation under English law) and the governing rules of the partnership can be written down and varied easily.

(2) *Tax transparency*. Tax transparency or "pass through" (with profits and losses being treated directly as those of the partners in their proportionate shares) may be advantageous for tax planning purposes and may enable the partners to obtain more effective tax relief for capital expenditure or losses.

(3) *No public filings.* The lack of any need to incur publicity or expense in making filings with any regulatory body (such as the Companies Registry) can be an advantage; but see para.19–02 below in the case of filings of audited accounts by UK corporate partners in a partnership.

3–12 The disadvantages of a partnership as a joint venture vehicle may include:

(1) *Absence of corporate identity.* A partnership can suffer in comparison with a corporate entity which can give the vehicle greater "identity" by separately owning the assets and liabilities of the joint business and provide an easier framework for a central management structure.

(2) *External finance.* A partnership provides fewer ways of obtaining external finance compared with a corporate entity (e.g. a partnership cannot create a floating charge as security under English law and non-recourse project finance will not usually be available).

(3) *Liability.* A disadvantage is the joint unlimited liability of each partner for liabilities incurred by the partnership or by any partner acting within the express or implied scope of the partnership business. Liability is not limited to the capital contributions of the parties. (However, the difficulties which unlimited liability might cause can largely be mitigated in practice by establishing a partnership between specially-formed subsidiary companies of the participants.)

These various disadvantages (taken with other practical considerations) mean that, in the absence of strong tax considerations or professional requirements, it is comparatively rare to find a commercial joint venture business intentionally organised in the UK on a partnership basis.

3–13 In some jurisdictions (particularly in the US and Germany), tax and other advantages can accrue from adopting the variant of a "limited partnership". This invariably involves having limited or sleeping partners who retain limited liability and at least one general partner, with unlimited liability, responsible for the management and conduct of the partnership's business. It is, however, important to note that a limited partner (which can be a company) often loses the protection of limited liability if it is engaged or involved in any way in the management of the business; see further para.5–27 et seq. below.

3–14 A further analysis of partnerships in the context of equity joint ventures appears in chapter 5.

CORPORATE JOINT VENTURES

3–15 A jointly owned corporate vehicle, holding the business assets of the joint venture, is generally viewed as the most appropriate legal form for the majority of equity joint ventures where a continuing business is to be operated. Such a corporate model is available in most jurisdictions worldwide.

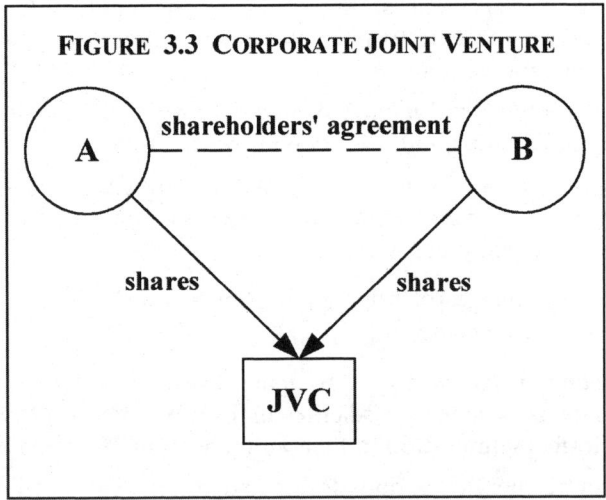

FIGURE 3.3 CORPORATE JOINT VENTURE

Advantages/disadvantages of a corporate structure

3–16 The advantages and disadvantages of a corporate vehicle for an equity joint venture are essentially the converse of those for a partnership or contractual alliance. The advantages include the following:

(1) *Identity*. A company has a strong, and potentially independent, identity for dealings with third parties and for creating a clear internal management and employment structure.

(2) *Limited liability*. Joint venture parties can have the benefit of limited liability since, in strict legal terms, their liabilities as shareholders will be limited to any unpaid sums in respect of their share capital (although in some situations there may be advantages in having an unlimited company).

(3) *Financing*. A company can own and hold assets in its own name and the structure generally offers more financing possibilities than an unincorporated venture; a company can (under English law) give floating charges as security for external finance and create charges

over future assets such as receivables—and enable finance to be raised on a non-shareholder recourse basis.

(4) *Continuity/transfer of interests*. A corporate structure enables sales of interests and introduction of new members to take place without affecting the direct legal ownership of the underlying assets.

(5) *Flexibility of share rights*. The share structure of a company can often provide useful flexibility. Under English law, for instance, preference shares may be issued which allow investors to obtain a priority return on the nominal value of their shares without having any voting rights over the management of the company. Shareholders may also be given the right to convert their preference shares into equity shares if certain situations occur.

(6) *Clear accounting structure*. A company provides a clear structure for internal accounting and reporting purposes.

(7) *Established laws*. In most countries worldwide, a company is a universally recognised entity with an established body of corporate laws and judicial precedents.

3–17 The disadvantages of using a company as a joint venture vehicle in some circumstances include:

(1) *Compliance requirements*. A company will be regulated by relevant corporate laws in its jurisdiction of incorporation and will require more formal administration than an unincorporated structure.

(2) *Publicity*. Generally, various forms and returns will need to be filed publicly. (In the UK, for instance, an annual return, details of directors and of share issues, audited accounts and other returns must be filed with the Companies Registry.) This can result in increased administration costs and some loss of confidentiality. An unlimited company may sometimes be considered with, usually, less stringent disclosure obligations.

(3) *Less flexibility*. A corporate venture generally involves less flexibility in its governance structure, and less freedom for change, than a contractual alliance. A party may also prefer to retain the more direct management control over its own employees and resources which a contractual alliance provides.

(4) *Formality*. A company generally involves more formality in incorporation (with a need for articles of association, by-laws or equivalent constitutional documents).

(5) *Complexity on winding-up of venture*. A company, as a separate legal entity, involves greater complexity if and when a party wishes to terminate or the venture is wound up and its assets realised or distributed.

3–18 A corporate structure is the most common legal form for an equity joint venture. An overview of different types of corporate entities available in Europe (including new European company models) and some of the key documentary issues arising out of a corporate joint venture are discussed more fully in chapter 5.

Location of the JVC

3–19 In the case of most joint ventures, it will be apparent from the circumstances of the venture where any joint venture company (JVC) is to be located. In other cases, and particularly many international ventures, two further structural questions may arise:

(a) in which jurisdiction should the joint venture vehicle be located?

(b) should the parties establish a single joint venture vehicle or more than one?

It will frequently be desirable, in the case of a joint venture with international operations, to have one or more operating subsidiaries in different jurisdictions in order to enable the group to operate efficiently. Alternatively, it may be desirable (usually for tax reasons) to consider having a series of joint venture companies or other jointly-owned vehicles in different jurisdictions. The analysis of the appropriate vehicle will therefore need to be examined on a country-by-country basis.

3–20 The location of an international JVC may be affected by tax or "political" considerations. There may be a desire for a location which is "neutral" as between two different national parties. For instance, a jurisdiction such as the Netherlands can offer attractions as a neutral location for the principal legal vehicle for many pan-European joint ventures—both for tax reasons and also because of its background of well-established and reasonably flexible corporate laws. In these cases, the way in which the overall joint venture structure is put together, or existing businesses are transferred to the JVC, will generally require careful tax planning (see chapter 15).

HYBRID AND OTHER STRUCTURES

3–21 There are an increasing number of legal forms which do not fall fully within the basic categories outlined above. Some are brought together in the remaining sections of this chapter for convenience.

Limited liability partnerships (LLP)

3–22 This important new form of business entity in the UK was created by the Limited Liability Partnerships Act 2000. It is potentially a significant legal form for equity joint ventures. The Act makes it possible to incorporate with limited liability while retaining the tax status, appearance and much of the flexibility of a partnership. The background to the legislation was concern arising from major negligence claims incurred by large professional partnerships and the need for some form of limited liability. The LLP is not, however, restricted to professional partnerships and is available as a vehicle for two or more persons (including companies) carrying on any trade or profession.

3-23 Key features[1] of a limited liability partnership include the following:

(1) *Body corporate.* An LLP is a body corporate with a legal personality separate from its members. It will own the assets of its business. It is subject to incorporation requirements similar to those of a company.

(2) *Membership agreement.* Dealings between the members of an LLP are governed by a membership agreement (termed here an LLP agreement) and by certain regulations under the 2000 Act.[2] There is considerable flexibility for the parties to establish their own constitutional and management structure.

(3) *Management.* There is no requirement to distinguish between "members" and "managers" of the business of the LLP. There is, however, no objection to the appointment of individual "managers" who may carry out functions similar to those of directors of a company (and may be given such titles as the members so wish).

(4) *Liability.* The LLP is liable to the full extent of its assets but the members have limited liability (so long as there is more than one member) irrespective of their involvement in management.

(5) *Finance.* Members will provide working capital and share any profits (or losses) in the manner set out in the LLP agreement. There are no capital maintenance rules. Any capital provided may be returned to the members at any time.

(6) *Members.* An LLP is not subject to any rule restricting the number of members. New members may be admitted by agreement of the existing members. A person may cease to be a member in accordance with the LLP agreement (or, in the absence of the matter being governed by that agreement, upon giving reasonable notice). Any entitlement, on leaving, to payment for its membership interest is left solely for any express agreement between the members. Expulsion of a member is only permitted if there is an express expulsion clause in the LLP agreement.

---

[1] For a more detailed discussion on the new LLP legislation see specialist texts, e.g. J. Whittaker and J. Machell, *The Law of Limited Liability Partnerships* (Bristol, Jordan Publishing, 2004).

[2] Principally the Limited Liability Partnerships Regulations 2001, SI 2001/90.

(7) *Overseas operations.* There is no restriction on foreign membership of an LLP. Similarly, there is no restriction on an LLP carrying on business outside Great Britain.

(8) *Default rules.* An LLP is not governed by partnership law. However, the LLP Regulations 2001 contain default provisions[3] relating, inter alia, to the mutual rights and duties of the members, many of which are derived from partnership law; these will apply unless displaced by agreement between the members. In the context of a joint venture, it will usually be appropriate for the parties to ensure that these default rules are so displaced in the LLP agreement.

(9) *Publicity.* An LLP has public filing requirements similar to those of a company (e.g. audited annual accounts, annual returns, notification of changes of members and any change to its registered office.)

(10) *Taxation.* In the UK at least, an LLP will be treated for tax purposes as if it were a partnership (i.e. profits and losses will accrue directly to the members in their relevant proportions). Assets of the LLP are treated as held directly by the members in partnership for tax purposes. Certain rules have been introduced to restrict the attraction of an LLP for tax purposes as a medium for property investment funds.

(11) *Winding-up.* A member of an LLP is potentially subject to a form of "claw-back", in the event of a winding-up of an LLP, if it has withdrawn property from the LLP in the two years prior to the winding up and it is proved that the member knew or had reasonable grounds for believing that the LLP was unable to pay its debts.

(12) *Unfair prejudice.* The LLP legislation applies to members the rights under the provisions of s.994 Companies Act 2006 (protection of members against unfair prejudice—see para.11–36 below). However, members may by unanimous agreement in writing exclude this right. In the case of an LLP between corporate partners, one may expect in practice such exclusion to be made in the LLP agreement.

Advantages of an LLP

3–24 The principal advantage of an LLP as a joint venture vehicle is the combination of the limited liability offered to its members and the flexibility and "pass-through" tax treatment of a partnership. It may therefore be of considerable interest as a joint venture vehicle in the UK primarily where there is a need for a fiscally transparent entity.

---

[3] Regs 7 and 8 of the Limited Liability Partnerships Regulations 2001. Section 4(3) of the 2000 Act also creates a default rule that a member of an LLP may cease to be a member by giving reasonable notice.

(1) In summary, compared with a general partnership, it offers:

    (a) limited liability for its members;
    (b) ability to grant security such as a fixed or floating charge;
    (c) no loss of limited liability for any member engaged in management and no requirement for a general partner (compared with a limited partnership);
    (d) separate legal personality; and
    (e) continuity in the event of transfers of interests by members in the LLP.

(2) Compared with a limited company, it offers:

    (a) tax transparency;
    (b) no rules regarding maintenance of capital;
    (c) flexibility in organisational rules and management structure; and
    (d) private constitutional documents.

Disadvantages of an LLP

3–25 What are the disadvantages of using an LLP for a joint venture? They are relatively few:

(a) reluctance of parties to adopt a new legal form until it has become more widely used;

(b) "claw-back": the risk of claim if any assets of the LLP are distributed to a member within two years prior to its winding-up if that member knew or had reasonable grounds for believing that the LLP was unable to pay its debts;

(c) the legal regulations are spread around a number of corporate law statutes and regulations and are not always easy to find;

(d) members have potential liabilities (e.g. for wrongful trading) in the same way as directors but not partners;

(e) there are a number of partnership-type "default rules" which, in the joint venture context, should be modified in a carefully prepared LLP agreement;

(f) accounts have to be filed publicly (but no more than for a partnership comprising corporate partners);

(g) certain tax pitfalls exist for investment LLPs;

(h) an LLP is not able to issue shares to the public (therefore its business would need to be transferred to a company if flotation is planned);

(i) the parties must maintain more than one member in order to retain the benefit of limited liability (therefore, in a two-party LLP, each runs a credit risk regarding its counterparty—this risk could, if wished, be mitigated by incorporation of a special purpose company as a third member).

3-26 The LLP therefore offers many potential attractions as a form of joint venture vehicle. It appears to be similar in many respects to the limited liability company (LLC) popular in many US states. However, there is likely to be some continuing hesitation in the UK in using an "unfamiliar" entity when much the same result can be achieved by a traditional partnership using special purpose subsidiaries as corporate partners. Experience so far suggests that the LLP is being used particularly for some infrastructure or project ventures but not yet widely in other commercial joint venture contexts. It will be interesting, however, to see if the LLP will attract increasing interest as a vehicle for joint ventures.

> An example of a Limited Liability Partnership Agreement is included as Precedent 8 in Part E.

US limited liability company (LLC)

3-27 A similar entity in the US which can offer both "tax transparency" or "pass-through" as well as limited liability is the US form of limited liability company (LLC). The LLC is frequently used as the legal vehicle for joint ventures in the US or for US parties entering into an international joint venture. Management arrangements are extremely flexible and are simply reflected in the terms of a written limited liability company agreement—see also Part D under "United States".

European Economic Interest Grouping (EEIG)

3-28 The European Commission initiated the European Economic Interest Grouping (EEIG)[4] in an attempt to encourage or assist cross-border alliances. An EEIG can now be established in most EU countries.[5] The advantages of an EEIG can include: relatively little expense in formation and administration; limited registration requirements; and flexibility regarding rules for managing and operating the EEIG which can be tailored to a particular collaboration. The EEIG has severe limitations, though, as a

---

[4] Council Reg (EC) No.2137/85
[5] The relevant regulations in the UK are the European Economic Interest Grouping Regulations 1989 (SI 1989/638). In the UK, although it is fairly informal and has many features of a partnership, an EEIG has an independent legal personality.

model for a business joint venture and will not be appropriate for an equity joint venture.[6] Based on the UK Regulations:

(a) an EEIG must have members based in at least two EU countries or, as now permitted, within the wider European Economic Area (EEA);

(b) only companies within the EEA can be members of an EEIG;

(c) the purpose of an EEIG must not be to make profits;

(d) the activity of an EEIG must be ancillary to the economic activities of its members (i.e. it must not operate in a different field nor itself carry on an independent business or practice);

(e) an EEIG cannot have more than 500 employees;

(f) an EEIG cannot (with limited exceptions associated with the EEIG's objects) hold shares in another undertaking;

(g) no single member of an EEIG can hold a majority vote;

(h) existing members must approve unanimously the introduction of any new members;

(i) the members of an EEIG have unlimited joint and several liability for its debts and liabilities;

(j) a member of an EEIG remains liable for debts incurred during its membership for a period of five years after its membership ends.

3–29 An EEIG is, therefore, of little use where the primary purpose of the joint venture is to carry on a profit-making business. It has nevertheless proved a suitable medium for cross-border trade associations and alliances involving accountants, solicitors and other professions. It may also be a suitable vehicle for cross-border R&D collaborations between European companies or other non-profit-making ventures. It can, on occasions, be used as a part of a larger joint venture structure. In the UK, use of the EEIG model has been relatively limited so far.[7] However, it is a model which will continue to deserve consideration in appropriate joint venture circumstances. Examples of its use in commercial situations include the following:

---

[6] The EU has also adopted a Statute for a European Co-operative Society (SCE) which will give co-operative businesses operating in more than one Member State the option of being established as a single entity under EU law (Council Reg (EC) No. 1435/2003). This may provide a vehicle for certain companies wishing to group together for their common benefit on the basis that each member should benefit from the activities of the SCE in relation to its volume of trade with the SCE and not its capital contribution. The Statute has been given effect in the UK by the European Cooperative Society Regulations 2006 (SI 2006/2078).

[7] The position contrasts with the French model of the Groupement d'Intérêt Économique (GIE) from which it was derived. This French model has been used by small and large firms, with the best known grouping being Airbus Industrie in which subsidiaries of UK, German and Spanish companies originally collaborated with Aerospatiale to build the Airbus range of aircraft.

- *EU Port EEIG* (2000). Established by members in the UK, Holland, Belgium, Germany and Italy, the grouping was formed to undertake: (i) joint research and development projects, (ii) exchange of technical information, (iii) co-operation in the field of enhanced safety in environmental management, (iv) co-operation in related training and (v) co-operation in related lobbying at European and international level. Its duration is indefinite.
- *European Engine Alliance EEIG* (1996). This is a co-operation between certain manufacturers of diesel engines (Cummins, a UK subsidiary of a US manufacturer, Iveco and New Holland) to establish a joint study for research and development leading to the design of new families of diesel engines of one litre per cylinder capacity. The EEIG is to continue until the year 2010.

3–30 An EEIG is formed by its members concluding a formation contract and registering the grouping with the appropriate registry in the chosen jurisdiction. A grouping has legal capacity as from the date of registration. The basic document will be a formation contract concluded by the members of the EEIG which is then filed with the Companies Registry. It is possible for this basic contract to be supplemented by more detailed operating rules as between the members. There may also be separate contracts (e.g. for services) between the EEIG and some or all of its members.

> An example of an EEIG Formation Agreement is set out as Precedent 7 in Part E.

Dual-headed structures

3–31 In some cases, companies may wish to conduct their businesses through a single merged venture for management purposes but, whether for tax reasons or for the sake of retaining clearer corporate or "national" identities, also wish to maintain their existing national companies for legal purposes. The tax costs of cross-border dividend payments or of transferring and merging the legal business interests (see chapter 15) can also lead to a call for imaginative structuring of international joint ventures.

3–32 Arrangements can be established whereby the principal corporate parties remain legally separate but are connected by contractual relationships relating to the joint venture businesses (such as profit-sharing or dividend equalisation arrangements) so that they can be operated as a single economic or business unit. Such a "dual-headed" structure may be used to bring together two listed companies (owned by different sets of national shareholders) in a way that the two companies can be run as a single business enterprise. An example of a "dual-headed" structure is:

- *GKN/Brambles*. GKN (of the UK) in 2001 demerged its support services activities into a new listed company which then combined with Brambles Industries (of Australia). Each company retains its own listing and public shareholders, but contractual links effectively give both sets of shareholders equivalent rights in the "combined business."

3–33 Features of such a "dual-headed" arrangement (which will have to be tailored to the particular circumstances) might include a framework or equalisation agreement providing for the following key principles:

(1) *Management*: identical boards of directors of the merged businesses (or at least a jointly appointed management committee) in order to ensure a common management for the business.

(2) *Accounting*: common accounting principles and a common method of determining the profits or losses of the merged businesses.

(3) *Profit sharing*: arrangements for pooling the profits and losses of the various businesses with profit sharing on an agreed basis (in which case the arrangement will often constitute a partnership in law) or arrangements for equalisation payments between the parties if one business incurs a loss or disproportionately low profit compared with the other.

(4) *Distributions*: distribution of dividends from the merged businesses to the respective joint venture parties to be made in equal or pre-agreed proportions.

(5) *Repayment of capital*: payment of capital or liquidation proceeds to the joint venture parties from the merged businesses to be made in the same pre-agreed proportions.

3–34 Any such structure will need to be examined carefully for, and will often be driven by, tax considerations. The contractual linking arrangements are likely to require review under partnership laws to assess if they cross the line and become a "partnership" in law. Such dual-headed structures have so far been used primarily at parent company level to merge the whole or significant parts of businesses of publicly quoted companies with shareholders based in different jurisdictions (giving rise principally to a range of public company or stock exchange issues such as the effect of rules relating to corporate governance, shareholder information or approval requirements). However, the development of similar techniques may be expected in the structuring of cross-border collaborations at subsidiary operating levels.

CONCLUSION

3–35 The choice of legal form for the joint venture or alliance will therefore depend on a variety of factors and their weighting in the circumstances of the particular venture. Figure 3.4 summarises the basic implications of the various principal legal "vehicles" available for joint ventures and alliances in the UK.

FIGURE 3.4 BASIC UK LEGAL STRUCTURES FOR JOINT VENTURES

	Contractual Alliance	Limited Company	Partnership	LLP	EEIG	European Company
Limited liability		✓		✓		✓
Sharing of net profits/losses		✓	✓	✓	✓	✓
Tax ("pass-through")	✓		✓	✓	✓	
Tax ("separate entity")		✓				✓
Clear separate management structure		✓				✓
Management control retained over party's own resources	✓					
Retained ownership by party of own assets/IPR	✓					
Ease of transferability of interests		✓				✓
Ease of termination and unwind	✓					
Non-recourse finance possible		✓		✓		✓
Separate "brand" identity for joint venture		✓		✓		✓
"Euro" identity					✓	✓
Little administration	✓	✓			✓	
Few reporting requirements	✓				✓	

This is a generalised summary only. Many of the different legal forms have elements of the "missing" characteristics or can be adapted to provide them—but more customised work is generally required to achieve this.

3–36 The choice of legal form will be a crucial step in the establishment of the joint venture or alliance. It will particularly affect the nature of the legal documentation required. Chapter 4 provides an overview of a range of typical arrangements established as "contractual alliances" and the key issues to be addressed. Chapter 5 similarly addresses in more detail the range of entities through which an "equity joint venture" may be conducted with particular emphasis on the documentary framework for a corporate joint venture.

CHAPTER 4

Contractual alliances: an overview

Many alliances do not involve the creation of any separate entity. The legal form rests simply on a contract between the parties. This offers advantages of relative flexibility, informality and ease of termination and unwind if and when the alliance comes to an end. It is a natural legal form for many of the diverse types of alliance which are now being formed. This chapter considers a range of typical contractual alliances, the type of legal documentation which may be involved and key issues to be addressed at the contracting stage.

Range of non-equity alliances

4–01 An unincorporated alliance, based solely on a contract between the parties detailing their co-operation, will be appropriate for many ventures and projects. The advantages/disadvantages of a purely contractual alliance are discussed more fully in chapter 3—see para.3–06 et seq. A contractual alliance does not involve the creation of an independent legal entity. Such an arrangement usually involves the sharing of certain costs and resources (and sometimes income) on terms which do not give rise to a "partnership" at law.

4–02 A contractual alliance will typically be suitable for a "non-equity" venture where parties are co-operating on a one-off project or where cost, information or output (rather than net profit) is being shared. Examples cover a wide range. Co-operative alliances have typically included situations such as:

(a) a collaboration agreement between parties to undertake joint research and development (R&D) or other forms of technology co-operation;

(b) a specialisation agreement whereby each party agrees to specialise in the development and/or production of a certain product and each party undertakes obligations to supply the other party with its product;

(c) a bidding agreement (often called a consortium) whereby different parties team together to bid to undertake a particular works project;

(d) a joint venture between natural resource companies to undertake the exploration and/or development of oil and gas or mining interests.

4–03 The contractual route is, however, flexible and is the basis of a diverse range of joint working arrangements or alliances between companies—often between competitor firms who undertake to provide complementary skills in a specific industry sector but not on a basis which creates a jointly-conducted business in which the parties share financial results on an equity basis. These are often termed "strategic alliances" although there is no special meaning to this term (the term "strategic" simply reflecting the importance of the collaboration to the strategic aims of the parties). These collaborative arrangements may include, for instance:

(a) key supplier/customer and other "partnering" arrangements for closer co-operation in technical, operational or commercial activities within the supply or distribution chain; and

(b) multi-party linkages where parties seek to establish a network which can provide services to customers on a pan-European or global basis or otherwise enable the parties to gain access to, or harness, a range of linked services or technologies.

The internet has, in particular, provided a transformation in connectivity between parties worldwide. This has greatly assisted, and indeed acted as a catalyst for, the formation of alliances integrated by sophisticated electronic information systems through which each party provides specialist products or services within an overall co-operative strategy. Some of these network alliances may, in effect, constitute a "virtual corporation".[1]

4–04 Examples of strategic alliances reported in the press or reviewed by the European Commission have included:

- *Autovaz/Renault*. Russia's largest car maker Autovaz has chosen Renault as a strategic partner and will offer it a blocking stake in the company, officials at both companies have announced. The deal will give Renault a foothold in one of the world's fastest growing car markets. Renault and its own alliance partner Nissan are scrambling to add capacity in emerging markets to offset slumping markets in western Europe and the US. [*FT:* 8.12.07].

- *BBC/IBM*. The BBC and IBM have forged a strategic alliance, following the signing of an agreement for a framework outlining several joint projects between the two companies. One of the first projects will focus on applying state-of-the-art image/video search technologies to BBC's massive TV and radio archive. [*FT:* 5.3.07].

---

[1] J. Child, D. Faulkner and S. Tallman, *Cooperative Strategy: Managing Alliances, Networks and Joint Ventures* (Oxford: Oxford University Press, 2005) p.164.

- *Microsoft/TiVo*. Microsoft has forged close links with consumer electronics companies in an attempt to boost the use of its software in digital media and entertainment. They include a partnership with TiVo, makers of digital video recorders. Co-operating with traditional consumer electronics companies, rather than competing with them head-on, has become central to Microsoft's plan according to industry analysts. [*FT:* 6.1.05].
- *MAN/Navistar*. Navistar (a US truckmaker) and MAN (Europe's largest truckmaker) signed a strategic alliance to jointly develop and manufacture truck components, including a range of diesel engines. It also underscored MAN's long-standing preference for co-operation agreements, rather than full-blown mergers, as a way of increasing the company's scale. [*FT:* 7.12.04].
- *Air France/Alitalia*. These two airlines agreed to build a long-term strategic bilateral alliance regarding air transport between Community airports. The agreement also integrated Alitalia into the world-wide SkyTeam Alliance. The co-operation agreements provide for the creation of a European multi-hub system, co-ordination of their passenger service operations and other areas such as cargo handling, maintenance, purchasing and training. The alliance was cleared by the European Commission. [Case COMP/38.2841D2 (2004)]
- *Esso/Tesco*. Tesco, the United Kingdom's biggest food retailer, announced that it was expanding its alliance with Esso to increase the roll-out of its Tesco Express outlets located in forecourts of Esso petrol stations. Both grocery retailers and forecourt operators benefit from these arrangements; the former through high-visibility 24–hour outlets and the latter through increasing sales of higher-margin non-fuel products. [*FT:* 5.2.00].
- *Banque Nationale de Paris/Dresdner Bank*. These two banks (being the fourth largest French bank and the second largest German bank) entered into a co-operation agreement that included exchange of information, certain developments on their home market and joint activity in third country markets. Each party had a right of veto if the other party wished to conclude a cooperation agreement with a competitor of the first party. The agreement was cleared for 10 years. [OJ 1996 L188/37].

4–05 Alliances can sometimes be so loose that there is no real legal form or, indeed, legal commitment. They may simply establish a "friendly" link as a framework for future co-operation on a project by project basis. Others may establish more concrete business links in terms of joint research, cross-supply arrangements, exchange of staff and/or sharing of resources—and, sometimes, minority equity investment. In some cases a joint venture entity may be formed to centralise or co-ordinate the alliance.[2] In very many

---

[2] See e.g. some of the examples of co-operative joint ventures referred to in para.5–08.

cases, they will be structured solely as an unincorporated contractual joint venture or alliance.

> One outline example of a Strategic Alliance Agreement appears as Precedent 4 in Part E.

BASIC ISSUES IN CONTRACTUAL ALLIANCES

Key basic issues

4–06 Alliances cover a wide range of business situations and market objectives. Each is different. The issues to be dealt with in each contractual negotiation will be specific to the particular venture and relationship. Key issues are, though, likely to centre around the following basic questions:

(1) *Objectives*. What are the key objectives of the alliance? What is its scope—in terms of territory, services, products and/or customers?

(2) *Responsibilities/Contributions*. What will be the key responsibilities of each party? What is each party to supply by way of services, facilities, personnel or products? Within what timetable and/or to what service standard level? What cash or resource commitments (including in-kind contributions) are to be made by each party?

(3) *Governance of the alliance*. How will any steering committee or board be established and what will be the structure for decision-making?

(4) *Operational management*. How will day-to-day operations be managed—including through the establishment of project committees or working groups? Will specific "alliance managers" be identified within each party with authority (and responsibility) to represent that party in the relationship? What management or organisational support is each party to provide?

(5) *Cost*. How are costs to be allocated and/or calls for finance to be structured? How are budgets to be adopted? Will a joint bank account be operated and who will be entitled to access and draw upon that account? What accounting and financial reporting systems will be put in place? Will there be a right for each party to require an audit?

(6) *Profits/income*. How is any income or profit (loss) to be shared?

(7) *Information flow*. What data or other information flows will be established? Will this involve the provision of "proprietary" information or technology of any party?

(8) *Patents/IPR*. Will each party grant licences in respect of existing background intellectual property rights (IPR) including software copyright, trademarks etc? How will IPR arising in the course of the

RANGE OF NON-EQUITY ALLIANCES

alliance be owned or dealt with? Will each party have a right to use IPR freely?

(9) *Rights to output.* What rights will each party have to market or distribute products, manufacture products or acquire or license technology developed by the alliance?

(10) *Confidential information.* How is confidential technical information developed by the alliance to be shared or its use restricted?

(11) *Non-compete/exclusivity.* Are restrictions to be imposed on the ability of the parties (or members of their corporate group) to engage in activities which "compete" with the activities of the alliance?

(12) *Inter-party transactions.* What principles and procedures are to apply in respect of costs and transfer pricing for goods/services supplied between the parties or between a party and the "alliance"?

(13) *Liability/indemnity.* Will each party remain responsible for its own activities in the alliance? Are there potential liabilities to customers or other third parties? If so, will each party indemnify the other party against any third party claims attributable to its activities (e.g. product liability, intellectual property infringement or employee claims)? Will there be any joint activities for which any liabilities should be shared—perhaps unless one party has been guilty of gross negligence or wilful default?

(14) *Term and termination.* Is there to be a specific term or "milestone" after which the alliance may be terminated? Will the alliance be for a fixed term with joint renewal (if agreed) thereafter? Will each party have a unilateral right to terminate on notice at any stage?

(15) *Consequences of termination.* Should any specific arrangements be pre-agreed in the event of termination—distribution of assets, entitlement to IPR or restrictions for a period on future competitive activity?

(16) *Anti-trust.* Do the parties have significant market shares in relevant areas? Are there likely to be anti-trust or other regulatory concerns?

(17) *Disputes and governing law.* How are disputes to be resolved? What should be the governing law?

Alliance agreements require careful "bespoke" contract drafting to meet the circumstances of the particular situation. No two will be the same. Contract drafting should normally be as simple and commercial as possible—avoiding the risk of "overlawyering": see generally the discussion at para.2–44 et seq. These should be business-orientated documents which are "owned" by the parties.

4–07 Many alliances will be substantially dependent on the personal relationship between the parties. The enforceability of contract provisions as a legal matter may well not be a high priority. Indeed, the parties may frequently consider that the commitment or structure of a legally-binding contract is not necessary or appropriate for the particular alliance. Rather than a formal contract, a commercial but non-binding "memorandum of understanding" ("MoU") may often suffice as the basis of the alliance— although any alliance documentation should, prudently, at least address in principle the basic issues.

Alliance charter

4–08 On occasions, it may be appropriate to accompany a more formal alliance agreement or MoU with an "alliance charter" of principles to which the parties agree to subscribe. Such a charter will address key principles of the particular alliance—e.g. commitments to joint preparation and annual review of a business plan; the achievement of measurable results (in terms of revenue growth or costs savings); allocation of resources and investment; an innovative approach to opportunities and problems; and behavioural principles such as regular and open communication. The primary role of such a charter will be to encapsulate, and promote, the key business philosophy underlying the "partnering" relationship rather than to establish legal commitment. The Association of Strategic Alliance Professionals (ASAP) offers the following as an example of a non-binding "alliance charter":

ASAP: EXAMPLE OF A CHARTER OF EXPECTATIONS

1. **Alliance Management.** The alliance managers are committed to using the Best Practices outlined in the [Alliance User Guide].

2. **Assignment of Personnel.** We will insist that high quality people are assigned to work in the alliance to help ensure high performance.

3. **Performance Review.** We will conduct a strategic and operational performance review every six months, and make corrections rapidly when required between reviews.

4. **Risk/Reward.** We will encourage informed risk taking in achieving the alliance shared vision.

5. **Urgency for Change.** Having asked our boards to support the alliance, we need to consider every decision's impact on achieving promised short-term results.

6. **Achievement.** We seek to reward shared achievement, balancing individual excellence with team accomplishment.

7. **Approval.** Middle and front line management will be able to make the investment decisions necessary to resolve customer issues on the spot.

8. **Power/Control.** We will share power with our customers. Customers will have the ability to modify orders (within parameters) up to 24 hours in advance without penalty.

9. **Learning.** Mistakes will not be punished or seen as failures, but be treated as learnings and opportunities to turn breakdowns into breakthroughs.

10. **Decision Making.** Decisions will be made at the lowest levels possible.

11. **Support.** We will engage all employees in the change process and work with those whose skills are no longer needed to seek gainful employment elsewhere.

12. **Conflict Resolution.** Immediate and aggressive handling of conflicts will be the norm. Disputants will candidly but constructively share concerns and grievances.

13. **Time Perspective.** We will focus our energy and talents on creating a shared future, not on advancing our individual organisations or living in their past successes.

14. **Relationships.** Teamwork and cross-process/cross-function collaboration must characterise all our interactions.

15. **Budget & Resources.** Alliance managers are committed to be strong advocates for sufficient resources to be allocated to the alliance to ensure its success.

Source: ASAP (Strategic Alliance Best Process Workbook)

4–09 In the remainder of this chapter we examine a number of arrangements which typically take the form of "contractual alliances" and identify material issues relating to them. Many joint ventures and alliances in real life will be sufficiently complex to include elements of more than one of these arrangements.

EXAMPLES OF CONTRACTUAL ALLIANCES

R&D/technology collaborations

4–10 A common form of contractual alliance is a co-operation between two or more parties to carry out a collaborative programme of research and/or development (R&D) in a particular field or to exchange and develop technical knowledge, skills and ideas. This generally falls short of carrying out a joint business undertaking—and will therefore usually avoid being a partnership under English law (see para.5–18 et seq. below). There are many varieties of technology collaboration agreements. They will generally take an unincorporated form but occasionally a corporate vehicle may be chosen. Types of collaboration agreement include the following:

(1) Two or more parties may collaborate by pooling existing know-how in a particular area of technology and/or agree a mutual research programme with the aim of sharing the costs and the results of that programme. This may be coupled with arrangements for joint production or exploitation of the results—or each party may be free to exploit separately.

(2) A number of parties, usually industrial companies, may sponsor a programme of work (e.g. by a university) and receive in return a right to the results of that work programme.

(3) A company may agree to collaborate with another in a particular field on the basis that it is given the right of first refusal to fund potential research projects on agreed terms including rights of subsequent exploitation.

4–11 Illustrative examples of technology collaboration agreements reviewed and cleared by the European Commission include the following:

- *Pfizer/Aventis*. Two pharmaceutical companies agreed to co-operate in research and development and then subsequent co-promotion of jointly-developed products to be sold under a single trade mark by the JV parents. (XXX1st Report on Competition Policy (2001), paras 241–243)

- *Asahi/Saint-Gobain*. An agreement between Saint-Gobain (France) and Asahi Glass (Japan) provided for research and development in the field of bi-layer technology and products derived therefrom (for car windows etc.). The parties agreed to share their past and future research. Pilot plants would be constructed by a JVC which would be licensed to carry out on behalf of the parties subsequent industrial exploitation of the results of the joint R&D. [OJ (1994) L354/87]

- *Continental/Michelin*. Two leading tyre manufacturers entered into a co-operation agreement to collaborate on pre-industrial development of a new design of tyre and wheel system for passenger cars with arrangements for subsequent joint licensing and administration of project-related intellectual property. If one party decided to terminate the co-operation, the other party could continue to use the other party's patents and know-how. [OJ (1988) L305/33]

4–12 Key issues which frequently arise in relation to R&D or technology collaboration agreements include those set out in the following checklist:

R&D/Technology collaborations: checklist of key issues

(1) *Scope of project.* What is the object and scope of the collaboration? A description in general terms should usually be accompanied by a more detailed technical annex.

(2) *Responsibilities of parties.* What is the responsibility of each participant? What contribution is each party to make in terms of personnel, facilities, equipment and materials? A detailed allocation of tasks as between the parties will usually be annexed.

(3) *Timetable.* Is there a planned timetable with basic benchmarks or "milestones" to be reached? Again a project timetable will normally be annexed.

(4) *Background technology.* Will existing or background technology need to be disclosed between the parties? Does this extend to any know-how developed independently by a party after commencement of the project but outside the scope of the project? Will each party indemnify the others against any liability for infringement resulting from use of its background technology?

(5) *Project know-how.* Will each party be obliged to disclose to each other know-how newly developed during the project? How will the parties report and communicate progress and results of work performed?

(6) *Use of know-how.* How freely may each party use existing know-how and/or newly developed know-how or results? Is use limited solely to the project during the term of the agreement?

(7) *Confidentiality.* Is a strict confidentiality obligation regarding the results of the programme to be imposed on each of the parties? Is any of the information or know-how proprietary to one party? Will there be prohibitions on publication or communications to third parties?

(8) *Structure.* How is the collaboration to be structured? Will there be a management and/or project committee? How often should it meet? Will there be a project leader? If so, what are his/its tasks and powers (including powers to represent the other participants)?

(9) *Project management.* How will the project be managed on a day-to-day basis? Will employees of each of the participants be working together as joint teams? Can sub-contractors be engaged and, if so, on what conditions? How will work be reviewed and, if necessary, verified?

(10) *Modifications.* How will changes to the project programme, including budgeted costs, be agreed?

(11) *Funding.* Will a budget or expenditure plan be adopted? Or will each participant bear its own research costs? Is the project dependent upon financial support to be obtained from a sponsoring agency or by each of the participants from their respective governments? What commitment will the parties have regarding payments to each other for services rendered or for reimbursement of project costs?

(12) *Ownership and exploitation of results.* It is vitally important to be clear on ownership of, and entitlement to use, know-how and other information associated with the project:

> — Will each participant remain owner of its existing know-how and inventions?
> — Will know-how or inventions resulting from the research programme (project know-how) become jointly-owned or remain the property of the particular participant carrying out the research?
> — How will results of the research programme be protected and/or intellectual property rights, such as patents, obtained and held?
> — What obligations will each participant have to maintain and defend any patents, or to protect know-how, resulting from the project?
> — Will each party be free, irrespective of ownership, to use the results of the research programme? Or are results going to be exploited jointly? (See also para.17–13 below.)
> — Will there be any co-branding or joint use of trademarks?
>
> (13) *Liability.* A number of issues arise in relation to liability:
>
> — Will each party be responsible for any damage or injury to property or persons of another participant resulting from its activities?
> — How will any potential product liability be shared or allocated?
> — Will there be inter-party remedies for defective or negligent performance? Or only for wilful default or perhaps gross negligence?
>
> (14) *Force majeure.* Is a force majeure or hardship provision appropriate?
>
> (15) *Termination.* Does the collaboration have a definite duration? Can it be brought to an end by notice of either party? What are the arrangements for use of IPR or other assets following termination?
>
> (16) *Exclusivity.* Will the parties be free to undertake independent research in the relevant area or to enter into co-operation agreements with third parties?
>
> (17) *Arbitration.* Is arbitration appropriate for dealing with any disputes?
>
> (18) *Competition law.* Are there restrictions which are likely to give rise to competition law concerns? Is it possible or desirable to bring the arrangements within the R&D Block Exemption published by the European Commission—see para.17–17.

The scope of each agreement will obviously vary with the nature and detail of the particular collaboration.[3]

An example of a multi-party R&D Collaboration Agreement appears as Precedent 5 in Part E.

Specialisation agreements

4–13 These are arrangements for specialisation at production level between competing or potentially competing manufacturers. Typical features are:

---

[3] Another precedent, for a two-party R&D collaboration agreement, is contained in *Practical Commercial Precedents*, vol.2 (London: Sweet & Maxwell, looseleaf).

(a) each party agrees to specialise in the production of certain products and excludes work on products to be produced by the other party;

(b) each party agrees to obtain exclusively from the other its requirements of those products which it has agreed not to produce;

(c) each party agrees to supply to the other party the products in which it has itself specialised.

4–14 Illustrative examples of specialisation arrangements which have been reviewed and cleared by the European Commission include the following:

- *BP Chemicals/ICI*. This was an agreement between ICI and BP, in the context of serious over-capacity in the petrochemicals industry, for rationalisation of plastics production between the parties whereby ICI would concentrate on production of LdPE and BP on production of PVC, each transferring to the other its main plant (and associated goodwill) relating to the product they were giving up. Each party agreed to buy at fair market price the relevant product from the other for a period of five years. [OJ (1984) 1112/1]

- *VW/MAN*. This was a co-operation agreement to enable VW and MAN to extend their respective product ranges. The parties undertook: (i) to develop, manufacture and distribute a joint range of commercial vehicles of between six and nine tonnes with each party specialising in specific development work (VW, inter alia, on the cab, clutch, gearbox and electrical systems and MAN, inter alia, on the engines, chassis, brakes and wheels); and (ii) to supply each other with sub-assemblies and parts for which it was responsible for fitting in the other party's commercial vehicle range. Each party accepted restrictions on use and licensing of IPR arising out of the joint development programme and provision was made for common distribution arrangements for the joint VW-MAN range. [OJ (1983) L376/11]

Works project joint ventures

4–15 A common example of a contractual joint venture or alliance is where two or more contractors combine for the purposes of submitting a bid for a works project (often in the construction and/or engineering field) and, if successful, carrying out the work. Such a joint venture (often called a "consortium") enables the participants to limit or spread risk associated with the project and/or to bring together skills of a variety of specialist contractors and, especially in the case of a project in a foreign jurisdiction, the opportunity to benefit from participation by one or more local contractors. Such joint ventures can broadly be categorised into two commercial types:

(1) *Integrated joint ventures:* where the joint venture itself is a profit centre and the parties accept joint and several liability vis-à-vis the principal third party employer and bear, as between themselves, agreed proportionate shares of any losses or liabilities; work may be carried out centrally on a pooled basis by the joint venture parties or, alternatively, by the placement of competitive sub-contracts.

(2) *Non-integrated joint ventures:* where the work is divided up into separate work segments with each party bearing its own cost of performance and, as between the parties, any liabilities associated with its own work segment; the joint venture will not itself be a profit centre.

4–16 In some cases, project joint ventures may take essentially an unincorporated form but be coupled with the formation of a company jointly-owned by the parties for certain purposes. Such a company may, for instance, provide management or administrative services to the parties or be used as the "front" vehicle for the contract with the employer (with the work being undertaken under sub-contract between the company and the unincorporated construction joint venture) or as the vehicle for raising of finance for the project.

4–17 Works project joint ventures of this kind call for careful drafting. A variety of issues need to be addressed; solutions will vary according to the circumstances of the particular venture. The following is a checklist of issues which will generally need to be considered:

WORKS PROJECT CONSORTIA: CHECKLIST OF KEY ISSUES

(1) *Identity of parties.* Who should be the parties? Will parent company guarantees be required? Will intra-group assignments be permitted?

(2) *Allocation of work.* Will work be carried out by the joint venture on a pooled basis or will work be sub-contracted in separate segments to the joint venture participants (or to third parties)? Will the EC procurement rules apply to the placement of contracts? If work is to be subcontracted, issues will arise, inter alia, concerning:

— scope of work;
— timing of performance;
— liability for defective performance and/or delay;
— remuneration, accounting and invoicing procedures.

(3) *Management.* Will a management committee be established with representatives appointed by each party? Will decisions be required to be unanimous? Will a two-tier structure be appropriate with delegation to a project committee responsible for the day-to-day co-ordination and execution of the work? Will a project director be appointed and will that individual be an appointee of a particular party? How can he be removed?

(4) *Project leader.* Will one of the parties have particular rights, and responsibilities, to represent the joint venture in negotiations with the employer and other third parties? What is the scope of its/his authority? What liability or responsibility will that party have to other members of the consortium? (Liability will often be limited to gross negligence or wilful default.)

(5) *Joint account.* Will a joint bank account be operated by the consortium and who will be entitled to access and draw upon that account?

(6) *Apportionment of profits/losses.* In an integrated-type joint venture, the agreement will need to deal with the method of apportionment and calculation of profits and losses of the joint operations.

(7) *Funding.* Will working capital essentially be provided by the third party employer through advance payments under the principal contract? Who can make calls upon the members of the consortium for cash contributions? Timing? Any maximum limit?

(8) *Bonds and sureties.* Will bonds and sureties for performance be given by the parties on a several basis or jointly and severally? Each party should be committed to provide its share of any bonds, guarantees or sureties (at least up to a stated limit).

(9) *Liability.* What responsibility or liability will each party have to the other party or parties for performance of its share of the work?

— If it is an integrated venture, the individual liability of each party to the other(s) will usually be very limited with the joint venture agreement excluding all claims as between the parties (and indeed containing cross-undertakings by all parties to share or contribute to third party claims in the agreed proportions).

— If it is a non-integrated venture, each party should indemnify the other joint venture parties against any claim or liability arising which is attributable to its performance or segment of the work. One issue which can arise is: what if it is unclear which party is to blame? Formulations differ but one approach, if there is material doubt, is for the claim to be met jointly (i.e. by all the parties) and for any dispute resolution mechanism to be operated only after completion of the project in order not to disrupt performance of the project by internal claims during the course of the venture.

(10) *Intellectual property.* Each party will normally grant a non-exclusive licence to the other parties in respect of its relevant existing IPR in order to ensure that all parties have the right of use for the purposes of the project. If the project is likely to result in arising IPR, it should be clarified whether each party has a free right of use of such IPR after termination of the venture. In some cases, the project will involve the transfer or licence of technology to the employer; in such event, more detailed provisions as to the timing and procedure for making available technical information and the provision of technical assistance will be necessary.

(11) *Staff/labour costs.* Will staff be seconded or dedicated to the joint venture and costs of employment charged to the venture account? If so, the basis needs to be clearly set out—including if there is a commitment on any party to make available the services of certain named individuals.

(12) *Exclusivity.* If it is a bidding agreement, should each party be restricted from bidding for the project independently or as part of a competing consortium? Will a party be free to join the winning consortium, or undertake sub-contract work for that consortium, in the event that the immediate joint venture fails to secure the project work? Note: competition laws may well apply.

(13) *Pricing.* Will each party price its own segment of the contract works (i.e. in a non-integrated venture)? How is the overall contract price to be established? Is that a decision requiring the unanimous approval of all the participants?

(14) *Termination.* The agreement should be clear as to when the joint venture comes to an end with provision for preparation of a final account if necessary. Termination will usually include the circumstances when it is agreed (or apparent) that the bid has failed.

(15) *Default.* Should the innocent parties have a right to terminate the joint venture vis-à-vis a party which is in material default? If so, the procedure and timing should be clearly stated. In most cases, the innocent parties should ensure that all rights, equipment, supply contracts etc. of the defaulting party are transferred or made available to the remaining parties to enable them to step in and take them over (or use them for sub-contracts) in order to complete the project works.

(16) *Force majeure/hardship.* In the case of a lengthy project, should a party escape liability in the event of force majeure? If so, how widely should that be defined; e.g. does it include strikes or other industrial action? Or is a hardship clause more appropriate, providing an opportunity for a party, suffering from unforeseen circumstances, to raise issues for change? If so, is any change to be left to agreement between the parties or to resolution by some form of independent umpire?

(17) *Insurance.* What risks and events are to be insured against at the cost of the joint venture? What is the responsibility of each joint venture party to cover its own liabilities?

(18) *Dispute resolution.* How are disputes to be resolved? Reference first to a management committee? Further reference to senior management within the parties? Is any alternative dispute resolution (ADR) procedure appropriate? Reference to arbitration, or to the courts, as a last resort? Are claims between the parties to be postponed until after completion of the project?

(19) *Choice of law.* What law is to govern the relationship between the parties? Although this may sometimes be potentially sensitive, it is desirable to be clear in order to avoid subsequent potentially complex issues of conflict of laws.

(20) *Accounting.* How will the assets, liabilities and results of the venture be accounted for in the accounts of the joint venture parties themselves—by equity accounting as a "joint venture entity" or a form of "proportionate" accounting? (See the discussion in chapter 19.)

(21) *Partnership.* A material legal issue is often whether the arrangement constitutes a partnership in law, see para.5–18 et seq. below. An integrated project venture may, in practice, do so. Principal legal consequences of a partnership will include under English law the following:

> — the parties will have joint and unlimited liability to third parties for claims in respect of the venture operations (joint and several liability may in any event be contractually required by the third party employer);
> — each party will be jointly bound by commitments entered into by another party within the apparent scope of the venture (this will need to be regulated in practice by appropriate internal contracting procedures and, if necessary, by indemnities against commitments entered into by a party outside the scope of authority).

4–18 The primary agreement will be the joint venture agreement between the parties coupled, in relevant cases, with a form of subcontract with one or more of the parties for the undertaking of specific work or services. In some cases, a bidding agreement may contain terms whereby, if the bid is successful, the parties agree to incorporate a company to enter into the prime contract with the employer; in such event, a shareholders' agreement will often be annexed to the initial joint venture agreement.

4–19 A number of standard or model forms exist.[4]

Joint operating agreements

4–20 A joint operating agreement (JOA) in the oil and gas industry is a well-established form of contract between two or more parties setting out the terms of a joint venture between them under which exploration, development and/or production operations will be conducted. It is the constitution by which the joint venture is governed. A JOA is needed in all cases where a relevant petroleum licence is held by two or more parties since the licence itself does not concern itself with the sharing of rights and obligations as between the licensees. A JOA is one of the longest-established forms of contractual joint venture.

4–21 Provisions developed in the context of JOAs are of interest in relation to a number of joint venture issues—such as financing commitments, funding default mechanisms, pre-emption provisions on transfer, management structure and duties owed between participants. These are referred to at other places in this book. Issues which need to be addressed in the context of a JOA itself are best considered by reference to specialist works on this topic.[5]

---

[4] Most of the major construction and engineering companies will have their own forms of agreement on which to base project or construction joint ventures in which they participate. For international projects, relevant model forms include (i) the Joint Venture (Consortium) Agreement prepared by the International Federation of Consulting Engineers (FIDIC) and (ii) the Model Form of Consortium Agreement published by ORGALIME.

[5] See e.g. Martyn David on *Upstream Oil and Gas Agreements* (London: Sweet & Maxwell, 1996). Examples of precedents of joint operating agreements also include (i) the Model Form Joint Operating Agreement published by the Association of International Petroleum Negotiators (AIPN); and (ii) the industry standard Joint Operating Agreement produced by Oil & Gas UK (2007).

Risk and revenue sharing

4–22 One specialised form of contractual joint venture is a risk and revenue sharing arrangement whereby two or more parties participate in the development and exploitation of a major product. This usually occurs where the parties operate in the same business area and wish to spread risk by sharing in each other's specific product developments. This can be particularly useful where a product is involved which requires substantial development expenditure, such as an aero-engine or pharmaceutical product. Under one example of such an arrangement:

(a) a minority party contributes to the cost of development and manufacture of the principal party's product in a pre-agreed proportion (with the minority party's contribution being paid in cash or "in kind" by carrying out specified work for the project);

(b) the principal party remains responsible for developing, marketing and selling the product; and

(c) revenues from eventual sales of the product are shared between the parties in pre-agreed proportions.

By sharing in revenue rather than profit, each party can benefit from the results of its own manufacturing efficiency. Insofar as it is genuinely a sharing of gross revenues at the production stage, rather than profits, such an arrangement may avoid being regarded as a partnership (with its potential consequences of joint and several liability). However, care must be taken and the analysis will often be difficult.

4–23 Issues arising from such an arrangement are likely to vary substantially with the specific circumstances of the particular venture. A risk and revenue sharing arrangement in respect of an engine or product development is likely to involve, inter alia, the following issues.

RISK AND REVENUE SHARING: KEY TOPICS

(1) *Participation/contribution.* The amount and timing of any cash payments should be established and/or the scope and extent of any development work contribution.

(2) *Design/development/work programme.* Detailed work schedules will normally be established together with provision for progress reports and contingency planning in the event of delay.

(3) *Responsibilities/cost-sharing.* Each party will be responsible for funding its specific share of the development programme and absorbing its own costs in relation to materials, labour, facilities and tooling including assembly and transportation costs.

(4) *Programme management.* The lead party will usually be responsible for programme management, marketing, sales and product support including responsibility for technical leadership and programme integration.

(5) *Pricing.* The lead party will be responsible for pricing, including negotiation of any marketing/financing concessions.

(6) *Revenue share.* The proportionate entitlements of the parties to revenue from sales will usually be established based on the proportion of the total value of the engine or spare parts which each party manufactures or funds.

(7) *Product warranty.* The lead party will normally be responsible for the administration of any product warranty programme vis-à-vis customers.

(8) *Exchange of information and data.*

(9) *Licences.* These will govern background technology licensed by each party to the other.

(10) *Warranty/indemnity.* Patent indemnity and/or arrangements for liability sharing are likely to be established as between the parties.

(11) *Liability.* Provisions should also be included regarding the scope of any liability as between the parties for defects, delays etc. or its exclusion (including consequential loss)—together with provision for liability sharing vis-à-vis third parties.

4–24 The arrangements will need to be carefully drafted in a risk and revenue sharing agreement or similar agreement between the parties. Issues will generally be commercial in nature and the detailed content will, of course, vary with the type of arrangement. The checklist of issues relating to R&D collaborations will frequently be appropriate (see para.4–12 earlier). In many cases, it will be advantageous if any such agreement can fall within the Specialisation Block Exemption (Regulation 2658/2000) published by the European Commission—see para.16–24 below.

Property development joint ventures

4–25 Recent years have seen the emergence of joint ventures as an important medium for property development. Joint ventures offer opportunities for developers to spread risk and to obtain finance which they could not raise alone. They provide landowners (who may lack development capital or expertise) with the ability to participate in increased land value consequent upon grant of planning permission or completion of a development project. Funding institutions and builders can similarly share in any potential development profit and/or rental growth.

4–26 Structures and arrangements for property development ventures vary considerably from project to project. Frequently a limited company will be used; however, disadvantageous tax treatment, particularly for a foreign investor, will often lead the parties towards a tax transparent arrangement.[6] A common arrangement in the UK is therefore some form of unincorporated joint venture which can be designed to reflect the different interests of the parties in the project including their different levels of participation in management and profits. Examples of contractual property development ventures in the UK include the following:

(1) *Joint venture between developers.* A contractual joint venture (sometimes, but usually not, constituting a partnership) may be established between developers, typically with different areas of expertise, to carry out a major development project. The parties will share the profits either through a one-off profit if the development is sold or an ongoing joint investment if the development is retained. This type of joint venture may frequently be used in combination with other structures mentioned below with a third party owning the land. Joint ventures of this type are often structured in such a way that the development or the interests in the joint venture vehicle are to be sold and the development profit crystallised as soon as possible. The trigger point for the sale will often be full letting but, more rarely, may be practical completion of construction.

(2) *Joint venture between developer, funding institution and others.* A contractual joint venture may be established between a developer and other participants (e.g. landowner, funding institution or building contractor) to carry out the development and to share, in a pre-agreed manner, in the profits of the resulting development. The route for sharing profits may take different forms and will vary according to the parties involved and their respective roles; for instance, the arrangements for carrying out the development may typically be combined with ongoing holding by the principal parties of different leasehold interests in the property (see "Profit-sharing lease", below). If the role of the developer, however, is to obtain a planning permission for a landowner, the developer's duties may be discharged once permission has been obtained and typically the agreement will then provide for the land to be sold and for the developer's payment to be met out of the sale proceeds.

(3) *Forward funding arrangement.* A forward funding arrangement is where an institution agrees (before development begins) to acquire a site from a developer and to fund all or part of the building cost. The developer is given a right to a share of profits depending on the success of the development with the developer's profit being represented by the difference between the agreed purchase price (which will include a rental formula) and the costs of development. The allocation of risk under such an arrangement may vary markedly; for example, the developer may on the one hand be required to under-

---

[6] Sometimes (subject to tax factors) a vehicle such as a limited partnership may be considered as a structure for investment and joint development or a US limited liability partnership.

write a guaranteed minimum rental income after a period of time and bear full responsibility of cost overruns, or on the other bear very little (if any) risk of cost overruns or voids beyond a downward adjustment in its profit share. The rewards available to the developer for bringing in a successful project to budget and on time will usually reflect the degree of risk which the developer has agreed to bear.

(4) *Profit-sharing lease*. This structure, also known as a side-by-side or "geared" lease, exploits different legal estates in land as a method for undertaking the development and sharing any subsequent rental profits. Under this arrangement the landowner (usually an institution) retains a long-term interest in the project by receiving a percentage of rental income following completion of the development. Steps may include:

(a) a sale by a developer of land to an institution;
(b) agreement for lease back to the developer containing development obligations (and an obligation on the institution to grant a full lease on completion);
(c) on completion, the institution will typically grant a long lease (say 125 years), for a premium, to the developer with rental calculated by reference to an agreed percentage of income from underlettings; and
(d) the developer will find sub-tenants and grant rack-rent leases to occupiers.

The co-venturers thus share, through their respective ongoing property interests, in profits from the development in the form of agreed percentages of the rental income. The discretions available to the developer will usually be balanced by the protections available to the landowner; e.g. a landowner may be more inclined to give the developer freedom of action in achieving lettings if the landowner is protected by guaranteed minimum rental levels. This type of arrangement is particularly attractive to local authority landowners who, under the terms of the agreement for lease, are able to control the nature of the development and, under the terms of the lease itself, enjoy an income geared to the success of the scheme and at the same time also impose a degree of control via the lease covenants over the quality and functioning of the development in a way which they would not be able to achieve by the use of their statutory powers alone.

4–27 For a more detailed examination of the advantages and disadvantages of these and other particular structures for property development joint ventures (including relevant property law factors and tax considerations), reference should be made to specialist textbooks.[7] Tax considerations will, in particular, be critical to the most effective structuring of the venture.

---

[7] See e.g. Alan Magnus and Robert Kidby (eds), *Property Joint Ventures* (London: Sweet & Maxwell, 2001). For a precedent for a single project, see *Practical Commercial Precedents* (London: Sweet & Maxwell, looseleaf), Vol.3.

Supplier/procurement "partnering"

4–28 In recent years there has been a growth in arrangements between employers and contractors (particularly in the construction and engineering industry) which incorporate "partnering" or "alliancing" philosophies. The parties express an aim to work together to achieve improvements such as cost reduction, speed to market and improvements in quality and safety. These "partnering" arrangements are somewhat different from other contractual alliances in that the "partnering" element is effectively an addition (although a very important addition) to a relatively defined employer/contractor or customer/ supplier relationship which usually falls short of an "alliance" in the usual sense. Broadly, "partnering" arrangements in this context may take two different legal forms:

(1) Non-binding arrangements constitute an expression of intent (often in the form of a "partnering charter") to behave in accordance with agreed principles—but not such as to be legally binding.

(2) Binding "partnering" arrangements will be more specific and reflected in the binding contract terms—with performance being evaluated against agreed standards and often including contractual incentivisation and formal risk/reward schemes.

Non-binding charter

4–29 A non-binding partnering charter will, in effect, be a "mission statement" which the parties declare should apply to their relationship—see also para.4–08 earlier. For example, parties may agree to conduct their relationship in a spirit of mutual trust and co-operation and to strive to avoid disputes by early communication of issues and shared problem-solving. It is common for a partnering charter to be drawn up which is designed to identify and align objectives and develop procedures for joint working by the parties. One author[8] has given the following as examples of topics to be addressed in a partnering charter:

TOPICS FOR A NON-BINDING PARTNERING CHARTER

- A general statement of commitment to abide by partnering principles.
- The key objectives jointly identified for project success.

---

[8] Sally Roe and Jane Jenkins, *Partnering and Alliancing in Construction Projects* (London: Sweet & Maxwell, 2003).

- Procedures for information exchange and joint working and a description of roles and responsibilities.

- Procedures for monitoring progress and building on lessons learned including the use of key performance indicators (KPIs), for example: reduced capital cost and whole life costs, reduced time to completion, reduced defects, increased productivity and improved quality.

- A commitment to discuss problems as soon as they arise and to work together to resolve them in a no-blame culture.

- Procedures for referring disputes to more senior levels of management if they cannot be resolved at site level.

- Allocation of responsibility for costs in relation to partnering workshops, seminars and facilitators.

Source: Roe and Jenkins, *Partnering and Alliancing in Construction Projects*.

4–30 The role of a charter of this kind is to address objectives and aspirations. It is generally not intended to be a contractual document nor to amend or override contractual arrangements. Many of the matters included in the charter are behavioural and conceptual, expressed in terms of general principles. The value lies as much in the process of drawing up the charter as in the charter itself. Such partnering arrangements are being used particularly in relation to procurement contracting for high value, complex projects and for certain joint research and development programmes and arrangements involving closer integration of the supply chain.[9]

Binding partnering arrangements

4–31 Binding partnering arrangements usually incorporate more specific risk/reward principles within the contractual terms for the relevant project. Benchmarks or key performance indicators (KPIs) are frequently agreed upon at the beginning of the contractual relationship and provide an objective measure of the progress and success of the alliance. The participants have the opportunity to derive quantifiable benefits from the specific incentive arrangements. The intention is that members of the alliance should be aligned to a set of common objectives through the use of a financial incentive scheme. As a matter of legal form, these specific partnering terms may be contained either:

(a) in an overall single contract relating to the project; or

---

[9] An example of a non-binding partnering charter in the construction industry is the "JCT Non-Binding Partnership Charter for Single Project" (Joint Contracts Tribunal, Practice Note 4, Series 2, Partnering).

(b) a "partnering" contract which is separate from a contract dealing more traditionally with the terms of delivery of the project.[10]

4-32 Key issues to address when parties are contemplating a binding partnering agreement on a specific project are likely to include the following:

TOPICS FOR A BINDING PARTNERING AGREEMENT

(1) *Objectives of the partnering arrangements:* key objectives in respect of quality, time for delivery and costs.

(2) *Organisational structure:* procedures for information sharing and management of the partnering arrangements, including role and powers of any alliance or management board.

(3) *Roles, responsibilities and liabilities:* clear definition of each of the partner's roles and its liabilities in relation to its own works.

(4) *Incentive arrangements:* establishing the risk/reward incentive arrangements:

— agreeing a suitable target cost against which out-turn costs should be measured and gainshare/painshare calculated;
— addressing caps on painshare/gainshare and percentage entitlements; identifying suitable performance targets (e.g. operational and maintenance costs after project completion);
— targets for staged and/or project completion;
— treatment of insurance proceeds, excess and deductibles; effect of project changes on the target cost and schedule.

(5) *Exclusions from the partnering arrangements:* circumstances when the partnering arrangements will not apply and/or provision for calculation of any painshare at the time of exit.

(6) *Confidentiality:* including arrangements for transfer of know-how and other confidential information from one "partner" to another and appropriate confidentiality undertakings.

(7) *IPR in project designs and information:* clarity as to ownership of, and right to use, designs and technology derived from the project.

(8) *Dispute resolution:* dispute resolution procedures and principles will often be a key part of the "partnering" arrangements, including early warning procedures and mediation and/or dispute review panels.

4-33 In establishing partnering arrangements, as with alliance arrangements generally, the parties have to be careful of not crossing the line into

---

[10] Certain standard forms for binding partnering arrangements which exist in the UK construction industry for use with other standard works contracts include (i) NEC Partnering Option X12, published in 2001 by the Institution of Civil Engineers as an option which can be added to a number of standard engineering contracts and (ii) ICE Partnering Addendum, published in 2003 by the Institution of Civil Engineers.

agreements or arrangements which improperly restrict competition. The principles are outlined more fully in chapter 16. The danger signs in the project partnering context are particularly where arrangements (or practices) lead to: bid rigging; information sharing on price or other commercially sensitive information not necessary for the project in question; market sharing arrangements for future projects; or long-term exclusive arrangements foreclosing new market entrants.

Conclusion

4–34 Partnering and collaboration arrangements of these kinds are evidence of the growth generally of the alliance philosophy in commercial arrangements. The contractual alliance is the "umbrella" legal form for a large proportion of these diverse collaborative arrangements which have become such a feature of the business landscape. The most integrated form of alliance structure is, though, an equity joint venture—to which we now turn.

Chapter 5

Equity joint ventures: the framework

Equity joint ventures have increased worldwide in recent years, particularly as a medium for cross-border collaborations and investments. Equity is the glue which binds the parties together and aligns their incentives where there is an ongoing business to be conducted. This chapter outlines certain business types of equity joint venture. It addresses—under the basic headings of "partnerships" and "companies"—the principal legal forms by which equity joint ventures are conducted. It then reviews, in broad terms, the typical content of the basic legal documentation relating to a joint venture company (JVC) and the status and role of the shareholders' agreement.

CATEGORIES OF EQUITY JOINT VENTURE

Equity joint ventures as a business form

5–01 An "equity joint venture" is not a legal term of art. It does, though, usefully describe a joint venture or alliance (and the term "joint venture" is generally used in this book in this context) which has the following characteristics, namely where (i) each party has an ownership interest in a jointly-owned business, (ii) the jointly-owned business has a distinct management structure in which each party directly participates and (iii) the parties share in the profits (or losses) of the jointly-owned business.

5–02 Equity joint ventures cover a wide range of different business arrangements. For present purposes, a useful distinction can be made between the following broad categories:

(a) full-function or merger-type joint ventures;

(b) limited-function or co-operative joint ventures; and

(c) minority equity investments.

Examples of these three different business categories of equity joint venture appear below.

Full-function or merger-type joint ventures

5–03 A "full-function" joint venture is a venture which is established by the parties with the intent that it should have (or have access to) its own employees, assets, facilities, funding and markets and generally carry on business as an autonomous economic entity without material recourse to its parents. The term "full-function" has been adopted by the European Commission and has important consequences for the treatment of joint ventures for competition law purposes—see para.16–08 et seq.

5–04 A full-function joint venture may, for instance, be created by the merger (through the medium of a JVC) of substantial existing businesses carried on by the parties. In many cases, this may be accompanied by a structure of operating subsidiaries or businesses in jurisdictions worldwide. Depending on tax considerations, one typical route is for the parties to form a new company (the JVC) by transferring their respective businesses or operating subsidiaries in the relevant field to the JVC in exchange for shares in the JVC.[1] Examples of full-function joint ventures include the following cases reviewed and cleared by the European Commission:

- *Fortis/Banco Comercial*. Fortis, a Dutch-led international banking and insurance group, has agreed to establish a joint company with Banco Comercial Portugu's (BCP). BCP is transferring four insurance companies in Portugal to the new company in which Fortis will hold 51% and BCP 49%. [Case M. 3556 (2005)]

- *Sony/BMG*. Sony and Bartlesmann agreed to merge their global recording music businesses into three or more newly created companies, to be operated under the name SonyBMG. It constituted a full-function joint venture and was cleared under the EC Merger Regulation. [Case COMP/M.3333 (2004)]

- *The Post Office/TPG/SPPL*. The Post Office (UK), TNT Post (the Netherlands) and Singapore Post (Singapore) formed two joint ventures for the provision of outbound cross-border mail services—one joint venture company providing those services in the Asia Pacific region and the other joint venture (Delta) elsewhere in the world. Each party contributed, directly or indirectly, its outbound international mail business to the joint venture. The joint ventures are jointly controlled by the three parents. The joint ventures are full-function. The European Commission has, subject to certain conditions, cleared the concentration. [Case No. COMP/M.1915 (2002)]

- *Kali & Salz/Solvay*. K&S (Germany) and Solvay (Belgium) agreed to combine their businesses for the production and sale of salt in a newly created joint venture to be named the European Salt Company. The

---

[1] See para.2–05 for a "road map" for this type of transaction.

joint venture has the sole responsibility for the production of salt and its sale to third parties. It obtains all financial, personnel and other resources (including IPR) necessary to operate on a lasting basis as an autonomous economic entity. It has its own independent management. [Case No. COMP/M.2176 (2002)]

- *De Beers/LVMH*. The parties established a new jointly-owned company, Rapids World, whose principal activity is the retail of diamond jewellery under a De Beers brand name with possible extension to associated luxury products. The new joint venture will source polished diamonds and other raw materials from third parties. It will control jewellery design in-house, outsource manufacturing activities and distribute products through its own distribution system. The parties have committed start-up finance, staff and assets. De Beers and LVMH will have joint control. The joint venture will perform, on a lasting basis, all the functions of an autonomous economic entity. [Case No. COMP/M.2333 (2001)]

5–05 The "full-function" nature of the joint venture does not affect the formal shape of the legal documents but it is likely to influence the way the parties approach the commercial terms in a number of significant areas, including in particular:

(a) governance and management structure—with the management of the JVC probably being given a greater degree of autonomy and independence than for a limited-function venture;

(b) transferability of interests—since it is more likely (compared with a limited-function venture) that one or more of the parties may wish to sell its interest in the future;

(c) ownership of intellectual property—since it is more likely that the JVC will develop and retain its own rights; and

(d) exit terms—including in some cases the possibility of an initial public offering (IPO) or eventual sale of the jointly-owned business but rarely any unilateral right of a party to terminate or wind-up the venture.

Limited-function or co-operative ventures

5–06 More frequently, perhaps, a joint venture entity will have a more limited role. It will not be an autonomous or independent unit but one which is designed to carry out a more specific and limited role under the direct control of its parents; e.g. to provide a new production plant for sourcing components for supply to the parties (sometimes termed an "input venture"). The European Commission has termed these "limited" or "partial function" joint ventures. They involve significant co-operation or co-ordination between the joint venture parents.

5-07 The "limited-function" nature of these joint ventures is likely to affect many of the commercial terms:

(a) the governance structure will usually provide for continuing close control of the parties over the operations of the joint venture entity;

(b) the terms of ancillary contracts (see chapter 6) will be crucially important in regulating dealings between the joint venture and each of the parties;

(c) there will be tighter restrictions on transferability of interests by the parties, compared with a full-function venture, since the continued participation of the same parties will usually be vital; and

(d) possibly more specific provisions may be included which contemplate termination if one of the parties wishes to end the venture.

A number of different types of "limited-function" or co-operative joint ventures are considered briefly below.

Production joint ventures

5-08 A JVC may be formed to establish a jointly-owned production plant which will manufacture components or raw materials to be supplied to each of the joint venture parties. Frequently, a first phase will be the pooling of technology and the undertaking, through the JVC, of further research and development. Examples of production joint ventures which have been reviewed and cleared by the European Commission include the following:

- *Solvay/Sisecam*. Solvay (of Belgium) and Sisecam (of Turkey) have created a joint venture for soda production in the form of a Bulgarian company, SOD I SPJCo. Solvay has a majority holding. The EBRD is a financial partner. Solvay and Sisecam have a right and off-take obligation on all production by SODI in proportion to their levels of capital contribution to the company. Marketing of the product is carried out in an autonomous way by Solvay and Sisecam separately. [OJ (1999) C272/14]

- *General Electric/Pratt & Whitney*. General Electric Aircraft Engines (GEAE) and Pratt & Whitney (P&W) agreed to form a joint venture company (the GE-P&W Engine Alliance LLC) to develop, manufacture, sell and support a new aircraft engine. The JVC does not itself produce the new engine but co-ordinates the parent companies' activities for design and production. Each party sells to the JVC the parts for which it has production responsibility at a price determined on the basis of a fixed formula. The profits and losses of the JVC are allocated between the parent companies at the end of each fiscal year. [OJ (1999) 0206/19]

- *Hydro Texaco/Preem*. These parties have created a co-operative joint venture through Scanlube in which each party holds 50 per cent of the capital. Preem transferred to Scanlube the lubricants plant it used to operate. Texaco has granted to the joint venture a licence to use Texaco's lubricating oil technology. The aim of the joint venture is to purchase base oils, additives, packaging materials and other supplies and to produce and package lubricants for sale to the shareholders. [COMPo REP 1997/108]

- *Fujitsu AMD Semiconductor*. Fujitsu and Advanced Micro Devices have entered into a joint venture agreement and five related agreements including a technology cross-licence agreement and a joint development agreement. A joint venture company has been established under Japanese law, Fujitsu AMD Semiconductor Limited, in which Fujitsu holds 50.05 per cent and AMD 49.95 per cent of the capital stock. Each party is entitled to purchase 45 per cent of the joint venture's total production of semiconductor wafers. The remaining 10 per cent of production is to be allocated as the board of directors of the joint company may decide, which may include sale directly in certain Asian countries. Separately, through a joint development committee, the parties collaborate in the development of product and process technologies; any IPR so developed will be jointly-owned by the parties. [OJ (1994) L341/66]

- *Exxon/Shell*. Chemical companies within the Exxon and Shell groups agreed to finance, construct, manage and operate a 50:50 production joint venture in France (to be formed as a GIE). Production of LLDPE (linear low-density polyethylene) is its main business. A large part of the feedstock is supplied by the parent companies. All polyethelene produced is supplied to the parents. The parties are jointly involved in budget decisions, investments and decisions on plant optimisation and product development. The co-operative venture was exempted by the European Commission for 10 years. [OJ (1994) L144/20]

An outline of a typical "limited-function" production joint venture is addressed further in chapter 6 including key issues likely to arise in supply and off-take agreements between the JVC and the respective parties.

Outsourcing joint ventures

5–09 Outsourcing of IT and numerous other services has become a common commercial arrangement for companies aiming at efficiencies. Sometimes, the outsourcing party forms a JVC with the outsourcing company in order to exercise more influence over the management of the outsourced activities or to benefit directly in the equity potential of the business (particularly if it is intended to grow as an independent business).

Appropriate assets and employees are transferred to the JVC by the "employer" and the other party contributes its outsourcing management expertise or local resources. The JVC then provides the outsourcing activities to the employer under an appropriate arm's length contract. The JVC may be in a position to provide services also to third parties. Examples of outsourcing joint ventures (including some considered by the European Commission) include:

- *NHS/Xansa*. Some of the finance, accounting and payroll functions of the NHS are to be outsourced to India through a 50:50 joint venture between NHS Shared Financial Services centres and Xansa. The deal could save the health service £220m over the next decade, according to health ministers. [*FT:* 22.11.04]

- *Telexis/EDS*. Telexis (a subsidiary of Fiat) and EDS Italia have set up a joint venture designed to provide call centre services. EDS was acquiring joint control of a subsidiary of Telexis. The principal client will be the provision of customer services for Fiat. [IP/99/715]

- *EDS/Lufthansa*. EDS agreed to acquire 25 per cent of the shares in Lufthansa Systems which provides IT and related services to Lufthansa. This business will account initially for a large proportion of the joint venture's work but, increasingly, the joint venture will play an active role in the market for IT services to the travel industry. [Case No. IV/M.560 (1995)]

- *IBM/Fiat*. IBM Italia and Fiat have agreed a 50:50 joint venture in IT services. The joint venture will mainly replace the captive outsourcing of services for Fiat (for which an initial guaranteed commitment was agreed) although the venture is expected to increase the proportion of third party customers. [Case No. COMPI M.2478 (2001)]

A joint venture can add a layer of complexity (and indeed potential conflict) into the outsourcing relationship—although provide potential benefits if the venture is likely to develop significant sales to third parties. Where such third-party business is developed, the joint venture may acquire a "full-function" nature (as in certain of the above cases). Commonly, though, the major client of the joint venture will be the outsourcing employer.

E-commerce platforms

5–10 Developments in telecommunications and the internet have opened up opportunities for participants in a specific industry to combine to form electronic and internet-based trading exchanges. These may be aimed at reducing procurement costs or generally at establishing a more efficient exchange for buyers and sellers in that market. They will usually be set up by certain "founders" incorporating a JVC which will own and operate an internet-based exchange in which other third parties may participate. An outline of such an e-commerce joint venture is addressed further in chapter 6. Some examples of e-commerce ventures include the following:

- *Covisint: General Motors/Ford/DaimlerChrysler.* These parties have created the world's largest electronics market place by linking to put their procurement needs on a single online trade exchange. Renault of France and Nissan Motors of Japan were also proposing to join. [*FT:* 28.2.00] The European Commission subsequently concluded that the agreements contain adequate provisions to eliminate potential competition concerns and did not fall within Art.81(1) of the EC Treaty. [OJ (2001) 49/04 and IP/Ol/1155 (2001)]

- *Opodo.* Opodo is an online travel agent created by nine of the largest European airlines as a joint venture. It offers its services on a pan-European basis and has launched websites in Germany, UK and France. The Commission cleared the joint venture subject to certain commitments by the shareholders. [Case COMP/D-2/38.006]

- *Volbroker.* Six major banks have formed a joint venture, called Volbroker.com, which will develop and market an electronic brokerage service for trading among banks in foreign currency options. The owners gave the Commission that they would set up 'Chinese walls' to impede any information flows between the parent companies and the joint venture. [Press Release IP/00/896 (2000)]

- *Indentrus.* A group of leading banks and financial institutes have established a network which will operate as "certification authorities" for securing electronic commerce transactions, initially in the business-to-business context. Indentrus was established in 1999 pursuant to a LLC Agreement governed by US Delaware law. No single equity owner will have control. [OJ 2001 2249/12]

- *Steel24–7.com and BuyForMetals.com.* Arbel of Luxembourg, Usinor of France, the Anglo-Dutch Corus and ThyssenKruper of Germany, Europe's four biggest steelmakers, have joined forces in a plan to set up two independent internet businesses which will use e-commerce to produce cost savings in the procurement of materials and services and to sell steel to customers. [*FT:* 23.6.00]

5–11 These multi-party joint ventures have given rise to a number of issues not normally a feature of more conventional "bricks and mortar" ventures. They include the following:

B2B E-commerce Ventures: Some Key Issues

(1) *Capital structure.* The founders may wish to develop a relatively sophisticated capital structure to cater for the different interests of equity participants. The original participants may seek a "founders' premium" in the form of entrenched rights to board representation or to receive a preferred dividend. Any such special rights will normally be attached to a separate class of shares. (See also the kind of preference rights discussed in para.7–12 et seq. below.)

(2) *New participants.* The capital structure will frequently allow for admission of new participants (e.g. trading members, suppliers, technology providers etc.) and the rights of such non-founding members may well be structured differently from those of the original founders.

(3) *Competition law.* At the structural level, these ventures attract careful review by competition authorities to ensure that the exchange is not being used as a framework for improper co-ordination between competitors. Competition law concerns often require the terms of these joint ventures to allow third parties open access to the relevant exchange and eliminate any non-arm's-length, preferential commercial arrangements with shareholders.[4]

(4) *Equity incentives.* There is frequently some form of equity incentive to encourage participants to trade over the exchange. Equity incentives may be offered in lieu of non-preferential commercial arrangements with shareholders. They can also be used as incentives for shareholders to use the exchange—particularly where they have been unable or unwilling to enter into non-compete covenants. Examples of equity incentives are warrants or options to subscribe for or convert into equity shares of the JVC based on usage over a designated period. The flexibility to do this may depend on the national corporate laws of the JVC.

(5) *IPO/trade sale.* Many participants will invest in the hope or plan that there will be a subsequent public offering or trade sale by which they may exit at a profit. Provisions to anticipate such an event will often be included.

(6) *Corporate governance.* Founder members (particularly if they are competitors) will frequently seek equal voting rights, and rights to appoint directors, and will seek to maintain that balance irrespective of changes in participation. One method (relevant national corporate law permitting) is to develop a capital structure which separates voting interests from economic interests in the JVC. Another consequence for multi-party joint ventures is that it may be difficult for the board to be structured and operate in an efficient manner "in the best interests of the company", with so many appointees having their own "member" interests as a primary consideration.

---

[2] See e.g. the clearance by the European Commission of the Covisint B2B automotive marketplace.

> (7) *Exit*. Provisions may be required to anticipate or discourage "bad leavers" who leave following a default or in situations not approved by an agreed majority of existing participants. In ventures where shareholders do not give non-compete covenants, voluntary exits can sometimes be treated as a "bad leaver" situation.

Acquisition vehicle

5–12 A JVC may be the route by which two or more parties combine for the purpose of making an acquisition of a business or company owned by a third party, frequently with the intention of subsequent division of the assets and liabilities of the relevant business after its acquisition. Examples considered by the European Commission include the following:

- *RBS/Fortis/Santander/ABN Amro*. RBS, Fortis and Santander were jointly running a €71bn break-up bid for Dutch bank ABN Amro. The consortium received approval from the European Commission. To meet the latter's requirements, Fortis is required to sell certain parts of the acquired business in the Netherlands. [*FT:* 4.10.07]

- *GEC Siemens/Plessey*. These were arrangements between GEC of the UK and Siemens of Germany to form a JVC (GEC Siemens Plc) which would bid to acquire Plessey Company Plc and subsequently reorganise Plessey's activities The arrangements allocated the various different Plessey's businesses between the parties; inter alia: (i) Plessey's defence systems business and radar systems business would be wholly owned by Siemens; (ii) Plessey's UK avionics and naval systems businesses would be wholly owned by GEC; (iii) Plessey's electronics components business would be owned by GEC and Siemens in equal proportions. [OJ (1990) C152/3]

Minority equity investment

5–13 A somewhat separate category of equity joint venture is minority investment where:

(a) one party takes a minority equity interest in another party (thereby sharing in the profitability or success of the investee entity—in some cases, each party may take a minority investment in the other); and

(b) the investment is part of a strategic relationship or alliance between the parties which extends beyond simply the equity investment and establishes other mutual commercial benefits to the parties.

In itself, this is frequently not a joint venture structure for a specific project or business but a framework on which specific business ventures between the parties can subsequently be developed and supported. Such links and alliances have become a feature, particularly, in the telecommunications field and other industries where participants are anxious to develop pan-European or global networks. Some examples of strategic equity investment reported in the press or reviewed by the European Commission include the following:

- *Autovaz/Renault*. Russia's largest car maker Autovaz has chosen Renault as a strategic partner and will offer it a blocking stake in the company, officials at both companies have announced. The deal will give Renault a foothold in one of the world's fastest growing car markets. Renault and its own alliance partner Nissan are scrambling to add capacity in emerging markets to offset slumping markets in western Europe and the US. [*FT:* 8.12.07]

- *DoCoMo/AT&T Wireless*. NTT DoCoMo, Japan's largest mobile phone operator, agreed to acquire a 16 per cent stake in AT&T Wireless. The investment was part of a broader alliance that would bring Japan's leadership in wireless internet technology to the United States. The AT&T unit would have exclusive rights to DoCoMo's i mode technology and marketing experience, as well as the i mode name, in North America. [*FT:* 1.12.00]

- *General Motors/Fiat*. Fiat and GM unveiled a cross-shareholding alliance aimed largely at reducing the two carmakers' costs through a series of joint ventures in the areas of powertrains (in particular, engines and gearboxes), purchasing of car components and R&D programmes relating to cars and light commercial vehicles. Both parties stressed that the deal would preserve their independence and separate identities: GM acquired a 20 per cent stake in the Fiat Auto car division in exchange for $2.45m GM common stock, giving Fiat a 5.1 per cent stake in the US group. Fiat acquired an option to sell the remaining 80 per cent of Fiat Auto to GM in three and a half years. [*FT:* 14.3.00] The European Commission approved the co-operation arrangements. [IP/00/931 (2000)]

- *Rolls-Royce/BMW*. BMW increased its holding in Rolls-Royce, the UK aero-engine manufacturer, from two per cent to 10 per cent under a reshaping of the close relationship between the companies. RR would take full control of a German joint venture which has developed the BR 700 engines for business and regional jets. The two companies planned to co-operate in research and technology, purchasing and logistics. BMW had no plans to increase its stake further. There was no discussion of its taking a seat on the board. [*FT:* 26.10.99]

- *Olivetti/Digital*. These parties entered into a co-operation agreement in the field of computer systems. Digital made available to Olivetti certain of its new microprocessor technology. Olivetti committed itself to the specified technology for its computer platform offerings and related software and agreed to purchase certain computer system products from Digital. This technological co-operation was accompanied by the acquisition by Digital of approximately eight per cent of Olivetti's share capital and by proportional representation of Digital on Olivetti's board of directors. The European Commission cleared the agreement for a period of 10 years. [OJ (1994) L309/24]

Other strategic minority investments may take the form of an acquisition by a larger corporate investor of an equity stake in a smaller company (with or without a listing). This may be a base from which to gain access to "niche" technology which the smaller company is developing or, possibly, as a first step to an eventual acquisition—see also "corporate venturing" discussed at para.1–05.

5–14 The legal issues involved in such strategic alliances where a minority equity investment is taken are both commercial and corporate in nature. They are discussed in more detail below in the context of minority investment and protection—see para.9–38 et seq.

Legal Form: Partnerships

5–15 We now turn to address in more detail the legal forms by which an equity joint venture may be conducted—principally (i) partnerships and (ii) companies. There are also some "hybrid" structures (particularly, in the UK, the limited liability partnership (LLP)) which are worthy of mention.

5–16 A partnership has, in particular situations, some advantages compared with a company as a legal form for an equity joint venture—see chapter 3. The structure offers relative informality and flexibility, with very few reporting or formal requirements. Partnerships are a recognised legal form in most jurisdictions. A primary feature is that a partnership will be a "fiscally transparent" vehicle for tax purposes—with the result that profits/losses/expenditure will accrue directly to the partners in their respective shares. This may be a more tax-efficient form than a separate corporate entity, particularly where early losses or expenditures are contemplated. Against these potential advantages, each partner will usually have joint and unlimited liability for the debts and obligations of the partnership and each partner can, as against third parties, commit the partnership as a whole. These risks can usually be mitigated by incorporating a special purpose subsidiary to act as the partner.

5–17 The types of partnership vehicles vary from jurisdiction to jurisdiction. The use of the partnership model in the UK is, in practice, relatively rare for a commercial joint venture business. However, partnership structures are frequently used in many continental European countries as a joint venture vehicle.

When does a partnership exist?

5–18 At law, a partnership is simply a form of unincorporated undertaking, founded in a contractual relationship between the parties, which has the requisite hallmarks for partnership applicable in the relevant country. What constitutes a partnership will, therefore, depend on the law of the relevant jurisdiction. In joint ventures, the test of "partnership" is generally met by contractual arrangements between parties who are establishing a common business or undertaking—particularly one in which the parties share in profits and losses. This relationship can lead to specific consequences under the partnership law of the relevant jurisdiction.

5–19 A partnership under English law is established when the statutory criteria of the Partnership Act 1890 are met, namely: "the relation which subsists between persons carrying on a business in common with a view of profit".[3] Where the courts are called upon to decide whether a partnership has been established, they will consider all of the circumstances of the relationship in order to apply these criteria to the facts including, particularly, the following:[4]

(1) A partnership cannot exist without a business. There must be some commercial venture, although "business" is widely defined to include "every trade, occupation or profession". It seems that a business can, for this purpose, exist without the element of continuity; accordingly, a single venture can in appropriate circumstances be a business. For a business to be carried on "in common", there must be participation in the business by two or more parties. The general view is that it is a business with a view of a profit which must be carried on in common, which implies that each of the partners must be entitled to a profit share.

(2) The profit criterion can cause particular difficulties. It may be necessary to decide, for instance, whether a financial return linked to profit from a business is that of a partner or a creditor or simply consideration under a contract for goods or services.[5]

---

[3] s.l(l) of the 1890 Act.
[4] *Cox v Hickman* (1860) 8 H.L. Cas 268. While s.l(l) of the 1890 Act lays down the criteria for a partnership, s.2 provides certain guidelines for determining whether or not those criteria have been met. These can be summarised as follows: s.2(1): co-ownership of property does not of itself create a partnership as to anything so held; s.2(2): the sharing of gross returns does not of itself create a partnership; and s.2(3): the receipt by a person of a (net) share of the profits of a business is prima facie evidence that he is a partner in the business.
[5] s.2(3) of the 1890 Act gives a number of specific examples where the receipt of a financial return does not of itself evidence a partnership. These include: s.2(3)(d): the payment of loan interest out of profits; and s.2(3)(e): payment for goodwill out of profits.

(3) The sharing of losses, if any, creates a strong presumption of partnership. The element of risk is an indication of true participation in a business. This is irrespective of any stipulation in the agreement between the parties.[6]

5-20 Partnership is a recognised legal relationship throughout Europe, founded on contract. Whilst the essential ingredients are generally similar, the particular legal requirements—and consequences—of partnership will depend upon the relevant jurisdiction. Most partnerships are established by means of a partnership agreement. The normal law of contract applies and thus, although the parties will often enter into a formal written agreement, an agreement can be inferred from a course of dealings. A partnership commences under English law when the criteria of the 1890 Act are met. This is a mixed question of law and fact. It follows that any commencement date which the parties stipulate is not conclusive.[7] Particular difficulty may arise when parties decide to form a joint venture company but commence the business in common before the company is formed.[8]

General partnerships

United Kingdom

5-21 The usual form of partnership in the UK is a general partnership under which each partner has unlimited liability for the debts and obligations of the firm (even if a creditor must look first to the firm's assets). This is to be distinguished, from a limited partnership—see para.5–27 et seq. below. Although, as a matter of procedure, it can sue and be sued in the partnership name, a partnership is not a legal entity separate from its individual partners under English law.[9]

Rest of Europe

5-22 Some continental European jurisdictions distinguish between civil partnerships (often applicable to land-based businesses such as farming or

---

[6] *Fenston v Johnstone (HM Inspector of Taxes)* [1940] 23 T.C. 29. One party wished to purchase and develop a piece of land. The other party advanced funds. The parties agreed to share in the profits and to be responsible for one half of any loss. The court decided that a partnership was created despite an express term stipulating that the arrangement should not constitute a partnership between them.

[7] *IRC v Williamson* (1928) 14 T.C. 335.

[8] *Keith Spicer Ltd v Mansell* [1970] 1 All E.R. 462. The parties agreed to form a limited company together to carry on a restaurant business. Before incorporation one party ordered goods for use by the company. The parties also opened a bank account in the name of the proposed company, without the word "Limited". It was held on the facts that they had not created a partnership.

[9] The Report of the Law Commission on "Partnership Law", Law Com No 283, November 2003, recommended reform but the UK Government has decided not to take forward this and other proposals regarding general partnerships.

building development) and commercial partnerships where the business involves recognised commercial activities. General commercial partnerships exist throughout Europe. Their individual legal features will, of course, depend upon the relevant national law. Some EU examples include:

Belgium:	*société en nom collectif (SNC/VOF)*
France:	*société en nom collectif (SNC)*
Germany:	*offene Handelsgesellschaft (OHG)*
Italy:	*società in nome collettivo (SNC)*
Netherlands:	*vennootschap onder firma (VOF)*
Spain:	*sociedad colectiva (SC)*

5–23 Illustrations of the partnership route being used for joint ventures between corporate entities include the following cases considered by the European Commission:

- *BP/Mobil*. The two parent companies agreed to combine their respective fuels and lubricants businesses throughout Europe by means of partnerships (or their local equivalent) in each national jurisdiction. There were to be two separate national partnerships for the combined fuels and lubricants businesses. For fuels, BP would hold 70 per cent and Mobil 30 per cent interests, while for lubricants Mobil would hold 51 per cent and BP 49 per cent. [1996 Case IV/M.727]
- *Corning/BICC*. Corning (of the United States) formed in 1981 a long-standing 50:50 joint venture in the UK with BICC which took the form of a general partnership, named Optical Fibres, whose principal purpose was the manufacture and sale of optical fibres. Other similar joint ventures with other European partners were formed in France and Germany. [OJ (1986) L236/30]

Particular issues

5–24 For a detailed analysis of partnership law in the UK, reference should be made to specialist textbooks on partnership law.[10] No special statutory provisions govern partnerships whose members are companies. The Partnership Act 1890 will apply in the normal way (save to the extent that its provisions are properly excluded by agreement). Many of the issues

---

[10] For instance, Lindley and Banks, *Law of Partnership*, 18th edn, (London: Sweet & Maxwell, 2002).

which arise in structuring a partnership between corporate partners are essentially the same as those for a corporate joint venture. Specific issues or factors which should be considered in relation to a partnership structure for a joint venture under English law include the following:

PARTNERSHIPS: KEY ISSUES FOR JOINT VENTURES

(1) *Is it a partnership?* This is often a first question, particularly where the parties do not document the arrangement as a conventional partnership. This will particularly apply if there are any elements of profit sharing. The test under English law has been discussed earlier (see para.5–18).

(2) *Liability.* Each partner is an agent of the firm and can bind the firm in the usual course. Each partner is jointly liable in law with the other partners for any obligations or liabilities incurred in the course of the partnership. A partnership therefore involves a credit risk for each partner. In addition, each partner will also have unlimited liability for the debts and obligations of the partnership. This can be mitigated to a significant extent by interposing a special purpose subsidiary, as a limited liability company, to act as the partner in the partnership. This will therefore provide an indirect shield of limited liability at a secondary level but will not affect that company's primary unlimited liability as a partner.

(3) *Management.* The arrangements for management will depend on contractual agreement. There is a "default" rule that each partner will have a right to participate in management unless otherwise provided—so, in a joint venture, it is vital that the agreement deals specifically with the management structure in order to avoid uncertainty and potential conflict.

(4) *Profits/losses.* The agreement should clearly set out the rules for division of any profit and the bearing of any losses. Unless otherwise agreed, the "default" rule is that both profits and losses will be divisible equally. The agreement should also make it clear when a contribution may be called from a partner to fund any loss.

(5) *Tax.* If a partnership is created, tax implications will need careful analysis. Sometimes, of course, tax will itself be the driving force behind the creation of a partnership by reason of a partnership's "transparency" for tax purposes compared with a corporate venture.

(6) *Implied terms.* The partnership medium leads to a number of other terms being implied, inter alia, under s.24 of the Partnership Act 1890 into the relationship between the parties. These terms can be excluded by appropriate provision in the partnership agreement. These "default" rules should always be considered. They include:

— where a partnership has no fixed term, a partner may determine it by notice;
— no new partner can be introduced without the consent of all existing partners;
— every partner is entitled to take part in the management of the partnership; loans to the partnership bear interest at five per cent per annum.

(7) *Fiduciary duties.* Partnership is a fiduciary relationship. Every partner is bound to render accounts and information to any partner (s.28). Every partner must account to the firm for any benefit derived by that partner, without the consent of the other partners, from any transaction concerning the partnership or from any use of the partnership property (s.29). A partner's use of information received in the course of the partnership business to secure a personal benefit will give rise to a similar obligation. A partner carrying on business of the same nature as the firm (without consent) must account to the firm for all profits which he makes from that business (s.30). Partners owe a duty of good faith towards each other which cannot effectively be excluded.

5–25 The UK Government considered the introduction of a new Partnerships Bill, by way of a re-statement and expansion of the law, following a Report in 2003 by the Law Commissions.[11] However, in 2006 the Government announced that it would not be taking forward any changes in relation to general partnerships. If the reforms had been enacted, partnership law would have been more up-to-date and accessible in codified form. This may have made it more popular as a legal structure for commercial businesses than is presently the case.

Documentation

5–26 The content and style of a partnership agreement will vary with the nature of the arrangement. In many cases, provisions comparable to a shareholders' agreement in the case of a corporate joint venture can be suitably adapted. Many of the specific issues discussed later in this book can, therefore, be adapted to apply to the partnership medium.

A precedent for a general Partnership Agreement under English law between corporate partners appears as Precedent 6 in Part E.

Limited partnerships

5–27 A limited partnership is a variant of the partnership model under which certain of the partners have limited liability. Such a model exists in most jurisdictions, although individual features will vary. In many ways it is a hybrid between a general partnership and a corporate structure. Its popularity and usefulness as a structure for joint ventures vary from jurisdiction to jurisdiction.

United Kingdom

5–28 Limited partnerships were first introduced into English law by the Limited Partnerships Act 1907. It is not a business structure which has been

---

[11] Partnership Law, Law Com No 283, Scot Law Com No 192, November 2003.

particularly well-used in the UK for joint ventures. Its principal features under English law include:

(a) the liability of some partners (limited partners) is limited to the amount contributed by them in cash or property to the partnership;

(b) at least one of the partners (general partner) must have unlimited liability; a general partner may nevertheless be a limited liability company;

(c) a limited partner has no implied authority to bind the firm, cannot be repaid any part of his capital contribution and (importantly) cannot take part in the management of the firm without forfeiting the benefit of limited liability;

(d) registration is required with the Registrar of Companies, including a statement of the sum contributed by each limited partner;

(e) unless agreed to the contrary, one or more new general or limited partners may be introduced at any time without the consent of the limited partners.

One advantage of using this structure is that a limited partner can enjoy limited liability but at the same time retain, in most respects, the benefit of "tax transparency" with profits and losses accruing directly to the partners by reference to their partnership shares.

5–29 A joint venture participant will, though, usually wish to have some influence over management beyond that permissible for a limited partner. In the context of joint ventures involving corporate partners, limited partnerships will rarely provide any additional advantage compared with a general partnership. The benefit of limited liability can probably be achieved in many cases through the formation of a special purpose subsidiary to act as a partner in a general partnership or, more recently, by the adoption of the LLP model. There may, though, be some situations where such a medium is attractive for tax purposes—particularly, it would appear, for US companies investing in joint ventures which are likely to involve initial losses or capital expenditure (e.g. in new technology fields) where tax efficiencies can be achieved through the partnership medium and they are accustomed to the limited partnership format.

5–30 The UK Government, following the review by the Law Commissions (see para.5–25 earlier), is proposing to proceed with certain useful changes to the 1907 Act which may increase the attractiveness of the limited partnership structure. In particular, the Law Commissions recommended that there should be a list of permitted activities in which limited partners may engage without loss of their limited liability, including:

(a) taking part in certain major decisions—including decisions regarding changes in the general nature of the partnership business, classes of investment by the partnership, disposal of the partnership business and winding up; and

(b) acting as a director or employee of, or a shareholder in, a corporate general partner.

The Government is consulting further with a view to any new law becoming effective in October 2009.

Rest of Europe

5–31 Limited partnership structures exist in most European civil law countries and, indeed, generally have more widespread use than in the UK. For instance, in Germany the GmbH & Co KG is a partnership model which combines a limited partnership (the KG) with a private company (the GmbH, which acts as the general partner); this model provides the management and organisational advantages of a corporate joint venture with the benefit of tax transparency. Some EU examples are:

Belgium: société en commandite par actions (SCA/CVA)

France: société en commandite par actions (SCA)

Germany: Kommanditgesellschaft (KG) (also the GmbH & Co KG)

Italy: società in accomandita per azioni[13]

Netherlands: commanditaire vennootschap (CV)

Spain: sociedad en comandita por acciones (S. Com.p.A.)

USA

5–32 In the US, partnerships are also a common model. In particular, the limited partnership laws of Delaware permit arrangements which enable the limited partners to be involved in certain key decisions on which their approval is required before the general partner is able to commit the partnership. The limited partnership has separate legal personality but is recognised as a "pass-through" or transparent vehicle for tax purposes.

UK limited liability partnerships

5–33 Mention should, lastly, be made here of the introduction in the UK of limited liability partnerships. This is a different animal from a limited

---

[12] Note, however, the limitation that a company cannot be a partner in an Italian limited or general partnership.

partnership, being in fact a new form of corporate entity primarily aimed at certain regulated professions in the UK. Its fiscal transparency for tax purposes may also offer potential use for commercial joint ventures—see para.3–22 et seq.

LEGAL FORM: JOINT VENTURE COMPANIES

5–34 A jointly owned corporate vehicle, holding the business assets of the joint venture, is generally viewed as the most appropriate legal form for the majority of equity joint ventures where a continuing business is to be operated—see chapter 3. A corporate structure offers advantages such as: separate identity and personality for the joint venture; limited liability; flexibility in designing share rights; an easier structure for raising finance; continuity in the event of share transfers; and well-established background laws. Against these advantages, there will be certain additional publicity, regulatory and compliance requirements. A corporate model is available in most jurisdictions worldwide.

Limited company

United Kingdom

5–35 In the UK formal distinctions are made between the following principal types of company:

(1) *Public limited company or Plc*. Only a plc may offer shares or other securities to the public. In return, a Plc is subject to tighter corporate law regulations in respect of maintenance of capital, distributions, transactions involving directors and certain other matters (e.g. a requirement for valuation of non-cash consideration before allotment of shares). There is rarely a need for a JVC in the UK to be a Plc unless such a public offering of securities is contemplated.

(2) *Private limited company or Ltd*. A private company limited by shares is the normal corporate vehicle for a JVC in the UK. Shareholders have the benefit of limited liability (i.e. liability only to pay up the full amount due in respect of the nominal amount of their shares and any share premium). There will be regular disclosure and public filing requirements. A private company can be converted to a Plc, if necessary, at a later stage.

(3) *Unlimited company*. This is essentially the same as a private limited company with the important exceptions that (i) each member has unlimited liability to contribute to any shortfall on a winding-up of the

company and (ii) on the other hand, an unlimited company in many circumstances is not required[13] to file publicly any annual accounts and this lack of publicity is sometimes seen as an advantage (although this exemption does not apply if it has a limited company as a subsidiary or its parent or, of more likely relevance to joint ventures, if two or more limited companies are its controlling shareholders).

Rest of Europe

5-36 Similar corporate entities can exist in all EU countries, although the type of company used will depend on the particular jurisdiction. Entities broadly corresponding to a UK private limited company include the following:

Belgium:	*société privée à responsabilité limitée (SPRL/CVBA)*
France:	*société à responsabilité limitée (SARL)* or *société par actions simplifiée (SAS)*[15]
Germany:	*Gesellschaft mit beschränkter Haftung (GmbH)*
Italy:	*società a responsabilità limitata (Srl)*
Netherlands:	*besloten vennootschap met beperkte aansprakelijkheid (BV)*
Spain:	*sociedad de responsabilidad limitada (SL)*

However, in certain countries the public company equivalent is more commonly used—for instance, in Spain the *sociedad anónima* (stock company), in Belgium the *société anonyme* (SA/NV) and in France the *société anonyme* (SA) may each be more frequently used for a large business undertaking than the private company—see further the summaries in Part D of this book.

USA

5-37 In most US states the stock corporation is a common and flexible form of business entity. Many foreign companies, for instance, choose to incorporate in Delaware because of its well-established corporate laws—and the fact that Delaware corporations are not required to have a

---

[13] See s.448 of the Companies Act 2006.
[14] The SAS, created by French law in 1994, offers many advantages for joint ventures compared with a SARL—see Part D.

principal place of business in Delaware. An even more flexible corporate entity is the limited liability company (LLC) which can now be established in all US states. Management arrangements for such companies are very flexible and are simply reflected in the terms of a written limited liability company agreement. An LLC frequently provides a convenient joint venture structure. A particular advantage is that an LLC may elect (by "checking the box") to be taxed in the US either as a corporation or as a tax transparent partnership. It is, in effect, a "hybrid" vehicle—see para.3–27 earlier.[15]

European companies

5–38 The European Commission has endeavoured to develop and promote certain new legal forms which, to a significant extent, are designed to have a common form throughout the EU—and thereby, the Commission hopes, facilitate cross-border trade and investment. Two legal forms designed to encourage collaborations of a somewhat specialised kind are the European Economic Interest Group (EEIG) and the European Co-operative Society—see para.3–28 earlier. Of much greater relevance in the context of equity joint ventures are the European Company (SE) and the proposal for a European Private Company (EPC).

Societas Europaea (SE)

5–39 The aim of the European Company Statute (ECS)[16] was to create a new type of public limited company (a *Societas Europaea*, or SE) which can be established as a single company under EU law able to operate throughout the EU with one set of rules and a unified management and reporting system. It is a corporate vehicle designed to assist further the breakdown of national barriers and the development of the single market. This new legal entity became possible in Great Britain from October 2004.

5–40 An SE can be set up in a number of specified situations. One of them is the creation of a joint venture "subsidiary" formed by companies from at least two different Member States. An SE is, therefore, a possible joint venture vehicle appropriate for a pan-European business and one which might overcome some of the difficulties derived from the present practice of having national subsidiary entities. Key features of the SE include:

---

[15] In addition, a Delaware LLC which does not carry on business in the US and has not elected to be treated as a corporation for tax purposes may, in certain circumstances, avoid fully the need to file US tax returns.
[16] Under SI 2004/2326 Council Regulation (EC) No. 2157/2001 on the Statute for a European Company and Council Directive 2001/86/EC with regard to the involvement of employees.

European Company (SE): Key Features

(1) *EU operations.* An SE must have operations in more than one Member State (and members from more than one Member State). An SE is able to operate on a European-wide basis and is governed to a substantial extent by Community law directly applicable in all Member States.

(2) *Means of creating an SE.* It is possible for companies within the EU to form an SE by certain specified means including: (i) a merger of two or more public limited-liability companies into a new company; (ii) the creation of a holding company with subsidiaries in several Member States; (iii) (more likely in the joint venture context) companies from at least two Member States forming a subsidiary as a joint venture; or (iv) transformation of a public limited-liability company into an SE. Companies and firms (including private limited companies in most EU jurisdictions) can therefore form a "subsidiary" SE by subscribing for its shares provided that at least two of them either (i) are governed by the laws of different Member States or (ii) have for at least two years had a subsidiary or branch in different Member States.

(3) *Registration in individual Member State.* Each SE must, nevertheless, be registered and have its head office in an individual Member State. An SE still has a strong "national" influence.

(4) *National laws.* An SE is similar to a public limited company in the relevant Member State in which it is registered. Indeed, rules applying to such public companies in that Member State are used to fill the gaps in the general framework provided by the Council Regulation. In particular, national law applies in such important areas as: auditing and accounting requirements; directors' duties and liability; raising, reducing and maintaining capital; insolvency; and (initially at least) tax treatment.

(5) *Share capital.* An SE may denominate its share capital in any currency it chooses (provided that, in the UK, at least £50,000 is denominated in sterling). No shareholder is liable for more than the amount it has subscribed.

(6) *Management structure.* An SE is free to adopt in its statutes either a one or a two-tier board system. The "organs" of an SE comprise (i) a general meeting of shareholders and (ii) either a supervisory body and a management body (two-tier system) or an administrative body (one-tier system) depending on the form adopted in its statutes:

— In the case of a two-tier system, the management body is responsible for managing the SE. The members are appointed (and removed) by the supervisory body or, depending on its statutes, by the general meeting. No person may be both a member of the management body and the supervisory body. The supervisory body (whose members are appointed by the general meeting) is responsible for supervising the work of the management body but may not exercise management powers.
— The supervisory body normally elects a chairman. If half of the members are appointed by employees, the chairman of the supervisory body is elected by the general meeting of shareholders.

>   - In the case of the one-tier system, the administrative body manages the SE.
>   - An SE's statutes should list the categories of transactions which require authorisation by the supervisory body (in the two-tier system) or an express decision by the administrative body (in the one-tier system).
>
> (7) *Employee participation.* There is no single model of employee involvement applicable to an SE. Under the Directive on employee involvement, the creation of an SE requires negotiations between management and a "special negotiating body" of employee representatives on arrangements for the ongoing involvement of employees (including, if applicable, representation on the SE's administrative or supervisory body):
>
>   - If negotiations fail, a set of "standard rules" set out in the Directive applies which contemplate an obligation on the management of the SE to provide regular reports on the progress and prospects of the SE as a basis for informing and consulting with a body representing the employees of the SE. This representative body is to receive the agendas of management and/or supervisory board meetings. Management meetings (at least once a year) with the representative body must cover, inter alia, the economic and financial situation, the probable development of the business and of production and sales, the probable trend of employment, investments, substantial organisational changes, introduction of new working methods, transfers of production, mergers, cut-backs, closures and collective redundancies.
>   - If, prior to the creation of the SE, relevant employees of the SE were employed by companies previously regulated by "worker participation" rules (e.g. including board representation), the principle is that the SE is obliged to continue these rules and provide equivalent participation of its workers (the "before and after" principle).
>
> (8) *Transfer to another Member State.* An SE is able to transfer its registered office to another Member State.
>
> (9) *Subsidiaries.* An SE may itself set up one or more subsidiaries in the form of SEs. (It seems clear that an SE can hold existing subsidiaries on its formation. Although not expressly stated, it is assumed that an SE will be able to form or acquire new subsidiaries, other than an SE, and indeed hold interests outside the EU.)

5–41 Advantages of an SE would appear to include:

(1) There is an "European flavour" to the corporate entity, free of specific national identity, which could offer some advantages for establishing a cross-border joint venture where a "neutral" vehicle is politically desirable.

(2) An SE offers the possibility of a single legal structure with a unified management and reporting system and avoids the need to set up a network of subsidiaries across Europe operating at national level—with, frequently, an awkward conflict of legal and operating reporting lines.

(3) An SE registered in one country can move its registered office within the EU, affording the opportunity for fast restructuring in response to trends in the internal market.

5–42 Disadvantages of adopting an SE structure include:

(1) The rules on employee participation are complex—and may involve a need (at least in the UK) for employee involvement in the corporate governance structure on a scale greater than that which some companies may be willing to concede.

(2) The Council Regulation produces an awkward combination of applicable laws—with many topics being governed by the ECS but significant other matters being governed by the relevant national law applicable to public limited companies (arguably, leading not to one uniform SE but potentially numerous different systems).

(3) Fiscal matters, such as accounting and tax, continue to depend significantly on national law.[17]

(4) There may be an inevitable reluctance on the part of commercial companies to use an "unfamiliar" entity unless there are clear substantive advantages.

In particular, there is still a need for careful tax structuring of a joint venture—with selection of the individual Member State for registration requiring careful tax analysis. An SE may provide some benefits since it may be possible (depending on the tax laws of the Member State where the head office is located) to set off losses from a permanent establishment in one country against profits derived from another. However, without greater EU corporate tax harmonisation, tax factors are still going to be crucial in establishing and locating an international joint venture.

5–43 The new rules for an SE may offer attractions as a vehicle for the establishment of a cross-border joint venture in some circumstances. However, its use for this purpose is likely to be restricted to a few major "pan-European" ventures.

European private company

5–44 Looking towards the future, the European Commission is embarking upon the introduction of a "European private company" (*Societas Privata*

---

[17] The Commission has been called upon to bring forward appropriate proposals to establish standard rules on taxation and accounting matters insofar as they affect SEs. The Centre for European Policy Studies has also issued a recent report (*Corporate Taxation and the European Company Statute*, January 2008) identifying issues and calling for the elimination of fiscal impediments to companies forming SEs.

Europea or EPC). The aim is to provide small and medium sized enterprises (SMEs) in Europe with a form of company which will make it easier, and less costly, for them to conduct cross-border business. Key elements of the initial proposals published by the European Commission are:

(1) The SPE will be a private company with a legal personality and share capital. There will be no requirement that founding shareholders come from different Member States.

(2) An SPE may issue both ordinary and priority shares with rights as designated in the SPE's articles. Consideration for the shares may be in cash or kind, including services. The minimum capital will be simply €1.

(3) A range of matters, in particular the SPE's internal organisation and decision-making structure, must be regulated by the articles. The shareholders will have a high degree of freedom to decide on these matters (including whether to adopt a one-tier or two-tier management structure).

(4) Any conditions or restrictions on transfer must be set out in the articles.

(5) Matters relating to tax, accounting and employment law will be governed by relevant national law of the country in which the SPE is registered.

The aim is that the SPE will, through a detailed governing EC Regulation and the SPE's own customised articles, have a more self-contained and understandable legal framework than the public European Company (SE) which suffers by a patchwork of references to national laws.

5–45 These are still only proposals. If adopted, the SPE will not become effective until 2010. No doubt there will be some hesitation in using a new structure. However, with its flexibility, "European feel" and similar structure in each EU country, the SPE may turn out to be of considerable practical interest as a legal form for cross-border European joint ventures.

LEGAL FORM: SOME "HYBRID" STRUCTURES

"Hybrid" structures

5–46 Various other vehicles or structures may be appropriate in certain circumstances for equity joint ventures. The availability of alternative vehicles for a particular venture should be reviewed on a jurisdiction-by-jurisdiction basis. In many cases, tax planning will play an important role in defining the required characteristics.

(1) *Limited liability partnership (LLP)*. The UK has now introduced this important new legal form. In fact, this is really a corporate entity with a separate legal status. Each partner has limited liability. The primary advantage is that an LLP is "tax transparent" and is treated for tax purposes as if it were a partnership (i.e. profits and losses accrue directly to the members in their relevant proportions). An LLP can carry on any type of business. Dealings between the members are governed by a membership agreement. Public filing requirements (e.g. annual accounts) apply on a basis similar to a limited company. The LLP may become an important medium for joint ventures in the UK—see para.3–22 et seq. earlier.

(2) *LLC*. Many companies requiring a US joint venture entity choose incorporation of a limited liability company (LLC)—frequently in Delaware. Such Delaware companies do not need to have a principal place of business in Delaware and have flexible constitutional arrangements. A particular advantage is that an LLC may elect (by "checking the box") to be taxed in the US either as a corporation or as a tax transparent partnership. An LLC may be a suitable vehicle for a joint venture with a US partner even if the operations of the venture will take place outside the US.

(3) *"Dual-headed" structures*. In some cases, companies may wish to conduct a combined business through a single merged venture for management purposes but, whether for tax reasons or for the sake of maintaining corporate identities, also wish to maintain their existing national companies. These "dual headed structures" have usually been established by publicly listed companies (owned by different sets of shareholders in each national entity respectively) but with contractual links so that the two companies can be run as a single business enterprise—such agreements covering management; accounting; profit sharing or equalisation; distribution; repayment of capital or liquidation proceeds.

Each of these "hybrid" structures is addressed in a little more detail in chapter 3. They will generally be considered where tax planning considerations are of high importance.

JVCs: Documentation and Key Issues

Shareholders' agreement for a JVC: outline issues

5–47 The choice of legal form will dictate to a large extent the formal shape of the joint venture documentation. Articles of association (or other formal constitutional documents) will be required for the establishment of a joint venture company (JVC). However, the commercial arrangements between the parties are likely to require contractual terms for a corporate joint venture which will inevitably go beyond purely constitutional matters. In the case of a corporate joint venture, a joint venture agreement or shareholders' agreement has become the principal commercial agreement between the parties establishing their relationship. This agreement supplements, and must be designed to inter-relate with, the formal constitutional documents. The shareholders' agreement, under English law, is a private agreement. It does not amend the articles of association and a corporate act undertaken in accordance with the articles of association will still be valid (and can be relied on by third parties) irrespective of the shareholders' agreement. However, as between the parties, the shareholders' agreement will have contractual effect.

5–48 In the UK the terms "joint venture agreement" and "shareholders' agreement" are often used interchangeably. The term "joint venture agreement" may in practice be more frequently used if it contains wider provisions relating to the initial establishment of the JVC, conditions precedent and the business contributions of the parties. A "shareholders' agreement" more commonly describes an agreement focusing on the ongoing relationship between the parties as shareholders in the JVC.

Key issues

5–49 The shareholders' agreement will deal with the establishment of the joint venture with emphasis on terms relating to the ongoing relationship of the parties as shareholders in the JVC. The commercial circumstances of each JVC will influence the particular issues to be addressed in any shareholders' agreement relating to that venture. Many specific issues affecting corporate joint ventures[18] are discussed generally throughout the remainder of this book.

SHAREHOLDERS' AGREEMENT: KEY ISSUES

The following basic topics are typically covered by a shareholders' agreement:

(1) *Parties*. Who will be the parties to the JVC? Will parent company guarantees be required?

---

[18] The following discussion relates to corporate joint ventures, although many of the principles can also be customised into partnership agreements.

SHAREHOLDERS' AGREEMENT FOR A JVC: OUTLINE ISSUES 123

(2) *Purpose.* What is the overall purpose and scope of the venture? Is there a business plan to which reference can be made (perhaps as an annex)?

(3) *Formation.* What are the key steps for formation of the JVC?

— what conditions precedent (e.g. regulatory approvals) must be satisfied prior to commencement and who will be responsible for satisfying or obtaining them?

— identify the name, registered office, initial directors etc.?

(4) *Capital.* What will be the initial share capital and equity interests? Will the parties have the same or different share rights (dividend, liquidation preference etc.)? How will initial contributions be made by the parties?

(5) *Additional financing.* What arrangements will be agreed for:

— procedures on new share issues?
— any commitments to contribute future finance? any provision for emergency funding?

(6) *Guarantees.* Will the parties undertake to give guarantees to support the JVC's financing or other commitments and agree sharing of any resultant liabilities?

(7) *Governance/board structure.* How will the JVC be governed? What arrangements will apply in respect of:

— board/management structure? appointment and removal of directors?
— matters requiring unanimity or super-majority at board level and/or reserved for decision to the shareholders?
— deadlock resolution procedures?

(8) *Financial matters.* What terms should be established regarding:

— dividend policy? accounts/accounting principles? auditors?
— preparation of budgets/business plans?

(9) *Reporting and information.* Will there be agreed procedures for reporting of financial and other management information to the shareholders?

(10) *Inter-party relationship issues.* Will undertakings or other arrangements be agreed regarding:

— non-compete restrictions on parents? secondment of staff and employment matters?
— provision by parents of any services, technology licensing, supply of products?
— co-operation on tax matters? confidentiality?

(11) *Transfers of interest.* What arrangements should be established regarding the ability of a party to transfer its interest:

— will consent be required prior to any transfer? will pre-emption rights apply?
— will any commercially agreed put or call options be negotiated?

(12) *Insolvency/default/change of control.* Will a party have a "call" or other special rights in the event of:

> — insolvency of the other party?
> — material default by the other party?
> — change of control?
>
> (13) *Governing law.* What governing law will apply?
>
> (14) *Arbitration.* How will any legal disputes be finally resolved?
>
> (15) *"Boiler-plate"* matters such as: amendments; non-assignment; invalidity; notices; entire agreement; announcements; costs; precedence over articles of association.

> The Joint Venture Checklists in Part F set out a fuller list of matters to be considered in establishing a joint venture. Part E contains a number of model precedents including:
>
> - a precedent of a 50:50 Shareholders' Agreement (short form) for a deadlock corporate venture as Precedent 9;
>
> - a precedent of a Multi-Party Shareholders' Agreement (long form) for a corporate venture as Precedent 10;
>
> - a model Corporate Joint Venture Agreement (Two-Party) developed for use internationally by the International Trade Centre and reproduced as Precedent 13.

Enforceability of shareholders' agreement

5–50 The shareholders' agreement therefore lies at the heart of the legal relationship between the joint venture parties. The courts had early doubts whether contractual arrangements between shareholders outside the scope of the articles of association (e.g. as to how votes will be exercised) should be enforced. However, it is now clear that a shareholders' agreement creates contractual rights and obligations between the parties which, under English law, should be enforced in the same way as any other contract. Remedies for breach may include not only damages but also (where available according to normal legal principles) equitable remedies such as an injunction[19] or specific performance.[20]

---

[19] An injunction may be prohibitive, preventing a shareholder from voting or acting in contravention of the agreement (e.g. *Greenwell v Porter* [1902] 1 Ch. 530) or mandatory (see e.g. *Puddephatt v Leith* [1916] 1 Ch. 200). The decision in *Russell v Northern Bank Development Corp* [1992] 1 W.L.R. 588 was a re-affirmation that a shareholders' agreement is enforceable as a contract between the shareholders who are parties to it. See also Australian authority, *Canatti Holding Co Pty Ltd v Zampatti* (1978) 52 A.L.J.R. 732, to the effect that a shareholders' agreement may be used to prevent parties acting on the basis of the articles of association but contrary to the terms of the shareholders' agreement.

[20] See e.g. *Peña v Dale* [2003] EWHC 1065 (Ch) where specific performance was ordered in relation to an option to acquire a minority party's shareholding. See also *Growth Management Ltd v Mutafchiev* [2006] EWHC 2774 (Comm) where the court confirmed that "commercial" canons, of interpretation applied to the construction of a shareholders' agreement.

5–51 This contractual position, and the scope for the shareholders' agreement to deal with a broader range of commercial matters than would be appropriate for a constitutional document, has led in practice to the shareholders' agreement being the primary mechanism under English law for establishing the rights and obligations of the parties in respect of a corporate joint venture.

5–52 In certain jurisdictions (including, particularly, civil law countries), there may still be uncertainties whether full effect should be given to an agreement between the shareholders, particularly if there is any conflict with the articles or by-laws. In some jurisdictions, remedies such as an injunction or specific performance may not be available—with breach giving rise only to a claim in damages. This is one reason why, in many jurisdictions, greater formal protection and legal certainty may be achieved by making more extensive provision for commercial matters in the constitutional documents than is customarily the case in the UK.

Parties to shareholders' agreement

5–53 For tax or other purposes, the actual shareholder in the JVC may in many cases not be the ultimate parent company but a subsidiary. In this situation, one approach is for the shareholders' agreement to be entered into by the actual shareholders—accompanied by a separate agreement or undertaking directly by the parent company(ies) since there will usually be a need for certain undertakings to be given at superior level by each parent, e.g. to observe confidentiality undertakings (applicable to its corporate group as a whole), to undertake non-compete obligations (similarly applicable to its corporate group as a whole) and to guarantee performance by its subsidiaries.

5–54 An alternative approach, particularly in the case of a major strategic venture, is for: (i) the shareholders' agreement to be entered into by the ultimate parent companies; (ii) provision to be included in the agreement to allow shares of the JVC to be issued, or transferred, to a wholly owned subsidiary within the relevant group; and (iii) each ultimate parent company to undertake to ensure performance by members of its corporate group of provisions of the joint venture agreement which are expressed to extend to them (e.g. non-compete and confidentiality undertakings).

JVC as a party?

5–55 Should the JVC itself be a party to a shareholders' agreement establishing a corporate venture? Practice varies. Under English law, advantages of the JVC being a party can be:

(1) If it is a party, the JVC can directly undertake obligations to observe relevant restrictions or procedures (e.g. non-compete or confidentiality undertakings) which could make enforcement easier. This

may be seen as an advantage in many cases—especially where it is a limited-function joint venture with important ancillary contracts between the JVC and the shareholders. It will generally be necessary, in any event, for the JVC to be party to ancillary contracts such as licence or supply agreements.

(2) A direct contractual right of enforcement against the JVC will also assist where there is judged to be a material risk that the individual directors of the JVC may not observe constraints or undertakings contractually agreed between the shareholders. The directors will no doubt in practice have regard to the wishes of the shareholders in fulfilling their duties as directors[21] but they will not be contractually limited or bound by commitments in the shareholders' agreement unless they are parties to it (or bound, indirectly, by contractual commitments made by the company).[22]

(3) In a multi-party joint venture, where the co-operation of several other shareholders is required in order to give effect to an undertaking relating to the company's conduct, it is more common for the JVC itself to be a party in order to assist enforcement.

(4) Where the alliance takes the form of a minority equity investment in a company, it is customary—and indeed necessary in most cases—that the company should be a party to give appropriate protections and strategic undertakings—see para.9.39 et seq.

On the other hand, factors against may be:

(1) The parties may prefer that the terms of their joint venture contract should not involve the JVC so that, in the event of disputes or variations, they can take any wider relationship issues into account without the consent of the JVC management being required.[23]

(2) If the JVC is party to a shareholders' agreement which contains terms which fetter the JVC's exercise of its statutory powers (i.e. a term which purports to restrict the company from passing a resolution

---

[21] It is doubtful whether, strictly, the directors are bound to observe limitations on their discretionary powers contemplated by provisions in a shareholders' agreement to which the JVC is not a party and which "reserve" to the shareholders certain decisions which would otherwise be within the domain of the directors (although it is arguable that, certainly where all the current shareholders are in agreement, the shareholders' wishes should be followed—consistent with decisions such as *Duomatic Ltd, Re* [1969] 2 Ch. 365 and *Cane v Jones* [1981] 1 W.L.R. 1451). If the JVC's constitution contains a provision comparable to reg.70 in Table A to the Companies Act, the shareholders (if in agreement) should also be able to issue a direction by special resolution to the directors which they would be obliged to follow. The issue rarely arises in practice but the analysis is not straightforward. For a further discussion, see K. Reece Thomas and C. L. Ryan, The *Law and Practice of Shareholders' Agreements* at p.75 et seq. (London: Butterworths, 2007).

[22] It is sometimes objected that the directors cannot fetter their future discretion. However, it is clear that a contract made by the company can have that effect subject to limited exceptions (see e.g. *Fulham Football Club v Cabra Estates* [1994] 1 B.C.L.C. 363).

[23] In the UK, if the JVC is not a party to the joint venture agreement, it should not normally be allowed any right to enforce any rights of the agreement under the new rules (modifying the doctrine of privacy of contracts) introduced by the Contracts (Rights of Third Parties) Act 1999. Appropriate wording to exclude the Act should be included in these cases.

pursuant to a specific right given to the shareholders by statute), it appears that under English law those terms will be unenforceable against the JVC—but may be enforceable as a voting agreement between the other parties if the terms which restrict the JVC can be severed. Although the "no fetter on statutory power" doctrine is limited in scope, it has become more common under English practice—particularly in a two-party joint venture—not to include the JVC as a party to the shareholders' agreement.

"No Fetter" Doctrine: UK Law

- In *Russell v Northern Bank Development Corp* [1992] 1 W.L.R. 588 a shareholders' agreement to which both the shareholders and the JVC were parties provided, inter alia, that the creation of new share capital should require the unanimous written consent of the shareholders and of the JVC (i.e. the JVC could not increase its authorised share capital without a unanimous resolution). The House of Lords held that this amounted to "an unlawful and invalid fetter on the statutory power of [the company] to increase its share capital" by ordinary resolution. The agreement was enforceable as a matter of personal voting contract between the shareholders themselves but not directly against the JVC.

- As a strict matter, the decision in *Russell* has no bearing in any event upon undertakings by a JVC which can be delivered or fulfilled without a decision of its shareholders (e.g. matters which fall within the decision-making authority of the directors rather than the shareholders). The better view is that the doctrine is restricted to "fetters" on such statutory shareholder powers as: increase of authorised share capital; consolidating, sub-dividing or reducing share capital; changing articles of association; removing directors or auditors; change of name; or winding-up of the company.

- The "no fetter" doctrine can be limited even further in the UK if use is made of the power to "entrench" rights in the JVC's constitution. It will be possible, as from October 1, 2009, under s.22 of the Companies Act 2006, to require unanimity or a super-majority for a shareholders' resolution to amend specified provisions of the articles. This could therefore "entrench" a requirement for a majority higher than that otherwise applicable under statutory corporate law for that resolution. The procedure for "entrenchment" set out in the Act must, however, be followed for the provision to be valid.

5–56 In some cases, where it is desirable for the JVC to be a party but it is not in existence at the time of original signature of the joint venture agreement, provision can be made in the joint venture agreement for the JVC to become a party after its formation and for the JVC to execute an addendum agreeing to "adhere" to the obligations, and to become entitled to the rights, as if it had been an original party.

Constitutional documents

5–57 In the case of a corporate entity, the constitutional documents will be a necessary and important part of the overall legal relationship between the parties. It is the shareholders' agreement and articles of association (or by-laws) which, together, define that relationship. The articles of association will therefore need to be tailored carefully to the requirements of the relevant law and will invariably be prepared by the local lawyers.

UK articles of association

5–58 In the case of a UK company, the articles of association will normally contain certain procedural and other regulations customary under corporate law and practice together with the constitutional matters applicable to the particular joint venture. The "special" joint venture provisions in the articles of association will usually address the following matters:

UK ARTICLES OF ASSOCIATION: KEY ISSUES

(1) *Classes of shares.* Commonly shares will be divided into separate "classes" to which the respective entrenched rights of the parties can attach.

(2) *Pre-emption provisions.* Pre-emption provisions will usually apply on share issues in favour of existing shareholders and possibly on share transfers (although practice varies as to whether transfer provisions are more easily left to the shareholders' agreement).

(3) *Directors.* Provisions will establish the respective rights of the parties to appoint (and remove) directors-and usually exclude any requirement for directors to retire by rotation.

(4) *Quorum.* Quorum provisions should be fixed for both board and shareholder meetings.

(5) *Shareholder meetings.* Procedural rules should generally be included for holding shareholder meetings.

(6) *Chairman's casting vote.* The articles should clarify whether the chairman has a casting vote or not at board meetings.

(7) *Alternate directors.* Provision (if applicable) may be included for appointment of alternate directors.

(8) *Resolutions.* Procedural provisions may be included to assist flexibility for shareholders' and/or directors' resolutions to be passed by "agreement" without formal meetings.

(9) *Conflict of interest.* Modifications to standard rules may be included to permit a director to vote on matters in which he may have an interest.

(10) *Notices.* In the case of a UK company, care will need to be taken about notice of meetings if any directors are based overseas; for example, reg.88 of Table A (which states that directors absent from the UK do not have to be given notice of meetings) may have to be amended.

5–59 The nature and extent of the contract created by the articles of association under English law is surprisingly still uncertain. The basic principle (under s.33 of the Companies Act 2006) is that the articles of association, as a statutory contract, confer rights and obligations between the company and its members and also[24] between the members *inter se*. Doubt, however, surrounds the enforceability of rights in the articles of association which relate to a shareholder personally rather than in its capacity as a member.[25] Although the practical scope of this limitation is probably narrow, this is another reason why the shareholders' agreement has become the primary document for the relationship between the parties as a whole.

An example of Articles of Association for a 50:50 joint venture company in the UK is set out as Precedent 11 in Part E. Precedent 11 in Part E also includes a description of modifications commonly made to reflect the joint venture context.

Relationship between shareholders' agreement and articles of association

5–60 The shareholders' agreement and the articles of association, together, contain the important legal rules governing the ongoing relationship of the parties as shareholders in the JVC. Preparing a consistent and easy-to-follow relationship between the two documents is an important part of the draftsman's task. Practice and drafting styles vary as to how much of the contractual arrangement should be reflected in the articles of association (or other constitutional documents) as well as, or in place of, the shareholders' agreement.

5–61 There are substantive legal differences between the two documents. The shareholders' agreement is governed solely by the ordinary rules of contract and only binds the parties to it. The articles of association are regulated in material respects by company law statute and will be binding automatically on all shareholders (including future shareholders). One consequence is that the articles of association under English law can

---

[24] See *Quin & Axtens Ltd v Salmon* [1909] A.C. 442.
[25] See e.g. *Hickman v Kent or Romney Marsh Sheep-Breeders Association* [1915] 1 Ch. 881.

normally be amended from time to time by shareholders holding 75 per cent or more of the voting rights.[26] The issue is potentially relevant for a minority shareholder whose rights, if only in the articles of association and not contractually protected by a shareholders' agreement, may therefore be vulnerable unless it holds more than a 25 per cent voting interest.

(1) Minority shareholders may, however, wish to entrench in the constitutional documents of the JVC their rights relating to such matters as the appointment of directors, pre-emption rights on transfer of shares and veto rights. This may also be the case where a "foreign" investor seeks to ensure maximum protection in relation to a JVC formed under the laws of a jurisdiction with which it is not familiar. In order to prevent amendment of those constitutional provisions without that party's consent, it will often be appropriate in these cases to create specific "class rights" in the articles of association (or relevant constitutional document)—e.g. by attaching the relevant rights to "A" and "B" shares held by the shareholders respectively.[27]

(2) One view is that veto and pre-emption rights in the constitutional documents of a JVC are also stronger rights for the shareholder than if solely in the shareholders' agreement. In particular, they are then rights enforceable directly against the JVC and its directors, who are bound by the provisions of the articles of association, rather than purely contractual rights against the other shareholder(s)—see para.5–55. Restrictions in the constitutional documents will also generally be in a public document, giving notice to third parties dealing with the JVC.[28]

5–62 Advantages, on the other hand, of incorporating veto and pre-emption rights solely in a shareholders' agreement—and not in the articles of association—in the case of a UK company include the following:

(1) The shareholders' agreement will generally not be a public document.[29]

---

[26] This is subject, under English law, to the power under s.22 of the Companies Act 2006—see para.5–55 earlier.
[27] See chapter 9 and, in particular, para.9–32 et seq. below.
[28] In the UK note that, in favour of a third party dealing with the JVC in good faith, the power of the directors to bind the JVC (or authorise others to do so) is deemed to be free of any limitation under the JVC's constitution (s.40 of the Companies Act 2006).
[29] It may, in some cases, be registrable with the Registrar of Companies either as part of the articles of association or under ss.29 and 30 of the Companies Act 2006 which requires registration of agreements made by all the members of a company which would otherwise require a special or ordinary resolution to be effective. A shareholders' agreement will, though, rarely attempt to amend the articles of association as such. The general view is that it is not registrable unless the shareholders' agreement is specifically referred to in the articles and the articles are not capable of interpretation without reference to the shareholders' agreement.

(2) The shareholders' agreement can set out rights and obligations enforceable between the members. Provisions in the articles of association relating to the same veto matters may, in certain circumstances, be invalid as fettering the company's statutory powers.[30]

(3) As a drafting matter, it can be awkward to try and make the detailed provisions regarding pre-emption on transfer the same in both documents. It is often easier and less cumbersome to leave such provisions solely to the shareholders' agreement. Alternatively, the articles of association could prohibit generally any transfers (other than intra-group transfers) except with the consent of all existing shareholders—and the shareholders' agreement could specify the detailed procedures governing transfers and the circumstances in which consent is, or must be, given by each party.

(4) Whilst there may be some comfort to be obtained from having express limitations on the powers of directors spelt out in a publicly available document, in many cases the parties will be reluctant to expose these internal commercial matters to the public eye.

(5) As a practical matter, it is the shareholders' agreement which is likely to be the more accessible and commercially important document for the principals on an ongoing basis. There is, therefore, advantage in having all material ongoing terms in a single document, rather than divided between the shareholders' agreement and the articles of association.

5–63 Any direct conflict between the provisions of the shareholders' agreement and the constitutional documents should be avoided. It will usually be sensible, however, to include a provision in the shareholders' agreement to the effect that the parties will co-operate to amend the articles of association (or other constitutional documents) if it should become reasonably necessary in order to ensure that the principles of the shareholders' agreement prevail. In an international joint venture, the documentary relationship (or overlap) between a shareholders' agreement and the constitutional documents is invariably a matter to be resolved with the local lawyers for the relevant jurisdiction.

CONCLUSION

5–64 Equity joint ventures are the most integrated and challenging forms of alliances. They provide the widest range of issues to challenge the lawyers—and the participants. The joint venture or shareholders' agree-

---

[30] See para.5.55.

ment lies at the centre of the legal relationship. We turn in Part B of this book to a detailed study of a number of specific issues—centred around capital, governance, duties of the parties, exit and termination—which particularly affect that relationship. Before that, we should not neglect the importance of ancillary commercial contracts in the initial planning of the overall joint venture arrangements.

CHAPTER 6

Importance of ancillary contracts

A joint venture vehicle is a structure for a business relationship and not an end in itself. Where the joint venture is structured as a joint venture company (JVC) or other separate legal entity, other legal contracts—usually involving one or more of the parties and the JVC—will be crucial to the overall business relationship. These other contractual relationships are, for convenience, here termed "ancillary contracts". This chapter considers a number of typical ancillary contracts and concentrates particularly on the issues raised by the joint venture context.

Importance of ancillary contracts

6–01 In many joint venture structures, it is the ancillary contracts which will be vital to the JVC's commercial and legal functioning. They may often be the parties' commercial focus. Indeed, in many instances a party may plan to make its commercial gain from the venture through its remuneration or receipt of goods or services under ancillary contracts rather than through its investment return as a shareholder in the JVC itself. It can therefore be vital for the parties, and the lawyers, to give as much attention to the ancillary contracts as to the foundation agreements establishing the joint venture vehicle itself.

6–02 It is not appropriate here to examine in detail the legal and/or commercial issues which can arise over the full range of potential ancillary contracts. In most cases, issues will be those common to the particular type of legal contract in question—irrespective of the overall joint venture context—and the issues (and precedents) are considered in detail in specialist textbooks relating to those particular types of contracts. This chapter therefore considers these types of contracts in outline only and provides, essentially, an initial checklist concentrating particularly on the issues raised by the joint venture context.

EXAMPLES OF OVERALL JVC STRUCTURES

Examples of overall JVC structures

6–03 The importance and role of ancillary contracts in joint ventures can be exemplified by examining four different types of joint venture situations:

(a) a technology joint venture;

(b) a "foreign" production joint venture;

(c) a B2B e-commerce joint venture;

(d) a joint venture to build and operate a power station.

Technology joint venture

6–04 An example of a technology venture is where a JVC is established to pool and develop the technologies of the parties in a particular area and to develop a component production plant utilising that joint technology—see also the examples in para.5–08.

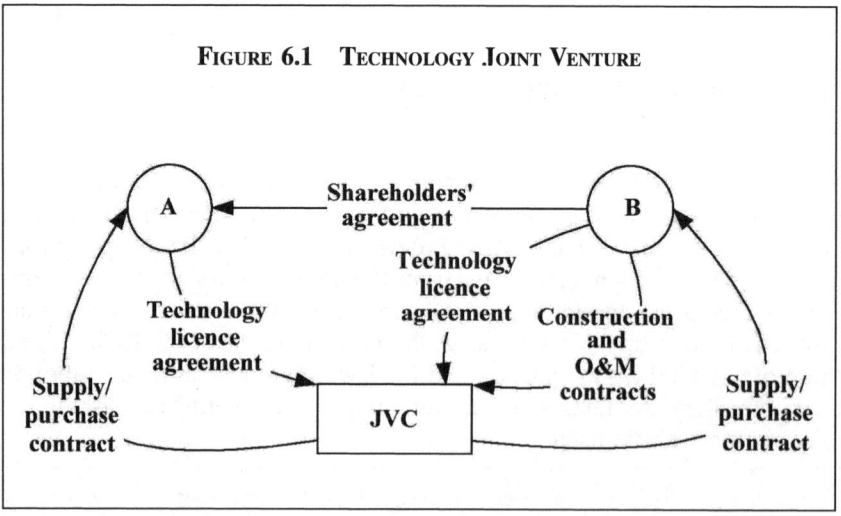

FIGURE 6.1   TECHNOLOGY JOINT VENTURE

6–05 In this joint venture, A and B agree to pool existing technology and (after undertaking further joint R&D) to share capital costs through the JVC in building a production plant which will manufacture components to be supplied to A and B. B is primarily responsible for construction and subsequent operation and maintenance (O&M) of the plant. The entire output of the JVC's plant is to be supplied to A and B for use in their separate manufacturing operations. Key ancillary contracts will therefore include:

(1) *technology licence agreements* between A and B, respectively, and the JVC for the provision of technology and technical assistance. It will be for negotiation whether there is substantial remuneration (e.g. lump sum fees and/or royalties) or whether the "value" of each party's technology will be taken into account in the capitalisation of the JVC;

(2) *supply/purchase contracts* between the JVC and A and B, respectively, whereby A and B agree to take (in equal shares subject to any formula agreed between them) the entire output of the JVC's production. Pricing will be a key issue for the JVC's profitability;

(3) *a construction contract* between B and the JVC for the construction (and possibly subsequent operation and maintenance) of the plant.

"Foreign" production joint venture

6–06 A joint venture may be established in a "foreign" country to build a production plant which will primarily be supplying product for that market and, possibly, for export sale of any surplus production.

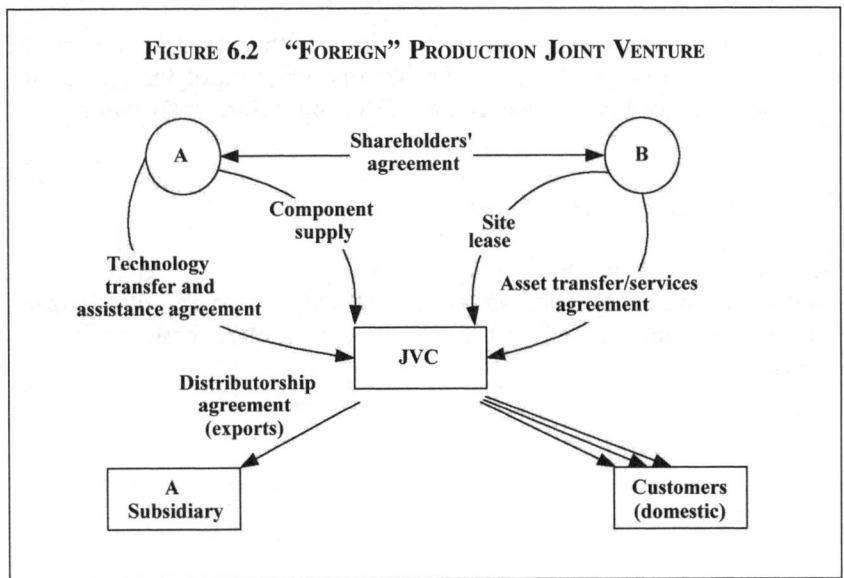

FIGURE 6.2 "FOREIGN" PRODUCTION JOINT VENTURE

6–07 In this example, the primary contributor of technology is party A. The JVC is based in an overseas jurisdiction and B is the local partner. The JVC will, using A's technology, construct a production plant for products which will be marketed domestically in that country by the JVC (either directly or possibly through B's distribution chain). If and to the extent that there are any exports, these will be channelled through A or A's distribution chain. B will provide land and certain other assets and resources. The joint venture agreement will be important but key ancillary contracts will include:

(1) a *technology licence agreement* between A and the JVC providing for the licence of A's technology, technical assistance to the JVC and A's remuneration and cost reimbursement;

(2) a *distributorship agreement* between the JVC and A (or another member of A's group) for the distribution of export sales of products manufactured by the JVC; and

(3) a *land transfer or lease* between B and the JVC for the availability of the site for the production facility.

Other ancillary contracts may include:

(4) an *asset transfer agreement* between B and the JVC for the transfer of specific assets (including possibly the proposed JVC's local workforce)—and probably extending to the provision of various ancillary services;

(5) a *component supply agreement* between A and the JVC for the supply (perhaps for an initial period) of components and/or raw materials to the JVC; and

(6) a *plant construction contract* relating to the construction of the production plant which may involve one or more of the parties and the JVC—or may be between the JVC and a third party contractor.

B2B e-commerce joint venture

6–08 The growth of the internet has spawned a wide variety of joint venture arrangements. One example is the development of electronic trading exchanges—initially set up on a joint venture basis by founder members.

EXAMPLES OF OVERALL JVC STRUCTURES

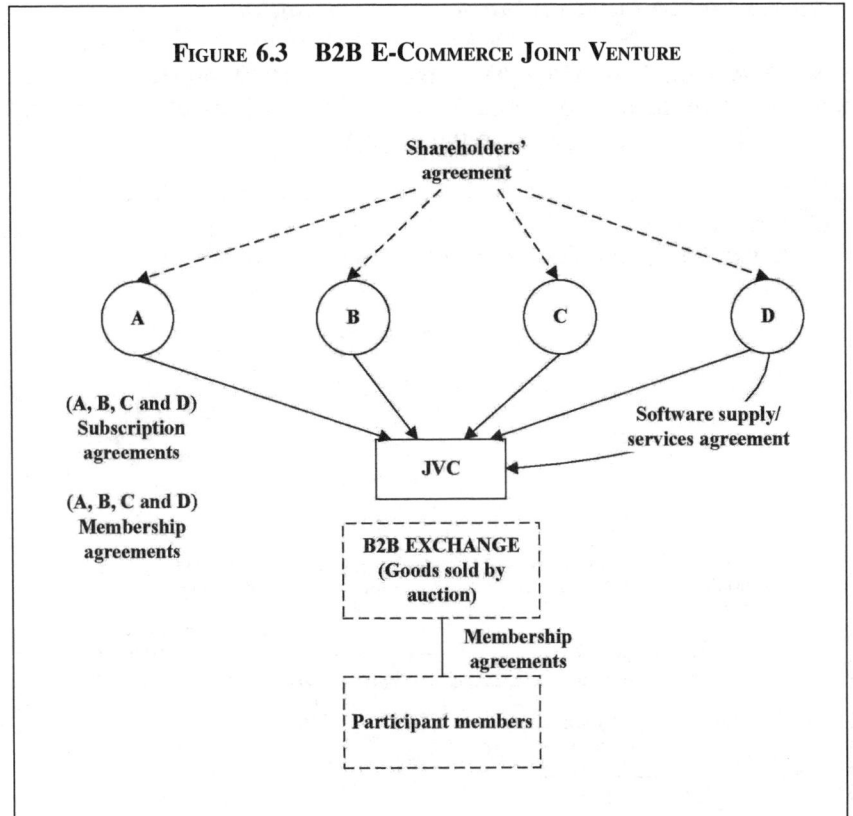

FIGURE 6.3 B2B E-COMMERCE JOINT VENTURE

6–09 The objective of this joint venture is to establish a business-to-business (B2B) electronic exchange or marketplace by which buyers and sellers trade goods and services online. Founder members (A, B, C and D in this example) establish the JVC. The JVC establishes, owns and administers the web-site based exchange. The shareholders and other outside participants sign up to be members of the exchange. Thereafter, the sales will be effected through the exchange—often by means of an auction process that can be initiated by either the buyer or seller and is administered by the JVC. The shareholders' agreement will be important and establish the JVC, including financing arrangements. Key ancillary contracts will be:

(1) *membership agreements* between each participant (including the founders) and the JVC whereby each participant signs up to the rules of the exchange (governing trading rules, confidentiality etc.) and, usually, setting the framework for fees and commissions for use of the trading platform;

(2) *software supply/services agreement* between one participant or technology supplier (D in this example) and the JVC for design, build and support of the software system for the exchange.

Joint venture to build and operate power station

6–10 Power stations and other large infrastructure projects are often constructed on the basis of a joint venture or consortium between different parties with a material interest in the project.

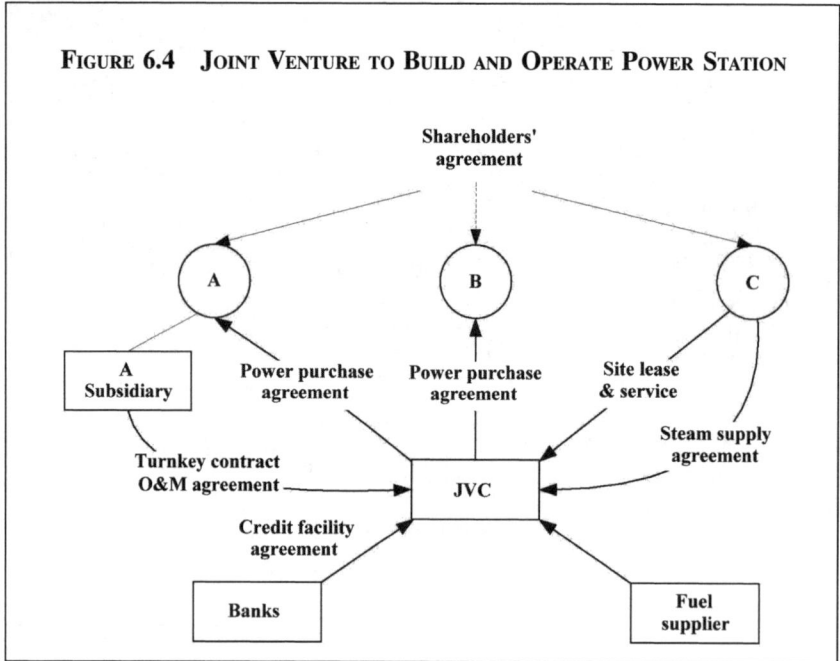

FIGURE 6.4 JOINT VENTURE TO BUILD AND OPERATE POWER STATION

6–11 The objective of this joint venture is to establish a "cogeneration" power station on the site of party C, an industrial company. Party A is leading the project and, through its construction subsidiary, will be responsible for plant construction and subsequent operation and maintenance (O&M) of the station. Party B is an electricity company which (together with party A) will commit to purchasing power produced by the plant. Steam heat produced by the plant will be supplied to the industrial party, C, for use in its neighbouring manufacturing facilities. Such a project includes a JVC at its heart but the various ancillary contracts provide the commercial core of the arrangements. They will include:

(1) a *turnkey contract* between A's subsidiary and the JVC for design, construction and installation of the plant. The terms of this contract must be satisfactory to support the project financing and to provide protection for the JVC against cost overrun risks or delays in meeting specified plant performance criteria;

(2) an *operation and maintenance contract* between A's subsidiary and the JVC for subsequent operation and maintenance of the plant;

(3) a *site lease and services agreement* between C and the JVC for provision of the site and associated site services and facilities (including, perhaps, appropriate environmental indemnities to protect the JVC);

(4) *power purchase agreements or contracts for differences* between A and B, respectively, and the JVC whereby A and B will commit to offtake electricity generated by the plant. The terms of these contracts will require a balance to be drawn between A and B's commercial interests and the interests of the JVC in limiting the effect of price fluctuations in order to assist bankability of the contracts.

Other ancillary contracts (not directly with any of the parties but crucial to the establishment and profitability of the JVC) will include:

(5) a *fuel supply contract* between a third party fuel supplier and the JVC for the sale of gas to the JVC. This contract will be aimed to ensure security of supply and mitigate the risk to the JVC of delays in delivery of gas;

(6) *credit facility agreements* between one or more banks and the JVC for the provision of project finance to the JVC to support the plant's construction and start-up costs.

ANCILLARY CONTRACTS: COMMON LEGAL ISSUES

Common issues in joint venture context

6–12 A number of common issues arise in a joint venture context which the parties should consider at the outset in relation to most ancillary contracts.

Conflicts of interest

6–13 In most cases, a party contributing goods, services, capital or technology to a joint venture will have a "conflict of interest", to a greater or lesser extent, insofar as the contributing party will naturally seek to protect its legal and commercial interests vis-à-vis the JVC. The other party(ies) to the joint venture (and indeed the JVC itself) will seek to ensure appropriate terms for the benefit of the JVC. In some situations, it may well be appropriate for the JVC to be separately represented in these negotiations; in most cases, the parties will be aware of the potential conflict and deal with it by appropriate allocation of tasks and negotiating responsibilities at the outset.

Enforcement by JVC

6–14 It will be important to ensure that legal obligations accepted by a joint venture party under an ancillary contract can, if necessary, be properly enforced. Whilst the directors of the JVC will, at least in theory, be under a duty to promote the success of the JVC—see para.8–49 et seq.—there remains a risk that enforcement may be "blocked" by the voting power or board representation of that party within the JVC. If there are significant ancillary contracts with the shareholders, the parties should consider the composition of the board of the JVC. The directors could find themselves in a difficult position. In some cases, it will be appropriate to ensure that there is a "strong" board, possibly having an independent non-executive chairman, enabling the JVC to carry out its role properly. Legal enforcement will, of course, be an extreme situation but the possibility should be protected. If a party has generally a right to veto major litigation proceedings, this veto should not apply to legal proceedings against that party itself. Other possible protective measures in relation to enforcement decisions against a majority party are considered in para.9–24.

Termination

6–15 The interrelationship between ancillary contracts and the principal joint venture agreement is vital and will often require careful thought, particularly in relation to termination.

(1) Should material breach of a particular ancillary contract give rise to a right for the non-defaulter to terminate the joint venture agreement as a whole?—see para.13–22. If so, the parties should be careful how any separately agreed put or call options arising on termination apply in these circumstances.

(2) If a party leaves the joint venture, should any ancillary contract under which it supplies goods or services, or licenses intellectual property, to the joint venture terminate—either automatically or after a period of notice? Even if the answer is "yes", it will often be appropriate to provide for a significant grace period to allow time for the JVC to obtain another contractor.

(3) Where a valuation of the JVC or its shares is necessary upon the exit of a party (see para.12–18), it will often be relevant for that valuation to take into account whether or not material ancillary contracts with the JVC will or can be terminated upon that exit.

6–16 If the JVC becomes insolvent or has a liquidator or receiver appointed, should the other party to an ancillary contract have a right of termination? This will depend on the contract—see para.13–26 et seq.—but there is an argument, in some cases, that the continuance of the contract for a period may enable the liquidator or receiver to realise the business more satisfactorily (thus benefiting the investment of the joint venture parties). In most cases, however, a licensor or supplier party will wish to reserve the right to terminate—with any decision to extend the contract being within its discretion at the time.

Separate contracts

6–17 Generally, it is preferable to structure these ancillary legal relationships as separate contracts—and not simply to incorporate detailed terms in the joint venture agreement. Reasons for this approach include the following.

(1) It is frequently easier (or less cumbersome) as a drafting matter to deal separately with a particular ancillary relationship. Covering matters relating to ancillary contracts in detail in a joint venture agreement can make the latter document over-lengthy and detract from ease of future reference to that agreement as one principally dealing with the management and operation of the joint venture vehicle.

(2) It will often render enforcement of an ancillary contract easier if it is documented separately, particularly if the JVC is a party to each ancillary contract but not to the joint venture agreement itself.

(3) Termination and default provisions can be particularly difficult and it is generally easier to deal with these separately, contract by contract, rather than for the principles—and drafting—to become too entangled with the parties' rights and obligations under termination provisions of the joint venture agreement itself.

However, even if they are structured as separate contracts, it will as a drafting matter generally be appropriate to refer to these ancillary contracts in the overall joint venture agreement (or sometimes in a "framework agreement"—see para.2–38 above) in order to provide overall cohesion between these various contracts.

Time for negotiation

6–18 It is sometimes tempting to leave the terms of the ancillary contracts to be settled at a much later stage than the principal joint venture agreement itself, on the alleged grounds that the terms of these contracts should be "standard" or "arm's-length" and not require early attention. This temptation should usually be resisted. These contracts will often be vital to the proper establishment and functioning of the joint venture—and identifying these contracts, and agreeing at least their basic commercial terms, should be undertaken at the same time as the establishment of the joint venture.

6–19 If there is a material time gap between the signing of the principal joint venture agreement and the formal commencement of the joint venture operations (e.g. because of the need to satisfy conditions precedent), it may be tempting to postpone dealing with the detail of some of these arrangements. However, it will still be prudent to agree the basic principles of these ancillary contracts and for these principles to be initialled or set out in (or scheduled to) the joint venture agreement at the time of signing of the latter in order to be clear that there are no fundamental commercial differences between the parties.

Governing law

6–20 It does not follow that the governing law of each ancillary contract should be the same as that of the joint venture agreement itself. Indeed, it will generally make sense for each ancillary contract to be governed by the law which is most appropriate to its subject matter—e.g. a contract for the supply of goods from a parent to the JVC may well be more suitably governed by the law of the country of the supplier/manufacturer. In practice, agreement by the parties as to the governing laws to be adopted in the various contracts relating to the joint venture may well be influenced by an express or implied trade-off in negotiations between the parties. It is preferable for this decision to be taken rationally but at an early stage. It can affect the practical choice of lawyers to draft and advise on a particular contract.

Dispute resolution

6–21 As a general rule, it will make formal dispute resolution procedures easier to implement if the same process (particularly any choice of institutional arbitration and/or place of arbitration) is adopted for the joint venture agreement and all material ancillary contracts. If legal action between the parties arises out of a joint venture, the question of fault or applicable legal rights and obligations can become entangled across a range of different contracts. Provision for multi-party arbitration, for instance, is not easy but the scope for sensible consolidation of arbitration claims will be made easier if this route is adopted.

Competition laws

6–22 Restrictions in contracts between one or more of the parents and the JVC—such as exclusivity terms in licence or supply agreements or "preferred supplier" arrangements—can be important in assessing the effect of competition laws on the overall joint venture arrangements. Under EU and UK competition laws, it is accepted that certain restrictions may be justifiable as being "ancillary" to the establishment of the joint venture, in particular:

(a) exclusive licences of intellectual property rights to a JVC or limitations on field of use or territory may be regarded as ancillary;

(b) long-term supply and purchase commitments between a JVC and its parents are likely to be regarded as "ancillary" if they are for a transitional period (e.g. up to five years) and for the purposes of safeguarding continuity of supplies.

More extensive restrictions may require closer review under competition laws—see para.16–16 et seq. and chapter 16 generally.

Establishing the Joint Venture

6–23 Many ancillary contracts may be necessary as part of the initial legal exercise of vesting in, or making available to, the JVC the assets, rights and facilities required to carry on the joint venture business. Described below, in outline, are a number of these contracts—together, in most cases, with an initial checklist which identifies material issues affecting that particular type of contract.

Sale and purchase/asset transfer agreements

6–24 Asset transfers to the JVC may comprise the transfer of a business as a whole (e.g. an undertaking in the UK falling within the Transfer of Undertakings Regulations) or the transfer of specific plant, equipment and other assets—or may take the form of the transfer of the share capital of a subsidiary holding the relevant assets/business. The transfer may be in consideration of the issue of shares by the JVC or be partly or wholly in consideration of a cash payment by the JVC. The structure of the documentation can similarly take various forms including a choice between:

(a) a separate, and relatively standard, sale and purchase contract between the transferor and the JVC for the sale and purchase of the relevant business and/or assets and/or shares; or

(b) an agreement to which both joint venture parents are parties (perhaps in order that relevant warranties can be given directly as between the joint venture parents themselves) as part of the overall agreement to establish the joint venture and the terms on which each party is to make its asset contribution.

In each case, many of the principal issues will be those common to sale and purchase contracts irrespective of the joint venture context. In the situation of a joint venture, key issues are likely to include the following:

TRANSFER OF ASSETS TO JVC: KEY ISSUES

(1) *Valuation.* How are the relevant assets etc. to be valued? By reference to a cost based formula or market value? Is this to be agreed between the parties or fixed by an independent valuer? Tactically, when should that valuation take place: at the time of, or after, the establishment of the joint venture? See generally para.2–30 et seq.

(2) *Warranties.* The nature of any warranties to be given by the seller will vary according to the subject matter of the transfer. The strength of each party's negotiating position will be important. Bringing a warranty claim against a joint venture party will, no doubt, be rare in practice. However, in the interests of the JVC (and the other co-venturer), certain basic warranties customary to that type of transfer transaction will normally be appropriate. A realistic view should normally be taken by setting appropriate minimum thresholds and time limits for claims.

Warranties and indemnities should generally be restricted to matters which go to the value of a party's contribution, which are likely to affect the financial performance of the venture or which provide reassurance that all corporate action has been duly taken. A typical list in the case of a contribution of a business may be:

— capacity/authorisation to enter into the joint venture;
— requisite governmental and regulatory approvals obtained;
— title to material assets being contributed;
— no material litigation;
— audited accounts give a true and fair view of the financial position (coupled, possibly, with a warranty that any management accounts supplied are not materially misleading);
— no material change in financial position of contributed business since last accounts date;
— business being contributed has been conducted in material compliance with all relevant laws;
— no material undisclosed liabilities including product liabilities (especially if not covered by insurance) and indemnity against any liabilities (except as reserved) for past trading or events;
— validity of IPR and no infringement claims by third parties (obviously important if technology is a crucial element of the contribution);
— where land is being contributed, appropriate environmental warranties or indemnities.

Where a company has initially been set up by one party alone in advance of participation by the other joint venture party or parties, one would normally expect the party setting up the company to give broad warranties to the effect that the company has never traded, has no assets or liabilities other than in respect of its share capital and has not entered into any transaction of any kind.

SALE AND PURCHASE/ASSET TRANSFER AGREEMENTS 145

(3) *Enforcement of warranties.* Should warranties be given directly to, and thus enforceable by, the JVC as the effective "purchaser" or should they be given "horizontally" to the other parent joint venture party? Practice varies and may depend on various factors:

(i) Do the joint venture parties prefer to sort out any problems for themselves without necessarily involving the JVC management (who may be keener to pursue remedies in order to compensate "their" business) on the basis that the two parents are more likely to reach a solution in the broad interests of their relationship?

(ii) Is it more appropriate (particularly where the subject matter of the claim affects the value of the business contributed to the venture) for the JVC itself to be compensated for the breach? Payment to the JVC will, of course, reflect the loss to the JVC as a whole—whereas payment to the joint venture party itself will be based on that party's proportionate shareholding in the JVC.

(iii) Tax considerations will often be important. Will any damages recovered for breach of warranty be taxable in the hands of the recipient? Will they be a deduction for the payer? (The position in the UK is that, if the warranty is given and sums are paid by the relevant party directly to the JVC, the receipt of such sums should not be immediately taxable in the hands of the JVC. If payment for a breach of warranty is made horizontally to the other joint venture party, such payment is likely to be taxable in the hands of the recipient.)

One approach is for warranties to be given primarily to the other joint venture party but, in the event of breach, for the "innocent" party to have the right to direct (at its option and in lieu of payment to itself) that financial compensation be paid by the "defaulting" party to the JVC to place the latter in the same financial position as it would have been had the relevant warranty been correct.

(4) *Non-cash consideration.* In many jurisdictions, particular procedures and rules will apply in respect of the valuation of non-cash assets where they constitute the consideration for shares to be issued by the JVC—often requiring an independent valuation. These procedures should be identified and understood at an early stage; see para.2–33.

(5) *Intellectual property.* Care should be taken to identify any intellectual property rights (IPR) being transferred or made available as part of the asset/business transfer and to clarify the rights and obligations of the parties in relation to IPR. These issues are addressed in more detail in chapter 17.

(6) *Employees.* A transfer of a business (or a change of control of a company) will invariably affect employees-and frequently trigger rights and obligations for the employer. A particular question now is whether the Information and Consultation of Employees Regulations 2004 (or equivalent legislation in other EU countries) will apply; see chapter 18.

(7) *Enforcement by JVC.* Will the JVC be able to bring an action, if necessary, against the transferor party—or will the latter (through its representatives on the JVC) in effect be able to block any such action? See para.9–24 for ways of dealing with this problem.

(8) *Tax/stamp duty*. Tax planning will play a crucial part in establishing the most cost-efficient method for transferring relevant assets to the JVC. This will be a vital consideration, particularly for the transferor, in assessing the cost of establishing the joint venture. Potential stamp duty on transfer documentation will be a concern for the purchaser. See chapter 15.

(9) *Timing of transfer*. Timing will often need to be considered carefully. There may be conditions precedent to be satisfied before a particular business can be transferred (e.g. as a result of regulatory approvals or third party consents required in a particular jurisdiction). It may be appropriate to include provisions which enable transfers of certain assets/businesses to go ahead in tranches to the JVC with delayed completion of "lesser" assets where delay is necessary for regulatory reasons. One party may, though, not be willing to transfer its assets! business unless that is simultaneous with the other party's contribution.

(10) *Formal transfers*. Other ancillary contracts may be necessary as part of the asset transfer arrangements-for example, documents to implement formal transfers of land or assignments of IPR.

(11) *Formalities of execution*. The formalities of execution should be carefully checked. Will notarisation be required in any jurisdiction? What will be the cost?

Funding agreements

6–25 Funding arrangements for the JVC will obviously be important. Documentation will depend on the source of the funding.

Third party borrowing

6–26 The JVC may obtain its funds from third party lending institutions. Terms of the borrowing will therefore be negotiated and entered into by the JVC as in any other similar financing situations. In certain circumstances, it may be the intention that the joint venture operations should be "project financed" without recourse, or with only limited recourse, to shareholder funds. Terms of any such financing, including the linking of repayment or security to any revenue stream of the JVC, will be a matter for specialist financing techniques. In other cases, the JVC may obtain more conventional borrowing-with or without guarantee support of the joint venture parties. See generally para.7–21 et seq. for issues which are likely to concern a third party lender to a JVC.

Shareholder loans

6–27 Financing will frequently take the form of debt/equity subscribed by the joint venture parties themselves. Funding obligations will usually be set out in the joint venture agreement itself. In the case of debt financing, it will be common for the financing to be represented, in addition, by a separate loan agreement (or loan note) between the lending shareholder and the JVC in order to enable more detailed terms attaching to that financing to be set out. Principal issues in relation to such financing arrangements are considered in para.7–19.

> An example of a Shareholder Funding Agreement to fund a JVC principally by way of loans from the shareholders is included as Precedent 16 in Part E

Venture capital

6–28 Financing may be raised, in effect, by venture capital with the lenders taking certain rights in relation to the JVC—often in the form of holdings of preference share capital. In the case of such share capital, these preferred rights will be spelt out in the rights attaching to the shares and set out (usually) in the JVC's articles of association. Such financing techniques have been common in management buy-out situations but are also increasingly applicable to other financings of a JVC—particularly in relation to a multi-party start-up joint venture in which an institution or venture capital provider participates. Specific issues which may concern such a venture capital provider in the context of an investment in a JVC are discussed in more detail in para.7–27 et seq. Many similar issues arise in the context of a strategic minority investment and the points raised at para.9–39 may be relevant also in this financing context.

6–29 Detailed rights and obligations relating to the venture capital financing will usually be contained in a subscription or investment agreement. Provisions and precedents relating to these types of agreements are best considered in conjunction with one of the specialist texts.[1]

Intellectual property/technology licence agreements

6–30 It will be crucial to many joint ventures for one or more parties to make available various intellectual property rights—e.g. by:

(a) transferring or making available its technology and know-how to the JVC (either generally within a particular field or for the purposes of a specific project to be undertaken by the JVC);

(b) granting rights to use various product or service trade marks in the course of the JVC's business; or

---

[1] For example, Maurice Dwyer, *Private Equity Transactions* (London: Sweet & Maxwell, looseleaf) and Darryl Cooke & James Dow, *Private Equity: Law and Practice* (London: Sweet & Maxwell, 2008). See also the model form subscription and shareholders' agreement produced by the British Venture Capital Association.

(c) granting rights for the JVC to use its "house" name or its "house" logo.

These important rights and obligations, and the legal issues raised in the context of joint ventures, are considered in more detail in chapter 17.

> An example of Technology Licence Agreement between a parent and the JVC is included as Precedent 19 in Part E. An example Trade Mark Licence appears as Precedent 20 in Part E.

Property agreements

6–31 It will often be necessary to establish the legal arrangements for the licence, lease or purchase of property (including office accommodation) to be used by the JVC where this property is being provided by one of the parties. Care may be needed to deal with the following issues:

PROPERTY AGREEMENTS: ISSUES

(1) *Costs.* It should always be clarified, as a commercial matter, what costs or charges will be borne by the JVC in respect of the property made available. If costs are to be shared between the JVC and the party which owns the property, the costs sharing arrangements need to be clearly defined. Often costs will be shared on an actual basis so that no party will make a separate profit from the joint venture outside the main agreed profit-sharing arrangements within the JVC itself. If, however, the JVC's occupation of premises is depriving one party of the opportunity to earn an income from the property, the parties may agree that the JVC should pay an arm's-length rent.

(2) *Common facilities/services.* The JVC will wish to ensure that it gains proper and continuing access to other facilities and services (e.g. computer, canteen, security, cleaning or property-related services) which are common to the premises made available to the JVC and any other neighbouring premises retained by the relevant parent for its separate business. If the JVC is to receive the use of serviced offices (e.g. including secretarial services or the use of other facilities over and above those required solely for the proper use of the premises themselves), then the party providing these services will usually require payment for them, unless the provision of services to the JVC forms part of its agreed contribution towards the joint venture.

(3) *Ownership.* It should be made clear whether the joint venture is to own the property or simply lease/license it. This can be particularly important if the joint venture is structured as a partnership and a party wishes to avoid the property becoming partnership property under the Partnership Act 1890, s.20.

(4) *Security of tenure.* A licence arrangement may be appropriate where space and facilities are genuinely shared and no particular area is exclusively allocated to the JVC. If, however, the JVC is given its own exclusive space, it is possible that the arrangements will in fact create a lease, even if the document is labelled a "licence"; the court will look at the substance of the arrangements, not their form or the labels the parties put on them. If the JVC in fact has a lease of space occupied for business purposes, it may be able to establish security of tenure under the Landlord and Tenant Act 1954 (and the parties cannot contract out of this unless their agreement to do so is approved by a prior court order). It may therefore be preferable in some cases to grant the JVC a lease to ensure from the outset that security of tenure is properly excluded.

(5) *Leasehold premises.* If the party making the property available has a leasehold interest, its landlord's consent may be required for the JVC's use of the property, particularly if the lease is to be assigned or there is to be a formal underletting to the JVC. Even sharing arrangements may require consent under modern forms of lease. The lease terms will always need to be checked to ensure that the intended arrangements are permitted. A landlord will often be in a position to require a guarantee as a condition of granting consent to an assignment or underletting to the JVC. If a guarantee is given by one party alone, the latter is likely to require a counter-indemnity to share liability with the other joint venture parties. Even if no guarantee is given, the party owning the lease will need to bear in mind that it will have a continuing liability to its landlord if there is an underletting to the JVC, and there may also be a continuing liability even if the lease is assigned. The leaseholder should therefore consider taking indemnities from its joint venture partners (as well as from the JVC itself).

Employee secondment agreements

6–32 In order to establish a joint venture, the JVC may well need the resources of staff (particularly senior executives) previously employed by one or more of the parents. These staffing and other employment arrangements with the JVC are considered in more detail in chapter 18.

Management agreements

6–33 In some joint ventures, one of the parties may have particular responsibility for management of the JVC's business. These will usually be reflected in a management agreement (sometimes termed a management services agreement) between that party and the JVC. Issues include the following:

Management Agreement: Key Issues

(1) *Manager's role and responsibilities.* It will, of course, be important to set out clearly the manager's duties for management and supervision of the business including the extent to which this is subject to instructions or policies from time to time laid down by the JVC board.

(2) *Limitations on manager's powers.* The scope of the manager's authority should be delineated. This includes identifying matters or decisions which require the prior approval of the full board of the JVC. Any limitations on the manager's power to enter into contractual commitments as agent for, or otherwise binding on, the JVC should be identified.

(3) *Employees.* Employment arrangements can vary. Will employees be seconded to the JVC or (more likely in these circumstances) remain with the manager? If certain individuals are key to the management operation, identify these and include an obligation on the manager to make available their resources.

(4) *Remuneration and costs.* Fees payable to the manager will no doubt be carefully negotiated. Will this be a lump-sum fee, or linked to the JVC's costs/revenues? Will there be any incentive fee linked to the JVC's profitability? Rules for invoicing and reimbursement of costs and expenses should be clearly stated, with provision for maintenance of proper records and accounts, and inspection rights for the JVC. The scope of reimbursable costs is, in particular, likely to require close scrutiny and negotiation. Will they cover salaries, wages and other employment costs, travel, lodging, subsistence and incidental expenses, property related costs, office overhead costs and litigation costs?

(5) *Liability.* Liability of the manager for its performance should be clarified. This will frequently be limited to wilful default or gross negligence and may be subject to an overall monetary limit.

(6) *Intellectual property.* It should be clarified whether any IPR developed by the manager in the course of its duties will belong to the manager or, more usually, to the JVC.

(7) *Reporting requirements.* Appropriate reporting mechanisms should be established, including the manager's duty to submit monthly or other regular reports to the JVC board/other joint venture party. The agreement should also normally deal with obligations and procedures for provision of budgets and estimates.

(8) *Termination.* Termination rights should be carefully considered. Each party will want to ensure that the management contract cannot be terminated easily-but will wish to preserve proper rights to terminate in the event of breach, or perhaps if there is a change in shareholdings of the JVC and/or the manager or, in some cases, simply if the arrangement is not working satisfactorily. A sensible procedure for notice and discussion between senior representatives of the joint venture parties should be facilitated before any unilateral termination is triggered which could seriously affect the JVC.

ONGOING BUSINESS CONTRACTS

6–34 The JVC's business will often be closely connected on an ongoing basis with the businesses of the joint venture parents. Indeed, the JVC's formation may be aimed specifically at providing a production or other facility to support the parents: see the examples at paras 5–08 et seq. and 6–04 et seq. These ongoing relationships are likely to be reflected in various ancillary contracts between the JVC and one or more of the parties. The following are typical examples.

Supply agreements

6–35 If the JVC is to operate a manufacturing facility, there will commonly be contracts between the joint venture parents (or one of them) and the JVC for the supply of goods, components or raw materials. These contracts give rise to issues common to all supply contracts. Key issues, within the joint venture context, are likely to include the following:

SUPPLY AGREEMENTS: KEY ISSUES

(1) *Pricing.* Pricing will no doubt be keenly negotiated. Will the supplier party agree to the JVC receiving a "most favoured customer" price—namely, an undertaking by the supplier to reduce the price (or render more advantageous other material terms) to the JVC if the supplier agrees a lower price (or more favourable other material terms) with any other customer? Price review and variation formulae will similarly be important for all parties.

(2) *Priority of supply.* Priority of supply will invariably be crucial for the JVC. The JVC will therefore seek a commitment from the supplier party that, in the event of a shortage of supplies, priority will be given to fulfilling the JVC's orders.

(3) *Exclusivity/preferred supplier.* Will the JVC undertake to acquire the relevant goods, components or materials exclusively from the supplier party? Will the obligation be to recognise the party as "preferred supplier"? Any exclusivity obligation will customarily contain an exception where the JVC (acting through its board) reasonably considers that the supplier's products are of inadequate quality or specification in a material respect or will be unduly delayed in delivery; usually such a situation will require prior notice to the supplier before the JVC can source from a third party. See also "Competition laws".

(4) *Warranty.* Will the supplier give its customary warranty in respect of the quality of the products? Is a special warranty required relating to compliance with any particular specification of the JVC? What remedies or procedures are to apply in the event of warranty claims? It may be necessary to consider whether the implied conditions of the Sale of Goods Act 1979 (or similar legislation in the relevant jurisdiction) apply or should be excluded, as far as permissible.

(5) *Ordering procedure.* A feature of most long-term supply arrangements will be the need to establish a sensible system for providing long-term forecasts of the JVC's requirements for the products, updating of these forecasts and converting them into binding purchase orders for requisite numbers of products. It should be clear whether or not the supplier has discretion to refuse any order; if so, a time limit after notification of the JVC's order should be specified. The supplier party may require that the JVC undertakes to purchase a minimum amount of products by value during a particular period.

(6) *Acceptance/rejection.* As with any other supply contracts, but importantly in a joint venture context in view of the relationship between the parties, the procedures (and commitments) for acceptance or rejection of the goods by the JVC as purchaser should be made clear.

(7) *Terms of payment.* Payment terms will probably be in standard form but should be clearly specified including currency of payment (and, if necessary, provision for any agreed adjustment in the event of material exchange rate fluctuations).

(8) *Title and risk.* Other issues customary to supply contracts which arise include: when is title in the goods to pass? when does risk in the goods pass to the purchaser? Insurance obligations should be clarified in order to ensure that there is no gap, or unnecessary overlap, in insurance coverage.

(9) *Export/import regulations.* The parties will need to comply with all applicable export/import regulations and allocate responsibility for establishing relevant clearances. In particular, an exporter from the UK will require an export licence for those categories listed in the Export Control Act 2002 and regulations made thereunder—see para.2–25 earlier.

(10) *Shipment.* Where goods are being shipped, it should be clear which party is to bear shipping costs, insurance, customs duties etc.

(11) *IPR indemnity.* The supplier party will normally provide an indemnity against damages and costs incurred by the JVC as a result of IPR infringement claims being brought by third parties against the JVC which are attributable to use of the supplied products.

(12) *Force majeure.* The scope of any exclusion of liability on the grounds of force majeure should be carefully considered.

(13) *Term and termination.* Termination rights should be clearly spelt out (e.g. whether the agreement is for a fixed term and/or subject to termination by notice (including for material breach or insolvency by either party)). Since termination of the supply contract could have a material effect on the JVC's operations, it will normally be sensible to ensure a built-in lengthy period of notice (and consultation at senior level) before any such termination is triggered.

SUPPLY AGREEMENTS 153

(14) *Group companies*. In appropriate cases, it should be clarified whether or not the relevant terms constitute a framework for supplies generally to all members of the JVC's group (e.g. if there are manufacturing subsidiaries of the JVC elsewhere in the UK or other parts of the world).

(15) *Competition laws*. Terms of any supply contracts (e.g. particularly regarding exclusivity, term and pricing) will need to be reviewed to ensure that they do not contravene applicable competition laws and are proportionate "ancillary restrictions"; see generally chapter 16.

6–36 For more detailed discussion and precedents relating to supply agreements generally, specialist texts should be consulted.[2]

Offtake/purchase contracts

6–37 The JVC's purpose may be to provide a production facility for particular goods or components required by the joint venture parents—and thus involve purchase contracts between the parents and the JVC. These contracts will raise equivalent or mirror issues to those in supply agreements considered in para.6–35 above. However, since the contracts will frequently relate to the JVC's entire output, they can raise additional issues. Decisions can obviously be taken by the parties within the JVC, but these are often such commercially important issues that the principles should be established at the outset. Issues which arise in this situation will frequently include the following:

OFFTAKE/PURCHASE CONTRACTS: ADDITIONAL ISSUES

(1) *Pricing*. Will pricing be negotiated by reference to an arm's-length market price or will it be a formula linked to the JVC's cost base? The latter may well be the most appropriate way of ensuring that the JVC's costs are covered if the purchase contracts relate to the whole or a substantial part of the JVC's production. However, the purchasing party (or parties) may well seek protection—perhaps after an initial period—that the price will not exceed a competitive market price (by perhaps an agreed margin), particularly if the parties have binding offtake commitments.

(2) *Offtake commitments*. If the contracts relate to the entirety of the JVC's output, the JVC's viability will depend on the parties being willing to take the output—in effect on a "take or pay" basis. The offtake commitment

---

[2] See, for instance, *Practical Commercial Precedents* (London: Sweet & Maxwell, looseleaf), Vol.3.

may be fixed by reference to the quantity of production forecast by the JVC or by reference to pre-agreed percentage shares (as between the parties) of the total production sometimes with arrangements for an "underage" or shortfall in a particular year to be compensated by an "overage" in a subsequent year—or with a penalty payment to compensate the JVC for additional costs attributable to any shortfall in offtake in any year. These arrangements will need to be carefully reviewed from the competition law viewpoint.

(3) *Shortage/non-production.* The purchasing party or parties will seek some "out" from their offtake commitments (or any exclusivity restriction against buying the relevant products from a third party supplier) if the JVC for any reason undergoes a shortage of production or is unable to supply sufficient quality products for the purpose. There should be provision for notice and consultation before any of these steps is taken, but recognising that the purchasing party will often have to act quickly to preserve supplies for its own operations.

Distributorship/marketing contracts

6–38 The JVC may be established as a distribution or marketing centre for products manufactured by one or more of the parents. Such an arrangement may, in particular, be the objective of an international joint venture where a party wishes to sell into countries where it cannot market effectively on its own—or where a joint venture is being established to take advantage of a local partner's access and connections. Alternatively, one or more of the parties may be responsible for distribution or marketing of goods manufactured by the JVC itself. In each case, the arrangements will normally be reflected in a separate distributorship or marketing agreement. Again, many of the key issues will be those common to these types of agreements generally.[3] Issues to be addressed are likely to include the following:

MARKETING AGREEMENTS: KEY ISSUES

(1) *Products.* The products covered by the arrangement should, of course, be clearly defined. Clarify whether the agreement will extend to new products developed from time to time by the JVC.

---

[3] For further discussion and precedents, see for instance: *Practical Commercial Precedents*, Vol.3 and R. Christou, *Drafting Commercial Agreements* (London: Sweet & Maxwell, 2004).

(2) *Territory.* The principal marketing territory should, in particular, be carefully defined. Restrictions imposed on the distributor party from dealing outside the territory may be subject to competition laws (see below).

(3) *Distribution/agency.* Clarify whether the party is to act as "agent" of the JVC or-as may be more usual-as a "distributor" (i.e. as a principal acquiring and selling goods in its own right).

(4) *Exclusivity.* Will the distributor be the exclusive distributor for that territory—as opposed to a sole distributor (where the supplier JVC retains the right itself to market directly) or a "non-exclusive" basis where other distributors in the territory may be appointed? See also "Competition laws" below.

(5) *Distributor/agent duties.* It is in the JVC's interests for the principal obligations on the agent/distributor to be clearly spelt out—for example, obligations to use best endeavours to promote and expand the sale of the products within the territory, to maintain adequate stocks, etc. Consider whether obligations in relation to specific campaigns, sales targets and/or marketing plans are appropriate, or whether these will in effect be dealt with through decisions on the marketing strategy to be undertaken within the organisation of the JVC itself.

(6) *Ordering procedure.* A clear forecasting, ordering and delivery procedure should be established.

(7) *Pricing.* Pricing will, as always, be important. In this instance, pricing policy will usually be determined by the board of the JVC (on which the relevant party will be represented). If the distributor party does not have a veto at that level, a separate mechanism for establishing the price should be clearly agreed. (In the case of an agency arrangement, pricing will take the form of commission payable in respect of sales.)

(8) *Terms of payment.* Payment conditions should be clear as to time, currency and method. If the goods are being exported by the JVC, an important factor may be the risk of any exchange rate fluctuations and which party is to bear that risk. One formula is for the distributor party to pay in the supplier JVC's currency but subject to a right to adjust if there is a major movement in exchange rates outside agreed bands.

(9) *Liability.* Usual clauses should deal with warranty (including principles of any warranty programme for customers to be operated by the distributor) and liability for defective products.

(10) *Shipment and delivery.* If product is being exported, it should be clear which party is responsible for shipment costs, insurance, customs clearance etc.

(11) *Trade marks.* Clarify whether the products are to bear only trade marks of the JVC—or whether they can be marketed under the distributor's own marks.

(12) *Termination.* The contract is likely to include normal provisions for termination for material default. An initial fixed term may be appropriate, followed by a mechanism for either party to give (probably a lengthy period of) notice of termination. Clarify whether it will automatically terminate in the event of termination of the joint venture agreement and/or the distributor party ceasing to hold a certain level of shareholding in the JVC. Any right of either party to terminate by notice should be carefully reviewed.

(13) *Force majeure.*

(14) *Title and risk.* Customary provisions should be included as to passing of title and risk. If the distributor party is in a foreign jurisdiction, it will be in the JVC's interest to check to establish to what extent a retention of title clause is valid in the relevant country. Insurance and risk should be properly dealt with.

(15) *Records.* The distributor party should be obliged to keep appropriate records, make them available for inspection, etc.

(16) *Non-compete.* Any restrictions on the agent/distributor from dealing in products which compete with those of the JVC should be clearly stated. If the agent/distributor is a joint venture party, any such restriction should be consistent with any non-compete restrictions in the joint venture agreement.

(17) *Governing law.* The governing law should be clear. It need not necessarily be the same as that governing the joint venture agreement.

(18) *Arbitration.* The procedure for resolution of disputes should be stated. It will generally be sensible to adopt the same procedure for all ancillary contracts as well as the joint venture agreement.

Services contracts

6–39 The establishment of a joint venture frequently involves the need for a wide range of services to be provided to the JVC in order to ensure that it has the facilities and resources to carry on business—particularly if its business was in whole or in part previously conducted by one of the parties. "Due diligence" prior to the transaction should establish the extent to which support services from the parents will continue to be necessary. In many cases, this support may be of an initial or temporary kind while the JVC's operations are established.

6–40 Some types of services have already been discussed; others which may need to be addressed include:

(a) administrative and commercial support services such as secretarial, commercial and accounting personnel, fax, telephone, photocopying and messenger services;

(b) accounting services such as book-keeping, ordering, invoicing, payroll, tax computations, payment and collection of accounts, preparation of accounts etc.;

(c) procurement and ordering of products and raw materials;

(d) security, cleaning or other property-related services—see para.6–31 et seq. above;

(e) professional support services such as IPR management, legal and company secretarial;

(f) computer/IT support services—continuity of IT systems (particularly during a transitional period) can be vital for a JVC; these may cover relatively administrative functions such as payroll, accounts, personnel records etc., but also include IT and communication systems central to the operations to be undertaken by the JVC and its technology.

In each case, key issues will be: clarity as to the scope of services to be provided; pricing (including price reviews); priority of service; liability; and rights of termination.

An example outline of a Support Services Agreement between a party and a JVC is included as Precedent 18 in Part E.

CONCLUSION

6–41 Ancillary contracts associated with the establishment of a joint venture can cover a wide range. Many will be vital to the functioning and potential success of the venture. Issues can be commercially important—and contentious. These contracts will generally require as much attention as the foundation agreements establishing the joint venture vehicle itself.

PART B

SPECIFIC ISSUES AFFECTING THE JOINT VENTURE RELATIONSHIP

7   Capital and funding

8   Governance and management

9   Minority investment and protection

10 Deadlock and breakdown

11 Duties between joint venture parties

12 Transfers of shares

13 Exit, termination and change

14 Dispute: mediation, litigation and arbitration

Part B addresses in more detail a range of important issues affecting the establishment of the venture and the subsequent relationship between the parties. What options are available for the capital structure and funding of the venture? What should be the governance and management structure? What protections are appropriate in the case of minority equity participant? What options are available in the event of deadlock or breakdown of the relationship? Do legal rights and remedies exist to counter the risk of opportunistic behaviour by a joint venture party? What transfer, termination or other exit provisions should be developed? How can any formal disputes be resolved?

CHAPTER 7

Capital and funding

How is the joint venture to be funded? What capital structure should be adopted? What is the desired balance between equity and debt financing? Initial contributions and ongoing financing obligations of the parties have vital implications for the joint venture arrangements as a whole. This chapter addresses the legal aspects affecting both the initial capital structure and funding of the venture and also subsequent financing. This can be one of the most complex parts of establishing a joint venture—and one of the most important.

Importance of initial capital contributions

7–01 The capital structure and funding arrangements will be a vital part of the commercial negotiations between the parties in establishing the venture. Initial contributions invariably create the opening shares or interests in an equity joint venture—which, in turn, are likely to affect management rights, voting rights, dividend rights and obligations to provide future financing (if the parties choose a pro rata basis for such financing).

7–02 The choice of capital structure and funding method will be particularly influenced by the legal form of the joint venture vehicle, the existing and future capital requirements of the joint venture and, importantly, tax considerations. The constitutional documents of the joint venture and/or appropriate funding agreements will, of course, need to be tailored to reflect the chosen capital structure and methods of funding.

OUTLINE CAPITAL STRUCTURES

Contractual alliances

7–03 Contractual alliances and their financing may take many forms. In some such ventures, funding may not be an issue—with each party being responsible for bearing its own costs and expenditure (e.g. on research) without any need to establish joint funding arrangements. There is no distinct entity to be funded and, in most such alliances, sophisticated financing arrangements will not be necessary. Indeed, the lack of capital commitment and investment risk may be a significant feature in choosing this legal form for the alliance or joint venture.

7–04 Where expenditure is to be incurred and shared between the alliance parties, they will usually agree what initial funding is required and, if appropriate, establish a joint account into which agreed funds are contributed and from which expenditure is paid out. Where subsequent funding of a joint account is required to meet project expenditure, rules for calling up contributions ("cash calls") will need to be developed in the alliance documents. These should make it clear who is entitled to call for funds and how the joint account is to be operated.

Joint operating agreements

7–05 Probably the most sophisticated rules for financing contractual joint ventures have developed in relation to joint operating or development agreements in the oil and gas industry—although similar principles are now being used in other major project ventures. A feature of these projects is that the capital investment programme may be spread over many years and timing may be unpredictable at the outset. Participants usually agree to an obligation to make cash contributions in proportion to their "percentage interests" in the underlying project. A typical funding structure under a joint operating agreement (JOA)[1] comprises the following:

(1) *Budget approval*. Budget approval is given by the operating or steering committee on behalf of the joint venture parties, followed by particular authorities for expenditure (AFEs) in relation to specific items.

(2) *Cash calls*. Cash calls may be made by the operator on all joint venture participants to fund items for which AFEs have been issued.

(3) *Payment*. A stated time is allowed for payment by the joint venture participants—followed by a short period of grace during which default interest will apply in the event of late payment.

(4) *Make-up of defaulter's share*. Often, an obligation will be accepted by the non-defaulting participants to make up the share of any defaulting party in order to ensure that the planned investment programme can be maintained.

(5) *Suspension of defaulter's rights*. A suspension will be imposed on any defaulter's rights (both as to voting and the right to take its share of oil or gas) during the period of default but with an opportunity for

---

[1] For a more detailed discussion and examples of a joint operating agreement incorporating this type of arrangement, see the precedents referred to in the footnote to para.4–21.

that party to cure the default by paying up the default amount (together with default interest) within a stated period.

(6) *Forfeiture.* Finally, forfeiture of the defaulting party's share in the joint venture will occur if payment is not made by a certain date—that forfeited share being taken up by the other joint venture parties.

7–06 One feature of joint operating agreements in the oil and gas industry is frequently the provision made for "sole risk" activity. This is activity (e.g. particular drilling activity) which has not been approved by a requisite majority of the operating committee for undertaking by the joint venture as a whole but which, under the rules of the joint venture, can be undertaken by one or more participants alone on the basis that:

(a) the participating parties are solely responsible for funding all costs (and meeting all liabilities) in connection with that activity; and

(b) the participating parties are solely entitled to the benefits or results from that activity.

JOAs can include sophisticated procedures whereby the non-participating parties can join the "sole risk" project later (e.g. at the development stage) upon payment of a premium. Whilst relatively unusual, it is possible to apply similar principles to other types of joint ventures.

Partnerships

7–07 In the case of a partnership, there are generally no fixed rules regarding contributions to capital or its maintenance. Under English law, for example:

(a) funding (including, if relevant, by the contribution of non-cash assets) will be represented by a capital account for each partner in such amount as shall be designated or agreed in accordance with the partnership agreement;

(b) a partner may under the partnership agreement be requested or required to inject further funding from time to time; if this is to be credited to its capital account, this should be stated; otherwise it will in effect be regarded as a loan;[2]

(c) there are no rules regarding the maintenance or repayment of capital—which may therefore be repaid at any time by requisite decision of the partners in accordance with the terms of the partnership agreement;

---

[2] On which, unless otherwise agreed, interest is payable at the rate of 5 per cent per annum—see s.24(3) of the Partnership Act 1890.

(d) no interest is payable on partnership capital unless otherwise agreed.[3]

Similar flexibility in relation to contribution and repayment of partnership capital applies in most other jurisdictions although, of course, the relevant national partnership laws should be reviewed in each particular case.

7–08 When a more sophisticated capital structure is desired for a joint venture taking the form of a partnership, it may be possible to adapt—by contractual provisions within the partnership agreement—some of the concepts of capital structure and financing discussed below in relation to corporate joint ventures.

Corporate joint ventures

7–09 Corporate joint ventures give rise to a variety of funding methods and structures. Contributions made by the parents to the new entity are the primary source of funding for most equity joint ventures. In many basic two party joint ventures, the capital structure may be straightforward and consist primarily of an equal holding by the parties of equity shares or their equivalent. In other ventures, particularly multi-party ventures where the entry of new participants or the exit of original participants may be contemplated, considerably more sophisticated financing techniques can be involved. Key issues when establishing the capital structure of a joint venture company (JVC) include the following:

(1) *Equity proportions.* What should be the proportionate holdings of equity in the JVC by the participants? Equity and voting rights will normally be in the same proportions but this need not necessarily be the case in most jurisdictions. The proportion of equity to be issued to each party may depend on the value of asset contributions to the JVC—see para.2–30 et seq. earlier.

(2) *Class rights.* Is it desirable to create different classes of shares—with different financial rights and obligations of the parties (e.g. as to dividends or return of capital) being established by reference to class of shares held?

(3) *Accounting treatment.* Will the capital structure be influenced by the accounting treatment which would result in the group accounts of each joint venture party or its parent? Will it result in consolidation as a "subsidiary undertaking" and require balance sheet consolidation of the debt of the JVC? Is such consolidation desirable—or is a structure which results in equity accounting a preferred treatment (see generally chapter 19)?

(4) *Debt/equity ratio.* What is the desired ratio of equity to debt for the balance sheet of the JVC? There may be advantages in debt financing. Loan interest is normally a deductible expense in computing the

---

[3] See s.24(4) Partnership Act 1890.

profits of the JVC for tax purposes. Subject to cashflow, a loan can normally be repaid by the JVC without the legal restrictions applying to dividend distributions and the return of equity share capital; and, unless subordinated, loans from the joint venture parties can usually rank *pari passu* with the other ordinary creditors of the JVC rather than behind the creditors as in the case of equity share capital. On the other hand, it may be important to demonstrate a strong balance sheet for the JVC for the purposes of market perception or the ability to raise outside finance.

(5) *Anti-dilution.* Is it desirable to protect any of the parties against the risk of dilution of its shareholding in the JVC (whether in terms of voting rights or value) upon subsequent share issues?

(6) *Loan finance: shareholder/outside loans.* How much debt finance should be raised by outside loans and how much (if practical) from the shareholders themselves? Where the rate of interest on an outside loan is less than the return which the JVC can generate on those funds, there may be attraction in allowing the JVC to "gear up" with outside loans. The rights of outside lenders (particularly in the case of venture capital or limited recourse finance) will need to be considered. Where shareholder loan finance is chosen, a variety of issues will need to be addressed as to the form and terms of such loans—see para.7–19 below. The effect of "thin capitalisation" rules should also be considered—see para.7–30.

(7) *Management incentives/rights.* Is it wished, in the case of a start-up venture, to give the management (or similar "founders") particular incentives or share rights-such as "warrants" or other entitlements to subscribe for or convert into additional equity share capital at particular levels depending upon the performance of the JVC? See also para.7–27 et seq. below in the case of venture capital-type finance.

(8) *Exit.* Are special terms required (e.g. for certain initial participants) to provide for exit or realisation of a particular party's investment at an early or pre-determined time? Various mechanisms may be considered: put options, redeemable shares, buy-back by the JVC or ability of the relevant shareholder to initiate a sale or public offering of the JVC as a whole. Again, these issues most frequently arise in the context of venture capital-type finance.

(9) *Default.* Are particular measures required to deal with financial default? Difficult issues can arise, but should be addressed, in the event of default by the JVC in paying interest or repaying capital on shareholder loans—and, importantly, in the event of default by a shareholder in performing any financing commitment; see para.7–44 et seq. below.

INITIAL FUNDING OF A JVC

Share capital

7-10 A straightforward subscription for ordinary equity shares in the JVC is perhaps the simplest and most common method for the parties to capitalise a new venture. Each party will agree at the outset to pay up a stated amount of equity capital on "start-up" of the JVC. Rights attaching to shares (e.g. as to votes, dividend and return of capital) will usually be the same for each joint venture party.

7-11 There may, though, be exceptions in particular circumstances when it is agreed that the parties should have differing financial or voting rights attaching to their respective shares:

(1) In some exceptional cases, despite one party having a greater proportionate equity ownership of the JVC, it may be agreed as part of the joint venture structure that voting rights—including rights to appoint directors—should be established on a different basis (e.g. on an equal 50:50 basis).

(2) A venture capital or similar finance provider taking equity in the JVC may seek special "preference" rights in relation to dividends and return of capital—see para.7–12 et seq. below.

(3) In some cases of a new multi-party "start-up" venture, where new entrants are likely to be introduced at a future stage, the parties may wish to create special rights for the "founders". These may include:
   (a) special rights to appoint directors;
   (b) special rights to veto or approve certain key decisions or enhanced voting rights on specified issues;
   (c) preferred rights to dividend;
   (d) rights to convert into or acquire additional ordinary shares in defined circumstances (e.g. on a sale or public offering of the JVC or if certain performance criteria are achieved); and/or
   (e) rights to prevent dilution of that shareholding.

These differing rights between the joint venture parties will usually require the creation of different "classes" of shares. The ability to do this, and the flexibility of share rights which can be adopted, will depend on the corporate laws of the relevant jurisdiction of the JVC.[4]

Preference shares

7-12 In many situations, it may be desirable to give certain parties a priority or "preference" right in relation to dividend entitlement or rights

---

[4] See para.9–36 for "class" rights under English law.

to repayment of capital on insolvency or winding-up of the JVC. Not all jurisdictions allow for shares of the JVC to be structured with different rights in a manner as flexibly as in the UK. However, where this can be done, forms of preference share capital provide useful possibilities to cater for the different interests which particular parties may have in funding a joint venture. Although not a term of art, these shares generally give their holders a right to receive dividends and/or to participate in a return of capital in priority to the holders of ordinary shares; they may or may not have voting rights equivalent to other shares.

7–13 The rights attaching to these "preference" shares will depend on the articles of association (or equivalent constitutional documents) of the JVC but may comprise:

(a) priority over other shares as regards dividends (possibly including both a fixed dividend and a participating dividend linked to profits);

(b) dividend rights which then rank *pari passu* with other ordinary shares (after the latter have received the same rate of dividend as the preferred shares);

(c) priority over other ordinary shares on a return of capital in a winding-up (up to the level of the subscription price); and

(d) rights which then rank *pari passu* with other ordinary shares in a distribution of surplus assets on a winding-up (after the other ordinary shares have received the same repayment of capital as the preferred shares).

United Kingdom

7–14 Types of preference shares used in the UK include the following:

(1) *Cumulative*. Cumulative preference shares entitle the holder to payment of arrears of dividend on those shares before dividends are paid to any other class of shareholders; they usually carry a fixed rate of dividend.

(2) *Participating*. Participating preference shares give the holder the right to a dividend (usually a dividend which "participates" in profits in addition to any fixed dividend) which is usually expressed by reference to a percentage of the JVC's annual pre-tax profits.

(3) *Redeemable*. Preference shares may by their terms be redeemable, either by the JVC itself or by the holder. These redemption rights are usually expressed to arise on a specified date or in specified circumstances; the redemption price will usually be specifically stated and may be at par or at a premium.

(4) *Convertible*. Convertible preference shares will entitle the holder to convert at a pre-agreed formula into shares of another class (usually ordinary equity shares) in specific circumstances—such as a public

offering by the JVC or a failure by the JVC to meet specified financial performance targets or if redemption does not take place on the agreed date; the effect of conversion will often be to dilute the equity interests of the other shareholders.

> **An example of Preference Shares with a variety of different rights under English law appears as Precedent 12 in Part E.**

7-15 Loan stock can also be used with rights comparable to those of preference shares (but not such as to amount to "shares"); often, these will be "convertible" at the option of the holder into ordinary equity shares. One reason for issuing loan stock, rather than shares, in the case of a JVC in the UK is that interest will commonly be allowable as a deduction in computing the profits of the JVC; preference share dividends will, on the other hand, be treated as distributions.

Outside the United Kingdom

7-16 The ability to use preference shares, or other special rights attaching to shares, differs from jurisdiction to jurisdiction. Preference shares are possible in most EU jurisdictions—but not always to the same level of sophistication as in the UK: see the various country-sections in Part D.

Non-cash contributions

7-17 Consideration for the issue of shares by the JVC may be either cash or, commonly, a non-cash contribution (such as the transfer of assets to the JVC or an undertaking to provide technology or other assistance to the JVC). Where non-cash consideration is provided, legal rules often apply in relation to valuation.

(1) Many countries impose a requirement for non-cash contributions to be independently valued.[5]

(2) In most countries, the directors of the JVC must be satisfied that the value of the non-cash contribution to the JVC is not less than the nominal value of the shares being issued in exchange for that contribution in order to avoid shares being allotted at a discount.[6]

7-18 Contribution of non-cash assets by one or more of the parties can give rise to complex valuation issues as between the parties. The parties will

---

[5] See, for example, the position in France and Germany. In the UK this is only obligatory in the case of public limited companies (see s.593 of the Companies Act 2006).
[6] In the UK, see s.580 of the Companies Act 2006. Note also that a public limited company cannot issue shares against an undertaking to provide future services.

need to negotiate and agree the most appropriate way to value such contributions. Sometimes a single independent valuation may be appropriate. On other occasions, there will be detailed financial negotiations—an exercise requiring careful consideration and analysis with the appropriate professional advisers; see para.2–30 et seq. earlier.

Shareholder loans

7–19 Equity share capital will often be supplemented by loans from the joint venture parties to the JVC. The debt/equity ratio for the JVC will depend upon factors such as tax considerations (e.g. thin capitalisation rules—see para.7–30 below), the desirability of ease of repayment (since loans can generally be repaid more easily than share capital) and the influence of market considerations which may lead to the need to demonstrate a sound equity base for the JVC. If loan capital is raised from the shareholders, issues which will need to be considered include the following:

(1) *Subordination*: whether or not the loan should be subordinated to the rights of third party providers of debt finance and, if so, the terms of subordination.[7]

(2) *Interest*: rate and timing of interest payments (sometimes an interest free period will be appropriate depending upon the projected cash-flow of the JVC but remembering the possible application of transfer pricing or similar tax rules in the case of non-commercial terms).

(3) *Repayments*: timing of repayments (including whether the loan is repayable at the option of the shareholder, or the JVC, and whether repayment must be equal or pro rata as between all shareholder loans).

(4) *Termination and/or transfer*: whether or not the loan should be repaid on termination or transfer of the shareholder's interest in the JVC (see para.7–20 below).

(5) *Security*: terms of any security.[8]

(6) *Forfeiture*: whether or not a shareholder's loan should carry the same risk of forfeiture as its equity interest (where applicable).

(7) *Timing of loan*: whether loan capital should be injected at the same time as equity capital (and in what proportion to equity).

---

[7] If the terms of subordination are satisfactory, third party lenders will frequently be prepared to regard subordinated debt as equal to equity; this is usually advantageous, for example, in relation to debt/equity ratios in financing covenants.

[8] In the case of a UK JVC, if parties have advanced loans to the JVC without security and subsequently wish to take security, the provisions of the Insolvency Act 1986 should be considered. Under s.240(1)(a), security established within a period of two years before the onset of insolvency may be set aside as a preference (instead of the usual period of six months) where the holder of the security is "connected" with the company.

(8) *Assignability*: the transfer of a shareholder's loan to an outside third party will not normally be acceptable (without consent of the other joint venture parties) unless accompanied by a permitted transfer of its shares.

(9) *Events of default*: events of default (which are usually more relaxed than in the case of an outside commercial loan) and, in such default event, whether a lending shareholder can take separate action to recover the loan (in most cases, the parties will wish all shareholder loans to be treated alike and enforcement decisions to be unanimous or require a specified majority).

(10) *Tranches*: where shareholder loans are to be provided in tranches, provisions may be necessary in the event of a failure by a lending shareholder to advance its tranche at the relevant time (see para.7–46) below.

(11) *Tax*: "thin capitalisation" and other tax considerations (see chapter 15 and also para.7–30 below).

These loan arrangements will usually be documented in a separate loan agreement between the lending shareholder and the JVC setting out the detailed terms of the financing. If there are multiple lending shareholders, it may be convenient for the JVC to issue a series of loan notes or loan stock which can therefore apply the same terms (including as to decisions or procedures required for enforcement) to all lending shareholders.

An outline example of a Shareholder Funding Agreement between shareholders and a JVC is included as Precedent 16 in Part E.

7–20 Where finance raised by the JVC includes shareholder loans, the question arises: how to treat these loans if the relevant party leaves the joint venture? In many situations, a party's holdings of equity shares and loans should be regarded, together, as essentially parts of its overall financial investment in the JVC. Therefore, in these situations it will commonly be appropriate to provide in the joint venture agreement that:

(a) assignment to a third party of the benefit of shareholder loans to the JVC should be subject to the same restrictions as apply to transfers of shares (in order to prevent an on-demand loan to the JVC falling under the control of a non-shareholder);

(b) if a shareholder transfers its shares (whether voluntarily or under a compulsory procedure), the transferee should be required to acquire the loans as well or, alternatively, the JVC should repay the loans—thus enabling a leaving shareholder to realise its entire investment in the JVC; and

(c) similarly, a transferee will normally be required to take over or replace any guarantees, counter-indemnities or other credit support to third parties given by the transferring shareholder—sometimes subject to the proviso that the transferring shareholder will remain liable for any liability attributable to events prior to the transfer.

Outside finance

7–21 The parties may, of course, seek to raise finance for the joint venture from outside banking or other funding sources. This may take several forms, including: bank overdraft for working capital, term loans from banks, capital market instruments, venture capital or project finance. Outside finance will be particularly appropriate where the JVC is intended to operate in an autonomous manner independently from its parents. Will lenders have regard to the "joint venture" background of the JVC? Aside from credit risk factors, considerations which a third party lender to a JVC is likely to take into account include:

(a) level of equity injected by the parties as shareholders;

(b) the debt/equity ratio and how much equity is to be injected before third party debt is called upon;

(c) existence of guarantees by the joint venture parents;

(d) how long the joint venture parties commit to retain their equity stakes (including whether there are any unusual or easy exit or termination provisions);

(e) the willingness of shareholders to accept any responsibility for cost overruns during the construction phase (in the case of project financing);

(f) the terms of subordination of shareholder loans;

(g) effectiveness of decision-making processes within the JVC;

(h) any provisions for resolution of deadlock;

(i) the availability of technical expertise needed by the JVC and the terms of material contracts between the JVC and particular shareholders (and whether or not claims under them are subordinated);

(j) any specific issues associated with public sector shareholders where the JVC is engaged in activities (e.g. infrastructure development) which may have political aspects in a particular country.

7–22 The debt funding of joint ventures frequently arises in the context of project finance—often where finance for new capital projects is provided on a "limited recourse" or "non-recourse" basis with the debt being primarily serviced from, and secured on, the income stream of the venture without parent company guarantees or credit support. The essential quality of this form of financing is that lenders do not have unrestricted access to the credit of the joint venture parents. Instead, the lenders must accept a degree of "project risk"; if the joint venture project is not successful, they may not recover their loan in full since their "recourse" is limited to project assets (i.e. the assets, including revenues, of the JVC).

7-23 In many infrastructure projects, there are three identifiable risk phases: an engineering and construction phase; the start-up phase; and the operational phase. In many cases, loans which are structured as "project finance" may not, during the construction phase, be possible without the support of guarantees or comparable support given by the joint venture parents or other related parties. Even during the later phases, third party lenders may endeavour to seek some form of "sponsor support" from the joint venture parents. Typically, project lenders wish equity to be injected in full before any project debt finance is raised, but it is not uncommon—particularly where the equity joint venture parties are sufficiently creditworthy—for lenders to accept that the funding should go in on a pro rata basis with equity.

Guarantees

7-24 Banks may not be prepared to lend to the JVC (at least not at acceptable rates) unless guarantees or counter-indemnities in support of such loans are offered by the "parent" shareholders. There should normally be provisions in the joint venture agreement governing the scope and extent of any such guarantees, including provisions to make it clear:

(a) whether there is an absolute commitment on the parents to provide such guarantees (or whether these will need to be agreed on a case-by-case basis);

(b) whether any such guarantees can, or should, be given on a "several" basis or a "joint and several" basis. (The essential difference is that on a several basis, the guarantor will only be liable for its percentage share of the guaranteed amount, whereas on a joint and several basis each guarantor could be liable for the full amount of the borrowing with a need to rely on its right of contribution from its co-guarantor(s) to recover any amount paid in excess of its share; this issue can give rise to severe difficulties where not all the shareholders are creditworthy); and

(c) that cross-indemnities will apply, as between the joint venture parties, to ensure that any residual liability called under any guarantee to a third party is borne in the correct proportions.[9]

---

[9] A guarantor will under English law normally have a right of recovery against the JVC as the principal obligor and a right of contribution against its co-guarantors under the Civil Liabilities (Contribution) Act 1978.

Charges

7-25 The issue may arise whether or not a joint venture party should be able to use its shares in the JVC by way of security for the purpose of raising finance itself. In many cases, the right to charge will be prohibited under the restrictions on transfer or other dealings in shares without the prior consent of the other shareholder(s) since, in the event of enforcement of the charge, a chargee exercising direct rights over the shares would become, in effect, a new joint venture party. In other cases, it may be appropriate to permit the charging of shares in the JVC for certain financing purposes—but subject to a requirement that, in the event of enforcement of that charge, the chargee must sell the shares as soon as reasonably practicable and be subject to the pre-emption procedures in favour of the other shareholder(s).

7-26 In the case of a JVC raising project finance, project lenders will nearly always require a charge over the shares of the borrower(s) as part of their standard security package. It is sensible for the joint venture documents to anticipate this.

Venture capital finance

7-27 Many start-up or early stage joint ventures now seek equity funding—as well as debt funding—in part from a venture capital or similar finance provider. Such equity funding arrangements use many of the same techniques as are employed in a typical corporate joint venture. The differences are essentially of emphasis in that the agreement with the equity finance provider (often called a "shareholders and subscription agreement") will focus specifically upon the needs of the equity provider rather than the joint venture as a whole. Detailed consideration of such transactions is outside the scope of this book and more specialist works should be consulted.[10] However, issues relating to capital structure addressed by such financing techniques are worth considering in many joint venture contexts—see, for instance, strategic minority investment discussed at para.9-38 et seq. below.

7-28 Key issues in venture capital-type equity financing include the following:

(1) *Exit*. Most venture capital providers will only invest if they can envisage an ability to sell their investment at a profit within a relatively short period. Exit routes will therefore be vital and may include:

---

[10] For a more detailed discussion in this area, see Darryl Cooke and James Dow, *Private Equity: Law and Practice* (London: Sweet & Maxwell, 2008).

- (a) a put option on the other joint venture parties at a predetermined formula and at particular times;
- (b) an entitlement to require redemption or buy-back of shares by the JVC (consistent with relevant corporate law requirements);
- (c) a right to call for or to initiate a sale or public offering of the JVC; see also para.13–39 below;
- (d) rights of "drag along" (i.e. to require other participants to join in a sale to a third party) or "tag along" (i.e. a right to join in any sale to a third party made by another joint venture party).

(2) *Income return before exit.* The equity provider will generally also seek an income return prior to exit. In order to establish priority rights over the ordinary shareholders, this will usually take the form of a preference share dividend. Frequently, the preference shares will be convertible into ordinary equity shares on or before exit. Different variants of preference share capital are discussed in more detail in para.7–12 et seq. earlier.

(3) *Anti-dilution.* A key interest of an equity provider will be to ensure that its equity stake in the JVC is not "diluted" by subsequent share issues. Dilution can be strategic (diminution in percentage voting influence) or result from loss of value (value per share being reduced by subsequent share issues to third parties at a more favourable subscription price per share than that at which the venture capitalist subscribed). Value protection is particularly important if the venture capital is provided at an initial stage of the JVC when pricing is more uncertain. Anti-dilution measures are discussed in more detail at para.9–15 et seq.

(4) *Incentives.* Techniques may be used to incentivise management or founders of the JVC. Although usually used to motivate individual participants, similar techniques can be developed in relation to other founding shareholders. These may include:
- (a) a "ratchet" under which the proportion of the equity share capital held by the management team is increased if the JVC's value on exit (e.g. sale or public offering) exceeds certain agreed parameters;
- (b) a "reverse ratchet" mechanism so that the management's proportion of the equity capital reduces if they fail to generate a defined performance return. This may be achieved by compulsory equity transfers or by adjusting the conversion rate of convertible preference shares held by the equity provider;
- (c) making a distinction between a "good leaver" and a "bad leaver" so that, if the management or other relevant founder party leaves prematurely or upon a default, the price payable to that party under pre-emption or option provisions is at a discount to market value.

(5) *Management rights.* The equity providers will commonly seek extensive rights of veto (or "consent rights") over material management decisions of the JVC.

(6) *Minority protection*. In addition, the equity provider is likely to require further "minority protection" rights such as board representation, information rights and other minority rights of the kind discussed in chapter 9.

Tax issues

7–29 A decision on the form of capital and the debt/equity ratio to be established for the JVC will often need to take account of tax factors particularly in the case of an international joint venture. These include:

(1) *Capital duties*. The cost of providing equity capital may in some jurisdictions be greater than loan capital since the former may attract duties on issue (although this is not the case in the UK).

(2) *Interest*. There are likely to be significant tax differences between paying interest on loans and distributing dividends on shares; e.g. a JVC may be able to deduct any interest paid on loans from its taxable profits whereas dividends are generally not tax deductible in computing the JVC's profits (but see para.7–30 below).

(3) *Place of borrowing*. It may be advantageous, from a tax viewpoint, for the joint venture parties to borrow the finance themselves and inject the money as equity into the JVC; e.g. the parties may have taxable profits against which the interest expense could be relieved whereas the JVC may, at least initially, be expected to have losses which could not be surrendered. Alternatively, if a joint venture shareholder is resident in a jurisdiction which has a higher tax rate than the country in which the JVC is based, it may prefer—in its overall tax planning interests—to reduce its own profits (and therefore the tax on them) by borrowing directly itself rather than to reduce the profits of the JVC.

(4) *Tax loss*. A party may wish to ensure (where feasible) that, if loan capital is provided and is eventually "lost", the lender will obtain tax relief for the bad debt. In the case of a joint venture, any loss by a corporate lender will generally be relievable against UK corporation tax—except that this will not normally apply if the joint venturer controls the JVC.

(5) *Thin capitalisation*. Many jurisdictions, on the other hand, have rules to prevent undue weighting towards debt rather than equity capital— see below.

Thin capitalisation

7–30 It will often be desirable to finance the JVC with a mixture of debt and equity. Tax rules on "thin capitalisation" in the relevant jurisdiction of the JVC will be relevant. These rules apply in most sophisticated tax systems. They limit the ability of a JVC to deduct interest in computing its taxable profits where the ratio of debt finance to equity finance exceeds a certain level. These rules therefore result in interest being effectively converted into a deemed dividend or distribution for tax purposes. Interest paid to a foreign shareholder which is treated as "excess" under thin capitalisation rules may also be excluded from exemption from withholding tax under relevant double tax treaties.

7–31 In the UK, "thin capitalisation" rules have been subsumed within the general transfer pricing rules. These now extend to transactions between UK residents as well as between UK and non-UK residents. Broadly, the transfer pricing rules apply to transactions, including loans, between connected companies where the terms (e.g. as to interest) differ from those which would have been made between independent companies. If the terms confer a potential UK tax advantage on a party, then the profits and losses of that party may be computed for tax purposes as if the transaction had been made on arm's length terms.[11]

7–32 The rules also apply if a loan to a JVC is supported by a guarantee from a related party which has the effect of increasing the amount which would otherwise be lent to the JVC. The interest on the "excessive" part of the loan may be disallowed (whether paid to a connected or independent lender). However, a UK resident guarantor can claim a compensating adjustment in the form of a tax deduction for the interest (which the borrower would otherwise have been entitled to claim).

7–33 There is a wide diversity of thin capitalisation rules internationally, even within the EU. Indeed, the Ruding Committee in 1992 recommended that the European Commission should take action to harmonise these within Member States. In the case of an international joint venture, the applicable rules of the particular jurisdiction of the JVC will need to be specifically considered.

Future Financing of the Venture

Future financing commitments

7–34 Future financing is a major area for potential inter-partner dispute. The parties in a joint venture should consider at the outset the likely needs of the joint venture for ongoing financing—and, in particular, how any future finance is to be provided for the joint venture operations. An agreed funding plan can avoid future uncertainty and dispute.

---

[11] See Sch.9, para.6, Finance Act 1996. The transfer pricing rules do, though, contain exemptions for small and medium enterprises (SMEs)—see also para.15–39.

Shareholder commitments

7–35 The parties should agree at the outset the extent to which they will be committed to provide future finance.[12] Broadly, options include the following:

(1) The parties may agree that they have no commitment to provide any further finance (i.e. any such future finance requires each party's prior agreement).

(2) Each party may accept a commitment to provide finance up to a specified maximum amount—either by payment up of instalments on partly paid shares or in tranches by an agreed cash call procedure.

(3) The parties may agree limited commitments for certain initial costs (e.g. during a "feasibility phase") followed by commitments, for significantly greater amounts, conditional on certain key criteria being satisfied.

(4) The parties may undertake an unlimited commitment to provide such finance as is necessary to keep the JVC solvent.

(5) The parties may agree undertakings to guarantee finance provided to the JVC by third party lenders (whether up to a limit or on an unlimited basis).

(6) The parties may agree a procedure for capital calls for funding on the basis that, although funding is not obligatory, if a party declines to fund:

　(a) the other shareholder has a right to provide the whole of the funding attributable to the "declining" shareholder; and if exercised

　(b) the other shareholder may, in some cases, have a right to acquire the "declining" shareholder's shares in the JVC (often at a price less than fair value).[13]

7–36 In many "start-up" ventures, financing commitments may be crucial. Where additional financing is contributed by the parties, this will commonly be contributed pro rata to their respective shares in the existing issued share capital (or partnership capital). When there are commitments in

---

[12] As a matter of corporate law in the UK, note that a shareholder cannot be required by an alteration in the articles of association after it has become a member to subscribe for further equity or pay money to the JVC (s.25 of the Companies Act 2006). Nor is it likely that any obligation to contribute additional finance will be construed as an implied term under the articles of association—see *Bratton Seymour Service Co Ltd v Oxborough* [1992] B.C.L.C. 693.

[13] See *Euro Brokers Holdings Ltd v Monecor (London) Ltd* [2003] EWCA Civ 105 where the court enforced such a provision (based on a price of 70 per cent of the consolidated net asset value of the company); the case was concerned with the validity of the capital call, not the purchase option.

advance by the parties to provide future financing, limitations on those commitments can be imposed. Common variants include the following:

(1) Specific time periods may restrict the "window" during which any joint venture party can be called upon to contribute according to its pro rata share—with financing obligations ceasing at the end of the period.

(2) Where funding requirements are certain, parties may agree on specific timing of payments in tranches over a number of years. A detailed schedule to the joint venture agreement may be used specifying the contribution, the form of financing (i.e. equity or debt) and the "trigger" points for any call.

(3) Alternatively, a monetary cap or limit may be fixed on financing obligations by reference to (i) sums advanced during the entire period of the joint venture or (ii) on a per year or per month basis.

(4) Time of payments may be fixed but the amount payable could vary according to a specific formula.

7–37 If long-term commitments are given to provide finance to the JVC, these should normally be given as between the shareholders themselves, and not directly to the JVC, in order to avoid the possibility of a liquidator or similar officer of an insolvent JVC being entitled to call for funds from a parent shareholder. However, arrangements involving outside lenders will frequently require commitments by the joint venture parties which can be enforced directly by those lenders.

Equity funding

7–38 Where future funding is by way of subscription for further shares of the JVC, a number of points arise. A principal issue is to make it clear by what authority and procedure the "call" for the subscription of further equity can be made. For example, should the decision be made:

(a) by a simple majority of the board of directors (assuming that there is sufficient authorised share capital for the issue)—or by unanimous or super-majority decision of the board of directors or general meeting of shareholders?

(b) subject to criteria that the board of directors must be reasonably satisfied that third party finance cannot be obtained on commercially acceptable terms (without recourse to the shareholders)?

(c) subject to a condition that the auditors (or another appropriate third party) should certify—or, upon request, be required to certify—that the issue price is fair?

(d) on the basis that, if shares are offered pro rata to existing shareholdings but some are not taken up, the balance will be re-offered in a further round to the shareholder(s) willing to take them up?

Similarly, there should be clarity as to circumstances (if any) in which the board of directors is authorised to issue new shares to a new, third party participant (and, if so, on what terms).

7–39 Call for new equity can be a critical decision, particularly if a party has a minority shareholding. In many cases, the parties may agree that no new equity shares are to be issued unless the parties agree unanimously. Equity funding calls can, of course, lead to changes in respective shareholding proportions in the JVC if a shareholder does not take up its proportion. There may be a need to anticipate the effect of significant shareholding changes by regulating in advance that certain rights (e.g. rights of board appointment or veto rights) will fall away if a party's shareholding falls below a certain percentage.

7–40 Corporate laws[14] may require that any new equity capital issued by the JVC for cash must be offered to shareholders pro rata to their existing shareholdings (i.e. by way of "rights issue") in order to give existing shareholders an opportunity to prevent their interests being diluted.

> One example of a procedure for "calls" and the issue of new shares in a multi-party venture is in clauses 4 and 5 of the Multi-Party Shareholders Agreement which appears as Precedent 10 in Part E.

Subsequent subscription obligations

7–41 In some joint venture situations (e.g. where a party does not have funds to invest significantly at the outset), it may be agreed that a particular party should be committed to making a subsequent subscription for equity. The obligation may require the under-invested party to use at least a portion of its subsequent returns from the joint venture to reinvest in the JVC. A greater equity stake may ensure greater commitment to the joint venture project. Such a subscription obligation could be limited by time or capped at a fixed monetary amount.

Emergency funding

7–42 It is not uncommon for joint ventures to include arrangements for shareholder financing in "emergency situations". A JVC, for instance, which operates in a fast changing industry may need commercially to react promptly to changes which call for financial investment. Emergency financing obligations can ensure that the funds are available and that the venture can respond in a timely manner. In other situations, emergency funding obligations which compel a party to contribute further funding may be inappropriate—simply throwing good money after bad. If emergency

---

[14] In the UK, see s.561 Companies Act 2006 (unless disapplied by s.570 or s.571).

financing obligations are established, they need to be carefully defined. Points to be addressed include:

(a) notice period;

(b) amount of contribution required and/or maximum funding which can be called; and

(c) method of decision-making for determining when an emergency situation arises for funding purposes.

Sole risk

7–43 On occasions, it may be appropriate to have a funding system which enables one or more parties to participate in a specific new project or business opportunity but allows another party not to participate. Alternative means to achieve this within a corporate joint venture include the following:

(1) Funding obligations relating to the new project may be undertaken by the participating party alone with an agreed increase in its equity share in the JVC.

(2) The project or opportunity could be carried out solely through a special purpose subsidiary (or other "ring-fenced" arrangement) whereby any distributable profit is structured to pass to the participating party—coupled, perhaps, with specific funding or indemnity obligations by that party in relation to that subsidiary.

(3) The participating party may be entitled to undertake the new project or opportunity itself, outside the joint venture, free of any non-compete restrictions.

This situation is, in effect, similar to a "sole risk" project in a natural resources JOA—see para.7–06 earlier.

Default

7–44 If financing commitments are central to the joint venture (as in a "start-up" venture involving significant planned capital expenditure), appropriate default procedures should be considered. Although default of financing obligations will usually trigger any general contractual default provisions, the importance of such commitments to the viability of the joint venture may mean that the non-defaulting parties should have additional rights—including a potential right to dilute the defaulting party's equity interest.

Unincorporated joint ventures

7–45 Again, the most sophisticated and perhaps draconian provisions for dealing with funding defaults are in JOAs in the oil and gas industry. The most significant features are that these will generally provide for:

(a) the non-defaulting parties to pay up the shortfall necessary to meet the cash calls made under the JOA; followed by

(b) outright forfeiture of the defaulting party's interest if it fails to remedy the default within a specified period of time (see para.7–05 et seq. above).

There is still debate as to whether such a forfeiture provision can amount to a "penalty" and be unenforceable under English law and/or entitle the court to exercise jurisdiction to grant relief against forfeiture. There is some judicial authority[15] to support the view that the English courts will generally uphold such a provision where it applies equally to each party and there are sensible commercial reasons for the parties to have agreed it in the circumstances of the particular venture.

Corporate joint ventures

7–46 Similar default principles can be applied to a corporate joint venture where heavy capital expenditure is planned at the outset. In these cases, future financing commitments of the joint venture parties will be central to the joint venture. Default will mean that the JVC will suffer a material shortage of funds. Appropriate default procedures should therefore be considered. These can include, usually in stages, the following:

(a) liability to pay default interest to the JVC;

(b) loss of rights to attend meetings and exercise voting rights (e.g. suspension of entitlement to exercise veto rights) and/or rights to appoint directors of the JVC;

(c) suspension, and possibly loss, of rights to dividends declared during the period of forfeiture (although this element may be more vulnerable to attack as a penalty—see below);

(d) after a prolonged failure by the defaulting party to cure the default, compulsory sale to the other joint venture parties of the whole or part of the defaulter's shareholding in the JVC.

In some cases, as in a JOA, it may be appropriate for the non-defaulting parties to have the right (or obligation) to take up the defaulting party's call and, if default is not remedied within a specific period, a right to call for transfer of the defaulting party's shares in the JVC.

7–47 A less drastic consequence is to allow non-defaulting parties to advance funds to the JVC on behalf of the defaulter at a specific rate of

---

[15] See, for example, *BICC Plc v Burndy Corp* [1985] 1 All E.R. 417 where the court did not regard a compulsory assignment clause in a commercial agreement for the maintenance of patent rights as a "penalty" but was prepared to grant relief against forfeiture in certain circumstances.

interest. This facilitates continuous funding of the venture without diluting the interests of any party. A non-defaulting party can be protected by:

(a) a contractual entitlement to receive the defaulting party's dividends on any additional shares so subscribed; or

(b) an obligation of the defaulting party to pay interest (at a high rate) and principal on a deemed inter-shareholder loan from the defaulting party; and/or

(c) a security interest ultimately exercisable over the defaulting party's shares.

7–48 If a compulsory inter-party transfer of a defaulting party's shares in the JVC takes place, a common practice is for the applicable transfer price to be designated as a percentage below the fair value (the latter being determined, if necessary, by an independent expert). It is still uncertain, under English law, whether or not the price on any such compulsory transfer can be contractually enforceable at less than fair value. Factors include:

(a) such a provision may be open to attack as a "penalty" if the primary purpose is to act *in terrorem* (and not as a genuine pre-estimate of the loss likely to flow from the breach) and, as a result, the court may have an equitable jurisdiction to grant relief; and

(b) if the power to require compulsory transfer is established in the articles of association and requires a shareholders' resolution, any resolution exercising that power must also pass the test of being bona fide in what the shareholders believe to be the interests of the JVC as a whole.

Whilst the position is not clearly established by judicial authority,[16] it is thought that the English courts will be reluctant to set aside such a provision in a joint venture as penal if the terms (i) are applicable on the

---

[16] In a Canadian case, *Ringuet v Bergeron* (1960) 24 D.L.R. (2d) 449, S.C. (Can), it was held that a provision in a shareholders' agreement requiring compulsory transfer of shares of a defaulting party, without consideration, following a material breach was valid and enforceable. In an Australian case, *CRA Ltd v New Zealand Goldfields Investments* [1989] V.R. 873, the court held that a term permitting the non-defaulter to purchase the defaulter's shares in a JVC for a gold mining project at 95 per cent of their fair value was not penal. The clause was described as "... accommodating a default in a fashion most conveniently suited to overcoming it in the interest of the progress of the joint venture project." See also *BICC Plc v Burndy Corp*, in relation to a forfeiture clause and *Euro Brokers Holdings Ltd v Monecor (London) Ltd*, where the court assumed the enforceability of a contractual option to purchase the shares of a party at 70 per cent of the consolidated net asset value of the JVC if that party declined to participate in a capital call for funding (rather than on a default as such). But compare *Jobson v Jobson* [1988] 1 W.L.R. 1026 where the court rejected as "penal" a right to purchase shares at a substantially reduced price upon a default under a share purchase agreement. Supporting a strict approach to these clauses under English law, see A. Chaplin on "Share sale penalty clauses", *The Company Lawyer* Vol.26 No.1 (2005).

same basis to all shareholders, (ii) represent a commercially justified and proportionate remedy for the non-defaulting shareholder(s) in the circumstances of the particular venture and (iii) have been negotiated at arm's length between the parties at the outset of the venture.

Conclusion

7–49 Capital and funding arrangements are crucial to the structure of an equity joint venture. The financial terms will inevitably form a fundamental basis to the commercial relationship between the parties. Establishing a clear funding plan is vital to commercial success and the avoidance of potential disputes. Negotiating the capital and funding arrangements can be one of the most complex aspects of establishing a joint venture—and also one of the most important.

Chapter 8

Governance and management

Effective governance and management will be crucial to success of the venture. Joint ventures and alliances present real management challenges. They frequently involve a need to integrate, or at least work with, different business cultures, personalities and (often) languages. For each of the "parents" in an equity joint venture, there will be the additional issue of ensuring appropriate supervision of its investment in the joint venture. This chapter addresses the key legal issues and options available in establishing the governance and management structure for the venture. It also examines the legal duties assumed by individual directors of a joint venture company.

Key governance issues

8–01 Effective governance and management are vital to the success of any joint venture or alliance. Management of joint ventures and alliances is increasingly being recognised as requiring a range of skills significantly different from the management skills involved in a wholly-owned operation.[1]

Key governance issues

8–02 The governance structure will lie at the heart of the joint venture or alliance arrangements. It is for the principal parties to design and implement the structure appropriate to their particular joint venture. For the lawyer, the task is to advise and to fit the desired structure into the framework of the chosen legal "vehicle" for the venture. Expressing the key issues in legal terms, a governance and management structure should address the following basic inter-related questions:

(1) *Role of alliance governing body*. What will be the role of the steering or governing body of the joint venture or alliance? What will be its composition and procedures? What will be its decision-making authority?

---

[1] Hence the importance of such bodies as the Association of Strategic Alliance Professionals (ASAP) which assist the sharing of experience and "best practice". See also para.1–23 and the various management studies and literature referred to in chapter 1.

(2) *Control*. Will one party essentially be in control of the overall direction and management of the joint venture company (JVC)—or is control to be shared?

(3) *Composition of the board of directors*. How is the board of directors to be appointed? Will each party appoint a certain number of board members? Will there be independent directors? Will the board include executive directors?

(4) *Governance by the joint venture or alliance "parents"*. What decisions will be reserved for the parent companies rather than the management organs of the joint venture? What reporting and/or approval mechanisms need to be established to ensure an appropriate balance between supervision and monitoring by the parents and autonomy for the joint venture?

(5) *Operational management*. What will be the structure for operational management, including the composition and role of any executive body and/or authority of individual executive officers?

(6) *Minority protection*. What influence or protection will each participant have in relation to the JVC's affairs—particularly in the case of a minority participant? Much may depend on the negotiating position or "strategic" role of each party.

(7) *Deadlock and dispute resolution*. Is it necessary or desirable to establish any formal "deadlock breaker" or dispute resolution procedures in the event of management deadlock between the parties?

These are the important areas for the lawyers. Addressing these issues at the outset—and, where necessary, building them into the governance structure reflected in the shareholders' agreement and/or constitutional documents—will help to avoid misunderstandings and create a firmer foundation for subsequent management of the venture.

8–03 There are likely to be important differences, both in terms of substance and form, between a governance structure for (i) an equity joint venture (particularly a corporate joint venture) compared with (ii) a contractual alliance. A contractual alliance will usually be a two-party relationship established solely by contract. An equity joint venture, particularly a corporate joint venture, brings into play the creation of a third "entity" and the need to establish the governance structure within the more formal, and often statutory, basis applicable to that legal form. In the case of a corporate joint venture, the governance structure will depend upon relevant national corporate laws relating to that venture. Whilst reference is made here to the position in certain countries outside the UK, the detailed legal rules and references relate to English law.

Role of joint venture or alliance governing body

8–04 The heart of the governance structure will be the governing or steering body of the venture. This will have a critical role in directing and driving the alliance. In terms of its business role, the Association of Strategic Alliance Professionals (ASAP) refers to five fundamental responsibilities of an overall steering committee or council:

ASAP: Key Responsibilities of an Alliance Governing Body

1. **Policy Guidance.** Developing and maintaining strategic and operational direction.
2. **Performance Review.** Controlling the alliance by measuring progress against planned results and milestones.
3. **Innovation and Transformation.** Motivating and empowering the alliance to encourage innovation and improvement.
4. **Problem sharing.** Overcoming difficulties in operations.
5. **Partnership relations.** Maintaining a win-win approach and keeping communications open.

Source: ASAP (Strategic Alliance Best Process Workbook)

Contractual alliance

8–05 In the case of a contractual alliance, the management structure will depend entirely on contract and the circumstances of the particular venture. The parties have a clean canvas on which to develop their chosen structure. The principal organ of the alliance will be the governing body representing the parties. The most common format in a straightforward alliance is the establishment of a management or steering committee[2] with each party having a right to appoint a stated number of individuals as representatives on that committee.

8–06 The role—or terms of reference—of any alliance management, advisory or steering committee should be clearly outlined. This will vary depending on whether it has essentially (i) a supervisory and co-ordinating role (monitoring and guiding the "partnering" relationship) or (ii) a management role with authority to make decisions and manage a distinct alliance project or activity. The terms of reference should clarify the scope of its authority, and that of any particular party, to commit the alliance parties in dealings with third parties. A common stipulation is that no party will be authorised to enter into commitments binding the other party to the alliance unless authorised or directed by the management committee.

---

[2] In many alliances, there may be a need at the outset to form terms of reference covering further committees or management structures, e.g. an operations or executive committee or other bodies with particular responsibilities.

8–07 A number of basic constitutional points and procedures should be addressed either in the original alliance agreement or in a subsequent protocol or supplementary agreement. They include:

(a) rights of appointment (and removal) of members of the committee;

(b) appointment of the chairman (including whether or not the chairman has, if necessary, a casting vote);

(c) whether individual members can appoint an "alternate" to attend any meeting in his or her absence;

(d) any formal requirement for a quorum for any meeting (e.g. the presence of at least one representative of each party);

(e) frequency of meetings—including flexibility to have meetings informally by telephone or videoconference.

> An example of provisions relating to a management committee to govern an R&D contractual alliance appears in Precedent 5 in Part E.

Equity joint ventures

8–08 Equity joint ventures, by their nature, invariably require a more formal and developed management structure. The governing body will not only have an overall leadership role but also responsibility for management of the resources, assets and employees of the joint venture entity itself. The governing body will be a formal "organ" of that joint venture entity and will need to comply with legal requirements applicable to that entity.

8–09 In the case of a partnership, the primary governing authority will be the partners' meeting (i.e. a meeting of the corporate partners themselves). The management structure of the partnership is a matter for contractual agreement between the parties—although certain default rules will apply if the parties fail to cover the situation in the partnership agreement. Under English law, these default rules include the following:

(a) each partner has a right to participate in management;

(b) each partner has authority to commit the other partners in dealings with third parties; as between the partners themselves, this rule may be modified by contract but this will not affect the theoretical position vis-à-vis third parties.

Some equity joint ventures which are established using a partnership structure may call for a more sophisticated management structure. Flexibility exists to adopt a "corporate" type structure within a partnership. Certainly under English law, there is nothing to prevent the parties agreeing to vest management authority in a partnership "board" or "committee". Rights of appointment of individuals to that board or committee may be agreed by the partners in much the same way as shareholders appointing a board of directors of a company.

> An example of a partnership governed by a partnership board appointed by the corporate partners is Precedent 6 in Part E.

8–10 In the case of a corporate entity such as a limited company, there is an important legal distinction between the shareholders (as owners of the enterprise) and the directors (responsible for management). The traditional constitution of a corporate entity will provide for substantial management powers to be vested in a board of directors and/or executive management. The shareholders will usually retain the power to change the board—and therefore the management—but, as shareholders, they will normally have little direct influence over the day-to-day running of the business of the company. This traditional model is not usually appropriate for a joint venture where the corporate shareholders are likely to play a more direct role in management of the venture.

8–11 The governance structure for a corporate joint venture will usually be reflected not only in the formal constitutional documents but also more fully in the arrangements established by the shareholders' agreement.

Control

8–12 A key commercial issue, shaping the governance structure, will be to establish the balance of "control" as between the shareholding parties. There are many different management models potentially available for joint ventures. One management study[3] has attempted to classify different business models for joint ventures by making a broad distinction between:

(a) the "transplant" model, where a dominant parent transplants its proven business formula and management practices into the environment of the JVC;

(b) the "dominant parent" model, where a domineering management style is led by the larger party with only a narrower, specialist minority role for the other party;

(c) the "independent roles" model, where each party has an equal share in management of the JVC but, in effect, separate "blocks of responsibility" for particular management functions are created; and

(d) the "shared management" model, where management of the JVC at the highest level is genuinely a shared task with joint accountability to each joint venture parent.

---

[3] Clifford Matthews, *Managing International Joint Ventures* (Kogan Page, 1999).

8–13 Whilst formal voting may rarely take place in most meetings, the respective voting rights of the parties represent the "control" position. The typical corporate joint venture model is for control rights to follow the respective ownership of shares by the parties in the venture. This usually results in an agreement that the voting rights of each party (as shareholder) should be in proportion to equity shares held and that each party should be given a right to appoint a number of directors broadly proportionate to its equity shareholding—with majority ownership therefore leading to board control.

8–14 Corporate joint venture structures are, however, capable of reflecting more varied ways of dealing with "control". The parties may consider, in some circumstances, that equal voting and control rights will create a stronger basis for the venture by encouraging consensus, co-operation and shared management responsibility. In these situations the parties choose to distinguish between "voting" rights and "economic" rights. At shareholder level, it may be possible to create voting rights which are held equally between the parties and not in the same proportions as their economic interests in the venture; e.g.:

(a) to issue voting shares equally between the parties and (as to the balance of the shares to be held by the majority shareholder) to create non-voting shares[4] which will solely have economic rights such as rights to dividend and return of capital; or

(b) to issue shares in the agreed economic proportions but giving enhanced voting rights to a particular class of shares so that, as between the two classes, the overall voting rights are equal.

At board level, it may then be provided that each party shall have the right to appoint an equal number of directors to the board.

8–15 It is not just board level appointments which are important. Control may also be exercised (even within a 50:50 venture) in more indirect and subtle ways at an operational level. Indeed, majority equity ownership or board voting rights may not always be an effective means of control at the operational level, particularly if operations are located in another party's country. Other mechanisms[5] for exercising influence or control include:

(1) *Appointment of key alliance management.* An important influence can be gained through appointment of managers running critical functions such as finance, marketing, R&D or human resources within the JVC.

(2) *Contractual arrangements.* A party's position may be enhanced by arrangements relating to specific activities of the JVC. These may include rights and obligations (and practical influence) under specific

---

[4] In some jurisdictions, though, non-voting shares may not be possible (e.g. the Netherlands) and more sophisticated measures may be required.
[5] See J. Child, D. Faulkner, and S. Tallman: *Cooperative Strategy: Managing Alliances, Networks and Joint Ventures*, p.221 et seq.

contractual arrangements between a parent and the JVC—e.g. relating to technology licensing, provision of management or financial systems, employment resources or use of brand names.

(3) *Relationships with parents.* Practical influence or control can be asserted through the reporting procedures established between the JVC and the joint venture parents (see para.8–30 below) and/or budget planning and approval processes.

(4) *HR programmes and systems.* One party may have or acquire a leading role in establishing systems for employment selection, training and development and remuneration structures. This can influence significantly the quality of the JVC's staff and its organisational culture.

(5) *Informal mechanisms.* Even more informal mechanisms can play a part such as maintaining regular personal relations with the alliance's senior managers or providing technical or advisory assistance on a non-contractual basis.

These more indirect methods of asserting control or influence can be of major practical importance. In many ventures, it may be possible (and effective) for control to be shared at the strategic level but for one party to have greater influence at operational level—either generally or in specific areas.

Composition of board of directors

8–16 Where two parties are contributing equally to the joint venture and take equal proportions of the equity, they will normally expect to nominate equal numbers of directors. This creates equality at board level but has an in-built potential for deadlock. Rights of appointment of directors may formally be reflected in the legal documents by either:

(a) a right for the particular shareholder to nominate a certain number of directors coupled with an undertaking by the other shareholder(s) to exercise its respective voting rights in support of the appointment or removal of the other party's nomination; or

(b) a direct right of appointment (and removal)[6] for the particular shareholder which is entrenched in the articles of association as a class right attaching to that shareholder's shares in the JVC.[7]

---

[6] Note that s.168 Companies Act 2006 in the UK provides that a director may always be removed by ordinary resolution. If a minority shareholder is concerned that the contractual protection of the shareholders' agreement is not sufficient, weighted voting rights can be created to give it a majority vote on any such resolution—see *Bushell v Faith* [1970] A.C. 1099.

[7] In certain countries (e.g. the Netherlands), a direct right of appointment may not be possible, so that a right of nomination (and a voting agreement to support that nomination) is the only practical route.

In order to preserve goodwill, it is often provided that the exercise of any such nomination or appointment will be subject to prior consultation with (and sometimes approval of) the other joint venture party.

8–17 Where one party is making a significantly greater equity contribution than the other, that party will usually seek the final control over matters to be decided at board meetings. This may be achieved through:

(a) the right to nominate or appoint a majority of the directors;

(b) the right to nominate or appoint a chairman with a casting vote; or

(c) its nominee directors having weighted voting rights on all (or at least specified) issues.

Where such dominance is established, a minority shareholder will frequently seek a right of veto (or at least a requirement for a super-majority vote) over certain important matters within the authority of the board.

8–18 In the case of a multi-party joint venture where it is contemplated that shareholdings may change during the life of the venture, a different formula is not to attach a right of appointment of directors to a particular named party or shareholder but for rights of appointment to apply if any shareholder (or sometimes a group of shareholders) holds not less than a specified percentage of the shares of the JVC.

8–19 As a practical point, it is important that the parties should consult early and agree the level within each parent organisation from which appointments to the board of directors will be made. Will they be senior officers within the parent organisations—or executives more closely associated with the operational management of the venture? A mismatch between the approach of the respective parties to board appointments can cause "political" friction as well as leading to dysfunctional management of the venture.

Chairman

8–20 A decision will also have to be taken as to choice of chairman and whether or not the chairman should have a casting vote at board meetings.[8] Usually, a casting vote will not be appropriate—unless in the context of an expressly agreed "deadlock-breaker" mechanism (see para.10–09). If wished, appointment of the chairman may rotate between the parties—e.g. on an annual basis—or sometimes the rather unsatisfactory formula is used of appointment of co-chairmen, with chairmanship rotating on a meeting-by-meeting basis (perhaps depending on the venue) or as agreed.

---

[8] Note that, by virtue of s.282 Companies Act 2006, it is not now possible for a chairman of a UK company to have a casting vote at shareholders' meetings—see para.10–10 below.

Alternates

8-21 The constitution should also make it clear whether or not a director can appoint an alternate to attend and vote in his place. Many parties take the view that the attendees at board meetings should always be the specifically appointed individuals. Others will be happy to permit alternates (perhaps if previously approved by the board). If alternates are not permitted, it is not uncommon to provide that those directors who are present and are appointed by a particular party shall have increased votes to take account of any "missing" director appointed by that party.

Independent directors

8-22 In larger-scale joint ventures, the parties may consider the appointment of additional executive or independent directors to the board—without specific allegiance to either joint venture party. Particularly for a JVC which is intended to act with "lasting autonomy" and possibly with a view to future flotation as a publicly quoted company, increasing influence of independent directors may be beneficial and give the JVC greater "identity". Such appointments may also assist the avoidance or resolution of deadlock between the joint venture parties—see para.10-11 below.

Two-tier board structures

8-23 The traditional UK form of corporate governance structure involves a single-tier board of directors which will often include senior executives. Continental European publicly held companies, on the other hand, typically have two boards: a supervisory board and a management board which reports to the supervisory board.[9] The supervisory board represents owners and employees (sometimes equally) while the management board is composed exclusively of key executives. Depending on where the JVC is incorporated, the parties may have to follow this model.

8-24 Although the existing UK company law framework formally only[10] recognises one level of director, it is possible to design by contract a comparable form of two-tier board structure in the UK. This may frequently be an appropriate model for a larger-scale joint venture. This may be achieved by one of the following structures:

---

[9] For example all German companies with more than 500 employees must have a two-tier board. All Dutch companies which have had, for three years, an issued share capital and reserves over €16m and more than 100 employees in the Netherlands, are similarly required to have a supervisory board.

[10] With the exception that a two-tier board system is recognised as a permissible structure for a European Company (SE) and may in due course be permissible in a European private company (EPC) if that proposal proceeds—see para.5-44.

(1) *Board/executive committee.* A board of directors could be established comprising appointees of the "parent" shareholders (possibly with a small number of key executives). This board could have wide powers to delegate management to an executive committee comprising senior management under the chairmanship of the chief executive. Senior management on the executive committee would not, as a legal matter, be directors of the company (although they may in practice be described or held out as "directors").

(2) *Advisory board/shareholders' committee.* Alternatively, a board of directors could be established comprising the key executives responsible for the management of the JVC and, separately, an advisory "board", committee or assembly comprising shareholder representatives which would play an advisory or limited supervisory role. Members of the advisory board or committee would not, as a legal matter, be directors of the JVC.[11]

(3) *Two-company structure.* A third option is to establish a corporate structure involving a holding company and a wholly-owned subsidiary operating company. The holding company board would assume an overall supervisory role and would also determine the overall strategy of the organisation. The operating company's board would consist of the senior management and would have a role similar to that of the management board in the continental European context. Members of the two boards would be full legal directors of their respective companies.

Owing to the administrative inconvenience of setting up a holding company/operating company structure and since the joint venture parties are likely to want more than a limited supervisory role, it is usually the first of these options that is pursued for a JVC in the UK in cases where a two-tier board structure is desired—unless there is some other compelling reason, such as tax considerations.

Supervision by joint venture parents

8–25 The joint venture parent companies will have their own "governance" issues in relation to the JVC—in addition to establishing the governance structure for the JVC itself. How best should a party ensure that structures and mechanisms are in place for it to monitor, and apply sufficient governance over, the joint venture operations? This may be achieved through a variety of mechanisms:

---

[11] Although there may be a significant risk that they will be "shadow directors" unless their role is clearly only advisory: see para.8–64.

(a) through representation on the board of directors of the JVC and ensuring full participation in (and, if necessary, blocking rights over) major decisions affecting the JVC;

(b) by ensuring that certain major "reserved matters" are subject to approval at shareholder level and not determined by the JVC board alone;

(c) by ensuring that appropriate reporting mechanisms and procedures, particularly relating to financial information, are in place so that it is properly informed on a regular basis about the JVC's affairs;

(d) through other internal "governance" disciplines and procedures adopted by the relevant parent company to monitor and supervise its investments in joint ventures and alliances.

For many companies with numerous joint ventures and alliances, there is also the additional management task of exercising prudent supervision over (and, where necessary, re-balancing) a "portfolio" of joint venture interests.

Decision-making authority of the JVC board

8–26 As to decision-making authority of the board of the JVC, much will depend on the scale of the venture, the seniority of the directors and the management reporting lines to be established. Formal "parental" shareholder control or direction will usually take the form of:

(a) a right for each party to appoint one or more members of the board of the JVC that will have responsibility for supervising the management of the business of the JVC; and/or

(b) reserving to the joint venture parties as shareholders (or to their appointees on the board of the JVC) the right to approve or veto certain key decisions ("reserved matters").

In many smaller joint ventures, on the other hand, the parties may be content to delegate the responsibility and discretion for all decisions relating to the joint venture to their appointee directors on the board of the JVC—usually with provisions to ensure that certain decisions require unanimity at board level (or at least the approval of an appointee director on behalf of each party).

8–27 Settling the list of "reserved matters" is often one of the most difficult issues to be resolved in establishing a governance structure for a JVC. A number of factors need to be balanced:

(a) the merit of giving the JVC autonomy to manage its own affairs and thereby empowered (and motivated) to drive the venture forward;

(b) the need for the business of the JVC to be conducted efficiently and expeditiously;

(c) the natural desire of the "parents" to exercise residual control over their "child", particularly where important decisions arise which materially affect their financial investment or the long-term strategy of the JVC; and

(d) the need to establish reasonable protections for any minority party where that minority party is making a significant contribution to the venture.

8–28 Reserved matters are frequently withdrawn from the authority of the board of the JVC and made subject to shareholder approval, either through the shareholders' agreement or (in some jurisdictions) through provision in the JVC's articles of association or other relevant constitutional documents.[12] The joint venture parties will thus have the opportunity to review such matters at their corporate level and need not rely simply on their appointees on the board of the JVC making the "right" decision. A list of matters commonly considered for attention in this context include the following:

GOVERNANCE: POSSIBLE "RESERVED MATTERS"

Items which may be considered as "reserved matters" include:

(1) any change to the articles of association or other constitutional documents of the JVC;

(2) any increase (or reduction) in the issued share capital of the JVC;

(3) any material change to the nature or scope of the business of the JVC (including any decision to expand or alter its field or the territory);

(4) approval of the annual budget and/or changes to the business plan;

(5) declaring or paying any dividend or making any other distribution to shareholders;

(6) borrowing or raising money which would result in the JVC's aggregate borrowing exceeding £_____;

(7) any capital expenditure in respect of any specific item or project in excess of £_____;

(8) acquisition or disposal (whether in a single transaction or series of transactions) of any business or shares in any company where the value of the acquisition or disposal exceeds £_____;

(9) entering into (or terminating) any material partnership, joint venture, profit-sharing agreement, technology licence or collaboration;

---

[12] Another reason for this structure is that, in exercising their votes, shareholders are generally free to vote in their own interests—whereas directors have a duty to promote the success of the company: see para.8–49 et seq. for a fuller discussion.

(10) entering into any material contract, liability or commitment (e.g. contracts of a long term or unusual nature or involving an obligation of a material magnitude or nature), unless a contract satisfies such authorisation criteria as the parties may approve from time to time as part of the procedures for the JVC entering into contracts;

(11) major decisions relating to the conduct (or settlement) of material legal proceedings;

(12) any significant inter-party transaction between the JVC and a member of the corporate group of a party to the JVC which is either (i) not on commercial arm's length terms or (ii) has a value in excess of £ _____;

(13) appointment (or removal) of the chief executive or other members of the senior executive team of the JVC;

(14) any charge or other security interest over any material part of the JVC's undertaking, property or assets;

(15) appointing or removing the JVC's auditors;

(16) approval of the JVC's statutory accounts and/or any change in the principal accounting policies of the JVC;

(17) material policies in respect of employees' remuneration, employment terms and/ or pension schemes;

(18) material policies in relation to environment and health and safety issues;

(19) any material acquisition or disposal (including any material licence) relating to intellectual property rights of the JVC;

(20) any proposal to wind up the JVC.

Monetary limits may be reviewed regularly by the parties and amended by agreement. Any "reserved matters" should, where a JVC has subsidiaries, normally extend to equivalent decisions taken within any subsidiary which affect the JVC group as a whole.

It is a separate question whether these "reserved matters" should then be decided by agreement (i.e. unanimously) between the parent shareholders—or whether special rules or majorities should be introduced.

8–29 An alternative approach in many substantial joint ventures—particularly where there are many different parties or a two-tier board structure has been put in place—is to retain many of these significant decisions as matters for the board of the JVC but to establish that certain major items require a "special" or "super" majority at board level. This has the significant merit of leaving business decisions within the scope of authority of the principal management organ of the JVC (and the individuals principally responsible for management). Drawing the distinction between shareholder matters and those requiring "super-majority" board decision would be for each venture but a distinction is frequently made in principle between:

(a) decisions relating to the business operations of the JVC—such as major acquisitions, capital expenditure, budgets, business plan, borrowings and key management appointments—which should remain with the board of directors of the JVC (albeit with a "super majority" requirement); and

(b) share structure and long-term investment decisions to be reserved to the shareholders of the JVC—such as constitutional changes, new share issues and material changes to the business of the JVC.

The more the parties are able to develop and agree a business/funding plan at the outset of the venture, the more the parties may be willing to permit the JVC to exercise substantial autonomy in carrying out that plan—with only "high level" strategic matters being reserved to the shareholders.

Reporting relationship between JVC and parents

8–30 Another area of challenge for management of a corporate joint venture is the establishment of appropriate co-ordination and reporting mechanisms between the JVC and its parents. An appropriate balance should be reached between supervision and monitoring by the parents and autonomy for the joint venture. At the practical level, it is important that each parent shareholder and the executive management of the JVC should understand, at the outset, how their relationship is to be co-ordinated and conducted. Issues include:

(a) what will be the reporting lines?

(b) what regular information, management reports and management accounts are to be provided, and when?

(c) how are budgets and business plans to be prepared and approved?

(d) is a parent entitled to exercise any direct rights to interview JVC executives, to inspect records or to initiate an audit?

Tensions can quickly arise if the parties have different expectations as to the degree and method of co-ordination and reporting to take place between the JVC and its parents.

Operational management

8–31 Operational management of the venture is the level at which the benefits and synergies of the alliance must be created. Day-to-day management within the context of a collaborative venture calls for demanding management skills. In some ventures, it may be appropriate for the board of the JVC to be directly responsible for operational management and for the executive team to be the directors of the JVC—with the shareholders exercising a supervisory role through a shareholders' committee or by "reserved matters" requiring shareholder decision. In other cases, the operational executives may form a looser management team under the supervision or direction of a "steering" board or committee.

Appointment of executives

8–32 A first point to stress is that it is not essential that the composition of the operational management team should reflect proportionate ownership shares of the parties in the joint venture. In establishing an operational management structure, the venture parties should address the practical position. Which party has effective management experience in the relevant area? Which party is willing to transfer top management personnel? Does one party have particular strengths or responsibilities which should be reflected in the management structure? Should members of management be recruited from outside? Different possibilities or formulae exist for the appointment of executive management. They include:

(1) *Appointments by board on case-by-case basis.* The parties may be content for appointments to executive posts to be made by the board of the JVC on a case-by-case basis—either on a "best man for the job" principle or by agreement being reached as to an appropriate mix of executives derived from the organisations of the parties.

(2) *Appointments to particular posts.* One party could be given the contractual right (and responsibility) under the shareholders' agreement to nominate appointments to particular management posts—e.g. chief executive, finance director, technical director, marketing director or human resources director.

(3) *Functional responsibility.* One party may be given the contractual right to control, or at least take leadership responsibility for, decisions falling within particular technical or management functions.

(4) *Management contract.* Alternatively, full day-to-day responsibility for management of the JVC may be allocated to a particular party under a management contract with the JVC—see para.6–33.

(5) *Appointment by chief executive.* In some ventures, the responsibility for the executive team will be vested in the chief executive who may be given the right to appoint (and remove) all other executives.

8–33 A particularly important appointment will be that of chief executive (or, in some cases, general manager). Studies indicate that a significant number of successful equity joint ventures depend on the drive, autonomy and strength of the chief executive. If the right of appointment of the chief executive (with extensive authority) is to be given to one party alone, the other party may seek some protective rights;

(a) the other party may be given the right of veto (or at least a right to be consulted) over any such appointment; or

(b) alternatively, and occasionally, the appointing party may be required to put forward, say, at least two potential candidates (expressing its own preference) and then allow the other party to select the chief executive from among those two candidates.

In some ventures, the chief executive may be given the delegated right and responsibility to appoint (and remove) the rest of the executive team.

Delegation of authority

8–34 How much authority should be delegated to the day-to-day executive management team of the JVC? How much authority should be vested in an individual chief executive? Decisions here are essentially the same as those which apply when establishing any corporate management structure. It is important that the principal parties agree the philosophy or approach. Getting the balance right for the particular venture raises issues similar to the question of what category of decisions should be "reserved" for the shareholders:

(1) Business issues requiring quick resolution (e.g. technology design issues or marketing decisions in highly competitive conditions) should normally be left for the decision of executive management. Matters involving specific expertise may also be referred to a smaller executive decision-making body.

(2) On the other hand, where decisions require or could lead to significant financial investment (such as material capital expenditure decisions or long-range strategic decisions), a more formal or methodical process involving the board of directors of the JVC should normally be used.

An ideal general principle is to establish a decision-making process by which the level of formality and degree of consensus required for a particular decision corresponds to the long-term importance of that decision.

8–35 Certain legal factors can affect questions of executive authority:

(1) If the management team is formally a management board (as in some continental European corporate models with two-tier boards), there will be statutory rights and responsibilities according to the laws of the relevant country which need to be taken into account.

(2) In some EU jurisdictions, the chief executive or equivalent officer will have—or will be expected to have—considerable formal authority to deal with third parties.

(3) In English law, irrespective of any delegation, the main board of directors will retain legal responsibility for the overall management of the JVC.

8-36 It will often be desirable, at the outset of the joint venture, to establish terms of reference or limits of authority for particular executives or bodies within the management structure—e.g. setting clear guidelines or thresholds for matters which must be handled at board level.[13] This can be particularly useful if a two-tier board structure is adopted in order to clarify what matters must be dealt with at the "supervisory" level compared with the "executive" board level. Some parties prefer this kind of clarification to be set out in the shareholders' agreement as part of the formal corporate governance structure of the JVC. This approach may be particularly useful in an international joint venture where there may be a strong practical need at the outset to clarify the limits of authority of executive management in order to avoid misunderstandings. In other cases, such terms of reference or authority limits may be adopted at an initial board meeting of the JVC and thereby become subject to more flexible procedures for subsequent amendment. A similar approach may be taken in relation to terms of reference or authority for particular executive managers.[14]

8-37 Generally, the greater the clarity which the governance structure can bring to the decision-making process, the less likely decision-making will become an ongoing—and potentially fatal—problem for the venture. A carefully constructed management structure can give all participants in the venture an "ownership stake" in the founding agreement to make strategic decisions in a particular way.

Tax issues

8-38 Commercial requirements may sometimes conflict with tax considerations when deciding the location of the administrative headquarters from which senior executives will run the joint venture. The tax issue will generally be one of central management and control. If it is desirable for tax purposes for the residence of the JVC to be in (or outside) a particular territory, care must usually be taken to ensure that the highest level of management control of the JVC is in practice exercised in an appropriate location in order to achieve this purpose.

8-39 Under the UK's tax rules, a company will normally be resident in the UK for tax purposes if it is either incorporated in the UK or its central management and control is located in the UK. One exception is that a

---

[13] Terms of reference might address, for instance, appropriate limits or division of authority regarding such matters as: acquisitions and disposals; capital expenditure; borrowings; material employment policies; commencement/settlement of material litigation; material dealings with IPR; key management appointments; employee benefits/remuneration policies; material transactions involving one of the parents; and other matters including procedures for preparation and approval of the annual business plan/budget.

[14] These limits will reflect internal authorities; they will not usually affect any "ostensible" authority which an executive may have to commit the JVC in dealings with third parties.

company which would otherwise be resident in the UK will not be treated as resident there if the company would be regarded as resident outside the UK under a "tie-breaker" clause in a double tax treaty. In practice, this will often mean that a company must have its effective place of management (i.e. its day-to-day affairs managed) in the UK in order to be tax resident in the UK.

Minority protection

8–40 Where a party in an equity joint venture has only a minority interest, a particular set of issues to be tackled in the governance structure relate to appropriate measures to "protect" that minority party. By the very nature of an equity joint venture, each participant (albeit in a minority) is likely to wish to participate in the management of the venture. The aim will be to ensure that proper checks or balances are in place but that additional "protections" for a minority party do not render procedures unduly cumbersome or restrictive. At a formal level, governance questions include:

(a) will the minority party have agreed rights of board representation?

(b) will the minority party (or its board representative) have a right of veto in relation to certain major decisions?

(c) will the presence of the minority party be necessary for a quorum at shareholder meetings—or of its board representative at board meetings?

These issues will reflect the balance of control between the majority party and the minority participant. The minority party may have a strategic role or be making a contribution which calls for specific rights and protections over a range of areas. This topic is more specifically addressed in chapter 9.

Management deadlock

8–41 How should the parties deal with the risk of potential deadlock in the management of a JVC? Potential deadlock—the inability of the parties or their representatives to agree on strategy or an important business decision—is an intrinsic feature of most joint ventures. It will be a challenge for the management team of the joint venture to develop systems, a culture and a relationship which reduces this risk. Although it is proper to view deadlock and dispute resolution mechanisms as an important part of the overall governance structure for a joint venture or alliance, it is convenient to address formal measures relating to "deadlock" separately— see generally chapter 10.

DUTIES OF DIRECTORS OF A JVC

General duties of directors to JVC

8–42 If the model of a corporate joint venture is chosen as the legal form for the venture, the individual directors of the JVC[15] will assume duties and responsibilities imposed by law. This is a direct consequence of adopting the corporate form. Directors of a JVC assume significant legal duties including fiduciary obligations. However, it is an area where, in relation to joint ventures, the theoretical requirements of the law frequently differ from the way things operate in practice. (These duties will, of course, be a matter for the relevant corporate law of the jurisdiction in which the JVC is incorporated. Although similar issues will arise in most jurisdictions, the following discussion relates to the position under English law.)

8–43 The general duties owed by directors to their company have now been codified in the Companies Act 2006. They replace the common law duties. The substance of these duties is nevertheless, apart from certain changes to the rules on directors' conflicts of interest, largely the same.

8–44 The general duties which came into force on October 1, 2007 are:

(a) to act in accordance with the company's constitution and to use powers only for the purpose for which they were conferred;

(b) to promote the success of the company for the benefit of its members (replacing, but largely similar to, the common law duty to act in good faith in the best interests of the company);

(c) to exercise independent judgement;

(d) to exercise reasonable care, skill and diligence.

The remaining general duties, which deal with conflicts of interest, come into force on October 1, 2008. These are:

(e) to avoid conflicts of interest (except where they arise out of a proposed transaction or arrangement with the company);

(f) not to accept benefits from third parties (e.g. secret profits obtained by virtue of his position as a director); and

(g) to declare to the company's other directors any interest a director has in a proposed transaction or arrangement with the company.

The same general duties are owed by all directors, both executive and non-executive.

---

[15] Individual members of a contractual alliance committee (or indeed a partnership management committee) nominated by the corporate "parents" do not assume, at least under English law, the more onerous duties borne by directors of a JVC.

8-45 It is important to remember that directors' duties are generally, as a matter of English corporate law, owed to the company of which they are directors and not directly to the shareholders.[16]

8-46 Consequently, legal claims arising out of an alleged breach of duty by a director will—perhaps fortunately—only arise in practice in relatively extreme circumstances; e.g. claims:

(a) upon an insolvency or liquidation of the JVC;

(b) where a minority party brings a claim using the new "statutory derivative action" under s.260 of the Companies Act 2006—see, para.11-31 et seq.; or

(c) in the context of a claim by a minority shareholder for "unfair prejudice" under s.994 of the Companies Act 2006.

Care, skill and diligence

8-47 All directors must exercise reasonable care, skill and diligence.[17] This includes both a subjective and an objective test. The 2006 Act refers to the care, skill and diligence which would be exercised by a reasonably diligent person with the general knowledge, skill and experience which may reasonably be expected of a director in his position (the objective element) and any additional general knowledge, skill and experience which that particular director has (the subjective element).

8-48 In the context of a joint venture, issues or questions which arise include:

(1) *Liability for acts of co-directors*. Shareholder-appointed directors will not be liable for the acts of other directors or employees of the JVC to whom authority has been delegated provided the board of the JVC exercises its powers of delegation of management reasonably. However, a director may still have liability where he has grounds for suspicion or ought to have supervised the activity or known that it was wrong.[18]

---

[16] s.170(1) Companies Act 2006 and, prior to the Act, *Percival v Wright* [1902] 2 Ch. 421 and *Towcester Racecourse Co Ltd v Racecourse Association Ltd* [2002] EWHC 2141. This does not preclude the recognition of a fiduciary duty to shareholders if a special factual relationship exists: *Peskin v Anderson* [2000] 2 B.C.L.C. 1. These circumstances may include "the situation where the company of which a person is a director is a company with a family character" per Lord Browne-Wilkinson in *Chez Nico (Restaurants) Ltd, Re* [1992] B.C.L.C. 192.

[17] s.174 Companies Act 2006.

[18] *Selangor United Rubber Estates Ltd v Cradock (No.3)* [1968] 1 W.L.R. 1555.

(2) *Liability of nominating shareholder.* A "parent" shareholder will rarely be liable under English law to the JVC or third parties for failure of its appointed director to show due care and skill.[19]

Fiduciary duties

Independent judgment and promoting the company's success

8–49 When acting as a director of the JVC, the director should exercise his powers (in particular, voting rights at board meetings) by applying "independent judgement" and act in the way he considers, in good faith, most likely to "promote the success of the company for the benefit of its members as a whole".[20] Amongst the factors to be taken into account is "the need to act fairly as between members of the company". The fact that he has been appointed by a particular shareholder is irrelevant.[21]

8–50 This is a tough, and often unrealistic, standard for directors of most JVCs. The concept of a director exercising "independent judgment" may fit the circumstances of an autonomous full-function JVC. However, very many JVCs are structured as a vehicle to co-ordinate or fulfil the respective interests of the joint venture parties—that is the purpose of the JVC within their business relationship. If a director is an individual shareholder in the JVC, he will naturally give priority to his interest as a participant in the joint venture. Where a director has been appointed by (and, in effect, represents) a particular joint venture "parent", he will inevitably take account of, and almost certainly give priority to, the interests of that "parent" shareholder in any decision or act within the JVC. It is therefore fortunate, perhaps, that the situations in which legal claims are likely to arise in the context of a JVC are limited.

8–51 Can this strict duty be modified? Historically, articles of a JVC in the UK have rarely attempted to define or limit the scope of this general duty (or its predecessor) of a nominee director. However, it seems

---

[19] In *Kuwait Asia Bank E.C. v National Mutual Life Nominees Ltd* [1991] A.C. 187 the Privy Council considered the potential liability of a substantial shareholder to a creditor of a company for acts and omissions of two directors it had nominated to the board of the company, and as a shareholder. The court concluded that the shareholder was not vicariously liable for the acts and omissions of its appointees, either as their employer or as their principal, and that a shareholder did not, by reason only of its position as such, have a duty to the company's creditors.

[20] ss.172 and 173 Companies Act 2006.

[21] In *Scottish Co-operative Wholesale Society Ltd v Meyer* [1959] A.C. 324, the House of Lords considered the conduct of three directors of a textile company appointed by a co-operative society which was its majority shareholder. The court summed up: "They [the three directors] probably thought that 'as nominees' of the co-operative society their first duty was to the co-operative society. In this they were wrong. By subordinating the interests of the textile company to those of the co-operative society, they conducted the affairs of the textile company in a manner oppressive to the other shareholders".

permissible and consistent with the Companies Act 2006[22] for the shareholders to agree in the JVC's articles of association that a director appointed to the board by a particular shareholder or class of shareholders shall not be taken to be in breach of this general duty by reason only that he has regard to the interests, and gives priority to the interests, of that shareholder or class—perhaps unless no reasonable director could have believed that he was acting in the interests of the company as a whole.

8–52 There are some interesting comparisons here with the position in certain other common law jurisdictions:

(1) In New Zealand, s.131(4) of the New Zealand Companies Act 1993 has dealt expressly with the position of a joint venture company and provides: "A director of a company that is carrying out a joint venture between the shareholders may, when exercising powers or performing duties as director in connection with the carrying out of the joint venture, *if expressly permitted to do so by the constitution of the company* [emphasis added], act in a manner which he or she believes is in the best interests of a shareholder or shareholders, even though it may not be in the best interests of the company".

(2) In Australia, certain case law[23] recognises that a nominee director may promote the interests of his appointor so long as he bona fide believes it is consistent with the interests of the company and that belief is not totally unreasonable.

(3) In the US, the rules applicable to the "hybrid" LLC structure in Delaware encourage giving "maximum effect to the principle of freedom of contract" and expressly permit the LLC agreement to restrict the duties (including fiduciary duties) and liability of members and managers of the LLC.[24]

It may also be noted that, in the UK, it is permissible to modify or waive fiduciary duties as between the members of a limited liability partnership (LLP) by express provision in the founding LLP agreement—see para.3–22.

8–53 One course which can avoid this often-theoretical problem is for matters involving a transaction or issue in which one of the parents is materially interested to be left as "reserved matters" for decision by the shareholders rather than taken by the board of the JVC—see para.8–28. It seems clear that shareholders do not generally owe a duty under English law to consider the interests of other shareholders when voting their shares.

---

[22] See s.173(2)(b) of the 2006 Act in relation to the duty to exercise independent judgment. There is no specific reference to a company's constitution qualifying the general duty to promote the company's success. However, an article framed to allow a director to give priority to his own or his appointor's interest would appear to fall within the ambit of s.180(4)(b) of the Act.
[23] See e.g. *Broadcasting Station 2 GB Ltd, Re* [1964–65] N.S.W.R. 1662.
[24] See e.g. s.18–1101 of the Delaware Limited Liability Company Act.

Disclosure of interest in proposed transactions with the JVC

8–54 The 2006 Act[25] imposes a duty on a director to declare to the company's other directors the nature and extent of any interest, direct or indirect, a director has in a proposed transaction or arrangement with the company. In the context of a JVC, this would include the situation where a director transacts directly with the JVC or, probably, where he has an interest as a significant shareholder in a company (e.g. a joint venture party) and that company or a subsidiary enters into a transaction with the JVC.

8–55 There are two important qualifications which soften the potentially serious implications[26] of a breach of this duty:

(1) The Act does not require declaration of an interest of which the directors are already aware or "of anything of which they ought reasonably to be aware".

(2) The duty can be modified by a company's articles of association. It has been common practice in the past to allow an "interested" director to attend and vote at any board meetings on a matter in which he is "interested"—provided that he makes full disclosure of the nature and extent of that interest; see Precedent 11 in Part E.

In practice, an appropriate course is for a director to give general notice at the outset that, for the purposes of the Act, he should be regarded as having an interest in any transaction or arrangement between the JVC and the joint venture parent (or member of its group) by whom he has been nominated.

Other conflicts/corporate opportunity

8–56 The Companies Act 2006[27] also contains a broad duty on a director to avoid any other situation in which he has an interest that conflicts, or may conflict, with the company's interests. This applies, in particular, to the exploitation of any property, information or opportunity (covering the so-called "corporate opportunity" doctrine). This means that a director, including a former director, of a JVC must not use for his own or anyone else's benefit (e.g. his appointing shareholder) any property, information or business opportunity of the JVC of which he became aware while a director

---

[25] See s.177 Companies Act 2006 re-stating, in effect, the principles of the previous law.
[26] If pursued, a director in breach could inter alia become liable to disgorge any profits received personally from the transaction in which he had an "interest". The contract may also be voidable, at the option of the company, against any party who had notice of the breach of duty.
[27] s.175 Companies Act 2006.

of the JVC. It is immaterial whether or not the company could take advantage of that property, information or opportunity.

8–57 There are two important qualifications:

(1) The Act makes it clear that there is no breach if the situation "cannot reasonably be regarded as likely to give rise to a conflict of interest".

(2) If a director (or a joint venture party) is concerned that the duty could apply to a particular activity or benefit in which he has an interest, there is scope for authorisation or ratification of the "conflict". There is an exception under the Act if the matter has been authorised by the board of the company (i.e. the JVC)[28]—provided that the authorisation would have been effectively agreed to (e.g. as to quorum and majority) without the participation of any "interested" director.[29] A cautious approach, using this "authorisation" regime, will often be sensible in this potentially difficult area.

The risk of a joint venture party taking advantage of a "corporate opportunity" relating to the JVC is addressed in more detail in chapter 11.

Confidential information

8–58 Information relating to the JVC acquired by its directors will have been acquired by them in their capacity as directors of the JVC and, therefore, will prima facie be information belonging to the JVC and not to the shareholders. Strictly, information may be disclosed to a "parent" shareholder only if the JVC's articles of association so permit or if the shareholders agree (in general meeting or otherwise). It is therefore common to include provisions in a JVC's constitution permitting a director to pass information back to his appointor for purposes related to its interest in the JVC.

> See Precedent 11 in Part E for a further discussion and examples of provisions for inclusion in a JVC's Articles of Association in the UK in relation to duties of directors.

Insolvency

8–59 Directors will have additional duties where the JVC is in financial difficulty. Directors can, importantly, incur specific liability in the event of a

---

[28] This assumes there is nothing in the JVC's constitution which invalidates the authorisation. In the case of a public company, board authorisation of the conflict is only effective if the company's constitution includes provision enabling the directors to give such authorisation.
[29] Where this is not possible (e.g. because the quorum provisions cannot technically be met), it seems that shareholder approval is still required. In addition, there are specific matters which require the approval of the shareholders (e.g. substantial property transactions under s.190 of the 2006 Act).

winding-up of a company. In particular, a director can become personally liable for the company's debts in the case of "wrongful trading" if the company continues to trade when insolvent.[30] If the JVC becomes insolvent, the interests of creditors become the principal consideration for the directors in discharge of their duties. The Companies Act 2006 recognises that the general duties of directors are subject to duties to creditors in the case of an insolvency. Consequently, if the JVC is insolvent, the directors should not pay dividends or repay shareholder loans if this would in effect distribute the JVC's assets without proper provision for all creditors.[31]

Indemnity to directors of JVC

8–60 A director may seek, as a safeguard, an indemnity to cover potential liabilities in the performance of his duties. Most jurisdictions impose restrictions on the ability of a company to indemnify its own directors. Under English law,[32] a JVC can only indemnify its directors against liability in limited circumstances. A company is prohibited from undertaking to indemnify a director against any liability "in connection with any negligence, default, breach of duty or breach of trust by him in relation to the company." Any provision in a company's articles of association or in any contract with the company or otherwise which seeks to do this is void.

8–61 However, a director can even if judgment is ultimately given against him be indemnified in proceedings brought by a third party both in respect of the claim itself and the cost of defending the proceedings, provided that the indemnity does not extend to the payment of criminal fines or regulatory penalties. A director can also be indemnified against costs incurred in defending proceedings brought by the company provided that the indemnity does not extend to cover (i) liabilities owing to the company itself or (ii) any liabilities incurred in defending those proceedings, if judgment is ultimately given against the director. An indemnity may also be available where a court decides to grant relief because the director acted honestly and reasonably and ought fairly to be excused. A company's articles of association will usually entitle a director to an indemnity to the fullest extent permitted by law.

8–62 The prohibition under the Companies Act 2006 prevents any group company within the UK[33] from giving an "unlawful" indemnity to the director of an associated company. (This would not, though, appear to prohibit a "parent" indemnifying a director of a company (e.g. a 50:50 JVC) which is not a subsidiary of the indemnifying company.)

---

[30] Under s.213 or s.214, Insolvency Act 1986.
[31] See *Macpherson v European Strategic Bureau Ltd* [2000] 2 B.C.L.C. 683.
[32] Under s.232 Companies Act 2006.
[33] Whether a member of the parent's corporate group outside the UK could give such an indemnity is a matter for the "foreign" corporate law.

8–63 Insurance is an alternative to the granting of an indemnity. A company under English law can take out insurance for the benefit of its directors against most of their liabilities; this can include claims for negligence, default, breach of statutory duty and costs of defending allegations or assisting any authorities with their investigations. In the case of a corporate group's "directors and officers" (D&O) policy, care should be taken to ensure that it covers any directors appointed by the group in any associated company in which the group has a defined percentage interest. For public policy reasons, insurance would not be available to cover loss due to fraud, wilful default or criminal behaviour.

Shadow directors

8–64 A "shadow director" under English law is a person in accordance with whose directions or instructions the directors of a company are accustomed to act.[34] Shadow directors have many of the same duties as directors.[35] The question can, in particular, arise whether a parent company which instructs a director of a JVC could assume any liability as a shadow director (e.g. for wrongful trading in the event of insolvency of the JVC). Earlier case law[36] suggested that this would rarely be the case unless the parent controlled and regularly directed the whole or a majority of the board. However, a more recent case[37] suggested that the doctrine of "shadow director" is wider in scope and can catch other individuals (or companies) who exercise real influence over the relevant company.

8–65 The Companies Act 2006[38] makes it clear, though, that a parent company will not be regarded as a "shadow director" of a subsidiary for the purposes of the general duties of directors by reason only that the directors are accustomed to act in accordance with its directions—and one may expect a similar result in the case of a parent shareholder of a 50:50 JVC or one in which it has a minority interest.

CONCLUSION

8–66 A carefully developed governance structure will be vital to the

---

[34] See s.251, Companies Act 2006.
[35] These do not, though, include the fiduciary duties of a director: *Ultraframe (UK) Ltd v Fielding* [2005] EWHC 1638 (Ch).
[36] *Unisoft Group Ltd, Re (No 2)* [1994] B.C.C. 766 where it was decided that, unless the whole of the board, or at least a governing majority of it, are accustomed to act upon the directions of an outsider, such a person could not be a shadow director. The case also clarified the point that the words 'accustomed to act' require there to have been a course of conduct and more than one act.
[37] *Secretary of State for Trade and Industry v Deverell* [2000] 2 W.L.R. 907.
[38] s.251(3) Companies Act 2006.

foundation of the venture and the relationship between the parties. The task of the lawyers will be to establish the formal structure within the chosen framework for the venture. The framework (particularly in the case of a corporate joint venture) will impose certain duties on the individual "directors". In the large majority of cases, these duties will be of academic interest only. They will become more relevant, though, if the relationship between the parties deteriorates or is abused by a particular party. Issues of deadlock, duties between joint venture parties and dispute resolution procedures are, ultimately, also issues of governance. For convenience, though, they are addressed separately in later chapters.

CHAPTER 9

Minority investment and protection

What rights or protections are appropriate for a minority participant in a joint venture company? Underlying statutory and corporate rights for a minority shareholder will generally be very limited and provide no realistic safeguards or influence in relation to a corporate joint venture. A minority party in a joint venture will expect stronger rights. This chapter addresses a range of possible structures and protections in the case of minority equity investment.

Background factors

9–01 In a joint venture context, all parties are likely to be participating directly to a material extent in the management and operations of the venture. A minority party will expect stronger rights than those granted by statutory or corporate law. The extent of any "minority rights" will therefore be a matter for contractual negotiation and vary from case to case. There are likely to be differences, for instance, between the rights to be negotiated by a minority party in:

(a) a 60:40 equity joint venture in which the minority party is providing substantial management and technical expertise;

(b) an 80:20 venture in which the minority equity participant is a "strategic partner" but the majority party has day-to-day operational control;

(c) a joint venture in which a venture capital or other private equity institution has a minority stake but may be the principal outside finance provider; and

(d) a multi-party venture in which a number of parties have comparatively small and passive shareholding interests.

There are a number of areas which will be of concern to a minority party. A range of protective measures may be considered. These protections will assist to prevent undue preference or misuse of control by a majority party. They will, though, rarely protect against simple bad management by the majority party or its nominee directors.

9–02 The interests of the minority participant(s) will, of course, need to be reconciled with those of the majority participant. The latter will often have different objectives—e.g. to maintain decisive power over management appointments; to ensure that clear decision-making processes exist by minimising minority veto rights and establishing "deadlock-breaker" devices where there are veto rights; and, frequently, to incorporate rights which support its ability to deliver a sale of the joint venture company (JVC) as a whole to a third party. A balance will have to be struck.

9–03 This chapter primarily addresses the position of a JVC under English law, but similar principles (at least in relation to the desirability and extent of contractual protection) are likely to be applicable to a JVC established in most jurisdictions worldwide.

STATUTORY AND CORPORATE LAW PROTECTION

9–04 Most legal systems offer some statutory or corporate law remedies for a minority shareholder in certain situations. However, these rights and remedies apply only in limited and relatively extreme circumstances. Under English corporate law, for instance, these rights are essentially confined to the following:

(a) (if the minority holds more than 25 per cent of the voting rights) the ability to block certain decisions[1] which require 75 per cent shareholder approval;

(b) statutory rights to call for meetings, information or formal regulatory investigations in certain limited circumstances;

(c) a right to initiate an action on behalf of the company (a "derivative action") against directors for breach of duty under s.260 of the Companies Act 2006—see para.11–31 et seq.;

(d) a right to seek a remedy under s.994 of the Companies Act 2006 in the event of "unfairly prejudicial" conduct by the majority party; and

(e) a right in certain circumstances to seek a winding-up of the JVC on the grounds that it is "just and equitable" under s.122(1)(g) of the Insolvency Act 1986.

The remedies under categories (c), (d) and (e) are addressed in more detail in chapter 11 in the context of possible claims arising from "misbehaviour"

---

[1] These are limited to such constitutional or formal matters as: change of articles or corporate name; reduction of share capital; disapplying statutory pre-emption rights on share issues; approval of financial assistance or purchase of own shares; voluntary winding-up. Under s.22 Companies Act 2006 the parties may agree in the JVC's articles of association that certain matters should be entrenched and require unanimity or a super-majority—see para.5.55.

by a joint venture party. They do not apply to give a minority shareholder direct "up-front" rights in the JVC of the kind that may reasonably be anticipated in the context of a joint venture or alliance in which that minority party seeks an active management participation.

CONTRACTUAL PROTECTION

Contractual protection: key aims

9–05 A minority shareholder will therefore look for express contractual rights and protections beyond those afforded by statute and corporate law. A minority participant will generally aim to protect its interests in the following principal areas:

(1) *Board representation*: to ensure its participation in management through representation on the board of directors of the JVC.

(2) *Major decisions*: to ensure, in any event, its involvement in major business decisions including, where feasible, that its consent is to be required on key matters (i.e. a right of veto).

(3) *Dilution*: to protect against its equity stake in the JVC being improperly diluted by subsequent share issues.

(4) *Profits*: to ensure that it receives a proper distribution of profits.

(5) *Information*: to ensure that it has adequate access to information regarding the JVC's affairs.

(6) *Claims*: to establish safeguards to enable the JVC to assert claims, where necessary, against the majority shareholder if the latter (or an affiliate) is in breach of its obligations to the JVC.

(7) *Exit*: to ensure it has an ability to "exit" the joint venture without remaining "trapped".

Numerous cases, particularly involving family companies and once "friendly" ventures, have illustrated where these issues have not been adequately addressed. We examine below each of these areas in more detail and discuss various rights and protections which may be available.

Board representation

9–06 Responsibility for management of the JVC will usually be vested in its board of directors. In order to participate directly in management, therefore, a minority shareholder will usually seek a right to appoint a director to the board of the JVC. This should ensure that, although the board may not be involved in day-to-day operations, the minority party is kept informed about the JVC's business through its appointed director and that it has a voice at board discussions on strategy and other key issues. Sometimes, rather than a formal right to appoint a director, a right is given for a party to send an "observer" (with no right to speak or vote).

9–07 In the case of a multi-party venture, it may not be appropriate for each minority participant to have a separate right to appoint a director. An alternative approach is for a number of minority shareholders, collectively, to be entitled to appoint a director. This can be achieved either by:

(a) identifying in the articles of association or shareholders' agreement the shareholders who are collectively (by agreement or other procedure established between them) to have this right; or

(b) specifying in the articles of association that this right of appointment will attach to the holders for the time being of a specific class of shares.

Another approach is to provide that any shareholder holding not less than X per cent of the voting share capital shall be entitled to appoint one director (and, possibly, two directors if holding not less than Y per cent).

9–08 Additional constitutional protections may be desirable to ensure that a minority party's right to participate in management is not circumvented. These could include:

(a) a requirement that the presence of its appointee is necessary for a quorum of the board[2];

(b) a right to prevent the delegation of key powers of the board (e.g. to an executive director or a committee) or, if delegation to a committee takes place, a right of representation on that committee;

(c) a requirement that reasonable notice is given of all board meetings and of the agenda items for discussion (including advance circulation of relevant board papers) and that no decisions can be taken (unless all directors agree) outside the scope of the matters on the agenda;

(d) a requirement that written resolutions require the approval of all directors.

These are formal protections. Most joint ventures will not, in practice, be managed through formal board meetings. Much therefore will continue to depend in practice on the "spirit" of the joint venture relationship and its practical management procedures in order to ensure appropriate participation by a minority party.

---

[2] See para.10–06 below for possible measures to avoid deadlock by boycott of meetings.

Consent rights

9–09 A minority party will usually wish to ensure that it is fully involved in certain major management and policy decisions affecting the JVC. Therefore, in addition to—or sometimes irrespective of—a right of board representation, a minority shareholder with sufficient bargaining strength will wish to have consent rights (i.e. a right of veto) over certain major decisions of the JVC. These decisions might include many of the matters discussed earlier in the context of "reserved matters" for shareholders or matters which may require a "super-majority" at board level—see para.8–26 et seq.

9–10 Even in a 50:50 joint venture with equality of board representation, it is common to ensure that certain "reserved matters" require unanimity between the parties—either at shareholder level or at board level—guarding, inter alia, against the possibility that a party's representative may be absent from a meeting at which the relevant decision is taken. These veto rights should usually be drafted, in a shareholders' agreement, to extend to any equivalent decision taken by any subsidiary of the JVC—or, sometimes, to those taken by "material" subsidiaries as defined in the particular case.

9–11 The strength of negotiated "consent rights" for a minority party may be balanced by other contractual provisions. A price for obtaining strong veto rights may be a right for the majority party to buy out the minority party if these veto rights are used persistently to block decisions. Alternatively, if a minority party has relatively weak contractual rights, then the minority party may have a stronger argument to establish a "put" option in its favour by way of a potential exit route—see para.9–27 below.

9–12 In addition to negotiating the substance of the matters over which the minority shareholder is to have consent rights, the parties must decide whether these rights should be entrenched at the level of board decisions or at the level of decisions by the shareholders themselves. In other words, should the unanimous approval or super-majority vote on these matters be required of (i) the directors of the JVC (including the minority shareholder's appointee) or (ii) the shareholders (including the minority shareholder)? In larger joint ventures, decisions on major matters may be reserved to the parties at shareholder level with more operational matters being left to board level (see also para.8–27 et seq. earlier). In smaller ventures, most major decisions may simply be taken at board level.

9–13 In the case of multi-party joint ventures, it may make decision-making too difficult and be inappropriate for each minority shareholder to have a separate right of veto. It is therefore relatively common, particularly in joint ventures where there are a large number of parties, for certain matters to require the approval of a "super-majority" of the shareholders (rather than unanimity). For example, certain fundamental matters could require the approval of 75 per cent (or sometimes 90 per cent) of the shareholder votes and other, less fundamental, matters could require approval of a lesser percentage.

9–14 Consent rights of a minority party are frequently subject to limitations:

(1) It is often sensible to provide that the rights will cease if the minority party's shareholding drops below a specified percentage level.

(2) It may be appropriate to recognise that frequent use of veto rights is likely to be a sign of permanent breakdown in the joint venture relationship. One approach is to provide that, if the minority veto is exercised on more than a specified number of occasions, the majority party shall have a right to buy out the minority in order to avoid future deadlock—see para.10–20.

Dilution

9–15 A minority party will wish to ensure that its equity stake in the JVC cannot be diluted (whether in strategic or value terms) by alterations to the share capital of the JVC such as:

(a) a subsequent issue of shares which is not made pro rata to existing shareholders and/or involves the introduction of new shareholders;

(b) an issue of shares to the other shareholders (and/or to a third party) at less than a fair price;

(c) a "rights" offer of shares to existing shareholders at a time when the majority party knows that the offer cannot in practice be taken up by the minority;

(d) a purchase by the JVC of its own shares at a price in excess of their fair value; and

(e) certain other reorganisations of share capital—such as a subdivision of share capital which alters the voting balance or an alteration in the rights attaching to certain shares and not to others.

9–16 Protections which it is customary for a minority party to seek, or at least consider, in this area include the following alternatives:

(1) The broadest protection would be a requirement that the minority party's consent is required if the JVC wishes to issue, allot, redeem, purchase or grant options over any of its shares or other securities or reorganise its share capital in any way.

(2) A more limited requirement would be that any issue of shares for cash should require the consent of the minority party—in order to avoid a share issue being made (without consent) at a time when the

minority party is unable to subscribe for its proportionate entitlement. A requirement for such approval will obviously be inappropriate in those joint ventures where it is always envisaged that substantial further funding will be required (perhaps up to a certain limit). This formula would not, therefore, restrict issues for a non-cash consideration (e.g. on an acquisition or introduction of a new shareholder in exchange for assets or services).

(3) It may simply, and commonly, be an agreed requirement that all new issues of shares in the JVC must be offered to existing shareholders pro rata to their existing holdings.[3] It will then be a decision for each shareholder whether or not to participate.

(4) A requirement could be included that any new shares must be offered at a fair value—with a right for a party to require certification by the company's auditors or an independent valuer that the offer price is fair.

9-17 Where these rights are not agreed in relation to new issues of shares or if the minority party chooses not to take up a particular rights issue, one possible protection to enable a minority party to preserve its percentage equity stake is for it to retain a "catch up" option—possibly for a specified period—to ensure that it can "buy back" its full equity stake by subsequently acquiring from the majority party (or the JVC) sufficient shares to take it back to an agreed percentage level. The price per share would typically be the current market or fair value or possibly be based on a "weighted-average" of the subscription prices of shares issued by the JVC since the relevant party's original subscription. This "catch up" right may be particularly appropriate where the minority party's original equity stake is sufficient to block special resolutions of the JVC.

9-18 Certain investors (particularly a venture capital investor taking an early stake in a JVC where subsequent financing rounds are anticipated) may seek even stronger rights by way of "price protection" to prevent the economic dilution of its shares which may occur if (i) a company issues ordinary shares (or instruments convertible into ordinary shares) after the protected investor has made its investment and (ii) the later issue is made at a lower effective price per share than the earlier issue—a so-called "down round" of financing. Anti-dilution provisions can require additional shares to be issued by the JVC (or transferred by other shareholders) to the protected investor upon certain dilutive events:

(1) A "full ratchet" provision entitles the protected investor to additional shares (at no additional cost or for a *de minimis* price) so that, overall, its average price per share is made equal to the price per share applicable in the subsequent "down round".

---

[3] Note that, under English law, an issue of shares for cash must be offered on a pro rata basis unless the statutory pre-emption rights under s.561 of the Companies Act 2006 are disapplied, which will require a special resolution.

(2) A "weighted-average" adjustment also entitles the protected investor to additional shares but takes into account the effect of the aggregate price of shares issued in all prior investment rounds as well as the price per share in the current round. A weighted-average formula applies a proportionate adjustment and is less favourable to the protected investor than a full ratchet.

These are specialist techniques,[4] more commonly negotiated by venture capitalist investors rather than by conventional participants in a corporate joint venture. However, the techniques may be considered in other circumstances during the initial phases of a JVC's development when share valuations are difficult to agree and the JVC's future is uncertain. If used, it is common to limit the period during which price-based anti-dilution provisions apply.

Dividend policy

9–19 The decision whether or not the JVC will declare dividends in any year, and the amount of each dividend distribution, will generally be made by the board of directors.[5] A minority party may wish to ensure that an agreed distribution policy is established at the outset—and, in some ventures, to ensure that profits cannot be diverted in a discriminatory manner to the majority shareholder by other methods such as excessive remuneration or management charges. Protective provisions may therefore include the following:

(1) The parties may agree that the JVC shall distribute not less than a stated percentage (or such other percentage as may from time to time be agreed) of its available distributable profits for any year—subject, usually, to the retention of such profits as the board considers prudent to meet the financing requirements of the JVC.

(2) Alternatively, in cases where the minority party is concerned that sufficient funds may not be retained to assist the development of the JVC, the formula could provide for a certain proportion of profits to be retained each year in the business of the JVC to fund future growth before there can be any distribution to shareholders.

(3) Where a minimum dividend policy is established, the auditors could be required to certify the amount of distributable profits available for that year.

(4) More broadly, a requirement could be imposed that the subsequent year's dividend policy should be included as part of the annual business plan or budget and that the minority party should have rights of approval over the annual adoption of that plan.

---

[4] Specialist textbooks should be consulted for more detailed discussions and examples of these techniques, such as Darryl Cooke & James Dow, *Private Equity: Law and Practice*.
[5] Under the articles of association of most UK companies, the board may pay interim dividends and the shareholders in general meeting cannot declare dividends in excess of those recommended by the board.

9–20 A minority party may be concerned that, even if a distribution policy is established, there may be improper "leakage" of profits to the majority shareholder by other means. Protective measures for this purpose could include:

(a) a requirement that the consent of the minority party is necessary for any management, services or royalty agreement to be entered into between the JVC and the majority shareholder (or connected parties) or any variation in the payment terms under any such agreements; and/or

(b) in some cases, a requirement that the terms (or limit) of any remuneration payable to directors appointed by the majority shareholder are also subject to prior approval by the minority party.

Right to information

9–21 Simply as a shareholder, a minority party has limited rights to information regarding the JVC's affairs.[6] In the case of a joint venture, a minority shareholder will invariably expect greater rights and access to information. In practice, this will often be implicit in the minority party's right (if negotiated) to appoint a director to the board of the JVC. A minority party should, though, consider whether it is desirable to establish specifically any of the following rights:

(a) an obligation for the board of the JVC to circulate monthly or quarterly unaudited management accounts and other regular financial information (budgets, cash flow forecasts etc.) to the shareholders, including the minority party, in such form as may be agreed;

(b) circulation in draft of annual budgets or business plans relating to the JVC for approval and/or comment by the minority party;

(c) in some ventures, an express right of access to inspect, and take copies of, accounting records and other documents of the JVC and, if thought appropriate, to visit the JVC's premises and interview its directors and senior staff (sometimes termed "visitation rights");

(d) a general obligation on the majority party and/or the JVC to keep the minority party informed, in advance, of material developments regarding the JVC's business.

An express right should be included to clarify that a director nominated by a particular shareholder can give his appointing shareholder such informa-

---

[6] Under English law, apart from the right to receive the annual audited accounts, a shareholder has no statutory right to inspect the accounting records of the company nor, as shareholder, a right to inspect the minutes of board meetings.

tion regarding the JVC's affairs as he thinks fit. It should be remembered that information regarding the JVC will invariably be confidential and there is no automatic right for a director to disclose that information within his parent organisation. A right to such disclosure, subject to continuing confidentiality restraints, should generally be made clear in the joint venture documentation.[7]

Other protective undertakings

9–22 The structure of the JVC may lead, and indeed be designed to lead, to the ability of a majority party to exercise rights which assist its own tax planning. Examples may include arrangements between the JVC and its shareholders concerning utilisation of group relief or consortium relief—see para.15–35 et seq. In most cases, the co-operation of the JVC itself will be required before any of these rights can be exercised. The minority party should ensure that these rights cannot be exercised to the prejudice of the JVC (and indirectly the minority party) and that provision is made for proper payment to the JVC by the majority party for any tax benefit obtained by it.

9–23 Other possible protections which a minority party may seek in appropriate cases include undertakings that the majority shareholder will ensure that the JVC:

(a) maintains proper insurance (particularly product liability insurance);

(b) prepares and maintains proper books of account;

(c) conducts its business in all material respects in accordance with applicable laws;

(d) concludes appropriate non-competition covenants, confidentiality agreements and employment contracts with key employees— including, in technology ventures, employment contracts which provide (so far as possible) that intellectual property devised by employees belongs to the JVC.

Claims against majority party

9–24 If the minority party considers that the majority party or any of its directors is in breach of any obligation to the JVC (e.g. breach of other ancillary contracts or breach of warranty under any asset transfer agree-

---

[7] Under English law, a director has a common law right to inspect the minutes of directors' meetings and the company's accounting records (*Conway v Petronius Clothing & Co Ltd* [1978] 1 W.L.R. 72) and probably a statutory right of access to accounting records for the purposes of compliance with s.386(1) Companies Act 2006.

ment at the time of formation of the JVC), the minority party needs to ensure that the right of claim of the JVC cannot simply be blocked by the majority. Common contractual solutions are:

(a) to provide that responsibility for pursuing any such claim against the majority party is delegated to a committee of the JVC board which excludes the appointees of the majority shareholder—or is delegated to the minority shareholder as agent of the JVC; or

(b) to provide, generally, a contractual principle that the majority shareholder (and/or its appointed directors) shall not vote on or interfere with or obstruct any such claim—but without prejudice to its rights as defendant to resist any such claim.

A minority party may, though, now be able in certain circumstances to bring a statutory derivative action on behalf of the JVC if the claim includes a breach of duty by a director appointed by the majority shareholder—see para.11–31 et seq.

Exit

9–25 A minority party is, absent specifically negotiated terms, in a weak position if it wishes to "exit" from the JVC—perhaps if it is unhappy with the JVC's financial performance or with its relationship with the majority party. It can find itself "locked" into a JVC without any effective exit route. In some ventures, it may always be envisaged that a minority party—perhaps investing on a venture capital basis—should have an exit route to enable it to realise its investment at a potential profit. Possible protective provisions include the following measures.

Transfer

9–26 A minority stake will rarely be marketable to a third party. However, a right to sell will commonly be preserved including provisions:

(a) ensuring that the minority party is free to transfer its shares to a third party, subject invariably to the other shareholder(s) being able to exercise a pre-emption right;

(b) ensuring that, where the pre-emption right is exercisable by the other shareholder(s) at fair value, it is made clear that there will be no discount in determining the value of the minority shareholding being sold (i.e. its value will be on a per share basis pro rata to the value of the JVC as a whole)—see para.12–18 below; and

(c) removing any right of the directors to refuse to register a transfer to a third party if the other shareholder(s) do not purchase the shares and a third party purchaser is found.

Put option

9-27 However, the reality remains that a sale of a minority interest to a third party purchaser is unlikely (absent positive co-operation from the majority party in finding a suitable alternative "partner"). One safeguard is for a minority shareholder to negotiate a "put option" whereby it can oblige the majority shareholder to buy-out its investment in the JVC, usually in accordance with a pre-determined price formula and at a defined time or times. Such an option will provide the surest protection against the risk of a minority shareholder being "locked in" if the joint venture is unsuccessful from its viewpoint or it wishes to exit. The negotiation of a put option may, for instance, be particularly appropriate if the minority party has conceded that it will have very limited voting or veto rights. Key issues relating to options are discussed more fully in para.13-33 et seq. below.

Redeemable shares

9-28 In some cases, one method of establishing a pre-determined exit route for a minority shareholder is for shares to be issued to the minority party which are redeemable at the option of the shareholder, usually at a stated price. Factors affecting the issue of redeemable shares under English law[8] include:

(a) redeemable shares must be issued at the outset since rights of existing shares cannot be altered so as to become redeemable;

(b) shares can only be redeemed out of distributable profits or a fresh issue of shares for that purpose although a private company can, subject to certain conditions, also redeem shares out of capital; since redemption on the due date may be impossible, it is sometimes provided that the company shall redeem the shares on the specified date or as soon as possible thereafter;

(c) the shareholder may wish to have a veto over transactions which could reduce the level of distributable reserves and therefore make redemption more difficult (such as bonus issues or dividends beyond a certain fixed or maximum level).

In the case of venture capital investors, it is common in the UK for part of the initial equity investment of such institutions to take the form of subscription for redeemable shares which are convertible into full equity shares (at certain times and in accordance with a pre-agreed formula) in order that they can benefit from any gain as a result of any sale or public offering of the JVC—see para.7-28. The ability to establish redeemable

---

[8] Other important constitutional limitations are set out in ss.684 to 686 of the Companies Act 2006.

preference shares depends on the local corporate law and many jurisdictions do not have the same flexibility in this respect as English law.

Buy-back by JVC

9–29 One of the simplest methods for a minority party to exit is for its shares to be bought-back by the JVC itself. However, it is rarely possible to structure this as a binding commitment in advance. If buy-back is to be a term of the shares themselves, the rules relating to redeemable shares must be satisfied. Buy-back by contractual arrangement will be subject to additional corporate law restrictions and procedures. It is therefore usually a route which can only be discussed at the time of proposed exit in the light of the JVC's then financial position and plans—see para.13–15. If a minority party wants certainty, a put option vis-à-vis the majority shareholder is the stronger route.

Tag-along

9–30 A minority shareholder will often wish to protect itself against the possibility that the majority party may seek at some stage to sell its interest in the JVC. A minority shareholder should consider establishing a "tag-along" right whereby it can oblige the majority shareholder to include the minority party's stake, at the same price per share, in any sale which the majority shareholder may make of its controlling interest to a third party. This right ensures that the minority shareholder cannot be left unwillingly as a minority party in a joint venture with a new majority partner.

9–31 The same principle, in appropriate cases, should apply to enable the minority party to "piggy back" and participate proportionately in any initial public offering or private placement of shares in the JVC (including, where applicable, participation in the US in any registration by the JVC of securities prior to any such potential US offering).

Shareholders' agreement or articles of association?

9–32 Once the basic protections for the minority shareholder have been agreed, the next question is: should they be set out in the shareholders' agreement or in the JVC's articles of association (or equivalent constitutional documents)? This issue will depend on a mixture of practice, drafting style, practitioner preference and legal considerations. In the case of English law and practice, the following distinctions can be made:

(1) *Share rights*. Rights attaching directly to shares (such as voting rights, dividend rights, rights upon a liquidation and rights to appoint directors) should be in the articles of association. These are an integral part of the "bundle of rights" constituting the shares.

(2) *Positive obligations.* Positive obligations on a majority shareholder (e.g. undertakings by the majority party to provide information or access rights to the minority) usually appear solely in the shareholders' agreement.

(3) *Veto rights.* Whether minority veto rights should appear in the articles of association and be established as "class rights", or be dealt with solely as contractual undertakings in the shareholders' agreement, is debated between practitioners. There are a balance of considerations. In theory, inclusion of such provisions in the articles of association as class rights provides certain advantages:

(a) it is generally accepted that class rights are capable of being enforced directly against the JVC[9];

(b) the directors are bound by the articles of association and the matters which are the subject of the veto are beyond their power to undertake unless the requisite consent is obtained (thus overcoming the difficulty of the recalcitrant director who is not technically bound by the shareholders' agreement).

On the other hand, there are strong practical considerations for keeping veto rights and similar matters to the shareholders' agreement:

(a) the articles of association are a public document and some or all matters governed by veto may best be kept as "internal housekeeping" in a non-public document[10];

(b) some veto matters may be difficult to express as a class right and, generally, it can often be difficult to draft matters in a way in which they will stand alone if the shareholders' agreement comes to an end;

(c) class rights in articles of association cannot effectively regulate actions or transactions carried out by subsidiaries of the JVC;

(d) generally, many parties prefer all such matters to be covered by a single agreement and there is usually little difficulty in practice in enforcing rights and obligations under the shareholders' agreement; many will prefer to keep to that route alone—perhaps coupled with a general obligation on the parties to make appropriate amendments to the articles of association in the event of any conflict or if reasonably required by any party.

9–33 Minority veto rights will usually take the form of an undertaking by the other party(ies) to use all respective votes and powers (including to

---

[9] See *Quin & Axtens Ltd v Salmon* [1909] A.C. 442 and, generally, the discussion at para.5–55 et seq.

[10] Joint venture agreements may in certain circumstances be registrable with the Registrar of Companies under ss.29 and 30 of the Companies Act 2006—see also para.5–62 above. However, the general view is that they are not registrable unless the joint venture agreement is specifically referred to in the articles of association and necessary for a proper interpretation of the articles.

procure that its nominated directors exercise their respective rights and powers) to ensure that the requisite action does not take place without the relevant minority party's consent. Where the party giving the undertaking does not have a majority shareholding, the undertaking will usually be given only "so far as it is able" or on a "best endeavours" basis. In the case of a multi-party joint venture where no single shareholder has a majority position and any contractual claim would involve many parties, there is a stronger argument that enforcement would be easier if the veto rights are established as class rights in the articles of association.

9–34 It is not uncommon for the JVC itself to be a party to the shareholders' agreement and to undertake to observe the veto rights. This preserves the advantage of enabling direct enforcement against the company—but there can be limitations to such a route. In particular, under English law, there are certain undertakings which may be regarded as an unlawful fetter on the statutory powers of the company and therefore unenforceable (see para.5–55 earlier for a further discussion of this principle).

9–35 This discussion has taken place within the context of English law. Practice and legal considerations may well vary in other jurisdictions—particularly in civil law countries (where there may be less flexibility to use a shareholders' agreement) or in a jurisdiction where the minority party is unsure of the law, or its enforcement, and prefers the maximum protection provided by establishing its rights in the public constitutional documents.

Variation of class rights

9–36 "Class" rights under English law comprise any rights conferred by the articles of association (or other terms of issue) on a particular class of shares in contrast to one or more other classes. They may, importantly in the joint venture context, include rights conferred on a shareholder by name under the company's articles of association even though they are not attached to a particular class of shares identified as such.[11] The Companies Act 2006[12] includes certain protections for the members of a class against any change in the rights attaching to shares of that class. Unless extended by specific provisions in the articles of association, however, these protec-

---

[11] In *Cumbrian Newspapers Group Ltd v Cumberland & Westmorland Herald Newspapers & Printing Co Ltd* [1986] 3 W.L.R. 26 the plaintiff was granted by the articles of association rights of pre-emption over other ordinary shares, rights in respect of unissued shares and the right to appoint a director. Although these were not rights expressed to be attached to any particular shares, it was held that they were conferred on the plaintiff as shareholder and these special rights could not be varied without its consent.
[12] s.630(2) of the Companies Act 2006 provides that such rights can only be varied if the variation is agreed in writing by the holders of 75 per cent in nominal value of the shares of that class or sanctioned by an extraordinary resolution at a separate class meeting.

tions only apply under English law to alterations which constitute a strict "variation" of legal rights attaching to a class of shares.[13]

Weighted voting rights

9–37 An alternative approach under English law, in situations where it is not appropriate to establish class rights but it is wished to entrench rights in the articles of association, is for a minority shareholder to have weighted voting rights (i.e. an increased number of votes) on particular matters on which it wishes to entrench its rights. This method has been used to ensure that a minority party's appointee as director cannot be removed by an ordinary resolution by the majority shareholders.[14] Although now rarely used, this approach appears to be a technique capable of general application to entrench rights of a shareholder under English law. It may, for instance, be appropriate where a particular shareholder (e.g. a founding shareholder) holds a "special share" designed to ensure that certain features of the JVC cannot be changed without its consent.

> The Multi-Party Shareholders' Agreement included as Precedent 10 in Part E incorporates examples of many of the minority protections discussed in this chapter.

STRATEGIC MINORITY INVESTMENT

Strategic equity investment

9–38 Issues of minority protection have so far in this chapter been addressed in the context of arrangements in a joint venture between a limited number of shareholders. A somewhat different category is where a party takes a minority equity investment in an existing company (perhaps even a listed company) as part of a strategic relationship with the company itself. In these cases, the relationship will extend beyond the equity

---

[13] For instance, in *White v Bristol Aeroplane Co Ltd* [1953] Ch. 65 it was held that the issue of new ordinary share capital ranking in priority to existing preference shares does not constitute a variation of the latter unless the company's articles of association specifically provide to the contrary. The variation of the rights of one class which has an adverse economic effect on the rights of another class of shares will not generally constitute a variation of the rights of that other class.

[14] *Bushell v Faith* [1970] A.C. 1099 is the case which sanctioned this approach. The articles of association provided that, on a resolution at a general meeting for the dismissal of a director, shares held by that director carried three votes per share—effectively meaning that he could not be voted out against his will. The House of Lords upheld this voting system and held that it was not inconsistent with the right of shareholders (now under s.168 of the Companies Act 2006) to remove a director by ordinary resolution.

investment and include commercial arrangements (e.g. technology licensing, resource sharing, supply or distribution arrangements) with the company which establish other strategic commercial benefits for the parties. Such strategic links and alliances appear in a wide variety of situations:

(1) Many such strategic alliances take the form of an investment by a larger corporate investor (with or without a listing) in a smaller company. This investment may be a base to gain access to "niche" technology which the smaller company is developing or, possibly, as a first step to an eventual acquisition—see also "corporate venturing" discussed earlier at para.1–05.

(2) Other alliances reflect international strategic "partnerships" between substantial companies (often publicly-listed companies) whereby a shareholding link or investment supports a significant technical or licensing collaboration aimed at assisting the development of the investee's business.

(3) Many multi-party strategic links and alliances have also become a feature, for instance, in the telecommunications field and other industries where participants are anxious to develop pan-European or global networks for the supply of goods or services. Cross-investment may provide additional "glue" to the relationship.

Some illustrative examples of strategic investments of these kinds are mentioned in para.5–13 earlier.

9–39 These kinds of strategic minority investment will bring together many of the issues of "minority protection" discussed earlier in this chapter. Since the investment is part of a larger strategic relationship, the minority party will often be in a position to negotiate relatively strong rights for its protection. There will also be a number of issues arising (for both parties) which are particularly important because of the strategic nature of the investment.

STRATEGIC MINORITY INVESTMENT: SOME KEY ISSUES

The legal issues involved in such strategic alliances where a minority equity investment is taken are both commercial and corporate in nature.

Commercial

A first set of issues for the strategic investor concerns the rights that it will have in relation to the business affairs of the JVC. These involve, in effect, many of the minority protection issues discussed earlier in this chapter:

(1) *Board representation.* The strategic investor will usually seek representation on the board of directors of the company.

(2) *Consent rights.* The investor, given its strategic objectives, will usually seek special rights to approve certain types of material transactions undertaken by the company. These will frequently take the form of special board majority requirements (e.g. requiring approval of a super-majority of the board or at least approval of the investor's appointee on the board). Given the fiduciary duties of directors, it may sometimes be more appropriate to structure these approval requirements as part of the rights of the shares to be issued to the investor. Since the company will be a party to the agreement, it may be necessary to check that any veto rights do not contravene any rules against "fettering the statutory powers of the company" or its equivalent in the relevant jurisdiction—see para.5–55 et seq. earlier.

(3) *Financial information and "visitation" rights.* The investor will seek regular financial information such as quarterly (or, in some cases, monthly) and annual information and annual budgets. An investor may also be granted rights to inspect the company's books and records and to meet with company executives or officers.

(4) *Confidential information.* The strategic investor is likely, whether through board representation or otherwise, to have access to sensitive information. In the commercial interests of the company, it may be appropriate to limit information which the company provides to the investor or, on occasion, to restrict its appointee's attendance at board meetings on certain items. If appropriate restrictions are negotiated on the investor's access to information, the company may wish to be able to disclose the terms of those restrictions to other customers in order to allay their concerns regarding the relationship between the company and the strategic investor.

(5) *Non-compete.* The investee company will normally want to ensure that the strategic relationship is "exclusive" and that the strategic investor does not enter into specified types of transactions (including other material equity investments) with a competitor in the relevant territory or field. In some cases, a restraint on the investee company's own competitive activities within a specified territory may be appropriate.

(6) *Non-issue of shares to a competitor.* Similarly, the strategic investor will frequently want to ensure that the investee company does not permit another competitor to acquire shares in that company (or at least to ensure that new shares are not issued by the company to any such competitor).

(7) *Technology/supply arrangements.* A strategic relationship is likely to be supported by important ancillary contracts between the two companies relating to technology, technical support, supply of materials or personnel. Commercial terms (including any termination rights) will require careful negotiation.

(8) *Redemption and other "rubber band" provisions.* Strategic alliances are typically entered into by the parties based on common mutual objectives and plans. Ultimately, if the alliance fails to develop as contemplated, the parties may agree to terminate the relationship. It is not uncommon to address these concerns with a "rubber band" provision pursuant to which each party may regain its contribution to the alliance, in whole or in part;

e.g. either the company or the strategic investor (or both) may regain technology contributed to the alliance. The company may, alternatively, have the right to redeem the strategic investor's shares on pre-determined terms.

Corporate/share rights

A further set of issues relate to the strategic investor's interest in protecting its shareholding stake in the JVC and, possibly, establishing rights which protect or enhance its ability to exit. In view of the strategic nature of the relationship, those rights will often be stronger than for a "simple" minority party. Many of the issues are similar to those addressed in venture capital investments—see para.7–27 et seq.

(1) *Dividends*. The investor may seek that at least part of its investment should be represented by shares with "preferred" dividend rights—either in the form of a non-cumulative dividend preference or by way of a fixed dividend to ensure an interest-like return on its investment.

(2) *Liquidation preference*. Similarly, "preference" shares to be held by the strategic investor may establish a preference over other shares on a liquidation (or sale of the company's business). The share terms will generally provide for a return of at least the original purchase or subscription price prior to any return of capital to the ordinary or common shareholders. Often, the terms may provide for the "preferred" shareholders then to participate on equal terms with the ordinary shareholders in any additional distributions by the company—perhaps up to a specified limit.

(3) *"Standstill" restraints*. The company may seek contractual restraints in relation to subsequent disposals or acquisitions of shares in that company by the strategic investor. For instance, a "standstill" commitment will often be appropriate whereby the investor undertakes not to acquire further shares in the investee company (or indeed not to dispose of its existing shares) for a certain period without the consent of the company.

(4) *Share issues*. A strategic investor will frequently seek a right of first refusal on future issues of equity securities by the company. (This "pre-emption" right may not apply on a public offering or on certain types of equity issues, e.g. to employees.) The principal purpose will be to avoid dilution—both in terms of value and also level of influence over management. The scope of any exceptions will therefore be important.

(5) *"Catch-up"*. An investor may seek a "catch-up" provision that allows it to maintain a fixed percentage equity interest in the company (irrespective of any security offerings in which the investor has not participated) by having a right to acquire further shares at certain times.

(6) *Registration rights*. Particularly in relation to US securities, an investor may seek two types of registration rights to ensure that it participates in any subsequent public offering by the JVC:

— "piggy-back" rights by which investors may elect to participate in a registration initiated by the investee company;

— "demand" rights by which the investor can cause the company to initiate registration for the benefit of the investors (in which case a material issue will be whether the investor can initiate demand registration unilaterally, without requiring consent from other shareholders)

(7) *Conversion: anti-dilution.* The investor may wish to have "conversion" rights attached to its preference shares—entitling it to convert in certain circumstances into ordinary shares according to a formula (often on a one-for-one basis). These may include a right to convert into ordinary shares automatically upon a public offering of a specified minimum size and at a specified minimum price per share. The conversion terms may include "price-based" anti-dilution provisions under which the conversion ratio of the preference shares is increased if the company issues shares at a price lower than the price of the original investment. These provisions will generally be structured as "weighted-average" formulae in which the increase in the conversion ratio takes into account the relative amounts of shares issued at various prices. On rare occasions, the anti-dilution protection may be structured as a "full ratchet" in which the conversion price is automatically adjusted to the price of the most recent issue of lower priced shares, irrespective of the number of shares issued.

(8) *Redeemable shares.* In some cases, the rights attaching to the shares of the investor may require the company to redeem the preference shares after a specified period of time. This provides an alternative liquidity route if the company does not achieve a public offering or sale within a specified period. Alternatively, the company may seek a provision enabling it to repurchase the investor's shares if specified objectives of the proposed strategic alliance are not satisfied.

(9) *Co-sale arrangements.* Venture capital investors often obtain an ancillary "co-sale" agreement with founders of the company—particularly in early rounds of financing. The co-sale agreement provides that the founder shareholder(s) will give each other principal shareholder an opportunity to participate on a pro rata basis in any sale of shares by that founder. This is equivalent, in effect, to a "tag-along" provision.

(10) *Acquisition of the investee company.* Often, the strategic investor's ultimate goal is to acquire, or have the right to acquire, the company in which it has taken a strategic equity interest. At a minimum, it will wish to prevent the acquisition of a controlling interest by one of its competitors. A number of alternatives may be used to address this issue:

(A) The investor may attempt at the outset to negotiate a commercial "call" option with the other major shareholders giving it the right to acquire majority control at a later date. Negotiations of such an option could, though, pose a number of problems. The existence of the option may restrict other alternative sale routes. It may adversely affect the company's relationships with other customers. The option may also pose accounting or tax problems which should be addressed with advisers at an early stage. The price at which the option may be exercised may also pose difficult valuation problems for both parties (see generally para.13–35 et seq. below).

(B) A different approach involves a "reverse auction" process—in which the investor has the right to offer a specific price to acquire the shares of the other shareholders on the basis that they must then either accept the offer or elect to buyout the investor at the same valuation. This puts the strategic investor in control of the price but may place it at risk that it will not be able to achieve its ultimate goal of acquiring the company.

(C) Another approach is for the other major shareholders to grant the investor a "right of first refusal" prior to any acquisition of their shares in the company. This provision can, though, cause a number of concerns. It may seriously restrict the company's flexibility to negotiate future transactions since other potential buyers may be reluctant to negotiate if they become aware that they will effectively be negotiating the purchase price for the strategic investor. One variant is to restrict the "right of first refusal" to a proposed acquisition by a specified list of competitors of the corporate investor.

(D) A different and more limited approach is to establish a "right of first discussion". This simply requires that the strategic investor must receive notice of any potential acquisition (and its terms) and be given a reasonable opportunity to make a counter bid or acquisition proposal. A "right of first discussion" requires the parties to negotiate in good faith for a specified time. If the parties are not able to come to terms regarding an acquisition within that period, the other shareholders are free to complete an acquisition transaction with a third party.

(11) *Right to purchase equity at time of IPO.* In some strategic alliances, in addition to its initial investment, the strategic investor may wish to establish a right to subscribe for further equity in the event of an initial public offering (IPO). From the company's perspective, a subscription of further equity by the strategic investor may give important support to the offering (provided the purchase price is substantially the same as that paid by public investors and the size of shareholding acquired is not so large as to impair future liquidity). The strategic investor, in turn, may thereby maintain a significant influence over the company's policies and direction. Compliance with securities laws will be important.

Regulatory and process factors

A strategic investment, particularly in a publicly-listed company, may also bring into play a number of procedural and regulatory issues:

(1) *Disclosure requirements.* If one of the parties is a publicly-listed company, stock exchange listing rules may apply—which can, inter alia, impose disclosure or announcement requirements in respect of material transactions entered into by the company (including disclosure of terms of that transaction on any subsequent share issue). Regulatory requirements or rules requiring notification of any substantial issues of shares or share purchases can apply; for example, the Rules Governing Substantial Acquisitions of Shares issued on behalf of the UK Panel on Take-overs and Mergers.

(2) *Mandatory bid rules.* Compulsory bid rules may also need to be watched in the case of a listed company; for instance, the City Code on Take-overs and Mergers in the UK requires a party to bid for all the shares in a UK public company once its shareholding reaches a 30 per cent level.

(3) *Stock exchange rules.* Corporate and regulatory requirements can apply to subsequent transactions between a listed company and a substantial or connected shareholder. For instance, transactions between the investee company and the strategic investor are likely to be "related party transactions" under the rules of the UK Listing Authority. Such requirements may call for special disclosure and, sometimes, shareholder approval.

(4) *Tax.* The tax position affecting dividends can create difficulties, particularly where cross-border payments are involved. However, no withholding tax applies to dividend payments between most EU countries.

(5) *Accounting.* The accounting implications for the strategic investor of its interest in the company will often be important-particularly if the size of the percentage share holding exceeds 20 per cent or otherwise triggers the "equity method" of accounting (see para.19–12 et seq).

9–40 Terms of the equity investment will usually be incorporated into a "subscription agreement" between the strategic investor and the investee company. If there are one or more significant shareholders, then they may also be joined as parties in a "subscription and shareholders agreement". It will, of course, be necessary to ensure that the terms comply with any applicable corporate laws in the jurisdiction of the investee company.

Some features of a minority equity investment are included in the Strategic Alliance Agreement which appears as Precedent 4 in Part E.

CONCLUSION

9–41 Minority investment and protection provisions can be amongst the most difficult issues to be negotiated in establishing a JVC. They require a balance to be drawn between the different interests of the parties—and the interests of the JVC in stability and effective decision-making structures. They are, in effect, a key part of the overall governance structure of the JVC. The existence of strong minority rights (especially veto rights) can, however, lead to greater risk of potential "deadlock" between the parties to which we now turn.

CHAPTER 10

Deadlock and breakdown

How should the parties deal with the risk of potential deadlock or breakdown in the management of a joint venture? It will be a challenge for the management team to develop systems, a culture and a relationship which reduces this risk. Potential deadlock is, nevertheless, an intrinsic feature of most joint ventures. Indeed, many equity joint ventures will deliberately be structured as 50:50 "deadlock companies". This chapter addresses a range of possible mechanisms to deal with this situation.

To deal with deadlock or not?

10–01 "Deadlock" in this context means the inability of the parties or their representatives to agree on strategy or other important decisions affecting the venture. This inability may be due to genuine disagreement between the parties or a fundamental breakdown in their relationship. Formal management deadlock in a joint venture company (JVC)[1] can arise in various different situations:

(1) *Board level*. A management deadlock can arise at board level where the directors appointed by the two shareholders take opposing views in a 50:50 joint venture or, if there is a minority shareholder, where that shareholder's appointee exercises an agreed veto right.

(2) *Shareholder level*. Similarly, deadlock can arise at shareholder level in relation to matters which require shareholder approval and either it is a joint venture where the parties have equal voting rights (e.g. a 50:50 venture) or a minority party has a veto right.

(3) *Boycott of meetings*. Sometimes a deadlock arises because one of the parties refuses to attend meetings (whether at board or shareholder level) and it becomes impossible to pass decisions or generally to conduct the affairs of the JVC.

10–02 Should the parties include provisions in the governance structure of the JVC to deal with deadlock or breakdown at all? Do they really assist?

[1] This chapter deals with deadlock in a corporate joint venture. Similar principles can apply in the case of a partnership. In a contractual alliance, apart from internal dispute resolution procedures, resolution of any deadlock or breakdown will usually involve termination of the alliance by one of the agreed contractual routes.

There are two primary schools of thought on the value of making special provision for deadlock resolution in joint venture agreements:

(a) those who actively try to establish governance rules which avoid a potential deadlock or which establish clear resolution procedures if deadlock or breakdown does arise;

(b) alternatively, those who would prefer to try and negotiate an appropriate resolution at the time of any deadlock, rather than anticipate in advance what this might be, and do not therefore provide for deadlock resolution procedures in the agreement.

10–03 Experience indicates that detailed "deadlock-breaker" provisions are rarely used in practice. Commercial pressures and negotiations will normally lead (if reluctantly) to agreement on the way forward without them. Many have considerable doubts as to their usefulness unless the parties have a strong commercial desire to ensure at the outset that a definite "exit" route exists in the event of breakdown. If they are included but not operated in full, these contractual provisions can nevertheless provide an important background against which each party must develop its tactical strategy in any dispute or deadlock situation.

MEASURES TO AVOID DEADLOCK ARISING

Management structures to avoid deadlock

10–04 One way of dealing with deadlock is to design the management structure in a way which endeavours to avoid it in the first place. Structural measures which help to avoid management deadlock arising include the following:

(1) It may be agreed at the outset that one party is to have clear voting and management control (e.g. generally, a majority voting interest at board and shareholder level).

(2) Alternatively, it may be agreed at the outset that a particular party shall have control or leadership over a particular area of management responsibility or decision-making (e.g. a named party to control decisions relating to technical matters). This can sometimes work well in practice in situations where each party is contributing a different skill or resource to the venture.

(3) A different approach is to establish a management structure whereby as many decisions as possible are taken at individual executive level (e.g. by the executive director responsible for the particular function or by the chief executive) without the matter requiring referral to the full—and potentially deadlocked—board of directors.

(4) Similarly, the parties may choose to restrict the list of "reserved matters" which must be referred or reserved to the decision of the shareholders themselves—as opposed to decisions which can be taken solely at operating board level (where those responsible for the joint venture's activities on a day-to-day basis may be readier to reach a compromise agreement).

10–05 These measures will all go to the management structure and scope of delegated authority within the particular venture. Much will therefore depend on the attitude of the parties when establishing that structure. In many cases, though, each party will be reluctant to give up its right to "agree" major decisions—which then leads back to the potential for a deadlock which will have to be broken by one means or another.

Boycott of meetings

10–06 Measures to avoid deadlock arising through boycott of meetings include the following:

(1) *Provision in constitutional documents.* One preventative measure frequently included in articles of association in the UK is to the effect that, if a meeting is adjourned because of absence of a quorum, at any subsequent meeting those members (or directors in the case of a board meeting) actually present shall constitute a quorum.[2] Another variant is to provide that this quorum is only required when the meeting proceeds to business; if one party walks out, the meeting may validly continue (so long as there are at least two members or directors present). Many joint venture parties may, though, be unwilling to contemplate any measure which would give the other party control in the event of any absence of its own representative(s).

(2) *Section 306 Companies Act 2006.* This is a re-enacted statutory provision under English law which entitles the court to order a meeting to be called, held and conducted in any manner the court thinks fit. This is potentially a useful power to unblock a deadlock where a minority shareholder is using the avoidance of a quorum to prevent a majority shareholder from exercising the majority voting rights attaching to its shares.[3] However, it is a limited remedy; it

---

[2] See, for example, the precedent Articles of Association as Precedent 11 in Part E.

[3] *Opera Photographic Ltd, Re* [1989] 1 W.L.R. 634. One party held 51 per cent of the shares of the JVC and the other party 49 per cent. The minority party refused to attend any meetings requisitioned to consider a resolution for his removal as a director. No quorum could therefore be obtained. The court made an order convening a meeting at which one member would constitute a quorum. If no order was made, the deadlock position would remain and the applicant would be denied his statutory right to remove the other party as director. See also *Union Music Ltd v Watson* [2003] EWCA Civ 180.

cannot be used to change substantive rights or shift the agreed voting balance between the parties.[4]

Mechanisms Enabling the Venture to Continue

10–07 Mechanisms for breaking deadlock where a business dispute between the parties has arisen tend to fall into two distinct categories:

(a) mechanisms enabling the venture to continue: these mechanisms are intended to provide a workable solution in order to permit the joint venture to continue;

(b) "divorce" mechanisms: these mechanisms, on the other hand, usually accept that the deadlock or breakdown is irreconcilable and provide a method by which the venture terminates as a joint enterprise—see para.10–15 et seq.

10–08 Possible mechanisms for resolving deadlock within the context of a joint venture which the parties wish to continue include the following:

(1) *Additional vote.* A party, or one of its appointees on the board, could have a second or additional vote in the event of a tie.

(2) *Independent director's swing vote.* An "independent" director, appointed from outside without prior allegiance to either joint venture party, may effectively be a "swing" director—whether chairman or not—capable of casting a vote which will decide what would otherwise be a deadlock between the parties.

Other mechanisms of this kind are essentially potential features of a general dispute resolution procedure for the joint venture:

(3) *Reference to the chairmen or chief executives of the joint venture parties.* The deadlock may be referred (perhaps in stages of escalation) up to the chairmen or chief executives of the joint venture parents themselves for resolution at the highest level within each party's management—particularly if it is a major strategic venture.

---

[4] *Harman v BML Group Ltd* [1994] 2 B.C.L.C. 674. The court held that the statutory power was not, however, intended to permit a meeting to be summoned which overrode quorum provisions which were created as, in effect, class rights. In *Ross v Telford* [1998] 1 B.C.L.C. 82 the company in question was owned by two shareholders, 50:50, with a deadlocked board. The Court of Appeal confirmed that the power does not enable the court to shift the voting balance so as to break a deadlock between two equal shareholders. Similarly, see *Manningtree v Easier Plc* [2005] EWHC 2578 and *Alvona Developments Ltd v Manhattan Loft Corp (AC) Ltd* [2005] EWHC 1567.

(4) *Reference to mediation/expert/arbitration.* A dispute may be referred to an independent "expert" or to mediation or other alternative dispute resolution (ADR) or arbitration procedure.

(5) *Dispute review panel.* In a potentially long-running or complex venture (e.g. a major infrastructure project), a standing dispute review panel may be established which will be available throughout the venture to assist with the resolution of disputes.

We review each of these possibilities in a little more detail.

Additional vote

10–09 In some ventures, it may be appropriate for one party in effect to have a casting or tie-breaking vote to resolve what would otherwise be a deadlock. A traditional mechanism has been to give the chairman of the meeting, usually appointed by one party, a second or casting vote. This gives that party a clear advantage (negating in effect, the concept of joint control). This is usually commercially unacceptable. One way of mitigating this effect to some extent in a 50:50 joint venture is to provide that the appointment of the chairman (with a casting vote) should alternate between the parties perhaps on a yearly basis—in order to retain some balance between the parties.

10–10 Such a mechanism may still be possible in most jurisdictions. In the UK, however, it is subject to new restrictions and must be carefully drafted. Under the Companies Act 2006,[5] a chairman's casting vote at a shareholders' meeting is no longer valid—unless such a right existed in the company's articles of association immediately prior to October 1, 2007. The effect is that, for new articles, any tie-breaker vote at a shareholders' meeting must be structured as an additional vote attaching directly to a share or shares held by a particular shareholder (i.e. as a class right) and not simply in the chairman of the meeting. The new restriction does not, however, apply to a chairman's casting vote at meetings of directors and may therefore continue to be used as a tie-breaker mechanism in that context.

Independent director's swing vote

10–11 Giving an independent third party a "swing" vote as an additional non-executive director will unlock deadlock at board level. The attractiveness of this approach will depend upon the structure of the board and

---

[5] s.282(3) and (4) Companies Act 2006 as modified by the Companies Act 2006 (Commencement No. 5, Transitional Provisions and Savings) Order 2007.

whether a suitable person with appropriate business expertise can be found. It may well be difficult for the parent shareholders to find a candidate who is acceptable to both of them. It is risky; each shareholder will obviously be concerned that the interests of the non-executive director may not always coincide with its own interests. In some ventures, it may be appropriate for the "independent" director to be an independent chief executive of the JVC where the other directors are non-executive representatives of the joint venture parents. As an alternative approach, the development of an increasingly "independent" board may, in certain circumstances, be a desirable aim if there is an intention in due course to develop the JVC for subsequent flotation as an independent public company.

Reference to mediation/expert/arbitration

10–12 Parties sometimes provide for any dispute or deadlock which arises in relation to the joint venture to be referred to an independent third party. This could be an expert in the relevant field or an arbitrator or could involve some form of alternative dispute resolution (ADR) procedure. These methods work well for legal or specialist disputes. They are less appropriate for business disputes because third parties will generally have insufficient knowledge of the business of the JVC. There may, however, be a role for a mediation structure in some ventures—particularly, perhaps, international joint ventures involving different cultures—where disputes may be partly managerial and partly legal and the role of the mediator(s) is not to determine the dispute but to assist the parties to do so: see a fuller discussion in chapter 14. Third party mechanisms will often, though, only provide a short-term solution which is unlikely to resolve more basic differences in approach between the parties (e.g. disputes over future funding or the strategic direction of the business).

Dispute review panel

10–13 Greater use is being made in some ventures (e.g. consortia to build major infrastructure projects) of establishing a "standing" panel at the outset in order to assist the speedy resolution of disputes. This could take a variety of forms, for instance:

(a) a board or panel could consist of senior executives from alliance members (sometimes with an "independent" member); or

(b) a named mediator or team of mediators may be appointed before the venture begins in order that they can become familiar with the venture, its members and objectives.

Such a panel, if adopted, will usually be a mechanism for resolution of disputes generally rather than specifically for a deadlock situation.

Reference to parties' chairmen or chief executives

10–14 A residual method, but often the most practical, is for the deadlock to be referred to the chairmen or chief executives of the parent shareholders (or, perhaps, to other specified directors with appropriate technical background). The chairmen/chief executives may be able to take a broader view of the dispute having regard to the overall interests of the parties. It may still be that they are unable to agree, but one advantage of this method is that the prospect of unresolved issues being referred to the highest authority within the organisations of the joint venture parties will concentrate the minds of the management of the JVC. This makes it more likely that they will find a solution for themselves. In practice, internal resolution at senior management level within the joint venture parents is likely to be the method by which most major disputes are resolved (whether or not provision is specifically made in the agreements).

"DIVORCE" MEASURES

10–15 Management deadlock, if serious, is likely to reflect a breakdown in relations between the parties which will inevitably lead to termination of the venture. The first question is to assess whether the express "exit" or termination provisions in the joint venture agreement are sufficient to deal with the situation. In many ventures, there may be express rights which provide an effective route to "divorce"; e.g. an express right for a party to terminate by notice, to call for a winding-up of the JVC, to exercise a "put" option or otherwise to exit from the venture—see chapter 13. It is only if the termination provisions do not provide an adequate solution that the parties need to consider whether special "divorce" measures should be introduced to provide for a situation of management deadlock or breakdown.

10–16 "Divorce" measures are often considered, but not always included, in equity joint venture agreements. They may act as a "nuclear deterrent"—the threat of their implementation assists to persuade the parties to agree a commercial solution. If adopted, it is highly desirable to allow sufficient breaks within the formal deadlock procedure before the strict provisions of the joint venture agreement are finally implemented. This allows the parties continuing opportunity to agree a commercial solution (even if reluctantly). The following are examples of measures which are sometimes used or considered. These measures recognise that an insoluble deadlock will inevitably lead to the break-up of the joint venture and that this cannot realistically be solved by sale of one party's interest to a third party.[6] The

---

[6] Note the finding by McKinsey & Co—see para.1–17 earlier—that, of equity joint ventures which terminate, nearly 80 per cent end with one party buying out the other. The measures discussed in this chapter are often simply background to inter-party negotiations for such a buy-out.

measures therefore result in buy-out of one party's interest or, in certain circumstances, winding-up of the JVC. In this scenario, upon the defined deadlock trigger event, a party would have a contractual right to initiate the relevant "divorce" measure. Possible measures include:

(a) *winding-up:* proceedings for voluntary winding up of the JVC;

(b) *sale of JVC:* to initiate (if viable) the sale of the JVC as a whole;

(c) *put/call options:* exercise of put/call options (including, where appropriate, buy-out of a minority party);

(d) *"shoot out" procedures:* commencement of a "Russian roulette" or other variant of a buy/sell "shoot out" procedure between the parties;

(e) *a "multi-choice" procedure:* commencement of discussions on a variety of options (possibly in order of preference).

Voluntary winding-up

10–17 One approach is for the parties to agree that a deadlock should trigger a specified period (say 90 days) for final negotiation between the parties. If no resolution is reached, this mechanism would then entitle either party to require the JVC to be wound up. The value of the JVC on a break-up basis is likely to be less than as a going concern, which should act as a restraint against a party initiating the process lightly. Winding-up would involve a sale of all the JVC's assets, the proceeds of which would then be distributed to the shareholders according to their respective equity interests.

10–18 If this stage is reached, it may be worth considering first holding a compulsory auction procedure in relation to the JVC's assets, at which each party (possibly along with third parties) would be able to make bids to a person acting as "auctioneer" for the JVC's assets (an auction shoot out). Alternatively, the parties may prefer to establish a pre-agreed termination plan whereby specified assets (or business) of the JVC are to be "returned" to the original contributing party—perhaps at a fair value to be determined by an agreed valuation procedure.

Sale of the JVC

10–19 In some circumstances, a party may have a right to initiate the sale of the JVC as a whole—and one of the "trigger" points for exercising that right could be a defined deadlock event. However, it is unusual for such a right to be linked specifically to deadlock; it is more likely to be a right which an equity finance provider (or possibly a founder shareholder) may have generally—see para.13–39 et seq. Such a right may be coupled with a "drag-along" right enabling that party to force through a sale of the JVC as a whole by acquiring shares in the JVC held by the other parties if an appropriate sale of the JVC to a third party is negotiated.

Put/call options

10–20 One source of deadlock may be the exercise of a veto right by a minority party. A term of the venture in favour of the majority party may be that, where the deadlock has arisen through persistent use by a minority party of its veto rights, the majority party shall have a call option on that party's interest in the JVC; possibly, in some cases, the minority party may have a put option. The buy-out right might be triggered, say, where the minority party (or its nominated director) has exercised a veto on resolutions on certain fundamental or "reserved" matters on more than a specified number of occasions or boycotted meetings at which such resolutions were to be considered.

10–21 Another possible use of call options in the event of deadlock is to initiate a call option procedure of one of the kinds contemplated in para.13–13 below following a notice of termination (with the right to serve such a notice being triggered by a deadlock event as well as other "termination" events). A more common alternative, in joint ventures between parties with roughly equal negotiating strength, is to structure put/call options within a termination "shoot-out" procedure of the kind discussed in para.10–22 below.

Shoot-out procedures

Russian roulette

10–22 The most dramatic solution (supported by some, but criticised by many as too arbitrary) is to establish a termination "shoot-out" or "buy/sell" procedure whereby, after the occurrence of a defined deadlock event and usually after a warning notice period:

(a) one party (A) has the contractual right to notify the other party (B) that it wishes to sell its shares in the JVC to party B (or to buy B's shares) at the price per share stated by A in its notice;

(b) within a stated period, party B must then elect either to sell its own shares in the JVC to A or to buy A's shares—in either case, at the price per share stated in A's notice;

(c) after the initial notice, there is therefore a compulsory sale and purchase between the parties as a result of which, in a two-party venture, the JVC will end up in the sale ownership of one party.

Figure 10.1 shows this process in flowchart form. Occasionally, party B is given the further option (instead of choosing to buy or sell) to elect that the JVC be put into liquidation.

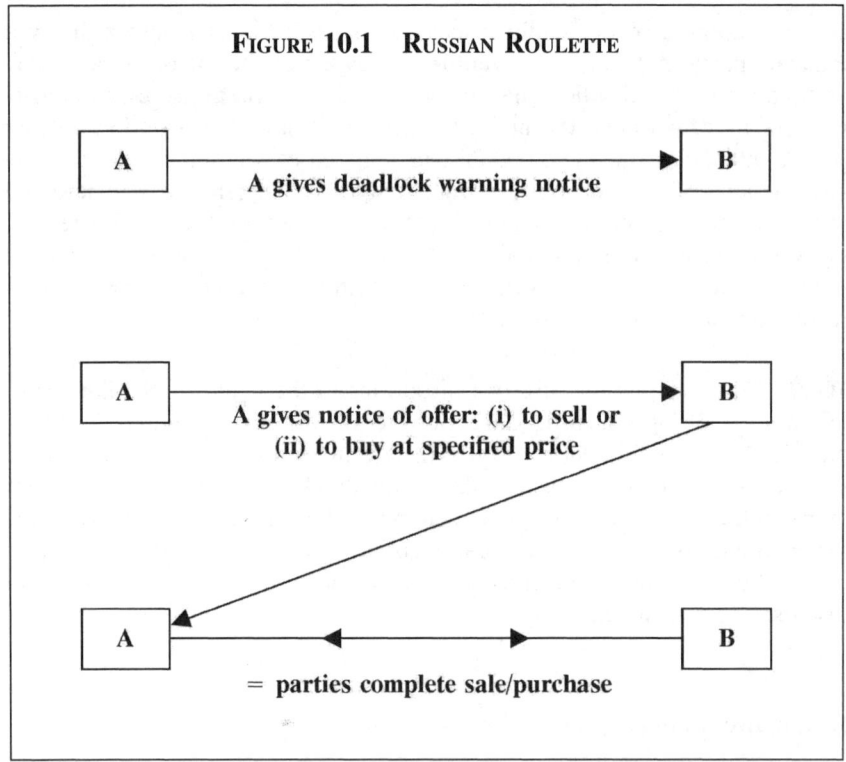

10–23 The theory is that the risk of reversal inherent in the process acts as an inducement for party A to put forward a fair price for the shares. "Russian roulette" should, however, be used with extreme care. It works reasonably well only if the proportionate shareholdings of the parties are roughly equal, and so long as there are no restrictions or circumstances which effectively prevent one party from being a buyer (such as restraints on foreign ownership in the country of the JVC or adverse tax consequences which would apply if that party were the acquirer). Disadvantages or difficulties, however, occur in many circumstances:

(1) A particular disadvantage of the process is that, where one party is in a stronger financial position than the other, or where it knows that any such restraints are likely to apply to the other party, it could invoke the "Russian roulette" procedure to buy out the other party

and set its proposed price in the knowledge that the other party could not fund or implement a counter-offer to buy.

(2) The mechanism is also difficult to operate where the JVC depends, or has depended, upon important services or facilities provided by one party or where part of the goodwill of the business of the JVC has arisen through use of one party's name which may no longer be available after termination.

10–24 Another disadvantage is that, because of the uncertainty of the outcome, it is not appropriate where a party definitely wants to exit from the JVC's business (unless it is confident that, if it is obliged to acquire the other party's shares in the JVC, it will be able to sell the JVC as a whole on to a third party buyer). It is therefore more commonly used following a deadlock event rather than as a mechanism associated with a right to exit.

"Trigger" event

10–25 If included, the conditions for the "trigger" to initiate the procedure need to be carefully defined. The parties may prefer that such a final and uncertain solution should only apply in extreme circumstances of clear breakdown of the relationship.[7] Trigger events might be:

(a) a failure to agree (i.e. each party voting in different ways) on specified "reserved matters", perhaps after at least two or three consecutive board or shareholder meetings at which the matter has been considered and a deadlock vote reached;

(b) a failure to agree a budget for the JVC within a stated period;

(c) a failure to reach a quorum at board or shareholder meetings on at least two or three consecutive occasions; or

(d) more generally, where a deadlock has been reached on a matter which a party has designated to be of material importance to the JVC.

Whatever the trigger event, there is much to be said for building into the procedure some initial warning notice that a party intends to implement the deadlock or "divorce" procedure if the matter is not resolved.

Texas shoot-out/highest sealed bid

10–26 In this variant, party A serves a notice on party B stating that it is willing to purchase B's shares in the JVC at a stated price. B has a period in

---

[7] *T–Mobile (UK) v Bluebottle Investments SA* [2003] EWHL 379 (Comm) is a case where a party, essentially in default, deliberately tried to engineer "no-fault" termination provisions in order to trigger a "shoot-out" procedure entitling either party to buy out the other. The court held, on the facts, that the party could not misuse an exit clause in this way.

which to elect either (i) to sell at that price or (ii) to indicate that it wishes to purchase A's interest at a higher price. If option (ii) is chosen, then:

(a) each party submits under a sealed bid (to a designated third party) a price per share which it would be prepared to pay the other party for the latter's shares in the JVC;

(b) the lower bidder is obliged to sell its shares to the higher bidder at the higher bidder's price.

Like the "Russian roulette" procedure, this mechanism tends to favour the party having greater financial strength. Figure 10.2 shows this mechanism in flowchart form.

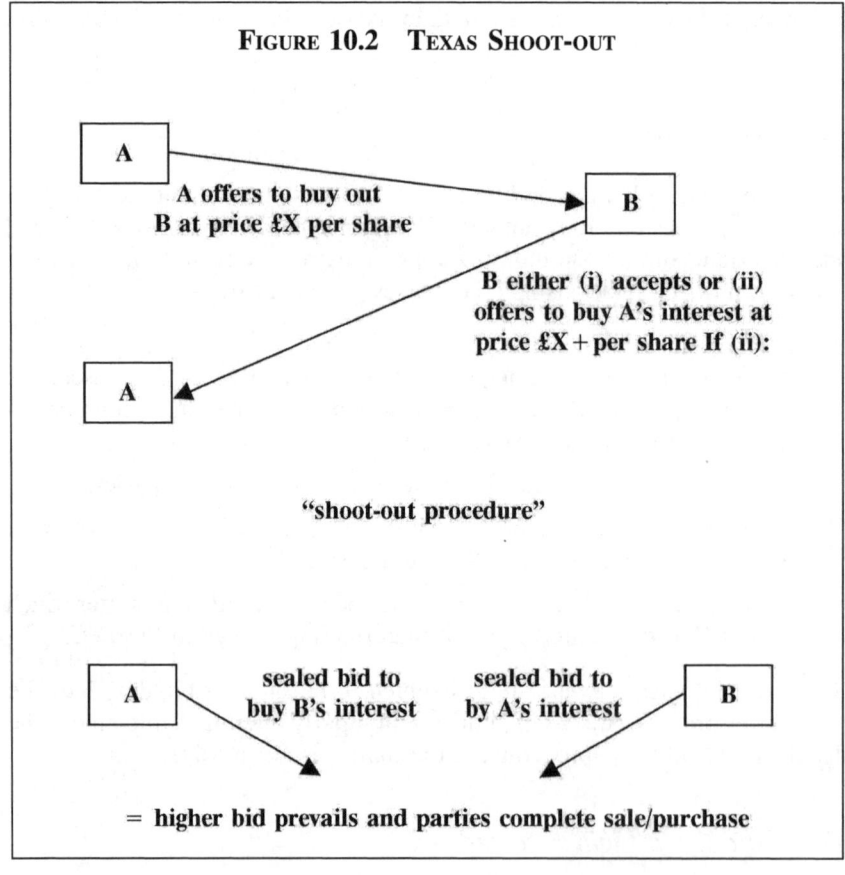

FIGURE 10.2 TEXAS SHOOT-OUT

If a bid auction is to be held, it may be necessary to develop further procedural rules to assist the process. In some cases, for instance, the parties may prefer to establish a procedure for a series of bid "rounds", with each bid being disclosed and with a requirement that any higher bid in the next "round" must exceed the previous highest bid by at least a specified percentage.

Fairest sealed bid

10–27 This is a more refined version of the "shoot-out" which does not rely solely on financial strength. Each party submits to an independent third party a sealed bid per share at which it is prepared to purchase the other party's shares in the joint venture. The independent third party then decides which of the bids represents the "fairest price" (i.e. the price closest to the price determined by such third party as the fair value or as the price based on the valuation method provided for in the joint venture agreement). The party losing the bid would then be required to sell its shares in the JVC at this price. Obviously, this method also involves a large element of risk, given the serious consequences of getting the bid price wrong.

Sale shoot-out

10–28 Another variant, serving also as an exit route, is for the "shoot-out" to operate on the basis of the price at which each party is willing to sell its interest in the JVC. For example:

(a) party A serves a notice on party B stating that it is willing to sell its shares in the JVC at a stated price;

(b) party B has a defined period in which to elect either (i) to buy at that price or (ii) to indicate that it wishes to sell its interest in the JVC to A at a stated price which must be lower than the price in A's notice;

(c) on receipt of party B's notice, if B has offered to sell its shares, A has a period in which to elect either (i) to buy at the price stated in B's notice or (ii) to indicate that it wishes to sell its interest in the JVC to B at a stated price which must be lower than that in B's notice.

The process goes on until one of the parties is a willing buyer (which will happen at some stage because the sale price is reduced each time). The procedure normally provides that the sale price has to be reduced by a specified percentage each time a notice is given in the process.

Deterrent approach

10–29 A different—and, in many ways, preferable—approach has two aims: (i) to enable a party to initiate a break-up of the joint venture in the event of major deadlock or breakdown but (ii) to provide a deterrent against this right being used too lightly or as a result of a deadlock being artificially engineered. Under this procedure, if there occurs a "deadlock event" and the parties fail (perhaps after a mediation procedure or other period for negotiation) to resolve the dispute:

(a) party A serves notice to initiate an agreed valuation procedure for determining the fair value per share of the JVC at the date of such notice (usually involving reference to a third party expert);

(b) after this valuation is determined, party B has a period in which to elect either: (i) to purchase A's shares in the JVC at a pre-agreed discount to the determined value per share (say, at 80 per cent of that valuation); or (ii) to sell its shares in the JVC to A at a pre-agreed premium to the determined value per share (say, 120 per cent of that valuation).

Such a procedure retains the advantage that it produces a resolution to the deadlock or breakdown. The price discount/premium acts, however, as a deterrent to the process being initiated lightly. It also acts as a strong incentive for a party wishing to end the venture to reach an amicable commercial resolution with the other party. If a "shoot-out" mechanism is included, this variant is one of the more attractive options.

"Multi-choice" approach

10–30 A realistic approach in many situations is to adopt a "multi-choice" provision whereby, upon the defined circumstances of deadlock or breakdown, a party can initiate by notice discussions of a variety of "divorce" routes (e.g. sale or purchase of one of the party's shares, possible buy-back of the relevant party's shares by the JVC, sale to a third party or break-up of the JVC's assets). A critical question is whether a party should have a residual right to call for winding-up of the JVC if the discussions have failed to produce an agreed solution after a defined period.

10–31 Such a "multi-choice" approach may not be linked specifically to a deadlock event. In many ventures, it may not be necessary or appropriate to have separate procedures for both termination and deadlock. If a residual right to call for winding-up of the JVC is contemplated, the easiest route may simply be to permit a party wishing to bring the venture to an end (whether for deadlock, breakdown or any other reason) to have a right to initiate "multi-choice" discussions with a right of either party thereafter to call for winding-up of the JVC but preferably only after a lengthy period during which the parties must endeavour to seek an agreed solution—see also para.13–18.

10–32 A "multi-choice" approach also works better than most other mechanisms in the context of a multi-party joint venture. Internal escalation and/or mediation procedures may work well within a multi-party joint venture—but the "shoot-out" varieties can rarely be structured to work properly or without undue complexity. Apart from trying to sell its shares, exercising any agreed put/call options or commencing inter-party discussions, the critical question in a multiparty venture is usually whether and in what circumstances a party should have a right to call for winding-up.

CONCLUSION

10–33 None of these measures is an ideal solution. The "shoot-out" variations can often be arbitrary and unsatisfactory in practice. Very few "divorce" resolution procedures are implemented and completed strictly in accordance with their contractual terms. Indeed, many consider that the in-built potential deadlock of a 50:50 joint venture company (e.g. through equality of voting rights at board and shareholder level) in itself provides the strongest structure for encouraging the parties to reach a commercially agreed solution. The severe commercial consequences to the business of the joint venture of an insoluble deadlock generally ensure that a sensible compromise will eventually be agreed between the parties.

10–34 If there is a prolonged and insoluble deadlock and no satisfactory termination procedure which can be triggered, the residual legal remedy is usually for a party to seek a winding-up of the JVC.[8] However, any such contested process is likely to be slow, costly and time-consuming. In any event, winding-up will invariably be a last resort and drastic remedy. A joint venture inevitably carries a commercial requirement for the parties to agree on certain matters. The parties need to agree when setting up the venture, and will invariably need to agree when terminating it.

> **Various examples of Deadlock Resolution Provisions discussed in this chapter are set out as Precedent 21 in Part E.**

---

[8] In English law, this would be under s.122(1)(g) of the Insolvency Act 1986, which gives the court power to order that a company be wound up where "the court is of the opinion that it is just and equitable that the company should be wound up"; see para.11–41 et seq., below. *Yenidje Tobacco Co, Re* [1916] 2 Ch. 426 is an example of a court exercising this power where there was a complete deadlock between two shareholders. The courts will be reluctant, though, to intervene if detailed provisions in the articles of association and/or joint venture agreement have been agreed at the outset of a venture setting out procedures for resolution in a deadlock situation.

Chapter 11

Duties between joint venture parties

The relationship between the parties is the foundation on which the success of any joint venture or alliance depends. Ideally, it should be a relationship of trust and confidence—with trust that the other party will act in the best interests of the venture. However, joint ventures and alliances can go wrong. There are inherent risks that one party may seek to act opportunistically in its own self-interest. Can these risks be reduced by terms in the joint venture or alliance contract? Are there underlying fiduciary duties between the parties? What statutory or other legal remedies are available in the event of a co-venturer's "misbehaviour"? This chapter addresses these issues.

Risk of self-interest and opportunistic behaviour

11–01 Opportunistic behaviour by a party in a joint venture or alliance may take a number of forms, for example:

(a) diverting some of the joint resources to its own activities;

(b) taking advantage of corporate opportunities which could have been exercised by the joint venture;

(c) using for its own ends confidential information belonging to the other party or built up jointly within the venture;

(d) engaging in activities competitive with the joint venture;

(e) poaching staff employed by the other party or seconded to the joint venture;

(f) unfair pricing in its dealings with the venture; or

(g) simply losing interest and commitment and concentrating on other activities.

11–02 A basic first protection for the parties against opportunistic behaviour is the commercial structure of the joint venture itself and the allocation of ownership, risk and reward between the parties. The aim should be to align the commercial incentives of each of the parties to act in the best interests of the venture. For instance, an "equity" joint venture (whether a jointly-owned company or a partnership) creates a profit-sharing model by which each party has an incentive to seek the profitable success of the venture. A 50:50 profit-sharing interest clearly creates equality of incentive. If only a minority share is allocated to one party, sufficient economic and commercial incentives should be established for that minority party to commit fully to the venture. If there are significant ancillary contracts, the economic terms should be sufficiently balanced so that a party's commitment and self-interest does not become excessively focused on its rewards from that contract rather than the success of the venture as a whole.

11–03 An equity joint venture also arguably enables a party (e.g. through the management structure of a joint venture company (JVC)) to exercise closer control and supervision over the contribution of the other party to the venture—compared with a contractual alliance where each party continues to own and manage its own resources. On the other hand, if there is a perceived risk of the other party not performing adequately or losing interest, a contractual alliance is easier to terminate and unwind than an equity joint venture.

Contractual Terms

Contractual responsibilities and incentives

11–04 Specifying clearly in the contract the responsibilities and obligations of each of the parties (e.g. as regards funding, provision of services, secondment of management personnel, supply of materials, licensing of technology or availability of research facilities) can also assist. This not only establishes legal commitment but also formulates each party's understanding and expectation of the other's behaviour. It reduces the chances of subsequent ambiguity or uncertainty and the potential for opportunistic behaviour being justified on the ground that it was not covered in the contract. Such an approach, though, is at the cost of increased time and intensity of joint venture negotiations. Insistence on excessive contractual detail can risk damaging the initial trust between the parties and may be too contentious and legalistic an approach. A balance has to be drawn.

11–05 In some alliances, incentives to promote the objectives of the venture can be built into the contractual terms for the venture as part of the specific allocation of risk and reward between the parties; for instance:

(a) allocation of joint venture profit to a party may be linked to performance or out-turn (e.g. as part of the remuneration for management or technical tasks undertaken by a particular party);

(b) where particular founders or shareholders have principal responsibility for management of the joint venture, "conversion" or "warrant" rights may be attached to their shares—entitling them to acquire additional equity shares at a future stage with the value of those rights being linked to performance of the JVC; or

(c) where a party has a "put" option as part of the agreed exit arrangements after an initial period, the price payable may be linked to financial performance of the JVC (see para.13–35 et seq.).

Misuse of confidential information

11–06 A major potential source of joint venture "misbehaviour" is misuse of confidential information. The danger is that a party will use for its own purposes confidential information or technology which derives either from (i) the other party's own "proprietary" information or (ii) technology or information developed by the joint venture and intended only for use in the joint venture business. Contractual terms cannot eliminate this risk but they are important measures to supplement any underlying legal protection in this area.

(1) *During negotiations*. During negotiations and throughout the formal due diligence process, a confidentiality agreement should be in place to protect the proprietary and business information that will be revealed by each party in the course of negotiations. Para.2–06 et seq. earlier describe both contractual and practical measures which may be considered appropriate at this stage to limit the risk of misuse by the other party.

(2) *During joint venture operations*. Once the venture has begun, initial obligations of confidentiality regarding each party's proprietary information should normally continue and be reflected in the shareholders' agreement—but may be revised to take account of the joint venture project (e.g. to reflect any specific technology licensing or similar arrangements agreed as part of the joint venture for which a properly drawn technology licence agreement may be appropriate-see chapter 17). The parties should also, importantly, address the manner in which newly-developed information within the joint venture will be treated. The important requirement is clarity:

(a) in some cases, the parties may agree that each participant is free to use jointly-developed information for its own business purposes; indeed this may be a central purpose of the collaboration. However, in such a case, it should still be clarified whether such information can be further disclosed by each party to third parties (e.g. through sublicences) or must be kept confidential and not sublicensed;

(b) in other cases, the use of joint venture-developed information may be restricted solely to use in the joint venture activity and not by the participants in their separate businesses. Tight practical measures within the joint venture's operations to support that confidentiality restriction will be appropriate if there is a risk of a party "abusing" that technology for its own purposes.

(3) *After termination or transfer.* The parties should also address contractually the manner in which information can be used following the termination of the joint venture or the sale or transfer of a party's interest. Underlying obligations of confidentiality, at common law at least, are often too hazy to provide an adequate remedy against misuse at this stage. Contractual terms should make it clear:

(a) whether, on termination, each party is freely entitled to use jointly-developed information or whether continuing confidentiality restrictions are to apply;
(b) whether rights to use specific confidential information or technology brought into the joint venture by one participant are to "revert back" solely to that participant;
(c) whether confidential documentary information, in the possession of a leaving party, is to be returned to the JVC and/or destroyed.

General legal obligations not "to breach confidence" may exist in many countries and provide some residual protection against abuse—but they are unlikely to assist in unravelling ambiguities or lack of clarity in the contractual arrangements. Clarity in the initial understanding of the parties is vital.

Non-compete

11–07 A related major potential source of inter-party dispute is unilateral competitive behaviour by one party. The extent of any general duties between joint venture parties at law—at least under English law—are, in very many cases, not sufficiently clear to provide any remedy. What are these general duties?

(1) The strictest duties exist where a partnership structure has been chosen for the venture since, as a default rule (*i.e.* unless specifically excluded) a partner must not compete with the partnership or use for its own benefit information confidential to the partnership.

(2) In relation to a corporate joint venture, on the other hand, general duties of good faith rarely apply under common law as between shareholders in a JVC and non-compete restrictions will not be implied as a matter of course. Competitive activity will not be

prevented in the absence of special circumstances—e.g. misuse by a majority shareholder-director for personal benefit of information derived from his position as a director of the JVC.[1]

It is therefore sensible, in most joint ventures, to be clear in the contract between the parties as to what can and cannot be undertaken by each party in its separate business.

11–08 The joint venture or alliance agreement (at least for any long-term venture) should accordingly address the scope of any non-compete or exclusivity obligation on each party. Issues to be addressed will commonly include the following:

(1) Is the non-compete obligation intended to apply to each "parent" undertaking and cover the activities of any subsidiaries within that parent's group?

(2) Is the non-compete obligation to have worldwide scope—or only specific territorial effect?

(3) What is the scope of the prohibited activity? This should be stated as clearly as practicable in order to avoid ambiguity and uncertainty.

(4) Are there any exceptions to the non-compete prohibition which should be spelt out (whether relating to existing or future activities of any party)? This is desirable if only to ensure that, if a party undertakes any such activity, it will not cause subsequent friction within the joint venture.

(5) Will the non-compete obligation apply to activities of any business acquired in future by a joint venture party or its "parent" even if the competing activity is only a small part of the acquired business—or are "carve-outs" to be allowed in order not to restrict unduly a party's flexibility in its future corporate activity? (If there are to be "carve-outs", these may be limited by size or turnover criteria—or by an obligation to offer the competing business to the joint venture.)

(6) Even if there are no non-compete obligations, will each party undertake an "exclusivity" obligation not to enter into a similar venture with any other party within a specified territory?

(7) Similarly, even if there is no non-compete obligation as such, is there to be any obligation on a party to offer first to the joint venture any "business opportunities" which arise within the scope of the joint venture's business?

(8) Is it intended that any non-compete undertakings should continue to apply—perhaps only for a limited period—after a party has ceased to be a partner or shareholder in the venture?

---

[1] See e.g. *Cook v Deeks* [1916] A.C. 554 and para.8–56 et seq. earlier.

(9) Is it appropriate to include an undertaking not to entice away or employ officers or employees of the JVC (or perhaps senior employees of the other joint venture party)?

There is a no substitute for clarity at the outset on these issues. The residual legal duties owed between joint venture parties will rarely be sufficient to provide a clear or prompt remedy—and, more importantly, it is vital to the trust and understanding between joint venture parties that these matters are clarified at the beginning of the relationship.

11–09 A warning must, though, be cautioned against excessive non-compete obligations. Competition law takes a keen interest in ensuring that any restraints are reasonable, proportionate and fairly related to the business of the venture itself—and not improper anti-competitive arrangements between the parties which go beyond restrictions "ancillary" to the establishment of the venture (see para.16–16 et seq. under "Competition and regulatory issues").

Contractual remedies

11–10 Additional protection against poor performance by the other party, or the venture generally, can sometimes be obtained by express contractual remedies "triggered" by specific circumstances linked to that performance. There are broadly two kinds:

(1) A party may preserve an ability "to cut its losses" by having a contractual right to terminate its interest in the joint venture or alliance in certain circumstances (irrespective of proof of any default by the other party).

(2) A shareholders' agreement or other alliance agreement may contain conventional provisions setting out or preserving remedies in the event of breach of contract by the other party (including possibly, in the event of material default, a right of termination and/or buy-out of the other party's interest in the venture).

Right of termination by notice

11–11 A simple and clear remedy, appropriate in many alliances, is for a party to have a discretionary right to terminate its participation in the venture by notice[2] at any time (perhaps after a minimum period of the venture or a failure by the venture to achieve certain specified "milestones" or performance targets). Such a provision does not in itself encourage performance or commitment levels by the other party—but it provides

---

[2] See generally para.13–09 et seq. for further discussion of termination rights.

some deterrent or "escape" route if the venture fails. It provides by far the easiest contractual form of protection since a party has no need to prove any default by the other party. Any such right of termination may, depending on the alliance, require further supporting provisions:

(a) possibly, terms providing for a "buy-out" of the terminating party's interest in the venture by the other party (usually at a fair value—although some discount to fair value may be the price which the terminating party should bear for having a clear exit route in these circumstances);

(b) alternatively, terms providing for winding-up of the venture—sometimes accompanied by a pre-agreed "break up" allocation between the parties of any of the assets or technology of the venture.

Default remedies

11–12 Contractual remedies will also apply in the event of a breach of contract. In any joint venture or alliance situation, any claim for breach will usually be a claim of last resort—but that, in itself, is not a reason for failing to include such a "stick" by way of contractual remedy for clear default. Default in performing obligations in a joint venture context may include not only obligations under the shareholders' agreement but also ancillary contracts between the JVC and the defaulting party. These contracts should normally contain their own regime for default. One important procedural point is to ensure that the defaulting party cannot block actions which are required to be taken by the JVC to enforce its contractual rights under any such ancillary contract—see para.9–24.

11–13 In addition to normal contractual remedies (e.g. damages), the shareholders' agreement may include an ultimate remedy for an innocent party to buy out the shares of the defaulting party in the JVC in the event of material default. In practice, it may be difficult to enforce such a buy-out provision prior to exhaustion of any formal dispute resolution process, such as litigation or arbitration proceedings, in which an issue is frequently whether there has occurred a default (and by which party) justifying the remedy. Another issue may be the price payable in the event of buy-out on default. It is sometimes agreed that the buy-out price should be at a discount to fair value—in order to provide a deterrent against breach. Although it is not beyond doubt, the general view is that such provisions should be upheld if part of an arm's length commercial agreement when establishing the joint venture arrangements—see para.7–48.

Alliance charter

11–14 Some parties prefer a different and more general approach. In the case of many alliances—particularly contractual alliances—the specific activities or responsibilities to be undertaken by each party may not be identifiable at the outset but will develop through the working of the venture. In these cases, a different approach is simply to establish in initial negotiations a "charter" of principles or expectations. This "charter" may not be legally enforceable but, if both parties have been engaged in its development, it can become a set of principles "owned" by both parties and thereby help to create a positive dynamic leading the parties to identify with and promote the venture—see also para.4–08 et seq.

UNDERLYING FIDUCIARY OBLIGATIONS BETWEEN PARTIES

Any underlying implied duties of good faith?

11–15 If structural or contractual measures fail to prevent a party to a joint venture or alliance from acting in a self-interested "opportunistic" way, does the general law provide the innocent party with any legal remedy? Is there any principle whereby —in the absence of express contractual terms—parties to a joint venture or alliance owe fiduciary or other general duties of good faith to each other in their dealings in relation to the venture and, if so, what is the extent of that duty? The variety of joint venture and alliance situations which exist means that no simple answers can be given.[3]

11–16 The existence and scope of any fiduciary obligations are, at least under English law, largely shaped by the legal form of the joint venture or alliance:

(1) *Contractual alliance*. It is doubtful whether parties to a simple contractual alliance owe under English law any inherent implied duties of good faith to each other beyond the scope of the specific terms of their relationship—partnership although, if the relationship strays into a "partnership" at law, the courts will be willing to supplement the relationship with implied terms and duties under partnership law.

(2) *Partnership*. Partners in a partnership, on the other hand, owe inherent duties of utmost good faith to fellow partners. Whilst these may be modified or clarified in the particular circumstances, it is unlikely that these fiduciary duties can be eliminated entirely.

(3) *Corporate*. A corporate joint venture involves, at law, a crucial distinction between duties owed in the capacity of shareholders and duties owed by directors. In simplistic terms, the orthodox view is that

---

[3] See further: Gerald Bean, *Fiduciary Obligations and Joint Ventures* (Oxford Clarendon Press, 1995) and John Birchall, *Duties of Good Faith in Commercial Joint Ventures? Contractual Duties, Fiduciary Duties and Shareholder Remedies* [2005] J.B.L. 269.

a shareholder owes no duty to other shareholders (or the company) when it exercises its rights whereas directors do owe significant duties to the company—see para.11–28 et seq. below.

(4) *LLP.* The new legal form of an LLP is a "hybrid" in many ways. Whilst there is no automatic duty of good faith between members, there will almost certainly be implied (unless clearly excluded) a number of quasi-partnership duties owed by each of the members.

We examine the position in relation to each of these principal legal forms in a little more detail in this chapter.

11–17 Questions of implied or underlying duties will also invariably be a matter for the governing law of the relationship. There appear, for instance, to be significant differences between the relatively narrow approach of the English courts compared with broader principles of civil law systems—with the latter being more willing to recognise general principles of good faith or loyalty in dealings between contracting parties. Each national law may have its own approach. The law is still in a developing state in many countries.

Contractual alliance

11–18 English law does not—at least under traditional principles—recognise a general duty of good faith between contracting parties (absent any added ingredient such as a "partnership").[4]

11–19 However, there are decisions in various common law countries which indicate that situations verging on partnership could result in the courts either imposing a general duty or interpreting contracts so as to include implied obligations of good faith.

(1) Most recently, in one particular case[5] an English court was prepared to decide that a term of good faith should be implied into an agreement (not reduced to writing) between two parties who established a property joint venture but never formed a JVC as such. The court judged that the relationship (though not a partnership in the strict sense) was a fiduciary one giving rise to a duty on both parties.

(2) There appears to be clear authority in the US (and in some Commonwealth countries such as Australia and New Zealand) for the proposition that participants in a natural resources joint venture owe fiduciary duties to one another in much the same way as partners.[6]

---

[4] See, for instance, *Interfoto Picture Library Ltd v Stiletto Visual Programmes Ltd* [1988] 1 All E.R. 348 where Bingham L.J. rejected any overriding principle that, in making and carrying out contracts, parties should act in good faith: " . . . English law has, characteristically, committed itself to no such overriding principle but has developed piecemeal solutions in response to demonstrated problems of unfairness."

[5] *Ahron Nathan v Zvi Smilovitch* [2002] EWHC 1629 (Ch).

[6] See Gerald Bean, *Fiduciary Obligations and Joint Ventures.*

(3) The US courts have traditionally found that, like a partnership, members of a joint venture owe to each other strict duties of good faith, fairness and honesty and one member may not secretly advantage himself over his partner(s). This duty is even clearer when a party has a position of managerial control[7] or stands in a position of trust and confidence in relation to, or control over, another's property.

11-20 It is doubtful whether the English courts will be willing to adopt any general implied duty of good faith in a contractual alliance but, in appropriate circumstances, they are likely to be prepared to imply obligations of good faith requiring full disclosure of material facts between the parties or obligations to prevent a co-venturer acting to the detriment of the alliance by abusing information or opportunities connected with the venture (irrespective of specific contractual terms). This is an area which is ripe for further judicial analysis and development given the range of contractual alliances which are now being established.

Partnerships

11-21 Perhaps unknowingly, by adopting a partnership structure for the venture, the parties will be adopting the duties of good faith owed between partners. These may vary between jurisdictions. Under English law:

(1) Partnership is a fiduciary relationship and partners owe a duty of good faith towards each other.

(2) Every partner must account to the firm for any benefit derived by that partner, without the consent of the other partners, from any transaction concerning the partnership or from any use of partnership property or information.

These principles provide a potentially powerful legal weapon for use by an "innocent" party to counter detrimental behaviour by another partner where the venture has taken the partnership form (particularly where there has been less than full disclosure by the other party).

Corporate joint venture

11-22 Duties in a corporate joint venture are more complex—with a legal distinction being drawn between duties as a shareholder and duties as a

---

[7] See e.g. *J Leo Johnson, Inc.*, 156 A. 2d 499, 503 (Del. 1959) and further *Dremco, Inc v South Chapel Hill Gardens, Inc.*, 654 N.E. 2d 501,504 (Ill. App. 1995): "The precise nature and intensity of the duty of loyalty depends, however, upon the degree of independent authority exercised by the fiduciary and the reasonable expectations of the parties at the beginning of the relationship." See also para.11-11 earlier.

director of a JVC. The orthodox view under English law, in relation to the duties of shareholders in a corporate joint venture, is that no such duty exists and that a shareholder is free to vote or act in such a way as it considers fit in its own interests without any duties (in its capacity as a shareholder) to the other shareholder(s) or without being required to consider the best interests of the JVC.[8] The approach taken by the law to the duties of shareholders contrasts (paradoxically in the context of joint ventures) with the more onerous duties imposed on directors.

11–23 However, there are several reasons for believing that this orthodox view may need qualification.

(1) The English courts are recognising that many corporate joint ventures are quasi-partnership in nature[9] and that, in some circumstances, this may give rise to partnership-equivalent principles. The traditional approach frequently fits uneasily with the structure of a corporate joint venture where there is a quasi-partnership relationship between the parties.

(2) The Court of Appeal has expressed the view—again in the context of a "quasi-partnership" relationship—that a duty of a shareholder-director to act in good faith to another shareholder can arise in certain joint venture circumstances.[10]

(3) Directors owe duties of good faith and other fiduciary duties to the JVC. Where the director is also a shareholder or a management representative of the shareholder, it can often be difficult or unrealistic to distinguish the capacity in which a person is acting.

(4) Other European (and indeed US) laws are comfortable with the concept of "good faith" in this context. The international nature of so many joint ventures may create further pressure on the English courts

---

[8] See *Percival v Wright* [1902] 2 Ch. 421 and *Northern Counties Security Ltd v Jackson & Steeple Ltd* [1974] 1 W.L.R. 1133.

[9] In *Yenidje Tobacco Co Ltd, Re* [1916] 2 Ch. 426, a case involving a claim for winding-up on the "just and equitable" ground, the court adapted principles to a jointly owned company which would have applied in the case of a partnership. "It is contrary to the good faith and essence of the agreement between the parties that the state of things which we find here should be allowed to continue . . .". *Ebrahimi v Westbourne Galleries Ltd* [1973] A.C. 360 was also a case involving a claim for winding-up on the "just and equitable" ground. Lord Wilberforce acknowledged that equity may enable the court to subject the exercise of legal rights to equitable considerations in circumstances "which may make it unjust, or inequitable, to insist on legal rights, or to exercise them in a particular way".

[10] *Elliot v Wheeldon* [1993] B.C.L.C. 53, where the Court of Appeal expressed the view that an obligation to act in good faith may arise in a joint venture context and stated: "Where A and B enter into a joint venture for the carrying on of a business through the medium of company C, with A as continuing guarantor of C's liabilities, it must, at the least, be arguable that B owes a duty to A to conduct himself as a director of C in such a way as not, except in good faith, to increase A's liabilities under his guarantee." The relationship between the joint venture parties does not appear to have been documented in this case. See also *Ahron Nathan v Zvi Smilovitch* and para.11–21 earlier; it is doubtful whether this decision would have been any different if the proposed JVC had actually been incorporated. Also, see *Murad v Al-Saraj* [2005] EWCA Civ 959 where the court established a fiduciary duty between parties proposing to establish a JVC and the defendant was liable to account for a secret commission obtained on the acquisition of a property for the new JVC.

to take a more flexible view and to base decisions not on the legal form of the venture but on the essential nature of the relationship.

(5) Even if earlier cases regarding free exercise by a shareholder of its voting rights are upheld,[11] the courts may be willing to draw a distinction between the exercise of such formal share rights and other acts or behaviour by that party in relation to the joint venture (e.g. independent commercial behaviour which is knowingly detrimental to the JVC's business).

11-24 It appears, though, that the English courts will look very carefully at the particular circumstances of the corporate joint venture concerned before implying or imposing any such general fiduciary duty on a party qua shareholder.[12] If (as in most large-scale joint ventures) the arrangements between the parties are the product of detailed and sophisticated contractual agreements entered into by companies having full access to legal advice, it is unlikely that the courts will be willing to imply any further or additional duties between them beyond the specific terms of any shareholders' agreement.[13]

Limited liability partnership (LLP)

11-25 The LLP structure raises some interesting issues in this context which have yet to be explored judicially. Conceptually different from a limited company, an LLP arguably reflects better the relationships in a corporate joint venture—it is the members themselves (i.e. the joint venture parties rather than the managers/directors) who are subject to the inter-partner duties implied by law. Each member will be in a fiduciary relationship with the LLP and must act in good faith towards the LLP. A member will, in particular, have certain "default duties"[14] including:

(a) an obligation to account to the LLP for any profits from a competing business undertaken without consent; and

---

[11] Some cases suggest there may also be equitable limits on the exercise of these rights—e.g. *Clemens v Clemens Bros Ltd* [1976] 2 All E.R. 268 per Foster J. at p.281.
[12] See *Button v Phelps* [2006] EWHC 53(Ch) where it was said that "a court should be wary of importing equitable obligations into a commercial relationship. A joint venture is not *per se* a relationship giving rise to fiduciary obligations in equity, although it might do so".
[13] In *Bond Corp Holdings Ltd v Granada Group* (unreported, May 17, 1991), the plaintiff claimed that the four other main shareholders in British Satellite Broadcasting Limited (BSB) had breached an implied contractual duty to act in good faith in their dealings with it, as a shareholder in BSB, by imposing allegedly unreasonable conditions on the plaintiff's freedom to find a purchaser for BSB shares allocated to it under a refinancing rights issue. Harman J. found it impossible to imply such an obligation: "I can't see there is any implied duty to act in good faith between these parties beyond the express duties [in the agreements] to act in good faith which arise . . . [T]his contract is exhaustive and exhausting to read and in the circumstances there is no reason to go any further and add additional terms by implication".
[14] Regs 7 and 8, Limited Liability Partnership Regulations 2001. See also the discussion on a member's duties in J. Whittaker and J. Machall *The Law of Limited Liability Partnerships* at p.134 et seq. (Jordans, 2004).

(b) an obligation to account to the LLP for any private benefit derived without consent from use of LLP property.

There is, though, no automatic or "default" duty of good faith on the members to each other—and there is no general application of partnership law to LLPs (although, arguably, a similar duty to act honestly and fairly may be implied). The "default" rules may be expressly excluded by the LLP agreement between the members or if it is clear from all the circumstances that particular duties were not intended to be applicable. In a joint venture between corporate partners, one may expect the LLP agreement to exclude these "default" rules. However, the LLP may develop as an entity which more closely reflects a principle of applying "quasi-partnership" duties to the inter-member relations of a corporate joint venture. Judicial attention to these issues in due course will be interesting.

Express good faith obligations

11–26 Many alliances and joint ventures do support the initial commitments of the parties by including express declarations that each party will act in "good faith" in "mutual co-operation", or similar expressions, to promote the venture or in their dealings with each other. What do these terms mean legally? English case law has so far offered only limited guidance.

(1) The English courts[15] have firmly concluded that an obligation to carry on negotiations in good faith is not legally enforceable as it lacks sufficient certainty or objectivity and also because of the court's inability to police any such obligation.

(2) Where the English courts have accepted an implied term of good faith, it has been narrowly construed—generally being interpreted as a negative requirement not to act in bad faith[16] or, where a discretionary power is exercised, to act fairly and reasonably in the exercise of that discretion. Although there is no clear judicial precedent, this could nevertheless act in some circumstances as a restraint on the ability of a party to exercise a right of termination for convenience.

(3) Where there is an express or implied duty under a contract to co-operate, the courts have been willing to imply a term that a party shall not prevent the other party from performing and, if co-operation is required for that other's performance, that it will reasonably co-operate.[17]

---

[15] *Walford v Miles* [1992] 2 A.C. 128.
[16] In *Medforth v Blake* [2000] Ch. 86, the Court of Appeal opined that "the concept of good faith should not be diluted by treating it as capable of being breached by conduct that is not dishonest or otherwise tainted by bad faith".
[17] See e.g. *Mackay v Dick* [1881] 6 A.C. 251 per Lord Blackburn at p.263 but "the law can enforce co-operation only in a limited degree—to the extent that it is necessary to make the contract workable": per Devlin J. in *Mona Oil Equipment & Supply Co Ltd v Rhodesia Railways Ltd* [1949] 2 All E.R. 1014.

(4) Where the contract allows a party room for discretion or further negotiation, the courts have been reluctant to deny that party the right to take into account its own financial and technical interests when operating these provisions.[18]

(5) Adopting partnership law principles, an obligation to act in good faith may impose duties of disclosure of facts or circumstances (or possibly the intentions of a joint venture party) where they are likely to affect materially the business of the joint venture.[19]

11–27 Other jurisdictions are noticeably happier with "good faith" concepts. Civil law jurisdictions recognise and enforce positive obligations of fair and open dealing including full disclosure in commercial negotiations—see para.20–13 et seq. In the US, the Uniform Commercial Code (UCC) s.1–203 provides: "Every contract or duty within this Act imposes an obligation of good faith for its performance or enforcement."[20] The Australian courts have regarded "good faith" and "acting reasonably" as overlapping concepts.[21] It will be interesting to see if the English courts are willing to develop firmer principles in this area. Certainly, the growth and variety of joint venture and alliance arrangements are likely to lead to more situations in which opportunistic behaviour is alleged to be contrary to express or implied "good faith" obligations.

ENFORCEMENT OF DUTIES OF DIRECTORS

Duties of directors to JVC

11–28 It is somewhat ironic in the joint venture context that, contrary to the position of duties between shareholders, directors of a JVC do assume significant underlying legal duties—including fiduciary obligations. They probably constitute, at least in theory, the strongest legal principles

---

[18] In *Phillips v Enron (Europe) Ltd* [1997] C.L.C. 329 the Court of Appeal concluded that a buyer could take its own interests into account despite a contractual obligation to "co-ordinate" commissioning. Potter L.J. stated: "I see no reason to suppose that ... in any area of activity in which room was left for manoeuvre or further negotiation, they were not at liberty to take into account their own financial position and act in a manner most beneficial to them, short of bad faith or breach of an express term of the contract."
[19] See e.g. *Ahron Nathan v Zvi Smilovitch* [2002] EWHC 1629 (Ch).
[20] The US Restatement (Second) Contracts, s.205 (not law but persuasive) includes a list of conduct which would be in bad faith which is wide in scope, including "evasion of the spirit of the bargain, lack of diligence and slacking off, wilful rendering of imperfect performance, abuse of power to specify terms and interference with or failure to co-operate in the other party's performance".
[21] See e.g. Finkelstein J. in *Garry Rogers (Aust) Pty Ltd v Subaru (Aust) Pty Ltd* (1999) A.T.P.R. 41–703: "provided the party exercising the power acts reasonably in all the circumstances, the duty to act fairly and in good faith will ordinarily be satisfied." Similarly, *South Sydney District Rugby League Football Club Ltd v News Ltd* (2000) 177 A.L.R. 611.

available to restrain "misbehaviour" within a corporate venture where a party's directors are involved in the offending acts or decisions. These duties will, of course, be a matter for the relevant corporate law of the jurisdiction in which the JVC is incorporated. Although similar issues will arise in most jurisdictions, the following discussion relates to the position under English law.

11–29 These duties can cause particular difficulties for a director of a JVC appointed by a "parent" shareholder.

(1) When acting as a director of the JVC, the director should under the strict doctrine exercise his powers (in particular, voting rights at board meetings) using independent judgement and to promote the success of the JVC as a whole. The fact that he has been appointed by a particular shareholder is irrelevant—see further para.8–49 et seq.

(2) An important duty[22] in this context is that a director must avoid a conflict of interest—particularly in relation to "the exploitation of any property, information or opportunity" of the JVC (e.g. use for his own or another's benefit an opportunity of which he became aware while a director). Under the general duty laid down by the Companies Act, it is immaterial whether or not the JVC could take advantage of the property, information or opportunity. This duty will not be infringed if the matter is authorised by the company's board of directors (provided, in this case, that such authorisation is agreed or would effectively have been agreed without the participation of any interested director).

(3) Remedies can be strict—including not only an injunction to prevent continuance of the breach but also a liability to account for benefits received as a result of the breach (a liability which may extend to any third party, e.g. a company employing the director, complicit in the director's breach of duty).

There have been a number of cases, prior to the 2006 Act coming into force, where the courts have addressed allegations of abuse of "corporate opportunity" or similar breach of fiduciary duty by a director and which have potential resonance in the context of joint ventures.

---

[22] s.175 Companies Act 2006.

CORPORATE OPPORTUNITY: SOME RECENT UK CASES

- *Director forced to resign and acting at client's request not in breach.* A director was excluded from a company's affairs and effectively forced to resign by the majority shareholder. He did not resign in order to divert any business opportunity from the company but agreed, at a major existing client's request, to work on that client's affairs after his departure. In the circumstances, he was not in breach of his fiduciary duies as director during his period of notice. *Foster Bryant Surveying Ltd v Bryant* [2007] EWCA Civ 200.

- *Director and his new company liable to account for benefits from diverted opportunities.* A director resigned and, through a company controlled by him, took over certain contracts which had been started with the claimant company. Both the director and his new company were held liable to account for all benefits received from the contracts. A director could not set the groundwork for diverting a corporate opportunity whilst a director and then take it for himself after he had ceased to be a director. It did not matter whether the company was in a position to exploit the opportunity. *Kingsley IT Consulting Ltd v McIntosh* [2006] All E.R. (D) 237. See also *Shepherds Investments Ltd v Walters* [2006] EWHC 836 (Ch).

- *Company participating in director's breach also liable to hand over sums.* A director was in breach of fiduciary duty by using a company's database and goodwill to divert business to another company. As regards the latter company, participating in the director's breach of duty, the court considered it unconscionable for that company not to be liable to hand over sums received as a result of the breach of duty. *Quarter Master UK Ltd (in liquidation) v Pyke* [2005] 1 B.C.L.C. 245.

- *No breach if opportunity outside scope of company's business.* The court said, in the circumstances of that case, a director who exploits an opportunity for his own benefit would not breach the "no conflict" rule if the corporate opportunity was outside the scope of the company's business by virtue of constitutional restrictions on the company's activities. *Wilkinson v West Coast Capital* [2005] EWHC 309.

- *Irrelevant that opportunity came to director privately if in company's line of business.* The claimants were members of a family company originally founded by two brothers. The company acquired properties for investment purposes. Relations broke down. One brother's family acquired on their own a property adjacent to an existing investment of the family company. It was held that this was in breach of his fiduciary duty as a director of the family company. It was irrelevant that the business opportunity came to him privately. A director is under a duty to make a business opportunity available to his company if it is in the company's line of business. *Bhullar v Bhullar* [2003] EWCA Civ 424.

- *Directorship of competitor: no breach in actual circumstances.* The Court of Appeal decided, on the particular facts, that there was no breach of fiduciary duty even though the defendant remained a director of the claimant company but set up a new competing company. The court stressed that the director must not make use of the claimant's property or confidential information to profit the second company. *In Plus Group Ltd v Pyke* [2002] EWCA Civ 370.

> - *Maturing business opportunity diverted to rival agency.* The first defendant resigned as a director and employee of the claimant which he had formed with two colleagues. He set up a rival advertising agency, with funding provided by a third party, and became managing director. Staff of the claimants later joined him and his rival agency took over a major client he had introduced to the original agency while a director. It was held that a maturing business opportunity of which he had knowledge as a director was to be treated as "property" of the company. He was liable to account for profits whether he exploited the opportunity personally, through a partnership or through a company controlled by him. *CMS Dolphin Ltd v Simonet* [2001] 2 B.C.L.C. 704.

11–30 The general rule is that a director's fiduciary duties are, as a matter of English corporate law, owed by him personally to the company of which he is a director and not directly to the shareholders.[23]

(1) A shareholder will not, therefore, itself have an individual claim against a director for breach of his duties to the company. A shareholder cannot recover damages from a wrongdoer for any loss which is merely a reflection of loss suffered by the company itself.[24]

(2) These cases apply to a breach of duty by a director of the JVC. A director common to both the JVC and a joint venture parent may be in a different, but nevertheless tricky, position. Whilst he may not be liable to account where a corporate opportunity (useful to the JVC) arises in his capacity qua director of the parent company rather than as director of the JVC, the dividing line will often be difficult to draw. He will be in a risky position if his potential "conflict of interest" is not fully disclosed.

(3) The ability of a minority shareholder to bring a derivative action on behalf of the JVC in respect of a breach of duty by a director (including a breach at the behest of a majority controlling shareholder) is now enhanced under English law by a new statutory derivative procedure—see para.11–31 et seq.

Any claim directly by one joint venture party against another (rather than the JVC) would, however, have to rely on the terms of the shareholders' agreement or on a breach of duty of the kind discussed at para.11–23 et seq. If no contractual remedy for termination or breach is available, the threat of a claim for "unfair prejudice" under s.994 of the Companies Act 2006 may be the residual route.

---

[23] Companies Act 2006, s.170(1). See *Percival v Wright* [1902] 2 Ch. 421 and *Towcester Racecourse Co Ltd v Racecourse Association Ltd* [2002] EWHC 2141 (although it appears that, in certain special factual circumstances, a limited fiduciary duty to members might arise: *Stein v Blake* [1998] 1 All E.R. 724 and *Peskin v Anderson* [2001] 1 B.C.L.C. 372).

[24] *Giles v Rhind* [2002] EWCA Civ 1428. Compare *Johnson v Gore Wood & Co* [2002] 2 A.C. 1 and *Gardner v Parker* [2004] B.C.L.C. 554.

Statutory derivative action

11–31 A "derivative action" is a claim brought by an individual shareholder, acting on behalf of the company, against one or more of the company's directors. The Companies Act 2006 contains an important new statutory derivative action—which effectively replaces and expands the previous common law. Whilst the new action has many limitations and is unlikely to lead to a flood of litigation, it is a potential weapon in the armoury of a minority shareholder seeking remedy against improper behaviour by a majority shareholder in a JVC involving the latter's directors.

11–32 In a joint venture context, there are three significant developments compared with the previous law:

(1) The new procedure broadens the circumstances in which a derivative action may be brought. It can be based on any "actual or proposed act or omission involving negligence, default, breach of duty or breach of trust by a director of a company". It therefore includes breach of the general duty to exercise reasonable care, skill and diligence.[25]

(2) The derivative action is based on a director's breach of duty—but it may also be brought against other persons involved in any such breach. So, in a claim based on misuse of the JVC's confidential information or abuse of a corporate opportunity which a director acquired through being a director of the JVC, the derivative action could extend to a claim against the corporate shareholder of whom that director was a nominee. (Such a doctrine probably existed under the previous law[26] but the route to challenge a majority shareholder may now be easier to pursue.)

(3) Any resolution to ratify a director's negligence, default, breach of duty or breach of trust will not be effective unless the votes of those members or directors personally interested in the ratification are disregarded. Ratification will be more difficult to achieve.

It should be stressed, though, that the statutory derivative action can only be brought as a remedy to prevent or recover damage or loss to the JVC—not as a means to recover loss to the shareholder itself.

---

[25] Under the common law, a claim would not lie merely for negligence: e.g. *Pavlides v Jensen* [1956] Ch 565.

[26] Under the doctrines of unconscionable behaviour, abuse of confidence or "accessory" liability of a third party who assists or procures a breach of duty: see e.g. *Bhullar v Bhullar* [2003] 2 B.C.L.C. 241 and *Quarter Master UK Ltd (in liquidation) v Pyke* [2005] 1 B.C.L.C. 245.

> **STATUTORY DERIVATIVE ACTION: PROCEDURE**
>
> The new procedure, under ss.260 to 263 of the Companies Act 2006,[28] involves a number of significant limitations and procedural steps:
>
> - *Stage 1.* A claim is made against the director (technically joining in the company itself) together with an application to the court for permission to continue.
> - *Stage 2.* There is an intermediate assessment by the court, based on filed evidence, to establish whether the shareholder has a prima facie case. This enables the courts to dismiss non-meritorious claims at an early stage. If the court decides against the shareholder, the latter can request an oral hearing.
> - *Stage 3.* If the action passes the intermediate hurdle, it proceeds as an interim application and the court considers further whether to grant permission to the shareholder to continue the claim. The court must take into account a number of factors. In particular:
>   — The court must refuse permission to continue if it concludes that (a) it would not be in the company's best interest to continue or (b) the relevant act has been authorised or ratified by the relevant decision-making body in the company (without participation of the interested shareholder or director).
>   — It may also refuse permission to continue if it considers that the shareholder is not acting in good faith or that the act will in future be authorised or ratified by the company's other shareholders.
>
> Only if court permission to continue is given will the action proceed to a full substantive hearing. There are, therefore, many procedural hurdles for an aggrieved shareholder to overcome. There is also the risk that, if the court declines permission to continue, the shareholder will become liable for the company's and/or director's costs of defending the application.

11–33 Despite these procedural hurdles, the new statutory derivative action is an important step. It is an alternative legal weapon which may be considered by a minority shareholder "wronged" by the misbehaviour of a majority shareholder and its directors. It will be interesting to see how its use develops in practice. It will only be practical, or indeed feasible, in relatively extreme circumstances of breakdown. It is unlikely to supplant an "unfair prejudice" claim under s.994 where the real aim is for the minority shareholder to be "bought out" of the JVC.

OTHER CORPORATE LAW REMEDIES

11–34 Most corporate law systems provide some residual remedies in the

---

[27] Procedurally, the rules are supplemented by the Civil Procedure (Amendment) Rules 2007 (SI 2007/2204).

event of oppressive or excessive behaviour by one shareholder towards another (generally behaviour by a "majority" shareholder towards a "minority" shareholder). These remedies have frequently been applied in the context of family owned companies but rarely in the context of joint venture relationships between corporate parties. However, these remedies do provide some background of protection in extreme circumstances.

Common law: fraud on a minority

11–35 The so-called rule in *Foss v Harbottle*[28] established the basic principle that a minority shareholder cannot sue for a wrong done to the company, or to remedy an internal irregularity, where the majority can lawfully ratify it. This is to prevent futile actions. Certain limitations or exceptions to this common law rule were developed. In particular, a minority shareholder could sue (by way of a derivative action on behalf of itself and other innocent members) where the conduct is a "fraud on the minority" and the wrongdoers were in control of the company. This extended to acts which, because of their nature, were incapable of ratification including:[29]

(a) expropriation by the majority shareholder-director of the company's property (including corporate business opportunities) for the shareholder-director's own benefit;

(b) negligent sale of assets at an undervalue to the directors themselves[30] (but note that this did not include negligence, however gross, where the shareholder—directors did not benefit—e.g. a sale of assets to a third party at an undervalue[31]).

Under English law, the common law action has now been replaced by the new statutory derivative action under the Companies Act 2006. Similar principles may, though, continue in other jurisdictions to support an action in extreme circumstances.

Unfairly prejudicial conduct: s.994

11–36 Many jurisdictions give limited statutory or equivalent rights to protect a minority party itself against extreme abuse of its position by a majority shareholder. The main statutory remedy for a minority shareholder which has developed under English law is under ss.994–996 of the Companies Act 2006 (replacing, in identical form, ss.459–461 of the 1985

---

[28] *Foss v Harbottle* [1843] 2 Hare 461.
[29] *Cook v Deeks* [1916] A.C. 554 and see para.11–29 et seq. earlier.
[30] *Daniels v Daniels* [1978] Ch. 406.
[31] *Pavlides v Jensen* [1956] Ch. 565.

Act). The court has wide discretion to grant such relief as it considers fit where any member can show that:

> "the company's affairs are being or have been conducted in a manner which is unfairly prejudicial to the interests of its members generally or of some part of its members (including at least himself) or that any actual or proposed act or omission of the company (including an act or omission on its behalf) is or would be so prejudicial."

Unfair prejudice

11–37 The concept of unfair prejudice is not clearly defined. It represents a level of misbehaviour or mismanagement which justifies intervention by the court. The assessment is whether a reasonable bystander would, having regard to the consequences of the conduct complained of, consider the member's interests as having been unfairly prejudiced.[32] This does act as a residual (but very residual) remedy against improper acts by a shareholder (usually a majority shareholder) in a joint venture.

11–38 The courts have continued to indicate that the test of "unfairness" will generally be whether or not the alleged conduct was contrary to the terms and agreements between the parties or (especially where the relationship is effectively a quasi-partnership) their legitimate expectations as to the conduct of the JVC's affairs. Terms of any shareholders' agreement between them will be important in establishing the interests and expectations of the parties.[33]

11–39 Numerous cases have been brought under this jurisdiction. The more detailed texts on company law should be consulted for a fuller analysis. Examples which may be of particular interest in the context of corporate joint ventures include the following:

---

[32] See *Noble A & Son (Clothing) Ltd, Re* [1983] B.C.L.C. 273.
[33] See e.g. *Vocam Europe Ltd, Re* [1998] BCC where the terms of the shareholders' agreement were given priority over the company's articles of association. See also *Astec (BSR) Plc, Re* [1998] 2 B.C.L.C. 556 where the alleged misconduct did not infringe a shareholders' agreement and a s.459 petition was refused.

Unfair Prejudice: Some UK cases under s.459

(now s.994 of the Companies Act 2006)

- *No right of unilateral exit.* In *O'Neill v Phillips* [1999] 1 W.L.R. 1092 the petitioner was brought into a company as a director and shareholder. The majority shareholder indicated that he was willing to increase the petitioner's shareholding and voting rights to 50 per cent. This did not happen. The House of Lords, in an important review of the scope of s.459, held that, although it might in certain circumstances be unfair for those conducting the affairs of a company to rely on their strict legal powers, a member "will not ordinarily be entitled to complain of unfairness unless there has been some breach of the terms on which he agreed that the affairs of the company should be conducted." There is no "stark right of unilateral withdrawal" when confidence and trust had broken down. See also *Phoenix Office Supplies Ltd v Larvin* [2002] EWCA Civ 1740: s.459 is not designed to provide for "no fault corporate divorce". Compare *Baumler (UK) Ltd, Re* [2005] 1 B.C.L.C. 92 where a cause of the loss of confidence was a breach by the majority shareholder of its duty to the company.

- *Claims as creditor as well as shareholder.* The Privy Council decided that, in a small two member joint company, an unfair prejudice application could proceed even though (if successful) the claim would benefit the applicant as creditor rather than as shareholder. *In Gamlestaden Fastfighter AB v Baltic Parties Ltd* [2007] BCC 272

- *Existing valuation procedure.* The fact that the parties had agreed in advance a valuation procedure in the event of breakdown of the relationship did not exclude an unfair prejudice petition where there was evidence of misconduct or genuine concern regarding the valuation process: *In Re Belfield Furnishings Ltd* [2006] EWHC 183 (Ch)

- *The company's affairs may include those of a subsidiary.* In *Citybranch Ltd, Gross, Re v Rackind* [2004] EWCA Civ 815, the court took a "group" approach and was willing to regard behaviour in relation to the affairs of a subsidiary as equivalent to affairs of the parent for the purposes of a s.459 claim, where the parent company and the subsidiary had directors in common.

- *Refinancing.* In *BSB Holdings Limited (No.2), Re* [1996] 1 B.C.L.C. 155 the court rejected an argument by a minority party that it had been substantially and unfairly prejudiced during a round of refinancings of the company and by a merger which had been negotiated without its consent.

- *Granting unduly favourable security.* In *Brenfield Squash Racquets Club Ltd, Re* [1996] 2 B.C.L.C. 184 three directors of the majority shareholder, who were also directors of the company, caused the company to grant security over its assets in favour of the majority party's bank and enter into arrangements which could have had the effect of transferring the company's assets to the majority shareholder. The court held that this amounted to unfair prejudice.

- *Excessive remuneration.* In *Saul D. Harrison & Sons Plc, Re* [1995] 1 B.C.L.C. 14 the petitioner alleged that the directors had been paid excessive remuneration and that also that the prospects for the business were so poor that any reasonable board would have closed it down and distributed the assets. The court dismissed the petition. Hoffmann L.J. said: " . . . The starting point in any case under s.459 will be to ask whether the conduct of which the shareholder complains was in accordance with the articles of association . . ." There may be cases where these or other agreements do not fully reflect the understanding of the parties but this is unlikely where the association is a purely commercial one. Neill L.J. confirmed: " . . . The court will be very reluctant to accept that managerial decisions can amount to unfairly prejudicial conduct . . .".

- *Removal of a party from management.* In *A Company (No. 002015 of 1996), Re* [1997] 2 B.C.L.C. 1 a party brought in a joint venture partner, with a majority share, to provide finance to his company. The original party was subsequently removed as chief executive. He argued that this was a quasi-partnership, he had a legitimate expectation to participate in the affairs of the JVC and his dismissal constituted unfairly prejudicial conduct. It was held that, although normally members of a company cannot have legitimate expectations beyond those conferred by exhaustive documentation, this was not impossible and, on the facts, it was arguable that there could exist "something more" in this particular case.

- *Exclusion from management, failure to pay dividends etc.* In *Quinlan v Essen Hinge Co Ltd* [1996] 2 B.C.L.C. 417 the court held that the petitioner's exclusion from management constituted unfairly prejudicial conduct. The case was stronger because of the company's failure to pay dividends and the retention of substantial (and unnecessary) reserves in the company.

- *Excessive remuneration, diversion of business etc.* In *Cumana Ltd, Re* [1986] B.C.L.C. 430 the court held that a majority shareholder had caused unfair prejudice to the minority shareholder by diverting business to another company, procuring a rights issue so as to reduce the minority's proportional holding and by paying himself an excessive salary. In valuing the minority's shares on a buy-out, it was appropriate in this case to take the date of the petition thereby excluding any subsequent decline in value of the shares.

- *"Unfair" rights issue.* In *A Company, Re* [1986] B.C.L.C. 362 an individual shareholder resigned as a director and left the company. He subsequently complained, inter alia, that a proposed rights issue was unfairly prejudicial since he did not have the funds and his interest would be significantly diluted if not taken up. It was held, on the facts, that the rights issue was genuinely motivated by a desire to raise capital and was not aimed at prejudicing the petitioner. Nevertheless, Hoffmann J. added: "if the majority know that the petitioner does not have the money to take up his rights and the offer is made at par when the shares are plainly worth a great deal more than par as part of a majority holding (but very little as a minority holding), it seems to me arguable that . . . the transaction in that form could . . . constitute unfairly prejudicial conduct."

The statutory right of a minority shareholder to petition for unfair prejudice under the Companies Act is inalienable and cannot be excluded by a term in a shareholders' agreement providing for arbitration of disputes.[34]

---

[34] *Exeter City AFC Ltd v Football Conference Ltd* [2005] 1 B.C.L.C. 238.

Remedies

11–40 If the court is satisfied that a petition is well founded, it may make such order under s.996 as it thinks fit for giving relief in respect of the matters complained of. Specific orders can include:

(a) requiring the JVC to refrain from or continuing to do a particular act;

(b) authorising civil proceedings to be brought in the name and on behalf of the JVC;

(c) regulating the conduct of the JVC's affairs in the future;

(d) ordering the purchase of the shares of any member(s) of the JVC by other member(s) or by the JVC itself.

A buy-out order is, though, the normal remedy.[35]

Price

11–41 In most cases, the aim of the petition will be to get one party to purchase the shares of another party in the JVC and the court is specifically empowered to make such an order. The main issue will then be the price to be paid for the shares. One reason for bringing an application under s.994 may be to force a sale at a price better than would otherwise be obtained.

(1) The general rule, certainly where the joint venture is a "quasi-partnership", is that it will be appropriate to fix the price pro rata according to the value of the shares in the JVC as a whole without any discount for the minority holding.[36] A discount might, however, be appropriate where the shareholding was acquired for investment purposes or in circumstances where the minority shareholder, although a victim of unfair prejudice, had acted in a way to deserve exclusion from the company.[37]

(2) The courts have been prepared to be flexible over the date of valuation to arrive at a fair result. Moreover, where the company is a going concern, the shares should normally be valued at the date on which the order to purchase is made.[38]

---

[35] See *Grace v Biagoli* [2005] EWCA Civ 1222. The Court of Appeal confirmed that a buy-out order should be the normal remedy. The trial judge had been too creative in trying to create alternative remedies.

[36] See *O'Neill v Phillips* [1999] 1 W.L.R. 1092 where Lord Hoffmann set out important guidance as to the principles governing an offer to buy the petitioner's shares as an answer to a petition under s.459. See also *Strahan v Wilcock* [2006] EWCA Civ 13 where the Court of Appeal re-iterated that this is the norm. The circumstances when a discounted valuation might be appropriate were discussed.

[37] See *Bird Precision Bellows Ltd, Re* [1984] B.C.L.C. 19.

[38] *Pro finance Trust SA v Gladstone* [2002] 1 W.L.R. 1024.

(3) The courts will, though, pay close attention to any terms agreed in the articles of association or shareholders' agreement. The more clearly the foundation documents of a JVC are drafted and provide remedies which can reasonably be pursued, the less likely it is that the court will intervene under s.994.[39]

Just and equitable winding-up

11–42 The other main remedy of a minority under English law is to seek a winding-up under s.122(1)(g) of the Insolvency Act 1986. This gives the court power to order that a company be wound up where "the court is of the opinion that it is just and equitable that the company should be wound up." Examples of where the courts have applied or considered s.122(1)(g) include the following:

WINDING-UP: SOME UK CASES UNDER S.122(1)(G)

- *Deadlock.* Two shareholders had equal voting powers. Differences arose between the parties and direct communications ceased (although the company continued, apparently, to make significant profits). It was held that the position amounted to a complete deadlock and, where there was in substance a partnership in the guise of a private company (and there would have been grounds for dissolution if it had been a partnership in law), it was just and equitable that the company should be wound up. *In Yenidje Tobacco Co, Re* [1916] 2 Ch 426.

- *Exclusion from management.* It was held by the House of Lords that, in a quasi-partnership type company established on the basis of mutual confidence, the exclusion of the petitioner from management or participation in the business of the company (where this participation had been understood and agreed, if not legally binding) may be grounds for a winding-up order under s.122(1)(g). *Ebrahimi v Westbourne Galleries Ltd* [1973] A.C. 360.

- *No participation in major decisions.* There had been a breakdown of an agreement that a shareholder would participate in all major decisions relating to the company's affairs. This might have constituted sufficient grounds although, in this case, the petitioner failed on the grounds that he had shown a lack of interest in the company's affairs. *Noble A & Son (Clothing) Ltd, Re* [1983] B.C.L.C. 273.

- *Unnecessary build-up of reserves.* The minority had been excluded from participation in profits by a board which had carried to reserves sums greatly in excess of those required to finance the business. It was held that this could provide a ground for a winding-up petition. *a Company, ex p. Glossop, Re* [1988] 1 W.L.R. 1068.

---

[39] *Pro finance Trust SA v Gladstone*, but compare *Belfield Furnishings Ltd, Re* [2006] EWHC 183.

- *No requirement to pursue pre-emption.* The Court of Appeal held that, in the circumstances, a shareholder could pursue its winding-up petition without first being required to pursue pre-emption provisions in the articles of association. *Abbey Leisure Ltd, Re* [1990] B.C.L.C. 342.

- *Scope of jurisdiction.* The jurisdiction to make a winding-up order under s.122(1)(g) is, however, not wider than the jurisdiction to grant relief under s.459 where it is based on the conduct of the respondent. Therefore, conduct which is not unfairly prejudicial cannot generally support a winding-up order on the just and equitable ground. *Guidezone Ltd, Re* [2000] 12 B.C.L.C. 321.

- *Reluctance to go beyond detailed agreements.* The petitioners claimed that they had been wrongfully excluded from management and sought various remedies. The court approved the striking out of the petition. It said that, on the facts, it could not be argued that there was any legitimate expectation that the petitioners would continue to participate in management. "The parties had not left the basis of their relationship only to the articles of association which were adopted as part of the transaction ... but had spelt out in detailed agreements all the matters which were to govern their relationship." This left "simply no room for the arising of any legitimate expectation" outside these agreements. *Ringtower Holdings Plc, Re* [1989] 5 BCC 82.

- *Court's discretion.* The courts have emphasised that they have a discretion not to make an order where the petitioner is acting unreasonably; for example, where the petitioner has been offered the chance to sell his shares at a fair value. See *a Company (No. 003843 of 1986), Re* [1987] 3 BCC 624 (and similarly *a Company (No. 002567 of 1982), Re* [1983] BCC [98,930]).

11–43 The court will look at all the circumstances where the claim is that the petitioner had a legitimate expectation that he would participate in the management of the company. The expectation need not be expressly provided for in the constitutional documents although the court will not normally accept that, where the parties have made an effort to set out in detail all the matters which are to govern their relationship, there are legitimate expectations beyond any rights spelt out between the parties. However, the principal limitation of this remedy is that the only action the court may take under s.122(1)(g) is to provide for the winding-up of the company. In some instances this may be unnecessarily drastic; hence, the popularity of an alternative claim under s.994 of the Companies Act 2006 which can offer a more flexible remedy.

CONCLUSION

11–44 The various principles and measures discussed in this chapter may provide some residual remedies for a party in a joint venture (particularly a minority party) against "excessive" oppression or misbehaviour by another party. However, remedies are limited and it is doubtful whether, individually or collectively, they amount to a serious restraint against opportunistic business behaviour. We await the development, through the courts, of stronger and broader principles. With the growth in the range of joint ventures and alliances and the plethora of situations which can arise, case law developments are still likely to occur.

11–45 The strongest protections against failure or opportunistic behaviour in a joint venture will not, of course, be legal in nature—they will lie commercially in the hands of the parties themselves. The initial selection of joint venture or alliance "partner", the establishment of an alliance structure which aligns the incentives of each party to commit to the venture, clear agreement on common goals and general diligence and communication both before and during the venture—these will all be crucial in forming, and maintaining, a relationship which diminishes the risk of "misbehaviour".

Chapter 12

Transfers of shares

An equity joint venture creates for each party a "share" in the joint venture vehicle. When and how can a share in the joint venture be transferred? What restrictions or conditions should apply in the case of a proposed transfer to a third party? These will be important policy decisions for the parties at the outset of the venture. This chapter addresses various structures and provisions for dealing with this potentially complex situation.

Effect of legal form on transferability

12–01 The legal form of the joint venture vehicle will be important in establishing the legal transferability of interests in the venture.

(1) A contractual alliance by its nature will rarely allow for assignment of rights (and/or obligations) to a third party without the consent of the other alliance party.

(2) In the case of a partnership, transfer of an interest in the partnership will also invariably require the consent of the other party or parties. Usually, the "exit" route will be termination and withdrawal from the partnership in accordance with notice provisions in a partnership agreement. This may or may not be accompanied by the introduction of a new partner.

(3) A corporate joint venture, on the other hand, creates an interest for each party as holder of shares in the capital of the joint venture company (JVC) which is legally separate from the JVC's ownership of its assets and business. It is this continuity of the JVC's legal ownership, alongside the transferability of shares in the JVC, which can often be a reason for adopting a corporate structure as the legal form for the venture in the first place.

In this chapter, we therefore focus on the different structures and provisions which may apply to transfers of shares in a JVC.

RANGE OF TRANSFER RESTRICTIONS

Range of potential transfer restrictions

12–02 Virtually all joint ventures do contain restrictions on transfer. An ability freely to transfer shares to any third party without constraint is contrary to the basic personal nature of a "joint" venture. The range of potential restrictions on transfer can cover the following spectrum outlined in Figure 12.1

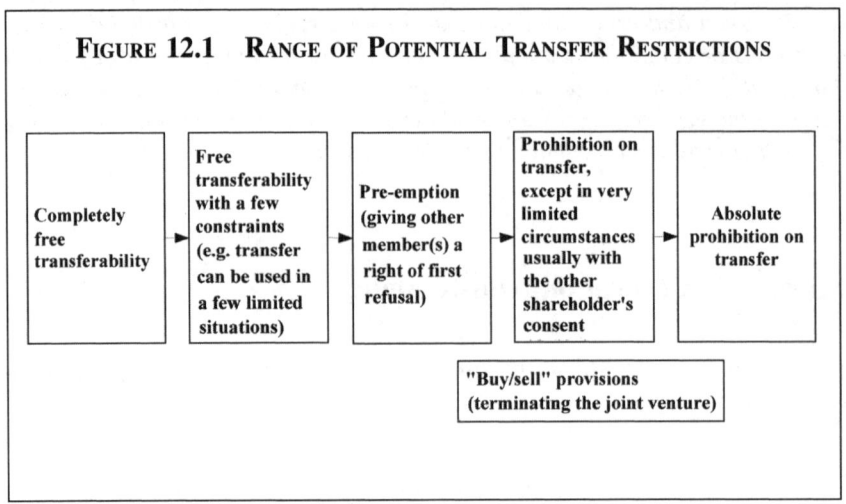

FIGURE 12.1 RANGE OF POTENTIAL TRANSFER RESTRICTIONS

12–03 A crucial first question is therefore: where, within this range, should transfer restrictions in this particular joint venture be pitched? Insufficient thought is sometimes given to this basic question. In many cases it is simply assumed that there should be a transfer regime (subject to pre-emption rights); then the parties sometimes add during negotiations provisions relating to "buy/sell" or other options if it is considered that transfers to third parties are unlikely in practice. This approach can lead to tortuous, and time-consuming, negotiations and drafting. Transfer restrictions should be viewed realistically in the context of exit and termination generally.

Free transferability

(1) In certain joint ventures, particularly multi-party ventures in which a number of parties may have largely a passive investment, a regime of relative freedom of transfer may be appropriate (subject only, for instance, to certain criteria such as credit-worthiness of the transferee or, perhaps, prohibition against transfer to certain competitors).

Prohibition on transfers

(2) In many corporate joint ventures, particularly limited-function or cooperative ventures where the personal relationship between the parties is crucial to the continuance of the venture, the simplest route may be to prohibit any transfers without consent of the other party or parties—certainly for a significant initial "lock up" period. For many ventures, this will meet the commercial realities. The exit route will then be one of the other exit mechanisms discussed in chapter 13, e.g.:

— notice leading to liquidation of the JVC;
— notice triggering "buy/sell" options as between the parties themselves;
— exercise of commercially agreed put and call options.

Given the rarity of transfers to third parties in the absence of consent and active cooperation of existing joint venture parties, it is surprising that parties in more joint ventures do not adopt this approach. (Note, though, that in some jurisdictions (e.g. the Netherlands) it may not be possible to have a legally enforceable prohibition on share transfers on a permanent basis. If so, methods to avoid or mitigate this rule may include (i) prohibition for a specified period or (ii) transfers being permitted only to narrow categories of "permitted" transferees.)

> **The short form 50:50 Shareholders' Agreement for a deadlock company as Precedent 9 in Part E adopts this approach.**

Pre-emption

(3) In very many ventures, however, the parties will choose to adopt an intermediate solution whereby transfers are permitted but subject to a "pre-emption" procedure. Pre-emption provisions give rise to the detailed issues discussed below in this chapter.

Agreed sales between the parties

12–04 Sales to third parties of joint venture interests are comparatively rare. Indeed, sales of such interests generally—even to the continuing party or parties—are, in practice, frequently not effected through implementation of the contractually agreed pre-emption provisions. These provisions more usually set the background against which a sale is commercially negotiated in the particular circumstances with relevant parties agreeing to waive the pre-emption procedure. These provisions can, nevertheless, play an important part in establishing each party's negotiating position. Where a sale is negotiated between the joint venture parties outside the scope of the formal pre-emption provisions, the terms will be solely a matter for commercial negotiation—not only as to price but also any warranties or indemnities.

(1) It is relatively rare for any warranties to extend beyond title to the shares being sold (unless the seller is a majority and controlling shareholder).

(2) It will be a matter for negotiation whether the selling party is to have any exposure (i.e. under an indemnity to the transferee) for a share of any liabilities arising from events and circumstances occurring during the period in which it was a shareholder (e.g. product liability, environmental liability, tax etc). More usually any risks will be taken into account in the negotiation of a price for a "clean" transfer of the transferring party's shares.

> A short-form precedent of a JVC Share Sale Agreement is included as Precedent 17 in Part E

Pre-Emption Rights

Pre-emption rights

12–05 The most common transfer restriction is a "pre-emption right" in favour of the other existing party or parties. This will usually entail a procedure along the following lines:

(a) a transfer notice is given to the other party setting out the selling party's wish to transfer shares in the JVC and the proposed price;

(b) the other joint venture party is given a period in which to decide whether or not to exercise a pre-emption right on the terms stated in the transfer notice;[1]

(c) in the case of a multi-party venture, each party is offered the selling party's shares pro rata to its existing interest in the JVC together with an opportunity to take up any excess shares not acquired by the other continuing parties;[2]

(d) if, and to the extent that the pre-emption rights are not exercised, the selling party is free to sell its shares to a third party within a defined period and at a price not less than that offered to the existing joint venture party or parties under the pre-emption procedure.

---

[1] Sometimes, the parties may only want the procedure to apply if there is a "real" third party purchaser in prospect and the continuing party can make its decision knowing the identity of the proposed purchaser. In this case, the transfer notice must give details of the proposed third party purchaser and the terms agreed with that potential purchaser. The procedure then becomes a "right of first refusal." It is also a simpler way of fixing the price for the pre-emption right—see para.12–15 below.

[2] In the case of a multi-party venture, the transfer notice will usually be given to the directors of the JVC who will undertake on behalf of the selling party the offer and allocation procedure with the other shareholders.

> A detailed example of a typical pre-emption procedure is set out in the Multi-Party Shareholders' Agreement as Precedent 10 in Part E.

Drafting of pre-emption provisions involves the consideration of a range of detailed points. This can be one of the most difficult areas to be dealt with in a shareholders' agreement. It is important to identify the main "structure" points before detailed drafting takes place.

Types of pre-emption right

12–06 First, and importantly, there are different types of "pre-emption rights". They most usually fall within one of the following basic types:

(a) a "right of first offer" (sometimes termed a "soft" pre-emption right);

(b) a "right of first refusal" (sometimes termed a "hard" pre-emption right).

Right of first offer

12–07 A "right of first offer" occurs where the selling party wishes to sell its shares but is not obliged first to identify a third party purchaser. It is a misnomer in the sense that it is usually the selling party who proposes the price. The non-selling party[3] has the first opportunity to take up that offer. The right arises at the "front end" of the sale process. If the offer is not accepted, then the selling party is usually free to sell its shares to a third party purchaser at a price not less than the previously offered price.[4] An advantage for the selling party is that this route avoids the initial costs and effort of marketing to third parties. A disadvantage for the non-selling party is that it may be forced in practice to make a decision whether or not to buy-out the selling party in circumstances where the sale to a third party may not be a real likelihood.

12–08 A right of first offer may be more acceptable to the non-selling party if it is bolstered by a "second bite of the cherry". In this event, the non-selling party can exercise a further pre-emption right when the identity of (and other sale terms with) the third party purchaser are known, even if it did not exercise the right the first time around. (The opportunity of such a second chance may, of course, be unacceptable to a selling party.)

---

[3] The singular "party" is used here. The same principles apply in the case of a multi-party joint venture—but see para.12–27 et seq. below.

[4] One variant, particularly used in some multi-party ventures, is to allow the non-selling parties (if they decline to accept themselves) a right to nominate any other person to purchase the selling party's shares, thus ensuring that the shares are acquired by someone of whom they approve.

12–09 A common variant rests on the premise that, if a joint venture party wishes to exit by transferring its shares, then it is appropriate for the other existing party to have a right to acquire those shares at a "fair" price—to be determined, if necessary, by an expert valuation—and not at an arbitrary or opportunistic price proposed by the selling party. The continuing party may therefore be given the right to call for an expert valuation. The process will then usually be:

(a) each party has a right to decide not to go ahead within a stated period after the valuation has been given (i.e. the selling party can withdraw its transfer notice if it considers the expert valuation is too low);

(b) unless the seller withdraws, the continuing party has the right to acquire the selling party's shares at the expert-determined price (or sometimes, if lower, the original offer price);

(c) if the pre-emption right is not exercised, the selling party is free to sell to a third party at not less than the expert-determined price.

12–10 Very occasionally, pre-emption provisions are drafted on the basis that the non-selling party is first invited to offer a price. The process is then, usually, that the seller can consider that "offered" price and decide whether or not to proceed with negotiations with the other party—or choose to proceed to find and negotiate with a third party purchaser (usually subject to a restriction that any price negotiated with a third party purchaser must not be less than the earlier "offered" price). Such a process will normally only be agreed where the selling party (e.g. a venture capital provider) is in a strong negotiating position.

Right of first refusal

12–11 A "right of first refusal" is where the selling party must identify a bona fide third party purchaser before the pre-emption right is exercisable by the non-selling party. The right arises at the "back end" of the sale process. In this situation, if the pre-emption right is not exercised, the only permitted sale will be to the specified third party purchaser at the price specified in the transfer notice. A "hard" right of this kind can make it very difficult in practice for a selling party in a JVC to find a purchaser. It will often not be feasible for a seller to obtain a firm offer from a third party in advance of the pre-emption process taking place, since the third party will usually prefer to wait and not waste time on potentially abortive negotiations until it has clarified whether any pre-emption rights will be taken up.

12–12 Another practical point to consider in relation to the involvement of any potential third party purchaser is: what right (if any) does the selling party have to provide the potential purchaser with information about the JVC? Some agreements, particularly where there is a "right of first refusal" approach, allow an exception to the confidentiality obligations for information disclosed to a bona fide potential purchaser of shares in the JVC, provided that the potential purchaser agrees to be bound by the relevant confidentiality provisions. If a sale to a third party is a real possibility, this is a sensible precaution. (One advantage of a "front-end" pre-emption right to a continuing party is that it should prevent any release of confidential information to potential third party purchasers whereas this would be likely to occur under a "back-end" pre-emption procedure.)

Price

12–13 Price is invariably a key issue. This will be affected by—and will indeed often be a principal reason for—the form of pre-emption right adopted for a particular venture. The price at which the non-selling party can buy the selling party's shares under pre-emption provisions could be:

(a) the price set by the selling party;

(b) the price offered by a third party purchaser; or

(c) a price determined by an independent valuation.

Set by seller

12–14 One common approach (i.e. under a right of first offer) is for the proposed seller simply to set out its proposed price in the transfer notice,[5] leaving the other joint venture party to decide whether or not to accept that price. If not accepted, the proposed seller is free to sell elsewhere to a third party, usually within a stated period (say three or six months) and at a price not less than that offered in the transfer notice. The seller should in practice be restrained from asking for a price which is manifestly too high because, if it does so, it is likely that neither the other shareholder nor any third party will be willing to buy at that price. (The selling party may on occasion, however, feel that it could find a third party prepared to pay a premium or relatively high price to gain a strategic foothold in the company and therefore decide to set the proposed price accordingly.)

Third party purchaser

12–15 An alternative approach is a "right of first refusal" where, in order to exit, an outgoing shareholder must first negotiate terms with a bona fide

---

[5] Note that the price must conform to any requirements for the transfer notice. In *EWE International Ltd v Philip Jones* [2004] B.C.L.C. 406 it was decided that a transfer notice did not comply with pre-emption provisions in the articles of association (which required the price to be "specified" in the transfer notice) when the price actually stated in the notice included a deferred element which was not capable of calculation at the date of offer to the existing shareholder.

third party purchaser but cannot complete without first giving the existing shareholder a right of refusal on the same terms (including price per share). If not taken up, the sale to the third party can proceed at the specified price. If this route is adopted, the non-selling party will be concerned to ensure that the price is a proper reflection of that third party price, with no side deal existing between the seller and the third party purchaser which makes it more attractive to the third party than the offer to the non-selling party. There are various protections which the non-selling party may seek—e.g. by requiring:

(a) that it should be a "bona fide" offer from a third party;

(b) that the identity of the third party should be specified in the transfer notice;

(c) disclosure of all material terms of the proposed sale to the third party purchaser;

(d) a warranty from the selling party that the information provided to the non-selling party is correct;

and sometimes pre-emption provisions go further and require:

(e) that there is no "connection" between the selling party and the third party purchaser;

(f) that a sale to a third party purchaser can only be effected for cash or, if the third party price is not expressed as a fixed cash sum, an independent valuation should determine an equivalent cash price;

(g) disclosure is made of the proposed sale and purchase agreement, including details of any warranties and indemnities to be given to the third party purchaser.

A non-selling party may wish to see the sale and purchase agreement because it may require, under the pre-emption provisions, that a sale to it from the selling party is on the same terms, including warranties, as the proposed sale by the selling party to the third party purchaser. There is an argument, at least in the case of a non-selling party which is not running or controlling the company, that it should have the benefit of the same warranty terms as are offered to the proposed third party purchaser.

12–16 An occasional variant of this alternative is to permit a selling party to obtain an offer from a third party purchaser for the JVC as a whole—but subject to the other joint venture party being given a right of first refusal to buy the interest of the selling party at the same price per share and on the same terms and conditions as those offered by the third party. However, if this right is not taken up by the other joint venture party, a common provision is that it can be "dragged along" and bound to sell its interest to the third party at the same time as the selling party.

12–17 Obviously, these types of provisions envisage that the negotiations with the third party purchaser will be well advanced by the time the selling party gives the transfer notice. In practice, a third party purchaser will usually want to be confident that the non-selling party will not seek to buy any of the selling party's shares under the pre-emption provisions, otherwise it will have wasted time and expense in negotiating its deal with the selling party.

Fair price determination

12–18 In some situations (see para.12–09), it may be agreed that the price should be determined by a third party expert such as an investment bank or the auditors. If so, the formula for valuation in such circumstances needs to be addressed carefully. Share valuation is a detailed topic and frequently controversial.[6] Settling the valuation formula and procedures will generally be a matter requiring the assistance of the parties' accountants or other financial advisers. Different bases for valuation of a party's shareholding in a JVC include the following:

(1) *Market value on a pro rata basis.* "Open market value" can be a dangerous term in relation to joint ventures. It should only be used in relation to the JVC as a whole. There will often be no outside "market" for the particular shares being sold, with the market for a partial shareholding being restricted in practice to the existing shareholders. Market value on a pro rata basis is often, though, a sensible basis. For this purpose, the valuer must first determine the market value of the whole JVC and then divide by the proportion which the shares being sold represent of the entire issued capital. It enables a party to realise a proportion of the total market value of the JVC equivalent to the proportion of its shareholding. It is appropriate if the selling party has paid the same price per share for its original equity stake as the other shareholders, irrespective of the size of that stake.

(2) *Fair value.* "Fair" value is different from "market" value. Under this concept, unless restricted by his terms of reference, the valuer has more flexibility to look at the particular circumstances. The valuer can allow in his determination for the rights or influence attached to the stake under the joint venture arrangements (e.g. a "discount" by reason of the minority holding). Where sale will give control to the buyer, the valuer could value and allocate an element of "control premium" to the price—unless otherwise directed by the parties. If a combined term such as "fair market value" is used, it is crucial to

---

[6] See specialist texts for a more detailed analysis; e.g. N. Eastaway *Practical Share Valuation* (Tottel Publishing, 2008).

clarify whether or not the valuer is to ignore any premium or discount by reference to the percentage shareholding being sold.

(3) *Other basis of valuation.* Other more specific bases of valuation are less common in pre-emption price formulae. They are more likely to be used in the course of commercial negotiations on valuation of initial contributions to the JVC where a party considers them to be an appropriate measure or in price negotiations as factors leading to a "fair" or "market" value. They include:

   (a) *Net asset value.* A valuation based on the net assets of the JVC may be appropriate for ventures which are not yet profitable or where a "break-up" basis is relevant. This will frequently establish a floor for the valuation overall. If adopted as a specific basis for determination of price, it will usually be desirable to spell out in more detail how, or if, specific assets (such as goodwill, real estate or inventory) are to be valued and the date at which the asset value is to be determined.

   (b) *Earnings basis.* A price/earnings (P/E) ratio is appropriate for valuing the entire issued share capital or a controlling interest where the business carried on by the JVC is a "going concern" (but noting that some element of premium for control should be added if comparisons are being made with the P/E ratios of quoted companies).

   (c) *Discounted cash flow.* The present value of estimated future cash flows is frequently regarded as an appropriate basis for valuing a company where the "buyer" acquires control over the cash flows generated by the business.

   (d) *Start-up cost.* In some cases, an appropriate level for fixing the price may be the start-up costs which have been incurred by the selling party and which a purchaser would have incurred if it had started from scratch with the investment.

   (e) *Dividend yield.* Dividend yield is sometimes an appropriate measure for valuing a minority holding where the shareholder does not have the ability to control the dividend policy of the JVC or exercise other significant minority influence over the JVC's policy. It will not usually be appropriate for a minority stake in a joint venture.

Sometimes, it may be appropriate for a different basis of valuation to "kick-in" after a defined period of the venture. For instance, a net asset or start-up cost basis (or perhaps a discounted valuation) may be appropriate during an initial period in order to discourage early use of the transfer/pre-emption provisions; then a business-related valuation mechanism may apply for transfers after an agreed initial period.

12–19 In some cases, a valuer may be given more specific instruction or guidance by the parties as to the basis to be adopted and/or the factors to take into account when assessing the value. For instance, it may be appropriate to give the valuer guidance on whether to take into account specific factors such as:

(a) the continuance (or non-continuance) of certain important ancillary support or licence contracts between the JVC and a joint venture party depending whether or not these contracts will terminate upon the sale;

(b) the impact of any default upon the business of the JVC (if the sale has been triggered by a material default of a party);

(c) the price and terms offered by any bona fide third party purchaser.

If so, the language of the instruction or guidance should be clear and normally pre-agreed with the valuer to ascertain that it is workable.

12–20 One variant which can act as an incentive to reach agreement on value (or at least encourage the parties to put forward reasonable proposals) is for the expert valuation to take the form of a "baseball" determination.[7] In this scenario, each party submits its own valuation to the independent expert. The role of the latter is to decide which party's valuation is closer to the expert's view; that party's valuation then prevails.

12–21 If share valuation is referred to an independent valuer, additional points which arise include:

(1) *Who should be the valuer?* Valuation is rarely an exact science; care should therefore be given to the choice of valuer. If the value is to be assessed by reference to the book or market value of the tangible assets, the auditors of the JVC would be a common choice. If a more judgmental business valuation is required, taking into account a range of market factors, an independent firm of accountants or an international investment bank may be regarded as more appropriate—particularly by a non-controlling party.

(2) *Costs.* The procedure should make it clear who is to pay the expert's fees and expenses—the JVC, the transferee, equally between the parties or should the expert be free to decide what is appropriate?

(3) *Submissions.* Each party should be given an opportunity to make written submissions to the expert on valuation. It will usually be left to the valuer to decide the procedure—although, in some cases, more specific procedural guidelines may be laid down in the joint venture agreement.

(4) *Challenging the valuer's decision.* If a valuer is appointed, it is sensible under English law to provide that he will act as an expert and not an arbitrator. This will generally mean that the valuer's deter-

---

[7] Named from the method used before the arbitrator in player salary negotiations in US major league baseball. This form is also known as pendulum or final offer arbitration.

mination is not subject to appeal under the Arbitration Act 1996. The valuer's determination (if expressed to be final and binding) is not open to challenge unless the valuer has departed from instructions to a material extent[8] or has committed a manifest error which obviously vitiates the result. Other factors include:

(a) if an expert reaches an incorrect valuation through negligence, he can be sued by an aggrieved party;[9]

(b) an aggrieved party will not be able to bring a petition under s.994 of the Companies Act 2006 on the basis of an incorrect valuation, unless there has been fraud or some other impropriety.[10]

Types of "transfer" to be covered

12–22 What types of "transfer" should be regulated? It is essential, at least under English law, to ensure that the drafting makes it clear that the pre-emption procedure applies to dealings in the equitable or beneficial interest in the shares as well as the legal interest. Unless the provisions state otherwise, a reference to a "transfer" refers only to an instrument of transfer passing the legal interest in shares and does not cover a transfer of the beneficial interest in shares.[11] Provisions are also commonly drafted to prevent the creation of any security interest or other encumbrance over shares—see below.

12–23 The time at which the pre-emption process is triggered will depend on the drafting of the provisions. Some traditional provisions under English practice are drafted on the basis that they apply when a shareholder "desires or wishes to transfer its shares". An alternative is simply to provide that the pre-emption procedure must be followed "before any transfer of shares (or any interest in shares)". It is arguable that the "desire to transfer" formula could be triggered at an earlier stage than the "before any transfer" alternative and may be slightly wider in scope.[12]

Charges

12–24 Should a party be able to charge its shares in the JVC by way of security? Pre-emption provisions commonly also provide that no charge,

---

[8] *Veba Oil Supply & Trading GmbH v Petrotrade Inc* [2001] EWCA Civ 1832.
[9] *Arenson v Casson Beckman Rutley & Co* [1977] A.C. 405.
[10] *Castleburn Ltd, Re* [1991] B.C.L.C. 89.
[11] *Safeguard Industrial Investments Ltd v National Westminster Bank Ltd* [1982] 1 All E.R. 449 and see also *Scotto v Petch* [2000] B.C.L.C. 211. Note also that the articles of association can only bind the shareholders themselves. A requirement to give a transfer notice under a pre-emption obligation cannot bind a non-member who holds an existing beneficial interest in shares: *Philip William Rose v Lynx Express Ltd* [2004] All E.R. (D) 143. A shareholders' agreement may, though, impose an obligation on a party to procure that all members of its relevant corporate group comply with the pre-emption provisions if they have an interest in shares in the JVC.
[12] See e.g. *Lyle & Scott Ltd v Scott's Trustees* [1959] 2 All E.R. 661 for interpretation of a "desire" to transfer and also *Macro (Ipswich) Ltd, Re* [1994] 2 B.C.L.C. 354.

pledge or other security interest may be created over the shares without the prior consent of the other party. The danger is that, if a charge is crystallised, the lender may step in and assume or direct the affairs of the shareholder in relation to shares in the JVC in the same way, in effect, as a transferee. There may be joint ventures where charges are permitted in certain circumstances—e.g. the freedom to charge shares in the JVC may well be essential to a party's ability to raise finance to support its participation in an infrastructure project to be carried out through a joint venture vehicle. In this case, one formula is to provide that a charge can be created so long as enforcement (if it occurs) by the chargee takes the form of sale of the shares as soon as is reasonably practicable after enforcement of the charge but only by going first through the pre-emption process.

Entire holding

12–25 Is a partial sale of a party's holding in the JVC to be permitted—or only its entire holding? It is usual to permit only the transfer of a party's entire holding. This prevents the dispersal of interests and the creation of small shareholdings in the JVC. It also prevents the transferor being left with a small residue of shares to sell if all the shares on offer are not taken up under the pre-emption procedure.

12–26 Partial transfers may, however, frequently be permitted in the case of some multi-party joint ventures as a way of enabling a party (particularly a financial party) to "sell down" its interest. If a party is able to sell part only of its shareholding, consideration needs to be given to the implications for other provisions of the shareholders' agreement and/or articles of association; e.g. the power of a particular party to appoint directors and accompanying veto rights to block resolutions or decisions. These rights may need to be adjusted if that party were to hold a substantially reduced stake following a transfer of shares.

Multi-party joint ventures

12–27 How are shares to be offered in a multi-party joint venture? The JVC's capital may be divided into different classes of shares. In a multi-party joint venture, the balance of rights between the various classes of shareholder may be carefully structured. In such cases, it is common to provide that, when shares of one class are being transferred, they should be offered first to those members holding shares of the same class and then (if any are remaining) to holders of shares of the other class or classes. It is also common to provide that, if a member of one class acquires shares of another class, the acquired shares are automatically re-designated as shares of the class held by the acquirer.

12–28 A variant in a multi-party venture is to provide that, on a sale, the continuing shareholders should be offered their proportionate entitlement and asked whether they wish to apply for any excess shares (if available) over that entitlement. If and to the extent that any non-selling party applies for less than its proportionate entitlement, any excess shares are then allocated to shareholders who wish to take up more—usually in proportion to their existing holdings until the excess is taken up. Sometimes, in a venture where there are a large number of shareholders, if any non-selling party does not take up its entitlement to the selling party's shares when initially offered, the JVC may administer the allocation process of the remaining selling party's shares through bidding "rounds".

12–29 In a two-party joint venture it is usual for a transfer notice to be given directly to the other shareholder. In multi-party joint ventures it is common to provide that the JVC will act as the agent of the selling party and receive the initial transfer notice and offer the seller's shares to the other shareholders. Other possible contractual variants which may be included in a multi-party situation are:

(a) a "total transfer condition" to the effect that, if continuing shareholders do not elect to take up all the shares on offer, their preemption rights cease to apply in respect of that offer and the selling party is free to sell all the shares on offer to a third party purchaser named in the original transfer notice (usually within a certain time at a price not less than the earlier offer price);

(b) a right for the non-selling party (or possibly the JVC) to nominate another person to purchase some or all of the shares which existing shareholders do not wish to take up—so that the latter can still stay in control of the identity of participants in the JVC;

(c) a right for the JVC to elect to buy back the balance of the selling party's shares if all are not taken up by the continuing shareholders.

An example of a pre-emption procedure in the context of a multi-party venture appears in the Multi-Party Shareholders' Agreement as Precedent 10 in Part E.

Revocation

12–30 Should it be possible to revoke a transfer notice? In theory (under English law), a transfer notice given under a pre-emption clause may, unless otherwise agreed, subsequently be revoked by the proposed transferor prior to any acceptance of the offer contained in it. This right of revocation should normally be negated by an express provision in the pre-emption procedure, unless such a right of revocation is specifically contemplated by the parties. A transfer notice is therefore usually made irrevocable so that, once the procedure has been started, the selling party is bound to go through with it; starting the process is a serious step. A right of revocation is, however, sometimes permitted in two circumstances:

(1) The selling party is frequently given the right to withdraw its transfer notice if the procedure involves an independent valuation of the shares being sold and it is dissatisfied with that valuation—see para.12–09.

(2) Another possible exception is if the transfer notice has a "total transfer condition". This allows the selling party to revoke the transfer notice if the existing shareholders are not prepared to buy all the shares comprised in the transfer notice. It may wish to do so, for example, if it has a stake which is capable of blocking a special resolution and would not wish to sell if existing shareholders only agree to buy a small proportion of that stake but sufficient to deprive the selling shareholding of its blocking ability.

Pre-emption provisions frequently provide that, if the seller revokes a transfer notice, it cannot initiate another transfer notice within a defined period after the date the first transfer notice is revoked.

Consent of continuing party still required?

12–31 If the continuing party decides not to exercise its pre-emption right, should the selling party then be entirely free to sell its shares in the JVC to any third party purchaser (i.e. without the continuing party's consent)? Usually the answer is "yes". There may, though, be some ventures where this is not feasible—particularly where the participation of the selling party (e.g. through ancillary supply contracts with the JVC) is an essential part of the overall joint venture operations. Possible options are therefore for:

(a) no transfer of shares in the JVC to be permitted in any event (without consent) to certain named, or specified categories of, competitors or buyers;

(b) no transfer to be permitted unless the transferee fulfils certain creditworthiness or other specified business criteria; or

(c) no transfer to any third party to be permitted without the consent of the continuing joint venture party (and/or for the directors of the JVC to have a discretion to refuse to register transfers in favour of a competitor or other unacceptable purchaser—see also para.12–43).

If the consent of the continuing party is required and refused, it is sometimes provided that the selling party should have a right to call for the liquidation of the JVC—although this is a draconian step which may not be justified or commercially appropriate in many ventures.

12–32 Alternatively, if a third party purchaser is not identified at the outset of the pre-emption procedure, the continuing party may sometimes be given "a second bite at the cherry" if, not having exercised its pre-emption right the first time around, it would wish to do so when the identity of the chosen buyer (and therefore its prospective joint venture partner) is actually known. It will, though, as a practical matter be difficult to advance a transaction with a third party while the threat of any pre-emption right still exists. If this type of formulation is desired, the simplest approach is probably to abandon the pre-emption approach and to adopt a straightforward formula that no transfers shall take place without the consent of the other party or parties—see para.12–03 earlier.

Tag-along

12–33 Is a "tag-along" right appropriate? If a party wishes to sell its interest in a JVC to a third party, the other joint venture party or parties may also want to have the opportunity to exit. (This is certainly a common requirement of private equity investors and may be a right appropriate for a minority party—see para.9–30.) This exit right may be preserved by giving the other party or parties a "tag-along" or "piggy-back" right whereby the selling party is obliged[13] to ensure that any third party purchaser must extend its offer so as to include, on the same terms, each other party's shares in the JVC. This is usually a sensible precaution for a minority party in order to ensure that, upon a sale by a majority party, the minority party is not deprived of the opportunity to obtain equivalent sale proceeds and that it does not get locked in as a minority in a joint venture with a new, unwelcome majority partner.

12–34 A party with a "tag-along" right may seek additional protection to ensure that:

(a) it is being presented with a bona fide third party transaction;

(b) all material terms offered by the third party are disclosed to it before its decision is required;

(c) if the selling party is accepting an element of non-cash consideration (in many cases, this may be excluded), a mechanism exists to verify that the price offered to the tag-along party has been fairly valued.

If the seller is able to, and does, dispose of part only of its interest in the JVC, the tag-along right will usually be expressed to apply to an equivalent pro rata proportion of the minority party's holding in the JVC.

Drag-along

12–35 Is a "drag-along" right appropriate? A "drag-along" right may be particularly appropriate for a majority party. In this case the selling party is

---

[13] It could be a "hard" right where the selling party is obliged to obtain such a third party offer (or itself to buy-out the minority party)—or a "soft" right where it is only under a "best endeavours" obligation to obtain a third party offer for the minority's shares.

given a right, if it is selling to a third party purchaser (and particularly if it has gone through a prior pre-emption process with the other joint venture party or parties), to oblige each other party also to sell its shareholding in the JVC to the third party (or to the selling party) at the same price per share as negotiated by the selling party. This enables the majority party to avoid any blocking of the sale by the minority and enables it to deliver the entire interest in the JVC to the third party purchaser usually, therefore, at a higher price per share than for a partial holding. The minority party may seek protections equivalent to those referred to in subparagraphs (a) to (c) in para. 12–34. It will not usually be required to give warranties or representations other than as to title.

Loans and guarantees

12–36 A joint venture party's investment in the JVC often includes debt (sometimes in the form of loan stock or loan notes) as well as shares. When a selling party wishes to sell its shares, how should any outstanding loans by it to the JVC be dealt with?

(1) One common approach is to require a transferee (whether it is an existing shareholder or a third party purchaser) to take over any loans made by the selling party for the benefit of the JVC. If the loans take the form of loan stock or loan notes, these may contractually be "stapled" to the shares held by the shareholders so that they must be transferred with the shares to the same purchaser. If a shareholder is entitled to transfer only part of its shareholding, it must contemporaneously transfer an equivalent proportion of its loans. It is common to stipulate that the price to be paid for any loans is their face value. (If it is more tax or cost-efficient for the loan to be repaid rather than assigned, the transferee should be obliged to make available equivalent finance in place of any such existing loans by the transferor.)

(2) An alternative approach (perhaps less common) is simply to provide that the outgoing party's loans should be repaid by the JVC on that party ceasing to be a shareholder.

12–37 How guarantees should be dealt with may depend on whether the selling party is selling its shares to an existing shareholder or to a third party purchaser and the terms agreed with the transferee.

(1) If another shareholder is buying the shares, a common approach is for the latter to undertake to use its best endeavours to procure the release of the guarantee obligations in question and, in the meantime, to undertake to indemnify the selling party against any claim made under it.

(2) Where the selling party is selling to a third party purchaser, it may be preferable to ensure that the third party purchaser provides a replacement guarantee as a pre-condition to the transfer of shares

taking place. It is common for the selling party to remain liable for any guarantees given by it insofar as liability under the guarantee is triggered by any default attributable to the period when it was a shareholder in the JVC.

Intra-group transfers

12–38 Are intra-group transfers of shares in the JVC to be permitted? Parties will commonly agree at the outset that intra-group transfers will be permitted as an exception from the requirement to go through the pre-emption or consent process. It will usually be sensible, though, to provide that:

(a) the transferor (or its parent) will continue to be liable for the performance by any transferee within its group of any obligations originally undertaken by the transferor in relation to the joint venture; and

(b) the transferor (or its parent) will be obliged to ensure that, if the transferee ceases to be a member of the same corporate group as the transferor, the latter must first re-transfer the holding in the JVC back to the parent or to another group member.

Where intra-group transfers are permitted, it is sensible to make clear at the outset whether the test is that the transferee must be a wholly-owned subsidiary—or whether a permitted transferee can include any subsidiary (including, therefore, the possibility of one in which a third party may have or acquire a significant shareholding or influence).

12–39 Another common provision is for the intra-group transferee to be required to enter into a deed of adherence, agreeing to be bound by the shareholders' agreement—see para.12–45. This will be the case if it is a straight substitution of a new party for the original party (which then ceases to have any liability in relation to the joint venture). It is arguably not necessary if the original party is the parent company within the group and it remains liable for the performance of its subsidiaries under the terms of the shareholders' agreement.

Shareholder/regulatory approvals

12–40 Pre-emption procedures in some ventures may need to take account of the fact that exercise of that pre-emption right by the continuing party could give rise to anti-trust or other regulatory issues. Any requirement for regulatory consents may affect timing and also determine whether or not a transfer can proceed. Shareholder approval under stock exchange or other regulations may also be required by one of the joint venture parties. In these cases, it will be prudent specifically to require each party to use all reasonable efforts to seek such approvals and/or take such other steps as are necessary or desirable to implement a transfer contemplated by the pre-emption procedure.

12–41 Pre-emption provisions should build in sufficient time to deal with regulatory consents and any shareholder approval which may be necessary for the transfer of shares. Sometimes there may simply be established a time period within which a transfer to an existing shareholder or third party must take place and, if it does not, the sale lapses. As a more formal approach, shareholders' agreements sometimes specify what are considered to be necessary approvals or "permitted conditions". Different time periods may be specified for different types of approvals. For example, a relatively short period (e.g. 30 days) may be set for any shareholder approval to be obtained, as the timing for this process is usually within the control of the relevant party. A longer period may be allowed for regulatory consents and clearances (e.g. 180 days). Although sufficient time should be allowed for approvals to be obtained, it is equally important to ensure that time periods are not too long or capable of being manipulated as a delaying tactic by the non-selling party.

12–42 It is also desirable to deal with the position if any necessary approval is not obtained. If a continuing party wishes to take shares offered for sale pursuant to the transfer provisions but does not obtain a necessary approval within the specified time period, then the usual consequence is that the selling party may sell to a third party purchaser.[14] If the sale is to a third party purchaser, there is usually a set time period within which the transfer must be completed; if this does not occur, then the selling party is no longer entitled to sell the shares without going through the pre-emption process again.

Directors' discretion to refuse registration?

12–43 Should the board of directors of the JVC have any continuing discretion to refuse to register transfers? Some pre-emption provisions or articles of association do give the directors a residual discretion, after the pre-emption machinery has been exhausted, to refuse the registration of a transfer to a third party purchaser. This could be drafted widely (e.g. they can refuse registration to any person of whom they do not approve) or perhaps on a limited basis (e.g. refused only if to a named competitor of the JVC or a transferee that is likely to have a material adverse effect on

---

[14] In a multi-party joint venture, a possible variation is that if any relevant conditions of any continuing shareholders who wish to buy shares have not been satisfied or waived, then their acceptances lapse and the remaining continuing shareholders who have satisfied or waived any necessary conditions can take up these shares.

the business of the JVC or if the transferee is likely to cause a problem with an important licence from a regulator).

12–44 Alternatively, and more commonly, no such discretion is reserved; the directors will be obliged to register a transfer made in accordance with the pre-emption provisions. It would usually be unfair to a shareholder, who has agreed a sale to a third party buyer and has complied fully with the prior pre-emption provisions, if the directors were allowed independently to refuse registration of the transfer[15] at this late stage.

Deed of adherence or replacement agreement

12–45 The rights and obligations under a shareholders' agreement do not automatically apply to a transferee of shares. A shareholders' agreement is only a contract between the existing parties. It will, therefore, usually be a condition of any transfer to a third party purchaser that the third party must first enter into an agreement (sometimes termed a "deed of adherence") with the continuing party or parties whereby the third party purchaser agrees to be bound by terms of the shareholders' agreement previously applicable to the transferring party. It is rare, though, for a joint venture party in practice simply to dispose of its interest in a JVC to a third party. If such a transaction takes place, there will commonly need to be a renegotiation or restructuring of the joint venture arrangements between the third party and the continuing party or parties. This is likely to lead, in practice, to a replacement or "restated" shareholders' agreement.

> **For an example of a Deed of Adherence, see Precedent 14 in Part E.**

Change of control

12–46 It is important to recognise the limitations of transfer restrictions. In particular, pre-emption provisions will usually only apply to catch dealings in shares held in the JVC itself. They will not apply to a change in control or ownership of the shareholding party itself or change of control of a holding company or ultimate holding company of that party (or the disposal or charging of shares in a company higher up in the shareholder's group structure). Rights in the event of any such change of control must be regulated, if at all, by different mechanisms:

(1) A common mechanism is to establish a right for the other shareholder party or parties to buy-out the "changed" party's shares in the JVC—see para.13—28 et seq.

---

[15] In any event, under English law, such refusal would only affect the transfer of the legal interest in the shares; it would not affect the transfer of the equitable or beneficial interest.

(2) An alternative to similar effect is to provide that, if a party suffers a change of control (as carefully defined for the purposes of the agreement), it is deemed to have given a transfer notice offering to transfer its shares under the pre-emption provisions at market value to the other party or parties. This works effectively but really only where the pre-emption provisions contemplate a purchase at market value—rather than at a specific price set out in the transfer notice.

Shareholders' agreement or articles of association, or both?

12–47 One common debate is whether pre-emption provisions should appear in the shareholders' agreement or in the articles of association of the JVC. In some cases, they may appear in both. Relevant factors have been raised earlier in para.5–55 et seq. They include the following:

(1) As a matter of drafting, it can be difficult to draft pre-emption provisions in the articles of association as fully or in the same commercial manner as in the joint venture/shareholders' agreement and some confusion can arise if the two sets of provisions are not identical. Incorporating the pre-emption provisions solely in the shareholders' agreement will often be the simplest course.

(2) Amendment of a shareholders' agreement usually requires the consent of all the parties to it. By contrast, articles of association can be amended by a special resolution (although rights can be entrenched by weighted voting rights or class rights).[16] A minority party who cannot block such a special resolution is therefore better protected by contractual provisions in a shareholders' agreement.

(3) The articles of association will automatically bind any person who becomes a shareholder. By contrast, a shareholders' agreement will only bind the parties to it. If it is a multi-party venture with numerous shareholders, the articles of association may be the easiest way to bind them and their successors-and, particularly, if it is anticipated that there may be many subsequent dealings in the shares. (It is therefore usual, in the case of a private equity-based venture, for provisions relating to pre-emption rights, drag-along rights and tag-along to be incorporated in the articles of association.)

(4) The articles of association will bind the JVC and the directors. Some think it is sensible to include the pre-emption provisions in the articles of association if the JVC or its directors or secretary are involved in the procedure of sending out transfer notices under the pre-emption provisions. Inclusion of the provisions in the articles of

---

[16] See also the power under s.22 Companies Act 2006 to entrench specified provisions of the articles of association so that unanimity or a super-majority is required for amendment.

association would impose obligations on the JVC (e.g. not to register transfers unless the procedure has been complied with) which could therefore be directly enforceable, if necessary, against the JVC and/or the directors of the JVC.

(5) Inclusion of such provisions in the articles of association may give greater public notice to third parties of their existence (although, as a matter of English law, it is doubtful whether this is a major advantage in practice).

The advantages of the latter two points may not be very significant in domestic ventures governed by English law and practice. They may have more weight, though, in reassuring a "foreign" joint venture party in an international joint venture. In many civil law countries, remedies of specific performance or an injunction may not be available to enforce a shareholders' agreement. In such cases, incorporating the transfer restrictions into the constitutional documents of the JVC will provide a more effective protection.

12–48 If the details of the transfer provisions are contained in a shareholders' agreement but the parties still wish to ensure that a transfer restriction appears in the articles of association, one formula is:

(a) for the articles of association to contain an absolute prohibition on transfers without consent of all shareholders (if such a provision is permitted by the local law as is the case under English law); and

(b) for the shareholders' agreement to set out the circumstances in which transfers can be made and to include an undertaking that, if the pre-emption procedure and other relevant conditions are satisfied, the other shareholders are obliged to give the requisite consent under the articles of association.

> **Different examples of pre-emption rights are contained in the following Precedents in Part E: the Multi-Party Shareholders' Agreement as Precedent 10; the ITC Model Corporate Joint Venture Agreement as Precedent 13; and the UK JVC's Articles of Association as Precedent 11.**

Consequences of "Wrongful" Transfer

Consequences of "wrongful" transfer

12–49 What happens if a transfer goes ahead in contravention of transfer restrictions? It is not certain, under English law, whether a purchaser can theoretically acquire the beneficial or equitable title to shares if they are

CONSEQUENCES OF "WRONGFUL" TRANSFER 297

transferred in contravention of a pre-emption provision. One case[17] has suggested that it will, unless someone can establish a prior equity. The following factors, however, assist the "innocent" joint venture party:

(1) A prohibition against assignment of a commercial contract (or of any benefit or interest therein) can be effective to prevent the assignee acquiring rights against the other parties.[18]

(2) An injunction should normally be granted by the courts to prevent an assignment, by a selling party in breach of a contractual prohibition, to an assignee who has knowledge of the pre-emption right (who would be committing the tort of knowingly interfering with contractual rights).

(3) Directors are under a duty to refuse to register transfers (i.e. transfer legal title) in breach of pre-emption provisions in the articles of association.[19]

(4) There are dicta in one case[20] which suggest that a purported agreement to transfer shares to a third party, in breach of a pre-emption provision, converts the pre-emption right into a call option in favour of the existing shareholder(s) which will be an equitable interest in the shares ranking ahead in time over the third party's claim.

(5) The courts[21] have been prepared to order rectification of the share register where a transfer (not to a purchaser for value) has taken place when the parties were unaware of the pre-emption provisions. In the case of a purchaser for value, rectification may depend on whether, at the time of transfer, the purchaser had actual or constructive notice that the pre-emption provisions in the articles had not been complied with.

12–50 Additional safeguards in the joint venture documentation to prevent "wrongful" transfer to a third party can include:

(a) a provision that, if a party attempts to dispose of its shares in contravention of such a pre-emption provision, it is deemed to have served an irrevocable transfer notice to the continuing party or parties;

---

[17] *Hawks v McArthur* [1951] 1 All E.R. 22.
[18] See e.g *Helstan Securities Ltd v Hertfordshire CC* [1978] 3 All E.R. 262 where the court held the purported assignment invalid and said " . . . there is no reason why the parties to an agreement may not contract to give its subject matter the quality of unassignability."
[19] *Tett v Phoenix Property and Investment Co Ltd* [1986] B.C.L.C. 149. The Court of Appeal also confirmed that, in construing the pre-emption provisions, an implied term could be introduced in order to give them business efficacy.
[20] *Tett v Phoenix Property and Investment Co Ltd* [1984] B.C.L.C. 599 per Vinelott J. at p.619 and supported in *Cottrell v King* [2004] 2 B.C.L.C. 413 at p.420.
[21] *Cottrell v King*. See also *Hurst v Crampton Bros. (Coopers) Ltd* [2003] B.C.C. 190.

(b) a requirement that each share certificate be endorsed with a note of the pre-emption restriction in order to give notice to a third party—a common protection in many jurisdictions[22];

(c) provisions entrenching the rights of pre-emption in the JVC's articles of association; although this may not constitute conclusive notice to third parties under English law, a third party will customarily review the articles of association before any acquisition of an interest in a JVC.

Conclusion

12–51 Transfer restrictions and pre-emption provisions can be complex. In many cases, they are catering for an unrealistic situation. In practice, detailed pre-emption procedures are likely to be more relevant in the circumstances of a multi-party venture rather than a two-party venture. In the case of a two-party venture, a simpler and more realistic approach is often simply to recognise that share transfers should not to take place without the consent of both parties.

12–52 Transfer provisions should be viewed as part of an overall "exit" structure—see generally chapter 13. Where pre-emption procedures are included, the parties should focus clearly on the basic component questions and build any pre-emption structure on that basis. As with most "exit" provisions, whilst it may be unlikely in practice that the provisions will need to be implemented fully in accordance with their terms, these provisions do provide an important background against which the parties are likely to undertake negotiations to reach a commercial agreement.

---

[22] This is of doubtful legal advantage under English law where the share certificate is only evidence of legal title and not itself part of the share transfer, although in practice the share certificate will generally be produced at the same time as the share transfer.

CHAPTER 13

Exit, termination and change

When, and how, should a party be able to exit from the alliance or joint venture? A high proportion of ventures have a relatively short life. Parties are often reluctant at the start of their relationship to discuss the possibility of its break-up or termination. A well-prepared joint venture should, nevertheless, provide for that possibility. Alliances and joint ventures should allow flexibility for change. "Exit" provisions are an important area for the lawyers.

Importance of exit provisions

13–01 A high proportion of joint ventures have a relatively short life.[1] It is important that this is recognised by the parties and that they plan sensibly for that possibility. A party that does not do so may be ill-protected if and when that eventuality arises. There are also some who argue that parties may be more willing to develop the joint venture if they have the knowledge that adequate provisions for termination of the relationship ("exit" mechanisms) are in place if necessary.

13–02 Exit provisions require careful thought. Even in the case of a contractual alliance, they will usually involve more than simple termination of contract. However, termination of a contractual alliance will generally be straightforward compared with an equity joint venture—where exit provisions will also need to deal with the interests of the parties in the joint venture vehicle itself (e.g. shares in a joint venture company (JVC)). The flexibility and ease of unwind of contractual alliances are, indeed, principal reasons for the popularity of that legal form as an alliance structure.

KEY ISSUES

Key issues in designing exit provisions

13–03 In designing appropriate exit provisions for a particular venture, a

---

[1] See para.1–16 et seq. above. In this context, it is interesting to note the finding of the McKinsey study (see para.1–17) which indicated that, of the joint ventures that terminated, nearly 80 per cent ended with an acquisition by one of the parties.

number of basic questions should be addressed. The answers will determine the structure of the formal contractual provisions:

(1) *Fixed term/joint renewal.* Is the joint venture or alliance to be established for a fixed term with automatic termination unless each of the parties agrees to renew? ("Our relationship is for a fixed term unless we both agree otherwise.") Such an approach is common for a contractual alliance and is often the simplest approach.

(2) *Termination for convenience.* Should a party have the right, simply by notice, to terminate its interest in the venture—irrespective of any "cause" attributable to the other party? ("I want out.") If so, what should be the exit mechanism following any such notice:

— winding-up of the JVC?
— buy-out of the exiting party's shares by the other party or parties?
— buy-out of the exiting party's shares by the JVC?
— implementation of a "buy/sell" or "shoot-out" mechanism between the parties?

(3) *Termination for cause.* Should a party have the right to terminate the venture (or its interest therein) in the event of specified circumstances or "cause"? ("We have agreed that these events should bring our relationship to an end.") If so, what should be the trigger events which entitle a party to exercise this right:

— material default by the other party?
— change of control affecting the other party?
— insolvency of the other party?
— failure of the JVC to reach a specified performance target?

(4) *Agreed put or call options.* Will a party have a direct right or option to "put" its shares in the JVC on the other party (or perhaps to "call" for the other party's shares) at specified times as part of a pre-agreed commercial deal? ("This is our commercial deal for exit.") Such arrangements may be particularly appropriate in a majority shareholder/minority shareholder relationship.

(5) *Sale or public offering of JVC.* Should a party have a right to initiate a sale of the JVC as a whole—either through an initial public offering (IPO) or through a trade or other secondary sale? ("Let's sell the company.") Such a route may be specifically contemplated as an objective or possibility when the JVC is established.

(6) *Transfer of interest.* Should a party have a right to sell its shares in the JVC to a third party purchaser? ("I want to sell my shares to a third party.") If so, should that right be:

— an entitlement which may be exercised "freely" without constraint?

KEY ISSUES IN DESIGNING EXIT PROVISIONS

— subject to a right of the other party to join in the sale?
— subject to pre-emption rights in favour of the other party or parties?
— subject always to the prior consent of the other party or parties?

(7) *Deadlock.* If there is a deadlock or breakdown in the relationship, should there be a right to trigger a specific deadlock resolution mechanism which will terminate the joint venture? ("We can't go on like this.")

(8) *Change or transformation.* Should a party have an express right to call for discussions which may lead to change in terms or scope of the venture? ("We can continue but it should be on a different basis.") If so, should this be linked to:

— changes in market conditions?
— alleged hardship?
— "milestone" events in the venture?

Importantly, are these simply discussions with no commitment to change unless agreed? Or can a party refer, if necessary, to a third party arbitrator or mediator to establish changes in the terms of the joint venture?

13–04 These are the basic questions. Any contractual provisions for exit, termination or change will be centred on these core issues. Within each of these scenarios, there are detailed questions and many different possible approaches. Transfer of shares in a JVC is discussed more fully in chapter 12 and various deadlock resolution mechanisms are discussed separately in chapter 10. The remaining scenarios are addressed in this chapter.

13–05 First, a warning. There is a danger that principles, and detailed rules in the joint venture documentation to reflect them, can become unduly complicated and commercially unworkable. In the large majority of cases, it may be unlikely that they will be used even if a dispute or breakdown arises. Generally, the parties will work out a commercially agreed solution at the time. Contractual provisions should, preferably, be kept as simple and commercially realistic as possible. However, principles or guidelines set out in the joint venture agreement can be useful—and important. They will often create the background against which the parties determine their tactics or relative strengths in the course of negotiations to arrive at an agreed solution.

FIXED TERM/JOINT RENEWAL

Fixed term/joint renewal

13–06 A common exit structure, particularly in the case of contractual alliances, is to establish a fixed term for the venture with automatic termination on expiry of that term—unless both (or all) parties agree to renew. This structure has the benefit of simplicity. The parties know clearly the position. It enables the parties to assess the success of the venture in the light of experience. Market conditions change; experience exposes weaknesses (and strengths); many ventures need to develop if they are to provide continuing benefits. Having those discussions against a framework of the venture coming to an end if no agreement is reached provides a clear and realistic focus. Renewal becomes a joint, and positive, act. It may, though, favour the negotiating power of the stronger party.

13–07 More detailed points to be addressed in this "renewal" scenario include the following:

(a) the term should normally be fixed so that it provides a realistic opportunity for the venture or alliance to achieve its initial goals—or perhaps be fixed by reference to a specific planned milestone or target;

(b) the time for commencing renewal discussions (or of any notice period to indicate that a party does not wish to renew) should be sufficiently in advance of the expiry date so that there is adequate opportunity to implement an alternative strategy;

(c) if the alliance involves dealings with third parties or the development of jointly-owned intellectual property rights or other assets, termination provisions dealing with those assets or contracts will often be necessary;

(d) it will usually be sensible to clarify the ability of the parties, post-termination, to compete freely with each other—although any restrictions on that freedom will almost certainly require review under competition laws.

13–08 A fixed-term route is particularly appropriate for many contractual alliances and some partnerships. Whilst this approach can be adapted to a corporate joint venture using the mechanisms outlined in para.13–09 et seq. below, it is less common. A corporate joint venture will usually have a more open-ended existence with termination mechanisms being of the kinds discussed later in this chapter.

TERMINATION FOR CONVENIENCE

Termination for convenience

13–09 Termination "for convenience" is used here to cover situations where a party can unilaterally, by notice, initiate a procedure for exit or termination of its interest in the joint venture—irrespective of any formal "trigger event" attributable to the circumstances of the other party.

13–10 First, a general point. A reasonable period should usually be allowed to elapse between (i) the initial notice to exit or terminate and (ii) the implementation of the mechanism for terminating that party's interest in the joint venture. In very many cases, the actual solution for dealing with the terminating party's interest will be worked out on a negotiated basis between the parties. The formal provisions setting out the exit or termination procedure in the joint venture agreement should allow time for these commercial negotiations.

13–11 The ability to terminate by notice (and the process) will be affected by the legal form of the joint venture vehicle.

(1) *Contractual alliance.* A party's interest under a contractual alliance will rest entirely on contractual rights and obligations. The general rule will therefore be that any right of a party to terminate will be a matter for the contract.[2] This will in any event fit the commercial background in those many cases where the venture is personal to the parties (such as an R&D collaboration) or has a natural lifespan.

(2) *Partnership.* Similarly, any right to terminate a partnership by notice will invariably be governed by the provisions of the partnership agreement.[3] If there is no such provision and the partnership is not for a fixed term, English law implies a right for a partner to determine the partnership by reasonable notice. Termination of a partnership will also involve arrangements for dealing with the value of a party's interest in the partnership and, if relevant, disposal and/or allocation of partnership assets. In some cases, this will be straightforward; in others, measures for realisation of assets similar to those for a corporate joint venture may have to be considered.

(3) *Corporate joint ventures.* A corporate joint venture creates for each party an interest in the JVC's shares which is legally separate from the JVC's ownership of the underlying assets and liabilities. Contractual exit or termination provisions must therefore deal with the sale or relinquishment of that party's interest. What mechanisms are available? The following basic routes may be considered in circumstances where a party has a right to initiate a procedure for exit or termination by notice:

  (a) *Liquidation/winding-up of the JVC.* It may be agreed that the appropriate, and sometimes only realistic, course is a notice to terminate which then leads to the liquidation or winding-up of the JVC and the realisation of its assets.

---

[2] Under some civil law jurisdictions, a more general, implied right to terminate may exist particularly in the case of a long-term relationship: see para.20–13.
[3] s.26 of the Partnership Act 1890.

(b) *Buy/sell options.* Provision may be made (usually in a two-party venture) for a notice to terminate by one party which then triggers a put/call option or "shoot out" procedure between the parties under which one party may end up as the sole owner of the JVC.

(c) *Buy-back by JVC.* In some circumstances, a suitable route may be buy-back of the outgoing party's shares by the JVC (either through purchase or redemption of those shares) after notice has been given by the exiting party.

(d) *Sale or public offering of JVC.* Provision may be made in some cases for a notice given by one party to initiate a process for the possible sale of the JVC as a whole to a third party or, in certain circumstances, the flotation of the JVC as a publicly listed company.

(e) *"Multi-choice" approach.* Alternatively, the parties may prefer not to be specific about the particular exit route and agree, following notice by one party, to discuss and pursue all or any of these routes sometimes in a specific order of preference.

These routes are not exclusive. In particular, winding-up of the JVC may be adopted as a residual "long stop" remedy if another route (such as buyback by the JVC or sale to another party) is not achieved. They will all, in practice, be subject to any arrangements commercially agreed between the parties at the time of termination. We now look at these various routes or mechanisms in a little more detail, focusing particularly on the situation of a JVC.

Liquidation/winding-up of JVC

13–12 The most extreme—but sometimes only practical—exit route is for a party who wishes to terminate to have a contractual right to require the JVC to be wound up and its assets realised. In certain cases, this may be accompanied by an agreed procedure for the disposal or break-up of the JVC's assets and/or the assumption of contractual obligations as between them prior to the formal winding up.

Buy/sell options on termination

13–13 In some cases,[4] the parties may contemplate put and/or call options as a method of resolving ownership of the JVC consequent upon a notice to terminate. There are a number of variants. Many are increasingly ingenious and complicated—and probably unrealistic. They should only be employed rarely and after careful consideration of the implications.

---

[4] These structures are usually only practical in the context of a two party venture. They can be very difficult to operate (and draft) in a multi-party venture.

(1) *Shoot-outs.* One route, in a two-party venture where the parties are of roughly equivalent financial strength and each is potentially a buyer or seller of the other's interest, is to adopt one of the stark "shoot-out" methods—see the discussion earlier at para.10–22 et seq. Since the outcome of these methods is so unpredictable, they are more usually employed as a form of resolution in cases of "deadlock" rather than consequent upon a right of unilateral termination. However, if such a right is agreed, it does provide a method—if somewhat arbitrary—of bringing the matter to a conclusion between the parties without the extra dimension of a third party valuation. There is perhaps a stronger argument for use in this context if the initiating party suffers a price detriment as a deterrent against commencing the process of termination too lightly (see the "deterrent" version discussed at para.10–29 whereby the party initiating the process suffers a price disadvantage on eventual sale/purchase).

(2) *Call options.* One alternative route involves call options only, as follows:

   (a) the terminating party (A) serves notice on the other party (B) requesting it to purchase the shares of the terminating party (A) at a price to be determined by an agreed valuation procedure;

   (b) the other party therefore has the first opportunity to buy or "call" A's shares but, if it fails to serve a counter-notice agreeing to do so within a certain time, the terminating party (A) then has the right to buyout that other party (B)—which it may do so in order to facilitate sale of the whole JVC to a third party.

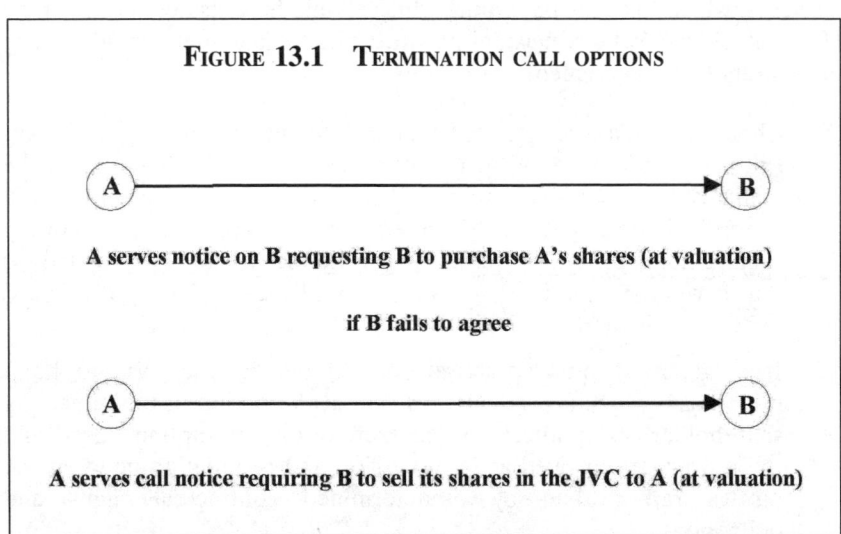

FIGURE 13.1 TERMINATION CALL OPTIONS

A serves notice on B requesting B to purchase A's shares (at valuation)

if B fails to agree

A serves call notice requiring B to sell its shares in the JVC to A (at valuation)

(3) *Call option/liquidation.* Another, perhaps simpler and more practical, variant is for the terminating party to give the other party the option to buy out the former's interest (at valuation) if it wishes the

business of the JVC to continue—and, if it does not exercise that right, the terminating party may initiate liquidation and dissolution of the JVC. Such a method may be appropriate after an initial minimum period for the venture has elapsed or if a certain milestone has not been achieved by a specified date.

> An example of this last route is contained in the 50:50 Shareholders' Agreement (short form) for a deadlock company set out as Precedent 9 in Part E.

13–14 Potential permutations of the various buy/sell termination options are numerous. Termination buy/sell options often appear attractive at the outset of a venture. Care must nevertheless be taken to ensure that the result is workable and takes account of the circumstances of the particular venture. It is vital, if one of these routes is chosen as a mechanism for terminating a party's interest in the joint venture, to take into account the effect of termination on ancillary contracts and other relationships between the JVC and the parents.

Buy-back of shares by JVC

13–15 One effective exit route is for the outgoing party's shares simply to be acquired by the JVC itself. This is attractive if no existing shareholder is able and willing to purchase the shares of a shareholder who wishes to exit and the sale of the shares to a third party is unlikely or unwelcome. However, whilst this may be a route which should be considered at the time of exit, it will rarely be a mechanism which can be guaranteed in advance in the shareholders' agreement.

(1) There are strict corporate law requirements in most jurisdictions (linked to rules relating to maintenance of capital) which affect the ability of a company to purchase its own shares. Consequently, it will be difficult or impossible to be sure in advance that the statutory requirements for such a purchase can be met by the JVC[5] or indeed that it will have the funds (or be able realistically to raise the funds) necessary for the buy-back.

(2) It is generally more practical for buy-out by the JVC to be a mechanism which is available, instead, at the option of the remaining shareholder (as an alternative to exercise of pre-emption rights) and to be a process arrived at in discussion and negotiation between the parties rather than by predetermined contractual rights and obligations.

---

[5] In the UK, a company must be given power to do so in its articles of association before purchasing its own shares and must comply with the requirements of s.690 et seq. Companies Act 2006.

13–16 An alternative method with a similar result may be the use of redeemable shares—discussed earlier in para.9–28. This may be an appropriate route where an investing party (such as a venture capital equity provider) wishes to have a certain exit route to cover its investment. The route needs to be established at the outset by the issue to the holder of redeemable shares (rather than by later alteration of the rights of existing shares).

Sale or public offering of JVC

13–17 Where it is contemplated that a JVC may subsequently be sold or perhaps floated on a public stock exchange, one possible exit is for a party (often a private equity investor) to require by notice that this sale process should be commenced. This will rarely provide certainty as an exit route—see para.13–39 et seq. for a fuller discussion.

"Multi-choice" approach

13–18 One other termination variant reflects the reality that the particular route is likely to be the subject of discussion and negotiations between the parties at the time of proposed termination. Without setting out the process for any particular route in detail, this approach provides that—following a notice of proposed termination—the parties will meet to discuss all or any of these routes (e.g. transfer of the outgoing party's shares to the other party, buy-back by the JVC, transfer of shares to a third party or sale or flotation of the JVC as a whole), sometimes in a specific order of preference, and will use all reasonable endeavours to agree an appropriate solution in the interests of the parties and the JVC.

13–19 Such a provision is given much more bite as an exit route if accompanied by a "long-stop" provision to the effect that, if no alternative route is achieved within a designated period, a party may then require that the JVC is wound-up. A "multi-choice" approach may also be used as a deadlock resolution formula in appropriate circumstances—see para.10–30 earlier.

TERMINATION FOR CAUSE

Termination for cause: general

13–20 The above mechanisms describe procedures for termination where a party can initiate the process simply by notice irrespective of default or other defined event. The following mechanisms apply where the termination is linked to the occurrence of some trigger event or "cause"—usually attributable to circumstances affecting the other party. Whether specific termination rights are required may depend upon the renewal or notice provisions discussed earlier. If the unilateral notice provisions are adequate for a party wishing to terminate, then additional terms may be unnecessary. If these do not suffice, there are a number of such situations where the joint venture parties may agree in advance that a party should be compulsorily required to sell (or offer to sell) its interest in the JVC.

13–21 Trigger events for termination may apply in the following circumstances:

(1) *Default.* Material breach by one party may give rise to an agreed right for the non-defaulting party or parties to purchase the defaulter's interest or, occasionally, to require the defaulter to buy out the interest of the non-defaulter(s).

(2) *Persistent use of veto rights.* Persistent use by a party of its veto rights may give rise to an agreed right for the other (usually majority) party to purchase the (minority) party's interest.

(3) *Insolvency.* An insolvency (or related event) affecting a party will usually give rise to an agreed right for the other party or parties to buy-out the insolvent party's interest.

(4) *Change of control.* Change of control or ownership of a party may, in certain ventures, be agreed as triggering a right for the other party or parties to purchase the changed party's interest (or, sometimes, to require the changed party to buyout the other party).

(5) *End of purpose.* End of the specific purpose of the joint venture (such as conclusion of a specific works project or loss of a basic regulatory licence or concession) may result in automatic termination or in a right for any party to terminate and call for winding-up of the JVC.

(6) *Performance target.* In some cases, a pre-determined profit or performance target may be agreed for the JVC and failure to meet the target may trigger a right for a party to commence a termination procedure. Any of the routes discussed previously in para.13–11 et seq. may be agreed to apply in this event.

We examine each of these scenarios in a little more detail.

Default

13–22 A right of purchase[6] for a party may be contemplated where the other party has committed a material breach (or perhaps persistent

---

[6] In some circumstances, it may decided that the non-defaulting party should have a choice of rights—either (i) to buy out the defaulter or (ii) to exit by selling its own shareholding to the defaulting party.

breaches) of the joint venture agreement. This may particularly be the case where a party has failed to meet an obligation to provide finance to the JVC (see para.7–46 et seq. above). In the case of non-financial breaches, such a provision is frequently seen in joint venture agreements but is generally more difficult to enforce in practice for a number of reasons:

(1) There will often be argument over whether there is a breach or whether it is sufficiently material (and frequently over which party is in breach) and this dispute will need to be resolved, either by litigation, arbitration or other dispute resolution procedure, before a party can effectively implement a compulsory buy-out in these circumstances.

(2) A recalcitrant party will often not be willing to participate in the buy-out process. If this is regarded as a material risk, it can be alleviated (in theory but often not in practice) by providing that:

   (a) a defaulting party is deemed to have served a transfer notice under the pre-emption procedure in the event of a material breach;
   (b) the non-defaulting party (or an officer of the JVC) is given an irrevocable power of attorney to complete any necessary sale documentation; and
   (c) any directors appointed by the defaulting party automatically cease to hold office or cease to be entitled to exercise voting rights which can prevent registration of the share transfer.

13–23 Provision in the joint venture agreement for a buy-out option in the event of default may be a useful deterrent where there are doubts that a co-venturer will perform its obligations. In deciding whether this is appropriate, a judgment should be made as to the nature of the obligations accepted by the joint venture parties under the joint venture agreement. The most material obligations (in addition to any funding commitments) may relate to non-competition or confidentiality. The need for a right of termination upon default may be more necessary or appropriate if used to deter a material default under ancillary contracts critical to the success of the joint venture's operations. In many cases, however, it will be considered inappropriate (as a "relationship" matter) to include such an option in the joint venture agreement except in circumstances of a funding default where there are significant funding obligations crucial to the venture.

13–24 Where there is a buy-out right upon default, the parties may agree that the price should be set at a discount to fair value. Although sometimes questioned, the general view is that these provisions should normally be upheld if they represent an arm's length agreement specifically negotiated in the circumstances of the particular venture—see para.7–48 as to the risk of unenforceability.

Persistent use of veto rights

13–25 We have discussed earlier the inclusion of a right (usually for the majority party) to buy-out the other party in certain circumstances following the persistent use by the other party of its veto rights—see para.10–20.

Insolvency

13–26 It is common to provide for a right of purchase (or a "call" option) in the event of insolvency or analogous circumstances affecting one of the joint venture parties. The definition of the applicable insolvency event should be drafted carefully so that it is clear when the call option can be enforced.

(1) Insolvency events can be drafted to have an early trigger (e.g. in the UK "any step taken with a view to the appointment of an administrator . . .") or a later trigger (e.g. "presentation of an application for the making of an administration order . . . "or, even later, "the making of an administration order . . ."). It will usually be appropriate, in a joint venture context, to have a reasonably certain trigger which is not unduly early—if only because it will often be unclear at the outset for whose benefit any call option rights will ultimately operate.

(2) Depending on the definition of the trigger event, a grace period for particular insolvency events may be included in order to protect a party against any vexatious or frivolous winding-up petition (which can then be discharged or removed during the grace period).

(3) A "carve out" may commonly be included so that the provision is not triggered by a solvent winding-up or corporate reorganisation (or, at least, that consent should not be unreasonably withheld in these circumstances).

(4) Should the insolvency trigger event apply only to the particular joint venture party—or catch also a similar event affecting other members of its corporate group? Sometimes, in a group situation, the definition is extended to include an insolvency or analogous event affecting a relevant parent company where there is a risk of a "domino" insolvency effect applying throughout the group.

In some jurisdictions, however, the enforcement of a termination right or call option upon an insolvency event of default may not always be enforceable under local bankruptcy laws.[7]

13–27 In cases where the option does apply, the relevant party will commonly be granted an option to acquire all the insolvent party's shares in

---

[7] Even in the UK, the option must be exercisable sufficiently early to avoid the statutory prohibition on disposal of assets following the presentation of a winding-up petition (s.127 Insolvency Act 1986) or the passing of a winding-up resolution (s.88 Insolvency Act 1986).

the JVC, usually at a fair value to be fixed by an expert.[8] The general view is that it would be unenforceable under English law against a receiver, administrator or liquidator for the price to be set at a discount to fair value in the circumstances of a compulsory buy-out linked to such an insolvency event.[9]

Change of control

13–28 A change of control of one of the parties can frequently bring about an unacceptable situation in which the other joint venture party is unwilling to continue the collaboration with the changed party under its new ownership. It creates a new situation. Such a change of control will not itself involve any transfer of shares by the changed party in the JVC—see para.12–46 earlier—and could, if not regulated, enable transfer restrictions to be circumvented. Any rights in this situation must, therefore, be negotiated in addition to any pre-emption procedures on transfer. Choices are:

(a) the non-changed party could have a "call" option to acquire the changed party's interest in the JYC (usually at a price[10] to be independently valued) or sometimes a proportion of the changed party's shares sufficient to give it control of the venture;

(b) the non-changed party could have a "put" option to sell its interest in the JVC to the changed party (usually at a price to be valued); or

(c) the parties could agree to do nothing (i.e. no legal rights to sell or buy are created in the event of such a change of control).

13–29 If a right to sell or buy is included, it is important to have a clear definition of what constitutes a "change of control" for this purpose. Many different approaches are possible.

(1) The "call" option may be triggered if the relevant party becomes a subsidiary of a third party—with "control" being defined, in effect, by reference to an ability to exercise more than 50 per cent of votes at a

---

[8] The option notice will, of course, have to comply with the shareholders' agreement. An offer notice was held invalid in *Martyn Rose Ltd v AKG Group Ltd* [2003] EWCA Civ 375 since the agreement did not contemplate deferred payment.

[9] In *Borland's Trustee v Steel Brothers & Co Ltd* [1901] 1 Ch. 279 Farwell J. upheld a provision which was a "fair agreement . . . binding equally upon all [shareholders]" but said: "If I came to the conclusion that there was any provision in these articles compelling persons to sell their shares in the event of bankruptcy at less than the price that they would otherwise obtain, such a provision would be repugnant to the bankruptcy law."

[10] There is some authority under English law to suggest that the parties could agree a price at less than market value (so long as it applies in equivalent circumstances to all parties): *Jarvis Motors Harrow Ltd v Carabott* [1964] 3 All E.R. However, it will rarely be in the best interests of the company to agree such a formula (particularly a listed company). A "discount" is therefore unusual; indeed, if such a call option applies upon a change of control, it is not unknown to require this to be exercised at a "premium".

general meeting or a right to appoint persons with the ability to exercise more than 50 per cent of votes at board level.[11]

(2) A different test is if a third party acquires control in the wider, and less specific, sense defined in the Income and Corporation Taxes Act 1988, s.840 ("power of a person to secure . . . that the affairs of [a body corporate] are conducted in accordance with the wishes of that person").

(3) In some cases, "control" may be deemed to pass if a third party acquires a specified lower percentage interest (e.g. 30 per cent or more) in the voting share capital of the changed party with this being expressly recognised as sufficient to constitute a change of control for the purpose of triggering an agreed option right.

(4) In some ventures, it may not be appropriate for a "call" option to be triggered by all changes of control—but only if a new "controller" is of a particular kind—e.g. only if a controlling interest is acquired by a "competitor" or specified category of buyer. Alternatively, the trigger may be expressed to apply if the change of control materially affects the joint venture party's ability to perform its obligations under the joint venture or the ability of the JVC to maintain a material regulatory licence.

(5) In some cases, it may not be ownership of share capital which is the concern but that the joint venture party (or a relevant parent) continues to carry on a particular type of business—particularly where there are important ancillary contracts to be performed. It may be necessary in some cases to guard against a party disposing of all or substantially all its assets, or a particular business, or perhaps ceasing to maintain a certain credit rating status.

(6) In some limited "personal" situations, a change of control may also be treated as occurring if certain specified individuals cease to be directors of the relevant joint venture party or engaged full-time in its management.

(7) A somewhat different scenario may apply in a multi-party joint venture. Two or more previously independent joint venture parties may merge and the merged entity may thereby have a controlling interest (or at least a majority interest) in the JVC. It is sometimes provided that, in such a situation, the minority parties should have a "put" option in respect of their shares in the JVC (or, occasionally, the majority party may have a "call" option on certain terms).

---

[11] In joint ventures between UK parties, this could be achieved by reference to the definition of a "subsidiary" in s.1159 of the Companies Act 2006. In international joint ventures, it is easier to state a substantive test rather than to refer obliquely to national legislation. If party X to the joint venture is only a subsidiary within the relevant corporate group of which the ultimate parent company is Y, a "change of control" provision will need to catch the situation of any change of control affecting Y itself as well as X ceasing to be a subsidiary of Y.

13–30 Whilst superficially attractive, change of control provisions can cause problems. The existence of a series of such provisions in agreements to which a company is party can cause delays or difficulties in later situations—e.g. if consents from joint venture counterparties have to be obtained in order for the parent company to be free to carry out a subsequent group reorganisation or major structural transaction. In addition, a publicly-quoted company may need to take into account other factors (e.g. whether the change of control provision could act as an improper "poison pill" to deprive its shareholders of the opportunity of considering an outside bid) before agreeing any such provision in relation to a joint venture affecting a major part of its activities.[12]

13–31 In certain circumstances, it may be desirable to establish a regime for a certificate of ownership (certified by an appropriate corporate officer) to be given by each party at regular intervals, or upon request, in order to ensure as far as possible that "control" of one party does not pass without knowledge of the other party.

End of purpose

13–32 Other situations where it may be appropriate for a party to have a right to bring the venture to an end are where the JVC's purpose has effectively ended; for example, where:

(a) the JVC has had a regulatory licence, crucial to its operations, revoked or not renewed; or

(b) the JVC was formed for a specific purpose which has come to an end (e.g. a joint venture to bid for a project which has not succeeded or where the resulting project has ended) or a significant technical or performance milestone has not been reached.

In these circumstances, an acquisition by one party of the other party's shares in the JVC may not be appropriate. A more likely solution is a right for a party to compel the JVC's liquidation.

PUT AND CALL OPTIONS

Put and call options

13–33 In some commercial circumstances the parties may agree, as part of

---

[12] A quoted company may also wish to consider, in some circumstances, whether a hostile offer could emerge from its own joint venture partner—and whether, in those circumstances, there should be provision releasing it from any pre-emption obligations to that party if it wishes to sell its stake in the JVC to a third party.

the up-front commercial deal, that one route of termination should involve the transfer of an existing party's interest between the joint venture parties themselves—irrespective of whether there is a triggering event such as default, insolvency or change of control. This route relies on "put" or "call" options:

(a) a "put" option is a right which entitles party A to require party B to purchase A's shares in the JVC—this may often be an appropriate exit protection if A is a minority shareholder;

(b) a "call" option is a right which entitles party A to require party B to sell B's shares in the JVC to A—and may be appropriate where A is a majority party and wishes to have a definite right to buy-out a minority.

13–34 The main disadvantage with put and call options is that a party may be forced to buy or sell shares at a time when it would not otherwise wish to do so (and this is particularly the case if the put/call price is fixed by reference to a pre-agreed formula and not a price negotiated independently at the time of transfer). Such options will therefore usually only be agreed at the outset of a venture in relatively exceptional circumstances—e.g. where it is recognised that one party (usually a minority party) must have a definite exit route or is only investing in the venture for a limited period or where a right enabling one party (usually a majority party) to buy-out the other is always envisaged.

13–35 Price will usually be the crux of any commercially agreed put/call option arrangements. In many cases, option price negotiations will call for specialist financial advice. Much will depend on the approach to be taken on certain key commercial issues—in particular:

(1) Should the price formula be largely independent of business performance of the JVC and be aimed at providing "downside" protection for a minority shareholder with a largely passive role—or should it include an element of "upside" opportunity to reflect (or incentivise) the relevant party's contribution to management of the JVC?

(2) Is there to be any adjustment to the price, or "deterrent" element, depending on which party initiates the put/call—perhaps by reference to the time at which the option is exercised (e.g. the price may be at a discount to fair value if the option is exercised before a certain period of the venture has elapsed)?

13–36 The possible price formulae, moving from maximum "downside" protection to more open-ended "equity" valuation and risk-sharing, may be illustrated by the following range:

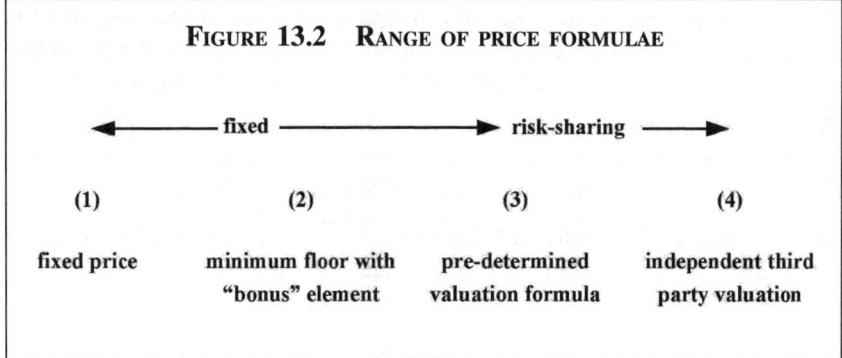

(1) A fixed price, particularly if it is linked to an agreed exit date, offers the greatest certainty for the parties. The party being bought-out has no "downside" risk (except the credit risk of the other party). Possible variations include a fixed price but with some adjustment for the time period until exercise of the option.

(2) A variation, still providing significant "downside" protection, would be a price comprising a minimum floor with an additional element by way of "bonus" if a pre-set financial target is achieved. The outgoing party can therefore benefit to some degree in "upside" financial performance by the JVC. The "bonus" element could be a fixed sum or a formula based, for example, on a multiple of profitability above a certain benchmark or threshold.

(3) Moving to a more "equity-based" approach, the option price may be determined by reference to a pre-agreed formula linked to the profitability of the business of the JVC—with no or only a low minimum floor. Such an approach is arguably more appropriate if the outgoing party has contributed significantly to the management of the JVC and should share in responsibility for financial performance.

(4) The most open-ended "equity" approach is for the price to be fixed at the time by reference to fair or open market value and for that price, if necessary, to be determined by independent valuation (see generally para.12–18 et seq. earlier).

There are, of course, numerous variations or specific formulae which may be negotiated in the particular circumstances within this broad range.

13–37 In a number of these routes, the parties should agree certain important points affecting the price formula, particularly if determination is to be referred to an independent valuer; for example:

(1) What financial metrics (if any) should be chosen as the basis for the price formula: EBITDA? net income? net assets? Financial advice will almost certainly be required to devise or negotiate the appropriate test for the particular venture.

(2) Are there specific accounting principles which should be assumed? Is it clear which GAAP or international accounting standards apply? Should there be specific assumptions regarding exchange rates?

(3) On which accounts should the price formula be calculated? Who will be the auditors? Should the financial metrics be defined by reference to a particular period—or averaged over a longer period?

(4) Selecting an appropriate third party valuer will be vitally important if significant discretion is left to the valuer to determine price—see also para.12–18 et seq. relating to expert valuation.

13–38 Put and call options will generally need also to take account of a number of other factors:

PUT/CALL OPTIONS: OTHER KEY ISSUES

(1) *Put or call?* Will the option be one way—or will each party have a right to terminate the joint venture?

(2) *Timing.* Will there be a fixed time period during which the relevant option is to be exercised?

(3) *Accelerated exercise.* Is exercise of the option to be permitted in circumstances of change of control, a third party offer for the share capital of the JVC or the listing of the JVC (in which event the option should be exercisable immediately before the sale or listing)?

(4) *Loans.* It should be made clear whether loans advanced by the shareholder to the JVC become repayable or whether certain loans are part of the total investment which is the subject of the put/call option.

(5) *Full/partial exercise.* Clarify whether the option is exercisable in respect of all shares or whether (rarely) partial exercise is permitted.

(6) *Undertakings.* Provisions will generally be appropriate—if not contained in other veto rights—to ensure that the JVC cannot, without the consent of the grantee of the option, enter into major transactions which may significantly affect the value of the JVC (e.g. substantial disposals or acquisitions).

(7) *Adjustment for capital reorganisation.* Protective provisions may be necessary to ensure that the formula applies appropriately following any reorganisation of the JVC's share capital.

(8) *Conflict with other provisions.* Ensure that the option takes precedence over pre-emption provisions or other restrictions on transfer in the articles of association and that the parties will take any action necessary to give effect to the exercise of the option, such as agreeing to any relevant pre-emption waivers or procuring the registration of a transfer.

(9) *Listed company.* Options can cause difficulties for UK listed companies where relevant transactions require approval of shareholders under chapter 10 of the Listing Rules. The UK Listing Authority takes the view that:

- where exercise of the option is solely at the listed company's discretion, the value of the transaction for the purpose of the "Class" tests will be assessed at the time the discretion is exercised (and the exercise may, therefore, have to be conditional upon obtaining shareholder approval if so required);
- where exercise is not solely at the listed company's discretion, the obligation is classified at the time it is agreed as if it has been exercised at that time. If the price payable on exercise could be higher than the Class 1 threshold, the consent of the shareholders of the listed company is likely to be required prior to the option being entered into. If the price payable on exercise is to be determined by reference to the future profitability of the JVC or an independent valuation at the time of exercise, then this will be treated as uncapped consideration. If the other class tests indicate that the transaction would be Class 2 but the consideration is uncapped, the transaction will be treated as Class 1 at the time it is entered into and the listed company will require prior shareholder approval. If the other class tests indicate that the transaction would be Class 3, it will be treated as a Class 2 transaction and there will be no need for shareholder approval.

The position is not, however, always clear and a UK listed company is well advised to consult the UK Listing Authority at an early stage if such put/call options are likely to be included in any substantial joint venture—see also para. 2–25 above.

(10) *Regulatory conditions.* Exercise of an option may be subject to the satisfaction of relevant regulatory or other conditions.

(11) *Voting rights and dividends.* It should be clarified which party is entitled to exercise the voting rights and to receive dividends in respect of the option shares during the period from date of exercise to completion.

(12) *Warranties and indemnities.* The selling party will generally warrant its title to the option shares but give no warranties regarding the affairs of the company.

(13) *Tax.* It may be necessary to check the impact of any put/call options on the ability of the parties to claim "consortium relief" or other tax treatment—see para.15–35.

(14) *Completion mechanics.* Provisions will usually be appropriate relating to completion of the sale and purchase of the shares under the option such as execution of share transfers, payment of price, registration of the transfer and removal of the selling party's board appointee(s).

An example of a Put and Call Option Agreement is Precedent 15 in Part E.

Sale or Public Offering of JVC

Sale or public offering

13–39 It is becoming increasingly frequent for participants in a joint venture to contemplate at the outset a subsequent exit through a sale or an initial public offering of the JVC itself after a number of years—particularly where there is substantial investment from a venture capitalist or similar equity provider. The viability of a sale or public offering will depend upon the performance of the JVC and the state of the market at the time. It will be impossible to structure a legally binding commitment to achieve such an exit. Any provisions will therefore inevitably be somewhat vague along the lines of:

(a) expressing the intention of the parties to co-operate to work towards achieving a sale or public offering within, say, a target period;

(b) possibly, enabling a party to call for the appointment of a financial adviser to give advice on the feasibility of, and measures to achieve, a sale and/or an initial public offering;

(c) possibly, requiring each party to co-operate in giving reasonable information and warranties upon any such sale or offering and generally to co-operate in the process.

> The Multi-Party Shareholders' Agreement at Precedent 10 in Part E includes a general clause contemplating a possible sale or public offering of the JVC.

13–40 Where there are venture capital or other private equity investors, they are likely to seek additional provisions in their investment agreement with the JVC and the other parties which will protect their interests in or promote a satisfactory exit.

VENTURE CAPITAL: IPO/SALE PROTECTIONS

If the desired exit is by way of an initial public offering (IPO) or sale of the JVC, the investors may wish to establish "piggy back" rights to join proportionately in, or sometimes to require the whole of their stake to be included in, any IPO, private placement or sale. (If an offering in the US is contemplated, the investors will commonly seek either "piggy back" rights to ensure that a company's registration statement with the US Securities and Exchange Commission (SEC) extends to cover the investors' shares in the company or, on occasions, "demand rights" compelling the company to file such a registration statement in anticipation of a possible future listing.)

In addition, the investors may (where appropriate) seek recognition from the other shareholders in advance, inter alia, on the following aspects:

— a statement that they (the investors) will not provide warranties and indemnities other than as to title to their shares;

— making it clear that any "drag along" provisions held by other parties should only apply if they extend to all shares and loans (i.e. the entire investment) of the institutional investor;

— an intention that any "lock-up" period required by a sponsor to a public offering should apply only to the management shareholders and not to the institutional investors;

— adjustment to any "ratchet" so that the proportion of the consideration receivable by management goes down the longer an exit takes to achieve;

— where the price from any sale of the JVC is less than sufficient to recover the whole of the institution's investment, a provision that the proceeds should be distributed on any preference shares held by the institution as if they were proceeds in a winding-up.

Specialist texts should be consulted for more detailed analysis and precedents. See also para.9–39 earlier for similar issues relating to minority strategic investment.

Third party offer

13–41 An alternative exit is a sale (not initiated under the joint venture arrangements) in response to an offer received from a third party (whether unsolicited or engineered by a shareholder who wishes to sell). In this situation, likely protections are:

(a) "tag-along" rights for the minority party, to ensure that the majority shareholder is obliged to ensure (or, in the softer version, must use reasonable endeavours to ensure) that the third party offer extends also to the minority shares and at the same price—sometimes with additional protection to ensure that a minimum price is obtained before the third party offer can be accepted by the majority;

(b) "drag-along" rights for the majority party to ensure that the sale is not obstructed or hindered by the minority stake.

13–42 In the case of a multi-party venture, it may be desirable to structure any "drag-along" provisions in the articles of association—rather than simply the shareholders' agreement. One formula is to require a general meeting of shareholders to be convened to approve any such third party offer (with the requisite majority being set at 75 per cent or other agreed majority) and, if approval is obtained, for all shareholders thereafter to be bound to accept the offer and transfer their shares accordingly.[13]

Transfer of Interest in JVC To Third Party

Transfer of interest to third party

13–43 One basic route for a party to terminate its interest in a JVC is for that party to sell (or attempt to sell) its interest to a third party. Such a route not only has practical difficulties in most joint venture situations but it will also be subject to detailed contractual and constitutional restrictions—frequently involving a pre-emption procedure in favour of the other shareholder(s) in the JVC. These are discussed separately in chapter 12. They should, however, be viewed in the overall context of the "exit strategy" available to the parties.

Deadlock

Deadlock

13–44 Provision may be made for specific termination or resolution mechanisms in the event of deadlock or breakdown between the parties. In many ventures, no specific mechanisms will be included—in which case exit procedures will depend on one of the various mechanisms discussed in this chapter. However, in some ventures, the parties may prefer to establish one of the specific termination or "divorce" mechanisms discussed in more detail in chapter 10.

Transformation or Change

Transformation or change

13–45 Joint ventures and alliances must be able to adapt to changing

---

[13] There is a slight doubt in the UK whether a drag-along provision in the articles of association is enforceable or whether it can be challenged as "expropriation" of a minority, but it is generally accepted as valid if already contained in the articles of association at the time of the minority party's subscription for shares and, preferably, if it is agreed by all shareholders.

circumstances.[14] A difficult question is the extent to which such change should be specifically contemplated in the contractual agreements—or simply left to discussions between the parties outside the contractual framework or to changes in the business plan within the governance structure. Different approaches can be taken:

(1) *Review*. Express provision may be included for a review of the joint venture or alliance (including the basic commercial terms of any ancillary contracts) by senior management at periodic intervals—e.g. every three years or even annually. This would simply be a non-binding review based on monitoring and communication without formal commitment to change. In many ways, this is simply contractual wording which reflects a "best practice" of keeping a joint venture or alliance under review and alive to the possibility of change.

(2) *Hardship or change of market conditions*. Provision may be included which expressly entitles a party to call for discussions, to be held in good faith, in the event that a party can demonstrate particular hardship—or perhaps change in market conditions or regulatory regime—which it considers justify a change in the scope or terms of the venture (or even termination).

(3) *Reference to mediator/arbitration*. Usually any "review" or "hardship" provisions will rely on good faith discussions—being a "peg" on which to hang the initiation of talks but without legal commitment to change. In some ventures, though, the parties may be prepared, or wish, to go further and to establish a firmer mechanism for review and change. This could include:

(a) reference to an executive panel or some other structured escalation of the issues to senior executives within the organisations of the joint venture parties;

(b) appointment of a mediator to assist the parties in reaching appropriate terms for change—in effect, as part of a mechanism for dispute resolution (see para.14–10 et seq. below for discussion of a greater role for third party mediation in joint ventures and alliances); or

(c) in some cases, if rarely, reference to an arbitrator or other third party with authority to impose "fair and reasonable" revisions to the joint venture arrangements.

An example of a provision for review in the event of "hardship" appears in the ITC Model Corporate Joint Venture Agreement included as Precedent 13 in Part E.

---

[14] Some commentators advocate regular review and change as a feature of successful growth, e.g., D. Ernst and J. Bamford *Your Alliances Are Too Stable* (Harvard Business Review, June 2005).

(4) *Fixed term/joint renewal.* Perhaps the simplest approach in many ventures (particularly contractual alliances) is to adopt the structure of a fixed term for the alliance—with "review" discussions being held against the background of the alliance coming to an end if the parties do not jointly agree to renewal: see para.13–06 earlier.

Change in terms of the venture (including the terms of any ancillary contracts) does not represent failure. We have seen that many joint ventures and alliances undergo a significant change after a few years. The flexibility to change can be part of the vitality and success of a venture.

CONSEQUENCES OF EXIT/TERMINATION

Consequences of exit/termination: general

13–46 Irrespective of whether termination of the joint venture is voluntary or compulsory (or results in a transfer of shares in a JVC), the following factors relating to termination will invariably have to be considered and dealt with in a well-prepared joint venture:

(1) *Non-compete.* It should be clearly established whether any undertaking by a party not to compete with the business of the joint venture should continue—at least for a short period after termination or transfer of the relevant party's shares. Beware, though, that competition laws may prevent any post-termination restraint in the case of ventures with appreciable market impact—see para. 16–17.

(2) *Confidentiality.* It would be usual to ensure that undertakings in respect of confidentiality, relating to information or the affairs of the joint venture or of the other joint venture parties, should survive transfer of a party's shares or the termination of the joint venture for whatever reason.

(3) *Intellectual property rights.* It should be clarified whether any party leaving the joint venture will continue to have the benefit of any licence to use the joint venture's IPR. Different considerations may apply following a sale by a party of its interest in the joint venture compared with a mutually agreed termination or winding-up of the venture. In the case of the former, it may commonly be provided that a leaving party should be entitled to use IPR developed by the JVC up to the time of termination but not to use any IPR originated by the JVC after that date—see generally chapter 17.

(4) *Name.* Frequently, the JVC will use under licence the name or trademarks of one or more of the joint venture parties. It should be made clear whether this right or use should continue or cease (perhaps after an appropriate grace period) if that party exits from

the joint venture. Loss of use of a name, or the benefit of other ancillary contracts, could have a significant effect upon the value of the JVC after such exit. It may well be appropriate to direct how this is to be taken into account if there is an agreed valuation process on a party's exit.

(5) *Loans.* It should be clarified also whether loans from the outgoing party to the JVC should be repayable by the JVC upon termination or whether they are required to be assumed by the continuing or incoming joint venture parties—see also para.12–36 earlier.

(6) *Guarantees/indemnities.* Similarly, is it to be an obligation of any transfer of shares in the JVC that the transferee must assume the transferor's obligations under any disclosed guarantees or counter-indemnities given by it for the benefit of the JVC (with an indemnity from the transferee to the transferor for any liability arising under any such guarantee or counter-indemnity unless and until replaced)? This indemnity may contain an exception for any liabilities attributable to circumstances arising prior to the date of transfer.

(7) *Ancillary contracts.* When designing termination rights, it is important to review the effect upon any other ancillary contracts (e.g. licences or contracts for the supply of goods) to assess whether they should continue uninterrupted—or whether either party should have a right of termination (or perhaps a right to require re-pricing) in the event of a party ceasing to be a party to the joint venture: see also para.6–15.

(8) *Warranties.* It will usually not be appropriate or required for a transferor party to give warranties on any transfer to an existing party (other than as to title to its shares). Terms of any sale to a third party will be a matter for commercial negotiation.

(9) *Completion mechanics.* Provisions will usually be appropriate relating to completion of the sale and purchase of shares (such as execution of share transfers, payment of price, registration of the transfer and removal of the transferring party's board appointees).

(10) *Deed of adherence.* Prior to completion of any transfer of interest to a third party, it will usually be important to ensure that the third party has executed a "deed of adherence" undertaking to be bound by the terms of the shareholders' agreement in place of the transferor (subject to such amendments as may be mutually agreed). In many cases, it may be more appropriate for a revised shareholders' agreement to be executed between the third party and the continuing party or parties.

(11) *Tax.* Steps to be taken on a winding-up or termination of a joint venture, particularly as regards the disposal of the JVC's assets, may be significantly influenced by tax considerations. These are referred to in more detail in para.15–40 et seq.

(12) *Realisation of assets.* Where a JVC is being wound-up or is to cease trading, the parties may wish to establish a procedure for dealing with outstanding contracts and/or realisation of assets prior to formal winding-up. In some cases, this may take the form of:

— an agreed "auction" procedure whereby each party can bid for identified assets and/or business of the JVC;
— a pre-agreed option for a particular party to reacquire the assets or business based on its original contribution (where still clearly identifiable), usually with some mechanism for independent valuation or determination of price; or
— occasionally, a dividend in specie to a particular party of an identifiable group of assets.

(13) *Good leaver/bad leaver.* In some joint ventures, it may be appropriate when providing for the consequences of termination—to make a distinction between the terms applicable to a "good leaver" (when circumstances are deemed to justify exit) compared with a "bad leaver" (when exit is premature or due to circumstances, e.g. default or insolvency, of the particular party). This is more likely to affect the terms applicable to conversion or warrant rights exercisable by, for instance, management shareholders.

This is a checklist of points to be considered. Generally, the break-up of a joint venture will inevitably involve detailed discussion between the parties—including, if necessary, negotiated arrangements for dealing with outstanding contractual obligations and the realisation (or carve-up) of the JVC's assets.

WINDING-UP OF JVC

13–47 Winding-up of the JVC will, of course, bring an end to a corporate joint venture. Winding-up may be brought about in circumstances of insolvency or may be initiated in certain circumstances by one or more of the parties. This is not the appropriate context for a detailed discussion of the law and procedure applicable to winding-up and further reference should, if necessary, be made to specialist texts. In the case of a JVC, it should be remembered that termination of the joint venture agreement does not necessarily mean that the JVC itself must be liquidated.

(1) If a joint venture between two parties comes to end upon a transfer of shares in the JVC to a third party, the JVC will of course continue and any arrangements between the new shareholders will be a matter of contract (including whether the new shareholder enters into a "deed of adherence" or revised shareholders' agreement with the continuing shareholder(s)).

(2) Similarly, if a voting or other contractual arrangement between existing shareholders comes to an end, the JVC can continue and the rights of the parties as shareholders in the JVC will, in that event, solely be governed by the memorandum and articles of association and relevant corporate law.

Voluntary winding-up

13-48 An extraordinary resolution of the shareholders (i.e. requiring a 75 per cent majority of those voting) is required under English law for a company to go into a members' voluntary winding-up—assuming, of course, that the necessary solvency test can be satisfied. A resolution to wind-up a JVC may not itself automatically bring a joint venture agreement to an end at that stage. This will depend upon its terms, but the parties may have contractually agreed:

(a) provisions which are in any event intended to operate between them on a continuing basis after winding-up (e.g. as to confidentiality or the use of intellectual property rights derived from the joint venture); and/or

(b) for a particular procedure to apply as to the disposal or break-up of the JVC's assets and/or the assumption of contractual obligations as between them.

In practice, the parties are likely to agree (either at the outset or at the time of the break-up) for a particular distribution or allocation to take place in respect of the joint venture's assets and liabilities. This will frequently be effected prior to the formal winding-up itself.

Compulsory winding-up

13-49 An order of the court is required for a compulsory winding-up of a UK company. In the context of a JVC, the most relevant ground is a petition that winding-up is "just and equitable" within the terms of s.122(1)(g) of the Insolvency Act 1986. This may commonly be brought by an aggrieved party as a measure of last resort. A more detailed review of this ground appears in the context of the remedies of a minority party discussed in para.11-41 et seq. above.

CONCLUSION

13-50 Provisions relating to exit and termination of a joint venture often appear complicated. The parties may regard a detailed contractual exercise unnecessary and counter-productive at the time of establishing the venture. In most ventures, however, it will be sensible to make appropriate provision for this eventuality. The recommendation is to "stand back" and assess the situation in the light of the key issues raised in para.13–03 at the beginning of this chapter. If appropriate thought is given to these key issues, then a sensible structure can be developed which could prove its value in later years.

Chapter 14

Disputes: mediation, litigation and arbitration

Joint ventures and alliances frequently give rise to inter-partner disputes. These may spill over into legal claims regarding the respective rights and obligations of the parties. Most disputes will be settled by negotiation. It will usually be in the interests of the parties to reach a settlement without undue acrimony and damage to the business. Parties are, however, not always able themselves to reach a negotiated solution. Third party intervention, whether in the form of alternative dispute resolution (ADR), arbitration or litigation, is sometimes unavoidable. This chapter[1] examines these dispute resolution mechanisms.

Why are dispute resolution provisions important?

14–01 Parties are often reluctant to give much thought to the possibility of disputes at the outset of their relationship. As a result, discussion of formal dispute resolution mechanisms in the joint venture or alliance agreement may receive less attention than is desirable—particularly in the case of international joint ventures. Consideration of dispute resolution procedures at the initial stage of a joint venture or alliance is, however, important.

(1) A dispute resolution structure, appropriately tailored to the venture, can help to catch problems early at a time when positions are not entrenched and problems are solvable. Having such a structure in place can facilitate dialogue within the joint venture and produce cost savings to the joint venture by preventing a formal dispute from arising or promoting the efficient management of a dispute once it has arisen. Indeed, many believe that resolution of differences can be a source of creativity and strength for the relationship going forward. A structure which helps to achieve this and avoid the bitterness of "divorce" can be a positive benefit.

(2) Even if termination of the venture is inevitable, there is still advantage in avoiding unnecessary conflict. Parties may still need to preserve good relations between themselves (possibly for alliances on other

---

[1] I am grateful to Nigel Rawding, Daniel Kalderimis and Devika Khanna of Freshfields Bruckhaus Deringer LLP for their review and update of this chapter.

projects). A company may also have a strong wish to maintain its reputation in the market as a good "alliance partner" and therefore its attraction for alliances and ventures with other potential partners.

(3) If a major dispute cannot be avoided and legal rights and obligations do have to be enforced, provisions relating to litigation or arbitration proceedings will become vital. Rights and obligations—however carefully defined in the contractual documents—are only as reliable, in the final legal analysis, as the courts or arbitral tribunals called upon to give effect to them.

INTERNAL DISPUTE RESOLUTION PROCEDURES

Executive level dispute resolution

14–02 Dispute resolution mechanisms will be likely to form part of the structure for governance of the joint venture and alliance.

(1) Measures will be designed in most alliances to create a culture and a regular communication system which endeavour to ensure that differences of opinion are addressed constructively and speedily. Frequently, particular alliance managers or "gatekeepers" appointed by each party will have a special role or responsibility for this purpose.

(2) More formally, the governance structure may itself be designed to assist a decisive resolution of differences—particularly if they relate to operational disputes (see generally para.10–04 et seq.). The board of the joint venture company (JVC) or management committee of the alliance will, of course, have a vital role in dealing with disputes which cannot be settled at an operational level.

(3) The next stage will usually involve some form of escalation of the dispute—sometimes in stages—to higher levels within the "parent" organisations. Variants will depend on the dynamics of the particular venture.

(4) In some cases, there may even be established a standing "dispute review panel", or similar, as a framework for assisting the speedy but considered resolution of disputes during the life of the venture—see para.10–13 earlier.

14–03 A final step is usually for the dispute to be referred ultimately to the chairmen or chief executives of the parent shareholders (or, perhaps, to other specified directors with appropriate technical background). A sensible provision is to enshrine in the joint venture agreement the principle that neither party shall proceed to litigation or arbitration proceedings until the expiry of a stated period after the dispute has been referred to the chairmen/chief executives of the parties. This provides both a "cooling off" period and an opportunity for the senior figures in each party's organisation to focus on the dispute and perhaps take a wider view. In many cases, such a provision will only reflect what would happen in any event in practice in the case of a serious dispute, but a formal provision to that effect can assist to clarify the process.

MEDIATION

Alternative dispute resolution (ADR)

14–04 Some disputes are not resolvable within the confines of purely internal procedures. This may particularly be so where a party is alleging non-compliance with its "rights" or breach by the other party of its "obligations". There has been increasing use of alternative dispute resolution (ADR) techniques—particularly mediation—as a way of avoiding full-scale confrontation in litigation or arbitration proceedings. The essence of ADR is that, if disputes arise which cannot be resolved through face-to-face negotiation, the assistance of an intervening third party may enable the parties to find a basis to do so. There are many forms[2] of ADR including conciliation, mediation, mini-trial and non-binding arbitration or a combination of more than one form, such as "Med-Arb" where parties agree that if mediation is unsuccessful, the mediator will then act as an arbitrator to reach a binding resolution of the dispute.

14–05 The ADR process (particularly mediation) is intended to encourage representatives of the parties to recognise the wider commercial implications of the dispute and their interests for the future as well as the weaknesses and strengths of the legal case. Concessions can be made and opportunities for compromise explored without prejudicing the parties" legal rights, at least until some form of binding agreement is reached. Mediators, coming independently to the problem, can bring additional value by suggesting creative "outside the box" (often commercial) alternatives that can facilitate the resolution of seemingly intractable disputes.

14–06 The primary advantages of ADR therefore include the following:

(1) *Speed*. The lack of formality means that the procedure can be as long or as short as the parties wish. Informality is encouraged.

(2) *Flexibility*. The parties have complete flexibility over the appointment of the neutral person to assist them in reaching a settlement, the procedures that person is to adopt and also the way in which that

---

[2] For an introductory guide, see J. Paulsson et al., *The Freshfields Guide to Arbitration and ADR* 2nd edn, (Kluwer Law International, 1999).

person is asked to come to a decision or recommendation (if at all). Strict rules of evidence and procedure are not required to be followed.

(3) *Costs.* There are opportunities for saving costs which would otherwise be incurred in litigation or arbitration. It should however be recognised that, if the parties are ultimately unable to agree a basis to settle their dispute, litigation or arbitration will be necessary and the costs of the ADR method may largely have been wasted. (In the UK however, the court's discretion to award costs may be influenced by a party's willingness to attempt dispute resolution through ADR[3].)

(4) *Party control.* The parties maintain a far greater degree of control over the procedure which is commercial and pragmatic rather than legalistic and formal. Each party also retains the power to refuse to agree to resolve the dispute at the end of the procedure. This psychological "investment" in the process can have a positive impact on the likelihood of a successful outcome.

(5) *Confidentiality.* Unlike litigation in the courts, ADR proceedings are carried out in private (as are arbitration proceedings). This avoids the possibility of adverse publicity and can also minimise the risk of disclosing business information and trade secrets to competitors.

(6) *Ongoing business relationship.* ADR provides an effective means of resolving disputes between parties who have an interest in maintaining an ongoing business relationship. The parties should approach the process in a spirit of negotiation and compromise, instead of adopting the adversarial positions associated with litigation. They are encouraged to focus on business objectives rather than legal positions.

Ultimately, however, the success of mediation will be determined by the goodwill of the parties and their relative degree of motivation to settle. Even if the dispute is not settled by ADR, the time and effort invested by the parties will in many cases not be entirely wasted. Mediation often focuses the parties on the real areas of dispute and narrows the outstanding issues of disagreement between them. It should also be borne in mind that ADR is always an option even after other more formal methods of resolving the dispute are underway.

14–07 Mediation or other ADR processes may not, however, be appropriate in all circumstances:

(1) ADR will not be appropriate where one party requires a remedy from the court such as an injunction (e.g. for breach of confidentiality or non-compete undertakings) or where one party may lose particular

---

[3] *Dunnett v Railtrack* [2002] EWCA Civ 302 was the first example of costs penalties being imposed on a successful litigant because of its unreasonable refusal to mediate. Parties litigating in the UK should expect questioning at case management conferences, pre-trial reviews and at the conclusion of a case as to whether mediation was considered and why it was turned down.

rights by a delay in bringing proceedings. Referring a dispute for resolution by ADR will not stop the clock running for limitation purposes.

(2) ADR may not be effective if the parties have already adopted extreme adversarial positions. In some cases, although ADR proceedings are generally confidential and conducted on a "without prejudice" basis (so that any statements made during the process cannot be disclosed in any subsequent proceedings), there may be a residual concern about disclosing too much during the ADR process in case that process later breaks down.

Application of different forms of ADR to joint ventures and alliances

14–08 With the growing popularity of mediation, as one might expect, there is an increasing trend to introduce mediation (or other ADR processes) as a dispute resolution mechanism for joint ventures. Parties may wish that the joint venture should continue after the particular dispute has been resolved (and this may be easier without the acrimony of litigation or arbitration which usually spells the end of the joint venture relationship). Generally, joint venture parties may prefer to keep their "matrimonial disputes" as low-profile and non-public as possible. Even if an ADR mechanism is not formally included in the joint venture agreement, there is, of course, nothing to prevent parties from applying such procedures when any dispute actually arises.

14–09 One area where such provisions have become more common is in the field of infrastructure and other project joint ventures and, in particular, those involving construction or engineering companies with experience of ADR in their separate contractual dealings. An increasingly frequent formula, in these cases, is the creation of a "project mediation panel" or a "dispute review board" consisting of senior managers from the alliance members—sometimes being executives not directly connected with the alliance operations and including, possibly, a named mediator or team of mediators—before the venture commences. This allows the panel to be familiar with the venture, its members and objectives. It also allows the alliance members to be familiar with the mediator(s), thus assisting a "kick-start" to any actual resolution process when needed.

14–10 Mediation clauses are also appearing more generally in international joint ventures, particularly those involving emerging market countries and different cultures, e.g. in many parts of Asia where business parties traditionally prefer a face-saving mutually-agreeable compromise than a public battle. Express reference in these cases to the availability of a mediation process, before a dispute is escalated to the level of formal arbitration or litigation, is often felt to be a useful and constructive principle to establish in the joint venture agreement. We are likely to see an increase in express provision for mediation in these types of joint venture situations.

14–11 Bodies active in the field of mediation include particularly the Centre for Effective Dispute Resolution (CEDR) based in London, Judicial Arbitration and Mediation Services (JAMS) in the US and the CPR Institute for Dispute Resolution in New York. Interestingly, CEDR has announced[4] an alliance with the Association of Strategic Alliance Professionals (Europe) Limited (ASAP) aimed at promoting effective dispute resolution as a key component of best practice in joint venture and alliance governance.

> **Precedent 22 in Part E includes mediation clauses recommended by CEDR and the CPR Institute.**

EXPERT DETERMINATIONS

14–12 Expert determinations are also commonly used particularly in disputes which require a specialist in a given technical field, e.g. disputes arising from the failure of the parties to agree on the valuation of non-cash contributions to a joint venture, the valuation of shares or particular items relating to the sale of a party's interest—see para.12–18 et seq.

14–13 An expert determination is usually expressed to be both final and binding by agreement of the parties. It is also common practice (at least in the UK) to agree that the expert shall act as an expert and not as an arbitrator in reaching a determination of the matter. This will generally mean that the methods of challenging arbitral awards[5] are not available to challenge the expert's determination. It also frees the expert of having to abide by some of the procedural constraints to which arbitrators are subject. Final and binding expert determination represents one end of the spectrum between speed and finality on the one hand and reviewability on the other. Parties are of course able to strike the balance they find appropriate to their needs, e.g. by making expert determination one stage in a multi-tier dispute resolution procedure. Such procedures require a clear delineation of when one form of dispute resolution is deemed to have failed and the next stage must begin.

---

[4] CEDR, Resolutions, Issue no.36, Autumn 2004. CEDR and JAMS have also recently announced a strategic alliance to assist clients involved in transatlantic disputes.
[5] Such as ss. 67–68 Arbitration Act 1996.

LITIGATION

14–14 Whilst the use of ADR may assist parties to reach a settlement, a dissatisfied party can always refuse to accept any compromise solution which may emerge through such a process. It is, therefore, never sufficient simply to provide for ADR as a means of resolving a dispute. It will always be necessary to provide, as a fall-back, a mechanism for achieving a binding solution to the dispute either by way of litigation in a selected national court or through arbitration.

Litigation in national courts

14–15 Where parties to a joint venture are from the same country, they may be willing to agree that the national courts of that country shall have jurisdiction to decide all legal disputes. In the case of many international joint ventures, there will often be pressure to accept the home jurisdiction of one party. This may be acceptable in many circumstances (particularly, say, in developed EU jurisdictions) or an inevitable consequence of doing business in that particular jurisdiction. However, the national courts of one party may not be commercially acceptable for many international joint ventures; a foreign party may be unwilling to permit disputes to be determined in another party's home territory.

Use of a neutral country

14–16 The courts of a third, neutral, country may also be inappropriate. It is often difficult to be certain that a neutral court, which otherwise has no connection with the disputing parties or the venture, will accept jurisdiction and hear the dispute. In litigating in the courts of a neutral country, significant expense may be incurred in instructing local lawyers, attending hearings and in complying with orders and procedures of that court. In addition, the network of treaties for the recognition of national court judgments is incomplete. In contrast to the position regarding the enforcement of arbitration awards (see para.14–22 below), there is no wide-reaching multilateral treaty regime in relation to the international enforcement of court judgments.[6] Where a neutral venue is desired, arbitration is likely to be the preferable alternative.

---

[6] There are certain multilateral treaties between groups of countries under which each country agrees to recognise and enforce court judgments rendered in other countries which are party to that treaty (e.g. under the Brussels Convention 1968 and the Lugano Convention 1988 in relation to countries within the EU). Where such treaties do not exist, enforcement of a judgment may be a difficult and lengthy process. The US, for example, is not a party to any bilateral or unilateral treaty allowing recognition and enforcement of judgments (although all US states have enacted uniform legislation providing for the enforcement of foreign money judgments).

Jurisdiction clause

14–17 Where it is agreed that disputes should be resolved by litigation rather than arbitration, it is important to establish which court will have jurisdiction. The parties may provide that such jurisdiction should be exclusive or non-exclusive. An exclusive clause cuts down the risk of prolonged and expensive forum disputes; a non-exclusive clause affords more flexibility (particularly if the location of relevant assets is likely to be uncertain).[7] So far as EU Member States are concerned, however, the courts of one EU Member State (even if jurisdiction purports to be exclusive in accordance with Article 11 of the Brussels Convention) cannot grant an anti-suit injunction to stop an action in another Member State.[8] It will invariably be sensible to take local law advice in the chosen jurisdiction as to the effectiveness of the jurisdiction clause.

14–18 Where the courts of England and Wales are selected and the joint venture includes a foreign party, it will generally be prudent to include a provision whereby an agent of that foreign party within the jurisdiction is appointed for service of process. This will then facilitate the commencement of any court proceedings and will obviate the need to obtain permission to serve those proceedings out of the jurisdiction, a process which can cause delay and further expense.

ARBITRATION

Litigation or arbitration?

14–19 There is continuing debate over the advantages and disadvantages of arbitration compared with litigation as a method of resolving commercial legal disputes. In the context of many joint ventures and alliances (and particularly international joint ventures), the balance of the arguments and the practicalities of negotiation will frequently lead to arbitration being chosen.

14–20 The advantages of arbitration in this context are generally perceived as the following:

---

[7] If an agreement conferring jurisdiction on the English courts is silent as to whether such a clause is exclusive or non-exclusive, case law suggests that the English courts are likely to construe it as exclusive; see e.g. *British Aerospace v Dee Howard* [1993] 1 Lloyd's Rep. 368 and *Continental Bank v Aeakos* [1994] 2 All E.R. 540.

[8] This follows two well-known ECJ decisions. In *Gasser GmbH v MISAT Srl* [2003] ECR I–14693, it was established that a court of an EU Member State on which exclusive jurisdiction had been conferred by agreement must stay its own proceedings if the court of another Member State has been first siesed. In *Turner v Grovit* [2004] ECR I–3565, the ECJ ruled that a court of a Member State could not issue an injunction restraining a party from pursuing proceedings in a court of another Member State even in circumstances where those proceedings had been commenced in bad faith.

(1) *Neutrality.* The arbitral tribunal, the procedure for the arbitration and the venue of the arbitration can be chosen by the parties so as to have a "neutral" or "non-national" character.

(2) *Enforcement of awards.* Arbitral awards are potentially more valuable to a successful party than court judgments because they tend to be more readily enforceable internationally through the New York Convention on the Recognition and Enforcement of Arbitral Awards ("New York Convention").

(3) *Confidentiality.* Commercial arbitration is undisputedly a private process. Confidentiality is a perceived advantage of arbitration compared to litigation and is of particular importance where the parties to the dispute are likely to have an ongoing relationship after the arbitration has been concluded and so are keen to ensure that trade secrets or know-how are not lost and that reputational damage is avoided. Whether confidentiality can be assured and to what extent varies, however, since different jurisdictions recognise confidentiality to varying extents.

(4) *Procedural flexibility.* The parties are free to choose the procedure which suits them best and are not bound by strict national rules of court procedure. Particular procedures (e.g. as to written submissions or discovery of documents) can either be established in advance by the parties or left to the discretion of the arbitrators. The element of party choice and control of the process adds to their confidence in the process.

(5) *Identity of the arbitrators.* The parties also have the opportunity to identify in the arbitration clause the number of arbitrators, the method by which those arbitrators will be appointed and whether they should have any particular characteristics (e.g. whether they should be, or not be, of a certain nationality or have certain technical knowledge, qualifications or experience). It also means that arbitrators with different skills and/or of different nationalities may appear on the tribunal, giving it a greater balance and breadth of knowledge and experience than a national court.

(6) *Speed and cost.* The flexibility of an arbitration procedure means that savings of time and money can be achieved. For example, it may be possible to agree a fast-track arbitration procedure with no oral hearing and the decision being made on the basis of a limited exchange of written submissions. However, the time and cost of an arbitration will depend upon the procedure adopted, the degree of co-operation between the parties and whether dilatory tactics are employed, the availability of the arbitrators and the fees charged by them. Where the chosen procedure is complex and there is extensive discovery of documentation, and/or where there is a three-member tribunal comprising people of different nationalities travelling from

different countries and staying in hotels for the duration of hearings in a neutral country, the time and costs involved can be very high.[9]

(7) *Finality of awards.* Court systems usually provide for a right of appeal from a lower court to a higher court. In contrast, arbitration awards in most developed jurisdictions are not subject to unfettered rights of appeal to the courts and the parties can usually agree to waive certain rights—see para.14–21 for the position in relation to England and Wales. In such circumstances, the parties can usually (subject only to those provisions of the law of the seat and/or in the chosen arbitration rules which may provide for limited jurisdictional, procedural and/or substantive challenges to awards) achieve a final result through arbitration and avoid the possibility of protracted appeals in the courts over a number of years. Of course, a waiver of any existing right of appeal may, with hindsight, not seem quite so attractive to the ultimate losing party.

(8) *Choice of place of arbitration.* The parties have the flexibility to agree where the arbitration proceedings should be held. This is a critical decision, not least because it will determine to some extent the enforceability of any award (see para.14–22 below on the New York Convention) and also because the mandatory provisions of the law of the place of arbitration will apply notwithstanding any choices (e.g. of arbitral rules) made by the parties. It will also be important to ensure that the chosen place of arbitration has a legal system which is supportive of the process but which does not unduly intervene or interfere with it.

14–21 There are some potential disadvantages in the use of arbitration as opposed to litigation, the significance of which will depend upon the circumstances of the particular case:

(1) *Limited powers of arbitrators.* Arbitrators have more limited powers than the courts since arbitrators (i) derive their authority from the underlying contract and (ii) do not have the power to enforce directly their own interim awards and orders. Arbitrators cannot themselves issue orders that are binding upon third parties. As a result, in complex matters involving numerous parties who are not bound by the arbitration agreement, it may still be advisable for the parties to have recourse to the national courts.

(2) *Multi-contract disputes.* One significant disadvantage of arbitration is the difficulty in consolidating multiple disputes among various parties involving the same basic set of facts or transactions. In general, an

---

[9] A recent empirical study conducted by PriceWaterhouseCoopers and Queen Mary School of International Arbitration found that 50 per cent of companies interviewed ranked the cost of arbitration as their primary concern. *Arbitration—Corporate Attitudes and Practices. 12 Perceptions Tested: Myths, Data and Analysis; Research Report*, 15 American Review of International Arbitration 525 (2005).

arbitral tribunal has no power to consolidate one dispute with another regardless of the fact that both disputes arise from the same event or series of events.

Enforcement of arbitral awards: New York Convention

14–22 It is clearly of critical importance that a court judgment or arbitral award is capable of being easily enforced in countries where the losing party has its assets. Generally, arbitration awards are more readily enforceable in other countries than court judgments. This is primarily due to the 1958 New York Convention. As at December 2007, 142 states were parties to the New York Convention.[10] The majority have adopted the so-called reciprocity reservation. This means that their courts will enforce an award under the New York Convention if it has been rendered within the territory of another state which has also adhered to the New York Convention.

14–23 The nationality of the parties is immaterial. It is the nationality of the award that counts. It is therefore important, for any arbitration agreement in an international joint venture, to identify explicitly one of the New York Convention countries as the place or legal seat of the arbitration proceedings. The grounds for refusal of enforcement are strictly limited by the New York Convention to matters generally relating to public policy and procedural irregularity in the conduct of the arbitration; the onus of persuading the court that the foreign award should not be enforced is upon the party seeking to resist enforcement.

Types of arbitration and leading arbitral institutions

14–24 Arbitration may broadly be conducted as either:

(a) *institutional arbitration* under the auspices of an international arbitral institution which, to a greater or lesser degree, carries out a supervisory and supportive role in the arbitration proceedings—the proceedings themselves being governed by the rules of the chosen institution; or

(b) *ad hoc arbitration*, either pursuant to the UNCITRAL Rules (see below) or pursuant to rules specially devised by the parties and the tribunal itself to govern the arbitration procedure—in an ad hoc arbitration, there is no arbitral institution to support the proceedings.

14–25 Ad hoc arbitration is occasionally preferred by parties on grounds that it may be quicker and cheaper than institutional arbitration. Since the

---

[10] A list of the countries which have ratified or acceded to the New York Convention appears at: *http://www.uncitral.org/uncitral/en/uncitral_texts/arbitration/NYConvention_status.html*.

parties are able to shape the procedure, it is often more flexible. However, in the case of international joint ventures, it will usually be easier to adopt institutional arbitration. It can prove expensive and time-consuming to draft special rules for an ad hoc arbitration.[11] The effectiveness of an ad hoc mechanism depends upon the voluntary co-operation of the parties in complying with the procedural rules, often at a time when they are already in dispute. In addition, it can be difficult or awkward for the parties to deal directly with the tribunal on logistical matters such as fees, costs and deadlines. There is therefore a risk that ad hoc arbitration may not proceed as smoothly as institutional arbitral proceedings. An institutional arbitration clause, negotiated when the transaction is entered into and before disputes have arisen, is generally the preferred option.[12]

Which arbitral institution?

14–26 Most arbitral institutions provide trained staff to administer the arbitration and to advise users. They ensure that the tribunal is appointed, that the basis of remuneration of the arbitrators is established, that advance payments are made in respect of the arbitrators' fees and expenses and, generally, that the arbitration remains on track. If there is no institution, the arbitration must be administered by the arbitral tribunal itself. There has been a proliferation of new arbitral institutions or arbitration centres in recent years. However, for transactions such as international joint ventures, the parties (and their advisers) should place great weight on institutional permanence and expertise. The most important and frequently used international arbitral institutions for business disputes include the following:

ARBITRAL INSTITUTIONS

(1) *International Chamber of Commerce.* The International Court of Arbitration of the International Chamber of Commerce (the ICC) remains the most important of the truly international arbitral organisations. The ICC Court does not actually decide disputes but appoints arbitral tribunals to deal with them. Such arbitral tribunals may comprise three arbitrators (two of whom are generally party nominated) or a sole arbitrator.

---

[11] This can, though, be made easier by adopting rules of procedure for ad hoc arbitrations developed in 1976 by the United Nations Commission for International Trade Law and known as the UNCITRAL Arbitration Rules—see para.14–37 below.
[12] In the PricewaterhouseCoopers' Report, 76 per cent of respondents said that their corporations opt for institutional arbitration—see para.14–20.

The ICC is based in Paris but arbitrations pursuant to its rules can take place anywhere in the world. It is still, perhaps, European in emphasis—although, with increasing participation in ICC arbitrations by developing countries, its constituency is changing and parties from 120 countries were represented in arbitrations under the auspices of the ICC in 2000 with places of arbitration in 43 countries.

It has a reputation for being more expensive than many of the other institutional arbitrations, both as a result of the fee basis applied (which is based on the amount in dispute) and due to the fact that it is more interventionist than other institutions (for example, it reviews all awards prepared by arbitrators before they are able to be issued to the parties). This process, known as "scrutiny", can also mean that awards in ICC arbitrations may be delayed. However, it also means that ICC awards are generally reliable. The institutional cachet of the ICC also may enhance the enforceability of its awards.

The latest version of the ICC's Rules (which apply to all ICC arbitrations) came into force on January 1, 1998.

(2) *LCIA* (formerly the London Court of International Arbitration—the name was abbreviated in order to avoid any misunderstanding as to the significance of the word "London" and to promote the LCIA's international reach). The LCIA has grown substantially in popularity over the last decade or so. LCIA arbitrations may take place anywhere in the world (although if the parties do not agree otherwise, the arbitration will be located in London unless the LCIA determines otherwise in the light of all relevant factors). Furthermore, the LCIA announced a joint venture with the Dubai International Financial Centre (DIFC) in February 2008 to open a new centre for the administration of international arbitration and mediation. The DIFC LCIA Arbitration Centre's rules are a close adaptation of the LCIA Rules with minor changes.

The LCIA has developed as an effective competitor to the ICC for international arbitrations. It also does not decide disputes but appoints arbitrators to do so. Its rules are modern and flexible and are designed for use in both common law and civil law countries. It is perceived as being less expensive than the ICC since its monitoring and administrative role is more limited and the basis upon which it charges for its services is on a time-cost basis. It does not scrutinise awards but has a good reputation for appointing skilled and reliable arbitrators and thus producing readily enforceable awards. The LCIA has also revised its Rules and these came into effect on January 1, 1998.

A number of other important regional or nationally-based arbitral institutions exist. Many of these have taken on an international role by extending their domestic services to include international arbitration of disputes between foreign parties. These should be considered whenever a dispute arises where the joint venture is based in a particular geographic area. Certain of the more prominent of these bodies or centres include the following:

(3) *The American Arbitration Association (AAA)*. Although the AAA is geared mainly to process an enormous volume of domestic US arbitrations, it also handles an increasing number of international cases due to the great number and strength of US businesses operating in the international arena. (In 2000, the AAA actually administered more international arbitrations than the ICC.) Revised rules were promulgated in

1997 for use in international arbitrations. The international division of the AAA is the International Centre for Dispute Resolution (ICDR) which has a European office in Dublin.

(4) *The Hong Kong International Arbitration Centre (HKIAC).* The HKIAC was formed to meet a growing need for arbitration services in South-East Asia. Hong Kong benefits from modern arbitration legislation (it has adopted the 1985 UNCITRAL Model Law). Parties may also avail themselves of the infrastructure benefits of the HKIAC by choosing it as a venue for arbitration under the ICC or LCIA Rules. Although (following the transfer of sovereignty of Hong Kong to the PRC in July 1997) doubts had existed regarding the suitability of Hong Kong as a venue for arbitrating disputes when the award would have to be enforced in China, such concerns have been allayed in the light of legislation passed in Hong Kong and China.

(5) *The Singapore International Arbitration Centre (SIAC).* The SIAC was founded in 1990 and maintains a panel of accredited local and international arbitrators. It is the designated appointing authority under Singapore's International Arbitration Act which adopts the UNCITRAL Model Law. SIAC's rules are based largely on the UNCITRAL Arbitration Rules and the LCIA Rules and may be adopted for use in any international arbitration, wherever located. If current rates of growth in its caseload are maintained, the SIAC is set to become a serious competitor to the HKIAC, particularly for South and South East Asian arbitrations.

(6) *The Arbitration Institute of the Stockholm Chamber of Commerce.* This has been used extensively in the resolution of East-West disputes. Historically, Stockholm has proved to be particularly acceptable in joint ventures and other contracts involving western European parties and parties from the former Soviet Union or China. New Stockholm rules became effective from January 1, 2007.

(7) *International Commercial Arbitration Court at the Chamber of Commerce and Industry of the Russian Federation.* This institution (ICAC) promulgated new rules in 1994. Awards rendered under its rules may, as a matter of practice, be easier to enforce than other arbitration awards against a Russian party within Russia—although the difficulties of enforcing arbitration awards in Russia and other CIS countries should not be underestimated.

(8) *The Dubai International Arbitration Centre.* The (DIAC) was created in 1994 but its rules were more suited to domestic arbitration. It has recently implemented new arbitration rules which came into effect in May 2007 and signify a major development for Dubai as a centre for international arbitration in the Middle East. The United Arab Emirates also ratified the New York Convention in November 2006.

(9) *China International Economic and Trade Arbitration Commission.* CIETAC's latest revised rules came into force in May 2005. It is fast-growing institution and is, at the time of writing, the busiest arbitration centre in the world in terms of case load. CIETAC has in effect a monopoly over the conduct of international arbitrations in China and it is also raising its international profile. CITEAC handles domestic arbitrations but its focus is international disputes. Local arbitration commissions, found in cities across China, are also permitted to hear international

> disputes. However, international parties often prefer CIETAC because of its reputation for having qualified arbitrators and the higher level of protection afforded to its awards by the Chinese courts.

Place of arbitration

14–27 The principal considerations from the legal viewpoint, when choosing the juridical place or "seat" of arbitration (which may in fact differ from the physical location of the actual hearings), should be as follows.

(1) *Enforceability of the award.* It will be important to ensure that a New York Convention country is chosen as the place of arbitration in cases where the arbitral award may need to be enforced in another country—see para.14–22 et seq. above.

(2) *A supportive legal system.* It is established that the choice of seat will determine the level of involvement of the national courts in the arbitral process.[13] Not all countries are supportive of international arbitration. Some have wide powers of judicial review or provide for excessive intervention by the courts with the arbitral process. The modern international consensus (as reflected in the 1985 UNCITRAL Model Law on International Commercial Arbitration) is that the courts at the place of arbitration should permit maximum party autonomy in determining the procedures of the arbitration and limit their review of arbitral awards to the grounds of excess of jurisdiction, failure to give a party an adequate opportunity to present its case or violation of public policy. Errors of fact and arguably law should be beyond the powers of review by national courts. The parties contract for arbitration and therefore should accept the arbitral tribunal's decision as final subject only to narrow exceptions.

Arbitration in England has been criticised in the past due, primarily, to the perception that the courts had excessive powers of intervention and to the availability of appeals to the court on questions of law. However, over time the courts have intervened more sparingly, seeing their function as being to support rather than displace the arbitral process. As a result, London has become an increasingly prominent centre for international arbitration. The Arbitration Act 1996 improved further the legal framework necessary for its continuing

---

[13] See, e.g. Colman J. in *A v B* [2007] 1 Lloyds Rep 237 and *A v B (No.2)* [2007] 1 Lloyds Rep 358 "... an agreement as to the seat of an arbitration is analogous to an exclusive jurisdiction clause. Any claim for a remedy going to the existence or scope of the arbitrator's jurisdiction or as to the validity of an existing interim or final award is agreed to be made only in the courts of the place designated as the seat of the arbitration."

presence as a significant arbitration venue.[14] Recent cases[15] have confirmed the courts' support for the arbitral process.

(3) *Geographical convenience.* The convenience of travelling to hearings by the parties, witnesses and arbitrators should not be ignored. The administering body need not be located in the forum chosen by the parties.

Establishing the arbitral tribunal

14–28 Arbitration clauses rarely designate arbitrators by name and, indeed, it would be unwise to do so since the chosen arbitrator may be otherwise occupied or deceased by the time a dispute arises. However, it is important to establish the criteria for constituting the arbitral tribunal if the parties are unable to agree on its composition.

Number of arbitrators

14–29 Many sets of institutional rules (including those of the ICC and the LCIA) provide that, if the arbitration clause is silent, the institution will designate a sole arbitrator unless the circumstances justify a three-member arbitral tribunal—although there is a clear trend (at least where significant sums are at issue) towards three-member tribunals. It is preferable, if possible, to resolve the question of the number of arbitrators in the arbitration clause itself.

(1) *Sale arbitrator.* The advantages of a sole arbitrator are self evident. Meetings and hearings can be arranged more easily; fees and expenses of only one arbitrator are incurred; and the arbitration should proceed more quickly since only one arbitrator has to make up his mind without consultation with colleagues.

(2) *Three-member tribunal.* On the other hand, particularly in international joint ventures, it may be preferable to provide specifically in the arbitration clause for a three-member tribunal and to set out the

---

[14] Although parties to an arbitration in London retain a limited right of appeal on a point of law, the circumstances in which such an appeal can be brought are now very restricted. In addition, parties to any arbitration agreement, whether domestic or international, have the right to exclude in advance any right of appeal on a point of law (Arbitration Act 1996, s.69). Such an exclusion can form part of the arbitration agreement itself or be made subsequently (e.g. when the dispute arises). Other rights of appeal are mandatory and so cannot be excluded by agreement.

[15] In *Lesotho Highlands Development Authority v Impregilo Spa* [2005] UKHL 43, the House of Lords gave a restrictive interpretation of when the tribunal would exceed its powers under s.68 of the 1996 Act. Most recently, in *Premium Nafta Products Ltd (20th Defendant) v Fili Shipping Company Ltd (formerly Fiona Trust)* [2007] UKHL 40, the House of Lords have held that a "fresh start" was needed in interpreting arbitration clauses; the starting point for interpretation is now a strong presumption that, unless there is precise wording to the contrary, commercial parties intend all disputes to be determined in the same forum.

procedure for its formation. The most usual procedure is to enable each party to appoint a member of the tribunal, the third member (the chairman) either being appointed by agreement of the parties (or, alternatively, of the party-appointed arbitrators) and, in default of such agreement within a limited period of time, by an identified appointing authority.

The advantage of each party being able to nominate an arbitrator is that both parties can then take some comfort from the composition of the tribunal and have some confidence in its deliberations. This is clearly important where the parties have different cultural and language backgrounds. It should also help to ensure that each party's case is properly understood by the arbitral tribunal. The act of appointing an arbitrator involves each party in the process and, therefore, arguably increases its likelihood of success. Arguably, a three-member tribunal should lead to a higher quality of justice. Against this, some consider that such a tribunal is likely to lead to more polarised views with the presiding arbitrator more likely to split the difference. Possible mechanisms to counter this are (i) to leave all three arbitrators to be appointed by the appointing authority or (ii) to provide that neither party may nominate an arbitrator of its own nationality.

14-30 Particular care needs to be taken as to the way in which the tribunal will be appointed where there are more than two parties. A mechanism by which all parties have the right to appoint an arbitrator to the tribunal will clearly result in an unwieldy (and expensive) tribunal. However, it will similarly be unacceptable to provide that some parties may appoint an arbitrator to the tribunal whereas others may not.[16] The simplest and most effective way round the problem is to provide that the tribunal (whether a sole arbitrator or a tribunal of three) be appointed by an independent appointing authority, such as the President of the ICC or the LCIA.[17]

Selection of presiding arbitrator

14-31 All arbitration rules contain provisions for the selection of presiding arbitrators. Most practitioners prefer to have the appointment made either (i) by agreement between the parties or (ii) by agreement between the arbitrators nominated by the parties or, in default of agreement, by a

---

[16] Indeed, in some countries (such as France), such a provision may result in any award subsequently made by that tribunal being set aside.
[17] See also art.8 of the LCIA Rules and art.10 of the ICC Rules which each empower multiple parties to group themselves into "Claimant" and "Respondent" groups, with each group collectively nominating an arbitrator. In the absence of a joint nomination, appointments of the tribunal can be made by the LCIA or ICC, respectively.

nominated appointing authority. Contractual provisions to cover appointment by the parties should always incorporate a deadline for agreement, upon the expiry of which either party may approach the appointing authority to make the appointment.

Interim measures

14-32 The ability to obtain interim relief (such as interim injunctions or orders for specific performance) is of particular importance in the context of disputes arising out of joint ventures or alliances. For example, a party may wish to seek interim measures in order to prevent breaches of non-compete or confidentiality undertakings or to preserve the assets of the joint venture company. Additional orders may be required to preserve evidence, to enforce the arbitration agreement or to obtain an order for security for costs. Applications for interim relief may generally be made to the arbitral tribunal[18] or, in certain circumstances, to a court of competent jurisdiction. The latter will be particularly relevant if relief is sought before the arbitral tribunal has been established.

14-33 Applications to the court for interim relief are generally permitted by most sets of arbitration rules, although some rules provide that recourse to the courts is available only in limited circumstances.

(1) Unless the parties otherwise agree, art.23 of the ICC Rules provides that application for interim measures may only be made to the court at a time before the constitution of the tribunal and only in exceptional circumstances thereafter (such as where an order is required against a party who is not a party to the arbitration).

(2) Similarly, art.25 of the LCIA Rules provides that a party shall have the right to apply to a court or other judicial authority for interim measures before the formation of the arbitral tribunal and in exceptional cases thereafter.

(3) Article 26 of the UNCITRAL Rules expressly provides that a request to the court for interim measures shall not be deemed incompatible with the agreement to arbitrate (even where the tribunal would have the power to make such an order).[19]

Where interim remedies are likely to be of importance, the arbitration agreement should clearly incorporate rules which provide the parties with the ability to obtain the required remedy-or to provide expressly to that effect in the joint venture agreement itself.

---

[18] Although in some jurisdictions, e.g. Italy, arbitrators are not empowered to grant interim measures of protection and parties must revert to the courts.
[19] This provision is currently under review.

Drafting the arbitration clause

14–34 Model arbitration clauses are recommended by most of the leading arbitral institutions and generally should not be tinkered with (so as to avoid disputes subsequently arising over the jurisdiction of the tribunal).

> Precedent 22 in Part E includes the model clauses recommended by the ICC, the LCIA and certain other arbitral institutions together with a few brief comments.

14–35 An alternative, general purpose, model clause for institutional arbitration is:

> "Any dispute, controversy or claim arising out of or in connection with this Agreement (including any question regarding its existence, validity or termination) shall be finally resolved by arbitration under the Rules of [name of institution] in force [at the date hereof/the date of request for arbitration], whose Rules are deemed to be incorporated by reference into this clause. The tribunal shall consist of [a sole/three] arbitrator[s]. The place of the arbitration shall be [city]. The language of the arbitration shall be [language]. [If not provided for elsewhere: 'The governing law of the Contract [is/shall be] the substantive law of [place]']"

14–36 In the case of an ad hoc arbitration clause, it is important to consider at the outset a range of questions which will depend upon, inter alia, the parties' identity and the contract's subject matter and to include express provisions to cater for them. Given that there is no institutional back-up to provide assistance, it is particularly important to cater for what is to happen in the event of one party's default during the course of the arbitration proceedings or deliberate obstruction of them. As a result, ad hoc clauses are inevitably somewhat lengthy.

14–37 Alternatively, parties can adopt the UNCITRAL Arbitration Rules. If disputes are to be resolved in accordance with the UNCITRAL Rules, then the parties will need to nominate an appointing authority to assist in the tribunal's formation. It is obviously important to ensure that the nominated appointing authority will remain in existence at the time any dispute arises. For this reason, it is not advisable to nominate a particular individual as the appointing authority. However, a number of institutional bodies, including both the ICC and LCIA, will act in this capacity.

> Precedent 22 in Part E includes a draft ad hoc arbitration clause by way of an example. It also sets out the model clause under the UNCITRAL Rules.

Conclusion

14–38 Fortunately, litigation and arbitration proceedings remain relatively rare for the resolution of joint venture disputes. They will invariably spell the death-knell for the venture. Generally, the strongest incentive and pressure to resolve joint venture disputes will come from the mutual interest of the parties in ensuring that the underlying business of the venture is not adversely affected by a simmering and acrimonious dispute. Most disputes will continue to be resolved commercially without recourse to legal process. It will then be a commercial, and separate, issue whether or not the dispute is so fundamental as to affect the ongoing viability of the joint venture relationship.

PART C

SPECIALIST ISSUES AFFECTING JOINT VENTURES

15　Tax planning

16　Competition and regulatory controls

17　Intellectual property and technology

18　Employment

19　Accounting

A challenge, and attraction, for lawyers engaged on joint venture and alliance transactions is the impact of different areas of law on their formation and subsequent operation. Particularly important "specialist" areas of law at the planning stage include: tax, competition and regulatory, intellectual property and technology, employment and accounting. This Part outlines the material issues impacting on joint ventures in these areas. These are not comprehensive reviews. They will not obviate the need to involve "specialist" advisers in particular situations. The aim is to provide the corporate/commercial lawyer with a grasp of the main issues and the applicable legal framework.

CHAPTER 15

Tax planning

The impetus for a joint venture or alliance will come from commercial factors. However, it is clearly undesirable for the viability of a commercially sensible and potentially profitable venture to be damaged by a disproportionate tax cost. Tax planning can therefore play an important, and often essential, role at the structuring stage—particularly for an international equity joint venture. This chapter[1] addresses the principal tax issues affecting joint ventures. It is important for the corporate and commercial lawyers to understand, in outline, the impact of these issues.

Key tax issues

15–01 What are the key tax "drivers" in planning a joint venture? Important issues—particularly where the transaction involves the transfer of substantial businesses/companies into an equity joint venture—include the following:

(1) *Choice of joint venture vehicle.* How should the joint venture or alliance be structured? Is a corporate entity (a JVC) appropriate—or does the ideal tax profile (perhaps in the light of anticipated heavy initial expenditure of the joint venture or financing costs) lead to a preference for a "fiscally transparent" vehicle such as a partnership or contractual alliance?

(2) *Location of the JVC.* Where should an international equity joint venture be set up? This may be influenced by a number of tax considerations (including tax costs on formation, basic corporate tax levels and tax costs on subsequent repatriation of funds). Sometimes a series of parallel joint venture vehicles in different countries may be desirable.

(3) *Costs of establishing the joint venture.* What are the most tax efficient steps for establishing the joint venture? This applies particularly where existing businesses or assets are being contributed through the transfer of a trade or the transfer of a subsidiary.

---

[1] I am very grateful to Jonathan Cooklin and Arun Birla of Freshfields Bruckhaus Deringer LLP who contributed most of the original material on which this chapter is based.

(4) *Financing costs.* How can a party maximise tax reliefs for financing costs? This may mean raising debt finance in a territory where taxable profits can be relieved at the highest possible rate (subject to relevant transfer pricing, thin capitalisation rules and other local restrictions).

(5) *Distribution of profits.* How can a party minimise tax on the distribution or repatriation of its share of profits from an equity joint venture? In an international joint venture, this may mean identifying a jurisdiction with double tax treaties (or which can benefit from relevant EU Directives) resulting in a nil or an acceptable level of withholding tax on dividends, interest or royalties paid not only to the parents by the JVC but also to the JVC from its operating subsidiaries.

(6) *Tax affecting ongoing operations.* How will tax factors affect the costs of ongoing operations of the joint venture? Will tax affect the transfer of assets or services between the parents? Where the joint venture makes losses, will the parties be able to take advantage of those losses to minimise the overall tax burden?

(7) *Termination.* Will the tax costs of "unwinding" the venture be significant? What will be the most tax efficient structure for disposal of assets in the event of termination of an equity joint venture?

15–02 Tax rules are invariably subject to detailed criteria and qualifications. Planning will always depend upon the tax profile of the particular parties concerned. The following chapter therefore highlights general issues and possible tax planning opportunities. Their application to any set of particular circumstances must, of course, be examined individually by the parties. Most detailed attention is given in this chapter to the position of corporate participants in a UK based joint venture company.[2] However, many of the tax issues discussed are of the kind which will arise internationally and reference is made to factors affecting other jurisdictions.

CHOICE OF JOINT VENTURE VEHICLE

Legal form of venture: corporate or "transparent"?

15–03 The choice of legal form for the joint venture vehicle will often be influenced by tax considerations—in particular, whether it should be a corporate entity or a "fiscally transparent" vehicle such as a partnership or a contractual alliance. The possibility of more than one legal form being

---

[2] References in this chapter to the "TCGA 1992" are to the Taxation of Chargeable Gains Act 1992, and to the "Taxes Act 1988" are to the Income and Corporation Taxes Act 1988.

adopted during the life of the joint venture should not be ruled out (e.g. set up as a partnership and incorporate later on). In more complex cases, tax planning objectives may sometimes be assisted by the use of a "hybrid" entity which is classified one way in one jurisdiction but differently in another jurisdiction.

Contractual alliance

15–04 A contractual alliance offers the simplest arrangement for tax purposes. This simplicity may be a substantial advantage. A contractual alliance has no separate status for tax purposes.[3] Thus, it will not be the alliance or joint venture itself that is taxed but rather the participants.

(1) Capital assets owned by a party which are used in the joint venture or alliance will usually remain owned by the party supplying them. There will, whether on setting up or on termination, normally be no disposal of the asset for tax purposes.

(2) Income (and expenditure) during the course of the joint venture will belong to (or be incurred by) the participants directly and not the jointly owned entity as in the case of a JVC. Each participant will be taxed on the results of its own trade or business.[4]

(3) Each UK joint venture party should be able to claim capital allowances for capital expenditure incurred by it on plant and machinery used in the trade (or other assets eligible for capital allowances). Similarly, tax relief for interest costs will normally be available to the party incurring those costs if they are incurred wholly and exclusively for the purposes of that party's trade.

Partnership

15–05 A UK trading partnership is largely transparent for tax purposes and is not itself liable to corporation tax on its trading profits. In broad terms, the profits and losses of the trade are computed for corporation tax purposes as if the partnership were a company. Each partner is then subject to tax on its share of the partnership profits or losses (subject to any applicable double tax treaty). Similar principles usually apply under local tax regimes in relation to the tax treatment of profits and losses of a fiscally transparent partnership based elsewhere in Europe. Somewhat more complex rules apply, though, in the case of tax on contributions of assets by the parties to the partnership business—see para.15–19 below.

---

[3] The position is more complex if the contractual alliance crosses the line into a "partnership" for legal purposes—see para.5–18 earlier. To avoid there being a partnership, the participants should ensure that each is entitled to a proportion of gross receipts (rather than net profit) and obliged separately to pay a proportion of expenses.

[4] A UK resident participant trading in the UK should be charged to tax under Sch.D Case I even if the joint venture operations are carried out overseas. This can be helpful from a loss relief perspective.

When is a "fiscally transparent" vehicle desirable?

15–06 Tax factors can lead to the preferred use of a "fiscally transparent" vehicle for the joint venture in some situations. They include the following:

(1) If the joint venture is likely to incur expenditure or losses which could be set off for tax purposes against profits of a joint venture party, a corporate vehicle may be tax inefficient. This particularly applies in a cross border structure.[5]

(2) Similarly, a corporate vehicle will not be tax efficient where a joint venture party has existing tax losses which could be used to shelter profits earned by the joint venture if those profits were received directly by the parties through a "transparent" vehicle rather than indirectly by dividend from a corporate joint venture entity.

(3) A corporate entity such as a JVC may result in a double level of taxation. Where relief is given by way of credit (and not exemption), tax paid by the JVC on profits earned by it may not reflect a full tax credit against taxes payable on subsequent distribution of those profits to the joint venture parties. The aggregate tax on foreign dividends, including withholding tax, may exceed the domestic tax against which credit may be obtained.

These factors may lead to a recommendation that, for tax planning purposes, a "fiscally transparent" vehicle should be adopted as the legal form of the venture or alliance—such as a purely contractual alliance, a partnership or a limited liability partnership. From the tax viewpoint, partnership-type structures often require serious consideration in many international joint venture situations. (If a partnership is being considered as the joint venture vehicle, it should be checked that it would also be recognised as "fiscally transparent" from the standpoint of the tax authorities in the jurisdiction of each joint venture party.)

Corporate entity

15–07 On the other hand, a corporate entity will often be favoured for a number of commercial reasons—see para.3–16 earlier. It may also be more tax efficient than a "fiscally transparent" vehicle if the joint venture operations are profitable but subject to a lower marginal rate of tax in a corporate entity than would be incurred if profits were received directly by its parents. This may occur, for instance, in the following situations:

(1) The corporate tax rate in the local jurisdiction of the JVC may be such that earnings can be accumulated in the JVC at a lower effective tax rate than that of each joint venture parent.

---

[5] In the case of a JVC in the UK, consortium relief may be available for the UK participating company—see para.15–35.

(2) A corporate structure will be beneficial if an acceptably low overall rate of tax is suffered even after distribution of profits (e.g. where a joint venture party benefits from a tax exemption on dividend receipts or a tax treaty provides for a refund of tax credit).

(3) If the JVC is in a country with a tax system which permits a "participation exemption" (e.g. the Netherlands or Luxembourg), there may be future tax savings on dividends received by the JVC from its subsidiary operations or on gains resulting from subsequent disposals of subsidiaries or other assets of the JVC.

(4) If the joint venture has operations in a number of jurisdictions, it could be tax efficient to have a single holding JVC located in an appropriate jurisdiction.

LOCATION OF THE JVC

Location of an international JVC

15–08 In most cases, the location for a JVC may be obvious from the commercial circumstances. In other cases, the choice of jurisdiction may depend on a number of factors (particularly if the JVC is to act as a headquarters or holding company of a group of subsidiaries worldwide). Important tax factors to be taken into account include the following:

(1) *Corporate tax rates.* The rate of tax on profits of the JVC will be a significant factor (for the obvious reason that this will have a major impact on the JVC's distributable post tax profits).[6]

(2) *Tax incentives/holidays.* Tax incentives to encourage investment may often be relevant. These can take a number of forms: e.g. reduced rates of taxation for given periods; full write off for tax purposes of certain types of expenditure (which would otherwise only be deductible over a specified period); and/or "holidays" from certain local taxes.

(3) *Repatriation of profits: withholding taxes.* The repatriation of profits from the JVC may be subject to a withholding tax (whether repatriation takes the form of dividends, interest payable on loans or royalties for the use of intellectual property). This will at best be a cash flow cost (in circumstances where the recipient can obtain an effective

---

[6] However, the tax rules of the jurisdiction in which the joint venture parties themselves are located will need to be investigated carefully—since those rules might effectively impose tax on a party by reference to the JVC's profits, particularly where the JVC is located in a low tax jurisdiction.

credit against its own tax bill for that withholding) and may at worst be an absolute cost (where no such credit is available). Accordingly, it will be desirable to locate the JVC in a jurisdiction which does not levy such withholding taxes or which has a favourable double tax treaty network providing reduced rates of withholding tax.

(4) *Dividends exemption.* A number of jurisdictions (typically European) offer an exemption from tax on dividends received from companies in which there is a threshold investment or "participation". A subsidiary of a JVC will normally qualify—although special rules may affect the exemption in cases where the subsidiary is located in a tax haven or held solely as a passive investment.

(5) *Capital gains exemption.* Some jurisdictions (e.g. the Netherlands or Luxembourg) also offer a "participation" exemption from capital gains which provides an ability for the JVC to dispose of operating companies free of any capital gains or analogous tax. In some cases, this may be dependent on a holding period or minimum value of the participation.

(6) *Indirect tax costs.* A comparison will need to be made of other indirect tax costs such as capital tax on issued share capital or stamp duty or similar transfer taxes. Local and municipal taxes may also be relevant.

(7) *Tax incentives for management.* Depending on the level of headquarters functions, the ability to provide tax effective incentives packages for management may be an important factor in particular situations.

(8) *Double tax treaties/EU Directives.* It may be important generally for the JVC to have access to a wide double tax treaty network or, where relevant, benefit from the EU Parent/Subsidiary Directive or the EU Interest and Royalties Directive. The rate of withholding tax levied on dividends, interest or royalties received by the JVC from its subsidiaries will often be reduced (or even eliminated) under the terms of a suitable treaty or EU Directive. Similarly, in circumstances where the JVC makes these kinds of payments, the withholding tax levied in the JVC's own jurisdiction may be reduced or eliminated.

UK as a location

15–09 The UK itself offers a number of advantages as a jurisdiction for the incorporation of a holding company for a joint venture with overseas operations. The main factors affecting the decision to use the UK as a suitable location for a JVC in the case of multi-national operations are set out below:

UK: LOCATION FOR AN INTERNATIONAL JVC

- *Rate of tax.* To the extent that taxable profits arise in the UK, the mainstream rate of corporation tax (for large companies) is now generally 28 per cent. Whilst many jurisdictions are steadily reducing their corporate tax rates, this (combined with no withholding tax on dividends) is regarded as a relatively favourable rate.

- *EU Directives.* A JVC in the UK can benefit from the EU Parent/Subsidiary Directive or the EU Interest and Royalties Directive. In broad terms, dividends, interest and royalties paid by subsidiaries of the JVC located in the EU should be capable of being paid to the JVC without withholding on account of tax.

- *Dividends.* Dividends paid by UK companies are not subject to withholding on account of UK tax. Nor is there any longer any requirement for a UK company paying a dividend to account for advance corporation tax (ACT).

- *Capital gains and the SSE.* A gain arising on the sale of a substantial interest in a qualifying company can be exempt from UK corporation tax (and similarly any loss arising on such a sale is unallowable for UK tax purposes). This exemption (SSE, the substantial shareholding exemption) has been a welcome development and greatly enhances the attractiveness of the UK as a favourable jurisdiction for the location of a JVC. The conditions for the SSE exemption are discussed further at para.15–16 et seq.

- *Transfer pricing.* The transfer pricing regime allows the UK Revenue to adjust, for tax purposes, the price paid for goods and services sold/supplied between connected parties, including interest paid on connected party debt, to an arm's length basis. The transfer pricing rules are discussed further at para.15–39.

- *Interest.* Various anti avoidance provisions can apply to deny a UK company tax relief on interest which it has paid (in particular the UK transfer pricing rules). There are also general, widely drafted, anti avoidance provisions which may need to be considered if borrowings are structured in an artificial way.

- *Controlled foreign companies (CFC) regime.* The UK's CFC rules are an anti avoidance regime designed to prevent UK companies rolling up profits in a non UK tax resident company which is subject to a lower level of tax than applies in the UK. Very broadly speaking, the rules operate by apportioning the profits of such a non-UK resident company where the requisite level of control exists. The rules can apply, by way of example, to joint ventures where a UK and foreign joint venturer each have a 40 per cent interest in the JVC.

- *Double tax relief.* Dividends received by a UK company from non UK subsidiaries may suffer local withholding tax although this may be reduced or eliminated by the EU Parent/Subsidiary Directive, applicable double tax

> treaties or unilateral relief. Nevertheless, the UK's complex double tax relief rules (combined with the general unavailability of tax rulings) have tended to hinder the development of the UK as the leading European jurisdiction of choice.

This section should, however, be read in the light of changes contemplated by a UK Revenue discussion document released in June 2007.[7] These changes should, in principle, increase the attraction of the UK as a jurisdiction for an international holding company (including by way of a JVC). Although the details remain to be finalised, in broad outline this document envisages the following elements:

(1) The UK would move to an exemption system under which dividends received by large and medium sized UK businesses (defined using EU law principles) from "participation shareholdings" (that is, shareholdings of 10 per cent or more) in foreign subsidiaries would be exempt from UK tax in circumstances where new controlled company rules apply to the foreign subsidiary paying such dividends.

(2) The UK would move from the current entity-based controlled foreign companies regime to an income-based "controlled companies" regime taxing the UK parent company on specifically defined "mobile income"—for "mobile income" which is passive in nature, the new "controlled companies" regime would apply whether such income arises in the UK or in foreign subsidiaries.

(3) There would also be changes to the existing regime governing relief for interest.

Use of a third-country jurisdiction for location of JVC

15–10 It may be advantageous, in an international joint venture, for a JVC to be located in a jurisdiction which is different from that of any of the joint venture parties, particularly where the JVC itself is to be a holding company. The choice of location of such a JVC will depend on many features—including the particular tax profile of the participants, the factors outlined in para.15–08 and, generally, any relevant double tax treaties between the country of each participant and that of the proposed JVC. There are now a number of European countries competing, in effect, for the business of being the location of European headquarters of international corporate groups.

(1) Many countries offer "participation exemption" regimes which essentially exempt from local tax foreign earnings derived from holdings in overseas companies. These earnings may be passed through to

---

[7] Taxation of the foreign profits of companies: a discussion document (HM Treasury/HM Revenue & Customs, June 2007).

another EU member without additional tax. Such a structure and location offer valuable opportunities when establishing a location for a JVC with operating subsidiaries in various European countries. "Participation" exemption regimes exist, for instance, in the Netherlands and Luxembourg. The Netherlands has been particularly successful in attracting companies due no doubt, in part, to its favourable tax regime—the Dutch "participation exemption" provides for both dividend and capital gains relief. Countries such as Spain, Sweden, Belgium and Denmark also have alternatives which may be considered. The accession of further EU Member States continues to expand the options available.

(2) Certain regimes currently offer basic rates of corporate tax which can be attractive inducements for locating a JVC where other factors render this feasible (e.g. Ireland). Several of the new EU Member States also offer low levels of taxation (e.g. Cyprus).

15–11 Tax will, of course, only be one of the relevant considerations in choosing the location of an international JVC. Non-tax issues (such as flexibility of corporate governance, international reputation of the legal system, availability of qualified staff, local accounting requirements and standards, adequacy of transportation and physical infrastructure) may be equally, or even more, important factors.

COSTS OF ESTABLISHING THE JOINT VENTURE

Tax costs of contributions to the joint venture

15–12 Tax planning will play a vital role in structuring the steps necessary to form an equity joint venture. Indeed, the costs involved may well be material to the decision whether or not to adopt a corporate structure or (in the case of an international joint venture) to locate the JVC in a particular jurisdiction. This is particularly so where there are existing assets and/or businesses to be contributed. Key tax issues in this context include the following:

(1) *Capital gains.* The contribution of assets to the JVC will normally constitute a disposal of those assets for tax purposes. If these assets have increased in value over the "base cost" since the original acquisition by the relevant party, profits or gains will arise which may give rise to a tax charge—which could be a material cost of establishing the JVC.

(2) *Income tax.* The transfer of certain assets to the JVC (such as intangible assets or trading stock) may give rise to income tax consequences.

(3) *Recapture of allowances.* Where the assets to be contributed include items on which the relevant joint venture party has claimed capital or depreciation allowances, the contributing party may incur a tax charge if the assets are transferred to the JVC at more than their tax written down value. There are usually provisions for substituting market value for the actual consideration where the transaction is between "connected" persons.

(4) *Transfer of losses.* Where a business to be contributed to the JVC has made past losses, it will often be important to structure the contribution so that the accrued losses can be used by the JVC and set off, for tax purposes, against subsequent profits of the JVC.

(5) *Transfer taxes.* A significant tax on formation of the JVC can be stamp duty or other transfer tax payable in respect of the transfer of particular categories of assets to the JVC (typically shares or land). Another potential tax item, in certain circumstances, is valued added tax on the transfer of assets to the JVC.

(6) *Capital tax.* In some jurisdictions, there may be a tax or duty payable on the value of the shares issued by the JVC in exchange for the contributed assets.

These tax issues will need to be considered in each case—whether it is a domestic or international joint venture. The particular tax consequences, and tax planning opportunities, will depend on the rules of the relevant taxing jurisdiction and may well affect the steps for establishing the particular JVC. They need to be addressed at an early stage in planning the joint venture. These issues are now examined in more detail.

Capital gains

15–13 The most significant potential tax cost is often tax on any chargeable gain triggered by the disposal of assets to the equity joint venture as part of a party's contribution. In the UK, corporation tax on chargeable gains (referred to here simply as "CGT") may arise. This can particularly affect the method for establishing the joint venture—and, if no tax efficient method can be found, may seriously affect the decision whether or not the equity joint venture is an affordable project. We look at various different ways by which assets may be contributed to the JVC and the UK tax consequences.

Transfer of trading assets to the JVC

15–14 If the contribution by a party takes the form of an asset or business transfer, the transfer of capital assets will be a disposal for the purposes of CGT. The consideration for the disposal will typically be the issue of shares by the JVC to the transferring company. (The same analysis will, though, apply if the transaction takes the form of a sale and purchase for a cash price—the cash being payable by the JVC out of funds subscribed by the joint venture parties.) Such a disposal will potentially trigger a charge to CGT or (subject to certain limitations) an allowable loss. This CGT cost can be a very material item. This cost may be mitigated in various circumstances, including as outlined below:

(1) The new substantial shareholding exemption (SSE) may apply to exempt any capital gain arising on the disposal by a party of assets which constitute shares or interests in shares—see para.15–16 below.

(2) Rollover relief on business assets may apply.[8] Broadly, if the price received by a party on the transfer into the JVC of particular types of assets (including buildings used for the company's trade and fixed plant and machinery) is reinvested in similar types of assets, no immediate gain will be realised on the disposal of the old asset. However, the tax base cost of the replacement asset will be reduced by the amount of the gain which would otherwise have crystallised and any liability to corporation tax on the chargeable gain is thereby deferred until a future sale of the replacement assets.[9]

(3) The gain may also be reduced where the joint venture party is able to take advantage of any allowable losses which it has available (or which a fellow member of a 75 per cent UK group of companies has available) to set off against the chargeable gain. It is no longer necessary for companies to transfer assets intra-group in order to "match up" chargeable gains and losses in the same entity before a disposal of the asset to the JVC.[10]

(4) In an international context, there are various provisions dealing with international reconstructions/mergers, notably those which implement the EC Directive 90/434/EEC (as amended) on cross-border mergers and those which deal with the European Companies Statute.

Transfer of a subsidiary to the JVC

15–15 From the perspective of a joint venture party, it will often be preferable for the transfer to the JVC to be structured as a transfer of a

---

[8] Under s.152 TCGA 1992.
[9] The fact that the relevant provisions require the joint venture party to "apply" the disposal "consideration" on the acquisition of new assets does not, as a matter of UK Revenue practice, appear to prevent rollover relief from applying where the party receives shares (rather than cash) from the JVC, provided that an equivalent amount is applied in reinvestment.
[10] Two members of a UK group of companies within 75 per cent ownership can elect that the transfer by one of them of an asset outside the group will be treated as made by the other with the available carried forward capital loss, without any actual intra group transfer of the asset taking place or being necessary (under s.171A TCGA 1992). For company law purposes, it is nevertheless likely that the transferor should pay compensation to the other company for use of its losses; any such payment can be received tax free.

subsidiary rather than as a transfer of assets. The transfer of a subsidiary will involve only a transfer of shares—for which reliefs from taxation of capital gains will commonly be available—and not a disposal of underlying assets on which various tax charges described above may arise. Commercial considerations, such as the maintenance of existing contracts, will also point frequently towards the contribution of a subsidiary as the preferred and easier route.

15–16 If the joint venture party contributes to the JVC shares in a company (whether UK or non-UK and termed here the "target company") in exchange for cash or the issue by the JVC of shares, there will prima facie be a disposal by the joint venture party for CGT purposes of its shares in the target company. Potential reliefs include:

(1) *SSE*. This exempts from UK corporation tax any gain on a disposal of shares in a qualifying company.[11] The principal conditions are as follows:

UK Substantial Shareholding Exemption: Conditions

The conditions for exemption under the SSE are detailed (and subject to various anti avoidance provisions) and it would be necessary to look closely at the structure and assets of the relevant transaction. The basic conditions for the exemption to apply are threefold, as follows:

(1) The shares disposed of must represent all or part of a "substantial shareholding" in the relevant company. A substantial shareholding will exist where, for a continuous period of 12 months during the two years prior to the disposal of the shares, the seller:

— has held at least 10 per cent of the ordinary shares of the relevant company;
— has been beneficially entitled to at least 10 per cent of the profits available for distribution to equity holders of the relevant company; and
— has been beneficially entitled to at least 10 per cent of the assets available for distribution to equity holders on a winding up of the relevant company.

(2) The seller must be a trading company or a member of a trading group (i) throughout the period beginning with the start of the latest 12 month period (within the period of two years prior to the disposal) in relation to which it met the substantial shareholding requirement and ending with the time of the disposal (the qualifying period) and (ii) immediately after the disposal.

---

[11] Sch. 7AC TCGA 1992.

> (3) The company whose shares are being disposed of must be a trading company or the holding company of a trading group or subgroup throughout the qualifying period and immediately after the disposal.
>
> The SSE provisions specifically deal with joint ventures in order to prevent participation in a "joint venture company" from adversely affecting the trading status of a company, group or subgroup. The significance of holding the requisite percentage of shares in a "joint venture company" is that it can be disregarded and the relevant participator treated as carrying on a fair proportion of the activities of the joint venture company. A company is a "joint venture company" for these purposes if (i) it is a trading company or the holding company of a trading group or trading subgroup and (ii) there are five or fewer persons who between them hold 75 per cent or more of its ordinary share capital.

(2) *Share for share rollover relief.* In the UK, rollover relief may be available in respect of the disposal. Broadly, if the JVC acquires in exchange for its own shares (or loan stock) more than 25 per cent of the ordinary shares of the target company or the majority of the voting power in the target company, then no charge to CGT should crystallise.[12]

15–17 Another risk is that the transfer of the subsidiary to the JVC could also crystallise a so-called "de-grouping charge" within the subsidiary under s.179 TCGA 1992. When assets have been transferred between members of a CGT group and the transferee leaves the group within six years of the transfer, the transferee is treated as if it had disposed of and reacquired those assets at their market value. This deemed disposal and re-acquisition is designed to bring into charge any gain latent at the time of the intra group transfer. This charge could therefore be triggered if the relevant subsidiary leaves the "seller's" CGT group on its transfer to the JVC. This can be a major potential cost—particularly where the business to be contributed to the joint venture has been hived down to a new subsidiary prior to the formation of the JVC. However, it should be appreciated that:

(1) The SSE can in principle apply to and exempt a de-grouping charge. If it does apply, the time of disposal is altered to the time when the transferee leaves the group. The consequence of this is that the shares in the transferee are re-based at that time rather than at the time of the original intra group transfer.

(2) It is possible (via a joint election) for s.179 TCGA 1992 gains to be reallocated to another company in the old group instead of being a liability of the company leaving the old group, potentially enabling losses of that other company to be accessed.

(3) S.179 TCGA 1992 gains may be eligible for rollover relief on the replacement of business assets—see para.15–14 earlier.

---

[12] By virtue of TCGA 1992, s.135. It will usually be sensible to obtain prior UK Revenue clearance that CGT rollover relief will not be prevented from applying by reason of any tax motivation underlying the transaction.

Structuring the transaction in order to avoid a "de-grouping charge" can be a challenge and will require detailed advice and tax planning in relation to the particular circumstances.

Transfer by both parties of companies into the JVC.

15–18 If there still remains a significant CGT or potential de-grouping charge, another method which can avoid these tax costs in the UK relies on a specific exemption[13] from certain CGT charges in the case of mergers—which can apply in the joint venture context if both parties are contributing companies to the JVC. The principles are:

(a) the joint venture party should ensure that the relevant business is contained within a subsidiary (including, if appropriate, first hiving down the relevant business into a newly established subsidiary);

(b) that subsidiary is then transferred to the JVC with the JVC issuing shares[14] to the joint venturer as consideration for the transfer; and

(c) the same procedure would apply to the other joint venture party in respect of its contribution.

Under this route, a transfer of assets between the joint venture party and its UK subsidiary (being a transfer within a CGT group) should not crystallise a CGT charge. The transfer of the shares in the subsidiary by the party to the JVC, in exchange for the issue of shares by the JVC, should not be treated as a disposal by the joint venture party for CGT purposes.[15] In addition and importantly, where s.181 TCGA 1992 applies (and the precise requirements of that section are both detailed and somewhat obscure), the potential de-grouping charge does not apply when the new subsidiaries leave their respective groups on the transfer to the JVC. This treatment should, in principle, apply to a joint venture which is not necessarily a 50:50 joint venture. In essence, the main requirement is that each party should receive shares in the JVC of a value equivalent to the value of the assets transferred by it to the JVC. Further, it is not necessary in practice for both joint venture parties to be UK companies for this treatment to apply.

Contributions to a partnership

15–19 The tax analysis, if a partnership vehicle is used, is by no means straightforward. In the UK, a major issue can be the potential CGT charge

---

[13] Under s.181 of the TCGA 1992 but, in practice, this will require UK Revenue clearance. The application of s.181 is not straightforward and the UK Revenue are known to consider transactions very carefully.

[14] At least 25 per cent of the consideration would need to be in ordinary shares with the balance in the form of shares (of any description) or debentures.

[15] It may, though, require UK Revenue clearance under s.138 TCGA 1992.

which might be incurred by a party upon contributing assets to the partnership. The disposal by a partner to a partnership is a disposal of a part share in that asset, the consideration for the disposal being the receipt of an interest in the assets contributed to the partnership by the other partner(s). Although there is no relief which specifically applies to the contribution of assets to a partnership, it is understood that as a matter of practice the UK Revenue is generally prepared to apply the principles set out in Statement of Practice SP D12 to the creation of partnerships.[16] The upshot of this approach is that the corporate partner will generally be treated as having disposed of its capital assets on a no gain/no loss basis for CGT purposes provided that (i) no consideration is provided outside the partnership accounts for the disposal, (ii) the asset is not revalued in the partnership accounts and (iii) it is a commercial arm's length transaction.

15–20 Any gain which is not protected by this UK Revenue practice may be relieved by the application of CGT rollover relief. Although the application of that relief is perhaps more problematic in the partnership context, as a practical matter the UK Revenue is understood to permit CGT rollover relief in certain circumstances.

Income tax consequences

15–21 The transfer of certain assets by a joint venture party to the JVC may, in certain circumstances, give rise to a taxable profit for the joint venture party. In the case of trading stock, in particular, the transfer pricing rules—see para.15–23—can operate to impute an arm's length price to the disposal by the transferor to the JVC. If that price exceeds book value, the transferor may recognise a taxable income receipt.

Recapture of allowances

15–22 The transfer to a JVC of assets which have previously attracted capital allowances may result in the recapture of all or part of the capital allowances previously given—in other words, the joint venture party may realise a so-called "balancing charge" on assets so transferred. It is also possible that where the disposal proceeds for the asset are less than its tax written down value (broadly, the cost of the asset less cumulative capital allowances), the party could realise a "balancing allowance", which has the effect of a trading deduction.

15–23 On a hive-down of a trade to a subsidiary prior to its transfer to a JVC, no balancing charge will arise. Instead, the relevant assets are treated

---

[16] By its terms, SP D12 only applies to pre-existing partnerships in respect of changes to profit sharing ratios.

as having been acquired by the subsidiary for capital allowances purposes at tax written down value.

Transfer of trading losses

15–24 One joint venture party may have accumulated past unused tax losses which the parties wish to preserve for the benefit of the joint venture. The transfer of a trade, which has generated tax losses, by one company to another does not generally carry with it the right for the transferee to utilise those losses. However, this may be achieved in certain circumstances. One possible route is for the joint venture party with the losses itself to form a company (to become later the JVC) and for that party to be the 100 per cent owner for a period of time during which it hives down the loss-making trade to it—with the other joint venture party or parties subsequently contributing their assets to the JVC in exchange for interests in the JVC (thereby diluting the first party's initial 100 per cent interest). This route is subject to some important qualifications, including:

(a) the UK Revenue tends to look at hive-downs closely;

(b) anti-avoidance provisions[17] will result in the ability to carry losses forward being lost if the incoming joint venture party or parties then acquire more than 50 per cent of the ordinary share capital of the JVC within three years of the transfer and, within that period, there is a major change in the nature or conduct of the trade in which the losses arose;

(c) the available trading losses may be reduced[18] where relevant liabilities of the trade are retained by the party transferring the business and they exceed the relevant assets transferred; the losses carried forward are reduced by the amount of the excess;

(d) as soon as the transferee company leaves the transferor's CGT group, a possible liability to CGT "de-grouping charge" may arise within the subsidiary in respect of assets acquired intra group by that subsidiary within the previous six years.[19]

Transfer taxes

Stamp duty

15–25 Transfer taxes (including, in the UK, stamp duty and stamp duty land tax) can be a material cost:

---

[17] See s.768 Taxes Act 1988.
[18] Under s.343(4) Taxes Act 1988.
[19] TCGA 1992, s.179. A similar charge could arise under the intangible assets regime. In addition, any clawback under the stamp duty/SDLT regimes should not be overlooked.

(1) The only types of property within the stamp duty charge in the UK are, broadly, shares, certain loans and interests in a partnership. Therefore, the transfer of assets such as book debts, moveable plant and contracts (at least to the extent not relating to shares or marketable securities) will not be subject to stamp duty or, indeed, any other stamp tax.

(2) Stamp duty land tax (SDLT) is chargeable on transactions in UK land. SDLT is a tax on a "land transaction", being any acquisition of a "chargeable interest" other than an "exempt transaction". Land transaction, chargeable interest and exempt transaction are all defined terms.

15-26 Since the scope of stamp duty has been significantly reduced, the planning techniques available to mitigate stamp duty costs have also become less applicable. However, stamp duty group relief may be available. Intra-group transfers of assets between members of a stamp duty group will usually be capable of being carried out free of stamp duty (and, in more restricted circumstances, SDLT).[20] The broad requirements for a stamp duty group are as follows:

STAMP DUTY GROUP: SUMMARY

- A joint venture party and the JVC will be members of a stamp duty group for this purpose if the party owns at least 75 per cent of the ordinary share capital (as defined in s.42(4) of the Finance Act 1930) of the JVC. This ownership test must be satisfied both before and after the transfer.

- In addition, the joint venture party must be beneficially entitled to at least 75 per cent of the profits and assets available for distribution to equity holders. The relief can be denied if there exist arrangements for a change of control of the JVC.

- Hive downs of assets by a joint venture party prior to a subsidiary being contributed to a JVC may not benefit from the "stamp duty group" exemption—notwithstanding that the transfer of assets by the joint venture party to its subsidiary is a transfer between members of a stamp duty group. There are certain stamp duty avoidance provisions which deny relief where there exist "arrangements" for the transferee to leave the stamp duty group or where there is a change of control. In many cases, the hive down will take place when arrangements exist for the subsidiary to be transferred to the JVC (unless the JVC is also a member of that group by reason of the joint venture party's ownership of the JVC)

VAT

15-27 Another potential transfer tax is value added tax (VAT). The transfer of business assets from a joint venture party to the JVC will often

---

[20] Although this will require the UK Revenue to confirm the existence of the relief by means of an adjudication under s.42 Finance Act 1930.

be a taxable supply for VAT purposes and will be the occasion of a charge to VAT—at least in the absence of the application of any relief. However, if the transfer is the transfer of a business as a going concern (and a number of other detailed requirements are satisfied),[21] the transfer will be outside the scope of VAT. Alternatively, it may be possible for the JVC and one of the joint venture parties to be grouped for VAT purposes, in which case the transfer to the JVC by that party will be outside the scope of VAT.

FINANCING THE JVC

Financing

15–28 Financing is an important factor in the structuring of any joint venture, especially a cross border transaction. Particularly important will be the capitalisation of the JVC and its equity/debt ratio. Those involved will usually aim to locate debt finance in a territory where taxable profits can be relieved at the highest possible rate. At its simplest:

(a) where interest expense is more valuable in tax terms in the territory of a joint venture party than in the territory of the JVC, equity financing of the JVC will be appropriate;

(b) on the other hand, where the joint venture is to be established for commercial reasons in a territory with a high level of corporate taxation, debt financing will normally produce a higher after tax return.

These simple calculations are useful as a starting point, but they will be affected by a number of factors including local interest relief or tax grouping restrictions, transfer pricing and thin capitalisation rules, foreign exchange gains or losses, and the expense of repatriating both interest and dividends to the parents. Some of these factors are discussed in more detail in chapter 7.

DISTRIBUTION OF PROFITS

Tax costs of distributions

15–29 The tax costs of repatriation of profits from the joint venture operations are frequently a material issue in planning an international equity joint venture. These costs can take, essentially, two forms:

---

[21] Art.5, VAT (Special Provisions) Order 1995.

(a) the tax authority of the paying company's jurisdiction may require that company to withhold and account for an amount from the dividend; and/or

(b) the recipient of the dividend may be taxed in its own jurisdiction on the dividend (unless exemptions or credits are available to minimise or avoid such taxes).

The overall cost of distributing dividends to the joint venture parties should be examined at an early stage when considering the proposed location of the JVC (see also para.15–08 earlier).

Tax liability of the JVC on dividend income from its operating subsidiaries

15–30 One material issue, where a JVC has multi-national operations, is to review the tax implications for the JVC of dividends received from its subsidiaries worldwide. In the case of a JVC located in the UK:

(1) Dividends received by the JVC from a UK tax resident subsidiary are not subject to UK tax.

(2) Dividends received by the JVC[22] from a non-UK resident subsidiary are subject to UK corporation tax. However, if the JVC's shareholding in the relevant subsidiary carries the right to at least 10 per cent of the votes of that subsidiary (as will usually be the case), the JVC will normally obtain relief against the UK tax payable on those dividends. The effect of this relief (known as relief for "underlying tax") is that, broadly speaking, provided the profits out of which the dividends were paid to the JVC have borne (foreign) tax at a rate equal to or greater than the rate of UK corporation tax, no further UK tax will be due by the JVC on those dividends.

Payment by JVC of dividends to its joint venture parents

15–31 In many jurisdictions, payment of dividends by a JVC to its joint venture parents will result in withholding taxes required to be deducted by the JVC as payer of the dividend. This can be an important factor.

(1) There is no withholding tax on dividends paid by a JVC in the UK wherever the joint venture parent is resident.

(2) Within the EU, the EU Parent/Subsidiary Directive eliminates withholding taxes on dividends paid from one EU country to another where, broadly speaking, the recipient owns more than 15 (to be reduced to 10) per cent of the company which pays the dividend.

---

[22] This section should be read in the light of the proposals set out in the UK Revenue discussion document mentioned in para.15–09 above.

368   TAX PLANNING

(3) In a country where there is a withholding tax, the position is often ameliorated by a double tax treaty between the payer's jurisdiction and that of the payee. Tax planning will often be appropriate to establish the most tax efficient treaty relationship.[23]

Income access structures

15–32 Where tax difficulties in relation to repatriation of profits from a cross-border venture still arise, an income access (or dividend access) structure is sometimes considered. A joint venture party may often prefer (if possible) to receive dividends from a company in its own jurisdiction, since this may reduce or eliminate withholding taxes and/or preserve imputation credits. The main principles or steps behind income access structures are as follows:

(a) each joint venture party has primary dividend access to profits of a subsidiary of the JVC resident in the party's own tax jurisdiction (such profits not being routed through the JVC);

(b) the joint venture party's dividend entitlement from the JVC is correspondingly reduced; and

(c) the income access shares in the JVC's subsidiary and the parent's shares in the JVC are "stapled" so that they cannot be held by separate owners.

Examples have included mergers between public companies (e.g. the Anglo-French merger of Wiggins Teape and Arjomari and the US-UK merger which established SmithKline Beecham). The same techniques can be applied to joint ventures where particular parts or subsidiaries within the joint venture party's overall businesses are being combined. An example:

FIGURE 15.1   INCOME ACCESS STRUCTURE: EXAMPLE

- Two joint venture parties (A and B) each have a company to contribute to a JVC (A Sub and B Sub). For political reasons it has been decided to locate the JVC in a neutral jurisdiction such as the Netherlands. In order to create an income access structure, each joint venture party:

---

[23] For instance, for investments into Russia, the Cyprus/Russia double tax treaty has historically been popular—partly because withholding tax rates have been reduced to 5 per cent or 10 per cent on dividends and 0 per cent on interest and royalties; similarly, the Mauritius/India treaty for investments into India.

- restructures its subsidiary's share capital into two classes of shares: one class carries the rights to substantially all the dividend income (income access shares) and the other class carries all voting rights and other economic rights in the joint venture (capital voting shares); and
- transfers the capital voting shares to the JVC in consideration of the issue of shares by the JVC.

• The end result is that the JVC owns the capital voting shares in A Sub and B Sub, and A and B own the income access shares in A Sub and B Sub, respectively. A and B also own the shares in the JVC.

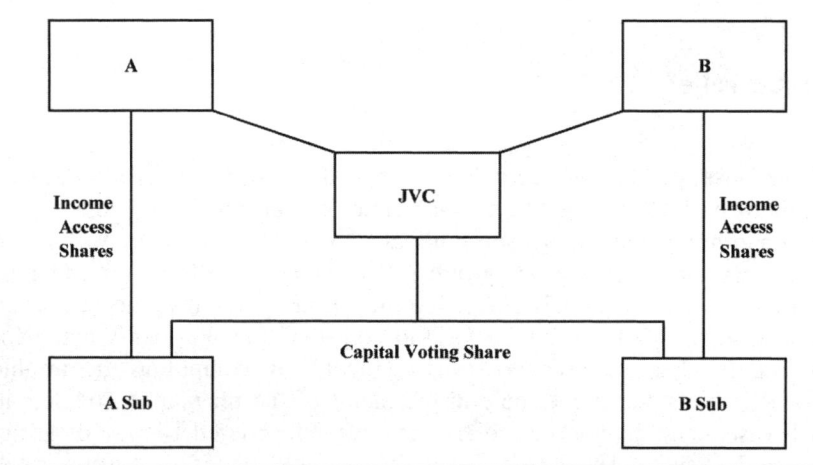

Such structures need careful planning. Whilst the right tax results can be achieved in a number of jurisdictions, constitutional and corporate law issues relating to share rights in particular jurisdictions (including a number of civil law countries) can create significant difficulties. For example, SmithKline Beecham replaced its dual share structure with a single class of ordinary shares in 1996.

ONGOING TAX ISSUES RELATING TO THE JOINT VENTURE

Ongoing tax issues: general

15–33 Tax considerations will continue to apply to the ongoing activities of the JVC and planning will be appropriate to ensure the most tax efficient arrangements. Particular objectives will be:

(a) to minimise the ongoing tax burden of the JVC; or

(b) where the JVC makes losses, to take advantage of those losses to minimise the overall tax burden of the joint venture parties.

One of the major tax planning issues for this purpose is likely to be the ability of the joint venture parties to surrender tax losses to the JVC and/or the ability of the JVC to surrender tax losses to the joint venture parties. If the offset of losses is a particular concern, it may be worth considering a tax "transparent" structure (such as a contractual alliance or partnership) where losses of the venture may accrue directly to the joint venture parties—see para.15–06 earlier. However, within a corporate structure, certain reliefs may be available which achieve this. In the UK, the important reliefs are (i) group relief and (ii) consortium relief.

Group relief

15–34 Group relief, where it is available after satisfying certain detailed conditions, allows in the UK the surrender of current trading losses (and certain other amounts) by one company to another company within the same corporate group. Since group relief enables a JVC to surrender its entire trading losses to a 75 per cent joint venture party, it would be normal for the surrender to be made for full consideration. Payments made for surrenders of group relief are not deductible in computing the taxable profits of the payer nor taxable in the hands of the recipient (provided, in each case, they do not exceed the amount surrendered by way of group relief). No surrender of losses will be possible under the group relief provisions between the JVC and a non-75 per cent joint venture party. If no joint venture party has a 75 per cent or greater interest in the JVC, group relief (as referred to herein) will not be available at all. Accordingly, the availability of consortium relief will generally be the more important relief in the context of joint ventures.

Consortium relief

15–35 Consortium relief is an important relief for many joint ventures in the UK—particularly 50:50 or multi party ventures where other "grouping" reliefs may not be available. It makes available the same treatment for losses, where a JVC is owned by several companies, as exist within a 75 per cent group. Features of this relief[24] are as follows:

---

[24] See s.402(3) Taxes Act 1988.

Consortium relief: summary

- Consortium relief is available between a joint venture party and the JVC if:

  — the JVC is a trading company or a holding company;
  — the JVC is not the 75 per cent subsidiary of any company; and
  — the JVC is owned by a consortium (i.e. 75 per cent or more of the JVC's ordinary share capital is owned beneficially by 20 or fewer companies, each owning at least 5 per cent of the JVC).

- It is not necessary that all the members of the consortium are UK tax resident nor does any residence requirement apply to the underlying subsidiaries. It is necessary, however, for both the claimant and surrendering company to be UK resident or carrying on a trade in the UK through a branch or agency.

- Consortium relief is available between a joint venture party and a trading company owned by the JVC if:

  — the JVC is a holding company;
  — the trading company is a 90 per cent subsidiary of the JVC and is not the 75 per cent subsidiary of a company other than the JVC; and
  — the JVC is owned by a consortium.

15–36 There are a number of detailed requirements (and anti-avoidance provisions) which can apply to restrict or deny the availability of consortium relief.

(1) The JVC can only surrender to each joint venture party (and vice versa) such part of the relevant losses as is proportionate to that party's share in the JVC. A party's share in the JVC is computed by reference to special rules.[25] The aim is to prevent artificial manipulation of a party's economic interest in another company and thereby artificially securing an increase in the availability of consortium relief.

(2) As with group relief, the relevant loss may only be set off against profits of the overlapping accounting period of the consortium company to which the amount is surrendered.

(3) Payments and receipts for the surrender are not deductible or taxable (provided they do not exceed the amount surrendered).

---

[25] See s.403C Taxes Act 1988.

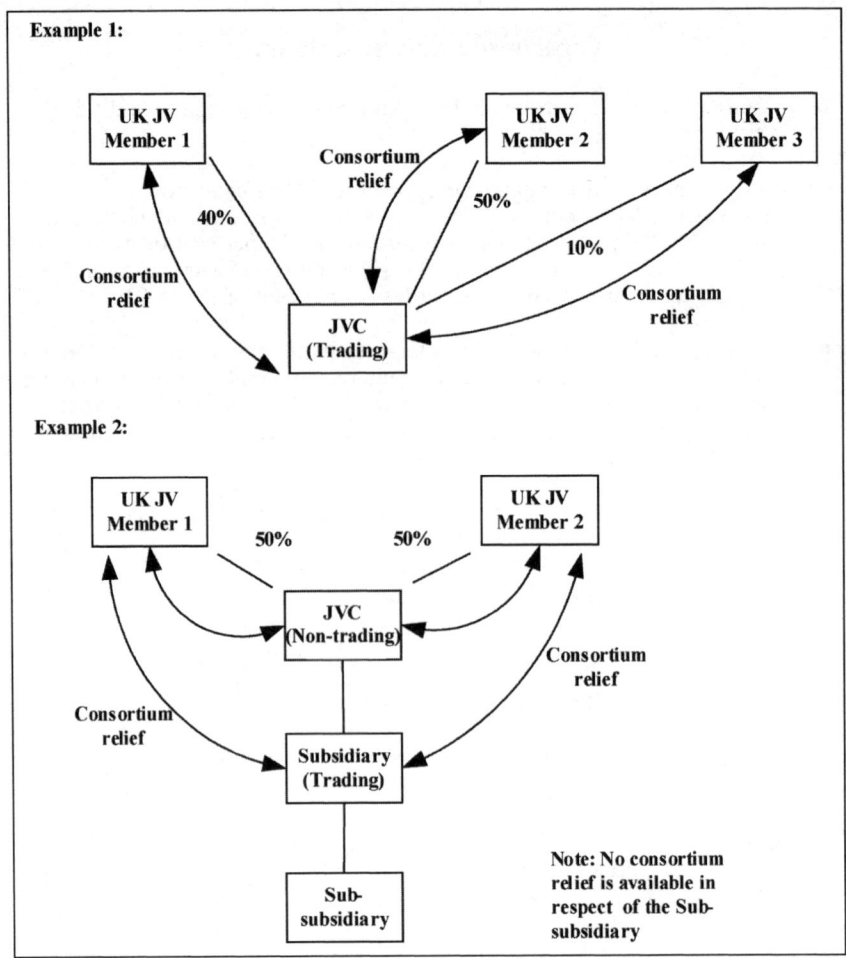

15–37 There are also anti-avoidance provisions principally designed to prevent the sale of tax loss companies. Consortium relief will be denied if there are "arrangements" by virtue of which (i) the JVC could become a 75 per cent subsidiary of a third company, (ii) a person holding less than 50 per cent of the JVC's ordinary share capital could obtain control of the JVC or (iii) any person, either alone or together with connected persons, controls or could control at least 75 per cent of the votes of the JVC. These provisions could technically be wide enough to catch many option type arrangements common in joint venture agreements. The UK Revenue has, however, issued a useful statement[26] which in practice excludes from the operation of the anti-avoidance legislation certain typical arrangements (including options) which could involve the transfer of shares in a JVC on

---

[26] Extra Statutory Concession C10 (as revised January 1993). Statement of Practice (SP3 1993).

or as a result of triggering events such as: insolvency, default or change of control affecting a member; deadlock resolution procedures; voluntary departure of a member; serious deterioration in financial condition of a member; or external change in commercial circumstances. This statement should be carefully reviewed where consortium relief is being relied on and the joint venture agreement contains unusual option or transfer arrangements.

15–38 Where consortium or group relief is available, the joint venture agreement should contain provisions regulating the process, as between the parties, of surrenders and claims. It is also sensible to provide some machinery for agreement as to whether, and to what extent, the JVC will utilise the losses first or whether it will surrender them.

Transfer pricing

15–39 Transfer pricing is another area which can be important in assessing the tax cost or efficiency of ongoing transactions between a JVC and its joint venture parents (e.g. sales of goods, recharging of overhead costs, supplies of services and, importantly, interest costs on loans). For instance, the UK's transfer pricing rules[27] may often apply in respect of transactions between a JVC in the UK and one of its joint venture parties if that joint venture party either controls the JVC or has a 40 per cent interest in it (where another joint venture party has a similar interest).[28] Where transfer pricing rules apply, they can operate to prevent (or limit) the joint venture profits being effectively realised in the most beneficial tax jurisdiction. In essence, where the transfer pricing rules apply, the transaction must be assimilated to an arm's length transaction between independent third parties.

TERMINATION

Termination: general tax issues

15–40 Termination of a joint venture or alliance can trigger significant tax consequences. Termination may take a number of routes, including, for example, the sale of some or all of the businesses or subsidiaries of the joint venture back to the joint venture parties. Key tax issues in this situation will be:

---

[27] Sch.28AA Taxes Act 1988.
[28] The Finance (No.2) Act 2005 has extended the transfer pricing rules to transactions where a number of persons "act together" in relation to the financing arrangements.

(a) to minimise, so far as is possible, the CGT costs incurred by the JVC upon the disposal by it of its capital assets;

(b) to establish the tax position of the joint venture parties (and whether they are treated as making a disposal for tax purposes upon the termination); and

(c) to identify or minimise the costs (e.g. in terms of stamp/transfer taxes) of transferring assets out of the joint venture to the joint venture parties.

In some cases, the likelihood of significant "unwinding" costs may be a material factor in deciding whether or not to establish an equity joint venture or, if so, its legal form. These potential costs should therefore be addressed at the outset.

Termination of a JVC: CGT

15–41 The termination of a JVC in the UK can result in a number of UK tax costs. For this purpose, it is assumed that the JVC is UK tax resident as is one (or more) of the joint venture parties. The principal potential cost is CGT.

(1) The route of "termination" may commonly involve the shares of one or more of the joint venture parties in the JVC being acquired by one of the other parties. If so, a UK tax resident party which disposes of its shares will make a disposal for CGT purposes and may have a chargeable gain or allowable loss. This is subject to the potential relief available under the SSE—see para.15–16 earlier.

(2) If the "termination" route takes the form of disposal of the assets of the JVC, this could result in a double layer of taxation: (i) the disposal of assets by the JVC is itself potentially subject to CGT; and (ii) the disposal, or deemed disposal, by a UK joint venture party of its shares in the JVC (e.g. upon the liquidation of the JVC) is also subject to CGT. Again the SSE may apply.

15–42 If a sale of assets or shares cannot be avoided, it may still under current law be possible to mitigate these tax costs by the JVC paying a pre-termination dividend (if resources permit) to its joint venture parents. A dividend received by a UK joint venture parent from a UK JVC is not generally subject to UK tax and foreign tax credits may be available to reduce or eliminate UK tax on a dividend from a non-UK JVC. Further, the reduction in value of the JVC as a result of paying that dividend will (subject to certain anti-avoidance provisions) reduce the gain realisable by the joint venture party upon the eventual disposal of its shares in the JVC.

15–43 The pre-termination dividend will not, though, reduce the gain realisable by the joint venture party in respect of the disposal of its shares in the JVC if the UK's CGT "value shifting" rules apply. These rules should in practice only be relevant in respect of a UK tax resident JVC.[29] Moreover, if the UK JVC is owned as to at least 75 per cent by a UK joint venture party, an exception to the "value shifting" rules will often apply in respect of pre termination dividends. In addition, as a matter of practice, it is understood that the UK Revenue may also apply that exception to dividends paid by a consortium owned JVC (i.e. a JVC owned by parties none of which has a 75 per cent stake but each of which owns at least five per cent of the JVC).

Termination of a partnership

15–44 A major issue on the termination of a partnership is likely to be the risk for the partners of a CGT charge in respect of assets disposed of by the partnership. Upon the distribution of assets by the partnership to the partners, the position is that, strictly, each partner whose share in an asset is reduced will be disposing of that share for the purposes of CGT. However, the CGT position is ruled to a large extent by the principles set out in UK Revenue Statement of Practice SP D12. Where a gain on an asset disposed of upon a partnership liquidation is allocated to the partner who actually receives the partnership asset, that partner is not charged to tax upon receipt of the asset. Instead, that partner's gain is deducted from its base cost in the asset. Other tax issues which need to be considered on the termination of a partnership include stamp duty, stamp duty land tax and VAT issues.

Termination of a contractual alliance

15–45 A contractual alliance is the most straightforward arrangement in terms of "unwinding" cost. The termination of a contractual alliance will not result in any disposal of assets by the joint venture parties and should not therefore lead to CGT costs. It therefore represents the simplest tax situation. However, if the termination were to constitute the cessation of a trade for UK tax purposes (and this may be a difficult question in some situations), there could be tax consequences including: (i) a deemed disposal of trading stock (with a potential for the crystallisation of a taxable profit); (ii) the clawback of capital allowances (again with the potential for realisation of taxable profits); and (iii) the effective loss of trading losses for tax purposes.

CONCLUSION

15–46 Tax will invariably play a key part in structuring a joint venture—

---

[29] If those rules, primarily in ss.29–34 TCGA 1992, were to apply, the joint venture party's consideration for that disposal could be treated by the UK Revenue as increased by a "just and reasonable amount", thus potentially undoing the benefit of the pre-termination dividend.

particularly an international joint venture. It will usually be important to involve tax specialists at an early stage. However, those dealing with the corporate and commercial aspects of the venture need to have a clear overview of the issues. Tax should rarely be the major "driving" force if commercial factors call for a different form of structuring. However, the costs involved can be significant—and in some cases critical. Sensible tax planning is commercially important.

CHAPTER 16

Competition and regulatory controls

Competition law and other regulatory controls have potentially a critical impact on the establishment of a joint venture. They can significantly affect the nature of conditions precedent required for the implementation of the venture, timing considerations and, not infrequently, the basic structure and terms of the joint venture or alliance itself. This chapter[1] addresses the broad framework of regulatory control and focuses, in particular, on the impact of competition laws in the EU and, domestically, in the UK

Range of regulatory controls

16–01 Joint ventures and alliances cover a wide diversity of collaborative arrangements. Many will be ventures between competitors or potential competitors. Most will be beneficial—not only to the parties but also to the economy and the consumer. They frequently lead to new or improved technologies, new products and enhanced competition and choice in the market place. Many will not be of sufficient size to have any material effect on market power. Some, however, do have the potential to restrict competition without creating any significant countervailing benefit.

16–02 Most jurisdictions therefore impose regulatory controls of some kind which affect joint ventures. Different types of control include:

(1) *Foreign investment review.* Many jurisdictions (in both developed and developing countries) impose governmental control over inward "foreign" investment—whether through political sensitivity or protection of national interests in particular industry sectors. The process of clearance will be a critical part of the establishment of the venture. The country summaries in Part D indicate some examples of strict procedures (e.g. China, Russia and India).

(2) *Industry regulation.* Many industries involve a particular licensing or regulatory structure controlling participation in that industry— whether by reference to qualifications, ownership criteria, competition

---

[1] I am very grateful to Andrew Renshaw and Jan Blockx (for the EU section), Alison Jones (for the UK section) and Victoria Harris (for the International Trade Regulation section) of Freshfields Bruckhaus Deringer LLP who contributed most of the original material on which this chapter is based.

or other public interest considerations. Some of these in the UK are addressed at para.16–44 et seq.

(3) *International trade regulation.* The operations of the proposed joint venture may trigger the application of important trade rules which should not be ignored in planning the venture. These include: export and/or import controls relating to products, components, raw materials and technology; trade remedy laws such as those relating to anti-dumping and countervailing duty actions; and rules against unlawful subsidies. Compliance with behavioural laws relating to anti-bribery and corruption must also be observed. These are discussed in outline at para.16–45 et seq.

(4) *Competition laws.* Joint ventures, by their nature, frequently involve collaboration between actual or potential competitors in a way which restricts their independent freedom of action. Competition authorities are therefore concerned to ensure, broadly, that the benefits to the public of collaboration outweigh the apparent detriments flowing from a reduction in competition. These laws are a principal focus of this chapter.

16–03 Competition laws exist worldwide. Since 1985, the number of countries around the world that have adopted antitrust laws has doubled. Well over 100 jurisdictions have now adopted antitrust laws in some form and nearly all of them have merger control regimes in place. A single transaction to establish a major international joint venture may be subject to multiple competition law regimes. Many competition authorities have formal or informal agreements for co-operation (including the exchange of information) in the investigation of mergers and joint ventures.

16–04 Competition law regimes tend to distinguish between two broad types of joint venture:

(1) *Merger-type ventures.* "Full-function" joint ventures, derived from mergers of existing businesses, result in a structural change in the market. They create a risk of increased dominance if market shares are high. They are generally judged under prior notification "merger control" regimes—e.g. in the EU under the EC Merger Regulation and in the UK under the Enterprise Act 2002.

(2) *Co-operative ventures.* Collaborative alliances involve the parties retaining their separate identities and businesses but with significant co-ordination or co-operation between them. Where the parties are actual or potential competitors, there is a risk of reduced competition and damage to interests of consumers. In the EU, the primary regulatory regime is Art. 81 of the Treaty of Rome and, in the UK, the Competition Act 1998. The competition law issues arising from these types of joint ventures must now typically be "self-assessed" by the parties to the transaction.

The critical issue in determining whether the joint venture requires notification or is subject to a "self-assessment" is how a jurisdiction defines a reportable "merger" under its legislation. The competition law regimes of a number of significant jurisdictions are outlined in Part D. This chapter concentrates on the position under EU and UK law. The scope and importance of EU law in this area is such that analysis of the competition law implications of a particular joint venture invariably requires EU law to be considered first.

EC MERGER REGULATION

EC Merger Regulation: when does it apply?

16–05 The structure of EU competition law is such that a first question is: does the EC Merger Regulation apply to the establishment of the joint venture? The EC Merger Regulation[2] is the main framework for merger control in the EU. It applies to a joint venture that satisfies the following three-prong test, namely where it: (i) is jointly controlled; (ii) is full-function; and (iii) has a Community[3] dimension.

Community dimension

16–06 It is convenient to take the size test first. The EC Merger Regulation, in this context, applies only to large-scale joint ventures or to joint ventures having a significant impact in at least three Member States.[4] The jurisdictional thresholds for "Community dimension" are set out below:

EC MERGER REGULATION: THRESHOLDS

(1) *Basic test*. A Community dimension arises if:

— the combined aggregate world-wide turnover of the parties exceeds €5bn (approximately US$6.85bn. at the relevant official exchange rates[6] applicable at the time of writing); and

---

[2] Regulation 139/2004.
[3] The EU Community now comprises 27 Member States.
[4] Since the monetary thresholds have not been amended to take into account inflation, an increasing number of transactions are subject to the EC Merger Regulation.
[5] 2007 average exchange rate of €1 = US$1.3705, based on rates set out in the European Central Bank's Monthly Bulletin (January, 2008).

> — the Community-wide turnover of each of at least two parties exceeds €250m (approximately US$343m)
>
> unless each of the parties achieves more than two-thirds of its aggregate Community-wide turnover in one and the same Member State.
>
> (2) *Alternative test*. A Community dimension will also arise if:
>
> — the combined aggregate world-wide turnover of the parties exceeds €2.5bn (approximately US$3.43bn); and
>
> — in each of at least three Member States, the combined aggregate turnover of the parties exceeds €100m (approximately US$137m); and
>
> — in each of at least these three Member States, the aggregate turnover of each of at least two of the parties exceeds €25m (approximately US$34.3m); and the aggregate Community-wide turnover of each of at least two of the parties exceeds €100m. (approximately US$137m)
>
> unless each of the parties achieves more than two-thirds of its aggregate Community-wide turnover in one and the same Member State.

In the case of joint ventures (i.e. those which are jointly controlled in accordance with para.16–07 below), the turnover[6] of the controlling joint venture parents (and the whole of the respective groups to which they belong) must be taken into account. Since the turnover tests are based on geographic turnover and not on the location of the parties, the Merger Regulation can apply to transactions which are essentially "foreign-to-foreign" joint ventures involving non-EU groups but which have the necessary turnover in the EU.

Joint control

16–07 If a Community dimension is possible, the other "tests" should be examined. For the purposes of the Merger Regulation, a joint venture is an undertaking which is jointly controlled by its parents. "Joint control":[7]

> ". . . exists where two or more undertakings or persons have the possibility of exercising decisive influence over another undertaking. Decisive influence in this sense normally means the power to block actions which determine the strategic commercial behaviour of an undertaking . . . It follows, therefore, that these shareholders must reach a common understanding in determining the commercial policy of the joint venture and that they are required to cooperate."

---

[6] For this purpose, turnover is the amount (excluding taxes) derived from the sale of products or the provision of services in the preceding financial year.
[7] Commission Consolidated Jurisdictional Notice OJ (2008) C95/1.

Joint control will normally exist (irrespective of whether the interests are 50:50) if the agreement of the joint venture parents is required in order to adopt major decisions in relation to the joint venture. This will apply if at least two parties have a blocking vote at board meetings or a right of veto over strategic matters. A veto right over strategic matters, such as the budget and the business plan as well as major investments or the appointment of senior management, will typically confer "control". Joint control may also exist de facto. The following are recent decisions[8] where the Commission has considered whether or not the parties had acquired joint control.

JOINT CONTROL: SOME RECENT CASES

- In *Alfa Acciai/Cronimet/Remondis/TSR Group*, the agreement of the directors appointed by all three shareholders was required for strategic decisions of the board of TSR. At the level of the shareholders' meeting, financial planning decisions could be blocked by any of the three shareholders. If no consensus could be reached by the three shareholders in the meeting, three arbitration rounds followed in which all three shareholders were equally represented. The fact that Remondis enjoyed a casting vote if no unanimous agreement could be found after these arbitration rounds, did not prevent the Commission from concluding that there was joint control. [M.4495 6.2.07]

- In *Arcelor/Oyak/Erdemir*, the Commission considered that a situation of de facto joint control can arise when the majority shareholder is a financial investor who is dependent on the minority industrial shareholder which is active in the same business as the joint venture. The fact that the industrial plan agreed between the shareholders was based on the integration of the commercial operations of the minority shareholder and the joint venture was also taken into account. [M.4085 13.2.06]

If the parents do not exercise joint control, the transaction will not be treated as a joint venture for the purposes of the Merger Regulation. Nevertheless, it may be regarded as an acquisition whereby one party acquires control of, or decisive influence over, another business. The transaction may therefore still fall within the Merger Regulation (on the basis of it being an acquisition) if the turnover of the acquirer and of the acquired business exceeds the threshold for Community dimension.

---

[8] Recent examples which involved unequal equity interests or multiple controlling parents include: *Scholz/voestalpine/Scholz Austria* (M.4469 22.3.07) where Scholz with a 60 per cent shareholding and voestalpine with a 33.41 per cent shareholding had joint control over Scholz Austria; and *Alfa Acciai/Cronimet/Remondis/TSR Group* (M.4495 6.2.07) where joint control was exercised over TSR by Remondis (60 per cent of the shares) and Alfa Acciai and Cronimet (each 20 per cent).

Full-function

16–08 A crucial element of the analysis under the Merger Regulation is to determine whether or not the joint venture is "full-function". These ventures bring about a structural change in the market. They are defined as: "performing on a lasting basis all the functions of an autonomous economic entity".[9] The Commission has given guidance[10] that, to be considered full-function, a joint venture:

> " . . . must operate on a market, performing the functions normally carried out by undertakings operating on the same market. In order to do so the joint venture must have a management dedicated to its day-to-day operations and access to sufficient resources including finance, staff, and assets (tangible and intangible) in order to conduct on a lasting basis its business activities within the area provided for in the joint venture agreement."

A joint venture will not be full-function if it remains dependent on its parents' activities and does not have independent access to the market. The upstream or downstream presence of the parents may affect this—although dependence on its parents for an initial start-up period should not affect its full-function nature. A joint venture with only a transitional impact will not bring about a lasting structural change in the market. (A right to dissolve or exit the joint venture will not normally affect this nor a provision which specifies a period of duration provided that this period is sufficiently long to create a lasting structural change; a duration of five to 10 years will frequently be sufficient depending on the structure of the market.)

16–09 In the following recent cases, the Commission considered the issue of whether or not a joint venture was full-function:

FULL-FUNCTION: SOME RECENT CASES

- *Sonae Industria/Tarkett/JV* involved the creation of two legal entities both jointly owned by Sonae and Tarkett: one producing, and the other distributing, laminate flooring. The Commission decided that the two entities together constituted one single joint venture as they served "mutually common economic purposes" and were subject to the same corporate governance rules. The Commission considered that this joint venture was full-function. The parents would transfer tangible and intangible assets to it. The fact that the two JVs would

---

[9] EC Merger Regulation, art.3(4).
[10] Commission Consolidated Jurisdictional Notice at para.94.

make use of the distribution network and outlet of the parent companies did not disqualify them from constituting, taken together, a full function joint venture. The JVs will be able to decide their own commercial, marketing and communication strategies independently from the parents, including pricing, rebates schemes and advertising campaigns. [M.4048 12.6.06]

- In *Fortis/BCP* a number of insurance companies were transferred by BCP to a newly established company, NHC, over which BCP and Fortis had joint control. The Commission noted that the joint venture was "full function", in part because it was made up of pre-existing companies and that, despite the fact that NHC would distribute its insurance products through BCP's banking network, NHC could also distribute its products through other channels (but not through other banking networks). [M.3556 19.1.05]

- In *Adecco/Manpower/Vediorbis/JV* three temporary work agencies set up a joint venture for the provision of extranet services between temporary work agencies (such as the parents) and companies employing temporary staff. Despite the fact that a relatively high proportion (up to 40 per cent) of the revenues of the joint venture was expected to come from its parents, it was considered to be full-function since it would provide its services independently from its parents and under the same conditions to other temporary work agencies (and their customers) as well. [M.3419 5.11.04]

One-stop-shop principle

16–10 The EC Merger Regulation procedure offers a "one-stop-shop" for merger control within the EU. If a merger or joint venture falls under the Merger Regulation, national competition rules within the EU will not apply to the establishment of the joint venture itself (save for certain limited rights of Member States referred to below). A benefit of the "one-stop-shop" is that it avoids the parties having to submit numerous national competition filings in EU jurisdictions affected by the joint venture.

16–11 The Merger Regulation allows for some added jurisdictional flexibility by entitling the parties (or indeed the Member States) to request the Commission that a merger which affects predominantly a local market should be reviewed by the local competition authority. Similarly, the parties to the transaction are also entitled to request a Member State to cede jurisdiction over a non-Community dimension merger to the Commission. Where the merger will be assessed depends on its "centre of gravity". Generally speaking, a joint venture which triggers merger filings in more than three countries and has cross-border effects is a likely candidate for review by the Commission even if the Community dimension test is not met. A Member State may also intervene to call for referral in certain narrow situations to protect its "legitimate interests" such as defence, public security, plurality of the media or the prudential supervision of financial institutions.

EC Merger Regulation: what is the test for clearance?

16–12 The Commission will approve a merger under the Merger Regulation if it:

> "would not significantly impede effective competition in the common market or in a substantial part of it, in particular as a result of the creation or strengthening of a dominant position".[11]

The Commission's focus is on whether the merger is likely to alter the competitive structure of a market by creating or strengthening the opportunity of one or more firms to exert market power (e.g. by increasing prices or changing the dynamics of supply).

(1) In its Horizontal Merger Guidelines,[12] the Commission explains its substantive approach to mergers between actual or potential competitors (so-called horizontal mergers). Post-transaction market shares and concentration levels provide a first indication whether or not a joint venture is likely to raise competition concerns. A market share of 50 per cent or greater will give rise to a (rebuttable) presumption of dominance; a post-transaction market share of 25 per cent or less will not normally raise concerns. The Commission is also concerned by link-ups between competitors in industries which have five or fewer major market participants.

(2) At the end of 2007 the Commission also adopted Non-Horizontal Merger Guidelines[13] in which it describes how it will assess vertical transactions (joint ventures between companies in vertically related industries, e.g. manufacturer and distributor of the same product) and conglomerate transactions (joint ventures between companies in closely related industries, e.g. producers of complementary products or products belonging to the same product range). The Commission states that non-horizontal mergers are generally less likely to raise competition concerns and that this is, particularly, the case if the market share of the parties in each of the markets concerned is below 30 per cent.

---

[11] Merger Regulation, art.2(2).
[12] Guidelines on the assessment of horizontal mergers OJ (2004) C3115.
[13] Guidelines on the assessment of non-horizontal mergers are available on DGComp's website at *http://ec.europa.eu/comm/competition/mergeers/legislation/legislation.html*.

16-13 The following are examples of recent joint ventures which fell within the jurisdiction of the Merger Regulation and were considered by the Commission:

SUBSTANTIVE ASSESSMENTS: SOME RECENT CASES

- In *Thales/Finmeccanica/AAS/Telespazio* Thales acquired the shareholding of Alcatel in AAS and Telespazio, which resulted in Thales acquiring joint control with Finmeccanica over these two entities active in the space industry. Since Thales was one of only two producers worldwide of Travelling Wave Tubes (TWT), a critical component of telecommunications satellites of which AAS was a leading manufacturer, the Commission had serious concerns about the transaction and initiated Phase II proceedings. The in-depth investigation showed that Thales' ability to restrict access to TWTs for rivals of AAS was constrained, in particular, by the buying power of its customers (as well as the credible competition of its rival). The Commission cleared the transaction unconditionally. [M.4403 4.4.07]

- In *APW/APSA/Nordic Capical/Capio* three private equity companies, all with subsidiaries active in the medical industry, acquired joint control of Capio, a provider of healthcare services via its acute private hospitals, diagnostic centres and private psychiatric hospitals in several EEA member states. In order to eliminate the Commission's concerns in relation to the UK, the parties committed to divest all of Capio's acute private hospitals in the UK and certain other services in order to remove the horizontal overlap with the private healthcare activities of APW in the UK. [M.4367 16.3.07]

- In *Bertelsmann/Springer/JV* a joint venture was created by Bertelsmann and Springer combining some of their rotogravure printing activities. The Commission considered that rotogravure printing was not substitutable for other printing techniques such as offset printing and, in light of the parties' near 50 per cent market share in Germany, decided to initiate Phase II proceedings. However, since the parties' competitors could readily expand their capacities and the parties had to face potential competitors from the Netherlands, France and Italy, the Commission approved the creation of the joint venture on an unconditional basis. [M.3178 3.5.05]

Full-function joint ventures with co-operative aspects

16–14 Many full-function ventures nevertheless involve "co-operative" aspects between the parent companies and may lead to co-ordination of competitive behaviour between the parents and/or the parents and the joint venture. These can give rise to some complex substantive assessments. If they have a Community dimension, they remain subject to the Merger Regulation. The general approach is that (i) the establishment of the joint venture itself and its structural aspects are to be judged in accordance with the substantive test applicable to mergers under the Merger Regulation and (ii) the co-operative aspects of the joint venture are to be appraised in accordance with art.81.

16–15 The Commission has stated that, for art.81 to apply, the co-ordination of competitive behaviour by parent companies (or co-ordination between the joint venture parties and the joint venture itself) must be both likely and appreciable and must flow directly from the creation of the joint venture. The following are two recent cases where the Commission has considered this difficult area:

Co-ordination Between Parents: Two Recent Cases

- *SES Astra/Eutelsat/JV* involved a joint venture between two satellite operators offering satellite based broadcasting services. The joint venture would be active in the provision of infrastructure for broadcasting and two-way communication services to mobile devices, an emerging market. Some respondents to the Commission raised the possibility of the parents coordinating their behaviour through the offering of bundled services with the joint venture. Since the market share of the joint venture would be small for a number of years and the customers and duration of the contracts envisaged by the joint venture were different from those of its parents, the Commission considered that no risk of coordination existed. [M.4477 25.7.07]

- In *Wegener/PCM/JV* two Dutch newspaper publishers contributed some of their national and regional newspaper titles to a joint venture which would publish a new "national-regional" daily newspaper in the Netherlands; its 19 editions would combine a national segment common to the Netherlands with local news. By publishing newspapers, Wegener and PCM would remain active, together with the joint venture, on the market for national advertisement space in daily newspapers. Since the combined market share of Wegener and PCM (including the joint venture) amounted to 45–55 per cent and their main rival, De Telegraaf, had 30–40 per cent, the Commission considered that the creation of the joint venture could lead to the coordination of the competitive behaviour of Wegener, PCM and their joint venture. To address the Commission's concerns, the articles of association of the joint venture were changed to ensure its independence from its shareholders and Wegener committed, for the duration of the joint venture, to refrain from selling or offering to national advertisers advertising space in its daily newspapers. [M.3817 7.7.05]

Ancillary Restrictions

16–16 Ancillary restrictions are restrictions "directly related and necessary to the implementation of the merger or joint venture". They are restrictions where, in their absence, the merger or joint venture could not be implemented or could only be implemented on more uncertain and unfavourable conditions—e.g. restrictions to protect the value transferred or continuity of supply or to enable the start-up of a new entity.

16–17 The concept of "ancillary restrictions" has been developed both in the context of the Merger Regulation and the analysis of agreements for the purposes of art.81. In merger cases, any clearance decision will also cover any ancillary restrictions. Guidance on what are generally acceptable as ancillary restrictions under the Merger Regulation is given by the Ancillary Restraints Notice[14] and certain decisions of the Commission.

ANCILLARY RESTRICTIONS

In order to be considered "ancillary", restrictions must be closely related to the merger or joint venture and necessary for its effective implementation. They must be proportionate—in duration, products or services covered and geographical field of application. Common clauses include the following:

(1) *Non-compete during JV*—restrictions on parents competing with the JV (or with each other) in relation to the specific activities of the JV. Such restrictions will typically be considered ancillary for the life-time of the venture. If a non-compete restriction goes beyond the JV's geographical field of operation or economic activity, it is unlikely to be ancillary. The same principles apply to non-solicitation and confidentiality clauses although the duration of confidentiality restrictions may be longer where necessary to protect valuable business secrets.

(2) *Non-compete after sale*—restrictions which apply for a limited period after the sale of a party's shareholding in a JV. Although not covered by the Ancillary Restraints Notice, these will usually be acceptable[16] for a limited period, on a basis comparable with a seller's standard non-compete undertaking, in order to protect the goodwill transferred to the other JV partner(s).

(3) *Purchase/supply obligations*—obligations on the JV to purchase from or supply to the parents (or vice versa between the parents and the JV). Such commitments, including on an exclusive basis, may be regarded as ancillary

---

[14] Notice on restrictions directly related and necessary to concentrations [OJ 2005 C56/24]
[15] See e.g. *Fujitsu/AMD/Semiconductor* [OJ 1994 L341/66] where two-year non-compete obligations after a sale within the first 10 years were upheld. See also *British Interactive Broadcasting Open* for a 12 month restriction after exit following a change of control [OJ 1999 L312/1].

> for a limited period e.g. where necessary to enable the start-up of the JV or to ensure continuity of supplies for the JV's activities or continuity of sales to the parents. Where the JV supplies the parents as a principal purpose of the venture, this would include an obligation to give the parties priority if there were capacity shortages. A "most favoured nation" obligation on the JV for the benefit of the parents may also be ancillary.
>
> (4) *Technology licence restrictions*—a licence (including an exclusive licence) by the parents to the JV of their technology or intellectual property rights. Such licences may be ancillary if limited to the field of activity of the JV. Licences from the JV to the parents may also be ancillary, although terms such as territorial limitations or manufacture may need to be assessed under art.81. Licences between the parents themselves will not, though, be regarded as ancillary. (Licences outside the Ancillary Restraints Notice may benefit, where applicable, from the Technology Transfer Block Exemption—see para.17–26 below.)
>
> (5) *Post-termination restrictions on licensing*—a restriction on a parent from licensing a third party to use technology or rights developed by the JV. Although not covered by the Ancillary Restraints Notice, such a restriction for a limited period, after dissolution of the JV or the parent's withdrawal, may be regarded as ancillary. (Note that this applies only to sub-licensing third parties, not to use by the parents themselves.)

Restrictions which go beyond the limits of the guidance given by the Ancillary Restraints Notice may be acceptable but it is necessary for them to be assessed by the parties under art.81(1) and justified, if necessary, under art.81(3)—see para.16–27 et seq.

Procedure and Commission powers

16–18 The notification process, timing and associated procedural consequences can be of considerable practical importance.

> **EC MERGER REGULATION: PROCEDURE AND TIMETABLE**
>
> (1) *Time for notification.* Joint ventures with Community dimension may be notified to the Commission at any time after the parties can demonstrate a good faith intention to conclude an agreement. The Commission strongly recommends that the parties meet with Commission officials—and provide a draft Form CO—in advance of filing a formal notification.
>
> (2) *Suspension.* The general rule is that a transaction must not be put into effect before notification or until a final decision is adopted following notification, unless a derogation is granted by the Commission. Fines can be, and have been, imposed (in theory up to 10 per cent of aggregate turnover of the undertakings concerned) for failure to comply with this suspension rule.

(3) *Form RS.* Prior to filing a Form CO, a notifying party can request either: (i) a joint venture with Community dimension be reviewed, in whole or in part, by a Member State(s) where the merger may significantly affect competition in a "distinct market" within that Member State(s); or (ii) that a joint venture which does not have Community dimension, but is reviewable under the merger control law of at least three Member States, be referred to the Commission for review. The request for a referral is made on Form RS.

(4) *Form CO.* Notification under the Merger Regulation is made on Form CO together with supporting documentation such as audited accounts and copies of relevant agreements. The Form CO must be complete to start the clearance clock running. (The Commission can, however, waive the obligation to provide required information where it considers that it is not necessary to its examination). Completing Form CO can be a major exercise. Protection for business secrets can be obtained.

(5) *Simplified procedure for routine cases.* A simplified procedure applies to notifications which do not raise competition concerns. This procedure allows the Commission to clear joint ventures falling within its scope by adopting a short-form (rather than a fully reasoned) decision. However, the actual notification process, from the parties' perspective, has not been altered.

(6) *Third parties.* Third parties can play a significant role in Merger Regulation proceedings—frequently as complainants. The Commission posts on its website the fact that a notification has been made. It also publishes a summary of all notifications in the EU Official Journal. This provides third parties with an opportunity to express their opinions on the likely impact of the transaction on the structure of competition. The Commission will also send out appropriate requests for further information to third parties (usually to customers and competitors).

(7) *Time limits for clearance.* Time limits are important for planning the transaction.

    (a) *Phase I.* The Commission must reach its preliminary decision within 25 working days from the effective date of a (complete) notification. This is extended by an additional 10 working days if the parties submit "commitments" intended to form the basis for a clearance decision or if a Member State has requested that all or part of the concentration be referred to it. Where the Commission believes that it will have "serious doubts" and is likely to initiate a Phase II investigation, it will hold a "state of play" meeting to allow the parties to address the Commission's concerns. A very large percentage of cases are cleared at the end of Phase 1.

    (b) *Phase II proceedings.* If the Commission decides that the merger raises serious doubts regarding the adverse impact of the joint venture on competition, it will commence an in-depth Phase II investigation to decide whether the concentration is compatible or incompatible with the common market. Where it runs its full course, the Phase II procedure may last between 90 working days and 125 working days. Additionally, the Commission can "stop the clock" where the parties have not fully complied with a request for the provision of information or documents or have not given Commission officials appropriate answers in a so-called "dawn-raid" inspection. Phase II investigations are very time-consuming.

16–19 If the Commission finds that a merger is incompatible with the common market, it may prohibit the transaction or accept remedies to address its concerns.

(1) The Commission will commonly accept "commitments" from the parties to remedy perceived competition concerns as a condition to receiving Commission approval. Such commitments are typically "structural" (e.g. divesting a business rather than contributing it to the joint venture) but may be "behavioural" (e.g. agreeing that relevant know-how or sensitive information will not be passed from the joint venture to its parents). An increasing number of transactions are cleared subject to conditions. Relatively few have been blocked outright.

(2) If the parties fail to comply with the conditions imposed or with a prohibition decision, the Commission may impose fines up to a level of 10 per cent of the aggregate turnover of the companies concerned and any transfer of shares may be voidable.

ARTICLE 81: CO-OPERATIVE JOINT VENTURES

Article 81: non-full-function joint ventures

16–20 Joint ventures which are not full-function (e.g. collaborative ventures and alliances) do not fall within the EC Merger Regulation. However, they may fall under art.81(1) of the EU Treaty as well as under the national competition laws of one or more Member States. art.81(1) prohibits:

> " . . . all agreements between undertakings, decisions by associations of undertakings and concerted practices which may affect trade between Member States and which have as their object or effect the prevention, restriction or distortion of competition within the common market."

It is up to the parties themselves to determine the extent to which art.81 applies to a non-full-function joint venture. If an agreement falls within art.81(1), it will nonetheless be excepted from the prohibition if it satisfies the conditions of art.81(3). If not, it will be void and liable to challenge.

Agreements falling outside article 81

16–21 Many joint ventures and alliances will fall outside the scope of art.81 altogether because they are too small or do not have sufficient market impact. The Commission has helpfully given guidance:

(1) *No appreciable effect on trade between Member States.* Will the joint venture affect trade between Member States? It is a requirement, to fall within art.81(1), that the joint venture must appreciably affect trade between Member States. This effect may be actual or potential, direct or indirect. It is not necessary to show that each restriction is capable of affecting trade; it is sufficient to show that the agreement taken as a whole is capable of doing so. (The EU competition laws can, though, apply to a joint venture between an EU company and a non-EU company including in relation to a joint venture entity established in a non-EU country if trade within the EU is capable of being affected.)

The Commission has published Guidelines to assist the determination whether an agreement is likely to be capable of appreciably affecting trade between Member States.[16] The Guidelines also set out both a market share and a turnover test to help the assessment.

APPRECIABLE EFFECT ON TRADE: THRESHOLDS

- Under the Guidelines, agreements are not, in principle, likely to affect trade between Member States appreciably if the following conditions are met:
    — the aggregate market share of the parties on any relevant market within the EU affected by the agreement does not exceed five per cent; and
    — in the case of horizontal agreements, the aggregate turnover in the EU does not exceed €40 million[17]; or
    — in the case of vertical agreements, the aggregate turnover in the EU of the supplier in the products covered by the agreement does not exceed €40 million.[18]

- The market share can be exceeded by up to two per cent, and the turnover threshold can be exceeded by up to 10 per cent, for up to two successive calendar years without the effect on trade being considered appreciable. For emerging markets where market share data is not available, the Commission will consider the position of the parties on related product markets or their strength in technologies related to the agreement.

---

(2) *No appreciable effect on competition/minor agreements.* Will the joint venture restrict competition to any appreciable extent? In principle, art.81 will not apply if the impact on competition is insignificant, in

---

[16] Guidelines on the effect on trade concept contained in art.81 of the Treaty OJ (2004) C/I01/81.
[17] In the case of agreements for the joint buying of products, the relevant turnover is the parties' combined purchases of the products covered by the agreement.
[18] In the case of a licence agreement, the relevant turnover is the aggregate turnover of the licensees in the products incorporating the licensed technology and the licensor's own turnover in those products.

particular where the position of the parties on the relevant product or geographic market is weak.

One way of determining that a joint venture will not restrict competition to an appreciable extent is to rely on the thresholds set out in the Minor Agreements Notice.[19] This is an important exception which, in practice, excludes many joint ventures between small and medium-sized enterprises as well as joint ventures which have limited effects on the market. According to the Notice, the Commission will not institute proceedings in respect of agreements that meet the conditions of the Notice.[20]

MINOR AGREEMENTS NOTICE: THRESHOLDS

According to the Minor Agreements Notice, those agreements which satisfy the following thresholds do not appreciably restrict competition within the meaning of art.81(1) of the EU Treaty:

- Where the aggregate market share of the parties on any relevant market affected by the agreement does not exceed:
    - 10 per cent for agreements between actual or potential competitors;
    - 15 per cent for agreements between undertakings who are not actual or potential competitors;
    - 10 per cent for agreements where it is difficult to classify whether or not the agreement is between actual or potential competitors.
- Where the relevant market is characterised as having a network of similar agreements (i.e. where 30 per cent or more of the relevant market is covered by parallel networks of agreements having the same effect), the concern is then over the cumulative effect of the agreement. In that case, the threshold will be exceeded where the parties have a market share that exceeds five per cent on any relevant market affected by the agreement, whether or not the parties are actual or potential competitors.

The calculation of market shares must include the groups to which the parties belong as well as the shares of the joint venture parties themselves. These market shares can be exceeded by up to two per cent for up to two successive years without the effect being regarded as appreciable.

The applicability of art.81 cannot, however, be ruled out where an agreement contains certain "hardcore" restrictions (such as price-fixing or customer sharing).

---

(3) *Minor sales/purchasing joint ventures.* The Horizontal Guidelines[21] give further guidance as to when horizontal co-operation agreements infringe art.81(1) and, if they do, when they satisfy the requirements of art.81(3).

---

[19] Notice on agreements of minor importance which do not fall within the meaning of Art. 81(1) of the Treaty establishing the European Community (*de minimis*) OJ (2001) C368/13.
[20] Technically, the Notice is not binding on the Member States or national courts but it is expected to be observed in practice.
[21] Guidelines on the applicability of art.81 of the EU Treaty to horizontal co-operation agreements OJ (2001) C3/02.

> **MINOR SALES/PURCHASING JOINT VENTURES: THRESHOLDS**
>
> Agreements which are unlikely to be regarded as falling within art.81(1) include:
>
> - purchasing joint ventures where the combined market share of the parties is less than 15 per cent; and
> - sales joint ventures (which do not involve price-fixing) where the parties' combined market share is also below 15 per cent.

(4) *Intra-group joint ventures.* Joint ventures formed by parties which belong to the same corporate group are outside the scope of art.81.

Material factors in assessing whether article 81 applies

16–22 The Commission's approach to horizontal co-operation agreements is set out in its Horizontal Guidelines.[22] These provide detailed and practical guidance as to the types of restrictions found in horizontal co-operation agreements which are likely to fall under art.81(1) and those likely to satisfy the conditions of art.81(3). Material factors may, broadly, be summed up in the following principal questions:

(1) *Actual or potential competitors.* Are the parent companies actual or potential competitors in relation to the activities of the joint venture? A review of the market in which each joint venture party operates (and their market shares) should be carried out early in the transaction. In general, the question is whether each party has, or would have had, the financial, technical and commercial resources to enter the market alone, at least in the medium term. The Commission has found it relatively easy to decide that parties are actual or potential competitors. Illustrative decisions include:

- In *GEAE/P&W* ("Engine Alliance") the Commission found that the joint venture partners were potential competitors since "it would be technically and economically feasible for both parties to develop the new engine independently", even if "it may be economically more efficient for the parties to develop the new engine in co-operation." [OJ (2000) L58/16]
- In *Eurotunnel* the Commission considered that art.81(1) did not apply to a joint venture set up to bid and operate a construction contract for the Eurotunnel because none of the parents was able by itself to execute the orders under the contract. [OJ (1988) L311/36]

---

[22] The Horizontal Guidelines should be read alongside the Commission's Guidelines on the application of art.81(3): Guidelines on the application of art.81(3) of the Treaty OJ (2004) CI01/97. The Guidelines also explain the Commission's analysis of art.81(1).

- In *Vacuum Interrupters*, each party had carried out R&D work in the past in relation to vacuum interrupters but had ceased independent research. The Commission concluded that they were potential competitors. [OJ (1977) L48/32]

(2) *Spill-over effects.* Are the parties actual or potential competitors in unrelated fields such that there may be spill-over effects of their cooperation which could adversely affect competition in those other fields? The Commission has been particularly concerned with the spill-over implications of certain strategic alliances between actual or potential competitors. These alliances may encourage the development of new services and/or pan-European networks but can also lead to diminution of competition if the co-operation becomes more general.
- In *BT/MCI* the strategic alliance involved the creation of a joint venture to develop and market international value-added telecom services for multinationals. It also included a reciprocal territorial non-compete clause. The Commission was concerned that the alliance could affect competition generally in the domestic markets and gave a limited exemption for five years in respect of the territorial non-compete clause. [OJ (1994) L223/36]

(3) *Network of joint ventures.* Is the joint venture part of a network of two or more competing joint ventures involving a common party?
- In *Optical Fibres* Corning had established a number of joint ventures with different parties in various EU countries. Each joint venture was dependent on Corning's technology. The Commission considered that this created a network of interrelated joint ventures with a common technology and they could not be expected to compete with each other to the same extent as if they were unrelated competitors. [OJ (1986) L236/30]

(4) *Foreclosure of opportunities.* Will the creation of the joint venture lead to foreclosure of opportunities for third parties?
- In *Olivetti/Canon* the joint venture limited opportunities for third party manufacturers who might otherwise have supplied the parties on an OEM basis and restricted the opportunities for competitors to acquire manufacturing licences from the parties. [OJ (1988) L 52/51]

(5) *Unnecessary restraints.* Do any terms of the arrangement go beyond restraints necessary to ensure the start-up and proper functioning of the joint venture and do they have any foreseeable anti-competitive impact on third parties?
- In *Elopak/Metal Box-Odin* an exclusive right for the joint venture to use relevant technology within the defined field was considered necessary for the joint venture's activities. [OJ (1990) L209/15]

- In *BP/Kellogg* BP entered into a joint development agreement with Kellogg to develop a process plant for ammonia production based on BP's catalyst. They were not actual or potential competitors. BP was restricted from disclosing information about its catalyst to third parties or supplying the catalyst to third parties without Kellogg's consent. The Commission nevertheless concluded that the restrictions were reasonable and necessary for the beneficial purposes of the venture. [OJ (1985) L369/6]

(6) *Hard-core restrictions.* Does the agreement contain any "hard-core" restrictions, such as fixing selling prices, limiting output or sales (including restrictions on passive sales) or allocating markets or customers?

A positive answer to any of these questions is likely, subject to factors outlined in para.16–21 earlier, to lead to an assessment that art.81(1) applies.

Exemptions/exceptions under article 81(3)

16–23 Even where co-operative joint ventures restrict competition within the meaning of art.81(1), the Commission recognises that they may still merit being upheld. Indeed, the Horizontal Guidelines generally acknowledge that:[23]

> "...horizontal co-operation can lead to substantial economic benefits. Companies need to respond to increasing competitive pressure and a changing market place driven by globalisation, the speed of technological progress and the generally more dynamic nature of markets. Co-operation can be a means to share risk, save costs, pool know-how and launch innovation faster. In particular, for small and medium-sized enterprises cooperation is an important means to adapt to the changing market place."

In other words, the economic benefits arising from co-operation between competitors frequently outweigh their resulting restrictive effects on competition. An agreement will still be upheld if it satisfies the conditions of a relevant "block exemption" or if it satisfies the criteria of art.81(3).

Block exemptions

16–24 The Commission has adopted block exemptions which set out the conditions under which certain categories of agreements automatically

[23] Horizontal Guidelines, at para.3.

benefit from an exemption. Block exemptions are directly applicable in national courts. They include the following:

(1) The R&D Block Exemption[24] provides for the automatic exemption of certain agreements relating to research and development.

(2) The Specialisation Block Exemption[25] provides for the exemption of certain agreements involving specialisation between the parties in the manufacture of products.

The Commission's aim in introducing these two block exemptions is to provide a clear and user-friendly legislative framework by which companies that do not hold significant market power can more easily determine for themselves whether art.81(3) applies. The market share threshold for exemption is set at 25 per cent for R&D agreements and 20 per cent for specialisation agreements. However, agreements which contain "hardcore" restrictions do not qualify for exemption under the block exemptions.

(3) The Technology Transfer Block Exemption applies under certain circumstances to the licence of intellectual property rights between one of the parents and the joint venture—see para.17–26 below.

(4) The Vertical Agreements Block Exemption[26] applies to various agreements relating to purchase, sale or resale of certain goods or services between undertakings operating at different levels of the production or distribution chain.

The terms of these block exemptions are still relatively narrow and many cooperative joint ventures will be unable to benefit from them.

Individual agreements satisfying art.81(3)

16–25 Non-full-function joint venture arrangements which fall under art.81(1) may also individually satisfy the conditions of art.81(3) and therefore be upheld. This is the case if the agreement:

" . . . contributes to improving the production or distribution of goods or to promoting technical or economic progress, while allowing consumers a fair share of the resulting benefit, and . . . does not:

— impose on the undertakings concerned restrictions which are not indispensable to the attainment of these objectives;
— afford the undertakings concerned the possibility of eliminating competition in respect of a substantial part of the products in question."

---

[24] Reg.2659/2000. See para.17–17 below.
[25] Reg.2658/2000.
[26] Regulation 2790/1999. See also the Guidelines on vertical restraints OJ (2000) C291/1.

These conditions are both cumulative and exhaustive. As part of its "modernisation package",[27] the Commission published Guidelines on the application of art.81(3). The Guidelines provide an analytical framework to assist parties in assessing whether their agreements satisfy the conditions of art.81(3). The Guidelines supplement—rather than replace—the Horizontal Guidelines and thus both should be consulted when assessing the consistency of a proposed non-full-function joint venture with EU Competition laws.

16–26 Under art.81(3), the economic and other benefits should be identified and an assessment carried out to determine whether these benefits outweigh the detriments to competition in the relevant market. Furthermore, such benefits must be passed on to consumers. The focus should be on the objective benefits (e.g. cost and qualitative efficiencies) which the joint venture will bring and whether these benefits could be achieved through less restrictive means or without unduly affecting third parties. There should be no substantial elimination of competition. Both the formation of the joint venture itself should be considered as well as the specific restrictions contained in the agreement.

Self-assessment and enforcement

16–27 Prior to the "modernisation" of EU competition law in 2003, parties who were in doubt as to whether their joint venture could restrict competition, could notify their agreement to the Commission. If the Commission considered that art.81(1) was applicable, it would then assess whether it could grant the notifying parties an individual exemption on the basis of art.81(3) or, more informally, provide a "comfort letter". As a result of "modernisation", parties can no longer notify their agreements to the Commission. Parties now have to assess themselves whether or not their agreement falls foul of art.81(1) and whether or not the exemptive conditions of art.81(3) are satisfied.

16–28 Self-assessment means that it has become more difficult for parties to a non-full-function joint venture to assess whether their agreement infringes competition law or not and whether the joint venture could be vulnerable to challenge by a third party before a competition authority or a national court. In some ventures, parties may decide to address this uncertainty by increasing the autonomy of a joint venture (and making it full-function) in order to obtain the legal certainty benefit provided for by the Commission's notification system for mergers.

16–29 It is the responsibility of national competition authorities (e.g. the OFT in the UK) to take action where they consider this necessary to

---

[27] Introduced by Regulation 1/2003.

enforce art.81. National courts can now hear and decide enforcement issues directly. The European Commission also retains power to initiate investigations into non-full-function joint ventures which restrict competition. In practice, it is likely to restrict its own intervention to more serious cases (e.g. price-fixing or market-sharing arrangements) but it will liaise closely with national authorities as part of the network that exists between competition authorities in Europe.

16–30 The consequences of an infringement of art.81 (and therefore the risks to be taken into account by the parties) are as follows:

(1) *Joint venture itself may be unlawful.* Joint ventures which have substantially adverse effects on competition, and do not give rise to appropriate countervailing benefits, will be prohibited in their entirety.

(2) *Restrictive provisions void.* Restrictive provisions in joint ventures which infringe art.81 are void and unenforceable as between the parties to the arrangements. The question whether these restrictive provisions are severable or not (or whether the agreement as a whole is void) is a matter of national law.

(3) *Interim measures and fines.* The Commission can adopt interim measures and, may impose fines of up to a level of 10 per cent of the global turnover of each of the parties concerned. In practice, the Commission is more likely to impose fines in relation to serious infringements such as export bans, market sharing and price fixing arrangements.

(4) *Third party claims.* Third parties may bring an action for an injunction and/or damages in national courts for breaches of EU antitrust laws. The risk may also exist that another party to the joint venture could plead that contractual obligations are not binding because of the application of the EU laws.

In making their self-assessment, the parties should, therefore, take into account not only the principles of EU competition law but also the risks and consequences of potential infringement action. The important consequences of infringement of the EU competition laws mean that self-assessment, certainly in any particular case of difficulty, should invariably be made in conjunction with lawyers experienced in this field.

MERGER CONTROL : UK

16–31 Joint ventures falling within the "one-stop shop" jurisdiction of the EC Merger Regulation cannot (subject to limited exceptions) be reviewed under UK merger control laws. However, if the EC Merger Regulation does not apply to a joint venture, the application of domestic UK competition law must then be considered. In theory, joint ventures may fall under two types of competition law control in the UK:

(a) merger-type joint ventures may fall under the merger control provisions of the Enterprise Act 2002; or

(b) collaborative joint ventures and alliances may fall within the prohibition of anti-competitive agreements in the Competition Act 1998.

UK Enterprise Act 2002

16–32 Under the Enterprise Act, the Office of Fair Trading (OFT) has a statutory duty to refer mergers to the Competition Commission where it believes that a relevant merger situation has resulted, or may be expected to result, in a "substantial lessening of competition".[28] Where a reference is made, the Competition Commission must decide whether a relevant merger situation has or will be created and, if so, whether the situation may be expected to result in a substantial lessening of competition. It can require action to remedy, mitigate or prevent the adverse anti-competitive effects and can even block the merger.

16–33 As a result, whilst pre-notification of mergers is not mandatory, it will usually be prudent to pre-notify any merger-type joint venture that raises material competition issues.[29] Confirmation that no reference will be made to the Competition Commission should normally be a pre-condition of any significant joint venture which constitutes a relevant merger.

Joint ventures caught by the Enterprise Act

16–34 The Enterprise Act applies to a wide range of joint ventures. A common feature of many joint venture arrangements is the allocation to the joint venture by one or more of the parties of some of its assets, business, intellectual property rights or personnel. This can lead to a merger situation

---

[28] The Act provides that the OFT may exercise its discretion not to refer a merger if it thinks that: the market involved is not of sufficient importance to justify an investigation; where any substantial lessening of competition would be outweighed by benefits to consumers; or where the OFT believes that the arrangements concerned are not sufficiently advanced or are not sufficiently likely to proceed to justify the making of a reference. The OFT has recently revised its substantive guidance to indicate that a market would not, subject to specified exceptions, be of sufficient importance to justify a reference where the market's size is less than £10 million, see OFT 516b Revision to Mergers—substantive assessment guidance: Exception to the duty to refer: markets of insufficient importance, November 2007.

[29] Although informal advice is available from the OFT, it is only given on rare occasions, see para.16–38 below.

qualifying for investigation if (i) two or more enterprises "cease to be distinct" and (ii) the threshold test in relation to turnover or market share is satisfied. Two or more enterprises "cease to be distinct" where they are brought under common ownership or common control.[30] The analysis is not straightforward. The Act in practice catches joint ventures where:

(a) existing activities (or enterprises) of two or more parties are brought together in a new, specially formed JVC;

(b) one party contributes an activity or business of its own to an existing company and acquires a material interest in that company which then becomes the JVC; or

(c) a party acquires a material influence or controlling interest in an existing company.[31]

The range of joint ventures which can fall within the Enterprise Act is therefore wider in scope than the "full-function" test for the EC Merger Regulation.

Joint ventures not caught by the Enterprise Act

16–35 The Enterprise Act does not catch all types of joint ventures. In particular, it does not apply:

(a) where a start-up business JVC is being established and no existing activities are transferred to it by any party-so that there are no enterprises which "cease to be distinct";

(b) to any other collaboration or co-operative joint venture where two or more enterprises do not "cease to be distinct";

(c) to any transaction caught by the provisions of the Merger Regulation (with certain limited exceptions referred to in para.16–11 earlier);

(d) to a "merger" which does not satisfy the jurisdictional thresholds of the Enterprise Act.

What are the jurisdictional thresholds?

16–36 The Enterprise Act only applies if the merger also satisfies a jurisdictional threshold test. It applies two alternative tests: a share of

---

[30] s.26, Enterprise Act 2002.
[31] The levels of control for this purpose are where one enterprise has: (i) the ability materially to influence policy (this may arise on acquisitions of as little as 10 to 15 per cent of the voting rights of an enterprise, or possibly as a result of contractual arrangements alone); (ii) the ability to control policy (which may arise on the acquisition of e.g. around 30 per cent of voting rights of an enterprise) (i.e. de facto control); or (iii) a controlling interest (which is unlikely to arise unless one enterprise holds more than 50 per cent of the shares carrying voting rights in the other).

supply test and a turnover test. (Although there is no UK nexus requirement, it is implicit in these jurisdictional criteria that at least one of the enterprises must be active within the UK. For the turnover test to be satisfied, the enterprise being taken over must be active in the UK and, for the share of supply test both must be).

RELEVANT MERGER SITUATION: THRESHOLDS

The Enterprise Act 2002 currently applies to a transaction where two or more enterprises "cease to be distinct" and either of the following conditions is satisfied, namely:

- *turnover:* the turnover test[32] is met if the annual value of turnover in the UK of the enterprise being taken over exceeds £70 million. Turnover is calculated by aggregating the total value of the turnover in the UK of the enterprises which cease to be distinct and deducting the turnover in the UK of any enterprise which continues to be carried on under the same ownership or control (e.g. the acquiring enterprise) or, if no enterprise continues to be carried on under the same ownership and control (e.g. on the formation of a new JVC), the turnover in the UK which, of all turnovers concerned, is the highest; or

- *share of supply*: the share of supply test[33] is met if, as a result of the merger, 25 per cent of all goods or services in the UK (or in a substantial part of the UK) are supplied by or to one and the same person or if the percentage share above 25 per cent is increased. The share of supply test is not a market share test and allows the OFT wide discretion in describing the goods or services, which need not amount to a relevant economic market.

The OFT is planning to publish guidance on how the turnover and share of supply tests are applied in joint venture cases.[34]

Mergers: substantive test for clearance

16–37 References to the Competition Commission are generally made on competition grounds. The OFT seeks to determine whether the merger is expected to weaken rivalry to such an extent that customers will be harmed.[35] When a merger is referred to the Competition Commission, it

---

[32] Enterprise Act, s.23(1)(b).
[33] Enterprise Act, s.23(1)(a). This is not a market share test and allows wide discretion in describing the goods or services, which need not amount to a relevant economic market.
[34] Its Mergers—Jurisdictional and Procedural Guidance was published in draft in March 2008: OFT 526 com.
[35] See OFT 516 Mergers: Substantive Assessment Guidance. The factors which are taken into account include: the relevant markets affected; the characteristics of the pre- and post-merger competition; possible new entry or expansion by existing competitors; other factors that may constrain post-merger behaviour such as buyer power; efficiency gains by the merged party which may increase rivalry within the market as a whole; and where one of the merging parties is failing, what would happen to the assets or business of that firm without the merger. Different analysis is required depending upon whether the merger raises horizontal, vertical or conglomerate issues.

must determine whether the merger has resulted or may be expected to result in "a substantial lessening of competition" within any market or markets in the UK. If it finds an anticompetitive outcome, it then considers remedies. Whilst many joint ventures fall within the scope of qualifying mergers, the Act (or its predecessor) has in practice not been used very often to regulate joint ventures. Relatively few have been referred for full investigation. These have generally constituted large-scale mergers (along the lines of full-function joint ventures falling within the EC Merger Regulation). Examples of joint venture cases considered by the Competition Commission (or its predecessor the Monopolies & Mergers Commission (MMC)) include the following:

Substantive assessment: competition commission

- *Kemira GrowHow Oyj/ Terra Industries.* This was a joint venture between Kemira and Terra Industries designed to merge the greater part of their UK fertilizer production and process chemicals businesses. Although the Competition Commission concluded that the joint venture would not be expected to lead to a substantial lessening of competition in the market for compound fertilizers, it did consider that a substantial lessening of competition could be expected in the markets for the supply of carbon dioxide and relevant process chemicals (nitric acid, aqueous ammonia and anhydrous ammonia). The Competition Commission considered that the parties had very high market shares in the identified markets (and would be monopoly suppliers in some) which would be unconstrained by other suppliers, importers or potential suppliers or importers. The Commission accepted undertakings involving both structural and behavioural remedies to address the substantial lessening of competition identified. (Competition Commission Completed Inquiry: July 11, 2007).

- *Stagecoach/Scottish CityLink.* The OFT referred to the Competition Commission a completed joint venture between Stagecoach Bus Holding Ltd and Braddell Plc in relation to the Scottish coach businesses operating as megabus.com, Motorvator and Scottish CityLink. The Competition Commission concluded that on two main routes, Glasgow-Aberdeen and Edinburgh-Inverness, the parties had been the two main coach competitors. As competitive constraints on the joint venture services from rail services, the car, third party coach service and threat of new entry were weak, the Competition Commission concluded that the joint venture would lead to higher fares and reduced service levels for passengers on these routes. The Competition Commission thus required Stagecoach and Scottish CityLink to sell some of their services on the routes to a competing operator in order to restore the competition that had existed previously. (Competition Commission Completed Inquiry: October 23, 2006).

- *P&O/Stena Line*. This reference concerned a joint venture between P&O and Stena Line to operate ferry services on the short sea routes between the UK and continental Europe. The MMC concluded that, whilst the joint venture would not operate against the public interest so far as it affected the freight market, it might be expected to lead to higher passenger fares which would be against the public interest. The MMC recommended that the merger should only be permitted if the companies gave undertakings designed to ensure sufficient competition from other ferry operators. (Monopolies & Mergers Commission Annual Review 1997).

Filing, procedure and timetable

16–38 There is no mandatory requirement to notify a relevant merger to the OFT and no sanctions apply if no notification is made. However, the OFT monitors UK merger and joint venture activity and may make enquiries of its own initiative. It may refer a merger to the Competition Commission at any time up to four months after the merger has taken place or it is made public. If a reference is made, the parties are prohibited from undertaking further integration without the consent of the Competition Commission.[36]

UK MERGER CONTROL: PROCEDURE AND TIMETABLE

(1) *Filing procedure.* Voluntary prenotification of a merger to the OFT may be made by the use of a pro forma Merger Notice, with a fixed statutory format, or by an informal submission in any format. A Merger Notice may only be used where proposed arrangements have been announced but have not yet been put into effect.

(2) *Information required.* The OFT has published guidance on the kind of information which is generally required. A Merger Notice must also be accompanied by the correct fee (currently ranging between £15,000–£45,000) in order to be valid. Small or medium-sized enterprises are exempted from the payment of fees in most cases.

Where an informal submission (rather than a formal Merger Notice) is made to the OFT, similar information should be provided since an application for clearance which contains less information than that required in a Merger Notice will probably result in a list of supplementary enquiries from the OFT. Pre-notification meetings may help to ensure that a submission is as complete as possible.

---

[36] Enterprise Act, ss.76 and 77. The Act also provides the OFT with powers, for the purpose of preventing pre-emptive action, to accept undertakings or to impose orders where it is considering whether to make a merger reference in relation to a completed merger, see ss.71 and 72.

> (3) *Informal advice.* The OFT will currently provide informal advice only for good faith confidential transactions which raise genuine issues. In contrast, it will not provide advice on transactions without apparent issues (and not hypothetical transactions or where there is no good faith intention to proceed). Any advice given does not bind the OFT or create any expectations as to the outcome. The advice and the fact that a party has applied is strictly confidential.
>
> (4) *Timetable.* The timetable for clearance will generally be an important factor in the overall timetable for establishment of the joint venture:
>
> (A) Merger Notice. Where a Merger Notice is filed, the initial period for the OFT's consideration is currently 20 working days, beginning with the first day after the Notice has been received and any relevant fee paid. The period may be extended by 10 working days.
>
> (B) Informal submission. There is no statutory timetable for dealing with informal submissions. The OFT states, however that companies can generally expect a decision within 40 working days from receipt by the OFT of a satisfactory submission.
>
> (C) Merger reference to Competition Commission. Where a merger is referred to the Competition Commission, it is required to publish its report within a statutory maximum period of 24 weeks. (In exceptional circumstances, the Competition Commission will be able to extend the maximum timetable by up to eight weeks. It will be required to publish the reasons for the extension.)
>
> In March 2008, the OFT published (OFT 526 com) its draft Mergers—Juridictional and Procedural Guidance which will provide further guidance on filing procedure, information required, informal advice and timetable before the OFT.

CO-OPERATIVE AGREEMENTS

16–39 Collaborative joint ventures and alliances may fall within the scope of the Competition Act 1998. The Competition Act is, however, aligned closely with the principles of EU law. Indeed, the general rule is that the UK authorities are obliged, in so far as is possible, to interpret questions arising under the Competition Act in relation to competition consistently with EU law.[37] EU law is given primacy so that (i) national law cannot be used to authorise an agreement which is prohibited by EU law and (ii) national law cannot lead to the prohibition of an agreement which affects trade between Member States and which is authorised by art.81. The Competition Act is in practice most relevant, therefore, where an agreement solely affects trade within the UK.

UK Competition Act 1998: Chapter I prohibition

16–40 The prohibitions of anti-competitive agreements and practices set out in the Competition Act are based on arts 81 and 82 of the EU Treaty.

---

[37] Competition Act 1998, s.60.

The Act contains a general prohibition against agreements which prevent, restrict or distort competition and which may affect trade in the UK (the "Chapter I prohibition"). This is potentially wide and, in theory, will catch many joint venture arrangements by virtue of restrictions expressly or impliedly accepted by the parties.

When the Act does not apply

16-41 The Act, however, has a number of qualifications and exceptions:

(1) *Appreciable effect*. As is the case under art.81, the Chapter I prohibition applies only to those agreements which have an appreciable effect on competition. OFT Guidelines[38] indicate that agreements will not appreciably affect competition unless (a) the agreement contains hardcore restraints (such as price or output restraints) or (b) in the context of agreements between competitors, the parties' combined share of the relevant market exceeds 10 per cent or, in the context of agreements between non-competitors, one of the party's share of a relevant market exceeds 15 per cent (see para.16–21(2) earlier for a corresponding principle under EC law).

(2) *Exclusion for mergers and ancillary restrictions*. There is an important exclusion for merger-type joint ventures. The Competition Act expressly does not apply to an agreement which results or, if carried out would result, in any two enterprises ceasing to be distinct for the purposes of the Enterprise Act 2002.[39] This exclusion applies irrespective of whether or not the turnover or market threshold for the Enterprise Act is met. The Competition Act will also not apply to any merger falling within the EC Merger Regulation.

The exclusion of mergers from the Competition Act also extends to any provision "directly related and necessary" to the implementation of the merger. As a result "ancillary restrictions" (such as non-compete provisions in joint venture agreements which are directly related to the setting up of a joint venture) will also fall outside the Chapter I prohibition. The OFT basically adopts[40] the same approach as that adopted by the European Commission when applying the EC Merger Regulation—see para.16–12 et seq. earlier.

The exclusion of "merger" joint ventures from the Competition Act can be withdrawn in certain situations. Broadly, this "clawback" provision allows the OFT to examine significantly anti-competitive

---

[38] Agreements and Concerted Practices: OFT 401.
[39] See Sch.1 para.1(1) to the Competition Act.
[40] OFT 516 Mergers: Substantive Assessment Guidance. In practice where a joint venture agreement falls within the UK merger control regime and includes ancillary restrictions these restrictions should normally be referred to in the submission made to the OFT. The aim in doing this is to obtain clearance of the transaction along with the ancillary restrictions (the result being that the Competition Act will not apply).

agreements (e.g. a price-fixing agreement) which would otherwise fall within the exclusion. In practice, the OFT is expected only to exercise this "clawback" power rarely.[41]

(3) *Exemptions and exceptions.* Joint venture agreements may be exempted or excepted from the Chapter I prohibition in certain circumstances. An agreement may be upheld if it meets the criteria under s.9 of the Act (modelled on art.81(3)) or be exempted by virtue of a UK block exemption or a parallel exemption, for example, where the agreement satisfies the conditions of one of the EC block exemptions—see para.16–24 above.

  (i) *Individual appraisal.* The criteria set out in s.9 of the Competition Act are almost identical to art.81(3). They apply to any agreement which: (a) contributes to (i) improving production or distribution, or (ii) promoting technical or economic progress, while allowing consumers a fair share of the resulting benefit, but (b) does not (i) impose on the undertakings concerned restrictions which are not indispensable to the attainment of those objectives, or (ii) afford the undertakings concerned the possibility of eliminating competition in respect of a substantial part of the products in question. The OFT does not grant individual exemptions. In general, parties must determine for themselves whether or not their agreements satisfy the exemption criteria. The OFT provides confidential informal guidance on an ad hoc basis and also operates a system of written opinions in cases where there is uncertainty (e.g. where the case raises novel or unresolved questions of law).

  (ii) *UK block exemptions.* The Secretary of State may, by order, provide for block exemptions for certain categories of agreement which are likely to fall within the statutory exemption criteria. Agreements which satisfy its conditions benefit automatically from block exemptions. To date only one block exemption has been adopted.[42]

  (iii) *Parallel exemptions.* "Parallel exemptions" apply to any agreements which are covered by a European Commission individual exemption decision or a Community block exemption under art.81(3) of the EC Treaty.[43] They also apply to any agreements which are not in fact covered by an EU exemption for the sole reason that they do not have an effect on trade between Member States. Agreements which benefit from a "parallel

---

[41] A joint venture agreement will be "protected" from the clawback provisions if (i) it relates to a merger which has been referred to the Competition Commission for investigation under the Enterprise Act or (ii) if it gives rise to a merger situation as a result of the acquisition of a controlling interest but does not qualify for referral because of the size threshold test.

[42] The Competition Act 1998 (Public Transport Ticketing Schemes Block Exemption) Order 2001 (SI 2001/1319).

[43] For example, the R&D Block Exemption and the Specialisation Block Exemption.

exemption" are automatically exempted from the Chapter I prohibition under the Competition Act.

Consequences of infringement

16–42 Provisions which breach the Chapter I prohibition are void and third parties may bring actions for damages. In addition, parties may be fined up to a maximum of 10 per cent of their total worldwide turnover. The Act does permit, though, the adoption of de minimis provisions whereby companies whose turnover falls below certain thresholds will be exempt from exposure to financial penalties. This applies to small agreements—i.e. agreements whose parties combined annual turnover does not exceed £20 million.[44]

Practical effect on joint ventures

16–43 The enactment of the Competition Act introduced a major change in the UK regulatory regime applicable to joint ventures and alliances. However, the exclusion of agreements which constitute qualifying mergers under the Enterprise Act (or which do not qualify solely because of the threshold tests) is a significant relaxation in regulatory control compared with the previous regime under the Restrictive Trade Practices Act. In assessing whether or not agreements fall under the general Chapter I prohibition or are excluded or excepted from it, techniques of analysis and approach relating to "local" agreements falling for review under domestic UK law have moved much closer to those applicable under EU law.

INDUSTRY-SPECIFIC REGULATION

Industry-specific regulation

16–44 Increasingly, particular industries are subject to specific licensing or other regulatory supervision—both in the UK and elsewhere, and particularly where previously state-owned industries have been opened up to privatisation. Joint ventures involving new entrants to such industries (or changes in identity or ownership of existing participants) may require (i) specific approval of a governmental or regulatory authority, or (ii) confirmation that the relevant authority does not intend to revoke a licence or similar enabling authority. Examples in the UK of such industry-specific regulation include the following:

---

[44] Competition Act 1998, s.39(1) and Competition Act (Small Agreements and Conduct of Minor Significance) Reg.2000 (SI 2000/262).

> **UK INDUSTRY-SPECIFIC REGULATION: EXAMPLES**
>
> - *Broadcasting Acts 1990 and 1996.* In the case of broadcasting licences (including television and radio), Ofcom is responsible for both licensing and licence enforcement. A licence is not transferable without the prior written consent of the ITC or the RA. Changes in control in levels of share holding (at prescribed levels) may need to be notified depending on the licence.
>
> - *The Financial Services and Markets Act 2000 (FSMA).* FSMA contains a general prohibition on a person carrying on a "regulated activity" in the UK unless that person is authorised by the Financial Services Authority (FSA) or is exempt; the activities which are regulated under FSMA include dealing in investments, accepting deposits and effecting and carrying out contracts of insurance. A person proposing to acquire "control" over an authorised firm must give advance notice to the FSA and may not proceed with the proposed action until the FSA has confirmed that it does not object.
>
> - *Consumer Credit Act 1974.* A business carrying out certain activities in the field of credit and hiring must obtain a credit licence from the Office of Fair Trading before carrying out such activities. A licence cannot be transferred. Changing the structure of a business usually means applying for a new licence.
>
> - *The Utilities Act 2000, Gas Act 1986, Electricity Act 1989 and Water Industry Act 1991.* Detailed licensing regimes apply in the gas, electricity and water industries. A new entrant in the relevant industry will invariably require a licence. A licence cannot generally be transferred. Changes in control of a licence are likely to require prior notification to the relevant licensing authority and, frequently, a power of revocation exists. In some circumstances, mergers of water or sewerage undertakings are subject to mandatory reference to the Competition Commission.

These are only examples. Detailed regulation also applies in a number of other industries. Each joint venture will need to be reviewed on an industry-specific basis to assess whether there are relevant regulatory controls which need to be taken into account.[45] A similar review of industry-specific regulation is likely to be necessary in any other jurisdiction materially affected by the proposed joint venture.

INTERNATIONAL TRADE REGULATION

16–45 An international joint venture can give rise to a variety of issues

---

[45] The Competition Act 1998 (Concurrency) Regulations 2000 contain provisions for the coordination of functions between relevant regulators. The OFT has published guidelines (Concurrent Application to Regulated Industries: OFT 405) which are designed to assist where an agreement falls under the concurrent jurisdiction of a relevant industry regulatory as well as the OFT.

under trade regulations which apply to the operations of the venture rather than its formation. These can significantly affect its prospects of success. Any problems should therefore be anticipated, so far as possible, in advance when the joint venture is formed.

Trade remedy laws

16–46 Trade remedy laws, such as anti-dumping, countervailing duty and safeguard actions, pose an increasing risk for international joint ventures. Trade tariffs have been lowered around the world following the successful completion of the Uruguay Round of the General Agreement of Tariffs and Trade (GATT) and the formation of the World Trade Organisation (WTO). Many developed and developing countries have turned to trade remedy actions as a means of protecting their domestic industries.

Anti-dumping

16–47 Anti-dumping actions are the most common of trade remedy actions. Under the WTO Anti-dumping Agreement,[46] government authorities may protect domestic industries from international price discrimination or "dumping" by imposing anti-dumping duties. Duties may be imposed if, following an investigation, a specific product is found to have been "dumped" by a foreign exporter which has exported it from one country to another at a price (the "export price") which is less than its "normal value" (i.e. its comparable price in the ordinary course of trade in the country of export). There must also be an investigation of "material injury" and "causation," to assess whether the imports in question are causing, or are threatening to cause, material injury to the domestic industry of the importing country.[47] Certain joint ventures are particularly subject to the risk of anti-dumping investigations:

(1) Joint ventures which rely on imports for key raw materials and components need to assess the risk of anti-dumping action affecting their access to the imports.

(2) If the joint venture will rely heavily on exports, a similar analysis should be undertaken in relation to key export markets—especially if exporters are highly reliant on a particular market where anti-dumping actions are frequent (e.g. India, Brazil, China, Japan, Korea, the US and Mexico).

---

[46] Agreement on implementation of art.VI of the General Agreement on Tariffs and Trade 1994.
[47] At the time of writing, WTO members are negotiating draft consolidated tests on anti-dumping and subsidiary and countervailing measures.

Subsidies/countervailing duty

16–48 National and regional authorities may approach possible joint venture parties with special offers of assistance if they locate facilities in that country or region (e.g. promises of improved infrastructure, duty rebates, low-interest loans etc). Such governmental assistance programmes can help the initial establishment of the joint venture. They can also be a source of subsidies and so potentially be subject to countervailing duty actions. The WTO Agreement on Subsidies and Countervailing Measures (the SCM Agreement) establishes rules allowing WTO members to impose "countervailing" duty measures against imports from other WTO members if, following a detailed investigation, the product is found to be subsidised by a prohibited or actionable[48] subsidy which causes material injury to the domestic producers in the country importing the product. Joint venture parties should work with the relevant governmental authority to ensure that the assistance is given in accordance with WTO rules and so reduce the risk of challenge by an importing WTO member under the WTO dispute settlement system.

Export/import controls

16–49 International joint ventures need to observe customs-related regulations affecting imported imports or exported finished products.[49] Costly issues can arise concerning the tariff classification of goods exported or imported. More significantly, the material export control laws may apply:

(1) In the US, the Bureau of Industry and Security (BIS) is responsible for the implementation of US export control policy for dual-use commodities, software and technology. Dual-use items subject to BIS regulatory jurisdiction have predominantly commercial uses but also have military applications. The BIS also promulgates and administers the Export Administration Regulations which impose controls on exports of dual-use items The BIS rigorously enforces these controls.

(2) In the UK, export controls apply pursuant to the Export Control Act 2002 and Control Orders made thereunder (including the Export of Goods, Transfer of Technology and Provision of Technical Assistance Control Order, Trade in Controlled Goods including those to Embar-

---

[48] A prohibited subsidy would typically require recipients to meet certain export targets, or to use domestic goods instead of imported goods. For a subsidy to be actionable, the complaining country has to show that it has no adverse affect on its interests.

[49] See also para.17–24 et seq relating to technology transfer.

goed Destinations Order and Trade in Goods Control Order). Amended Orders came into force on March 28, 2005.[50]

(3) Particular care must be taken in the EU to comply with the Dual-Use Regulation (Regulation (EC) No. 1334/2000 as amended[51]) which stipulates licensing requirements and procedures for the export and transfer of "dual use" items which could be used for both civil and military purposes.

16–50 Exports to certain countries may be affected by US and international embargoes prohibiting business transactions or activities with those regimes. US sanctions regulations, in particular, may govern the conduct of "US persons" and purport to have wide extraterritorial effect. The Office of Foreign Asset Controls (OFAC) administers and enforces trade and economic sanctions regulations against a range of designated foreign countries and individuals based on US foreign policy—particularly in support of national security goals against targeted foreign countries, terrorists, international narcotics traffickers and those engaged in activities related to the proliferation of weapons of mass destruction. (The US also maintains "anti-boycott laws" (e.g. under its Export Administration Regulations) which prohibit US companies and individuals from supporting or participating in boycotts of countries friendly to the US.)

16–51 Joint venture parties which rely on imports or exports should also be aware of the risk of WTO safeguard measures being taken by national authorities in the event of an emergency level of imports (e.g. a sudden increase of imports). Under the WTO Agreement on Safeguards, a WTO member is permitted temporarily to restrict imports of a product if its domestic industry is injured or threatened with injury caused by a surge in imports. As the use of safeguard action is intended to be limited and temporary in nature on account of its being a "fair" trade remedy (unlike anti-dumping and countervailing duty actions, which aim to correct "unfair trade"), a higher standard of "serious injury" must be met for measures to be imposed.

Behavioural laws

16–52 An international joint venture party also needs to ensure compliance with "behavioural" regulations—not only by itself but also by its

---

[50] The UK government has amended secondary legislation on export and trade controls as follows: The Export of Goods, Transfer of Technology and Provision of Technical Assistance (Control) (Amendment) Order 2005; The Trade in Goods (Control) (Amendment) Order 2005; and The Trade in Controlled Goods (Embargoed Destinations) (Amendment) Order 2005. The amending Orders came into force on March 28, 2005. Further, at the time of writing, the export control legislation introduced in 2004 under the Export Control Act 2002 is under review (the review was launched on June 18, 2007 and the public consultation period ended on September 30, 2007). The UK Government published its initial response on February 6, 2008. The UK Government aims to finalise its position on all areas of ongoing research during 2008.

[51] Amendments to EC Regulation 1334/2000 are generally made on an annual basis.

joint venture partners. Misdeeds of a joint venture partner may not only create bad publicity for an innocent party—they can also result in liability. Examples are compliance with anti-bribery and corruption laws relating to dealings with foreign public officials (the most well-known and aggressively enforced being the US Foreign Corrupt Practices Act). In some situations, a joint venture partner may need to ensure that anti-money laundering laws are satisfied in relation to funds establishing the venture.

Trade-related intellectual property controls

16-53 Joint venture parties with activities involving significant intellectual property rights should also be aware of the WTO Agreement on trade-related aspects of Intellectual Property Rights (TRIPS), which establishes minimum levels of protection that each WTO member government has to provide to the intellectual property of other WTO members. The TRIPS Agreement covers copyright, trademarks, geographical indications, industrial designs, patents, the layout-designs of integrated circuits and undisclosed information, including trade secrets. It applies basic WTO principles such as non-discrimination, including national treatment (equal treatment of one's own nationals and foreigners) and "most-favoured nation" treatment (equal treatment for nationals of all WTO member trading partners) as well as the additional principle that intellectual property protection should contribute to technical innovation and the transfer of technology, benefiting both producers and users and enhancing economic and social welfare. The TRIPS Agreement also sets out provisions dealing with domestic procedures and remedies for the enforcement of intellectual property rights and allows WTO members to bring disputes between WTO Members concerning the respect of the TRIPS obligations before the WTO's dispute settlement system. Reliance on the TRIPS Agreement may in particular be relevant for those joint venture parties seeking to protect their developments when entering foreign markets. Use of this agreement can be relied on to ensure international trading standards are upheld.

CONCLUSION

16-54 Competition and regulatory issues can be critical to the planning of any joint venture or alliance—particularly one involving actual or potential competitors with significant market shares. Identification at an early stage of the key issues in relation to the particular venture, and developing a strategy for dealing with any required clearances or consents of regulatory authorities, will be a vital task.

CHAPTER 17

Intellectual property and technology

Acquiring and developing technology is an objective which lies at the heart of many joint ventures or alliances. Intellectual property rights (IPR) are crucial to the "ownership" and use of technology. Rights and obligations relating to IPR are therefore integral to the legal and commercial structure of many ventures—from the stage of pre-contract negotiations to the period after the venture has ended. This chapter[1] outlines the material issues by way of an overview for the corporate/commercial lawyer.

Importance of IPR in joint ventures

17–01 Learning is a central objective of many joint ventures and alliances: learning new ideas, technologies and ways of working which a "partner" can bring to the venture—or developing and learning new technologies by collaborative efforts through the venture itself. Intellectual property rights (IPR) are the legal rights which enable a party to "own" technology or key features of it. A vital aspect of many ventures is therefore (i) to understand the legal rights involved in making available technology for use in the venture and (ii) to establish appropriate rights and obligations of the parties (including any joint venture entity) in respect of the use of intellectual property rights.

17–02 In this chapter, these issues are addressed primarily in the context of three common situations in which the joint development or exploitation of technology is at the heart of the joint venture or alliance:

(a) a contractual alliance between X and Y to carry out a jointly agreed programme of collaborative research with a view to the parties sharing the results of that research (some programmes may be partly funded by a body such as the European Commission under a Community Research Programme or by another sponsoring governmental body);

---

[1] I am very grateful to Chris Forsyth, Hannah McCann and Laurence Kalman of Freshfields Bruckhaus Deringer for their contribution to this chapter.

(b) an equity joint venture where X and Y merge their existing activities in a particular field in a joint venture company (JVC) with a view to pooling and developing their existing technologies through the JVC and carrying on thereafter joint production and exploitation;

(c) an international joint venture where X (possessing technology in a particular field) wishes to exploit that technology in an overseas market through a production joint venture with a "local" partner Y who will provide capital, manpower and/or local market connections; technology transfer to the JVC will be required to enable the production plant to be constructed and/or the JVC's business to be undertaken in the relevant overseas jurisdiction.

IDENTIFYING IPR

What IPR exists in technology?

17–03 Technology is not a legal term of art. It comprises a miscellany of ideas, inventions, processes, techniques, information, data, trade secrets, software, documentation and know-how. It may or may not be protected in the particular circumstances by various intellectual property rights. A first legal task is therefore to identify what intellectual property rights exist in any technology being contributed by a party to the joint venture. Technology may be protected by a combination of rights (or applications for such rights). These may include: copyright in data, plans, computer programs etc.; database rights; design right in designs and semiconductor topography; patents in any underlying inventions; confidential information in respect of technical information and know-how; trade marks in relation to marks under which the resulting products are branded; and analogous rights in countries where relevant rights have been registered (or otherwise protected). Reference should be made to specialist intellectual property textbooks for a detailed description and analysis of these respective rights. Such an identification exercise is appropriate not only to ensure that the contributing party's interests are protected in the joint venture arrangements but also as the basis of appropriate "due diligence" where a party is relying on the technology being contributed by the other party for the success of the venture.

Proprietor/licensee

17–04 In each case, these rights may be held by a party either as "proprietor" or as a "licensee" under licence or similar agreement with a third party proprietor. If held under licence, the terms of the licence will need to be carefully reviewed to assess whether consent is required for any sub-licence or assignment to the joint venture. In some circumstances, it may be preferable for a separate licence in favour of the joint venture to be negotiated—particularly if the joint venture's operations relate to part only of the subject matter of the head licence.

National rights

17–05 It is important to recognise that (except for the Community trade mark and Community design right) intellectual property rights are essentially national rights. They enable the holder to take action to prevent (or obtain compensation in the event of) infringement that occurs within the territory for which the right is registered. Therefore, any company doing business on the international stage will need to address how most appropriately to protect its technology and intellectual property rights in all countries where it is likely to be disclosed or used—in each case, well before reliance on those rights is intended for a joint venture or otherwise. Reference should again be made to specialist textbooks and advice in relation to procedures for protecting rights internationally. Broadly:

(1) Most countries have systems for the protection of intellectual property in the relevant jurisdiction (although the enforceability of those rights in some less-developed jurisdictions can be a serious issue for a party in a technology-based international joint venture).

(2) International conventions exist (relating to various types of intellectual property right) which enable a holder in one convention country to have a right of priority for a period of time to obtain registration in another convention country in respect of the underlying right—or, where there is no registration, as in the case of copyright, to receive recognition of that prior right in that other country.

(3) The European Patent Convention (EPC) promotes a system whereby, under a single application to the European Patent Office, an applicant may obtain a suite of national patents valid in each of the EPC signatory states (at a significant saving compared to multiple applications in each state).

(4) The Community trade mark and Community registered design right systems enable an applicant to obtain protection of a trade mark or a design in every EU Member State under a single application. The resulting registration provides, subject to conditions, a unitary right that is valid in every Member State.

It should certainly not be taken for granted that a set of intellectual property rights held in the UK will be equally enforceable in another jurisdiction. A review of the legal position in that other jurisdiction, and identification of the appropriate steps (if necessary) to be taken in order to protect rights in that jurisdiction, will be part of the "due diligence" for an international technology-based joint venture.

Foreground/background technology

17–06 In many joint ventures, it is convenient to classify IPR by different labels—since the rights and obligations of the parties to be negotiated for the purposes of the venture may differ depending upon the classification. Common classifications or distinctions for this purpose include the following:

(1) *Existing/future.* A basic distinction is between (i) rights and technology existing at the outset of the joint venture and (ii) those arising after its establishment (whether in the course of the operations or, perhaps, through independent activities of the joint venture parties themselves).

(2) *Background/foreground.* Another common distinction, particularly in relation to research and development collaborations, is between background and foreground rights or information. "Background" describes rights or information which are of broad application or relevance to the operations of the joint venture but have not been specifically developed for that purpose. "Foreground" rights or information are those which relate directly to the activities to be carried out by the joint venture; where these latter rights arise after the establishment of the joint venture, particularly if it is for a specific project, they are sometimes described as "project" rights or "project deliverables".

KEY IPR ISSUES

Key issues in different phases

17–07 Regulation of the intellectual property aspects of a joint venture involves a combination of commercial, competition law, tax and "pure" IPR legal considerations. These issues arise at different stages in the life of a joint venture:

(1) *Pre-contract.* The issue during this phase is primarily the need to ensure the confidentiality of technical information disclosed during the course of joint venture negotiations. From the legal viewpoint, it will be important to ensure that a proper confidentiality agreement or information exchange agreement is established at the outset (see para.2–08 et seq. above). This agreement should bind the recipient party, inter alia, (i) to keep the technical information confidential and not to disclose the same to any third parties; (ii) to use the information solely for purposes relating to the evaluation, negotiation and establishment of the proposed joint venture; and (iii) to return the information if negotiations break down.

> An example of an Information Exchange Agreement is included as Precedent 1 in Part E.

From a practical viewpoint, it will usually be sensible to ensure that a party's most sensitive technical information is not disclosed until as late a stage as possible in the negotiations in case of breakdown.

(2) *Establishment of the joint venture.* The primary issues on establishment of the joint venture are: (i) identifying IPR required for use in the joint venture activities; (ii) deciding the most appropriate method and basis for "vesting" in the joint venture (or the other party) rights relating to the use of a technology and/or IPR held by one or more of the parties; and (iii) establishing terms for transfer to the joint venture of any information, know-how and documentation representing that technology.

(3) *Operation of the joint venture.* Intellectual property issues will continue to arise during the operational life of the joint venture, including principally:

 (a) the need to establish arrangements for proper management of IPR of the joint venture; this will essentially involve principles of good industry practice in order to ensure that existing rights are properly administered and, when necessary, enforced; and to ensure that appropriate policies and procedures are in place to deal with the protection of newly developed technology arising during the course of the joint venture's operations;

 (b) the need to define clearly the rights and obligations of the parties in relation to the ownership and use of any developments in technology derived from activities conducted through the joint venture; these principles should, as a general rule, be clearly agreed at the outset on the establishment of the joint venture relationship.

(4) *Termination of the joint venture and changes in law.* An important issue (and frequently contentious, particularly if not addressed until it becomes "live") is the need to establish the rights and obligations of the parties—including those of any joint venture company—consequent upon the withdrawal (e.g. by transfer of shares) of a party originally providing technology or the termination of the joint venture or alliance itself, or upon a change in law which affects a party's participation in the joint venture or the benefits it may derive from the IPR.

Competition law

17–08 Intellectual property rights by their very nature create exclusive rights for the holder and provide means for the holder to prevent use by non-authorised parties. Joint ventures commonly involve further restrictions on the ability of the parties to develop or exploit intellectual property. There is a potential conflict with competition law which seeks to encourage free, independent and open competition by as many different "players" as possible in the market. Competition laws generally recognise, however, that intellectual property rights encourage innovation and new developments and can increase technologies available to the market—and therefore enhance consumer choice and product quality. A balance therefore has to be drawn between these objectives. EU law, in particular, has developed a sophisticated network of principles, and exemptions, which tries to draw this balance. These competition laws must therefore be taken into account when establishing the commercial principles in a joint venture relating to the development and exploitation of IPR and associated technology.

R&D/Technology Collaborations

R&D/technology collaborations

17-09 A common form of joint venture is a collaboration between two or more parties to carry out a jointly agreed research programme in a particular field of technology and to share the results of that research (and sometimes thereafter to engage in joint development and/or exploitation of those results). These arrangements will frequently be agreed in the form of contractual alliance between the parties. Commercial/legal issues which are typically addressed in collaborations of this kind, including in relation to IPR, are summarised in para.4–12 et seq.

Identifying IPR required from each party

17-10 The scope of the R&D programme should be clearly defined—not only to set the goals of the project but, importantly in the IPR context, to establish the scope of the rights to be licensed by each party to the other (or to any JVC carrying out the project) for use in the collaborative programme. The scope may include limitations as to "field of use" or territorial limits on the activities of the joint venture. Each party will normally disclose and license its "background" technology and associated IPR. It should be clarified whether this is restricted to technology necessary for the parties' obligations under the work programme—or includes any existing technology which may be useful or relevant to the programme.

17-11 Each party may, in its independent activities, acquire "future" technology or IPR relevant to the collaborative work programme. It should be clarified whether a party is under a continuing obligation to make such "future" rights available and, if so, on what terms. Additional compensation may well be appropriate as a term of such future provision.

Access to results

17–12 Access to the results of the joint programme is, of course, a vital interest of each party. Normally there will be an agreed system of technical meetings and reports. The right of each party to use the results of the R&D programme should be clarified—including the right to use and exploit technology and related IPR developed by other parties to the collaborative project. A central principle of EU competition law in this area is that all parties should have access to the results of the joint R&D in order that, individually if wished, each party can use those results after the venture including in further research or exploitation.

Ownership of the results

17–13 Ownership of "foreground" or "project" technology developed through the R&D collaboration must be addressed. Assuming there is no jointly owned "entity" to own the IPR, two basic possibilities exist.

(1) Each party can become the "owner" of rights derived from work carried out by it during the collaboration. Indeed, this will prima facie be the legal position where a party carries out a discrete segment of the work. (The basic position under English law is that IPR generated by employees in the course of their employment will belong to their employer; contractual provision will, however, be necessary to assign IPR to a party commissioning work carried out by non-employees (e.g. third party contractors).) Provision can then be made for cross-licensing of IPR between the parties for the purposes of the collaboration.

(2) An alternative is that the parties can become "joint owners" of arising IPR. This will generally be the position where the work has been jointly generated by the parties (e.g. by their respective employees working together). If the work has not been jointly generated, express assignments will be necessary in the collaborative arrangements in order to create the "joint ownership".

Joint ownership appears fair but its implications need to be carefully examined. These implications can vary between jurisdictions.[2] The consequences (unless otherwise agreed between the parties) in the UK are generally that each joint owner is free to use and exploit the relevant IPR in the course of its own business (note that copyright is an exception—the consent of all joint owners is required even to exploit the copyright)—but that it will require the consent of the other joint owner(s) if it wishes to

---

[2] In the UK, joint ownership of most IPR is possible (see, inter alia, Patents Act 1977, s.36, Copyright, Designs and Patents Act 1988, s.10(1) and Trade Marks Act 1994, s.23).

exploit the IPR by assignment or licensing to any third party. The latter requirement could be a severe constraint on a party's future conduct of its business. It will invariably be prudent, therefore, to set out clearly in advance the respective rights of the parties relating to exploitation (and any restrictions thereon) in the collaboration agreement.

17–14 Another problem with joint ownership is where one party wishes to pursue registered intellectual property protection (e.g. a patent application) in respect of arising IPR—either generally or in a particular jurisdiction—but the other "owners" of the project technology do not wish to do so (whether on grounds of expense or other reasons). It can sometimes be necessary to develop contractual principles whereby particular parties can become "participating" members in such registered IPR with others having a right to opt out (and therefore ceasing to have any contribution obligations or subsequent rights of exploitation of that particular IPR).

> **An example of a Collaboration Agreement containing such provisions is included as Precedent 5 in Part E.**

Competition law

17–15 Competition law issues can affect the terms of R&D collaborations. Most R&D collaborations create benefits. The European Commission, for instance, seeks to encourage co-operation in R&D but is concerned to ensure that the arrangements (particularly if they extend to joint production and/or exploitation) do not unduly prejudice potential competition between the collaborators within the EU. The formal test is whether or not art.81 of the Treaty of Rome applies—see para.16–20 et seq.

17–16 The Commission takes the view[3] that most R&D agreements do not fall within the scope of art.81(1), including particularly:

(a) arrangements relating to co-operation at a theoretical stage of research, far removed from the exploitation of possible results;

(b) collaborative arrangements between non-competitors; if the parties are not realistically able to carry out the R&D independently, there is no competition to be restricted;

(c) outsourcing of R&D to specialised companies, research institutions or academic bodies which are in the business of providing R&D services but are not active in the exploitation of the results;

(d) co-operation to the development stage but which does not include the joint exploitation of possible results by means of licensing, production and/or marketing; such "pure" R&D agreements are generally only

---

[3] Guidelines on the applicability of art.81 of the EU Treaty to horizontal co-operation agreements OJ (2001) C3/02.

likely to cause a competition problem if effective competition with respect to innovation is significantly reduced.

17–17 The revised Research and Development Block Exemption exempts a further range of R&D collaborative agreements (including those involving joint production) so long as no significant market shares are involved (e.g. no more than 25 per cent of the relevant market).

R&D BLOCK EXEMPTION: SUMMARY

(1) *Application.* This block exemption applies to agreements for joint R&D (whether or not coupled with joint exploitation) and to agreements for joint exploitation relating to results of R&D jointly carried out by the parties under an earlier agreement. The following are basic requirements:

- all parties must have access to the results of the R&D and, where the agreement does not include joint exploitation of the R&D, the parties must be free to exploit the results independently—although research institutes or academic bodies may agree to confine their use of the results only to further research;
- an obligation to exploit jointly must relate only to results which are protected by IP rights or constitute know-how which substantially contribute to technical or economic progress; the results must be decisive for the manufacture or provision of products or processes;
- undertakings charged with manufacture by way of specialisation in production must be required to fulfil orders for supplies from all the parties, except where the agreement also provides for joint distribution.

(2) *Market share threshold and duration.* Exemption applies for the entire period of the R&D where there is no joint exploitation of the R&D. It also applies for a further seven years from the time the product is put on the market in the EU if joint exploitation is involved in the following cases:

- where the agreement is between non-competitors; or
- where the agreement is between competitors and, at the time of the R&D, the parties' combined market share does not exceed 25 per cent of the relevant market for the products capable of being improved or replaced.

The exemption continues to apply at the end of the period if the combined market share of the participating undertakings does not exceed 25 per cent of the relevant market.

(3) *Agreements not covered by the exemption.* Any agreement which (directly or indirectly) has as its object any of the following restrictions is not covered by the exemption:

- restriction on independent R&D in unconnected fields;
- prohibition, after the completion of the R&D, against challenging the validity of IPR held by the parties which are relevant to the R&D;
- limitation of output or sales (except the setting of production or sales targets where the exploitation of the results includes the joint production of the contract products);

- fixing of prices (except where the exploitation of the results includes the joint distribution of the contract products);
- restriction as to the customers which the parties may serve after a period of seven years from the time the contract products are first put on the common market;
- prohibition of passive sales of contract products in territories reserved for other parties;
- prohibition of active sales of contract products in the common market territories reserved for other parties after a period of five years from the time such products were first put on the common market;
- restriction on granting licences for the manufacture of contract products;
- restriction on meeting demand from users who would market the contract products in other common market territories;
- restrictions which make it difficult for users to obtain the contract products from other resellers within the common market, particularly through the exercise of IPR.

(4) *Withdrawal of exemption.* The exemption may also be withdrawn by the Commission if third parties are substantially restricted from carrying out R&D in the relevant field; if the parties fail to exploit results without objective reason; and/or if there is lack of effective competition in the relevant market.

Many significant R&D agreements may fall outside the relatively narrow parameters of the Block Exemption. They may still qualify for exemption—but the assessment will be based on the criteria for applying art.81(3) discussed at para.16–23 et seq.

JVC: Pooling of Technology

Technology-based JVC

17–18 Many joint ventures involve the formation of a JVC into which existing business activities are transferred. These will often include the benefits of existing technical research and technology. From the intellectual property viewpoint, the principal issues relate to the vesting in that JVC of rights relating to the parents' technology so that technology can be pooled and/or developed jointly through the JVC.

Ownership or licensing?

17–19 How are relevant intellectual property rights best vested in the JVC? Broadly, the choice is between a route which will result in the JVC being owner of the rights or one whereby it becomes a licensee.

(1) Direct ownership can be achieved by means of an assignment of the relevant rights to the JVC. Indirect ownership can be achieved by transfer to the JVC of the share capital of the company or companies in which ownership of the relevant rights is vested.

(2) A licence could take the form of (i) a direct licence to the JVC or (ii) a licence to a company whose share capital is transferred to the JVC.

17–20 The best route for any particular venture is likely to depend on a range of factors, including:

(a) whether the rights form part of an existing business or company where the whole business or company is being contributed to or vested in the JVC (thus suggesting the "ownership" route);

(b) whether the rights are likely to be used by the existing joint venture party in its own independent operations after the formation of the venture (in which event it would be common for that party to retain ownership of such "shared" or "background" rights and to license them to the JVC);

(c) whether maintenance and enforcement of those rights is to continue to be the responsibility of the existing joint venture party, or whether these responsibilities are to be transferred to the JVC;

(d) whether the joint venture is likely to be for the short term only (with the result that retention of ownership in the parent, and licensing to the JVC, will generally be the easier route);

(e) tax factors: a detailed examination is beyond the scope of this book but the decision to transfer or license could also be affected by tax considerations e.g. a licence not granted for a capital sum may avoid a claw-back of capital allowances previously obtained by the transferor or royalties paid under a licence by the JVC may be tax deductible in circumstances where a capital sum paid to acquire the right would not have been.

Key IPR issues

17–21 Where technology is to be pooled, the relevant rights and obligations of the parties will normally be contained either in the joint venture agreement (perhaps in a separate schedule to that agreement) or in a separate intellectual property agreement to which the JVC is a party. There is advantage in the latter if the JVC is not a party to the principal joint venture agreement. Other technology/IPR issues to be addressed on establishment of the joint venture, as between the parties and the JVC, are likely to include the following:

(1) *Business IPR.* Definition will be needed of intellectual property rights to be assigned to (or, through ownership of a company, owned by) the JVC. These will commonly include all rights exclusively or predominantly used in the operations to be vested in the JVC. Where rights are licensed to the JVC, a careful "field of use" definition

relating to the JVC's activities may be required. Registered rights may be listed or scheduled, where practicable, but such lists will rarely be exhaustive.

(2) *Grant-back.* Will there be grant-back rights to the relevant joint venture party to use the "business IPR" in its independent activities—subject to any non-compete provisions in the joint venture agreement? It should be clarified whether such grant-back rights are to be royalty-free, irrevocable, non-exclusive, worldwide, non-transferable and/or carry the right to sublicense.

(3) *Payment.* A key issue is, inevitably, price. It should be made clear whether the originating party is to receive any separate payment for the "transferred" technology. In many cases, this will be inappropriate; it will be part of its contribution in exchange for its "share" of the capital of the venture. In others, the originating party may receive an initial lump sum—or subsequent royalties linked to production by the JVC or (more likely) a share of royalties received by the JVC on any sub-licensing of the originating party's IPR to third parties.

(4) *Maintenance and enforcement.* Should an obligation be imposed on the JVC to maintain and enforce its registered rights? Possibly, if it ceases to maintain such rights, an obligation may be imposed on the JVC to offer to reassign them to the relevant joint venture party free of charge.

(5) *Shared IPR.* An important area is to establish the need for any licence to the JVC by each party in respect of any "shared IPR" (i.e. background IPR applicable to the joint venture activities but also used significantly by the parent in its independent activities). Again, it should be clarified whether any such licence is to be royalty-free, non-exclusive, non-transferable, irrevocable etc. Responsibilities should be defined for prosecution, maintenance and protection of such shared IPR—usually, this responsibility will remain with the owning party with assistance from the JVC (although, possibly, with an obligation on the owning party to bring proceedings if so requested by the JVC); similarly, whether any maintenance or enforcement costs are to be shared and the respective entitlement to any damages received from infringement proceedings.

(6) *Arising IPR.* A vital requirement is to clarify the rights and obligations of the parties, and the JVC, in relation to intellectual property arising in the course of the JVC's operations after its formation. Will it be owned (and maintained) by the JVC? Will each party be granted a licence to use that arising IPR in its independent activities? If so, are the terms to be negotiated on an arm's-length and case-by-case basis, or will such licence be royalty-free and/or agreed as a pro forma licence?

(7) *Future IPR of the parties.* Future intellectual property may be generated by the parties, in the course of their independent activities, which may have application to the JVC's operations. The extent of

any obligation on each party to keep the other party (and the JVC) informed as to any such developments and/or rights so generated should be clarified—and any obligation to grant (or negotiate) a licence to the JVC to use such future IPR; will this be royalty-free or on commercially negotiated terms?

(8) *Warranties/indemnities.* Agreement should be reached on the scope of any warranty or representation to be given by a joint venture party as to the validity of any IPR transferred to the JVC or as to its performance. Each party may have a similar interest. Generally, the scope of any such warranties will be extremely limited and the JVC will take such rights on an "as is" basis. In some circumstances, however, it may be appropriate for a joint venture party to give an indemnity to the JVC in the event that the operations of the JVC, based on technology contributed by that party, infringe the IPR of a third party. (If an indemnity is given, the relevant party will usually wish to ensure that it has conduct of all third party proceedings and has an opportunity to remedy or mitigate the effect on the JVC.)

(9) *Termination.* The position on termination of the joint venture should be addressed. This can become contentious and, wherever possible, it is advisable to establish the principles at the outset. Different scenarios can again be envisaged. Typical principles may include the following:

    (a) *Voluntary sale by a party of its JVC interest.* A withdrawing party will normally cease to benefit from any licence in respect of IPR arising in the JVC after its withdrawal. Any licence to the JVC of its existing technology would normally continue. Similarly, any licence to the withdrawing party from the JVC in respect of IPR created in the JVC prior to the date of termination would normally continue; it will be a separate question whether any non-compete or field of use restrictions should apply.

    (b) *Termination due to one party's circumstances* (e.g. default, insolvency or (possibly) change of control). This scenario is more difficult. Again, the right of a party leaving the JVC to any licence of future-generated IPR by the JVC would normally cease. The question whether that party should cease to have the benefit of any licence from the JVC in respect of prior-generated IPR (or of cross-licences from the other parties) is more debatable; in cases of default and insolvency (but possibly not change of control) such a right will often cease. Any licences to the JVC (or the other parties) in respect of existing technology of the leaving party would, however, normally continue.

    (c) *Mutual termination/break up of the JVC.* Detailed arrangements here will, in practice, probably be left for mutual agreement at the time of termination. Generally, one would expect each party to be free to use and exploit (by non-exclusive licence) IPR generated through the JVC—and for cross-licences in respect of all existing IPR to continue. If there are to be restrictions (perhaps by reference to field of use or territory) on a particular party, these would need to be carefully examined from the competition law viewpoint.

(10) *Competition laws.* Arrangements regarding IPR may significantly affect the competition law analysis of the joint venture—see chapter 16 generally. The Technology Transfer Block Exemption (see below) can apply to arrangements for transfer of technology between a party and the JVC—but note that harsher restrictions on the availability of the exemption apply if the parties are competitors.

Technology Transfer

International technology venture with a "local" party

17–22 A somewhat different scenario is where the principal requirement is a specific technology "transfer" to the JVC by one of the joint venture parties. The purpose of the joint venture may be, in conjunction with a "local" partner, to build a production plant based on that technology or otherwise to exploit that technology in a particular territory or region. This may, for example, be the situation in an international joint venture where the "foreign" party is essentially providing skills and technology and the "local" party in an overseas jurisdiction is providing land, local manpower and/or market access and connections—e.g. the situation discussed at para.6–06 et seq earlier.

17–23 In such circumstances, a fundamentally important contract will be the technology licence or similar agreement between the party providing the technology and the JVC. Although often termed technology "transfer", the principal IPR will generally be licensed. Its essential purpose will be to set out the legal rights and obligations (and often many of the practical steps) relating to the transfer of technical information to the JVC, the provision of technical assistance and the JVC's right to use the technology and any associated IPR. Many or most of the issues will be those common to technology transfer agreements generally (and will overlap with the issues raised in other forms of technology joint venture discussed earlier). Reference should be made to specialist text books for more detailed discussion. The following is a summary, by way of a checklist, of some of the more important items to be addressed:

(1) *Supply of technical information.* Describe in broad terms the technical and engineering information and know-how to be provided; the gateways for the transfer; the protocols for maintaining secrecy; the nature of any "excluded" information; whether or not access to

"source codes" is permanently excluded or available in specified circumstances; the nature of documentation; the number of copies and the form and language in which the information is to be provided.

(2) *Exclusivity.* State whether the licence is non-exclusive or exclusive for a particular territory.[4] If non-exclusive, there are still likely to be relevant noncompete provisions in the joint venture agreement itself which will restrict a licensor party.

(3) *Improvements/developments.* Clarify whether any obligation on the "transferring" party to provide technology extends to improvements and/or new developments made by that party (or possibly other members within its corporate group) in the future. Clarify particularly the position in relation to any products or other technology currently under development.

(4) *Right to use.* The agreement should specify clearly the grant of licence to the JVC and its right to use the technology and/or to manufacture, assemble, use and/or sell products. This should cover any field of use restriction, any territorial limitation and any restrictions on assignment or sub-licences.

(5) *Fees/royalties.* Set out the basis of any fees payable by JVC to the licensor. Clarify whether the licence is royalty-free or set out the basis of subsequent royalties (e.g. percentage of gross selling price of subsequent products sold by the JVC). It will be an important structural decision whether a party's technology contribution should be in exchange for its allocation of shares in the JVC (and therefore "valued" at the outset) or an arm's-length commercial arrangement on more conventional terms. In some cases, royalty terms may be "soft" for an initial period to assist the JVC to become established.

(6) *Warranty.* Clarify that the licensor makes no warranty or representation in relation to the technical information (except perhaps to verify that such information is the same as that used by the licensor in its own business and that any documentation has been prepared in accordance with good industry standards).

(7) *Technical assistance.* Establish provisions relating to supply of technical assistance to the JVC and scope of the licensor's obligation to provide technically qualified personnel (subject to availability). Distinguish between:

(a) assistance at the facilities of the JVC: provision for notice; scope; arrangements for travelling, living and other expenses; any maximum obligation on the number of man-working days

---

[4] Under a non-exclusive licence, the licensor is not precluded from granting the same rights to other persons or from using the licensed IPR itself. In contrast, a licensee under an exclusive licence has the right to use the licensed IPR to the exclusion of all other persons including the licensor. A licence may also be expressed to be sole, in which case the licensee has the right to use the licensed IPR to the exclusion of all other persons except the licensor.

(perhaps distinguishing between pre-production period, a period after commencement of commercial production, and thereafter); indemnity for any employee liability; and

(b) assistance at the facilities of the licensor: notification of proposed names and period by JVC; obligation to reimburse all expenses; fees payable; no unreasonable disturbance with operations of the licensor; any maximum limit on the numbers of man-days' technical assistance.

(8) *Patents.* Establish terms of any patent licence to the JVC. Clarify whether the licence extends to any new patents acquired by the licensor (including e.g. from any third party). Establish the procedure in the event of any third party infringement claims; also responsibility for renewals.

(9) *Infringement claims.* The position should be clarified if any third party alleges infringement of its IPR. In many cases, no warranty or indemnity will be given that use of technology or the products manufactured will not infringe third party rights. It is not uncommon, though, for a licensor to provide a qualified indemnity to the JVC against any liabilities incurred to third parties. In such event, the licensor will normally insist upon rights to conduct any legal proceedings. The position regarding proceedings against unlicensed activities of third parties should also be addressed; again, these would normally be left to the licensor.

(10) *Confidentiality.* Establish an obligation on the JVC to observe confidentiality. Set out relevant standards and measures (including limiting disclosure of technical information to officers and employees whose duties require such information and who have given binding undertakings not to disclose confidential information). Include standard exceptions where information has fallen within public domain etc.

(11) *Payments.* Establish provisions relating to payment including: invoicing procedures; time of payment; currency; no deduction of taxes; grossing-up in case withholdings or deductions are required to be made by law; default interest etc.

(12) *Statements/records.* Establish obligation on the JVC to maintain accurate records and to provide certified statements. Establish right of the licensor to examine and audit.

(13) *Commencement date.* Specify any conditions precedent or approvals required prior to commencement date. These may include approvals of any superior licensor (where rights derive from a licence from a third party). Governmental approval may also be required, in some cases, for export of particular types of sensitive technology—see below.

(14) *Term and termination.* The licence agreement may have a fixed term or continue indefinitely (although the requirement to pay royalties may be limited in term). Rights of earlier termination require careful thought in the joint venture context.

(a) The licensor party will usually reserve "arm's-length" rights to terminate in the event of material breach or insolvency of the JVC. There is an argument that (having regard to that party's own interest in the JVC) there should be a reasonably long period of grace to enable the JVC's business to be re-organised—particularly if the licensor's technology is key to the JVC's business.

(b) It should be made clear whether the agreement continues (or is capable of termination by either party) if the licensor party transfers its shares in the JVC. It will usually be in the JVC's interest for the agreement to continue—although sometimes this may be on the basis that the licensor can require the financial terms to be re-negotiated or increased to an arm's-length royalty basis.

(c) The consequences of termination also require thought and clarity. Normally any licence to use technology (apart from non-confidential know-how) will cease and technical documentation returned to the licensor. However, there may become a point at which the licence should be regarded as "paid-up" and, whilst terminating future obligations (e.g. as to improvements), termination should not affect rights to use previously disclosed information. Obligations of confidentiality or non-disclosure to third parties will normally continue.

(15) *Product liability claims.* Provide for an indemnity by the JVC to the licensor for any third party claims that are attributable to operations of the JVC including use of technical information.

(16) *Severability.* Clarify severability (e.g. if any provision is held unenforceable due to competition law or other regulatory action).

(17) *Disputes.* IPR disputes are likely to be material to the joint venture. Dispute procedures should therefore be co-ordinated with those under the principal shareholders' agreement. While the licensor is a shareholder in the JVC, it is sensible to involve a leading representative of the other shareholder(s)—particularly before any notice of termination for breach.

(18) *Standard provisions.* Include "boiler-plate" provisions such as governing law; arbitration; no assignment; and entire agreement.

An outline example of a Technology Licence Agreement between a party and a JVC is included as Precedent 19 in Part E.

Export controls

17-24 Many countries have regulatory controls on the outward flow of technology. In the UK, the primary control of exports is through the Export

Control Act 2002 together with Export Control Orders which impose a system of licensing, supervised by the Department for Business, Enterprise and Regulatory Reform and the Export Control Organisation, in respect of the export of wide categories of goods (including technology relating to those goods). Whilst a general licence applies to the export to most countries (including all countries within the EU) of a wide range of industrial goods and technology, certain types of goods and sensitive technology may require a specific licence, and a number of destinations are subject to specific licensing procedures.[5]

17-25 The US also imposes, under the US Export Administration Acts, tight controls on the export of certain commercial commodities, software and technology—including the re-export of goods or technology originating in the US. These regulations will apply generally to US corporations and their affiliates. They are intended to serve national security, foreign policy, non-proliferation and short supply interests of the US. If an export or re-export of technology is subject to the regulations, a licence may be required or other requirements satisfied.

Technology Transfer Block Exemption

17-26 Technology transfer agreements may require review under competition or other regulatory controls. Certain emerging market countries have specific laws that regulate the terms on which technology may be licensed to a JVC in that country. Technology transfer agreements between a joint venture party and a JVC with operations in the EU will in particular need to take account of the provisions of the Technology Transfer Block Exemption.[6]

TECHNOLOGY TRANSFER BLOCK EXEMPTION: SUMMARY

(1) *Application.* The Block Exemption applies to licences of patents and know-how and also to licences of copyright in software and design rights (including licences of a mixture of these rights and agreements with ancillary provisions relating to the licensing of other IP rights) where the agreement permits the production of goods or services ("contract products").

(2) *Non-application.* The Block Exemption does not, inter alia, apply:
- where the parties to the technology transfer agreement are competing undertakings and their combined market share exceeds 20 per cent;

---

[5] The principal order made under the Export Control Act 2002 is the Export of Goods, Transfer of Technology and Provision of Technical Assistance (Control) Order 2003. This also implements the EU-wide system of control in respect of dual-use items and technology, whereby a Community authorisation may be required for the export outside the EU of certain sensitive goods/technology designed for civil use but where there are grounds for suspecting military or similar use.

[6] Regulation No 772/2004.

- where the parties to the technology transfer agreement are not competing undertakings and the market share of either of the parties exceeds 30 per cent.

If the market shares of the parties rise above the thresholds during the course of the agreement, then the Block Exemption continues to apply for a period of two years following the year in which the threshold was first exceeded.

(3) *Withdrawal of exemption.* The exemption may also be withdrawn in certain circumstances, in particular where access of third parties' technologies or potential licensees to the market is restricted (e.g. by the cumulative effect of parallel agreements) or where, without any objectively valid reason, the parties do not exploit the licensed technology.

(4) *Prohibited clauses ("hardcore restrictions").* The Block Exemption will not apply if the agreement contains certain prohibited clauses:

(a) For agreements between competitors, hardcore restrictions include:

- restriction on a party's ability to determine selling prices to third parties;
- output limitations, except limitations on the output of contract products imposed on the licensee in a non-reciprocal agreement or imposed on only one of the licensees in a reciprocal agreement;
- any restriction on the licensee's ability to exploit its own technology or any restriction on the ability of either party to carry out research and development, unless such latter restriction is indispensable to prevent the disclosure of the licensed know-how to third parties;
- allocation of markets or customers except:

    — field of use or product market restrictions imposed on the licensee;
    — restrictions on the licensee or licensor in respect of fields or product markets or exclusive territories reserved for the other party;
    — an obligation on the licensor not to license the technology to another licensee in a particular territory;
    — bans on active and/or passive sales by the licensee or licensor into exclusive territories/customer groups allocated to the other;
    — bans on active sales by the licensee into territories or customer groups allocated to another licensee (provided that the latter was not a competitor of the licensor at the conclusion of its own licence);
    — a requirement that the licensee produce the contract products only for its own use provided that the licensee is not restricted from selling the contract products actively and passively as spare parts for its own products (captive use restrictions); and
    — an obligation to produce the contract products only for a particular customer, where the licence was granted in order to create an alternative source of supply for that customer (second source provisions).

(b) As regards non-competitors, hardcore restrictions include:

- restriction on a party's ability to determine selling prices (without prejudice to the possibility of imposing a maximum sale price or recommending a sale price provided it does not amount to a fixed or minimum sale price);
- any restriction on the territory into which, or of the customers to whom, the licensee may passively sell contract products, with certain exceptions including:
    — restriction of passive sales into an exclusive territory or to an exclusive customer group reserved for the licensor;
    — second source provisions.

The Block Exemption clarifies that when undertakings are not competing at the time that the agreement is entered into, but become competing undertakings afterwards, then the rules on hardcore restrictions applicable to non-competing undertakings will continue to apply during the life of the agreement, unless it is materially amended.

(5) *Excluded restrictions.* Where an agreement contains any of the "hardcore" restrictions then the benefit of the Block Exemption is withdrawn in its entirety. In addition, the Block Exemption lists certain "excluded restrictions". These are not covered by the Block Exemption (and so need to be individually assessed by the parties), although their inclusion will not prevent the rest of the agreement benefiting from the Block Exemption. The "excluded restrictions" include:

- obligations on the licensee to grant an exclusive licence to the licensor (or a third party designated by the licensor) in respect of its own severable improvements to, or its new applications of, the licensed technology;
- obligations on the licensee to assign to the licensor or a third party designated by the licensor rights to improvements to, or new applications of, the licensed technology;
- no-challenge clauses; and
- where the parties are not competing undertakings, limitations on the licensee's ability to exploit its own technology or on the parties' ability to carry out R&D.

(6) *Duration.* The Block Exemption will remain in force until April 30, 2014.

A technology transfer arrangement which affects trade within the EU but falls outside the parameters of the Block Exemption may still qualify for exemption but this must be assessed against the general exemption criteria of art.81(3)—see para.16–21 et seq. This may be a difficult assessment in many cases.

TRADE MARKS

Trade mark licences

17–27 Trade marks are a somewhat different category of IPR. They are not part of the underlying technology itself but their use can be vital to the "branding" of the products or the public profile of the proposed joint venture. Trade marks will often be owned by one or more of the joint venture parents and licensed to the JVC. The terms of that licence may, in some cases, be spelt out in the joint venture agreement itself—or, particularly in the case of important trade marks or a long-term venture, spelt out in greater detail in a separate licence agreement between the trade mark owner and the JVC.

17–28 A particular area of concern for a joint venture party may be to ensure proper protection of its "house marks" (i.e. marks bearing the corporate name of the owning party or its key brands); these will often be used in the JVC's corporate name. In many cases, house marks may not be owned by the actual shareholding participant in the JVC but by another member of its corporate group, which will therefore make a separate licence agreement necessary. Registration of domain names by the JVC and the terms on which the JVC will use the parties' trade marks on websites may also need to be addressed.

17–29 Matters to be addressed in a trade mark licence with a JVC will be those common to such agreements generally. Key issues in the joint venture context will often include the following:

(1) *Exclusivity.* Usually the licence to the JVC will be non-exclusive in order to enable the trade mark owner to use the marks outside the field of the joint venture (subject to any non-compete provisions agreed in the joint venture agreement).

(2) *Royalty.* The licence may be royalty-free and, if so, this should be clarified. Alternatively, the basis of any royalty—with supporting obligations on the JVC for accounting and reporting—should be spelt out. If there is no consideration, the licence may need to be executed as a deed.

(3) *Scope.* Particularly if the owning party does not have a controlling or blocking position in the JVC, it will be important to spell out any field of use or other restrictions (including territorial scope) applicable to the use of the trade marks by the JVC.

(4) *Control/directions on use.* The owning party will typically wish to reserve a formal right to approve and/or direct the way in which the marks are used by the JVC. In some jurisdictions, a reservation of a right to assert quality control will be necessary or desirable in order to ensure that the JVC obtains no independent rights in the marks and that the validity of the latter is not diluted.

(5) *Form and style.* Similarly, a party may wish to ensure that the marks (particularly its house marks) are used in a particular form or style, and in accordance with its brand guidelines or standards. It may wish to set out procedures for monitoring compliance with those brand guidelines.

(6) *Acknowledgement of title.* There will usually be an acknowledgement by the JVC that it will not obtain any independent goodwill or title in the marks and that it will execute any documents required to confirm this, nor (without the owner's consent) take any steps to register the marks or marks which are similar to, or which incorporate elements of, those marks, in any jurisdiction.

(7) *Infringements.* Provisions will include an obligation on each party to give notice to the other if it becomes aware of infringements—whether infringements by third parties or claims by third parties alleging that the marks infringe their own rights.

(8) *Conduct of claims.* It will normally be provided that the owner will have exclusive conduct of claims relating to its trade marks, although a JVC may wish to have a right to take enforcement action against infringements if the owner does not do so with in a certain period. Unless the licence provides otherwise, a licensee has certain enforcement rights under English law under s.30 of the Trade Marks Act 1994.

(9) *Termination.* Crucially, the owner will want to establish a clear right to terminate the licence and use of any marks by the JVC (particularly of its house marks) in certain specified events. These are likely to include: (i) material breach; (ii) insolvency of the JVC; and (iii) the owner (or a member of its corporate group) ceasing to be a shareholder in the JVC, or perhaps its shareholding falling below a defined level. Termination of the right to use trade marks could have a serious effect on the JVC, particularly if it is a continuing business. It will therefore usually be practical to provide for a relatively lengthy procedure, or notice period, before any such termination becomes effective—e.g. one formula may be that the owner cannot exercise a right of termination unless a prior period of notice has been given specifically to the chairman/chief executive of the other joint venture party since, usually, any question of termination will arise in the context of discussions about the future of the joint venture itself.

An example of a Trade Mark Licence Agreement in the context of a joint venture is included as Precedent 20 in Part E.

Conclusion

17-30 Intellectual property rights, in their various forms, are critical to the operation of most ventures—particularly those based on the development of new technology, products and services. Establishing appropriate rights and obligations relating to IPR at the outset of the venture is vital—

both to ensure an adequate legal foundation for the venture's activities and also in the interests of clarity to avoid potential disputes at a later stage. Terms may be significantly influenced by competition law constraints. The rights of the parties at the end of the venture will determine their subsequent freedom to exploit the knowledge acquired through the venture. Careful attention should be given to the intellectual property implications of most joint ventures and alliances.

Chapter 18

Employment

Any joint venture or alliance will require personnel to be engaged on the venture's activities. Where there is a separate joint venture entity, the employment law implications can be significant and will need to be carefully handled. Issues may arise relating to employee consultation, transfer of employees, secondment arrangements, harmonisation of employment terms and establishment or maintenance of benefits under pensions or share schemes. This chapter[1] outlines the key issues by way of an overview for the corporate/commercial lawyer.

Key employment issues

18–01 Any joint venture or alliance will involve employees engaged on its activities. Where the venture takes the form of a contractual alliance, there will be no change in the employment relationship; the employees will remain employees of each party respectively. This simplicity may be part of the attraction of using this legal form for the alliance.[2] Where the joint venture vehicle is a separate entity such as a company, the employment situation will be more significant. The joint venture's personnel will usually, at least at the start, come from one or more of the joint venture parties. These personnel will either:

(a) become employees of the joint venture company (JVC); or

(b) remain employees of one or more of the joint venture parties and be seconded to work for the joint venture.

In either case, the employment implications of the establishment, operation and (in some cases) the eventual termination of the joint venture should be considered at the outset.

18–02 Employment issues, particularly in the case of most equity joint ventures, include the following:

---

[1] I am very grateful to David Pollard and Kathleen Healy of Freshfields Bruckhaus Deringer who contributed most of the original material on which this chapter is based.
[2] Even in this situation, of course, there may be proposed exchanges of staff between the parties, in which case issues relating to secondment of employees may arise.

(1) *Identification.* Which employees will work in or for the joint venture?

(2) *Employee consultation.* Will the formation of the joint venture trigger the application of laws relating to employee participation? Are there consultation obligations in relation to setting up the joint venture? Will the JVC be required to establish a national works council or, perhaps, a European works council under the European Works Council Directive?

(3) *Transfer.* Will employees transfer automatically to the JVC with any business being contributed to the joint venture, or will individual consents to transfer be needed? If employees are to be seconded, what terms will apply to the secondment arrangements?

(4) *Terms of employment.* What terms and conditions will apply to the employees while they work for the joint venture? Will there be a wish by the parties to harmonise terms and conditions?

(5) *Control procedures.* What will be the control procedures or mechanisms within the joint venture for hiring and firing employees, for managing the employees and/or for approving employment terms?

(6) *Work permits.* In the case of work in a "foreign" jurisdiction, will work permits be required? What will be the process for obtaining any such permits?

(7) *Employee benefits.* What employee benefits will be provided for the joint venture employees?

(8) *Pensions.* What pension benefits will be provided for the joint venture employees?

(9) *Share incentives.* What will be the impact on share scheme or other incentive arrangements for the employees? How will any existing rights be affected when they start work for the joint venture? How can new rights be offered to employees working for the JVC itself?

18–03 These issues are addressed in this chapter primarily in the context of UK employment laws. However, similar issues will need to be considered in the context of the laws of the JVC's particular jurisdiction. Employment laws are a significant factor affecting transactions in many jurisdictions, particularly within the EU. Most EU countries now have a sophisticated set of laws protecting employees' rights which can have a material impact on the establishment and operation of a proposed joint venture. These laws not only protect employees' rights in situations where they may be required to work in a joint venture operation (thereby transferring their employment to a new employer) but frequently also give employees (or works councils on their behalf) rights to be informed and consulted in advance of any such transfer taking place. They will also be relevant to what happens to the employees of the JVC on its eventual termination.

Employee Consultation

EU Information and Consultation Directive

18–04 The EU Information and Consultation Directive[3] obliges Member States to introduce procedures requiring employers (whether multinational or domestic) to inform and consult with staff representatives on a number of issues including:

(a) the recent and probable development of the undertaking;

(b) the probable development of employment and any "anticipatory measures" envisaged, in particular where there is a "threat to employment";

(c) decisions likely to lead to "substantial changes in work organisation or in contractual relations."

The Directive was generally required to be implemented in EU Member States by March 2005 with a longer lead-in time in certain situations. Since March 2008, all companies with at least 50 staff in any Member State have been covered. The Directive provides for a mechanism whereby staff can require their employer to set up a works council so that staff representatives can be informed and consulted on issues affecting employees. A proposal to set up a JVC may prompt a request that a works council be set up for that JVC, which would then need to be kept informed of any matters affecting the employees in the JVC. Alternatively, employees who are to work in or for the JVC may already be covered by an existing works council which may need to be consulted about the proposed joint venture. Finally, a proposal to disband a JVC may also give rise to information and consultation obligations.

18–05 The Directive was brought into effect in the UK through the Information and Consultation of Employees Regulations 2004.[4] In summary, the Regulations provide that if 10 per cent or more of the workforce in an undertaking make a valid request to the employer to set up information and consultation procedures, then the employer must initiate negotiations to agree what procedures should be put in place. In the absence of agreement, "standard" information and consultation procedures will apply. If the employer already has an agreement in place providing for information and consultation with staff, then it may be that this "pre-existing agreement" negates the need to set up new procedures. Failure to respond to a workforce request to set up an information and consultation procedure (or to comply with it once established) can result in a fine of up to £75,000.

---

[3] Directive 2002/14/EC.
[4] SI 2004/3426. The Regulations came into force in April 2005.

European works councils

18–06 The formation of the JVC may itself trigger the application of other employment laws—including both domestic laws in the JVC's jurisdiction and (particularly in the case of an international joint venture merging businesses cross-border) laws which have cross-border application, such as the European Works Council Directive.[5] This Directive has been implemented into law by separate legislation in each of the relevant Member States, including the UK.[6] The requirement is to establish a European works council (EWC) in entities where there are more than 1,000 employees across the European Economic Area, and more than 150 in two or more Member States. The Directive envisages that corporate groups to which it applies will either voluntarily agree to establish a European-wide works council or, alternatively, will be required to go through a negotiation procedure triggered by a request from at least 100 employees from two Member States. An EWC, once established, will normally have the right to be consulted about matters affecting employees on a Europe-wide basis, or involving establishments or undertakings in two different Member States. Joint ventures can be affected by the EWC Directive in several ways:

(1) The proposed joint venture may trigger a consultation obligation under the terms of an existing EWC agreement within the joint venture parents themselves.

(2) The formation of the joint venture may trigger an obligation on a joint venture parent to establish an EWC. Generally, national legislation should be checked to see if joint ventures which are not subsidiaries may still be treated as falling within a "group of undertakings" for these purposes on the basis of exertion of a "dominant influence".[7]

(3) The establishment of the joint venture may trigger an obligation on the JVC itself to establish an EWC.

One consequence of establishing an EWC, under the Directive, is that at least one meeting of the EWC must be held a year to consider the report prepared by central management for the purpose of the meeting, covering issues such as structure, financial situation of the business and its probable development.

18–07 As previously indicated, in many European countries it is likely that there will be local works councils with elected union or employee repre-

---

[5] Directive 94/45/EC.
[6] The Transnational Information and Consultation of Employees Regulations 1999 (SI 1999/3323).
[7] Directive 94/45/EC, Arts 2.1 and 3.

sentatives who may represent the JVC employees in relation to country-specific issues. Particularly in countries such as the Netherlands and France, local works councils are common, and the relationship between the employer and the works council is key to the successful operation of the business. In addition to the requirement to inform and consult the works council, there may also be a requirement to consult with unions representing certain categories of employees. There may therefore be two layers of employee representation—at local and European level. Each layer will need to be involved in any decision-making process which affects employees in more than one jurisdiction. The process, and timing, of any information and consultation exercise will need to be carefully considered in the context of relevant national laws. This process can be a material requirement both prior to the establishment of the joint venture and subsequently.

Transfer of Employees

Transfer of existing business to JVC

18–08 Where an existing business is to be contributed to the joint venture (either in the form of a company or by the transfer of a business as a going concern), the relevant employees in that business will usually also transfer to the JVC (unless a specific structure is adopted to prevent this). This transfer will occur in one of two ways:

(1) If the shares of the employer company are transferred to the joint venture, then the employees will pass with the company to the JVC group. This is the most straightforward route from an employment law viewpoint.

(2) If the business of the employer company is contributed to the joint venture by way of a transfer of assets, then in EU Member States it is likely that the Acquired Rights Directive[8] will apply so as automatically to transfer the employment of existing employees employed in that business to the transferee (the JVC). All rights and liabilities connected with the employment of those employees (with some limited exceptions, depending on the jurisdiction in which the employees are based) will usually also transfer to the transferee.

Business transfers in the UK

18–09 The Acquired Rights Directive is implemented in the UK by the Transfer of Undertakings (Protection of Employment) Regulations 2006

---

[8] Council Directive 77/187 EC, consolidated in Directive 2001/23 EC.

(TUPE).[9] TUPE will apply to the transfer of a business or part of a business that constitutes an identifiable, stable economic entity which retains its identity following the transfer. TUPE will also apply where there is a "service provision change". This could be the case e.g. where a joint venture parent ceases carrying out certain activities in order to outsource those activities to the JVC which then provides a service to the joint venture parent by undertaking those activities on its behalf.

(1) Where business assets are transferring and the business will retain its identity post-transfer, then TUPE will invariably apply.

(2) Where assets are not transferring, the position is more complex. The European Court of Justice (ECJ) previously distinguished between a business which is asset-reliant and one which is labour-intensive. This distinction meant that, if the business being transferred required substantial tangible assets and those assets were not transferring, this might preclude the application of TUPE.[10] However, in more recent cases and since TUPE was amended in 2006, there has been a move away from this asset-reliant/labour-intensive analysis in favour of a "multifactoral approach" when deciding whether TUPE applies with the focus on whether there has been a transfer of a stable economic entity.[11]

18–10 In the UK, if there is a TUPE transfer, then:

(1) All rights, powers, duties and liabilities under or in connection with contracts of employment of the individuals employed in the business (with only limited exceptions) will transfer to the JVC.

(2) The only present exceptions are criminal liabilities and, importantly, certain liabilities relating to occupational pension schemes. However, rights to enhanced redundancy payments or early retirement severance payments may transfer to the transferee company, even if the underlying occupational pension scheme is not transferring. In addition, under provisions of the Pensions Act 2004[12] there is now an obligation on the transferee to set up specified levels of future pension arrangements based on certain minimum standards (see para.18–27) for those employees who have transferred across under a TUPE transfer from an occupational pension arrangement (although it is possible to agree otherwise with the relevant employees).

(3) Subject to (2) above, employees have the right to continue to benefit from the same terms and conditions of employment. The JVC will therefore have to replicate the employees' existing terms and condi-

---

[9] SI 2006/246, which replaced the 1981 Regulations (SI 1981/1794) on April 6, 2006.
[10] *Ayse Süzen v Zehnacker* [1997] I.R.L.R. 255 followed by the Court of Appeal in England in *Betts v Brintel* [1997] I.R.L.R. 459.
[11] See e.g. *P&O Trans European Ltd v Initial Transport Services Ltd* [2003] I.R.L.R. 128 and *Scottish Coal Company Ltd v McCormack* [2005] CSI 11 68.
[12] ss.257 and 258, Pensions Act 2004.

tions. This can prove problematic where certain terms and conditions, such as share option plans, cannot sensibly be replicated. In the UK, employers who are unable to replicate benefits following a TUPE transfer must put in place something which is of "substantial equivalence".[13]

(4) Certain employee representation arrangements will also transfer (e.g. any trade union recognition arrangements if the undertaking (or part) which has transferred retains a distinct identity). Similarly, if the transferring employees have established a works council under the Information and Consultation of Employees Regulations 2004, then the works council may transfer across with the employees (unless the works council covers a wider group of employees who remain behind following the transfer).

(5) Representatives (either a recognised trade union or elected employee representatives) of any employees affected by the transfer must be informed in advance of the transfer and consulted about any "measures" that are proposed in connection with the transfer. If there are no existing representatives, then the employer must arrange elections (following the detailed guidelines set out in TUPE).[14] "Affected" employees may encompass not only those employees whom it is intended will transfer and work for the JVC but also those employees remaining in the business of the joint venture party.

(6) There will be no break in the employees' continuity of service—periods of service with the old employer will count for all purposes (e.g. statutory qualification periods for unfair dismissal rights).

(7) The consent of employees is not needed for the transfer. However, if they wish, employees can choose to object to the transfer—in which case they are treated as having resigned. This may be a particular issue if there are key employees whom it is desired to transfer to the JVC. Employees wishing to leave (but constrained by long notice periods) could take this opportunity to be released from their employment. It is not common for employees to choose to leave by this route, however, as objecting has the effect of terminating their employment at the time of the transfer with no right to pay in lieu of notice or compensation. In addition, employees can also resign if the proposed transfer involves or would involve a substantial change in working conditions to the employee's material detriment.[15]

18–11 In certain other EU jurisdictions, the prior consent of, or a formal opinion from, the works council and/or the relevant unions representing

---

[13] *French v Mitie Management Services Ltd* [2002] All E.R. 150.
[14] Failure to comply with these obligations could result in an award of up to 13 weeks' pay (uncapped) for each affected employee being made by an employment tribunal.
[15] TUPE, reg.4(9). In this case, the employee remains entitled to bring an unfair dismissal or breach of contract claim against the employee's employer (although such a claim cannot be brought purely on the basis that the transfer will result in the loss or reduction of rights under an occupational pension scheme).

affected employees may be needed before employees can transfer into the JVC—see para.18–07 earlier. For example, in the Netherlands, a formal written opinion of the works council must generally be obtained by which the works council gives a positive opinion of the proposals in relation to the employees. Failure to obtain such an opinion could result in the works council seeking an injunction to prevent the transfer going ahead or to reverse a transfer which may already have taken place. In France, the information and consultation process must be completed and the opinion of the works council obtained before a final decision to effect an employee transfer is made (although the opinion is not required to be positive as it does in the Netherlands).

Non-TUPE transfers

18–12 In the UK, if there is no business transfer, with the result that TUPE does not apply, then:

(1) Employees will need to consent to the transfer of their employment from a joint venture party to the JVC (unless there is an express power of assignment in the employment contract which can be used). Consent may be implied if the employee is informed of the change of employer and accepts this by continuing to work for a period without objection. However, it is preferable to obtain express written consent to the change of employer.

(2) Periods of service with the old employer will not count for statutory purposes where the transfer is made outside TUPE (but with consent) unless the JVC is "associated"[16] with the original employer (i.e. the joint venture party). The association test generally requires voting control by a majority of shares.[17] Accordingly, unless care is taken to structure the transaction (e.g. by transferring employees before shareholdings are changed), a transfer to a JVC which is not more than 50 per cent owned will not be a transfer to an associated employer and:

 (a) employees will lose statutory continuity of employment;
 (b) the requirement to pay statutory redundancy pay may be triggered[18]; and
 (c) the right to receive contractual redundancy payments may also be triggered (depending on the terms of any applicable policy or previous custom and practice of payment).

It may well be possible to structure matters to avoid this problem—e.g. by arranging for the employees to transfer, by consent, to a new wholly-owned subsidiary of their current employer. Shares in this

---

[16] Within the meaning of s.218(6) of the Employment Rights Act 1996.
[17] See *South West Launderettes Ltd v Laidler* [1986] I.C.R. 455 and *Payne v Secretary of State* [1989] I.R.L.R. 352.
[18] Any offer of alternative employment by the JVC will not satisfy the exclusion in ss.141(1) and 146(1) of the Employment Rights Act 1996 which requires suitable employment to be offered by an associated employer.

wholly-owned subsidiary would then be sold to the JVC; following the sale, employment would be transferred (again with consent) from the subsidiary up to the JVC.

Harmonisation of terms and conditions

18–13 The JVC may acquire employees from various joint venture parties. Particularly if employees are working side by side, there may be a desire to harmonise terms and conditions amongst all the employees within the JVC. However, changing employment terms is not straightforward.

Consent of employees to change of terms

18–14 Generally, any change to terms and conditions will, under English law, require the consent of the employees concerned. Even if there is a specific power in the contract of employment allowing amendment without consent, UK employment tribunals are reluctant to accept the enforceability of such a power to change anything other than relatively minor provisions of the employment contract. Consent of the employees to change terms and conditions will also be required in similar circumstances in other countries in the EU. In practice, any harmonisation exercise which the JVC wishes to implement in these other EU countries will usually need to be negotiated with the relevant employee works council, employee representative body or with the involvement of any relevant union.

18–15 If consent is not forthcoming from the employees in question, there are a number of possible alternatives:

(1) Threatening dismissal if consent is not given, and thereby forcing consent, will rarely be appropriate. Such a course may give rise to claims that the employee was constructively dismissed and may also give rise to potential claims for breach of contract (depending on whether notice is given). The industrial relations impact of taking such a step would also need to be considered carefully.

(2) It can be a difficult question whether an employee who does not object following notification of a change in terms and conditions, but continues to work, is deemed to have accepted the change. If it does not have an immediate impact (e.g. a change to a notice provision or a restrictive covenant), then consent is unlikely to be implied.[19]

(3) The position is more complex where a TUPE transfer is involved. If the change in terms and conditions is by reason of the transfer or for a reason connected with the transfer and there is no economic,

---

[19] See e.g. *Aparau v Iceland Frozen Foods Plc* [1996] I.R.L.R. There may be an exception if the employee is someone of "experience and sophistication": *Armstrong v Credit Suisse Asset Management* [1996] CR 882.

technical or organisational reason for the change which entails changes in the workforce, it will be void as being an attempt to contract out of the rights conferred on employees by TUPE.[20] This would mean that the employee would not be bound by his agreement to the new terms and conditions—even if, after the contract changes, the employee is overall better rather than worse off and is given substantial consideration for his agreement to the new terms. Indeed, that employee may even be legally able to "cherry-pick" from both the old and the new terms and conditions of employment.[21]

(4) Any dismissal of an employee for failure to agree to the new terms and conditions will be deemed automatically unfair unless the change relates to the job function itself. An employee may only be able to agree to changed terms and conditions (and any dismissal not be rendered automatically unfair) if the changes are for an "economic, technical or organisational reason entailing changes in the workforce".[22] Generally, this must mean that there is a real change to the structure of the workforce as well as to the job concerned, not merely a desire to "harmonise" terms and conditions in a manner that does not impact on the job itself.[23]

(5) Dismissal and offering new terms is likely to be the most expensive option because it gives rise to possible unfair dismissal claims.[24]

(6) Dismissing and offering new terms and conditions of employment will also count as a dismissal for the purposes of the redundancy consultation legislation. If 20 or more employees are to be dismissed and offered new terms, the employer will be obliged to engage in collective consultation with the staff for a minimum of 30 days before the first of such dismissals takes effect.

Decision-making by JVC

18–16 It will be important, going forward, to consider the decision-making process within the JVC for determining the terms and conditions on which employees are employed by the JVC. Are key decisions regarding material employee issues or policies to require super-majority board or shareholder consent? The terms of the joint venture agreement may need to include various veto or consent provisions in favour of one or more of the joint venture parties in certain key employment areas (e.g. hire or dismissal of particular employees or setting up incentive or pension arrangements).

---

[20] See the ECJ decision in *Martin v South Bank University* (C-4/01).
[21] *Regent Security Services Limited v Power* [2007] EWCA Civ 1188.
[22] TUPE, reg.7(6).
[23] *Berriman v Delabole Slate* [1985] I.C.R. 546 and *London Metropolitan University v Sackur & Others* [2006] UKEAT/0286/06.
[24] The maximum compensatory award (in the UK) for unfair dismissal is currently £63,000.

Restrictive covenants

18–17 If the services of particular key individuals are crucial to the success of the joint venture, then consideration should be given to obtaining suitable restrictive covenants from those individuals—both to set out their duties during employment and to provide protection following employment. The validity of such covenants will need to be reviewed under relevant local law. Restrictive covenants in existing employment contracts may not protect the interests of the JVC, as references to "group companies" may not catch the JVC itself (depending on the particular structure of the JVC arrangements).

18–18 As a matter of general English law, a restrictive covenant (e.g. against competition or soliciting clients or employees) is only enforceable, following termination of employment, if the employer has a legitimate business interest to protect and the restrictive covenant goes no further than is reasonably necessary to protect that interest. The onus will be on the employer to show that this test is satisfied. If it is not, then the covenants will be struck down as being in restraint of trade. The same principles generally apply in other European jurisdictions. However, in a number of EU Member States (notably Germany and France) payment must usually be made to the employee during the period for which the employee is restricted; a failure to provide for payment can render the covenant unenforceable.

18–19 A joint venture party may need to ensure that it is in a position, if necessary, to require the JVC to enforce employee covenants if the other joint venture party is not willing to agree to such an enforcement (e.g. if it is benefiting from the services of the individuals concerned). One method of avoiding this problem is for the restrictive covenants to be given directly to the joint venture parties themselves (as well as the JVC). In suitable circumstances, the English courts will allow a joint venture party to enforce covenants given for the benefit of a JVC in which it holds shares.[25]

18–20 The creation of the joint venture may also mean that the terms of any existing restrictive covenants applicable to key employees should be reconsidered and suitable amendments sought in order to make them more

---

[25] In *Dawnay, Day & Co Ltd v De Braconier D'Alphen* [1997] I.R.L.R. 442 and [1998] I.C.R. 1068, the claimants entered into a shareholders' agreement with three individual brokers. A JVC was formed. The brokers were senior employees of the JVC. They gave notice of termination of their employment and subsequently joined a competitor. Both the shareholders' agreement and the individual employment contracts contained non-compete and non-solicitation of clients covenants extending, under the shareholders' agreement, for one year after cessation of employment. It was held that the claimants had sufficient interest to bring proceedings (even though the JVC, as employer, was deadlocked) and that the covenants (but not a wider covenant against solicitation of staff in the shareholders' agreement) were enforceable against the brokers as reasonable restraints of trade. See also *TSC Europe (UK) Ltd v Massey* [1998] I.R.L.R. 22.

SECONDMENTS

Secondments

18–21 In some situations it will not be appropriate for some or all of the employees of the joint venture parties to become employees of the JVC itself. Instead, the employees may remain employed by the respective joint venture parties with their services being provided or "seconded" to the JVC. (This should be distinguished from the situation, also sometimes loosely called "secondment", where the employees become employed by the JVC itself but on the basis that they will ultimately return to the joint venture party). Care needs to be taken if this structure is intended to be used. If there is a business transfer to the JVC, then TUPE (or its equivalent European legislation) will automatically transfer to the JVC the employees who are employed in that business. Ways of avoiding this result will, therefore, need to be considered (e.g. obtaining individual employee consents not to transfer or moving relevant employees out of the business before the business transfer to the JVC).

18–22 The advantages of secondment can include the following:

(1) *Continuity of benefits.* It may be easier for the joint venture party to continue to provide various employee benefits such as share options (see para.18–38).

(2) *Control.* The joint venture party may wish to retain control over the relevant employees. If the employees are to return to that party at the end of the joint venture, it may be easier if they always remain employed by the joint venture party rather than by the JVC itself.

(3) *Fluctuating secondments.* If a fluctuating workforce is required, the joint venture party may find it easier to retain all employees, choosing for secondment only those who are needed by the JVC from time to time.

(4) *Non-TUPE situations.* In situations where TUPE does not apply, it should be easier to deal with issues such as statutory continuity of employment and avoidance of potential redundancy issues if the employees remain employed by the joint venture party rather than transfer to the JVC.

18–23 A variety of other issues can arise in relation to secondments. They include the following:

(1) *Consents.* If secondment is to be considered, the employee's terms of employment must be checked to see if such a secondment is permitted. Otherwise, the employee's consent will be needed in order for the secondment to be permissible.

(2) *Liability to employee.* Care also needs to be taken with secondment arrangements to deal with liabilities owed to employees and the division of responsibility between the JVC and the joint venture party—e.g. if the employee is injured at work, is the JVC to be liable (in which case it will need to indemnify the joint venture party) or will it remain the responsibility of the joint venture party? Who will arrange for relevant insurance to be taken out? Commonly, it will be easier for employee liability (and insurance) to remain the responsibility of the joint venture party.

(3) *Indemnities between joint venture parties.* Care needs to be taken with the terms of any relevant indemnities apportioning ultimate economic liability between the parties. Unless expressly stated, such indemnities under English law will generally be interpreted as not applying in circumstances where the party seeking to rely on the indemnity is negligent.[26]

(4) *Authority of employees to bind JVC.* The secondment arrangements will also need to deal with the scope of the employee's authority to bind the JVC and any vicarious liability owed by the joint venture party for the employee's actions. There may be regulatory considerations here as well (e.g. if the joint venture business is regulated under the Financial Services and Markets Act 2000).

(5) *Control of seconded employees.* Ultimately, there may be difficulties if the JVC is able to give directions and control the actions of the employees whilst they still purport to remain employed by the joint venture party. Care must be taken that the actual day-to-day situation does not diverge so much that it could be in the interests of the employee (or the tax authorities) to claim that the employee has actually become employed by the JVC instead of the joint venture party. All relevant documentation should reflect that the employment, and ultimate control, of the employee remains with the joint venture party.

(6) *Payment.* The JVC will need to make payment to the joint venture party for the services of the seconded employees, usually on a cost or cost plus basis.

(7) *VAT.* The value added tax (VAT) implications of a secondment arrangement need to be considered. Generally, employers do not pay VAT on payments of remuneration to employees. However, in the

---

[26] See *EE Caledonia Ltd v Orbit Valve Plc* [1995] 1 All E.R. 174, applied in *Campbell v Conoco (UK) Ltd* [2003] 1 All E.R. (Comm) 35.

situation where an employee is seconded by a joint venture party to a JVC, the joint venture party (as employer) will pay the employee's remuneration with the JVC paying a fee to the employing party for the employee's services. As such, both the fee and the employment costs would, in the UK, be liable to VAT.[27] This may not be an issue where the JVC is able to recover all the VAT it pays. However, if it is unable to achieve full VAT recovery (e.g. if its business is wholly or partially exempt, such as banking or financial services), then this would be an additional cost. VAT is chargeable on payments made by the JVC for a seconded employee's remuneration or other obligations relating to the employee unless:

(a) the JVC exercises exclusive control over the allocation and performance of the employee's duties during the period of secondment; and

(b) the supplying business (i.e. that of the employing party) does not derive any financial gain from the placement.

(8) *Intellectual property rights.* Care should also be taken in the secondment arrangements to deal with the issue of ownership of any intellectual property rights developed by the employee while on secondment. Normally, these will belong legally to the joint venture party rather than the JVC unless specifically assigned.

(9) *Pensions.* In relation to pensions, one distinct advantage of the secondment route is that the JVC will not need to become a party to the pension arrangements of the supplying joint venture party (although the Pensions Regulator's "moral hazard" powers may apply—see para.18–35). The joint venture party will remain the employer and, accordingly, responsible for the relevant pension arrangements (even if the cost is to be refunded by the JVC).

(10) *Return at end of secondment.* It may be appropriate to provide that the employee will resume full-time duties for the joint venture party at the end of the secondment. Sufficient flexibility should be created to redeploy the employee where there is no certainty that he will get the same job back.

WORK PERMITS

Work permits

18–24 Where the location of an employee's employment duties are to be transferred to a "foreign" jurisdiction as part of the arrangements for

---

[27] Customs and Excise Statement of Practice of March 25, 1997.

undertaking the joint venture activities, it may be necessary to obtain a work permit or other licence for the employee. This will depend on the particular jurisdiction:

(1) For an employee recruited from overseas to work in the UK, the employee will require a work permit if he is not a resident of the European Economic Area (EEA). The joint venture party will have to demonstrate reasons why an EEA resident worker is not able to fill the position. If the employee is resident in the EEA, then no work permit will be required.

(2) For an employee being recruited to work outside the UK but in another EEA Member State, no work permit should be required if the employee is resident in an EEA Member State. Non-EEA residents who wish to move to an EEA Member State will, however, need a work and residency permit in order to do so. Note that in some EU jurisdictions (e.g. France), stricter rules apply to the employment of nationals from the ten new members of the EU and will continue to do so for a transitional period of up to seven years from the date of their accession. The rules applying to the employment of Swiss nationals also vary between the EU jurisdictions.

(3) Other jurisdictions will have their own regulations (often quite strict) regarding requirements for work permits.

Where work permits are required for employees who are critical to the venture's operations, the process for obtaining them should be built into the arrangements and timing for establishing the venture.

PENSIONS AND SHARE SCHEMES

Pensions for joint venture employees

18–25 An issue of growing importance is whether the JVC can, or should, provide pension benefits for employees of the JVC. Pension arrangements and practice differ significantly from jurisdiction to jurisdiction, including within the EU. However, the growth of multinational operations is leading to an increasing review of the regulations and practice affecting pension provision.

18–26 In September 2003, the EU Pensions Directive[28] regarding occupational retirement provision came into force, with a view to facilitating

---

[28] Directive 2003/41/EC on the Activities and Supervision of Institutions for Occupational Retirement Provision.

management of cross-border pension schemes. The Directive applies to funded pension schemes, but not to state pensions or to pure personal savings plans. The Directive provides for greater security for beneficiaries, investment and regulation of domestic and cross-border pension schemes. It is one of the Commission's first initiatives in its long-term plan to promote social protection in the EU, including plans to reduce the cost to employers of running pension schemes, encouraging workers to opt out of state-run schemes and tackling the ageing population problem.

18–27 There is an exclusion from the TUPE provisions in the UK in relation to occupational pension rights and obligations. However, the Pensions Act 2004 introduced a minimum standard of occupational pension protection entitlement to be afforded to all transferred employees who had such an entitlement prior to a TUPE transfer. Sections 257 and 258 of the Pensions Act 2004 provide that the minimum level will be either (i) a final salary scheme which satisfies the "reference scheme test" for contracting-out purposes or (ii) a money purchase scheme under which the employer matches employees' contributions up to six per cent of basic pay.

18–28 Several practical questions arise where the JVC wishes to put in place pension arrangements for its employees which are similar (or, if feasible, identical) to those they enjoyed when employed by the joint venture party. Should the joint venture employees remain in the existing pension scheme of the joint venture party, if possible, or should a new scheme be set up by the JVC and a transfer payment made into it from the schemes of the joint venture parties?

Using existing scheme of a joint venture party

18–29 One option that may be available is for the JVC to participate in the existing group pension arrangements of one (or more) of the joint venture parties. This may be attractive in relation to the employees supplied by that joint venture party.

18–30 There is no longer a requirement that companies participating in the same pension scheme must be in the same corporate group so long as they have a sufficient "business association". There may be advantages of continued participation in existing pension arrangements of a UK joint venture party. There is less need to set up new arrangements. It is easier to explain to transferring employees (in particular, the consultation on any TUPE transfer should be more straightforward). Possible economies of scale can be achieved. It is possible for the JVC to share in any current contribution reduction (compared to normal costings) in the joint venture party's scheme.

18–31 However, there are a number of potential disadvantages to such a route which need to be considered:

(1) The JVC is likely to have a potential funding liability in respect of the joint venture party's scheme.[29]

(2) There will be a need to document the terms of the participation by the JVC. What level of contributions will it pay? Will it be able to take advantage of any contribution reduction or holiday? Will it have to pay additional contributions if liabilities increase (e.g. larger pay rises than anticipated, or discretionary benefits granted)?

(3) The parties will need to consider the implications if the JVC should ultimately cease to be associated with the sponsoring employer for the pension scheme. At that stage, the JVC must cease to participate in the pension scheme, and the exit terms may need to be negotiated from the outset (e.g. if the exit incurs involuntarily as a result, say, of option rights applying under the joint venture agreement, or if sale or subsequent flotation is a realistic possibility). What special provisions should apply for the transfer of pension liabilities? How should any existing funding defect in the scheme be covered? The JVC will assume a statutory obligation to fund, if necessary, the scheme in respect of its employees and/or former employees.[30]

JVC's own scheme

18–32 If it is decided that employees of the JVC should not remain in a scheme of one of the joint venture parties, the alternative route is to review the possibility of the JVC establishing its own pension arrangements. Much will depend on the laws and practice of the relevant jurisdiction of the JVC. Actuarial advice on the costs involved in this should also be obtained.

18–33 In the UK, it would be common to negotiate for an enhanced transfer payment from the pension scheme of the joint venture party in relation to those employees who transfer to the JVC and who consent to a transfer of their pension benefits being made. This is designed to enable the JVC to offer broadly equivalent benefits to such employees, notwithstanding that they cease to remain in pensionable service in the joint venture party's scheme. If such special transfer terms are not negotiated, there is a risk in a final salary (defined benefit) scheme that the employees will be left with statutory minimum preserved benefits and statutory cash equivalent transfer rights. These are calculated on the basis of salary at the date of leaving the existing scheme and may well result in a reduction of antici-

---

[29] There is a statutory funding obligation on employers under s.75 of the Pensions Act 1995.

[30] When the JVC ceases to participate in the pension scheme, a statutory debt obligation will be triggered under s.75 of the Pensions Act 1995. Since September 2005, the Occupational Pension Schemes (Employer Debt) Regulations 2005 (SI 2005/678) modified the way in which the debt obligation is calculated; it is calculated on a buy-out basis, i.e. the cost of securing benefits based on purchasing annuity policies from an insurer. Amendments to the Employer Debt Regulations are currently being considered.

pated benefits for the employees concerned (given that their benefits previously were tied to their ultimate final salary). It is usual for the terms of the transfer to be set out in a pension schedule in an agreement between the JVC and the relevant joint venture party. This schedule will include a set of actuarial assumptions detailing how the transfer payment ought to be calculated. Actuarial advice should be taken on this by both parties.

18-34 It is also possible to arrange for the JVC to participate in the UK joint venture party's scheme either on a permanent or temporary basis. This is often structured as an interim solution to enable time for the JVC to set up its own scheme and seek consents to transfer. Where the JVC participates in the UK joint venture party's scheme, care needs to be taken to deal with any residual liabilities which arise (by statute or under the terms of the scheme) in relation to funding of the old scheme. Indemnities and/or confirmations may be desirable.

Joint venture party liability for JVC pensions

18-35 The UK Pensions Regulator has powers under the "moral hazard" provisions of the Pensions Act 2004 to ignore the corporate veil and impose funding obligations on third parties in relation to occupational pension schemes of an employer. These provisions are designed to protect pension benefits. Joint venture parties may potentially be at risk of such funding orders in relation to the pension benefits of the JVC's employees.

(1) Broadly, the Pensions Regulator is able[31] to issue contribution notices and financial support directions imposing liability on a person "connected with or an associate of" the employer. Such connected and associated persons are widely defined and include members of the same group of companies, a shareholder holding at least one-third of the company's voting capital and companies who are connected to a director of the JVC (e.g. because the JVC director is also an employee or director of the joint venture party). In relation to a corporate JVC employer, associated parties will therefore often include the joint venture parties themselves.

(2) Liability is not automatic just because a party is connected or associated with the employer. The relevant notices and directions can only be issued if the Pensions Regulator considers it to be reasonable. In determining reasonableness, the Pensions Regulator will consider, amongst other factors, the degree of involvement of that party, the relationship that party has with the employer and the party's financial circumstances. The reasonableness requirement means that, in practice, liability is only likely to be imposed if the connected person has

---

[31] Under s.38 and s.43 Pensions Act 2004 respectively.

been actively involved with the employer or has benefited from the activities of the employer.[32]

The potential liability under the "moral hazard" provisions should be considered in the context of the arrangements for establishing the JVC. It may be that any risk can, and should, be reduced by appropriate indemnities between the parties. It is also possible to seek (on a voluntary basis) clearance from the Pensions Regulator that it would not be reasonable for it to exercise its power to issue contribution notices or financial support directions in the particular circumstances described in the application.

Employee share schemes

18–36 Increasingly, employees in corporate groups headed by a publicly quoted company participate in company or group-wide share incentive schemes. The granting of options and/or share awards has been popular both in the UK and other European countries for a number of years. Giving employees the opportunity to participate in share schemes is seen as a good way of building worker loyalty and cohesion. Two main issues arise in relation to share incentivisation arrangements for employees transferred to a joint venture:

(1) What is the impact of a transfer of employment to a JVC on any existing employee share incentives (e.g. share options) which relevant employees may have received from their existing employer?

(2) Will the JVC itself be able to offer share incentivisation arrangements in future to its employees?

Participation in existing schemes

18–37 The impact on existing share option arrangements of a participant's change of employment to work for a JVC will depend on the terms of the existing schemes which have been put in place. In the UK, schemes adopted by publicly-quoted companies frequently include the following types of arrangements:

(1) *Company share option plans ("CSOPs")*. Options under a CSOP will normally become exercisable on the employee moving to the JVC. The CSOP will usually provide for an exercise period (typically six

---

[32] In June 2007 the Pensions Regulator exercised its "moral hazard" powers for the first time in the case of *Sea Containers Services Ltd*. The Pensions Regulator stated that an additional factor to be taken into account in determining the reasonableness of issuing a direction is the "value of any benefits received directly or indirectly" by the recipient from the employer under the scheme.

months), triggered either by a transfer of the business or company in which the employee is employed out of the group, or, in appropriate cases, by redundancy. The transfer of a business to which TUPE applies may result in a technical redundancy for the purposes of the option scheme, even though it will not normally trigger a statutory redundancy payment.

— There will usually be a provision that early exercise under a CSOP is on a pro-rated basis. In addition, income tax and National Insurance contributions (NICs) may be chargeable on the employee if, as a result of the change of employment, options are exercised within three years from the date of grant. The income tax and NICs due must be collected through the PAYE mechanism.

— The combination of pro-rating for early exercise and the potential for income tax and the NICs charges means that early exercise is often regarded as unfavourable. It may be that the rules do not provide for early exercise on transfer to the JVC because of the continued shareholding in (or other form of control of) the JVC by the relevant joint venture party—e.g. rules often provide for an exercise trigger where an employee ceases to be employed by an "associated company", which includes any company which is "controlled" by the company which stands behind the scheme. The definition of control for these purposes is a broad one[33] and may mean that transfer to the JVC does not result in any cessation of employment for this purpose. While this may be favourable to the individual employees since it enables them to continue to hold their options until normal maturity, at which time they are exercised on a tax efficient basis, the rules should be checked to ensure that the JVC employees will be able to exercise on normal maturity—e.g. faultily drafted rules may provide that only employees of a "subsidiary" of the parent company can exercise at normal maturity, and the JVC may not come within this definition.

— If the terms of the existing CSOPs provide for early exercise, it may be possible, in limited circumstances, to amend them to provide that the options remain in force and do not become exercisable by virtue of the change in employment.[34]

(2) *HMRC approved savings related share option schemes ("SAYE schemes")*. The position here is similar to an executive scheme. The joint venture parties may be treated as controlling the JVC provided the joint venture is either a 50:50 company or is otherwise controlled by two persons together. Note that employees of the JVC may then be

---

[33] Income Tax (Earnings and Pensions) Act 2004, Sch.4, para.35.
[34] See e.g. *IRC v Reed International Plc* [1995] S.T.C. 889.

eligible to participate in future option grants made under an SAYE scheme operated by one of the joint venture parties since the JVC will be a constituent company of that party's group. (Early exercise (e.g. on business transfer) is particularly disadvantageous for SAYE schemes because employees can exercise only in respect of the number of shares that can be purchased using the savings and interest in the underlying savings account up to the date of exercise, not including the terminal bonus.)

(3) *HMRC approved share incentive plan ("SIP")*. Depending on the structure of the JVC and the drafting of the rules of the SIP, shares awarded under a SIP may cease to be subject to the plan on the employee moving to the JVC. If the JVC is "controlled" by the former parent company after JVC implementation, the shares will be able to remain within the plan because the JVC employees will not cease to be in "relevant employment". If the JVC is not "controlled" in this sense, the shares will "cease to be subject to the plan" but there should be no charge to income tax.

In relation to future grants, the joint venture parties will be treated as controlling the JVC provided the joint venture is either a 50:50 company and is not controlled by one person. This provision is different from the equivalent provision which applies in the case of CSOP and SAYE schemes in that it only applies where the shareholding is split on a 50:50 basis between the joint venture parents. Since many JVCs are structured in such a way that the shareholding is not split in this way, it may be that employees of the JVC may not be eligible to participate in future share awards made under a share incentive plan operated by one of the JVC parties, where they would have been able to participate in a CSOP or a SAYE scheme operated by either party.[35]

(4) *Unapproved share option arrangement/incentive plans*. The position here will depend entirely on the rules of the relevant plan.

Generally, care needs to be taken if a JVC which is not a subsidiary continues to participate in an existing scheme. Participation of a non-subsidiary could mean that the share scheme ceases to be an "employees' share scheme" (as defined in s.1166 of the Companies Act 2006) and this could have company law and other implications.[36]

18–38 If there is difficulty in arranging for continuation of share incentives and their termination could have a severe industrial relations impact on employees, it may be possible to avoid this adverse effect by arranging

---

[35] Income Tax (Earnings and Pensions) Act 2003, s.498.
[36] The definition under s.1166 limits such schemes to employees of the relevant company and its subsidiaries (although it may be possible to extend the definition to apply to those employees who were formerly employed by the company or its subsidiaries).

for the employees to remain employed by their existing employer but seconded to the JVC until the option or award becomes exercisable in the normal course (see para.18–21 et seq. earlier in relation to secondment).

Enterprise Management Incentive (EMI) Options

18–39 Enterprise management incentive (EMI) options attract very favourable tax treatment. They are specifically targeted at small, higher-risk trading companies to assist such companies in attracting and retaining high-performing individuals. If a company owns 50 per cent or less of the shares in another company which is a joint venture, it is likely that it will not qualify to grant EMI options. This is because EMI options can only be granted over shares in companies which have only "qualifying subsidiaries".[37]

JVC's own share incentive arrangements

18–40 It may be appropriate for the JVC to establish its own share incentive arrangements (although the cost implications should be considered). Two possible arrangements include:

(1) A scheme based on shares in the JVC itself. The joint venture parties would obviously need to consider the dilution implications of any issues of shares by the JVC under such arrangements. It may also be appropriate to introduce a valuation mechanism and perhaps an exit for participating employees. In addition, if there are institutional investors in either joint venture party, they are likely to consider this route undesirable.[38]

(2) A scheme based on shares in one or more of the "parent" companies participating in the joint venture.[39]

CONCLUSION

18–41 Employment law implications when establishing a joint venture will need to be carefully handled. Increasing regulation, particularly within the

---

[37] Para.11 Sch.5 ITEPA 2003. For EMI purposes, a subsidiary is any company which the company controls, either on its own or with a connected person. Broadly, to be a qualifying subsidiary, the subsidiary needs to be a 51 per cent subsidiary. A joint venture arrangement will probably be interpreted, for this purpose, as giving the company control of the joint venture company together with "connected persons". As a result, the joint venture company will be treated for EMI purposes as being a "subsidiary". However, since it is not a 51 per cent subsidiary, the joint venture company cannot be an EMI "qualifying subsidiary".

[38] See the Association of British Insurers' Guidelines for Executive Remuneration for 2008.

[39] This is permitted by para.48 of Sch.3 of the Income Tax (Earnings and Pensions) Act 2003 in relation to SAYE schemes and by para.36 of Sch.4 in relation to executive share option schemes provided the relevant parties between them beneficially own at least 75 per cent of the JVC's ordinary shares and none of them beneficially owns less than five per cent.

EU, has brought compliance with obligations of consultation to the forefront of legal planning considerations for the venture. Terms of employment, including pension and other benefits, will inevitably be important for employee relations. Whilst legislation in the UK is making the establishment of pension and share scheme benefits easier for JVC employees, this is accompanied by greater regulation and significant potential liabilities. Employment law has become increasingly technical and remains an important issue to consider.

CHAPTER 19

Accounting

How should a joint venture party account for its interest in a joint venture? The accounting treatment of the venture's assets and liabilities, and profits and losses, can significantly affect the financial results for each party—particularly the presentation of those results in a parent group's consolidated accounts. This involves a mixture of law and accounting practice. This chapter[1] provides an overview of the basic rules under UK GAAP and International Accounting Standards (IAS).

Overview of accounting issues

19–01 Accounting issues arise in relation to joint ventures and alliances in a number of different, but all significant, areas:

(1) As part of the initial inter-party commercial negotiations, specific issues are likely to include (i) the accounting principles and policies to apply on the valuation of any contribution made to the joint venture by any of the parties (see para.2–30 et seq) and (ii) the value to be attributed to a party's share in the joint venture on its subsequent transfer or disposal (see para.11–19).

(2) The joint venture vehicle itself must adopt accounting policies and principles in preparing its own accounts.

(3) For the joint venture parents, there is the important issue of how each parent should account, particularly in its consolidated group accounts, for its interest in the joint venture or alliance.

This chapter first addresses the position of the joint venture vehicle and then, particularly, the implications for the accounts of the joint venture parents.

Joint venture's own accounts

19–02 The accounting requirements in relation to the joint venture's own accounts will depend on the legal structure of the joint venture or alliance itself. As far as the UK is concerned:

---

[1] I am very grateful to Janet Milligan of PricewaterhouseCoopers for her contribution to the update of this chapter. The corresponding chapter in an earlier edition of this book was based on the PricewaterhouseCoopers Manual of Accounting.

(1) *Corporate vehicles.* If the joint venture takes a corporate form (including an LLP), the joint venture company (JVC) will be subject to the applicable statutory rules of the Companies Acts and UK generally accepted accounting principles (UK GAAP). There are also rules in the Companies Acts that permit reporting under International Accounting Standards (IAS).

(2) *Partnerships.* The Partnership and Unlimited Companies (Accounts) Regulations 1993 apply to a partnership, governed by the laws of any part of Great Britain, in which inter alia all the members are (i) limited companies, (ii) unlimited companies or (iii) comparable undertakings formed under the laws of another country. These corporate-owned partnerships must prepare annual accounts, an annual report and an auditor's report in the same way as a registered company. Each corporate partner must append these accounts to its own accounts for filing purposes (unless it can take advantage of the exemption in SI 1993/1820 because the partnership is consolidated by one of its members or by a parent of one of the members).

(3) *Other unincorporated ventures.* No statutory rules apply in the UK to the accounts of an unincorporated joint venture or alliance (other than a partnership). The form of accounts (if any) will depend on any agreement between the parties, and their accountants, as to what is desired or appropriate for that particular case. In many contractual alliances, there will be no separate accounts; each parry's income and expenditure will simply be reflected in that party's "own" accounts.

19–03 Accounting principles frequently allow some discretion or variation of accounting treatment on particular issues (e.g. depreciation or amortisation policies). Where two joint venture parties forming a JVC have different accounting policies, it will be necessary as part of the establishment of the JVC for the parties to agree harmonised accounting policies for the JVC itself. This can be a matter of some significance and potential conflict. The issue should be resolved before the JVC is established.

Accounting treatment for the joint venture parents

19–04 How should a party account for its joint venture interest in its (i.e. that party's) own accounts and, where relevant, that party's consolidated group accounts? Broadly, there are four basic types of accounting treatment which, depending on the circumstances, could be applied by a party in relation to its interest in a joint venture (using the term "joint venture" in a broad sense).

(1) *Consolidation.* Consolidation requires:

ACCOUNTING TREATMENT FOR THE JOINT VENTURE PARENTS 461

(a) the results of the joint venture to be included in full on a line-by-line basis in the group's consolidated profit and loss account; and

(b) the assets and liabilities of the joint venture to be included in full on a line-by-line basis in the group's consolidated balance sheet.

An appropriate amount is attributed to minority interests for their share of results, assets and liabilities representing interests in shares in the joint venture not owned by the parent but held by outside minority participants.

(2) *Proportionate consolidation.* This is consolidation on a line-by-line basis in the group's consolidated accounts of the parent's proportionate share of the joint venture's individual assets and liabilities as well as of its profits and losses. The difference from full consolidation is that in proportionate consolidation the minority interest (i.e. the equity interest of the other party) is deducted directly from each asset, liability, revenue and expense. This leaves only the percentage equity interest of the reporting party in each individual item shown in its balance sheet and income statement.

(3) *Equity method.* In this case, the participating company's share of the joint venture's operating profit/loss is reflected as a one-line item in the group's consolidated profit and loss account. Similarly, its share of the joint venture's net assets (and any premium or discount arising on acquisition) is included in the group's consolidated balance sheet as a one-line item—which may then be expanded by additional disclosure in the notes to the accounts.

The "gross equity method" now applies in some circumstances under UK accounting standards. This is identical to equity accounting but requires in addition:

(a) the participating company's share of the turnover of joint ventures to be shown in its profit and loss account (and in the segmental analysis of turnover); and

(b) the participating company's share of the aggregate gross assets and liabilities underlying the net equity investment in joint ventures to be shown on the face of its consolidated balance sheet.

(4) *Investment.* In this case, the investing company simply shows in its profit and loss account the amount of any dividend income received or receivable from the joint venture for the particular year—and, unless revalued (under the alternative accounting or fair value accounting rules of the Companies Act), the investment in the joint venture will appear at cost less any provisions for impairment in its balance sheet.

19–05 In deciding the relevant accounting treatment for a reporting entity, UK GAAP and International Accounting Standards (IAS) distinguish broadly between three types of strategic participation, namely interests in:

(a) entities controlled by the reporting entity (i.e. subsidiaries);

(b) entities jointly controlled by the reporting entity and one or more third parties (it is this category which is generally termed "joint ventures" within accounting terminology);

(c) entities which are not controlled or jointly-controlled but over which the reporting entity has significant influence (termed "associates" for accounting purposes).

19–06 However, precise definitions of these categories and the resulting accounting treatment vary. The Seventh Company Law EC Directive attempted some harmonisation but, importantly, permitted both proportionate consolidation and equity accounting for joint ventures. In the UK, proportional consolidation is permitted by the Companies Acts only in the case of unincorporated joint ventures. It is not permitted by UK accounting standards. The introduction of IAS does, though, also permit proportionate consolidation and introduces certain other detailed variances between UK GAAP and IAS—see para.19–22 et seq.

UK GAAP

Distinctions drawn by UK GAAP

19–07 The most relevant sources for UK GAAP are the Companies Act 2006 and the ASB's Financial Reporting Standard (FRS) 9: "Associates and Joint Ventures" and Financial Reporting Standard (FRS) 2: "Accounting for Subsidiary Undertakings". The basic distinctions which these UK accounting rules have drawn are between:

(a) subsidiary undertakings;

(b) associates;

(c) joint venture "entities"; and

(d) joint arrangements which are not entities.

In summary, and at the risk of some simplification, the UK accounting treatment for different types of joint venture is illustrated in the following chart.

UK Accounting Treatment For Joint Ventures: Summary

Form of venture

Accounting treatment

(1) *Corporate JV.* A owns 60 per cent and B owns 40 per cent of JVC. Voting rights correspond to equity interests. JVC is a "subsidiary undertaking" of A.

A: consolidation (with B's interest being shown as a minority interest). *B:* its interest in the JVC might simply be an investment but, if B has "significant influence", then equity accounting as an associate should be adopted.

(2) *Corporate JV.* A owns 60 per cent and B owns 40 per cent of JVC. Voting/board appointments are 50:50 or joint venture agreement contains severe long-term restrictions which limit A's voting powers.

A and B: gross equity accounting.

(3) *Corporate JV.* Deadlock JVC held 50:50 between A and B.

A and B: gross equity accounting.

(4) *Multi-party JV.* Corporate JVC jointly controlled by A and B who each owns 45 per cent. C owns 10 per cent and has no "significant influence".

A and B: gross equity accounting. *C:* an investment.

(5) *Partnership.* Corporate-owned partnership carrying on a business in which each of A and B has a 50 per cent interest and joint control.

A and B: gross equity accounting.

(6) *Contractual JV.* Contractual unincorporated joint venture for sharing project costs/risks in which each of A and B has a 50 per cent share.

A and B: each accounts directly for its share of assets, liabilities and cashflows under the "joint arrangement".

(7) *Contractual JV.* Contractual unincorporated joint venture for oil and gas exploration and development in which A has a 75 per cent interest and B a 25 per cent interest in assets and operations.

If the undertaking is an "entity" (see para.19–14) then probably consolidation for A as a subsidiary undertaking and equity accounting for B as an associate. If not an "entity", then each of A and B accounts directly for its share of assets, liabilities and cashflows.

> *International Accounting Standards (IAS)*. Importantly, when a company (e.g. a listed Plc) is required to adopt IAS—or where a company chooses to adopt IAS—the company may now adopt an accounting policy of either proportional consolidation or the equity method of accounting for its interest in a JVC. JVCs are not accounted for using the gross equity method under IAS. Whether the company adopts proportional consolidation or the equity method, a consistent policy must be applied in respect of all its interests in JVCs.

SUBSIDIARY UNDERTAKINGS

What is a subsidiary undertaking?

19-08 A crucial question is whether or not the particular joint venture vehicle constitutes a "subsidiary undertaking" of one of the parties. If it does, it will generally require consolidation in that party's group accounts. In some situations, particularly where the joint venture is carrying a high level of debt, a party may wish to avoid the JVC being a "subsidiary undertaking" and the requirement of consolidation. This assessment is often difficult. It can be an issue for both the lawyers and the accountants. A "subsidiary undertaking" for accounting purposes in the UK is of wider scope than a "subsidiary" for other purposes under the Companies Acts.[2]

> **WHAT IS A SUBSIDIARY UNDERTAKING? UK RULES**
>
> Section 1162 and Schs 6 and 7 of the Companies Act 2006 detail the situations in which an undertaking is a "subsidiary undertaking" of a parent undertaking for accounting purposes:
>
> (1) *Majority of voting rights*. An undertaking is a subsidiary undertaking of the parent undertaking if the latter "holds a majority of the voting rights in the undertaking". This is the definition which will apply most frequently in practice to identify joint ventures which are to be treated as subsidiary undertakings for accounting purposes. "Voting rights" means the rights conferred on shareholders to vote in respect of their shares at the undertaking's general meetings on all, or substantially all, matters. Options will generally only be taken into consideration, for this purpose, when the option has been exercised.

---

[2] The primary definition is in s.1162 of the Companies Act 2006 which gave effect to the Seventh Company Law EC Directive. This is supplemented by the ASB's FRS 2, "Accounting for subsidiary undertakings".

(2) *Appointment or removal of majority of board.* An undertaking is a subsidiary undertaking where the parent "is a member of the undertaking and has the right to appoint or remove a majority of its board of directors." In this circumstance, "the right to appoint or remove the majority of the board of directors" means the right to appoint or remove directors who have a majority of the voting rights at board meetings on all or substantially all matters (without the need for any other person's consent or concurrence). Where an undertaking has the right to appoint a director with a casting vote in the event of a board deadlock and that undertaking controls half of the voting rights on the board, it will effectively control the board. (However, if the parties in a 50:50 joint venture rotate between them the appointment of a chairman with a casting vote, this is likely to be treated as a joint venture with shared control and covered by the gross equity accounting principles described below).

(3) *Right to exercise a dominant influence.* An undertaking is a subsidiary undertaking of a parent if the parent "has a right to exercise a dominant influence over the undertaking (i) by virtue of provisions in its memorandum or articles or (ii) by virtue of a control contract". "Dominant influence" is defined by FRS 2 as "influence that can be exercised to achieve the operating and financial policies desired by the holder of the influence, notwithstanding the rights or influence of any other party". A "control contract" is a contract in writing that confers a right to dominant influence which is authorised by the memorandum or articles of the relevant undertaking and which is permitted by the local law. The concept is alien to UK practice (as opposed to some continental European jurisdictions); a "right" to exercise a dominant influence is unlikely to apply to UK companies since directors have, generally, an overriding duty under UK law to act in the company's best interests.

(4) *Member and controls a majority of voting rights.* An undertaking will be *subsidiary* undertaking where the parent "is a member of the undertaking and controls alone, pursuant to an agreement with other shareholders or members, a majority of the voting rights in the undertaking." This test overlaps with test (1) outlined above but will also apply where a party (not holding a majority shareholding itself) has a voting agreement with another shareholder whereby it is able to exercise the votes of that other shareholder and thereby control a majority of the voting rights.

(5) *Power to exercise or actually exercises dominant influence.* An undertaking is a *parent* undertaking in relation to a subsidiary undertaking if "it has the power to exercise, or actually exercises, dominant influence or control over it". This test has now been substantially widened (to bring it more in line with IAS 27) to include not only the "actual" exercise but also the "power" to exercise dominant influence. A "participating interest" is no longer required. FRS 2 defines "actual exercise of dominant influence" as follows:

> "The actual exercise of dominant influence is the exercise of an influence that achieves the result that the operating and financial policies of the undertaking influenced are set in accordance with the wishes of the holder of the influence and for the holder's benefit whether or not those wishes are explicit. The actual exercise of dominant influence is identified by its effect in practice rather than by the way in which it is exercised."

> The interpretation of this test has often proved difficult in practice, principally because of the degree of judgment involved. The operating and financial policies of an undertaking will normally be set by the board of directors in the case of a company or a similar body for unincorporated undertakings. A power of veto (or other reserve power) may give the holder a basis for exercising a dominant influence. The nature of the power of veto will be of critical importance.
>
> (6) *Managed on a unified basis.* An undertaking is a parent in relation to a subsidiary undertaking if "...it and the undertaking are managed on a unified basis." A participating interest is no longer required for this test. The Companies Act provides no definition of "managed on a unified basis". However, FRS 2 defines it as follows:
>
> "Two or more undertakings are managed on a unified basis if the whole of the operations of the undertakings are integrated and they are managed as a single unit. Unified management does not arise solely because one undertaking manages another."
>
> The application of this definition in practice requires considerable judgment. Characteristics of unified management could include: adoption of an overall management strategy for the group which includes the undertaking in question; the group treating the undertaking as if it were a subsidiary, for example, by determining its dividend policy; or common management teams, both at board level and operationally.

Subsidiaries excluded from consolidation

19–09 The general rule is that all subsidiary undertakings should be included in the consolidated financial statements. However, in certain situations relevant accounting rules may permit—or, in certain cases, require—exclusion of a particular subsidiary from consolidation. In the UK, the Companies Act permits exclusion of a subsidiary from consolidation where:

(a) inclusion is not material for the purposes of giving a true and fair view;

(b) the information necessary for the preparation of consolidated financial statements cannot be obtained without disproportionate expense or delay;

(c) the parent's interest is held exclusively with a view to resale (although FRS 2 restricts this exclusion and only allows it if the subsidiary has not previously been consolidated); or

(d) there are severe long-term restrictions which substantially hinder the exercise of the parent's rights over the assets or management of that subsidiary.

19–10 The concept of "severe long-term restrictions" can be particularly important in the context of joint ventures. Consolidation of a subsidiary undertaking is optional under the Companies Act where severe long-term restrictions substantially hinder the exercise of the parent company's rights over the assets or the management of the undertaking.[3] However, FRS 2 considers that, where the parent's rights are restricted in this way, the subsidiary concerned definitely should be excluded from consolidation.[4] In these cases, the effect of FRS 9 would be to require the gross equity accounting method to be used if the joint venture parties share "joint control" of the joint venture. The test of "severe long-term restrictions" is, nevertheless, likely to be difficult to apply in many cases. It is an important issue since the conclusion will significantly affect the accounting treatment. The onus should be on a parent company to justify non-consolidation of a "subsidiary undertaking". (Note that IAS 27 does not have such an exclusion exemption—although severe restrictions should be considered in determining whether control exists.)

19–11 The scope of "subsidiary undertaking" is therefore crucial in establishing whether a joint venture's results are to be consolidated in the accounts of a UK parent. Essentially the same test of "control" of a subsidiary, requiring full consolidation, applies under International Accounting Standards: IAS 27 ("Consolidated and Separate Financial Statements"). Where joint ventures do not constitute "subsidiary undertakings", the appropriate accounting treatment varies internationally. As a result of the publication of FRS 9, although not strictly required by the Companies Act, it is necessary under UK GAAP to distinguish between:

(a)   associates;

(b)   joint ventures which are "entities";

(c)   joint arrangements which are not "entities".

Associates

What is an associate?

19–12 Where a joint venture party has a significant but only a minority stake in a JVC, an accounting treatment which recognises only dividend income actually received from the JVC (as if it were an investment) is unlikely to be sufficient to give a fair view of the group's involvement. Consequently, a different basis of accounting known as "equity accounting" has developed for associated undertakings or "associates" as more commonly called.

---

[3] s.405(3)(a), Companies Act 2006.
[4] FRS 2, para.25. See also para.19–14 below.

> **WHAT IS AN ASSOCIATE? UK RULES**
>
> (1) An "associated undertaking" is defined pursuant to the Companies Act 2006 (SI No 410 Sch.6 para.19(1)) as ". . . an undertaking in which an undertaking included in the consolidation has a participating interest and over whose operating and financial policy it exercises a significant influence, and which is not (a) a subsidiary undertaking of the parent company, or (b) a joint venture dealt with in accordance with paragraph 18."
>
> — "Participating interest" is defined (SI No 410 Sch.10 para.11(1)) as "an interest. . . which it holds on a long-term basis for the purpose of securing a contribution to its activities by the exercise of control or influence arising from or related to that interest".
> — It is often difficult in practice to determine whether significant influence exists and therefore whether there is an associate relationship. FRS 9 provides added guidance.
>
> (2) FRS 9 defines "significant influence" as being where the investor ". . . is actually involved and is influential in the direction of [the JVC] through its participation in policy decisions . . . including decisions on strategic issues such as: (a) the expansion or contraction of the business, participation in other entities or changes in products, markets and activities of [the JVC]; and (b) determining the balance between dividend and reinvestment."
>
> (3) The investor must generally have a substantial basis of voting power. A holding of 20 per cent or more of the voting rights creates a presumption of associate status but does not in itself ensure this level of influence. In order to gain the level of influence necessary, representation on the board of directors (or its equivalent) is essential in most circumstances.
>
> (4) FRS 9 provides in effect that, once an investor has actually exercised significant influence over an entity, to maintain that relationship requires merely the ability to exercise significant influence.

19-13 The Companies Act 2006 requires that associated undertakings should be accounted for by the equity method of accounting, whereby the investing group's share of the associate's operating profit/loss, and of its net assets, is shown as a one-line item in the group's profit and loss account and balance sheet respectively. FRS 9 goes further than the Companies Act and adds an important subdivision of "joint venture entities" to which additional disclosure requirements apply. The basic concept is that additional disclosure—under the gross equity method—should be required where the level of investment goes beyond "significant influence" and becomes one of "joint control".

JOINT VENTURE ENTITIES

Joint venture entities under FRS 9

19-14 It is therefore important, under FRS 9, "Associates and Joint

Ventures", to establish whether an investment in what would otherwise be an "associate" is in a "joint venture". The level of detail that participants in such joint ventures are required to give in their consolidated financial statements is greater than for investments in associates and is what FRS 9 terms "gross equity accounting".

JOINT VENTURE ENTITIES UNDER FRS 9: SUMMARY

(1) *Joint venture*. FRS 9 defines "joint venture" as an "entity" in which the relevant participant holds an interest on a long-term basis and which is jointly controlled by that participant and one or more other venturers under a contractual arrangement.

(2) *Entity*. "Entity" is defined for this purpose as a body corporate, partnership or unincorporated association carrying on a trade or business with or without a view to profit. The trade or business must be its own trade or business and not just part of those of the venturers. Indications of this are the ability to pursue its own commercial strategy within agreed objectives, trading directly with the market in its own right and evidence that it is a continuing activity rather than a one-off project.

(3) *Joint control*. "Joint control" exists under FRS 9 "if none of the entities alone can control that entity but all together can do so and decisions on financial and operating policy essential to the activities, economic performance and financial position of that venture require each venturer's consent". The venturers must play an active role in setting the operating and financial policies of the joint venture but this involvement can be at quite a high level—e.g. setting the general strategy of the venture. It seems clear that the venturers do not have to have equal shares in the entity; for example, it would be possible to have an arrangement whereby the investors' interests are 30:35:35 so long as there is joint control including the ability for one party to veto the interests of the other parties. It is also possible for certain parties to be in "joint control" while certain other minority shareholders are not.

(4) *Subsidiaries with "severe long-term restrictions"*. A joint venture may fall within this category even if it is a "subsidiary undertaking"—if contractual arrangements with the other shareholder mean that in practice the shareholders have "joint control" over the joint venture entity. In this type of situation, the interests of the minority shareholder would amount to "severe long-term restrictions" which would substantially hinder the exercise of the parent's rights over the assets or management of its legal subsidiary (see para.19–10 earlier); the subsidiary should not be consolidated but should instead be treated as a joint venture and be gross equity accounted. This may apply if unanimous agreement is required before the joint venture can pay a dividend, change direction of the JVC's business, incur capital expenditure over a specified level, pay its directors and other employees, change other major operating and financial policies, etc. It appears that FRS 9 may open a wider exemption from consolidation than intended (or, some argue, permitted) by the Companies Act. However, where an entity is a subsidiary undertaking of one party, the test of "joint control" is likely to be applied sparingly for this purpose.

19–15 As a broad generalisation, most corporate joint ventures (unless a parent/subsidiary undertaking relationship is created) are likely to fall within this category of "joint venture entity". Most unincorporated joint ventures are unlikely to fall within this categorisation unless (as often in the case of partnerships) there is a separate "undertaking" or "entity".

19–16 Under FRS 9, joint venture "entities" require more specific detail of the participant's share of the joint venture's turnover and assets and liabilities on the face of the profit and loss account and balance sheet respectively—see para.19–04 earlier. This is referred to as the gross equity method. Other features include:

(1) *Turnover.* For joint ventures entities, the gross equity method requires that the participant's share of turnover for joint ventures must be shown separately. This turnover cannot simply be shown as part of group turnover. In addition, in the segmental analysis required by SSAP 25, turnover in respect of joint ventures must be distinguished clearly from group turnover.

(2) *Operating results.* The share of operating results of joint ventures and associates must be included immediately after the group's operating result. Any amortisation or write-down of goodwill (which arose on the acquisition of a joint venture or an associate) must be disclosed.

(3) *Exceptional items.* The participant's share of exceptional items relating to its joint ventures and associates (i.e. those appearing after operating profit) must be disclosed.

(4) *Other line items.* As with associates, any items in the profit and loss account or balance sheet which relate to joint ventures should be clearly distinguished from those for the group (e.g. the participant's share of taxation relating to its joint ventures and associates).

(5) *Consolidated balance sheet.* The group's consolidated balance sheet should disclose the gross assets and gross liabilities underlying the net amount attributable to joint ventures. This disclosure cannot be relegated to the notes to the financial statements and must appear on the face of the balance sheet.

(6) *Financial statements used.* The financial statements used for the results of joint ventures and associates should be either co-terminous with those of the group or, where this is not practicable, made up to a date not more than three months *before* the investing group's period end. (IAS is different—being three months before or after the investing group's period end.)

(7) *Transactions between associates and joint ventures and the reporting entity.* FRS 9 also regulates the accounting treatment for transactions between a reporting entity and a joint venture, including a requirement that the reporting entity's share of any profit arising from

those transactions should be eliminated in the consolidated accounts. The Urgent Issues Task Force has issued further guidance for consolidated financial statements on this topic by its UITF Abstract 31 on "Exchanges of business or other non-monetary assets for equity in a subsidiary, joint venture or associate".

Participating company's individual financial statements

19–17 In the case of the participant's individual financial statements, investments in both joint venture entities and associates should be treated as fixed asset investments and shown either at cost (less amounts written off) or at valuation (under either the alternative accounting or fair value accounting rules of the Companies Act). In its individual profit and loss account, it will simply show dividend income received from the investment, not share of profit.

Additional disclosure

19–18 Certain additional information must be disclosed, under FRS 9 and the Companies Act 2006, in the consolidated financial statements in relation to a group's investments in its joint ventures and associates:

(1) *15 and 25 per cent threshold information.* Particular disclosures arise where associates and joint ventures are material—namely where the group's share in its associates or joint ventures in aggregate exceeds 15 per cent of the group's gross assets, gross turnover or (on a three-year average) operating results. In addition, where the group's share in any of its individual joint ventures and associates exceeds 25 per cent of certain thresholds individually, then additional disclosures have to be given for that entity under FRS 9.[5]

(2) *Trading balances.* Information is required to be disclosed concerning the trading balances with joint ventures and associates.

(3) *Excessive disclosure.* Where the directors are of the opinion that the number of undertakings in respect of which the company is required to disclose the above information required by Companies Act 2006 would result in excessive disclosure being given, the information need only be given in respect of joint ventures and of associates whose results or financial position, in the opinion of the directors, principally affect the figures shown in the financial statements.[6]

---

[5] IAS 31 does not require the same detailed disclosure requirements as FRS 9; however, a venturer which recognises its interest in a joint venture using the line-by-line reporting format of proportionate consolidation or the equity method should disclose the aggregate amounts of (respectively) current assets, long-term assets, current liabilities, long-term liabilities, income and expenses relating to its interests in joint ventures.

[6] Under IAS, the exemptions referred to in para.19–18 (3) and (4) are only available in respect of disclosure requirements which are additional to those required by IAS 31 (and IAS 27 for separate financial statements). The exemptions are not available in respect of the specific disclosure requirements of IAS 31 (or IAS 27).

19–19 The ASB, in publishing FRS 9, supported the equity accounting method and rejected proportional consolidation for "joint venture entities". It believed that it would be misleading to represent each venturer's joint control of a joint venture as being in substance equivalent to it having sole control of its share of that entity's assets, liabilities and cash flows. There is now, though, an awkward inconsistency with IAS—see below.

JOINT ARRANGEMENTS WHICH ARE NOT ENTITIES ("JANES")

What is a JANE?

19–20 FRS 9 introduced a new category of "joint arrangements which are not entities" (JANEs). These are contractual arrangements under which co-venturers engage in joint activities which do not create a separate "entity". Joint arrangements of this type are required to be accounted for in a different way from associates and joint venture entities—namely, interests in such arrangements should not be equity accounted but each participant should account directly for its own assets, liabilities and cash flows, measured according to the terms of the agreement governing the arrangement. Most contractual alliances will, in practice, fall within this category.

WHAT IS A JANE? SUMMARY

(1) A "joint arrangement that is not an entity" is defined by FRS 9 as ". . .a contractual arrangement under which the participants engage in joint activities that do not create an entity because it would not be carrying on a trade or business of its own. A contractual arrangement where all significant matters of operating and financial policy are predetermined does not create an entity because the policies are those of its participants, not of a separate entity."

(2) Therefore, a "joint arrangement that is not an entity" can be an undertaking such as a partnership or an unincorporated undertaking or it may be a simple arrangement between the parties where a separate entity is not established. It is the nature or substance of its trading relationship (not the legal form) which determines whether or not it falls within the definition for FRS 9, not how it is constituted.

(3) It is theoretically possible under FRS 9 for a limited company to be a "joint arrangement" where the undertaking is a mere "shell" or acts solely as an agent of its participants and it is clear that the undertaking's business is just an extension of the separate businesses of the co-venturers without access to the market in its own right.

> (4) Many contractual alliances—such as cost-sharing or risk-sharing arrangements, a one-off construction project consortium and many joint marketing or distribution arrangements—will not be entities but "joint arrangements" for this purpose. Joint arrangements of this nature encompass what are sometimes termed "jointly controlled operations" and "jointly controlled assets". Many activities in the oil, gas and mineral extraction industries, for instance, involve the use of jointly controlled assets.

19-21 FRS 9 requires that each participant in such a "joint arrangement" should account for its own assets, liabilities and cash flows, measured according to the terms of the agreement governing the arrangement. Participants should therefore recognise their own assets, liabilities and cash flows (together with their proportionate shares of assets or liabilities held jointly under the arrangements) directly in their individual accounts as well as on consolidation. Where treatment as a JANE is permitted, this generates an end-result similar to that of proportional consolidation.

INTERNATIONAL ACCOUNTING PRACTICE

International Accounting Standards (IAS)

19-22 International Accounting Standards (IAS)[7] are now mandatory for the consolidated accounts of all EU listed companies.[8] In addition, all other UK companies now have the option of preparing their accounts using IAS. The relevant IAS standards for this purpose are currently:

(a) IAS 27: "Consolidated and Separate Financial Statements";

(b) IAS 28: "Investments in Associates"; and

(c) IAS 31: "Interests in Joint Ventures".

These Standards are having an increasingly significant effect on the accounting treatment for joint ventures in the UK. The primary difference between IAS and the previous UK GAAP is that IAS permits (indeed has, until recently, encouraged) the use of proportional consolidation for most joint ventures.

IAS 27: Subsidiaries

19-23 IAS 27's definition of subsidiary is simply "an entity, including an unincorporated entity such as a partnership, that is controlled by another entity (known as the parent)".

---

[7] These are strictly termed International Financial Reporting Standards (IFRS) although the existing terminology is being retained for existing international standards.

[8] Listed companies no longer have to comply with the accounting rules set out in the Companies Acts. Listed companies traded on the London Stock Exchange became required to comply with IAS for financial years beginning on or after January 1, 2005. Companies traded on the Alternative Investment Market (AIM) have been mandated to use IAS for financial years beginning on or after January 1, 2007.

> **WHAT IS CONTROL? IAS RULES**
>
> Control is defined as the "power to govern the financial and operating policies of an entity so as to obtain benefits from its activities". IAS 27 specifies situations where a parent has control over another entity. In particular, control will arise where the parent:
>
> (a) owns more than half of the voting power of an entity, in which case control is presumed to exist unless in exceptional circumstances it can be clearly demonstrated that such ownership does not constitute control; or
>
> (b) owns half or less of the voting power of an entity when there is:
>
> — power over more than one half of the voting rights by virtue of an agreement with other investors;
> — power to govern the entity's financial and operating policies under a statute or an agreement;
> — power to appoint or remove the majority of the members of the board of directors or equivalent governing body and control of the entity is by that board or body;
> — power to cast the majority of votes at meetings of the board of directors or equivalent governing body and control of the entity is by that board or body.

The circumstances where there is control are similar, in effect, to most of the situations covered by FRS 2. Although there are subtle differences in IAS 27 in some of the provisions[9] which explain how an entity might be controlled, they should not affect significantly the situations in which companies are required to be consolidated by UK groups on their transition to IAS.

IAS 28: Associates

19-24 The definition of an "associate" under IAS 28 is similar to that under UK GAAP. However, under IAS 28 an undertaking is an investor's associate if the investor is able to exercise significant influence—i.e. has the power to do so rather than necessarily actually exercising this power and irrespective of the existence of a participating interest. IAS 28 also takes into account potential voting rights (options and convertible instruments) that are currently exercisable or convertible when assessing if there is significant influence. More investments may therefore now be classified as associates under IAS 28 than previously under FRS 9.

---

[9] For instance, IAS 27 states that the existence and effect of potential voting rights that are currently exercisable or convertible should be considered when assessing whether an entity controls another entity. This is a subtle difference from the UK GAAP position where options are taken into account in determining whether a party has a majority of the voting rights only when the option has been exercised. However, in practice, other factors (such as dominant influence) may well make the decision to consolidate the same under both sets of accounting standards.

19–25 Both IAS 28 and FRS 9 use the equity method of accounting for associates. Under IAS the reporting entity presents its share of the associate's profits or losses (i.e. profits or losses net of tax and minority interests) in its income statement as a one-line item after finance costs but before tax expenses. However, FRS 9 is more detailed and requires the investor's share of the associate's operating profit, exceptional items, interest and tax to be presented separately. This is a significant difference since, under IAS, the share of an associate's results is net of interest and tax and no longer shown as part of operating profit.

IAS 31: Joint ventures

Categories under IAS

19–26 IAS 31 is more complex than UK GAAP and distinguishes three types of joint venture which involve a contractually agreed sharing of control:

(1) *Jointly controlled entities.* These involve the establishment of a corporation, partnership or other entity which is jointly controlled by the venturers. Most equity joint ventures (unless there is a parent/subsidiary relationship) will fall within this category. Jointly controlled entities may be accounted for in group accounts either by proportional consolidation (recognising the attributable share of assets, liabilities, income and expenses) or by equity accounting.[10] Importantly, the view of the International Accounting Standards Board (IASB) has been, until recently, that proportional consolidation is the preferred route as better reflecting the substance of a party's interest in a joint venture. There are two reporting formats for proportionate consolidation: (i) combining the venturer's share of assets, liabilities and income on a line-by-line basis with similar items or (ii) reporting the share as separate line items.

(2) *Jointly controlled operations.* These involve the use of the assets and other resources of the venturers themselves rather than the establishment of a corporation, partnership or other entity (e.g. where two or more venturers combine on joint development, production and marketing of a product or for a construction joint venture). A participant in a jointly controlled operation should recognise its attributable assets, liabilities, income and expenses directly in its own financial statements. Most contractual alliances will fall within this category.

(3) *Jointly controlled assets.* This is intended to cover assets such as shared oilfields or pipelines or jointly-owned real estate. These should be accounted for on a proportional basis in the participant's individual accounts.

---

[10] Gross equity accounting, as described in FRS 9, does not feature in IAS 31.

An example of an income statement for joint ventures and associates under IAS, using the equity method of accounting, is the following:

BALFOUR BEATTY PLC: ANNUAL REPORT AND ACCOUNTS 2006 [Extract]	
Group income statement for the year ended 31 December 2006	**Total** **£m**
Revenue including share of joint ventures and associates	5,852
Share of revenue of joint ventures and associates	(1,365)
Group revenue	4,487
Cost of sales	(4,121)
Gross profit	366
Net operating expenses	
— amortisation of intangible assets	(1)
— other	(304)
Group operating profit	61
Share of results of joint ventures and associates	63
Profit from operations	124
Investment income	26
Finance costs 124	(25)
Profit before taxation	125
Taxation	(34)
Profit for the year attributable to equity shareholders	91

Individual company accounts

19–27 The rules under IAS for individual company accounts, insofar as they relate to investments in associates and jointly controlled entities, are more complex than under FRS 9. (The latter simply requires the investment to be carried at cost less amounts written off or valuation.) Broadly, proportionate consolidation or equity accounting applies under IAS in individual accounts (termed economic entity financial statements in IAS) unless the reporting entity is exempt from preparing consolidated accounts. Where it is exempt, the investment is accounted for either at cost or at fair value in accordance with IAS 39: "Financial Instruments: Recognition and Measurement".

Transactions with joint venture parties

19–28 IAS 31 has also developed guidance for the accounting treatment of certain transactions between a venturer and a joint venture. When a venturer contributes or sells assets to a joint venture and the assets are retained by the joint venture, the venturer should generally recognise only the proportion of the gain or loss that is attributable to the interest of the other venturer(s). Further guidance (in SIC-13 "Jointly Controlled Entities—Non-Monetary Contributions by Venturers") is given on the application of these general principles to the specific situation of a transfer of non-monetary assets to a jointly controlled entity in exchange for equity.

Future developments

19–29 The introduction of IAS has been an important development. However, some of the inconsistencies between IAS and UK GAAP—and also with US GAAP (see below)—are awkward and the rules are complex. The IASB is reviewing the position. It published in 2007 draft proposals, "Exposure Draft ED 9 Joint Arrangements", to replace IAS 31. Main points in the proposals are:

(1) The accounting treatment should depend more on the contractual rights and obligations agreed by the parties in relation to the venture rather than the legal form or entity in which the activities take place. At present, IAS 31 can lead to the recognition of assets that are not controlled and liabilities that are not obligations.

(2) The choice of accounting treatment should be eliminated since this makes it difficult to compare financial reports. The IASB is moving away from proportional consolidation. ED 9 would require parties to recognise both the individual assets to which they have rights and the liabilities for which they are responsible—even if the joint arrangement operates in a separate legal entity.

(3) On the other hand, if the parties only have a right to a share of the outcome of the activities (e.g. dividends), their net interest in the arrangement should be recognised using the equity method.

(4) Enhanced disclosure requirements would be introduced setting out additional information to be disclosed by a reporting entity in respect of operations carried out through "joint arrangements".

(5) ED 9 proposes the use of the terminology "joint arrangement" rather than "joint venture", "joint operations" rather than "jointly controlled operations" and "joint assets" rather than "jointly controlled assets".

(6) The proposals would, as one of its intentions, achieve convergence in principle with US GAAP which (see below) generally requires the use of the equity method rather than proportionate consolidation.

The IASB proposals have received mixed reactions. Although change is likely, it is not certain that they will go forward in the current proposed form. This is still an area where debate is continuing on the best way of reflecting a party's interest in joint ventures and collaborative arrangements.

Other European countries

19–30 There is no consistent approach to accounting for joint ventures in other EU countries, since the Seventh Company Law EC Directive allowed Member States the option to permit proportionate consolidation for joint ventures. This option was taken and proportionate consolidation is the more common practice in Belgium, Germany, the Netherlands, Spain and Italy. In France, proportionate consolidation has been mandatory for joint ventures, irrespective of whether or not they take a corporate form. French listed companies are now required to comply with IAS but an example of a French company continuing, within IAS, to use the proportionate method is Thales S.A.:

ANNUAL REPORT 2006 OF THALES S.A.

1. Accounting Policies [Extract]

In application of European regulation No. 1606/2002 pertaining to international standards, issued on 19 July 2002, the consolidated financial statements of the Thales Group are prepared, since 1 January 2005, in accordance with IAS/IFRS standards (International Financial Reporting Standards) as approved by the European Union.

The Group previously applied French accounting standards, as defined notably in regulation 99–02 of the French accounting rules and regulations committee (*Comite de Reglementation Comptable* or C.R.C.).

a) Consolidation

The financial statements of significant subsidiaries directly or indirectly controlled by Thales have been fully consolidated. Companies in which Thales does not have a controlling interest but over which it exercises significant influence, directly or indirectly, are accounted for under the equity method. Companies under joint control are accounted for under the proportionate method.

[NOTES] [Extract]

% Control
31/12/2006

[2.] Accounted for under the proportionate method	
Aircommand Systems International SAS (ACSI) (France)	50%
Amper Programs SA (Spain)	49%
Armaris (France)	50%
Citylink Ltd (UK)	33%
Diehl Avionik Systeme GmbH (Germany)	49%
Faceo (France, UK, Spain, Italy, Belgium)	50%
Samsung Thales Company (Korea)	50%
Stesa (Saudi Arabia)	49%
Navigation Solutions (USA)	22%
Thales Raytheon Systems (France, Ireland, USA)	50%
United Monolithic Semiconductors (France, Germany)	50%
[3.] Accounted for under the equity method	
Arab International Optronics (Egypt)	49%
Aviation Communications & Surveillance Systems (USA)	30%
Camelot (UK)	20%
Elettronica S.p.A. (Italy)	33%
ESG (Germany)	30%
Dpix (USA)	20%

US GAAP

19–31 US GAAP has broadly followed a similar approach to UK GAAP and requires (i) consolidation for subsidiaries and (ii) equity accounting for associates in which the relevant party exercises significant influence. Proportionate consolidation is not regarded as appropriate for corporate joint ventures. There is less specific guidance in relation to unincorporated joint ventures, although proportionate consolidation is common—e.g. practice in relation to oil and gas ventures is for the relevant participant to account for its pro rata share of the assets, liabilities, revenues and expenses of a joint venture in its own financial statements.

19–32 One area where some important guidance has been given concerns the criteria for excluding consolidation of subsidiaries—recognising that, under certain circumstances, a majority party in a joint venture may not be able to exercise control even though it has more than a 50 per cent voting interest. The assessment of whether or not the rights of a minority shareholder are such as to overcome the presumption of consolidation is a matter of judgment that depends on facts and circumstances. The Emerging Issues Task Force of the Financial Accounting Standards Board (FASB) has issued guidance that:

"the framework in which such facts and circumstances are judged should be based on whether the minority rights, individually or in the aggregate, provide for the minority shareholder to effectively participate in significant decisions that would be expected to be made in the 'ordinary course of business'. Effective participation means the ability to block significant decisions proposed by the investor who has a majority voting interest. That is, control does not rest with the majority owner because the investor with the majority voting interest cannot cause the investee to take an action that is significant in the ordinary course of business if it has been vetoed by the minority shareholder."

The Task Force believes that certain minority rights would not overcome the presumption of consolidation by the investor with a majority voting interest since they are considered "protective rights"—even if they allow the minority shareholder to block certain corporate actions (e.g. acquisitions and disposals of assets greater than 20 per cent of the fair value of the JVC's total assets). However, the following corporate actions will be regarded as overcoming the presumption of consolidation since they are considered "substantive participating rights":

"1. Selecting, terminating, and setting the compensation of management responsible for implementing the investee's policies and procedures;
2. Establishing operating and capital decisions of the investee, including budgets, in the ordinary course of business."

These criteria will therefore frequently affect the scope of minority rights which a majority US participant is willing to concede if it wishes to ensure consolidation of the joint venture in which it holds a majority interest.

Conclusion

19–33 Accounting law and practice will affect the financial results which a party can demonstrate for its participation in a joint venture. Accounting principles are therefore important, particularly for parent companies in preparing group accounts. Accounting treatment for joint ventures is by no means consistent internationally. Given the increase in cross-border joint ventures and alliances, one may expect—or hope—that greater convergence and clarity will be brought to international accounting law and practice in this important area over the coming years.

PART D

INTERNATIONAL JOINT VENTURES AND SELECTED JURISDICTIONS

    20   International joint ventures

Selected Jurisdictions:

    (1)   Brazil

    (2)   China

    (3)   Czech Republic

    (4)   France

    (5)   Germany

    (6)   India

    (7)   Italy

    (8)   Japan

    (9)   The Netherlands

    (10)   Poland

    (11)   Russia

    (12)   South Africa

    (13)   Spain

    (14)   United States

Many joint ventures and alliances involve parties from different jurisdictions or operations in more than one jurisdiction. Many of the topics discussed in previous Parts of this book (including tax, competition laws, transaction planning and commercial issues) apply equally to international joint ventures. Additional issues arise, however, where the joint venture is with a local partner for investment in a "foreign" jurisdiction. This Part addresses issues in these transactions—and includes summaries of the legal framework in a number of selected jurisdictions of importance for international joint ventures.

CHAPTER 20

International joint ventures

Joint ventures and alliances have become an integral part of international business. Economic trading barriers between nations are being eliminated; industries are becoming global in nature; new markets are opening up; developing economies are seeking foreign capital and technology; and, in many countries, the most effective means of market entry is through a collaboration with a local partner. This chapter highlights issues which require particular attention for parties participating in international joint ventures with a "local" partner.

GENERAL BACKGROUND

Growth in international joint ventures

20–01 A large number of joint ventures and alliances are international in nature—in the sense that they involve parties from different jurisdictions or operations in more than one jurisdiction. Different types include:

(1) *Cross-border mergers.* Cross-border joint ventures are frequently the medium whereby two or more parties combine or merge existing activities in a common field. These invariably involve subsidiaries or activities in many jurisdictions worldwide. These are complex transactions which involve a wide range of the issues discussed earlier in this book. A key issue will often be: where should the joint venture company (JVC) be located?[1] Will it be desirable to have a single JVC with operating subsidiaries in different countries—or (whether for tax or other reasons) a series of "parallel" joint ventures in different jurisdictions?[2]

(2) *Complementary skills joint ventures and alliances.* Many international joint ventures are established where two or more parties, multinational or based in different jurisdictions, agree to collaborate and

---

[1] See para.15–08 et seq. for a discussion of tax issues relating to location of an international JVC.
[2] Or, possibly, one of the new types of European company may be considered—see para.5–38 et seq.

bring together complementary skills (e.g. technology, construction, production, marketing and/or distribution) in a new joint venture. Some joint ventures will be to undertake a single project; others will be to establish an ongoing jointly-owned business.

(3) *Multi-national strategic alliances.* In many service industries, there is pressure to provide a global service for customers. There are many examples in the airline, automotive and services fields of strategic alliances between parties from different jurisdictions whereby they agree to ally and provide mutual customers services on a pan-European or global basis.

(4) *Joint ventures with "local" partners.* A common form of international joint venture is where one party (the "foreign" company) combines with a party from another jurisdiction (the "local" party) in order to undertake a joint venture business based principally in that jurisdiction. Much of the remainder of this chapter deals with issues relating to international joint ventures of this last kind, particularly in the context of ventures in developing market economies.

20–02 Joint ventures and alliances with local partners in "developing" markets have become a major feature of international business. Developing countries contain over three-quarters of the world's population and, therefore, potential consumers. Economies in countries such as China, India, Russia and Brazil have been growing at rates significantly greater than in the industrial "developed" economies. Joint ventures and alliances between companies from developed countries and emerging market companies have an obvious attraction:

(1) The growing economies of these and other developing countries have led to high demand for consumer and industrial products and services—creating significant opportunities for companies from developed countries to expand their markets, benefiting from the use of a local party's existing distribution system and guidance in adapting their goods to local customer demands.

(2) Many emerging countries have been attracting inward investment on the basis that they can offer a highly competitive low-cost production or service-provision base for the foreign party (e.g. China for manufacturing and India for software and communication services).

(3) Host governments in many of the emerging markets have, during this developing phase, had a strong preference that "local" firms should share in the ownership of foreign-funded ventures and increase their opportunities to acquire new technology, management skills and other expertise.

(4) A joint venture may, strategically, be a way for a foreign party to start in an overseas jurisdiction and to gain experience in the local conditions and customs—with, not infrequently, a subsequent phase being a move to full acquisition and to integrate more fully the local company into the foreign party's production, sales and marketing plans.

(5) Importantly, joint ventures with local companies may be perceived by many foreign investing companies as reducing their exposure to risk and providing some commercial protection in situations where laws and business practices create risk levels higher than those normally acceptable in the West.

At the macro-economic level, international joint ventures may be regarded as performing an important role in bringing the businesses of developed and emerging market countries together and, by so doing, assisting in the continuing development of a global marketplace.

20–03 A sample of press announcements over the last year or so illustrate the range of activity:

- *Citigroup/China.* Citigroup has signed an agreement with a Chinese partner, Central China Securities, to establish a mainland investment banking venture, ahead of an expected opening of the sector to more overseas participation. Credit Suisse and Morgan Stanley have recently each signed similar agreements with Chinese partners. The agreements come as Beijing is poised to relax a two-year ban on foreign investment in the country's booming domestic securities industry. [*FT*: 28.1.08]

- *Vodafone/India.* Vodafone has finalised a mobile phone infrastructure sharing agreement with rivals in India that should accelerate wireless coverage across the country and provide the participating companies with significant cost savings. Vodafone, Bharti Airtel (India's largest mobile operator) and Idea, a smaller rival, have agreed to pool network infrastructure in a joint venture that may in the future seek a stock exchange listing. [*FT*: 8.12.07]

- *Nissan/Ashok Leyland.* Nissan and Ashok Leyland, a truckmaker owned by the Indian Hinduja Group, have announced an agreement to form three joint ventures in light-truck and engine production in India. One venture would be majority-owned by the Indian company and produce light commercial vehicles. In the second venture, controlled by Nissan, the companies will produce engines and gearboxes. A third, 50:50 joint venture, will develop light trucks and engines for local and export markets. [*FT*: 30.8.07]

- *Iraq.* Iraq's ministry of industry and minerals declared plans to open up all 65 of its state-owned enterprises to joint ventures with international investors by the end of the year. Attracting foreign investment is seen as vital to the reconstruction of the economy, to creating employment and, the Iraqi government hopes, reducing sectarian violence. [*FT*: 30.8.07]

- *ABF/China*. Associated British Foods is to spend L70m on launching a sugar beet joint venture in the north east of China with the Hebel Tinn Lu Sugar Group. The UK-based food and retail group will own 51 per cent of the joint venture while Tinn Lu will contribute its existing beet sugar business and hold the remainder of the shares. [*FT*: 25.8.07]

- *Fiat/China*. China has deepened its alliance with Chery Automobile of China, signing a letter of intent for a joint venture that will manufacture 175,000 cars a year from 2009. The agreement is a further step for the Italian industrial group as it seeks multiple alliances worldwide to offset research and production costs while preserving its independence. [*FT*: 8.8.07]

- *Wal-Mart/India*. Wal-Mart of the US has succeeded in getting its toe in the door of the Indian market via a long-planned joint venture with local partner Bharti Enterprises, one of India's largest companies. The 50:50 joint venture, called Bharti Wal-Mart, is a "wholesale cash-and-carry" business that will use Wal-Mart's logistics technology, inventory systems, truck tracking and fuel management. [*FT*: 7.8.07]

- *Generali/PPF*. Generali, one of Europe's largest insurers, announced a joint venture with PPF, a Netherlands-based group with operations in the Czech Republic and other parts of eastern Europe as the Italian insurer continues its run of deals in emerging markets. Generali will own 51 per cent of the joint venture. The venture will combine the two groups' insurance markets in central and eastern Europe. [*FT*: 27.4.07]

- *Argos/India*. Home Retail Group has announced plans to launch its Argos chain in India. It is expected to open an initial 20 to 30 stores in a joint venture with two Indian parties. [*FT*: 24.2.07]

- *Tata/Fiat*. Tata Motors, India's largest automaker, is poised to strengthen its presence in Latin America through a partnership with Italian carmaker Fiat, adding to its portfolio of global markets. The pair unveiled an $80m agreement to build Tata pick-up trucks under the Fiat brand at the Italian carmaker's plant in Argentina. It expands the joint collaboration "beyond the shores of India". [*FT*: 15.2.07]

- *Aegon/Romania*. Aegon, a Dutch insurance company, has announced plans to establish pension and life assurance operations in Romania as it seeks opportunities in central and eastern Europe, including Ukraine. It will launch a joint venture business with Bucharest-listed Banca Transilvania, the country's fifth-largest commercial lender. [*FT*: 19.1.07]

20-04 Yet, despite the activity and attraction, joint ventures and alliances between global and emerging market companies are often unstable—more so than alliances between companies from similar economic and cultural backgrounds. Many have failed to meet expectations or have required extensive restructuring. Potential tensions or conflicting priorities enhancing the risk of failure are many:

(1) Culture and management styles can lead to frustrating negotiations and relationships. State-owned enterprises can be difficult partners for multinationals because there is often no simple decision-maker or approvals have to be sought from a range of internal constituencies.

(2) Contributions by the parties to the joint venture may have different life-spans. The foreign company may be contributing intangible assets such as technology, brands and skills that grow in importance and size. The local party's contribution is more likely to be local market knowledge, relationships with regulators and/or an initial distribution network—assets that may fade in importance as the foreign company becomes more knowledgeable about the local market.

(3) The underlying objectives of the joint venture parties may often be different. The foreign partner may be looking at the venture as an opportunity to develop a new market with good prospects for medium to long-term profitability. The local partner may be placing greater weight on a short-term opportunity to learn expertise or to acquire technology.

(4) The role of government in emerging economies tends to be significant, involving greater bureaucracy, political interference and risk of changing regulatory background or governmental support.

(5) A political area of conflict may also be the venture's net contribution to the developing country's foreign trade. Many emerging country companies are keen to export on the world market. The foreign company, on the other hand, may be more concerned about building a strong position in the local market.

One commentator[3] expresses these potential tensions and conflicting priorities in the following summary:

---

[3] J. Child, D. Faulkner and S. Tallman, *Co-operative Strategy*: *Managing Alliances, Networks and Joint Ventures* (Oxford: Oxford University Press, 2005).

> **FIGURE 20. Conflicting priorities between developed and emerging economy partners**
>
> | Foreign partner | | Local partner |
> |---|---|---|
> | Local market | >< | Export market |
> | Access local market | >< | Protect local market |
> | Safeguard technology | >< | Transfer technology |
> | Import components | >< | Develop local supplies |
> | High quality standard | >< | Cost savings |
> | Long term focus | >< | Short term focus |
> | Foreign management style | >< | Local management style |
>
> Source: J Child, D. Faulkner and S. Tallman, *Cooperative Strategy*

20–05 Adopting a similar analysis, one group of commentators[4] has identified that alliances with emerging market partners tend to evolve along one of four paths:

(1) The joint venture may develop into a successful long-term alliance (possibly expanding into neighbouring countries and industry sectors).

(2) The relationship may lead to a power shift towards the foreign company (often followed by a buy-out after a foreign partner has succeeded in getting the organisation up-and-running and the local party's contribution has ceased to be so significant).

(3) The third path sees a shift of power towards the emerging market party with the local operations building up strength and the local party increasing its ownership stake.

(4) The fourth path leads to break-up and competition between the parties, involving dissolution or acquisition of the joint venture by one of them.

20–06 Indeed a vital first question for the foreign party—in the light of this background—is whether the choice of the joint venture option is the right one commercially. Establishing an international joint venture (and, if necessary, unwinding it) is likely to involve considerable management time and effort—even greater than for a domestic joint venture. A foreign party should consider whether any alternative option of gaining market entry may be easier and preferable; e.g.: (i) setting up a wholly owned subsidiary or branch; (ii) acquiring a local entity; (iii) using a representative office to facilitate a supply or licensing relationship without creating a local legal entity; (iv) involving a local party as a manager or adviser rather than an

---

[4] A. Adarkar, A. Adil, D. Ernst and P. Vaish in *Mastering Alliance Strategy* (eds. J. Bamford, B. Gomes-Casseres and M. Robinson, John Wiley & Sons, 2003) at p.51.

equity partner; or (v) hiring a limited number of specialist or key local employees.

20–07 This is general background. All is not gloom and failure. Many joint ventures in emerging markets do provide significant benefits. Each joint venture will, of course, be different and have its own dynamics. It will be for the principal parties to decide whether or not a joint venture is the right course and to resolve the central commercial issues. However, the lawyers should be aware of the commercial background and, with the client, anticipate the areas likely to be of key importance going forward; e.g.:

— strategic and operational control[5] (if the foreign party seeks a dominant influence over the business in the longer-term);

— measures to control the release of technology[6] to the JVC, protection of confidential information and rights of use of IPR (if the foreign party's participation may not be long-term);

— rights to terminate and consequences of termination,[7] particularly in relation to ownership and use of IPR (if the local party is likely to become more dominant or independent).

Preparing for an International Venture

Convergence of approach—or national differences?

20–08 An international joint venture with a "local" party is not in essence different from any other joint venture. The commercial and legal issues addressed in other chapters of this book apply equally—both in relation to the content of the joint venture agreement and also the overall transaction process. The globalisation of business is leading in many respects to a convergence of practice, approach and solutions in the way these types of transactions are structured and documented.[8]

20–09 However, an equity joint venture vehicle must be founded in the jurisdiction of one country[9] and national laws (and practice) will continue

---

[5] See para.8–12 et seq. for different ways (direct and indirect) by which "control" may be established at operational level (including nomination of particular executive posts, control of financial reporting systems, provision of resources under contract, licensing and setting standards for use of brand names etc).
[6] See para.17–22 et seq. for a general discussion of technology transfer in a venture with a "local" party.
[7] See para.13–46 et seq. The high-profile dispute between Danone and Wahaha (see para.1–19) is an example where these issues have come to the fore, including the right to use a strong brand name.
[8] The International Bar Association (IBA) is also contributing to the growth of joint venture experience for lawyers internationally through its distance-learning International Practice Diploma course on "International Joint Ventures".
[9] Even a new European Company must be formally registered in a selected jurisdiction—see para.5–38.

to be important. There are still a significant number of national differences which may affect the structuring and negotiation of joint ventures and alliances. Some derive from differences between common law and civil law systems. International joint ventures are also likely to involve additional process and transaction issues for the "foreign" party.

20–10 It is not possible in a book of this kind to give solutions, or indeed to raise issues, applicable to all jurisdictions. The approach here is to raise questions, warnings and issues which should then be specifically addressed in the context of the particular venture and the particular jurisdiction. It is convenient in this chapter to address separately the following topics:

(a) issues relating to preparation and commercial due diligence;

(b) understanding the local law regime;

(c) some differences, of a general nature, in law and practice relating to joint ventures under civil law systems compared with common law jurisdictions;

(d) a range of additional issues or factors which arise in joint ventures with local parties in developing market economies such as China, Russia, Latin America and Central and Eastern Europe; and

(e) some issues relating to governing law and arbitration.

Preparation and commercial due diligence

20–11 Turning to international joint ventures more generally, good preparation and due diligence are crucial—particularly where a foreign party is proposing to enter into a joint venture in a jurisdiction, or with a party, with which it is not familiar. International joint ventures require considerable preparation by the parties (and their advisers) if the parties are to establish a framework for success and avoid unexpected problems—whether of a commercial or legal nature.

20–12 Preparation for a joint venture transaction involving a "local" jurisdiction should involve the same transaction-planning principles as discussed in chapter 2. Where the venture is in a "new" country or with a "new" partner for the foreign investor, this should also include proper investigation into the following areas:

(1) *Culture and background of local party.* A well-prepared joint venture party will make efforts to understand both the legal nature and social and business culture of its prospective partner. Parties should be aware of cultural differences which may affect the nature and outcome of negotiations. Often there is a need to investigate the background of the local party, particularly if the entity is or has been government-owned. What is its legal status? Has it been privatised?

(2) *Local party's existing business.* Where the local party has an existing business or assets which are being vested in the joint venture, appropriate due diligence should be undertaken into that business or those assets. What other business activities does the local party undertake? What negotiations or transactions has it undertaken with other foreign companies? Is it listed on a local stock exchange and subject to local information and reporting requirements? What is the local party's decision-making process? Is it centralised and likely to involve delays before final decisions can be made? Are individual officers of the local party relatively experienced or inexperienced in international business transactions and practices?

(3) *Financial.* Initial due diligence prior to any equity joint venture with a new partner should include, wherever possible, access to review operational, asset and financial information concerning the local party. Getting quality financial information in some emerging markets can often be a real problem; there may be a general reluctance to share information, including on the part of the government (if enterprises are state-owned), and often a lack of public record. Even if information is forthcoming, local accounting and valuation principles may fall short of international standards. In appropriate cases, an independent audit should be considered.

(4) *Currency fluctuation and convertibility.* Currency risks are common in international joint ventures. The value of the "investing" currency relative to the currency of the local jurisdiction affects the value of the joint venture's assets and earnings. Currency fluctuations and problems of inconvertibility have been the cause of the failure of many international joint ventures in emerging markets.

(5) *Political environment.* Understanding the political environment in the "local" country is important, particularly in the case of economies operating on a centralised basis and still moving towards a market economy. If the establishment of the joint venture is part of the privatisation process, what are the basic features of that process? Are special governmental permissions required for it to undertake transactions? How great is the political risk of governmental instability or even of potential nationalisation of the venture's assets?

(6) *Compliance and corporate policies.* Association with a local partner can carry reputational and legal risks for the foreign party. It is becoming increasingly common, and important, for a foreign party (particularly one with US legal or SEC obligations) to investigate whether the local party has adequate compliance and anti-corruption policies in place. Does it have any history of actual or alleged misconduct? Do any of its owners, directors or employees hold positions as government officials? Is it a "high risk" or "low risk" environment?

Understanding the local law regime

20–13 More specifically for the lawyers, attention should be given to key areas of local law and practice which could materially affect the investment by the foreign party and the establishment or ongoing operations of the proposed joint venture. These issues vary from jurisdiction to jurisdiction. Engagement of lawyers experienced in the local jurisdiction will almost certainly be necessary. The following is a checklist of key questions of local law which frequently arise in relation to international joint ventures, particularly those involving emerging market economies:

(1) *Structure*. What types of legal structure are available for the joint venture vehicle? Chapter 3 has addressed the particular factors which should be taken into account when structuring a venture, but the exact nature of the options available in the particular jurisdiction should be carefully reviewed.

(2) *Tax*. What are the basic corporate tax rates applicable to the operations of the joint venture? What are the rules permitting deduction or set-off of losses and expenditure? Are tax-free "holidays" or customs zones being offered to encourage investment in particular industries or locations? Will withholding taxes apply to dividends? Many countries create free trade areas or economic zones. Foreign companies and international joint venture companies registered in such a zone may have privileges relating to tax, repatriation of profits or capital or export-import incentives. It may be possible, and desirable, to seek advance rulings on the tax status of the proposed joint venture.[10]

(3) *Regulatory controls on foreign participation*. Are there restrictions on foreign participation (including as to the percentage size of any shareholdings) in particular industries? Are there any foreign investment or other governmental/regulatory approvals required for participation by the foreign party or for undertaking of the joint venture operations? Who should make the necessary application? What documentation (e.g. feasibility study) is required? How long is the approval procedure likely to take? Special registration procedures for international joint ventures are required in many countries and, depending on the business sector, authorisation and licensing are frequently required. China and India are two important countries with highly-structured foreign investment review procedures. Russia has recently enacted important laws affecting foreign participation in many industries.

(4) *Industry regulation*. Many industries—such as defence contracting, insurance, telecommunications, media, air and maritime transportation, energy and natural resources—may be closely regulated and involve particular registration and licensing requirements.

---

[10] In some cases, tax planning may lead to structuring the foreign investment through an intermediate country with a favourable double tax treaty with the local jurisdiction (e.g. Cyprus for investment into Russia).

(5) *Exchange control restrictions.* Are there governmental or central bank restrictions, or approvals required, in relation to the foreign acquisition of shares or the payment of dividends by the JVC, or the payment by the JVC for management services or raw materials or goods supplied by the foreign party? Are there restrictions on the conversion of the local currency into hard currency and the use of hard currency for dividend payments? Can capital be repatriated and the venture's profits be distributed to the partners? Do currency controls limit the amount of the loans or foreign borrowings which can be raised? Failure to comply with currency exchange regulations can result in blocked funds which can be used only for domestic payments and not repatriated. In some countries, exporters may be required to deposit all payments in foreign currency with the central bank and have such payments converted into local currency.

(6) *Real property and land rights.* Is property owned by the state? What are the nature of land rights held by the local party or planned to be vested in the JVC? Are these limited in time or subject to restrictions or potential withdrawal? Can land rights be used as security to support borrowings by the JVC? How are any land rights contributed by a local party to be valued?

(7) *Environmental laws.* What laws apply to regulate environmental pollution or abuse? What powers does any governmental authority have to require clean-up or to impose fines or damages? What approvals are required for any new plant? What indemnities or comfort against environmental clean-up costs can realistically be obtained by a foreign investor?

(8) *Capital requirements.* Are there any minimum capital requirements or any maximum permitted debt/equity ratio? Does a capital contribution require registration with any governmental authority? Does a non-cash capital contribution require to be valued by a governmental authority or an independent valuer?

(9) *Management structure.* Are there any specific laws or practices which regulate the form of management structure for a joint venture with a local party? Is there any requirement that a particular management post (e.g. general manager) must be occupied by a national of the local jurisdiction? Are there any requirements relating to nationality or residence of directors?

(10) *Technology transfer.* If the foreign party is to contribute technology or know-how, are there any restrictions on such an arrangement—particularly as regards royalty payments?[11] Can restrictions on use by the local party be imposed or enforced by the foreign party after termination?

---

[11] India is a jurisdiction which imposes constraints on royalty payments.

(11) *Employment laws.* Companies intending to operate through joint ventures need to clarify their obligations to their prospective employees abroad. Are there any material employment laws, such as laws relating to minimum wages; procedures or approvals before making any redundancies or dismissals; requirements for employment of local staff or management; or immigration laws affecting secondments or employment from the foreign party? Are there requirements to employ a specific percentage of local apprentices? Are work permits required for the employment of foreign nationals?

(12) *Intellectual property rights.* Are intellectual property rights (IPR) recognised in the local jurisdiction? Are they capable of effective enforcement? Is the local jurisdiction a party to any international conventions recognising IPR created in another country? Are developments or innovations generated by the JVC capable of independent protection under local law? Are there laws protecting confidential information disclosed to the JVC or later developed by the JVC?

(13) *Liability.* Will the parent joint venture parties have any "vicarious" liability under the local laws for the actions or obligations of the JVC?

(14) *Dispute resolution.* Is there any standard practice as to form of dispute resolution for joint ventures in that jurisdiction? Is arbitration in a venue outside that jurisdiction legally and commercially acceptable? Is the local jurisdiction a signatory to the 1958 New York Convention on the Recognition and Enforcement of Foreign Arbitral Awards? Is enforcement of any award practical?

(15) *Process.* It is important, in any international joint venture, to understand the basic legal documentation which will be required and the formal processes in the particular jurisdiction:

   (a) Is a feasibility study or business plan required as part of the formal process required for obtaining governmental approvals?
   (b) There will usually be by-laws or a charter or other equivalent constitutional document. Is this required to be approved in advance by a local corporate or commercial registry?
   (c) There will also usually be a joint venture agreement or shareholders' agreement. Does this also need to be approved in advance by any governmental body'? Is there a standard or usual form on which this should be based or can it be prepared or adapted by the foreign party? Does it need to be governed by the local law? Does it need to be in the local language?
   (d) Will notarisation be required? In many civil law jurisdictions, in particular, documents are executed in the presence of a public authenticating officer; the degree of formality (e.g. will all documents need to be produced in the local language for the notary?) can add not insignificant delay and expense in establishing the joint venture.

Awareness of the basic rules in these areas at an early stage of planning the joint venture will greatly assist the negotiations and legal process. The country summaries later in this Part D address many of these introductory questions in selected jurisdictions worldwide.

Differences in civil law systems

20–14 Where an international joint venture involves a European civil law country or party, differences encountered are often more of culture and style than legal rules and processes. There is growing similarity between the structures and approach under English common law and continental European civil law systems in relation to joint ventures. The growth of international transactions (and perhaps the influence of UK/US style techniques in this field) has led to increasing convergence in practice and documentation.

20–15 However, important differences remain—sometimes of emphasis and style rather than substance. The following discussion runs the risk of over-generalisation but there are a number of issues or practices where civil law systems tend to differ from the common law approach. It is important, in international joint ventures, for lawyers (whether common law or civil law) to recognise these differences. The following is a discussion on various selected points of comparison.[12]

(1) *Contract drafting.* A broad, philosophical difference underpins a difference in approach to contractual drafting. It is not simply that common law-derived contracts are usually longer and more detailed. As one civil law commentator[13] has remarked:

> "Common law practitioners will attempt to create their own independent little contract world. Statutes and case law are not seen as background law to rely on, but rather as rules which will be incorporated in the terms if deemed useful, or circumvented with great skill if considered a nuisance. Civil law practitioners, on the contrary, tend to see a contract as a means to fit an individual legal situation into a grid of legal rules which consist of entire codifications, such as civil or commercial codes, other statutes and court decisions. They will concentrate on making adjustments to this background law as required by the individual case... Common law contracts will attempt to cover the possibility of possibilities. Civil law contracts will most likely

---

[12] Many of the comparisons are illustrated here by reference to laws in Germany: see generally Eva Micheler and D.D. Prentice (eds), *Joint Ventures in English and German Law* (Hart Publishing, 2000). Each country will, of course, be different and legal advice on a particular transaction should be taken from lawyers in the relevant jurisdiction.
[13] Dr Gerhard Dannemann in *Joint Ventures in English and German Law*, p.2.

outline the main obligations of both parties and cover those situations which have in the past proven to be important, in particular where the draftsperson feels that the position of his or her party is not adequately covered by the background law."

As a consequence, contracts governed by civil law systems tend to be shorter, with more reliance on implied terms or other provisions of the relevant civil code to supplement, or apply "reasonableness" to the interpretation of, the express rights and obligations of the parties.

(2) *Pre-contractual liability in civil law.* Not all joint venture negotiations end in an agreement. Whilst English law has concepts of misrepresentation and confidentiality, many civil law jurisdictions[14] have broader doctrines which may lead to liability for pre-contractual behaviour. For instance, failed negotiations may lead to liability in German law (and most other civil law systems) under the doctrine of *culpa in contrahendo*, or pre-contractual liability, which establishes liability for negligence during contractual negotiations. Liability may also arise if one party leads the other to believe that an agreement is certain, so that costs and management time are expended, but then breaks off the negotiations without any good reason.

(3) *Duty of good faith and equal treatment.* Similar notions of good faith in contractual dealings give rise to wider potential for liability as between shareholder participants in a joint venture company than is traditionally considered to be the case under English law; e.g.

— in Germany, shareholders are subject to a "duty of loyalty" (*Treuepflicht*). This concept sets certain limits to the pursuit of an individual shareholder's interest where that is detrimental to that of the company—although the issue of when a majority shareholder may compete with the company is still unresolved; closely related to a shareholder's "duty of loyalty" is a broad principle of "equal treatment" (*Gleichbehandlungsgrundsatz*) whereby a shareholder may not be treated less preferentially than other shareholders of a particular class without his consent;

— additional duties beyond those expressly set out in the contract may also arise (irrespective of whether a "partnership" exists) due to the concept of "good faith" (*Treu und Glauben*) under the German Civil Code which imposes a general obligation on contractual parties to act in good faith. This may include, for instance, an obligation to inform the other joint venture party of certain developments and events which might materially affect the common undertaking.

(4) *Approach to contract interpretation.* Civil law courts may not apply as literal an approach to contract interpretation as common law courts. In addition to a greater readiness to imply terms or fall back on

---

[14] The Netherlands is a jurisdiction with well developed principles of pre-contractual liability if negotiations are conducted in bad faith.

general principles of the relevant civil code, many civil law courts are willing to investigate more deeply behind the scenes (including looking at past correspondence and conduct) in order to ascertain the true purpose and intent of the parties and/or the most "reasonable" interpretation in the circumstances.

(5) *Due diligence/warranties.* For the reasons outlined earlier, the extent of warranties and indemnities (or associated issues of due diligence) can be a vexed issue in many jurisdictions. A detailed due diligence exercise in a joint venture transaction can seem a mistrustful and, some say, unnecessary approach imported as a result of US/UK style acquisition techniques. Similar arguments apply in relation to the quest for detailed and lengthy warranties. However, in international transactions, there is growing acceptance of the practice. One reason for the conceptual difference in approach is that under English law a seller has no positive obligation to disclose adverse matters—subject to there being no material misrepresentation. Under German law, on the other hand, any party contributing assets in a joint venture transaction will be under an implied duty to disclose information which could have a material negative effect on the valuation of such assets; this disclosure obligation cannot, in principle, be excluded in the joint venture documentation.

(6) *Termination.* Under English law, rights of termination of the joint venture will depend on the terms of the contract (or narrow statutory rights relating to "unfair prejudice" or winding-up on just and equitable grounds). Many civil systems have a more general right of termination. For instance, a principle of the German Civil Code is that any long-term agreement may be terminated by either party for "good cause" (*wichtigerGrund*)—including if the relevant party cannot reasonably be expected to continue its shareholder relationship with the company or the other shareholders. In such an event, unless agreed otherwise, a withdrawing shareholder may be entitled to be compensated by the company in an amount equalling the market value (*Verkehrswert*) of his shares.

(7) *Enforcement and procedural law.* As one commentator[15] has remarked:

> "The differences between common law and civil law in terms of procedure are no less striking, and certainly no less economically relevant, than substantive law differences."

Differences in enforcement and court procedures include:

— one of the more striking differences between common law and civil law litigation relates to the procedure for discovery or disclosure of documents. This just does not exist in the same

---

[15] Dr Gerhard Dannemann in *Joint Ventures in English and German Law*, p.8.

way in the civil law tradition and this procedure can greatly affect the length (and conduct) of litigation proceedings;
— common law courts are more respectful of the wording of statutes and of precedents, whereas civil law courts are more likely to come to a decision which accords with their judicial instincts;
— civil law courts will normally also be more actively involved in the establishment of facts—and frequently become actively involved in the negotiation of an in-court settlement between the parties; litigation is generally cheaper under civil law systems. Many practitioners' fees will be governed by, or influenced by, a fee scale rather than charged by the hour.

(8) *Use of partnership structures.* Turning to structure, although the corporate joint venture is the most popular form, civil law systems generally make greater use of partnerships in planning joint venture structures than in the UK. This is attributable not only to tax and other factors but also to a greater acceptance of and familiarity with the partnership model. Partnerships also offer greater flexibility (e.g. as to contribution of non-cash assets in exchange for capital on formation). Many varieties of partnership are available under civil law systems. These also include a wider use of limited partnerships (such as the GmbH & Co. KG under German law) compared with the UK.

(9) *Governance/management structure.* Whilst most civil law systems enable some modifications to be made to standard governance structures to reflect joint venture arrangements, there is generally less flexibility and certain mandatory rules have to be observed. Using German law again as an example:
— compulsory rules apply, in certain circumstances, for the establishment of a supervisory board (including representation of employees) within a formal two-tier board structure; e.g. in Germany, a company with 500 or more employees must have a supervisory board comprising at least three members, one of whom is appointed by the employees. If a joint venture involves more than 2000 employees, half the members of the supervisory board must be appointed by employees, although the chairman is elected by the shareholder members and has a casting vote;
— duties of directors are strict and no material deviation is allowed from the principal responsibilities of directors to serve the company as a whole and to treat shareholders equally rather than acting in favour of one particular shareholder;
— directors sometimes have a degree of independence which is perhaps greater than that of their UK counterparts. In a German AG, for instance, the directors are not subject to specific instructions from either the shareholders' meeting or the supervisory board. Members of the management board can only be removed by the supervisory board (not the shareholders).

(10) *Articles of association/constitutional documents.* Although the basic documentation in joint ventures is similar, it is perhaps fair to generalise that more provisions (e.g. those relating to minority veto rights or restrictions on transfers of shares) tend to be incorporated into the articles of association or relevant constitutional documents of a joint venture company formed in a civil law country compared with the UK (although practice in the UK does itself vary). This is partly style and tradition, but also recognises under civil law that:

— inclusion of terms in the constitutional documents generally gives more formal notice to third parties than in the UK;
— it is the only way in which directors of the JVC can legally be bound to observe the restrictions (compared with a shareholders' agreement to which they are not usually a party) and this may be appropriate where the directors perhaps have a degree more independence than their UK counterparts of a JVC.

(11) *Remedies for enforcement of shareholders' agreements.* Remedy for breach of the shareholders' agreement will, under certain civil law systems, often be limited to a claim for damages rather than specific performance.[16] A view also prevails in many civil law countries that the articles of association (or other relevant constitutional document) will be given primacy in the event of any conflict with the shareholders' agreement which affects enforcement.

(12) *Process of forming a JVC.* There can also be important differences in the procedures for forming a JVC which have a significant effect on timing and cost of formation. These include rules relating to valuation of non-cash assets contributed to the venture. Regulatory procedures frequently apply in relation to contributions in kind, which can affect both substance and timing; e.g. contributions in kind to both a GmbH and an AG in Germany involve a formal valuation by an independent auditor and the filing of respective certificates with the Commercial Register.

ISSUES IN EMERGING MARKET VENTURES

Joint ventures in "emerging markets"

20–16 Where the joint venture is with a local party in a developing or "emerging market" country, particular issues arise for the lawyers which

---

[16] France is a country where damages, rather than specific performance, will be the primary remedy for breach of a shareholders' agreement. (Elsewhere, India and Japan are other countries where specific performance is an unlikely remedy.)

impact on the content of joint venture documentation as well as the transaction-planning process.

20–17 Issues to be addressed in the contract negotiations and documentation are again not different in kind from those arising in domestic ventures. The precedents and checklists discussed elsewhere in this book will continue to be relevant. However, certain issues frequently cause particular concern and sometimes call for different or special treatment—particularly in the case of ventures involving jurisdictions with less developed legal systems. Particular issues may include the following:

(1) *Identity of contracting party.* This is sometimes not as straightforward as it sounds. The joint venture agreement should identify the full legal name and address of the local party. In the case of a state enterprise, or a state-controlled enterprise, particular attention to detail may be required. The party's foundation documents should be investigated and the authority of the individual or individuals committing the enterprise clearly established. Be clear exactly who is giving warranties and undertakings and/or entering into other legal commitments.

(2) *Representations and warranties.* It may sometimes be difficult (particularly in certain emerging economies) to obtain information about the other contracting party in a manner equivalent to that available for Western companies. Although no substitute for prior due diligence, representations and warranties will often be appropriate. A foreign party should also be prepared to give them on a reciprocal basis. Warranties and representations may operate to affirm that:

— the local party has obtained all requisite authorisations for its participation and has the requisite power to transfer assets to the joint venture and to undertake the joint venture activities contemplated by the agreement;

— no third party has any legal claim, or grounds for claim, against the local party which might hinder or prevent the fulfilment of its obligations under the joint venture arrangements;

— the local party's obligations under the joint venture agreements are valid, binding and enforceable;

— the local party has disclosed all material facts about itself (and its related entities) which are likely to affect its participation in the joint venture arrangements and that specified documents and information provided by the local party during negotiations are not misleading in any material respect.

On the other hand, the foreign party should be wary of being drawn into undue warranties on its part, particularly warranties relating to the performance of technology—e.g. that any production plant to be developed by the joint venture with the foreign party's technology will achieve a specific rate of production or quality or that particular export levels will be achieved (which may all be dependent on many factors outside the foreign party's control).

(3) *Limitations affecting the JVC's operations.* It is important to establish any territorial or other limitations on the intended scope of the JVC's activities in order that this is commercially clear between the parties and to prevent the JVC subsequently competing (e.g. in relation to distribution of products) with the foreign party elsewhere in the world.

(4) *Capital contributions.* The agreement should clearly specify any obligations of the local party to transfer to the joint venture any rights to land or buildings (or to procure the grant of land use rights); the same applies to any obligation to transfer equipment to the JVC. Any agreed mechanism for valuing these contributions should be clearly spelt out.

   (i) Valuation of in-kind contributions of the local party may be difficult—particularly in the case of land, buildings and plant where traditional methods may not be feasible.

   (ii) The timing and pre-conditions (and any cash limit) of the respective contributions of the parties should be clear. In many cases, the foreign party will wish to ensure that its own contribution to the capital of the JVC is not made until the local party has made a contribution of similar value and that the timing of funding is tied to the real financial needs of the joint venture business.

   (iii) Although valuation is usually a matter for commercial negotiations, consider in appropriate cases a verification of value of in-kind contributions by an independent third party (e.g. one of the leading international accounting firms) with, possibly, an obligation on the local party to "make good" any shortfall in value by injection of fresh capital into the JVC.

(5) *Capital structure.* The same issues as regards capital structure and funding arise as for domestic ventures but these can be particularly contentious in the case of some international ventures—leading to the need for clear and unambiguous obligations. What will be the parties' respective equity shares in the JVC? How will the parties finance the JVC on an ongoing basis? Will financing need to be obtained from third parties? What will be the JVC's registered or authorised capital? Howe will future issues of equity capital be authorised?

(6) *Financing guarantees.* As with other joint ventures, it is important to establish what obligation (if any) the parent shareholders—and particularly the foreign party—will have to enter into guarantees, bonds or indemnities to support the provision of finance to the JVC. In this situation, the joint venture agreement should be careful to establish the principle of sharing of any liability incurred under any such guarantees, bonds or indemnities.

(7) *Management structure.* The management and decision-making procedures will be vital and not necessarily as flexible or straightforward as under English law. The process for nominating and electing

directors and officers should be clearly established. It may be desirable to establish that the appointment of certain officers or executive managers (e.g. general manager, chief financial officer, technical manager etc.) will be the entitlement of a particular party. If the foreign party wishes to ensure that it can maintain or assert operational control of the JVC if necessary, this needs to be clearly established—not only in commercial understanding but also in the joint venture documentation. This should apply to each level of management (general meeting, supervisory board, management board, etc.).

(8) *Real property/land.* The local party will often be contributing or leasing land and buildings to the joint venture. Establishing ownership rights to real property can be complex under the laws of some jurisdictions (e.g. Russia). The agreement should be clear as to the rights the JVC will be acquiring and what are the rights of the respective parties on termination.

(9) *Environmental issues.* Controlling a foreign party's exposure to environmental costs and liabilities is frequently a crucial factor of joint venture negotiations in particular regions (e.g. upon privatisations in eastern Europe). A variety of measures may be taken to minimise this risk including:

— undertaking an environmental audit in order to quantify the risk and determine a negotiating policy vis-à-vis the local government or partner;
— establishing an escrow account at the outset whereby a portion of any purchase price paid for assets or other financial contribution by the foreign party is placed in escrow for use in the event of environmental clean-up costs being required within a certain period; and negotiating an indemnity if the local partner or privatising government ministry is prepared to give it; this will sometimes be on the basis of the parties agreeing to share environmental costs or liabilities in specified proportions (i.e. a partial shifting of risk).

(10) *Intellectual property.* Intellectual property laws may not be particularly developed in the local jurisdiction. If the foreign party is making technology available to the JVC or the local party, the terms for that technology transfer and its use should be clearly set out and procedures developed for its orderly transfer.

(i) In order to guard against the risk of "leakage", consider the JVC receiving only a simple (and non-transferable) right of usage of relevant know-how/IPR without access to source code or "black box" technology. Non-disclosure and restricted use obligations should be spelt out contractually (and consider provision for substantial financial payment[17] in the event of breach in order to give added "bite").

---

[17] In some jurisdictions, such provisions may be of doubtful enforceability if construed as a "penalty" (see para.2–09) but may still have value *in terrorem*.

(ii) It will be important that rules regarding use by the parties of intellectual property created by the JVC and its employees are addressed. Employees of the JVC should be obliged to protect the intellectual property of each of the parties and of the JVC itself.
(iii) The position on use of technology after termination of the venture should be clearly established—see generally para.17–23 et seq.

(11) *Accounts*. Accounting standards in many jurisdictions may not be regarded as adequate for the foreign party. In addition to dealing with the appointment of auditors, the joint venture agreement should establish the requirement of the JVC to maintain proper accounts and to provide accounting information on a regular basis to the parent companies. Where practicable, it is desirable to provide that accounts be prepared in accordance with US, UK or international accounting standards as well as any local accounting requirements.

(12) *Dividends*. Provisions relating to dividend policy may depend on whether the foreign party can receive dividends in convertible currency. Foreign investment laws may provide that enterprises are entitled to repatriate profits in hard currency only to the extent that sales have been made in hard currency. One possibility is to provide that no distributions of profit by the JVC should be made unless the foreign party can receive its dividends in convertible currency.

(13) *Compliance/anti-corruption*. The foreign party may (for legal and/or reputational reasons) need to ensure clear commitment to compliance and anti-corruption procedures. These may include provisions:

— to ensure that the JVC adopts corporate policies with regard to compliance and anti-corruption and does not engage in improper activity or influence with government officials;
— representing or warranting that none of the contracts or other assets to be contributed to the JVC by the local party have been procured in violation of applicable anti-corruption or other laws;
— establishing adequate internal controls, compliance procedures and rights to audit;
— regulating the appointment of agents and/or representatives of the JVC (e.g. only to be appointed by the board of the JVC after agreed procedures and undertakings);
— giving the foreign party a right to withdraw or terminate in the event of material breach of any anti-corruption or corporate conduct rules (or, sometimes, if it has reasonable cause to suspect such behaviour).

(14) *Termination/deadlock*. Obviously this is a crucial element of any joint venture but it is particularly important for a foreign party to establish appropriate exit routes. In addition to the customary issues and since transfer of its interest in the JVC to a third party transferee

will generally not be a practical option, the foreign party may seek to establish a put option on a termination or dissolution of the JVC in particular circumstances such as:

— deadlock over a particular period or failure to agree an updated business plan;
— failure of the JVC to make a profit, or to meet certain minimum performance targets, or to meet a technical or construction milestone, within a specified time;
— material breach of corporate compliance and anti-corruption procedures; or
— possibly, a material change in the local regulatory regime applicable to the foreign party and/or the JVC's operations.

Procedures on termination may well not be clear under the local law. A foreign party should ensure that, where necessary, reasonably specific provisions are agreed to clarify the method of dissolution and disposal of assets, including terms to ensure that the JVC's assets are not undervalued and do not pass by default at a favourable price to the local party.

(15) *Dispute settlement.* The dispute resolution provisions will be important since the agreement is unlikely to cover as much ground, or be in as much detail, as might conventionally be desired. Resolution of business disputes will invariably have to be reached between the parties themselves although, on occasions, the inclusion of a mediation procedure may be considered. If a dispute arises regarding the rights or obligations of either party, it will frequently be advisable to provide for arbitration of disputes which cannot amicably be resolved by the parties. If arbitration is chosen, the agreement should specify clearly: the arbitration institution and rules to be used; the number of arbitrators and how they are to be selected; the procedural law to be applied; and the language of the arbitration. See chapter 14 for a further discussion in relation to international arbitration.

20–18 It is frequently not possible, or indeed desirable, in many international joint venture situations to establish joint venture documentation with the same detail as that customarily achieved in most UK/US style transactions. However, the practice and requirements relevant to the particular jurisdiction will always require specific attention. The documentation often has to be guided by the "art of the possible". There is no standard form for such transactions—although there is increasing convergence of practice and approach in many international transactions.[18]

---

[18] The International Trade Centre (ITC) (an agency of the United Nations Conference on Trade and Development and the World Trade Organisation) has, though, been working on certain Joint Venture Model Agreements which may be used by small and medium-enterprises (SMEs) as a "fair" basis in many situations. A copy of the ITC Incorporated Joint Venture Model/Agreement (two party) is reproduced as Precedent 13 in Part E.

Importance of process

20–19 As to transaction process, a joint venture in many developing or "emerging market" countries will be affected by local regulatory requirements, customs and processes. These can be lengthy, bureaucratic and demanding. They will be critical to the successful formation of the venture.

20–20 An example[19] is the highly-regulated process for establishing a joint venture in the People's Republic of China (PRC):

ESTABLISHING AN EQUITY JOINT VENTURE IN THE PRC

The procedures outlined below are based on national regulations and are generally applicable to PRC equity joint ventures, but there are local variations and joint ventures in specific sectors (e.g. financial services) have somewhat different approval requirements.

1. **Letter of intent.** First, there is usually a letter of intent (or project agreement) setting out the salient points of the proposed project. The PRC party is required to submit it to the relevant approving authorities for review with the project proposal. Generally, the letter of intent indicates the willingness of the parties to co-operate in the future and sets out in broad terms the basic parameters of the project. Information regarding the site (if located) and the basic operation and management structure may also be included.

2. **Application report.** This report is submitted to the relevant level of the National Department and Reform Commission (NDRC) for verification and should include a description of the project including:

    (a) name, term, and basic situation regarding the investors:
    (b) scope of the project to be established, products and product market, principal technology and planned number of employees;
    (c) location, requirements with respect to land, water, energy and raw materials;
    (d) environmental impact assessment; and
    (e) total amount of investment, registered capital, capital contribution by parties, financing, and equipment to be used.

    Other supporting materials that must be submitted include (i) incorporation documents for the parties, financial statements of the parties, and a letter of creditworthiness for each party: (ii) letter of intent; (iii) letter of intent from a bank; and (iv) opinion on project location and site to be used by the project.

3. **Approval Authority and limits.** The PRC State Council has given the Ministry of Commerce (MOFCOM) the authority to examine and approve the establishment of FIEs (joint ventures and wholly foreign-owned enterprises) in the PRC. Guidelines for approval of foreign investment projects have been published by the National Development and Reform Commission (NDRC). Broadly, the limits for central and approval are set out below:

---

[19] See the country summaries later in this Part D for outlines of the regulatory process in India, Russian and other countries.

Total Investment and Investment Category	Approval Authority Amount
Projects with investment of $100m, or above and which are in the Encouraged/Permitted Category. Projects with investment of $50m or above and which are in the Restricted Category.	State Council (in respect of projects with a total investment amount of $500m or more) and NDRC for the verification of the project and MOFCOM for the approval of the JV contract and articles of association.
Projects with investment below $100m, and which are in the Encouraged/Permitted Category. Projects with investment below $50m and which are in the Restricted Category.	Provincial/City level of NDRC for the verification of the project and Provincial/City level of MOFCOM for the approval of the JV contract and articles of association.

The approval limits apply specifically to foreign investment projects of a "productive nature." After a project has been approved at the local level, the approval must be filed for the record with central government authorities.

4. **Evaluation of the PRC party's assets.** PRC law requires that State-owned assets being contributed to a joint venture be evaluated by the State Administration of Stateowned Assets. This process will need to be carried out and completed before the joint venture contract is signed.

5. **Enterprise name registration.** All PRC enterprises, including FIEs, are required to register their Chinese enterprise names.

6. **Approval and verification of joint venture contract and articles of association.** Approval and verification of the joint venture contract and articles of association must be obtained from the Approval Authority. The joint venture parties are required to submit the following:

   (a)   application for establishment of joint venture;
   (b)   application report;
   (c)   joint venture contract (generally including as annexes various ancillary contracts, e.g. technology transfer contract, land use agreement, equipment purchase contracts, etc.);
   (d)   articles of association;
   (e)   list of appointments to the board by each party (including chairman and vice chairman);
   (f)   favourable written opinions of the department in charge and provincial or local government; and
   (g)   other required documents and information not listed in the regulations but required in practice, which can include:

   — application report verification and other related documents; business licence of the parties, with seal of original issuing authority (which for the foreign party means the certificate of incorporation or equivalent document from the foreign party's jurisdiction);
   — list of equipment to be imported; and
   — letter of authorisation from the parties' respective legal representatives to their personnel handling the project.

In general, MOFCOM checks a joint venture to ensure three principles: (i) the joint venture conforms to the requirements of PRC foreign investment laws and regulations; (ii) the joint venture's terms and conditions follow the application report as approved by the planning authorities; and (iii) the terms and conditions accord with the principles of equality and mutual benefit. There are, of course, numerous specific rules and guidelines for approval of foreign investment projects. The Approval Authority will examine and either approve or reject the joint venture contract and the articles of association within 30 days. If approved, an approval certificate for the project is then issued, normally to the PRC party who will provide a copy to the foreign party.

7. **Obtaining the business licence.** The PRC party must then file with the provincial or local office of the SAIC for registration certain documents within one month after the receipt of the approval certificate from MOFCOM in order to obtain a business licence. Under PRC law, an enterprise comes into existence upon the issue of the business licence.

8. **Foreign Exchange Registration Certificate (FERC) and bank accounts.** The State Administration of Foreign Exchange (SAFE) issues a FERC, which is needed to open a foreign currency account. The FERC must be applied for within 30 days of obtaining the business licence. A FERC and a "Notice to Open an Account" (issued by SAFE) are required to open a foreign currency account with the local bank. FIEs may also open foreign exchange special purpose accounts for capital account transactions, which still require Safe approval. (The special account may include sub-accounts for registered capital, foreign loans, principal and interest payments etc.) Ceilings on the amount of foreign exchange that may be held in a basic operating account are imposed by PRC regulations.

9. **Contributions by parties.** The parties' capital contributions to a joint venture's registered capital may take a variety of forms, including cash, buildings, land use rights, machinery and equipment, technology and trademarks. Machinery, equipment and other items contributed by a foreign party must be: (i) indispensable to the production of the joint venture; (ii) incapable of being produced in the PRC, or only producable in the PRC at excessively high price, or of unreliable quality and supply; and (iii) priced no higher than the current international market price for similar items. The local bureau of the State Administration of Import and Export Commodity Inspection will appraise, among other things, the "foreign investment property" contributed by foreign investors to the registered capital of the joint venture and property purchased from overseas by foreign investors on behalf of the joint venture.

10. **Investment verification report and certificates.** After the parties have made their investments, an investment verification is carried out by a PRC registered accountant (who may be associated with an international accounting firm) who will issue an investment verification report. The joint venture will then issue investment verification certificates to the parties showing the company's name and date of establishment, the parties' names, investment contributions, date of contributions, and certificate date. The investment verification certificate is also filed with the Approval Authority and the SAFE.

11. **Other authorities.** It may also be necessary for the joint venture to deal with and/or seek approval from other authorities, including:

    (a) the local Labour Bureau on employment issues;

(b)	the local Real Property Administration Bureau, Land Administration Bureau or Building Administration Bureau on real property matters;
(c)	the local Environmental Protection Bureau for environmental appraisals;
(d)	the Technology Import/Export Division of MOFCOM or its local branch on technology transfers;
(e)	the local Tax Bureau for tax registration;
(f)	the local Public Security Bureau for registration of the company and registration of expatriate personnel working for the joint venture;
(g)	the local Customs Bureau to confirm import/export procedures and obtain approval documents;
(h)	the local Finance Bureau for finance registration; and the relevant Administration of Technology Supervision to obtain a "Nationwide Organizations and Institutions Unified Code Certificate".

20–21 Tact, perseverance and discipline will often be required for the negotiation of joint venture arrangements in many developing countries (and the conduct of the venture thereafter). The UK/US style of detailed attention to terms of legal contracts (with comprehensive "what if?" questions) may be alien to the culture of the local party. Judgments will have to be made as to whether an "acquisitive" or "collaborative" approach to negotiations is to be adopted—invariably the latter will be more constructive. At a practical level, thought should be given to the process:

(1) What should be the language of negotiations? How prepared should a foreign party be to undertake negotiations in the local language?

(2) Is a good translator necessary and/or available? Translation is more of an art than a science, and misunderstandings of language can easily arise. Should the translator be present in negotiations? In most cases, such a translator will be important.

(3) Is it feasible to aim to negotiate using the foreign party's own documents as the basis and with English as the governing text, perhaps by demonstrating that it is easier for the foreign party to generate speedy revisions of the text in both English and the local language?

(4) Will it be advantageous to use lawyers with offices in the country where the project or joint venture is to be located?

GOVERNING LAW AND ARBITRATION

Governing law

20–22 Choice of governing law is important in international joint ven-

GOVERNING LAW 509

tures. Even if a detailed contract has been drafted which attempts to set out the rights and obligations of the parties fully, there will often still be gaps to be filled or substantive questions of interpretation which can arise. The governing law of the contract (which will then be the law applicable to the substance of the dispute) should therefore be clearly specified.[20]

(1) *Local law.* It is common, and generally desirable, to select the law of the country in which the JVC is incorporated as the governing law. The law of the place of incorporation will almost certainly govern all matters relating to the powers and constitution of the JVC. The choice of another law may cause extra complications, although this may be preferred where the local law is not considered suitable (or sufficiently developed) to govern the relationship between the joint venture parties.

(2) *"Trade-off" with venue of arbitration.* In the course of negotiations, there may often be a commercial "trade-off" between choice of a national law favoured by one party and choice of a place of arbitration (or institutional arbitration) favoured by another. Factors relating to arbitration and other forms of dispute resolution are discussed in chapter 14.

(3) *Ex aequo et bono.* In some exceptional cases, parties may wish to avoid reference to a national law altogether or to modify a governing law clause by reference to "general principles of law" or by giving the arbitral tribunal power to decide *ex aequo et bono* (in equity and good conscience). These formulations lack certainty, are now rare and should only be used as a last resort.

(4) *Amiable compositeurs.* Another possibility in some exceptional cases, particularly in ventures involving civil law countries, is to give an arbitral tribunal powers to act as *amiable compositeurs*. Under this concept (better understood in civil law countries such as France, where it originated), the tribunal need not apply strict legal rules of interpretation to the obligations of the parties, if they consider that a strict legal approach would lead to an inequitable result.[21]

20–23 Many international joint ventures involve a state agency as a party. A private entity will be under considerable commercial pressure to agree

---

[20] The law of the place of arbitration will almost invariably govern the conduct of the proceedings, but it will not govern the substantive dispute (unless the parties expressly provide for that to be the case). In the interests of certainty, a governing national law should therefore be specified in any international joint venture.
[21] The UK Arbitration Act 1996 (s.46) expressly recognises that parties may agree that their dispute is not to be decided in accordance with the recognised law of a particular country but in accordance with "such other considerations as are agreed by them"—in other words, pursuant to general principles of equity and fairness. The 1996 Act does not specifically refer to the principle of *ex aequo et bono* or *amiable compositeurs*, but it clearly envisages that the parties should be able to give the tribunal the power to act in this way, if they choose to do so.

that the law governing the contract should be that of the state concerned. This sometimes raises the fear (perhaps less now as the importance of an international trading reputation has grown for developing countries) that the state party may subsequently use its powers to alter the law, and hence the contractual regime, without the consent of the private party.

(1) One technique to protect the foreign party (but now rarely seen) is to couple the law of the state party with a reference to public international law or to general principles of law (see para.20–22 earlier).

(2) Another used to be to attempt to "freeze" the law of the state party so that the relevant law is expressed to be the law in force at the date of the contract—thus (theoretically at least) preventing any subsequent change in the law to the detriment of the private party. However, these provisions will need specific local advice to establish if the state can so restrict its future legislative policy. They will rarely be attainable.

(3) A more reliable and practical approach is to include specific provisions in the joint venture agreement which trigger a review (or, preferably, termination) in the event of any significant change in the law or regulatory regime—or provide for compensation if the law is changed so as to affect adversely the foreign party's interests.

In most cases, though, risk of local regulatory change must be accepted as part-and-parcel of doing business in that jurisdiction.

20–24 In some rare cases, it may be convenient for matters relating to the powers and the constitution of the JVC to be governed by the mandatory provisions of the local law and for all other matters between the parties to be expressed to be governed by a (more acceptable or suitable) foreign law.

(1) In this regard, art.3(1) of the 1969 Rome Convention on the Law Applicable to Contractual Obligations contemplates that different parts of the same contract may be governed by different laws; the rationale being that severability should be allowed provided that the choice of different laws is logically consistent (i.e. the choice must relate to elements in the contract which can be governed by different laws without giving rise to contradictions). "Split laws" have also been upheld by the English courts.[22]

(2) However, it can never be certain that such a "split law" will be upheld by the relevant court or arbitral tribunal in the particular situation. Even if different parts of a contract are said to be governed by different laws, difficulties may arise—e.g. if the issue whether one party may terminate or withhold performance on account of the other

---

[22] See *Libyan Arab Foreign Bank v Bankers Trust Company* [1989] 3 All E.R. 252.

party's breach and the underlying contractual obligation itself are purportedly governed by different laws.

(3) It is highly desirable, if a "split law" is chosen, that the agreement should set out precisely which law is to govern which provisions of the agreement. Any ambiguity can lead to expensive and time-consuming disputes in future.

Arbitration

20–25 Arbitration, as a method of final dispute resolution, is a common feature of international joint venture agreements. Arbitration in a neutral venue can provide some protection or comfort for a foreign party. There is much merit in such an approach. Care should nevertheless be taken with the choice of arbitral institution. A fuller discussion of the advantages/disadvantages of arbitration and possible arbitral institutions to be considered appears in chapter 14.

SELECTED JURISDICTIONS

20–26 It is not practical in a work of this kind to provide a comprehensive review of, or indeed to summarise, the joint venture laws of all jurisdictions worldwide. There follows in the remainder of Part D of this book summaries of the legal framework affecting joint ventures in a selected number of important jurisdictions, namely:

1. Brazil
2. China
3. Czech Republic
4. France
5. Germany
6. India
7. Italy
8. Japan
9. The Netherlands
10. Poland
11. Russia
12. South Africa
13. Spain
14. United States

These summaries are, of course, in outline only. Many details, conditions and qualifications may affect a particular situation and specific advice should always be taken in relation to each joint venture.

(1) Brazil

Authors: Syllas Tozzini and Renato Berger
Tozzini, Freire, Teixeira e Silva Advogados, São Paulo

1. General background

Are joint ventures popular as a form of foreign investment into your jurisdiction?

The major forms of direct foreign investment in Brazil are the creation of a wholly-owned subsidiary, the acquisition of an existing Brazilian company and the formation of a joint venture. All are popular. The choice will be primarily motivated by business factors.

Are there restrictions on foreign participation?

As a general rule, foreigners may invest in any and all activities not expressly restricted under the Federal Constitution.

Foreign investment restrictions remain in certain areas, however, such as nuclear energy, rural property ownership, border activities, health care services, mail and telegraph, domestic aviation and aerospace. Also, foreigners cannot hold more than 30 per cent of Brazilian press and broadcasting companies.

In addition, until the enactment of a new law regulating the Brazilian financial system, the opening of new branches of foreign financial institutions and increases in the percentage participation of foreign individuals or legal entities in the corporate capital of Brazilian financial institutions are prohibited. However, the Brazilian President may authorise new investments from foreign investors or increases in existing levels of participation of foreign investors in Brazilian financial institutions.

An Amendment passed in 1995 to the Federal Constitution removed foreign investment restrictions in certain other economic sectors (including petroleum, mining, domestic transportation and local gas service activities).

What (if any) are the major legal problems which a foreign investor in a joint venture faces in your jurisdiction?

Foreign investors should not expect to face major legal problems solely by virtue of participating in a joint venture or as a result of their nationality. The legal treatment accorded to those participating in a joint venture, regardless of nationality, is substantially the same, and foreign investors in general are not faced with major legal difficulties.

2. Governmental/regulatory approvals

What principal governmental or regulatory approvals are required (excluding competition law) for establishing a joint venture?

A joint venture does not require any different or specific regulatory approvals compared to any other enterprise. These depend on the activities to be undertaken on a case-by-case basis. No specific approvals result from foreign participation in the joint venture.

Are there local anti-trust laws which might apply to the formation of the joint venture?

In general terms, Brazilian law follows the US competition law model. In Brazil, though, there is no bar on closing and no mandatory waiting period, thereby allowing the parties to close the transaction at their own risk. The Brazilian anti-trust authority (*Conselho Administrativo de Defesa Economica-CADE*) nevertheless has the discretionary power to impose whatever measures it deems necessary to remedy any anti-competitive consequences resulting from a given transaction. A brief summary appears below:

Filing requirement/ trigger	Timetable for clearance	Test for clearance
Applies to a JV which qualifies as full-function. Test: the combined market share is 20 per cent or more of a relevant market or the group of one of the controlling parents has a turnover in Brazil of at least BRL 400 million (approx. €115.2 m).	The Brazilian decision is handled by four distinct offices and ministries, so that in total, the full assessment can take up to 120 days from filing. Fast track: 90 days. These deadlines, however, are suspended if a request for additional information is issued. In practice, less complex cases: four months. For more complex cases: six months-one year. The JV may be implemented before a clearance decision is received. However, suspension can be ordered where there is a high level of market concentration.	Whether the JV will create or strengthen a dominant position or whether it will lead to a lessening or restriction of competition. *Mandatory/voluntary Penalties* Filing is mandatory within 15 working days starting from the first binding document signed by the parties. Failure to notify or late notification: fines averaging approx. BRL 200,000 (approx €50,000 m).

3. Types of joint venture vehicle

What are the principal types of joint venture vehicle commonly used with foreign investors?

Joint ventures are usually structured through the establishment of a joint venture company. Brazilian laws provide for several types of company forms, of which the *Sociedade Limitada* ("Limitada": a limited liability company) and the *Sociedade Anonima* ("SA": a corporation) are most commonly used. Other legal forms have little use, particularly because most of them provide for unlimited liability of their members.

As a consequence of the Brazilian Civil Code enacted in 2002, which replaced the existing regulations dealing with a Limitada, the use of this type of company for joint ventures may reduce. This is because certain fundamental matters affecting the company will require approval from partners representing at least 75 per cent of its capital, which may not be appropriate depending on the intended capital structure and division of powers among prospective participants in a joint venture. For instance, if the joint venture has a minority party holding at least 25 per cent of the Limitada capital, a number of major decisions could not be taken without the approval of that party, which may be contrary to the structure envisioned by the participants.

However, if these requirements are not an obstacle to the specific joint venture, the Limitada (in contrast to the SA) is not required to publish financial records and statements—resulting in cost savings and confidentiality benefits for the Limitada. Unlike the Limitada, the SA may issue securities to the public to fund its activities. The Limitada and SA are accorded the same treatment under Brazilian tax legislation.

4. Capital structure and funding

Is it common to have different "classes" of shares (e.g. A and B shares) to reflect different initial contributions or financial interests of the parties?

Limitada. The capital of a Limitada is represented by units called "quotas", with no issuance of certificates of ownership. Owners of quotas are normally designated "quotaholders". The capital is denominated in Brazilian currency and recorded in the articles of association, as amended from time to time to reflect any assignment and transfer of quotas and capital increases and reductions. There are generally no different classes of quotas.

SA. The capital of the SA is divided into shares. There is no issuance of share certificates. Share ownership is evidenced by record in the registered share book or through a statement issued by a financial institution acting as depositary agent. The shares of the SA may be divided into several share classes based on the rights and obligations attached to each specific class. A publicly-held SA may have different classes of preferred shares, but only one class of common shares. A privately-held SA may have different classes of preferred shares, and also more than one class of common shares, which may (i) be convertible into preferred shares, (ii) restrict ownership to Brazilian citizens or (iii) grant a separate right to appoint members of management bodies.

Is it common to have "preference" shares which give a party a priority on payment of dividends or on a return of capital?

Limitada. In the Limitada, there are usually no preferred quotas and all quotas generally confer the same rights over dividends and on a return of capital. However, the articles of association of the Limitada may provide for profit distributions which are not in proportion to the quota interests of quotaholders and result in dividend structures that resemble a preferred share.

SA. In the SA, preferred shares are common. Preferred shareholders whose shares are not admitted for trading in the securities market are entitled to: (i) priority distribution of fixed or minimum dividends, which may be cumulative or not; (ii) priority in the reimbursement of capital upon liquidation of the company, with or without a premium; or (iii) a combination of items (i) and (ii).

Are "redeemable" shares permitted (i.e. shares that can be repaid and cancelled)?
The by-laws or the general shareholders meeting of the SA may authorise the company to use accumulated profits or profit reserves in the redemption of shares. Unless the by-laws provide otherwise, the redemption of shares can only be effected if approved in a prior special meeting by shareholders representing at least half of the affected shares.

Are "non-voting" shares permitted?

Limitada. The law does not provide for non-voting quotas in a Limitada.

SA. The SA, both publicly-held and privately-held, may have more than one class of preferred shares without voting rights. For an SA incorporated after October 31, 2001 (date of approval of a major revision of the Brazilian Corporation Law), the number of non-voting or restricted voting preferred shares cannot exceed 50 per cent of the total number of issued shares.

Are there any local laws which require an independent valuation of any non-cash assets to be contributed to the joint venture?

Limitada. In a Limitada, the value of moveable or immovable property contributions is not subject to expert appraisal, and may be established by mutual agreement of the quotaholders. However, all quotaholders are jointly liable for five years with respect to any deficiency between the actual value of the assets and the value attributed to them at the time of the capital contribution.

SA. In a SA, assets to be contributed as capital must have their value determined by expert appraisal and approved by the shareholders.

If a foreign party is to contribute technology to the joint venture, are there any special requirements for valuation of that technology?
Although the foreign party may transfer technology to the joint venture in exchange for royalty payments, technology may not be contributed as capital to a joint venture company.

Are there exchange control regulations which materially affect the establishment of the joint venture-or the subsequent repatriation of profits or dividends from the joint venture to a foreign party?
Registration of foreign capital must be made with the Central Bank of Brazil (abbreviated as "BACEN"). Current legislation guarantees equal treatment of foreign and national capital. Foreign capital is defined to mean currency or goods (machinery, equipment, trademarks, patents and technology) which belongs to individuals or legal entities resident, domiciled or with a head office abroad. Capital and profit repatriations relating to foreign capital duly registered with BACEN may be made at any time without the prior authorisation of BACEN, subject to compliance with applicable corporate and tax legislation.

5. Tax

Are there any particular tax laws or incentives which significantly affect the establishment of joint ventures in this jurisdiction by a foreign investor?

There is no extra tax benefit and/or extra burden directly related to the establishment of a joint venture in Brazil by a foreign investor. However, depending on the type of activities to be developed, as well as the region in Brazil in which the businesses will be carried out, it is possible for any company established in Brazil (whether a joint venture or not) to apply for certain tax benefits.

Profits arising from activities carried out in Brazil or abroad by a Brazilian company are subject to corporate income tax and a tax called social contribution on profits. For any company with a taxable income exceeding BRL 240,000 per year, the respective rates of these taxes are presently 25 per cent and nine per cent, resulting in a combined rate of 34 per cent. In addition to corporate income taxes, Brazilian companies are subject to certain other types of taxes, including taxes on revenues, taxes on production and circulation of goods etc.

Will withholding taxes apply to dividends paid by a joint venture company?

Dividends with respect to profits earned on or after January 1996 are currently exempt from withholding income tax.

6. Board and management

Are there local law rules which affect the board or management structure of the joint venture? May a two-tier board be required?

Limitada. Management of the Limitada must be vested in one or more resident individuals, appointed in the articles of association or in a separate document. Managers may or may not be quotaholders, but in the latter case the articles of association must expressly authorise the appointment of non-quotaholder managers. Whenever the articles of association establish that all quotaholders will be managers of the company, such attribution does not apply automatically to new quotaholders. The Limitada is liable for all acts performed on its behalf by managers acting within the scope of their powers.

SA. Management of an SA is vested in a *conselho de administraçao* (board of directors) and a diretoria (executive officers). The board of directors is optional in the case of a privately-held S.A., provided that its by-laws do not specify an authorised capital level. Members of the board of directors are elected at a general shareholders meeting and are known as *conselheiros*. The board of directors of an SA is empowered inter alia to direct the company's business, elect and remove the company's officers, establish their duties and responsibilities and supervise their activities, approve certain issuances of shares, decide on the disposal of assets, encumbrances, guarantees and obligations assumed on behalf of third parties, unless the by-laws provide otherwise.

Each SA must have at least two executive officers (*diretores*), who may or may not be shareholders. Executive officers must be elected by the board of directors, if one exists, or otherwise at a general shareholders meeting. Up to one-third of the members of the board of directors may also serve as executive officers. The duties of the officers may be established by the board of directors or in the by-laws.

Are there local law constraints on persons who can be directors or managers of the joint venture (e.g. only local residents or nationals)?

Management of the *Limitada* must be vested in resident individuals. The board of directors of the SA must comprise at least three individual shareholders, who need not be resident in Brazil. Non-resident directors must be represented in Brazil by an attorney-in-fact. Executive officers of the SA must be resident in Brazil.

Does a shareholder in a joint venture company owe a duty of good faith (or similar duty) to other shareholders in the way it behaves in relation to the joint venture?

All shareholders must exercise their voting rights in the best interests of the company.

The exercise of voting rights will be deemed abusive whenever aimed at harming the company or other shareholders or at generating any undue benefits to the relevant shareholder at the expense of the company or other shareholders. Shareholders may be liable for exercising voting rights in an abusive manner, even if their vote did not prevail in the applicable deliberation.

Can you modify the legal duties of directors so that they can expressly take into account the interests of their "appointer" when voting or acting as director-or must they always act objectively in the best interests of the company?

The law recognises the validity of a shareholders' agreement which regulates the votes to be cast by members of the board of directors. During the relevant board meeting, any votes that are not compatible with the provisions of the shareholders' agreement shall not be counted.

However, some construe this rule independently from the duties applicable to directors. On this interpretation, the directors should always vote according to what they believe is in the best interests of the company (even if such vote will not be counted on the basis of the earlier rule). By doing this, the director would ensure that no liability will attach to her/ him as a consequence of harmful or illicit deliberations.

7. Transfer of shares

In the case of a joint venture company, can a permanent restriction on transfer of shares be imposed under the local law (e.g. no transfer without the consent of the other shareholder)?

SA. Yes. In the SA, a shareholders' agreement may be executed to regulate the transfer of shares held by the parties to the agreement. In such agreement, a number of structures can be created by the parties, ranging from simple transfer restrictions to tag along rights, drag along rights etc. Once the shareholders' agreement is filed with the company and annotated in its books, it becomes valid and binding with respect to the company and third parties.

Limitada. Yes. The parties to a Limitada may also establish restrictions on the transfer of quotas by virtue of specific provisions inserted in the articles of association.

8. Protection for minority shareholders

Are there any statutory rules or remedies which help significantly to protect a minority shareholder in a joint venture company?

SA. There are various legal provisions affecting the rights of minority shareholders in the SA. The law ensures that all shareholders are entitled to participate in the company's profits and proceeds of dissolution, may inspect the business of the company, have pre-emptive rights on the subscription of new shares and other securities that are convertible into shares (save for certain exceptions if the SA is publicly-held), and have dissent and withdrawal rights in certain circumstances provided by law, including major changes to the company structure (reduction of compulsory dividends, changes in corporate purposes, certain mergers etc.) and changes that are prejudicial to a given class of shareholders (creation of a more favoured preferred class, modifications in redemption terms etc).

Limitada. In the Limitada, quotaholders are entitled to general dissenting and withdrawal rights, are entitled to participate in the company's profits as established in the articles of association, and may be protected by virtue of voting quorums specified in the articles of association, or as a result of the mandatory quorum of at least 75 per cent in certain fundamental matters as indicated below.

Does the law require any major business decisions to be approved by a special resolution or super-majority (whether at board or shareholder level)-or must a minority party protect itself by contract?

SA. In the SA, the following matters require approval from shareholders representing at least half of the voting shares, which quorum may be increased in the by-laws of a privately-held SA: (i) the creation of preferred shares or a disproportionate increase in existing classes, unless contemplated in the by-laws, (ii) a change in the redemption or amortisation terms of one or more classes of preferred shares or the creation of a new, more favoured class, (iii) the reduction of compulsory dividends, (iv) merger, (v) participation in a group of companies, as defined by law, (vi) a change in corporate purposes, (vii) cessation of liquidation procedures, (viii) the creation of securities known as beneficiary parts, (ix) spin-off and (x) dissolution.

Limitada. In the Limitada, the following matters require approval from quotaholders representing at least 75 per cent of the total capital: (i) amendments to the articles of association, (ii) merger, (iii) dissolution and (iv) cessation of liquidation procedures.

9. Employment laws

Are there any material employment laws (compared with the UK) which are likely to affect the ongoing operations of the joint venture?

Brazilian labour laws always apply to any employment relationship, regardless of the company form adopted by the employer, thus including any type of joint venture. The basic principles concerning labour relations are consolidated in the Labour Code of 1943. Since then, however, various statutes have been passed covering wage increases, social security and pension funds, strikes, health and safety standards, and protection of certain specific classes of workers. The 1988 Federal Constitution also granted certain rights to city and rural workers, which overruled some of those provided for in the Labour Code.

As far as labour liabilities are concerned, the concept of economic group is of particular importance to joint ventures. Companies belonging to a group of legal entities under the same control, direction or management are jointly liable for the obligations of any company belonging to the group in connection with any employment relationship. In addition, parties to a joint venture may be liable for labour obligations of the joint venture company whenever the company is unable to fulfil them.

10. Accounts

Is there a requirement on the joint venture company to file accounts with any authority where they are publicly available?

Limitada. Financial statements of the Limitada need not be published or filed with any authority.

SA. Financial statements of the SA, including an annual balance sheet, accumulated profit and loss statement, income statement and source and application of funds statement, must be published in the official gazette and in one widely circulated newspaper. A privately-held SA with less than 20 shareholders and a net capital of less than BRL 1,000,000 is exempted from such publication, but in that case the financial statements must be filed with the commercial registry. The financial statements of a publicly-held SA must also be filed with the Brazilian Securities Commission (CVM).

11. Dispute resolution

Is there any standard local practice as to form of dispute resolution in relation to joint ventures with foreign investors? Is arbitration in a venue outside that jurisdiction acceptable?

The selection of arbitration as the preferred form of dispute resolution has been growing considerably in the past years. At the end of 2001, the Brazilian Supreme Court issued a major decision affirming the constitutionality of the Brazilian Arbitration Law of 1996, thereby recognising the enforceability of arbitration clauses inserted in private agreements. This decision significantly encouraged the use of arbitration in Brazil. In addition, the selection of a venue outside Brazil for arbitration proceedings relating to a joint venture with a foreign party would be valid and legal.

Is the local jurisdiction a signatory to the 1958 New York Convention on the Recognition and Enforcement of Foreign Arbitral Awards?

Yes.

12. Legal documents and formalities

Is there any special form of legal documentation required under local law for establishment of a joint venture company? What are the usual principal documents?

To constitute a *Limitada*, at least two individuals or legal entities must sign a contrato social (articles of association) and comply with the registration requirements of the state in which the head office of the company is to be located.

An SA is constituted by the public or private subscription of the company's capital by at least two individuals or legal entities. Upon full subscription of the capital, the formation of the SA must be approved at a general shareholders meeting. Private subscription is subject to the approval of subscribers of capital at a general shareholders' meeting or to the execution of a public deed, including approval of the proposed by-laws of the company. Once approved, the by-laws must be registered and published. Corporate documents of the SA are registered with the competent state commercial registry.

Does the joint venture documentation need to be in the local language and/or governed by the local law?

Both the articles of association of the Limitada and the by-laws of the SA must be written in Portuguese and governed by Brazilian law.

Are there any commonly-accepted "standard forms" for joint ventures with foreign investors in your jurisdiction?

There are no standard forms for the creation of a joint venture with a foreign party, since the details and characteristics of each joint venture will have to be reflected and established in the articles of association of the Limitada or the by-laws of the SA. In Brazil, the articles of association and the by-laws are not mere formalities but major documents which support most of the joint venture relationship together with any shareholders' or quotaholders' agreement.

Are agreements between shareholders (e.g. as to appointment of directors, conduct of the business of the company or voting majorities required for certain decisions etc) enforceable under local law? In the event of breach, is specific performance or a similar remedy available-or only damages?

The validity and enforceability of shareholders agreements in the SA are expressly recognised by law, and specific performance is available if the agreement is breached. The company will be required to comply with shareholder agreements on file at its head office.

Although not expressly provided by law with respect to a *Limitada*, quotaholders agreements are generally deemed valid and enforceable as well. As far as specific performance, it is also possible to construe that a general provision of the Brazilian Civil Procedure Code recognising specific performance as a legal remedy shall apply in relation to a quotaholders agreement.

Are restrictions relating to (a) transfers of shares and/or (b) minority "veto rights" commonly included in the articles of association or by-laws of the company-or included in a separate shareholders' agreement?

In the SA, restrictions relating to transfer of shares and exercise of voting rights are normally included in a shareholders' agreement.

In the Limitada, it is advisable to include the rules governing the transfer of quotas in the articles of association. This is because the law expressly states that the transfer of quotas shall be regulated in the articles of association, which may lead to the interpretation that a quotaholders agreement may not be enough to ensure the enforceability of the applicable restrictions. Supermajority requirements which effectively confer veto rights upon minority quotaholders are also normally included in the articles of association.

Are there any formalities (e.g. notarisation or registration) which are material and which may affect the timing involved in forming the joint venture?

In general, no prior governmental consents or approvals are required for the formation of the joint venture company. Consequently, the filing of the articles of association or the by-laws with the competent state commercial registry will be enough to ensure the legal creation of the company.

However, there are certain registration requirements that must be observed before the company can legally initiate its activities. Such requirements include registration with the tax authorities, registration with the Ministry of Labour, payment of the applicable trade union tax, registration with the social security authorities, as well as the receipt of a municipal licence to do business.

(2) China

Authors: Carl Cheng, Tianfu Liu and Andrew Gardner
Freshfields Bruckhaus Deringer LLP, Shanghai

1. General background

Are joint ventures popular as a form of foreign investment?
The joint venture (JV) was the first form of foreign investment permitted by law in 1979 in the People's Republic of China (PRC) and has been much used since then. In recent years, however, the wholly foreign-owned enterprise (WFOE) has become the more popular form of foreign invested enterprise (FIE).

Are there restrictions on foreign participation?
Yes. For a joint venture to qualify as an FIE, the foreign party is required to contribute at least 25 per cent of the joint venture's registered capital. In principle, there is no upper limit, except that establishment of a WFOE may be restricted or prohibited in certain industry areas.

Industries or service sectors in which foreign investment is restricted or prohibited are set out by the National Development and Reform Commission (NDRC) (formerly the State Development and Planning Commission) and the Ministry of Commerce (MOFCOM) in the *Foreign Investment Guidance Catalogue* which is updated from time to time. The Catalogue classifies industries and services into "Encouraged", "Restricted" and "Prohibited" Categories. Those not listed are simply "Permitted". In certain sectors, the Catalogue places specific caps on the proportion of equity that can be held by foreign investors in an FIE, whereas in certain other sectors the Catalogue simply states that foreign investment may only take the form of a JV without providing a specific cap on foreign participation. WFOEs are permissible in a wide range of areas, particularly under the Encouraged Category. Under the Prohibited Category, foreign investment is barred completely.

In the most recent version, effective December 1, 2007, the Encouraged Category has been expanded significantly. Modern logistics and service outsourcing have been added to the Encouraged Category, bringing China further into line with its World Trade Organisation (WTO) commitments. Projects bringing in new technology, high-tech equipment manufacturing and management expertise are further encouraged, while certain conventional manufacturing areas in which China already possesses sufficient capacity have now been placed in the Restricted Category. State control over media and publishing is further strengthened by the addition of various internet businesses to the Prohibited Category.

Another major focus of the revisions is the environment. A range of environmentally friendly and "green-tech" sectors have been included under the Encouraged Category, while mining rare or non-renewable minerals, and industries with high resource or energy usage (like paper, steel, aluminium, and cement) have become restricted or prohibited.

What (if any) are the major legal problems which a foreign investor in a joint venture faces in your jurisdiction?
Some of the major legal problems include the following:

- *Control of foreign investment*. The Chinese government controls the level of foreign shareholdings in companies. The Foreign Investment Guidance Catalogue sets the permissible level of foreign investment. As a part of China's WTO commitments, the restrictions on foreign investments have been relaxed in certain industries. However, certain types of investments are still prohibited and the level of foreign investment in others remains restricted.

- *Governmental approvals*. Foreign investments require governmental approval and verification, which can be time-consuming. Depending on whether the investment is classified as restricted, encouraged or permitted and the amount of the investment, approvals and verifications from the central, provincial, or local branches of MOFCOM and NDRC may be required. Additionally, investment in certain industries requires the approval of the relevant industry regulator.

- *Land*. China has complex land legislation; e.g. agricultural land cannot be used for industrial purposes without obtaining approval from the competent local authority to convert it into industrial land. Land is also divided into state owned land and collectively owned land.

- *Foreign exchange control*. China has complex foreign exchange controls. Although the local currency, the Renminbi (RMB) is convertible on the current account, current account transactions may require extensive documentation. RMB is not convertible for capital transactions unless an approval has been obtained from the State Administration of Foreign Exchange.

- *Intellectual property enforcement*. Enforcement of legal rights remains a serious problem in China, however. Although since as early as 1994 the Supreme People's Court has encouraged lower courts with many intellectual property cases to set up specialised intellectual property divisions, the courts can vary significantly in the quality of personnel. In addition, a local court receives most of its funding and services from its local government, and is therefore often susceptible to local pressures.

2. Governmental/regulatory approvals

What principal governmental or regulatory approvals are required (excluding competition law) for establishing a joint venture?

A joint venture involving foreign investors requires various planning, environmental and foreign investment approvals or verifications. In addition, construction and various industry-specific approvals may also be necessary. Authority to approve JVs may be delegated to the provincial, or local level, depending on the size of the project, its categorisation under the Foreign Investment Guidance Catalogue and other conditions. (See the more detailed description of the approval process in chapter 20 at para.20–18.)

Previously, NDRC or its local commission was responsible for evaluating a proposed foreign investment project in the context of China's macroeconomic policy (the so called "Five-Year Plans") and the Foreign Investment Guidance Catalogue, and would examine and approve the project proposal and feasibility study report for the project. MOFCOM or its local bureau was responsible for examining the contractual terms of the foreign investment, and would examine and approve the JV contract and articles of association. However, the "State Council Decision on the Reform of the Investment System" promulgated on July 17, 2004 (the State Council Decision) has somewhat changed the foreign investment approval process.

The State Council Decision provides that all foreign investment projects will be subject to a verification process. The verification process, like the former approval process, is conducted at the level of the central government or the local government depending on the size of the project's total investment amount as follows:

(1) For foreign investment projects which are encouraged or permitted in accordance with the Foreign Investment Guidance Catalogue, central government verification is required when the project's total investment is US$100m or above.

(2) For foreign investment projects which are restricted in accordance with the Foreign Investment Guidance Catalogue, central government verification is required when the project's total investment is US$50m or above.

Currently, NDRC is in charge of verification of the "application report" (in the place of the project proposal and the feasibility study report as required in the old regime) while MOFCOM is responsible for approval of the contracts and the articles of association. However, the main difference seems to be that the project proposal and the feasibility study report under the old regime have been merged into the new "application report". Note that the verification requirement is not currently being implemented in all localities.

Total Investment and Investment Category	Approval / verification authority
Projects with investment of $100m or above in the Encouraged/Permitted Category.	State Council (in respect of projects with a total investment amount of $500m or more) and NDRC for the verification of the project and MOFCOM for the approval of the JV contract and articles of association.
Projects with investment of $50m or above in the Restricted Category.	
Projects with investment below $100m in the Encouraged/Permitted Category.	Provincial/City level of NDRC for the verification of the project and Provincial/City level of MOFCOM for the verification of the JV contract and articles of association.
Projects with investment below $50m in the Restricted Category.	

The main steps in the approval process include: (i) preliminary approval for the project including consent from relevant industry departments and planning authorities; (ii) verification of the project by NDRC or its local commission; (iii) formal approval of the signed JV contract and articles of association by MOFCOM or its local commission; and (iv) the issuance of the business licence by the state or local Administration of Industry and Commerce (the SAIC).

Are there local anti-trust laws which might apply to the formation of the joint venture?

China recently adopted its first comprehensive competition law, the Antimonopoly Law (AML), on August 30, 2007. The AML will become effective on August 1, 2008.

The AML contains merger control provisions which provide that a concentration of undertakings that meets the "relevant thresholds" will be required to file a notification with the Anti-Monopoly Enforcement Authority, failing which the undertakings will be prohibited from implementing the concentration. The AML does not set out the specific thresholds for notification filing but indicates that such thresholds will be stipulated by the State Council in subsequent implementation regulations. It is expected that these implementation regulations will be published by August 1, 2008.

The Anti-Monopoly Enforcement Authority may also block, or approve subject to restrictive conditions, concentrations that have or may have the effect of eliminating or restricting competition.

A "concentration of undertakings" is defined to mean any of the following: mergers; acquisition of control of other undertakings through means of acquisition of shares or assets; or acquisition of control or the capability of imposing decisive influence over other undertakings by contract or other means. However, "control" or "decisive influence" are not defined in the AML. The State Council is expected to publish implementation regulations which should also help clarify these terms.

If the local party is a public company, when might the approval of its shareholders be required under stock exchange or similar rules?

If the investment in the JV is deemed a "significant investment", then according to the standard articles of association of the typical PRC listed company (any deviations from the standard articles of association would need to be explained to the relevant authorities), the board of directors of such listed company is responsible for organising an evaluation by experts and also reporting the investment to the shareholders meeting for approval. There are also disclosure requirements for the making of "significant investments" by PRC listed companies under the relevant rules issued by China Securities Regulatory Commission.

3. Types of joint venture vehicle

What are the principal types of joint venture vehicle commonly used with foreign investors?

There are two forms of joint venture: the equity joint venture (EJV) and the cooperative joint venture (CJV), each governed by a separate law and implementation regulations. Each of these laws has been amended to bring China's joint venture rules into line with WTO requirements.

(i) **EJV**

An EJV is similar to a limited liability company in that a legal entity is formed to which the parties contribute capital and take equity interests in proportion to the size of their investment. There are no shareholders in an EJV; instead, the investors control the operation of the company directly through their appointees to the board of directors.

An EJV may have an unlimited term of duration; this is, however, dependent on the business of the EJV and other circumstances. Since government policy plays a large role in the granting of such rights, EJVs with unlimited terms are still fairly rare. For the majority of EJVs, a fixed term of years is still the norm, although the term may be up to 50 years.

Parties to an EJV share the EJV's net profits in accordance with the ratio of their capital contributions to the enterprise after payment of taxes and contributions to the required reserve funds.

(ii) **CJV**

There are two types of CJV. The first type is often referred to as a "co-operative" enterprise and is very much like the EJV in that a legal entity similar to the limited liability company is created. The co-operative entity is managed by a board of directors. Certain fundamental matters require the unanimous decision of the board of directors, such as amendment of the articles of association, increase or decrease in registered capital, dissolution, merger or restructuring. In the second type of CJV, no legal entity is created and all aspects of business relations between the parties are to be stipulated in the JV contract. CJVs without legal status must be directed by a joint management committee rather than a board of directors. This type of CJV is often called a "contractual" joint venture. The use of this second form of CJV has become quite restricted, as government authorities are reluctant to approve a venture which does not result in the establishment of a legal person formed under PRC law.

Variable arrangements for profit sharing remain one of the distinguishing features of CJVs. Profits from a CJV may be shared in any manner specified in the JV contract. Provided that the contractual provisions are clear, the parties may choose to share net profits, gross revenues or products manufactured or produced. A reasonable method for the payment of taxes and operational expenses must also be stipulated. Furthermore, the parties' profit sharing ratio in a CJV may vary during the term of the CJV.

One important characteristic of a CJV is the possible reversion of CJV assets to the PRC party and the return of investment during the term of the CJV. The parties may provide in the JV contract for the "reversion" of all fixed capital assets to the PRC party at the end of the JV term without compensation to the CJV. At the same time, there may be an accompanying right of the foreign party to take priority in recovering its investment during the term of the CJV, if the parties have so agreed in the JV contract and subject to the foreign party not being permitted to recover its investment before any losses of the CJV have been made up. The fixed assets of the CJV which the PRC party is permitted to receive at the end of the venture term are those that remain after the settlement of debts through required liquidation procedures.

If a partnership structure is chosen, does this lead to (a) joint and several liability to third parties and/or (b) duties of good faith as between partners?

For EJVs and "co-operative" CJVs, the JV entity created will be a limited liability company, and each party's liability is limited to its capital contribution to the JV. For a "contractual" CJV, no separate legal entity is created, and the joint venture parties' liability to third parties could be potentially unlimited. Furthermore, a "contractual" CJV may arguably be regarded as being a partnership as defined by the PRC General Principles of Civil Law, under which partners are subject to joint and several liability for partnership debts. The PRC Partnership Enterprise Law, effective June 1, 2007, introduces limited liability partnerships with between two and fifty partners, but at least one partner must be a general partner with unlimited liability.

Duties of good faith between partners are derived from the General Principles of Civil Law and the Contract Law, both of which require contractual parties in general to exercise their rights and perform their obligations pursuant to the principles of honesty and good faith. However, in practice, it is not uncommon for partners to take into account their own interests in preference to the interests of the JV.

4. Capital structure and funding

What principal local law issues affect the capital structure and funding of the joint venture?

The concepts of authorised and issued capital are not used in the PRC. The term employed in the capitalisation of EJVs and CJVs is registered capital, which refers to the equity contributed by the parties and registered with the government authorities. The registered capital represents the parties' equity investment and is to be distinguished from the concept of total investment amount, which represents the sum of registered capital plus the maximum permitted amount of external borrowings. The registered capital and total investment amount of a project are stated in the project documents, and once approved cannot be increased without approval by the relevant government authorities. Registered capital may not be reduced during the term of a JV unless the scale of the company's activities has been reduced and approval given by relevant government authorities.

Capital contributions may take a variety of forms, including cash, machinery, equipment and intangible property such as proprietary technology, trademarks and other industrial property rights. In addition, the PRC party may contribute buildings, premises and the right to use a site as part of its contribution. PRC regulations provide that the JV contract must set forth a timetable for contributions to registered capital.

Is it common to have different "classes" of shares (e.g. A and B shares) to reflect different interests or contributions of the parties?

While Chinese joint ventures in the form of a limited liability company do not issue "shares" as such, it is possible to structure cooperative joint venture contracts to afford one party more preferential voting and profit distribution rights than the other party or parties. Equity interests in EJVs, on the other hand, are equivalent to one class of shares, with voting and distribution rights being in direct proportion to the parties' equity holdings.

Are there any "thin capitalisation" or similar rules which affect the equity/debt ratio for the capital structure?

Yes. Certain minimum equity requirements are imposed on both EJVs and CJVs. These requirements are outlined as follows:

Total Investment	Minimum equity (% of total investment)
Up to $3m	70%
$3–10m	50% or $2.1m (whichever is higher)
$10–30m	40% or $5m (whichever is higher)
Over $30m	33.3% or $12m (whichever is higher)

Is there capital or similar duty payable in respect of issued share capital?

Not applicable to EJVs and CJVs.

Is it common to have "preference" shares which give a party a priority on payment of dividends or on a return of capital? Are "redeemable" shares permitted (i.e. shares that can be repaid and cancelled)? Are "non-voting" shares permitted?

EJVs and CJVs do not issue shares as such, and all rights under EJVs must be proportionate to the parties' equity holdings. CJV contracts, on the other hand, may be structured so as to afford one joint venture party preferential voting and profit distribution rights over the other party or parties, or, subject to the foreign party not being permitted to recover its investment before any losses of the CJV have been made up, allow the foreign party to take priority in recovering its investment during the term of the CJV, provided that the CJV's assets pass automatically to the Chinese party (without compensation to the CJV) upon expiration of the term of the CJV.

Is there any capital or similar tax payable in respect of issued share capital?

Not applicable. EJVs and CJVs do not issue shares. There is no tax imposed on contributions to registered capital.

Is a separate "contribution agreement" or other formal document (other than formal property transfer agreements) required or usual under the local law to document the contribution of assets to the joint venture?

A JV contract, which functions as a shareholders' agreement, is required. The terms and conditions for the foreign and PRC parties' contribution to the JV will be included as part of the JV contract, with details of the contributions attached as annexes to the contract. In some cases where the contribution of plant, equipment and other assets raises complex issues of valuation, representations and warranties and/or environmental conditions, a separate asset transfer agreement or asset contribution agreement will also be used. This is not, however, obligatory.

Are there any local laws which require independent valuation of any non-cash assets to be contributed?

Yes, when state-owned assets and/or co-operative conditions are used by the PRC party as investment, a valuation must be conducted and certified by a PRC-registered accounting firm in accordance with the requirements of the State-owned Assets Supervision and Administration Commission, which will issue a verification.

Under separate regulations, contributions in kind by the foreign party to a joint venture must also be appraised. The local bureau of the State Administration of Import and Export Commodity Inspection will appraise, among other things, the "foreign investment property" contributed by foreign investors to the registered capital of FIEs and property purchased from overseas by foreign investors on behalf of FIEs. An investment verification report from a PRC registered accountant based on the appraisal certificates issued by the local inspection bureau is required to verify the investments made by the parties.

The foreign party can avoid this appraisal procedure and possible under-valuation of its contributions in kind by making contributions in cash. The joint venture can then purchase the machinery and equipment itself at market price or whatever price the joint venture and foreign party negotiate.

Are there exchange control regulations which affect the establishment of the joint venture or the subsequent repatriation of profits or dividends for the joint venture to a foreign party?

Yes. The Renminbi is not freely convertible on the capital account. The approval of the State Administration for Foreign Exchange must be obtained before Renminbi may be converted into foreign currency and transferred abroad for the payment of capital account items such as repayment of foreign loans, loans to an overseas borrower, remittance of proceeds from the disposal of an investment in China and remittance of capital remaining after liquidation of a JV.

A system has been in place for current account convertibility since 1996. Current account convertibility provided for under existing regulations means that no formal approvals are required from the State Administration of Foreign Exchange when converting Renminbi into foreign currency, provided that the foreign currency will be used for bona fide trade in goods and services and certain other legitimate uses as defined by the relevant regulations. Processing and documentation requirements can, however, be significant.

If a foreign party is to contribute technology to the joint venture, are there any special valuation requirements?

The Sino-foreign EJV Law contains the principle that the parties to the joint venture shall determine the value of contributions through joint assessment. While this general principle has been supplemented by regulations requiring the valuation of contributions in the form of State-owned assets and foreign in-kind contributions, the valuation of technology and know-how is still subject more to the pressures of policy guidelines than published regulations.

Technology licences, know-how transfer contracts, technical assistance contracts and other types of technology contracts must be separately examined by the relevant division of MOFCOM or its local branch, and then filed for the record. It is during this approval process that government officials will make policy preferences known through requests for changes to the contract.

Similarly, although there are no restrictions affecting the payment of royalties by a JV to the foreign party for the use of technology, the terms and conditions for the payment of royalties and methodology for calculation of royalties will be examined closely during the approval process.

5. Tax

Are there any particular tax laws or incentives which significantly affect the establishment of joint ventures in this jurisdiction by a foreign investor?

JVs are subject to several kinds of taxes, including income tax, value-added tax, customs duties, business tax, urban building tax, and vehicle and vessel licence tax. Expatriate employees are also subject to individual income tax.

For over two decades, China operated a dual tax system which gave favourable tax treatment to FIEs. While the standard rate of enterprise income tax was 33 per cent (30 per cent national tax plus 3 per cent local tax), the national tax rate was reduced to 24 per cent for production-oriented FIEs in Coastal Open Economic Zones or in old urban districts of cities where Economic and Technological Development Zones (ETDZs) and Special Economic Zones (SEZs) are located. The national tax rate was 15 per cent for (i) FIEs in the SEZs, (ii) production-oriented FIEs located inside the ETDZs, and (iii) production-oriented FIEs and FIEs engaged in projects such as ports, airports, transport, energy and communications in Pudong and certain other locations. Tax holidays were available for production-oriented FIEs scheduled to operate for a period of 10 years or more, including a complete exemption from enterprise income tax in the first two profit-making years and a 50 per cent reduction in tax in the following three years.

The new PRC Enterprise Income Tax Law (EIT Law), effective as of January 1, 2008, imposes a flat enterprise income tax rate of 25 per cent for foreign and Chinese enterprises alike. Incentives and deductions are mostly industry-based, with a few reductions based on geography. A rate of 15 per cent applies to new-tech ventures and enterprises in "encouraged" sectors (such as technological development, energy conservation and infrastructure), with a rate of 20 per cent for qualifying small and "thin-profit" companies. The new rates will be phased in over a five-year period for FIEs established prior to March 16, 2007 (the promulgation date of the EIT Law), and unused tax holidays will be triggered on January 1, 2008 and will continue until they expire. Once these preferential treatments expire, the only tax advantage of FIE status seems to be that FIEs in the Encouraged Category will be entitled to certain import VAT and customs duty exemptions or deductions in respect of their imported machinery.

Other relevant taxes include VAT, business tax on turnover from services not subject to VAT, customs duties, urban building tax, land appreciation tax and land use tax.

Will withholding taxes apply to dividends paid by a joint venture company?

Under the old dual tax regime, profit distributions received by a foreign investor from an FIE were exempted from withholding tax. At the time of writing, the detailed EIT implementation guidelines have not been published, although it is expected that this general exemption may be rescinded and that a unified withholding tax rate may apply. The withholding tax rate is expected to range from five per cent to 20 per cent, depending on the tax treaty applicable (if any) between the jurisdiction of the foreign investor and China. Exemptions may be available for new/high-tech FIEs.

6. Board and management

Are there local law requirements which affect the board or management structure of the joint venture? May a two-tier board be required?

Yes, there are some local requirements. A two-tier board is not required. In EJVs, as well as CJVs with legal person status, the board of directors is the highest decision-making authority of the JV. In EJVs, the interests of the parties are represented by their appointees to the board, and the distribution of seats on the board generally follows the ratio of investment contributions. The boards of CJVs can be constituted in accordance with the contractual arrangements of the parties, and do not have to be in proportion to the capital contributions of the parties. For both EJVs and CJVs, the chairman of the board is the legal representative of the company.

In both the CJV and EJV, a general manager is usually appointed for the day-to-day running of the JV. The right to appoint the general manager and other management posts are set by agreement of the parties, without reference to investment ratios. The parties may adopt a management structure that suits their business needs.

Are there local law constraints on persons who can be directors or managers of the joint venture (e.g. only local residents or nationals)?

No, the directors and managers may be foreign nationals. However, in certain specially regulated sectors such as banking and insurance, managers and directors are required to meet certain qualification requirements which a foreign national may be unlikely to satisfy.

Does a shareholder in a joint venture company owe a duty of good faith (or similar duty) to other shareholders in the way it behaves in relation to the joint venture?

Both the General Principles of Civil Law and the Contract Law require shareholders in a joint venture, as contractual parties, to act pursuant to the principles of honesty and good faith. However, as a practical matter, it is common for the directors appointed by a party to take instructions from the party which appointed them.

Can you modify the legal duties of directors so that they can expressly take into account the interests of their "appointer" when voting or acting as director, or must they always act objectively in the best interests of the company?

PRC law on this point is rather weak and only broadly states that directors shall be "faithful to his duties, protect the company's interests and shall not use his power and position in the company for his personal gain." However, in practice, directors not infrequently take into account the interests of their the party which appointed them.

7. Transfer of shares

In the case of a joint venture company, can a permanent restriction on transfer of shares be imposed under the local law (e.g. no transfer without the consent of the other shareholder)?

If one party to an EJV intends to transfer all or part of its equity interest to a third party, consent must be obtained from the other party. The other party or parties have a pre-emptive right, and any transfer by one EJV partner to a third party must be on terms no more favourable than those offered to the other EJV party or parties. For CJVs, transfers require the written consent of the other party or parties.

8. Protection for minority shareholders

Are there any statutory rules or remedies which help significantly to protect a minority shareholder in a joint venture company?

For an EJV, minority shareholders are protected by the requirement of unanimous consent of the board of directors for the following: (i) amendments to the JV's articles of association; (ii) termination and dissolution of the EJV; (iii) increase or decrease in the EJV's registered capital; and (iv) merger or division of the EJV.

Similarly, for a CJV, the following require unanimous consent by the directors or joint management committee members: (i) amendments to the JV's articles of association; (ii) increase or reduction of the CJV's registered capital; (iii) dissolution of the CJV; (iv) mortgage of the CJV's property; or (v) merger, dissolution or amendment to the organisational structure of the CJV.

In either case, the parties to an EJV or CJV may provide in their JV contract for additional decisions requiring unanimous approval.

Does the law require any major business decisions to be approved by a special resolution or super-majority (whether at board or shareholder level)—or must a minority party protect itself by contract?

Sino-foreign joint ventures do not have shareholders' meetings. The major business decisions mentioned in the previous section must be approved by unanimous consent of the directors.

9. Employment laws

Are there local law obligations requiring a "local" party to consult with, or obtain the approval of, employees or employee representatives on a contribution of its business to the joint venture?

No, there are no such requirements. However, for foreign investors purchasing interests of domestic enterprises, a plan of "re-settlement of local employees" is required as part of the application to be submitted to the Chinese approval authorities. This will be relevant where the JV is formed by way of an acquisition of an equity interest in an existing Chinese entity.

Are there any material employment laws (compared with the UK) which are likely to affect the ongoing operations of the joint venture?

Yes, the PRC has a developing body of labour and safety laws, in particular the Employment Contract Law which was recently passed by the Standing Committee of the PRC National People's Congress and effective as of January 1, 2008.

Under PRC law, personnel must be hired pursuant to either a collective labour contract signed with the JV's labour union or to individual labour contracts entered into with each staff member. Industrial or regional collective labour contracts may also be concluded between the labour unions and representatives of enterprises in industries such as construction, mining and catering services.

The JV must support the establishment of a labour union, an obligation which was strengthened in recent amendments to the law. The Employment Contract Law further requires that the JV consult with its labour union in relation to certain matters including the establishment of its rules and regulations. Approved labour unions are often subject to significant government or party control.

PRC law regulates the termination of employment. In general, a JV may terminate an employee only under certain conditions set out in the PRC Labour Law. The Employment Contract Law further stipulates that were the employer to dismiss either 20 or more, or 10 per cent or more, of its employees, the JV would have to explain such dismissals to its labour union (or all its staff) 30 days prior to the dismissal. In addition, the JV would have to submit a report to the relevant labour administrative authorities regarding such dismissals.

10. Accounts

Is there a requirement on the joint venture company to file accounts of the joint venture company with any authority where they are publicly available?

If a JV becomes a publicly-listed company, then it must comply with the standard public disclosure rules for listed companies. Otherwise, a JV has no legal obligation to make any registration making its accounts publicly available.

11. Dispute resolution

Is there any standard practice as to form of dispute resolution in relation to joint ventures with foreign investors? Is arbitration in a venue outside that jurisdiction acceptable?

Parties to a JV may stipulate a dispute resolution process in their JV contract, including: (i) conciliation; (ii) mediation; and (iii) litigation or arbitration. It is typical for the JV contract to stipulate arbitration as the means for resolution of disputes.

The arbitration of disputes arising from the JV contract between foreign and Chinese parties or the technology licence agreement between a foreign party and the JV company may be conducted outside the PRC.

Is the local jurisdiction a signatory to the 1958 New York Convention on the Recognition and Enforcement of Foreign Arbitral Awards?

Yes.

12. Legal documents and formalities

Is there any special form of legal documentation required under local law for establishment of a joint venture company? What are the usual principal documents?

The following are the basic documents required for the formation of an EJV and CJV:

- *Letter of intent or memorandum of understanding.* These documents contain a brief summary of the parties' negotiations to date or a statement of their intention to pursue the establishment of an EJV or CJV. The PRC party will often submit the document to its department in charge and relevant government authorities as part of the "project establishment" process, i.e. the process of obtaining a preliminary approval for the JV.

- *JV agreement.* This is an interim agreement (as distinguished from the JV contract) which is not legally binding. A JV agreement will often be used in large-scale projects, especially where agreement is needed on sharing costs for an extensive feasibility study. A JV agreement is often dispensed with in more routine JVs.

- *Application Report.* This sets forth the economic and technical assumptions under which the JV will operate. It must include a description of the scope of the project, the products to be produced, the target market, proposed investment by the parties, and basic information concerning the parties. An environmental impact statement is a required part of the application. The report will be used by PRC authorities to evaluate the project and for planning purposes. Depending on the size and nature of the project, a financing plan and an energy savings analysis report may be required as part of the application report.

- *JV contract.* This contract is the fundamental document which provides for the establishment of the JV, and is binding on both the foreign and PRC parties. PRC law requires that certain specified provisions be contained in the JV contract.

- *Articles of association.* This document is the equivalent of the articles of incorporation and by-laws of many foreign jurisdiction companies. PRC law also requires certain specified provisions to be contained in the articles of association.

- *Ancillary contracts.* Although not required by law, a number of ancillary contracts are generally referenced in the JV contract or attached as annexes thereto.

Does the joint venture documentation need to be in the local language and/or governed by the local law?

Yes. The above documents must be in Chinese and may be in a foreign language as well. The JV contract must be governed by PRC law.

Are there any commonly accepted "standard forms" for joint ventures with foreign investors in your jurisdiction?

Yes. The government has recommended standard forms and the joint venture contracts developed by law firms follow the broad outlines of the government forms but are more detailed. Negotiations remain important to settle "fair" trade terms for the venture.

Are agreements between shareholders (e.g. as to appointment of directors, conduct of the business of the company or voting majorities required for certain decisions etc.) enforceable under local law? In the event of breach, is specific performance or a similar remedy available, or only damages?

The agreement between the shareholders is contained in the joint venture contract. In the event of breach, the arbitral tribunal or court may order specific performance. If a party does not voluntarily comply with the arbitral award or court judgment, in theory, court enforcement may be sought. However, courts are generally reluctant to enforce specific performance.

Are restrictions relating to (a) transfers of shares and/or (b) minority "veto rights" commonly included in the articles of association or by-laws of the company, or included in a separate shareholders' agreement?

Restrictions relating to (a) transfers of shares and (b) minority "veto rights" (as reflected in provisions requiring unanimous decision for certain matters) are generally included in both the articles of association and the JV contract.

Are there any formalities (e.g. notarisation or registration) which are material and which may affect the timing involved in forming the joint venture?

In addition to the approval processes previously discussed, JVs requiring central level approval will usually take considerably longer to accomplish and be more burdensome than JVs requiring only local approval. Also, some localities require the foreign party to have copies of its corporate documents submitted as part of the approval application package, consularised or notarised.

(3) Czech Republic

Author: Marketa Zachova
Vejmelka & Wuensch, Prague

1. General background

Are joint ventures popular as a form of foreign investment into your jurisdiction?

Joint ventures are increasingly popular in the Czech Republic, in particular as a form of foreign investment. Establishment of a relatively high number of joint ventures over the last decade or so has been prompted by substantial movement of western producers into the Czech Republic, enabled by opening of eastern markets and the wish of foreign investors to expand in the newly available territories.

Foreign investors can expect financial support based on various bilateral and multilateral agreements encouraging joint ventures that meet specific conditions in terms of the volume and value of the intended activity (e.g. the Joint Venture Program PHARE (JOPP) supports creation of new and extension of existing joint ventures between western European entrepreneurs and their eastern European counterparts). Financial support can also be sought from the European Bank for Reconstruction and Development and the European Investment Bank. The possibility of receiving investment incentives from the Czech government should also be mentioned.

Are there restrictions on foreign participation?

Generally, there are no restrictions on foreign participation.

What (if any) are the major legal problems which a foreign investor in a joint venture faces in your jurisdiction?

Czech business law is based on the principle of equal treatment. This means that a foreign investor should not basically face any other legal problems than its Czech partners do.

There are, of course, rules and practices that might seem unusual to foreign investors. For instance, foreign investors have formerly complained of long drawn-out processes for company registrations in the Czech Republic. However, the situation has significantly improved and nowadays it is a rule that a company is registered within 10 business days of the submission of an application for registration, provided that the application meets all the legal requirements. Nevertheless, the registration process is still very formal and even minor formal deficiencies may cause certain delays in execution of the registration, or later changes in the registration. The process of company registration has been simplified by partial amendments to the provisions of the Commercial Code which became effective in July 2005. Where a foreign investor is going to be a party to the registration proceedings, it is advisable to have a Czech person (counsel) empowered to represent it, as otherwise all official papers would be delivered to the investor's address abroad, which could considerably protract the whole process. However, members of company bodies (such as managing directors or supervisory board members) are no longer regarded as participants of the registration proceedings.

Another problem is lengthy court proceedings in civil disputes. Again, the situation is improving gradually and especially higher courts decide their cases promptly and efficiently. However, if a foreign investor wants to be sure of prompt assertion of its rights, there is always the possibility of agreeing on the exclusive jurisdiction of an arbitration tribunal or an ad hoc arbitrator; this is generally perceived as a more flexible dispute resolution alternative.

2. Governmental/regulatory approvals

What principal governmental or regulatory approvals are required (excluding competition law) for establishing a joint venture?

There are no material governmental or regulatory approvals required under Czech law for establishing a joint venture other than those required in particular significant areas (banking, insurance, etc.) where regulatory approvals are indispensable.

Are there local anti-trust laws which might apply to the formation of the joint venture?

Concentration joint ventures (i.e. those exercising all functions of a business entity independently of the controlling entities) are subject to anti-trust laws regulating merger control. Such concentrations must be approved by the competent Czech anti-trust authority (Office for Protection of Economic Competition). A brief summary appears below:

Filing requirement/ trigger	Timetable for clearance	Test for clearance	Mandatory/ voluntary Penalties
Applies to a JV that qualifies as full function. *Test:* (i) combined turnover of the joint venture parties in the Czech Republic exceeds CZK 1.5bn (approx. €47.1m); and (ii) turnover of at least 2 parties in the Czech Republic exceeds CZK 250m (approx. €7.8m). *or:* the turnover achieved by at least one party in the Czech Republic exceeds CZK 1.5bn and the worldwide turnover of another parent exceeds CZK 1.5bn.	Stage 1: 30 days from filing (15 additional days if remedies are submitted). Stage 2: five months from filing (15 additional days if remedies submitted). No implementation in the Czech Republic before clearance is received. A derogation from the obligation to suspend completion may be possible in some cases.	Whether the JV will significantly impede competition on a relevant market, in particular as a result of creation or reinforcing of a dominant position.	Filing before completion of the transaction is mandatory and can be made prior to a legally binding agreement having been concluded. Breaches of the law (including implementation before clearance): fine up to CZK 10m (approx. €314,000) or up to 10 per cent of net turnover in preceding calendar year.

Co-ordination joint ventures (i.e. those not meeting the above criteria) are regarded, from the competition law point of view, as agreements that could possibly distort economic competition and the parties should thus do their own assessment of the compatibility of co-ordination joint ventures with the competition rules. However, as a result of elimination of a notification system, they no longer need to notify co-ordination joint ventures restricting competition to the anti-trust authority in order to benefit from an individual exemption.

If the local party is a public company, when might the approval of its shareholders be required under stock exchange or similar rules?

The formation of a joint venture by a local company having publicly traded shares is not subject to approval of its shareholders, unless such pre-condition is explicitly envisaged by the relevant company's articles of association (stock exchange rules do not apply in this context).

3. Types of joint venture vehicle

What are the principal types of joint venture vehicle commonly used with foreign investors?

"Concentration joint ventures" (or "equity joint ventures") are those, which take the form of a separate business entity independent of the controlling entities. For this purpose, all types of business companies regulated by Czech law (i.e. joint stock company, limited liability company, general partnership and limited partnership), as well as cooperatives, civil associations and other conceivable types of legal entities are generally eligible. Nonetheless, a *joint stock company* and, to a lesser extent, a *limited liability company* are the most popular forms.

"Co-ordination joint ventures" (or "contractual joint ventures") are usually single-purpose arrangements and, therefore, do not lead to formation of a new legal entity.

Shareholders are not liable for the obligations of a joint stock company. Shareholders of a limited liability company are (vicariously) liable up to the total of unpaid investments into the registered capital, as entered in the Czech Commercial Register. If an enterprise, or a part thereof, is to be contributed by one parent joint venture party, that party is by virtue of law liable (as a surety) for all liabilities contributed to the joint venture as part of the enterprise.

If a partnership structure is chosen, does this lead to (a) joint and several liability to third parties and/or (b) duties of good faith as between partners?

If the parties to the joint venture conclude an agreement on association pursuant to the Czech Civil Code, all parties involved become, by virtue of law, liable for any acts of the association jointly and severally, regardless of who is acting. Partners in a general partnership and general partners to a limited partnership are liable, without limitation, jointly and severally.

Irrespective of the joint venture type, there is a general duty of good faith as between the partners to the joint venture. Different forms of misconduct may lead to different consequences based on the chosen form of the partnership and the particular arrangements agreed between the partners. In extreme cases, the court may dissolve a "malfunctional" joint venture or expel a "non-obedient" partner from a partnership. Should a joint liability of partners arise due to damage caused by some of the partners only, the partners in default are obliged to compensate the other partners for what has been incurred by them in connection with that joint liability. The statutory duty of good faith may be broadened or made stricter by the particular partnership agreement.

4. Capital structure and funding

Is it common to have different "classes" of shares (e.g. A and B shares) to reflect different initial contributions or financial interests of the parties?

Generally, shares and different "classes" of shares are possible only in relation to joint stock companies. If the articles of association so stipulate, a joint stock company may issue shares to which priority rights in relation to dividends or liquidation shares are attached ("preference shares"), provided that the total nominal value of such preference shares does not exceed one half of the company's registered capital. The right to issue preference shares is not vested in joint stock companies engaged in specific significant areas such as investment funds, pension funds, stock exchanges, etc.

Other types of company do not issue any "shares" but the rights of the parties may reflect their different initial contributions or financial interests, for example, by preferential voting rights, shares in profit or preferential rights in a liquidation.

Is it common to have "preference" shares, which give a party a priority on payment of dividends or on a return of capital?

Preference shares are quite common in the case of joint stock companies. In the case of a limited liability company or other forms of partnerships, it is possible to agree that some shareholders will have priority in dividend payments or will be entitled to dividends to a greater extent than the other parties. Such agreement must be part of the company's memorandum of association. Any such arrangements must not be contrary to good morals and unequal dividend distribution should always be reasonably justified.

Are "redeemable" shares permitted (i.e. shares that can be repaid and cancelled)?

Redeemable shares are not recognised by Czech law. Nonetheless, apart from usual ways of cancellation of a shareholder's partnership, leading to "cancellation" of its share(s), in certain cases there is the possibility of cancelling a shareholder's share(s) as a result of its default in payment of its capital contribution.

Are "non-voting" shares permitted?

Non-voting shares are permitted only if they are provided for in the articles of association of a joint stock company, and only in relation to preference shares which may be deprived of voting rights (so far as a preferred dividend is actually paid). Any agreement on restricted voting rights must not be contrary to good morals or establish (unjustifiable) unequal treatment.

Are there any "thin capitalisation" or similar rules which affect the choice of equity/ debt ratio for the capital structure?

In the Czech Republic, there are certain "thin capitalisation" rules aimed at prevention of a bankruptcy situation (which is deemed to occur, inter alia, if the company is overdebted, i.e. it has more creditors and its due liabilities exceed its assets) such as a ban on division of profit where the net business assets are or could thereby become lower than the company's registered capital.

Is there any capital or similar tax payable in respect of issued share capital?

No capital or other tax is payable directly in connection with issued share capital.

In respect of a limited liability company, the Czech Commercial Code envisages the duty of shareholders to contribute to the creation of the company's equity capital by a monetary contribution, in excess of the amount of the shareholders' investments, up to one half of the company's registered capital in proportion to the respective shareholders' investments. The payment of this contribution does not affect the amount of the shareholders' existing investments. This obligation must, however, be explicitly stated in the company's memorandum of association.

Is a separate "contribution agreement" or other formal document (other than formal property transfer agreements) required or usual under the local law to document the contribution of assets to the joint venture?

Unless the parties' contributions are in cash, certain formalities must be met in connection with capital contributions (introduced by amendments to the Czech Commercial Code with effect from January 1, 2001): Non-cash contributions (contributions in kind) can only comprise assets which can be appraised in money and used by the future joint venture company in relation to its registered scope of business. Contributions consisting of work or services are not allowed.

Unlike cash contributions, contributions in kind must be paid in full before the joint venture company is entered into the Czech Commercial Register. Movable assets are deemed paid up on their handover to the company's investments administrator designated in the company's memorandum of association (it can be either one of the founders or a bank), unless the memorandum of association states otherwise. As far as immovable assets are concerned, the contributing party is supposed to produce a written declaration (with its signature being officially certified) based on which the company's ownership title can be entered into the Cadastral Land Register, and then (symbolically) to hand over to the investments administrator the relevant real estate being contributed.

All other non-cash contributions require the conclusion of a written "contribution agreement" between the investor and the future company (acting through the investments administrator) and, in case (a part of) an enterprise or know-how is being contributed, also handover of (a part of) the enterprise or documents containing such know-how. The handover of (a part of) an enterprise, or the handover of documents containing know-how, must be recorded in a special protocol.

Receivables from third parties can be contributed (providing that they fulfil the above conditions) on the basis of an assignment agreement. On the other hand, receivables from the joint venture company itself can be contributed only as part of a capital increase (by means of an offset of mutual counterclaims) following the company's incorporation.

Are there any local laws which require an independent valuation of any non-cash assets to be contributed to the joint venture?

The value of non-cash contributions must be stated in the memorandum of association. Moreover, the value of a non-cash contribution to a limited liability company or to a joint stock company must be determined on the basis of a valuation opinion of an independent expert to be appointed by the competent court on motion of the (future) founders. The costs of the expert's opinion are borne by the (future) joint venture company.

Are there exchange control regulations which materially affect the establishment of the joint venture—or the subsequent repatriation of profits or dividends from the joint venture to a foreign party?

Under the Czech foreign-exchange regulations, foreigners are generally entitled to acquire all foreign-exchange values and to import and export Czech/foreign currency without any limitations, unless the Act explicitly states otherwise ("free convertibility" rule). There are currently no foreign-exchange restrictions that could affect the establishment of a joint venture or the repatriation of profits, dividends and/or liquidation shares to the relevant foreign joint venture party.

If a foreign party is to contribute technology to the joint venture, are there any special valuation requirements?

Technology may be contributed into the registered capital of a joint venture as a non-monetary investment, provided that it is appraisable in money and capable of being used by the joint venture company in relation to its registered scope of business. The value of the relevant technology to be contributed must be stated in the memorandum of association and, in case of a limited liability company or a joint stock company, assessed by an expert.

5. Tax

Are there any particular tax laws or incentives which significantly affect the establishment of joint ventures in this jurisdiction by a foreign investor?

If a new company is established in the Czech Republic, it is subject to the same tax law regulations as any other legal entity. In other words, joint ventures in the Czech Republic do not enjoy any preferred tax treatment. Possible losses incurred by the joint venture company cannot be transferred for tax purposes to any of its parent companies (though different regulation is under preparation); however, it may be carried forward (not back) in time for up to five years.

Investment incentives are provided, pursuant to the Act on Investment Incentives, to investors meeting both the general and specific conditions set out therein, while joint ventures are generally eligible as well. Incentives consist of tax reliefs, subsidies, insurance of suitable land, financial assistance in connection with creation of new jobs and staff training.

Will withholding taxes apply to dividends paid by a joint venture company?

Apart from the corporate income tax to be paid by the joint venture company itself, any dividends paid by the company to its shareholders are subject to a withholding tax of 15 per cent, applicable to both Czech residents and non-residents, unless otherwise provided for by a relevant double taxation treaty.

6. Board and management

Are there local law rules which affect the board or management structure of the joint venture? May a two-tier board be required?

In the Czech Republic, there are no specific rules for the board or management structure in respect of joint venture companies. Therefore, the general rules applicable to the respective company form will apply (e.g. the board of directors of a joint stock company must have at least three members, the statutory body of a limited liability company is formed by one or more managing directors, etc.). A two-tier board is not required.

It is a usual practice that both joint venture parties having a 50:50 shareholding in the joint venture are entitled to nominate one half of members of all decision-making bodies so that "joint" control of the joint venture company is guaranteed. Similarly, if the proportion of the parties' shareholdings is other than 50:50, the number of members of the company's bodies to be nominated by each party usually corresponds to such proportion.

Are there local law constraints on persons who can be directors or managers of the joint venture (e.g. only local residents or nationals)?

There are several conditions which have to be satisfied by members of a statutory body of a company before they can be appointed such as: full legal capacity;

satisfying the integrity test, i.e. does not have any criminal record in the Czech Republic (in the case of Czech citizens) and/or abroad (in the case of non-EU/EU-citizens) in relation to crimes enumerated in the Czech Trade Act; and is not prevented from performing this function by the occurrence of an impediment to carrying out a trade within the meaning of the Trade Act (e.g. initiation of bankruptcy proceedings in relation to the respective person's assets). Satisfaction of these conditions must be documented by appropriate evidence to be presented to the Registry Court.

Apart from these formal conditions, non EU-nationals to be registered as persons entitled to act on behalf of the company in the Commercial Register were previously required to submit to the Registry Court a valid residence permit for the Czech Republic. In the case of EU nationals, an amendment to the Commercial Code has been passed by the Czech Parliament as a result of which no residence permit was required from EU nationals as from January 1, 2005. As from July 1, 2005, no residence permits are required at all, including from non-EU nationals.

Does a shareholder in a joint venture company owe a duty of good faith (or similar duty) to other shareholders in the way it behaves in relation to the joint venture?

Shareholders are obliged to obey all rules set forth either by law or by the memorandum of association and/or articles of association (in the case of a corporation joint venture) or the partnership contract (in the case of a co-ordination joint venture). The duty of good faith between shareholders is not expressly formulated by Czech law but such a duty follows from general legal principles and especially from the duty of each person to act in accordance with good morals.

Can you modify the legal duties of directors so that they can expressly take into account the interests of their "appointer" when voting or acting as director, or must they always act objectively in the best interests of the company?

A director, as a member of the statutory body of a company, must always act objectively in the best interests of the company. He is neither obliged, nor entitled, to obey instructions given to him by individual shareholders. Nevertheless, if the general meeting issues an order or gives an instruction to the director, the director is obliged to follow such instruction, unless it is contrary to law. If the director is given an instruction by the general meeting which is contrary to law and the director obeys such instruction, the director is obliged to compensate the company for any damage caused by such unlawful act. Directors are not bound to follow any instructions, even those of the general meeting, which concern the business management of the company.

7. Transfer of shares

In the case of a joint venture company, can a permanent restriction on transfer of shares be imposed under the local law (e.g. no transfer without the consent of the other shareholder)?

In the case of a limited liability company, a business share may be transferred to another party that is not a current shareholder of the company only if the memorandum of association so admits (unless the company has only one shareholder, where the share is freely transferable). Thus, where the memorandum of association does not state anything regarding the transfer of shares, the shares are non-transferable to another party.

In the case of a joint stock company, the shares are always transferable. The articles of association may restrict the transferability of registered shares (shares registered in the name of a specific shareholder as opposed to "bearer shares") e.g. by requiring the consent of a company body, but the transferability of shares may never be excluded.

The memorandum of association or articles of association, as applicable, of both a limited liability company and a joint stock company may make the transfer of shares subject to specific conditions or approval of the general meeting.

The shares in a general partnership or (in respect of general partners) in a limited partnership are non-transferable without the approval of all partners by way of an amendment to the memorandum of association.

8. Protection for minority shareholders

Are there any statutory rules or remedies which help significantly to protect a minority shareholder in a joint venture company?

There are no special rules aimed at protection of minority shareholders in a joint venture company. Therefore, the general rules on protection of minority shareholders will apply. The Czech Commercial Code grants a number of specific (but relatively limited) rights to minority shareholders.

In the case of a limited liability company, shareholders whose contributions exceed in total 10 per cent of the registered capital are entitled to request the convocation of a general meeting. If the managing directors fail to convene it within one month as of the delivery of such request, the shareholders themselves may convene the general meeting.

Even more extensive protection is provided to minority shareholders of a joint stock company. For example, minority shareholders (holding a certain minimum of the registered capital) are entitled inter alia to:

(a) ask the board of directors to convene an extraordinary general meeting to discuss specified matters;

(b) convene an extraordinary general meeting if the board of directors fails to do so;

(c) ask the supervisory board to examine the performance of the board of directors in respect of specified matters and/or to assert the right to compensation for damage which the company has against a member of the board of directors;

(d) file a lawsuit with the competent court for the appointment of an expert to review a report on the relations between a controlled person and related persons ("intra-group report").

If the board of directors or the supervisory board fails to comply with the relevant request, the minority shareholder(s) may assert the right to damages themselves with the competent court.

The abuse of minority rights is prohibited by Czech law. The company is entitled to assert damages suffered due to "harassing" execution of minority shareholders' rights.

Does the law require any major business decisions to be approved by a special resolution or super-majority (whether at board or shareholder level)--or must a minority party protect itself by contract?

Both in the case of a limited liability company and a joint stock company there are a number of material corporate matters that have to be decided by a two-thirds or three-quarters majority. A "super-majority" (qualified majority) is thus required, in particular, in the case of any amendments to the memorandum of association/ articles of association, increase or reduction in the registered capital, winding-up of the company with liquidation, etc. In some cases (such as changing the class or type of shares or the rights attached to a particular class of shares, restricting the transferability of registered shares, cancellation or restriction of the pre-emptive rights attached to convertible bonds or bonds with share warrants attached, increasing the registered capital by non-monetary contributions, etc.) a qualified majority of votes of shareholders possessing the relevant class of shares is required. The memorandum of association or the articles of association, as applicable, may provide for stricter conditions and thus require a qualified majority even in cases not stipulated by law, or set higher percentages of votes necessary for adopting certain resolutions at a general meeting.

9. Employment laws

Are there local law obligations requiring a "local" party to consult with, or obtain the approval of, employees or employee representatives on a contribution of its business to the joint venture?

Pursuant to the newly adopted Czech Labour Code, effective as of January 1, 2007, employees are entitled to receive appropriate information from the employer and/or to consult with the employer on all substantial affairs of the company including information on intended structural changes, rationalisation and/or organisational measures, especially if such measures could affect the future existence of the employees' employment relationships (e.g. intended transfer of employees to the newly established joint venture company as part of the contribution of an enterprise, cancellation of existing jobs due to organisational measures, etc.).

Are there any material employment laws (compared with the UK) that are likely to affect the ongoing operations of the joint venture?

There are many employment-related issues of which a foreign joint venture party should be aware (e.g. in relation to the establishment and termination of employment relationships, working hours, wages, requirements on working environment, etc.).

10. Accounts

Is there a requirement on the joint venture company to file accounts with any authority where they are publicly available?

The financial statements (and auditor's reports thereon) of a joint venture company—like any other company—must normally be filed with the competent Registry Court.

11. Dispute resolution

Is there any standard local practice as to form of dispute resolution in relation to joint ventures with foreign investors? Is arbitration in a venue outside that jurisdiction acceptable?

Basically, resolution of disputes between foreign and local joint venture partners can be regulated at the parties' free discretion, i.e. disputes can be resolved either by local or foreign courts (depending also on the governing law) or by a local or foreign arbitration body (arbitration court or single arbitrator). In this context, arbitration in accordance with the UNCITRAL Arbitration Rules is frequently agreed upon.

Is the local jurisdiction a signatory to the 1958 New York Convention on the Recognition and Enforcement of Foreign Arbitral Awards?
Yes.

12. Legal documents and formalities

Is there any special form of legal documentation required under local law for establishment of a joint venture company? What are the usual principal documents?

Although the applicable laws do not require the execution of any special form of legal documentation, formation of a joint venture company involves in practice a three or four step procedure:

- A letter of intent is usually concluded, containing basic rules about the future structure and operation of the joint venture and proving the parties' readiness to cooperate.

- Thereafter (or as a first step), a joint venture agreement or a co-operation agreement (shareholders' agreement) is concluded, being a comprehensive document regulating all substantial rights and obligations of the parties and setting out business, technical and commercial objectives of the parties' co-operation. As a rule, the parties also agree upon the governing law.

- A memorandum of association or a document equivalent thereto is concluded in accordance with the chosen legal form of the joint venture company (this document may be attached, in rough outline, to the joint venture agreement).

- Finally, supplementary agreements are concluded, such as supply contracts, know-how/trademark exchange agreements, technical/administrative services agreements, etc. Since it is important that all these documents are duly interconnected with the joint venture agreement/co-operation agreement, they are usually referenced therein or even attached as annexes.

Does the joint venture documentation need to be in the local language and/or governed by the local law?

Except for the memorandum of association of a limited liability company or a joint stock company, which need to take the form of notarial deed, none of these joint venture documents needs to be executed in the Czech language. However, as far as the founding documents (memoranda of association) of all company forms are concerned, the registry court would normally require at least an official Czech translation to be able to register the company and an official Czech translation should be deposited in the public records of the Commercial Register.

The joint venture documentation may be governed by either Czech or foreign law, providing that each party comes from a different jurisdiction. However, the Czech joint venture company itself must be established and governed by Czech law.

Are there any commonly-accepted "standard forms" for joint ventures with foreign investors in your jurisdiction?

There are no commonly-accepted "standard forms" for joint ventures. Each will be structured and documented in accordance with its particular circumstances.

Are agreements between shareholders (e.g. as to appointment of directors, conduct of the business of the company or voting majorities required for certain decisions etc.) enforceable under local law? In the event of breach, is specific performance or a similar remedy available—or only damages?

Valid and effective agreements between shareholders, including the memorandum of association, articles of association and other specific agreements, unless contradictory to Czech law, are fully enforceable under Czech law. Some provisions are, however, enforceable only if made part of the company's memorandum of association or articles of association.

Certain provisions could, nonetheless, not be enforceable even if made part of the company's memorandum of association or articles of association. For instance, any agreements are void that would bind a shareholder to (a) follow instructions given by the company or any of its bodies on how to vote; or (b) vote for proposals presented by the company bodies; or (c) use its voting right in a predetermined manner, or not to vote, in exchange for advantages granted to him by the company. Also, any provisions of articles of association that would provide for different number of votes pertaining to shares with the same nominal value, or that would distribute the votes pertaining to shares disproportionally to the nominal value of the shares, would not be enforceable. It is, however, possible to determine in the articles of association a maximum number of votes assigned to one shareholder, or to one shareholder and persons controlled by him.

In the case of a breach of an enforceable agreement, it is always possible to file an action for fulfilment of the particular contractual duty, as well as suit for damages, providing that fulfilment of the duty is still practically possible.

Are restrictions relating to (a) transfers of shares and/or (b) minority "veto rights" commonly included in the articles of association or by-laws of the company—or included in a separate shareholders' agreement?

Restrictions on transfers of shares and minority veto rights must always be included in the memorandum of association or articles of association. It is, of course, possible to agree in principle in the letter of intent or a joint venture agreement on restrictions relating to transfers of shares and minority veto rights. However, if the restrictions are not reflected in the memorandum of association or articles of association, they would not be enforceable and the statutory provisions would apply instead.

Are there any formalities (e.g. notarisation or registration) which are material and which may affect the timing involved in forming the joint venture?

The joint venture documentation does not need to be drawn up in the form of a notarial deed (except for the memorandum of association of a limited liability company or a joint stock company). With regard to other company forms, the parties' signatures on the memorandum of association or document equivalent thereto must be certified by a notary public. The company is incorporated upon its entry into the Czech Commercial Register.

(4) France

Authors: Jean-Claude Cotoni and Thomas Rabain
Freshfields Bruckhaus Deringer LLP, Paris

1. General background

Are joint ventures popular as a form of foreign investment into your jurisdiction?

Foreign investments in France commonly take the form of direct acquisitions, mergers or joint ventures. The choice will depend on strategic, financial and commercial considerations. Joint ventures are frequent.

Are there restrictions on foreign participation?

French regulations applicable to direct foreign investments have been considerably simplified during the last decade and restrictions reduced, particularly as regards investments by EU nationals. The principle applicable to non-French investors is that of freedom to invest subject to filing a simple administrative declaration with the French ministry of economy upon completion of the investment. An administrative declaration is required in particular in case of creation of a new company, acquisition of more than one-third of the shareholding or voting right of a company and even the conclusion of credit or commercial agreements with a French company resulting in a de facto control. However, an authorization by the French Ministry of Economy is still required as a condition precedent to closing in case of investments in certain sensitive sectors of the French industry (see Section 2 below). Also, specific prior authorisation may be required in certain cases depending on the nature of activity of the proposed investment. In addition, there are other requirements applicable to investments in certain industry sectors (such as press, insurance, banking, transportation or audiovisual sectors); these may entail restrictions such as the size of the foreign shareholding or the nationality of the directors. Careful consideration should be given to investments in "sensitive" sectors.

What (if any) are the major legal problems which a foreign investor in a joint venture faces in your jurisdiction?

The major concerns probably relate to France's labour laws (see below) and, in particular industry sectors, the investment controls and regulations referred to above. Otherwise, there are no major legal problems.

2. Governmental/regulatory approvals

What principal governmental or regulatory approvals are required (excluding competition law) for establishing a joint venture?

Investment in strategic industry sectors, such as weapons and ammunitions, contracts with French ministry of defence and, generally, equipment used for military purposes require a prior authorization by the French Ministry of Economy in case of investments by non EU nationals amounting to more than one-third of the share capital of a company (for EU nationals, the authorization is only required when the investment amounts to a change of control of the joint venture company). The filing of an application must be done prior to completion, the ministry of economy having two months to render its decision. The Ministry of Economy has the power to approve subject to specific prior conditions or declare void a transaction completed without its approval (and in the latter case impose a substantial fine).

Are there local anti-trust laws which might apply to the formation of the joint venture?

The establishment of a joint venture in France must be examined in terms of competition law in respect of both (i) merger control and (ii) anti-competitive practices.

(i) **Mergers**. French merger control law has undergone substantial modification through the adoption of the New Economic Regulation Act (NERs) which came into effect on May 18, 2002. The following is a brief summary:

Filing requirement/ trigger	Timetable for clearance	Test for clearance	Mandatory/ voluntary Penalties
Applies to a JV that qualifies as full-function. *Test:* (i) combined worldwide turnover of all concerned undertakings is greater than €150m; and (ii) the turnover achieved in France by at least two parties is greater than €50 m.	*Phase 1*: five weeks from complete filing with DGCCRF (extended by three weeks where commitments are submitted). *Phase 2*, if requested: four weeks to three months. Transaction cannot be completed before clearance has been received.	Whether the JV will create or strengthen a dominant position as a result of which effective competition will be significantly impaired in France.	Filing is mandatory. Failure to notify can result in fines of up to five per cent of turn over in France during previous financial year.

Notification of the creation of a JV is compulsory and suspensive where the JV constitutes a concentration and where the turnover thresholds are met. A concentration that meets the EU thresholds requires notification before the European Commission, but not before the French Competition Authority (the DGCCRF). In France, the final decision is taken by the Ministry of Economy. Phase 2 (in-depth review by the *Conseil de la Concurrence*) is only open when the concentration is likely to raise competition concerns. In practice, most of the concentrations are cleared in Phase 1. Except in specific cases, notifiable concentrations cannot be closed (i.e. no effective implementation) before clearance.

(ii) **Anti-competitive practices**. When a co-operative joint venture is considered to constitute an anti-competitive agreement (e.g. if its purpose or effect is to restrict or distort competition), it can be examined by the *Conseil de la Concurrence* and/or by the relevant courts. In opposition with merger control, there exists no formal "notification procedure" (requiring for exemption) for anti-competitive agreements. Agreements that appear anti-competitive can be exempted in specific cases, notably if the parties show that the agreement contributes to economic progress. The courts may declare an anti-competitive agreement to be void and may impose damages. The *Conseil de la Concurrence* has notably the power to impose heavy fines, up to 10 per cent of the worldwide turnover achieved by the infringing companies group.

3. Types of joint venture vehicle

What are the principal types of joint venture vehicle commonly used with foreign investors?

There are three main structures for setting up joint ventures in France. These may take the form of (i) a corporation, (ii) a partnership or (iii) a purely contractual alliance or relationship. Generally, a distinction is made between joint ventures which give rise to a legal entity and those which do not.

Contractual joint ventures. The main feature of a contractual venture is that it is a "simple" co-operation agreement directly between parties pursuing a common objective, such as the pooling and supply of resources.

Partnerships. *Sociétés de personnes* (the equivalent to partnership) are characterised by legal personality, the joint and unlimited liability of the partners and restrictions on the transfer of shares. A range of partnership-type forms exist. The main forms of partnerships for use in joint ventures include the following:

- A *société civile* is generally chosen as a vehicle for real estate activities. Its main advantage is its tax transparency which involves profits and losses flowing directly to its members who will each be taxed on their own share in the profits in compliance with their own tax regime. The main disadvantage is that partners are jointly liable, pro rata to each partner's contribution, for the partnership's debts.

- A *société en nom collectif* (SNC) is only suitable for joint ventures between a limited number of partners, among whom trust prevails. Its main advantage is that there is no minimum level of capital required and the partners benefit from tax transparency (unless the SNC elects for corporation tax). The main disadvantage is that the partners are indefinitely jointly and severally liable for the partnership's debts.

- A *société en commandite* is generally used when one of the venturers seeks control over the management and the others only have a share in the profits. General partners have joint and several unlimited liability but have control over the management. Limited partners' liabilities are limited to the amount of their financial contributions but they are not permitted to take an active part in management. The main disadvantage is the unlimited joint and several liability of the general partners. From a tax viewpoint, the part of the profits or the losses corresponding to the general partner's share will benefit from the tax transparency whereas the part of the profits or losses corresponding to the limited partners' share will be subject to corporation tax.

- A hybrid vehicle, having legal personality, is the *groupement d'intérêt économique*, which is similar to a non-profit-making association; the aim is for the members to share costs. It is transparent in terms of taxation and liabilities.

Corporations. The main advantage of a corporation is its legal independence from the joint venturers and the limited liability of the shareholders. The principal forms are:

- The *société anonyme* (SA) is the most common form of French commercial company with limited liability. It must have at least seven shareholders and has to be managed by a board of directors and a directeur général. French company law, however, determines the content of the articles of association with little scope for the flexibility of a *société par actions simplifiée*. There are significant difficulties in enforcing classic joint venture corporate governance provisions (such as veto rights or weighted voting) in a *société anonyme*.

- The *société en commandite par actions* is a *société en commandite* whose share capital is divided into shares (*actions*). The regime of the société en commandite par actions is very similar to that of the *société anonyme* except that there are two categories of shareholders: general partners and limited partners.

- The *société par actions simplifiée* (SAS) was introduced under French law in 1994 and simplified in 1999. It is the most flexible form of company as regards its organisation and operation of its management bodies. Most of the provisions that are ordinarily included in shareholders' agreements may be included in the articles of association and therefore be subject to specific performance (such as prior approval of the sale of shares, pre-emption rights, right to exclude a shareholder under certain circumstances, inalienability of the shares for a certain period of time). This form of company cannot be listed (although it may be re-registered as a société anonyme for the purposes of listing). It is the most appropriate vehicle for structural joint ventures.

- There also exists the *société à responsabilité limitée* (SARL) which was the simplest form of commercial company with limited liability until the introduction of the SAS into French law. However, it is generally not chosen for joint ventures as it presents several disadvantages such as the impossibility of having different classes of shares, complicated formalities and the payment of relatively high registration duties on transfer of shares.

If a partnership structure is chosen, does this lead to (a) joint and several liability to third parties and/or (b) duties of good faith as between partners?

A partnership structure implies a joint and several liability as regards general partners to third parties in the case of the *société civile*, the *société en nom collectif*, the *société en commandite* and the *groupement d'intérêt économique*. The by-laws of a partnership may be considered as a contract which must be performed in good faith in accordance with the French Civil code.

4. Capital structure and funding

What principal local law issues affect the capital structure and funding of the joint venture?

Funding techniques are numerous. Usually the most common method is a straightforward subscription for shares (either in cash or for a non-cash consideration). However, joint ventures with outside investors not engaged in the management of the company may involve more complex funding: methods such as preference share capital or convertible loans, both of which are possible under French law. It is, for example, possible to have non-voting preference shares.

The minimum capital for a non-listed *société par actions* (e.g. an SA or SAS) is — 37,000. At least one half of the nominal value of the capital of an SA or SAS (one-fifth for a SARL) has to be paid up on incorporation and the balance in any event within five years. Shares subscribed for non-cash or mixed consideration must be paid up in full on issue.

Is it common to have "preference" shares which give a party a priority on payment of dividends or on a return of capital?

It is common to have preference shares in joint venture companies. Before a law dated June 24, 2004, there were various categories of preference shares. Such categories have now been unified under a single regime.

Are "redeemable" shares permitted (i.e. shares that can be repaid and cancelled)?

Under French law, it is possible for a *société par actions* to buy its own shares from its shareholders under certain conditions. The most common purpose for such transaction is to reduce the share capital of the company. In such case, any shares of the company may be redeemable. The creation of shares redeemable at the option of an individual shareholder is difficult (and would require co-operation or agreement of all shareholders).

Are "non-voting" shares permitted?

Yes, such shares are permitted.

Is it common to have different "classes" of shares (e.g. A and B shares) to reflect different initial contributions or financial interests of the parties?

Yes. The share capital of most of the French companies (*société par actions*) may be divided into classes of shares with special rights allocated to each of them (although not weighted voting rights-generally each share gives one vote). In practice, the allocation by class appears to be the best method to provide protection for each joint venturer and minority shareholders in particular. Since the law dated June 24, 2004, such classes of shares will be created under the preference shares regime.

Are there any "thin capitalisation" or similar rules which affect the choice of equity/debt ratio for the capital structure?

From a tax viewpoint, French companies are not obliged by law to respect a particular debt to equity capitalisation ratio. However, there are rules which restrict the deduction of part of the amounts of interest paid by companies in respect of funds advanced as a loan by its shareholders or by an enterprise related to the borrower. For that purpose, an enterprise is deemed to be related to the borrower either when (i) one owns directly or through interposed persons the majority of the share capital of the other or holds in fact the power of decision, or (ii) both the borrower and the lender are related to the same third person. In particular, interest paid to a shareholder or a related enterprise must not exceed an average rate periodically published by the French tax authorities (however, where the borrower is a related enterprise, this limitation does not apply if it demonstrates that the rate applied is at arm's length).

In addition, interest paid in respect of funds advanced by a related enterprise to a French company that is subject to corporation tax is generally deductible only to the extent that the borrower is not considered as thinly capitalised (subject to a number of safe harbour rules). A company will be viewed as "thinly capitalised" if none of the three following tests are satisfied: (i) the related party debt does not exceed one and a half times the net assets of that company, (ii) the interest paid to related enterprises does not exceed 25 per cent of the adjusted pre-tax operating profits of the borrower, and (iii) the interest paid to related enterprises does not exceed the amount of interest received by the borrowing company from other related enterprises. Non-deductible interest, may under certain conditions and limitations, be carried forward. Specific rules apply where the borrower and the lender are members of a tax consolidation group.

Under French law, the net assets of a *société à responsabilité limitée*, a *société anonyme*, a *société en commandite par actions* and a *société par actions simplifiée* must be, at all times, in excess of one half of the amount of its share capital. If the net assets of the company are below such threshold, a shareholders' meeting must be convened (to decide whether to wind up the company or to carry on) and the situation must be regularised in the two years following the year in which the undercapitalisation has been acknowledged.

Is a separate "contribution agreement" or other formal document required under the local law?

A separate contribution agreement is usual in the case of contribution in kind although it is not a requirement under French law.

Are there any local laws which require independent valuation of any non-cash assets to be contributed?

A contribution in kind to a company against the issue of shares is subject to a prior valuation made by an independent appraiser (*commissaire aux apports*) appointed by the commercial court. The procedure is relatively simple and the names of the appraiser which the parties wish to be appointed may be proposed to the commercial court.

Are there exchange control regulations which materially affect the establishment of the joint venture-or the subsequent repatriation of profits or dividends from the joint venture to a foreign party?

As indicated in section 2 above, certain investments in a French entity whose activity relates to or may affect public policy, public safety or defence is subject to the prior consent of the Ministry of Economy which may grant or withhold its approval at its discretion. Repatriation of profits or dividends is not restricted.

If a foreign party is to contribute technology to the joint venture, are there any special requirements for valuation of that technology?

Intellectual property rights contributed in kind to the joint venture need to be valued as any other asset contributed in kind.

5. Tax

Are there any particular tax laws or incentives which significantly affect the establishment of joint ventures in this jurisdiction by a foreign investor?

There are no particular tax regulations which significantly affect the establishment of joint ventures in France. The corporate income tax (*Impôt sur les Sociétés*) is levied at the normal rate of 33.33 per cent. A social contribution at a rate of 3.3 per cent may apply to the amount of corporate income tax.

If the joint venture is set up in order to purchase a French company subject to corporate income tax, it might benefit under certain circumstances from the so-called "participation exemption" regime with respect to dividends if it holds at least five per cent of the voting rights and share capital of the French company. A tax consolidation group (*intégration fiscale*) may also be set up between the joint venture and that French company if the former owns at least 95 per cent of the voting rights and share capital of the latter. Capital gains realized upon the disposition of shares (except shares in real estate companies) are exempt from corporation tax provided the shares have been held for at least two years and qualify, and are booked, as a controlling interest (titres de participation).

Will withholding taxes apply to dividends paid by a joint venture company?

A 25 per cent withholding tax is levied on dividends paid by a French resident company to a non resident (company or individual), unless reduced under a tax treaty or exempt under the EU Parent/Subsidiary Directive as implemented by French law.

6. Board and management

Are there local law rules which affect the board or management structure of the joint venture? May a two-tier board be required?

A board system or a two-tier management structure may be freely chosen in an SA. The first type of management structure consists in entrusting the management to a single body (board of directors) whereas the second consists in creating a separation between a management board (directoire) and a supervisory board. A two-tier management is cumbersome (and is not often used) but has the advantage of offering more independence and stability to the directoire (whose members cannot be revoked without motive, contrary to the members of a board of directors; in certain circumstances, this can be a disadvantage), which assumes the day-to-day management. In an SAS, the management structure is defined by the parties; the only mandatory organ of management is the President of the SAS, who holds all its powers vis-a-vis third parties. The SAS has the advantage of allowing the shareholders to adapt the management organisation to their specific needs and requirements.

Are there local law constraints on persons who can be directors or managers of the joint venture (e.g. only local residents or nationals)?

They are few legal requirements as regards nationality. However, if the proposed president or managers are not French, EU or OEeD nationals, they must hold a residence permit.

Does a shareholder in a joint venture company owe a duty of good faith (or similar duty) to other shareholders in the way it behaves in relation to the joint venture?

If a shareholders' agreement has been entered into, each party to it must perform that agreement in good faith. Otherwise, there is no specific duty of good faith between shareholders although they must not commit any fraud while acting as shareholders.

Can you modify the legal duties of directors so that they can expressly take into account the interests of their "appointer" when voting or acting as director, or must they always act objectively in the best interests of the company?

Under French law, directors must always act objectively in the best interests of the company and the shareholders.

7. Transfer of shares

In the case of a joint venture company, can a permanent restriction on transfer of shares be imposed under the local law (e.g. no transfer without the consent of the other shareholder)?

In both a *société anonyme* and a *société par actions simplifiée*, the by-laws as well as a shareholders' agreement may provide for a permanent restriction consisting in a share transfer approval by a corporate body. However, a restriction consisting in a lock-up (i.e. no right to transfer) cannot be permanent: in a *société anonyme*, such lock-up although not provided by law is deemed to be valid only if it is provided for a limited period of time and if it is justified as regards the corporate interest of the company. In a *société par actions simplifiée*, the law specifically allows the by-laws to provide that the shares of the company are not transferable for a period of up to 10 years.

8. Protection for minority shareholders

What protections exist for a minority shareholder in a joint venture company?

Aside from statutory rules (see below), a minority shareholder in a joint venture may protect itself mostly through the shareholders' agreement (lock-up, veto rights regarding certain management decision) but also by pushing for a corporate form allowing *intuitu personae* relationships (e.g. SAS or partnership) since provisions in by-laws are easier to enforce when breached than those in a private shareholders' agreement.

Are there any statutory rules or remedies which help significantly to protect a minority shareholder in a joint venture company?

In a *société anonyme*, a minority shareholder holding one share will receive permanent information on the company and may (i) commence liability proceedings on its own behalf and/or on behalf of the company against its officers (also the case in a SAS and SARL) (ii) request the court to order the nullity of a corporate decision or of the company or to appoint a representative to convene a shareholders' meeting in case of emergency. Shareholders with at least five per cent may request the inclusion of a new item in a shareholders' meeting agenda and request the court to appoint an expert to review a management decision (also the case in a SAS and SARL). In addition, any decision increasing the obligations of the shareholders will require their unanimous approval.

If it holds at least one third of the share capital and one share, a minority shareholder benefits from a blocking right as it can oppose all shareholders' extraordinary resolutions (e.g. capital increase or decrease, merger, liquidation, change of the by-laws).

Does the law require any major business decisions to be approved by a special resolution or super-majority (whether at board or shareholder level)—or must a minority party protect itself by contract?

Per law, a special majority is required for certain formal acts (such an amendment of the by-laws). However, these do not extend to business decisions such as acquisitions, disposals, capital expenditure etc., which may, however, be specifically covered in the by-laws (preferable in terms of efficiency) or in the shareholders' agreement (preferable in terms of confidentiality). However, in case of sale of most or all of the assets of a company, which could be interpreted as a change of corporate purpose, such divestiture may have to be authorised by the shareholders with a two-thirds majority even in the absence of contractual provision. Likewise, the President of a *société par actions simplifié* deciding the sale of a subsidiary will often in practice seek a formal approval by the shareholders of the company.

9. Employment laws

Are there local law obligations requiring a "local" party to consult with, or obtain the approval of, employees or employee representatives on a contribution of its business to the joint venture?

The contribution of a French company's business to a joint venture triggers the prior obligation to inform and consult the French company's works council (if any). Indeed, the works council has to be informed and consulted in case of a change to the legal or economic organisation of the business, notably in the event of sale, merger or significant changes to the structure. The works council must render an opinion on the transaction be it positive or negative, prior to the execution of a binding agreement. A negative opinion cannot prevent a transaction from going forward. However, failure to consult the works council is a criminal offence and may result in a civil action being brought by the employee representatives in order to suspend completion of the transaction until the works council deems itself sufficiently informed.

Any company with more than 50 employees during any 12 months over a three year period must have a works council (*comité d'enterprise*). Two representatives of the works council must be invited to attend all board meetings (in which they have a consultative role but no right to vote) and may be invited to shareholders' meetings.

Are there any material employment laws (compared with the UK) which are likely to affect the ongoing operations of the joint venture?

Once the joint venture has been set up it will be necessary to determine which collective bargaining agreement will apply to the employees. Staff representative bodies will need to be set up for the joint venture, which would be likely to affect ongoing operations. In the event of a mass layoff plan, attempts must be made to offer the affected employees new positions throughout the entire group, including with the parent company. Recent French legislation has softened the impact of the 35 hours working week with notably a decreased cost for overtime. This matter is highly regulated by industry wide and company collective bargaining agreements

In addition, French labour law provides for mandatory profit-sharing for employees in any company having more than 50 employees. Employer and employee social security contributions are higher than in the UK.

10. Accounts

Is there a requirement on the joint venture company to file accounts with any authority where they are publicly available?

Annual accounts must be filed each year with the companies' clerk of the local commercial court and therefore become publicly available.

11. Dispute resolution

Is there any standard local practice as to form of dispute resolution in relation to joint ventures with foreign investors? Is arbitration in a venue outside that jurisdiction acceptable?

Arbitration outside France is acceptable. However, many dispute resolution clauses provide for the competence of the ICC, the seat of which is in Paris.

Is the local jurisdiction a signatory to the 1958 New York Convention on the Recognition and Enforcement of Foreign Arbitral Awards?

Yes

12. Legal documents and formalities

Is there any special form of legal documentation required under local law for establishment of a joint venture company? What are the usual principal documents?

The usual principal documents will be those required for any company: the by-laws, which set the organizational rules of the company, a certificate from a bank acknowledging receipt of the share capital in the bank account of the company, a lease agreement or domiciliation agreement (e.g. for letter-box registered office), a declaration of non-conviction by the President or directors of the company and a letter from the statutory auditors accepting their duties. As the by-laws are public documents, the shareholders of a joint venture will in practice also resort to a private shareholders' agreement which will set out in detail the contractual relationships between the parties in the context of their joint venture.

Does the joint venture documentation need to be in the local language and/or governed by the local law?

Official documents such as by-laws must be drafted in the French language and subject to French law. Private agreements that are not required to be registered (e.g. a shareholders' agreement) may be drafted in any language and may be regulated by a foreign law.

Are agreements between shareholders (e.g. as to appointment of directors, conduct of the business of the company or voting majorities required for certain decisions etc.) enforceable under local law? In the event of breach, is specific performance or a similar remedy available-or only damages?

Agreements between shareholders are enforceable under French law provided that they do not contravene any public policy provision. However, by-laws prevail over a shareholders' agreement since the former set out imperative rules for the company's corporate bodies whereas the latter set out contractual relationships between shareholders. In practice, the French courts are extremely reluctant to award specific performance in the case of a breach of a shareholders' agreement (although, in one case involving a breach of a "drag-along" provision, a defaulting party was ordered by the court to sell its shares and in another case the court ruled that the beneficiary of a breached preemption right, not notified of a share transfer, was the rightful transferee of the share transfer).

Are restrictions relating to (a) transfers of shares and/or (b) minority "veto rights" commonly included in the articles of association or by-laws of the company-or included in a separate shareholders' agreement?

Given the reluctance of the courts to order specific performance (rather than damages) for breach of a shareholders' agreement, it is common to include restrictions on the transfer of shares in the by-laws of the company. A transfer in breach of the by-laws will be null and void.

Are there any formalities (e.g. notarisation or registration) which are material and which may affect the timing involved in forming the joint venture?

The transfer of real estate requires a notarial deed. The procedure for valuation of contributions in kind also involves certain unavoidable periods for disclosure formalities.

(5) Germany

Authors: Hildegard Bison and Johanna Schrammen
           Freshfields Bruckhaus Deringer LLP, Germany

1. General background

Are joint ventures popular as a form of foreign investment into your jurisdiction?

Joint ventures are fairly popular as a means of foreign investment into Germany. Germany has a highly developed free market economy with hardly any restrictions on foreign investment. It is legally and commercially closely linked to its partners in the EU. It offers significant freedom in the establishment of a joint venture. However, Germany is also a country with complex rules (e.g. on employment, environment and consumer protection) that can be alien to foreign investors.

Are there restrictions on foreign participation?

Germany has no controls discriminating against foreign investment (except for rarely enforced restrictions under the Foreign Trade Act).

What (if any) are the major legal problems which a foreign investor in a joint venture faces in your jurisdiction?

German law provides for strict rules regarding the raising and maintenance of the share capital of companies which should be considered before setting up the finance structure of the joint venture vehicle.

2. Governmental/regulatory approvals

What principal governmental or regulatory approvals are required (excluding competition law) for establishing a joint venture?

The setting-up of most businesses is free of regulation subject only to a notification to the local governments and tax authorities. Some businesses are subject to prior authorisation including, inter alia, banking, insurance and investment funds. Authorisation may sometimes not be required if the founder of the business is already authorised in another EU country. Therefore, regulatory control is primarily through competition laws—applicable to both foreign and German parties.

Are there local anti-trust laws which might apply to the formation of the joint venture?

If a joint venture is set up as a legal entity (in contrast to an alliance only by contract) it may require pre-closing clearance by the German Federal Cartel Office (*Bundeskartellamt—FCO*) under the merger control procedures laid down in the German Act against Restraints on Competition (*Gesetz gegen Wettbewerbsbeschränkungen—GWB*), provided that the German turnover thresholds are met. Alternatively, a joint venture set up in Germany may require (pre-closing) clearance by the European Commission if the thresholds laid down in the EC Merger Regulation (*ECMR*) are met.

In addition, potential spill-over effects of a joint venture on its parent companies and the potential of co-ordination between the parent companies may also be subject to regulation for anti-competitive behaviour in the GWB. These regulations for anti-competitive behaviour may also apply if a joint venture is set up and governed by contract only (without establishing a legal entity) e.g. as a "strategic alliance".

(i) **Mergers.** The following is a brief summary of this German merger control law:

Filing requirement/ trigger	Timetable for clearance	Test for clearance	Mandatory/voluntary Penalties
German merger control applies to an acquisition of (joint) control or an acquisition of 25 per cent or more of the shares or the voting rights in a joint venture (provided that the turnover thresholds are met).

The turnover thresholds are met if: (i) the combined worldwide turnover of the undertakings concerned is at least €500m; and (ii) at least one of the undertakings concerned has a local turnover of €25m or more in Germany. It should be noted that an "undertaking concerned" is any entity acquiring more than 25 per cent in the joint venture and the joint venture company itself if it already generates turnover.

Lower thresholds may apply to certain media and trade companies. The test is also subject to certain de minimis exemptions designed to ensure a sufficient nexus to Germany. | Stage 1 (in straightforward cases): one month after filing.

Stage 2 (in cases which require an in-depth competition assessment): four months after filing. However, this deadline can be extended if the parties agree.

There is a suspension obligation, i.e. the transaction cannot be implemented until the respective waiting period has expired or a clearance decision has been received. A derogation can be granted in case of extraordinary circumstances. | The FCO will assess whether a joint venture will create or strengthen a dominant market position, which is not outweighed by an improvement of the market conditions in other markets.

There is a statutory presumption of single-firm dominance where the joint venture will hold a share of one third of the market (33.3 per cent) or where the joint venture is part of an oligopoly of not more than three undertakings which holds a share of 50 per cent or an oligopoly of not more than five undertakings which holds a share of two thirds (66.66 per cent).

The FCO will also assess possible spill-over effects between the JV and the parent companies of the JV partners and the possibility of coordination between these parent companies. | Filing is mandatory, and documents can be submitted any time before the completion of the transaction.

Failure to file and implementation without clearance: fines of up to —1m or, in case of undertakings, 10 per cent of the turnover generated in the preceding business year.

Incomplete/incorrect filing: fines of up to —100,000.

In addition, from a German civil law point of view a transaction is invalid until clearance has been granted. |

(ii) **Provisions for anti-competitive behaviour.** A joint venture can also fall within the ambit of the provisions for anti-competitive behaviour. The FCO will assess whether the joint venture will restrict competition between the activities of the parent companies of the JV partners or between the joint venture and its parent companies (in particular, if they are active on the same markets as the joint venture).

If certain criteria are met, the provisions for anti-competitive behaviour in the GWB can in particular apply to non-compete undertakings or other ancillary restrictions of competition. The FCO does not issue comfort letters. However, even if the FCO does not take up alleged breaches of the provisions for anti-competitive behaviour on its own initiative, the competent courts can (in the case of dispute) still hold any such arrangement void.

If the local party is a public company, when might the approval of its shareholders be required under stock exchange or similar rules?
There are no stock exchange or similar rules which would require a prior consent of the general meeting of a stock corporation (AG) for the establishment of a joint venture—although reporting requirements may apply. However, according to the judicature of the German Federal Court of Justice in the *Holzmüller* and in the *Gelatine* case, the approval of the general meeting of an AG is required for structural measures of extraordinary importance. In the *Holzmüller* case (1982), an AG contributed approximately 80 per cent of its assets to a subsidiary. In its 2004 decision of the *Gelatine* case, the German Federal Court of Justice confirmed that the *Holzmüller* rule should apply to cases where the structural measures touch the core competence of the general meeting to decide matters concerning the constitution of the AG: The general meeting must consent to structural measures that result in changes which are comparable to changes requiring a modification of the statutes of the AG. The Court also held that the approval by the general meeting of such structural measures requires 75 per cent of all votes cast.

Exact criteria for such "structural measures" have not yet been defined by the German courts. Against this background, there is a substantial risk that the intention of the management board to implement structural measures of a certain importance in a publicly listed company in Germany could lead to a minority shareholders' action based on the *Holzmüller/Gelatine* judicature.

3. Types of joint venture vehicle

What are the principal types of joint venture vehicle commonly used with foreign investors?
The joint venture vehicle mostly used in setting up an international joint venture domiciled in Germany is either (a) a limited liability company (*Gesellschaft mit beschrankter Haftung—GmbH*) or (b) a limited partnership (*Kommanditgesellschaft—KG*) with the general partner being a GmbH (*GmbH & Co KG*). The stock corporation (*Aktiengesellschaft—AG*) is rarely used due to its more rigid rules of corporate law. If the involvement of a joint venture partner is limited to its capital contribution, a silent partnership (*stille Gesellschaft*) might also be considered. Furthermore, the European public limited-liability company (*Societas Europaea—SE*) is available as a vehicle for international joint ventures incorporated in Germany.

(1) *GmbH.* A GmbH is a private limited liability company. It can be set up by one or more persons and has to be registered in the commercial register of the competent local court at its seat. The shareholders' liability is, in principle, limited to the amount of the share capital subscribed for. The GmbH statutes

can be tailored closely to the needs of the shareholders who have ultimate control over the GmbH's affairs.

(2) *GmbH & Co KG.* A GmbH & Co KG is a limited partnership (KG). Necessary for its establishment are a sole general partner and one or more limited partners. The general partner, which incurs full liability as against the KG's creditors, is a GmbH which usually holds no capital in the partnership. The limited partners are usually the GmbH's sole shareholders. The liability of the limited partners is limited to the nominal amount of their partnership interest as registered with the commercial register of the competent local court at its seat. The GmbH & Co. KG therefore allows for a partnership structure but still offers limited liability to its partners. The partnership agreement may be structured to reflect the partners' specific needs.

(3) *AG.* An AG is a stock corporation and, generally speaking, only AGs can be listed on one of the German stock exchanges. It may be set up by one or more persons under a somewhat formal procedure and it also requires registration in the commercial register of the competent local court at its seat. Compared to a GmbH, it offers less flexibility as to the provisions of its statutes. In addition, the influence of the shareholders with respect to management decisions is limited since the managing board has extensive competence.

(4) *Silent partnership.* The silent partnership is a contractual agreement between one or several "silent" partners and a business entity. The silent partners have no influence and only limited information rights against the business entity. The silent partnership is generally aimed at profit-sharing. Under specified circumstances, it might offer tax advantages compared with a loan to the business entity.

(5) *SE.* A SE *(Societas Europaea)* is a European public limited-liability company. The foundation of a SE follows the harmonised rules established by the European Union in Council Regulation (EC) No 2157/2001 on the Statute for a European company (SE) *(SE Regulation)*, but also particular German rules established for the SE. To the extent no particular legislation has been created for the SE, the SE follows the rules applicable to a German AG. The most distinctive differences between a SE and an AG are the choice between a two-tier and a one-tier administrative system as regards the structure of the SE, and the possibility to deviate from the—otherwise mandatory— German rules concerning the co-determination rights of employees in the company (as described under 9 below). The forming of a joint venture is a particular method of foundation of a SE under the SE Regulation.

If a partnership structure is chosen, does this lead to (a) joint and several liability to third parties and/or (b) duties of good faith as between partners?

Yes. The partners are jointly and severally liable for the debts and other liabilities of the partnership. In case of a KG, however, the liability of the limited partners is limited to the amounts registered with the commercial register. There are no specific duties of good faith between the partners other than the general duties of good faith which apply under German corporate law. However, a liability for any violation of the partnership agreement or under mandatory law may apply.

4. Capital structure and funding

Minimum capital requirements are as follows:

(1) *GmbH.* The minimum share capital of a GmbH is €25,000. Non-cash capital contributions are subject to a valuation by an independent expert, usually a certified auditor. They have to be registered as such with the commercial

register and are subject to particular procedures. The registration of the company cannot be effected before (i) each cash contribution has been paid in by at least one fourth and (ii) the sum of all paid-in cash contributions and the shares for which non-cash contributions are made amount to €12,500.

(2) *GmbH & Co KG.* A GmbH & Co KG as such is not subject to any minimum capital requirement; however, the GmbH as its general partner must have a minimum capital of €25,000. Non-cash capital contributions to the KG may be freely valued by the partners for internal purposes (e.g. to calculate voting rights or profit-sharing) but liability towards third parties can arise if the fair market value of the non-cash capital contribution is less than the registered partnership interest.

(3) *AG.* The minimum share capital of an AG is €50,000. Non-cash contributions are subject to similar rules as apply to a GmbH.

(4) *Silent partnership.* A silent partnership has no minimum capital requirement.

(5) *SE.* The minimum share capital of a SE is €120,000. Non-cash contributions are subject to similar rules as apply to an AG.

Is it common to have different "classes" of shares (e.g. A and B shares) to reflect different initial contributions or financial interests of the parties?

In general, it is not common in Germany to have different "classes" of shares. Nevertheless, AGs may introduce two different "classes" of shares pursuant to the German Stock Corporation Act (*Aktiengesetz*) and issue (i) ordinary shares and (ii) preference shares. Although the Limited Liability Companies Act (*GmbH-Gesetz*), which governs the GmbH, does not provide for such classes of shares, it is not uncommon for different classes of shares to be created in a GmbH—either in the articles of association or in a shareholders' agreement.

Is it common to have "preference" shares which give a party a priority on payment of dividends or on a return of capital?

AGs may issue (i) ordinary shares and (ii) preference shares. The holders of preference shares are precluded from voting in the general meetings but are, on the other hand, entitled to receive a preferred dividend. During recent years, the number of AGs that have issued preference shares has continuously decreased. In particular, the pressure of institutional investors might have caused a trend to abolish preference shares.

In the statutes of a GmbH, it is possible to provide for special rights of individual shareholders that grant them a claim for a priority on the distribution of profits or on the return of capital.

Are "redeemable" shares permitted (i.e. shares that can be repaid and cancelled)?

No, AGs and GmbHs cannot issue redeemable shares. Shares may, however, be subject to a share-buy-back or the cancellation by shareholders' resolution if the statutes authorise such cancellation.

Are "non-voting" shares permitted?

Yes. Holders of preference shares in an AG are precluded from voting at general meetings. The same rules apply to a SE. In a GmbH, the statutes may provide for voting shares and non-voting shares. However, even the holder of non-voting shares has certain veto rights that cannot be excluded by the statute, in particular where a fundamental change of the company is envisaged (e.g. a change of the purpose of the company, such as the decision to give up the realisation of profit and to act as a non-profit-making entity instead).

Are there any "thin capitalisation" or similar rules which affect the choice of equity debt ratio for the capital structure?

Yes. Basically, interest payments on shareholder loans are fully deductible for corporate tax purposes. For trade tax purposes, 75 per cent of the interest payments are deductible.

The Business Tax Reform 2008 intended to limit the possibilities of reducing taxable income. A key component of the new law is the introduction of a general limitation on the tax deductibility of interest expenses (*Zinsschranke*). The general rule is that interest expenses will be deductible without limitation only if interest expenses do not exceed interest income in the same year. Otherwise interest expenses may be deducted without limitation only if (i) the interest expenses exceed the interest income less than the exempt threshold of —1m, (ii) the company is not or only partially an affiliated company within the meaning of the German Income Tax Act (*Einkommensteuergesetz*), or (iii) the company is an affiliated company, but the equity capital ratio of the company claiming the deduction of interest is not more than one per cent lower than the equity capital ratio of the group as a whole.

If these conditions are not satisfied, the deduction of interest expenses exceeding interest income is limited to 30 per cent of taxable income as increased by interest expenses, depreciation and amortisation and as reduced by interest income. Any additional non-deductible interest may only be claimed in subsequent years.

The new law applies to all types of borrowed capital. It does not make any difference whether the corporation has borrowed the capital from a shareholder or from a bank.

Is there any capital or similar tax payable in respect of issued share capital?

No.

Is a separate "contribution agreement" or other formal document (other than formal property transfer agreements) required or usual under the local law to document the contribution of assets to the joint venture?

In general, it is not required by law but common practice to conclude a separate written agreement of the contribution of existing assets to a joint venture. Only the transfer of specific assets is subject to formal requirements under German law. Inter alia, the transfer of shares in a GmbH or land has to be recorded by a notary.

Are there any local laws which require an independent valuation of any non-cash assets to be contributed to the joint venture?

In cases where the non-cash contribution is treated as payment for issued shares of an AG, SE or a GmbH, an independent valuation is required since the contribution has to cover (at least) the nominal value of the shares. Therefore, it is necessary to prove the value of the contributed non-cash assets by the statement of an independent expert, usually a certified auditor. The local courts must dismiss an application for the registration of an AG, SE or a GmbH or the increase of the share capital with the commercial register if the value of non-cash assets has not been correctly determined. If the contribution is booked to the capital reserves of the company, such valuation is dispensable.

Are there exchange control regulations which materially affect the establishment of the joint venture—or the subsequent repatriation of profits or dividends from the joint venture to a foreign party?

Foreign-held companies may freely import and export currencies and pay dividends, licence fees, etc. However, significant reporting requirements do apply to such payments if they exceed certain thresholds.

5. Tax

Are there any particular tax laws or incentives which significantly affect the establishment of joint ventures in this jurisdiction by a foreign investor?

The German tax system is fairly complicated. However, the rates of several taxes have recently been cut significantly and Germany now provides for a 95 per cent dividend and capital gains exemption. Therefore, an international joint venture should not rule out Germany as a location for the joint venture entity. However, German external tax audits (which are performed by the German tax authorities on a regular basis if the joint venture company reaches certain turnover and/or profit thresholds) are quite onerous compared to the level of investigation in other countries.

German taxation comprises taxes on income and profits and taxes on the transfer of real estate. Profits are subject to trade tax on income as well as corporate income tax.

(1) *Trade tax on income.* Trade tax is a municipal tax which is levied by each municipality where a permanent establishment is maintained. The municipality has the right to determine the tax rate. Currently, the rate of trade tax on profit ranges from approximately 15 to 22 per cent. Trade tax is deductible when calculating the corporate income tax.

(2) *Corporate income tax.* Corporations resident in Germany are subject to corporate income tax at a rate of 15 per cent. In addition, a so-called solidarity surcharge of 5.5 per cent on the corporate tax amount applies. The overall tax burden of profits (including trade tax, corporate tax and solidarity surcharge) amounts to approximately 30 per cent. Capital gains from the disposal of shares in corporations are 95 per cent tax exempted for corporate as well as for trade tax purposes if the seller is a corporation. Further, dividends paid to corporate shareholders are 95 per cent tax exempted. Thus, the overall tax burden on capital gains and dividends deriving from an investment in a corporation amounts to approximately 1.5 per cent (30 per cent tax on five per cent of the dividend or the capital gain).

(3) *Partnership income.* If a corporation is a partner in a partnership, the income deriving from the partnership is taxed in the hands of the partner(s), i.e. the partnership is transparent for corporate income tax purposes (but not for trade tax).

Will withholding taxes apply to dividends paid by a joint venture company?

Dividends paid by corporations resident in Germany are, generally speaking, subject to a 25 per cent withholding tax. In addition, a solidarity surcharge on the withheld amount becomes payable. For non-resident taxpayers this rate may be lowered in certain circumstances. If a double taxation treaty applies, the rate (including the solidarity surcharge) is usually reduced to 15 per cent for portfolio shareholders and often to five per cent for corporate shareholders with a direct substantial shareholding.

In the case of dividend payments made to corporations resident in EU countries holding at least 20 per cent (10 per cent in the case of reciprocity) of the shares for at least one year prior to the distribution, withholding tax is reduced to zero. If the one year holding period is fulfilled after distribution, withholding tax has to be withheld on distribution but will be refunded to the shareholder on request.

6. Board and management

Are there local law rules which affect the board or management structure of the joint venture? May a two-tier board be required?

The requirements for management structure differ according to the joint venture vehicle:

(1) *GmbH*. A GmbH has one or several managing directors (*Geschäftsführer*) who are appointed, and may be removed by, shareholders' resolution at any time. They are subject to instructions from the shareholders meeting. If the GmbH is subject to the co-determination laws (see section 9 below), it also has to have a supervisory board. Otherwise a supervisory board is optional.

(2) *GmbH & Co KG*. The GmbH & Co. KG is managed by its general partner, the GmbH, to which the above principles apply.

(3) *AG*. Each AG must have a supervisory board (*Aufsichtsrat*) and a board of managing directors (*Vorstand*). The two boards are separate and no individual may be a member of both boards. The board of managing directors is responsible for managing the AG's business and is accountable to the supervisory board. The supervisory board is also responsible for appointing and removing the members of the board of managing directors. The general meeting (*Hauptversammlung*) of an AG appoints and removes the members of the supervisory board representing the shareholders. The supervisory board of a major AG also includes employees' representatives (see section 9 below). Neither an AG's general meeting nor the supervisory board may give any instructions to the board of managing directors regarding the day-to-day management of the AG. However, certain consent requirements must be established according to which management decisions of major importance for the company (which must be listed in detail) may not be implemented without the prior consent of the supervisory board. Furthermore, certain transactions may require the prior consent of the general meeting (see 2 above).

(4) *Silent partnership*. A silent partnership does not have a management organ.

(5) *SE*. A SE can be established with either a one-tier or a two-tier administrative system. In case of the one-tier system, there is one administrative organ, the so-called administrative board (*Verwaltungsrat*), which is responsible for the management of the SE. However, for the carrying out of the day-to-day business of the company and for its representation, there are also managing directors (*geschäftsführende Direktoren*), which are appointed and removed by the administrative board and bound by the instructions of the administrative board. A member of the administrative board may be a managing director of the SE at the same time. In case of the two-tier system, a management organ and a supervisory organ must be established. To the two-tier system, the rules of the AG apply with minor variations. Thus, there is a board of managing directors (*Vorstand*) and a supervisory board (*Aufsichtsrat*).

Are there local law constraints on persons who can be directors or managers of the joint venture (e.g. only local residents or nationals)?

There are no age limits and no nationality requirements. The law only requires that a managing director of a GmbH or a member of the managing board of an AG or SE has unlimited legal capacity. Individuals who are convicted of bankruptcy offences or who are prohibited by a court or a public authority from exercising a profession or pursuing a trade are disqualified by law from acting as a managing director.

Does a shareholder in a joint venture company owe a duty of good faith (or similar duty) to other shareholders in the way it behaves in relation to the joint venture?

There are no specific duties of good faith to other shareholders. However, the general duties of good faith under German corporate law apply and the shareholders may be liable for any infringement of the statutes of the company, the joint venture agreement or mandatory law.

Can you modify the legal duties of directors so that they can expressly take into account the interests of their "appointer" when voting or acting as director, or must they always act objectively in the best interests of the company?

Generally, the directors owe duties only to the company and not to certain shareholders. These duties cannot be modified, in particular they cannot be modified in favour of one shareholder. In a GmbH, however, the shareholders may adopt shareholders' resolutions by which the managing directors are instructed to take certain action. Furthermore, a shareholders' agreement may provide for certain instruction rights vis-a-vis the management in favour of one shareholder. In contrast to that, the board of management of an AG or SE is independent and not obliged to take measures upon instruction by the company's shareholders.

7. Transfer of shares

In the case of a joint venture company, can a permanent restriction on transfer of shares be imposed under the local law (e.g. no transfer without the consent of the other shareholder)?

Yes. Unless otherwise agreed in the partnership agreement, the transfer of the interest in a KG always requires the consent of all partners. Furthermore, the shareholders of a GmbH can agree in the statutes that the transfer of shares is subject to the consent of the shareholders' meeting, other shareholders or the company itself. The statutes of an AG or SE may require the transfer of the shares to have the approval of the board of managing directors if the shares are issued as registered shares. A requirement for the consent of other shareholders to the transfer of shares in an AG or SE may only be implemented by a separate shareholders' agreement.

8. Protection for minority shareholders

Are there any statutory rules or remedies which help significantly to protect a minority shareholder in a joint venture company?

Again, the position varies according to the type of joint venture vehicle:

(1) GmbH. A shareholder of a GmbH has broad information rights relating to all matters concerning the company, including the right to inspect the books and records of the company. The holders of 10 per cent or more of the share capital are entitled to request that management call a shareholders' meeting and, if such request is not complied with, to call the meeting themselves.

A minority shareholder may also be in the position to exercise a veto right in shareholders' resolutions. Shareholders' resolutions generally require a simple majority vote only. However, structural changes, in particular changes to the articles of associations, need the approval of 75 per cent of all votes cast. A very limited number of decisions may even require the unanimous approval of all shareholders (disputed among the legal authorities), e.g. resolutions changing the fundamental purpose of the company and resolutions concerning affiliation agreements, such as domination agreements and profit and loss pooling agreements to which the GmbH is party as the dominated or controlled company. In all cases where—pursuant to the applicable law—only a simple majority is required for shareholders' resolutions, it is possible to tighten the majority rule by including in the articles of association an increased majority requirement that e.g. correlates with the participation quota of the minority shareholder. This allows the minority shareholder to exercise a veto right. Furthermore, the articles of association, the rules of procedure for the management or the managing directors' service agreements can provide for a list of management measures which shall require the consent of the shareholders' meeting (for which the same increased majority requirement applies). Again, a minority shareholder is protected by a veto right.

Apart from that, the articles of association may establish certain rights for minority shareholders, e.g. preferential treatment of individual shareholders in terms of preferential dividends, veto rights, the right to appoint managing directors etc.

(2) *GmbH & Co KG.* The limited partner of a KG only has limited information and control rights and has no say in the company's business. Structural changes require its approval. However, these rules may be substantially altered by the partnership agreement and are of less significance for a GmbH & Co KG in which the limited partners are also the shareholders of the general partner.

(3) *AG.* A shareholder of an AG has limited information rights, which are considerably less extensive as in a GmbH. Each shareholder has, however, the right to request information in a general meeting for evaluating an agenda item. Furthermore, the management board must provide special reports to the shareholders when certain measures (e.g. a merger or the conclusion of a domination agreement or a profit and loss pooling agreement) are submitted for approval in general meeting.

The holders of five per cent of the share capital may request the convocation of a general meeting. Furthermore, shareholders holding five per cent or €500,000 of the share capital may request the inclusion of a particular item in the agenda for a general meeting. Just as in a GmbH, a minority shareholder may also be in the position to exercise a veto right in shareholders' resolutions. In an AG, a wide range of matters require—pursuant to the German Stock Corporation Act (*Aktiengesetz*)—a majority of 75 per cent of the represented share capital. This 75 per cent majority applies in particular to changes to the statutes, including decisions concerning the share capital (e.g. the creation of conditional or authorised capital or the issuing of convertible bonds). In most cases, it is possible to tighten the majority rule by including in the statutes a higher majority requirement that correlates with the participation quota of the minority shareholder, which allows the minority shareholder to exercise a veto right. In many cases, it is, however, also possible to lower the majority requirement in the statutes—with the effect that the veto right of a minority shareholder can be extinguished. A very limited number of decisions require the unanimous approval of all shareholders (e.g. resolutions changing the fundamental purpose of the company), which gives every minority shareholder a veto right, irrespective of its precise participation quota.

(4) *Silent partnership.* A silent partner has only limited information rights and no say in the business. However, the partnership agreement may provide otherwise.

(5) *SE.* Similar rules apply as to an AG.

Does the law require any major business decisions to be approved by a special resolution or super-majority (whether at board or shareholder level)—or must a minority party protect itself by contract?

Structural changes require the consent of all partners of a KG or a silent partnership and a 75 per cent vote of the shareholders of a GmbH. Which changes are to be considered as "structural" always depends on the circumstances of the individual case. In exceptional cases (e.g. a change of the purpose of the company), a unanimous decision may be required.

The shareholders of an AG or SE are not involved in business decisions but merely in changes of the statutes which require a 75 per cent vote of the shareholders (unless this majority is modified in the statutes of the company). Furthermore, in exceptional cases the shareholders' meeting must approve important management decisions with major structural impact under the *"Holzmüller/ Gelatine"* judicature of the German Federal Court of Justice (e.g. sale or spin-off of more than 70–80 per cent of the companies' assets). See also section 2 above.

9. Employment laws

Are there local law obligations requiring a "local" party to consult with, or obtain the approval of, employees or employee representatives on a contribution of its business to the joint venture?

Perhaps one of the most distinctive features of German law is its high level of employees' co-determination and protection—see further below. However, this has helped the relative peace between the management and the workforce in German companies and is considered one of the reasons for the rarity of strikes in Germany.

Are there any material employment laws (compared with the UK) which are likely to affect the ongoing operations of the joint venture?

(1) *Supervisory boards.* The supervisory board of an AG (with more than 500, but fewer than 2,000, employees) must have one-third of its members elected by the workforce. Certain other entities with at least 500 employees, including a GmbH, are required to establish a supervisory board to which the same rules apply as for an AG. All companies (including a GmbH & Co KG) with more than 2,000 employees (potentially including the employees of subsidiaries) are required to have a supervisory board with one-half employee representation of which two members must be trade union representatives. The chairman of the supervisory board, who is usually a shareholder representative, has a casting vote in the case of a tied vote. Different rules apply, however, for the SE: as the co-determination rights of employees are subject to an agreement between the administrative organ of the SE and representatives of the workforce of the SE and its affiliates, the parties have the opportunity to deviate from the aforementioned rules (see also 3 above).

(2) *Works councils.* Another element of co-determination is the so-called works councils (*Betriebsräte*). In each workplace with more than five employees, a works council may be elected by the workforce which has certain co-determination or consultative rights in social and personnel matters, notably in the dismissal of employees. If an enterprise has more than one workplace, a central works council should be established and, in addition, a group works council must be formed if the enterprise has subsidiaries. Both such works councils have mainly co-ordinating functions. In enterprises having, as a rule, more than 100 employees, a business committee must be established which has information and consultation rights in relation to commercial matters of the enterprise.

(3) *Social security.* German employees benefit from a well-established social security system. As a general rule, the employer has to contribute half of the costs of the mandatory health care and nursing insurance, retirement insurance and unemployment insurance. In addition, the employer has to bear the costs of industrial injuries insurance.

(4) *Redundancies.* German employees enjoy a high level of protection against redundancy. Redundancies, generally speaking, need to be strictly justified and need prior consultation with the works council if one exists. Large-scale redundancies caused by changes in the operations, such as the closing down of factories, are often accompanied by substantial payments to affected employees under a social plan. Large-scale redundancies must be notified to the labour office.

(5) *Trade Unions.* Trade unions play an important role in labour relations, not only due to the membership of trade union representatives on supervisory boards but also due to the practice of industry-wide collective agreements between trade unions and employers' associations. These agreements ordinarily regulate the wages, benefits, daily working hours and annual holidays of the employees. These agreements may, under certain circumstances, be declared mandatory for all companies in the field of business in question even if a company is not a member of the relevant employers' association.

10. Accounts

Is there a requirement on the joint venture company to file accounts with any authority where they are publicly available?

All companies (GmbH & Co KG, GmbH, AG and SE) are required to publish their annual financial statements in the electronic Federal Gazette (*elektronischer Bundesanzeiger*). Depending on their size, certain companies also have to file their financial statements with the commercial register. Companies listed on a stock exchange in Germany are required to prepare and publish a detailed annual report of their business under the Securities Trading Act (*Wertpapierhandelsgesetz*). Additionally, the Exchange Rules for the Frankfurt Stock Exchange (*Börsenordnung für die Frankfurter Wertpapierbörse*) require the filing of detailed annual, biannual and quarterly reports of their business with the stock exchange, where they are made publicly available.

11. Dispute resolution

Is there any standard local practice as to form of dispute resolution in relation to joint ventures with foreign investors? Is arbitration in a venue outside that jurisdiction acceptable?

Litigation in Germany is efficient and, compared to common law systems relatively inexpensive. Injunctive relief can be sought and obtained promptly. However, a civil procedure brought to the second and third instance might also easily take years to reach a final decision. Therefore, arbitration is a common and accepted means of dispute resolution in all areas of commercial and corporate law. Arbitration in a venue outside Germany is accepted under German law.

Is the local jurisdiction a signatory to the 1958 New York Convention on the Recognition and Enforcement of Foreign Arbitral Awards?

Yes. Germany will, broadly, recognise arbitral awards unless minimum standards of fair procedure are not adhered to or the award is contrary to public policy.

12. Legal documents and formalities

Is there any special form of legal documentation required under local law for establishment of a joint venture company? What are the usual principal documents?

The setting-up of an international joint venture in Germany will typically involve the following documentation:

(1) A joint venture agreement between the parties laying down the joint venture's basic structure and rules regarding shares in profits and losses, participation in the management, termination etc. The joint venture agreement as such is not subject to any requirements of form. However, if it obliges the parties to contribute real property or shares in a GmbH, it must be recorded by a notary to become valid.

(2) If a German joint venture company is to be established, its founding documents need to be prepared. The incorporation of a GmbH and an AG need to be recorded by a notary. Each of an AG, SE, GmbH and GmbH & Co KG has to be registered with the commercial register of the competent local court at the company's seat. In the case of an AG, SE or GmbH, the articles of association and the appointment of managing directors need to be filed with the commercial register when application for registration is made.

(3) Additional documents might be needed for non-cash contributions of the joint venture partner(s), to the joint venture company, e.g. a land transfer agreement or an agreement on the transfer or use of intellectual property rights. These may again require to be recorded by a notary.

(4) If required, a pre-merger notice to the FCO will need to be filed.

(5) The local governments and the tax authorities have to be notified of the setting-up of the business. For specific businesses, additional notification or prior authorisation requirements may apply.

Does the joint venture documentation need to be in the local language and/or governed by the local law?

Generally, the joint venture agreement, the founding documents of the company and any additional agreements between the shareholders need not be in German. However, any documents to be filed to, and any communication with, German courts and public authorities need to be in German. If documents to be filed have been prepared in foreign languages, e.g. the articles of association, they need to be translated. The German version will be the governing version. The courts and public authorities may require the translation to be attested by a sworn translator. The founding documents of the company need to be governed by German law. Other agreements may, in principle, be governed by foreign law.

Are agreements between shareholders (e.g. as to appointment of directors, conduct of the business of the company or voting majorities required for certain decisions etc.) enforceable under local law? In the event of breach, is specific performance or a similar remedy available—or only damages?

A shareholders' agreement is a contract between the shareholders and contains binding provisions, which are, in principle, enforceable. However, the freedom of contract is limited by the mandatory law. Thus, contractual obligations that are contrary to mandatory legal provisions are neither binding nor enforceable. In the event of the breach of a shareholders' agreement by one party to such agreement, the other parties may claim either specific performance of the contractual obligations by the breaching party or damages for non-performance under the general provisions of German contract law. The shareholders' agreement may also provide for a contractual penalty for breach by which the details of the claim for damages and the amount to be paid are defined.

Are restrictions relating to (a) transfers of shares and/or (b) minority "veto rights" commonly included in the articles of association or by-laws of the company—or included in a separate shareholders' agreement?

Since the articles of association have to be filed with the commercial register of the competent local court and are accessible to third parties, critical provisions such as restrictions to the transfer of shares, pre-emption rights or specific shareholders' rights are mostly included in shareholders' agreements, rules of procedure or even in the managing directors' service agreements.

Are there any formalities (e.g. notarisation or registration) which are material and which may affect the timing involved informing the pint venture?

Yes—see earlier. The requirement of notarisation should not affect any timetables if the appointment with the notary is arranged in good time. Some local courts tend to be slow in processing applications for registrations with the commercial register, which is of particular importance as a GmbH, an AG and a SE only come into existence upon such registration. Anybody who acts, before the registration, in the name of a GmbH, an AG or a SE has personal and unlimited liability for those actions.

(6) India

Authors: Pratap Amin and Bharat Anand
Freshfields Bruckhaus Deringer LLP, London

1. General background

Are joint ventures popular as a form of foreign investment into your jurisdiction?

Joint ventures are a popular means of foreign investment into India. Their importance has declined somewhat owing to progressive liberalisation of the Indian economy now permitting 100 per cent foreign ownership in a number of sectors. Nevertheless, joint ventures are used frequently—especially in sectors where foreign ownership is restricted (e.g. insurance and telecommunications) or where the foreign party seeks to rely on special skills of the local party (e.g. a local distribution network).

Are there restrictions on foreign participation?

India has exchange control regulations that place restrictions on foreign investment in certain industries. The acquisition of existing shares by a foreign party is also subject to certain restrictions (mainly relating to price). An overview of the principal routes and applicable rules for investing in joint ventures in India is set out in section 2 below.

What (if any) are the major legal problems which a foreign investor in a joint venture faces in your jurisdiction?

Major legal problem areas for foreign investors in an Indian joint venture are:

(i) *Enforcement, uncertainty and expense*:

- Since the Supreme Court of India decision in the case of *VB. Rangaraj v Gopalakrishnan* (AR 1992 SC 453), there is a risk that an Indian court would not give effect to at least some of the provisions of a shareholders' agreement relating to an Indian company (e.g. restrictions on share transfers).

- Under the Securities Contracts and Regulation Act 1956, the transfer of shares must be implemented on a "spot delivery basis" i.e. payment should be made on the same day or the next day as the date of the contract. This has cast some doubt over the validity of options—particularly where "public" listed/unlisted companies are concerned.

- Winding up is not an effective remedy for deadlock or exit and few companies are successfully wound up.

- Indian courts tend to be interventionist even in circumstances where the parties have provided for dispute resolution outside India. Enforcement in India is time consuming and expensive.

(ii) Foreign exchange laws:

- In case of exit by a foreign party in favour of an Indian party, remittance of sales proceeds outside India to the foreign party can be somewhat problematic with the Indian tax authorities insisting upon the Indian party withholding tax on any capital gains (determination of the amount of tax to be withheld by seeking an order from the Indian tax authorities is possible, but, in practice, requires the cooperation of the Indian party).

- The government has introduced regulations that restrict the ability of a foreign investor with a joint venture or investment in India to make another investment in the same field unless it obtains a "no-objection" certificate from its local joint venture partner. (There is, however, an exemption for the IT sector.) This has resulted in some "blackmail" risk for the foreign investors.[1] Although the regime has purportedly been liberalised in relation to ventures, technical collaborations and trademark agreements entered into after January 12, 2005, the position is not entirely free from doubt (not in the least on account of the fact that the body of supplemental regulations, guidelines, circulars and press notes governing foreign investment in India have not been uniformly and consistently modified to reflect the purported relaxation and the rules are not properly drafted and open to interpretation).

(iii) Structuring limitations on loans and preference shares

An Indian company seeking to borrow monies from a non-resident needs to comply with the Guidelines on External Commercial Borrowings (ECB) issued by the RBI. Through a series of policy initiatives raising ECBs (which includes shareholder loans) has generally been tightened making structuring transactions more complicated. For example, ECBs cannot be used for onward lending, investing in capital markets and real estate (except development of townships and construction and development activities), working capital purposes and repayment of rupee loans. Borrowers raising ECBs more than US$20million are required to park the ECB proceeds overseas for use as foreign currency expenditure and not remit the funds into India. If ECBs up to US$20million are raised for Rupee expenditure, the drawdown of such funds into India requires prior RBI approval.

Owing to changes in the Indian foreign investment regulations, preference shares issued to non-residents must be compulsorily convertible into equity. If preference shares are not converted into equity but are redeemed then for exchange control purposes the preference shares are treated in a manner akin to debt and the terms of the preference shares must adhere to the guidelines on ECB by residents from non-residents.

---

[1] These rules were introduced through Press Note 18 of 1998. Under Press Note 18, where a foreign party had a previous joint venture or trademark agreement or technical collaboration in the same or allied field (as its proposed new investment) in India, it was not entitled to invest under the "automatic" approval route and prior approval of the FIPB was required. The FIPB, in turn, would seek the view of the local party and require a no objection certificate before granting its approval. However, Press Notes 1 and 3 of 2005 have amended Press Note 18. The "net effect" of Press Notes 1 and 3 is that: (a) prior approval of the FIPB is not required if the existing joint venture, collaboration or trademark agreement in India relates to an allied field as the proposed investment; and (b) investments, technical collaborations and trademark agreements entered into after January 12, 2005 will not be taken into account.

2. Governmental/regulatory approvals

What principal governmental or regulatory approvals are required (excluding competition law) for establishing a joint venture?

Foreign investment in joint ventures is principally made through the "foreign direct investment" (FDI) route and is subject to fairly detailed government regulation. Under the FDI route, foreign investment in most sectors is freely permitted (under what is commonly referred to as "automatic approval") except for the following:

- proposals that require an industrial licence;

- proposals for greater foreign investment than is automatically permissible in certain sectors; governmental guidelines set down the freedom, and restrictions, for FDI in many sectors (e.g. a limit of 49 per cent in many telecom-related sectors; 26 per cent in defence industries; 26 per cent in insurance; restrictions in non-banking financial sectors; 74 per cent in private sector banking); these guidelines and associated detailed requirements must be considered before any foreign investment decision;

- proposals by a foreign collaborator who has an existing joint venture or trademark agreement or technical collaboration in the same field in India.

Prior approval of the government, granted through the Foreign Investment Promotion Board (FIPB), is needed if a foreign investment proposal is ineligible for "automatic approval". The eligibility criteria for "automatic approval" tend to be strictly administered and proposals continue to be cleared by the government acting through the FIPB.

Where fresh shares are issued to a foreign investor under "automatic approval", the shares must be priced in accordance with the guidelines issued by the Reserve Bank of India (which are not generally regarded as onerous). The guidelines essentially set a "floor price" for the shares. Broadly, in case of an unlisted company, a fresh issue of shares must be valued in accordance with the guidelines issued by the erstwhile Controller of Capital Issues. These guidelines prescribe a formula based on the net asset value or the profit earning capacity to calculate the per share price for the target. Where the target is listed, a fresh issue of shares must be made at market price. Once shares have been issued, the issuer is required to make certain filings with the Reserve Bank of India within 30 days of the receipt of subscription proceeds and the allotment of shares.

Although a particular investment may have been approved by the FIPB or may otherwise be eligible for "automatic approval", depending upon the nature of the business to be undertaken, various other operational approvals may have to be obtained and maintained (e.g. investments in insurance require registration with the Insurance Regulatory and Development Authority).

Are there local anti-trust laws which might apply to the formation of the joint venture?

Indian competition law is in a stage of development. The existing Monopolies and Restrictive Trade Practices Act 1969 ("MRTPA") does not apply specifically to merger and JV transactions but can be invoked to prohibit transactions which create a monopolistic position. The MRTPA will be replaced by a new Competition Act in the near future.

Filing requirement/ trigger	Timetable for clearance	Test for clearance
Once the Competition Act is in force, transactions can be reviewed by the Competition Commission of India (CCI) if they involve companies with: (i) assets of more than INR 10bn or turnover of more than INR 30bn in India, or (ii) in or outside India, assets of more than US$500m including at least INR 5bn in India or turnover of more than US$1500m, including at least INR 15bn in India. For transactions involving groups of companies, the review thresholds are different: (i) with operations in India: INR 40bn asset value or INR 120bn turnover; and (ii) US$2bn asset value, including at least INR 5bn in India or US$6bn turnover, including at least INR 15bn in India. There are no specific provisions for joint ventures	Under the Competition Act, filings can be made to the CCI. If the CCI does not pass an order or issue a direction following 210 days from the day of the receipt of the notice of the merger, permission is deemed to have been obtained.	Under the MRTPA: prejudice to the public/company's/shareholders' interest, or likelihood of adoption of monopolistic or restrictive trade practices. Under the Competition Act: whether the transaction causes or is likely to cause an appreciable adverse effect on competition within the relevant market in India. **Mandatory/voluntary Penalties** Optional but, under the Competition Act, if it is determined later that the combination has or is likely to have an adverse effect on competition, the combination would be void. The CCI may prohibit or amend the transaction.

It should be noted that while the Competition Act restricts anti-competitive "horizontal" and "vertical" agreements there is an express safe harbour for agreements entered into by way of "joint ventures" if such agreements increase efficiency in production, supply, distribution of goods or services.

3. Types of joint venture vehicle

What are the principal types of joint venture vehicle commonly used with foreign investors?

The usual vehicle for a joint venture in India is a company limited by shares. The company could be a "public" company or a "private" company. (In India, a public company could be listed or unlisted.) An overwhelming majority of the parties prefer a "private" company due to the less onerous regulatory regime under the Companies Act 1956 as compared to a "private" company. Where a public listed Indian party owns the majority of an Indian joint venture, there are doubts over whether the Indian joint venture company can properly be incorporated as a "private" company and may be deemed to be a "public" company. This is potentially disadvantageous because, in addition to a more onerous corporate compliance regime, the enforcement of options and restrictions on transfers of shares is less certain in case of a "public" company and "public" companies are not entitled to issue different classes of shares unless they comply with a rolling three year profitability requirement.

If a partnership structure is chosen, does this lead to (a) joint and several liability to third parties and/or (b) duties of good faith as between partners?

Yes. The general position under the Partnership Act 1932 is that partners are jointly and severally liable for debts due to third parties and are bound to act in good faith.

4. Capital structure and funding

What principal local law issues affect the capital structure and funding of the joint venture?

Under the Companies Act, a "private" company must have a minimum paid up share capital of Rs 100,000 and a "public" company must have a minimum paid up share capital of Rs 500,000. In addition, under the FDI regime, minimum capitalisation norms would be applicable in respect of certain industries (e.g. non-banking finance companies and investments in insurance).

Is it common to have different "classes" of shares (e.g. A and B shares) to reflect different interests or contributions of the parties?

In theory, it is possible to have different "classes" of share capital. Under the Companies (Issue of Share Capital with Differential Voting Rights) Rules 2001 a "public" company must fulfil a (rolling) three-year profitability criteria before it can issue equity shares with disproportionate rights. In practice, joint ventures in India rarely have more than one class of equity shares although there are signs that this might change as the regime for issuing preference shares to non-residents has become more restrictive (see below).

Is it common to have "preference" shares which give a party a priority on payment of dividends or on a return of capital?

Foreign investors are permitted to invest in "preference" shares. The holders of "preference" shares are not allowed to vote at general meetings (save in respect of resolutions that directly affect their rights). "Preference" shareholders are entitled to receive a fixed rate of dividend provided this is paid out of the profits or reserves of the company. If a foreign party holds "preference" shares, the rate of dividend payable cannot exceed 300 basis points above the prime lending rate of the State Bank of India as at the date of the board resolution approving the issue (unless prior approval of the FIPB is obtained). Following changes to the Indian exchange control regulations in June 2007, unless fully converted preference shares are deemed to be "debt" under Indian exchange control rules and subject to the ECB Guidelines. This raises complex exchange control issues since it is not clear whether the RBI would seek to regulate the "conversion ratio" for preference shares. For example, conversion of ECBs (such as shareholder loans) into equity is regulated by the RBI and must adhere to the RBI's minimum pricing guidelines (as opposed to par or a contractually specified value).

Are "redeemable" shares permitted (i.e. shares that can be repaid and cancelled)?

Under the Companies Act, "preference" shares are mandatorily redeemable within 20 years of their issue. Preference shares can only be redeemed out of distributable profits or the proceeds of a fresh issue of shares. (See above in relation to the implications of issuing.) The Act does not contemplate the issue of redeemable equity shares.

Are "non-voting" shares permitted?

While equity shares with "differential" voting rights are permitted, it appears that the Act does not contemplate "non-voting" equity shares. However, "preference" shares do not carry voting rights (except in the limited circumstances mentioned above).

Are there any "thin capitalisation" or similar rules which affect the choice of equity/ debt ratio for the capital structure?

Strictly speaking, there are no "thin capitalisation" or similar rules under the Income Tax Act 1961. However, under that Act, any expenditure for which payment is made to a related party is liable to be disallowed if the expenditure is regarded as excessive or unreasonable having regard to the fair value of the relevant goods/ services and the legitimate needs of the business. Furthermore, under the Indian "transfer pricing" regime, transactions between an Indian entity and its "associated undertakings" (which would cover a parent-subsidiary relationship) must take place on an "arm's length basis". If not, the Indian tax authorities can impute an arm's length price and charge tax accordingly.

Is there any capital or similar tax payable in respect of issued share capital?

A company is liable to pay ad valorem certain fees to the relevant Registrar of Companies on an increase in its authorised share capital (not its issued capital).

Is a separate "contribution agreement" or other formal document (other than formal property transfer agreements) required or usual under the local law to document the contribution of assets to the joint venture?

Although there is no legal requirement (other than formal property transfer agreements), it would be common to have an agreement to record the terms and conditions surrounding the "contribution" of assets/investments by the local partner. Under the Act, where shares are issued for consideration other than cash, various documents including a copy of the contract for the transfer of assets/provision of services to the Indian company (duly verified and stamped) must be filed with the Registrar of Companies.

Are there any local laws which require an independent valuation of any non-cash assets to be contributed to the joint venture?

Although there is no legal requirement to obtain an independent valuation report where shares are "contributed" to the joint venture, in certain circumstances the directors of the joint venture company may consider it advisable to obtain a valuation report before shares are allotted on this basis (owing to their fiduciary duties to the company).

Furthermore, a valuation report may be desirable where there is doubt over the amount of stamp duty payable for the "contribution" of the relevant assets. (The transfer of assets or investments by a local partner would attract stamp duty at the applicable rate which could be as high as eight per cent on an ad valorem basis depending upon the asset and its location.)

Are there exchange control regulations which materially affect the establishment of the joint venture or the subsequent repatriation of profits or dividends from the joint venture to a foreign party?

India's exchange control regulations also regulate foreign investment into India. An overview of some key aspects of the FDI route are described in section 2. The RBI's pricing guidelines set a *cap* (determined by reference to the lower of two third party valuations) on the price that can be paid by a resident to a non-resident for the transfer of existing Indian shares and a *floor* (determined by an Indian chartered accountant) on the price that must be paid by a non-resident to a resident for existing Indian shares. It is not permissible for parties to "contract out" of these provisions.

Generally, Indian companies can freely repatriate dividends to equity shareholders. In the case of preference shares, the rate of dividend cannot exceed 300 basis points above the prime lending rate of the State Bank of India (on the date on which the shares are issued).

Remittance of share sale proceeds can be a problem if remitting bank insists upon a tax clearance certificate (demonstrating that the foreign party has discharged its tax obligations) before permitting the repatriation of funds outside India.

If a foreign party is to contribute technology to the joint venture, are there any special requirements for valuation of that technology?

There are no special requirements regarding valuation of technology contributed by a foreign party to a joint venture. As previously mentioned, a joint venture company would not be freely permitted to issue shares to a foreign party in exchange for technology contributed by the foreign party and such a transaction would require regulatory approval.

Indian foreign exchange laws place restrictions on the royalty that is payable by an Indian joint venture company to its foreign participants for intellectual property (e.g. trademarks or technology) provided by the foreign partners. Royalty payments in excess of these limits would require prior approval of the FIPB. (Currently royalties on technology transfer agreements cannot exceed five per cent of domestic sales or eight per cent of exports and royalties on trademarks cannot exceed two per cent of exports and one per cent of domestic sales.)

5. Tax

Are there any particular tax laws or incentives which significantly affect the establishment of joint ventures in this jurisdiction by a foreign investor?

Although there are no tax laws or incentives that affect joint ventures specifically, the following points may be relevant to foreign investors:

- India has double tax treaties with a number of countries. The treaty with Mauritius is particularly favourable especially as it eases the obligation to pay Indian capital gains tax at the time of exit (from an Indian joint venture).

- In order to promote exports from India, the government has introduced some tax incentives under the Software Technology Park (STP) Scheme and the Export Oriented Units (EOU) Scheme. Broadly, subject to the satisfaction of certain conditions, companies engaged in the export of certain services/goods and registered under these schemes are entitled to certain tax exemptions.

- India has introduced transfer pricing rules which require transactions between a multinational and its Indian subsidiary to be on arm's length terms. If not, the tax authorities are entitled to impute a price that represents the arm's length price and tax the transactions accordingly.

Will withholding taxes apply to dividends paid by a joint venture company?
Under the Income Tax Act 1961 dividends (in the hands of the recipient) are not subject to tax and therefore there would be no withholding at the time dividends are paid. However, Indian companies declaring a dividend are required to pay a "corporate dividend tax" at the rate of approximately 14.025 per cent (including surcharge) on the gross amount of dividend declared.

6. Board and management

Are there local law rules which affect the board or management structure of the joint venture? May a two-tier board be required?
There are no specific rules relating to the board or management structure of a joint venture and there is no requirement for a two-tier board. Under the Companies Act, a "private" company must have at least two directors, whereas, a "public" company must have at least three directors. The quorum for a board meeting is the higher of one-third of the "total strength" of the board or two directors. Further, Indian companies must have at least four board meetings in a year, with one meeting each quarter.

The Act provides that at least two-thirds of the directors of a "public" company must be appointed by the shareholders in general meeting and that their office must be liable to retirement by rotation. One-third of the "retiring" directors must retire at every annual general meeting. The Act also provides that a maximum of one-third of the board could comprise of "non-retiring" directors.

Where a joint venture is listed, the board must comprise an optimum combination of "executive" and "non-executive" directors. If the chairman is "non-executive", at least one-third of the board should be "independent"; if the joint venture has an "executive" chairman, a majority of the board should comprise "independent" directors.

Are there local law constraints on persons who can be directors or managers of the joint venture (e.g. only local residents or nationals)?
There is no requirement for Indian nationals to be appointed as directors of a "private" company. However, managing directors, whole time directors and managers of a "public" company must be "resident in India" (as contemplated under Sch.XIII of the Companies Act), unless approval of the central government is obtained. Furthermore, a body corporate cannot be appointed as a director. It should be noted that all directors need to obtain a specific Director Identification Number from the Ministry of Company Affairs prior to being appointed to the board of directors of an Indian company.

Does a shareholder in a joint venture company owe a duty of good faith (or similar duty) to other shareholders in the way it behaves in relation to the joint venture?
Whilst shareholders in a joint venture do not owe any statutory duty of good faith to their joint venture partners, there is some risk (especially where the foreign party has majority ownership) that an Indian minority party may approach local courts claiming that it has been treated "unfairly" or in a manner that is "oppressive". In practice, this means that specific legal advice is needed where a foreign shareholder seeks to take any action that could prove detrimental to the interests of the joint venture company or hurt the interests of its local partner.

Can you modify the legal duties of directors so that they can expressly take into account the interests of their "appointer" when voting or acting as director, or must they always act objectively in the best interests of the company?

The principles of Indian law relating to directors' duties are similar (but not identical) to the relevant principles of English law. Broadly, directors must exercise their powers honestly, in good faith and for the benefit of the company and avoid a conflict of interest. Directors owe their duties to the company and not to their "appointer" and therefore a director's fiduciary duties to the company cannot be modified.

7. Transfer of shares

In the case of a joint venture company, can a permanent restriction on transfer of shares be imposed under the local law (e.g. no transfer without the consent of the other shareholder)?

The enforceability of restrictions on transfer is a complex area under Indian law. A useful starting point would be the Supreme Court decision in the case of *VB Rangaraj v Gopalakrishnan*, which casts doubts over enforceability of agreements between shareholders in an Indian company unless the provisions (especially in relation to the transfer of shares) are incorporated into the articles. Even if the provisions are incorporated in the articles, there is a risk that some of the provisions may be construed as an unlawful fetter on the statutory powers of the Company and held to be unenforceable.

Section 111A of the Act provides that the shares of a "public" company must be "freely transferable". This requirement has cast further doubt on the validity of restrictions on transfer of shares of a "public" company (even if these restrictions are included in the articles).

However, notwithstanding the above, parties often use contractual restrictions on transfer (such as, for example, pre-emption rights or a prohibition on transfer unless consent is obtained). The effectiveness of these measures is not free from risk.

8. Protection for minority shareholders

Are there any statutory rules or remedies which help significantly to protect a minority shareholder in a joint venture company?

The approach of minority protection under Indian law is similar (but not identical) to that under English law. It would be possible for a minority shareholder to bring a claim against the majority alleging unfair prejudice/fraud on the minority. A minority shareholder could also exert pressure on the majority by making complaints to relevant regulatory bodies.

Does the law require any major business decisions to be approved by a special resolution or super-majority (whether at board or shareholder level) or must a minority party protect itself by contract?

Under Indian law, certain matters (such as amendments to the company's constitution, issue of shares (other than on a pre-emptive basis to existing shareholders), reduction of capital, winding-up etc.) require a special resolution of the members (i.e. 75 per cent majority). These do not include major business decisions such as acquisitions or disposals.

Typically, Indian minority parties insist upon a list of "reserved" matters that goes beyond the above-mentioned list. This is normally a matter for negotiation.

9. Employment laws

Are there local law obligations requiring a "local" party to consult with, or obtain the approval of, employees or employee representatives on a contribution of its business to the joint venture?

In theory, it is possible to structure a "contribution" in a manner that prior approval of employee/employee representatives is not required. (Broadly, this could be achieved if employees are transferred as a part of the sale of a business on terms "no less favourable" than the terms previously offered to them provided continuity of service is maintained.) However, in practice, the employer would have to persuade the employees to accept the joint venture company's offer and this would require the relevant employee's acceptance. This is a delicate issue, especially if labour is unionised, and could be one of the reasons why such "contributions" are rare in India.

Are there any material employment laws (compared with the UK) which are likely to affect the ongoing operations of the joint venture?

Under the Industrial Disputes Act 1948, if employees can be categorised as "workmen" and over 100 are employed, central government approval is required to terminate their employment. In practice, approvals are rarely granted. In addition, persons last employed should be the first to be terminated and, at the time of new/fresh employment, previously terminated employees must be given first preference.

The consequences of breaching the above provisions can be quite onerous. The Labour Court can re-instate the workman and/or can order the employer to pay back wages from the date of termination until the date of the order. In extreme cases, breaches can be punishable with six months of imprisonment. Typically, companies proposing to fire employees adopt voluntary retirement schemes and then payoff the workforce.

10. Accounts

Is there a requirement on the joint venture company to file accounts with any authority where they are publicly available?

Under the Companies Act, both "public" and "private" companies must file their balance sheets and profit and loss statements with the Registrar of Companies annually. However, in case of a "private" company, members of the public are not entitled to obtain copies of its profit and loss account from the Registrar.

"Public" companies listed on a stock exchange must comply with additional disclosure requirements (e.g. to file annual audited accounts with the relevant stock exchanges and the Indian securities regulator, the Securities and Exchange Board of India).

11. Dispute resolution

Is there any standard local practice as to form of dispute resolution in relation to joint ventures with foreign investors? Is arbitration in a venue outside that jurisdiction acceptable?

There is no standard practice as to the form of dispute resolution. This is usually a matter for negotiation between the parties. Courts in India tend to be slow and the system is inherently inclined to favour the local party. The majority of foreign parties insist upon dispute resolution outside India. A common compromise position is arbitration in a neutral jurisdiction outside India.

Is the local jurisdiction a signatory to the 1958 New York Convention on the Recognition and Enforcement of Foreign Arbitral Awards?

Yes. Enforcement of a "foreign" arbitration award may, however, be refused by an Indian court at the request of the party against whom it is invoked if it can prove certain grounds (e.g. improper notice was given of the proceedings or the party was otherwise unable to present its case or the arbitral authority or procedure was not in accordance with the agreement of the parties).

A "foreign" arbitration award will also not be enforced if the court finds that the subject matter is not capable of settlement by arbitration under the law of India or the enforcement of the award would be contrary to "public policy" in India.

12. Legal documents and formalities

Is there any special form of legal documentation required under local law for establishment of a joint venture company? What are the usual principal documents?

In order to incorporate a "private" limited company in India the following documents must be registered with the Registrar of Companies: (i) a copy of the name availability letter issued by the Registrar[2]; (ii) memorandum of association; (iii) articles of association; (iv) agreements with any managing or whole-time director or managers; (v) fees based on the authorised share capital; (vi) statutory declaration (Form 1); (vii) details of the company's registered office (Form 18) and board constitution (Form 32). Although the steps involved in setting up a "private" company are relatively straightforward, typically it takes approximately five to six weeks to incorporate.

Does the joint venture documentation need to be in the local language and/or governed by the local law?

It is not mandatory for the joint venture agreement or constitutional documents of the joint venture company (e.g. memorandum and articles of association) to be in a local language (depending upon the state in which the company is incorporated). (On the contrary, legal documents of this nature tend to be in English.) While it is also not mandatory for the joint venture agreement to be governed by Indian law, foreign parties commonly concede this point for tactical reasons or practicality.

Are agreements between shareholders (e.g. as to appointment of directors, conduct of the business of the company or voting majorities required for certain decisions etc.) enforceable under local law? In the event of breach, is specific performance or a similar remedy available—or only damages?

Subject to the doubts that have been caused by the Supreme Court's decision in the case of *VB Rangaraj v Gopalakrishnan*, such contracts would be enforceable. Specific performance is a discretionary remedy and it is not possible to advise with certainty as to whether the remedy would be available. Generally, a court would grant specific performance only where damages are an inadequate remedy.

---

[2] The party responsible for incorporating the company should reserve the proposed name (of the joint venture company) with the Registrar. This could take two-three weeks.

Are restrictions relating to (a) transfers of shares and/or (b) minority "veto rights" commonly included in the articles of association or by-laws of the company-or included in a separate shareholders' agreement?

Normally provisions relating to transfers of share and/or veto rights are found in a shareholders' agreement. However, following on from the Supreme Court decision in the case of *VB Rangaraj v Gopalakrishnan*, it is not unusual to have the principal rights or provisions of a shareholders' agreement (including restrictions on transfer or voting rights) incorporated into the articles of association.

Are there any formalities (e.g. notarisation or registration) which are material and which may affect the timing involved in forming the joint venture?

If the foreign party is responsible for or has control over incorporation of the joint venture (this is not unusual especially where the joint venture will have a hybrid name or a name that incorporates any trademark/tradename of the foreign party), incorporation documents executed outside India will have to be notarised and apostilled by the relevant Indian High Commission before they can be filed with the Registrar of Companies in India. This could be a time consuming exercise and lead to some delay (especially if the Registrar makes supplemental information requests). Consequently, it is sometimes advisable to appoint a local director (acting for and on behalf of the foreign company) who incorporates the company and retires at the first board meeting (if necessary). A local lawyer assisting the foreign company could be used for this purpose.

(7) Italy

Author: Mario Ortu, Ida Bassano and Giovanna Rossi
          Freshfields Bruckhaus Deringer LLP, Milan

1. General background

Are joint ventures popular as a form of foreign investment into your jurisdiction?

Equity joint ventures have become increasingly important in Italy as a means through which companies undertake significant business activities including major industrial projects. Foreign investors have also used joint ventures in order to enter certain business areas where the "outsider" perception of a foreign investor on the Italian market may have an adverse effect (e.g. the fashion industry).

Are there restrictions on foreign participation?

In principle, Italian legislation does not limit the size of foreign interests in an Italian business entity. However, pursuant to the Italian Civil Code, foreigners (including foreign companies) enjoy the civil rights granted to Italian citizens on condition that there is reciprocity for Italians in the foreigner's home jurisdiction. If this is met, 100 per cent foreign ownership of Italian corporations is generally permitted.

What (if any) are the major legal problems which a foreign investor in a joint venture faces in your jurisdiction?

Agreements among shareholders of a company governing certain matters (such as the exercise of voting rights, the transfer of shares or dominant influence on the company) may not have a duration greater than three years, for a listed company, and five years, for a non-listed company. For listed and non-listed companies the agreement shall be deemed to have been concluded for such duration even if the parties provided for a longer term; such agreements are, however, renewable. Agreements may also be concluded for an indeterminate period; in such case each party may withdraw on giving six months' notice.

2. Governmental/regulatory approvals

What principal governmental or regulatory approvals are required (excluding competition law) for establishing a joint venture?

There is no specific legislation or governmental regulation governing foreign participation in joint ventures based in Italy. With respect to certain commercial activities with a "public interest" component (e.g. certain types of transport, banking finance, insurance, telecommunications and utilities), there is special legislation imposing certain limits, or notification procedures, which would apply to foreign investment in these areas.

Are there local anti-trust laws which might apply to the formation of the joint venture?

Regulatory control is primarily effected through competition laws, which are applicable to both foreign and Italian parties. Italian competition rules are set out in Law no.287 of 1990, which established the Italian Antitrust Authority (*Autorità Garante della Concorrenza e del Mercato*). The creation of a joint venture company may give rise either to a "concentrative joint venture" (which would fall under the Italian merger control regime) or to a "co-operative joint venture") (which, on the contrary, might be deemed by the Italian Antitrust Authority as an agreement under the art.2, Law no.287 of 1990 or art.81 of the EC Treaty).

(i) **Concentrative joint ventures: merger control**. The Italian merger control regime is summarised, in general terms, below:

Filing requirements/ trigger	Timetable	Authority's evaluation
The creation of a JV could be considered "concentrative" if the following conditions are met: (i) the JV is provided with its own financial, human, physical and intellectual resources; (ii) a JV management body has been set forth; (iii) the JV is able to carry own an economic activity autonomously; (iv) JV activity appears stable and lasting. In this case the transaction would be notified and consequently assessed as a merger by the Italian Antitrust Authority if: —the combined turnover of the controlling undertakings concerned exceeds €440 m in Italy; or: —in the case of a joint acquisition of an existing company (or, alternatively, contribution of assets from the parent companies to the JV), the turnover realised by the acquired company (or the turnover attributable to the assets being contributed) is above €44m in Italy. [Note: turnover thresholds are updated annually]	Stage 1: the first evaluation of the transaction can last up to 30 days after the merger filing. This time frame could be extended if the information provided therein is not sufficient. Within this term the Authority could either decide to start the investigation or to issue to the notifying party a letter for clearance. Stage 2: If a decision to start the investigation is adopted, the Authority proceeding shall end within a period of 45 days (extendible up to a further 30 days terms in case of insufficient information).	The Authority shall verify whether the JV transaction will create or strengthen a dominant position in Italy or in a substantial part thereof in a way that threatens to eliminate or reduce competition to a considerable and lasting extent. If the competition rules are breached, the Authority shall forbid the creation of the JV. **Mandatory/voluntary Penalties** Parties are forbidden to implement the transaction before having filed the communication to the Authority. Nevertheless, whilst the proceeding is pending, the effectiveness of the merger could be suspended. In case of failure, file fines up to one per cent of parents' overall turnover may be applied. Unless the Authority orders to suspend the effectiveness of the transaction, in case of implementation before clearance, no penalties apply, except the order to break up the JV if it is later prohibited.

While the Italian Antitrust Authority has prohibited very few transactions, sometimes its clearance has been subject to the some conditions (such as asset divestiture or undertakings cession to be complied with by the parties).

(ii) **Co-operative joint ventures: restrictive practices.** When the above mentioned conditions concerning the "concentrative" JV are not satisfied, the new company should be considered as a "co-operative" joint venture. This will be evaluated under the rules prohibiting restrictive agreements that have a significant effect on free competition in the market. The Italian Antitrust Authority may authorize (for a limited period) individual agreements which otherwise fall within the scope of these provisions if the benefits are judged to outweigh the restrictive effects on free competition. The Italian Antitrust Authority must issue a decision within 120 days of the relevant notification.

3. Types of joint venture vehicle

What are the principal types of joint venture vehicle commonly used with foreign investors?

A number of possible structures exist under the Italian Civil Code:

(i) **Contractual arrangement.** No corporation is set up and the co-venturers set out the terms of their co-operation in a properly drafted agreement.

(ii) **Corporate structures.** Foreign investors wishing to operate in Italy using a joint venture company generally choose from among three main types of corporate forms, all of which can provide limited liability benefits:

- *società per azioni* (an SPA) (joint stock company) in which the liability of the shareholders is limited to the par value of their shares;

- *società a responsabilità limitata* (an SRL) (limited liability company) in which the quotaholders' liability is limited to the par value of their quotas (shareholdings);

- *società in accomandita per azioni* (SAPA) (partnership limited by shares) in which the liability of certain of the managing partners (*soci accomandatari*) is unlimited, while the liability of the other partners (*soci accomandanti*) is limited to the par value of their quotas (shareholdings).

Generally speaking, the SPA is the most appropriate corporate form for medium and large companies which intend to raise funds through the equity and debt capital markets. The law offers a choice of three different corporate governance models. The SRL is the most appropriate corporate form for small-to-medium sized companies. In particular, the rules offer the possibility of including in the by-laws restrictions on transfer of quotas (such as pre-emption rights, or, subject certain conditions, approval by the management, quotaholders or third parties). There is a new regime governing quotaholder financing; a substantial development is that SRLs are now permitted to issue debt securities. In general terms, the rules applicable to SRLs provide for less disclosure and procedural rigidity than those applicable to SPAs.

(iii) **Patrimonio destinato.** An SPA may create a *"patrimonio destinato"*, which permits the establishment (within the SPA) of segregated pools of business assets dedicated to a specific business activity. These could include establishing a joint venture with a third party without incurring the costs inherent in the creation of a new company.

If a partnership structure is chosen, does this lead to (a) joint and several liability to third parties and/or (b) duties of good faith as between partners?

The *"società in nome collettivo"* has characteristics similar to a general partnership. Each partner is jointly liable for the debts and other liabilities of the business. Although Italian law has no direct equivalent to the UK limited partnership, the *"societa in accomandita per azioni"* is similar to it. A limited partner may not participate in the management of the SAPA, or otherwise it would lose the benefit of limited liability. The SAPA is seldom used. Only individuals can hold the position of managing partner.

A substantive principle of Italian law is that each party to a contract (including an agreement to set up a company) has a duty to carry out the contract in good faith.

4. Capital structure and funding

What principal local law issues affect capital structure and funding?

Generally, an SPA has access to a broader range of corporate financing sources than an SRL. Differences between SRLs and SPAs concerning capital structure include:

(i) Equity

- An SPA must have a minimum capital of €120,000, while an SRL requires a minimum capital of only €10,000; the capital of an SPA is composed of shares, while the capital of an SRL is composed of quotas; only shares (and not quotas) may be issued to the investing public.
- Only shares (and not quotas) can be listed on recognised stock exchanges.
- In the case of an SRL, pre-emption rights in respect of a capital increase may be excluded only if provided for by the deed of incorporation, while in an SPA such rights may be excluded by a majority vote of the shareholders (provided that certain requisites are satisfied). In companies with listed shares the bylaws may also provide the possibility to exclude the option right within the 10 per cent of the pre- existing capital stock, provided that the issue price corresponds to the market value of the shares and this is confirmed in a special report of the company entrusted with the auditing.

(ii) Debt

- SRLs may issue debt instruments only if subscription is reserved exclusively to certain categories of "qualified investors"; this does not, generally, apply to SPAs.
- The rules applicable to SPAs expressly provide for the option of issuing convertible bonds; the rules applicable to SRLs do not.

Is it common to have different "classes" of shares (e.g. A and B shares) to reflect different initial contributions or financial interests of the parties?

Under the Italian law there is the flexibility to create a wide range of different classes of shares. All shares of the same class, however, must bear the same rights. Types of shares may include: subordinated shares (*"azioni postergate"*); shares with disproportionate profit and loss sharing rights; non-voting shares (*"azioni senza diritto di voto"*) and shares with limited voting rights (*"azioni con diritto di voto limitato"*); redeemable shares (*"azioni riscattabili"*) which entitle their holders to have them redeemed by the company or shareholders; tracking shares (*"azioni correlate"*) which entitle their holders to track the performance of a separate business segment or revenue stream.

Is it common to have "preference" shares which give a party a priority on payment of dividends or on a return of capital?

Yes. The Italian law provide that a listed company may issue "preference shares" (*"azioni di risparmio"*) that have complete "economic" priority over any ordinary and preferred shares, both in relation to a final dividend and return of capital on a winding-up; however, they do not carry voting rights.

Another category is that of "preferred shares" (*"azioni privilegiate"*) which rank ahead of ordinary shares in the event of a winding up. They may carry (i) a fixed cumulative dividend in addition to a pro rata participation, along with ordinary shares, in surplus profits, and/or (ii) a "participation dividend", entitling such shares to an increased share of the profits if certain targets are achieved. They usually rank pari passu with the ordinary shares in terms of voting rights.

Are there any "thin capitalisation" or similar rules which affect the choice of equity/debt ratio for the capital structure?

Yes. The Italian tax laws contain rules which may limit the deductibility of interest expense in certain circumstances.

Is a separate "contribution agreement" or other formal document (other than formal property transfer agreements) required or usual under the local law to document the contribution of assets to the joint venture?

Non-cash contributions are quite common in Italy. Both in the case of SPAs and SRLs, a deed of contribution must be executed before a notary public.

If assets and liabilities transferred to the joint venture vehicle are deemed to constitute a business as a going concern or a branch thereof (*a ramo d'azienda*), not only are any debts of the transferor transferred with that going concern but also any third party contingent claims relating to employment, social security or tax obligations of that going concern.

Are there any local laws which require an independent valuation of any non-cash assets to be contributed to the joint venture?

SPA. In the case of a non-cash contribution to an SPA (including assets but not work performed or services provided), the value of the consideration must be assessed by an independent appraiser to be appointed by the President of the court having jurisdiction over the area in which the company has its registered office. The time and costs involved with these proceedings should not be underestimated. There is no fixed period within which the expert must provide his report; however, he or she usually takes between 30 and 50 days. Moreover, the Italian Civil Code does not specify the valuation criteria to be used by such expert appraiser. The board of directors must then confirm the expert valuation within 180 days of registration of that contribution in the relevant Companies Register.

SRL. In relation to SRLs the law provides different types of non-cash contributions, including assets, work performed and services provided as well as other items having economic value (such as the goodwill of a going concern, a mortgage over real property or non-competition covenants). An appraisal is required by an expert or a registered auditor to be appointed directly by the relevant contributing person (and not by the court as described above).

Are there exchange control regulations which materially affect the establishment of the joint venture or the subsequent repatriation of profits or dividends from the joint venture to a foreign party?

Dividends are freely payable by an Italian joint venture company to non-resident companies and are not subject to any exchange control restrictions (except for information to be provided by the banks to the Ufficio Italiano Cambi-the Italian Exchange Office for mere statistical purposes).

5. Tax

Are there any particular tax laws or incentives which significantly affect the establishment of joint ventures in this jurisdiction by a foreign investor?

Both SPAs and SRLs are liable to pay both corporate income tax (IRES) (at a current rate of 33 per cent) and regional tax (IRAP) (generally levied at a rate of 4.25 per cent). IRES is basically due on before-tax profits, as adjusted for tax purposes. IRAP is due on the difference between production value and production costs, on the basis of the balance sheet, as adjusted for tax purposes. (Some Italian regions have increased the IRAP base rate and/or instituted special IRAP exemptions or IRAP tax rate relief for certain activities). Both SPAs and SRLs may generally benefit from a 95 per cent IRES exemption on dividends received on profits from any subsidiary which is not resident in a tax haven jurisdiction.

Both SPAs and SRLs may also benefit from the "participation exemption" regime, which provides a 84 per cent exemption from IRES on capital gains arising from the disposal of a participation in a company if a number of conditions are met.

Any SRL or SPA resident in Italy for tax purposes and participated in by Italian resident companies (or foreign entities provided that they are able to take advantage of the Italian withholding tax exemption on Italian source distributions paid out of profit) may elect to be treated as a "tax-transparent" entity whereby the taxable income (or deductible loss) of that company is allocated for IRES (not IRAP) purposes to its shareholders in proportion to the share of profits assignable to each of them, irrespective of whether the profits have been distributed or not.

Starting from tax year 2008 it is proposed that: (i) IRES will apply at the reduced rate of 27.5 per cent; (ii) IRAP will apply at the reduced rate of 3.9 per cent; (iii) the determination of the IRAP tax base will be simplified; (iv) the "participation exemption" regime will provides for a 95 per cent exemption from IRES on capitals gains arising from the disposal of a participation in a company.

Will withholding taxes apply to dividends paid by a joint venture company?

Dividends paid by an Italian SPA or SRL to a non-resident company are subject in principle to an Italian withholding tax. However, many double tax treaties entered into by Italy reduce the level of dividend withholding tax rates. Moreover, if the parent company is an EU resident company, no withholding tax is levied on dividends provided that the relevant requirements are met.

6. Board and management

Are there local law rules which affect the board or management structure of the joint venture? May a two-tier board be required?

SPAs. For SPAs three alternative corporate governance systems exist: the standard model, the so-called "dualistic model" (based on the German corporate governance system) and the "monistic model" (based on the Anglo-Saxon governance corporate system).

- The standard model is based on the existence of a managing body (usually a board of directors) and a board of statutory auditors. Unless otherwise specified in the by-laws, the standard model is automatically applicable to SPAs.

- The dualistic model contemplates the co-existence of a management board ("*consiglio di gestione*") and a supervisory board ("*consiglio di sorveglianza*") without a board of statutory auditors. The management board is vested with the exclusive responsibility for managing the company's activities; the supervisory board is responsible for appointing members of the management board and for approving the annual financial statement. The management board is appointed by the supervisory board and must have at least two members.

- The monistic model does not envisage a board of statutory auditors; this is replaced by a "committee for management control" (*"comitato per il controllo sulla gestione"*). This committee is part of the board of directors and is charged with: (i) determining the adequacy of the company's organisational structure, internal corporate governance system and administrative and accounting system, as well as determining the suitability of the company to enter into certain business transactions; and (ii) carrying out other tasks assigned to it by the board of directors.

SRLs. In line with this very flexible structure, the managing body of an SRL—which may also be composed of non quotaholders—may be freely shaped by quotaholders in accordance with their needs. Alternatives, for instance, include: (i) a sole director; (ii) a traditional board of directors collectively acting as a committee, with a chairman and, if the sole director decides, by one or a more managing directors; or (iii) a board of directors not acting as a committee but consisting of a plurality of members having the same powers.

Are there local law constraints on persons who can be directors or managers of the joint venture (e.g. only local residents or nationals)?

In principle, any directors or members of the management board or the supervisory board (under the dualistic system) or the committee for management control (under the monistic system) may be foreign citizens residing abroad (provided that they obtain a tax code from the Italian tax authorities). The monistic model requires that at least one-third of the directors must meet the independence requirements for statutory auditors set out in the Italian Civil Code.

For the listed company the law provide that a member of the board of statutory auditors may not act as director or statutory auditor for more than a specified number of companies.

In addition, cannot be appointed as statutory auditors of the companies individuals with employment, economic or professional relationships with any director of the company or any member of his family.

Directors of a listed company have to meet the good standing requirements that are already applicable to statutory auditors, such as not having been convicted of financial, bankruptcy-related or other crimes. In the standard model where the board of directors of a listed company has less than seven members at least one director must be independent, if the board has more than seven members, at least tow director must now meet certain independence requirements. For the listed companies applying the dualistic model whose board comprise more than four members, at least one member must fulfil the independence requirements.

Does a shareholder in a joint venture company owe a duty of good faith (or similar duty) to other shareholders in the way it behaves in relation to the joint venture?

A general and substantive principle of Italian law is that each party to a contractual agreement has a duty to carry out the contract in good faith.

Can you modify the legal duties of directors so that they can expressly take into account the interests of their "appointer" when voting or acting as director, or must they always act objectively in the best interests of the company?

Italian corporate law on directors' duties is not dissimilar to corporate law in other European jurisdictions. Directors owe duties of diligence, honesty and good faith (including the duty to avoid conflicts of interest) to the company. However, a transaction that cannot be justified in the interests of the company, but which is undertaken for the benefit of certain shareholders, is not ipso facto unlawful.

7. Transfer of shares

In the case of a joint venture company, can a permanent restriction on transfer of shares be imposed under the local law (e.g. no transfer without the consent of the other shareholder)?

Yes. In Italy it is common practice to restrict transfers of shares in a joint venture company. Common restrictions include: pre-emption rights in favour of other shareholders; transfer of shares subject to prior approval by board of directors; and new shareholders being required to comply with certain qualifications. These restrictions are usually provided for under the company's by-laws. Provisions of the by-laws which condition the transfer of the shares on the agreement of the other shareholders are not valid if they do not also contemplate an obligation of the company or of the other shareholders to purchase. The normal remedy for a "prohibited" transfer is that the transfer of share cannot be registered on the company register. If the restrictions are part of a shareholders' agreement, the agreement may contain specific liquidated damages. By-laws or a shareholders' agreement may also prohibit (even totally) the transfer of shares but in this case for no more than a five year term (three years, in the case of a shareholders' agreement for a listed company).

Restrictions on transfer of shares contained in the by-laws are enforceable also against third parties (including any purchaser of the shares) and vis-à-vis any future shareholders. Restrictions contained in shareholders' agreements alone are enforceable only among the contracting shareholders and, if any shares were sold irrespective of any such restrictions, the sale would be valid and binding.

8. Protection for minority shareholders

Are there any statutory rules or remedies which help significantly to protect a minority shareholder in a joint venture company?

In the absence of a specific provision in the shareholders' agreement or in the by-laws of a joint venture company, a minority shareholder has a number of protections under Italian law. In broad summary, these include the following:

- Action can be taken against resolutions of shareholders' meeting in certain situations where there is a conflict of interest (eg. where the vote of the director or shareholder with a "conflict" has been decisive).
- Annulment (and set aside) of resolutions of a shareholders' meeting if that resolution was taken by the majority shareholders with the exclusive purpose of (i) harming the rights of the minority shareholders or (ii) achieving interests different from those of the company. Scholars and courts derive this right from general principles of law, most notably principles of good faith.
- Right of withdrawal. As regards SPAs, a shareholder can withdraw from a company in certain limited circumstances (e.g. significant change of the company's corporate purpose; or change of quorum requirements and voting rights). Shareholders also have a right to withdraw from the company, unless the by-laws provide otherwise, if, inter alia, a resolution introduces or removes limitations on the transfer of shares.

As regards SRLs, quotaholders may withdraw from the company in all those cases indicated in the deed of incorporation. In addition, the quotaholders which have not given their consent to certain decisions are entitled to withdraw from the company (e.g. a change in the rights granted to the quotaholders concerning the management of the company or the distribution of profit.)

The withdrawal right is also granted to the quotaholders where the company has an indefinite duration. In this case, as for SPAs, the quotaholders may withdraw at any time by giving six months' prior notice. Such term may be extended by the deed of incorporation up to one year.

For the companies subject to the direction and co-ordination of companies, the law provides three cases in which shareholders are entitled to withdraw: a) in the event that the parent company is transformed; b) in the event that the parent company is found to be liable vis-à-vis the shareholder; c) when such direction starts or ends.

In SRLs, every quotaholder may apply to the court, if there are serious irregularities in the management of the company, in order to audit the company's management at his (the quotaholder's) own expense, make a claim for damages and/or remove a director or directors from office.

- Minority shareholders representing at least 2.5 per cent of the company's capital may institute legal proceedings relating to the liability of any director(s). Shareholders representing at least 20 per cent of the share capital of a non-listed company or five per cent of a listed company can block the waiver or the settlement by the company of any action against the directors, statutory auditors or general managers.

- Shareholders representing at least 2.5 per cent of the capital stock of a listed company may add matters to the shareholders' meeting agenda.

- If requested by as many shareholders as together representing at least one tenth of the company's capital or the lower percentage provided for in the by-laws and if the agenda to be dealt with is specified in the request, the directors or the management board must call a shareholders' meeting without delay.

- In the listed companies a system of cumulative voting must be adopted for the election of directors. These voting systems must ensure that at least one member of the board is elected from the slate presented by minority shareholders. Similarly, at least one statutory auditor of the company will have to be designated by minority shareholders, and this statutory auditor will act as the chairman of the board of statutory auditors.

- For making list the law provides that the by-laws could determine the minimum participation quota at no more than 2.5 per cent of the corporate capital however the bylaws could determine a different participation quota provided by regulations from financial regulator CONSOB.

Does the law require any major business decisions to be approved by a special resolution or super-majority (whether at board or shareholder level), or must a minority party protect itself by contract?

Minimum voting majorities are required by statute for a number of corporate actions. As regards extraordinary shareholders' meetings, minimum voting majorities do not cover operational business decisions. However, at ordinary shareholders' meetings, the attendance quorum of not less than 50 per cent of the share capital is required and the absolute majority of those in attendance is required for any resolution at that meeting.

9. Employment laws

Are there local law obligations requiring a "local" party to consult with, or obtain the approval of, employees or employee representatives on a contribution of its business to the joint venture?

The contribution of a local business to the joint venture may trigger mandatory union consultation requirements, which should be factored into the formation timetable. If a transferor contributing its business employs (in the aggregate) more than 15 employees (irrespective of the number of employees assigned to the part of the business being transferred), the transferor and, where possible, the relevant recipient of the business (or part of the business) will be required to comply with compulsory notification of and/or consultation with the relevant works councils and unions. Failure to comply with these notification/consultation obligations may be grounds for the works councils/unions to claim an "anti-union behaviour" (*condotta antisindacale*) and may result in a court ordering the suspension of the transfer until the process has been properly carried out.

Are there any material employment laws (compared with the UK) which are likely to affect the ongoing operations of the joint venture?

Employment contracts are subject to general Italian law and to any national collective bargaining agreement governing the industry involved. Employees enjoy a relatively protected status in Italy.

- Under the Labour Law, a company may terminate employment only if there is a "just cause" or "a subjective or objective justified reason" for not continuing the employment relationship. Where a just cause or justified reason is not proven, the judge may order reinstatement and award the employee an indemnity (or, if reinstatement is not possible, an indemnity equal to 15 months' salary).
- The rules requiring a justified reason for dismissal also apply to executives (*dirigenti*), except that the employer is not obliged to reinstate the dismissed executive (who, where just cause is not proven, would only receive protection by damages under any applicable collective bargaining agreement).
- In all cases involving the termination of the employment relationship, a statutory severance payment is also due, for whatever cause, to all affected employees.

10. Accounts

Is there a requirement on the joint venture company to file accounts with any authority where they are publicly available?

In relation to SPAs or SRLs, the joint venture company must file its financial statements for each financial year with the relevant Companies Register.

11. Dispute resolution

Is there any standard local practice as to form of dispute resolution in relation to joint ventures with foreign investors? Is arbitration in a venue outside that jurisdiction acceptable?

It is common practice for both the by-laws and the shareholders' agreement to provide for dispute resolution terms. In many cases, disputes are submitted to arbitration.

Arbitration clauses contained in the deed of incorporation or, more commonly, in the by-laws of a company may provide that any dispute arising among the company's members, or between the company and any of its members, may be settled by arbitration, with certain minor exceptions. Resolutions concerning arbitration clauses do not have to be passed by the totality of members, but only by a qualified majority (two-thirds of the corporate capital).

An arbitration clause will be binding on the company and all of its members, including those whose capacity as member is in dispute. New members are also bound by the clause, even without a specific approval. The by-laws may extend the arbitration clause to disputes commenced by or against the company's directors, liquidators and internal auditors, in which case the clause will be binding upon them following their formal acceptance of appointment, without a specific approval of the clause. The arbitration clause may also be extended to disputes regarding the validity of the members' resolutions.

It is important to note that arbitration clauses of this type must require that all members of the arbitral tribunal be appointed by a third party who is unrelated to the company (including an arbitral institution), otherwise the clause is null and void. If the third party called to act as the appointing authority fails to do so, then the arbitrators will be appointed, at a party's request, by the president of the court in the place of the company's registered offices.

Italy has also enacted special provisions applicable to international arbitration proceedings which take place in Italy and follow Italian procedural law. The advantages are that formalities are fewer than in national arbitration proceedings (e.g. video conference is allowed for the meetings of the arbitrators) and a lesser number of grounds for challenging an international arbitral award are available than for a national arbitral award.

Is the local jurisdiction a signatory to the 1958 New York Convention on the Recognition and Enforcement of Foreign Arbitral Awards?
Yes.

12. Legal documents and formalities

Is there any special form of legal documentation required under local law for establishment of a joint venture company? What are the usual principal documents?

A company may be incorporated by agreement or by unilateral act. In both cases, the company's deed of incorporation must be filed as a public deed with the Companies' Register at the Chamber of Commerce where the company has its registered office. The deed of incorporation must be in the Italian language. However, there are no requirements that the joint venture agreement be in Italian or for it to be governed by Italian law.

Shareholders' agreements are not legally required but they are usually adopted to govern the relationship between co-venturers. Shareholders' agreements are not usually registered with the Companies' Register although in certain cases they have to be publicly disclosed, e.g. those relating to (i) listed companies or (ii) companies acting in certain commercial activities with a "public interest" component—such as telecommunications.

Does the joint venture documentation need to be in the local language and/or governed by the local law?

Any deed for notarisation must be in the Italian language and any document presented to an Italian notary for notarisation must be translated into Italian (e.g. by notarised proxies granted abroad).

Are agreements between shareholders (e.g. as to appointment of directors, conduct of the business of the company or voting majorities required for certain decisions etc.) enforceable under local law? In the event of breach, is specific performance or a similar remedy available—or only damages?

As a result of the Corporate Law Reform, agreements regarding voting rights, restrictions on share transfers and joint management relating to SPA may only last for a maximum duration of five years (although renewable at the relevant expiry date). There is no equivalent limitation on the duration of quotaholders' agreements for SRLs.

While the deed of incorporation and the by-laws bind the company and its members, a company is not bound by the terms of a shareholders' agreement. The only remedies for breach of a shareholders' agreement are damages, as the agreement is not enforceable against the joint venture company and does not override the company's constitutional documents. Consequently, shareholders' agreements usually contain very specific indemnity clauses. Members may be able, in limited circumstances, to obtain provisional protective measures (preliminary injunctions) if a shareholders' agreement is breached until the legally qualified court decides the merits of the case.

In case of a conflict between the provisions of a shareholders' agreement and the constitutional documents (i.e. by-laws) of a joint venture company, the following apply: (i) vis-à-vis the joint venture company, the by-laws prevail; and (ii) as between shareholders, a valid provision of the shareholders' agreement prevails over a conflicting clause in the bylaws. However, once again, the only remedy for breach of a shareholders' agreement is an action for damages.

Are restrictions relating to (a) transfers of shares and/or (b) minority "veto rights" commonly included in the articles of association or by-laws of the company, or included in a separate shareholders' agreement?

Restrictions on the transfer of shares and/or on minority veto rights may be included in the by-laws and/or in shareholders' agreements.

- If the restrictions are included in the by-laws, any transfer of shares which is not in compliance with the restrictions cannot be accepted and registered in the shareholders' ledger by the company. Therefore, the transferee will not be entitled to exercise the rights attaching to such shares (voting, sharing in profits, etc.).

- If the restrictions are only contained in a shareholders' agreement, the only remedy for the continuing shareholder(s) is likely to be an action for damages against the selling shareholder. Any good faith third party purchaser can normally exercise all the rights attached to the transferred shares in the joint venture company. Nevertheless, the shareholders could claim damages against the third party if it was aware of the restrictions but actively co-operated with the seller in breaching them.

Are there any formalities (e.g. notarisation or registration) which are material and which may affect the timing involved in forming the joint venture?

The deed of incorporation must be executed before a notary public.

(8) Japan

Authors: Junzaburo Kiuchi and Tatsuhiro Kubo
Freshfields Bruckhaus Deringer, Tokyo

1. General background

Are joint ventures popular as a form of foreign investment into your jurisdiction?
Yes. Due to the relative complexity of entering the Japanese market, many foreign investors have preferred to pair up in joint ventures with local Japanese partners. In the post-war period, the Japanese government promoted joint venture relationships rather than foreign direct investment. In 2006, the Japan Investment Council, which is chaired by the Prime Minister and the members of which include ministers such as the minister of state for economic and fiscal policy, pronounced that foreign investment should be accelerated and targets are to be doubled by 2010.

The Companies Act, which came into effect in May 2006 and replaced the Commercial Code, liberalised to some extent the environment for establishing joint ventures in Japan. Under the Companies Act, there are two types of limited liability companies called *"kabushiki kaisha"* ("KK") company and *"godo kaisha"* ("GK") company. A KK company is a joint stock company and is the most general entity used for joint ventures. A GK company is a newly established entity under the Companies Act and is similar to a limited liability company (LLC) in the US. A special law for a Limited Liability Partnership ("LLP") (*yugen sekinin jigyo kumiai*) also came into effect in August 2005. A LLP is a pass-through entity for taxation purposes.

Unless otherwise specified, this section relates to a joint venture by way of a KK company.

Are there restrictions on foreign participation?
Not generally—although there are a number of government-regulated industries in which foreign participation is limited. (For example, terrestrial and radio broadcasters must be less than 20 per cent and domestic airline companies must be less than one-third foreign owned.)

What (if any) are the major legal problems which a foreign investor in a joint venture faces in your jurisdiction?
Previously, under the old Commercial Code, the key legal considerations for foreign investors who intended to establish a KK company type joint venture in Japan were likely to be (i) the validity of the terms of the joint venture agreement and its enforceability, (ii) avoiding Japanese asset valuation rules and (iii) ensuring that labour issues in connection with assigning employees to the joint venture company ("JVC") are managed to avoid triggering retirement and pension liabilities. However, the new Companies Act has eased the regulations relating to (i) and (ii).

First, foreign investors need to be aware that provisions of a joint venture agreement that are inconsistent with the Companies Act or the principle of equality of treatment between shareholders may be void or unenforceable. However, the

Companies Act gives flexibility with regards to the management structure etc. and, consequently, there are now less mandatory statutory provisions which place structural and administrative restrictions on a JVC. However, even if the terms of the joint venture agreement are valid, remedies for breach of such terms by another party are likely to be limited to damages rather than enforcement of the other party's performance of its obligations.

Secondly, in certain circumstances, valuation rules are applicable to Japanese companies. For example, if certain assets (such as technology or securities) are contributed in-kind to the JVC in exchange for shares and if the value of such assets exceeds JPY5 million, an appraisal process may be required under which a court-appointed appraiser assesses the value of the in-kind contribution. Appraisals generally take around two months to complete, with the JVC prevented from engaging in business during the appraisal period. However, an appraisal is not required if the assets are acquired by the JVC after it has been incorporated. This is because the Companies Act has abolished the old valuation rule regarding the acquisition of a certain amount of assets by companies who are less than two years old.

Finally, on the issue of employees, in Japan it is not possible to transfer employees as part of a joint venture contribution unless the employees first resign and are re-hired by the JVC. This may trigger retirement allowance and pension payments to departing employees. Such issues can be avoided by seconding the employees to the JVC. This would also not apply to joint venture companies that are formed through a statutory demerger (or acquire businesses through a statutory demerger), as in this case employees relating to the demerged business would generally be automatically assigned.

2. Governmental/regulatory approvals

What principal governmental or regulatory approvals are required (excluding competition law) for establishing a joint venture?

Prior government notifications are required for foreign investment in certain industries that could constitute a threat to national security, obstruct public order or threaten public safety or are categorised as belonging to industries which Japan has not yet liberalised. Furthermore, foreign investment from certain countries sometimes requires prior notifications.

If the foreign investment takes the form of foreign direct investment (e.g. the investment is by a foreign corporation or a Japanese subsidiary of a foreign corporation in shares of a listed Japanese company or is for shares in an unlisted domestic company acquired from a domestic shareholder), a prior or subsequent notification to the Ministry of Finance and the Minister in charge of the industry concerned (through the Bank of Japan) will be required, depending on the industry in which the investment is made. Examples of industries in which foreign investment requires prior notification include aircraft manufacturing, agriculture, forestry, pharmaceutical manufacturing, electricity and gas production and distribution, fixed and mobile telecommunications, commercial broadcasting, rail, sea and air transport and security services.

A small number of industries, such as the financial services industry, have enacted industry-specific legislation that requires the approval of operations established by foreign investors.

Are there local anti trust laws which might apply to the formation of the joint venture?

Under the Japanese Anti-Monopoly Law, a business combination (merger, share acquisition, asset acquisition, demerger, etc.) is prohibited where it is likely to substantially restrain competition in the relevant market. The Guidelines Concerning Review of Business Combinations issued by the Japanese Fair Trade Commission ("JFTC") outline the approach the JFTC takes in assessing whether a business combination is prohibited. The JFTC's Guidelines Concerning Joint Research and Development may also be applicable in assessing whether a particular joint venture is permitted under Japanese law. Further, it is necessary to check whether any provisions in the joint venture agreement and ancillary agreements or arrangements among the joint venture parties are in violation of Japanese antitrust legislation concerning private "monopolisation," "unreasonable restraint of trade" or "unfair trade practices."

In relation to joint ventures by way of acquisition of businesses or assets of an existing company (*jigyo joto*), a brief summary of the merger controls appears below:

Filing requirement/trigger	Timetable for clearance	Test for clearance
Pre-transaction notification of acquisitions of businesses or assets required if: (i) acquirer (and its parent and subsidiary companies in Japan) has total gross assets of more than JPY10bn.; and (ii) target is the whole business of a Japanese company with total gross assets of more than JPY1bn.; target is partial business or assets of Japanese company with a worldwide turnover of more than JPY1bn.; target is the whole or part of the business or assets of a foreign company with a turnover in Japan of more than JPY1bn. However, no filing requirement if (i) the acquirer already holds more than 50 per cent of the shares in the acquired company, (ii) the acquired company holds more than 50 per cent of the shares in the acquirer, or (iii) more than 50 per cent of the shares in both the acquirer and the transferor company are held by the same company.	Filing must be made to the Fair Trade Commission (FTC) 30 days prior to the closing of the transaction. The parties cannot close the transaction for a period of 30 days following the filing, although the FTC may shorten or lengthen the waiting period. The FTC may still take action even after the expiry of the waiting period in certain circumstances.	Whether transaction will result in a "substantial reduction of competition" in the relevant market. **Mandatory/voluntary Penalties** Filing is mandatory. Failure to file may result in fines of up to JPY2m (although rarely applied in practice). Other possible sanctions are: divestiture and proceedings to nullify the acquisition. Measures to restore competition may also be imposed.

Currently discussions are underway regarding amending the law to require pre-transaction notification for share acquisitions for which only post-transaction notification is required under the current law.

If the local party is a public company, when might the approval of its shareholders be required under stock exchange or similar rules?

Shareholder approval is unlikely to be required—unless the transaction involves a transfer of an important business into a JVC or a demerger (which would require a special shareholder resolution). In addition, if the joint venture investment will be a significant investment for the local company, board approval will be required under the Companies Act.

3. Types of joint venture vehicle

What are the principal types of joint venture vehicle commonly used with foreign investors?

The most common form of vehicle presently used for joint ventures is a KK company. As we mentioned above, a KK company is a joint stock company regulated primarily by the Companies Act, and has no limitations on the number of its shareholders. Before May 2006, a KK company under the old Commercial Code was designed to be used for a large sized company whose governance system was determined strictly and whose capital could not have been less than JPY10 million. However, the regulations on governance systems have been eased (it is now possible to choose one of various governance systems permitted under the law) and minimum capital requirements have been abolished under the Companies Act. Consequently, a KK company has become a more useful entity, regardless of the size of the joint venture. Other types of corporate entities or partnerships, etc. sometimes used in joint venture arrangements include:

(a) GK company;

(b) partnerships and unincorporated associations (*kumiai*);

(c) LLP; or

(d) a business alliance (*gyomu teikei*) without forming any partnership or legal entity.

The choice of vehicle will depend on the size and purpose of the venture and the tax status/needs of the parties and the joint venture entity. If the parties choose a GK company, they can give the power to bind the company to all or any of the equity holders. A GK company has legal personality and is taxable. In order to avoid double taxation a partnership structure rather than company structure should be used. It should be noted that the *yugen kaisha* entity, a type of a limited liability company for small sized companies, available under the old Commercial Code has been abolished.

If a partnership structure is chosen, does this lead to (a) joint and several liability to third parties and/or (b) duties of good faith as between partners?

Partnerships (*kumiai*) in Japan are regulated by the Civil Code, the provisions of which provide for several and unlimited liability to third parties and for a duty upon a managing partner to all other partners to manage the partnership affairs with due care. Under the Civil Code a *kumiai* grouping is not afforded the status of an independent legal entity and, as a result, this form is rarely utilised.

LLPs are regulated by the Limited Liability Partnership Act and liability to third parties is limited, unless damages to a third party are caused by the bad faith or gross negligence of a party to the LLP. The duties of partners may be determined in the partnership agreement, but are subject to the duty of good faith under the Civil Code.

4. Capital structure and funding

Is it common to have different "classes" of shares (e.g. A and B shares) to reflect different initial contributions or financial interests of the parties?

It is common for a KK JVC to have different classes of shares. Under the Companies Act, a KK company may issue classes of shares that differ with respect to (i) payment of dividends or interest, (ii) distribution of residual assets, (iii) any matters on which voting rights are exercisable at a shareholders' meeting, (iv) restriction on transfer of shares, (v) right of the shareholder to request that the issuing company acquire the shares, (vi) mandatory redemption by the issuing company or (vii) the right to appoint directors or corporate auditors at a shareholders' meeting of each class of share.

A company having different classes of shares may provide in its articles of incorporation that certain matters (such as share transfers) require the passing of a resolution by shareholders' meeting of a particular class of shares in addition to a resolution by the board of directors meeting and/or shareholders' meeting. As such, it is possible to give a shareholder of a particular class of shares a veto right in respect of certain matters by issuing shares of a particular class.

Is it common to have "preference" shares which give a party a priority on payment of dividends or on a return of capital?

Yes.

Are "redeemable" shares permitted (i.e. shares that can be repaid and cancelled)?

Yes.

Are "non voting" shares permitted?

Yes.

Are there any "thin capitalisation" or similar rules which affect the choice of equity/ debt ratio for the capital structure?

There are "thin capitalisation" rules in Japan which only allow for the tax deductibility of interest payments on loans made by a foreign parent company where the capital to loan ratio of the borrowing company exceeds one:three.

Is there any capital or similar tax payable in respect of issued share capital?

A registration tax is payable upon filing for the incorporation of a KK with the Legal Affairs Bureau in the amount of 0.7 per cent of the issued share capital (with a JPY150,000 minimum). A further registration tax is payable on registration of any capital increase (or decrease) in the amount of 0.7 per cent of the additional issued capital (with a JPY30,000 minimum).

Is a separate "contribution agreement" or other formal document (other than formal property transfer agreements) required or usual under the local law to document the contribution of assets to the joint venture?

No special contribution agreement is required. However, if assets are being contributed to a company as part of the incorporation process, a description of the in-kind contribution must be included in the company's initial articles of incorporation.

Are there any local laws which require an independent valuation of any non cash assets to be contributed to the joint venture?

Yes. In-kind contributions of assets in exchange for shares are subject to independent appraisal under the following circumstances:

- KK companies being newly incorporated: if the assets being contributed are worth more than JPY5 million and, in the case of securities, more than the market value; and

- Previously existing KK companies: if the assets being contributed are worth more than JPY5 million, more than the market value in the case of securities, and the shares to be issued in exchange for such assets are more than 10 per cent of the total outstanding shares. Under the Companies Act, certain contributions in-kind by way of a debt-equity swap will not trigger an independent appraisal procedure. In addition, no independent appraisal is required for the sale (i.e. not contribution in-kind) of non cash assets to a KK company.

No court appraisal will, however, be required if a certification by professionals such as an attorney-at-law, certified public accountant, tax accountant or incorporated professional services firm employing such individuals certifies that the value of the assets being contributed is fair (in the case of real estate (land or buildings) an additional certified valuation by a special real estate appraiser (*fudosan kantei nin*) is required). For newly incorporated companies, such information must also be specified in the articles of incorporation.

Are there exchange control regulations which materially affect the establishment of the joint venture or the subsequent repatriation of profits or dividends from the joint venture to a foreign party?

Restrictions in relation to financial transactions between a resident and a non-resident of Japan have been deregulated in the past few years. Consequently, prior approval from or registration with the Ministry of Finance for such transactions is no longer required (with some exceptions described below) and generally repatriation of profits or dividends is easily achieved.

The Foreign Exchange and Foreign Trade Law now only requires that a resident of Japan file an after-the-fact report after engaging in certain financial transactions with a non-resident. Examples of such transactions include loans and the purchase or sale of securities. There are certain exceptions where prior notification is still required.

An inbound cross-border financial transaction will require prior notification if: (a) the nationality of the foreign investor in the transaction is other than those listed in Sch.1 of the Ordinance regarding Foreign Direct Investments; or (b) the investment destination of the transaction includes any industry the investment in which is subject to prior notification, such as agriculture, electricity, gas, water, communications or finance.

If a foreign party is to contribute technology to the joint venture, are there any special requirements for valuation of that technology?

If the technology is contributed in exchange for shares in the KK JVC, in certain circumstances the technology may have to be valued as described earlier. If the value of the technology, etc., triggers the requirement for a valuation appraisal, it is possible to avoid the appraisal if the technology is merely licensed to the JVC or is acquired after the JVC has been incorporated.

5. Tax

Are there any particular tax laws or incentives which significantly affect the establishment of joint ventures in this jurisdiction by a foreign investor?

Japanese companies (including subsidiaries of foreign companies) are taxed on aggregate yearly corporate income (including both domestic and foreign-sourced income). Japanese subsidiaries receive tax credits for tax paid in other jurisdictions on foreign sourced income.

Foreign companies having a permanent establishment in Japan such as a branch office are taxed by the Japanese tax authorities only on domestic-sourced income. Foreign branches and subsidiaries are subject both to a national corporate tax and local enterprise and inhabitant taxes. Japan also imposes consumption tax on non-exempt transactions in Japan.

Will withholding taxes apply to dividends paid by a joint venture company?

The Japanese Income Tax Law applies a 20 per cent withholding tax on dividends, interest, royalties and rents payable to a non-resident of Japan. Bilateral tax treaties (including with the UK) reduce this rate on dividends, interest and royalties.

6. Board and management

Are there local law rules which affect the board or management structure of the joint venture? May a two tier board be required?

Under the Companies Act, the governance system of a KK company depends on (i) whether such company is a private company or not and (ii) whether such company is a large sized company or not. A private and non-large sized company is given more flexibility with regards to its governance system; it is only required to have at least one director and is not required to have a board of directors, board of statutory auditors or accounting auditor. Non-private and large sized companies are, however, required to have a board of directors and an accounting auditor and a board of statutory auditors or three committees (i.e. nominating, compensation and audit committee). For this purpose, a "private company" means a company that has a restriction on the transfer of its shares and a "large sized company" means a company whose capital amount is JPY500 million or more or whose total liabilities are JPY20 billion or more.

Two-tier boards are not required under Japanese law.

Are there local law constraints on persons who can be directors or managers of the joint venture (e.g. only local residents or nationals)?

At least one of the representative directors of a KK company must be resident in Japan (but who may be a foreign national).

Does a shareholder in a joint venture company owe a duty of good faith (or similar duty) to other shareholders in the way it behaves in relation to the joint venture?

Shareholders of KK companies do not have a specific duty of good faith to the company or to other shareholders under the Companies Act. However, the principle of good faith is a term generally implied into contracts such as the shareholders' agreement by operation of the Civil Code. Thus, shareholders who are party to the shareholders' agreement have a general duty of good faith and fair dealings with the other parties.

Can you modify the legal duties of directors so that they can expressly take into account the interests of their "appointer" when voting or acting as director—or must they always act objectively in the best interests of the company?

Directors of a KK company have various duties under the Companies Act to the company on whose board they serve, including the duty faithfully to perform their duties in the interest of the company "as a good manager" and to refrain from competing with the company. Failure to comply with such duties (e.g. by considering the interests of their appointer over those of the company) can subject the director to civil liability. Therefore, best practice is for a director to act objectively in the best interests of the company.

7. Transfer of shares

In the case of a joint venture company, can a permanent restriction on transfer of shares be imposed under the local law (e.g. no transfer without the consent of the other shareholder)?

Under the Companies Act, the JVC's articles of incorporation can have a provision, for example, that the approval of shareholders or approval by the board of directors or a representative director for share transfers is required. It is possible to include in the articles of incorporation a provision that any approval by the shareholders/directors of a share transfer must be unanimous. However, if no express disapproval is given to a proposed transfer or if no alternative purchaser is nominated within two weeks, the transfer will be deemed to be approved. It is possible to establish transfer restrictions on a particular class of shares.

8. Protection for minority shareholders

Are there any statutory rules or remedies which help significantly to protect a minority shareholder in a joint venture company?

The Companies Act does provide some material protections. In particular, a KK JVC will be unable to take a number of corporate actions without super-majority approval (two-thirds or more) of the shareholders, including: any amendment of the JVC's articles of incorporation; share buy-backs from specific shareholders; a transfer of the whole or a substantial part of the company's business; acquiring the whole business of any other company; new share issues at significantly below market price; new share issues by a private company; grant rights to subscribe for new shares to directors and/or employees (e.g., share option plans); stock-for-stock exchanges (*kabushiki kokan*); share transfers to a new holding company (*kabushiki iten*); mergers or demergers; capital reductions; company dissolution; and releasing a director from any liability owed to the company in certain circumstances.

Therefore, a shareholder with greater than one-third of a JVC's voting shares would essentially have a veto right over any of the above matters (provided, however, that such shareholder attended the shareholders' meeting at which such items were discussed since only a simple majority quorum is required). The articles of incorporation may be drafted to require unanimous consent of all shareholders with regard to certain matters.

Does the law require any major business decisions to be approved by a special resolution or super-majority (whether at board or shareholder level), or must a minority party protect itself by contract?

As mentioned above, the law requests a super-majority approval at shareholder level for certain matters. There is no super-majority matter at board level provided under the Companies Act. However, it is possible to have provisions requiring an increased quorum or approval threshold (e.g. two-thirds) for certain matters at board or shareholder level. It also is common practice in Japan for joint venture partners to supplement these statutory rights by providing for additional protections in the shareholders' agreement.

9. Employment laws

Are there local law obligations requiring a "local" party to consult with, or obtain the approval of, employees or employee representatives on a contribution of its business to the joint venture?

If the local party is unionised, the provisions of its collective bargaining agreement with its union may require consultation in good faith with the union in advance of certain material business decisions such as a decision to establish a new company or business line.

Are there any material employment laws (compared with the UK) which are likely to affect the ongoing operations of the joint venture?

The Japanese Labour Standards Law and Employment Contract Law sets out the mandatory requirements that will be applicable to all employees (other than directors) of the JVC.

Most importantly, termination of the employment of an employee will only be valid if it is based on objectively "reasonable" grounds and cannot be considered to be "socially inappropriate". Japanese court precedent has identified only a limited number of circumstances in which reasonable grounds will be held to exist. Most relevantly, dismissals on the grounds of extreme poor performance or in the case of absolute business necessity (e.g. when a business needs to reduce its staff in order to survive) will be more likely viewed as valid. Further, Japanese law imposes an obligation to avoid dismissals, so even a poorly performing individual would need to be given an opportunity to rectify that performance before the employer proceeds with the dismissal. As a result, workforce restructurings are less easily achieved than in other jurisdictions. Joint venture partners should, therefore, consider whether to transfer or second employees into the joint venture and where liability will fall for any costs associated with the termination of employees.

10. Accounts

Is there a requirement on the joint venture company to file accounts with any authority where they are publicly available?

Japanese KK companies and foreign companies who are registered in Japan (including branch offices) are technically required to publish their balance sheet annually in the official gazette, a national newspaper or on the internet. In practice, a number of companies do not comply with this requirement.

11. Dispute resolution

Is there any standard local practice as to form of dispute resolution in relation to joint ventures with foreign investors? Is arbitration in a venue outside that jurisdiction acceptable?

There is no standard practice as to form of dispute resolution in relation to joint ventures. Popular approaches include prior negotiation between high level officials of the shareholders, submission to the Tokyo District Court, or arbitration under the rules of the ICC or the Japan Commercial Arbitration Association (JCAA). Arbitral awards issued outside of Japan will be enforceable by Japanese courts (provided that certain procedures for their enforcement are followed).

Is the local jurisdiction a signatory to the 1958 New York Convention on the Recognition and Enforcement of Foreign Arbitral Awards?

Yes, subject to the reservation that it will only apply the Convention to awards made in the territory of other parties contracting to the Convention.

12. Legal documents and formalities

Is there any special form of legal documentation required under local law for establishment of a joint venture company? What are the usual principal documents?

There is no special form of documentation required. The principal documents involved will include incorporation documents (e.g. board and shareholder minutes and articles of incorporation) as well as a shareholders' agreement between the joint venture parties and possibly the JVC. There may also be supporting commercial agreements such as technology licensing agreements, employee secondment agreements and marketing and distribution agreements.

Does the joint venture documentation need to be in the local language and/or governed by the local law?

The shareholders' agreement can be governed by a foreign law and be in any language.

Documentation to be filed with the relevant local Legal Affairs Bureau such as the articles of incorporation must be in Japanese.

Are agreements between shareholders (e.g. as to appointment of directors, conduct of the business of the company or voting majorities required for certain decisions etc) enforceable under local law? In the event of breach, is specific performance or a similar remedy available, or only damages?

Such agreements are enforceable unless the agreement is inconsistent with the mandatory provisions in the Companies Act. However, agreements that are inconsistent with such mandatory provisions can still be valid as between the parties. A joint venture party can only seek compensatory damages and not specific performance, although injunctive relief is available in limited circumstances. Joint venture agreements may contain provisions for liquidated damages.

Are restrictions relating to (a) transfers of shares and/or (b) minority "veto rights" commonly included in the articles of association or by laws of the company, or included in a separate shareholders' agreement?

Under the Companies Act, it is common that share transfer restrictions and veto rights are included in the articles of incorporation. In addition, it is common that these restrictions and rights are also included in the shareholders' agreement.

Are there any formalities (e.g. notarisation or registration) which are material and which may affect the timing involved in forming the joint venture?

It can take two or three weeks to form a KK company. The time required depends on (i) whether or not the incorporator is a Japanese resident and (ii) whether or not the incorporator has a bank account in Japan. As a matter of practice, it is difficult to purchase a suitable shelf company. The articles of incorporation must be prepared in Japanese, notarised and filed with the Legal Affairs Bureau. If the JVC is being formed by way of demerger, a number of other procedural requirements (including consultation with and notification to employees and notice to creditors) will be involved which affect timing.

(9) The Netherlands

Authors: Dirk-Jan Smit (corporate) and Machiel Lambooij (tax).
Freshfields Bruckhaus Deringer LLP, Amsterdam

1. General background

Are joint ventures popular as a form of foreign investment into your jurisdiction?

Joint ventures are quite popular as a form of foreign direct investment. The Netherlands is, however, particularly popular as a jurisdiction in which to locate a holding company of a joint venture—particularly where the parties are based in different jurisdictions and/or have subsidiaries operating internationally. The popularity of Dutch companies internationally is due to many reasons—e.g. its tax laws including its treaty network and its participation exemption and the absence of capital tax and stamp duties, which are all attractive in an international context; an established and respected system of corporate law; an efficient business and service infrastructure; and a jurisdiction well-placed geographically and in business outlook for an international role within Europe.

Are there restrictions on foreign participation?

No. There are no material restrictions on foreign participation.

What (if any) are the major legal problems which a foreign investor in a joint venture faces in your jurisdiction?

There are no major legal problems as such. The most difficult areas for a foreign investor may be: (i) strict Dutch employment laws; (ii) the requirement for a two-tier "structure regime" in certain circumstances (see below); and (iii) certain restrictions relating to the content of share rights and the articles of association (e.g. no permanent restriction on transfer of shares in a BV and no non-voting shares, although more flexibility is likely to be introduced in the course of 2008). The Netherlands offers, overall, a flexible and attractive jurisdiction for international joint ventures.

2. Governmental/regulatory approvals

What principal governmental or regulatory approvals are required (excluding competition law) for establishing a joint venture?

The incorporation of a limited liability company (BV or NV) requires the prior approval of the Ministry of Justice. Financial information about the initial shareholders and proposed members of the management board must be inter alia submitted for this purpose.

Are there local anti-trust laws which might apply to the formation of the joint venture?

Yes. Assuming that the EC Merger Regulation does not apply, notification prior to closing of a joint venture with the Dutch competition authority (*Nederlandse Mededingingsautoriteit*, "*NMa*") is required if that joint venture is "full function", i.e. if it performs on a lasting basis the functions of an autonomous economic entity, and certain turnover thresholds are met. A brief summary is set out below:

Filing requirement/ trigger	Timetable for clearance	Test for clearance	Mandatory/ voluntary Penalties
Applies to the formation of a "full function" JV; Test: (i) combined worldwide turnover of the parties that set up the JV (i.e. the future parents) exceeds approx. €113m; and (ii) two or more parties that set up the JV have individual turnover in the Netherlands exceeding €30m.	Within four weeks from the notification the NMa must decide whether a licence is required. If so, an application for a licence must be made and the NMa must decide within 13 weeks from the application. Transaction cannot be implemented until a clearance decision has been received. A derogation may be possible.	Whether the JV would lead to a significant impediment of competition on the Dutch market, or part thereof, in particular as a result of the creation or strengthening of a dominant position.	Filing mandatory prior to JV becoming effective. Failure to file/ implementation before clearance: fines of up to €22,500 and the transaction is void.

3. Types of joint venture vehicle

What are the principal types of joint venture vehicle commonly used with foreign investors?

A corporate entity (BV or NV) is the most popular legal form, although a limited partnership is sometimes employed. Principal distinguishing features are:

(i) **BV.** The BV (*besloten vennootschap met beperkte aansprakelijkheid*) is probably the most common, and most flexible, form of corporate entity. Features include: some restrictions on transfer of shares must be included in the articles of association of a BV; minimum issued and paid-up capital of €18,000 is required; only registered shares may be issued; a BV may, subject to certain restrictions, repurchase up to a maximum of 50 per cent of its issued and outstanding shares; prohibition of financial assistance: BV may, subject to restrictions, grant loans for the acquisition of its own shares by third parties. Some of these, and a number of other, restrictions will be abolished once a legislative proposal to that effect is enacted (likely to happen in the course of 2008). As a result the BV will be even more flexible.[1]

---

[1] Given that the exact changes are not fully clear at this stage, the paragraphs in this chapter reflect the current legislation.

(ii) **NV**. The NV (*naamloze vennootschap*) is necessary where shares are likely to be issued to the public or in case of a bank or insurance company. Features include:

- shares are freely transferable, unless provided otherwise in the articles of association;
- minimum issued and paid-up capital of €45,000 is required; registered shares and/or bearer shares may be issued;
- an NV may, subject to certain restrictions, repurchase up to a maximum of 10 per cent of its issued and outstanding shares;
- prohibition of financial assistance; granting of loans is prohibited in this context.

(iii) **Limited partnership**. There are two types of limited partnership: *vennootschap onder firma* or *vof* and *commanditaire vennootschap* or *CV*. These are occasionally used, mainly for tax purposes:

- no legal entity as such is created (although this will change as a result of new legislation, likely to be enacted in the course of 2008) but merely a contract between parties;
- at least one of the parties acts as general partner with unlimited liability.

A regular partnership (*vof*) is transparent for income tax purposes. A limited partnership may qualify as an entity subject to corporate income tax for the profits allocable to the limited partners (open limited partnership; *open CV*) if the partnership interests can be transferred (or new partners can accede) without the permission of all partners. Only if the permission of all partners is required for such acts, a limited partnership will be considered transparent for income tax purposes (*besloten CV*). The interest of the general partner in the limited partnership is directly allocated to such partner and taxed in his hands. The new legislation mentioned above should not affect this tax treatment.

If a partnership structure is chosen, does this lead to (a) joint and several liability to third parties and/or (b) duties of good faith as between partners?

In a *vof*, all partners are jointly and severally liable towards thirds parties. In a CV, the general partners are jointly and severally liable towards third parties. The liability of the limited partners in a CV is in principle limited up to the amount of their contribution. The new legislation will not materially change this.

The relationship between the partners is governed by the partnership agreement as well as the dictates of reasonableness and fairness (*redelijkheid en billijkheid*). The latter means that an acting partner should not only take his own interests into account but also those of his partners and the partnership as a whole.

4. Capital structure and funding

What principal local law issues affect the capital structure and funding of the joint venture?

The issued capital must at all times be at least one-fifth of the authorised share capital. Minimum issued and paid-up capital requirements are: €18,000 in the case of a BV; €45,000 in the case of an NV. If contribution takes place in kind, a detailed description of the contribution and an auditor's statement are required.

Transactions between shareholders and the joint venture company within a period of two years after the registration of the incorporated joint venture company at the

Chamber of Commerce may also be subject to further disclosure and approval requirements.

Is it common to have different "classes" of shares (e.g. A and B shares) to reflect different initial contributions or financial interests of the parties?

Yes. Dutch law is relatively flexible as to the creation of special classes of shares and rights attributable to them. Shares may have different rights attaching to them, including different rights to dividend and/or capital and different nomination rights for the appointment of members of the management board. Shares may be created with special voting rights. Non-voting shares are, however, not yet permitted. Also, it is not possible yet to exclude a particular class of shares fully from a share in the profit (although this may be a very small, nominal profit share only).

Is it common to have "preference" shares which give a party a priority on payment of dividends or on a return of capital?

Yes, these are often used in joint venture structures.

Are "redeemable" shares permitted (i.e. shares that can be repaid and cancelled)?

Yes.

Are "non-voting" shares permitted?

Non-voting shares are not yet permissible under Dutch law. However, through a structure whereby a special purpose entity (*stichting administratiekantoor*) holds the shares in trust and issues depository receipts in exchange, the voting rights and the dividend rights attached to the shares can in effect be separated.

Are there any "thin capitalisation" or similar rules which affect the choice of equity/ debt ratio for the capital structure?

Dutch corporate law only provides for minimum capital requirements (see above). There are no formal equity/debt ratio requirements.

For corporate income tax purposes, thin capitalisation legislation is applicable, generally requiring a debt-to-equity ratio of not more than three-one unless the Dutch entity is part of a larger group of companies that has a de facto debt-to-equity ratio on the basis of its commercial consolidated balance sheet that is higher (group ratio). In case of excess debt, only interest payable on debt due to related parties is not tax deductible; the excess interest is not subject to dividend withholding tax. Third party interest benefiting from a related party guarantee may qualify as related party interest for purposes of these rules.

Is there any capital or similar tax payable in respect of issued share capital?

Capital tax has been abolished. There are no stamp duties. Under specific circumstances, real estate transfer tax may be due on the transfer of shares in a company mainly holding (interests in) real property located in the Netherlands for portfolio investment purposes.

Is a separate "contribution agreement" or other formal document (other than formal property transfer agreements) required or usual under the local law to document the contribution of assets to the joint venture?

In the case of contribution of non-cash assets, a separate contribution agreement will be required. For certain assets, e.g. registered shares or real estate, a notarial deed of contribution is required.

Are there any local laws which require an independent valuation of any non-cash assets to be contributed to the joint venture?

If non-cash assets are contributed in exchange for shares, an auditor must state that the value of the contribution at least equals the amount of payment obligations in respect of the shares. The auditor's statement must be filed with the trade register of the Chamber of Commerce. Timing very much depends on the auditor.

Are there exchange control regulations which materially affect the establishment of the joint venture or the subsequent repatriation of profits or dividends from the joint venture to a foreign party?

No. There are no exchange control regulations.

5. Tax

Are there any particular tax laws or incentives which significantly affect the establishment of joint ventures in this jurisdiction by a foreign investor?

Tax plays a significant role in attracting companies to use the Netherlands as the location of a joint venture holding company. In short, Dutch tax law has: an extensive double tax treaty network, which reduces the foreign and domestic applicable withholding tax rates substantially; various reorganisation facilities (in accordance with the EU Merger Directive); no withholding tax on interest and royalties; and a "participation exemption", which creates a full exemption for dividends received from, or capital gains realised on disposal of, qualifying participations (i.e. qualifying interests in subsidiaries or other companies held by the joint venture holding company).

The participation exemption is subject to a number of conditions: (a) the parent company must meet the five per cent threshold test (see below); (b) the subsidiary must have "capital" that is "divided into shares"; and (c) the subsidiary must not constitute a low-taxed investment company.

The *five per cent threshold test* requires that the parent company:

(i) owns at least five per cent of the shares in the subsidiary ("the five per cent shareholding threshold"); or

(ii) owns less than five per cent of the shares in the subsidiary but (a) a company related to the parent company (whether resident in the Netherlands or elsewhere) owns at least five percent of the shares in the subsidiary or (b) it has owned for an uninterrupted period of at least one year at least five per cent of the shares in the subsidiary and three years have not yet passed after the shareholding by the parent company in the subsidiary dropped below five per cent; or

(iii) if the subsidiary is resident for Netherlands tax purposes in an EU Member State with which the Netherlands has concluded a treaty for the avoidance of double taxation that provides for a reduction of Netherlands dividend withholding tax on the basis of the number of voting rights, then the five per cent shareholding threshold described above may be replaced by a threshold requiring an interest of five per cent in the voting rights in the subsidiary.

A low-taxed investment company for this purpose is a subsidiary:

(i) the assets of which (and of any subsidiary in which the subsidiary holds an interest of at least five per cent) consist for more than 50 per cent (in terms of fair market value) of or a combination of: (a) portfolio investments that do not have a function in the enterprise of the subsidiary; (b) interests of less than five per cent in companies, certain funds and certain limited partnerships that do not have a function in the enterprise of the subsidiary; and (c) assets used for finance transactions with related parties (which includes the granting of loans and the financing otherwise of business assets and business activities of related parties), unless the foreign finance company is sufficiently "active"; (d) shareholdings of five per cent or more in a company that is primarily (for 50 per cent or more) engaged in finance transactions with related parties; and

(ii) is subject to an income/profits tax at an effective rate of less than 10 per cent on its profits calculated in accordance with Netherlands tax principles with the exception of loss carry-overs and tax grouping rules;

except if the assets of the subsidiary (and of any subsidiary in which the subsidiary holds an interest of at least five per cent, but calculated on a consolidated basis) consists of 90 per cent or more (in terms of fair market value) of real property and neither the subsidiary nor its subsidiaries are portfolio investment institutions (*fiscale beleggingsinstelling*).

The participation exemption rules no longer make a distinction between resident and non-resident subsidiaries.

Will withholding taxes apply to dividends paid by a joint venture company?

The Netherlands levies under its domestic laws a dividend withholding tax at a rate of 15 per cent. This is also the rate that applies under most tax treaties that the Netherlands have entered into applicable to portfolio investors. This means that no formalities are any longer required to obtain the benefits of the reduced treaty rate. Due to EU law developments, a full exemption now applies to most EU resident corporate shareholders holding five per cent or more of the shares in a Dutch company, provided they are eligible for application of the EU Parent-Subsidiary Directive. Other EU resident entities that are not subject to tax, but would have been entitled to a refund of Dutch dividend withholding tax were they to have been resident of the Netherlands are entitled to a full refund (this may apply to pension funds, charitable institutions, etc.). Otherwise, non-resident corporate shareholders, holding an interest of—generally—25 per cent or more may benefit from a reduced rate of five per cent (or in some cases zero per cent).

6. Board and management

Are there local law rules which affect the board or management structure of the joint venture? May a two-tier board be required?

Where there is a distinction between executive and non-executive functions, Dutch companies typically have a two-tier system. This system consists of a management board performing executive functions as opposed to a supervisory board performing supervisory and advisory functions, with each board having its own responsibilities, powers and duties. The establishment of a supervisory board, however, is generally optional unless, according to the Dutch Civil Code, the company is obliged to adopt the so-called "Structure Regime". A one-tier board with both executives and non-executives is also possible.

In general, a company is obliged to adopt the Structure Regime if for a period of three consecutive years (i) it has a capital of at least €16m, (ii) it has a works council and (iii) the group employs on a regular basis at least 100 employees in the Netherlands.

The most important feature of the Structure Regime is the broad authority of the supervisory board; they appoint and dismiss managing directors and approve important management board decisions. In addition, they have the same advisory and supervisory function as they have in "ordinary" companies.

In the Structure Regime, the members of the supervisory board are appointed by the shareholders' meeting on the basis of nominations drawn up by the supervisory board. The works council has the right to make a binding recommendation of one-third (rounded down) of the supervisory board. Unless the recommended person is unsuitable for the performance of the duties of a supervisory board member or if, as a result of the appointment, the supervisory board will not be suitably composed, the supervisory board is required to nominate the individual recommended by the works council.

Are there local law constraints on persons who can be directors or managers of the joint venture (e.g. only local residents or nationals)?

No corporate constraints. For tax purposes it may be advisable in order to ensure tax residency in the Netherlands that the joint venture company has a certain balanced composition of the board of directors and/or that actual decision making takes place predominantly in the Netherlands.

Does a shareholder in a joint venture company owe a duty of good faith (or similar duty) to other shareholders in the way it behaves in relation to the joint venture?

Shareholders must conduct themselves towards other shareholders, board members and the company in accordance with the dictates of reasonableness and fairness—the so called good faith principle. This does not mean that shareholders should always act in the interests of the company or that they necessarily have obligations towards other shareholders. Violation of this principle, though, could form a ground to challenge resolutions.

Can you modify the legal duties of directors so that they can expressly take into account the interests of their "appointer" when voting or acting as director, or must they always act objectively in the best interests of the company?

This is problematic as the directors must always act in the best interests of the company.

7. Transfer of shares

In the case of a joint venture company, can a permanent restriction on transfer of shares be imposed under the local law (e.g. no transfer without the consent of the other shareholder)?

The articles of association of a BV must provide for restrictions on transfer of shares.

There are two possibilities: either (i) an obligation to first offer the shares to the other shareholders or (ii) an obligation to request the shareholders' meeting (or any other corporate body) for approval on the basis that if the shareholders' meeting does not grant approval and fails to specify the name(s) of one or more designated parties who is/are willing to acquire the relevant shares for cash, the selling shareholder is free to transfer its shares to a third party during a certain period.

The contents of such a transfer restriction are very much based on mandatory Civil Code provisions. Dutch mandatory law does not permit a right permanently to prohibit a transfer—although it is considered that, in a joint venture situation, a prohibition for a defined period of time (in practice, usually two to five years) will be enforceable. It may be possible to limit the categories of persons to whom transfers may be made. (Although not required, the articles of association of an NV could also have restrictions on transfer of shares.)

Often the shareholders' agreement has more detailed provisions on share transfer restrictions than set out in the articles.

8. Protection for minority shareholders

Are there any statutory rules or remedies which help significantly to protect a minority shareholder in a joint venture company?

Minority shareholders are entitled to the general rights attributed by statutory law and by the articles of association to individual shareholders. Generally, a shareholder holding voting rights sufficient to appoint or dismiss the management board is in full control of the company. A controlling shareholder must observe the principles of reasonableness and fairness which play an important part in Netherlands law generally.

There are some provisions in the Netherlands Civil Code offering specific protection to minority shareholders, such as the right of holders representing 10 per cent of the issued share capital to convene a general meeting if the management board of the company refuses to do so. Certain formal resolutions (if less than 50 per cent of the issued capital is represented at the shareholders' meeting) require a special majority of votes including: restriction or limitation of pre-emption rights in an NV; reduction of share capital in an NV; merger/division of an NV or a BV. Minority shareholders also have a veto right in respect of resolutions in the following circumstances: resolutions adopted at a general meeting held outside the Netherlands are only valid if the entire issued share capital is represented at that meeting; also, if the notice period before a shareholders' meeting is shorter than 15 days, no valid resolution may be adopted unless the resolution is adopted by unanimous vote at a meeting at which the entire issued share capital is represented.

Shareholders representing at least 10 per cent of the issued share capital of a Dutch company may file a request with the Enterprise Chamber of the Court of Appeal in Amsterdam (the Enterprise Chamber) to start an investigation into whether the company is, or has been, properly managed. If the Enterprise Chamber finds indications of improper management, it may appoint experts to carry out an investigation. If the Enterprise Chamber finds that there is or has been mismanagement, the Enterprise Chamber may take certain measures in order to address the mismanagement found.

The Netherlands Civil Code also provides for a dispute resolution procedure to resolve disputes between shareholders. In summary, if a shareholder damages the interest of the company, one or more shareholders representing one-third of the issued share capital may request the Enterprise Chamber to force the shareholder to transfer his shares to the innocent shareholder(s) or may seek to force the other shareholder to acquire the shares of the innocent shareholder(s). This statutory procedure does not apply to listed NV companies and is not applicable in cases where a shareholders' agreement or the articles of association contain a specific dispute resolution procedure, unless it can be demonstrated that this specific procedure cannot be applied in the particular case.

Does the law require any major business decisions to be approved by a special resolution or super-majority (whether at board or shareholder level), or must a minority party protect itself by contract?

For an NV, board resolutions that have an important impact on the identity or nature of the company require shareholders' approval. Unless the articles stipulate differently, an ordinary majority will be sufficient.

The law does not otherwise provide for any special majorities for business decisions (such as acquisitions etc.). For both the BV and the NV, however, the articles of association often provide for a list of board decisions that require prior approval of the shareholders meeting or the supervisory board. The articles could require a supermajority.

9. Employment laws

Are there local law obligations requiring a "local" party to consult with, or obtain the approval of, employees or employee representatives on a contribution of its business to the joint venture?

If a works council has been established, in principle, its advice must be obtained. It is important that the advice is asked for at an early stage, i.e. at such a time that the works council's opinion could still have an impact upon the decision. A negative advice of the works council can seriously delay the transaction.

If one or more of the joint venture parties employs 50 employees in the Netherlands or if it forms part of a group of companies employing 50 or more employees in the Netherlands, then the relevant trade unions and the Social Economic Council must, in principle, be notified. This notification should also take place at an early stage.

Are there any material employment laws (compared with the UK) which are likely to affect the ongoing operations of the joint venture?

Generally, the Netherlands has strict employment laws. Features include:

- A works council must be established if, basically, an enterprise in the Netherlands has at least 50 employees.
- In the event of a transfer by a shareholder of (one of) its undertakings to the joint venture company, the rights and the obligations under contracts for employment are transferred by operation of law if the transfer is considered as a transfer of undertaking within the meaning of the Acquired Rights Directive as implemented in the Dutch Civil Code. A transfer of undertaking will exist in the case of a transfer of an "economic entity" that retains its identity.
- If a works council has been established, it may have a right to give its advice on a proposed appointment or dismissal of a managing director or concerning certain decisions relating to the financing of the transaction. If the Structure Regime rules apply, the works council has additional rights (see section 8 earlier).
- Strict laws apply to protect employees against dismissals. The main rule is that employees cannot be dismissed without the approval of the Central Organisation for Work and Income or court permission.

10. Accounts

Is there a requirement on the joint venture company to file accounts with any authority where they are publicly available?

Accounts (both in the case of an NV and a BV) must be filed with the trade register of the Chamber of Commerce where the joint venture company has been registered.

11. Dispute resolution

Is there any standard local practice as to form of dispute resolution in relation to joint ventures with foreign investors? Is arbitration in a venue outside that jurisdiction acceptable?

There is no real standard practice. Reference is frequently made to the Rules of the Netherlands Arbitration Institute. Arbitration outside the Netherlands is acceptable.

Is the local jurisdiction a signatory to the 1958 New York Convention on the Recognition and Enforcement of Foreign Arbitral Awards?

Yes.

12. Legal documents and formalities

Is there any special form of legal documentation required under local law for establishment of a joint venture company? What are the usual principal documents?

The documents required will usually comprise: (i) joint venture/shareholders agreement; (ii) notarial deed of incorporation; (iii) Ministerial "declaration of no objection"; (iv) statement from a bank, if the contribution is in cash; (v) description of the contribution, auditor's statement and notarial deed of contribution, if a contribution in kind.

Does the joint venture documentation need to be in the local language and/or governed by the local law?

The joint venture agreement or shareholders' agreement need not be in the Dutch language. The notarial deed of incorporation must, however, be executed in the Dutch language. If there is a conflict between a translation of the articles of association and the Dutch wording, the latter shall prevail.

Although there is no specific case law on the issue, the general view is that it is not essential for a shareholders' agreement of a Dutch company to be governed by Netherlands law. However, the use of a foreign law may give rise to enforcement difficulties in relation to certain provisions relating to the organisation of the company, such as provisions relating to voting, dissolution, appointment of managing and supervisory board members, etc.

Are there any commonly-accepted "standard forms" for joint ventures with foreign investors in your jurisdiction?

No.

Are agreements between shareholders (e.g. as to appointment of directors, conduct of the business of the company or voting majorities required for certain decisions etc.) enforceable under local law? In the event of breach, is specific performance or a similar remedy available, or only damages?

Shareholders' agreements are generally enforceable. Remedies include specific performance and damages.

Are restrictions relating to (a) transfers of shares and/or (b) minority "veto rights" commonly included in the articles of association or by-laws of the company, or included in a separate shareholders' agreement?

Restrictions on transfer of shares are typically included in the articles of association; for the BV this is even mandatory. Restrictions relating to minority "veto rights" are commonly included in the articles as well. The shareholders' agreement often repeats these restrictions and/or provides for more detail. The main advantage of having these in the articles of association as well—except to comply with mandatory law, if applicable—is that a share transfer or a resolution in violation of the articles is null and void.

Are there any formalities (e.g. notarisation or registration) which are material and which may affect the timing involved in forming the joint venture?

The deed of incorporation and the deed of contribution, if any, must be executed before a Dutch civil law notary. The notarisation itself will not significantly affect the timing. The procedure for a "declaration of no objection" from the Ministry of Justice, however, may take some time. Normally, the procedure takes approximately ten business days; under certain circumstances, an expedited procedure can be applied for.

(10) Poland

Authors: Prof. Grzegorz Domanski and Marek Swiatkowski
Domanski Zakrzewski Palinka sp.K, Warsaw

1. General background

Are joint ventures popular as a form of foreign investment into your jurisdiction?

Joint ventures continue to be a popular way for foreign entities to invest. Agreements on co-operation between partners are becoming more and more complex. Very often a joint venture is chosen by foreign investors as the first step in the Polish market. After a successful start-up (which may last several years), the foreign investor frequently chooses to take over the whole undertaking, if given the opportunity.

There are no specific legal provisions governing joint ventures in Poland. The joint venture will be regulated by the provisions applicable to the "vehicle" chosen by the parties (e.g. contract, partnership, company).

Are there restrictions on foreign participation?

Most of the restrictions on foreign participation in joint ventures have been lifted over the last few years. The restrictions which are still applicable concern particular sectors and relate to investors which have their registered seats outside the EU or the European Economic Area.

What (if any) are the major legal problems which a foreign investor in a joint venture faces in your jurisdiction?

There are no major legal problems that would differ Poland from most other European countries. Some procedural requirements (see e.g. section 15 below regarding legal formalities) can, though, be cumbersome and take time to complete.

2. Governmental/regulatory approvals

What principal governmental or regulatory approvals are required (excluding competition law) for establishing a joint venture?

If a foreigner which has its registered seat outside the EEA intends to take up more than 50 per cent of shares in a company owning real estate, a permit from the Minister of Internal Affairs and Administration will be required. No other government or regulatory approvals are required for a joint venture to be set up with foreign participation.

Are there local anti-trust laws which might apply to the formation of the joint venture?

Under the Law on the Protection of Competition and Consumers, the President of the Office for Competition and Consumer Protection must be notified of any intention to carry out large transactions which may affect the standing and development of competitive businesses. This obligation should be met by a notification being filed within seven days of an agreement being executed or any other action by which a concentration is to be effected. The Law requires the following events to be reported to the President of the Office: (i) merger of two or more independent entrepreneurs; (ii) take-over in any manner of direct or indirect control over another entrepreneur; (iii) establishment of a common entrepreneur by several entrepreneurs; (iv) acquisition of part of a business, if the turnover of the acquired part of the business exceeded €10 million in either of the two years preceding the take-over. The Law provides for a number of exceptions to these requirements, the most important being that no filing is required if the annual turnover of the target did not exceed €10 million in either of the two years preceding the take-over. A brief summary of merger law is given below:

Filing requirement/ trigger	Timetable for clearance	Test for clearance	Mandatory/ voluntary Penalties
Applies to both co-operative and concentrative JVs. Combined worldwide turn-over exceeds €10m or combined turn-over in Poland exceeds €50m (there is a de minimis exception).	Two months from filing. A transaction cannot be completed until a clearance decision has been received or the waiting period has expired.	Whether the JV would significantly impede the effective competition in the market, in particular as a result of the creation or strengthening of a dominant market position. There is a presumption of dominance when the market share is greater than 40 per cent.	Filing is mandatory. Failure to fine/failure to suspend implementation: fines of up to 10 per cent of the turnover achieved by the undertakings in the last financial year. A separate fine may be imposed on a person acting on behalf of the undertaking of up to 50 times the average remuneration in Poland (approx. €35,000). Implementing of a prohibited transaction or not fulfilling commitments: daily penalty up to €10,000 and a revocation of the clearance in the case of commitments.

If the local party is a public company, when might the approval of its shareholders be required under stock exchange or similar rules?

Although there is no legal requirement for a local public company to obtain the approval of its shareholders' meeting to enter into a joint venture, there may be such an obligation under the company's statutes. A public company entering into a joint venture must notify the Securities and Exchange Commission.

3. Types of joint venture vehicle

What are the principal types of joint venture vehicle commonly used with foreign investors?

The most popular vehicles for equity joint ventures are a limited liability company (similar to the German GmbH) and a joint stock company (similar to the German *Aktiengesellschaft*). A limited liability company is more frequently used since there are fewer formal requirements for its management. Investors rarely decide to use partnerships.

The parties sometimes decide to conduct certain activities jointly without incorporating a separate entity. In such cases, the parties execute agreements which may differ significantly from each other in all aspects and are dependent on the wishes of the persons involved—called joint venture agreements (although this name has recently become less popular), co-operation agreements, consortium agreements, agreements on a common undertaking, etc.

If a partnership structure is chosen, does this lead to (a) joint and several liability to third parties and/or (b) duties of good faith as between partners?

If the investors decide to structure their joint venture in the form of a partnership, they will be jointly and severally liable to third parties (with certain exceptions).

The law provides that the partners in a partnership must co-operate to achieve a common goal.

4. Capital structure and funding

Is it common to have different "classes" of shares (e.g. A and B shares) to reflect different initial contributions or financial interests of the parties?

The articles of association or the statutes may grant preferences to certain shares. The most common type of share preference concerns the number of votes at the shareholders' meeting, dividends or post-liquidation assets. The Code of Commercial Companies provides that not more than three votes can be attached to a share in the case of a limited liability company and not more than two votes in the case of a joint-stock company. The Code also sets limits for preferential dividend rights in both types of company, e.g. the maximum preference cannot be more than 50 per cent of the dividend due to shareholders who do not hold preference shares. There are no limitations on preferences concerning post-liquidation assets.

Is it common to have "preference" shares which give a party a priority on payment of dividends or on a return of capital?

The provisions of the Code of Commercial Companies allow a shareholder to be given priority in respect of payment of dividends or a return of capital in both a limited liability company and a joint-stock company with one condition: this right must be set out in the company's articles of association or statute. Although there is such a possibility, investors rarely take advantage of it.

Are "redeemable" shares permitted (i.e. shares that can be repaid and cancelled)?

The shares in both a limited liability company and a joint-stock company may be redeemed if the articles of association or the statutes so provide. A share may be redeemed with or without the shareholder's consent. The conditions for redeeming shares and the procedure should be set out in the articles of association or the statutes.

Redeeming shares usually requires a shareholders' resolution. However, if an event provided for in the articles of association or the statutes takes place, the management board may be entitled to redeem the shares.

Are "non-voting" shares permitted?

Non-voting shares are only permitted in a joint-stock company. The Code of Commercial Companies provides that shares with dividend preferences may be deprived of voting rights (similar to German *Vorzugsaktien*). Holders of non-voting shares may be granted the following additional rights (which are not available to holders of other shares):

- priority of satisfaction over other shares;
- lack of limitation on maximum level of dividend preference;
- right to compensation paid out of profit in subsequent years if the holder does not receive the full dividend due to it in a given financial year.

Are there any "thin capitalisation" or similar rules which affect the choice of equity/debt ratio for the capital structure?

According to the current Polish rules, interest on loans granted to a company by:

- a shareholder holding at least 25 per cent of the company's shares is not tax deductible if the loan amount due to shareholders holding at least 25 per cent and to other entities holding at least 25 per cent of the shares in the share capital of such shareholder is more than three times the company's share capital;
- another company (if the same shareholder holds in both companies at least 25 per cent of the shares) is not tax deductible if the amount due from the company to shareholders holding at least 25 per cent and to other entities holding at least 25 per cent of the shares in the share capital of such shareholder and the company providing the loan is more than three times the company's share capital.

The interest on the part of the loan that exceeds the debt to equity ratio referred to above as at the interest payment date is not tax deductible.

Is there any capital or similar tax payable in respect of issued share capital?

Issued share capital is subject to 0.5 per cent civil transactions tax, which is payable within 14 days of the date on which the shareholders' meeting is held. However, if the minutes of the meeting are taken by a notary, the notary is obliged to collect the tax on the day the meeting is held.

Civil transactions tax (of 0.5 per cent) is also levied on additional payments and loans granted to a company by its shareholders.

Is a separate "contribution agreement" or other formal document (other than formal property transfer agreements) required or usual under the local law to document the contribution of assets to the joint venture?

The law does not require a separate contribution agreement to be executed between the company and the investor, although, if the assets are to be contributed at a later stage, then an agreement documenting the transfer would be needed.

Are there any local laws which require an independent valuation of any non-cash assets to be contributed to the joint venture?

The Code of Commercial Companies provides that, if the share capital of the joint-stock company is to be covered by in-kind contributions, the management board should draw up a report specifying in particular the nature of the in-kind contributions as well as the number and classes of shares allotted in exchange. The report must be audited by a certified auditor appointed by the company's local registry court.

The above requirement does not apply to limited liability companies and partnerships.

Are there exchange control regulations which materially affect the establishment of the joint venture or the subsequent repatriation of profits or dividends from the joint venture to a foreign party?

There are no such exchange control restrictions.

If a foreign party is to contribute technology to the joint venture, are there any special requirements for valuation of that technology?

Unless the technology is contributed to the share capital of a joint-stock company, there are no legal requirements for valuation (see section 5 above). However, investors often decide to have an independent valuation carried out in order to be able to present arguments if any doubts are raised in the future (particularly by the tax authorities).

5. Tax

Are there any particular tax laws or incentives which significantly affect the establishment of joint ventures in this jurisdiction by a foreign investor?

There are no tax laws which apply specifically to joint ventures, irrespective of whether they are "equity" or "non-equity".

Will withholding taxes apply to dividends paid by a joint venture company?

The payment of dividends and other revenues from sharing in profits is subject to 19 per cent tax withheld by the payer. The payee is not liable to any further taxes on the dividend received. Dividends paid abroad are also subject to 19 per cent withholding tax unless a relevant tax treaty provides otherwise. A reduced rate provided in a double tax treaty may be applied only if the recipient (foreign entity) supplies the required certificate issued by its domestic tax authority showing that it is tax resident or has its registered office abroad.

The EU Parent/Subsidiary Directive has been implemented into Polish tax law. From May 1, 2004 payments of dividends and other revenues from sharing in profits of Polish entities are exempt from taxation in Poland if the following conditions are jointly met:

- dividends are paid to a non-resident company;
- the beneficiary is subject to income tax on its worldwide income in an EU Member State;
- the beneficiary has directly held at least 25 per cent of the shares in the Polish company for an uninterrupted period of not less than two years.

The amount of tax withheld by the Polish dividend payer may be credited against the payee's tax liabilities (other than those resulting from sharing in corporate entities' profits) and carried forward without limitation.

6. Board and management

Are there local law rules which affect the board or management structure of the joint venture? May a two-tier board be required?

The same rules for management boards apply to joint ventures as to other limited liability or joint-stock companies. The management board may be composed of one or more members. In a limited liability company the members are appointed by the shareholders' meeting and in a joint-stock company by the supervisory board, unless the articles of association or the statutes provide otherwise.

Permanent supervision of the company's activities in all aspects of its business is exercised by the supervisory board with the reservation that the supervisory board is not allowed to issue binding instructions to the management board in respect of managing the company's affairs. The Code of Commercial Companies provides that a supervisory board must be appointed:

- in all joint-stock companies;
- in limited liability companies if (a) the share capital exceeds PLN 500,000 and there are more than 25 shareholders or (b) the articles of association so provide.

The supervisory board must comprise at least three persons. A supervisory board member may not be a member of the management board at the same time.

Companies whose shares are traded on the stock exchange may decide (at their sole discretion) to apply corporate governance rules which inter alia regulate the composition of the management board and their relations with the other authorities of the company.

It is also possible to incorporate a European Company in Poland (also for joint venture purposes) and to appoint a one-tier board.

Are there local law constraints on persons who can be directors or managers of the joint venture (e.g. only local residents or nationals)?

There are no requirements for Polish nationals to be directors or managers of joint ventures. Nationals of certain countries require a work permit if certain conditions are not met (this does not apply to most EU countries).

Does a shareholder in a joint venture company owe a duty of good faith (or similar duty) to other shareholders in the way it behaves in relation to the joint venture?

Unless required under a contract, shareholders do not owe a duty of good faith to each other. However, each shareholder has the right to appeal against a shareholders' resolution which is contrary to the articles of association or good practice and which at the same time is detrimental to the company's interests or aimed at harming a shareholder.

Can you modify the legal duties of directors so that they can expressly take into account the interests of their "appointer" when voting or acting as director, or must they always act objectively in the best interests of the company?

No binding instructions can be given to the management board nor can their duties be modified to take into account the interests of any entity other than the company.

7. Transfer of shares

In the case of a joint venture company, can a permanent restriction on transfer of shares be imposed under the local law (e.g. no transfer without the consent of the other shareholder)?

The articles of association or the statutes may make the disposal or pledge of a share contingent upon the consent of the management board, the shareholders' meeting, the supervisory board or the other shareholders. The law does not contain any time limitations on this restriction.

Shareholders may also execute agreements under which they restrict the transferability of shares. In the case of a joint-stock company the restriction cannot apply for more than five years. Law provisions do not contain any time limit for the validity of such restrictions in limited liability companies, but the general civil law rule will apply under which the transferability of a right cannot be excluded for an indefinite period.

8. Protection for minority shareholders

Are there any statutory rules or remedies which help significantly to protect a minority shareholder in a joint venture company?

The general rule in the Code of Commercial Companies is that a company's shareholders must be treated equally in the same circumstances.

Irrespective of this general rule, minority shareholders holding at least 10 per cent of the shares have certain rights, such as (i) the right to request that a shareholders' meeting be convened or that certain matters be put on the agenda, and (ii) the right to request that the registry court appoint an auditor to audit the company's accounts. Furthermore, each shareholder may appeal against a shareholders' resolution which he feels is contrary to the articles of association or good practice and is detrimental to the company's interests or aimed at harming a shareholder.

Does the law require any major business decisions to be approved by a special resolution or super-majority (whether at board or shareholder level), or must a minority party protect itself by contract?

The Code of Commercial Companies requires that the consent of the shareholders' meeting is necessary for (i) any disposal of the lease of the enterprise or an organised part thereof, or establishment of a property right thereon, (ii) any acquisition and disposal of real property or interest therein, unless the articles of association or the statutes provide otherwise, (iii) any contract under which the company acquires real property or fixed assets at a price exceeding a quarter of the company's share capital, executed within two years of the company being registered and (iv) any issue of convertible bonds or bonds with priority of conversion into share capital (only in a joint-stock company). If any of the above actions are taken by the company without consent being given by way of a shareholders' resolution, these actions will be invalid.

Unless the articles of association or the statutes provide otherwise, resolutions are adopted by the shareholders' meeting by an absolute majority of votes. Exceptions apply to e.g. resolutions amending the articles of association or the statutes, disposing of the enterprise, winding up or redeeming share capital, which require a majority of two-thirds in a limited liability company and three-quarters in a joint-stock company.

A resolution amending the articles of association or the statutes by imposing a broader scope of shareholder duties or restricting the personal rights conferred upon individual shareholders requires the consent of all the shareholders affected.

9. Employment laws

Are there local law obligations requiring a "local" party to consult with, or obtain the approval of, employees or employee representatives on a contribution of its business to the joint venture?

There is no obligation to obtain the approval of any employee representatives when contributing a business to a joint venture with one exception: the director of a state-owned enterprise must obtain the approval of the board of employees before making the contribution. In view of the fact that there are few state-owned enterprises left (most have been transformed into limited liability or joint-stock companies, with the state being the sole or majority shareholder), the effect of this restriction has decreased significantly.

Are there any material employment laws (compared with the UK) which are likely to affect the ongoing operations of the joint venture?

Polish labour laws are rather complex, as are those of most other European countries.

This means that, on the one hand, most labour law directives have already been implemented or will be implemented in the near future and, on the other, the rights of employees and trade unions are similar to those guaranteed in other European countries.

10. Accounts

Is there a requirement on the joint venture company to file accounts with any authority where they are publicly available?

Financial statements must be filed with the company's local registry court and tax office.

All entities which by law have to be audited must also publish elements of their financial statement in a special economic bulletin. Listed companies are obliged to file their financial statements with the Securities and Exchange Commission.

11. Dispute resolution

Is there any standard local practice as to form of dispute resolution in relation to joint ventures with foreign investors? Is arbitration in a venue outside that jurisdiction acceptable?

There are no particular rules on dispute resolution in relation to joint ventures with foreign investors. Arbitration is very often an alternative. The parties may choose between a permanent arbitration court or arbitration ad hoc, either in Poland or abroad.

Is the local jurisdiction a signatory to the 1958 New York Convention on the Recognition and Enforcement of Foreign Arbitral Awards?

Yes. Poland has been a signatory to this Convention from the very beginning.

12. Legal documents and formalities

Is there any special form of legal documentation required under local law for establishment of a joint venture company? What are the usual principal documents?

To establish a limited liability company the shareholders must: (i) draw up articles of association and execute them before a notary, (ii) appoint members of the company's authorities and (iii) pay up the entire amount of share capital. Appointments can be made in the articles of association or by way of a shareholders' resolution or in any other way stipulated in the articles of association (e.g. nomination by a certain shareholder).

Together with the application (in the form set by the law) to the registry court, management board members have to file a set of documents which must be signed by them—in particular, specimen signatures made before a notary, a statement that contributions to share capital have been paid up, list of shareholders, etc.

The same procedure generally applies to the incorporation of a joint-stock company.

However, if any in-kind contributions are made, the management board must in addition apply to the registry court with a request to appoint an independent auditor to confirm that the in-kind contribution was valued properly.

Does the joint venture documentation need to be in the local language and/or governed by the local law?

Formal corporate joint venture documentation must be drawn up in Polish. However, this does not apply to agreements such as shareholders' agreements, joint venture agreements, or commercial agreements.

Are there any commonly-accepted "standard forms" for joint ventures with foreign investors in your jurisdiction?

There are no standard forms for joint venture agreements, though shareholders' agreements are sometimes similar.

Are agreements between shareholders (e.g. as to appointment of directors, conduct of the business of the company or voting majorities required for certain decisions etc.) enforceable under local law? In the event of breach, is specific performance or a similar remedy available, or only damages?

The enforceability of shareholders' agreements depends on the nature of the obligations provided therein. As there are no specific legal provisions which regulate these matters, there is a great deal of controversy about this issue in legal literature. However, in enforcing obligations relating to e.g. appointing directors, running the company's business or voting majorities required for certain decisions, specific performance is not available and the investor may only seek damages. Of course, other contract instruments may be used to secure and enforce these obligations (e.g. powers of attorney to vote which can only be used in certain circumstances, etc.).

Are restrictions relating to (a) transfers of shares and/or (b) minority "veto rights" commonly included in the articles of association or by-laws of the company, or included in a separate shareholders' agreement?

Restrictions on transferring shares are usually set out in the articles of association and the statutes. This is due to the fact that transferring shares without the consent required under the articles of association or the statutes is ineffective with respect to the company. On the other hand, if the transfer is performed in breach of the shareholders' agreement, the investor may only claim damages from the party in breach for liquidated damages, if such damages were stipulated in the agreement.

Issues concerning minority "veto rights" have recently been widely discussed in Polish legal literature and there are different opinions in this respect. It can generally be stated that it would be against the rule for shareholders to be treated equally in similar circumstances for one shareholder to be given the right to veto shareholders' resolutions. On the other hand, the interests of a minority shareholder may be secured in the articles of association or the statutes by requiring a higher majority for the adoption of resolutions.

Are there any formalities (e.g. notarisation or registration) which are material and which may affect the timing involved in forming the joint venture?

The articles of association (and the statutes), all resolutions passed by the shareholders' meeting of joint-stock companies and limited liability companies amending the articles of association must be executed in the form of a notarial deed. This requirement is not time consuming but it does involve additional costs.

Furthermore, amendments to the articles of association (statutes) and changes in the company's authorities and other changes must be registered with the registry court. Although the procedure is usually quick, it can sometimes take several weeks.

(11) Russia

Authors: Michael Schwartz, Maxim Pogrebnoy and Alexander Viktorov
Freshfields Bruckhaus Deringer LLP, Moscow

1. General background

Are joint ventures popular as a form of foreign investment into your jurisdiction?

Joint ventures are popular. Increasingly, however, more foreign investors prefer to establish wholly-owned subsidiaries in Russia. Joint venture structures and practices in Russia are still relatively new and, as result, there continues a degree of legal and judicial uncertainty for any foreign investor. Many practical difficulties are experienced.

Are there restrictions on foreign participation?

Effective in May 2008, a significant Federal Law (No. 57–FZ) has been adopted: "The Procedure for Making Foreign Investments in Business Entities Having Strategic Value for the Defence of the Country and Security of the State". Under this Law, the Russian Federation has rights to approve or control transactions whereby foreign investors acquire interests in Russian companies engaged in a wide variety of important business activities including (subject to detail): military equipment; cryptographic and communication facilities; aviation and space exploration; TV and radio broadcasting; nuclear; certain communication and telephony services; mineral exploration or extraction; and printing. A foreign investor must provide the state authority with information. Breach of the approval procedures can mean the transaction being declared invalid and/or the foreign investor being deprived of voting powers.

Moreover, there are certain restrictions that affect joint ventures operating in the banking and insurance fields. Restrictions relating to the percentage of foreign participation may also result from the conditions imposed in licences necessary for the activity in question (e.g. in the area of oil and gas). For certain Russian companies, further restrictions on foreign participation are established by law (e.g. for certain companies in the oil and gas or defence sectors).

What (if any) are the major legal problems which a foreign investor in a joint venture faces in your jurisdiction?

Following the liberalisation of the process of state registration of joint ventures and foreign currency legislation, the establishment and operation of joint ventures are easier for foreign investors. However, the following problems should be noted:

- option rights (put and call options) and voting agreements between shareholders are, in most cases, unenforceable in Russia against a Russian shareholder even if they are governed by foreign law; this makes it difficult to establish a reasonable mechanism for the resolution of deadlock-situations in joint ventures as well as extended minority protection rights for a specific shareholder;
- frequent change of legislation;

- failure by the state authorities (especially the Anti-Monopoly Service) to comply with established terms and procedures for provision of consents, approvals, registration, issuance of licences etc.

It is not uncommon for investment in a Russian company to be made through a jointly-owned foreign holding company with shareholder/joint venture issues being dealt with at that level (see section 12 below).

2. Governmental/regulatory approvals

What principal governmental or regulatory approvals are required (excluding competition law) for establishing a joint venture?
There are a significant number of registrations and approval requirements:

(a) State registration as a legal entity with the RF Ministry of Tax and Duties;

(b) registration with the State Statistics Committee, tax authorities (as a taxpayer), the State Pension Fund, the Employment Fund, the Medical Insurance Fund and the Social Insurance Fund;

(c) obtaining work permits from the Immigration Service for foreign employees and obtaining licences, if required, for specific types of activities (e.g. banking, dealing in securities, insurance, transportation, production of natural resources, the trading of certain goods, the provision of audit, etc.);

(d) in certain cases where there are restrictions on the participation of foreign investors in the capital of Russian companies, the Federal Finance Markets Service must be notified of acquisitions by foreign investors of shares in Russian joint stock companies.

Are there local anti-trust laws which might apply to the foundation of the joint venture?
Yes. The general merger control rules apply to joint ventures.

> The most important events **triggering merger control** are inter alia:
>
> - the acquisition of (direct or indirect) rights to determine the business activities of another company by one or several enterprises (through shareholdings, agreements, voting arrangements, rights etc);
>
> - the acquisition of certain packages of shares in another company, resulting in the acquirer and its group holding in total over 25 per cent, over 50 per cent or over 75 per cent of voting shares in a joint-stock company or over 33.3 per cent, over 50 per cent or over 66.6 per cent of the shares in a limited liability company;
>
> - the incorporation of a company by contribution of assets or shares, or rights in another company.
>
> Mergers and takeovers may be subject to either a pre-acquisition filing or a post-completion notification if the relevant thresholds are met.
>
> A **pre-acquisition filing** is required if: (i) the aggregate book value on a worldwide basis of all companies within the acquirer's group and the target's group exceeds 3 billion roubles (approximately €88 million) and the aggregate book value on a worldwide basis of all companies within the target's group

> exceeds 150 million roubles (approximately €4.4 million); (ii) the aggregate turnover on a worldwide basis of all companies within the acquirer's group and the target's group exceeds 6 billion roubles (approximately €176 million) and the aggregate book value on a worldwide basis of all companies within the target's group exceeds 150 million roubles (approximately €4.4 million); or (iii) any company within the acquirer's or the target's group is recorded in the Russian register of dominant businesses and businesses with a market share exceeding 35 per cent.
>
> A **post-completion notification** may be required if the thresholds for a pre-acquisition filing are not met. The threshold for a post-completion notification is 200 million roubles (approximately €6 million) both for the aggregate assets and the aggregate revenue tests mentioned above if, in addition, the aggregate value of assets of the Russian target and the companies of its group exceeds 30 million roubles (approximately €880,000).

Foreign mergers are subject to Russian merger control if they have or may have an impact on competition in the Russian Federation. However the FAS position is that only the antimonopoly authorities are entitled to determine whether the transaction has or may have an impact on competition in the Russian market. While direct or indirect control over a Russian company, as well as the direct acquisition of shares in a Russian company, has always been caught by Russian merger control rules irrespective of where the transaction takes place, the FAS now applies a broader concept of effect on the Russian market which includes consideration of market shares and actual market presence. As a result, more foreign-to-foreign mergers are subject to clearance by the FAS.

Completion of transactions before clearance may result in fines and invalidation of the transaction. Failure to submit a filing can be penalised by fines on legal entities and individuals. In addition, the FAS may apply to a court to invalidate, in full or in part, agreements and other transactions for which its prior authorisation or subsequent notice was required but has not been obtained or given.

If the local party is a public company, when might the approval of its shareholders be required under stock exchange or similar rules?

The approval of the shareholders will be required if the company proposes to contribute to the joint venture more than 50 per cent of its assets. In other cases, the decision to participate in the joint venture must be taken by the board of directors.

3. Types of joint venture vehicle

What are the principal types of joint venture vehicle commonly used with foreign investors?

The principal types of joint venture vehicle are (i) limited liability companies (LLC) where participation is based on participation interests (*doli*), and (ii) joint stock companies (JSC) where participation is based on shares (*aktsii*).

Each type has its advantages and disadvantages, and which type would be preferable for a foreign investor should be determined on a case-by-case basis. The protections for shareholders, particularly minority shareholders, are greater in the case of a joint stock company than for participants in a limited liability company; in certain circumstances, for example, the shareholders would have the right to require the company to purchase their shares at market value (see also section 8 below). However, joint stock companies must register the shares with the Federal Finance Markets Service and comply with other statutory requirements which do not apply to limited liability companies.

Other specific features of a limited liability company include a participant's right to withdraw from the company at any time irrespective of other participants' consent (and to receive after such withdrawal the book value of its share) and a greater degree of flexibility in foundation documents. The charter of a limited liability company may provide for prohibition on the transfer of participation interests to third parties; in other cases the participants have a pre-emptive right to acquire participation interests disposed of by another participant.

There are closed joint stock companies and open joint stock companies. The main differences are that shareholders of a closed joint stock company have pre-emptive rights in respect of proposed transfers of shares; the company may not have more than 50 shareholders and may not issue shares to the public; also, there are fewer public reporting requirements imposed upon a closed joint stock company. Generally, closed joint stock companies are preferred over open joint stock companies for joint ventures.

A party to the joint venture may be held vicariously liable for the obligations of a bankrupt joint venture if (i) the bankruptcy was due to the faulty actions or inaction of that party and (ii) the assets of the joint venture are not sufficient to satisfy its debts.

Partnership structures are not popular in Russia and are almost never used.

4. Capital structure and funding

What principal local law issues affect the capital structure and funding of the joint venture?

The following requirements may be relevant:

- A joint stock company may have both issued and authorised (but unissued) shares.

- 50 per cent of a joint stock company's charter capital must be paid up within three months after its registration, and the remainder within one year after the registration. 50 per cent of a limited liability company's charter capital must be paid before its state registration, and the remainder within one year after the registration.

- A stock company must establish a reserve fund equal in value to not less than five per cent of its charter capital, to be used for payment of losses, redemption of bonds and purchases of its own shares.

- If at the end of the second and each subsequent fiscal year the value of the net assets of a joint venture is less than (a) the amount of its charter capital, the joint venture must decrease its capital by the amount of the deficit; and if less than (b) the statutory level (see "thin capitalisation" below), the joint venture must be liquidated.

- Additional issues of shares by a stock company (other than the primary issue made when the company is being established) must be made at market value as determined by the board of directors.

- The charter capital of a joint venture company may not be less than the amount established by law: 1000 times the minimum monthly wage for open stock companies (currently, about $4,200) and 100 times the minimum monthly wage for closed stock companies and limited liability companies (currently, about $420). The charter capital of a joint venture company must be stated in Russian roubles.

Is it common to have different "classes" of shares (e.g. A and B shares) to reflect different initial contributions or financial interests of the parties?

No. Sometimes, however, in order to attract funding without giving an investor voting rights, joint stock companies issue preference shares (which may have different classes) in addition to ordinary shares. As for limited liability companies, the participants may establish in the charter that the number of votes to which a participant is entitled may be other than pro rata to its participation share.

Is it common to have "preference" shares which give a party a priority on payment of dividends or on a return of capital?

There can be preference shares of different types. In the case of preferred shares, the company's charter must provide for (i) the amount of dividends payable on a preference share and/or (ii) the amount payable on a preference share upon liquidation of the company or the procedure for determining such amounts. The amount of dividends and liquidation amount can be defined as a percentage of the nominal value of a share or as a lump sum. In practice, however, preference shares are not widely used in Russia.

As a general rule, holders of preference shares cannot vote, except for on certain matters such as the liquidation or reorganisation of the company and in certain other cases e.g. if dividends on a preference share have not been paid.

If provided for by the charter, preference shares may be converted into preference shares of another type or ordinary shares.

Are "redeemable" shares permitted (i.e. shares that can be repaid and cancelled)?

"Redeemable" shares are not permitted. However, if provided for by its charter, a joint stock company can have the right itself to buy the issued shares upon the decision of the shareholders to reduce the company's charter capital. If provided by its charter, a company may also buy back a maximum of 10 per cent of its issued shares (calculated on the basis of their nominal value) in order to on-sell those shares within one year after their acquisition. In such a case, shareholders will have the right to sell their shares (or part thereof) to the company in proportion to their shareholdings, but are not obliged to do so.

The company must acquire the shares of any holder of voting shares in certain circumstances (e.g. upon the latter's request, in the event of reorganisation of the company, entry by the company into a "major transaction", amending the charter etc.), if that shareholder voted against the particular decision or did not participate in the particular vote. The shares in this case must be redeemed at the price established by the board of directors; the price must not be less than the market value of such shares. The company is only obliged to repurchase the shares up to a total purchase price of 10 per cent of the balance sheet value of its assets.

However, there are certain restrictions in respect of acquisitions of shares by the company itself (e.g. if the charter capital is not paid in full, the shares cannot be redeemed).

There are no comparable regulations for an LLC. In an LLC, the participants have a right of withdrawal at any time without having to obtain the consent of the other participants or the company, and can also demand upon exit that the company pays them the book value of their stake.

Are "non-voting" shares permitted?

There are no "non-voting" shares apart from "preference" shares. However, holders of "preference" shares may vote on the liquidation and reorganisation of a company. In certain circumstances, holders of "cumulative preference" shares are entitled to vote on all matters at the general shareholders meeting. Holders of "preference" shares of any type are entitled to vote on amendments to the charter where such amendments restrict the rights of holders of that type of "preference" shares.

Are there any "thin capitalisation" or similar rules which affect the choice of equity / debt ratio for the capital structure?
Yes. The practical effect could be that a certain part of interest paid by the joint venture for loans granted by its foreign shareholder is not tax-deductible.

Is there any capital or similar tax payable in respect of issued share capital?
No tax is payable on issues of shares. However, state duties will be paid on each action connected with an issue of shares (e.g. registering the prospectus, registering the report on the results of the securities issue etc.). Such state duties vary from 1000 roubles to 10,000 roubles (approximately $40-$4,200).

Is a separate "contribution agreement" or other formal document (other than formal property transfer agreements) required or usual under the local law to document the contribution of assets to the joint venture?
Usually, no separate agreement is required except the formal corporate and other related documents (decision of shareholders meeting etc.). The fact of contribution must be confirmed by a bank confirmation for cash contributions or a delivery and acceptance certificate (signed by the contributing shareholder/participant and the joint venture company) for in-kind contributions. In practice, a joint venture agreement is often entered into by the parties to the joint venture, which can also cover the contribution issues. The transfer of real estate must be registered by the federal registration services.

Are there any local laws which require an independent valuation of any non-cash assets to be contributed to the joint venture?
Yes. In-kind contributions to the charter capital of a joint venture must be valued by an independent evaluator licensed to do so. There are no specific timing or other requirements for such valuation and in practice it does not present a problem for the joint venture partners. If the actual value of the contribution is less than the value established by the evaluator, all shareholders/participants (and not only the contributing one) may be held liable for the shortfall.

Are there exchange control regulations which materially affect the establishment of the joint venture--or the subsequent repatriation of profits or dividends from the joint venture to a foreign party?
Russian legislation in this area changes frequently. Currently, foreign currency may be contributed to the charter capital of a Russian joint venture company without the necessity to obtain a licence from the Central Bank of Russia.

If a foreign party is to contribute technology to the joint venture, are there any special requirements for valuation of that technology?
No, except for independent valuation (see above). A contribution of technology must, nevertheless, comply with Russian law requirements.

5. Tax

Are there any particular tax laws or incentives which significantly affect the establishment of joint ventures in this jurisdiction by a foreign investor?

The taxation system in Russia is complex and comprises a broad range of taxes at federal, regional and local levels. Foreign investors should anticipate the need to spend what they might consider as being considerably more time and effort than normal in structuring their joint ventures so as to maximise tax efficiency in Russia. Relief from withholding tax (imposed on dividends paid to a foreign investor or on the sale of shares in the joint venture by the foreign investor to a Russian resident) may be available for the foreign investor pursuant to an applicable double taxation treaty. To benefit from such a treaty, the foreign investor will need to register with the Russian tax authorities. Generally, in-kind contributions to the charter capital of a joint venture company are exempt from customs duties and import VAT subject to approval(s) to be granted by the Russian customs authorities.

Will withholding taxes apply to dividends paid by a joint venture company?

In general, dividends paid to the foreign party to the joint venture will be subject to Russian withholding tax, which will be withheld at source by the joint venture (subject to any applicable double taxation treaty).

6. Board and management

Are there local law rules which affect the board or management structure of the joint venture? May a two-tier board be required?

A board of directors is obligatory for stock companies having 50 or more shareholders (evidently, this is not relevant for joint ventures). For other stock companies and for limited liability companies a board of directors is optional. The board has areas of exclusive authority which cannot be delegated. If there is no board, decisions within its exclusive authority must be referred to shareholders. A board is elected for a definite time period and may be re-elected an unlimited number of times. All members of the board may be removed by shareholders. The chairman of the board is elected by the members of the board. The chairman of the board has no casting vote (unless otherwise specified in the company's charter). A director cannot be represented at a board meeting by another director. The general director may not be chairman of the board.

There are no requirements for a two-tier board (and there is no concept of a two-tier board as such), although a company may have a management committee—a collective executive body supervised by the board and led by the General Director as its chairman. Members of the management committee may not comprise more than one fourth of the members of the board of directors.

Typically, the General Director is entitled to represent the joint venture company alone. However, accounting and payment documents as well as credit and finance obligations are not valid without the signature of the Chief Accountant of the company, who is usually appointed by the General Director. Any relevant restrictions on the power of the General Director to represent the company alone contained in the charter are only valid in relation to third parties if such third parties knew or should have known about them.

Are there local law constraints on persons who can be directors or managers of the joint venture (e.g. only local residents or nationals)?

Generally, no. However, there are such requirements for businesses operating in certain sectors, e.g. the General Directors and Chief Accountants of insurance companies must be Russian citizens.

There might also be restrictions of other kinds—e.g. certain officers (the General Director, Chief Accountant, etc.) of a credit organisation must have a higher legal or economics education and experience of working in a credit organisation. Officers of insurance companies must have a higher economics or finance education and also work experience in insurance of not less than two years. No one with a criminal record is allowed to hold a managerial position in a credit or insurance organisation.

In any case, a working permit is required for a (resident) foreign General Director and the foreign members of a management committee of a Russian company.

Does a shareholder in a joint venture company owe a duty of good faith (or similar duty) to other shareholders in the way it behaves in relation to the joint venture?

No. However, members of a company owe a duty of good faith to the company itself. If the bankruptcy of a company is caused by the actions (omissions) of its founders (members), they may be held secondarily liable for the obligations of the company if its assets are not sufficient to meet the claims of the creditors.

Can you modify the legal duties of directors so that they can expressly take into account the interests of their "appointer" when voting or acting as director—or must they always act objectively in the best interests of the company?

Directors must always act in the best interest of the company and, while enjoying their rights and performing obligations, directors must act reasonably and in good faith. Directors are liable to the company for losses of the company caused by their wilful actions (omissions). Moreover, a contractual obligation on directors to act pursuant to directions given by a shareholder could, under certain circumstances, lead to a liability of that shareholder for obligations of the joint venture.

7. Transfer of shares

In the case of a joint venture company, can a permanent restriction on transfer of shares be imposed under the local law (e.g. no transfer without the consent of the other shareholder)?

Transfer restrictions cannot be imposed on the shareholders of an open joint stock company. In closed joint stock companies and limited liability companies the shareholders/participants have a pre-emptive right to purchase shares being sold by other shareholders/participants. The charters of closed joint stock/limited liability companies may provide that if the shareholders/participants have not exercised their pre-emptive right to purchase the shares/participation interest, the respective company will exercise its pre-emptive right.

Charters of limited liability companies may provide for the prior consent of participants when one participant wishes to sell or otherwise dispose of its participation interest to another participant of the company as well as prohibit participation interests being disposed of to third parties.

8. Protection for minority shareholders

Are there any statutory rules or remedies which help significantly to protect a minority shareholder in a joint venture company?

The following rules may provide some element of protection in particular circumstances:

(1) Transactions involving a value ranging from 25 per cent to 50 per cent of the balance sheet asset value of the company require the board's prior approval; transactions involving a value over 50 per cent (or in certain cases lower than 50 per cent) require the prior approval of the general meeting of shareholders.

(2) Members of the board of directors of a JSC are elected by cumulative voting.

(3) 25 per cent, plus one share, in a JSC (or one-third of the voting rights in a LLC) gives a shareholder a blocking minority to prevent certain formal changes, e.g. changes to the company's charter, the company's voluntary liquidation or reorganisation.

(4) Certain transactions of a company may be "interested party transactions" and require approval by uninterested directors or, if it has a value exceeding two per cent of the company's assets, uninterested minority shareholders.

(5) A shareholder may challenge the lawfulness of a decision of the general shareholders meeting if such shareholder did not participate in the relevant meeting or voted against such decision.

(6) One per cent of the shares in a JSC gives a shareholder the right to file a claim with the court against a member of the board of directors or the general director, accusing them of causing damages to the company through their actions.

(7) A shareholder of a JSC holding not less than two per cent of the shares may propose matters to be included in the agenda of a meeting and also propose candidates for the management bodies of the company.

(8) 10 per cent of the shares in a JSC gives a shareholder the right to call a general shareholders' meeting and demand an audit of the company by the internal audit commission.

(9) If a shareholder voted against a substantial transaction or reorganisation of the joint venture or did not participate in voting, but the decision to enter into such transaction or to reorganise was nevertheless taken, the shareholder will have the right to demand that the joint venture company purchases such shareholder's shares at their market value (subject to a maximum purchase price equal to 10 per cent of the balance sheet value of the company's assets).

(10) There are a number of special rules about so-called "squeeze out" relating to an open JSC according to which a majority shareholder has the right, as well as an obligation, to redeem the shares held by the other shareholders.

As for limited liability companies, the principal protection for a minority participant is the right to withdraw at any time from the limited liability company. Then, the withdrawing participant's participating share would pass to the company, and the company would pay the participant the actual value of its participation share, being a proportion of the value of the company's net assets pro rata to the participation share of the participant concerned. The right to withdraw from the company cannot be excluded by agreement. Further minority protection rights can be provided for in the charter of an LLC. In particular, the required majority for shareholders resolutions may be increased.

Does the law require any major business decisions to be approved by a special resolution or super-majority (whether at board or shareholder level)—or must a minority party protect itself by contract?

Russian law defines "major" transactions as transactions which have a value equal to or exceeding 25 per cent of the balance sheet value of the company's assets determined on the basis of its latest balance sheet.

As a general rule, transactions which have a value equal to or exceeding 25 per cent of the balance sheet value of the company's assets but less than 50 per cent must be approved by the board of directors unanimously. Transactions with a value over 50 per cent must be approved by a three-quarters' majority of shareholders participating in the meeting.

Limited liability companies are more flexible in respect of the approval of major transactions: (i) the threshold may be increased by the charter, (ii) the quorum for approval is established in the charter, and (iii) the charter may provide that no prior approval of major transactions by the board of directors or shareholders is required.

9. Employment laws

Are there local law obligations requiring a "local" party to consult with, or obtain the approval of, employees or employee representatives on a contribution of its business to the joint venture?

No, there are no such law obligations, but they may be contained in the local collective bargaining agreement.

If, however, such a contribution results in a change of organisational or technological terms of labour at the joint venture, the employer may unilaterally change the employment terms and conditions with two months' notice to each affected employee.

Are there any material employment laws (compared with the UK) which are likely to affect the ongoing operations of the joint venture?

The foreign JV partner should bear in mind that all foreign employees transferred to the joint venture must have Russian law employment contracts, be on local payroll and have work permits. The concept of employee secondment is not recognized in Russia and therefore is difficult in implementation.

Dismissal of employees is also heavily regulated and as a rule employees may be dismissed by the employer only for cause (CEOs are an exception) and in accordance with prescribed statutory procedures.

10. Accounts

Is there a requirement on the joint venture company to file accounts with any authority where they are publicly available?

There is such a requirement for joint stock companies. Any open stock company which registered a prospectus must file accounts with the Federal Finance Markets Service on a quarterly basis. Moreover, the open joint stock companies must file lists of their affiliated persons on a quarterly basis.

The annual accounts of joint ventures must be published in the newspapers and magazines available to users of the accounts or must be distributed to such users in the form of brochures and booklets.

11. Dispute resolution

Is there any standard local practice as to form of dispute resolution in relation to joint ventures with foreign investors? Is arbitration in a venue outside that jurisdiction acceptable?

Disputes between the parties to the joint venture are resolved by a state commercial court (*arbitrazhnyi sud*) or arbitral tribunal, depending on the dispute resolution clause of the foundation agreement, if any. If the agreement has no arbitration clause, the disputes are resolved by the state commercial court. Disputes between the joint venture and its parties) are also resolved by the state commercial court, unless it is agreed to refer such disputes to an arbitral tribunal. An arbitration venue outside

Russia is acceptable. The enforcement of a foreign arbitral award in Russia requires a decision of a Russian court.

Is the local jurisdiction a signatory to the 1958 New York Convention on the Recognition and Enforcement of Foreign Arbitral Awards?
Yes.

12. Legal documents and formalities

Is there any special form of legal documentation required under local law for establishment of a joint venture company? What are the usual principal documents?

There are no specific forms for the foundation and other documents of the joint venture, but there is a mandatory list of issues required by law which must be included in such documents.

For the joint venture itself, the following documents are required for state registration: application to register the joint venture in a mandatory form to be signed by a founder's CEO and notarised; minutes of the founders' meeting; foundation documents; evidence of payment of the state duty for registering the joint venture; and an extract from the trade register in respect of any foreign legal entity which is a founder of the joint venture.

Does the joint venture documentation need to be in the local language and/or governed by the local law?

The joint venture documentation required by law must be in Russian and must be governed by Russian law. The (optional) joint venture agreement may be governed by a foreign law and may be executed in a foreign language. There are no commonly-accepted standard forms.

Are agreements between shareholders (e.g. as to appointment of directors, conduct of the business of the company or voting majorities required for certain decisions etc.) enforceable under local law? In the event of breach, is specific performance or a similar remedy available—or only damages?

No. Such shareholders' agreements if governed by Russian law are not enforceable in the Russian Federation and, if governed by foreign law, specific performance in Russia is not possible either. (Therefore, it is quite common not to have a Russian joint venture company as such—but to establish a foreign holding company holding 100 per cent of the shares in the Russian company and to deal with the usual shareholder issues in the foreign law-governed shareholders' agreement at the level of the foreign holding company.)

According to Russian law, the foundation agreements of a joint stock company and a LLC are (i) the foundation agreement (agreement among the shareholders determining the size of the company's charter capital, the number, categories and classes of shares subject to distribution among the founders or, respectively, the nominal value of the participation share, the amount of and the procedure for payment for such shares, and the founders' rights and obligations regarding the establishment of the company) and (ii) the charter of the company. These foundation documents have to be governed by Russian law.

In practice, there may be an additional shareholders' agreement (joint venture agreement) usually governed by foreign law and providing for additional rules and regulations of the relationship between the shareholders.

Are restrictions relating to (a) transfers of shares and/or (b) minority "veto rights" commonly included in the articles of association or by-laws of the company, or included in a separate shareholders' agreement?

Restrictions relating to the transfer of shares are included in the charter of the company as this is the most important company document. Provisions of the charter will prevail over other internal documents of the company (provided they do not contradict the provisions of legislation).

Are there any formalities (e.g. notarization or registration) which are material and which may affect the timing involved in forming the joint venture?

Yes. All foundation and other documents submitted for the registration of the joint venture must be originals or notarised copies. All foreign documents must be notarised by a foreign notary public, apostilled (or legalised by a Russian consulate) and accompanied by a notarised Russian translation. There are other issues which may affect the timing (e.g. opening the bank accounts of the joint venture, making contributions to its charter capital, ordering its seal, etc.). A name search as to the uniqueness of the joint venture's name must be carried out prior to the registration of the joint venture.

(12) South Africa

Author: Charles Douglas
Bowman Gilfillan, Johannesburg

1. General background

Are joint ventures popular as a form of foreign investment into your jurisdiction?

Joint ventures, which are not currently regulated by specific statute, are regularly used as a form of foreign investment into South Africa. Many recent large scale foreign investments have, however, generally been through direct investment in the share capital of the South African entity, rather than by way of joint venture.

Are there restrictions on foreign participation?

There are various relevant regulations which affect potential foreign participation:

(i) *Exchange control*. The Exchange Control Department of the South African Reserve Bank ("the SARB") imposes exchange controls on South African residents and currency cannot be transferred by a South African resident into or out of South Africa except in accordance with the Exchange Control Regulations made in terms of the Currency and Exchanges Act No.9 of 1933 ("Currency and Exchanges Act"). Further detail regarding exchange control regulation is set out in section 6 below.

(ii) *Foreign directorships*. Currently there is no requirement that either shareholders or directors be South African citizens or residents. However, this is likely to change when the proposed draft Companies Bill 2007 comes into force (which is currently estimated to occur by 2010) ("Companies Bill"). The Bill is intended to replace the existing Companies Act No.61 of 1973 ("Companies Act"), in order to align South African corporate statutes with international jurisdictions. The current draft of the Companies Bill disqualifies a person acting as a director if that person does not reside in South Africa, unless the company has more than one director and at least one of the other directors resides in South Africa.

(iii) *Black economic empowerment* ("BEE"). BEE is an important component of the South Africa's transformation strategy. The main elements of BEE are direct empowerment through equity ownership, employment equity and indirect empowerment through preferential procurement. The central legislation relating to BEE is the Broad-Based Black Economic Empowerment Act No.53 of 2003, and certain codes of good practice made in terms of that Act.

Several industries (e.g. ICT sector, mining sector, legal sector) have, in addition to the measures set out above, set up industry specific BEE targets which have been incorporated into transformation charters. The transformation charters each contain a scorecard against which industry members will be measured. The scores achieved are important in tendering for government and private sector business, each of which will set certain BEE targets for the company concerned in order to be considered for the tender. There are certain BEE targets in the scorecards from which foreign-owned companies will be excluded (e.g. financial services sector), and the codes of good practice also make provision for 'equity equivalence' programs, which are specifically aimed at foreign companies that are not able to implement local BEE equity transactions (although such programs have not been regularly implemented and require regulatory approval).

What (if any) are the major legal problems which a foreign investor in a joint venture faces in your jurisdiction?
Other than the exchange control restrictions referred to in the previous question, there are no major legal problems facing investors.

2. Governmental/regulatory approvals

What principal governmental or regulatory approvals are required (excluding competition law) for establishing a joint venture?
No general governmental or regulatory approvals are required. An acquisition of banks, pharmaceutical companies, insurers and aircraft transport companies, among certain others, has special requirements and conditions.

Are there local anti trust laws which might apply to the formation of the joint venture?
The test for determining if a transaction is a notifiable merger has two main components. Firstly, it is necessary to determine whether the transaction constitutes a merger, as defined in the Competition Act No.89 of 1998 ("Competition Act"). Section 12 of the Competition Act defines a merger broadly and states that a merger occurs when "one or more firms directly or indirectly acquire or establish direct or indirect control over the whole or part of the business of another firm", which could include the formation of a joint venture. Secondly, it must be established whether the parties to the transaction meet the threshold values of assets and turnover in, and/or attributable to, South Africa. Notification of a merger is compulsory when the thresholds of turnover and assets of the firms involved are met or exceeded.
Joint ventures, which fall within the broad definition set out above, which take place in South Africa or outside South Africa with an effect in South Africa, fall within the ambit of the Competition Act.

If the local party is a public company, when might the approval of its shareholders be required under stock exchange or similar rules?
The Listings Requirements of the JSE impose obligations on listed companies in addition to those imposed by the Companies Act. A transaction is categorised by assessing its size relative to that of the issuer proposing to make it and the listed holding company of such issuer, if applicable. The comparison of size is made by the use of the percentage ratios, being consideration to market capitalisation and dilution.
Approval of shareholders may be required in certain circumstances (e.g. certain "related parties" transactions or in a "category 1 transaction" which occurs where any of the percentage ratios is 25 per cent or more of the total consideration).

3. Types of joint venture vehicle

What are the principal types of joint venture vehicle commonly used with foreign investors?

(i) *Partnership*. A partnership consists of two or more entities and can be created by either written or oral agreement. The relationship between partners and third parties is governed by the relevant agreement and common law.

Generally, each of the partners makes a contribution to the partnership or binds themselves to contribute something. The contribution by the respective partners must be capable of being valued, but need not be of the same character, value or quantity. The contribution may be monetary, labour or skills related. The business should be carried on for the joint benefit of the partners, as opposed to an arrangement where each partner acts independently in their own interest and individual benefit.

A partnership is not a legal entity and cannot conduct transactions in its own name. Therefore the partners conduct transactions on behalf of the partnership.

(ii) *Joint venture company ("JVC")*. A joint venture may also be created through an incorporated separate legal entity whereby the contributing parties each contribute certain assets and share in profits and losses to the joint venture. Therefore, a legally independent and separate corporate entity is created through which the business is operated, as opposed to a co-operation arrangement (see below) which is generally created for the performance of a particular contract.

(iii) *Unincorporated joint venture*. This is a co-operation arrangement constituted by two or more entities by either written or oral agreement. The relationship between the parties is contractual, and is governed by agreement and the common law. A separate legal entity is not created.

An unincorporated joint venture is usually utilised by parties to pursue a common objective, whilst confining their obligations between each other. The parties agree to associate as independent contractors, as opposed to shareholders of a company or partners in a partnership. Co-operation agreements are used for specific projects, for example to tender for and negotiate a contract and fulfil the terms of the tender.

A co-operation arrangement is distinguishable from a partnership. Partners may be co-owners of given assets, however, this is not necessarily the case with a co-operation agreement. Co-ownership of assets does not necessarily establish the existence of one. Parties must be cautious that a co-operation agreement is not deemed a partnership contrary to the intention of the parties. It is therefore advisable to specifically express the non intention to establish a partnership in the co-operation agreement.

Differences between a partnership and a co-operation arrangement include: (i) a co-operation arrangement does not necessarily involve the sharing of profit and loss, whereas partnership does; (ii) a co-participant can dispose of its interest in a jointly owned asset without the consent of other co-participants, whereas a partner cannot; and (iii) each partner is deemed an agent of the other partner/s, whereas a co-owner is not.

If a partnership structure is chosen, does this lead to (a) joint and several liability to third parties and/or (b) duties of good faith as between partners?

A partnership does not have separate legal personality and as such there is no limited liability protection for the partners. The partners of a partnership are jointly and severally liable for the debts of the partnership.

The individual partners can regulate their liability amongst each other by agreement. Partners can be sued by a third party creditor for the joint venture debts. Partners have a right of recourse against the other partner or partners (if more than one). On dissolution of the partnership, the partners become liable *singuli et solidum* (i.e. each for the whole debt) for the partnership debts.

A partnership is a contract of *uberrimae fidei*. The relationship between partners is one of mutual trust and confidence. The duty to observe good faith is not confined to partners in an existing partnership. The fiduciary duties of partner include the due acceptance and fulfilment of partnership obligations; duty not to compete with the firm; duty to guard against a conflict of interest and duty of full disclosure.

4. Capital structure and funding

Is it common to have different "classes" of shares (e.g. A and B shares) to reflect different initial contributions or financial interests of the parties?

Yes, it is common to issue different classes of shares to reflect different financial interests. South African company law allows parties the flexibility to create different classes of shares on the spectrum of pure equity to pure debt.

Is it common to have "preference" shares which give a party a priority on payment of dividends or on a return of capital?

It is common for preference shares to be issued to give priority on payment of dividends to a shareholder. The Companies Act provides that the share capital of a company may be divided into shares having a par value or may be constituted by shares having no par value, provided that all the ordinary shares or all the preference shares shall consist of either the one or the other.

A company having a share capital, if so authorised by its articles, may issue preference shares which are, or at the option of the company are liable, to be redeemed. No such shares may be redeemed except out of profits of the company which would otherwise be available for dividends or out of the proceeds of a fresh issue of shares made for the purposes of the redemption, and in such manner as shall be provided by the articles of the company.

Are "redeemable" shares permitted (i.e. shares that can be repaid and cancelled)?

Yes, with preference shares being redeemable on the basis set out above.

In terms of the proposed changes in terms of the Companies Bill, the company may establish for a particular class of shares, in terms of its memorandum of incorporation, preferences, rights, limitation and other terms that (a) confer special, conditional or limited voting rights or no voting rights; or (b) provide for shares of that class to be redeemable or convertible: (i) at the option of the company, shareholder or another person; or (ii) for cash, indebtedness, securities or other property; or (iii) at prices or amounts specified or determined in accordance with a formula; or (iv) subject to any other terms contained in the company's memorandum of incorporation.

Are "non voting" shares permitted?

Under the Companies Act, and subject to what is set out below regarding preference shares, every holder of shares shall have the right to vote at meetings of that company in respect of each share held, and hence, non voting shares are not permitted. However, in respect of private (as opposed to public) companies, it is possible to load the votes of a certain class of shares, which can reduce or nullify the voting rights held by other classes of shareholder.

The Companies Act permits the articles of the company to provide that the preference shares shall not be voted at meetings of the company except during any period when dividends remain in arrears and unpaid; and in regard to any resolution proposed which directly affects any of the rights attached to such shares, including a resolution for the winding-up of the company or for the reduction of capital.

The proposed Companies Bill provides that if there is more than one class of shares, the memorandum of incorporation must provide that at least one of the classes of shares has a right to be voted on every matter that may be decided by shareholders of the company.

Are there any "thin capitalisation" or similar rules which affect the choice of equity/debt ratio for the capital structure?

South Africa does have thin capitalisation rules which affect the choice of equity/debt ratio. These rules are contained in s.31(3) of the Income Tax Act No.58 of 1962 ("Income Tax Act"). The inclination to thinly capitalise a company generally arises because non-resident investor does not pay income tax on interest derived from the loan while the local company is generally entitled to deduct the interest which it pays to the investor. Dividends on the other hands are not deductible by the South African company and are subject to Secondary Tax on Companies ("STC") at a rate of 10 per cent. The thin capitalisation rules provide for a "safe haven" ratio of three:one. What this means is that, provided the debt portion is not more than 75 per cent of the total financing, the full interest will be deductible by the local company.

Is there any capital or similar tax payable in respect of issued share capital?

On increasing its share capital, an amount of ZAR5 for each ZAR1000, or part thereof, is payable by the company. There is no stamp duty on the issue of shares.

Is a separate "contribution agreement" or other formal document (other than formal property transfer agreements) required or usual under the local law to document the contribution of assets to the joint venture?

No. The joint venture/relationship/co-operation agreement may contain details of each party's contribution.

Are there any local laws which require an independent valuation of any non cash assets to be contributed to the joint venture?
No.

If a foreign party is to contribute technology to the joint venture, are there any special requirements for valuation of that technology?

There are no special requirements for the valuation of technology. The valuation methodology remains the same. The valuator will take into account that the ownership of the technology is based with a foreign party and deal with any relevant implications on the value.

5. Tax

Are there any particular tax laws or incentives which significantly affect the establishment of joint ventures in this jurisdiction by a foreign investor?
No.

It should be noted that a partnership, unlike a JVC, is not a person either under the South African common law or the Income Tax Act. Accordingly, for tax purposes a partnership is not regarded as a taxpaying entity. The parties making up the partnership are subject to tax in their individual capacities, with the South African Revenue Services apportioning the taxable income from the partnership amongst the partners in their profit sharing ratio, and each partner is taxed on his share of the profits. Notwithstanding the fact that the partners are taxed in their individual capacities, the Income Tax Act requires them to submit a joint tax return at the end of any year of assessment.

Any capital gain or capital loss accruing to the partnership on the disposal of an asset will be accounted for in the hands of the partners. Further, the initial capital contributions made by the individual partners to the partnership have been held to be a "disposal" for purposes of capital gains tax.

A secondary tax on companies (STC) is only paid by South African resident companies when they declare dividends. A partnership is not a company and is not subject to STC on any profits which are distributed to the partners.

Will withholding taxes apply to dividends paid by a joint venture company?

A JVC will be liable for income tax on its income in accordance with the rules contained in the Income Tax Act. A company is liable for 10 per cent STC on all dividends declared, if any, and income tax at a rate of 28 per cent tax on all its income. Please note that STC is not a withholding tax on dividends. It is a tax on the profits of the company declaring dividends. The assessed losses of a company are ring-fenced in the company and there are anti-avoidance provisions in the Income Tax Act which prohibit companies from trading in assessed losses.

However, South Africa is in the process of changing the way in which dividends will be taxed. The intention is to replace STC with a withholding tax on dividends. According to the budget speech delivered by the Minister of Finance on February 20, 2008, the withholding tax, the liability for which will fall on the shareholder and not the company as is the case with STC, will be introduced in 2009. There is as yet no legislation detailing the manner in which this tax will apply but we expect that amended legislation will be drafted during the course of 2008.

6. Exchange control regulation

Are there exchange control regulations which materially affect the establishment of the joint venture or the subsequent repatriation of profits or dividends from the joint venture to a foreign party?

The Exchange Control Department of the SARB imposes exchange controls on South African residents and currency cannot be transferred by a South African resident into or out of South Africa except in accordance with the Exchange Control Regulations made in terms of the Currency and Exchanges Act.

A non-resident may acquire any South African shares or other assets. Under the exchange control regulations, no person is entitled to transfer South African shares from or into the name of a non-resident without the approval of the SARB. The approval which requires a demonstration that there is no prejudice to the South African fiscal reserves (e.g. the purchase price was paid off-shore) is evidenced by the endorsement of the share certificate in the name of the non-resident with the words "non-resident". This endorsement ensures that sale proceeds of the shares, which belong to a non-resident, can be transferred abroad. Any income, such as dividends and interest, derived from the South African shares or assets is freely transferable by the non-resident and may be remitted out of South Africa into any foreign currency at prevailing exchange rates. Where a non-resident sells any South African asset, the proceeds of the sale can be transferred on the same basis into any foreign currency at prevailing exchange rates.

No foreign currency commitments may, in terms of the regulations, be entered into by residents without prior approval from the SARB. However, dealers authorised by the SARB to deal in foreign exchange (most commercial banks in South Africa are authorised dealers) are sometimes authorised by the SARB to remit funds abroad without specific permission from the SARB. These include the remittance of funds abroad for the purposes of: the payment for imported goods; the remission of dividends declared by a South African company; interest earned on loans to a non-quoted South African company; profits distributed by a non-quoted South African company; the payment of directors' fees; and the payment of legal and other fees (i.e. advertising fees).

Agreements by South African companies to pay royalties, licence and patent fees to non-residents in respect of the local manufacturing of a product are subject to the approval of the Department of Trade and Industry. Agreements by South African companies to pay royalties, licence and patent fees to non-residents where no local manufacturing is involved are subject to the approval of the SARB. Any advance payments of royalties, even if such payments may be recouped from future royalties payable, will be declined. The SARB is also not in favour of minimum payments should the royalty not reach a certain amount during a specific period (i.e. the royalty payable should be in proportion to the production and sales achieved).

The following factors, inter alia, are taken into account when considering an application for approval: the strategic importance of the product; the economic importance of the product in the furthering of industrial development by means of import replacement, export promotion or expansion of the domestic market and its contribution to national income and employment; the new technological know-how entering the country through the manufacturing process in question; the domestic content of the particular product; the financial interest of the licensor in the local venture; the duration of the contract; and the nature of any restrictions contained in the agreement, i.e. on the exportation of South African products.

7. Board and management

Are there local law rules which affect the board or management structure of the joint venture? May a two tier board be required?

The management structure of the partnership can be more flexible than that of the JVC, with a management committee (in the case of a partnership) instead of a board of directors (in the case of a JVC) managing the joint venture. A board of directors, unlike a management committee is less flexible due to the structures imposed by the Companies Act on company directors.

No, a two tier board is not a requirement.

Are there local law constraints on persons who can be directors or managers of the joint venture (e.g. only local residents or nationals)?

There are no restrictions on the persons who may be a director or manager of a joint venture. There is no requirement that directors be South African citizens or residents. That being said, as stated above, the current draft of the Companies Bill disqualifies a person acting as a director if that person does not reside in South Africa, unless the company has more than one director and at least one of the other directors resides in South Africa.

Does a shareholder in a joint venture company owe a duty of good faith (or similar duty) to other shareholders in the way it behaves in relation to the joint venture?

South African corporate law recognises that a company has a separate and independent entity which is capable of acquiring its own rights and incur its own duties and obligations. Responsibility remains that of the company and not its shareholders or directors.

However, in certain circumstances South African courts have disregarded the separate legal entity of the company so as to hold shareholders and/or directors liable for the actions of the company. This is referred to as the "piercing" or "lifting" of the corporate veil. This means that shareholders and/or directors can be held personally liable for certain infringements of corporate legislation or for acting negligently or fraudulently. Although the courts do not have a general discretion to look beyond the personality of the company, fraud, dishonesty or improper conduct are considered sufficient grounds to do so.

Can you modify the legal duties of directors so that they can expressly take into account the interests of their "appointer" when voting or acting as director—or must they always act objectively in the best interests of the company?

Yes. Directors' duties can be amended to suit the relevant joint venture, but any deviations must not conflict with the Companies Act and a director's fiduciary duties under the common law.

8. Transfer of shares

In the case of a joint venture company, can a permanent restriction on transfer of shares be imposed under the local law (e.g. no transfer without the consent of the other shareholder)?

Yes, a limit on the transfer (e.g. lock-in or pre-emptive rights) can be included in the co-operation/shareholders or relationship agreement between the parties. In a private limited liability company which may have between one and 50 shareholders, the right to transfer shares is usually restricted and offers to the public for the subscription of shares or debentures are prohibited.

Please refer above for exchange control restrictions.

9. Protection for minority shareholders

Are there any statutory rules or remedies which help significantly to protect a minority shareholder in a joint venture company?

Any member of a company who complains that any particular act or omission of a company is unfairly prejudicial, unjust or inequitable, or that the affairs of the company are being conducted in a manner unfairly prejudicial, unjust or inequitable to him or to some part of the members of the company, may make an application to the court for an order altering the memorandum of the company; reducing the capital of the company; any variation of the rights in respect of the shares; or conversion of a private company into a public company or vice versa.

Does the law require any major business decisions to be approved by a special resolution or super majority (whether at board or shareholder level)—or must a minority party protect itself by contract?

The Companies Act requires shareholders approval, being 75 per cent of the shares voted on the resolution, for certain decisions, although it is also market practice for parties to expand this list contractually through "reserved matters". Examples of matters requiring a special resolution under the Companies Act include: disposal by a company of the whole or a large portion of its assets; amendment of the company's memorandum and articles of association; increase by the company of its share capital; company's acquisition of its own shares; voluntary winding up of the company.

The current draft of the Companies Bill permits a smaller percentage of shares, subject to a minimum of 65 per cent, to be voted in support of a special resolution (provided the memorandum of incorporation provides for a smaller percentage).

10. Employment laws

Are there local law obligations requiring a "local" party to consult with, or obtain the approval of, employees or employee representatives on a contribution of its business to the joint venture?

A contribution of a business to a joint venture would in most instances result in a portion of a business being transferred as a going concern. In these circumstances the provisions of section 197 of the Labour Relations Act No.66 of 1995 ("Labour Relations Act") are applicable. Section 197 of the Labour Relations Act has a dual purpose. On the one hand, and contrary to the common law, it permits an employer to transfer its employees to another employer, without their consent where it is transferring the business as a going concern. On the other hand, it protects the employees by ensuring that where they are transferred without their consent, this must be done without affecting their terms and conditions of employment or their length of service. Ultimately no consultation is required in law, however, there are provisions requiring disclosure of information to employees and their representative trade unions. This dual purpose of facilitating the commercial transaction while, at the same time, protecting the workers against unfair job losses has been recognised by the Constitutional Court.

In the event of a sale of shares, the employees' employment relationship with the company is normally unaffected. This is because apart from the change in ownership at the shareholder level, the business itself should continue to operate as before. The employees' employment contracts should therefore simply continue in force. No consultation process with the employees is legally required. It may, however, from an industrial relations perspective, be advisable to inform the employees of the anticipated change and the effect thereof.

In the event of retrenchments for operational requirements the Labour Relations Act prescribes a consultation that is peremptory. "Operational requirements" are defined as the structural, economic, technological or similar needs of the employer. However, a retrenchment process should not be embarked on if entering into the joint venture can be classified as a transfer as a going concern as prescribed by s.197, as it would be considered an automatically unfair dismissal in terms of the Labour Relations Act.

Are there any material employment laws (compared with the UK) which are likely to affect the ongoing operations of the joint venture?

The following statutes regulate different aspects of the employment relationship and hence must be complied with:

o The Labour Relations Act No.66 of 1995 provides a framework for among other things, collective bargaining, the granting of organisational rights, dispute resolutions, dealing with strikes and lock-outs.

o The Basic Conditions of Employment Act No.75 of 1997 deals with, for example, regulation of ordinary working hours, overtime, work on Sundays and public holidays, annual leave, sick leave, maternity leave and termination of employment. In addition there are a number of sectoral determinations and bargaining council agreements that affect employees and employers in different sectors.

o The Employment Equity Act No.55 of 1998 deals with the elimination of unfair discrimination and the establishment of specific measures to accelerate the advancement in the workplace of black people, women and people with disabilities.

o The Skills Development Act No.97 of 1998 sets out a framework for devising and implementing skills development programmes and learnerships to improve the skills of a workforce.

- The Broad-Based Black Empowerment Act No.53 of 2003 provides the framework for policies, strategies and codes designed to increase broad-based and effective participation by black people in the economy and to promote a higher growth rate, increased employment and more equitable income distribution. As far as employment is concerned, the BEE Act focuses on employment equity (especially affirmative action) and skills development.

- The Regulation of Interception of Communications and Provision of Communications-Related Information Act No.70 of 2002 regulate the interception of certain communications, the monitoring of certain signals and radio frequency spectrums and the provision of certain communication-related information. In terms of this Act, no one may intercept "direct" (oral communications or utterances by a person) or "indirect" communications. The said Act authorises interception or attempted interception in a number of circumstances.

- The Occupational Health & Safety Act No.85 of 1993 brings the country's legal framework for regulating occupational health and safety closer to international standards and contemporary approaches in other countries. This is particularly true of the systems for worker participation and the definition of the employer's general duty which is to provide and maintain, as far as is reasonably practicable, a working environment that is safe and without risks to health.

- Health and safety in the mining industry is regulated by the Mine Health and Safety Act No.29 of 1996.

- The Compensation for Occupational Injuries and Diseases Act No.130 of 1993 provides a system of compensation for work related injuries and diseases. Employers are assessed according to a tariff calculated on the basis of the annual earning of employees and are obliged to pay that assessment. The consideration for this is that employers are protected against any liability to an employee or his or her dependants in respect of any occupational injury or disease resulting in the disablement or death of the employee.

- The Occupational Diseases in Mines and Works Act No.78 of 1973, regulates the payment of compensation in respect of certain diseases contracted by persons employed in mines and works.

- The Unemployment Insurance Act No.63 of 2001 and the Unemployment Insurance Contributions Act No. 4 of 2002 provide a system of limited unemployment, illness, maternity and other benefits. These are funded by levies paid by employers and employees.

- The Pension Funds Act No.24 of 1956 regulates the operation of pensions and provident funds, while providing pensioners and employees with statutory entitlements to these funds.

11. Accounts

Is there a requirement on the joint venture company to file accounts with any authority where they are publicly available?

All companies have to make an annual return for each financial year and all public companies must also submit a full set of audited annual financial statements for each financial year.

In terms of the Companies Act a private company is not required to file its accounts with the Registrar of the Companies' Office. However, public companies are required to file accounts with the Registrar.

The 2006 Corporate Laws Amendment Act which amended the current Companies Act with effect from December 14, 2007 provides the framework for the imposition of a uniform set of accounting standards to ensure compliance with GAAP and/or IFRS.

The Corporate Laws Amendment Act establishes a Financial Reporting Standards Council ("FRSC"), whose objective is to "establish financial reporting standards which promote sound and consistent accounting practices" and it also establishes a Financial Reporting Investigations Panel. This Panel is charged with the duty to investigate alleged non-compliance with financial reporting standards and recommend "appropriate measures for rectification or restitution". Its report may, "if it is in the interests of users", be published in the news media and must be made available for public inspection.

12. Dispute resolution

Is there any standard local practice as to form of dispute resolution in relation to joint ventures with foreign investors? Is arbitration in a venue outside that jurisdiction acceptable?

Alternate forms of dispute resolution (arbitration) are governed by the Arbitration Act No.42 of 1965. Professional bodies specialising in mediation services and alternate dispute resolution have been formed and are used extensively, particularly in labour related matters.

Parties are free to agree on a governing law and to the jurisdiction of international arbitration forums.

Certain procedures must be followed to procure the enforcement of foreign judgments, including foreign arbitral awards. Under the Protection of Businesses Act, 1978, the consent of the Minister of Trade and Industry is required for the recognition and enforcement by South African courts of a judgment or arbitration award rendered by a court or arbitral tribunal outside South Africa. Enforcement is also subject to compliance with the requirements of South African law for the enforcement of foreign judgments. Generally, a foreign judgment may be enforced in South Africa.

Is the local jurisdiction a signatory to the 1958 New York Convention on the Recognition and Enforcement of Foreign Arbitral Awards?

Yes.

13. Legal documents and formalities

Is there any special form of legal documentation required under local law for establishment of a joint venture company? What are the usual principal documents?

A JVC is normally constituted by two types of agreements, the memorandum and articles of association (which are lodged with the Registrar of Companies) and the shareholders' agreement. A joint venture agreement for an incorporated joint venture does not need to be registered.

An incorporated joint venture must be registered in accordance with the Companies Act No.63 of 1973 by lodging the required documentation with the South African companies' office. Incorporation proceedings in South Africa are not complicated. On registration, the Registrar of Companies will issue a certificate of incorporation and a certificate to commence business. Only when the latter certificate has been issued, may the company commence business. However, it is possible for pre-incorporation contracts to be concluded by persons acting as trustees for the company to be formed. Such a contract must be in writing, must be disclosed in the memorandum of association and must be ratified by the company on incorporation.

Does the joint venture documentation need to be in the local language and/or governed by the local law?

Joint venture documentation can be governed by a foreign law and be in any language. However, documents filed/lodged with a South African regulatory authority should be in English. For purposes of the Competition Act, submissions to the competition authorities are made in English. Ordinarily, the merger agreement (joint venture agreement, sale agreement, and shareholders' agreement.) is submitted as part of the submission.

Are agreements between shareholders (e.g. as to appointment of directors, conduct of the business of the company or voting majorities required for certain decisions etc.) enforceable under local law? In the event of breach, is specific performance or a similar remedy available, or only damages?

Such agreements are enforceable unless the agreement is inconsistent with mandatory legislation. A party can seek damages and specific performance as a remedy for breach.

Are restrictions relating to (a) transfers of shares and/or (b) minority "veto rights" commonly included in the articles of association or by laws of the company-or included in a separate shareholders' agreement?

The articles of association of private companies generally contain restrictions on the transfer of shares, as must be applicable to private companies, in order to reflect the position under the Companies Act. Minority "veto rights" are, however, generally contained in the shareholders' agreement, although they can be incorporated into the articles of association. If included in the shareholders' agreement and not the articles of association, it is acceptable to include a provision in the shareholders' agreement stating that, in the event of a conflict between the two documents, the provisions of the shareholders' agreement will prevail.

Are there any formalities (e.g. notarisation or registration) which are material and which may affect the timing involved in forming the joint venture?

The only formalities relate to the establishment of a JVC. Incorporation of a new company is effected by lodging various documents with the Registrar of the South African Companies Office.

Thereafter, the Registrar of the South African Companies Office will register the company, allocate a registration number to the company concerned and issue a certificate of registration to the company. The certificate of registration issued by the Registrar of the South African Companies Office is conclusive evidence that the registration requirements in terms of the Companies Act have been complied with. This process generally takes about three weeks.

(13) Spain

Authors: Antoni Valverde and Carlos Bas
Freshfields Bruckhaus Deringer, Barcelona

1. General background

Are joint ventures popular as a form of foreign investment into your jurisdiction?
Spain has witnessed a significant amount of inward investment in the last decade through joint ventures.

Are there restrictions on foreign participation?
There are almost no restrictions on the ownership percentage foreign investors may hold in Spanish joint ventures. In general, foreign investments only need to be communicated to the Spanish exchange control authorities (*Direccion General de Politica Comercial e Inversiones Exteriores*) for statistical and economic purposes once they have been established. Exceptionally, prior administrative clearance is required if the investment relates to national defence matters, strategic mining interests or certain specific sectors regulated by law (e.g. gaming, radio, television, private security, air transport, telecommunications and manufacturing).

What (if any) are the major legal problems which a foreign investor in a joint venture faces in your jurisdiction?
Generally speaking, there are no major legal problems as such for a foreign investor to form part of a Spanish joint venture. Investors may find, however, that the process of negotiating a joint venture is slightly different as a result of (i) certain cultural differences between the approaches of Spanish businessmen and their advisers compared with those of the US or the UK and (ii) differences in the legal system, which comprises several layers of authority (national, regional and municipal).

2. Governmental/regulatory approvals

What principal governmental or regulatory approvals are required (excluding competition law) for establishing a joint venture?
Many economic activities in Spain are subject to a variety of governmental regulatory approvals, applicable irrespective of whether the parties to the joint venture are Spanish or foreign. Examples include: travel agencies, motorways, private banking, financial and credit institutions, casinos and bingos, insurance, securities' companies, temporary employment agencies, television, radio, electricity, oil and gas, etc. In a number of former state-owned privatised companies, notification to the Spanish authorities is required in respect of transactions which result in the acquisition of shares representing 10 per cent or more of the relevant company's shareholding.

Are there local anti-trust laws which might apply to the formation of the joint venture?

If a joint venture is determined to be of a "concentrative" nature but falls outside the scope of the EC Merger Regulation, the new Spanish Competition Act (in force since 2007) will apply and may require a mandatory filing with the Spanish competition authorities (*Comisión Nacional de la Competencia*). A brief summary of the merger control law appears below:

Filing requirement/ trigger	Timetable for clearance	Test for clearance	Mandatory/ voluntary Penalties
Applies to "full function" JV's. To qualify as "full function", the JV must be an autonomous economic entity resulting in a permanent structural market change, regardless of any resulting co-ordination of the competitive behaviour of the parents; or the parents' combined market share in Spain (or in a defined market within Spain) exceeds 30 per cent.	Stage 1: one month after filing. Stage 2: two months from stage 1. Stage 3: one month from stage 2. Transaction cannot be completed until a clearance decision has been received. A derogation may be sought at the time of filing and decided upon at the end of stage 1.	Whether the JV prevents the maintenance of effective competition in whole or in part of the national market	Filing mandatory prior to completion. Failure to file: fines up to 1 per cent of the annual turnover of the parent companies. Failure to notify after having been requested to file by the authorities: fines of up to approx. €12,000 per day of delay. Implementation before clearance: fines of up to five per cent of the annual turnover of the parent companies.

3. Types of joint venture vehicle

What are the principal types of joint venture vehicle commonly used with foreign investors?

The *sociedad anonima* (SA) and the *sociedad de responsabilidad limitada* (SL) are the most common types of company used in Spain. The SA is generally used for businesses of any material size, whereas the SL is more suitable for small businesses. Nonetheless, the SL has become the most common type of business entity for non-listed companies since it is more flexible than the SA and has fewer formal requirements. The share capital of the SA is divided by shares and that of the SL is divided by participaciones; both are limited liability entities. The principal differences are:

- The SA must have a minimum of approx. €60,000. The SL, on the other hand, needs to have a minimum capital of only approx. €3,000. *Participaciones* in an SL must be fully paid up, whilst shares of an SA need only initially be paid up

- to a minimum of 25 per cent of their nominal value. The SA's corporate by-laws should establish how and when the remainder should be paid up.
- The requirements for filing information are less onerous for an SL than for an SA, and it is easier to amend the by-laws of an SL.
- *Participaciones* in an SL are not "securities" under Spanish law, and therefore may not be listed on a securities exchange.

The *cuenta en participacion* (participation account or silent partnership) is also used as a joint venture structure in Spain. It is simply a contractual and accounting arrangement by which an investor (i.e. the silent partner) makes a capital contribution to a third party's (i.e. the manager's) business and enters into a profit and loss sharing agreement in the proportion agreed between the parties. The main disadvantages of the *cuenta en participacion* are that one per cent capital duty is payable on contribution and return of capital; in addition, the tax treatment has changed a number of times over recent years. Given the uncertainty, the structure is suitable only for short-term ventures.

The *agrupacion de interes economico* (AIE)—the Spanish version of the EEIG—is also used as a joint venture structure in Spain. It is a non-profit legal entity whose purpose is to facilitate its partners' activities (an AIE must have as its corporate object ancillary activities to those of partners). It is characterised as being a very flexible and efficient legal entity. However, partners of an AIE are, residually, personally and jointly liable. Spanish tax legislation tries to promote the incorporation of AIEs by means of tax advantages (e.g. tax transparency in direct taxes and unlimited allocation of losses).

Additionally, the following type of companies may also be used as joint venture structures in Spain in certain limited circumstances: general partnership (*sociedad colectiva*), limited partnership (*sociedad comanditaria simple*), and partnership limited by shares (*sociedad comanditaria por acciones*). Differing from UK partnerships, these types of companies enjoy full legal personality under Spanish law and, thus, constitute legal entities separate from their partners and are not tax transparent.

If a partnership structure is chosen, does this lead to (a) joint and several liability to third parties and/or (b) duties of good faith as between partners?

The general rule is that partners are jointly and severally liable for the partnership's debts. (A limited exception is in the case of a limited partnership (*sociedad comanditaria*) and a partnership limited by shares (*sociedad comanditaria por acciones*), since in these forms, in addition to "general partners" whose liability is unlimited, there must be at least one "limited partner" whose liability is limited to his/her contribution. "General partners" can be limited liability companies.)

Unless otherwise provided in the company's by-laws, under Spanish law "general partners" are subject to a non-compete obligation. In addition, both general and limited partners are subject to duties of good faith.

4. Capital structure and funding

What principal local law issues affect the capital structure and funding of the joint venture?

In determining the capital structure and funding of the joint venture, the following factors should be taken into account:

(i) *Shares.* In a *sociedad anonima* (SA) shares may be divided into classes and series, where classes are defined by the granted rights and series by the nominal values. Share rights are relatively rigid under Spanish corporate law; for instance:

- the issue of shares with interest-related dividends is not generally permitted;
- voting rights must be related to the nominal value of the shares (i.e. enhanced rights cannot be conferred, except by adjusting the nominal value);
- preference shares must have a voting right attached and their dividends must be satisfied before sharing benefits among ordinary shares;
- non-voting shares must carry a right to a minimum nominal dividend (in addition to any other dividend the company declares) fixed in the by-laws, and have in all respects (other than voting) similar rights as other shares; the nominal value of non-voting shares must represent not more than half of the issued share capital; and
- public companies may issue redeemable shares (*acciones rescatables*) which must not represent more than one quarter of the issued share capital.

In a *sociedad de responsabilidad limitada* (SL), under a strict interpretation of the law, participaciones may not be divided into classes and series, although they may attach different voting (non-voting shares can also be issued by an SL) and/or economic rights—recently there has been a move towards more flexibility in this area; in addition, they are subject to transfer restrictions and thus offer less flexibility than shares in an SA.

(ii) *Non-cash contributions.* The following issues arise where non-cash assets form all or part of the consideration for shares in the joint venture vehicle:

In a *sociedad anonima* (SA) an expert (appointed by the Mercantile Registry) is required to make a valuation of non-cash contributions through an established procedure whilst in the *sociedad de responsabilidad limitada* (SL) this valuation procedure is not imposed (but the contributing shareholders will be jointly and severally liable to the company and its creditors for the value given to the non-cash contribution in the relevant public deed).

The investors may opt for a special tax regime where the non-cash contribution for shares constitutes the transfer of a business as a going concern or where the consideration shares represent at least five per cent of the issued share capital of the transferee. The possible advantages include a deferral of Spanish capital gains tax which would otherwise be payable by the transferor in respect of the assets transferred. (Although the option for this special regime might be an advantage for the Spanish party, who would therefore be able to pass on its potential capital gain to the joint venture vehicle, it might not be so advisable for a foreign investor who is resident in a country with a tax treaty with Spain under which the capital gains are taxable only in the state of the transferor).

Is it common to have different "classes" of shares (e.g. A and B shares) to reflect different initial contributions or financial interests of the parties?

Yes. Please see "capital structure" issues under section 4 above.

Is it common to have "preference" shares which give a party a priority on payment of dividends or on a return of capital?

Preference shares, giving a party a priority on payment of dividends and on the return of capital, can be created by *sociedades anonimas* (SA) and by *sociedades de responsabilidad limitada* (SL). Certain limitations apply in the case of an SA (e.g. the preference right may not entitle the shareholder to receive a fixed interest.)

Are "redeemable" shares permitted (i.e. shares that can be repaid and cancelled)?

Redeemable shares (*acciones rescatables*) may only be issued by listed *sociedades anonimas* (SA) and must not represent more than one quarter of the company's issued share capital. The redeemable shares must be fully paid-up when subscribed. If the redemption right is only granted to the company, it cannot exercise such right until three years have elapsed from the issue of the redeemable shares.

Are "non-voting" shares permitted?

Yes. Both *sociedades anonimas* (SA) and *sociedades de responsabilidad limitada* (SL) may issue non-voting shares with a nominal value not exceeding half of the paid-up share capital. Non-voting shares carry a right to a minimum nominal dividend set out in the company's by-laws (in addition to any other dividend the company declares), and have in all respects (other than voting) similar rights as other shares. When there is no dividend to pay, voting rights are temporarily granted.

Are there any "thin capitalisation" or similar rules which affect the choice of equity/debt ratio for the capital structure?

The Spanish "thin capitalisation" rules provide for restrictions on the debt/equity ratio when the direct or indirect interest-bearing indebtedness of a Spanish company (excluding financial entities) in respect of a connected party which is not resident in Spain exceeds three times the equity of the Spanish company (i.e. the Spanish debt-to-equity ratio is three:one) on a yearly average basis. The interest paid in relation to the excess indebtedness would be recharacterised as dividends and, therefore, would not be tax deductible. It is possible to submit a (duly supported) proposal to apply a higher ratio, provided the lender is not resident in a country or territory classified as a tax haven for Spanish tax purposes. This "thin capitalisation" rule does not apply when the lender is resident in the EU, unless it is resident in a country or territory classified as a tax haven for Spanish tax purposes (i.e. Andorra, Cyprus, Gibraltar, Isle of Man and the Channel Islands (Guernsey and Jersey), Liechtenstein, Luxembourg (only in respect of income received by companies subject to the special holding company status), Monaco and San Marino).

Is there any capital or similar tax payable in respect of issued share capital?

Capital tax is payable at the rate of one per cent in respect of the share capital contributed by the shareholders (at incorporation or any time thereafter).

Is a separate "contribution agreement" or other formal document (other than formal property transfer agreements) required or usual under the local law to document the contribution of assets to the joint venture?

If assets or a business are being contributed in consideration for new issued shares of the joint venture vehicle, a public deed of increase in share capital will be required. Additionally, if the assets or business contributed by the local party as a going concern are the result of spin-off or winding-up of an existing company, a public deed must also be formalised with a notary public to that effect. In addition, an investment or contribution agreement will normally be entered into by the parties.

Are there any local laws which require an independent valuation of any non-cash assets to be contributed to the joint venture?

Contributions in kind by the shareholders to the joint venture vehicle require, in the case of a *sociedad anonima*, an expert (appointed by the Mercantile Registry) to make a valuation of non-cash contributions through an established procedure. Such a valuation procedure is not required for a *sociedad de responsabilidad limitada*.

Are there exchange control regulations which materially affect the establishment of the joint venture or the subsequent repatriation of profits or dividends from the joint venture to a foreign party?

Establishment of a joint venture by a foreign party will need to be communicated to the Spanish foreign investment and exchange control authorities (*Direccion General de Politica Comercial e Inversiones Exteriores*) for statistical and economic purposes once it has been established. Repatriation of profits and dividends to a foreign party (provided the above requirements have been fulfilled) is fully liberalised subject to certain general conditions. Payments and collections between residents and non-residents, as well as transfers to or from abroad, whether in Euros or foreign currency, have to be made through a bank or financial entity registered with the Bank of Spain.

If a foreign party is to contribute technology to the joint venture, are there any special requirements for valuation of that technology?

If a foreign company were to contribute technology directly to the joint venture, it will be considered as a non-cash contribution and a valuation by an expert would be required as described above.

5. Tax

Are there any particular tax laws or incentives which significantly affect the establishment of joint ventures in this jurisdiction by a foreign investor?

Joint venture companies conducting activities within certain economic sectors may be favoured by special industry-oriented tax regimes, and there is a special economic and tax regime aimed at attracting foreign investment to the Canary Islands. In addition, Spanish corporate tax law includes several tax reliefs and incentives aimed at promoting certain activities (e.g. investment in R&D, exportation of goods and services abroad, etc.). Such tax relieves and incentives are being reduced progressively and will no longer be applicable as of year 2011, 2013 or 2014, as the case may be.

Additionally, Spanish law provides for a "participation exemption" regime and for a special tax regime (covering dividends and capital gains) for Spanish holding companies with foreign interests (*Entidades de tenencia de valores extranjeros, the ETVE Regime*), irrespective of whether the shareholders in the Spanish holding company (the *She*) are Spanish or not. These exemption regimes make Spain a more attractive location for holding companies (including joint ventures) with international operations.

Will withholding taxes apply to dividends paid by a joint venture company?

As a general principle, Spanish law provides for an 18 per cent withholding on dividends distributed by Spanish companies to non-residents with no permanent establishment in Spain. However, in the cases of dividends paid by a Spanish company to an EU company, the exemption under the EU Parent/Subsidiary Directive applies provided the necessary requirements are met. In the case of companies resident in non-EU countries, double tax treaty reduced rates may be applicable.

6. Board and management

Are there local law rules which affect the board or management structure of the joint venture? May a two-tier board be required?

For a *sociedad anonima* or *sociedad de responsabilidad limitada*, the management structure could be any of the following:

- A *sociedad anonima* can be managed by (i) a sole director; (ii) two directors acting jointly; (iii) several directors acting jointly and severally; and (iv) a board of directors (minimum three members). It is necessary for the by-laws to establish which of the different systems of administration will be applicable. Directors are appointed for a maximum of five years (although they can be re-elected) and they need not to be shareholders unless the by-laws provide otherwise.

- A *sociedad de responsabilidad limitada* can be managed by (i) a sole director; (ii) several directors acting jointly or jointly and severally; and (iii) a board of directors (minimum three members, maximum 12 members). The by-laws can contain alternative administration systems, it being possible for the members' general meeting to decide which administration system will be applicable (without the need to amend the by-laws in case of change). Directors may be appointed for an indefinite term and need not be members (unless otherwise provided in the by-laws).

The directors, in any of these cases, may be foreign individuals or corporations (and in the latter case an individual should be appointed to act on behalf of the appointed corporate director). A two-tier board is not possible, except for a European Company domiciled in Spain (SE). Companies frequently delegate some of the board powers to an executive committee in charge of taking day-to-day management decisions and making proposals to the board.

Are there local law constraints on persons who can be directors or managers of the joint venture (e.g. only local residents or nationals)?

Eligibility for the position of director is the same for *sociedades anonimas* (SA) and *sociedades de responsabilidad limitada* (SL). Both individuals and corporations are eligible for the position of director. Being Spanish or having a domicile, primary residence or primary place of work in Spain is not a requirement to be appointed as a director (unless otherwise provided in the by-laws).

Does a shareholder in a joint venture company owe a duty of good faith (or similar duty) to other shareholders in the way it behaves in relation to the joint venture?

Regulations of *sociedades anonimas* (SA) and *sociedades de responsabilidad limitada* (SL) do not expressly provide a duty of good faith of shareholders in relation to other shareholders or to the joint venture itself. However, according to general civil law, good faith must prevail in all legal relationships. In addition, the regulation of *sociedades de responsabilidad limitada* (SL), prevents shareholders from exercising their voting rights at general meetings in some specific situations where conflicts of interest may arise.

Can you modify the legal duties of directors so that they can expressly take into account the interests of their "appointer" when voting or acting as director, or must they always act objectively in the best interests of the company?

The legal duties of directors (which are now set out in some detail in the regulation of *sociedades anonimas* (SA)) cannot be modified expressly to take into account an obligation to act in the interest of their "appointer". Directors must always act objectively in the best interests of the company. The general duty imposed on directors of *sociedades anonimas* (SA) and *sociedades de responsabilidad limitada* (SL) is to act at all times in good faith and honestly, discharging their duties as directors with the diligence of an "organised businessman and a loyal representative" (*ordenado empresario y representante leal*).

7. Transfer of shares

In the case of a joint venture company, can a permanent restriction on transfer of shares be imposed under the local law (e.g. no transfer without the consent of the other shareholder)?

(i) *SA*. Share transfer provisions in the by-laws of a limited liability company in the form of a *sociedad anonima* (SA) are void if in practice they render the shares non-transferable. Such provisions could be included in the shareholders' agreement but would only be binding between the parties and not vis-à-vis third parties. Restrictions on the free transferability of shares (i.e. pre-emption rights) are only be valid vis-à-vis the company where they apply to registered shares and are expressly established in the company's by-laws. In an SA, the transferability of shares may only be subject to prior authorisation of the company when the company's by-laws specify the grounds on which such authorisation may be refused. Prohibitions on transfers (i.e. "lock-ups") are permitted in the by-laws up to two years from the company's incorporation.

(ii) *SL*. As regards a *sociedad de responsabilidad limitada* (SL), share transfer restrictions will be established in the by-laws (with the law providing a fall-back regulation). Having said this, share transfer provisions forbidding the voluntary transfer of shares are only valid if the company's by-laws grant a withdrawal right to the shareholder which can be exercised at any time. The adoption of these provisions in the company's by-laws requires the consent of all the shareholders. In addition, Spanish law prohibits provisions in the by-laws of an SL which (i) would in practice result in voluntary inter vivos share transfers being free or (ii) would compel a shareholder (offering some or all of its participation in the company) to transfer a different number of shares from the number initially offered. Any such provision will be null and void. The by-laws may, though, prohibit voluntary transfers of shares (i.e. establish a "lock-up") for a maximum period of five years from the company's incorporation (or, in the case of shares arising from a share capital increase, from the date of the deed of share capital increase).

8. Protection for minority shareholders

Are there any statutory rules or remedies which help significantly to protect a minority shareholder in a joint venture company?

The primary protection for minority shareholders in both *sociedades anonimas* (SA) and *sociedades de responsabilidad limitada* (SL) is by setting in the company's by-laws special majority requirements for particular resolutions. Additionally, by-laws of an SL may require the favourable vote of a determined number of shareholders.

The consent of individual shareholders in SA and SL is required for certain decisions, such as (i) any amendment to the by-laws entailing new obligations for the shareholders or affecting their individual rights; (ii) the reduction of the share capital not affecting all shareholders equally; or (iii) the increase of the shares' nominal value, except when carried out against the company's reserves or income.

Does the law require any major business decisions to be approved by a special resolution or super-majority (whether at board or shareholder level), or must a minority party protect itself by contract?

There is no requirement for special majorities for business decisions such as major acquisitions or disposals. However, certain formal corporate acts require special shareholder majorities—e.g. in the case of an SL, resolutions for the transformation, merger, de-merger, suppression of pre-emption rights in capital increases, exclusion of any shareholder and the authorisation to directors to compete with the company require the favourable vote of at least two thirds of the voting rights of the company's share capital. The by-laws cannot establish the requirement that decisions are adopted unanimously.

9. Employment laws

Are there local law obligations requiring a "local" party to consult with, or obtain the approval of, employees or employee representatives on a contribution of its business to the joint venture?

Employee rights on business transfers in Spain are governed by the Workers Statute (*Estatuto de los Trabajadores*). Where there is a transfer of a business as a going concern, employees will transfer automatically on their existing terms and conditions of employment to the purchaser of the business. The purchaser will become liable for all employee liabilities both prior and subsequent to the transfer. In addition, the vendor will be jointly liable with the purchaser for the three-year period following the transfer for any outstanding employee liabilities accrued prior to the transfer.

Both the transferor and the transferee have an obligation to inform the employees' legal representatives, whenever a transfer of a business is proposed, a "sufficient time" before the transfer takes place. In addition, if the adoption of employment measures is envisaged because of the transfer (e.g. restructuring), the transferor or the transferee (whoever is planning to adopt any such measures) will also need to consult in good faith with the legal workers representatives in respect of the relevant measures. The employees' representatives cannot, though, prevent the business transfer from taking place.

Are there any material employment laws (compared with the UK) which are likely to affect the ongoing operations of the joint venture?

Employment law in Spain is complex and, despite recent changes, strongly biased towards the employee. There are various levels of legal protection for employees that need to be considered in order to understand the overall position. These include:

- the Workers Statute, which is the basic law setting out the minimum employment conditions which must be adhered to by employers;
- collective bargaining agreements (*convenios colectivos*) negotiated between employers and representatives of the trade unions. These agreements govern working conditions in certain industrial sectors and geographical areas and are mandatory for those employers. Every Spanish sector business is governed by a specific collective bargaining agreement; and
- specific agreements (*convenios*) negotiated between employees and a single, (usually) large-scale employer.

An employee cannot be freely dismissed without a reason. The employee's legal rights upon dismissal are expressly set out by statute. The amount which an employee is entitled to receive as a redundancy payment depends on the length of service, the type of contract, the reason for dismissal and the salary of the individual concerned.

10. Accounts

Is there a requirement on the joint venture company to file accounts with any authority where they are publicly available?

Sociedades anonimas (SA), *sociedades de responsabilidad limitada* (SL) and several other entities must file annual accounts (i.e. balance sheet, profit and loss account and annual report) with the Mercantile Registry. Documents at the Mercantile Registry are publicly available.

11. Dispute resolution

Is there any standard local practice as to form of dispute resolution in relation to joint ventures with foreign investors? Is arbitration in a venue outside that jurisdiction acceptable?

Litigation in Spain has traditionally been slow and costly. A more speedy and common alternative to a judicial action is therefore for parties to agree to submit to arbitration. It is common for joint ventures to refer to foreign arbitration—under the rules of the International Chamber of Commerce (ICC) being a particular favourite.

From September 1, 2004, the newly created mercantile courts are competent to deal with corporate claims. These new specialised courts have so far been functioning efficiently and have enhanced the speed and reduced the length of court procedures and increased the predictability of court decisions in this area.

Is the local jurisdiction a signatory to the 1958 New York Convention on the Recognition and Enforcement of Foreign Arbitral Awards?

Yes. Spain is a party to the New York Convention.

12. Legal documents and formalities

Is there any special form of legal documentation required under local law for establishment of a joint venture company? What are the usual principal documents?

Documentation will include:

- *Shareholders' agreement.* This agreement will be similar to UK/US-style shareholders' agreements. There are limits as to how far the contractual protections can be entrenched in the by-laws of the joint venture vehicle. Shareholders' agreements (or some of their provisions) can be deposited with the Mercantile Registry provided they meet certain requirements—thus having publicity but not necessarily the same enforceability as by-laws; this responds to recent changes in this area and implications are still unclear.

- *Investment/acquisition agreement/warranties.* Traditionally, it was uncommon for specific warranty protection to be agreed between the parties to a joint venture in Spain. Where the assets or a business are being acquired from one of the parties, however, recent trends towards US/UK-style warranties are now starting to prevail. Time and financial limits on warranty claims are negotiated in much the same way as in the UK. However, Spanish courts have not yet been sufficiently tested on the issue of assessing damages awards under warranties and indemnities, and a conservative estimate of recovery should be taken.

- *Deed of incorporation and by-laws.* The incorporation documents of the joint venture vehicle must be executed as a public deed. The role of the Mercantile Registry at which the joint venture company is to be registered may impact on timing and cost. The relevant registrar will qualify all documents submitted for filing at the Registry.

- *Ancillary documentation.* These may include: supply agreements, intellectual property rights and technology licence agreements, agreements for provision of management and services and other documents.

Does the joint venture documentation need to be in the local language and/or governed by the local law?

The shareholders' agreement and joint venture/acquisition agreements do not need to be in Spanish. The deed of incorporation and the by-laws must, however, be in Spanish since they are executed before a Spanish notary and thereafter filed for record with the Mercantile Registry.

The joint venture/shareholders' agreements are usually governed by Spanish law, although this is not compulsory. The incorporation of the company and its corporate existence and governance (in formal terms) will, however, be governed by Spanish law.

Are agreements between shareholders (e.g. as to appointment of directors, conduct of the business of the company or voting majorities required for certain decisions etc.) enforceable under local law? In the event of breach, is specific performance or a similar remedy available, or only damages?

Shareholders' agreements are binding amongst the parties to them. Under the Spanish Civil Code, in the event of breach, the non-defaulting party would be entitled either to require specific performance or, in appropriate circumstances, to terminate the agreement. The non-defaulting party would be entitled to damages. The application of these regulations may be added to, or excluded, by terms in the shareholders' agreement.

Are restrictions relating to (a) transfers of shares and/or (b) minority "veto rights" commonly included in the articles of association or by-laws of the company-or included in a separate shareholders' agreement?

Provisions related to share transfer restrictions and minority voting rights are commonly included in the company's by-laws. However, if restrictions do not comply with corporate regulations (for example, veto rights requiring unanimity to approve certain decisions), they can only be included in the shareholders' agreement. Generally speaking, it is advisable to consult on a case-by-case basis whether such provisions can be included in the by-laws of the company prior to its filing with the Mercantile Registry.

Are there any formalities (e.g. notarisation or registration) which are material and which may affect the timing involved in forming the joint venture?

The degree of formality required by the Spanish notarial system (where documents are formalised as public documents in the presence of a public authenticating officer, i.e. a Spanish notary public) can involve both delay and unforeseen expense in establishing the joint venture structure. In addition, the interventionist role of the Mercantile Registry can have a significant impact on the timing of the deal.

(14) United States

Author: Charles Peet
Freshfields Bruckhaus Deringer, New York

1. General background

Are joint ventures popular as a form of foreign investment into your jurisdiction?

Joint ventures are common in the US. However, they are probably not quite as popular for foreign direct investment as in many other jurisdictions since direct investment and/or 100 per cent ownership by foreign entities is not generally prohibited.

Are there restrictions on foreign participation?

There are no general restrictions on participation by non-US nationals or companies.

What (if any) are the major legal problems which a foreign investor in a joint venture faces in your jurisdiction?

The principal legal problems or risks for foreign investors are probably: US Federal withholding tax; product liability laws (depending upon the business involved); antitrust; and, if the business is in a regulated industry (such as banking, insurance, mining, power generation and transmission, public transportation or securities), the degree of government regulation and supervision in particular industries. The actual legal process of establishing a joint venture in the US is, though, relatively straightforward.

2. Governmental/regulatory approvals

What principal governmental or regulatory approvals are required (excluding competition law) for establishing a joint venture?

Generally, no prior approvals are required for merely establishing a joint venture.

Moreover, if the business of the joint venture is in a regulated industry (such as banking, insurance, mining, power generation and transmission, public transportation, or securities), there can be material governmental or regulatory approvals and supervision involved in engaging in such business.

Are there local antitrust laws which might apply to the formation of the joint venture?

Yes. The formation of a joint venture can implicate a number of US antitrust laws, especially if the joint venture involves collaboration between horizontal competitors. Certain forms of joint ventures also trigger pre-merger notification requirements of the HSR Act. Depending on how it is structured, a joint venture may be subject to ss.1 and 2 of the Sherman Act and s.5 of the Federal Trade

Commission Act, which prohibit anti-competitive agreements and monopolisation, and s.7 of the Clayton Act, which prohibits anti-competitive mergers and acquisitions.

(i) **Joint ventures analysed as mergers**

Where a joint venture involves extensive integration of all aspects of a line of business, it will be analysed under the same standards as if it were a merger between the parties. For example, the formation of a new independent entity in which the joint venture parties will acquire shares, or the acquisition by one party to the joint venture of an interest in the other party, are likely to be treated as mergers. A brief summary of merger controls under the HSR Act appears below:

Filing requirement/trigger	**Timetable for clearance**
(i) Corporate JVs The acquisition of voting securities in the formation of a corporate joint venture is potentially subject to the notification requirements of the HSR Act if (i) the acquiring person will hold voting securities of the JV valued at greater than $59.8m, and (ii) certain size criteria are met. *(ii) Partnership and Limited Liability Company JV's* Formation of a new joint venture partnership or LLC is potentially reportable if (i) any party will hold a controlling interest in the joint venture entity, (ii) that party's interest will be valued at greater than $59.8m, and (iii) certain size criteria are met. Control of a partnership or LLC is defined as having the right to receive 50 per cent or more of the profits of the entity, or 50 per cent or more of the assets of the entity on dissolution.	The US has two federal enforcement bodies, the Antitrust Division of the Department of Justice (DOJ) and the Federal Trade Commission (FTC), both of which are responsible for the review of mergers and JVs. The allocation of cases is, broadly speaking, based on the industry experience and expertise of each agency. Initial Waiting Period: 30 days after filing. Parties may request an "early termination" of this period. Extended Waiting Period: 30 days following compliance by all parties with the government's "second request" for additional information. The JV cannot be implemented until the waiting period has expired or been terminated by the government agency. **Test for clearance** Whether the effect of the JV may be substantially to lessen competition, or to tend to create a monopoly. **Mandatory/voluntary Penalties** Filing is mandatory. Failure to file or implementation before clearance: $11,000 per day, plus the possibility of divestiture.

There are a number of exemptions available under the HSR Act, including an exemption for certain mergers and acquisitions by foreign persons of foreign assets and of voting securities of foreign issuers. Determining whether HSR notification is required for a particular joint venture requires a very fact-specific analysis.

(ii) **Joint ventures analysed as agreements**

Many joint ventures do not involve such complete integration. Instead, they are based on contractual arrangements between the parties. These joint ventures are analysed under s.1 of the Sherman Act, which prohibits unreasonable restraints of trade.

The first inquiry into such joint ventures is whether the collaborative activity is so likely to harm competition and have no significant benefits that it should be condemned per se. Generally, the key question regarding a joint venture among actual or potential competitors is whether it involves an economic integration sufficient to preclude censure as a per se unlawful cartel. Where a joint venture appears likely to lead to efficiency gains, it will be evaluated under the rule of reason test.

Second, where the agreement is not condemned as per se illegal, a determination will be made as to whether it is likely to harm competition by enhancing the ability of the competitors to reduce service, quality or output, or to raise prices, to a greater extent than they could in the absence of the joint venture. The extent of the antitrust analysis required of a joint venture varies depending on several factors, including the venture's structure and purpose, as well as the competitive relationship between the companies forming the joint venture.

Taking an overview, the federal anti-trust agencies recognise that collaborations—including between competitors—are often not only benign but pro-competitive. It will only be in relatively rare cases that they will intervene. Indeed, the Federal Trade Commission and the US Department of Justice have published "Antitrust Guidelines for Collaborations Among Competitors" (2000) to this effect. In particular, these recognise a general "safety zone" when the market shares of the collaboration and its participants collectively account for no more than 20 per cent of each relevant market in which competition may be affected. (The "safety zone" will not apply, though, to arrangements which are per se illegal or where a merger analysis is applicable.)

If the local party is a public company, when might the approval of its shareholders be required under stock exchange or similar rules?

Unless the US public company is contributing a material amount of its own stock into the joint venture, it is highly unlikely that shareholder approval would be necessary for a US public company to enter into a joint venture arrangement.

3. Types of joint venture vehicle

What are the principal types of joint venture vehicle commonly used with foreign investors?

Joint ventures may take the legal form of corporations; limited liability companies ("LLC"); general and limited partnerships; limited liability general and limited partnerships; and purely contractual arrangements.

An LLC is particularly popular as a legal form for joint ventures. It is not a corporation. It is a statutory hybrid between a corporation and a partnership with some elements of each; its equity holders (called members) are not liable for the debts of the LLC (like a corporation but unlike a general partnership). An LLC can elect to be either tax transparent (like a partnership) or taxed like a corporation pursuant to the so-called "check the box" regulations of the US Internal Revenue Service. There is no requirement for the formal separation between ownership and management (as with a corporation). An LLC is generally preferred over a partnership (even a limited partnership) because there is much less risk of owner liability even than in a limited partnership.

A joint venture entity will need to be incorporated or established in a particular US State. The entity formation laws of the State of Delaware (as well as its tax laws) are regarded as particularly flexible and convenient for many international ventures—Delaware law does not require the joint venture's operations (or headquarters) to be based in Delaware.

If a partnership structure is chosen, does this lead to (a) joint and several liability to third parties and/or (b) duties of good faith as between partners?

Generally, yes. However, in certain States (e.g. Delaware) general partnerships and limited partnerships may be established with limited liability (called limited liability general partnerships and limited liability limited partnerships), and an obligation incurred while a partnership is a limited liability partnership is solely the obligation of the partnership and a partner is not personally liable for such an obligation solely by reason of being a partner. In addition, the duties of partners may be restricted or eliminated in the relevant partnership agreement—but subject always to an overriding duty of good faith and fair dealing.

4. Capital structure and funding

Is it common to have different "classes" of shares (e.g. A and B shares) to reflect different initial contributions or financial interests of the parties?

Yes. Different "classes" of shares are not uncommon (including in an LLC).

Is it common to have "preference" shares which give a party a priority on payment of dividends or on a return of capital?

Yes. The use of "preference" shares (generally referred to as "preferred" stock, interests or units) is not uncommon (including in an LLC).

Are "redeemable" shares permitted (i.e. shares that can be repaid and cancelled)?

Yes, particularly in the case of corporations. "Redeemable" shares, or their equivalent, are also possible in the case of an LLC, although less common.

Are "non-voting" shares permitted?

Yes (including in an LLC).

Are there any "thin capitalisation" or similar rules which affect the choice of equity/debt ratio for the capital structure?

Yes. The US has principles under which, for US Federal income tax purposes, an investment may be treated as debt (and distributions treated as deductible interest) or as equity (and distributions treated as non-deductible dividends) if a corporation's debt to equity ratio is too high. A debt to equity ratio of three:one or less is usually acceptable provided the entity can adequately service its debt without the help of related parties.

Another principal "thin capitalisation" concern involves "piercing the corporate veil". "Thin capitalisation" is a factor in determining whether, in exceptional cases, the owners will be liable for the debts of a corporation, limited partnership or a limited liability company.

Is there any capital or similar tax payable in respect of issued share capital?

For corporations, an annual franchise tax in a nominal amount is payable by a corporation usually based upon its stated capital. No such tax applies in the case of an LLC.

Is a separate "contribution agreement" or other formal document (other than formal property transfer agreements) required or usual under the local law to document the contribution of assets to the joint venture?

It is customary where substantial assets are involved. However, it is not generally required by law and can be built into the other operative documents, such as the joint venture agreement, the operating agreement, shareholders' agreement, etc.

Are there any local laws which require an independent valuation of any non-cash assets to be contributed to the joint venture?

No. However, a corporation may not issue shares except for money paid, labour done or personal or real property actually acquired by the corporation. An agreement to provide future services is not sufficient consideration for the issue of fully-paid and non-assessable shares of a corporation. The consideration for shares must be paid in such form and in such manner as the board of directors determines and, absent actual fraud, the judgment of the board of directors as to the value of the consideration is conclusive.

The contribution to an LLC by a member of the LLC may be in cash, property or services rendered, or a promissory note or other obligation to contribute cash or property or to perform services. There are no formalities if contributions are made other than in cash.

Are there exchange control regulations which materially affect the establishment of the joint venture-or the subsequent repatriation of profits or dividends from the joint venture to a foreign party?

There are no foreign exchange control regulations.

5. Tax

Are there any particular tax laws or incentives which significantly affect the establishment of joint ventures in this jurisdiction by a foreign investor?

A US corporation is basically liable as a separate entity to corporate tax on its worldwide income. The standard rate of federal corporation tax is currently 35 per cent. Many States and localities levy income or capital-based taxes.

An LLC may, however, elect to be tax transparent (i.e. taxed as a partnership) pursuant to the so-called "check-the-box" regulations of the US Internal Revenue Service.

Will withholding taxes apply to dividends paid by a joint venture company?

Dividends, interest and royalties paid by a US corporation to foreign persons are generally subject to US withholding tax at a current rate of 30 per cent. This rate may be reduced or eliminated by the application of a double tax treaty.

6. Board and management

Are there local law rules which affect the board or management structure of the joint venture? May a two-tier board be required?

The structure of governance and management will depend entirely in the legal form of the joint venture entity. A corporation must have a board of directors but a two-tier board will never be required legally (although there may be committees of the board of directors). The governance and management structure of other types of joint venture vehicles, such as LLCs and general and limited partnerships, is extremely flexible and dependent on the wishes of the parties.

Are there local law constraints on persons who can be directors or managers of the joint venture (e.g. only local residents or nationals)?
Generally not.

Does a shareholder in a joint venture company owe a duty of good faith (or similar duty) to other shareholders in the way it behaves in relation to the joint venture?
A majority corporate shareholder can owe certain fiduciary duties to a minority shareholder. The duties (including fiduciary duties) of members or managers of an LLC may be restricted or eliminated by contract in the LLC agreement, subject always to an overriding duty of good faith and fair dealing. Partners owe certain fiduciary duties to each other, except that the duties (including fiduciary duties) of partners may be restricted or eliminated by contract in the partnership agreement, subject always to an overriding duty of good faith and fair dealing.

Can you modify the legal duties of directors so that they can expressly take into account the interests of their "appointer" when voting or acting as director, or must they always act objectively in the best interests of the company?
In a corporation, the directors owe a fiduciary duty to the corporation and must act in the best interests of the corporation, unless and until the corporation becomes insolvent, whereupon the directors also owe fiduciary duties to the creditors of the corporation as well.
The duties (including fiduciary duties) of managers of an LLC and of partners may be restricted or eliminated by contract in the LLC or partnership agreement, subject always to an overriding duty of good faith and fair dealing.

7. Transfer of shares

In the case of a joint venture company, can a permanent restriction on transfer of shares be imposed under the local law (e.g. no transfer without the consent of the other shareholder)?
Yes, a permanent restriction on transfer (without consent) is possible. Usually it is included in a shareholders' agreement and not in the organisational documents of the joint venture.

8. Protection for minority shareholders

Are there any statutory rules or remedies which help significantly to protect a minority shareholder in a joint venture company?
Statutory rules provide limited protection in practice for minority corporate shareholders (notably appraisal rights in connection with mergers and some ability to seek judicial relief to compel directors to comply with the fiduciary duties).

Does the law require any major business decisions to be approved by a special resolution or super-majority (whether at board or shareholder level), or must a minority party protect itself by contract?

Not under the general law. The organisational documents can, though, require that certain actions require shareholder approval (either simple majority or super-majority) and/or super-majority approval of the board of directors.

9. Employment laws

Are there local law obligations requiring a "local" party to consult with, or obtain the approval of, employees or employee representatives on a contribution of its business to the joint venture?

No, there are no material employment law obligations of this nature.

Are there any material employment laws (compared with the UK) which are likely to affect the ongoing operations of the joint venture?

No. Employees in the US receive less statutory protection than employees in the UK.

Employment laws are not onerous for an employer. Most private employees in the US may terminate their employees without any statutory breach, as long as termination is not discriminatory based on membership of a protected class (e.g. gender, race, religion, national origin etc.).

10. Accounts

Is there a requirement on the joint venture company to file accounts with any authority where they are publicly available?

No. There is no requirement to file accounts with an authority where they are publicly available—unless the joint venture is a public company.

11. Dispute resolution

Is there any standard local practice as to form of dispute resolution in relation to joint ventures with foreign investors? Is arbitration in a venue outside that jurisdiction acceptable?

There is no standard practice in the US with respect to dispute resolution in joint ventures with foreign investors, although arbitration is one of the most commonly used methods chosen by parties in those circumstances. Certainly, it is acceptable in the US for the joint venture parties to elect to conduct their arbitration outside of the US. Frequently, however, the US party will insist upon arbitration in the US for reasons of convenience. A great deal depends on the relative bargaining power of the foreign investor versus the US party.

Is the local jurisdiction a signatory to the 1958 New York Convention on the Recognition and Enforcement of Foreign Arbitral Awards?

Yes.

12. Legal documents and formalities

Is there any special form of legal documentation required under local law for establishment of a joint venture company? What are the usual principal documents?

No. The form of the documentation will, of course, depend upon the legal structure of the joint venture entity.

- For a corporation, the two basic organisational documents are a Certificate of Incorporation and by-laws.

- For a limited liability company (LLC), the two basic organisational documents are a Certificate of Formation and a Limited Liability Company Agreement.

- For a limited partnership, the two basic organisational documents are a Limited Partnership Agreement and a Certificate of Limited Partnership.

In Delaware, only the Certificates need to be filed publicly. Limited liability partnerships must file a statement of qualification for limited liability. All other documents are private.

There would also customarily be subscription or capital contribution agreements; and there may be shareholders' or joint venture agreements. In the case of an LLC, shareholders' agreement matters can be, and usually are, incorporated into the Limited Liability Company Agreement itself.

Does the joint venture documentation need to be in the local language and/or governed by the local law?

The publicly filed documents probably have to be in English—although the law does not expressly so provide.

Are there any commonly-accepted "standard forms" for joint ventures with foreign investors in your jurisdiction?

No.

Are agreements between shareholders (e.g. as to appointment of directors, conduct of the business of the company or voting majorities required for certain decisions etc.) enforceable under local law? In the event of breach, is specific performance or a similar remedy available, or only damages?

Shareholders' agreements are generally enforceable (subject to enforceability concerns around topics such as non-compete clauses). The same rules that generally apply to the availability of specific performance for contracts would apply to shareholders' agreements.

Are restrictions relating to (a) transfers of shares and/or (b) minority "veto rights" commonly included in the articles of association or by-laws of the company-or included in a separate shareholders' agreement?

Share transfer restrictions are not usually included in publicly filed documents but in the shareholders' agreement or the LLC agreement.

Are there any formalities (e.g. notarisation or registration) which are material and which may affect the timing involved in forming the joint venture?
   Not for private entities.

PART E

PRECEDENTS

1	Information Exchange Agreement
2	Memorandum of Understanding
3	Legal Due Diligence Questionnaire
4	Strategic Alliance Agreement
5	R&D Collaboration Agreement
6	General Partnership Agreement
7	EEIG Formation Agreement
8	Limited Liability Partnership Agreement
9	50:50 Shareholders Agreement (short form)
10	Multi-Party Shareholders' Agreement (long form)
11	Articles of Association (UK Company)
12	Preference Share Rights
13	ITC Model Corporate Joint Venture Agreement (Two-Party)
14	Deed of Adherence
15	JVC Share Sale Agreement
16	Shareholder Funding Agreement
17	Put and Call Option Agreement
18	Support Services Agreement
19	Technology Licence Agreement
20	Trade Mark Licence Agreement
21	Deadlock Resolution Clauses
22	Arbitration and Mediation Clauses

Precedents can provide a useful starting point for the preparation of joint venture documents. Provisions will always have to be tailored to the circumstances of each particular joint venture. The following precedents should be regarded as an initial base only. Independent legal advice should be sought or used before entering into any agreement whether based on the precedent documents contained in this publication or otherwise.

Precedent 1

Information Exchange Agreement

> *The following is a basic Information Exchange Agreement applicable where two parties are agreeing to exchange confidential information prior to the conclusion of any binding joint venture agreement. Other provisions may be appropriate in particular circumstances e.g.: a "standstill" undertaking not to acquire shares in the other party (if its shares are publicly-traded) and/or an undertaking not to solicit or entice away any employee of the other party who has participated in negotiations regarding the transaction or has access to relevant confidential information. An exclusivity undertaking (clause 8) should, of course, only be included if it is appropriate for the particular circumstances.*

THIS AGREEMENT is made on _____200__

BETWEEN:

(1) _____, whose registered office is at _____ (*X*)

(2) _____, whose [principal] office is at _____ (*Y*)

WHEREAS:

(A) X and Y have each requested the other to make available certain confidential information for the purposes of evaluating a possible joint venture between them [in the field of _____] (the "**Transaction**").

(B) The parties, for their mutual benefit, wish to exchange such confidential information on and subject to the terms of this Agreement.

IT IS AGREED AS FOLLOWS:

Definitions

1. In this Agreement, unless the context otherwise requires, the following expressions shall have the following meanings:

"**Approved Representatives**" means those Representatives of either party approved by the other in accordance with the provisions of clause 3.1 (a);

"**Affiliate**" means, in relation to either party, any company within the same Group as such party;

"**Group**" means, in relation to any party, that party and any other company which, at the relevant time, is that party's holding company or subsidiary or a subsidiary of any such holding company;

["**holding company**" and "**subsidiary**" shall bear the meanings as ascribed to them by section 1159 of the Companies Act 2006, as amended from time to time;]

"**Information**" means, in relation to either party, any and all information which is now or at any time after the date of this Agreement is in the possession of that party and is disclosed to the other pursuant to this Agreement (including any information or analysis derived from that Information); [Information shall include, but not be limited to, the information more particularly described in Parts 1 and 2 of the Schedule] [together with the Information described in Parts 3 and 4 of the Schedule which has been disclosed prior to the date of this Agreement];

"**Purpose**" means any discussions and negotiations between the parties concerning or in connection with [the Transaction] [the evaluation or establishment of a business relationship between the parties in the field of _____];

"**Representatives**" means, in relation to either party, its directors, officers, employees and consultants or those of other companies within its Group and its professional advisers consulted in relation to the Purpose;

"**writing**" includes fax, e-mail and other forms of written material transmitted electronically.

Obligations of confidentiality

2. In consideration of the mutual exchange and disclosure of the Information, each party undertakes in relation to the other party's Information:

(a) to maintain the Information confidential and to use the Information exclusively for the Purpose and for no other purpose;

(b) not to copy, reproduce or reduce to writing any part of the Information except as may be reasonably necessary for the Purpose; and

(c) not to use, reproduce, transform or store any of the Information in an externally accessible computer or electronic information retrieval system or transmit it in any form or by any means whatsoever outside its usual place of business.

Confidentiality measures

3.1 To maintain the confidentiality of the disclosed Information each party shall:

(a) not disclose the Information to anyone other than to such Representatives of the receiving party [who have been previously approved in writing by the disclosing party and] who require access to the Information for the Purpose and who are aware of the obligations of confidentiality relating to the Information and are obliged by their contracts of employment or service (or other binding obligations) not to disclose the same to any third party ("**Approved Representatives**");

(b) keep separate all Information (including all information generated by the receiving party which derives from the Information) from all other documents and records of the receiving party;

(c) apply to the Information no lesser security measures and degree of care than those which the receiving party applies to its own confidential information;

(d) keep a written record of (i) any document or other Information received from the other in tangible form, (ii) any copy made of all or part of the Information and (iii) the Approved Representatives of the receiving party having possession or control of the Information or any part of it;

(e) ensure that any document or other records containing Information shall be kept at its premises at _____ and shall not remove or allow to be removed such document or other records from its premises without the prior written approval of the other party; and

(f) ensure that its Representatives do not contact any Representatives (other than the Approved Representatives) of the other party with a view to obtaining information about the other party, its Group or its business.

3.2 If and to the extent that any Information is stored within a computer system or is stored in machine-readable form, the receiving party shall ensure that the Information is secured so that access may not be gained and copies may not be made other than in accordance with this Agreement.

3.3 The receiving party shall enforce the obligations set out in this clause at its own expense and at the request of the disclosing party insofar as any breach of such obligations relates to the unauthorised disclosure of the other party's Information.

Excepted Information

4.1 The undertakings contained in clauses 2 and 3 shall not apply to any Information which the receiving party can prove by documentary evidence:

(a) was, is or has become lawfully available to the public otherwise than through breach of this Agreement; or

(b) was previously known to and at the free disposal of the receiving party (or any of its Affiliates or Representatives); or

(c) was disclosed to the receiving party by a third party having the right to make such disclosure free of any confidentiality obligation.

4.2 If either party is required to disclose any of the Information pursuant to any legal requirement of any country which has jurisdiction over that party [or any regulation or rule of any recognised stock exchange on which that party's shares are listed] [or any governmental or quasi-governmental authority] [or the Panel on Takeovers and Mergers or its equivalent] [or is required to make any announcement concerning the Purpose], it will be entitled to do so *provided that* the party required to make such disclosure shall advise the other party of the circumstances in which the disclosure is [alleged to be] required and [use all reasonable efforts to] agree with the other the extent and timing of such disclosure.

Return of Information

5.1 Each party shall immediately on the written request of the other return all documents and materials containing the Information or, if so required at the request of the other, shall destroy all material containing the Information (including any copies, analysis, memoranda or other notes made by the receiving party, its Representatives or Affiliates) in its possession or under its custody or control and shall in addition [take all reasonable steps to] remove any Information stored within any computer or word processing system whether or not in machine-readable form and (by a director of that party) certify in writing to the other that all such material has been destroyed.

5.2 Notwithstanding completion of the Purpose or return or destruction of the documents and materials containing the Information, each party shall continue to be bound by the undertakings set out in this Agreement.

Disclaimer and warranty

6.1 Each party reserves all rights in its Information and no rights or obligations other than those expressly granted are to be implied from this Agreement. In particular, no licence is granted directly or indirectly under any patent, invention, discovery, copyright or other intellectual property right now or in the future held, made or obtained by either party prior to or after the date of this Agreement whether or not contained in the Information.

6.2 Nothing in this Agreement or its operation shall constitute an obligation on either party to enter into the business relationship contemplated by the Purpose.

6.3 Each party warrants that it is entitled to disclose its Information to the other and to authorise the party to use the same for the Purpose.

Announcements

7. Each party agrees to keep the existence and nature of this Agreement confidential. Any announcement or circular relating to this Agreement or the possible Transaction shall (subject in the same manner as set out in clause 4.2) first be approved by both parties as to its content, form and manner of publication.

Exclusivity

8.1 The parties have agreed to a period of exclusivity in respect of negotiations relating to the Transaction which shall end at [noon] (London time) on _____.

8.2 During this exclusivity period, each party undertakes to ensure that none of its directors or officers will:

(a) directly or indirectly solicit, initiate or participate in discussions or negotiations with any third party in relation to a business combination [or disposal] involving [the whole or any substantial part of] its respective _____ business; or

(b) provide any information to any third party with a view to that third party investigating or entering into such a transaction.

Each party shall also each ensure that none of its employees or professional advisers who are aware of the Transaction do anything referred to in (a) and (b) above.

8.3 The obligations of the parties under this clause 8 will terminate upon the earlier of (i) either party confirming to the other in writing that the negotiations relating to the Transaction have terminated and (ii) [*e.g. insert end of exclusivity period*].

Remedies

9. The parties acknowledge and agree that:

(a) damages would not be an adequate remedy for any breach of the provisions of this Agreement;

(b) the disclosing party shall be entitled to the remedies of injunction, specific performance and other equitable relief for any threatened or actual breach of the provisions of this Agreement; and

(c) no proof of special damages shall be necessary for the enforcement of this Agreement.

Waiver

10.1 No waiver by a party of a failure or failures by the other party to perform any provision of this Agreement shall operate or be construed as a waiver in respect of any other or further failure whether of a like or different character.

10.2 The rights, powers and remedies provided in this Agreement are cumulative and not exclusive of any rights, powers or remedies provided by law.

Assignment

11. Neither of the parties may assign any of its rights or obligations under this Agreement in whole or in part.

Entire agreement

12. This Agreement constitutes the whole agreement and understanding between the parties with respect to the subject matter of this Agreement and supersedes all prior discussions between the parties and/or their Representatives and all representations, warranties or undertakings with respect to the subject matter of this Agreement [except as expressly incorporated in this Agreement].

Governing law

13.1 This Agreement shall be governed by [English law].

13.2 Each party submits to the [non-]exclusive jurisdiction of the courts of [England] and waives any objection to proceedings in such court on the grounds of venue or on the grounds that the proceedings have been brought in an inconvenient forum.

AS WITNESS this Agreement has been executed by the duly authorised representatives of the parties.

SCHEDULE

Part 1—X's Information
Part 2—Y's Information
[Part 3—X's previously disclosed Information]
[Part 4—Y's previously disclosed Information]

Signed by _____   }
for and on behalf of **X**   }

Signed by _____   }
for and on behalf of **Y**   }

Precedent 2

Memorandum of Understanding

> *This precedent is a framework only for a memorandum of understanding for a joint venture where each party will contribute a business and/or subsidiaries. It contemplates the formation of a joint venture company. It is likely to need substantial adaptation to fit the circumstances of the particular transaction.*
>
> *Consider carefully the governing law for the Memorandum. Unlike English law, an agreement to negotiate in good faith may be enforceable or give rise to liability in many civil law jurisdictions (e.g. France, Italy, the Netherlands and Spain).*

_____ ("*A*") and _____ ("*B*") wish to set out in this Memorandum the principles of a proposed joint venture in the field of _____. Each party has various interests in the field [in the _____ region.] The parties wish to establish a 50/50 joint venture to consolidate their interests in the field so as to enable them to develop the business more effectively [and to take advantage of the opportunities arising in the field [throughout the _____ region.]

The parties believe that the joint venture will be in their mutual best interests. They recognise that the various arrangements regarding their existing interests will need careful review but each will endeavour in good faith to agree the detailed terms of the joint venture, on the basis of the principles set out in this Memorandum, and to take all necessary actions in order successfully to establish the joint venture.

Joint venture company

1. The parties intend to establish a 50/50 joint venture company for [the manufacture and sale of _____ as more particularly described in Annex 1 (the "Products")].

2. The preferred intention of the parties is to create a new jointly-owned company into which their existing interests would be transferred. The parties will nevertheless consider appropriate alternative structures if that becomes necessary or desirable on the grounds of tax and cost efficiency.

3. The name of the joint venture will be '_____' or such other name as the parties shall agree.

4. [The headquarters of the joint venture company will be based in _____.]

Activities of the joint venture

5. [The territory of the joint venture will be _____ as per the [plan][list] set out as Annex 2 (the "**Territory**").]

6. The business of the joint venture will be the development, manufacture and sale [in the Territory] of [the Products]. The business may include such other technologies and products as the parties may subsequently agree.

7. The parties shall draw up and approve an initial business plan [to be attached to the joint venture agreement]. The business plan will be reviewed by the board of the joint venture company (the "**Board**") at regular intervals and updated annually.

Interests to be vested in the joint venture

8. The parties will contribute to the joint venture all their relevant interests [in the Territory]. These include the following existing interests: _____ .

9. Pending establishment of the joint venture, each party shall ensure that its business and interests to be vested in the joint venture are carried on in the ordinary and usual course. No new venture or material transaction likely to have a material effect on the joint venture shall be entered into by either party (or any member of their respective groups) without prior consultation between the parties.

Technology

10. Each party will make available to the joint venture the benefit of all its existing technology relating to the Products. The parties will discuss the most appropriate structure and arrangements by which this is to be achieved. These arrangements will include detailed terms covering:

(a) [royalty or other fair and reasonable commercial terms to be agreed;]

(b) availability of improvements and new technology developed or acquired by either party specifically relating to the Products;

(c) improvements and/or new technology developed by the joint venture to be made available (on commercial terms) to A and B for use outside the Territory;

(d) appropriate controls to prevent use of the technology by third parties outside the joint venture;

(e) A's trade marks and name to be licensed to the joint venture.

Valuation

11. Valuation negotiations in respect of their respective contributions to the joint venture will be finalised by the parties before signature of the joint venture agreements. A and B will use all reasonable efforts to agree an appropriate valuation process and methodology [in accordance with the outline principles set out in Annex 3]. [The intention is that an independent valuer should be jointly appointed by the parties to undertake the valuation exercise (supervising, if necessary, appropriate specialist valuers in particular areas). The independent valuer shall have regard to valuation principles agreed between the parties and to submissions and materials provided by them.]

12. Each party will make available to the other party [(and the valuer)] all such information (including financial information) regarding the interests to be vested in the joint venture as the other party [(or the valuer)] may reasonably request in order to facilitate the valuation process.

13. If there is a material difference in the valuations of the respective contributions of the parties, the parties will use all reasonable efforts to agree an appropriate cash payment or alternative cost-efficient arrangement for bridging any difference in order to maintain the 50/50 equity relationship within the joint venture.

14. The parties agree that the definitive legal agreements will set out appropriate warranties and indemnities (subject to limits and qualifications to be agreed) in relation to the interests being contributed by each party. [There will be appropriate provisions for compensation or value adjustment arising from any material change in the information provided or representations made by each party for valuation purposes.]

Capital and funding

15. Equity capital of the joint venture shall be held 50/50 by the two parties.

16. It is the intention of the parties that the joint venture should be self-financing and should obtain additional funds from third parties without recourse to its shareholders. Neither party shall be obliged to contribute further funds. Each party nevertheless acknowledges its intention to support the business of the joint venture in accordance with the current business plan, and [will] provide such guarantees and undertakings as may reasonably be required to enable the joint venture to obtain funds. Any new equity capital shall (unless otherwise agreed) be raised on a 50:50 basis.

Board and management

17. Overall management and supervision of the joint venture shall be the responsibility of the Board. Each party shall appoint an equal number of directors to the Board and have equal voting rights. The chairman of the Board shall not have a casting vote. A quorum shall require at least one director appointed by each party.

18. The initial appointments to the Board shall be:

A: _____ B: _____

_____ _____

_____ _____

19. The first chairman of the Board shall be _____ with the first deputy chairman being _____. [The chairmanship shall rotate between the two parties on a _____ yearly basis.]

20. The initial senior management appointments shall be:

Chief Executive: _____;

Chief Financial Officer: _____;

Chief Operating Officer: _____.

[Successor appointments will be made on the basis of "the person best qualified for the position" regardless of whether the person is currently employed by the joint venture, one of the parties or a third party. Appointments (and removals) of senior management shall be a matter for the parties.]

21. Certain key decisions affecting the joint venture shall be reserved for mutual agreement between A and B as shareholders [(or require unanimity between their respective appointees on the Board)]. [Final identification of these matters will be for the definitive agreement but they are likely to include:

— material change in scope or nature of the business;

— approval of the annual budget;

— making (or terminating) any material joint venture, collaboration or technology licence;

- any material contract or transaction outside the ordinary course of business;
- major asset or business acquisitions/disposals;
- appointment/removal of the Chief Executive [and other senior management];
- capital expenditure in excess of £_____;
- borrowings exceeding an aggregate level of £_____;
- changes in dividend policy;
- material dealings between the joint venture and the [A] or [B] groups;
- appointment/removal of the auditors.]

Shareholders' Agreement

22. The Shareholders' Agreement shall also include appropriate provisions in respect of the following matters:

(a) dividend policy (the joint venture shall adopt a maximum distribution policy subject to its internal operation, cash flow and funding requirements and to applicable laws and regulations);

(b) the auditors of the joint venture (who shall be _____);

(c) the financial year of the joint venture (which shall be _____);

(d) monthly management accounts to be produced in respect of the operations of the joint venture and made available to the Board and the shareholders (together with such additional financial information as they may from time to time require);

(e) each party to have pre-emption rights if the other party wishes to transfer its shares in the joint venture (which, save for intra-group transfers, shall not be permitted for an initial period of _____ years);

(f) appropriate undertakings to be given by the parties not to compete with the business of the joint venture [and clarifying the territorial scope of the joint venture business (including in relation to exports outside the territory of the joint venture)];

(g) [deadlock and] dispute resolution.

Third party approvals

23. The parties will use all reasonable efforts to identify [and obtain] as soon as possible any third party consents or approvals which may be required, including (i) consents of relevant regulatory authorities, (ii) any tax clearances reasonably required by either party in relation to the proposed joint venture structure and (iii) consents of [other joint venture partners] [specific major customers].

24. Material third party consents or approvals will be a pre-condition of completing the joint venture. Each party will endeavour to obtain them as speedily as possible and each will co-operate with the other for this purpose.

[**25.** The arrangements set out in this Memorandum of Understanding are subject to the approval of the boards of directors of A and B. Such approvals will be sought as soon as practicable [with a view to such approvals being obtained by no later than _____.]]

Confidentiality and announcements

26. [The Confidentiality Agreement dated _____ shall continue in force.] [Each of the parties shall keep confidential and shall not disclose to any other person, nor use for any purpose except the purposes of the joint venture, any information obtained from the other party as a result of negotiating, entering into or implementing the joint venture other than information which:

(a)   is required to be disclosed by operation of law or any stock exchange regulations or any binding judgment or order, or any requirement of a competent authority;

(b)   is reasonably required to be disclosed in confidence to a party's professional advisers for use in connection with the joint venture and/or matters contemplated herein;

(c)   is or becomes within the public domain (otherwise than through the default of the recipient party).]

27. No public announcement or press release in connection with the subject matter of this Memorandum of Understanding shall be made or issued by or on behalf of either party without the prior written approval of the other, except such as may be required by law or by any stock exchange or by any governmental authority.

[Governing law

28. This Memorandum of Understanding shall be governed by English law.]

Procedure

29. Following signature of this Memorandum of Understanding, the parties will proceed as rapidly as possible with the due diligence and valuation process and the preparation and negotiation of the legally definitive agreements. [An outline timetable is set out in Annex 4.]

Status

30. This Memorandum of Understanding represents the good faith intentions of the parties to proceed with the proposed joint venture but is not legally binding and creates no legal obligations on either party (save for clauses [26], [27] and [28].) Its sole purpose is to set out the principles on which the parties intend in good faith to negotiate legally definitive agreements.

Dated:………………………

Signed:

for A   for B

_____   _____

ANNEX 1: DESCRIPTION OF THE [PRODUCTS] [BUSINESS]

ANNEX 2: THE TERRITORY

[ANNEX 3: OUTLINE VALUATION PRINCIPLES]

[ANNEX 4: OUTLINE TIMETABLE]

Action **Target Date**

1. Valuation process agreed.
2. Structure of JV company (including tax issues) agreed.
3. Business plan agreed.
4. Drafts of definitive legal agreements (Asset Transfer Agreements, Shareholders' Agreement, Articles of Association, Technology Licence Agreement).
5. Third party approvals identified and sought.
6. Valuation process completed and any valuation differences resolved.
7. Definitive legal agreements negotiated and ready for signature.

Precedent 3

Legal Due Diligence Questionnaire

> *This is a relatively "high level" Questionnaire appropriate where a company/business is being contributed by a party to the joint venture. It should be adapted if a more limited set of assets is being contributed. This Questionnaire relates to "legal" due diligence and should be co-ordinated with other areas of due diligence being carried out. In particular, information regarding accounts, financial and tax matters will usually be the subject of separate investigations.*

QUESTIONNAIRE

- References to "the *Business*" mean the activities to be contributed to the joint venture. References to "the *Companies*" mean the companies carrying on the Business. "*JV*" means the joint venture proposed to be established between the parties.

- Please supply information in response to this Questionnaire in as much detail as possible. Where necessary, only *"material"* matters should be disclosed: but please specify the level of materiality adopted for this purpose. *"Material"* should be judged by an appropriate monetary amount or the possible effect of the contract **or** item in question on the Business.

1. Corporate

1.1 Corporate details of the Companies (Name, office, share capital, Chamber of Commerce No, Statutes etc.).

1.2 A structure chart of the Companies.

1.3 Details of principal corporate transactions over the last five years affecting the Companies, including: mergers, joint ventures, corporate reorganisations, company or business acquisitions and disposals.

1.4 Details of any branches or places of business outside [*country*] of the Companies.

1.5 Details of any charges, encumbrances, options or pre-emption rights over the shares of any of the Companies.

2. Licences

2.1 List any licences, permits, accreditations or regulatory approvals which are material to the carrying on of the Business.

2.2 Give details of any alleged violations of the terms of any such licences or approvals in the last five years including details of any investigations by licensing or regulatory bodies.

2.3 Are any such licences or approvals subject to termination, or a need for consent, on a change of control of the Companies or the Business?

3. Employees

3.1 Details (by number, grade or other appropriate category) of the employees engaged in the Business.

3.2 Details of material agreements affecting the relationship between the Companies and the employees including: collective bargaining or similar agreements with unions; standard employment contracts currently used in the Business; staff handbooks.

3.3 Details of service contracts (including consultancy contracts) of all senior executives or managers earning in excess of [£_____] per annum.

3.4 Details of all relevant employee benefit schemes or arrangements, including those relating to:

— pension schemes

— profit sharing

— stock options

— savings plans

— bonus schemes

— life/medical insurance

— loans (or subsidies) to employees.

Supply copies of latest annual reports or accounts of any such plans. Provide latest actuarial valuations of any pension schemes. Copies of all documents currently governing any pension scheme including explanatory booklets.

3.5 Give details of any changes in pension contribution rates currently proposed or recommended.

3.6 Details of any charges, investigations, proceedings or orders against any of the Companies during the last three years relating to labour standards or employment laws, including any material claims asserted by unions or employees.

3.7 Give details of all material labour disputes relating to the Business during the last five years.

3.8 Give details of any loans, transfers of assets or similar arrangements within the last five years between the Companies and any directors of those Companies or persons "connected" with them.

4. Material contracts

4.1 Give details of all material contracts relating to the Business where the establishment of the JV will or may trigger a right for another party to the contract to terminate or otherwise alter the terms (i.e. change of control provisions/prohibition against assignment).

4.2 List (or provide copies of) all other material contracts relating to the Business including:

— joint ventures, joint R&D, distributor, agency, franchise or similar contracts;

- contracts outside the ordinary and usual course of business;
- contracts or understandings purporting to limit the freedom of any of the Companies to compete in any particular line of business or in any particular geographic area;
- any contracts having a value/or involving expenditure in excess of £ _____;
- contracts which are likely to be "loss-making";
- long-term contracts (over [3] years) or those which contain material obligations or restrictions of an exceptional or unusual nature;
- contracts granting any options or similar rights over any assets of the Business;
- outstanding tenders or bids which (if accepted) would fall in any of the above categories;
- any other contract or arrangement which has, or is likely to have, a material effect on the Business.

4.3 List of all guarantees and other credit support obligations in favour of the Companies—or given by any of the Companies.

4.4 Details of any material defaults (or alleged defaults) under contracts on the part of the Company—or by any other party to the contract.

4.5 Details of standard terms of business with principal customers.

5. Borrowings

5.1 List of all agreements evidencing borrowings and credit facilities of the Companies in excess of £_____ (and indicate whether secured or unsecured). Details of any finance leases relating to plant and equipment.

5.2 Details of any alleged event of default (or event which by notice or lapse of time may become an event of default) or breach of covenant in respect of any such borrowings.

6. Intra-group arrangements

6.1 Details of existing intra-group agreements or arrangements between (i) the Business and (ii) any other companies or parts of the retained business of [the relevant party] not included in the Business, including:

- management or administrative services arrangements
- "shared" services arrangements (e.g. computer systems or services)
- site support facilities relating to properties
- intellectual property or licensing arrangements
- financing arrangements
- marketing or sales arrangements
- insurance.

6.2 Details of intra-group arrangements (of the kind set out in 6.1) which will need to be established to enable the JV to carry on the Business as previously carried on.

7. Intellectual property

7.1 Provide details of intellectual property rights (*IPR*) worldwide of the Business in the form of appropriate schedules covering:

— patents (including applications)

— trade marks (including applications)

— registered designs

— analogous rights

Such details to include: a brief summary; countries covered by registrations; and expiry date of registrations.

7.2 Give an outline summary of any material areas of proprietary but unpatented know-how developed by the Business. Do the Companies seek patents wherever possible or rely on maintaining confidentiality of trade secrets and know-how?

7.3 List all significant intellectual property licences (including material software licences) affecting the Business—distinguishing between (a) licences to the Business and (b) licences out to third parties.

7.4 Distinguish, if applicable, between (a) IPR which is used predominantly in the Business and (b) IPR which is used by the Business but is also used by remaining parts of the Group which will not form part of the JV.

7.5 Give details of any significant claims (or threatened claims) [in the last five years] relating to intellectual property, including (a) claims against the Business by third parties alleging infringement and (b) claims by the Companies against third parties.

7.6 Give details of any IPR (including licences of IPR/computer software) which may be "lost" to the Business, or the terms of use by the Business adversely affected, on a change of control or establishment of the JV.

8. Real property

8.1 List all properties owned or occupied for the purpose of the Business, including details of: interest held (freehold, lease etc); rent payable; rent review terms; any licences or sub-leases to third parties; any contracts for the acquisition of property.

8.2 Details of all mortgages, security interests or material restrictions affecting any of the properties used for the purpose of the Business.

8.3 Have the Companies complied in all material respects with the terms of any applicable leases, planning conditions, orders or laws relating to the properties? Give details of any material claims.

8.4 Details of continuing liabilities (if any) of any of the Companies for lease or other covenants relating to properties no longer occupied by the Companies.

9. Environmental

9.1 Details of any breach (or alleged breach) of any law, code, regulation, licence or order affecting the Business concerning health, safety, pollution or protection of the environment.

9.2 Details of all environmental surveys, audits or similar reports, in the last five years, relating to any property used for the purpose of the Business.

9.3 Details of any material spill, leakage, emission or discharge of pollutants, contaminants or hazardous or toxic substances in the last five years at any of the properties owned or occupied by the Company.

10. Litigation and claims

10.1 Details of all litigation, arbitration or government proceedings (current or pending) involving an amount in excess of £_____ to which any of the Companies is a party or otherwise relating to the Business.

10.2 If and to the extent not previously covered under this Questionnaire, provide details of all material claims during the last five years relating to the Business alleging:

— infringement of patent or other intellectual property rights;

— product liability;

— infringement of environmental laws;

— breach of contract or inadequacy of contract performance by the Company.

Where a claim is purely monetary (i.e. no other material effect upon the business) the same threshold as in 10.1 should apply.

10.3 Are any facts or circumstances known to exist which are likely to lead to any such litigation or claim?

10.4 Provide a brief summary of the policy of the Business in respect of product warranty claims, including: "standard" warranties given; insurance; claims history over last five years; any exceptional "ex gratia" payments by the Companies to meet claims.

11. Insurances

11.1 List of all insurance policies relating to the Business. Identify which of these insurance policies will terminate on the establishment of the joint venture.

11.2 List any claims [in excess of £_____] which (i) have been made under the insurance policies in relation to the Business during the last [3] years or (ii) are still outstanding.

Precedent 4

Strategic Alliance Agreement

> *There is no standard model for a "strategic alliance". This precedent is an example of a contractual framework for a close working relationship between two parties primarily operating in different countries and/or fields. It is "strategic" because of the importance of the relationship to the future strategic direction of the parties. It contemplates a number of different features including (i) the establishment of an alliance board or committee responsible for overall direction of the alliance; (ii) specific technical assistance by one party to the other; (iii) a framework for joint research projects; (iv) a minority equity investment by one party in the other (in some cases there may be mutual cross-equity investment).*
>
> *A "strategic alliance" will rarely incorporate all these elements. Each agreement must be tailored to the circumstances of the particular alliance. It will generally be a "business" document stressing principles on which the relationship is to be based rather than comprise fine legal detail. The important legal protections will relate particularly to (i) IPR, (ii) termination rights and (iii) any funding commitments.*

THIS AGREEMENT is made on _____

BETWEEN:

(1) _____ whose registered office is at _____ ("**ABC**")

(2) _____ whose registered office is at _____ ("**XYZ**")

WHEREAS:

(A) ABC is primarily based in _____ and has particular technical expertise in the field of _____.

(B) XYZ is primarily based in _____ and is engaged principally in the field of _____. Given the increasing convergence of _____ technology with technologies in related fields, XYZ wishes to broaden its technological and product base with the benefit of ABC's expertise.

(C) Both parties believe that there are potentially many synergies and mutual benefits to be achieved by working together and have agreed to establish a strategic alliance on the terms of this Agreement.

IT IS AGREED AS FOLLOWS:

Scope and objectives

1. The parties agree to establish an alliance (the "**Alliance**") whose objectives are:

(a) to make ABC's technical expertise in the field of _____ available to XYZ in order to develop its business in _____;

(b) to explore the various synergies which may be obtained by working together, particularly in the field of _____;

(c) to undertake particular joint research projects as may be agreed from time to time;

(d) to consider the joint commercial exploitation of any particular new technologies or products resulting from their joint research;

(e) to establish ABC as the preferred [supplier to] [distributor for] XYZ in respect of _____ products;

(f) generally, to explore commercial arrangements between them which will be for the mutual benefit of both parties as strategic partners.

Alliance Board

2.1 The parties shall establish an Alliance Board responsible for overall direction, co-ordination, organisation and implementation of the Alliance. Its role will include:

(a) developing and maintaining strategic and operational direction of the Alliance;

(b) approving particular projects to be carried out through the Alliance and any funding commitments of the parties for these approved projects;

(c) developing targets and milestones in order that progress of the Alliance can be measured;

(d) ensuring that communications between the parties are maintained actively and in a co-ordinated manner;

(e) providing a forum in which any problems can be addressed constructively and resolved.

2.2 Each party shall appoint three representatives to be members of the Alliance Board (and shall consult with the other party before any such appointment). The first members of the Alliance Board shall be: _____, _____, _____, _____, _____ and _____. Each member shall have one vote. [_____ shall be the initial chairman (but shall not have any casting vote).]

2.3 The Alliance Board shall meet regularly (either telephonically, by video conference or in person) and, unless otherwise agreed, not less than quarterly during the initial period of the Alliance. Unless otherwise agreed, the venue (if the meeting is physical) shall alternate between the parties [and a representative of the "host" party shall act as chairman (but with no casting vote)].

2.4 Communication on a regular basis by e-mail, telephone and/or video-conference shall be encouraged between members of the Alliance Board.

2.5 Any decision made by the Alliance Board in relation to the Alliance (provided that it is supported by a majority of the members of the Alliance Board appointed by each party) shall be binding and carried into effect by the parties.

Technical assistance

3.1 ABC has particular technical expertise in the field of _____. In the light of technical developments and convergence of technologies, XYZ wishes to access ABC's technical expertise. The parties have accordingly agreed to enter into the

Technical Assistance Agreement [in the agreed form]. [*See Precedent 17 (Technology Licence Agreement)*.]

3.2 The parties will actively explore whether there are other areas where technical exchange may be beneficial (whether through joint research projects under clause 4 or otherwise).

Joint projects

4.1 A particular objective of the Alliance is to identify appropriate projects for joint research or other collaboration, particularly in the field of _____ [and other areas where the respective technologies of the parties potentially converge]. These projects will be aimed at technology improvements and developments where the results will be of benefit to each party. These projects may lead, in appropriate cases, to arrangements for joint exploitation.

4.2 A Project Committee will be established. The members will be appointed by the Alliance Board from time to time. The initial members will be _____, _____ , _____ and _____. The initial chairman will be _____.

4.3 The Project Committee's functions shall (unless otherwise decided by the Alliance Board) include: (i) establishing specific proposals for research or collaborative projects which shall (where funding in excess of £_____ is required) be submitted to the Alliance Board for approval; (ii) assignment of financial resources and personnel to approved research projects (including appointment of project team leaders); (iii) approval of specific research plans including operational objectives; (iv) developing specific performance criteria and targets; and (v) review and evaluation of progress of specific research projects. Decisions of the Project Committee shall be taken, if possible, by unanimous vote. If no decision is reached, the matter shall be put to the Alliance Board for final decision.

4.4 [It is contemplated that, for each approved project, the parties through the Project Committee will identify one of the parties to be the project leader responsible for organising and leading the project under an individual project manager appointed by that party.]

4.5 The parties agree that a particular area of joint research through the Alliance will be _____. The particular arrangements for that research shall be determined by the Project Committee but the parties agree in principle that:

(a) the project leader shall be [XYZ];

(b) each party shall make available its background IPR relating to _____;

(c) nothing shall affect the ownership by either party of its intellectual property rights existing prior to the commencement of the research project;

(d) each party will make available, at its own site or (if agreed) by cross-exchange of staff, appropriate research personnel;

(e) each party shall be entitled to use in its business all know-how and other rights derived from the research collaboration;

(f) costs shall be shared equally (to be monitored and approved in a manner determined by the Project Committee).

4.6 A particular Project Agreement shall be entered into, where considered appropriate, in relation to a joint research or other collaborative project to be funded by the parties. A Project Agreement shall be approved by the Project

Committee and shall be based (as far as practicable) on [the principles set out in Schedule _____] [the agreed form]. [*See Precedent 5 (R&D Collaboration Agreement)*.]

4.7 After approval of the research plans for particular projects by the Project Committee, the respective project teams shall co-ordinate and implement all day-to-day activities of the parties. The project teams shall work openly and co-operatively and shall meet periodically, as the project manager determines to be necessary, to co-ordinate their activities. Each party shall, through the project manager, periodically submit to the Project Committee progress reports in relation to its activities under each joint research project.

Preferred supplier/distributor

5. It is anticipated that XYZ's business, if it develops in the field of _____ , will create a need for _____ [*products*]. Any decision to develop that business shall be solely for XYZ. If XYZ does develop this business, it is agreed that:

(a) ABC shall become a "preferred supplier" to XYZ for _____ [*products*] subject to price, specification, quality and delivery times being agreed and no less favourable than other potential comparable suppliers;

(b) if XYZ decides to distribute _____ [*products*] internationally, the parties shall negotiate in good faith for the appointment of ABC as exclusive distributor in [territories] for an initial period of _____ years (renewable by agreement) on commercial terms to be agreed.

Secondments and personnel

6.1 The parties recognise that secondments of staff (and other sharing of personnel resources and know-how) are likely to be an appropriate means to develop the Alliance. The parties will actively develop a programme for staff secondments. The terms of any such secondments shall be agreed between the parties (if necessary through the Alliance Board).

6.2 Any employees of either ABC or XYZ who are seconded or sent to visit the premises of the other party under this Agreement shall remain employed by the party sending them. That party shall (i) be responsible for ensuring that its employees comply with all security and site regulations applicable at those premises and (ii) indemnify the other party against any property damage or any personal injury caused by the negligent act or omission of any such employee at the other party's premises.

6.3 During the period of the Alliance, neither party (nor any member of its group) shall entice away for employment any individual who was an employee of the other party (engaged in a senior management or technical role) at any time within the previous [12 months].

Equity investment

7.1 Having regard to the strategic relationship being established between the parties by this Agreement, it is agreed that ABC will become an equity investor in XYZ. Accordingly:

(a) XYZ warrants to ABC in the form of the warranties set out in Schedule _____ ; [*warranties relating to* e.g.: *a good standing; accounts/financial information provided; regulatory compliance; no material litigation*]

(b) ABC shall subscribe for ———— ordinary shares of ———— each in the capital of XYZ for a total subscription price of ————, payable for value in cash on ———— ————;

(c) XYZ shall issue ———— ordinary shares to ABC credited as fully paid (being equal to ————% of the total issued ordinary share capital of XYZ).

7.2 For so long as ABC holds not less than ————% of the issued ordinary share capital of XYZ:

(a) ABC shall be entitled to appoint (and/or remove) one director of the board of directors of XYZ;

(b) XYZ shall not issue any equity shares in the capital of XYZ without the prior consent of ABC [unless it is an offer of new shares in cash made to all existing shareholders (including ABC) pro rata to their shareholdings];

(c) no decision to proceed with any of the matters specified below (whether by the shareholders or board of directors of XYZ or any subsidiary thereof or any of their respective officers or managers) shall be made without the prior written consent of ABC, namely:

(i) any material change in the nature or scope of the business of XYZ;
(ii) any proposal that XYZ be wound-up, liquidated or dissolved;
(iii) the transfer, assignment or sale by XYZ of its ———— business or any substantial part thereof;
(iv) any proposal that XYZ should enter into any merger, acquisition, joint venture or partnership with (or issue shares to) a Competitor or an associated party of a Competitor;
(v) any proposal that XYZ acquire any shares in a Competitor or an associated party of a Competitor.

For this purpose: a "**Competitor**" means a company, person or firm whose [principal business is in the ———— industry]; and "**associated party**" means, in relation to a Competitor, a person in which that Competitor directly or indirectly owns [15%] or more of the voting interests or securities of any class of such person;

(d) [if an offer is made by any third party for the whole or a majority of the issued share capital of XYZ, XYZ shall notify ABC promptly and shall (so far as it is able) give ABC all relevant information and an opportunity within a reasonable time to make an offer to acquire all the issued share capital not held by ABC.]

7.3 ABC undertakes that [, for a period of ————,] it will not acquire any further shares in XYZ except through an offering of new shares by XYZ in accordance with clause 7.2(b). This undertaking shall terminate automatically if an offer is made by any third party to acquire the issued share capital of XYZ or a Controlling Interest (as defined in clause 12.4) in XYZ.

Confidentiality and announcements

8.1 Each party shall use all reasonable efforts to keep confidential all commercial and technical information which it may acquire in relation to the customers, business or affairs of the other party (including any information acquired pursuant to clauses 3 and 4). No party shall use or disclose any such information except with prior consent of the other party. This restriction shall not apply to any information:

(a) which is publicly available or becomes publicly available through no default of the party wishing to use or disclose the information;

(b) which that party can demonstrate was already in its possession or was independently developed by that party;

(c) which is obtained from a third party which did not acquire or hold the information under an obligation of confidentiality; or

(d) to the extent that it is required to be disclosed by law or by the rules of any recognised stock exchange or regulatory body.

8.2 Clause 8.1 shall not restrict or prevent a party from using, in the course of its business, any know-how or technical information acquired pursuant to the arrangements contemplated by clauses 3 and 4 of this Agreement provided that (i) such use shall not include sub-licensing, (ii) appropriate measures to ensure confidentiality shall be maintained and (iii) no disclosure to third parties shall take place except as permitted by clause 8.1. This shall be subject to the provisions of the Technical Assistance Agreement or any specific Project Agreement which (in the event of any conflict) shall prevail over this clause 8 in respect of the use of information disclosed pursuant to those Agreements.

8.3 Each party shall use all reasonable efforts to ensure that its employees and agents and any affiliates (including its employees and agents) observe these confidentiality obligations.

8.4 No announcement in connection with the Alliance or this Agreement shall be made by either party without the prior approval of the other party (such approval not to be unreasonably withheld or delayed) except as may be required by law or by any stock exchange or by any governmental authority.

8.5 The provisions of this clause 8 shall survive any termination of this Agreement.

Non-compete

9. [It is the intention of the parties to work closely and collaboratively with each other in developing the Alliance. Therefore, during the period of the Alliance:

(a) ABC shall not enter into a similar alliance with any other party with operations in the field of _____ or (directly or indirectly) carry on business [in the field of _____] in a manner competitive with XYZ in _____ [*territory*];

(b) XYZ shall not enter into a similar alliance with any other party with operations in the field of _____ or (directly or indirectly) carry on business [in the field of _____] in a manner competitive with ABC in _____ [*territory*].]

Indemnity

10.1 Neither party shall have any responsibility for any liabilities arising or incurred to third parties in the course of the other party's business. Each party (the "**indemnifying party**") shall at all times indemnify the other party against all or any liabilities, claims or damages (including legal or other professional expenses reasonably incurred in connection with any claim) incurred by that other party in respect of products or services supplied by the indemnifying party or other activities carried on by that party in the course of its business.

10.2 During the course of this Agreement, it is contemplated that the parties (and their employees and representatives) may provide recommendations and advice to each other in many areas outside the scope of any specific Project Agreement and/ or the Technical Assistance Agreement as part of the relationship between the parties. It is acknowledged by both parties that any such recommendations and advice are given freely and without any warranties or liability. Neither party shall have any claim, liability or cause of action against the other party in respect of any such recommendation or advice.

10.3 Clauses 10.1 and 10.2 are subject to any specific terms regarding liability agreed in the Technical Assistance Agreement and/or any specific Project Agreement.

No partnership

11.1 The relationship between the parties is not intended to create a legal partnership.

11.2 Neither party shall have any authority to commit or bind the other party [except in accordance with principles and procedures agreed through the Alliance Board].

Duration and termination

12.1 The Alliance shall commence on the date hereof. It shall continue indefinitely subject to termination in accordance with this clause 12. The parties shall, nevertheless, keep the Alliance under regular review and not less than [every two years].

12.2 The Alliance may be terminated by agreement between the parties at any time.

12.3 Either party may give not less than [three months'] written notice at any time to terminate the Alliance, provided that no such notice shall be given prior to _____ [*e.g. two years after commencement*].

12.4 Either party shall have a right to terminate the Alliance if any of the following shall occur in relation to the other party (the "**Defaulting Party**"):

(a) if the Defaulting Party commits a material breach of this Agreement (or any agreement entered into pursuant to this Agreement) and fails to remedy the breach within [45] days after being given notice by the other party to do so (and such notice specifies that the notifying party intends to exercise its rights under this clause); or

(b) if the Defaulting Party goes into liquidation (whether compulsory or voluntary) except for the purposes of a *bona fide* reconstruction with the consent of the other party (such consent not to be unreasonably withheld) or if a petition is presented or an order is made for the appointment of an administrator, receiver, manager or similar officer over any substantial part of its assets or undertaking (and such petition or order is not discharged within 30 days); or

(c) a third party acquires a Controlling Interest in that party (and, for this purpose, a "**Controlling Interest**" means (i) the ownership or control (directly or indirectly) of more than 50 per cent of the voting capital of that party or (ii) the ability to direct the casting of more than 50 per cent of the votes exercisable at general meetings of that party on all, or substantially all, matters or (iii) the right to appoint or remove a majority of the directors of that party).

12.5 In the event of termination:

(a) the parties shall consult and use all reasonable efforts to agree an orderly programme for winding-up the activities of the Alliance;

(b) the terms of this Agreement and (unless otherwise agreed between the parties) the terms of the Technical Assistance Agreement and any outstanding Project Agreement shall automatically terminate except that:

   (i) the provisions of clause 8 (Confidentiality), 10 (Indemnity) and 16 (Disputes) shall continue as surviving provisions together with any provisions specified in any Project Agreement or the Technical Assistance Agreement as surviving termination;

   (ii) each party shall remain liable for any breach of its obligations which has occurred prior to termination;

   (iii) (save as specified in any Technical Assistance Agreement or specific Project Collaboration Agreement) each party shall be entitled to use any know-how developed or acquired prior to termination through the joint operations contemplated by this Alliance.

Trade marks

13. Except as specifically agreed in writing between the parties, neither party shall use the trade marks or trade names of the other party in the course of its business or in any form of publicity relating to this Agreement.

General

14.1 No waiver by a party of a failure by the other party to perform any provision of this Agreement shall operate or be construed as a waiver in respect of any other failure (whether of a like or different character).

14.2 No amendment or variation of this Agreement shall be effective unless in writing and signed by a duly authorised representative of each party.

14.3 If any provision of the Agreement is found invalid or illegal, the parties shall use all reasonable efforts to agree a substitute provision having (as closely as possible) the commercial effect intended by the parties.

14.4 This Agreement is personal to the parties and neither party shall assign any of its rights or obligations under this Agreement without the prior written consent of the other party.

14.5 Any notice given under this Agreement shall be in writing addressed to the party at its address set out below or at such other address as the party may designate in writing:

ABC:	Address:	XYZ:	Address:
	Fax No:		Fax No:
	For the attention of:		For the attention of:

Key principles

15.1 Each party acknowledges that the success of the Alliance will require a co-operative working relationship established upon good communications and "team working" between the parties at all levels.

15.2 Each party similarly recognises that it is vital for the success of the Alliance to maintain flexibility and to respond to changing circumstances and practical experience. Each party will consider in good faith any proposals put forward by the other party for the development of the Alliance.

15.3 This Agreement sets out the basic principles on which, in good faith, the parties agree to develop more specific arrangements for the development of the Alliance. Any more detailed or definitive legal agreements between the parties, if necessary, shall require the prior approval of the parties through the Alliance Board.

15.4 The parties confirm their intention to establish and develop the Alliance in accordance with the principles set out in this Agreement with a view to achieving the success of the Alliance in their mutual best interests.

Entire agreement

16. [This Agreement (taken with the agreements referred to herein) constitutes the entire agreement and understanding of the parties in relation to the subject matter of this Agreement.] No party has entered into this Agreement in reliance upon any representation, warranty or undertaking by or on behalf of the other party which is not expressly set out in this Agreement.

Disputes

17.1 The parties shall use all reasonable efforts to ensure that any disputes or conflicts between them shall be addressed speedily and constructively on an amicable basis. Any material dispute shall be resolved through the Alliance Board (or, if necessary, through the respective Chairmen or Chief Executives of the parties). The parties shall, in that event, consider an appropriate mediation procedure.

17.2 Any dispute which cannot be resolved amicably shall be determined by arbitration in [London] by [three] arbitrator[s] appointed under the Rules of the [International Chamber of Commerce].

Governing law

18. This Agreement shall be governed by English law.

AS WITNESS the parties have executed this Agreement

SIGNED BY_____   SIGNED BY _____
for **ABC**   for **XYZ**

....

Precedent 5

R&D Collaboration Agreement

Collaboration agreements vary greatly. This precedent is essentially a framework which will need to be tailored to the particular circumstances. Greater detail may be needed in many areas. Features of this precedent include the following.

(1) *This precedent is structured as a research project to be carried out as a consortium by a number of parties described as "Members". It should be adapted, and the terminology changed, if there are fewer parties agreeing to undertake a co-operative research programme on a less formal basis.*

(2) *The Agreement contemplates the "free" exchange of existing technology between the Members. In some circumstances, royalty provisions or other monetary compensation in respect of existing work may be appropriate. It also contemplates that the research programme will be co-ordinated by a Project Manager with invoicing and re-imbursement through a joint account. In other circumstances, the parties may simply bear their own costs.*

(3) *Each Member is to have free use of project technology. However, the Agreement contemplates a two-year restriction on individual commercial licensing by any Member to third parties after completion of the project. This and similar provisions will obviously depend on the commercial terms and may need review under competition laws.*

(4) *In some collaborations it will be left to each individual party to obtain, and own, IPR in technology developed by it under the project—and to cross-license the other party(ies). This Agreement contemplates that project technology (and any related IPR) should be held jointly—except that a Member may choose to opt out of obtaining registered IPR in any particular jurisdiction; if so, only participating Members would be entitled to exploit those rights by licensing third parties.*

(5) *The Agreement also contemplates that funding may be sought from a specific third party body. In practice, the terms of any funding agreement are likely to affect the terms of this Agreement.*

THIS AGREEMENT is made on _____ 200—

BETWEEN:

(1) _____, whose [registered] office is at _____ *(A)*

(2) _____, whose [registered] office is at _____ *(B)*

(3) _____, whose [registered] office is at _____ *(C)*

WHEREAS:

(A) The parties (individually referred to in this Agreement as a "**Member**" and collectively as the "**Members**") desire to participate in a project with the aim of undertaking pre-competitive research in the field of ——————— as more particularly described in Schedule 1 (the "**Project**").

(B) The Members desire by means of this Agreement to establish their respective rights and obligations in relation to their collaboration.

IT IS AGREED AS FOLLOWS:

Interpretation

1.1 In this Agreement the following words and expressions have the following meanings unless the context otherwise requires:

"**Affiliate**" means a company or firm which, in relation to the specified Member, is (i) a company or firm in which more than 50% of the issued share capital or voting interests are owned or held directly or indirectly by that Member; (ii) a company or firm which directly or indirectly owns or holds more than 50% of the issued share capital or voting interests in that Member; or (iii) a company or firm in which more than 50% of the issued share capital or voting interests are owned or held directly or indirectly by a company or firm falling within (ii);

"**Chairman**" means the chairman for the time being of the Project Committee;

["**Aggregate Contribution Commitment**" means the aggregate contribution to the costs of the Project to be made by each Member;]

"**Existing Technology**" means, in relation to each Member, any Technology held by any Member (or any Affiliate) at the date of this Agreement which relates to the subject matter of the Project [and which it is free to disclose to the other Members pursuant to clause 8.1];

["**Funding Agreement**" means any agreement with ———————, as contemplated by clause 4, for the funding of any part of the Project;]

["**Funding Share**" means, in relation to a Member, the share of the costs of the Project to be borne by that Member being the proportion which its Aggregate Contribution Commitment bears to the Aggregate Contribution Commitments of all Members;]

"**Intellectual Property Rights**" means any patent, copyright, registered design, unregistered design right or other intellectual property protection (including any application for any such protection) and all rights in any secret process, know-how or other confidential information; and "**Registered Intellectual Property Rights**" means any Intellectual Property Rights which are protected by registration in any jurisdiction;

"**Joint Account**" means the joint account more particularly described in clause 6.4;

"**materials**" means any model, prototype, material or substance (including, without limitation, any living organism or genetic material);

"**Member(s)**" means the party or parties to this Agreement;

"**Project**" means the programme of joint research and development work to be carried out pursuant to this Agreement, a brief description of which is set out in Schedule 1;

"**Project Budget**" means the budget of estimated expenditure on the Project in each Year set out in Schedule 3 [(as varied from time to time by the Project Committee)];

"**Project Committee**" means the committee to be constituted by the Members pursuant to clause 5;

"**Project Manager**" means the full-time manager of the Project in accordance with clause 5.11;

"**Project Technology**" means any Technology acquired, developed or produced by or on behalf of any Member (or the Members collectively) during and in the course of carrying out the Project;

"**Quarter**" means each calendar period of 3 months (whether during this Project or thereafter) during the continuance of the Agreement ending on 31 July, 30 October, 31 January and 30 April in each Year; and "**Quarterly**" has a corresponding meaning;

["**Spokesman**" means such person as the Project Committee shall appoint to act, unless otherwise agreed by all the Members, as the main spokesman of the Members during the negotiation of the Funding Agreement;]

"**Technology**" means any discovery, invention, development, technical information, data, know-how, techniques, processes, systems, software, formulae, results of experimentation, designs, statistics, records, substances and/or materials (including, without limitation, living organisms and genetic material);

"**Territory**" means [any country of the world];

"**Year**" means each 12 month period during which this Agreement, or any part of it, continues in force.

1.2 Each reference in this Agreement to:

[(a) a statute or a statutory provision shall be construed as a reference to that statute or provision as amended or re-enacted at the relevant time;] and

(b) a "**licence**" in respect of any Technology includes, unless the context otherwise requires, a reference to a sub-licence; and "**license**" (as a verb) shall be construed accordingly.

1.3 The headings in this Agreement are for convenience only and shall not affect its interpretation.

Scope of collaboration

2.1 The Members agree to form a collaboration, in accordance with the terms of this Agreement, in order to undertake the Project.

2.2 The Members shall fully co-operate with each other in relation to the Project in accordance with the provisions of this Agreement and act at all times in such a way as to further the common interest of the parties as Members of the collaboration.

2.3 [This Agreement shall in no way restrict any Member from engaging independently in any activities of any kind whether involving the subject matter of the Project or otherwise (but subject to the restrictions of clause 10 and clause 11).] or [During the term of this Agreement no Member (or any Affiliate) shall (without the prior written consent of the other Members and whether directly or indirectly or by agreement with any third party) undertake or participate in any research and development project which is in the same field as the Project or in research or development relating to any technology similar to or closely connected with any Project Technology.]

2.4 In no event shall the Members consider the collaboration to be, or in any way act as though it were, a corporation, partnership or any other form of entity having any independent legal personality whatsoever. Nothing in this Agreement shall entitle any of the Members to pledge the credit or incur any liabilities or obligations binding upon any other Member except insofar as may be expressly agreed by each of those Members.

The Project

3.1 The Project shall have the objectives referred to in the Project Profile set out in Schedule 1 and, so far as practicable, shall be carried out in accordance with the timetable and outline programme contained in the Project Outline/Timetable set out in Schedule 2.

3.2 The Project shall be carried out at the premises of A at _____, the premises of B at _____ and the premises of C at _____ or such alternative or additional premises (including those of research bodies) as the Members may from time to time agree in writing.

3.3 Each Member shall, in furtherance of the objectives of the Project, carry out the tasks and contribute the resources and facilities respectively allotted to or required of it under Schedules 1 or 2 [(or by the Project Committee)] for the performance of the Project.

3.4 Each Member shall:

(a) co-operate in ensuring that the Project is carried out on its part by properly qualified personnel;

(b) submit to the other Members (through the Project Manager) on a regular Quarterly basis a written report of the work carried out by it in the course of the Project during the previous Quarter and of its results;

(c) ensure that properly qualified and authorised representatives of the other Members are allowed reasonable access (in accordance with policies and procedures approved by the Project Committee) to the work carried out by it in connection with the Project and to the personnel involved in that work from time to time;

(d) promptly notify the Project Manager and the other Members if there is any unforeseen technical or scientific problem which is likely to cause a material delay or difficulty in achieving any of the objectives of the Project or result in any material increase in the costs of the Project.

3.5 If at any time the Members believe that:

[(a) there is no reasonable prospect of obtaining funding as contemplated by clause 4;]

(b) there is no reasonable likelihood of success of the Project;

(c) there has been a failure to achieve any of the material steps of the Project set out in the Project Profile; or

(d) the objectives of the Project have been substantially achieved by research outside the Project;

they shall [, if a majority of them so agree,] re-define the Project or terminate this Agreement.

Negotiation of Funding Agreement

[**4.1** The Members acknowledge their intention to enter into negotiations with _____ with a view to entering into a Funding Agreement.

4.2 The terms of the Funding Agreement shall be negotiated by the Project Committee under the leadership of the Spokesman. The Members agree to give full assistance to the Spokesman for this purpose. Each Member agrees that throughout the period of negotiations for the Funding Agreement it will act quickly on all matters and shall at all times co-operate with the Spokesman to ensure that the negotiations proceed in a satisfactory manner.

4.3 The Funding Agreement shall require signature on behalf of each Member by its duly authorised representative.]

Project Committee

5.1 The direction and overall management of the Project shall be vested in a Project Committee.

5.2 Each Member shall appoint a representative (and an alternate) to represent that Member at meetings of the Project Committee. Such representative (or, in his absence, his alternate) shall be counted for the purpose of determining whether a quorum is present and shall have one vote on any matter requiring a decision. Each Member shall be entitled to change that representative (or alternate) at any time by written notice to the Project Manager.

5.3 The Project Manager shall also attend such meetings but shall not be entitled to vote on any decision to be made at such meetings.

5.4 Meetings of the Project Committee shall be convened by the Project Manager on a Quarterly basis or at such other times as may be agreed by the Project Committee or at any time upon a Member so requesting the Project Manager. Any Member may propose agenda items for consideration at a meeting of the Project Committee provided that such items are notified to the Project Manager at least 14 days in advance of a proposed meeting of the Project Committee. The Chairman of the Project Committee shall be elected by the Project Committee.

5.5 A quorum for a meeting of the Project Committee shall only be present when the authorised representative (or alternate) of each of the Members is present.

5.6 [Except as provided in clause 5.10,] all decisions at meetings of the Project Committee shall require a [majority] vote of the representatives entitled to attend and vote thereon. In the case of an equality of votes, the Chairman shall [not] be entitled to a second or casting vote.

5.7 The authorised representative of a Member shall (unless specific notification to the contrary is given) be authorised to make decisions on behalf of that Member on all matters connected with the Project. All decisions made at meetings of the Project Committee in connection with the Project shall be binding on all Members.

5.8 The Project Committee shall review the Project each Quarter and recommend to the Members any variations to the objectives of the Project, or to the timetable of the work to be carried out or to any proposed expenditure, which seem desirable to the Project Committee from time to time. The Members shall give consideration to any recommendations made by the Project Committee [provided that any such variation shall be subject to their prior agreement [in writing]].

5.9 The Project Manager shall prepare minutes of each meeting of the Project Committee which shall be distributed as soon as possible after the end of each meeting to, and shall be confirmed by, each Member or its representative on or before the next meeting. Agreed minutes shall be signed by the Chairman and each Member shall be supplied with a copy.

5.10 None of the following matters shall be proceeded with unless [all of] [a majority of not less than three-quarters of] the representatives of those Members entitled to attend and vote thereon shall have so resolved or agreed in favour at a meeting of which at [least 30] days' notice has been given, namely:

(a) acceptance of a new entrant as a Member (including terms of admission of any new Member); and

(b) approval of expenditure on any particular item which would be more than [10 per cent in excess of budget for that particular item].

5.11 The Project Manager shall be such person as shall be so appointed by the Project Committee. The Project Manager shall act as a co-ordinator of the combined activities of the Members and shall carry out his duties in order to facilitate the successful implementation of this Agreement, with particular responsibility for the overall technical and commercial planning of the Project. The terms of such appointment, including as to remuneration and expenses, shall be determined by the Project Committee.

5.12 The Project Committee may delegate any of its powers to a sub-committee consisting of the authorised representative(s) of one or more Members.

Project costs

6.1 Each Member shall contribute [its Funding Share] towards the costs of the Project on a Quarterly basis in accordance with the Project Budget [up to, in each case, its Aggregate Contribution Commitment].

6.2 Not less than 30 days before the end of each Quarter, the Project Manager shall submit to each Member an invoice in respect of that Member's contribution to the costs of the Project which is due pursuant to clause 6.1 in respect of that Quarter and each Member shall pay into the Joint Account the amount shown by that invoice on or before the last day of the Quarter in question.

6.3 Not less than 60 days before the end of each Year, the Project Committee shall review the future funding of the project so as to procure its successful completion within the Project Budget. No Member shall be obliged to provide funds in excess of [its Aggregate Contribution Commitment].

6.4 Unless otherwise agreed between the Members:

(a) all invoices to be submitted pursuant to this clause 6 shall be sent to the address of the relevant Member as specified in or pursuant to clause 20;

(b) all payments pursuant to this clause 6 shall be made by each Member in [pounds sterling] in cleared funds to such joint bank account in such name as the Project Committee may from time to time nominate (the "**Joint Account**");

(c) [any payment which is in default or delayed by any Member shall bear interest at the rate of _____ per cent above the base lending rate for the time being of _____ Bank PLC during the period from the due date of payment until the actual date of payment.]

6.5 Payments from the Joint Account shall only be made, whether to any of the Members or any other person, for work carried out or provided in connection with the Project. [Invoicing and payment procedures to reimburse Members for work carried out by them on the Project shall be [as set out in Schedule 4 or] as [otherwise] determined from time to time by the Project Committee.]

6.6 Any cheque or other payment drawing on funds from the Joint Account shall require the signature or written authorisation of the Project Manager or other person authorised by the Project Committee. Any cheque or other payment in excess of £_____ (or such other sum as the Project Committee may from time to time decide) shall also be countersigned by such other person as shall be authorised by the Project Committee. Any cheque or payment in excess of £_____ shall, in addition to the above signatures, require express authorisation by the Project Committee.

Accounts

7.1 Full and proper books of account and records relating to the Project shall be kept in accordance with standard accounting practice under the supervision of the Project Manager. Such books and documents shall be available at all times for inspection by the Members or their duly authorised representatives.

7.2 [An audit of the Joint Account shall be undertaken every 12 months by an independent auditor and a report (in a form to be established by the Project Committee) shall be prepared and submitted to each of the Members. The audit fee shall be paid out of the funds authorised by the Project Budget.]

7.3 If following the completion or prior termination of the Project there remains a credit balance on the Joint Account (all outstanding fees, costs and expenses of the Project having been met), such balance shall be distributed among the Members *pro rata* to their respective [Funding Shares/Aggregate Contribution Commitments].

Existing Technology

8.1 Promptly following the execution of this Agreement [and under arrangements to be co-ordinated by the Project Manager], each of the Members shall disclose to the other Members such of its Existing Technology as is necessary or desirable to be disclosed in order to enable the Project to be carried out in accordance with Schedules 1 and 2. Such disclosure shall, if appropriate, include reasonable arrangements for the instruction of suitably qualified personnel of the other Members in the use and application of such Existing Technology.

8.2 All Existing Technology of each Member (and all related Intellectual Property Rights) shall remain the exclusive property of that Member. The other Members shall not use or disclose any of such Existing Technology (or related Intellectual Property Rights) except for the specific purposes of the Project or as expressly permitted by clauses 9 and 10 of this Agreement.

8.3 Each Member shall be entitled to use the Existing Technology (and, by way of non-exclusive licence, any related Intellectual Property Rights) of any other Member in order to enable it to carry out the Project in accordance with this Agreement.

8.4 [Each Member warrants to the other Members that, so far as it is aware, the use of its Existing Technology by any other Member in accordance with this Agreement will not infringe any Intellectual Property Rights of any third party.] A Member gives no [other] warranty or representation of any kind to any other Member in relation to its Existing Technology (including but not limited to its suitability for any particular use or application).

Project Technology and Intellectual Property

9.1 During the Project, the Project Manager shall be responsible for ensuring full disclosure to each Member of all Project Technology. Each Member shall co-operate with the Project Manager in ensuring disclosure of all Project Technology arising from work carried out by or on behalf of that Member.

9.2 Any disclosure pursuant to clause 9.1 shall be in writing or, if made orally, confirmed as soon as practicable thereafter by way of written report and shall be subject to the confidentiality provisions of clause 9.3.

9.3 All Project Technology (and, subject as provided in this clause 9, all related Intellectual Property Rights) shall belong to all the Members as joint owners. [Each Member shall, if requested by any other Member, enter into such assignments or other formal documentation as may be necessary or desirable to record or effect such joint ownership.]

[**9.4** During the period of this Agreement, the procedure for obtaining initial Registered Intellectual Property Rights in respect of any Project Technology, up to and including first filing, shall be implemented by the Project Manager acting on his own initiative or at the request or direction of the Project Committee. The costs of obtaining or applying for any such initial protection (including the costs of first filing) shall be met from the Project Budget.

9.5 Any steps to obtain further Registered Intellectual Property Rights shall so far as possible be taken by agreement between the Members (but on the basis that, if a Member does not wish to proceed with any such further Registered Intellectual Property Rights (including in any particular Territory) but a majority of Members do so wish, it shall become a "**Non-Participating Member**" in respect of those Registered Intellectual Property Rights and shall have no rights under clause 10 to exploit the same by licensing third parties.]

9.6 In the event of any alleged infringement by a third party of any Intellectual Property Rights or of any alleged infringement by any Project Technology of any Intellectual Property Rights of any third party, the Members shall meet to decide by majority vote the best course of action and shall thereafter be bound to take steps to implement that action [(except that a Non-Participating Member shall not be bound to participate in, or bear any costs of, pursuing any infringement action relating to Registered Intellectual Property Rights for which it is not a participating **Member**)].

Commercial exploitation

10.1 Each Member shall be entitled [both during and] after the completion of the Project and without any payment to the other Members:

(a) to use and exploit any Project Technology (and, subject to clause 10.5, any related Intellectual Property Rights) in any part of the Territory and for any purpose;

(b) to use any Existing Technology (or, by way of non-exclusive licence, any related Intellectual Property Rights) of any other Member as may be reasonably necessary in order to enable it to use and exploit any Project Technology; and

(c) to license third parties to use any Project Technology in any part of the Territory (together with any such Existing Technology or, by way of sub-licence, any related Intellectual Property Rights of any other Member as may be reasonably necessary to use and exploit any Project Technology).

10.2 Each Member undertakes that (without the consent of the other Members) for a period of [2] years after the termination of the Project:

(a) it shall not grant (other than to its Affiliates) any licences in respect of any Project Technology (or any related Intellectual Property Rights); and

(b) it shall not make public (and shall procure that its Affiliates do not make public) any Project Technology other than for the purposes of the Project (provided that this shall not apply to information which the receiving Member can show was developed wholly independently of the Project or which was generally available to the public otherwise than through default on the part of the receiving Member).

10.3 In relation to any licence to an Affiliate under clause 10.2, the relevant Member shall ensure that:

(a) the terms of licence or disclosure impose an obligation of strict confidentiality on the Affiliate in respect of Project Technology; and

(b) no right of use or exploitation of Project Technology shall be permitted to any other shareholder or participant in the company or firm which is the Affiliate in question (except for use and exploitation through that Affiliate) and the relevant Member shall take steps diligently to ensure that such terms are observed.

10.4 For the avoidance of doubt, clause 10.2 shall not apply to prevent a Member making available Project Technology to a third party sub-contractor to carry out research and development work for that Member provided that:

(a) the terms of contract impose an obligation of strict confidentiality on that third party in respect of Project Technology; and

(b) such third party shall not acquire or be granted any right to use Project Technology except for the purposes of that contract or for the purposes of other research and development work for that Member;

and the relevant Member shall take steps diligently to ensure that such terms are observed.

[**10.5** Each Member acknowledges that it shall have no rights to disclose or licence any Registered Intellectual Property Rights in respect of which it is a Non-Participating Member and agrees to surrender and assign in favour of the participating Members all rights of ownership in respect of such Registered Intellectual Property Rights. For the avoidance of doubt, each Non-Participating Member shall have an irrevocable, royalty-free, non-exclusive licence to use any such Registered Intellectual Property Rights (and associated Project Technology) for its own purposes but shall have no right to disclose or sub-licence the same to third parties.

10.6 The participating Members shall be entitled to grant licences on such terms as they think fit in respect of any Registered Intellectual Property Rights obtained pursuant to clause 9.5 and any royalties received shall be shared between the relevant participating Members.]

[**10.7** For the purposes of the preceding provisions of this clause 10, each Member shall adopt such security procedures as may be reasonably necessary or prudent in accordance with good industry practice to ensure the safe custody of any materials forming part of any other Member's Existing Technology or Project Technology.]

Confidentiality

11.1 Each Member shall use its best efforts to keep in strict confidence, and shall bind all its employees and agents to keep in strict confidence, all commercial and technical information in whatever form acquired by it (whether directly or indirectly) concerning any other Member in consequence of this Agreement ("**Confidential Information**"). No Member shall, except as provided in this clause, use or disclose any such Confidential Information other than for the purposes of the Project or as expressly permitted by this Agreement. This restriction shall not apply to:

(a) information which at the time of disclosure is generally available to the public;

(b) information which after disclosure becomes generally available to the public through no fault of the receiving Member;

(c) information which the receiving Member can show was in its possession prior to the disclosure and which was not acquired directly or indirectly from any other Member;

(d) information which the receiving Member can show was received by it after the time of disclosure from any party without any obligation of confidentiality and which was not acquired directly or indirectly from any other Member(s).

11.2 The confidentiality obligations set out in this clause shall survive [indefinitely] or [for a period of 5 years after the termination of the Project].

11.3 Each Member shall impose the same confidentiality obligations set out in this clause 11 upon its Affiliates, sub-contractors, suppliers and other third parties who are in association with it and may have access to any Confidential Information during the term of this Agreement.

11.4 No Member shall make any press or other public announcement concerning any aspect of this Agreement without first notifying the other Members of the proposed text of that announcement and [(unless such announcement is required by law or any stock exchange or by any governmental authority)] obtaining their consent.

Liability

12.1 No Member shall have any liability of any kind whatsoever to any other Member for any damage, loss or expense of any kind of any other Member arising out of or in connection with the Project except as a result of death or personal injury caused by the negligence of the first-mentioned Member or its employees or agents.

12.2 Each Member (the "**indemnifying Member**") shall indemnify each of the other Members, its employees and agents from and against:

(a) all actions or claims which may be brought or made against any such other Member (or any of its employees or agents) by any third party; and

(b) all damages, costs or expenses which may be incurred by any of them in respect of any such action or claim

if and to the extent that such action or claim arises out of or in connection with the use by the indemnifying Member (or any of its employees or agents or Affiliates) of any Existing Technology or Project Technology including, but not limited to, the manufacture, use or sale of any products by or on behalf of the indemnifying Member (or any of its Affiliates).

Duration and termination

13.1 This Agreement shall be effective as from _____ and, except as provided in this Agreement, shall continue until each Member has completed and settled all its obligations and liabilities under this Agreement.

13.2 This Agreement shall be terminated upon a decision of the Members in the circumstances contemplated by clause 3.5.

13.3 The participation of a Member in the Project may be terminated forthwith by written notice from all of the other Members who are not in breach of this Agreement in any of the following circumstances, namely:

(a) if such Member has committed a material breach of any of its obligations under this Agreement and (in the case of a breach which is capable of remedy) has failed to remedy it within a period of 60 days after receipt of written notice giving full particulars of the breach and requiring it to be remedied;

(b) [if such Member makes any arrangement or composition with its creditors or goes into liquidation (except for the purposes of amalgamation or reconstruction in such manner that the company resulting therefrom effectively agrees to be bound by or assume the obligations imposed on that Member under this Agreement) or if an encumbrancer takes possession of, or a receiver, administrator or administrative receiver is appointed over, the whole or any substantial part of the property or assets of such Member;] or

(c) if such Member ceases, or threatens to cease, to carry on business.

In the event of any such notice, the Member whose participation in the Project is thereby terminated shall cease to have any rights of any kind to Project Technology thereafter developed or acquired [and neither it (nor any Affiliate) shall thereafter have any right to [use or] exploit any Project Technology (or related Intellectual Property Rights)].

13.4 For the purposes of clause 13.3(a), a breach shall be considered capable of remedy if the Member in breach can comply with the provision in question in all respects other than as to the time of performance (provided that time of performance is not of the essence).

13.5 The provisions of clauses 8.2, 9.3, 10 and 11 shall continue to be binding on each of the Members notwithstanding termination of this Agreement or of a Member's participation in the Project and (subject to clause 13.3) any licences or sub-licences granted pursuant to this Agreement by any Member to any other Member prior to such termination shall continue in force in accordance with their respective terms.

13.6 Upon the termination of this Agreement for any reason, the Members shall take such steps as may be necessary in order to wind up the Project in a fair and orderly manner.

Force majeure

14.1 No Member shall be considered in breach of its obligations under this Agreement or be responsible for any delay in carrying out its obligations, if performance is prevented or delayed wholly or in part as a consequence (direct or indirect) of war (whether war be declared or not), emergency, strike, industrial dispute, accident, fire, earthquake, flood, storm, tempest, any act of God or any other cause beyond the reasonable control of the Member affected.

14.2 If the performance of a particular Member's obligations under this Agreement is in the opinion of that Member likely to be hindered, delayed or affected by a reason falling within clause 14.1, then the Member so affected shall promptly notify the other Members in writing.

Assignment

15. No Member shall have the right to assign or in any way transfer any of its rights or obligations under this Agreement to any other company, firm or person without first obtaining the consent in writing of all the other Members.

Entire agreement

16. This Agreement constitutes the entire agreement between the Members in relation to the Project and cancels or supersedes all prior negotiations, representations or agreements, whether written or oral, between the Members prior to the date of this Agreement.

Governing law

17. This Agreement shall in all respects be construed and interpreted in accordance with the laws of [England].

Arbitration

18.1 Any difference or dispute between the parties (or their respective representatives) which at any time arises out of or in connection with this Agreement shall, failing any agreement to settle it in any other way, be referred for decision to an arbitrator to be agreed among the parties. In the event of failure to agree an arbitrator, the difference or dispute shall be referred to and finally resolved by arbitration appointed under the Arbitration Rules of the _____. The number of arbitrators shall be _____ and the place of arbitration shall be _____.

18.2 The costs of any arbitration pursuant to clause 18.1 shall be met equally by each party to the dispute and not from the Project Budget.

Waiver and amendments

19.1 No waiver by a Member of a failure by any other Member to perform any provision of this Agreement shall operate or be construed as a waiver in respect of any other failure whether of a like or different character.

19.2 This Agreement shall not be amended or modified in any way other than by an agreement in writing executed by a duly authorised representative of each of the Members.

Notices

20.1 All notices and communications required or permitted to be given to any Member under this Agreement shall be sent to the following addresses or fax numbers (and a copy shall also be sent to the Project Manager):

A:

B:

C:

20.2 Each Member shall promptly notify the other Members of any change in any such details.

Costs

21. Each of the Members shall bear its own costs of and incidental to the preparation, execution and implementation of this Agreement.

AS WITNESS the parties have caused this Agreement to be duly executed by their duly authorised representatives.

SCHEDULE 1: PROJECT PROFILE

[*This Schedule should describe, inter alia, the objectives and scope of the work programme to be carried out.*]

SCHEDULE 2: PROJECT OUTLINE/TIMETABLE

[*This Schedule should describe, inter alia, the tasks to be carried out by each of the Members and the time scales applicable to each of those tasks.*]

SCHEDULE 3: BUDGET

[*This Schedule should set out the Project Budget including the Aggregate Contribution Commitment of each Member.*]

SCHEDULE 4: [INVOICING PROCEDURES]

[*This Schedule should set out any invoicing procedures, inter alia, for reimbursement to Members of costs incurred in carrying out work on the Project. The definition of "costs" and principles of reimbursement should be carefully spelt out.*]

Signed by _____ }
for and on behalf of **A** }

_____

Signed by _____ }
for and on behalf of **B** }

_____

Signed by _____ }
for and on behalf of **C** }

_____

Precedent 6

General Partnership Agreement

> *This precedent assumes that the two parties will both be companies and that the partnership (a general partnership) will be established under English law. It provides a basic framework. It has been structured in many ways in terms comparable to a "deadlock" joint venture company. Features include the following:*
>
> *(1) The initial contributions of capital may take the form of cash and/or assets. Details should be spelt out or referred to in clause 4.*
>
> *(2) The partnership is managed principally through what is termed a partnership "board" and by "directors". This has no legal status—and the terminology of a "management committee" or the like may be preferred.*
>
> *(3) The Agreement provides for certain standard "reserved matters" which will require unanimity—either at the partnership board or by separate agreement of the partners, as appropriate.*
>
> *(4) The Agreement contemplates that a partner may only sell its partnership interest to a third party with the consent of the other partner. It is possible to include a pre-emption procedure comparable to that in a JVC but this is likely to be unrealistic. It may be easier (if more drastic) to provide for termination and dissolution of the partnership.*

THIS PARTNERSHIP AGREEMENT is made on ─────── 200

BETWEEN:

(1) ─────────, having its [registered] office at ─────── (***ABC***); and

(2) ─────────, having its [registered] office at ─────── (***XYZ***).

WHEREAS:

(A) ABC and XYZ wish to establish a partnership under the name of ─────── (the "**Partnership**") for the purpose of ─────── .

(B) ABC and XYZ wish to regulate their relationship as partners in the Partnership and the management of the Partnership in accordance with the terms of this Agreement.

IT IS AGREED:

Interpretation

1.1 In this Agreement the following terms shall, except where the context otherwise requires, have the following meanings:

"**ABC's Capital Account**" means an account in the name of ABC to which there are credited the sum referred to in clause 4 and all sums contributed by ABC to the Partnership in respect of capital in accordance with clause 5;

"**ABC Director**" means a member of the Partnership Board appointed by ABC;

"**Affiliate**", in relation to any Partner, means any subsidiary or holding company for the time being of that Partner and any other subsidiary for the time being of that holding company (and "**holding company**" and "**subsidiary**" shall be construed in accordance with section 1159 of the Companies Act 2006);

"**Accounts**" means the accounts of the Partnership audited by the Auditors in accordance with clause 12;

"**Auditors**" means _____ or such other firm as may subsequently be appointed by the Partnership Board;

"**Budget**" means the budget for each Financial Year of the Partnership prepared pursuant to clause 13;

"**Business**" means the business and affairs of the Partnership as set out in clause 3 of this Agreement;

"**Business Day**" means a day on which banks generally are open in London [and _____] (excluding Saturdays) for a full range of business;

"**Business Plan**" means a rolling business plan for the Partnership relating to the current Financial Year and [four] succeeding Financial Years, as approved from time to time by the Partnership Board;

"**Director**" means any member of the Partnership Board;

"**Effective Date**" means the date of this Agreement;

"**Event of Default**" has the meaning set out in clause 15.2;

"**Executive**" means [the Chief Executive and any other member of the senior management team of the Partnership];

"**Financial Year**", with respect to the Partnership, means the period from and including 1 April in any calendar year to and including 31 March in the following year or such other period or periods as the Partners may determine;

"**Partners**" means ABC and XYZ and "**Partner**" means either of them;

"**Partnership Board**" means the Partnership Board constituted pursuant to clause 7;

"**Partnership Interest**", when used in relation to a Partner, means the Partner's Percentage Share and the Partner's rights and obligations under this Agreement;

"**Partnership**" means the partnership between ABC and XYZ constituted by this Agreement and known as '_____';

"**Percentage Share**" means, in relation to a Partner, the proportion [which its Capital Account bears to the aggregate Capital Accounts of all the Partners;] or [the respective percentage set opposite its name in the Schedule (or such other Percentage Shares as may be agreed from time to time in writing by the Partners)];

"**XYZ's Capital Account**" means an account in the name of XYZ to which there are credited the sum referred to in clause 4 and all sums contributed by XYZ to the Partnership in respect of capital in accordance with clause 5;

"**XYZ Director**" means a member of the Partnership Board appointed by XYZ.

1.2 Clause and other headings are for convenience only and shall not affect the construction of this Agreement.

1.3 Any reference to a statute, order or regulation shall, unless the context otherwise requires, include references to such statute, order or regulation as amended, replaced, supplemented or re-enacted from time to time.

Commencement

2. This Agreement shall be effective from the Effective Date and shall continue until terminated in accordance with the terms of this Agreement.

Business of the Partnership

3.1 The Business shall be _____.

3.2 The Business shall be conducted in the best interests of the Partnership on sound commercial profit-making principles in accordance with the Business Plan. The initial Business Plan is set out [in Annex XX] and the Partners shall use all reasonable efforts to procure its prompt and effective implementation.

3.3 The name of the Partnership shall be "_____" (or such other name as the Partners shall agree).

Partnership capital

4.1 The Partners shall respectively make initial contributions to the capital of the Partnership as follows:

(a) ABC: [*describe or refer to commitment to provide initial contribution: cash, assets, transfer of property etc.*]

(b) XYZ: [*describe or refer to commitment to provide initial contribution: cash, assets, transfer of property etc.*]

4.2 The Partners acknowledge and agree that, following the initial contributions referred to in clause 4.1:

(a) ABC's Capital Account shall be credited with the sum of £_____;

(b) XYZ's Capital Account shall be credited with the sum of £_____.

[**4.3** The Percentage Shares of the Partners shall accordingly be _____ per cent for ABC and _____ per cent for XYZ (or such other percentages as may from time to time be a consequence of any sale, assignment, transfer or disposal of the whole or part of a Partner's Partnership Interest pursuant to this Agreement).]

Further finance

5.1 Each Partner undertakes that it will during the term of this Agreement contribute its Percentage Share of all funding required by any relevant Budget approved by the Partnership Board.

5.2 [Each Partner undertakes that, if the Partnership Board resolves that further funding from the Partners is required in addition to any finance provided for in any relevant Budget and/or obtained from any third party borrowing, it will contribute its Percentage Share of the additional required funding on such terms as the Partnership Board shall agree].

5.3 All capital contributed by ABC or XYZ to meet funding pursuant to clause[s] 5.1 [or 5.2] shall (unless otherwise agreed by the Partners) be treated as a capital contribution and credited to its respective Capital Account.

5.4 The Partners shall not be obliged to provide guarantees to support the Partnership's financing commitments. If they do so, such guarantees shall be given in proportion to each Partner's Percentage Share. The liabilities of the Partners under such guarantees (so far as possible) shall be several and not joint and several. If a claim is made under any such guarantee against a Partner, it shall be entitled to such contribution from the other Partner as will ensure that the aggregate liability is borne by the Partners in their respective Percentage Shares.

Profits and losses

6.1 The amount of profits and losses in respect of any Financial Year shall be determined from the Accounts of the Partnership. All profits and losses of the Partnership for any Financial Year shall, unless otherwise agreed by the Partners, be allocated to the Partners in proportion to their Percentage Shares.

6.2 All profits and losses allocated to the Partners under clause 6.1 shall be respectively credited or debited to current accounts of the Partners.

6.3 Any cash available to the Partnership which the Partnership Board determines is surplus to the requirements of the Partnership shall, at the request of any Partner, be distributed to ABC and XYZ in accordance with their respective Percentage Shares.

Directors and partnership board

7.1 Overall supervision of the Business shall be the responsibility of the Partnership Board, which shall have authority to act on behalf of the Partnership in all matters in connection with the Business and shall carry out its duties in such manner as the Partnership Board considers to be in the best interests of the Partnership.

7.2 The Partnership Board shall comprised [a non-executive, non-voting Chairman and] four (4) non-executive Directors consisting of:

(a)   2 Directors nominated by ABC; and

(b)   2 Directors nominated by XYZ.

7.3 Any appointment or removal of a Director shall be effected by notice in writing to the Partnership signed by or on behalf of the Partner that appointed such Director and shall take effect, subject to any contrary intention expressed in the notice, when the notice is delivered to the Partnership.

7.4 If ABC ceases to be a Partner for any reason, the ABC Directors shall immediately resign their post. If XYZ ceases to be a Partner for any reason, the XYZ Directors shall immediately resign their post.

7.5 ABC shall be entitled to appoint the Chairman. The first Chairman shall be _____.

7.6 The Partnership Board shall meet quarterly. In addition, any Partner shall have the right to convene a meeting of the Partnership Board at any time. Any meeting of the Partnership Board shall be called by the [Chairman] and conducted in accordance with the provisions of this clause 7.

7.7 The quorum for any meeting of the Partnership Board (other than an adjourned meeting) shall be a majority in number of the Directors, including at least 1 ABC Director (or his alternate) and at least 1 XYZ Director (or his alternate). If such a quorum is not present within 30 minutes from the time appointed for the meeting or if during the meeting such quorum ceases to be present, the meeting shall be adjourned for 7 Business Days [and at that adjourned meeting any 2 Directors (or their alternates) present shall constitute a quorum.]

7.8 At least 10 Business Days' written notice shall be given of any meeting of the Partnership Board, provided that a shorter period of notice may be given with the written approval of at least 1 ABC Director and at least 1 XYZ Director. Any such notice shall include an agenda identifying in reasonable detail the matters to be discussed (in particular, of any matter set out in clause 7.12) and shall be accompanied by copies of any relevant papers to be discussed at the meeting and any resolutions to be tabled. A meeting of the Partnership Board may consist of a conference between Directors who are not all in one place, but of whom each is able (directly or by telephonic communication) to speak to each of the others and to be heard by each of the others simultaneously; and the word "**meeting**" in this Agreement shall be construed accordingly.

[**7.9** Any Director shall be entitled to require the Chief Executive or any other Executive to attend (but not vote at) all or part of any meeting of the Partnership Board in order to provide information or views, provided that the Director notifies the relevant Executive and the Chairman and the other Directors within [2] Business Days from receipt of the notice of meeting that the Executive's attendance is required and specifies the items on which his information or views will be required.]

7.10 Resolutions of the Partnership Board shall be passed as follows:

(a) Each Director shall have one vote. Any Director who is absent from the meeting may nominate any other [Director] who is present to act as his alternate and to vote in his place at the meeting.

(b) The Chairman shall not have a casting vote. If the Chairman is not present at any meeting of the Partnership Board, those Directors present (if constituting a quorum) shall nominate a chairman for that meeting. Any Director acting as such a chairman shall continue to have his vote in accordance with this clause 7.10.

(c) Subject to clause 7.12, resolutions of the Partnership Board shall be passed by simple majority.

(d) A written resolution signed by all the Directors (whether in a single document or in counterpart) shall be binding as a resolution passed at a meeting of the Partnership Board.

7.11 In the event of deadlock on any vote taken pursuant to clause 7.10 which cannot be resolved after a further meeting of the Partnership Board, the matter shall be referred to the [Chairmen/Chief Executives or other senior representatives of the Partners] whose determination (if unanimous) shall bind the Partnership Board.

7.12 The following Reserved Matters shall in any event require unanimity of the [Partnership Board] [the Partners]:

(a) any change in the nature or scope of the Business (including any material business acquisition or disposal exceeding £_____ in value or any material partnership or joint venture);

(b) any material change in the organisation of the Partnership;

(c) the appointment or removal of the Chief Executive [or other Executive] or any material change in their respective terms of employment;

(d) approval of the Business Plan and Budget or any material deviation from the Business Plan or Budget;

(e) any expenditure on any particular item which is [_____ per cent] more than that provided for in the relevant Budget;

(f) the disposal of (including the grant of any security interest or other encumbrance over) any Partnership property where the value of such property exceeds £_____;

(g) any transaction with a Partner or its Affiliate [having a value in excess of £_____] (or any material amendment to any contract with a Partner or its Affiliates);

(h) the removal of Auditors and appointment of new Auditors;

(i) any [material] change in the accounting policies of the Partnership;

(j) the commencement, settlement or cessation of any litigation or arbitration involving the Partnership other than any litigation or arbitration involving (i) a dispute pursuant to this Agreement or (ii) a claim of less than £_____;

(k) any decision whether cash available to the Partnership is surplus to the requirements of the Partnership;

(l) any resolution to terminate or dissolve the Partnership under clause 18.2.

7.13 [The ABC Directors (acting unanimously) shall be empowered to bind ABC in matters relating to the Partnership. The XYZ Directors (acting unanimously) shall be empowered to bind XYZ in matters relating to the Partnership.]

Executive management

8.1 The Partnership Board shall delegate day-to-day executive management of the Business to the Chief Executive, who shall carry out such responsibilities in accordance with the then current Business Plan and Budget and such policies as shall be laid down by the Partnership Board.

8.2 The Chief Executive shall be responsible to the Partnership Board and shall be assisted in his duties by the other Executives.

8.3 The appointment and terms of reference of the other Executives will be proposed by the Chief Executive but will be subject to the prior approval of the Partnership Board.

Partnership property

9.1 The property and assets of the Partnership shall be beneficially owned by the Partners in the proportions of their respective Percentage Shares and shall comprise:

(a) _____;

(b) _____;

(c) _____;

(d) all other property (whether tangible or intangible) hereafter owned, developed, produced, created or acquired by the Partners in the course of the Partnership.

9.2 Any property of the Partnership which is held by one of the Partners (or an Affiliate) shall be held by such Partner (or Affiliate) on trust for the benefit of the Partnership and such Partner shall (if required) enter into or procure appropriate declarations of trust in respect of such property.

Undertakings by Partners

10.1 Neither Partner (nor any Affiliate) shall (whether solely or jointly with any other person, firm or company or whether directly or indirectly) carry on or be engaged in or interested (except as the holder for investment of securities dealt in on a stock exchange and not exceeding [5] per cent in nominal value of the securities of any class) in any Competing Business during the period of this Agreement. For this purpose, "**Competing Business**" means _____. [*Consider whether undertaking against non-solicitation of employees is also appropriate*].

10.2 Each Partner undertakes to the other that, in addition to its other obligations under this Agreement, it shall:

(a) promote the best interests of the Partnership and consult fully on all matters materially affecting the development of the Business; and

(b) act in good faith towards the other in order to promote the success of the Partnership, including considering in good faith any proposals made by any other Partner for the modification of this Agreement.

Expenses

11. A Partner shall be entitled to be reimbursed by the Partnership for costs and expenses reasonably incurred by the Partner in the due performance of its obligations as a partner in the Partnership. Such reimbursement shall be in accordance with and subject to arrangements and procedures approved by the Partnership Board.

Accounts

12.1 The initial Auditors of the Partnership shall be _____.

12.2 The [Partnership Board] shall be responsible for maintaining proper accounting records for the Partnership. These records shall be available for inspection by any Partner during normal business hours and upon reasonable notice.

12.3 The [Partnership Board] shall be responsible for arranging the preparation of a balance sheet, profit and loss account, and a statement of source and application of funds relating to the Partnership as at the end of and for each Financial Year in accordance with generally accepted accounting standards and principles in the [United Kingdom]. The Accounts shall be audited by the Auditors.

Budgets and information

13.1 The Chief Executive shall have responsibility for the production of a draft Budget for each Financial Year and updating the Business Plan. The draft Budget and updated Business Plan shall be submitted to the Partnership Board for approval not less than [45] Business Days prior to the commencement of the following Financial Year. In any event, the draft Budget and Business Plan (in each case with such amendments as may be agreed by the Partnership Board) shall be adopted by the Partnership Board prior to the commencement of the relevant Financial Year.

13.2 The Chief Executive shall:

(a) as soon as reasonably practicable after the end of each [calendar month], ensure that management accounts, and a management report relating to the business of the Partnership during that period, are prepared in such a manner and format as shall be approved by the Partnership Board;

(b) following any request from any Partner, prepare all information relating to the affairs of the Partnership as may reasonably be required by that Partner.

13.3 Each Partner will promptly, following any request from the other Partner, submit to the Partnership Board all information relating to the affairs of the Partnership in the possession of that Partner and which may reasonably be required by the requesting Partner.

Indemnities

14. Each Partner (the "**Indemnifying Partner**") undertakes to indemnify the other Partner against any and all losses, demands, damages, charges, claims, actions, costs, expenses and other liabilities ("**Liabilities**") of whatsoever nature suffered or incurred by such other Partner arising out of:

(a) any breach by the Indemnifying Partner of any of its obligations under this Agreement; or

(b) any act (including but not limited to the making of any contract or commitment) by the Indemnifying Partner outside the scope of its authority as established by this Agreement, the Partnership Board or by express prior written authorisation of the other Partner;

provided that:

(i) the Indemnifying Partner shall be permitted to take in the name of the other Partner such action as the Indemnifying Partner may reasonably require to defend or avoid any such Liabilities or to recover the same from any third party (but subject to the other Partner being indemnified to its satisfaction by the Indemnifying Partner against all losses, liabilities, costs, damages, and expenses thereby incurred or to be incurred); and

(ii) the other Partner shall (subject to such indemnity) give all such assistance to the Indemnifying Partner as the latter may reasonably require.

Default

15.1 If a Partner (the "**Defaulting Partner**") commits an Event of Default, then:

(a) the other Partner shall have a right to serve a notice ("**Default Purchase Notice**") requiring the Defaulting Partner to sell its Partnership Interest to that other Partner;

(b) any Default Purchase Notice shall be served within [30] days of the Event of Default;

(c) the price at which the Partnership Interest of the Defaulting Partner shall be sold under this clause 15 shall be negotiated between the Partners or, failing agreement, shall be the fair value of the Partnership Interest as determined by an independent firm of chartered accountants appointed by the Partners (or, failing agreement, appointed by [the President for the time being of the Institute of Chartered Accountants in England and Wales]) taking into account all factors it considers relevant. Any such independent firm shall act as experts (and not as arbitrators) and its decision shall be final and binding on the Partners.

15.2 For the purposes of this clause 15 an "**Event of Default**" shall occur:

(a) if the Defaulting Partner shall commit a material breach of its obligations under this Agreement and shall fail to remedy it (or implement plans to the reasonable satisfaction of the other Partner to prevent the recurrence of such breach) within 90 days after being given notice by the other Partner to do so (such notice to indicate the notifying Partner's intention to exercise its rights under this clause 15); or

(b) if the Defaulting Partner [(or any holding company of the Defaulting Partner)] shall go into liquidation whether compulsory or voluntary (except for the purposes of a bona fide reconstruction with the consent of the other Partner, such consent not to be unreasonably withheld) or if a petition shall be presented or an order made for the appointment of an administrator in relation to the Defaulting Partner or if a receiver, administrative receiver or manager shall be appointed over any substantial part of the assets or undertaking of the Defaulting Partner.

15.3 If an Event of Default shall occur in relation to a Partner, then (irrespective of whether or not a Default Purchase Notice is served on the Defaulting Partner) the Directors appointed by the Defaulting Partner shall, for as long as the Event of Default exists, cease to be entitled to vote at any meeting of the Partnership Board and the approval of such Directors shall no longer be required under clause 7.12 and no such Directors appointed by the Defaulting Partner shall be required for the purposes of a quorum.

Assignment

16.1 No Partner shall transfer, assign, encumber or otherwise deal with any of its Partnership Interest (except in accordance with clause 16.2) without obtaining the prior written consent of the other Partner.

16.2 A Partner shall be entitled at any time to transfer all (but not some only) of its Partnership Interest to an Affiliate provided that (i) the Affiliate shall first have entered into an agreement with the continuing Partner agreeing to be bound (in terms reasonably satisfactory to the continuing Partner) by the provisions of this Agreement [and (ii) the selling Partner shall remain liable for the performance by such Affiliate of its obligations under this Agreement].

Confidentiality and announcements

17.1 Each Partner shall at all times use its best efforts to keep confidential all commercial and technical information which it may acquire in relation to the Partnership or the Business or in relation to the customers, business or affairs of the other Partner or its Affiliates. No Partner shall use or disclose such information except with the consent of the other Partner or, in the case of information relating to the Partnership, for the purpose of advancing the Business. This restriction shall not apply to any information:

(a) which is publicly available or becomes publicly available through no act of the Partner wishing to use or disclose the information;

(b) which that Partner can demonstrate was already in its possession or was independently developed by that Partner or on its behalf;

(c) which is obtained by that Partner from a third party which did not acquire or hold the information under an obligation of confidentiality; or

(d) to the extent that it is required to be disclosed by law or by the rules of any recognised stock exchange or regulatory body.

17.2 Each Partner shall use all reasonable efforts to ensure that its employees and agents and any Affiliate (including its employees and agents) observe this confidentiality.

17.3 No announcement in connection with the subject matter of this Agreement shall be made or issued by or on behalf of either of the Partners without the prior written approval of both Partners (such approval not to be unreasonably withheld or delayed) except as may be required by law or by any stock exchange or by any governmental authority.

17.4 The provisions of this clause 17 shall survive any termination of this Agreement.

Termination and deadlock

18.1 If a Partner considers that a fundamental deadlock or difference in relation to the conduct or development of the Business is arising between the Partners, it shall give as early an indication as practicable to the other Partner of that concern so that orderly arrangements for the continuation of the Business can, if possible, be agreed on an amicable basis.

18.2 If the Partners agree that the financial results of the Business are substantially lower than contemplated or that the Business is no longer viable for any reason, then (i) the [Partnership Board] may resolve that the Business should be terminated; and (ii) (subject to any arrangements agreed between the Partners), the Partnership shall terminate upon the date agreed by the [Partnership Board].

18.3 In the event of termination:

(a) the Partners shall consult and use all reasonable endeavours to agree an orderly programme for winding-up the business of the Partnership and the realisation and distribution of its assets;

(b) the assets of the Partnership shall upon termination be realised and distributed to the Partners in the manner agreed between them or, failing agreement, *pro rata* to [their Percentage Shares] [the amounts standing to the credit of their respective Capital Accounts] (subject to the payment of the debts and liabilities of the Partnership);

(c) [the Partners may agree on a full or partial distribution of the assets of the Partnership in kind and/or they may agree a procedure whereby each Partner may make an offer to acquire a specific group of assets or interests of the Business (including all liabilities relating thereto); the other Partner may offer to acquire the same assets or interests and the acquisition shall be made by the Partner which is prepared to make the higher offer or (absent any such counter-offer) following such independent valuation procedure as shall be agreed.]

18.4 Upon termination, the Partners shall prepare a balance sheet relating to the Partnership as at the date of termination and a profit and loss account for the period from the end of the last Financial Year up to the date of termination. Such accounts shall be audited. The provisions of clause 6.1 shall apply to any profits and losses of the Partnership shown in the profit and loss account for the period up to the date of termination as if such period were a Financial Year.

Waivers and amendments

19.1 No failure or delay on the part of any Partner in exercising any power or right under this Agreement shall operate as a waiver of any agreement or undertaking to be performed by the other Partner or in any way restrict or prejudice the rights and powers of the first-mentioned Partner.

19.2 Save as expressly provided herein, no amendment or variation of this Agreement shall be effective unless in writing and signed by a duly authorised representative of each Partner.

Severability

20. If any provision of this Agreement is found invalid or illegal, the remainder of this Agreement shall be binding on the Partners and shall be construed as if the invalid or illegal provision had been deleted from this Agreement. The Partners shall use all reasonable efforts to agree any substitute provisions for the invalid or illegal provision having, as close as practicable, the same commercial effect.

Notices

21.1 Any notice required or permitted to be given under this Agreement shall be in writing addressed to the party at its address set out below or at such other address as the party may designate in writing:

ABC:	XYZ
Address: _____	Address: _____
Fax No: _____	Fax No: _____
For the personal attention of:	For the personal attention of:
_____	_____

21.2 Any such notice shall be delivered by hand or sent by fax or post (recorded delivery, post or airmail prepaid). Any notice sent by fax shall be deemed to have been received at the opening of business on the first business day (in the country of intended receipt) following despatch, and if sent by letter shall be deemed to have been received 72 hours (in the case of any letter sent to and from an address in the United Kingdom) and 8 days (in any other case) after the time of posting.

Governing law

22. This Agreement shall be governed by and construed in accordance with the laws of [England]. The Partners agree that, subject to the prior procedures in clause 23 below, all disputes in relation to this Agreement shall be subject to the non-exclusive jurisdiction of the [English] courts.

Settlement of disputes

23. If there shall be any dispute, controversy or claim ("**dispute**") between the Partners arising out of this Agreement, or the breach, termination or invalidity of this Agreement, the Partners shall use their best efforts to resolve the matter on an amicable basis. If one Partner serves formal written notice on the other that a dispute has arisen and the Partners are unable to resolve the dispute within a period of [30] days from the service of such notice, then the matter shall be referred to the [Chairmen/Chief Executives of the Partners]. No legal proceedings shall be commenced unless and until these procedures have been followed.

Entire agreement

24. This Agreement [(taken with _____)] constitutes the entire agreement and understanding of the Partners with respect to the subject matter of this Agreement and none of the Partners has entered into this Agreement in reliance upon any representation, warranty or undertaking by or on behalf of any Partner which is not expressly set out herein.

AS WITNESS the parties have duly executed this Agreement.

SCHEDULE: [PERCENTAGE SHARES OF THE PARTNERS]

ABC: _____ %

XYZ: _____ %

Signed by_____ }
for and on behalf of **ABC** }

Signed by_____ }
for and on behalf of **ABC** }

Precedent 7

EEIG Formation Agreement

Precedents for an EEIG vary in length and detail. This precedent is an intermediate version which includes the essential features and records certain other formal matters for the benefit of Members. It is drafted on the basis of three Founder Members but contemplates the addition from time to time of new Members. The EEIG is termed an "Association". This is simply a matter of terminology; the term "Grouping" is frequently used instead.

This Agreement contemplates that most decisions will be taken through a management committee and that each Member will appoint a Manager. There is provision for matters to be decided by majority vote—except, essentially, for those matters requiring a unanimous resolution or special resolution of the Members under the EU Regulation and/or the UK Statutory Instrument. This voting procedure could be simplified (e.g. by requiring unanimity in all cases) where this is appropriate.

This Agreement includes provision for more detailed Rules to be adopted to regulate internal dealings of the Members. This may be useful if more detailed provisions (e.g. regarding licensing of IPR, exchange of information or personnel, invoicing procedures or other matters) are contemplated; in more simple cases, simply delete.

THIS AGREEMENT is made _____ 200__

BETWEEN:

(1) _____ whose [registered] office is at _____ ("**A**");

(2) _____ whose [registered] office is at _____ ("**B**"); and

(3) _____ whose [principal place of business] is at _____ ("**C**")

WHEREAS:

A, B and C (together the "**Founder Members**") have decided to form a European Economic Interest Grouping, pursuant to European Council Regulation No. 2137/85 of July 25, 1985 and Statutory Instrument 1989 No. 638, for the purpose of _____.

IT IS AGREED AS FOLLOWS:

Interpretation

1.1 In this Agreement, the following terms shall (unless the context requires otherwise) have the following respective meanings:

"**Association**" means the EEIG established by this Agreement;

"**Date of Admission**" means, in respect of any Founder Member, the date of this Agreement and, in respect of any other Member, the date on which a unanimous resolution of the Members for the time being approving the admission of that person as a member of the Association is passed pursuant to clause 7;

"**EC Regulation**" means Council Regulation (EEC) No.2137/85 of July 25, 1985 as implemented in the United Kingdom by Statutory Instrument 1989 No.638 (the "**Statutory Instrument**");

"**Management Committee**" means the committee of Managers constituted in accordance with clause 10;

"**Founder Members**" means A, B and C and each of them is a "**Founder Member**";

"**Manager**" means a manager (as the term is used in the EC Regulation) of the Association appointed in accordance with clause 9;

"**Members**" means the persons who from time to time are the members of the Association in accordance with clause 7, and "**Member**" shall be construed accordingly;

["**Rules**" means the rules relating to the Association as more particularly described in clause 6.] [*Omit if not needed.*]

1.2 Unless the context otherwise requires, in this Agreement:

(a) reference to any statute or statutory provision (including, for the avoidance of doubt, the EC Regulation and/or the Statutory Instrument) includes any statute or statutory provision which amends or replaces, or has amended or replaced, it and includes any subordinate legislation made under the relevant statute;

(b) references to "**writing**" include any mode of reproducing words in a legible and non-transitory form;

(c) references to "**persons**" include individuals, bodies corporate, unincorporated associations and partnerships.

1.3 The headings to the clauses in this Agreement are for ease of reference only and shall not affect its interpretation.

Name

2. The name of the Association shall be _____ **EEIG**.

Official address

3. The official address of the Association shall be situated in England and Wales at _____.

Objects

4.1 The objects of the Association are to _____. The Association may take all such actions or do all such other things as may be reasonably necessary or conducive to achieve its objects.

4.2 The objects of the Association are related to the economic activities of the Members and shall, throughout the duration of the Association, remain ancillary to those activities. The primary purpose of the Association is not to make a profit.

Duration

5. The duration of the Association shall be indefinite but subject to termination in accordance with the provisions of this Agreement and/or the EC Regulation.

[**Rules** [*Note. This may not be necessary or appropriate. If so, omit.*]

6.1 Certain rights which may be enjoyed by the Members by reason of their membership of the Association, and certain obligations which may arise between the Members, and/or between the Members and the Association, may from time to time be set out in internal rules of the Association (the "Rules"), subject to the adoption of such Rules by the Members pursuant to clause 12.

6.2 The Rules shall constitute an agreement entirely separate from this Agreement and shall not amend any provision of this Agreement. However, for the avoidance of doubt, in the event of any conflict between the Rules and the provisions of this Agreement, the provisions of this Agreement shall prevail.]

Members of the Association

7. The Members shall (subject to termination of membership pursuant to clause 14) be the Founder Members and any person who is admitted as a member of the Association following:

(a) a unanimous resolution of the then current Members of the Association; and

(b) the completion by the proposed new Member of any further requirements of admission as may be required by the Management Committee on behalf of the Association.

Liability of Members

8.1 Each Member shall (subject to clause 8.2) be jointly and severally liable for all debts and other liabilities of the Association which arise in respect of the period during which the Member is a member of the Association. As between themselves, the Members shall contribute to the payment of the debts and other liabilities of the Association which arise in respect of the period during which the Member is a member of the Association in [equal proportions]. The obligations of the Members as set out in this clause 8.1 shall (subject always to Article 37 of the EC Regulation) be continuing obligations of the Members and shall survive (i) any Member ceasing to be a member of the Association or (ii) the termination of this Agreement, in either case, for any reason whatsoever.

8.2 A Member's instrument of admission to the Association may include a provision to the effect that such Member will not be held jointly and severally liable for any debts or other liabilities of the Association incurred prior to the Date of Admission of that Member (provided that, if such a provision is included in the instrument of admission of a Member, it shall be binding as between the Members but may not be relied upon as against third parties unless notice of such provision is published in accordance with the provisions of Article 8 of the EC Regulation).

Managers

9.1 Each Member shall be entitled to appoint a natural person to act as a Manager and shall give notice of such appointment promptly to the other Members. Particulars of the Manager shall be the subject of the filing provisions of Article 7(d) of the EC Regulation and of regulation 5 of the Statutory Instrument.

9.2 A Manager may be removed from office by the Member who appointed him, whereupon the Member shall promptly serve notice of such removal on the other Members and, as soon as is reasonably practicable thereafter, designate a replacement in accordance with clause 9.1. Upon cessation of any Member's membership of the Association, the Member's right to appoint a Manager under clause 9.1 shall immediately terminate. A Manager's appointment shall terminate automatically if the Manager is prohibited by any applicable law or regulation preventing him from acting as a Manager.

9.3 Each Manager shall disclose by notice in writing to the Association the nature and extent of any material interest which the Manager may have in any transaction or arrangement with the Association, and such disclosure shall be made prior to the Association's entry into such transaction or arrangement. A Manager shall not be entitled to vote on any matter in which the Manager has a material interest which is required to be disclosed hereunder and which has not been disclosed in accordance with the provisions of this Agreement.

9.4 Each Manager shall be indemnified by the Association against all costs, liabilities and expenses which the Manager may incur whilst acting in the proper performance of the Manager's duties.

[**9.5** The Association shall only be validly bound as against third parties by two or more Managers acting jointly and in accordance with the objects of the Association, except where a single Member acts under the express authorisation of the Association (pursuant to a resolution of the Management Committee) and adduces evidence to such effect. The Members shall procure the appropriate filing in respect of the foregoing under Article 7(d) of the EC Regulation.] [*Note: Include this provision only if the authority of a Manager to act alone on behalf of the Association vis-à-vis third parties is to be limited.*]

Management Committee

10.1 The Management Committee shall be responsible for pursuing the objects of the Association and, in particular, shall (i) administer and manage the activities of the Association and (ii) take such decisions as may be necessary or desirable to achieve the objects of the Association.

10.2 The Management Committee shall be made up of the Managers appointed in accordance with clause 9.1, who shall each have the right to attend, speak and vote at all meetings of the Management Committee (subject to the provisions of this Agreement).

10.3 Meetings of the Management Committee shall be convened by a Manager giving not less than [14] days' notice to all the other Managers for the time being, such notice to be given in writing and to set out the date, time and place of the meeting and an agenda describing the matters to be considered at the meeting. The period of notice stipulated for the calling of the meeting may be reduced or waived with the consent of all the Managers. Meetings of the Management Committee shall be held at least [once in every calendar quarter]. The normal venue for meetings of the Management Committee shall be in _____ but may be held elsewhere by agreement of the Managers.

10.4 [A meeting of the Members] may, by ordinary resolution, appoint a particular Manager to be the chairman at meetings of the Management Committee.

10.5 A Manager may upon 24 hours' written notice to the Association appoint an alternate (who need not be a Manager) to attend and vote in his place at a meeting of the Management Committee.

10.6 A Manager or his alternate shall be entitled to one vote at meetings of the Management Committee. Resolutions put to the vote at a meeting of the Management Committee shall be decided by a majority of votes upon a show of hands. Each Manager who is also an alternate shall be entitled to a separate vote on behalf of his appointor in addition to his own vote.

10.7 No business shall be transacted at any meeting of the Management Committee unless a quorum is present. The quorum for meetings of the Management Committee shall be not less than [half in number] of the Managers for the time being and, in any event, not less than 2 Managers present at the same time. Alternates shall be counted in the quorum. If such a quorum is not present within half an hour from the time appointed for the meeting of the Management Committee, or if during such meeting such a quorum ceases to be present, the meeting shall stand adjourned to the same day in the next week at the same time and place or to such time and place as the Managers may determine.

10.8 The secretary for each meeting of the Management Committee shall [be appointed by _____ and shall] shall have the right to attend each meeting of the Management Committee. He shall record the proceedings of such meetings and will prepare minutes. Any such minutes, if purporting to be signed by the chairman of the meeting to which they relate or of the meeting at which they are read, shall be sufficient evidence, without further proof, of the facts therein stated.

10.9 A resolution in writing signed by or on behalf of each Manager who would have been entitled to vote upon that resolution if it had been proposed at a meeting of the Management Committee at which he was entitled to be represented shall have effect as if it had been passed at a meeting of the Management Committee properly convened and held and may consist of several instruments in like form each executed by one or more of the Managers.

10.10 A meeting of the Management Committee may consist of a conference between Managers who are not all in one place but each of whom is able (directly or by telephone or other medium of communication) to speak to each of the others and to be heard by each of the others simultaneously; the word "**meeting**" in this clause 10 shall be construed accordingly.

10.11 The Management Committee may delegate (and grant the power to subdelegate) any of its powers, duties, obligations and discretions to any committee, board, employee, agent or person [(provided that the Management Committee may not so delegate its power to represent the Association in respect of dealings with third parties which power may only be exercised by the Managers in accordance with clause 9.5)].

10.12 The Management Committee, through the Managers, shall provide (or procure that there is provided) to any Member any information which that Member may reasonably require in relation to the business of the Association and shall provide or procure access at all reasonable times to any Member for the purpose of inspecting the Association's books and records.

Meetings of Members

11.1 Meetings of the Members shall be held at such intervals as may be agreed by the Members provided that such a meeting shall take place not less than once in each calendar year. A Member may call a meeting of the Members by not less than 21 clear days' notice in writing sent to every Member (provided that a meeting may be held on shorter notice if every Member so agrees).

11.2 No business shall be transacted at any meeting of the Members unless a quorum is present. The quorum for a meeting of the Members shall require the presence of a duly authorised representative of [each Member].

11.3 [Except as provided in clause 12 or by the EC Regulation,] all decisions at a meeting of the Members shall [be passed by ordinary resolution] [require a unanimous vote].

11.4 A resolution in writing signed by a duly authorised representative of each Member shall have effect as if it had been passed at a meeting of the Members properly convened and held and may consist of several instruments in like form each executed by one or more duly authorised representatives of the Members.

11.5 A meeting of the Members may consist of a conference between duly authorised representatives of all the Members who are not all in one place but each of whom is able (directly or by telephone or other medium of communication) to speak to each of the others and to be heard by each of the others simultaneously; the word "**meeting**" in this clause 11 shall be construed accordingly.

Reserved matters for Members

12.1 The following matters shall be decided upon at meetings of the Members and shall be passed:

(a) (in the case of matters specified in clause 12.2) by unanimous resolution ("**unanimous resolution**") requiring the votes of all the Members entitled to vote; or

(b) (in the case of matters specified in clause 12.3) by special resolution ("**special resolution**") requiring not less than 75 per cent of the votes of all the Members in attendance and entitled to vote.

12.2 The following matters may only be decided upon by the passing of a unanimous resolution of the Members, namely any decision:

(a) to alter the objects of the Association;

(b) to transfer the official address of the Association;

(c) to admit a new Member to the Association;

(d) to alter the number of votes allotted to each Member;

(e) to alter the basis of contribution of any Member to the Association's financing;

(f) to alter the conditions for the taking of decisions;

(g) to alter the duration of the Association;

(h) to authorise the assignment of a Member's participation;

[(i) to authorise a single Manager to bind the Association as against a third party; [*note: omit unless clause 9.5 is included*]]

(j) to transform the Association from a European Economic Interest Grouping into another legal form;

(k) on any other matter requiring a unanimous decision by the Members in accordance with the EC Regulation and/or the Statutory Instrument.

12.3 The following matters may only be decided upon by the passing of a special resolution, namely any decision:

[(a) to adopt (or amend) the Rules; or]

[(b)] to amend this Agreement.

Budget and costs

13.1 At the first meeting of the Management Committee in any financial year of the Association, an annual budget in respect of the running costs and expenditure of the

Association for the forthcoming financial year shall be approved. The financial year of the Association shall commence on [1 January] and end on [31 December] in each calendar year.

13.2 The Members shall contribute in equal shares to the payment of any amount by which the expenditure of the Association at any time exceeds the income of the Association. Any call on the Members for funding to meet such expenditure shall be made by the Management Committee.

13.3 Any incidental profits arising from the activities of the Association shall be divided among the Members in equal shares.

13.4 Proper books of account and records relating to the affairs of the Association shall be kept under the supervision and authority of the Management Committee. Such books and records shall be available at all times for inspection by the Members or their duly authorised representatives.

[**13.5** An audit of the books of account of the Association shall be undertaken every 12 months by an independent auditor and a report (in a form to be established by the Management Committee) shall be prepared and submitted to each of the Members.] [*Omit if not required.*]

Termination of membership

14.1 A Member may terminate its membership of the Association upon giving not less than [6 months'] notice in writing to each of the other Members, such notice to expire in any event at the end of a financial year of the Association. The consent of the other Members shall not be required.

14.2 A Member shall cease to be a member of the Association on the passing of a unanimous resolution (such Member not being entitled to vote thereon) to that effect at a meeting of the Members if any of the following events or grounds shall occur, namely:

(a) if it makes any composition or arrangement with its creditors or shall go into liquidation (whether compulsory or voluntary) or if a provisional liquidator, administrator, receiver or administrative receiver is appointed over a substantial part of its assets or undertaking or if anything analogous to any of the events specified in this sub-paragraph (a) occurs in respect of such Member under the laws of any applicable jurisdiction;

(b) if it ceases to be a person who is entitled to be a member of a European Economic Interest Grouping in accordance with Article 4 of the EC Regulation;

[(c) if any person (other than a person who was a holding company of that Member at its Date of Admission) becomes a holding company of that Member;] [*review carefully before including this "change of control" ground of termination*]

(d) if it has persistently breached this Agreement or otherwise seriously failed in the obligations which it is required to discharge by reason of its membership of the Association; or

(e) if it has caused or threatens to cause serious disruption to the operations of the Association.

14.3 [If a Member ceases to be a member of the Association (save by reason of the Association being wound-up), no distribution shall be required or made by the Association to that Member from the assets of the Association by reference to the value of the ceasing Member's rights and obligations in the Association.]

14.4 All Members shall cease to be members of the Association upon completion of a winding-up pursuant to clause 15 of this Agreement.

14.5 Upon the termination of this Agreement, no Member shall have any continuing right or obligation under it (except as expressly provided under this Agreement or to the extent that such right or obligation has accrued prior to termination).

Winding-up

15.1 The Association may be wound up at any time by a [unanimous] resolution of its Members resolving to that effect.

15.2 The Association shall be wound up:

(a) by a special resolution of its Members resolving to wind-up if the objects of the Association have been accomplished or it becomes impossible to pursue the objects of the Association any further (and any such resolution shall note the relevant ground accordingly); or

(b) by a unanimous resolution of its Members (or of the remaining Member) when the conditions set out in Article 4(2) of the EC Regulation are no longer fulfilled.

Confidentiality

16.1 Each Member shall keep confidential (and shall ensure that its officers, employees, agents and professional and other advisers enter into undertakings to keep confidential) and shall not disclose to third parties nor use for any purpose (save for disclosure or use in the course of accomplishing the objects of the Association) any information relating to the clients, business or affairs of any other Member (or any subsidiary of any other Member) unless such information:

(a) is acquired from a third party with the right to divulge it; or

(b) is required to be disclosed by operation of law or any regulation or binding judgment or order, or any requirement of a competent authority (provided that, where a Member is required to make a disclosure under this sub-paragraph (b), it shall use its reasonable efforts to obtain a waiver or exemption from such obligation in respect of that confidential information); or

(c) is information which the Members have jointly decided to disclose; or

(d) is reasonably required to be disclosed, in confidence, to such of the Member's officers, employees, agents and professional and other advisers as need to know the same for use in connection with accomplishing the objects of the Association;

(e) is or becomes within the public domain (otherwise than through the default of the relevant Member);

(f) was in the Member's possession prior to the date of its receipt from the Association or the disclosing Member.

16.2 A Member shall promptly notify the Association and/or the relevant Member if it becomes aware of any breach of confidence by any person or body to whom the Member divulges any confidential information and shall give the Association, and/or the Member whose information is the subject of the breach of confidence, all reasonable assistance in connection with any proceedings which the Association and/or the relevant Member may institute against such person for breach of confidence.

16.3 The obligations as to confidentiality under this clause 16 shall remain in full force and effect notwithstanding any termination of a Member's membership of the Association or any termination of this Agreement.

Notices

17.1 Notices served under this Agreement shall only be valid if in writing and in English, and shall be delivered to the official address of the Association (made out to the attention of the Secretary) and to the address for service of the other Members (as set out in the Schedule). A Member may designate, by notice given in accordance with the provisions of this clause 17 to all other Members and to the official address of the Association, another address for service of notices.

17.2 Any notice served under this Agreement may be delivered by hand or by first class pre-paid letter or fax and shall be deemed to have been served: if by hand, when delivered; if by first class post, 48 hours after posting; and if by fax, when despatched.

Assignment

18. A Member shall not be entitled to assign, sub-license or otherwise transfer any of its rights or obligations under this Agreement.

No partnership or agency

19. Nothing in this Agreement (or any of the arrangements contemplated by this Agreement) shall be deemed to constitute a partnership between the Members nor, except as may be expressly set out herein, constitute any Member the agent of any other Member for any purpose.

Waiver and amendments

20.1 A waiver (whether express or implied) by a Member of any of the provisions of this Agreement or of any breach by any other Member in performing any of those provisions shall not constitute a continuing waiver and shall not prevent the waiving Member from subsequently enforcing any of the provisions of this Agreement.

20.2 Except as expressly provided in this Agreement, this Agreement may be amended only by an instrument in writing signed by a duly authorised representative of each Member.

Invalidity

21. If any of the provisions of this Agreement is or becomes invalid, illegal or unenforceable, the validity, legality or enforceability of the remaining provisions shall not in any way be affected or impaired. Notwithstanding the foregoing, the Members shall thereupon negotiate in good faith in order to agree the terms of a mutually satisfactory valid provision (achieving so nearly as possible the same commercial effect) to be substituted for the provision found to be void or unenforceable.

Entire agreement

22. This Agreement constitutes the entire agreement and understanding of the Members with respect to the subject matter hereof and no Member has entered into this Agreement in reliance upon any representation, warranty or undertaking by or on behalf of any other Member which is not expressly set out herein.

Disputes and arbitration

23.1 The Members shall use all reasonable endeavours to resolve any dispute amicably in good faith in the best interests of the Members of the Association.

23.2 All disputes arising in connection with this Agreement shall be finally settled under [the Rules of Conciliation and Arbitration of the International Chamber of Commerce by one or more arbitrators appointed in accordance with the said Rules.] The arbitration shall be in [London] and the language of the arbitration shall be English.

Governing law

24. This Agreement shall be governed by and construed in accordance with English law.

AS WITNESS the hands of the duly authorised representatives of the parties.

SCHEDULE: ADDRESSES OF MEMBERS

Signed by _____   **Signed** by _____   **Signed** by _____

for and on behalf of **A**   for and on behalf of **B**   for and on behalf of **C**

....

Precedent 8

Limited Liability Partnership Agreement

> *The limited liability partnership (LLP) is a new legal vehicle in the UK. Its constitution is very flexible. There is no fixed terminology. In the following Agreement, the parties are described as "Members" with individual "directors" being appointed to a "Board" which is responsible for management of the LLP. "Designated Members" are individuals within certain specific responsibilities under the Act. The Agreement is modelled fairly closely on the structure for a partnership agreement (see Precedent 6) with the important difference that the LLP is a corporate entity and the "Members" have limited liability. Some of the duties as between members of an LLP under the general law remain uncertain. This precedent excludes the application of the "default" duties under the 2000 Act with the intent that the rights and duties should be those expressly set out in the Agreement.*

THIS LIMITED LIABILITY PARTNERSHIP AGREEMENT is made on _____

BETWEEN:

(1) _____, whose registered office is at _____ (*"A"*)

(2) _____, whose registered office is at _____ (*"B"*)

(3) _____, whose registered office is at _____ (*"C"*)

WHEREAS:

(A) _____ (the "**LLP**") was registered on _____ as a limited liability partnership under the Limited Liability Partnerships Act 2000.

(B) A, B and C are entering into this Agreement to set out the terms governing their relationship as members of the LLP.

IT IS AGREED AS FOLLOWS:

Interpretation

"**the Act**" means the Limited Liability Partnerships Act 2000;

"**Affiliate**" means, in relation to a Member, any subsidiary or holding company for the time being of that Member and any other subsidiary for the time being of the holding company (and "**holding company**" and "**subsidiary**" shall be construed in accordance with section 1159 of the Companies Act 2006);

"**Board**" means the Board of Directors of the LLP constituted pursuant to clause 9;

"**Budget**" means the budget for each Financial Year of the LLP prepared pursuant to clause 11;

"**Business**" means the business and affairs of the LLP as set out in clause 3 of this Agreement;

"**Business Day**" means a day on which banks generally are open in London [and _____] (excluding Saturdays) for a full range of business;

"**Business Plan**" means a rolling business plan for the LLP relating to the current Financial Year and [four] succeeding Financial Years, as approved from time to time by the Board;

"**Companies Act**" means the Companies Act 2006 as amended by the Act for the purposes of limited liability partnerships;

"**Designated Members**" means such Members, being not less than two in number, as shall be specified by the Board as designated members for the purposes of the Act;

"**Director**" means any member of the Board;

"**Event of Default**" has the meaning set out in clause 17.1;

"**Executive**" means [the Chief Executive and any other member of the senior management team of the LLP];

"**Financial Year**" means the period from and including 1 April in any calendar year to and including 31 March in the following year or such other period or periods as the Members may determine;

"**Insolvency Act**" means the Insolvency Act 1986 as adjusted by the Act for the purpose of limited liability partnerships;

"**LLP Interest**" means the total interest of a Member in the LLP;

"**Members**" means A, B and C and "**Member**" means any of them;

"**Member's Share**" means, in relation to a Member, the proportion which the amount standing to the credit of that Member's Capital Account bears to the total amounts standing to the credit of all Capital Accounts;

"**Registered Office**" means _____ or such other address as shall from time to time be registered by the LLP with a Registrar of Companies as its registered office;

"**Regulations**" means the Limited Liability Partnerships Regulations 2001.

1.2 References to any profits or losses of the LLP include a reference to profits and losses of a capital nature.

1.3 References to the winding-up of any Member shall include the dissolution or striking off the register of that Member.

1.4 Words and phrases which are contained or defined in the Act or the Companies Act (including as amended in relation to limited liability partnerships by the Regulations) shall have the respective meanings so attributed to them.

Commencement

2. This Agreement shall be deemed to be effective from the date of registration of the LLP and shall continue until terminated in accordance with the terms of this Agreement.

Business of the Partnership

3.1 The Business shall be _____.

3.2 The Business shall be conducted in the best interests of the LLP on sound commercial profit-making principles in accordance with the Business Plan. The initial Business Plan is set out [in the Annex to this Agreement].

Designated Members

4.1 The initial Designated Members for the purpose of the Act shall be [specify at least two individuals].

4.2 The Designated Members shall be responsible for ensuring compliance with all registration and other requirements of designated members under the Act and the Regulations.

4.3 Any Designated Member may cease to be so by giving notice to the LLP to that effect. Such notice shall take effect immediately provided that, if there would be only one Designated Member then remaining, the notice shall not take effect until such time as the Board shall have specified a replacement Designated Member.

Name

5.1 The name of the LLP shall be "_____ LLP" (or such other name as the Members shall agree).

5.2 Each Member acknowledges that all proprietary and other rights in the Name are vested exclusively in the LLP and agrees that no Member shall use the Name (or any name which may be substituted for it or which is so similar to any such name that it is likely to be confused with it) for any purpose other than for the purposes of the Business whilst it is a Member.

Capital Accounts

6.1 The Members shall respectively make initial contributions to the capital of the LLP as follows:

(a) A: [*describe or refer to commitment to provide initial contribution: cash, assets, transfer of property etc.*]

(b) B: [*describe or refer to commitment to provide initial contribution: cash, assets, transfer of property etc.*]

(c) C: [*describe or refer to commitment to provide initial contribution: cash, assets, transfer of property etc.*]

6.2 The Members acknowledge and agree that, following the initial contributions referred to in clause 6.1, their respective Capital Accounts shall be credited as follows:

Member	Capital
A	£_____
B	£_____
C	£_____

6.3 No Member shall have any right, directly or indirectly, to withdraw or receive back any part of the amount standing to the credit of its Capital Account except (i) following a decision of the Board under clause 6.4 or (ii) upon winding-up of the LLP.

6.4 If the Board determines (taking into account the working capital requirements of the LLP) that all the Members may withdraw a *pro rata* proportion of their respective capital contributions, each Member shall be entitled to make such a withdrawal from its Capital Account accordingly.

6.5 No interest shall be payable by the LLP on amounts credited to the Capital Accounts of the Members.

Further funding

7.1 Each Member undertakes that, if the Board resolves that funding from the Members is required pursuant to any relevant Budget approved by the Board, it will contribute its Member's Share of the required funding on such terms as the Board shall determine to apply to all Members.

7.2 All capital contributed by a Member to meet funding pursuant to clause 7.1 shall (unless the Members otherwise agree) be treated as a capital contribution and credited to its respective Capital Account.

7.3 The Members shall not be obliged to provide guarantees to support the LLP's financing commitments. If they do so, such guarantees shall be given in proportion to each Member's Share. The liabilities of the Members under such guarantees (so far as possible) shall be several and not joint and several. If a claim is made under any such guarantee against a Member, it shall be entitled to such contribution from the other Member as will ensure that the aggregate liability is borne by the Members in their respective Member's Shares.

Profits and losses

8.1 The amount of profits and losses in respect of any Financial Year shall be determined from the audited accounts of the LLP. All such profits and losses shall, unless the Members otherwise agree, be allocated to the Members in proportion to their Members' Shares and shall be respectively credited or debited to current accounts of the Members.

8.2 The Members may withdraw amounts credited to their current accounts in cash pro rata, if the Board determines that such cash is available and surplus to the requirements of the LLP.

Directors and Board of the LLP

9.1 Overall supervision of the Business shall be the responsibility of the Board, which shall have authority to act on behalf of the LLP in all matters in connection with the Business and shall carry out its duties in such manner as it considers to be in the best interests of the LLP.

9.2 The Board shall comprise [a non-executive, non-voting Chairman and] non-executive Directors of which (i) 2 Directors shall be nominated by A; (ii) 2 Directors shall be nominated by B; and (iii) 1 Director shall be nominated by C.

9.3 Any appointment or removal of a Director shall be effected by notice in writing to the LLP signed by or on behalf of the Member which appointed that Director and shall take effect, subject to any contrary intention expressed in the notice, when the notice is delivered to the LLP. If a party ceases to be a Member for any reason, its nominated Director(s) shall immediately resign their post.

9.4 A shall be entitled to appoint the Chairman. The first Chairman shall be _____.

9.5 The Board shall meet quarterly. In addition, any Member shall have the right to convene a meeting of the Board at any time. Any meeting of the Board shall be called by or on behalf of the Chairman and conducted in accordance with the provisions of this clause 9.

9.6 The quorum for any meeting of the Board (other than an adjourned meeting) shall be a majority in number of the Directors, including at least 1 A Director (or his alternate) and at least 1 B Director (or his alternate). If such a quorum is not present within 30 minutes from the time appointed for the meeting or if during the meeting such quorum ceases to be present, the meeting shall be adjourned for 7 Business Days [and at that adjourned meeting any 2 Directors (or their alternates) present shall constitute a quorum].

9.7 At least 10 Business Days' written notice shall be given of any meeting of the Board, provided that a shorter period of notice may be given with the written approval of at least 1 A Director and at least 1 B Director. Any such notice shall include an agenda identifying in reasonable detail the matters to be discussed (in particular, of any matter set out in clause 9.10) and shall be accompanied by copies of any relevant papers to be discussed at the meeting and any resolutions to be tabled. A meeting of the Board may consist of a conference between Directors who are not all in one place, but of whom each is able (directly or by telephonic communication) to speak to each of the others and to be heard by each of the others simultaneously; and the word "**meeting**" in this Agreement shall be construed accordingly.

9.8 Any Director shall be entitled to require the Chief Executive or any other Executive to attend (but not vote at) all or part of any meeting of the Board in order to provide information or views, provided that the Director notifies the relevant Executive and the Chairman and the other Directors within [2] Business Days from receipt of the notice of meeting that the Executive's attendance is required and specifies the items on which his information or views will be required.

9.9 Resolutions of the Board shall be passed as follows:

(a) Each Director shall have one vote. Any Director who is absent from the meeting may nominate any other [Director] who is present to act as his alternate and to vote in his place at the meeting.

(b) The Chairman shall not have a casting vote. If the Chairman is not present at any meeting of the Board, those Directors present (if constituting a quorum) shall nominate a chairman for that meeting. Any Director acting as such a chairman shall continue to have his vote in accordance with this clause 9.9.

(c) Subject to clause 9.10, resolutions of the Board shall be passed by simple majority.

(d) A written resolution signed by all the Directors (whether in a single document or in counterpart) shall be binding as a resolution passed at a meeting of the Board.

9.10 The following Reserved Matters shall in any event require unanimity of the [Board] [the Members], namely:

(a) admission of a new Member;

(b) any change in the nature or scope of the Business (including any material business acquisition or disposal exceeding £_____ in value or any material partnership or joint venture);

(c) any material change in the organisation of the LLP;

(d) appointment or removal of the Chief Executive [or other Executive] or any material change in their respective terms of employment;

(e) approval of the Business Plan and Budget or any material deviation from the Business Plan or Budget;

(f) any expenditure on any particular item which is [_____ per cent] more than that provided for in the relevant Budget;

(g) disposal of (including the grant of any security interest or other encumbrance over) any LLP property where the value of such property exceeds £_____;

(h) any transaction between the LLP and a Member or its Affiliate [having a value in excess of £_____] (or any material amendment to any contract with a Member or its Affiliates);

(i) removal of Auditors and appointment of new Auditors;

(j) any [material] change in the accounting policies of the LLP;

(k) the commencement or settlement or cessation of any litigation or arbitration involving the LLP other than any litigation or arbitration involving (i) a dispute pursuant to this Agreement or (ii) a claim of less than £_____;

(l) any decision whether cash available to the LLP is surplus to the requirements of the LLP;

(m) any resolution to terminate or dissolve the LLP under clause 19.

9.11 In the event of deadlock on any vote taken in relation to a Reserved Matter which cannot be resolved after a further meeting of the Board, the matter shall be referred to the [Chairmen/Chief Executives or other senior representatives of each of the Members] whose determination (if unanimous) shall bind the Board.

9.12 No Director shall be liable or accountable in damages or otherwise to the LLP (or any of the other Members) in respect of performance of his duties as a Director unless guilty of bad faith, wilful default [or gross negligence].

Executive management

10.1 The Board shall delegate day-to-day executive management of the Business to the Chief Executive, who shall carry out his responsibilities in accordance with the then current Business Plan and Budget and such policies as shall be laid down by the Board. The Chief Executive shall be responsible to the Board and shall be assisted in his duties by the other Executives.

10.2 The appointment and terms of reference of the other Executives will be proposed by the Chief Executive but will be subject to the prior approval of the Board.

Budgets and information

11.1 The Chief Executive shall be responsible for the production of a draft Budget for each Financial Year and updating the Business Plan. The draft Budget and updated Business Plan shall be submitted to the Board for approval not less than [45] Business Days prior to the commencement of the following Financial Year. In any event, the Board shall adopt a draft Budget and Business Plan (in each case with such amendments as the Board may agree) prior to the commencement of the relevant Financial Year.

11.2 The Chief Executive shall (i) as soon as reasonably practicable after the end of each [calendar month], ensure that management accounts, and a management report relating to the business of the LLP during that period, are prepared in such a manner and format as the Board shall approve and (ii) following any request from any Member, prepare all information relating to the affairs of the LLP as that Member may reasonably require.

11.3 Each Member will promptly, following any request from the other Member, submit to the Board all information relating to the affairs of the LLP in the possession of that Member and which the requesting Member may reasonably require.

Rights, duties and liabilities as Members

12.1 The aggregate liability of each Member to the LLP shall not exceed its outstanding obligations (if any) to make capital contributions under this Agreement in respect of its Capital Accounts. Notwithstanding any other provision of this Agreement, it is the intention of the parties that, in accordance with the Act and to the fullest extent permitted by law, no Member shall have any personal liability for the LLP's obligations because of its status as a Member.

12.2 No Member shall have any liability under this Agreement or as a Member except as expressly provided in this Agreement or under the Act.

12.3 The Members shall not owe fiduciary duties to each other or to the LLP (except for such fiduciary duties to the LLP as are implied by their status as agents of the LLP [and for their duties under clause 13.2]).

12.4 The default provisions under Regulations 7 and 8 of the Regulations shall not apply.

12.5 The right contained in section 994(1) of the Companies Act 2006 is excluded.

12.6 A Member shall be entitled to be reimbursed by the LLP for all costs and expenses reasonably incurred by it in the due performance of its obligations as a Member of the LLP or in respect of anything necessarily done by it for the preservation of the Business or the property of the LLP. Reimbursement shall be in accordance with and subject to procedures approved by the Board.

Undertakings by Members

13.1 No Member (nor its Affiliates) shall (whether solely or jointly with any other person, firm or company or whether directly or indirectly) carry on or be engaged in or interested (except as the holder for investment of securities dealt in on a stock exchange and not exceeding [5] per cent in nominal value of the securities of any class) in any Competing Business during the period of this Agreement. For this purpose, "**Competing Business**" means _____. [*Consider whether undertaking against non-solicitation of employees is also appropriate*].

13.2 Each Member undertakes to the other that, in addition to its other obligations under this Agreement, it shall (i) promote the best interests of the LLP and consult fully on all matters materially affecting the development of the Business and (ii) act in good faith towards the other Members in order to promote the success of the LLP, including considering in good faith any proposals made by any other Member to modify this Agreement.

Indemnity

14. Each Member and its officers, directors, and employees (an "**indemnified party**") shall be entitled to be indemnified out of the assets of the LLP against any liability, damage, cost or expense (including legal fees and expenses reasonably incurred in defence of any claims or legal proceedings) arising from any act or omission in the course of the Business or activities authorised by or on behalf of the LLP (unless and to the extent due to bad faith, wilful default [or gross negligence] of the indemnified party). This right to indemnification and payment of legal fees and expenses shall not be affected by the termination of the LLP.

Accounts

15.1 The initial auditors of the LLP shall be _____.

15.2 The Board shall be responsible for maintaining proper accounting records for the LLP. These records shall be available for inspection by any Member during normal business hours and upon reasonable notice.

15.3 The Board shall be responsible for arranging the preparation of a balance sheet, profit and loss account, and a statement of source and application of funds relating to the LLP as at the end of and for each Financial Year in accordance with generally accepted accounting standards and principles in the [United Kingdom]. The accounts shall be audited by the auditors.

Confidentiality and announcements

16.1 Each Member shall at all times use its best efforts to keep confidential all commercial and technical information which it may acquire in relation to the LLP or the Business or in relation to the customers, business or affairs of any other Member (or its Affiliates). No Member shall use or disclose such information except with the consent of the other Members or, in the case of information relating to the LLP, for the purpose of advancing the Business. This restriction shall not apply to any information:

(a) which is publicly available or becomes publicly available through no act of the Member wishing to use or disclose the information;

(b) which that Member can demonstrate was already in its possession or was independently developed by that Member or on its behalf;

(c) which is obtained by that Member from a third party which did not acquire or hold the information under an obligation of confidentiality; or

(d) to the extent that it is required to be disclosed by law or by the rules of any recognised stock exchange or regulatory body.

16.2 Each Member shall use all reasonable efforts to ensure that its employees and agents and any Affiliate (including its employees and agents) observe this confidentiality.

16.3 No announcement in connection with the subject matter of this Agreement shall be made or issued by or on behalf of any of the Members or the LLP without the prior written approval of all the Members (such approval not to be unreasonably withheld or delayed) except as may be required by law or by any stock exchange or by any governmental authority.

16.4 The provisions of this clause 16 shall survive any termination of this Agreement.

Default

17.1 For the purposes of this clause 17 an "**Event of Default**" shall occur in relation to a Member (the "Defaulting Member"):

(a) if the Defaulting Member commits a material breach of its obligations under this Agreement and fails to remedy the breach (or implement plans to the reasonable satisfaction of the other Members to prevent the recurrence of such breach) within 60 days after being given notice by the other Members to do so (and such notice indicates that the notifying Members intend to exercise their rights under this clause 17); or

(b) if the Defaulting Member [(or any holding company of the Defaulting Member)] goes into liquidation whether compulsory or voluntary (except for the purposes of a bona fide reconstruction with the consent of the other Member, such consent not to be unreasonably withheld) or if a petition is presented or an order made for the appointment of an administrator in relation to the Defaulting Member or if a receiver, administrative receiver or manager is appointed over any substantial part of the assets or undertaking of the Defaulting Member.

17.2 The LLP may (by a unanimous decision of [the Board]) [the Members] (other than the Defaulting Member (or its nominated Director(s)) resolve to expel any Defaulting Member by 30 days' notice in writing following an Event of Default.

17.3 If the Defaulting Member on whom such expulsion notice is served shall within 14 days of the date of service of that notice serve on the LLP a counter-notice denying the allegations and declaring that it wishes to refer the dispute to arbitration in accordance with clause 23, the operation of the notice shall be suspended and only re-instated if (i) the Member agrees or (ii) the arbitration confirms the Event of Default by the Defaulting Member.

17.4 If a Defaulting Member is expelled under this clause 17, the LLP Interest of the Defaulting Member shall be allocated to the other Members (unless otherwise agreed, in proportion to their respective Members' Shares). The expelled Defaulting Member shall be entitled to a price in respect of its LLP Interest which shall be negotiated between the Members or, failing agreement, shall be the fair value of the Member's LLP Interest as determined by an independent firm of chartered accountants appointed by the Members (or, failing agreement, appointed by [the President for the time being of the Institute of Chartered Accountants in England and Wales]) taking into account all factors it considers relevant including the effect of the Event of Default. Any such independent firm shall act as experts (and not as arbitrators) and its decision shall be final and binding on the Members.

17.5 If an Event of Default occurs in relation to a Member, then (irrespective of whether or not an expulsion notice is served on the Defaulting Member) the Director(s) appointed by the Defaulting Member shall, for as long as the Event of Default exists, cease to be entitled to vote at any meeting of the Board and the approval of such Director(s) shall no longer be required in respect of any of the Reserved Matters and no such Director(s) appointed by the Defaulting Member shall be required for the purposes of a quorum.

Assignment

18.1 No Member shall transfer, assign, encumber or otherwise deal with any or all of its LLP Interest (except in accordance with clause 18.2) without obtaining the prior written consent of the other Members.

18.2 A Member shall be entitled at any time to transfer all (but not some only) of its LLP Interest to an Affiliate provided that (i) the Affiliate shall first have entered into an agreement with the other Members agreeing to be bound (in terms reasonably satisfactory to the other Members) by the provisions of this Agreement [and (ii) the transferring Member shall remain liable for the performance by such Affiliate of its obligations under this Agreement].

Termination and winding-up

19.1 If a Member considers that a fundamental deadlock or difference in relation to the conduct or development of the Business is arising between the Members, it shall give as early an indication as practicable to the other Members of that concern so that orderly arrangements for the continuation of the Business can, if possible, be agreed on an amicable basis.

19.2 This Agreement shall continue in full force and effect for so long as at least two Members hold their respective interests in the LLP or until the LLP is wound-up or dissolved pursuant to law, by mutual agreement of the Members or in accordance with this Agreement.

19.3 In the event of the winding-up of the LLP, no Member (past or present) shall be obliged to contribute to the assets of the LLP under section 74 of the Insolvency Act.

19.4 In the event of termination or a voluntary winding-up of the LLP:

(a) the Members shall consult and use all reasonable efforts to agree an orderly programme for the winding up of the business of the LLP and the realisation and distribution of its assets;

(b) [the Members shall be entitled to be allocated such profits of the LLP, for the period from the commencement of the Financial Year in which the resolution for voluntary winding-up was passed to the date such resolution was passed, to which they would have been entitled in accordance with clause 8;]

(c) the assets of the LLP remaining after payment of its liabilities [(and the operation of clause [_____] sub-paragraph (b))] shall be applied in returning to the Members the amounts standing to the credit of their Capital Accounts (and, if there are insufficient assets to return such amounts in full, then the available assets shall be applied pro rata as between the Members in proportion to the amount standing to the credit of their respective Capital Accounts); and

(d) any remaining assets of the LLP shall be distributed amongst the Members in the proportions [in which they would be allocated profits in accordance with clause 8] [in their respective Members' Shares];

(e) [the Members may agree on a full or partial distribution of the assets of the LLP in kind and/or they may agree a procedure whereby each Member may make an offer to acquire a specific group of assets or interests of the Business (including all liabilities relating thereto); the other Members may offer to acquire the same assets or interests and the acquisition shall be made by the Member which is prepared to make the higher offer or (absent any such counter-offer) following such independent valuation procedure as shall be agreed.]

Waivers and amendments

20.1 No failure or delay on the part of any Member in exercising any power or right under this Agreement shall operate as a waiver of any agreement or undertaking to be performed by the other Member or in any way restrict or prejudice the rights and powers of the first-mentioned Member.

20.2 Except as expressly provided in this Agreement, no amendment or variation of this Agreement shall be effective unless in writing and signed by a duly authorised representative of each Member.

Severability

21. If any provision of this Agreement is found invalid or illegal, the remainder of this Agreement shall be binding on the Members and shall be construed as if the invalid or illegal provision had been deleted from this Agreement. The Members shall use all reasonable efforts to agree any substitute provisions for the invalid or illegal provision having, as close as practicable, the same commercial effect.

Notices

22.1 Any notice required or permitted to be given under this Agreement shall be in writing addressed to the party at its address set out below or at such other address as the party may designate in writing:

A:

Address: _____

Fax No: _____

For the personal attention of: _____

B:

Address: _____

Fax No: _____

For the personal attention of: _____

C:

Address: _____
Fax No: _____
For the personal attention of: _____

22.2 Any such notice shall be delivered by hand or sent by fax or post (recorded delivery post or airmail prepaid). Any notice sent by fax shall be deemed to have been received at the opening of business on the first business day (in the country of intended receipt) following despatch, and if sent by letter shall be deemed to have been received 72 hours (in the case of any letter sent to and from an address in the United Kingdom) and 8 days (in any other case) after the time of posting.

Settlement of disputes

23.1 If there shall be any dispute, controversy or claim ("dispute") between the Members arising out of this Agreement, or the breach, termination or invalidity of this Agreement, the Members shall use their best efforts to resolve the matter on an amicable basis. The parties shall consider the use of mediation. If one Member serves formal written notice on the other that a dispute has arisen and the Members are unable to resolve such dispute within a period of [30] days from the service of such notice, then the matter shall be referred to the [Chairmen/Chief Executives of the Members]. No legal or arbitration proceedings shall be commenced unless and until these procedures have been followed.

23.2 If a dispute cannot be resolved amicably, it shall be referred for resolution to arbitration by [three] arbitrators appointed under the [Rules of Arbitration of the LCIA]. The arbitration shall be held in [London].

Entire agreement

24. This Agreement [(taken with _____)] constitutes the entire agreement and understanding of the Members with respect to the subject matter of this Agreement and none of the Members has entered into this Agreement in reliance upon any representation, warranty or undertaking by or on behalf of any Member which is not expressly set out herein.

Governing law

25. This Agreement shall be governed by and construed in accordance with the laws of [England].

As WITNESS the Members have executed this Agreement.

Signed by _____	**Signed** by _____	**Signed** by _____
for A	for B	for C
....	....	....

Precedent 9

50:50 Shareholders' Agreement (short form)

> *This Agreement provides the framework for a relatively straightforward 50:50 "deadlock" company. See Precedent 10: Multi-Party Shareholders' Agreement (long form) or Precedent 13: ITC Model Incorporated Joint Venture Agreement for various additions and/or alternative provisions which may be appropriate in more complex cases.*

THIS AGREEMENT is made on _____ 200_____

BETWEEN:

(1) _____ ("*A*") whose [registered] office is at _____

(2) _____ ("*B*") [registered] office is at _____

WHEREAS:

(A) The parties have agreed to form _____ a new jointly-owned company (the "**JVC**") which will acquire certain rights and assets, and otherwise be established and carry on business, in the manner set out in this Agreement.

(B) The parties have agreed that their relations as shareholders in the JVC shall be governed by the terms of this Agreement.

IT IS AGREED AS FOLLOWS:

Interpretation

1.1 In this Agreement the following terms shall, unless the context otherwise requires, have the following meanings:

"**A Director**" means a director of the JVC appointed by A pursuant to clause 5.1;

"**A Shares**" means A ordinary shares of £1 each in the capital of the JVC;

"**B Director**" means a director of the JVC appointed by B pursuant to clause 5.1;

"**B Shares**" means B ordinary shares of £1 each in the capital of the JVC;

"**Board**" means the board of directors of the JVC;

"**Business**" means the business to be carried on by the JVC as _____ in accordance with the Business Plan as updated by the [Board] from time to time;

"**Closing**" means completion of the establishment of the JVC in accordance with clause 3;

"**Conditions Precedent**" means the conditions precedent to establishment of the JVC set out in clause 18;

"**JVC**" means _____, the company to be incorporated pursuant to the terms of this Agreement;

"**member of the A Group**" means A and any subsidiary or holding company for the time being of A and any other subsidiary for the time being of that holding company; and "**holding company**" and "**subsidiary**" shall be construed in accordance with section 1159 of the Companies Act 2006);

"**member of the B Group**" means B and any subsidiary or holding company for the time being of A and any other subsidiary for the time being of that holding company;

"**Memorandum and Articles**" means the Memorandum and Articles of Association of the JVC;

"**parties**" means A and B.

1.2 Headings are inserted for convenience only and shall not affect the construction of this Agreement.

1.3 Any reference to an "**agreed form**" is to the draft form of the relevant document agreed between the parties and signed on their behalf for the purpose of identification before the signature of this Agreement (with such amendments, if any, as may subsequently be agreed in writing between the parties).

1.4 Any reference in this Agreement to an amount in pounds sterling shall include its market rate equivalent at the relevant time in any other currency.

Business of JVC

2.1 The parties agree to establish the JVC in accordance with this Agreement. The establishment of the JVC shall be subject to the Conditions Precedent.

2.2 The business of the JVC shall be _____ and shall be conducted in the best interests of the JVC in accordance with the then current Business Plan. [The initial Business Plan is annexed to this Agreement.]

Establishment of JVC

3.1 [The parties] [A] shall take appropriate steps to arrange for the formation of the JVC in _____. The JVC shall not trade or carry on business in any manner prior to Closing. Closing shall take place on _____ (or, if later, within 7 days after the fulfilment or waiver of all the Conditions Precedent) when the following events and matters set out in this clause 3 shall take place.

3.2 If not previously formed under clause 3.1, the parties shall cause the JVC to be incorporated with the following characteristics:

(a) the JVC shall be formed in [England as a private company limited by shares];

(b) the Memorandum and Articles of the JVC shall be in the agreed form [attached as an Annex to this Agreement];

(c) the JVC shall have an authorised share capital of £_____ divided into _____ A Shares and _____ B Shares;

(d) the name of the JVC shall be "_____";

(e) the registered office shall be at _____;

(f) the directors of the JVC shall be:

| A Directors: | [ ] | B Directors: | [ ] |
| | [ ] | | [ ] |

(g)　the first auditors of the JVC shall be _____ .

3.3 A shall subscribe unconditionally for _____ A Shares in cash [at a subscription price of £_____ per share] [at par], payment for which shall be made in cleared funds for the account of the JVC. B shall subscribe unconditionally for _____ B Shares in cash [at a subscription price of £_____ per share] [at par], payment for which shall be made in cleared funds for the account of the JVC. The parties shall procure that the JVC allots and issues credited as fully paid:

(a)　_____ A Shares to A [(to include the initial _____ ordinary shares of £_____ each in the JVC subscribed for by A upon incorporation)]; and

(b)　_____ B Shares to B;

and that the names of A and B are entered in the register of members of the JVC as the respective holders of the shares subscribed by them and that share certificates are issued to A and B in respect of such shares.

3.4 The parties shall cause the following ancillary agreements to be entered into, namely:

[(a)　the Asset Transfer Agreement/Sale and Purchase Agreement (in the agreed form) between _____ and the JVC for the transfer of _____ ;]

[(b)　the Distributorship Agreement (in the agreed form) between _____ and the JVC relating to the distribution of _____ ;]

[(c)　the Technology Licence (in the agreed form) between _____ and the JVC for the licensing of _____ ;]

[(d)　the Supply Agreement (in the agreed form) between _____ and the JVC for the supply of _____ ;]

[(e)　the Services Agreement (in the agreed form) between _____ and the JVC for the provision of services to the JVC as therein provided;]

[(f)　the Trade Mark Agreement(s) (in the agreed form) between _____ and the JVC for licensing of the use of the _____ mark.]

Capital and further finance

4.1 The JVC shall, in accordance with and following completion of the events and transactions referred to in clause 3, have an issued share capital of £_____ consisting of _____ A Shares owned by A and _____ B Shares owned by B.

4.2 The share capital of the JVC may from time to time be increased by such sum as shall be mutually agreed but so that in any event (unless otherwise agreed) such increased share capital shall be held in the proportions of 50 per cent by A (or other member of the A Group) and 50 per cent by B (or other member of the B Group).

4.3 If the JVC shall in the opinion of the Board require further finance, the JVC shall first approach its own banking sources. If finance cannot be obtained from the JVC's own banking sources, neither party shall be obliged to provide any such further finance to the JVC. Any such finance which the parties do agree to provide shall (unless otherwise agreed) be provided by the parties in equal proportions (whether by way of subscription of share capital, loan stock or otherwise). [*See Precedent 10 if the parties are committed to provide further funds to the JVC.*]

4.4 The parties shall not be obliged to provide guarantees for the JVC's liabilities in respect of such finance but, if they do so, they shall be given in equal proportions. The liabilities of the parties under any such guarantees shall (so far as possible) be several and, if a claim is made under any such guarantee against a party, that party shall be entitled to a contribution from the other party of such amount as shall ensure that the aggregate liability is borne in equal proportions.

4.5 Upon either party ceasing to be a shareholder in the JVC, the continuing party shall procure that any finance provided by the leaving party by way of loan under clause 4.3 shall be repaid to it and that it shall be relieved of its obligations under any guarantees provided under clause 4.4 (provided that, notwithstanding the termination of this Agreement, a party ceasing to be a shareholder shall remain liable under any such guarantees for any claims arising in respect of any default by the JVC occurring during the period during which that party was a shareholder in the JVC).

Directors and management

5.1 The business and affairs of the JVC shall (subject to the Reserved Shareholders Matters set out in clause 6) be managed by the Board of the JVC. The Board shall consist of 6 persons of which:

(a) A shall be entitled to appoint and maintain in office 3 Directors (and to remove any Director so appointed from office and to appoint another in the place of any Director so removed); and

(b) B shall be entitled to appoint and maintain in office 3 Directors (and to remove any Director so appointed from office and to appoint another in the place of any Director so removed).

5.2 Every appointment and removal by A or B of a Director pursuant to its entitlement shall be notified in writing to the other party and the Secretary of the JVC. A and B shall each use their respective votes in the JVC to ensure that the Board of the JVC is constituted by persons appointed in the manner set out in this Agreement.

5.3 The quorum for the transaction of business at any meeting of the Board shall be at least 1 A Director and at least 1 B Director present at the time when the relevant business is transacted.

5.4 At any meeting of the Board, each Director shall be entitled to one vote. Any decision of the Board in favour of a resolution, to be valid, shall require the positive vote of at least 1 A Director and at least 1 B Director. If the parties are not represented at any meeting of the Board by an equal number of A Directors and B Directors, then one of the Directors present nominated by the party which is represented by the fewer Directors shall be entitled at that meeting to such additional vote or votes as shall result in the Directors present representing each party having in aggregate an equal number of votes. The Chairman shall not have a casting vote.

5.5 At least 14 days written notice shall be given to each member of the Board of any meeting of the Board, provided always that a shorter period of notice may be given with the written approval of at least 1 A Director and at least 1 B Director. Any such notice shall include, an agenda identifying in reasonable detail the matters to be discussed at the meeting and shall be accompanied by copies of any relevant papers.

50:50 SHAREHOLDERS' AGREEMENT (SHORT FORM)

Reserved Matters

[*Note: list of matters to be reviewed in light of authority proposed for the Board.*]

6.1 The following matters ("**Reserved Matters**") shall require the prior approval of A and B:

(a) any issue of shares (or securities convertible into shares) of the JVC other than an issue of shares to A and B in equal proportions as specified in clause 4.2;

(b) any alteration to the Memorandum and Articles;

(c) any sale of the whole or any substantial part of the JVC;

(d) any borrowing by the JVC which would result in the aggregate borrowings of the JVC being in excess of £_____ or such other amount as the parties shall from time to time determine;

(e) approval of the annual budget and operating plan of the JVC;

(f) any expansion of the marketing territory of the JVC beyond _____;

(g) any development of the product line of the JVC beyond _____ (as improved or enhanced from time to time);

(h) the purchase by the JVC of the shares or other securities, stock or debentures of any other company;

(i) the formation of any subsidiary of the JVC;

(j) any contract or commitment by the JVC having a value or likely to involve expenditure by the JVC in excess of £_____ (or such other limit as the parties shall from time to time agree);

(k) the appointment (or removal) and the terms of reference of [the Chief Executive] [any executive Director];

(l) the approval of, or any [material] change to, the service/employment contracts with _____ or _____;

(m) the appointment (or removal) of the auditors of the JVC;

(n) [the commencement, settlement or abandonment of litigation or admission of liability by the JVC involving a dispute in excess of £_____ (other than a claim against a member of the A Group or a member of the B Group);]

(o) any repayment by the JVC of any loan made by a member of the A Group or the B Group;

(p) filing by the JVC for liquidation, receivership or reorganisation under any insolvency laws or any similar action.

6.2 Approval for the purposes of clause 6.1 may be given:

(a) in the case of items 6.1[(a), (b) and (c)] ("**Reserved Shareholder Matters**"), by A and B either in writing or by unanimous resolution at a general meeting of the shareholders of the JVC or by written resolution;

(b) in the case of the remaining Reserved Matters, by unanimous agreement of all the Directors (either by written resolution or by unanimous resolution at a meeting of the Board).

6.3 The provisions of clause 6.1 shall apply equally to any matters undertaken by a subsidiary of the JVC as if references therein to "the JVC" included, where appropriate, any such subsidiary.

Transfer of shares

7.1 Unless it is a transfer made with the prior written consent of the other party, neither A nor B shall sell, transfer, pledge, charge, dispose of or otherwise deal with any right or interest in any of its shares in the JVC (including the grant of any option over or in respect of any shares).

7.2 Consent shall not unreasonably be withheld to a transfer by a party to a member of its respective Group. Each of A and B respectively undertakes to procure that, if any member of its Group which holds shares in the JVC ceases at any time to be a [wholly-owned] subsidiary of that party, that subsidiary shall prior to so ceasing transfer beneficially all its shares in the JVC to the relevant party (or another member of its Group).

7.3 No transfer of shares of the JVC shall in any event be registered or become effective unless the transferee shall first have entered into an Agreement undertaking to be bound by this Agreement (including this clause 7) to the same extent as the transferor would have been bound had the transfer not been effected.

Confidentiality

8.1 Each of the parties shall at all times use all reasonable efforts to keep confidential (and to ensure that its employees and agents keep confidential) any confidential information which it may acquire in relation to the JVC and its subsidiaries or in relation to the clients, business or affairs of the other party (or any member of its respective Group) and shall not use or disclose such information except with the consent of the other party or, in the case of information relating to the JVC (or any of its subsidiaries), in the ordinary course of advancing the Business. The restriction in this clause 8.1 shall not apply to any information which is:

(a) publicly available or becomes publicly available through no fault of that party;

(b) in the possession of that party prior to its disclosure;

(c) disclosed to that party by a third party which did not acquire the information under an obligation of confidentiality;

(d) independently acquired by that party as the result of work carried out by an employee to whom no disclosure of such information had been made;

(e) disclosed in accordance with the requirements of law, any stock exchange regulation or any binding judgment, order or requirement of any court or other competent authority.

8.2 Each party shall use all its respective powers to ensure (so far as it is able) that the JVC and its subsidiaries (and the officers, employees and agents of each of them) observe a similar obligation of confidence in favour of the parties to this Agreement.

8.3 The provisions of this clause 8 shall survive any termination of this Agreement.

Restrictions on the parties

9. Neither A nor B nor any member of its respective Group shall (directly or indirectly or solely or jointly with any other person, firm or company) carry on or be engaged in or interested (except as the holder for investment of securities dealt in on a stock exchange and not exceeding [5] per cent in nominal value of the securities of any class) in any Competing Business [in the Territory] during the

50:50 SHAREHOLDERS' AGREEMENT (SHORT FORM) 751

period of this Agreement. For this purpose: "**Competing Business**" means _____; and "Territory" means _____.

Deadlock or termination

10.1 In the event of a deadlock, breakdown or other circumstances in which a party wishes to terminate or substantially change the structure of the relationship of the parties through the JVC, the matter shall be referred to the respective chairmen/chief executives of the parties who shall seek to resolve the matter on an amicable basis.

10.2 If the matter cannot be resolved, then either party may give notice that it wishes formally to resolve the situation [within 90 days]. The parties shall continue to negotiate in good faith with a view to resolving the matter including by one of the following methods:

(a) the purchase by the JVC of the disaffected party's shares on terms acceptable to the parties (provided that the purchase by the JVC can lawfully be made and is financially practicable);

(b) the purchase by the other party of the disaffected party's shares in the JVC (or the sale of that party's shares to one or more third parties);

(c) the sale of the whole of the issued share capital of the JVC to a third party; or

(d) winding-up of the JVC.

10.3 If no such method of resolution has been agreed [within 90 days] after the notice is given under clause 10.2, a disaffected party may serve notice requiring the JVC to be wound-up. No notice requiring the winding-up of the JVC may, however, be served by either party within the initial 5 years after the establishment of the JVC.

10.4 Upon or as soon as practicable after notice under clause 10.3, the parties shall use their respective powers and votes to cause the JVC to be placed in liquidation. The parties shall co-operate to ensure that all existing contracts entered into by the JVC (or any subsidiary thereof) prior to such winding-up shall be duly completed subject to such arrangements as the parties may mutually agree. The parties shall endeavour to agree an appropriate allocation of the assets of the JVC prior to any such winding-up.

Supremacy of this Agreement

11. A and B shall each use its respective powers (including its votes in the JVC) and all other means at its disposal to ensure that this Agreement is duly observed and performed. If there is any conflict between this Agreement and the Memorandum and Articles, this Agreement shall prevail as between the parties and they shall make such changes to the Memorandum and Articles as shall be necessary to give effect to this Agreement.

Costs

12. The costs of and incidental to the incorporation of the JVC shall be borne and paid by the JVC. The costs of each of the parties incurred in the preparation, execution and performance of this Agreement shall be borne by such party.

No partnership or agency

13. Nothing in this Agreement shall be deemed to constitute a partnership between the parties or constitute either party the agent of the other for any purpose or entitle either party to commit or bind the other (or any member of its respective Group) in any manner.

Entire agreement

14. This Agreement [and [*any other Agreements entered into on Completion pursuant to clause 3*]] set[s] out the entire agreement and understanding between the parties with respect to the subject matter hereof. [This Agreement supersedes [the Confidentiality Undertaking/any Heads of Agreement or Memorandum of Understanding], which shall cease to have any further force or effect.] Neither party has entered into this Agreement in reliance upon any representation, warranty or undertaking of the other party which is not expressly set out or referred to in this Agreement. This clause shall not exclude any liability for fraudulent misrepresentation.

Mutual consultation and goodwill

15.1 The parties confirm their intention to promote the best interests of the JVC and to consult fully on all matters materially affecting the development of the Business. Each party shall act in good faith towards the other in order to promote the JVC's success.

15.2 The parties shall keep the organisation and progress of the JVC under regular review and shall consider, in good faith but without any obligation to agree, any amendments proposed by either to improve the prospects for success of the JVC.

Notices

16. Any notice under this Agreement shall be in writing signed by (or by some person duly authorised by) the person giving it and may be served by leaving it or sending it by fax, prepaid recorded delivery or registered post to the address of the other party as follows (or to such other address as shall have been duly notified in accordance with this clause). The details for notices are:

A: _____	B: _____
Fax:	Fax:
Attention:	Attention:

Assignment

17. Neither of the parties (nor any member of its respective Group) shall be entitled to assign this Agreement or any of its rights or obligations hereunder except to a transferee of that party's shares in the JVC in accordance with clause 7 of this Agreement.

Conditions Precedent

18.1 Closing under clause 3 shall be conditional upon each of the following conditions having first been satisfied or waived:

(a) —————;
(b) —————.

18.2 Each party shall use all reasonable efforts to ensure that the Conditions Precedent are fulfilled as soon as possible. If they are not fulfilled (or waived) by —————, this Agreement (other than the provisions of clause 8 (*Confidentiality*)) shall, unless otherwise agreed, thereupon automatically cease and terminate and neither party shall have any claim of any nature whatsoever against the other party.

Disputes

19.1 If a dispute arises out of this Agreement, the parties shall seek to resolve it on an amicable basis. They shall, if appropriate, consider the appointment of a mediator to assist in that resolution. No party shall commence legal or arbitration proceedings unless 30 days' notice has been given to the other party.

19.2 If the dispute cannot be resolved, it should be referred to and finally resolved by arbitration under the [Rules of Arbitration of the London International Court of Arbitration] by [a sole arbitrator] [three arbitrators] appointed in accordance with those Rules. The arbitration shall be held in [London].

Governing law

20. This Agreement shall be governed by [English] law.

As WITNESS this Agreement has been executed by the parties.

Signed by————   }
for and on behalf of **A**   }
Signed by————   }
for and on behalf of **A**   }

Precedent 10

Multi-Party Shareholders' Agreement (long form)

> *The following is a long-form Shareholders' Agreement where there are three or more shareholders in the JVC. Compared with a 50:50 venture, these Agreements frequently involve a wider range of options including particularly in relation to: (i) commitments and procedures on issues of new shares (clause 5.3); (ii) whether particular decisions require unanimity or can be resolved by, say, two parties holding a majority interest (clause 8); (iii) arrangements for possible public listing of the JVC's shares (clause 10); (iv) scope of restrictions and/or procedures on transfer of shares (clause 16); and (v) procedures on buy-out for default, insolvency or change of control (clause 17). This particular Agreement is drafted on the basis that there is a single class of shares (with rights depending on the percentage interest held) rather than each party being issued with a separate class of shares (e.g. A Shares, B Shares) with various rights being attached to each class of shares. Where there are subsidiaries of the JVC, the term "JVC Group" may be appropriate in many places instead of "JVC". Many of these provisions may, of course, be adapted to a two-party joint venture.*

THIS AGREEMENT is made on _____ 200—

BETWEEN:

(1) _____, whose [registered] office is at _____ ("**A**");

(2) _____, whose [registered] office is at _____ ("**B**");

(3) _____, whose [registered] office is at _____ ("**C**");

(4) _____, whose [registered] office is at _____ ("**D**");

[(5) _____, whose [registered] office is at _____ (the "**JVC**")].

WHEREAS:

(A) The parties have agreed to form a new jointly-owned company (the "**JVC**") which it is intended will be established and organised in the manner set out in this Agreement.

(B) The parties are entering into this Agreement in order to set out the terms governing their relationship as shareholders in the JVC.

IT IS AGREED AS FOLLOWS:

The JVC

1.1 The Shareholders agree to establish the JVC in accordance with the provisions of this Agreement.

1.2 The business of the JVC shall be ——————.

1.3 The business of the JVC shall be conducted in the best interests of the JVC in accordance with the general principles of the then current Business Plan approved by the Shareholders.

Conditions to Closing

2.1 Closing is conditional on the following conditions being fulfilled (or waived):

(a) [refer to any specific governmental or regulatory approval or licence, to be given in a relevant jurisdiction or by a relevant industry regulator];

(b) [all [other] government, governmental body or regulatory authority (including any stock exchange) consents (including the expiry of any period following a notification such that consent is deemed to be given or no consent is required) which are required for the actions contemplated by this Agreement being obtained in terms satisfactory to each of the [Shareholders]];

(c) [refer to any specific tax clearances];

(d) [refer to any specific waivers by third parties of share pre-emption rights or rights to terminate contracts (upon assignment or change of control) which are of material importance and are required from third parties before Closing];

(e) [refer to the execution of any other agreement to be concluded by the parties or involving the JVC, or any other matter which is sufficiently material to be a Condition.]

2.2 Each Shareholder shall use its reasonable efforts to ensure (so far as it is able) that the Conditions are fulfilled as soon as possible.

2.3 If any Condition is not fulfilled (or waived) on or before ——————, this Agreement (other than the Surviving Provisions) shall automatically terminate. No party shall have any claim against any other under this Agreement (except in respect of any rights and liabilities which have accrued before termination or in relation to any of the Surviving Provisions).

Closing

3.1 Closing shall take place at —————— (or such other venue as may be agreed between the Shareholders) on 10 Business Days' notice given by [the JVC] to the Shareholders after the fulfilment (or waiver) of the Conditions. The events set out in the remainder of this clause 3 shall take place on Closing.

3.2 Each Shareholder shall subscribe unconditionally for the number of Shares set out against its name in column (2) of Schedule 1, to be subscribed at Closing for [cash at par] [for a total issue price set out in column (3) of that Schedule]. Each Shareholder shall advance the amount of Loans set out against its name in column (4) of Schedule 1, to be subscribed at Closing for [cash at par value]. Payment shall be made by each Shareholder in cleared funds to the account of the JVC at ——————.

3.3 The JVC shall allot and issue, credited as fully paid, the number of Shares for which each of the Shareholders has subscribed under clause 3.2, and shall enter the names of the Shareholders in the register of members as the respective holders of the Shares subscribed by them. The JVC shall issue share certificates to the Shareholders accordingly and Loan Notes in respect of the Loans.

3.4 The Shareholders shall procure that the necessary board or general meetings of the JVC are held in order to:

(a) change the name of the JVC to "_____";

(b) approve the allotment and issue of the Shares to the Shareholders in accordance with clause 3.3;

(c) adopt the Memorandum and Articles of Association in the agreed form;

(d) appoint the following as Directors of the JVC: _____; _____; _____; _____; _____; _____;

(e) appoint _____ as the Chairman;

(f) appoint _____ as the Chief Executive; and

(g) conduct such other business as shall be unanimously agreed by the Shareholders for the establishment of the JVC.

3.5 [A/B/C/D] shall execute, and the JVC shall execute, the following ancillary agreements [in the agreed form]:

(a) the Asset Transfer/Sale and Purchase Agreement relating to _____;

(b) the Distributorship Agreement relating to _____;

(c) the Technology Licence relating to _____;

(d) the Supply Agreement relating to _____;

(e) the Services Agreement.

3.6 Each Shareholder undertakes with the JVC and each other Shareholder that, immediately on execution of this Agreement, it will (if it is not an ultimate holding company) procure that its ultimate holding company delivers to the JVC a Parent Company Guarantee.

Additional funding

[Note: This is one simple approach. For alternative approaches, including a commitment of each Shareholder to provide finance to the JVC up to a stated limit, see the various provisions of Precedent 15: Shareholder Funding Agreement.]

4.1 If the Board determines at any time that the Business requires additional finance beyond the initial capital subscribed under clause 3, the Board will consider whether or not to approach the JVC's bankers or other financial institutions or, in appropriate circumstances, to seek such further finance from the Shareholders. No Shareholder shall be required to contribute any loan or equity capital to the JVC or to guarantee any debt of the JVC without that Shareholder's prior written consent.

4.2 If the Board determines that the appropriate method of obtaining additional finance is to issue new Shares, then the Shareholders will give serious consideration to any proposals of the Board but on the basis that (i) no new Shares shall be issued unless the requisite consent is obtained in accordance with clause 8.2(b), and (ii) if that consent is obtained, the Shareholders shall (in accordance with the Articles and any applicable law including any provisions regarding pre-emptive rights) procure the passing of all necessary resolutions to complete such issue of Shares.

Issue of new shares

5.1 If the JVC proposes to issue new shares (the "**New Shares**") in accordance with clause 4.2:

(a) the New Shares shall be offered for subscription in cash and on the same terms to each Shareholder pro rata to its Equity Proportion (as nearly as may be) as at the close of business on the date prior to such offer (a Shareholder's

MULTI-PARTY SHAREHOLDERS' AGREEMENT (LONG FORM) 757

"**Pro Rata Entitlement**") on the basis that each Shareholder may take up all or part or none of the New Shares offered to it;

(b) each offer shall be made by notice from the JVC (the "**Issue Notice**") specifying (i) the number of New Shares to which the relevant Shareholder is entitled, (ii) the price per New Share (the "**Subscription Price**") which shall be established in accordance with clause 5.2 and (iii) a time (being not less than 21 days from the date of the Issue Notice) within which, if the offer is not accepted, it will be deemed to be declined;

(c) each Shareholder who accepts the offer by notice to the JVC shall, in addition, state either (i) that it would accept, on the same terms, New Shares (specifying a maximum number) that are not accepted by other Shareholders ("**Excess Shares**") or (ii) that it would not accept any Excess Shares (and, if a Shareholder who accepts the offer fails to make a confirmation in the terms of (i) or (ii), it shall be deemed to have made a confirmation in the terms of (ii));

(d) on expiry of the acceptance period, New Shares shall be allocated to each Shareholder who has applied for its Pro Rata Entitlement (or less than its Pro Rata Entitlement);

(e) Excess Shares shall be allocated to each Shareholder, who has indicated that it will accept Excess Shares, pro rata to the Equity Proportions of all those Shareholders who have indicated that they would accept Excess Shares (provided that no Shareholder shall be allocated more than the maximum number of Excess Shares it has indicated it is willing to accept);

(f) if (after the first allocation of Excess Shares) there remain Excess Shares which have not been allocated and one or more Shareholders (the "**Remaining Shareholders**") have indicated in their response to the Issue Notice that they will accept more Excess Shares than they have been allocated, the remaining Excess Shares shall be allocated to the Remaining Shareholders pro rata to the Equity Proportions of the Remaining Shareholders; Excess Shares shall continue to be allocated on this basis until either all Excess Shares are allocated or all requests for Excess Shares have been satisfied;

(g) on expiry of the acceptance period pursuant to clause 5.1(b) or upon receipt by the JVC of an acceptance or refusal of every offer made by the JVC, the Board shall be entitled to issue to any person any New Shares offered to Shareholders and which have not been taken up in accordance with the provisions of this clause 5.1; such issue by the Board shall be on the same terms as those offered to the Shareholders and made in such manner and to such third party or parties as the Board may think most beneficial to the JVC;

(h) where any allocation under this clause 5.1 would result in a fractional allotment of New Shares, the Board may, in its absolute discretion, round up or down such fractional allotments so that the offers and/or allotments of New Shares by the JVC are of whole numbers of shares (totalling the number of shares for which the Shareholders have given approval for issue).

5.2 The Subscription Price shall be determined as at the date consent is given to the issue by the Shareholders under clause 8.2 (the "**Consent Date**"). The Subscription Price shall be such price as shall be [determined by the Board] [agreed by [all] [a Qualifying Majority of] the Shareholders on or prior to the Consent Date or, if not so agreed, a fair price determined by an Expert appointed in accordance with clause 18].

5.3 It shall be a condition of the issue of any New Shares to a third party or third parties (a "**Third Party Subscriber**") pursuant to clause 5.3(g) that the Third Party Subscriber enters into a Deed of Adherence and (if it is not an ultimate holding company) delivers to the JVC a Parent Company Guarantee.

5.4 Promptly after completion of the allocation process pursuant to clause 5.1, the JVC shall allot and issue (credited as fully paid) the relevant New Shares, enter the relevant allottees in the register of members and complete and despatch to the relevant allottee(s) certificates for the New Shares.

Guarantees

6.1 No Shareholder (nor any member of its respective Group) shall be obliged to participate for the benefit of the JVC in any guarantee, bond or financing arrangement with any bank or financial institution, whether as a guarantor or in any other capacity whatsoever.

6.2 If and to the extent that all the Shareholders agree to participate (or agree to procure that members of their respective Groups participate) in any such guarantee, bond or financing arrangement then, unless the Shareholders agree otherwise, any liability or obligation to be assumed by them in relation to that guarantee, bond or financing arrangement shall be borne in their Equity Proportions. If a Shareholder (or a member of its Group) incurs any liability under any such guarantee, bond or financing arrangement, that Shareholder shall be entitled to a contribution from the other Shareholders to ensure that the aggregate liability of the Shareholders or members of their respective Groups (as the case may be) is borne by them in their Equity Proportions at the time the relevant guarantee, bond or financing arrangement is made.

Directors and management

[Note: Management structures vary considerably. The management structure for the JVC in this Agreement has been drafted on the following basis: the board of the JVC comprises shareholder-appointed directors and a Chief Executive; the Chief Executive is responsible for the day to day management of the JVC and preparation of the business plan and budget; the Chief Executive is assisted by an Executive Committee compromising the Chief Executive and senior management of the JVC; a number of matters are reserved for a decision of the board (clause (8.3); a number of matters are reserved for a decision of the shareholders (clause (8.2). This is only one possible option. In settling the most appropriate structure, much will depend on the respective proportionate interests of the parties and also on the number of parties. In addition, it will also be necessary to take into account the autonomy to be given to the JVC and its senior management to run the JVC.]

7.1 The Board shall (subject to the requirements of clause 8) be responsible for the overall direction and supervision of the JVC. The Board shall not, however, take any decision in relation to the Reserved Shareholder Matters or Reserved Board Matters without the requisite approval under clause 8.1.

7.2 The Board shall consist of up to _____ (_____) Directors. Any Shareholder shall be entitled to appoint:

(a) 1 Director for so long as such Shareholder holds at least 10 per cent but less than 20 per cent in nominal value of the Shares from time to time;

(b) 2 Directors for so long as such Shareholder holds at least 20 per cent in nominal value of the Shares from time to time.

7.3 Any Shareholder who holds less than 10 per cent in nominal value of the Shares may aggregate its shareholding with that of any other Shareholder(s) who also hold(s) less than 10 per cent in nominal value of Shares. If the resulting aggregate shareholding is 10 per cent or more in nominal value of the Shares, then those

Shareholders shall be entitled to appoint 1 (but only 1) Director and will not be entitled to appoint more than 1 Director even if their aggregate shareholding is equal to or exceeds 20 per cent in nominal value of the Shares.

7.4 If a Shareholder's holding of Shares falls below 10 per cent in nominal value or the requisite higher percentage to entitle it to appoint the number of Directors appointed by it pursuant to clause 7.2, then the Shareholder shall promptly give a notice to the JVC removing one or more of the Directors appointed by it so that the total remaining number of Directors appointed by it (if any) does not exceed its entitlement under clause 7.2. If the aggregate shareholding of relevant Shareholders falls below 10 per cent for the purposes of clause 7.3, those Shareholders shall promptly give a notice to the JVC removing the Director appointed by them.

7.5 A Shareholder (or Shareholders) may appoint or remove a Director nominated by it (or them) by notice to the JVC. The appointment or removal shall take effect when the notice is delivered to the JVC, unless it indicates otherwise. Each Shareholder shall use its respective votes in the JVC to ensure that the Board is constituted by persons in the manner set out in this Agreement. A Shareholder (or Shareholders) removing a Director shall indemnify the JVC against any liability arising from the removal. A Shareholder shall consult with the others before appointing or removing a Director.

7.6 The initial Directors shall be:

Appointed by A:	[ ][	]
Appointed by B:	[ ][	]
Appointed by C:	[ ]	
Appointed by D:	[ ]	
Chief Executive	[ ]	
[Others	[ ]]	

7.7 The quorum for transacting business at any Board meeting shall be [2] Directors appointed by 2 or more different Shareholders holding together not less than 50 per cent in nominal value of the Shares. If such a quorum is not present within 30 minutes from the time appointed for the meeting or if during the meeting such a quorum is no longer present, the meeting shall be adjourned for 5 Business Days to the same place and time and at that adjourned meeting any 2 Directors present appointed to the Board by at least 2 different Shareholders shall be a quorum. At least 2 Business Days' notice of the adjourned meeting will be given to each of the Directors, and any such notice will be given in the same manner, and specifying the same agenda, as for the original meeting.

7.8 At least 10 Business Days' notice shall be given to each Director of any meeting of the Board (except for an adjourned meeting) unless all the Directors (or their alternates) or [all] [a Qualifying Majority] of the Shareholders approve a shorter notice period. Any such notice shall include an agenda identifying in reasonable detail the matters to be discussed at the meeting and shall, wherever practicable, be accompanied by copies of any relevant papers to be discussed at the meeting. If any matter is not identified in reasonable detail, the Board shall not decide on it unless all of the Directors or [all] [a Qualifying Majority] of the Shareholders agree in writing.

7.9 Meetings of the Board shall take place at least 4 times in each year.

7.10 The Chairman of the Board shall be one of the Directors nominated by _____ [or _____] pursuant to clause 7.2. [Such appointments shall be annual (except for the first appointment) and shall be rotated between _____ and _____ in that order.] If the shareholding of [either] _____ or _____ falls below _____ ( ) per cent of the Shares of the JVC, that Shareholder shall not be entitled to appoint a Chairman. If no one Shareholder is entitled to appoint a Chairman pursuant to this Agreement, then the Board shall appoint the Chairman.

7.11 Any Director may appoint any other Director [or any other person [approved by a resolution of the Board and willing to act],] to be an alternate director and may remove from office an alternate director so appointed by him. An alternate director shall [not] count as a Director for the purposes of a quorum.

7.12 The Board shall decide on matters by a simple majority vote. Each Director present, whether in person or (where relevant) represented by an alternate, shall have one vote (and, for the avoidance of doubt, any alternate present at a meeting shall be entitled (in the absence of his appointor(s) to a separate vote on behalf of each Director he represents in addition to his own vote (if any) as a Director). The Chairman shall not have a casting vote.

7.13 Subject to the provisions of clause 8, the authority and responsibility for implementing the Business Plan and each Budget, together with day-to-day management of the JVC, shall be vested in the Chief Executive. The Chief Executive shall be appointed by the Board.

7.14 The Executive Committee shall assist the Chief Executive in the execution of his duties and such other duties as may be specified by the Board from time to time. The Executive Committee shall comprise the Chief Executive [, a Deputy Chief Executive] and such other persons (not being Directors) as are appointed by the Board upon the recommendation of the Chief Executive. It shall be chaired by the Chief Executive and shall meet regularly in _____ (or such other place as the Chief Executive may determine). The initial Executive Committee shall be: _____, _____, _____, and _____.

7.15 The terms of reference of the Executive Committee, and the manner of its proceedings, shall be determined by [the Chief Executive subject to such directions or limitations as may be given by] the Board from time to time.

Reserved Matters

[Note. This list is illustrative only and should be reviewed in each case. It divides Reserved Matters between Shareholder and Board matters. The split is likely to vary on each transaction. In some ventures, "business--type" decisions—including acquisitions/ disposals—may be regarded as more appropriately Board matters. It may be that, in relation to Reserved Shareholder Matters there should be different levels of approval e.g. ordinary majority and super majority and/or even unanimity.]

8.1 The Shareholders shall use their respective powers to ensure, so far as they are legally able, that no action or decision is taken (whether by the Board, the JVC, any Subsidiary of the JVC or any of the officers or managers of the JVC) to proceed with any of the matters:

(a) specified in clause 8.2 ("**Reserved Shareholders Matters**") unless it is approved by Shareholders holding at least [75 per cent] of the Shares present and entitled to vote at the relevant general meeting or the prior written consent has been obtained of Shareholders holding at least [75 per cent] by nominal value of the Shares;

(b) specified in clause 8.3 ("**Reserved Board Matters**") unless it is approved by at least [three-quarters] of the Directors in number present and entitled to vote at the relevant Board meeting or the prior written consent has been obtained of at least [three-quarters] in number of the Directors; and

8.2 The Reserved Shareholder Matters are:

(a) *Memorandum and Articles*: altering the Memorandum and/or Articles or other constitutional documents of the JVC;

(b) *changes in share capital*: changing the authorised or issued share capital of the JVC (including any reduction of capital);

(c) *change in nature of Business*: materially changing the nature or scope of the Business (as described in clause 1.2) of the JVC [including any decision to change or extend the Field];

(d) *acquisitions and disposals*: the JVC acquiring or disposing (whether in a single transaction or series of transactions) of any business (or any material part of any business) or any shares in any company where the value of that business or those shares exceeds £_____;

(e) *partnerships and joint ventures*: the JVC entering into (or terminating) any material partnership, joint venture, profit-sharing agreement, technology licence or collaboration;

(f) *charges*: creating any mortgage, charge, encumbrance or other security interest of any nature in respect of all or any material part of the undertaking, property or assets of the JVC;

(g) *auditors*: appointing or removing auditors of the JVC; or

(h) *winding-up*: any proposal to wind-up the JVC (other than pursuant to clause 20.3) or commence any other proceedings seeking liquidation, administration (whether out of court or otherwise), reorganisation or relief under any bankruptcy, insolvency or similar laws.

8.3 The Reserved Board Matters are:

(a) *Business Plan and Budgets*: adopting the Business Plan or Budget for the JVC;

(b) *borrowings*: the JVC borrowing or raising money (including entering into any finance lease, but excluding normal trade credit and borrowings or raising of capital from Shareholders pursuant to clause 4) which would result in the aggregate borrowing of the JVC exceeding £_____ (or such other amount as the Shareholders may agree from time to time);

(c) *capital expenditure*: the JVC incurring any capital expenditure in respect of any item or project in excess of £_____ (or such other amount as the [Shareholders] may agree from time to time);

(d) *material contracts*: the JVC entering into any contract, liability or commitment which:

    (i) could involve a liability for expenditure in excess of £_____ or any other obligation of a material magnitude or importance in the context of the Business; or

    (ii) is outside the ordinary course of business of the JVC
unless a contract satisfies such authorisation criteria as the [Shareholders] [Board] may approve from time to time as part of the procedures for the JVC entering into contracts;

(e) *transactions with Shareholders or their Groups*: the JVC entering into, renewing or amending any transaction with any Shareholder or a member of its Group which is either (i) outside the ordinary course of business or (ii) within the ordinary course of business but has a value of more than £_____ or is not on commercial arm's length terms;

(f) *Intellectual Property Rights*: the JVC making any material acquisition or disposal (including any grant of any material licence) relating to any Intellectual Property Rights;

(g) *material litigation*: decisions relating to the conduct (including the settlement) of any legal proceedings to which the JVC is a party; for this purpose "**material**" means a potential liability or claim of more than £_____;

(h) *Chief Executive and senior management*: appointing or removing any person as the Chief Executive, the Chief Financial Officer [or the Secretary] of the JVC or settling or changing any of their respective [conditions of employment] [terms of reference];

(i) *accounts and accounting policies*: approving the JVC's statutory accounts and/or any change in the [principal] Accounting Principles of the JVC and/or any change in the end of the Financial Year of the JVC;

(j) *employee policies*: adopting (or varying) the material policies of the JVC in respect of employees' remuneration, employment terms and/or pension schemes;

(k) *dividends*: the JVC declaring or paying any dividend or other distribution.

8.4 General meetings of Shareholders shall take place in accordance with the applicable provisions of the Articles including on the basis that (i) the quorum shall be duly authorised representatives of at least _____( ) Shareholders holding, in aggregate, not less than _____( ) per cent in number of the Shares and (ii) the notice of meeting shall set out an agenda identifying in reasonable detail the matters to be discussed (unless the Shareholders agree otherwise). Any matters requiring a general meeting of or approval by the Shareholders under relevant corporate laws shall be dealt with in accordance with the Articles and applicable corporate laws.

Financial matters

9.1 The auditors of the JVC shall be such firm of accountants as may be agreed from time to time by the Shareholders [in accordance with clause 8].

9.2 The JVC's Financial Year shall be _____, unless [the Shareholders] agree otherwise.

9.3 Each Shareholder may examine the separate books, records and accounts to be kept by the JVC. Each Shareholder shall be entitled to receive all information, including [monthly] management accounts and operating statistics and other trading and financial information, in such form as [the Board determines] [a Shareholder reasonably requires] to keep it properly informed about the business and affairs of the JVC and generally to protect its interests as a Shareholder.

9.4 Without prejudice to the generality of clause 9.3, the JVC shall supply the Shareholders with copies of:

(a) audited accounts for the JVC (complying with all relevant legal requirements) (which shall be prepared and reported on by the Auditors within [5] months after the end of the Financial Year in question);

(b) a Business Plan and itemised revenue and capital Budgets for each Financial Year [covering each principal division of the JVC] [and showing proposed trading and cash flow figures, manning levels and all material proposed acquisitions, disposals and other commitments for that Financial Year]; and

(c) monthly/quarterly management accounts of the JVC [; these shall include a profit and loss account, balance sheet and cash flow statement broken down according to the principal divisions of the JVC (including a statement of progress against the relevant Business Plan, a statement of any variation from

MULTI-PARTY SHAREHOLDERS' AGREEMENT (LONG FORM) 763

the [quarterly] revenue Budget and up-to-date forecasts for the balance of the relevant Financial Year and itemising all transactions referred to in the capital Budget entered into by [each principal division of] the JVC during that period).

9.5 The distribution of profits of the JVC shall be made by a decision of the Shareholders in accordance with clause 8. [No distribution shall be made in respect of the Shares without the consent of the holders of all of the Loan Notes for the time being in issue until the Loans shall have been repaid in full including all accrued interest)]. [Subject to this,] the parties shall, unless they agree otherwise in relation to any Financial Year, take all steps to ensure that in respect of each Financial Year the JVC distributes not less than 50 per cent (or such other percentage as the parties may agree from time to time in writing) of the profit (after taxation and extraordinary items) of the JVC as shown by the JVC's financial statements for that Financial Year and available for distribution in accordance with applicable law. The JVC's constitutional documents shall provide for the ability to pay interim dividends whenever legally permitted.

9.6 The JVC shall prepare its financial statements in accordance with the Accounting Principles.

Listing

10.1 Each of the Shareholders acknowledges that it is the intention that the Business should be developed so that, as soon as is practicable, the Shares in the capital of the JVC are admitted to trading on one or more recognised investment or stock exchanges which provide a reasonable and genuine market for such shares of sufficient liquidity and upon which Shares can be freely traded (a "Listing").

10.2 Without prejudice to clause 10.1, at any time after _____ Shareholders together holding _____ ( ) per cent or more of the Shares of the JVC may give notice to the Board and the other Shareholders (a "**Listing Notice**") that they require the JVC and the other Shareholders to take such steps as may be necessary to obtain a Listing.

10.3 Following a Listing Notice, the JVC shall appoint an internationally recognised firm of investment bankers in [London] (and reasonably familiar with the markets and sector in which the JVC operates) [, independent of all of the Shareholders,] to advise on the viability of obtaining a Listing and which, if it determines that a Listing is viable, will be appointed to act as sponsor in relation to the Listing (the "**Sponsor**"). If the Sponsor advises that a Listing is not viable, then the provisions of this clause 10 shall cease to apply. No Shareholders shall be entitled to give another Listing Notice until after 1 year from the date of the previous Listing Notice. If the Sponsor advises that a Listing is viable, then:

(a) the Shareholders will co-operate fully with each other and the JVC and their respective financial and other advisers in relation to the timing of, and actions to achieve, the Listing in accordance with the rules and regulations of the relevant recognised investment exchange or listing authority;

(b) the Shareholders will provide all necessary assistance and information as the JVC or the Sponsor may reasonably require in relation to the preparation and verification of any prospectus, listing particulars or registration statement in respect of the JVC;

(c) if Shares are to be placed or offered for sale in connection with the Listing, any Shares to be placed or offered shall be drawn from the respective shareholdings of Shareholders pro rata to their respective Equity Proportions; for this purpose, each Shareholder shall agree to the placing or offer for sale of so many of its Shares as the Sponsor shall advise is necessary or advisable in order to obtain the Listing [, subject to a maximum of [10 per cent] of that Shareholder's holding of Shares immediately prior to the Listing;]

(d) the Shareholders shall execute all such documents and deeds, and do all such acts and things, as the JVC or the Sponsor may request as being reasonably necessary or expedient for the purpose of obtaining the Listing and which are in accordance with market practice at such time (including entering into any agreement to be bound by dealing restrictions, approving the appointment and removal of Directors and/or the giving of customary warranties (including as to title to any shares) by the parties or Directors).

10.4 No Shareholder shall be obliged to subscribe for any new securities of the JVC issued pursuant to any placing or offer for sale in connection with a Listing.

Confidentiality

11.1 Each Shareholder shall use all reasonable efforts to keep confidential any information:

(a) which it may have or acquire (whether before or after the date of this Agreement) in relation to the customers, business, assets or affairs of the JVC;

(b) which it may have or acquire (whether before or after the date of this Agreement) in relation to the customers, business, assets or affairs of any other Shareholder (or member of its Group) as a result of (i) negotiating this Agreement, (ii) being a shareholder in the JVC, (iii) having appointees on the Board or (iv) exercising any of its rights or performing any of its obligations under this Agreement; or

(c) which relates to the contents of this Agreement (or any agreement or arrangement entered into pursuant to this Agreement).

No Shareholder shall use for its own business purposes or disclose to any third party any such information (collectively, "**Confidential Information**").

11.2 The obligation of confidentiality under clause 11.1 does not apply to:

(a) disclosure (subject to clause 11.3) in confidence by a Shareholder to a company which is another member of the relevant Shareholder's Group or to that Shareholder's (or that member's) directors, officers, employees, agents and professional or other advisers ("**Representatives**") on a "need to know" basis where the recipient, in the reasonable opinion of the disclosing Shareholder, requires access to the information for a purpose reasonably incidental to the Shareholder's investment in the JVC;

(b) information which is independently developed by the relevant party or acquired from a third party with the right to disclose the same free of confidentiality;

(c) disclosure of information to the extent required by law, any stock exchange regulation or any binding judgment, order or requirement of any court or other competent authority;

(d) disclosure of information to any tax authority to the extent reasonably required for the purposes of the tax affairs of the party concerned or any member of its Group;

(e) disclosure of information to a bank or financial adviser of a Shareholder [or a bona fide potential purchaser of securities in the JVC or in a Shareholder (or its holding company),] provided that, before any such disclosure, the relevant

Shareholder obtains from the bank or potential purchaser an undertaking in favour of the JVC and the other Shareholders in terms equivalent to this clause 11; or

(f) information which comes within the public domain (otherwise than as a result of a breach of this clause 11); or

(g) any announcement made in accordance with the terms of clause 29.

11.3 Each Shareholder shall inform (and shall ensure that any member of its Group informs) any Representatives to whom it provides Confidential Information that such information is confidential and shall instruct them (i) to keep it confidential and (ii) not to disclose it to any third party (other than those persons to whom it has already been disclosed in accordance with the terms of this Agreement). The disclosing party is responsible for any breach of this clause 11 by a Representative to whom it provides any Confidential Information.

11.4 If a party ceases to be a Shareholder, it shall (if required by notice from the JVC or any other Shareholder) return to the JVC or that other Shareholder the Confidential Information of the JVC or the relevant Shareholder (as the case may be). If so required to return Confidential Information, the relevant party shall (and shall ensure that members of its Group and its Representatives shall): (i) return all documents containing Confidential Information which have been provided by or on behalf of the party demanding the return of Confidential Information; (ii) destroy any copies of such documents and any document or other record reproducing, containing or made from or with reference to the Confidential Information; and (iii) take reasonable steps to expunge all confidential information from any computer, hard processor or other device containing Confidential Information (save, in each case, for one copy of any submission to or filings with governmental, tax or regulatory authorities). Any destruction of Confidential Information shall be certified in writing to the relevant party by an authorised officer supervising it.

11.5 The JVC shall (and shall ensure that its Representatives shall) observe a similar confidentiality obligation in favour of each of the Shareholders in respect of Confidential Information relating to each Shareholder or any member of the Shareholder's Group.

11.6 The provisions of this clause 11 shall continue to apply if this Agreement is terminated and/or a party ceases to be a Shareholder.

Tax matters

12.1 Each of the Shareholders agrees to co-operate to such extent as may be reasonably requested in connection with the making of any returns, claims, or elections for taxation purposes (i) by the JVC in relation to the taxation affairs of the JVC or (ii) by any Shareholder in relation to the taxation affairs of any member (or former member) of its Group for any period ending before Closing.

12.2 [Unless the Shareholders agree otherwise in writing, each Shareholder shall ensure that all of the JVC's trading losses and other amounts eligible for relief from corporation tax under Chapter IV of Part X of the Income and Corporation Taxes Act 1988 ("**ICTA**") ("consortium relief") are surrendered or made available to the Shareholders in their Equity Proportions. For this purpose, the Shareholders shall procure that:

(a) the JVC and each Shareholder shall give all consents and take such other action (including, in the case of the JVC, submission of computations) as may reasonably be required to ensure that surrenders are promptly and effectively made within any relevant time limits;

(b) in respect of each surrender, the relevant claimant company makes a payment in relation to the amount surrendered (as referred to in s.402(6) ICTA) to the relevant surrendering company within 1 month of the date on which corporation tax becomes (or but for the utilisation of relevant relief would have become) payable by the claimant company for the claim period;

(c) the amount of any payment referred to in paragraph (b) shall be equal to [100%] of the [sum obtained by multiplying the amount so surrendered by a percentage equal to the effective percentage rate of corporation tax applicable in the United Kingdom to companies generally in respect of income profits for the claimant company's accounting period in question. For the avoidance of doubt, the small companies' rate as defined in s.13 ICTA is excluded];

(d) any payment made pursuant to paragraph (b) shall be subject to return if and to the extent that it is determined that relevant losses or other amounts surrendered are not available for surrender for reasons other than insufficiency of profits of the claimant or other members of the relevant party's Group.]

Non-competition

13.1 Each Shareholder agrees that, for so long as it holds Shares, neither it (nor any member of its Group) shall compete with the JVC [in the Field]. For this purpose, "**compete**" means to undertake or carry on or be engaged or interested in any business or activities in competition with the JVC (or any of its Subsidiaries) [within the Field] (whether alone or jointly with others or whether as principal, agent, shareholder or otherwise and whether for its own benefit or that of others).

13.2 The restriction contained in clause 13.1 does not prohibit any Shareholder (or any member of its Group):

(a) acquiring or holding shares amounting to less than [5 per cent] of the capital of a company quoted on any recognised investment or stock exchange and engaged in activities [within the Field] [which compete with the JVC]; or

(b) acquiring or holding shares in a company or undertaking (listed or non-listed) engaged in activities which compete with the JVC provided that the annual turnover of the competing activities amounts to less than [£_____] [10 per cent of the turnover of the JVC].

13.3 The relevant Shareholder shall keep the other Shareholders and the JVC promptly informed when any acquisition or holding referred to in clause 13.2 occurs.

Regulatory matters

14.1 The Shareholders shall co-operate with each other to ensure that all information necessary or desirable in connection with any notification, filing or request from a regulatory authority made in relation to this Agreement is supplied accurately and promptly.

14.2 If any material regulatory action is taken or threatened, the Shareholders shall promptly meet to discuss (i) the situation and the action to be taken as a result and (ii) whether any modification to the terms of this Agreement should be made in order that any requirement (whether as a condition of giving any approval, clearance or consent or otherwise) of any regulatory authority may be reconciled with the business arrangement contemplated by this Agreement.

Possible changes in relationship

15. If a Shareholder considers that circumstances have arisen (whether due to deadlock, breakdown, change in market conditions, circumstances affecting a particular party or other reasons) which lead to a wish on its part to alter the relationship established by this Agreement and/or that Shareholder's participation in the JVC, the Shareholder may raise the issue with the other Shareholders (whether through the Board or by direct discussions). The parties shall in good faith discuss the Shareholder's concerns and seek to resolve the issue on an amicable basis in the best interests of the JVC. The parties acknowledge that any such discussions shall not involve any obligation to reach agreement. Any such discussions shall not prejudice or affect a Shareholder's right at any time to exercise any rights, or to initiate any procedures, specifically set out in this Agreement.

Transfers of Shares

16.1 Unless it is (i) a transfer of Shares permitted by this clause 15 or Schedule 2 or (ii) a transfer made with the prior written consent of the other Shareholders (each being a "**Permitted Transfer**"), no Shareholder shall sell, transfer, pledge, charge, dispose of or otherwise deal with any right or interest in any Shares (including the grant of any option over or in respect of any Shares).

16.2 Each Shareholder (the "**Transferor**") is free to transfer its Shares to any [wholly-owned] member of its own Group. If the Transferor transfers its Shares to a member of its Group (the "**Transferee**") pursuant to this clause 16.6, then (i) the Transferor shall procure that, if the Transferee ceases or proposes to cease to be a [wholly-owned] member of the Transferor's Group, the Transferee shall immediately transfer all of its interest in any Shares to the Transferor or to another member of the Transferor's Group and (ii) the provisions of clause 19 (as specified in that clause) shall apply.

16.3 The provisions of Schedule 2 shall apply in relation to any transfer, or proposed transfer, of Shares and Loans in the JVC by a Shareholder to a third party.

16.4 [Except for a Permitted Transfer, no Shareholder shall transfer any Shares and/or Loans during a period of 3 years from the date of this Agreement.]

Termination events triggering option to purchase

17.1 It is a Termination Event in relation to a Shareholder (the "**Affected Shareholder**") if:

(a) a court of competent jurisdiction makes an order or a resolution is passed for the dissolution, liquidation or administration (whether out of court or otherwise) of that Shareholder [(or any holding company of that Shareholder)] (otherwise than in the course of a reorganisation or restructuring previously approved in writing by [all] the other Shareholders, such approval not to be unreasonably withheld or delayed) or a receiver, administrator, administrative receiver or other similar officer is appointed (and not discharged within 30 days) in respect of any assets which include [either (i)] the Shares held by that Shareholder or any Subsidiary of it [or (ii) shares in that Shareholder or any holding company of that Shareholder]; or

(b) a third party (together, if applicable, with persons acting in concert with any such third party) acquires a Controlling Interest in that Shareholder which it does not have at the date of this Agreement;

(c) that Shareholder (or a member of its Group) commits a breach of this Agreement or any other agreement with the JVC which [all] [a Qualifying Majority] of the other Shareholders consider is materially prejudicial to the

JVC and/or the ongoing relationship between the Shareholders (a "**Material Default**") where (i) notice of that breach has been given by [all] [a Qualifying Majority] of the other Shareholders to the defaulting Shareholder and declared their intention to treat the breach as a Termination Event under this clause and (ii) the defaulting Shareholder has failed to remedy that breach within a period of [45] days after that notice.

17.2 Upon a Termination Event, [all] [a Qualifying Majority] of the other Shareholders ("**Non-Affected Shareholders**") may serve notice on the Affected Shareholder [and the JVC] specifying that they (i) wish to exercise their rights under the remaining provisions of this clause 17 and (ii) request that the Fair Price of the Shares be determined in accordance with clause 18 and Schedule 4.

17.3 Within [7] days of receipt of the Certificate of the Fair Price in accordance with [Schedule 4], the JVC shall (i) give notice to the Affected Shareholder of the Certificate and (ii) give notice (a "**Right to Purchase Notice**") to each of the Non-Affected Shareholders of their right to purchase the Shares [and Loans] of the Affected Shareholder (the "**Affected Shares**") (i) at the Fair Price if the Termination Event is not a Material Default or (ii) at an amount equal to [80 per cent.] of the Fair Price if the Termination Event is a Material Default, in each case pro rata to their Equity Proportions (as at the close of business on the date prior to the date of the Right to Purchase Notice). The Right to Purchase Notice shall (i) specify the number of Affected Shares that are offered to each of the Non-Affected Shareholders and the price per Share [and Loan Note] at which the Affected Shares are offered, (ii) be expressed to be open for acceptance for [30] days from the date of service of the Right to Purchase Notice (the "**Right to Purchase Period**"), (iii) be irrevocable except as set out in clause 17.5 and (iv) be subject to no other terms other than as set out in clause 19.

17.4 Any Non-Affected Shareholder may, at any time before the expiry of the Right to Purchase Period, serve a written notice upon the JVC (i) stating its wish to purchase all or any of the Affected Shares offered to it on the terms set out in clause 17.3 and (ii) if it wishes to purchase Affected Shares in excess of its pro rata entitlement (its "**Entitlement**"), specifying the number of Affected Shares in excess of its Entitlement that it is prepared to purchase. If any Non-Affected Shareholder fails to serve a notice before the expiry of the Right to Purchase Period, it shall be deemed to have declined the offer constituted by the Right to Purchase Notice. A notice served pursuant to clause 17.4 shall be irrevocable without the written consent of the Affected Shareholder.

17.5 If any Non-Affected Shareholder has applied for less than its Entitlement, the excess shall be allocated to each Non-Affected Shareholder wishing to purchase Affected Shares in excess of its Entitlement, in proportion to the Equity Proportions of the Non-Affected Shareholders who have applied for any part of such excess as at the close of business on the date prior to the date of the Right to Purchase Notice (provided that any allocation made under this clause shall not result in any Non-Affected Shareholder being allocated more Affected Shares than it wishes to purchase). Any excess Affected Shares shall continue to be allocated on this basis until either all the Affected Shares have been allocated or all requests for extra Affected Shares have been satisfied.

17.6 [Subject only to the fulfilment of such specified [regulatory] conditions as may be required in order to enable the Non-Affected Shareholder to acquire the Affected Shares without breach of any relevant law or regulation as specified in the relevant Non-Affected Shareholder's notice of its desire to purchase Affected Shares,] the Affected Party shall be bound to sell and the relevant Non-Affected Shareholders shall be bound to buy such of the Affected Shares that have been allocated to them pursuant to this clause (i) at the Fair Price (or, if the Termination Event is a Material Default, at an amount equal to [80 per cent] of the Fair Price) and (ii) within 15 days of allocation of the Affected Shares [(or, if conditions have been specified, within 45 days from the date of the expiry of the Right to Purchase Period)] and otherwise on the terms of clause 19.

17.7 [If a Material Default occurs, then [all] [a Qualifying Majority of] the non-defaulting Shareholders shall (in addition to any other rights under this clause 17) be entitled (after the expiry of the 45 day period referred to in clause 17.1(c)) by notice to the defaulting Shareholder to require that:

(a) the defaulting Shareholder shall not exercise its right to attend and vote at general meetings of the JVC; and

(b) the consent of the defaulting Shareholder or of any Director appointed by the defaulting Shareholder shall no longer be required (if otherwise applicable) under clause 8; and

(c) the defaulting Shareholder shall cease to have the right to appoint any Director and any Director(s) appointed by it shall not be entitled to vote at any Board meeting and, for the purposes of clause 7.7, the quorum for a Board meeting shall not be required to include the Director(s) appointed by the defaulting Shareholder. Any Director(s) appointed by the defaulting Shareholder shall promptly resign or be removed by the defaulting Shareholder, failing which any such Director(s) may be removed from office by notice to the JVC by [all] [a Qualifying Majority of] the Non-Affected Shareholders.]

17.8 If a Material Default is treated as a Termination Event and the defaulting Shareholder's Shares are acquired pursuant to this clause 17, the provisions of clause 13 (Non-Competition) shall continue to apply to the defaulting Shareholder for a period of [2] years after the disposal of its Shares.

17.9 Nothing in this clause 17 shall affect any party's right to claim damages or other compensation under applicable law for a breach or, where appropriate, to seek an immediate remedy of an injunction, specific performance or similar court order to enforce the defaulting Shareholder's obligations.

Determination of Fair Price

18. The price for the subscription for any Shares on issue of new shares under clause 5.6 or the sale and purchase of any Shares following a Termination Event under clause 17 shall be a fair and reasonable price ("**Fair Price**") determined (unless otherwise agreed by all the parties) by an expert (the "**Expert**") in accordance with the provisions of Schedule 3.

Transfer terms

19.1 In this clause:

(a) "**Buyer(s)**" means the Non-Affected Shareholders, the Transferee, the Continuing Shareholders or a Third Party Purchaser (as the case may be) acquiring the Seller's Shares;

(b) "**Outgoing Party's Loans**" means any Loans owing at that time from the JVC to the Seller or any member of its Group;

(c) "**Relevant Notice**" means the relevant Transfer Notice, Right to Purchase Notice or other equivalent notice (as the case may be);

(d) "**Sale Proportion**" means the proportion which the Seller's Shares to be transferred to the Buyer (or, where more than one, to each Buyer) bears to the number of Seller's Shares held by the Seller prior to the transfer;

(e) "**Seller**" means the Shareholder selling, or required to sell, its Shares in the JVC;

(f) "**Seller's Shares**" means the shares in the JVC being sold or transferred.

19.2 Any transfer of Seller's Shares pursuant to clause 16 and Schedule 3 (*Transfers of Shares*), clause 17 (*Events Triggering Option to Purchase*) [or] shall be on the following terms:

(a) the Seller's Shares shall be sold free from all liens, charges and encumbrances and third party rights, together with all rights of any nature attaching to them including all rights to any dividends or other distributions declared, paid or made after the date of the Relevant Notice;

(b) with effect from the completion date the Buyer shall (i) take an assignment of, or make available equivalent finance in place of, the Outgoing Party's Loans in the relevant Sale Proportion and (ii) assume any obligations of the Seller and any member of its Group (in the relevant Sale Proportion) under any guarantees, indemnities, letters of comfort and/or counter-indemnities to third parties in relation to the business of the JVC. This is without prejudice to the right of the Buyer(s) to receive a contribution from the Seller and any member of its Group for its share of any claims attributable to any liabilities arising in respect of the period before the completion date;

(c) the Seller shall deliver to the Buyer a duly executed transfer in favour of the Buyer (or to such person as it may direct) together with any appropriate certificate(s) for the Seller's Shares and a certified copy of any authority under which such transfer is executed and, against delivery of the transfer, the Buyer shall pay the consideration for the Seller's Shares (in the relevant Sale Proportion) to the Seller in cleared funds for value on the completion date;

(d) the Seller shall do all such other things and execute all other documents as the Buyer may reasonably request to give effect to the sale and purchase of the Seller's Shares;

(e) if requested by the Buyer, the Seller shall ensure that the relevant Directors appointed by it resign and the resignation(s) take effect without any liability on the JVC for compensation for loss of office or otherwise (except to the extent that the liability arises in relation to any service contract with a Director who was acting in an executive capacity);

(f) if any Buyer is not a party to this Agreement, it shall enter into a Deed of Adherence and, if it is not an ultimate holding company, deliver to the JVC a Parent Company Guarantee.

Deadlock

20.1 In the event of a Deadlock, the matter shall be referred to the respective [Chairmen] [Chief Executives] of the Shareholders with a view to it being resolved as early as possible in the best interests of the JVC. If the Deadlock cannot be resolved [within 30 days of that referral], any Shareholder may give notice (a "**Warning Notice**") that it intends to implement the deadlock procedure contemplated by this clause.

20.2 If the Deadlock cannot be resolved within a further 30 day period after service of a Warning Notice, then [any] Shareholder (the "**Disaffected Shareholder**") may give notice to the other Shareholders that it wishes to terminate the joint venture and/or to sell its Shares in the JVC. On receipt of the notice, the Shareholders shall negotiate with each other in good faith and co-operate with a view to achieving the sale of that Shareholder's Shares by one of the following methods (or a combination of them) or resolving the Deadlock in another manner acceptable to the Shareholders. The methods are:

(a) the purchase by the JVC of the Disaffected Shareholder's Shares on terms acceptable to all the Shareholders (provided that such purchase by the JVC can lawfully be made and is financially practicable); or

(b) the purchase by one or more of the other Shareholders of the Disaffected Shareholder's Shares; or

(c) the purchase by one or more third parties of the Disaffected Shareholder's Shares; or

(d) the sale of the whole of the issued share capital of the JVC to a third party.

20.3 If no such method has been agreed [or completed] by _____ _____, [the Disaffected Shareholder] [a Qualifying Majority of Shareholders] may serve a written notice on the other Shareholders requiring the JVC to be wound-up. All the Shareholders shall be bound to join in all steps necessary for that purpose.

Winding-up of JVC

21.1 Prior to any resolution for winding up the JVC being passed, the Shareholders shall endeavour to agree a suitable basis for dealing with the interests and assets of the JVC in such event. For this purpose:

(a) the Shareholders shall co-operate (but without any obligation to provide any additional finance) with a view to enabling all existing trading obligations of the JVC to be completed insofar as its resources allow. The Shareholders shall consult together with a view to the JVC novating or re-allocating outstanding contracts within the Business in a suitable manner;

(b) the JVC shall not assume any new contractual obligation for the supply of products or services;

(c) unless the Shareholders agree otherwise, the Shareholders shall ensure that the JVC is wound up as soon as practicable;

(d) each Shareholder shall promptly deliver up to each other Shareholder, and the JVC shall as soon as reasonably practicable deliver up to each Shareholder, all drawings, notes, copies or other representations of confidential information proprietary to and/or originating from that other Shareholder or its Group;

(e) the Shareholders shall be free upon winding-up to compete in any way [within the Field] [with the Business];

(f) [each Shareholder shall have free access to, and use of, any technology or products developed by the JVC (whether by transfer of design and manufacturing rights or by appropriate non-exclusive licences). The JVC shall deliver to each Shareholder, and not to any third party, copies of drawings, notes or other representations of confidential information proprietary to and/or originating from the JVC.]

This Agreement shall terminate upon completion of such winding-up except that winding-up shall not affect the obligations of the parties under clause 11 (Confidentiality) which shall remain in full force and effect

21.2 [If [A, B, C or D] [a party] ceases or is about to cease to be a Shareholder or to have any of its Subsidiaries as a Shareholder, each Shareholder shall on the request of that party exercise its powers with a view to ensuring that the JVC's name (or that of any other relevant JVC Member) is changed so that it no longer includes the name, initials or trade mark, or any reference to the name, initials or trade mark, of the Shareholder making the request.]

Further assurances

22.1 So far as it is legally able, each Shareholder agrees with the others to exercise all voting rights and powers (direct or indirect) available to it in relation to any person and/or the JVC to ensure that the provisions of this Agreement (and the other agreements referred to in this Agreement) are duly fulfilled and generally that full effect is given to the principles set out in this Agreement.

22.2 Each Shareholder shall ensure that its Subsidiaries comply with (i) all obligations under this Agreement which are expressed to apply to members of its respective Group and (ii) all obligations under any agreement entered into by any of its Subsidiaries pursuant to this Agreement. The liability of a Shareholder under clause 22.2 shall not be discharged, or impaired by any amendment to or variation of this Agreement any release of or granting of time or other indulgence to any of its Subsidiaries or any third party or any other act, event or omission which but for this clause would operate to impair or discharge the liability of such Shareholder under clause 22.2.

Claims by JVC against Shareholders

23. If the JVC has or may have any claim against a Shareholder or any member of its Group arising out of any agreement entered into by a Shareholder or any member of that Shareholder's Group, that Shareholder will ensure that its nominated Directors shall not do anything to prevent or hinder the JVC asserting or enforcing the claim and that they shall, if necessary, enable all decisions regarding such claim to be taken by the Directors nominated by the Shareholders wishing to assert or enforce the claim. This is without prejudice to any right of the defendant Shareholder itself to dispute the claim.

Non-assignment

24. No party shall (nor shall purport to) assign, transfer, charge or otherwise deal with all or any of its rights and/or obligations under this Agreement nor grant, declare, create or dispose of any right or interest in it in whole or in part (otherwise than pursuant to a transfer of Shares in accordance with the terms of this Agreement).

Waiver of rights

25. No waiver by a party of a failure by any other party to perform any provision of this Agreement operates or is to be construed as a waiver in respect of any other failure whether of a like or different character.

Amendments

26. A variation of this Agreement (or of any of the documents referred to in it) is valid only if it is in writing and signed by or on behalf of each party [(except that a variation of any provision of this Agreement which only affects the respective rights and obligations of the Shareholders as between themselves does not need the JVC's agreement)].

Invalidity

27. If any provision of this Agreement is or is held to be invalid or unenforceable, this shall not invalidate any of the remaining provisions of this Agreement. The parties shall use all reasonable efforts to replace the invalid or unenforceable provision by a valid provision the effect of which is as close as possible to the intended effect of the invalid or unenforceable provision.

No partnership or agency

28. Nothing in this Agreement (or any of the arrangements contemplated by it) shall be deemed to constitute a partnership between the Shareholders nor, except as may be expressly set out in it, constitute any party the agent of any other party for any purpose. Unless the Shareholders agree otherwise in writing, none of them shall (i) enter into any contract or commitment with third parties as agent for the JVC or for any of the other Shareholders or (ii) describe itself as such an agent or in any way hold itself out as being such an agent.

Announcements

29.1 No formal public announcement or press release in connection with this Agreement shall (subject to clause 29.2) be made or issued by or on behalf of any party or any member of its Group without the prior written approval of all the Shareholders (such approval not to be unreasonably withheld or delayed).

29.2 If a party has an obligation to make or issue any announcement required by law or by any stock exchange or by any governmental authority, the relevant party shall give the other parties every reasonable opportunity to comment on any announcement before it is made or issued (provided that this shall not prevent the party making the announcement from complying with its legal and/or stock exchange obligations).

Costs

30.1 Each of the Shareholders shall pay its own costs, charges and expenses (including taxation) incurred in connection with negotiating, preparing and implementing this Agreement and the transactions contemplated by it.

30.2 The costs of and incidental to the incorporation and the establishment of the JVC shall be borne and paid by the JVC and the JVC shall reimburse to the Shareholders all expenditure incurred by them in relation to the JVC and agreed [in writing] by the Shareholders to be reimbursed by the JVC.

Entire agreement

31. This Agreement [and [*any other Agreements entered into on Closing pursuant to clause [3]*]] set[s] out the entire agreement and understanding between the parties with respect to the subject matter of it. [This Agreement supersedes [the Confidentiality Undertaking/any Heads of Agreement or Memorandum of Understanding], which cease to have any further force or effect.] No party has relied or has been induced to enter into this Agreement in reliance on any representation, warranty or undertaking which is not expressly set out or referred to in this Agreement. This clause shall not exclude any liability for fraudulent misrepresentation.

Conflict with Articles

32.1 If the provisions of this Agreement conflict with the Memorandum and Articles of Association or the JVC's other constitutional documents, the provisions of this Agreement shall prevail as between the Shareholders. The Shareholders shall (i) exercise all voting and other rights and powers available to them to give effect to the provisions of this Agreement and (ii) (if necessary) ensure that any required amendment is made to the Memorandum and Articles of Association or other constitutional document of the JVC.

32.2 [Without prejudice to the generality of clause 32.1, the provisions of this Agreement shall prevail in relation to the transfer of Shares and accordingly:

(a) no Shareholder shall use the provisions of Article _____ of the Articles to frustrate the operation of [clauses 16 or 17 or Schedule 3] of this Agreement; and

(b) each Shareholder shall promptly give (or ensure that any member of its Group promptly gives) any approval under Article _____ of the Articles which is necessary or appropriate to give full and immediate effect to the procedure contemplated by the provisions of [clauses 16, 17 or Schedule 3] and/or any transfer of Shares permitted under this Agreement.]

32.3 The JVC is not bound by any provision of this Agreement to the extent that it constitutes an unlawful fetter on any statutory power of the JVC. This shall not affect the validity of the relevant provision as between the Shareholders or the respective obligations of the Shareholders as between themselves under clause 32.1.

Notices

33.1 Any notice or other formal communication to be given under this Agreement shall be in writing and signed by or on behalf of the party giving it. It shall be sent by fax to the relevant number set out in clause 33.3 or delivered by hand or sent by prepaid recorded delivery, special delivery or registered post to the relevant address in clause 33.3. In each case it shall be marked for the attention of the relevant party set out in clause 33.3 (or as otherwise notified from time to time in accordance with the provisions of this clause 33).

33.2 The addresses and fax numbers of the parties for the purpose of clause 33.1 are:

A:	B:	JVC:
Address:	Address:	Address:
Fax No:	Fax No:	Fax No:
For the attention of:	For the attention of:	For the attention of:
C:	D:	
Address:	Address:	
Fax No:	Fax No:	
For the attention of:	For the attention of:	

33.3 All notices or formal communications under or in connection with this Agreement shall be in the English language or, if in any other language, accompanied by a translation into English. In the event of any conflict between the English text and the text in any other language, the English text shall prevail.

Dispute resolution

34.1 If any dispute, controversy or claim [(other than a Deadlock)] arises out of or in connection with this Agreement, including the breach, termination or invalidity thereof ("**Dispute**"), any party may serve formal written notice on the other parties that a Dispute has arisen ("**Notice of Dispute**").

34.2 The parties shall use all reasonable efforts for a period of 30 days from the date on which the Notice of Dispute is served (or such longer period as may be agreed in writing between the parties) to resolve the Dispute on an amicable basis.

34.3 If the parties are unable to resolve the Dispute by amicable negotiation within the time period referred to in clause 34.2, the Dispute shall be referred to the respective [Chairmen] [Chief Executives] of [the ultimate holding companies of the Shareholders] who shall attempt, for a period of 30 days from the expiry of the time period referred to in clause 34.2, to resolve the Dispute. Mediation shall be considered. If the respective [Chairmen] [Chief Executives] of [the ultimate holding companies of the Shareholders] are unable to resolve the Dispute within the stated time period (or such longer period as may be agreed in writing between the parties), the Dispute shall be [referred to arbitration in accordance with clause 34.4].

34.4 Subject to clauses 34.1 to 34.3, the Dispute shall be referred to and finally resolved by arbitration under the Rules of Arbitration of the International Chamber of Commerce by [a sole arbitrator] [three arbitrators] appointed in accordance with those Rules. The seat of arbitration shall be [London, England]. The language to be used in the arbitral proceedings shall be English. The parties shall have the right to seek interim relief from a court of competent jurisdiction, at any time before and after the arbitrator has been appointed, up until the arbitrator has made his final award.

Counterparts

35. This Agreement may be executed in any number of counterparts and by the parties to it on separate counterparts, each of which shall be an original but all of which together shall constitute one and the same instrument.

No rights under Contracts (Rights of Third Parties) Act 1999

36. [A person who is not a party to this Agreement shall have no right under the Contracts (Rights of Third Parties) Act 1999 to enforce any of its terms.]

Governing law

37. This Agreement shall be governed by the laws of [England].

AS WITNESS this Agreement has been signed by the duly authorised representatives of the parties.

Schedule 1

Shareholder Interests and Commitments on Closing

Shareholder	(1) Equity Proportion at Closing %	(2) Number and Type of Shares	(3) Total Issue Price £	(4) Amount of Loans £
A				
B				
C				
D				

Schedule 2

Transfer of Shares

[*Note. These transfer pre-emption provisions have been drafted on the basis that: (i) the seller has an identified third party purchaser for all its shares and has agreed the price (which must be cash) and material terms with that purchaser; (ii) the other shareholders have the opportunity to buy their proportionate share of those shares at the same third party price and on the same terms (a "right of first refusal"); (iii) the other shareholders can apply for shares in excess of their proportionate entitlement; and (iv) if not all of the shares on offer are accepted by the other shareholders, the seller can withdraw its transfer notice and retain its shares or transfer all of its shares to the third party (a "total transfer condition"). There is no provision for an expert to determine the "Fair Price" of the shares. If it is appropriate for an expert to be appointed, the expert determination provisions in clause 18 and Schedule 4 could be adapted accordingly.*]

Right of first refusal

1. Before a Selling Shareholder makes any transfer of the Seller's Shares to a third party it shall first give a written notice (a "**Transfer Notice**") to the other Shareholders (the "**Continuing Shareholders**") offering to sell the Seller's Shares to each of the Continuing Shareholders. Each Continuing Shareholder shall be offered (as nearly as may be) such proportion of the Seller's Shares as corresponds to the proportion which the number of Shares held by that Continuing Shareholder bears to the total number of Shares held by all the Continuing Shareholders as at the close of business on the date prior to the date of the Transfer Notice (a "**Proportionate Entitlement**"). A Transfer Notice shall specify:

(a) the number of Seller's Shares which the Selling Shareholder is proposing to sell and each Continuing Shareholder's Proportionate Entitlement;

(b) the proposed price for the relevant transfer, which must be cash (the "**Specified Price**");

(c) the identity and address of the person(s) to whom the Selling Shareholder proposes to sell the Seller's Shares (the "**Third Party Purchaser**"); and

(d) any other material terms of the proposed sale (the "**Offer Terms**").

2. A Transfer Notice shall be irrevocable (except as provided by paragraphs 7 and 8 of this Schedule) and shall constitute an offer by the Selling Shareholder to sell the

Seller's Shares to the Continuing Shareholders at the Specified Price and on the Offer Terms and shall be open for acceptance by each of the Continuing Shareholders for 30 Business Days from the date of despatch of the Transfer Notice (the "**Acceptance Period**").

3. Each of the Continuing Shareholders may at any time before the expiry of the Acceptance Period give notice (a "**Buy Notice**") to the Selling Shareholder of (i) its wish to purchase all or any of the Seller's Shares offered to it by the Selling Shareholder at the Specified Price and on the Offer Terms and (ii) if applicable, its wish to apply for Seller's Shares in excess of its Proportionate Entitlement by specifying in its Buy Notice the number of Seller's Shares in excess of its Proportionate Entitlement which it is prepared to purchase. If any of the Continuing Shareholders fails to serve a Buy Notice before the expiry of the Acceptance Period, it shall be deemed to have declined the offer by the Selling Shareholder constituted by the Transfer Notice. A Buy Notice shall be irrevocable unless agreed in writing by the Selling Shareholder and all the Continuing Shareholders giving Buy Notices.

4. If any Continuing Shareholder has applied for less than its Proportionate Entitlement, the excess shall be allocated (as nearly as may be) to each Continuing Shareholder who has applied for Seller's Shares in excess of its Proportionate Entitlement, pro rata to the number of shares held by the Continuing Shareholders who have so applied as at the close of business on the date prior to the Transfer Notice. Any allocation made under this paragraph shall not, however, result in any Continuing Shareholder being allocated more Seller's Shares than it has applied for; any remaining excess shall be apportioned between the other Continuing Shareholders by applying this paragraph without taking account of such Continuing Shareholder.

5. [A Buy Notice may be expressed to be subject to the fulfilment of such specified [regulatory] conditions as may required in order to enable the Seller's Shares to be acquired without breach of any relevant law or regulation. The right may be reserved to waive all or any of such conditions, whether in whole or in part, provided that a Buy Notice must provide that it will cease to be effective if all relevant conditions are not fulfilled or waived within a specified period not exceeding 45 Business Days from the date of the Buy Notice (the "**Condition Period**").]

6. If Buy Notices [(for which all specified conditions are fulfilled or waived within the Condition Period)] are served by Continuing Shareholders for all of the Seller's Shares, the Selling Shareholder shall be bound to sell, and the relevant Continuing Shareholders shall be bound to purchase, all of the Seller's Shares at the Specified Price and upon the Offer Terms and otherwise in accordance with clause 19. Completion shall take place within 10 Business Days from [the end of the Condition Period].

7. [If Buy Notices are served by Continuing Shareholders for all of the Seller's Shares but all of the specified conditions in the Buy Notices are not fulfilled within the Condition Period, the Selling Shareholder shall be entitled at its discretion either to (i) withdraw its Transfer Notice and retain all the Seller's Shares or (ii) transfer all of the Seller's Shares to the Third Party Purchaser at not less than the Specified Price and on the Offer Terms provided that the transfer is completed within 60 Business Days of the end of the Condition Period. The Selling Shareholder shall indicate whether it elects for option (i) or option (ii) by notice to the Continuing Shareholders and the JVC within 5 Business Days of the end of the Condition Period. If it does not so elect, it shall be deemed to have elected for option (i).]

8. If Buy Notices are served by Continuing Shareholders for less than all of the Seller's Shares, the Selling Shareholder shall be entitled at its discretion either to (i)

withdraw its Transfer Notice and retain all the Seller's Shares or (ii) transfer all of the Seller's Shares to the Third Party Purchaser at not less than the Specified Price and on the Offer Terms provided that the transfer is completed within 60 Business Days of the end of the Acceptance Period. The Selling Shareholder shall indicate whether it elects for option (i) or option (ii) by notice to the Continuing Shareholders and the JVC within 5 Business Days of the end of the Acceptance Period. If it does not so elect, it shall be deemed to have elected for option (i).

9. If the Selling Shareholder withdraws the Transfer Notice under paragraph 7 or paragraph 8, the Selling Shareholder shall not be entitled to serve a further Transfer Notice in respect of the Seller's Shares until the expiry of a period of 12 months after the end of the Acceptance Period.

Non-Sellers' tag-along right

[*Note: a tag-along right for the non-Sellers may be appropriate. If not appropriate, exclude.*]

[**10.** If the Seller proposes to sell its Shares on a *bona fide* arm's length sale to a Third Party Purchaser in accordance with this Schedule 3, it shall not complete such sale unless it ensures that the Third Party Purchaser offers to buy all the Shares [and Loans] held by the Continuing Shareholders on the same terms (including price per Share [which must be cash]) as apply to the purchase of the Seller's Shares. The offer shall:

(a) be irrevocable and unconditional (except for any conditions which apply to the proposed transfer of the Seller's Shares);

(b) fully describe all material terms and conditions (including terms relating to price, time of completion and conditions precedent) agreed between the Seller and the Third Party Purchaser;

(c) be open for acceptance by each Continuing Shareholder during a period of not less than [21] days after receipt of such offer.

If the offer is accepted by a Continuing Shareholder, the sale shall be conditional upon completion of the Seller's sale to the Third Party Purchaser and shall be completed at the same time as that sale [or, if later, within [7] days after acceptance by the Continuing Shareholder of the offer by the Third Party Purchaser.] The sale of the Continuing Shareholder's Shares shall otherwise proceed in accordance with the terms of clause 19 as if that party was "the Seller".

Drag-along right

[*Note: this drag-along right may be appropriate in some circumstances e.g. if the Seller is a majority party. If not appropriate, exclude.*]

[**11.** If [A is] the Seller [and] proposes to sell all its Shares on a bona fide arm's length sale to a Third Party Purchaser in accordance with this Schedule 3], it shall be entitled to give all (but not some only) of the Continuing Shareholders [not less than [30] days'] notice requiring them to sell all (but not some only) of their respective Shares [and Loans] to the Seller (or its nominee which may be the Third Party Purchaser) at a price per Share equal to [the greater of]:

(a) the value of the consideration per Share being offered to the Seller by the Third Party Purchaser; [and

(b) the Fair Price if a Continuing Shareholder elects, within [10] days of that notice, to have that Fair Price determined in the same manner as set out in accordance with Schedule 4.]

No Continuing Shareholder shall be obliged to make any representation or warranty or to incur any liability to the Third Party Purchaser other than in respect of a warranty as to title to its Shares. The sale of the Continuing Shareholders' Shares shall be completed at the same time as that sale [or, if later, within 7 days of determination of the Fair Price.] The sale of the Continuing Shareholders' Shares under this Schedule shall otherwise proceed in accordance with the terms of clause 19 as if that party was "the Seller".

Schedule 3

Valuation by Expert

1. The price for any Shares to be valued for the purposes of clauses [5 or 17] of the Agreement (the "**Valuation Shares**") shall be determined by an Expert in accordance with this Schedule.

2. The Expert shall be such internationally recognised firm of investment bankers as [a Qualifying Majority of] the Shareholders may agree or, if they fail to agree, such internationally recognised firm of investment bankers, independent of all of the Shareholders, as the [International Centre for Expertise of the International Chamber of Commerce] shall appoint at the request of any Shareholder. The Expert shall act as an expert and not as an arbitrator and its decision, which shall be incorporated in a certificate (the "**Certificate**") (a copy of which will be provided to each of the Shareholders and the JVC), shall be final and binding on the Shareholders (and the JVC) and not subject to appeal to any court or tribunal on any basis whatsoever and the Shareholders and the JVC must comply with the Expert's decision. The Expert's fees and expenses shall be borne by the JVC.

3. The Expert shall exercise its independent professional judgment in arriving at a determination of the Fair Price (which shall be expressed in [currency]) of any Valuation Shares by (i) assessing the historical and projected financial performance of the JVC, (ii) applying generally accepted methodologies for valuing the JVC, including discounted cash flow analysis, comparisons with any similar companies whose shares are traded on any stock exchange and comparisons with any publicly disclosed sales of similar companies or significant pools of similar assets, and (iii) such other valuation methods as the Expert shall consider to be appropriate in the circumstances.

4. The Expert shall determine the Fair Price of the Valuation Shares on the following basis:

(a) by valuing the JVC on a going concern basis for an arms' length sale between a willing buyer and a willing seller and on the assumption that the subject matter of the valuation is exposed to an open market;

(b) by valuing the Valuation Shares by reference to the value of the JVC as a whole (and therefore without regard to the size of any relevant holding);

(c) making no allowances for any expenses that might be incurred in connection with the issue, sale or purchase of the Valuation Shares;

(d) in the case of an issue of Shares under clause 5, (i) without regard to the size of the issue of the New Shares, (ii) on the assumption that the share capital of the JVC has been increased by the issue of the New Shares and that the proceeds of the issue of such shares have been received, (iii) without any discount which would normally be taken into account in the case of a rights issue by a listed company; and

(e) in the case of a sale and purchase of Shares following a Termination Event, taking into account the likely effect on the JVC's business of the loss of the Affected Shareholder as a shareholder in the JVC and that the JVC will [not] continue to benefit from the terms of the [*describe ancillary agreement(s)*] (to the extent that it/they terminate as a consequence of the exercise of any rights under clause 17) and taking into account the impact (if applicable) of the Material Default in question on the business of the JVC and on the value of the Valuation Shares.]

The Fair Price of the Valuation Shares may also reflect any other factors which the Expert [reasonably] believes should be taken into account. The Expert shall have access to all accounting records or other relevant documents of the JVC which it requests for the purposes of its determination, subject to any existing confidentiality provisions.

SCHEDULE 4

DEFINITIONS AND INTERPRETATION

1. In this Agreement, and in the Recitals and Schedules, the terms set out below shall (unless the context requires otherwise) have the following respective meanings. Other defined terms shall have the meaning set out in the clause or Schedule in which that term is first used.

"**Accounting Principles**" means the accounting principles and policies to be adopted by the JVC [in the agreed form];

"**Auditors**" means the auditors of the JVC from time to time;

"**Board**" means the board of directors of the JVC;

"**Business**" means the business to be carried on by the JVC, as described in clause 1.2;

"**Business Day**" means a day (other than a Saturday) on which banks generally are open in London for a full range of business;

"**Business Plan**" means the business plan referred to in clause 9;

"**Chairman**" means the chairman from time to time of the Board;

"**Chief Executive**" means the chief executive from time to time of the JVC;

"**Closing**" means closing of the establishment of the JVC in accordance with clause 3;

"**company**" means any body corporate, wherever incorporated;

"**Controlling Interest**" means: (a) the ownership or control (directly or indirectly) of more than 50% of the voting share capital of the relevant undertaking; or (b) the ability to direct the casting of more than 50% of the votes exercisable at general meetings of the relevant undertaking on all, or substantially all, matters; or (c) the right to appoint or remove directors of the relevant undertaking holding a majority of the voting rights at meetings of the board on all, or substantially all, matters;

"**Deadlock**" means the occurrence of any of the following circumstances, namely if:

(a) [any of the Reserved Board Matters or Reserved Shareholder Matters is proposed for decision at a meeting of the Board or a general meeting of the JVC in writing by one or more of the Shareholders and there is no relevant majority or approval for the matter as specified by clause 8.2 (in respect of Reserved Shareholder Matters) or clause 8.3 (in respect of Reserved Board Matters) or otherwise;] or

(b) a quorum is not present at two successive duly convened general meetings by reason of the absence of the same Shareholder or at two successive duly convened meetings of the Board by reason of the absence of a Director

MULTI-PARTY SHAREHOLDERS' AGREEMENT (LONG FORM)   781

nominated by the same Shareholder being, in each case, a meeting at which a Reserved Board Matter or Reserved Shareholder Matter was on the agenda to be decided;

"**Deed of Adherence**" means a deed in the agreed form [set out in Schedule [   ]];

"**Directors**" means the JVC's directors;

"**Equity Proportions**" means the respective proportions in which the Shares are held from time to time by each of the Shareholders (initially being the percentages as set out in Schedule 1 save that, if the expression "**Equity Proportion**" is used in the context of some (but not all) of the Shareholders, it shall mean the respective proportions in which Shares are held by each of those particular Shareholders;

["**Field**" means_____];

"**Financial Year**" means a financial period of the JVC (commencing, other than in the case of its initial financial period, on _____ and ending on _____);

"**Group**" means, in relation to the JVC or a Shareholder, that company and its Subsidiaries for the time being;

"**holding company**" means, in relation to a company, any company of which the latter is a Subsidiary;

"**Loan Noteholders**" means the holders of the Loan Notes;

"**Loan Notes**" means unsecured loan notes to be issued by the JVC in the agreed form [set out in Schedule [   ]]; [*See also Precedent 16*]

"**Maximum Commitment**" means the maximum amount which each party is obliged to subscribe for Shares [and/or advance by way of Loans] as set out against its name in Schedule 1;

"**Ordinary Share**" means an ordinary share of £_____ each in the capital of the JVC having the rights set out in the Articles;

"**Parent Company Guarantee**" means a guarantee in the agreed form [set out in Schedule [   ]];

"**parties**" means the JVC and the Shareholders, and any other person who at the relevant time is a party to, or has agreed (by executing a Deed of Adherence) to be bound by, this Agreement;

"**Qualifying Majority**" means shareholders whose aggregate Equity Proportions exceed [75%] of the total issued Shares from time to time;

"**Shares**" means shares in the equity share capital of the Company;

"**Shareholders**" means those parties to this Agreement which at the relevant time hold Shares (and "**Shareholder**" means any one of them), including any person to whom Shares have been transferred or issued and who has agreed to be bound by this Agreement by executing a Deed of Adherence;

"**subsidiary**" means, in relation to a company (the "**holding company**"), any other company in which the holding company for the time being directly or indirectly holds or controls either: (a) a majority of the voting rights exercisable at general meetings of the members of that company on all, or substantially all, matters; or (b) the right to appoint or remove directors having a majority of the voting rights exercisable at meetings of the board of directors of that company on all, or substantially all, matters; and any company which is a subsidiary is also a subsidiary of any further company of which that other is a subsidiary;

"**Surviving Provisions**" means clause 11 (*Confidentiality*), clause 13 (*Non-Competition*), clause 25 (*Waiver of Rights*), clause 27 (*Invalidity*), clause 28 (*No*

Partnership or Agency), clause 29 (*Announcements*) clause 30 (*Costs*), clause 31 (*Entire Agreement*), clause 33 (*Notices*), clause 34 (*Dispute Resolution*), [clause 36 (*No Rights under Contracts (Rights of Third Parties) Act 1999*)] and clause 37 (*Governing Law*);

"**Termination Event**" has the meaning set out in clause 17.1;

"**ultimate holding company**" means a holding company which is not a subsidiary.

2. The headings in this Agreement do not affect its interpretation.

3. Any reference to document in the "**agreed form**" is to a document agreed by the parties and initialled by them or on their behalf for identification purposes.

4. Where any obligation in this Agreement is expressed to be undertaken or assumed by any party, that obligation is to be construed as requiring the party concerned to exercise all rights and powers of control over the affairs of any other person which it is able to exercise (whether directly or indirectly) in order to secure performance of the obligation.

5. References to an English legal term or concept shall, in respect of any jurisdiction other than England, be construed as reference to the term or concept which most nearly corresponds in that jurisdiction to it.

SIGNED by _____ }
for and on behalf of **A** }

SIGNED by _____ }
for and on behalf of **B** }

SIGNED by _____ }
for and on behalf of **C** }

SIGNED by _____ }
for and on behalf of **D** }

SIGNED by _____ }
for and on behalf of **JVC** }

Precedent 11

Articles of Association for a UK Joint Venture Company

> The following precedent is a set of Articles of Association for a joint venture company (JVC) which is established as a private company limited by shares in the UK. The Articles of Association are based on the final draft of the Model Articles published under the Companies Act 2006 (see below). They reflect relevant parts of the 2006 Act which will be in force as at October 1, 2009. A number of changes to "standard" articles for a private company are usually made for a JVC. Section A below contains explanatory background relating to the proposed Model Articles and the issues commonly considered in the case of a JVC. Section B contains the precedent Articles of Association.

A. GENERAL

1. Purpose of Articles of Association. The constitution and internal regulations of a company in the UK are set out in its articles of association. The articles are the primary regulations relating to the company's internal management and administrative structure. Under the Companies Act 2006, the constitutional significance of a company's memorandum of association will be significantly reduced as from October 2009. It will record only the names of subscribers and the number of shares each subscriber has agreed to take. In the case of a then existing company, the objects clause and all other provisions in its memorandum as at October 2009 will be deemed to be contained in its articles of association (but the company can remove these by special resolution).

2. Model Articles. The Companies Act 1985 offered model forms of articles of association which could be adopted in whole or in part by companies incorporated in Great Britain. Table A has been commonly used for limited companies. The Companies Act 2006 provides for new model articles to be developed for use by a private company limited by shares (the **Model Articles**). These will replace Table A for private companies incorporated under the new Act after October 2009. A final draft of the Model Articles was published on April 7, 2008[1] with the intention that the implementing regulations will be made in Autumn 2008.

3. Modifications for a JVC. After October 2009, the Model Articles can be adopted by any company and, if a private company limited by shares fails to register any articles on incorporation, will be its articles by default. However, as with Table A, the Model Articles are unlikely, without amendment, to be wholly appropriate in the context of a JVC. Modifications are likely to be necessary to reflect the JVC's shareholding and management structure. It is often a matter of debate and drafting style, or preference, as to what matters should be addressed in the articles—see generally para.5–55 et seq. of Part A of this book. The most usual changes to be considered in the case of a JVC are described below.

---

[1] A copy of the draft Companies (Model Articles) Regulations 2008 can be obtained on the BERR website: *www.berr.gov.uk/files/file45533.doc*.

Prior to October 2009, modifications to a JVC's articles of association should be made by reference to Table A. After October 2009, a pre-existing company can continue to adopt articles by reference to Table A or, if it wishes, then by reference to the new Model Articles.

A precedent set of Articles of Association by reference to the proposed Model Articles accompanies this explanatory section. Numbered references in the right-hand column are to the numbered Articles in the accompanying precedent.

MODIFICATION/SPECIFIC JVC ISSUE	REF IN ARTICLES
Directors' general authority/shareholders' reserve power	
The Model Articles (Model Article 3) contain the general principle that, subject to the articles, the directors are responsible for the management of the company's business. It is possible formally to set out limitations on the directors' authority in the articles by specifying certain decisions to be reserved for shareholder decision—but such "reserved matters" are usually dealt with solely in the shareholders' agreement. Model Article 4 preserves the "reserve power" of share-holders, by special resolution, to direct the directors to take or refrain from specified action.	
Directors: maximum number	
Provision is sometimes made for a maximum number of directors.	4
Directors: appointment and removal	
Power to appoint and remove directors will often be attached to different classes of shares held by each of the parties. A straightforward method of appointing (and removing) directors is by written notice given by the shareholder to the registered office of the company (i.e., without the need for a shareholder or board meeting). It is common to provide that the appointment or removal takes effect simply on receipt of the notice at the registered office or such later time as may be specified in the notice itself. These provisions are set out in Article 5.	5
Alternate directors	
It is common to provide for directors to be able to appoint alternates who can attend meetings in their place (although in some ventures it may be important that only the "true" directors should attend). The Model Articles do not provide for alternates, although the model articles for a plc do so. The latter wording could be adopted. However, there are some amendments that are commonly made to such provisions in this respect:	
• Consider whether a proposed alternate should be subject to prior approval by the board if he is not already a director of the company. In a joint venture where the parties often appoint whoever they wish as their nominated directors, it is unlikely to be appropriate for the representatives of the other parties to have to approve the appointment of alternates.	6.1
• A common addition, included here [in square brackets] in Article 6.2, is to make it clear that one person can act as the alternate for more than one director and can cast votes for every director whom he is representing, although he only physically counts as one person for quorum purposes.	6.2

Directors' meetings

A number of modifications may be made in relation to meetings of directors in order to provide flexibility. They include:

- Specifying a minimum period of notice for board meetings (e.g. seven days); under the general law, only reasonable notice need be given.   7.1

- A requirement limiting business transacted at a meeting to that specified in the notice convening the meeting, unless all the directors attending agree otherwise.   7.1

- Provision that the quorum should comprise at least one nominated director from each of the parties.   7.2

- If appropriate, provision that matters may only be decided upon if one, or perhaps all, of each party's nominated directors vote in favour.   7.2

- In order to prevent abuse of the quorum provisions as a means of disrupting board meetings, provisions similar to those described above in respect of shareholder meetings should be considered. This would allow an adjourned board meeting to be held despite only one director being present.   7.3

- To provide that meetings of any board committee require at least one director nominated by each party to be present throughout the meeting. It is also common to provide that a decision of any such committee should require at least one nominated director of each party, or perhaps all directors who are present, to vote in its favour.   7.6

The Model Articles make basic provision, in a more adequate form than the old Table A, for (i) resolutions in writing (Model Article 8) and (ii) meetings of directors in direct communication if not the same physical location (Model Article 10). No specific provision has therefore been included in the Precedent. Similarly, the Model Articles (see Model Article 9) permit notices of board meetings by email and also word of mouth; if the latter is not regarded as appropriate for the JVC, Model Article 9 should be modified.

Board chairman

In a deadlock joint venture, the appointment of a chairman and whether or not he is to have a casting vote will be important. Whatever is agreed should be reflected in the articles.   7.5

Directors' duties and interests

The Companies Act 2006 includes extensive, and somewhat complex, provisions relating to director's interests and potential conflicts—see generally the discussion in chapter 8 of this book. Standard practice has yet to develop in relation to terms of the articles and the provisions of the new Act. It is likely that, for convenience, articles for a JVC should be as permissive and flexible as possible recognising that directors may have other "interests" inherent in the joint venture relationship and giving the board powers under the Act, where appropriate, to authorise conflicts of interest.

(i) *Duty to promote the company.* The Act imposes a general duty on each director to exercise independent judgment and to promote the success of the company for the benefit of its members as a whole. This is not easy to apply in the case of a JVC where a director is likely to give priority to the interests of his appointing shareholder (see the general discussion at para.8–49 et seq. earlier in the book). Although not common, it seems possible under the Act to modify a director's general duties in this respect. One possibility is to include a provision along the lines:

> "A director appointed by the A Shareholder(s) or the B Shareholder(s) (as the case may be) shall not be taken to be in breach of his general duties under sections 172 and 173 of the Companies Act 2006 by reason only that he has regard to, and gives priority to, the interests of the shareholder or class of shareholders by whom he was appointed."

This will not be appropriate if the parties wish the directors always to act in the objective best interests of the JVC. It has not yet been general practice to include such a provision in the UK and is untested.

(ii) *Arrangements with the company and "interests of directors".* Section 177 of the 2006 Act imposes a duty on a director to declare the nature and extent of any interest, direct or indirect, a director has in a proposed transaction or arrangement with the company. This may impact on joint ventures where a director of the JVC may well have an interest in a shareholder in the JVC (or a member of that shareholder's group) and therefore be indirectly "interested" in transactions or other arrangements between the JVC and members of that group: 8.1 8.2

- Article 8.1 confirms that various relatively common interests are permitted (although disclosure of the general interest is still required in accordance with s.177 of the Companies Act 2006).
- Article 8.2 provides that an "interested" director can still participate and vote, and be included in a quorum, at directors' meetings of the JVC notwithstanding his "interest" in a transaction or arrangement with the Company.

Whilst permitting the director to have such other "interests" and to act in the normal course of them, these provisions should not be interpreted as authorising an abuse such as exploitation of the JVC's property, information or opportunity in favour of that other "interest". Any such direct conflict would still require authorisation (if appropriate) under s.175 of the 2006 Act.

(iii) *Other conflicts of interest.* The 2006 Act, s.175, contains a broad duty on a director to avoid any other situation (i.e. not involving an arrangement with the company) in which he has an interest that conflicts, or may conflict, with the company's interests. The Act permits a board of directors of a private company to authorise such a conflict or potential conflict (provided there is nothing in the company's articles to invalidate such an authorisation). A JVC would normally wish to take advantage of this route—with appropriate modifications. There are safeguards which apply when directors decide whether, under the powers of the Act, to authorise a conflict or potential conflict. One of these is that only those directors who have no interest in the matter being considered will be able to take the relevant authorisation decision. For a board of a JVC to use this power to authorise a conflict involving one of the joint venture parents or its representatives, this is likely to require a relaxation to the quorum and voting provisions for directors' meetings—see Article 8.3(a).   8.3

(iv) *Chairman's ruling.* Article 8.4 preserves a "safety" mechanism which confirms that, for the purpose of the meeting, the chairman's ruling is conclusive in relation to any entitlement of a director to vote.   8.4

(v) *Information.* Another addition which is commonly made is a provision clearly permitting directors nominated by shareholders to pass information obtained whilst a JVC director to the nominating shareholder.   8.5

Share rights

In a JVC it is common to have separate classes of share (e.g. "A" and "B" shares or perhaps using the initials of the names of the joint venture parties) to which to attach certain specific rights of each shareholder such as voting rights and rights of appointment of directors.   9

Share issues: authority

Directors of private companies can allot shares without authorisation where the company has one class of share (unless the articles provide otherwise). If the company has more than one class of share, the directors must be authorised by the articles or shareholders' resolution. A provision could therefore be added giving the directors a general and unconditional authority to allot shares for the purposes of s.551 of the Companies Act 2006. The authority must state the maximum amount of shares which may be allotted under it and must be for no longer than five years. It may be renewed by ordinary resolution.   10

Pre-emption rights on new share issues

There are no common law pre-emption rights (or first refusal rights) in favour of existing shareholders on new issues of shares (*Mutual Life Insurance Co of New York v Rank Organisation Ltd* [1985] B.C.L.C. 11). Shareholders may, however, be bound by pre-emption rights in articles of association or by separate agreement. The Companies Act 2006 (s.561 and following sections) sets out a detailed and often cumbersome statutory pre-emption procedure on new issues of shares; the statutory provisions are also limited in scope—they only apply in respect of shares issued for cash. These provisions are often excluded in favour of specific pre-emption provisions in the articles. This is done by Article 10 in the following precedent.   10

Partly paid shares and liens

The Model Articles do not include provision for issue of partly paid shares nor for liens or shares. The model articles for a Plc under the Companies Act 2006 will, though, provide for partly paid shares and for the company to have a lien on those shares in respect of sums payable on them. This wording can be adopted and extended, in the case of a private company, to include a lien also over fully paid shares and for this lien to extend to *any* monies (not just sums owing in respect of the shares) owing from shareholders to the company. This can sometimes be a useful mechanism for a JVC, in the event of defaults, particularly if shareholders are committed to provide funding in tranches to the JVC. If such a regime is desired for a JVC, the provisions of the Plc model articles could be adapted.

Shareholder meetings: quorum

It is often appropriate, in the case of a JVC, to provide that a representative of each shareholder must be present for a quorum. If there are more than two shareholders and they all wish to ensure that they are represented at shareholder meetings, this will need to be specified in the quorum provision. 12.1

In order to prevent an *impasse* situation where one shareholder refuses to attend a meeting and the meeting is adjourned but the shareholder still refuses to attend when the meeting is re-convened, it may be appropriate to add wording that deems business transacted with only one shareholder present at that re-convened meeting to constitute business transacted at a meeting for all purposes. The wording in Article 12.2 seeks to achieve this. (It is thought that this should work for company law purposes, although it is not entirely free from doubt.) 12.2

Even if there are only two shareholders, it may still be considered appropriate to provide that there only need be a quorum (comprising a representative from each of the shareholders) when the meeting *starts*—see the first sentence of Article 12.1. The purpose of this is to seek to prevent a dissatisfied shareholder from disrupting company business by leaving a meeting and thereby rendering it inquorate. 12.1

Voting

It is sometimes convenient to provide that, where shares of a particular class are held by more than one shareholder (e.g. by different companies within the same group) and one or more of such shareholders is not present in person or by proxy at the meeting, then the votes of the shareholder of the class which is present are increased on a poll by the number of "absent" shares—ensuring that the total votes of that particular class can always be cast. This mechanism avoids the necessity for formal proxies and is provided for [in square brackets] in Article 13.2. 13.2

Proxies

Another common amendment is to shorten the time within which proxies should be deposited at the company's registered office before the time appointed for the meeting and, in the case of a poll, after it is demanded (see s.327(2) Companies Act 2006). It is usually thought sufficient, and will often be administratively easier to enable meetings at short notice, for a proxy to be deposited at any time before the meeting or the taking of the poll, as the case may be. 9.3

Transfers of shares

The Model Articles do not specify grounds for directors to refuse to register transfers. Provisions might be considered whereby directors could refuse to register a transfer of shares in certain circumstances—but, even then, it may not be effective to prevent the transfer of beneficial interests or voting rights in (as opposed to legal ownership of) the shares. Usually, therefore, specific pre-emption provisions will be agreed between the parties in a JVC to prevent transfers of *any* interest in shares taking place without the consent of the other shareholder or the other shareholders having a right of first refusal to acquire them. For a discussion as to what might be included in transfer pre-emption provisions, see generally chapter 12 of this book. For an example of such a pre-emption procedure to be included in the Articles, see the version set out as an option in Article 14 of the following precedent. 14

If the parties prefer not to set out the detailed pre-emption rights in the articles but still want a restriction on transfer to appear on the face of the articles (e.g. to warn third parties), one route is to have (in the articles) a total restriction on any such transfers without the consent of each of the other shareholders and for the joint venture agreement to oblige each shareholder to give its consent under the articles to a transfer permitted under the contractual procedures of the joint venture agreement. 14

Compulsory transfers

It may, in some circumstances, be appropriate to include in the articles provisions requiring a shareholder to transfer its shares (or at least to offer to transfer its shares) in certain circumstances; e.g. if the shareholder suffers a change of control or becomes insolvent or if that shareholder's continuing interest in the JVC would lead to the JVC being in breach of any statutory or regulatory requirements. See chapter 13 for a fuller discussion of this area. In most circumstances, though, it will be more convenient to leave these triggering events to be dealt with purely as a contractual matter in the joint venture agreement.

B. PRECEDENT

Note: The following Articles of Association are appropriate for a deadlock 50:50 joint venture company established after October 2009 where (unless otherwise agreed between the two parties) shareholdings are intended to be maintained in that proportion. If Articles of Association are to be prepared for a multi-party joint venture where the shareholding proportions may change, principal adjustments to this precedent are likely to include: (i) expansion to Article 5.3 in relation to new issues of shares; (ii) principles of appointment of directors (Article 5); (iii) careful consideration of the quorum requirements for board meetings (Article 7) and general meetings (Article 12); and revision of Articles 14.1 to 14.7 in relation to transfers of shares.

Where the inclusion or exclusion of provisions will clearly depend on a policy decision, the relevant provisions appear in square brackets in the precedent. The Articles of Association will, of course, always need to be tailored to the circumstances of the particular joint venture.

A PRIVATE COMPANY LIMITED BY SHARES

ARTICLES OF ASSOCIATION of
_____ LIMITED
(as at _____)

Model Articles

1. The articles in the model articles for private companies limited by shares prescribed under section 19 of the Companies Act 2006, as amended and in force at the date of adoption of these Articles (in these Articles referred to as the **Model Articles**), shall, except to the extent they are excluded or modified by these Articles, apply to the Company.

2. The following provisions of the Model Articles shall not apply to the Company:

— article 11(2) (*quorum for directors' meetings*)
— article 12 (*chairing of directors' meetings*)
— article 14 (*conflicts of interest*)
— article 17 (*methods of appointing directors*)
— article 39 (*quorum for general meetings*)

Interpretation

3. In these Articles, where the context so admits:

"**A Director**" means any person appointed as a director in accordance with the provisions of Article 5.1;

"**B Director**" means any person appointed as a director in accordance with the provisions of Article 5.2;

"**A Shares**" means the issued A ordinary shares of £1 each in the capital of the Company;

"**B Shares**" means the issued B ordinary shares of £1 each in the capital of the Company;

"**A Shareholder(s)**" means the registered holder(s) for the time being of the A Shares;

"**B Shareholder(s)**" means the registered holder(s) for the time being of the B Shares;

"**holding company**" and "**subsidiary**" shall be construed in accordance with section 1159 of the Companies Act 2006;

"**A Group**" means A and its subsidiaries for the time being;

"**B Group**" means B and its subsidiaries for the time being.

"**Articles**" means these articles of association incorporating the Model Articles (as applicable to the Company), as altered from time to time by special resolution.

Number of directors

4. The directors shall not be more than _____ (_____) in number of whom not more than _____ (_____) shall be A Directors and not more than _____ (_____) shall be B Directors.

Appointment and removal of directors

5.1 The A Shareholder(s) shall be entitled at any time and from time to time to appoint a total of _____ (_____) directors as A Directors and to remove or replace any director so appointed.

5.2 The B Shareholder(s) shall be entitled at any time and from time to time to appoint a total of _____ (_____) directors as B Directors and to remove or replace any director so appointed.

5.3 Every appointment and removal of a director under Article 5.1 or 5.2 shall be effected by notice to the Company executed by or on behalf of the A Shareholder(s) or the B Shareholder(s), as the case may be. The appointment or removal shall take effect when received by the Company or on such later date (if any) specified in the notice.

Alternate directors

6.1 Any director (the "appointor") may appoint as an alternate any other director or any other person to (a) exercise that director's powers and (b) carry out that director's responsibilities in relation to the taking of decisions by the directors in the absence of the alternate's appointor. Any appointment or removal of an alternate must be effected by notice to the Company signed by the appointor, or in any other manner approved by the directors. [The appointment or removal shall take effect when received by the Company or on such later date (if any) specified in the notice.] The notice must identify the proposed alternate and, in the case of a notice of appointment, contain a statement signed by the proposed alternate that the proposed alternate is willing to act as the alternate of the director giving the notice.

6.2 An alternate director has the same rights, in relation to any directors' meeting or directors' written resolution, as the alternate's appointor. [A director or any other person may act as an alternate director to represent more than one director, and an alternate director shall be entitled at meetings of the directors or any committee of the directors to one vote for every director whom he represents in addition to his own vote (if any) as a director.]

6.3 A person who is an alternate director but not a director (a) may be counted as participating for the purposes of determining whether a quorum is participating (but only if that person's appointor is not participating), and (b) may sign a written resolution (but only if it is not signed or to be signed by that person's appointor). No alternate may be counted as more than one director for such purposes.

6.4 An alternate director is not entitled to receive any remuneration from the Company for serving as an alternate director [except such part of the alternate's appointor's remuneration as the appointor may direct by notice in writing made to the Company].

6.5 An alternate director's appointment as an alternate terminates: (a) when the alternate's appointor revokes the appointment by notice to the Company in writing specifying when it is to terminate; (b) on the occurrence in relation to the alternate of any event which, if it occurred in relation to the alternate's appointor, would result in the termination of the appointor's appointment as a director; (c) on the death of the alternate's appointor; or (d) when the alternate's appointor's appointment as a director terminates.

Proceedings of directors

7.1 Any director may call a directors' meeting (or may authorise the company secretary (if any) to do so). At least [seven (7)] days' notice of every meeting of the directors shall be given (unless the written approval of at least one (1) A Director (or his alternate) and at least one (1) B Director (or his alternate) is obtained) and no business except that in respect of which the notice has been given shall be transacted at that meeting unless all the directors otherwise agree.

7.2 Subject to Articles 7.3 and 7.4:

(a) the quorum for the transaction of the business of the directors shall be one (1) A Director and one (1) B Director throughout the meeting; and

(b) questions arising at a meeting shall only be capable of resolution if [at least one (1) of the] A Directors and [at least one (1) of the] B Directors who are present vote in favour of the resolution.

7.3 If a quorum is not present within 30 minutes from the time appointed for the meeting of the directors or if during the meeting such a quorum ceases to present, the meeting shall be adjourned to the same day in the next week at the same time and place. [If a quorum is again not then present at such adjourned meeting, [any two directors] present shall form a quorum and a resolution will be valid if passed by majority vote irrespective of which directors vote in favour of its being passed (provided that this shall only be the case for the purpose of the transaction of the business specified in the agenda contained in the notice of the meeting).]

7.4 If and so long as the number of the directors is reduced below the quorum prescribed by Article 7.2 (except in the circumstances provided for in Article 7.3), the continuing directors may act for the purpose of convening a general meeting of the Company but for no other purpose.

7.5 Unless the A Shareholder(s) and the B Shareholder(s) agree otherwise, directors may appoint one of their number to be the chairman of the board of directors and may at any time remove him from that office. The director so appointed shall preside at every meeting of directors at which he is present but in the absence of such a director, or if such director is unwilling to preside or is not present within [fifteen (15)] minutes after the time appointed for the meeting, the directors present may appoint one of their number to be chairman of the meeting. The chairman shall [not] have a second or casting vote.

7.6 A committee of directors shall always consist of [at least one (1) A Director and one (1) B Director] who shall be present throughout any committee meeting. A committee of directors may meet and adjourn as it sees fit. No decision of a committee shall be effective unless [at least one (1) A Director and one (1) B Director] vote in favour [(save that the provisions of Article 7.3 applicable to meetings of directors shall apply, *mutatis mutandis*, to meetings of any committee of directors)].

Duties and interests of directors

8.1 A director, notwithstanding his office, may:

(a) be a director or employee of, or otherwise interested in, any body corporate (i) which is a shareholder in the Company or a holding company or subsidiary of any such shareholder or (ii) in which the Company is otherwise (directly or indirectly) interested;

(b) may act by himself or his firm in a professional capacity for the Company (otherwise than as auditor) and he or his firm shall be entitled to remuneration for professional services as if he were not a director;

(c) be a party to, or otherwise interested in, any transaction or arrangement with the Company *provided that* (unless the circumstances referred to in section 177(5) or section 177(6) of the Companies Act 2006 apply) he shall be required to disclose to the board the nature and extent of his interest. Any such disclosure may be made at a meeting of the board, by notice in writing or by general notice or otherwise in accordance with section 177 Companies Act 2006.

8.2 Without prejudice to his duties of disclosure under the Act or these Articles, a director may be counted as participating in the decision-making process for quorum, voting or agreement purposes at any meeting of the directors (or committee of the directors) concerning a transaction or arrangement with the Company or any other matter relating to the Company, notwithstanding that he is interested in that transaction, arrangement or matter.

8.3 For the purposes of section 175 Companies Act 2006 (*conflicts of interest*), the board may authorise any matter proposed to it in accordance with these Articles which would, if not so authorised, involve a breach of duty by a director under that section including, without limitation, any matter which relates to a situation in which a director has, or might have, an interest which conflicts or might conflict with the interests of the Company.

(a) Any such authorisation under this Article 8.3 will be effective only if:

  (i) any requirement as to quorum for the meeting at which the matter is considered is satisfied without counting the director in question or any other interested director (a "*Conflicted Director*"); and
  (ii) the matter was agreed to without any Conflicted Director voting or would have been agreed to if his vote had not been counted.

  For these purposes, the quorum for transaction of business shall be any two (2) non-Conflicted Directors and the provisions of Article 7.2 requiring [at least one (1) of the] A Directors and [at least one (1) of the] B Directors to be a quorum or vote in favour of the resolution shall not apply.

(b) The board may (whether at the time of the giving of the authorisation or subsequently) make any such authorisation subject to any limits or conditions it expressly imposes but such authorisation is otherwise given to the fullest extent permitted. The board may vary or terminate any such authorisation at any time.

8.4 If a question arises at a meeting of directors (or of a committee of directors) as to the right of a director to vote, the question may, before the conclusion of the meeting, be referred to the chairman of the meeting whose ruling is to be final and conclusive.

8.5 A director appointed under Article 5 (or his alternate) may provide to the member which appointed him any information which he receives by virtue of his being a director.

Secretary

9. Subject to the provisions of the Act, the directors may decide from time to time whether the Company should have a secretary and, if they so decide, the secretary shall be appointed by the directors for such term, on such remuneration and upon such conditions as they may think fit; and any secretary so appointed may be removed by them. In these articles references to the secretary shall be construed accordingly.

Share capital

10. The share capital of the Company is £_____ divided into _____ A Shares and _____ B Shares. Such shares shall entitle the holders to the respective rights and privileges, and subject them to the respective restrictions and provisions, contained in these Articles. Save as otherwise provided in these Articles, the A Shares and the B Shares shall rank *pari passu* in all respects.

Allotment of shares

11.1 The directors are hereby generally and unconditionally authorised to allot shares or grant rights (pursuant to section 551 of the Companies Act 2006) up to an aggregate nominal amount of £_____ share capital of the Company for a period (unless previously renewed, varied or revoked by the Company in general meeting) expiring five years after the date of adoption of these Articles. Before the expiry of the authority granted by this Article, the Company may make an offer or agreement which would or might require relevant securities to be allotted after that expiry and the directors may allot relevant securities in pursuance of the offer or agreement as if that authority had not expired.

11.2 The pre-emption provisions in sections 561 and 562 of the Companies Act 2006 shall not apply to the allotment of the Company's equity securities.

11.3 Any shares for the time being unissued shall (unless otherwise agreed by all the members) only be offered [and issued] to the members: (i) as to [one-half] of such additional shares, as A Shares to the A Shareholder(s); and (ii) as to [one-half] of such additional shares, as B Shares to the B Shareholder(s).

{*Option*: *An offering process may be appropriate, particularly in the case of a multi-party JVC. An example is the following*:

11.4 *Unless otherwise agreed by all the members of the Company, any shares for the time being unissued shall, before they are issued, be offered to the members holding ordinary shares in proportion as nearly as the circumstances admit to their existing holdings of ordinary shares in the Company. This offer shall be made by a notice in writing which shall specify: (i) the number of shares offered; (ii) the subscription price; and (iii) a period [of not less than thirty (30) days] within which the offer, if not accepted, will be deemed to be declined.*

11.5 *[After the expiry of such period, any shares declined (or deemed to be declined) shall be offered to the members who have, within such period, accepted all the shares offered to them. This further offer shall be made as between such members in proportion to their existing holdings of ordinary shares in the Company and shall be made in the same manner, and limited by the same period, as the original offer.]*

11.6 *Any shares not accepted pursuant to such offer [or further offer] shall be under the control of the directors who, subject to the provisions of the Act and Article 11.1, may allot, grant options over or otherwise dispose of the same to such persons, on such terms and in such manner as they think fit (provided that such shares shall not be disposed of on terms which are more favourable to the eventual subscribers than the terms on which they were offered to the original members).*

11.7 *Shares which are issued to A Shareholders shall be designated as A Shares and those which are issued to B Shareholders shall be designated as B Shares. Where shares are issued to a person not previously a member, the shares shall be given the designation which they would have received if they had been accepted by the original member to whom they were offered.*}

Proceedings at general meetings

12.1 No business shall be transacted at any general meeting unless a quorum is present at the time when the meeting proceeds to business. The quorum at a general meeting shall consist of [one (1)] A Shareholder and [one (1)] B Shareholder each of whom is present in person or by proxy or, in the case of a corporation, by a duly authorised representative.

12.2 If a quorum is not present within [30 minutes] from the time appointed for a general meeting, the meeting shall be adjourned to the same day in the next week at the same time and place. If a quorum is then not present, it shall stand adjourned likewise to the following week. [If a quorum is again not present, then at such [re-]adjourned meeting, the member or members present shall form a quorum and business transacted with only one (1) member present in accordance with this Article 8 shall be deemed for all purposes to constitute business transacted at a meeting and a resolution shall be valid if passed by a majority vote irrespective of which member or members vote in favour of its being passed (provided that this shall only be the case for the purpose of the transaction of the business specified in the agenda contained in the notice of the meeting).]

Votes of members

13.1 No shares of either class shall confer any right to vote upon a resolution for the removal from office of a director appointed by holders of shares of the other class.

[**13.2** If any holder of shares is not present in person or by proxy at any meeting, the votes exercisable on a poll in respect of the shares of the same class held by members present in person or by proxy at that meeting shall be *pro tanto* increased (fractions of a vote by any member being permitted) so that those shares collectively entitle such members of that class to the same aggregate number of votes as could have been cast in respect of all shares of that class if all the holders of those shares were present at that meeting.]

13.3 The appointment of a proxy and any document necessary to show the validity of, or otherwise relating to, the appointment of a proxy shall be received by the Company: (a) before the time appointed for holding the meeting or adjourned meeting; (b) where a poll is taken more than 48 hours after it was demanded, after the poll has been demanded and before the time appointed for the taking of the poll; (c) in the case of a poll taken not more than 48 hours after it was demanded, be delivered at the meeting at which the poll was demanded to the chairman or to any director.

Transfer of shares

14. No sale, transfer, pledge, charge or other disposition of any shares or any interest in any shares shall be effected without the consent of [at least one (1) A Shareholder and at least one (1) B Shareholder] [all members for the time being].

> {*Option*: Instead, a pre-emption procedure may be appropriate particularly in a multi-party JVC. An example follows:

14.1 Except as permitted by this Article or with the prior written consent of the other members, no member shall: (i) transfer any shares; (ii) grant, declare, create or dispose of any right or interest in any shares; or (iii) create or permit to exist any pledge, lien, encumbrance, charge (whether fixed or floating) or other security interest over any shares.

14.2 Except for transfers for which prior written consent is given by [all members for the time being] or for intra-group transfers permitted under Article 14.7, no shares held by a member may be transferred otherwise than pursuant to a transfer by that member (the "**Seller**") of all (and not some only) of the shares which are held by the Seller and all (and not some only) of the shares which are held by any member of the Seller's Group and for this purpose the Seller shall act as agent for all such members of the Seller's Group (as the case may be) (all such shares being herein termed, together, the "**Seller's Shares**").

14.3 Before the Seller makes any transfer of the Seller's Shares, the Seller shall first give notice in writing (a "**Transfer Notice**") to the Company irrevocably appointing the Company as its agent for the sale of the Seller's Shares and specifying the price per share at which the Seller is prepared to sell the Seller's Shares. A Transfer Notice shall be irrevocable once given to the Company.

14.4 Within seven (7) business days of receiving the Transfer Notice, the Company shall by notice in writing offer the Seller's Shares at the price specified in the Transfer Notice to all members other than any member of the Seller's Group. The offer shall invite the member to state in writing to the Company within thirty (30) days of the date of the offer (the "**Acceptance Period**") the number of shares in respect of which it wishes to accept the offer. If a member wishes to accept the offer (an "**Accepting Member**"), it shall give written notice to the Company.

14.5 If the total number of shares in respect of which Accepting Members wish to accept the offer exceeds the number of the Seller's Shares, then on expiry of the Acceptance Period the Seller's Shares shall be allocated as follows:

(a) an Accepting Member shall be entitled to that proportion of the Seller's Shares that its then shareholding bears to the total shareholdings of all Accepting Members (its "**Proportionate Entitlement**"), or the amount of shares in respect of which it has accepted the offer, whichever is less;

(b) an Accepting Member who, in its notice, has notified a wish to accept the offer in respect of more than its Proportionate Entitlement (its "**Excess Proportion**") shall receive that proportion of any remaining unallocated shares as its Excess Proportion bears to the total Excess Proportions on any Accepting Members.

14.6 The Company shall within seven (7) business days of the end of the Acceptance Period notify the Accepting Member(s) of their respective allocations and shall inform the Seller of the identity of the Accepting Member(s) and the number of shares allocated to them under this Article. If there are no (or insufficient) acceptances of the offer, the Company shall inform the Seller within seven (7) business days of the end of the Acceptance Period and the Seller may then proceed to transfer all the Seller's Shares (but not some only) to a bona fide third party purchaser at a price not less than the price stated in the Transfer Notice, provided that such transfer must be completed within [one hundred and eighty (180)] days of the notice from the Company.}

[Note. If Articles 14.3 to 14.6 are adopted, additional provisions may be necessary to deal with the possibility of regulatory or other approvals being required. It is also an important decision whether the right of the Accepting Members to purchase should terminate if there are not sufficient acceptances to acquire all the Seller's Shares.]

14.7 A member shall be entitled at any time to transfer any of the shares held by it to a company which is either: (i) the wholly-owned subsidiary of the transferor; or (ii) a holding company of which the transferor is a wholly-owned subsidiary; or (iii) a wholly-owned subsidiary of any such holding company of the transferor.

Precedent 12

Preference Share Rights

> *Share rights under English law are very flexible and enable "special" rights to be granted to particular shareholders—e.g. founders or, more typically, venture capital investors. The following precedent is a framework for different share rights to be included in the articles of association of the JVC.*
>
> (1) The preference shares give a priority right to the holders, over all other shareholders, for a fixed dividend and for a return of capital on a winding-up. In this case, the preferential dividend is "cumulative" so that (if not paid in any year) arrears of this yearly fixed dividend accrue and are paid in later years.
>
> (2) In this case, the preference shares are also "participating" and, after a specified level of profits/return of capital, share pari passu with ordinary shareholders.
>
> (3) Preference shares may be "convertible" into ordinary shares. Conversion may serve different purposes:
>
> — It enables the holder to benefit if the profitability of the JVC improves so that ordinary shares become more valuable than continuing to hold simply preference shares.
> — Conversion enables the holder to benefit if there is an IPO or sale of the JVC from which the holders of preference shares wish to benefit in the same way as ordinary shareholders.
> — The conversion rate formula can be structured to protect the holder of preference shares if subsequent financing is at a lower effective rate than the subscription price for the preference shares. Complex formulae may be employed to protect against this dilution. Article 7 below is a more general formula for adjustment.
> — In some ventures, the conversion rate formula may be subject to adjustment in order to incentivise management and/or the ordinary shareholders. The rate may be adjusted so that preference shareholders will receive fewer ordinary shares on conversion if the profitability and financial success of the JVC has exceeded a specified level. Venture capital investors frequently tie this to a (complex) formula for a specified internal rate of return (IRR). Article 6 is simply a possible framework for a performance--related adjustment.
>
> (4) Preference shares may also be "redeemable" at the option of the holder and thereby provide the holder with protection for its investment through an ability to exit at a specified price (usually at the amount paid up on the shares).
>
> *This precedent is intended as a framework for developing "special" rights for particular capital investors in a JVC. Further specific provisions are likely to be necessary to tailor the share rights to the particular case.*

1. The respective rights attaching to the Preference Shares and the Ordinary Shares are as follows:

Income

2. The holders of the Preference Shares shall be entitled, in priority to the holders of any other class of Share, to receive out of the distributable profits of the Company a fixed cumulative preferential dividend (the "**Preference Dividend**") at the rate of _____ per cent per annum on the capital (including any share premium) from time to time paid up or credited as paid up on each Preference Share respectively held by them.

(i) If and to the extent that there are distributable profits, the Preference Dividend shall be paid before the transfer of any sums to reserves. The right of the Preference Shareholders to the Preference Dividend has priority over the rights of the holders of any other class of Shares to receive a dividend.

(ii) The Preference Dividend shall accrue from day to day and shall be payable yearly on 30 June.

(iii) For the purposes of calculating the amount of the Preference Dividend in respect of any financial period, the amount of any arrears or accruals of the Preference Dividend at the commencement of such period shall be deemed to form part of the amount paid up on the Shares in question.

(iv) Where the Company has had insufficient distributable profits and is in arrears with the payment of the Preference Dividend, distributable profits arising thereafter shall first be applied in or towards paying all accruals and/or unpaid amounts of Preference Dividend.

(v) [If the Company fails to pay any dividend on the date specified by these Articles, interest thereon shall accrue from that date until payment at the rate of _____ per cent per annum above the base rate of _____ Bank plc from time to time.]

(vi) If the Company is precluded by law from paying in full any Preference Dividend on the date specified by these Articles, the Company shall pay on that date the maximum sum (if any) which can then lawfully be paid by the Company on account of such Preference Dividend and, as soon as the Company is no longer precluded from doing so, the Company shall continue to pay the maximum amount which it may lawfully pay on account of such Preference Dividend and any accrued interest until the whole of the Preference Dividend (together with any accrued interest) has been paid in full.

3. After the Preference Dividend has been paid in full, all distributable profits of the Company in respect of each financial year which are resolved to be distributed shall belong to and be distributed amongst the Ordinary Shareholders [and the Preference Shareholders as follows:

(i) Until the Ordinary Shareholders have received in respect of that financial year an amount per Ordinary Share equal to _____ per cent of the amount (including any premium) paid up or credited as paid up on such Ordinary Shares, all amounts so resolved to be distributed will be distributed amongst the Ordinary Shareholders according to the amounts paid up or credited as paid up on the nominal amount of the Ordinary Shares.

(ii) Any further amounts so resolved to be distributed in respect of that financial year will belong to and be distributed amongst the Preference Shareholders and the Ordinary Shareholders pari passu as if they were all shares of the same class.]

Capital

4. On a return of capital on the making of a winding-up order by a competent court or the passing of a special resolution by the Shareholders or otherwise, the assets of the Company available for distribution among the members shall be applied:

(i) First, in repaying to the holders of the Preference Shares:
   (a) the amount (including the amount of any share premium) paid up or credited as paid up in respect of such Preference Shares; and
   (b) a sum equal to any arrears, deficiency or accrual of the Preference Dividend thereon calculated down to the date of the return of capital and to be payable irrespective of whether or not such Preference Dividend has been earned or declared.
(ii) Next, in repaying to the holders of the Ordinary Shares the amounts (including any premium) paid up or credited as paid up on their Ordinary Shares.
(iii) Finally, and subject always to (i) and (ii) above, the balance (if any) of such assets shall belong to and be distributed amongst the Ordinary Shareholders and Preference Shareholders *pari passu* as if they were all shares of the same class.

Conversion

5. At the option of the holder of the relevant Preference Shares, exercisable by notice (a "**Conversion Notice**") given at any time after _____ and before [*final redemption date under Article 9*], the Preference Shares shall be convertible into Ordinary Shares at the rate (the "**Conversion Rate**") (subject to adjustment in accordance with Article[s] [6 and] 7 below) of one Ordinary Share for each Preference Share held.

(i) A Conversion Notice shall be effected in writing, signed by each of the Preference Shareholders in respect of which the conversion rights are to be exercised and sent to the Company.
(ii) Forthwith after the service of a Conversion Notice, the holders of the Preference Shares being converted shall send to the Company the certificates in respect of their respective holdings of Preference Shares and the Company shall issue to such holders respectively certificates for the Ordinary Shares resulting from the conversion.
(iii) The Ordinary Shares arising on conversion shall rank pari passu in all respects with the Ordinary Shares in the capital of the Company for the time being in issue.
(iv) [Any conversion of Preference Shares shall be without prejudice to the right of the holders of those Preference Shares immediately before conversion to be entitled to claim and pursue any previously declared but unpaid arrears of dividend prior to conversion.]

6. [If the [earnings per Ordinary Share (as determined by the auditors, acting as experts) shall exceed _____ for each of the [three] financial years of the Company immediately preceding [*the first conversion date*]], the Conversion Rate for the purposes of Article 5 shall be adjusted and the Preference Shares shall thereafter be convertible into Ordinary Shares at the rate of [one] Ordinary Share for every [two] Preference Shares held.]

7. The Conversion Rate shall be subject to [further] adjustment on such basis as may be agreed with the holders of 90 per cent of the Preference Shares (or, failing such agreement within 14 days after the event in question, on such basis as may be determined by the auditors, acting as experts, to be appropriate) to preserve the economic value of the conversion right attaching to the Preference Shares in the event of any consolidation or subdivision of any of the Company's share capital, or any issue of shares by way of capitalisation of reserves or of profits, or any repurchase or redemption of shares (other than Preference Shares) or any variation in the subscription price or conversion rate applicable to any other outstanding convertible security or warrant issued by the Company for the time being outstanding, or any offer of shares, debentures, options, warrants or other securities made either by the Company or by any other person to the holders of Ordinary Shares by way of rights.

8. So long as any conversion rights of the Preference Shareholders remain exercisable the following provisions shall apply: (i) the Company will not do any act or thing resulting in an adjustment of the Conversion Rate if in consequence this would involve the issue of Ordinary Shares at a discount; (ii) none of the shares in the capital of the Company shall be subdivided or consolidated; and (iii) the Company shall send to the Preference Shareholders a copy of every document sent to its Ordinary Shareholders at the same time as the same is sent to the Ordinary Shareholders.

Redemption

9. On or after _____, every holder of Preference Shares in respect of which no Conversion Notice has been served may require the Company to redeem all or any of his Preference Shares at par by serving a notice (a "**Redemption Notice**") upon the Company signed by him requiring such redemption.

10. All Preference Shares remaining unconverted and unredeemed on [final redemption date] shall be redeemed at par on that date.

11. For the purposes of Articles 9 and 10:

(i) Upon receipt of a payment in respect of a redemption, the holder of the Preference Shares which are to be redeemed shall deliver to the Company for cancellation the certificate(s) for those Preference Shares or an indemnity in a form reasonably satisfactory to the Company in respect of any missing share certificate in order that they may be cancelled.

(ii) Within 14 days of the Redemption Notice (or, in the case of final redemption, on [the *final redemption date*]) the Company shall pay to each registered holder of Preference Shares which are to be redeemed on that date an amount equal to the amount paid up or credited as paid up (including any premium) on the Preference Shares concerned together with a sum equal to all arrears, deficiency or accruals of the Preference Dividend (whether earned or declared or not) calculated down to and including the date of redemption.

Voting

12. As regards voting:

(i) On a show of hands, every Ordinary Shareholder and Preference Shareholder who (being an individual) is present in person or by proxy or (being a corporation) is present by a duly authorised representative or by proxy shall have one vote.

(ii) On a poll, every Ordinary Shareholder who (being an individual) is present in person or by proxy or (being a corporation) is present by a duly authorised representative or by proxy shall have one vote per Share or, in the case of any Preference Shareholder, one vote for each Ordinary Share which he would hold on a conversion of all his Preference Shares at the applicable Conversion Rate at that time.

Precedent 13

ITC Model Incorporated Joint Venture Agreement

© International Trade Centre UNCTAD/WTO

> *The following is a model form agreement for an Incorporated Joint Venture (two parties) published by the International Trade Centre (ITC)—an agency of the United Nations Conference on Trade and Development (UNCTAD) and the World Trade Organisation. It is intended for use internationally. A similar model form has been published for use where there are three or more parties. The only change here from the ITC version is the use for convenience of "JVC" in place of "Joint Venture Company". This version is reproduced with the kind permission of the ITC. See www.jurisint.org*

THIS AGREEMENT is made _____ 200—

BETWEEN:

(1) [**Specify for individuals**: _____ [*surname and first name*], _____ [*status*], residing at _____ [*address*], _____ [*profession*], _____ [*nationality*], _____ [*(possibly) identity card or passport number*]]

(2) [**Specify for corporations**: _____ [*name of company*], _____ [*legal form (e.g., limited liability company), country of incorporation, trade register number*], having its seat at _____ [*address*], represented by _____ [*surname and first name, address, position*]]

WHEREAS:

Party 1: is active in [_____];

has at its disposal _____ [*mention if appropriate one or several distinctive assets, abilities, specific know-how or intellectual property rights necessary to its activity and/or to the objectives of the Joint Venture*] which it is prepared to place at the disposal of the joint enterprise;

has the following objectives _____ [*complete*];

is interested in _____ [*describe the development that the Party expects from this Agreement, its contractual expectations*].

Party 2: _____

In the light of their activities, abilities and objectives, as described above, the Parties wish to form a Joint Venture by incorporating and operating a Joint Venture Company (the "**JVC**") through which their joint business enterprise will be conducted.

IN CONSIDERATION OF THE ABOVE, THE PARTIES AGREE AS FOLLOWS:

1. Contractual Definitions

"Affiliate"
in relation to a Party, a corporation in which that Party (directly or indirectly) owns more than 50 per cent of the issued share capital or controls more than 50 per cent of the voting rights;

"Ancillary Agreements"
agreements entered into between a Party and the JVC (including those referred to in Article 4);

"Auditors"
the external auditors of the JVC;

"Board of Directors"
the principal executive body of the JVC referred to in Article 9;

"Contributions"
the contributions (whether in cash or in-kind) to be made by the Parties to the JVC pursuant to Article 4;

"Deadlock"
the inability of two successive meetings (whether a Meeting of the Shareholders or of the Board of Directors) to reach a decision by reason of the non-attendance of the same Party or its appointed representatives (when there is a requirement of minimum attendance) or lack of agreement on a matter material to the strategic or continuing operations of the JVC;

"Director"
a member of the Board of Directors;

"Fair Price"
the fair price for the sale and purchase of Shares under this Agreement without any premium or discount for the size of holding of Shares concerned (determined, if necessary, by an Independent Expert);

"Fiscal Year"
the fiscal year of the JVC as defined in Article 11;

"Force Majeure"
an impediment to performance beyond a Party's control as defined in Article 25;

"Independent Expert"
an expert appointed, in connection with a determination or dispute relating to valuation, pursuant to the terms of this Agreement.

"Joint Venture"
the relationship between the Parties as regulated by this Agreement and the corporate instruments of the JVC;

"Joint Venture Intellectual Property"
intellectual property or know-how relating to technical developments acquired or developed in the course of its activities by the JVC;

"JVC"
the corporation which the Parties intend to create and operate to carry on their joint business enterprise;

"Meeting of the Shareholders"
the ultimate authority of the JVC, comprising the Parties or their representatives as referred to in Article 8;

"Party"
each of the Parties (whether an individual or a corporation) being signatories to this Agreement and those adhering to it subsequently;

"President"
the chairman of the Meeting of the Shareholders appointed in accordance with Article 8.6;

"Regulatory Approvals"
governmental or regulatory approvals required by the Parties for the establishment of the JVC in [specify country];

"Share"
a share in the capital of the JVC;

"Shareholder"
a Party (or its representative) in its capacity as a holder of Shares in the JVC;

"Statutes"
the corporate instruments of the JVC.

Object of the Joint Venture

2.1 The Parties hereby agree to pool their resources and efforts by establishing jointly a corporation to be known as _____ [*name of the JVC*] (referred to as the "**JVC**").

2.2 The object of the JVC shall be to [*develop, exploit, research, produce, distribute, etc.* _____].

2.3 The business of the JVC shall be developed in accordance with the business plan adopted by the Parties (as revised from time to time by the Board of Directors under Article 9.6).

Establishment, capital and seat of the JVC

3.1 The Parties agree to act with diligence and care to establish the JVC as promptly as practicable in accordance with this Agreement and all Regulatory Approvals.

3.2 The JVC shall be established pursuant to the laws of _____ [*country*].

3.3 The seat of the JVC shall be _____. The JVC shall be registered with the Trade Register/Company Register/Corporations Office of _____.

3.4 The duration of the JVC is unlimited in time.

> {*Option: delete Article 3.4 if there is no requirement under local law to specify duration.*}

3.5 The JVC shall be endowed with an initial capital of _____, divided into _____ shares [registered/registered with limited transferability/bearer] with a par/face value of _____. The initial Shares shall be issued to the Parties in accordance with Article 4.

Contributions to the JVC upon its establishment

4.1 The Parties intend that, by their contributions under this Article 4, the Shares of the JVC shall be owned in the following proportions:

Party 1 _____%
Party 2 _____%

4.2 The Parties agree to subscribe for initial Shares of the JVC and pay-in funds in cash by way of payment for such Shares as follows:

Party	Number of Shares	Cash Payment
Party 1:	_____ Shares	_____
Party 2:	_____ Shares	_____

Payment in full for such Shares shall be made by each Party in cash, for the account of the JVC, at such time as shall be fixed by the Board of Directors after all Regulatory Approvals have been obtained.

{*Option: delete Article 4.2 and use solely Article 4.3 if initial contributions will be a mixture of cash and in-kind contributions*}

4.3 The Parties shall make the following further {*Option: delete "further" if Article 4.2 is deleted*} respective contributions—in cash, real estate, personal property including machinery and tools, intellectual property, services or other in-kind contributions (referred to as Contributions)—by way of payment for further {*Option: delete "further" if Article 4.2 is deleted*} Shares of the JVC to be issued to each Party as follows:

Party	Contributions	Value (value/currency)	Number of Shares
Party 1:			
Party 2:			

[*Complete the list as required.*]

These Contributions shall be made at times fixed by the Board of Directors and, in the case of in-kind Contributions, in accordance with Ancillary Agreements to be entered into between the contributing Party and the JVC as set out in the Appendices to this Agreement. The Parties shall enter into the relevant Ancillary Agreements promptly upon the formation of the JVC after all Regulatory Approvals have been obtained. Each Party to an Ancillary Agreement with the JVC undertakes to the other Party that it will perform its obligations under that Ancillary Agreement.

The corresponding Shares shall be issued at such time or times as shall be fixed by the Board of Directors.

4.4 Each Party represents and warrants that the Contributions described in Article 4.3 and relevant Ancillary Agreements (a) are at its free disposal and that it is entitled to contribute them to the JVC for the agreed use; (b) are of the described quality; and (c) may be used for the purpose and duration provided or implied in the Contribution (subject only as stated in the relevant Ancillary Agreement).

4.5 If the use of a Contribution to the JVC is materially restricted or rendered impossible due to a defect, claim by a third party or other reason due to the fault of the contributing Party, the contributing Party shall replace the Contribution and provide to the JVC another in-kind Contribution which meets, as closely as possible, the needs of the JVC for which the original Contribution was intended.

The contributing Party shall compensate the JVC for any loss and damage suffered as a result of any defect in its Contribution and any restriction affecting its use contrary to the representations and warranties of that Party in Article 4.4 and the relevant Ancillary Agreement.

> {*Option*: in some cases, it may be appropriate to have an independent valuation of in-kind Contributions:
>
> "The Board of Directors shall arrange for the in-kind Contributions to be valued by such method as the Board of Directors shall determine (or, failing agreement, by an Independent Expert appointed in accordance with Article 10.4). The valuer shall certify whether or not, in its opinion, the value of the in-kind Contribution is at least equal to the value attributed under Article 4.3 to the Shares which are to be issued by the JVC to the contributing Party.
>
> If the valuer certifies that the value of the in-kind Contribution is not sufficient, the contributing Party shall be obliged to make up the shortfall in cash (unless the Parties agree to an adjustment in the number of Shares to be held by them respectively)."}

4.6 Any amendment to any of the Ancillary Agreements shall require the approval of both Parties.

Additional funding of the JVC, new issues of shares and guarantees

5.1 The issued share capital of the JVC may be increased from time to time by such amount as the Parties may agree in accordance with this Article 5. Unless the Parties agree otherwise, the JVC shall not issue any Shares unless such additional Shares are issued in the following proportions:

Party 1 _____%
Party 2 _____%

5.2 If the Board of Directors considers at any time that the JVC requires further finance, the Board of Directors will discuss whether or not to approach third party lenders or, in appropriate circumstances, to seek such further finance from the Parties. The Parties are not obliged to provide any further finance unless they both agree on the amount and method of providing the finance. Unless they agree otherwise, they shall contribute finance to the JVC (whether by subscribing for Shares or by way of loan or otherwise) at the same time and on the same terms and in the same proportions in which they then hold Shares.

> {*Option*: include 5.3 below if the Parties do accept a commitment to provide further finance—in which case, more detailed provisions as to financing programme, timing, limits and/or consequences of failure to provide such finance may need to be included:
>
> "**5.3** Each Party undertakes that it will:
>
> (a) not later than _____, subscribe unconditionally for an additional_____ Shares and pay _____ in cash for those Shares at such time as shall be fixed by the Board of Directors;
>
> (b) not later than _____, advance in cash to the JVC a loan in the principal amount of _____ on such terms as shall be agreed with the Board of Directors."}
>
> {*Option*: include alternative 5.3 below if a more formal procedure is appropriate following a call for finance by the Board of Directors:
>
> "**5.3** If the Board of Directors considers at any time that additional funding is required for the development of the JVC and that such finance cannot, or should not commercially, be raised from third party lenders:

(a) the Board of Directors shall notify each of the Parties of the need for additional funding;

(b) the Parties shall (unless otherwise agreed by all Parties) provide such additional funding by contributions in proportion to their Shares;

{*Option 1*: add:

the obligation of each Party to provide additional funding (whether in Shares or loans) is subject to the following maximum limit:

Party	Limit
Party 1	_____
Party 2	_____ }

{*Option 2*: replace (b) entirely with:

no Party shall be obliged to provide any such further finance to the JVC unless approved by the Parties jointly {*Option*: a unanimous vote of a Meeting of the Shareholders.} Any such finance which the Parties do agree to provide shall (unless otherwise agreed) be provided by the Parties in the same proportions in which they then hold Shares (whether such additional finance is provided by way of subscription for new Shares, loans or otherwise)}

(c) any new Shares shall be offered to the Parties in the same proportions in which they then hold Shares (and shall not be issued to any third party unless approved in accordance with Article 16);

(d) if any Party so requests, the Board of Directors shall provide a certificate from the Auditors or an Independent Expert (appointed in accordance with Article 10.4) that the issue price for the new Shares is fair and reasonable in the circumstances.}

5.3 The Parties shall not be obliged to provide guarantees for any borrowings of the JVC. If they do agree to do so, such guarantees shall be given in the same proportions in which they then hold Shares. The liabilities of the Parties under any such guarantees shall (so far as possible) be several and, if a claim is made under any such guarantee against a Party, that Party shall be entitled to a contribution from the other Party of such amount as shall ensure that the aggregate liability under that guarantee is borne by the Parties in proportion to their holdings of Shares.

{*Option*: shall be obliged to provide guarantees to support borrowings of the JVC up to a maximum amount of _____}

5.4 Funding of the JVC may (if agreed by both Parties {*Option*: if decided by the Board of Directors}) take the form of loans by the Parties to the JVC on such terms, which shall be the same for each Party, as the Parties may agree {*Option*: the Board of Directors may determine}.

5.5 If a Party shall default in making any payments under this Article 5 to the JVC, that Party shall pay to the JVC interest on the outstanding amount at the rate of _____ (without prejudice to any other rights which a Party may have in respect of a breach of this Agreement by the other Party).

Administrative steps, expenses and pre-incorporation undertakings

6.1 The administrative steps required for the establishment and registration of the JVC shall be carried out by the Parties jointly.

{Option: appointment of a representative to be chosen among the Parties or external third parties}

6.2 The expenses related to the establishment and registration of the JVC shall be paid by the Parties, in equal proportions, as and when required.

{Option: the payments related to establishment and registration shall be made by the Parties in the same proportions in which they will hold Shares in the future JVC}

As soon as it is established, the JVC shall reimburse to the Parties the agreed expenses paid by them in relation to the establishment and registration of the JVC.

{Option 1: instead of a reimbursement, the advance payment could be credited to the Parties against the subscription price of their Shares (subject to any local law restrictions)}

{Option 2: payment by the Parties, in equal proportions or in proportion to the Shares they will hold in the JVC, without reimbursement by the JVC at a later stage}

6.3 Any undertaking made, by agreement between the Parties, in the name of the new JVC before its creation shall give rise to joint and several liability of the Parties in equal shares. *{Option: in proportion to the Shares they will hold in the JVC.}*

6.4 The JVC may assume an undertaking made explicitly in its name before its creation. In that case, the persons having made such undertaking shall be released and the JVC shall indemnify them against any liability under that undertaking.

Statutes of the JVC

7.1 The Parties agree to adopt the Statutes of the JVC. These shall provide for the following:

— Meeting of the Shareholders;

— Board of Directors; and

— Auditors.

7.2 The Statutes shall be in a form agreed by both Parties and shall conform in substance with the provisions of Articles 8 to 11 below.

7.3 The Statutes will regulate the rights and obligations of the Parties in the JVC. Nevertheless, the Parties' rights and obligations remain governed by the present Agreement which, with respect to the internal relationship between the Parties, shall take precedence over the Statutes. If there is any conflict between this Agreement and the Statutes, the Parties shall take all steps necessary to amend the Statutes.

Meeting of the shareholders

8.1 The Meeting of the Shareholders is the ultimate authority of the JVC. Its decisions are binding on both Parties.

8.2 The Meeting of the Shareholders has the non-transferable authority to:

— adopt and modify the Statutes;

— approve any change in the name or objectives of the JVC;

— appoint and remove the Directors and the Auditors;

- approve the issue of any new Shares (or any options or securities convertible into new Shares) of the JVC;
- approve the annual accounts and the payment of any dividends;
- grant any release of liability of the Directors;
- establish the remuneration of the members of the Board of Directors (including the remuneration of any executive Director); and
- decide on the dissolution of the JVC.

8.3 An Ordinary Meeting of the Shareholders is to be held _____ [*specify frequency*] a year, but at least once a year within the period of six months following the end of the Fiscal Year.

An Extraordinary Meeting of the Shareholders shall be called at any time the Board of Directors deems it useful or necessary or at the request of one or more Shareholders representing at least _____ per cent [*e.g., 10%*] of the issued share capital of the JVC.

> {*Option 1: Shareholders whose Shares have a value of _____ .*}
> {*Option 2: Auditors may also call an Extraordinary Meeting of the Shareholders*}

8.4 The Notice of the Meeting of the Shareholders must be sent not less than _____ days [*e.g., 20 days*] before the date fixed for the Meeting of the Shareholders. The Notice must contain the Agenda of the Meeting and any proposals of the Board of Directors and, if applicable, any proposals of the Shareholders who have requested the Meeting or that a particular item be placed on the Agenda.

No decision may be taken on items that are not on the Agenda, except in the circumstances of Article 8.5.

8.5 If all Shareholders are present or represented and if there is no objection, a Meeting of the Shareholders may be held without observing the formalities set forth in the previous Article.

For as long as they are all present, and there is no objection, the Meeting of the Shareholders may deliberate and decide on all items within its competence.

8.6 The Chairman of the Board of Directors or, if that person is not present, a Director approved by the Meeting of the Shareholders, shall preside over the Meeting of the Shareholders (such person being referred to herein as the President).

> {*Option: instead of "the President" use the term "Chairman"*}

The President of the Meeting of the Shareholders shall designate a Secretary who is responsible for taking the Minutes of the Meeting.

8.7 A Shareholder may be represented at the Meeting of the Shareholders by another Shareholder or a third party. For such representation, the Shareholder shall issue a power of attorney or similar evidence of authority to be submitted to the President of the Meeting before the start of the Meeting.

> {*Option 1: exclude representation (i.e. a Shareholder must be present)*}
> {*Option 2: exclude representation by a third party*}

If a Shareholder is a corporate entity, evidence of the authority of its representative at any Meeting of the Shareholders shall be provided at the request of the President.

8.8 The Meeting of the Shareholders is legally constituted if at least one authorised representative of each Party is present and/or represented and the notice requirements established by this Article 8 have been met.

ITC MODEL INCORPORATED JOINT VENTURE AGREEMENT 809

8.9 Each Share gives the owner the right to one vote at the Meeting of the Shareholders.

8.10 Decisions on any of the matters set out in Article 8.2 shall require unanimity at a Meeting of the Shareholders.

8.11 In addition, the following matters (Reserved Matters) shall also require the prior approval of both Parties either at a Meeting of the Shareholders or by written agreement between the Parties:

— approval (or revision) of the business plan;
— any material change to an approved budget;
— acquisition or disposal of a material business or asset;
— any capital expenditure or investment project likely to involve expenditure in excess of _____;
— a material contract likely to involve expenditure in excess of _____;
— any financing resulting in aggregate borrowings in excess of _____;
— appointment (or removal) of any chief executive, general manager [*or other senior executive*];
— any major partnership or alliance;
— any proposal to issue new shares (or options or securities convertible into shares);
— remuneration of senior executives;
— any contract (with a value in excess of _____) to be entered into with a Party or any of its Affiliates;
— any material licence or other dealing in Joint Venture Intellectual Property;
— formation of any subsidiary;
— repayment to a Party (or its Affiliate) of any loan.

{*Option 1*: delete or amend Article 8.11 if one Party is in majority control and it is not intended that the minority party should have significant veto rights.}

{*Option 2*: delete or amend Article 8.11 if the Parties are content for all or any of these decisions to be taken by the Board of Directors under Article 9.15.}

8.12 All other decisions shall require a majority vote of the total Shares held by the Parties.

{*Option 1*: qualified majority, e.g., two-thirds vote. Consider any other decisions listed in Article 8.2 which should require a special majority}

{*Option 2*: majority (or qualified majority) of the votes attributed to Shareholders present or represented (i.e. excluding those not present or represented)}

8.13 In case of a tie, the President of the Meeting of the Shareholders shall not {*Option*: delete "*not*"} have a second or decisive vote.

8.14 The Parties shall endeavour to consult before a Meeting of the Shareholders with a view to establishing a common voting position on each Agenda item.

8.15 The Secretary shall arrange the taking of the Minutes of the Meeting of the Shareholders. The Minutes shall record the Shareholders present or represented and a reasonable summary of the discussions and any decisions taken at the Meeting. The President {*Option: and the Secretary*} shall sign the Minutes of the Meeting.

8.16 A written resolution signed by both Shareholders (whether in a single document or in separate counterparts in equivalent terms) shall be binding as a resolution passed at a Meeting of the Shareholders.

Board of Directors

9.1 The JVC is managed by a Board of Directors of not more than _____ [*specify number*] Directors, who need not be Shareholders.

9.2 Members of the Board of Directors are appointed by the Meeting of the Shareholders. The Meeting of the Shareholders may remove a member of the Board of Directors at any time.

9.3 Each Party shall be entitled to nominate the following number of Directors (and to replace any Director so nominated):

    Party 1   _____%
    Party 2   _____%

Each Party shall, at the Meeting of the Shareholders, vote to support the appointment (or replacement) by another Party of any Director which that Party nominates under this Article 9.3.

9.4 A Director shall begin his/her term at the Meeting of the Shareholders at which he/she is appointed, and shall continue in office until the end of any agreed term, or until removed at a Meeting of the Shareholders, or until resignation or death. A Director may be re-elected.

9.5 The Board of Directors shall designate the persons to act as Chairman, Vice-Chairman and Secretary. The Secretary need not be a member of the Board of Directors.

> {*Option 1*: "The Leader shall be entitled to nominate the Director to be Chairman, and the Deputy Leader shall be entitled to nominate the Director to be Vice-Chairman, in accordance with Article 12."}

> {*Option 2*: "The position of Chairman will be held, taking it in turn in alternate years, first by a Director nominated by Party 1 and then by a Director nominated by Party 2."}

9.6 The Board of Directors has all the powers not reserved by the Statutes or this Agreement to the Meeting of the Shareholders or to any another body. In particular, it shall have the following functions:

— responsibility for the management of the JVC;

— approval (or revision) of the business plan and associated budgets;

— establishment of rules of procedure for the making of any commitments binding on the JVC;

— establishment of the structure of the accounting systems and financial controls of the JVC;

— appointment and removal of the executives entrusted with the day-to-day management or representation of the JVC;

— preparation of the annual report and accounts;

— compliance with the Statutes and instructions given by the Meeting of the Shareholders.

9.7 The Board of Directors may delegate some or all of the management of daily business to one or several of its members or to executives employed by the JVC.

9.8 The Board of Directors may delegate powers of representation of the JVC vis-à-vis third parties to one or several of its members or to any employees (or other third parties) to which it may grant authority to bind the JVC.

> {*Option*: joint or collective signature of at least two Directors (or other designated signatories) for any contract or commitment vis-à-vis third parties.}

9.9 The Board of Directors shall ensure that the Parties are kept adequately informed about the affairs of the JVC and shall inform each Party (at its reasonable request) in writing about the details of the JVC's organisation and management.

9.10 The Board of Directors shall meet as often as the JVC's affairs require. A meeting of the Board of Directors may be called by its Chairman or by any of its members. Notice of the meeting must be sent [by _____ [*means of communication to be determined*] at least _____ days [*e.g., 10 days*] before the meeting; this deadline can be shortened with the approval of all Directors].

> {*Option*: with the approval of at least one Director nominated by each Party.}

The notice must contain the agenda of the meeting including reasonable details of the matters to be discussed. No decision may be taken on items that are not on the agenda, except in the circumstances of Article 9.11.

9.11 If all the Directors are present and if there is no objection, the Board of Directors may hold a meeting without observing the formalities set forth in the previous Article.

> {*Option:* "If at least one Director nominated by each Party is present and if there is no objection..."}
>
> {*Option:* if added flexibility is required, consider:
> "A meeting of the Board of Directors may also be held if all the Directors are in simultaneous telephonic or video-conference communication during which each Director can both listen and speak to the other Directors."}

9.12 A meeting of the Board of Directors is legally constituted if at least one Director nominated by each Party is present at the time when the relevant business is transacted.

9.13 At any meeting of the Board of the Directors, each Director shall be entitled to one vote. Any Director who is absent from any meeting may nominate any other Director to act and to vote in his place at the meeting.

9.14 Decisions of the Board of Directors are (except as provided in Article 9.15) taken by a majority of the votes cast by its members.

> {*Option:* "Decisions of the Board of Directors are taken by a majority of the votes cast by its members provided that the majority includes the approval of at least one Director nominated by each Party". If this option is included, Article 9.15 is not strictly necessary.}

Each Member shall have one vote. In case of a tie, the Chairman shall not {*Option: delete "not"*} have a second or casting vote.

9.15 The following matters shall require the approval of a two-thirds majority {*Option: unanimity or other specified majority*} of the members of the Board of Directors (including for this purpose any Director not in attendance):

{*Option*: replace with "The following matters shall require a majority vote which includes the approval of at least one Director nominated by each Party:"}

— approval (or revision) of the business plan;

— approval of the annual budget or any material change to an approved budget;

— acquisition or disposal of a material business or asset;

— any capital expenditure or investment project likely to involve expenditure in excess of _____;

— a material contract likely to involve expenditure in excess of _____;

— any financing resulting in aggregate borrowings in excess of _____;

— appointment (or removal) of any chief executive, general manager [*or other senior executive*] and their terms of reference;

— any major partnership or alliance;

— any proposal to issue new shares (or options or securities convertible into shares);

— remuneration of senior executives;

— any contract (with a value in excess of _____) to be entered into with a Party or any of its Affiliates;

— any material licence or other dealing in Joint Venture Intellectual Property;

— formation of any subsidiary;

— repayment to a Party (or its Affiliate) of any loan.

{*Option 1*: decide whether all or any of these decisions should be taken by the Parties as Shareholders under Article 8.11—or by the Board of Directors under this Article. Co-ordinate the content of Article 8.11 and this Article accordingly.}

{*Option 2*: if the Option under Article 9.14 is selected so that all decisions of the Board of Directors in any event require the vote of at least one Director nominated by each Party, then Article 9.15 could be omitted entirely.}

9.16 The decisions of the Board of Directors shall be recorded in the minutes of the meeting, signed by the Chairman or in his/her absence by the Vice-Chairman.

9.17 A written resolution signed by all the Directors (whether in a single document or in separate counterparts in equivalent terms) shall be binding as a resolution passed at a meeting of the Board of Directors.

Auditors and Independent Expert

10.1 The Meeting of the Shareholders shall appoint Auditors to serve for a one year period. The Auditors must possess sufficient competence and technical qualifications to undertake an audit of the accounts and related tasks. The Auditors must be independent of the Board of Directors and the Parties. The Auditors may be re-elected.

ITC MODEL INCORPORATED JOINT VENTURE AGREEMENT

10.2 The Auditors shall, after the end of each Fiscal Year, present to a Meeting of the Shareholders a written report with the results of an audit of the accounts undertaken in accordance with good accounting practice and all applicable legal requirements.

10.3 The Auditors must be present at each Ordinary Meeting of the Shareholders, unless the Meeting of the Shareholders unanimously decides to waive this requirement.

10.4 The Parties or the Auditors (if requested by the Parties) may appoint an Independent Expert for such valuation purposes as may be required under this Agreement.

10.5 If an Independent Expert is appointed for any purpose under this Agreement, the fees and costs of that Independent Expert shall (unless otherwise agreed between the Parties) be borne by the Parties in equal proportions {*Option:* add: "or in such other proportions as the Independent Expert considers to be appropriate in the circumstances".}

Accounts and Dividends

11.1 Accounts of the JVC shall be prepared and maintained, under the supervision of the Board of Directors, in accordance with good accounting practice and all applicable legal requirements.

> {*Option*: _____ with generally accepted accounting principles in _____}

11.2 The Fiscal Year of the JVC shall (unless otherwise decided by a Meeting of the Shareholders) commence on the first day of January and end on the thirty-first of December of each year.

> {*Option:* choose different accounting period for Fiscal Year.}

The first accounting period of the JVC shall (unless otherwise decided by a Meeting of the Shareholders) commence on the date on which the JVC is created and end on the thirty-first of December of the same year.

11.3 The Meeting of the Shareholders shall decide on the payment of any dividends after the audit of the accounts and after consultation with the Board of Directors.

A dividend may only be distributed from profits legally available for distribution (including any retained profits).

The payment of any dividend, after approval of the Meeting of the Shareholders, shall be made at a time fixed by the Board of Directors.

11.4 The Parties agree that (unless the Parties agree otherwise in relation to a particular Fiscal Year) it is their intention that the JVC should distribute by way of dividend at least _____ [*e.g. 50*] per cent of the audited after-tax profit in relation to each Fiscal Year.

11.5 Each Party (and its authorised representatives) will be allowed access at all reasonable times to examine the books and records of the JVC.

Leadership

> {*Option:* omit Article 12 if no single Party is to be designated as the Leader of the Joint Venture.}

12.1 The Party _____ [name] is designated as the Leader of the Joint Venture. The Leader has the right to nominate a Director on the Board of

Directors who shall be the Chairman of the Board of Directors. The other Party agrees to vote (or to procure that its nominated Directors on the Board of Directors vote) accordingly upon any relevant election of the Chairman.

> {*Option*: provide that the Leader shall be entitled to nominate the person to act as chief executive/general manager of the JVC and that the other Party will support that appointment by the Board of Directors; if so, amend list in Article 9.15.}

12.2 The Party _____ [*name*] has the right to nominate a Director on the Board of Directors who shall be the Vice-Chairman of the Board of Directors. The other Party agrees to vote (or to procure that its representatives on the Board of Directors vote) accordingly upon any relevant election of the Vice-Chairman.

12.3 The remuneration of the Chairman and the Vice-Chairman is decided by the Meeting of the Shareholders in accordance with Article 8.2.

Technical and Administrative Services to the JVC

> {*Option*: delete Article 13 entirely if the Parties will have no specific duties to provide services beyond their initial Contributions under Article 4 and all functions of the JVC are to be organised and established through the Board of Directors.}

13.1 The Parties agree respectively to be responsible for providing or organising the following technical or commercial services within the scope of the JVC's activities:

(a) Party 1 shall _____ [*specify*];

(b) Party 2 shall _____ [*specify*].

[*Complete the list of services or functions as required (e.g. relating to administrative or IT support, tax or other professional services, supply of materials, marketing or distribution services etc.*]

13.2 Provision of these technical or commercial services shall be additional to any in-kind Contributions required to be made under Article 4. Such technical or commercial services shall be provided free of charge.

> {*Option 1*: _____ on such terms, including payment, as shall be approved by the Board of Directors}
> {*Option 2*: _____ on such terms, including payment, as shall be reflected in an appropriate Ancillary Agreement entered into with the JVC and approved by the Board of Directors}

13.3 The cost of any persons seconded by the relevant Party to work for the JVC in connection with such services or functions shall be borne by the JVC on such terms as shall be approved by the Board of Directors.

13.4 Each Party shall use reasonable care and skill in providing and/or organising such technical or commercial services.

Intangible Assets and Intellectual Property Rights

14.1 The contribution by each Party of intangible assets and/or intellectual property rights relating to technical developments, patents, software or know-how to the JVC shall be made in accordance with:

(a) the relevant Ancillary Agreement (attached as Appendix _____) between that Party and the JVC; and/or

(b) such other agreements as may be entered into between that Party (or its Affiliates) and the JVC on such terms as both Parties may agree.

14.2 Intellectual property rights which are developed by the JVC during the course of the Joint Venture (referred to as Joint Venture Intellectual Property) belong to the JVC and shall be used exclusively for the purposes of the Joint Venture. No private use or exploitation by either Party is allowed unless agreed by both Parties (and subject to such terms as may be approved by the Board of Directors).

> {*Option*: "Each Party is entitled to use Joint Venture Intellectual Property for its own business purposes [free of charge] (subject to its confidentiality obligations under Article 22 and to the restraints of Article 23.6)".}

Transfer of shares

15.1 A Party shall not transfer or pledge all or any of its Shares (or any interest therein) without the prior approval in writing of the other Party. The other Party does not need to justify any refusal.

No notice of any proposed transfer (except to an Affiliate) shall be given by either Party within an initial period of _____ [*e.g. three*] years after the establishment of the JVC.

15.2 If the other Party approves the transfer of Shares to an Affiliate of the transferor or to a third party non-member of the Joint Venture, such transfer is subject to that Affiliate or third party unconditionally agreeing in writing to all the terms of the present Agreement (as modified or supplemented by such other terms as may be agreed with the other Party).

In the case of a transfer to an Affiliate, the transferor Party is obliged to procure that such transferee re-transfers the Shares to that Party if at any time the transferee ceases to be an Affiliate of that Party.

> {*Option*: if the Parties wish to include a formal pre-emption procedure whereby a Party proposing to transfer its Shares must offer them to the other Party but still on the basis that any sale to a third party requires unanimous approval, add Articles 15.3, 15.4 and 15.5 as follows:
> "*15.3* If a Party (the Selling Party) wishes to transfer all or any of its Shares in the JVC (referred to as the Sale Shares), it must give notice in writing (a Transfer Notice) to the other Party at least _____ [specify] months prior to the end of the Fiscal Year. The following procedure shall then apply:
>
> (a) the Selling Party shall (except where the proposed transfer is to an Affiliate) offer the Sale Shares to the other Party (the Continuing Party), who has a right of first refusal;
>
> (b) if the Continuing Party wishes to exercise its right of first refusal, it must give notice to the Selling Party within _____ days after the date of the Transfer Notice;
>
> (c) the purchase price of each of the Sale Shares shall be determined according to Article 15.5.
>
> *15.4* If all the Sale Shares are not agreed to be acquired by the Continuing Party under this procedure, the Selling Party may proceed to sell the remaining Sale Shares {*Option*: all the Sale Shares} to a third party buyer provided that:

(a) such sale takes place within _____ months of [the completion of the process under Article 15.3;

(b) the sale takes place at a price per Sale Share which is not less than the Fair Price;

(c) the sale is approved by the Continuing Party pursuant to Article 15.1; and

(d) the third party unconditionally agrees in writing to all the terms of this Agreement (as modified or supplemented by such other terms as are agreed with the Continuing Party).

15.5 The price of each of the Sale Shares to be offered under the right of first refusal shall be established by common consent of both Parties.

If the Parties do not agree on the price, the Parties agree that an Independent Expert shall fix the Fair Price for each of the Sale Shares and the price so determined shall be final and binding.

When determining the Fair Price of the Sale Shares, the Independent Expert shall fix a price per Sale Share based on the market value of the JVC as a whole or, if there is no real market price, a "fair" price of the JVC as a whole. The Fair Price shall be fixed without any premium or discount for the size of the holding represented by the Sale Shares. {*Option:* delete last sentence and replace with: "When determining the Fair Price of the Shares, the Independent Expert shall fix a price per Share based on the market/fair price of the Shares being sold".} If there is a bona fide potential buyer, the Independent Expert shall take that price into account in determining the Fair Price of the Sale Shares.

Each of the Selling Party and the Continuing Party has the right (by notice in writing within _____ days after the Independent Expert's determination) to withdraw from the proposed sale/purchase if it does not wish to proceed on the basis of the Fair Price per Sale Share fixed by the Independent Expert.

15.6 The transfer of Shares shall (unless otherwise agreed by both Parties) take place at the end of the Fiscal Year for which notice of intention to transfer was provided. If only some of the Shares are acquired by the other Party and/or a third party, the transferor maintains and enjoys all corporate and financial rights related to the remaining Shares and remains a full Party with all of the rights and duties provided in this Agreement."}

Entry of new parties into the Joint Venture

16. The entry of a new Party into the Joint Venture requires the joint approval of both Parties including agreement on the number of Shares that the new Party must purchase or acquire in the JVC (and the price). The entry of a new Party is subject to its unconditional agreement in writing to all the terms of this Agreement (as modified or supplemented by such other terms as the existing Parties may agree).

Termination for breach, change of control, force majeure or insolvency of a party

17.1 A Party shall be entitled to terminate this Agreement by notice in writing to the other Party in the following cases:

(a) if the other Party or an Affiliate commits a material breach of this Agreement (or any agreement with the JVC) which the first Party considers is likely to prejudice materially the business or success of the Joint Venture, provided that:

(i) notice of that breach has been given by the first Party to the defaulting Party including its intention to treat the breach as a terminating event if unremedied within a reasonable period; and

(ii) the defaulting Party has failed to remedy that breach (or establish steps to prevent any recurrence) to the satisfaction of the first Party within a reasonable period;

(b) if an important change takes place in the control or the ownership {*Option: or management*} of the other Party within Article 20; or

(c) if the other Party has been excused for non-performance on grounds of Force Majeure for a period exceeding that specified in Article 25; or

(d) if the other Party goes into or suffers bankruptcy or insolvency or an act or order is made by a court or other public authority which materially restricts that Party's capacity to perform its obligations in the Joint Venture.

17.2 If a Party terminates this Agreement by notice under Article 17.1, it shall be obliged to acquire the Shares of the other Party at their Fair Price as established by an Independent Expert.

When determining the Fair Price of the Shares, the Independent Expert shall fix a price per Share based on the market value of the JVC as a whole or, if there is no real market price, a "fair" price of the JVC as a whole (taking into account the effect of the excluded Party's breach and exclusion from the Joint Venture). The Fair Price shall be fixed without any premium or discount for the size of the holding of Shares concerned.

Completion of the sale and purchase shall take place within _____ [*e.g. thirty*] days after agreement on the price or its determination by the Independent Expert.

17.3 An exclusion does not relieve a Party in breach of its obligations under this Agreement (or any Ancillary Agreement) from its liability to damages for such breach.

Withdrawal of a party

18.1 If a Party wishes to withdraw from the Joint Venture, it shall give written notice to the other Party at least three months before the end of a Fiscal Year. No notice shall be given within an initial period of _____ [*e.g. three*] years after the establishment of the JVC.

18.2 The Board of Directors (or other representatives of the Parties) shall discuss the situation in good faith and shall consider any or all of the following:

(a) whether the Party wishing to withdraw should offer its Shares to the other Party in accordance with Article 15 prior to a possible sale of its Shares to a third party;

(b) whether it is feasible or desirable for the Shares of that Party to be acquired by the JVC;

(c) whether the withdrawal of that Party is prejudicial to the affairs of the Joint Venture and should be refused or deferred for consideration until a later time;

(d) whether the Joint Venture should be terminated and the JVC wound up;

(e) whether there is any other solution for dealing with the situation.

{*Option*: add "If no solution is agreed within _____, the Party wishing to withdraw may require the JVC to be dissolved and the Joint Venture to terminate".}

18.3 For the avoidance of doubt, the Joint Venture shall continue and the Party wishing to withdraw shall remain a Party to the Joint Venture unless either:

(a) a transfer of all of its Shares takes place under Article 15; or

(b) the Parties agree another solution for that Party's withdrawal pursuant to discussions under this Article 18.

{*Option*: if Option under Article 18.2 is selected, add: "(c) the JVC is dissolved"}

Death of a party

{*Option*: delete Article 19 entirely if neither Party is an individual.}

19.1 In the event of the death of a Party, the other Party may decide to continue the Joint Venture with those heirs who request it and unconditionally agree in writing to all terms of this Agreement (as modified or supplemented by such other terms as the Continuing Party may agree).

{*Option*: automatic continuation of the Joint Venture with those consenting heirs who unconditionally agree in writing to all terms of the present Agreement and any other agreements and decisions of the Parties concerning the Joint Venture.}

19.2 Failing such a request or consent of the heirs or in the event of a refusal by the other Party, the other Party is obliged to purchase the Shares of the deceased Party. The price per Share shall be agreed with the heirs or, failing agreement, determined by an Independent Expert in the same manner as specified in Article 17.2.

19.3 The heir(s) or any Party that acquires the Shares of the deceased Party shall participate in any dividends paid in respect of the Shares after the date of death of the deceased Party.

19.4 In the period between the death of a Party and the transfer of the deceased Party's Shares, all votes shall be counted without considering the Shares of the deceased Party.

Change in control to a party to the Joint Venture

20.1 A Party which is a legal entity must notify the other Party immediately of any important change in its control or ownership {*Option*: add "or management"}.

20.2 In such a case, the other Party has the right to exclude the Party concerned if it believes that the change in control of the Party is likely to prejudice materially the business or success of the Joint Venture. {*Option*: add "or is prejudicial to the interests of that other Party"}. Its decision in this respect must be notified to the Party concerned within _____ [*specify time*] of the notification under Article 20.1.

20.3 The provisions of Article 17 governing termination apply to any decision to exclude a Party under this Article 20.

End of the Joint Venture

21.1 The Joint Venture will come to an end if:

(a) both Parties agree that its objectives have been realised or have become impossible to realise or that it is otherwise appropriate to terminate the Joint Venture; or

(b) an Arbitral Tribunal (or other competent authority to which a dispute is referred under Article 31) decides that the Joint Venture should be terminated.

21.2 Upon termination of the Joint Venture under Article 21.1, the Parties shall take all steps necessary to dissolve the JVC and to distribute or sell its assets. To this effect, the Parties shall proceed in particular by taking the following steps:

(a) terminating all legal relationships of the JVC with third parties;

(b) selling the assets of the JVC at the best possible price; a Party having a justified interest in the return of a Contribution it has made in a form other than cash shall have a right of first refusal to re-acquire this Contribution at market value;

(c) settling the debts of the JVC;

(d) where applicable, refunding any loans made by the Parties;

(e) at the end of the liquidation, distributing any remaining cash surplus to the Parties according to their Shares.

If both Parties wish to take over the assets and activities of the JVC, they shall seek in good faith to agree a reasonable allocation of assets; failing agreement, an Arbitral Tribunal (established under Article 31) shall decide.

21.3 Upon termination of the Joint Venture under Article 21.1, the Parties agree (subject to any contrary arrangements agreed or established under that Article) that:

(a) each Party shall be free to carry on business in the same products, services and market as the business previously carried on by the JVC prior to termination;

(b) each Party shall have a non-exclusive right (free of charge) to use any Joint Venture Intellectual Property;

(c) any commercial exploitation of Joint Venture Intellectual Property by licence or assignment to a third party shall, nevertheless, require the prior approval of both Parties;

{*Option*: *delete (c) if each Party will be completely free to use such Joint Venture Intellectual Property including by commercial exploitation with third parties.*}

21.4 The Joint Venture will also come to an end:

(a) if a Party transfers all its Shares to the other Party under Article 15 (Transfer of Shares) and there is no new Party;

(b) if a Party terminates this Agreement under Article 17 (Termination for Breach, Change of Control, Force Majeure or Insolvency of a Party) and acquires the Shares of the other Party;

(c) if a Party gives notice of withdrawal under Article 18 (Withdrawal of a Party) and the Parties agree that the Joint Venture should be terminated;

(d) on the death of an individual Party without an heir replacing that deceased Party under Article 19 (Death of a Party).

21.5 Upon termination of the Joint Venture, this Agreement shall automatically terminate except for:

(a) any rights or obligations of either Party in respect of any breach of this Agreement prior to termination; and

(b) the provisions of this Article 21 and Article 22 (Confidentiality).

Confidentiality

22.1 Each Party agrees to keep confidential all business and technical information relating to the JVC or the other Party and acquired in the course of its activities in connection with the Joint Venture. This obligation is not limited in time, and shall continue after a Party has left the Joint Venture or the Joint Venture has been terminated. The only exceptions to this confidentiality obligation are:

(a) if the information is or becomes public knowledge (without fault of the Party concerned); or

(b) if and to the extent that information is required to be disclosed by a Party to a regulatory or governmental authority or otherwise by law (in which case that Party shall keep the other Party informed of such disclosure).

22.2 Each Party shall use all reasonable efforts to ensure that its employees, agents and representatives (and those of its Affiliates) comply with these confidentiality obligations.

Good faith, consultation and duty to promote interests of the Joint Venture

23.1 Each Party shall use all reasonable efforts to promote the best interests of the JVC and to consult fully on all matters materially affecting the development of the business of the JVC. Each Party shall act in good faith towards the other Party and the JVC in order to give effect to the spirit of this Agreement and to promote the success of the Joint Venture.

23.2 When consent or approval is required of a Party under this Agreement or in the course of the activities of the JVC, such consent or approval shall not unreasonably be withheld.

23.3 Each Party undertakes to ensure that its representative(s) attend Meetings of the Shareholders and/or meetings of the Board of Directors and do not to create a Deadlock by non-attendance.

23.4 A Party (or any Director nominated by it) is not entitled to vote on any matter that relates to any claim or dispute between the JVC and that Party or any of its Affiliates. This is without prejudice to any right of the relevant Party itself to dispute the claim.

23.5 Each Party shall ensure that any contracts between the JVC and that Party (or any of its Affiliates) are made on an arm's length commercial basis and on terms that are not unfairly prejudicial to the interests of the other Party or the JVC.

23.6 The Parties, while pursuing their own respective rights and interests, shall further their common interest in the Joint Venture and its activities. In particular, each Party undertakes that during the term of this Agreement it (and each of its Affiliates) will:

(a) not carry on any business or activity which competes {*Option: add "in any material respect"*} with the business of the JVC {*Option: in* _____ *[specify territory]*};

(b) refrain from any other activity, behaviour or steps which would be {*Option: add "materially"*} detrimental to the interests of the JVC.

Upon a Party ceasing to hold any Shares following any transfer under Articles 15, 17 or 18, the leaving Party shall continue to be under an obligation not to compete with the business of the JVC (as carried on at the exit date) for a period of _____ [*specify period, say 2 years*] after the leaving Party's exit date.

23.7 Each Party undertakes with the other Party that it will (so far as it is legally able) exercise all voting rights and powers available to it in relation to any person (including the JVC, any Affiliate and any Director of the JVC nominated by it) to ensure that the provisions of this Agreement and any relevant Ancillary Agreement are fulfilled and performed and generally that full effect is given to the principles set out in this Agreement.

Hardship and review

24. The Parties recognise that business circumstances change and that factors may arise which cause hardship to one Party by fundamentally affecting the equilibrium of the present Agreement or which make it desirable to review the structure and objectives of the Joint Venture. Each Party will in good faith consider any proposals seriously put forward by the other Party in the interests of the relationship between the Parties and/or the business of the JVC. Neither Party shall be under any obligation to agree any revision. No amendment shall be effective unless agreed by both Parties in accordance with Article 28.

> {*Option*: If the Parties fail to reach agreement on the requested revision, any Party may resort to the proceedings contemplated by Article 31. The Arbitral Tribunal shall have the power to make any revision to this Agreement that it finds just and equitable in the circumstances.}

Relief from performance and liability in case of force majeure

25.1 Non-performance by a Party under this Agreement (or any Ancillary Agreement) is excused if that Party proves that the non-performance was due to an impediment beyond its control and that it could not reasonably be expected to have taken the impediment into account at the time of the signing of the Agreement or to have avoided or overcome it or its consequences (such circumstances being referred to herein as "Force Majeure").

25.2 Force Majeure within the meaning of Article 25.1 does not include the lack of any authorisation, licence, permit or approval necessary for the performance of this Agreement (or any Ancillary Agreement) and required to be issued by a public authority of any kind whatsoever in the country of the Party seeking excuse for non-performance.

25.3 When the Force Majeure is only temporary, the excuse for non-performance shall have effect for such period as is reasonable, having regard to the effect of the Force Majeure on the performance of this Agreement (or any Ancillary Agreement) by that Party.

25.4 The Party which suffers any such Force Majeure must give notice to the other Party of the circumstances of the Force Majeure and its effect on that Party's ability to perform.

> {*Option*: add: "If the notice is not given to the other Party within a reasonable time after the affected Party knew or ought to have known of the circumstances of the Force Majeure, the affected Party is liable for damages resulting from such non-notification."}

25.5 As soon as notice according to Article 25.4 has been given, the Parties shall consult about the consequences of the Force Majeure for the operations of the Joint Venture. Both Parties shall make all reasonable efforts to overcome any obstacles to the activities of the Joint Venture that may result from Force Majeure.

25.6 If the circumstances of Force Majeure continue to affect the Party for a period exceeding _____ _____ [*specify period, say one year*], the other Party shall be entitled to give notice to terminate this Agreement whereupon it shall be obliged to acquire the affected Party's Shares in accordance with Article 17.

Consequences of partial invalidity

26.1 If any of the provisions of this Agreement are found to be null and void, the remaining provisions of this Agreement shall remain valid and shall continue to bind the Parties unless it is clear from the circumstances that, in the absence of the provision(s) found to be null and void, the Parties would not have concluded the present Agreement.

26.2 The Parties, if necessary with the assistance of an Arbitral Tribunal pursuant to Article 31, shall replace all provisions found to be null and void by provisions that are valid under the applicable law and come closest to their original intention.

Notices

27.1 The addresses for formal notices and service of process under this Agreement are the following:

> Party 1: [*specify*].
> Party 2: [*specify*].

Unless and until a new address has been notified to the Board of Directors and the other Party, all communications to a Party are validly made when sent to its address as specified above.

27.2 Notices under this Agreement shall be sent by registered mail or by fax with confirmation by mail. They may also be validly sent by electronic mail provided the sender takes precautions necessary to ensure that the notice has been received.

Amendments

28. This Agreement may be varied or modified only by a written amendment signed by both Parties.

No assignment

29. Neither Party can assign its rights or obligations under this Agreement without a corresponding transfer of the Shares of that Party and the approval of the other Party. {*Option: majority vote of the Meeting of the Shareholders in accordance with Article 15.*}

Applicable law

30. This Agreement is governed by the laws of _____ [*specify country*].

Resolution of disputes

31.1 If a dispute (including a Deadlock) arises between the Parties in relation to this Agreement or any Ancillary Agreement or in the course of the activities of the Joint Venture, both Parties shall seek to resolve it amicably.

31.2 In the course of their attempts at amicable settlement of any dispute seriously affecting the Joint Venture, either Party may request (in writing to the other Party) that the dispute be brought before the most senior decision-making persons in their respective organisations. If such a request is made, the decision-makers in the organisations concerned shall meet at least once to consider the dispute and possible ways to resolve it.

31.3 If the dispute has not been resolved within one month after the request under Article 31.2, either Party may request that it be brought to mediation or any other form of alternative dispute resolution (ADR). The other Party shall give constructive consideration to such request but, with the exception of the meeting of senior decision-makers pursuant to Article 31.2 above, neither Party shall be obliged to engage in ADR procedures unless (and then only for so long as) it agrees to it.

31.4 If a Party has come to the conclusion that the attempts at amicable resolution are to no avail, it may give notice to the other Party of this failure and, thereupon, may commence arbitration pursuant to Article 31.5 et seq. Except to the extent that urgent interim measures of protection are required which the Arbitral Tribunal cannot provide effectively and for the enforcement of an arbitral award, the Parties exclude recourse to the courts.

> {*Option:* If a Party has come to the conclusion that the attempts at amicable resolution are to no avail, it may give notice to the other Party of this failure and, thereupon, may submit any legal claim in the courts of [specify place/country], which shall have exclusive jurisdiction.}

31.5 The arbitration proceedings shall be conducted under the Rules of [*specify an Arbitration Institution (e.g. the International Chamber of Commerce or UNCITRAL or other Rules)*]. The place of arbitration shall be [*specify*]. The language of the arbitration proceedings shall be _____ [*e.g. English*].

31.6 In the resolution of the dispute, the arbitrators shall give effect to the letter and the spirit of this Agreement and, where necessary, reconcile conflicting provisions of this Agreement (or any Ancillary Agreement) in this spirit. In the event of any conflict between this Agreement and the applicable law, the arbitrators shall act as *amiable compositeurs* and, subject to public policy, shall give effect to this Agreement and the reasonable intentions and expectations of the Parties.

31.7 If any such dispute relates to a question of valuation not otherwise determined under this Agreement, either Party may request the appointment of an Independent Expert according to proceedings to be agreed by the Parties. If the Parties fail to agree on the appointment of the Independent Expert and on the applicable rules, the Rules for Expertise of the International Chamber of Commerce's International Centre for Expertise shall apply. The Independent Expert's valuation shall be final and binding on the Parties.

The present Agreement is signed in [*specify number*] copies, each of which is an original.

> [*Add place and date*;
>
> signature by both Parties to the Joint Venture Agreement.]

Appendix 1

Ancillary Agreement on Real Estate

XXX [*identify the name and address of the Party in question*] (referred to as "the Contributing Party")

YYY [*identify the name and address of the JVC*] ("the JVC")

This Agreement is entered pursuant to an Agreement dated _____ between [*names of the Parties to the Joint Venture*] ("the Joint Venture Agreement").

It is Agreed as Follows:

1. The Contributing Party has rights as [*identify the nature of the rights (e.g. owner, tenant, lease holder, etc.)*] with respect to the following property (referred to as "the Property"):

   [*describe the property*]

2. The JVC wishes to use the Property for the following purpose:

   [*describe the purpose for which the Property is to be used*]

3. Further to the Joint Venture Agreement and pursuant to its terms and conditions, the Contributing Party undertakes to place the Property at the disposal of the JVC for the described purpose.

   {*Option:* add: "This Agreement does not transfer ownership of the Property to the JVC but gives the JVC solely the right of use as herein specified."}

4. The use of the Property by the JVC shall be subject to the following terms:

   [*specify any particular terms and conditions, e.g. as to rent, compliance with any covenants or planning conditions applicable to the Property, etc.*]

5. This Ancillary Agreement shall be treated as supplemental to the Joint Venture Agreement including, in particular, Article 4 (Contributions to the JVC). The provisions of Article 24 (Hardship), Article 25 (Force Majeure), Article 30 (Applicable Law) and Article 31 (Resolution of Disputes) in the Joint Venture Agreement shall apply *mutatis mutandis* to this Agreement.

[*Add place and date;*

signature by XXX and the JVC.*]

Appendix 2

Ancillary Agreement on Intangible Assets/Intellectual Property Rights

XXX [*identify the name and address of the Party in question*] (referred to as "the Contributing Party")

YYY [*identify the name and address of the JVC*] ("the JVC")

This Agreement is entered into pursuant to an Agreement dated _____ between [*names of the Parties to the Joint Venture*] ("the Joint Venture Agreement").

It is Agreed as Follows:

1. The Contributing Party has rights as [*identify the nature of the rights (e.g. owner, licensee, assignee, etc.)*] with respect to the following Intangible Assets and/or Intellectual Property Rights (referred to as "the Rights"):

   [*describe the Intangible Assets/Intellectual Property Rights (e.g. inventions, patent, industrial designs and models, designs, get-up, trademark or service mark, software, copyright)*].

2. The JVC wishes to obtain use {*Option: ownership*} of the Rights for the following purpose:

   [*describe the purpose for which the Intangible Assets/Intellectual Property Rights are to be used/owned*].

3. Further to the Joint Venture Agreement and pursuant to its terms and conditions, the Contributing Party grants to the JVC an exclusive {*Option: a non-exclusive*} licence to use the Rights within the following territories [*specify*] of the Joint Venture, for the described purpose.

{*Option: instead of granting a licence, the Contributing Party assigns the Intangible Assets/Intellectual Property Rights to the JVC.*

If this option is chosen, add:

In such event, if the Intangible Assets can be registered, the JVC shall undertake all necessary steps for registration, at its cost, of such Intangible Assets.}

4. The Contributing Party agrees to use all reasonable efforts to maintain the Rights in force in all countries where they are registered {*Option: provide a list of countries*}.

5. The JVC agrees to pay all administrative costs, taxes and fees necessary for the registrations to remain in force in the above-mentioned countries.

{*Option: in the event that the Contributing Party uses the Rights to a greater extent than the JVC, consider a different distribution of the costs.*}

6. If and to the extent that the Contributing Party continues to use the Rights in territories in which the JVC is also active, the Contributing Party shall do so subject to Article 23 (Duty to Promote the Interests of the Joint Venture) of the Joint Venture Agreement.

7. This Ancillary Agreement shall be treated as supplemental to the Joint Venture Agreement including, in particular, Article 4 (Contributions to be Joint Venture) and Article 14. (Intangible Assets/Intellectual Property Rights). The provisions of Article 24 (Hardship), Article 25 (Force Majeure), Article 30 (Applicable Law) and Article 31 (Resolution of Disputes) in the Joint Venture Agreement shall apply *mutatis mutandis* to this Agreement.

[*Add place and date*;

signature by XXX and the JVC]

Appendix 3

Ancillary Agreement on Know-How

XXX [*identify the name and address of the Party in question*] (referred to as "the Contributing Party")

YYY [*identify the name and address of the JVC*] ('the JVC')

This Agreement is entered into pursuant to an Agreement dated _____ between [*names of the Parties to the Joint Venture*] ("the Joint Venture Agreement").

It is Agreed as Follows:

1. The Contributing Party, as [*identify the nature of the rights (e.g. owner, licensee, assignee, etc.)*], has knowledge and experience in [describe broadly the Know-How] (referred to as 'the Know-How').

2. The JVC wishes to use the Know-How for the following purpose:

[*describe the purpose for which the Know-How is to be used*]

3. Further to the Joint Venture Agreement and pursuant to its terms and conditions, the Contributing Party grants the JVC an exclusive {*Option: a non-exclusive*} licence to use the Know-How within the following territories [*specify*] for the described purpose.

{*Option*: instead of granting a licence, the Contributing Party assigns the Know-How to the JVC}

4. If and to the extent that the Contributing Party continues to use the Know-How in territories in which the JVC is also active, the Contributing Party shall do so subject to Article 23 (Duty to Promote the Interests of the Joint Venture) of the Joint Venture Agreement.

5. This Ancillary Agreement shall be treated as supplemental to the Joint Venture Agreement including, in particular, Article 4 (Contributions to the JVC) and Article 14 (Intangible Assets/Intellectual Property). The provisions of Article 24 (Hardship), Article 25 (Force Majeure), Article 30 (Applicable Law) and Article 31 (Resolution of Disputes) in the Joint Venture Agreement shall apply *mutatis mutandis* to this Agreement.

[*Add place and date*;

signature by XXX and the JVC]

APPENDIX 4

ANCILLARY AGREEMENT ON EQUIPMENT AND PRODUCTION TOOLS

XXX [*identify the name and address of the Party in question*] (referred to as "the Contributing Party")

YYY [*identify the name and address of the JVC*] ("the JVC")

This Agreement is entered into pursuant to an Agreement dated _____ between [*names of the Parties to the Joint Venture*] ("the Joint Venture Agreement").

IT IS AGREED AS FOLLOWS:

1. The Contributing Party has rights as [*identify the nature of the rights (e.g. owner, lessee, lease holder, etc.)*] with respect to the following equipment, machines and production tools (referred to as "the Equipment"):

   [*describe the Equipment*]

2. The JVC wishes to use the Equipment for the following purpose:

   [*describe the purpose for which the Equipment is to be used*]

3. Further to the Joint Venture Agreement and pursuant to its terms and conditions, the Contributing Party undertakes to place the Equipment at the disposal of the JVC for the described purpose.

4. This Ancillary Agreement shall be treated as supplemental to] the Joint Venture Agreement including, in particular, Article 4 (Contributions to the JVC). The provisions of Article 24 (Hardship), Article 25 (Force Majeure), Article 30 (Applicable Law) and Article 31 (Resolution of Disputes) in the Joint Venture Agreement shall apply *mutatis mutandis* to this Agreement.

[*Add place and date;*

signature by XXX and JVC]

APPENDIX 5

ANCILLARY AGREEMENT ON CONTRIBUTIONS IN SERVICES

XXX [*identify the name and address of the Party in question*] (referred to as "the Contributing Party")

YYY [*identify the name and address of the JVC*] ("the JVC")

This Agreement is entered into pursuant to an Agreement dated _____ between [*names of the Parties to the Joint Venture*] ("the Joint Venture Agreement").

IT IS AGREED AS FOLLOWS:

1. The Contributing Party is competent and experienced in [*describe the Services*] (referred to as "the Services")

2. The JVC wishes to benefit from the Services for the following purpose:

    [*describe the purpose for which the Services are to be used*].

3. Further to the Joint Venture Agreement and pursuant to its terms and conditions, the Contributing Party undertakes to provide its Services to the JVC for the described purpose.

4. The following rules shall govern the Services:

    [*describe the general rules to which the Services are to be subject*]

5. The Party which has made the Services receives no special compensation for this activity. {***Option:*** *specify any payment or other terms.*}

6. This Ancillary Agreement shall be treated as supplemental to the Joint Venture Agreement including, in particular, Article 4 (Contributions to the JVC). The provisions of Article 24 (Hardship), Article 25 (Force Majeure), Article 30 (Applicable Law) and Article 31 (Resolution of Disputes) in the Joint Venture Agreement shall apply *mutatis mutandis* to this Agreement.

7. This Agreement terminates if the Joint Venture Agreement is terminated or the Contributing Party ceases to be a Party to the Joint Venture Agreement or hold any Shares in the JVC.

    [*Add place and date;*

    signature by XXX and JVC]

Precedent 14

Deed of Adherence

> This is a Deed of Adherence to a Joint Venture Agreement to be executed upon a transfer by one party of its shares in the JVC to a third party transferee. It takes the form of a novation to be executed by the Transferor, the Transferee and the Continuing Party or Parties. The Transferor is released from its obligations under the Joint Venture Agreement and the Transferee assumes those obligations together with the right of the Transferor.
>
> The parties should consider whether the Transferor should be released from all its obligations. Should liability remain for antecedent breaches? In addition there may be particular provisions which should survive the transfer, e.g. confidentiality and non-compete provisions. Clause 3 of the Deed provides for this.

THIS DEED is made on _____ 200 _____

BETWEEN:

(1) _____ of _____ ; and _____ of _____ (together the "**Continuing Parties**")

(2) _____ of _____ (the "**Transferor**")

(3) _____ of _____ (the "**Transferee**")

WHEREAS:

(A) The Continuing Parties and the Transferor are parties to a Joint Venture Agreement dated _____ in relation to the affairs of [*name of JVC*] (the "**Company**") (such Agreement, as varied, supplemented, novated or amended from time to time, herein termed the "**Joint Venture Agreement**").

(B) The Transferor intends to transfer [shares] in the capital of the Company to the Transferee subject to the Transferee entering into this Deed.

(C) The Transferee wishes to accept such shares subject to such condition and to enter into this Deed.

NOW IT IS AGREED AS FOLLOWS:

Interpretation

1. Words and expressions defined in the Joint Venture Agreement shall, unless the context otherwise requires, have the same meanings when used in this Deed.

Novation

2.1 With effect from [*the effective date*] the Continuing Parties hereby release and discharge the Transferor [(save in relation to any antecedent breach)] from all its obligations under the Joint Venture Agreement and [(without prejudice to the rights of the other parties to the Joint Venture Agreement in respect of any antecedent breach),] the Transferor shall cease to be a party to the Joint Venture Agreement.

2.2 The Continuing Parties agree that, with effect from [*the effective date*], the following shall apply:

(a) the Transferee shall assume all the rights of the Transferor pursuant to the Joint Venture Agreement; and

(b) the Transferee shall be subject to and shall perform the obligations from which the Transferee is released and discharged pursuant to clause 2.1 as if the Transferee had at all times been a party to the Joint Venture Agreement in place of the Transferor.

[Transferor provisions

3. With effect from [*the effective date*] the Transferor, in consideration of the other parties entering into this Deed, hereby agrees (as a separate, independent and collateral contract with all the other parties to this Deed) to be bound by the provisions of clause _____ and clause _____ of the Joint Venture Agreement as if it had remained a party to the Joint Venture Agreement.]

Notices

4. For the purposes of the Joint Venture Agreement, the Transferee's address for notices shall be as follows:

Address:
Fax No:
Addressed for the personal attention of:

Counterparts

5. This Deed may be executed in any number of counterparts and by the parties to it on separate counterparts, each of which shall be an original, but all of which together shall constitute one and the same instrument.

Governing law

6. This Deed shall be governed by and construed in accordance with English law.

IN WITNESS this Deed has been duly executed and delivered by the parties.

Executed as a **Deed** by _____	} }	**Executed** as a **Deed** by _____	} }
acting by two Directors/ a Director and the Secretary		acting by two Directors/ a Director and the Secretary	
Executed as a **Deed** by _____	} }	**Executed** as a **Deed** by _____	} }
acting by two Directors/ a Director and the Secretary		acting by two Directors/ a Director and the Secretary	

Precedent 15

JVC Share Sale Agreement

> *This Agreement provides the framework for a straightforward sale by one party of all its shares in a JVC to another party (e.g. thereby terminating say a 50:50 venture). It assumes that only a warranty of title will be given—unless exceptionally an indemnity is given by the selling party for "its share" of any specified liabilities arising out of pre-Closing operations of the JVC.*

THIS AGREEMENT is made on _____ _____ 200____

BETWEEN:

(1) _____ _____ _____ ("**Seller**")

(2) _____ _____ _____ ("**Purchaser**")

WHEREAS:

(A) _____ _____ _____ is a company incorporated in _____ _____ (the "**JVC**"). The issued share capital of the JVC is beneficially owned [in equal shares] by the Seller and the Purchaser. The Seller's shareholding in the JVC comprises _____ [Ordinary Shares of £1 each] (the "**Shares**").

(B) The Seller and the Purchaser are parties to a Shareholders' Agreement dated _____ _____ in respect of the JVC (the "**Shareholders' Agreement**").

IT IS AGREED:

Sale and Purchase

1. The Seller shall sell, and the Purchaser shall purchase, the Shares with effect from Closing with all rights then attaching to them including the right to receive all dividends declared or paid in respect of the Shares on or after Closing. The sale and purchase of the Shares shall be on the terms of this Agreement.

Price

2. The price for the Shares shall be £_____ (the "**Price**") which shall be payable on Closing.

Conditions precedent

3. Completion of the sale and purchase ("**Closing**") shall be conditional on _____ _____ (and all other regulatory consents required for completion of the transaction) being obtained either unconditionally or on terms reasonably satisfactory to the Purchaser.

Closing

4. Closing shall take place at _____ _____ on such date as the Seller and the Purchaser may agree in writing (and in any event within 7 business days after the fulfilment or waiver of the conditions set out in clause 3). On Closing:

(A) The Seller shall deliver (i) duly executed share transfers of all the Shares into the name of the Purchaser or its nominee, (ii) share certificates in respect of all the Shares and (iii) resignations of all directors of the JVC appointed by the Seller (acknowledging that they have no claims of any kind against the JVC).

(B) The Purchaser shall pay the Price to the Seller for value in immediately available funds.

(C) [The Purchaser shall cause the JVC to repay to the Seller the outstanding loan of £_____ due from the JVC to the Seller (together with accrued interest to the date of repayment).]

Warranty as to title

5. The Seller warrants that it has, and will at Closing have, the right to sell and transfer full legal and beneficial ownership of the Shares free from all third party rights or claims. The Seller gives no other warranty, representation or indemnity of any kind save as expressly set out in this Agreement.

Transitional arrangements

6.1 [*Specify any transitional arrangements which may apply for a period after Closing e.g. regarding*:

— continued provision of services/facilities by the Seller to the JVC or vice versa;

— use/removal of trade marks on JVC stocks of products (see clause 10 in Precedent 18).]

6.2 The Seller shall, upon reasonable notice, be given such access for inspection (and copying, at the Seller's expense) of the books and records of the JVC relating to the period up to Closing as it shall reasonably require for the sole purpose of dealing with its tax affairs and financial reporting requirements. Such right of inspection shall last for a period of six years for the purpose of its tax affairs and one year for the purpose of financial reporting.

Indemnity

[In certain circumstances, the Seller may agree some continuing indemnity in respect of pre-Closing liabilities of the JVC. Clauses 7 and 8 are a framework. This will rarely be appropriate in the case of a sale by a minority party. In most cases, all risk of liability will be with the Purchaser and simply be reflected in the Price.]

7.1 The Seller undertakes to the Purchaser that it will, by way of indemnity, pay to the JVC [fifty per cent] of any liability incurred by the JVC to any third party (a "**Third Party Claim**") if and to the extent that it is in respect of:

(i) a liability for tax for which the JVC is or becomes liable for any period prior to Closing;

(ii) a liability for damages caused by any products or services supplied by the JVC, or activities undertaken by the JVC, in the course of operations of the JVC during any period prior to Closing; or

(iii) *[other specific matters]*.

The Seller's indemnity under this clause 7.1 shall include any reasonable costs incurred by the JVC in respect of the relevant Third Party Claim.

7.2 The Seller shall only be liable under clause 7.1 if and to the extent that the amount of the JVC's liability in respect of the particular Third Party Claim is not covered by (i) any relevant provision in the management accounts of the JVC as at _____ _____ or (ii) insurance held by the Purchaser and/or the JVC.

7.3 The Seller shall not be liable for any claim under clause 7.1 unless (i) the Seller receives from the Purchaser a notice containing reasonably specific details of the Third Party Claim on or before _____ _____ and (ii) the amount of the Seller's liability under clause 7.1 in respect of that particular Third Party Claim exceeds £_____. The aggregate amount of the liability of the Seller under its indemnity under clause 7.1 shall not in any event exceed £_____.

Conduct of claims

8.1 If the Purchaser or the JVC becomes aware of any potential Third Party Claim after Closing which is likely to result in a claim being made under clause 7.1 of this Agreement, the Purchaser shall as soon as reasonably practicable give notice of the Third Party Claim to the Seller and shall:

(a) ensure that the Seller is given all reasonable facilities to investigate the Third Party Claim;

(b) not (and ensure that the JVC shall not) admit liability or make any settlement or compromise with any person in relation to that Third Party Claim without the prior consent of the Seller.

8.2 The Seller's liability (if any) under clause 7.1 in respect of any relevant Third Party Claim shall not arise unless and until (i) consent to pay or settle that claim is given by the Seller in accordance with clause 8.1 or (ii) a final, binding, non-appealable judgment is made against the JVC by a court or arbitral body in respect of that Third Party Claim.

Guarantees

9. The Purchaser shall use all reasonable efforts to ensure that, as soon as reasonably practicable after Closing, the Seller is released from all guarantees [listed in Annex _____] given by it in respect of obligations of the JVC. Pending release of any such guarantee, the Purchaser shall indemnify the Seller against any liabilities or costs arising after Closing under or by reason of that guarantee.

Protective post-Closing covenants

10.1 Neither the Seller nor any of its subsidiaries (collectively, the "**Seller's Group**") shall (whether alone, jointly with another, directly or indirectly) carry on or be engaged or interested in any Competing Business in the Protected Territories for a period of 2 years after Closing. For this purpose:

(a) "**Competing Business**" means a business which [involves the manufacture and/or sale of _____ or] competes with any business carried on by the JVC at any time during the 12 months preceding Closing; and

(b) "**Protected Territories**" means [*list territories*]

Nothing in this clause 10 shall prevent, after Closing, any member of the Seller's Group from owning purely for financial investment purposes securities in any company provided that they do not exceed 10 per cent. in nominal value of the securities in that company (or of any class of its securities).

10.2 Neither the Seller nor any member of the Seller's Group shall (whether alone, jointly with another, directly or indirectly), for a period of 2 years after Closing, offer to employ or seek to entice away from the JVC any person who was employed by the JVC in skilled or managerial work at Closing.

Confidentiality

11.1 The provisions of clause _____ (*Confidentiality*) of the Shareholders' Agreement shall continue to apply and shall survive termination of that Agreement. [*See clause 8 of Precedent 9 or clause 11 of Precedent 10*]

11.2 The Seller shall return to the JVC, or destroy, all documents containing confidential information of the JVC [in accordance with the provisions of clause _____ of the Shareholders' Agreement]. [*See clause 11.4 of Precedent 10*]

Shareholders' Agreement

12. The Shareholders' Agreement shall terminate and cease to have any effect after Closing except for clause _____ (*Confidentiality*) [*and other specified provisions, if relevant, e.g. regarding use of IPR*]. [*Also review/confirm position in relation to any ancillary agreements.*]

Announcements

13. [Until 3 months after Closing,] neither the Seller nor the Purchaser shall make any public announcement in connection with this Agreement without the prior written approval of the other party (such approval not to be unreasonably withheld or delayed). This restriction shall not apply if and to the extent that the announcement is required by law or by any stock exchange or governmental, regulatory or supervisory body or authority of competent jurisdiction. If this exception applies, the party making the announcement shall use its reasonable efforts to consult with the other party in advance as to its form, content and timing.

Further assurances

14. At any time on or after Closing, each of the Seller and the Purchaser shall take all reasonable steps to execute such documents, and take such further action, as the other may reasonably require for the purpose of giving effect to the provisions of this Agreement.

Costs

15.1 Subject to clause 15.2, the Seller and the Purchaser shall each be responsible for its own costs, charges and other expenses incurred in connection with negotiating, preparing, entering into and completing this Agreement [(including any notarisation and/or registration fees)].

15.2 Any stamp duty or other transfer taxes (including interest and penalties) payable in respect of the transfer of the Shares shall be borne by [the Purchaser].

Entire agreement

16. This Agreement sets out the entire agreement and understanding between the parties in respect of the sale and purchase of the Shares. This Agreement supersedes all prior agreements, understandings or arrangements (whether oral or written) relating to the sale and purchase of the Shares. No party has entered into this Agreement in reliance upon any statement, representation, warranty or undertaking made by or on behalf of any other party other than those expressly set out in this Agreement. Nothing in this Agreement shall exclude any liability for, or remedy in respect of, fraudulent misrepresentation.

Governing law

17. This Agreement shall be governed by English law.

AS WITNESS this Agreement has been signed by duly authorised representations of the parties.

Precedent 16

Shareholder Funding Agreement

> *This Precedent contains a series of provisions for funding a JVC by way of loans from one or more of the Shareholders. Each provision can be used singly—or in combination with others—to meet the circumstances. These provisions could be contained in a self-standing Agreement between the Shareholders and the JVC or the provisions could be included in the principal Shareholders Agreement (e.g. in clause 4 of Precedent 10: Multi-Party Shareholders' Agreement (Long Form)).*

Shareholder loans on Closing

1. Each Shareholder shall on Closing advance to the JVC by way of loan the sum set opposite its name in column (2) of Schedule 1. Payment shall be made in immediately available funds to the account of the JVC at _____. The JVC shall issue a Loan Note to each Shareholder in respect of its loan.

Loan facility

2. The JVC shall arrange a loan facility or facilities ("**Loan Facility**") for its working capital needs with such bank(s) as the Board shall select and on such terms as the Board considers appropriate. Each of the Shareholders shall, if requested by the Board, guarantee the Loan Facility in their respective Equity Proportions up to an aggregate principal amount under the Loan Facility of £_____.

Capital commitments

3.1 The Shareholders acknowledge that the JVC may require further capital and finance for the purposes of carrying out its agreed Business Plan. During the period until _____ (the "**Commitment Period**"), the Shareholders agree to provide such further capital in their respective Equity Proportions up to a maximum aggregate amount of £_____. The maximum commitment ("**Maximum Commitment**") of each Shareholder, based on its existing Equity Proportion, is set out in column (3) of Schedule 1.

3.2 At any time and from time to time during the Commitment Period, the JVC may (following a decision of the Board) notify each Shareholder in writing in the form set out in Schedule 2 (a "**Call Notice**") that it requires capital from the Shareholder (a "**Call**") *provided that* the Call, together with any Calls already made pursuant to this clause 3, does not exceed the Shareholder's Maximum Commitment. A Call shall (unless all the Shareholders agree) be met by loans provided on the terms and conditions of, and be represented by, Loan Notes issued by the JVC. Each Call Notice shall set out the amount that it requires by way of additional loans from that Shareholder but always on the basis that:

(a) each Call shall be made on the Shareholders pro rata to their Equity Proportions immediately prior to the Call Notice; and

(b) the Call shall require payment from each Shareholder in the same currency and by the same date (the "**Due Date**") which shall not be less than 7 business days after the Call Notice.

3.3 Following receipt of a Call Notice, each Shareholder shall pay by the Due Date in immediately available funds, to the account of the JVC referred to in the Call Notice, the amount required to be paid or advanced pursuant to the Call.

3.4 Promptly after receipt of any sums pursuant to a Call, the JVC shall issue a Loan Note to each Shareholder for the principal amount advanced by that Shareholder and register the relevant Shareholder in the Register of the Noteholders.

Additional funding

4.1 If the Board determines at any time that the Business requires additional finance beyond the capital committed under clause 3, the Board will consider whether or not to approach the JVC's bankers or other financial institutions or, in appropriate circumstances, to seek such further finance from the Shareholders (whether by way of further loans, issue of new shares or otherwise).

4.2 The Shareholders will give serious consideration to any financing proposals of the Board but on the basis that: (i) no new Shares shall be issued unless the requisite consent is obtained in accordance with clause _____; and (ii) (subject to each Shareholder's obligation to provide finance up to its Maximum Commitment in accordance with clause 3), no Shareholder shall be required to contribute any loan or equity capital to the JVC or to guarantee any debt of the JVC without that Shareholder's prior written consent.

Alternative. The following is an alternative set of provisions specifying a preferred order for financing the JVC (unless otherwise agreed by the Shareholders):

4.1 The Shareholders intend that [(beyond the capital committed under clause 3)] the activities of the JVC shall be self-financed and that the JVC should obtain additional funds from third parties without recourse to the Shareholders. The Shareholders shall not be obliged to contribute any loan or equity capital or issue any guarantees or provide security or issue any comfort letters in favour of the JVC.

4.2 If the Board determines by a simple majority that the JVC requires additional financing, the Shareholders agree that such additional funding should be obtained from sources in the following order of priority on the basis that, unless the Board is satisfied that it will not be possible to raise money from an earlier source on terms reasonably satisfactory to the Board, a later source will not be used:

(i) obtaining an overdraft with the JVC's usual banks on normal commercial terms;

(ii) entering into external unsecured financing (whether in the form of bilateral or syndicate loans) on market terms;

(iii) entering into external secured financing (whether in the form of bilateral or syndicate loans) on market terms;

(iv) entering into external secured or unsecured financing (whether in the form of bilateral or syndicated loans) on market terms guaranteed by the Shareholders *pro rata* to their Equity Proportions (provided that each Shareholder agrees to give such guarantee); and

(v) requesting that the Shareholders provide unsecured shareholder loans to the JVC on arm's length terms (including as to payment of interest) pro rata to their Equity Proportions. Any such loans shall accrue interest at normal commercial rates, have a maximum term of three years, shall rank pari passu with other unsecured creditors and shall be repayable in accordance with their terms and no dividend shall be paid by the JVC until such shareholder loans (including accrued but unpaid interest) have been repaid in full.

If the Board determines, having exhausted all possible sources of financing under clause 4.2, that additional equity share capital is required from the Shareholders by means of the issue of new ordinary shares of the JVC, then the provisions of *[see e.g. clause 5 of Precedent 10: Multi-Party Shareholders Agreement (Long Form)]]* will apply.

Guarantees

5.1 [Except as specified in clause 2,] no Shareholder shall be obliged to participate for the benefit of the JVC in any guarantee, bond or financing arrangement with any bank or financial institution.

5.2 *[Provision to ensure that liability under any guarantees (if given) are borne by the Shareholders in their Equity Proportions—see e.g. clause 6.2 of Precedent 10: Multi-Party Shareholders Agreement (Long form).]*

Defaulting Shareholder

6.1 If any Shareholder (a "**Defaulting Shareholder**") fails to advance by way of loan the sums required on the Due Date pursuant to any Call Notice:

(i) the Defaulting Shareholder shall become liable to pay interest to the JVC on the overdue amount at the rate of _____ from the Due Date until the date of payment;

(ii) if the Defaulting Shareholder is still in default after a period of _____ from the Due Date for payment under the Call Notice, the non-defaulting Shareholders (the "**Funding Shareholders**") shall be [entitled, but not bound,] [obliged] to advance to the JVC the Defaulting Shareholder's contribution in their respective Equity Proportions (or in such proportions as they may agree);

(iii) any advance by a Funding Shareholder pursuant to sub-clause (ii) shall bear interest at the rate of _____ payable in arrears by the JVC at three-monthly intervals from the date of the advance. If and when the Defaulting Shareholder pays its outstanding contribution (together with interest thereon), the JVC shall repay pro rata, to those Funding Shareholders who have advanced sums under sub-clause (ii), an amount equal to the Defaulting Shareholder's actual contribution.

6.2 If a Defaulting Shareholder remains in default of its obligation to advance sums pursuant to a Call Notice for a period of _____ [(and the amount of the default, including interest, at the end of the period exceeds £_____)], then [all] [a Qualifying Majority] of the Funding Shareholders shall be entitled to give notice to the Defaulting Shareholder requiring that:

(i) any directors appointed by the Defaulting Shareholder shall resign from the Board (and shall not be replaced) and such directors shall cease to be required for the purposes of any quorum;

(ii) the consent of the Defaulting Shareholder, or of any director appointed by the Defaulting Shareholder, shall no longer be required for any of the Reserved Shareholder Matters or Reserved Board Matters set out in clause _____ [of the Shareholders' Agreement];

(iii) any dividend due from the JVC in respect of the shares of the Defaulting Shareholder shall not be paid directly to the Defaulting Shareholder but shall be held by the JVC and set-off against any funding default of the Defaulting Shareholder then outstanding.

7.3 If a Defaulting Shareholder remains in default of its obligation to advance sums pursuant to a Call Notice for a period of _____ [(and the amount of the default, including interest, exceeds £_____)], then the Funding Shareholders shall (following a decision of [all] [a Qualifying Majority] of them) be entitled to acquire all the shares of the Defaulting Shareholder in the JVC [in accordance with the procedure and terms applicable upon a Termination Event for a Material Default under clause _____ of the Shareholders' Agreement]. *[Refer to terms of purchase e.g. at a discount to a Fair Price Valuation—see e.g. clause 17.6 in Precedent 10: Multi-Party Shareholders' Agreement (Long form).]*

General

8. The Loan Note, representing the terms of each advance by a Shareholder under clause 1 or clause 3, shall be in the agreed form set out in Schedule 2.

9. No repayment of any Loan Note shall be made by the JVC unless:

(i) repayment is made pro rata to each of the Shareholders in proportion to the principal amount of the laws represented by their respective Loan Notes;

(ii) repayment shall be made to each Shareholder at the same time and in the same currency.

10. The obligations of any Shareholder under clause 3 to make advances up to its Maximum Commitment shall automatically cease if a resolution is passed by the shareholders or creditors, or an order is made by a court or other competent body or person, instituting a process to wind up the JVC. This shall not affect any outstanding obligation of a Defaulting Shareholder to remedy a funding default.

Schedule 1

Shareholder Loans and Commitments

Shareholder	(1) Equity Proportion at Closing %	(2) Amount of initial Loan £	(3) Maximum Commitment
A			
B			
C			
D			

Schedule 2

Call Notice

To: *[Shareholder]*

We refer to clause 3.2 of the Shareholders' Agreement dated _____ between, amongst others, the JVC and yourselves (the "**Agreement**"). Terms defined in the Agreement have the same meaning in this notice.

We hereby give you notice pursuant to clause 3.2 of the Agreement that we require you, in the manner set out in clause 3 of the Agreement, to subscribe in cash (by electronic funds transfer to the JVC's bank account at [*name of bank*] at [*branch address*], sort code _____, account number _____) for [£ _____ nominal of Loan Notes] of the JVC at the price of [£ nominal of loan stock], amounting to a total price of £_____ by _____ Business Days from the date of this notice.

Signed by: ....

                                        Duly authorised for and on behalf of [JVC]

Schedule 3

Form of Loan Note

Note No: _____

Amount: £_____

Holder: _____

Unsecured Loan Note

This Note is made on _____ by _____ (the "**Company**").

1. The Company will pay to the above-named registered holder the principal amount of £_____ subject to and in accordance with the Conditions endorsed on this Note.

2. This Note is issued subject to the Conditions endorsed on it which form part of it.

3. This Note and the Conditions endorsed on it shall be governed by, and construed in accordance with, the laws of the Netherlands.

The Company has caused this Note to be executed on _____.

Executed as a **Deed**   )
_____ _____ _____ _____   )
for and on behalf of [the Company]   )

Loan Note issued pursuant to a resolution of the Directors of the Company passed on _____ authorising the issue of up to £_____ Unsecured Loan Notes.

Conditions

Definitions

1.1 In this Note (including these Conditions):

"**Insolvency Event**" means, in relation to the Company, if:

(a) a court of competent jurisdiction makes an order or a resolution is passed for the dissolution or administration of the Company (otherwise than in the course of a reorganisation or restructuring previously approved in writing by the Noteholders, such approval not to be unreasonably withheld or delayed); or

(b) any person other than the Company takes any step (and it is not withdrawn or discharged within ninety (90) days) to appoint a liquidator, manager, receiver, administrator, administrative receiver in respect of its assets; or

(c) the Company convenes a meeting of its creditors or makes or proposes any arrangement or composition with, or any assignment for the benefit of, its creditors;

["**Interest Rate**" means _____ _____ _____ _____;]

"**Noteholders**" means the persons for the time being entered in the Register of Noteholders as holder of the Notes;

"**Notes**" means this series of £_____ Unsecured Loan Notes (and any other Unsecured Loan Note issued on identical terms with it) or, as the case may be, the amount for the time being outstanding;

"**Shareholders' Agreement**" means the agreement dated _____ between [*names of signatories to the shareholders' agreement*] relating to the establishment of the Company as a jointly-owned company.

1.2 Capitalised terms in this Note, which have not been otherwise defined in condition 1.1, shall have the same meanings as set out in the Shareholders' Agreement.

1.3 Words denoting the singular only include the plural also and vice versa. Words denoting the masculine gender include the feminine and vice versa. Words denoting persons only shall include corporations.

Creation and Issue of Notes

2.1 The amount of this series of Notes is £_____. Power is however reserved to the Company by resolution of the Directors of the Company at any time and from time to time to create and issue additional notes identical in all respects to and forming a single issue with this Note or carrying such rights as the Company may determine.

2.2 All Notes as and when issued shall rank pari passu and rateably without discrimination or preference and as unsecured obligations of the Company.

Repayment

3. The Notes shall become repayable in full at par (i) upon a resolution of the Directors of the Company to repay the Notes or (ii) on the occurrence of an Insolvency Event [(but subject always to Condition 4.2)].

Status of Notes [and Subordination]

4.1 The Notes when issued will rank pari passu equally and rateably without discrimination or preference as between the Noteholders and with all other indebtedness of the Company except to the extent provided by law [and subject to Condition 4.2].

4.2 [If an Insolvency Event occurs, the Notes shall be a subordinated obligation of the Company and no payment of principal [or interest] in respect of the Notes shall thereafter be paid to any Noteholder unless and until all other creditors of the Company have been paid in full during any administration, liquidation or other process commenced as a result of the Insolvency Event.]

Interest

5. [Interest shall not be payable by the Company in respect of any Loan Note.] [Interest, at the relevant Interest Rate, shall be paid by the Company in respect of the principal amount of the Note. Interest shall be payable _____.]

Register of Noteholders

6.1 The Company shall at all times keep a register showing the names and addresses of the Noteholders together with the amount of their respective holdings of Notes and the dates upon which they were respectively registered as holders.

6.2 The Noteholders or any of them (and any person authorised in writing by any of them) may at all reasonable times during office hours inspect the register and take copies of it and extracts from it or any part of it.

Title of Noteholders

7.1 The Company will recognise the registered holder of any Note as the absolute owner of it and shall not be bound to take notice of any express, implied or constructive trust to which any Note may be subject. The receipt of the registered holder for the time being of any Note for any moneys payable in respect of it shall be a good discharge to the Company.

7.2 Every Noteholder will be recognised by the Company as entitled to its Note free from any equity, set-off or cross-claim on the part of the Company against the original or any intermediate holder of the Note.

Transfers of Notes and restrictions on transfer

8.1 [A Note may only be transferred in accordance with the terms of clause _____ of the Shareholders' Agreement.]

8.2 In circumstances where a transfer of a Note is permitted, the following provisions shall apply:

(a) A Note is transferable by instrument in writing in the usual common form or in such form as the Board may approve in amounts and in multiples of £_____. Where the transfer is of only part of a Note, a fresh Note in respect of the balance will be issued to the transferor free of charge.

(b) Every instrument of transfer must be signed by or on behalf of the transferor and the transferor shall be deemed to remain the owner of the Note to be transferred until the name of the transferee is entered in the register in respect of them.

(c) Every instrument of transfer shall be delivered to the registered office of the Company accompanied by (i) the Note to be transferred and (ii) such other evidence as the Board or other officers of the Company authorised to deal with the transfer may require to prove the title of the transferor or its rights to transfer the Notes.

Renewal of Notes

9. If any Note is defaced, worn out lost or destroyed, it may be renewed on payment of a fee not exceeding £_____ and on such terms (if any) as to evidence and indemnity as the Board may require. If the Note is defaced or worn out, the defaced or worn out Note shall be surrendered before the new Note is issued.

Notices

10.1 Any notice under this Note may be given to the Company or to any Noteholder by sending it by post in a prepaid letter addressed to the Company at its registered office.

10.2 Every such notice sent by mail shall be deemed to have been served forty-eight (48) hours after the time of posting. In proving service it shall be sufficient to prove that the letter containing the notice was properly addressed, stamped and posted.

Precedent 17

Put and Call Option Agreement

> *An option agreement is often entered into in the context of a joint venture in order to protect a minority shareholder who wishes to be assured of an exit from the venture. The terms will often be included as part of the original Shareholders' Agreement. The price formula will, of course, be carefully negotiated and tailored to the specific venture. This Agreement provides for a minimum price. Clear designation of the Accounting Principles is vital; these will normally be based on the accounting principles and policies of the JVC consistently applied.*

THIS PUT AND CALL OPTION AGREEMENT is made _____ 200__

BETWEEN:

(1) _____, whose registered office is at _____ ("**ABC**"); and

(2) _____, whose registered office is at _____ ("**XYZ**").

WHEREAS:

(A) [JVC] is a [private limited] company with an authorised share capital of _____ divided into _____ shares of [£1] each.

(B) ABC and XYZ have agreed to enter into certain option arrangements on the terms of this Agreement.

IT IS AGREED AS FOLLOWS:

Interpretation

1.1 In this Agreement, the following expressions shall have the following meanings:

"**Accounting Principles**" means the principles and policies set out in the Schedule;

["**After Tax Earnings**" means (based on the Accounting Principles) the actual [consolidated] after tax earnings of the JVC [Group] before the payment of dividends [(including its share of the after tax earnings of associated companies and, for the avoidance of doubt, including any extraordinary profits and losses as disclosed in the audited accounts)];]

"**Business Day**" means a day (other than a Saturday) on which banks generally are open in London [and _____] for a full range of business;

"**Call Option**" has the meaning set out in clause 2;

"**Completion**" means completion of the transfer of the Option Shares in accordance with clause 5;

"**Controlling Interest**" means: (a) the ownership or control (directly or indirectly) of more than 50% of the voting share capital of the relevant undertaking; or (b) the ability to direct the casting of more than 50% of the votes exercisable at general meetings of the relevant undertaking on all, or substantially all matters; or (c) the right to appoint or remove directors of the relevant undertaking holding a majority of the voting rights at meetings of the board on all, or substantially all, matters;

"**Group**" means, in relation to the JVC or a party, that company and its subsidiaries for the time being, and "**subsidiary**" has the meaning set out in the Companies Act 2006;

"**JVC**" means _____ Limited, a [private limited] company incorporated in England and Wales;

["**Net Tangible Assets**" means the [consolidated] fixed assets and current assets of the JVC [Group] (including cash and including investments in and loans to associated companies) less [consolidated] current liabilities of the JVC (including, for the avoidance of doubt, both current and deferred tax liabilities);]

"**Option Notice**" means a notice given in accordance with clause 3.1 or 3.2;

"**Option Period**" means the period beginning on _____ and ending on _____;

"**Option Price**" has the meaning given to it in clause 4;

"**Option Shares**" means shares fully paid and beneficially owned by and registered in the name of ABC and, if the Put Option or the Call Option is exercised after any Reorganisation has taken place, any shares, stock or other securities constituting ABC's interest in the JVC as ABC at the time of such exercise may hold (including any shares acquired since the date of the Option Notice under clause 3) after every such Reorganisation;

"**persons acting in concert**" means persons who, pursuant to an agreement or understanding (whether formal or informal), actively co-operate, through an acquisition by any of them of shares in a party, to obtain a Controlling Interest in relation to that party, or agree so to co-operate;

"**Put Option**" has the meaning given to it in clause 2;

["**Regulatory Approvals**" means any necessary approvals required by any competent supranational, governmental or regulatory agencies or authorities;]

"**Reorganisation**" means every issue by the JVC by way of capitalisation of profits or reserves and every issue by way of rights and every consolidation or sub-division or reduction of capital or capital dividend or other adjustment relating to the equity share capital (or any shares or stock derived therefrom) and to any amalgamation or reconstruction affecting the equity share capital (or any shares or stock derived therefrom);

"**Shares**" means ordinary shares of [£1] each in the capital of the JVC;

1.2 The Schedule comprises a schedule to this Agreement and forms part of this Agreement.

Put and call options

2. XYZ hereby grants to ABC an option to require XYZ to purchase (the "**Put Option**"), and ABC grants to XYZ an option to purchase (the "**Call Option**"), ABC's entire interest in Shares in the JVC and in each case on the terms of this Agreement.

Exercise of options

3.1 The Put Option may be exercised by ABC by notice to XYZ given at any time during the Option Period.

3.2 The Call Option may be exercised by XYZ by notice to ABC given at any time during the Option Period.

3.3 The Put Option and the Call Option may be exercised in respect of all (but not some only) of the Option Shares.

3.4 An Option Notice, once served, shall not be revoked.

Option price

4.1 The price payable for the Option Shares under the Put Option or the Call Option (the "**Option Price**") shall be:

(a) the sum certified by the Auditors of the JVC in writing (the "**Auditor's Certificate**") to be equal to _____ per cent of the greater of:

    (i) [_____ times the average Net Tangible Assets; or
    (ii) _____ times the average After Tax Earnings;]

such average being calculated in each case by reference to the audited accounts of the JVC [Group] for the last _____ years ended prior to the date of the exercise of the Put/Call Option; or

(b) £_____

whichever shall be the greater.

4.2 The cost of obtaining the Auditors' Certificate shall be borne by the parties [equally] [in proportion to their respective shareholdings in the JVC].

4.3 For the purpose of calculating the Option Price, the same accounting principles and policies shall be applied for all periods up to the exercise of the Put/Call Option. The accounts of the JVC shall be drawn up in accordance with the Accounting Principles.

4.4 Within 7 days of receipt of the Auditor's Certificate either ABC or XYZ may give a written notice to the other (a "**Counter-Notice**") stating that it disputes the sum set out in the Auditor's Certificate. ABC and XYZ shall use all reasonable endeavours to meet and discuss the objections of the other party and to reach agreement.

4.5 If the parties are unable to agree within 21 days of receipt of a Counter-Notice, the matter shall be referred to an internationally recognised firm of accountants (independent of the parties and agreed by them) to determine the dispute. In the absence of agreement, the internationally recognised firm of accountants shall be appointed by [the President for the time being of the Institute of Chartered Accountants in England and Wales] on the application of either party. The internationally recognised firm of accountants is referred to in this Agreement as the "**Expert**".

4.6 The parties shall ensure that there is made available to the Expert such information about the JVC as the Expert reasonably requires to determine the dispute. The Expert shall be deemed to be acting as an expert and not as an arbitrator and its decision shall be final and binding on the parties. The cost of obtaining the Expert's certificate (the "**Expert's Certificate**") shall be borne as directed by the Expert or, if there is no such direction by the parties, equally.

4.7 Interest at a rate of _____ per cent per annum above the base rate for the time being of _____ Bank plc shall be payable to ABC on the Option Price from [the expiry of the day on which Completion ought to take place in accordance with clause 5.1] to the date of actual payment.

Completion

5.1 Completion of the sale and purchase of the Option Shares shall take place at a venue to be agreed by the parties and, in default of agreement, at the JVC's registered office on:

(a) the [fifth] Business Day following:

  (i) agreement by ABC and XYZ of the Option Price based on the Auditor's Certificate; or
  (ii) if a Counter-Notice has been received by either party and the matter is referred to an Expert, receipt by the parties of the Expert's Certificate; [or if later

(b) the fifth Business Day following the day on which all Regulatory Approvals have been obtained.]

5.2 The following events shall take place at Completion:

(a) XYZ shall cause the Option Price to be paid by electronic funds transfer to ABC's bank account at _____ [details];

(b) ABC shall deliver, or procure that there is delivered, to XYZ a transfer or transfers in respect of the Option Shares duly completed in favour of XYZ (or as XYZ may direct) together with the share certificates relating to the Option Shares (and such other deeds and documents as may be necessary to transfer the unencumbered beneficial ownership of the Option Shares);

(c) [ABC shall deliver, or procure that there is delivered, to XYZ a waiver of any applicable rights of pre-emption, duly executed by all the other members of the JVC;] and

(d) the parties shall procure that the transfer or transfers are registered subject to their being duly stamped (all stamp duty to be paid by XYZ);

(e) the obligations of any member of the ABC Group under any guarantees and/or counter-indemnities to third parties in respect of obligations of the JVC (other than those incurred by any member of the ABC Group in the ordinary course of business) shall be assumed by XYZ.

Dividends and voting

6. Following the exercise of the Put Option or the Call Option, ABC shall (i) account to XYZ for all dividends or other distributions of the JVC declared or paid after the date of service of the Option Notice and (ii) exercise all voting and other rights at the direction of XYZ.

[or]

[ABC shall be entitled to all dividends or other distributions declared and/or paid on the Option Shares, and to exercise all voting rights in respect of the Option Shares, in the period prior to Completion.]

Warranties

7.1 ABC warrants to XYZ that it is and will remain, until the exercise of the Put Option or the Call Option or the expiry of the Option Period, the beneficial owner of the Option Shares (subject only to the Put and Call Options) and has and will have full power and authority to grant an option in respect of the same upon the terms and conditions of this Agreement.

7.2 ABC shall not, prior to the exercise of the Put Option or Call Option or the expiry of the Option Period, transfer, dispose of, charge, pledge or encumber in any way its interest in any of the Option Shares.

7.3 The Option Shares shall be sold free from all security interests, options, equities, claims or other third party rights (including rights of pre-emption) of any nature whatsoever and with all rights attaching to them at the date of exercise of the Put/Call Option.

Change of control

8. If a Controlling Interest in ABC or XYZ is acquired by a third party (together, if applicable, with persons acting in concert with any such third party), then the party not suffering any change of control shall be entitled to exercise its Put Option or Call Option (as the case may be) under clause 2 irrespective of the time of such change of control (provided that notice of any exercise of such Put Option or Call Option shall be given no later than 14 days after notice in writing of such change of control from the party suffering the same).

Non-assignment

9. Neither party may assign or transfer any of its rights or obligations under this Agreement in whole or in part.

Amendments

10. This Agreement may be amended only by an instrument in writing signed by duly authorised representatives of each party.

Entire agreement

11. This Agreement sets out the entire agreement and understanding between the parties with respect to its subject matter. Neither party has entered into this Agreement in reliance upon any representation, warranty or undertaking of the other party which is not expressly set out or referred to in this Agreement. This clause shall not exclude any liability for fraudulent misrepresentation.

Notices

12.1 Any notice to be given under this Agreement shall be in writing and signed by or on behalf of the party giving it. Any such notice may be served by sending it by fax to the number set out in clause 12.2, or delivering it by hand or sending it by pre-paid recorded delivery, special delivery or registered post to the address and for the attention of the relevant party set out in clause 12.2 (or as otherwise notified from time to time in accordance with the provisions of this clause 12).

12.2 The addresses and fax numbers of the parties for the purpose of clause 12.1 are as follows:

ABC: **XYZ:**

Governing law

13. This agreement shall be governed by and construed in accordance with English law.

AS WITNESS this Agreement has been signed by authorised representatives of the parties.

SCHEDULE

ACCOUNTING PRINCIPLES

[   ]

Signed by _____   }
for and on behalf of **XYZ**   }

Signed by _____   }
for and on behalf of **ABC**   }

Precedent 18

Support Services Agreement

> This precedent Agreement contemplates that a range of administrative and commercial services may be supplied by one party to the JVC, possibly for a transitional period. Particular points:
>
> (1) The Services may be described in a general manner—or specifically described in the Schedule.
>
> (2) There may be different categories of Services which may have their own term and charging basis (and the JVC may be able to terminate certain categories of the Services before others).
>
> (3) No specific service levels are designated. Liability will normally be subject to low limits.
>
> (4) Rights of termination (and dispute resolution) should be co-ordinated with the position under the Shareholders' Agreement. If the Agreement has potentially a long or indefinite term, consider: (i) should either party have a right to terminate all or any of the Services if ABC ceases to be a shareholder in the JVC (see clause 11.6)? (ii) should the JVC have rights of termination if a third party acquires control of ABC (see clause 11.4)? (iii) should the JVC be able to terminate by notice at any time (see clause 11.5)? (In this latter case, ABC may wish to continue to charge for a period for costs which cannot be avoided (see clause 12.2). In some cases, more detailed provisions on termination (e.g. as to the cost of redundancy payments etc.) may be appropriate.

THIS AGREEMENT is made on ＿＿＿＿＿ 200＿

BETWEEN:

(1) ＿＿＿＿＿("**ABC**") whose registered office is at ＿＿＿＿＿; and

(2) ＿＿＿＿＿ ("**JVC**") whose registered office is at ＿＿＿＿＿.

WHEREAS:

(A) ABC is a shareholder in the JVC and a party with [XYZ] to a Sharcholders' Agreement dated ＿＿＿＿＿ ("**Shareholders Agreement**").

(B) As part of the arrangements for establishing the JVC in accordance with the Shareholders' Agreement, ABC has agreed to provide various administrative and commercial services to support the JVC's business.

(C) The Services are being provided by ABC [for a transitional period] with the expectation of the parties that the JVC will, in due course, develop resources to undertake itself some or all of the Services.

IT IS AGREED AS FOLLOWS:

Interpretation

1.1 The following terms shall, unless the context otherwise requires, have the following respective meanings:

"**Affiliate**" means, in relation to a party, any subsidiary or holding company of that party, or any subsidiary of a holding company of that party;

"**Business Day**" means a day (other than a Saturday or Sunday) on which banks are generally open for normal banking business in London;

"**Business Hours**" means the hours of _____ am to _____ pm (inclusive);

"**Charges**" means the charges for the Services specified in the Schedule or, if no charge is specified for a Service, the Charge means the [direct costs incurred by ABC in providing the Service plus _____ per cent];

"**Effective Date**" means _____;

"**Force Majeure**" means, in relation to either party, any circumstances beyond the reasonable control of that party (including any strike, lockout or other form of industrial action);

"**Intellectual Property Rights**" means patents, trade marks, service marks, logos, get-up, trade names, internet domain names, rights in designs, copyright (including rights in computer software) and moral rights, database rights, semi-conductor topography rights, utility models, rights in know-how and other intellectual property rights, in each case whether registered or unregistered and including applications for registration, and all rights or forms of protection having equivalent or similar effect anywhere in the world;

"**JVC Board**" means the board of directors of the JVC;

"**Proprietary Software**" means software owned by ABC and used in the provision of the Services;

"**RPI**" means the index of retail prices published by the Office for National Statistics (or by any governmental department upon which duties in connection with the index have devolved) and, in the event of any change in the reference base used to compile the index, such adjustment shall be made as the auditors of the JVC (acting as experts and not arbitrators) determine;

"**Services**" means the services to be provided by ABC to the JVC in accordance with clause 2 [and more particularly set out in the Schedule];

"**Service Term**" means [, in relation to each category of Services,] the term specified for those Services in the Schedule (or, if no term is specified, the Service Term means [6] months starting on the Effective Date);

"**the Site**" means _____; and

"**Third Party Software**" means software owned by a third party which is licensed to ABC and used in the provision of the Services.

1.2 References to any English legal term or concept shall, in respect of any jurisdiction other than England, be construed as references to the term or concept which most nearly corresponds in that jurisdiction to it.

1.3 The headings in this Agreement do not affect its interpretation.

Scope of Services to be provided by ABC

2.1 ABC shall provide to the JVC [during Business Hours on each Business Day] the following administrative and commercial services (the "**Services**"):

(a) [*office and administrative services*: such office services (on or adjacent to the Site) and other administrative and commercial support services as the JVC may from time to time reasonably require (including secretarial, commercial and accounting personnel, fax, telephone, photocopying, computer support and messenger services);

(b) *accounting services*: such range of accounting services as the JVC may from time to time reasonably require (including book-keeping, ordering, invoicing, payroll, tax computations, preparation of accounts, budgeting control, reporting, payment and collection of accounts, together with such assistance and information in relation to the foregoing as the JVC's statutory auditors may reasonably require);

(c) *purchasing*: the ordering of products and raw materials for the account of the JVC in the course of the JVC's business and arranging for their delivery to and/or reception at the Site in accordance with the JVC's reasonable requirements from time to time;

(d) *personnel*: the secondment of personnel for the sale and distribution of products in [_____]; and

(e) *other*: such other related administrative and commercial services as may appropriately be carried out by ABC and as shall be agreed by the JVC to form part of the Services under this Agreement.]

or

[**2.1** ABC undertakes to provide to the JVC the various services more particularly described in the Schedule (together, the "**Services**").]

2.2 ABC may from time to time change operational aspects of the Services or the way in which they are provided, or substitute them with other services. If changes or substitutions are made, ABC shall use its reasonable efforts to ensure that (i) the business of the JVC is not disrupted to a material extent and (ii) the change or substitution does not result in an increase to the Service Charges unless the JVC has agreed to the increase in advance.

2.3 [ABC shall give priority to the provision of the Services over the undertaking by ABC of any other activities for any other party comparable to the Services.]

2.4 Except as agreed between the parties in writing, ABC shall have no obligation to provide any Services to the JVC outside Business Hours.

2.5 Where the consent of a third party is required for the provision of a Service, ABC shall use reasonable efforts at the JVC's cost to obtain the consent, but shall not be in breach of this Agreement if a third party refuses to give it.

ABC's rights and obligations

3.1 ABC shall use all reasonable efforts to ensure that the personnel providing the Services are suitably qualified.

3.2 ABC shall [use reasonable efforts to] ensure that the Services are, in all material respects, provided to the same standards and with the same level of efficiency as comparable services were provided or undertaken within the ABC Group immediately prior to the Effective Date.

3.3 [ABC shall, in supplying the Services at the Site, comply with such practices and procedures as are reasonably required by the JVC and generally act in accordance with guidelines from time to time laid down by the JVC Board or other authorised representatives of the JVC.]

3.4 ABC shall provide the JVC from time to time in writing with such up-to-date and accurate information in relation to the Services as the JVC Board may from time to time reasonably request.

3.5 [ABC may suspend the JVC's access to the information technology or communications systems used by the ABC Group if, in ABC's reasonable opinion, the integrity, security or performance of the systems (or any data stored on them) is being or is likely to be jeopardised by the activities of the JVC.]

JVC's obligations

4.1 The JVC shall ensure that all relevant personnel of ABC have such access to the Site and to any information or records kept by, or under the control of, the JVC in relation to its business as is reasonably necessary to enable ABC to provide the Services. In particular, the JVC shall ensure that appropriate payroll data is supplied, as required, to ABC on a timely basis each month.

4.2 The JVC shall take all reasonable steps to ensure the safety of any of ABC's personnel [or contractors] who visit any premises of the JVC.

4.3 The JVC shall use all reasonable efforts to (i) ensure that those of its personnel whose decisions are necessary for the performance of the Services are available at all reasonable times for consultation on any matter relating to the Services and (ii) respond promptly to any requests for guidance, instruction or information reasonably required by ABC to enable it to perform the Services.

4.4 The JVC shall not cause ABC to breach any obligation (contractual, tortious or otherwise) which ABC owes to any third party supplier notified to the JVC.

4.5 The JVC shall not use, or attempt to access or interfere with, any communications systems, information technology systems or data used by ABC unless authorised to do so under this Agreement and shall co-operate with ABC in any reasonable security arrangements which ABC considers necessary to prevent the JVC, or any unauthorised third party, accessing a system or data in an unauthorised manner.

4.6 The JVC shall use all reasonable efforts, as soon as practicable after the Effective Date, to acquire its own information technology and communications systems and services and to migrate off the systems used by ABC.

Charges

5.1 The JVC shall pay to ABC the charges set out in the Schedule in respect of the provision of the [relevant] Services (the "**Charges**").

5.2 [The Charges shall be reviewed on [each anniversary of this Agreement.] The parties shall negotiate in good faith and use all reasonable efforts to agree charges to be set for the following year which shall then replace those set out in the Schedule. If the parties are unable to reach agreement on the Charges for that following year, they shall be an amount equal to the Charges [for the relevant Services] for the year which is ending [together with an amount equal to those Charges multiplied by the percentage increase (but not decrease) in RPI during the year which is ending].

5.3 If ABC's services are requested for any matter not covered by the Services (such services being "**Additional Services**"), the JVC shall be liable to pay ABC's standard charges from time to time in force in respect of such Additional Services (or, if no standard charges are in force, such charges as shall be fair and reasonable for the relevant Additional Services).

5.4 All charges and other sums payable by the JVC under this Agreement are exclusive of any applicable value added tax.

5.5 Payment of the Charges shall be made in the manner specified in the Schedule. If payment terms are not specified in the Schedule, payment shall be made within 30 days from and including the date of ABC's invoice for the Charges.

5.6 If any third party costs associated with the provision of any of the Services increase, ABC shall be entitled, on prior written notice to the JVC, to increase the charges for those Services to reflect that cost increase.

5.7 Interest shall be payable by the JVC on any amounts which are not paid by the due date for payment. Interest shall accrue and be calculated on a daily basis (both before and after any judgment) at the rate of _____ per cent per annum above the base rate of _____ from time to time for the period from the due date for payment until the date of actual payment.

5.8 [If the JVC disagrees with any invoice or statement delivered by ABC pursuant to clause 5, ABC shall supply the JVC with such information as is reasonably necessary to support the calculations contained in that invoice or statement. ABC shall also permit the JVC to have such access as it may reasonably request to the books and records maintained by ABC in connection with the provision of the Services to enable the JVC to verify that information. The parties shall use all reasonable efforts (in conjunction with their respective accountants) to resolve any dispute. If they fail to reach agreement, then (unless the parties agree otherwise) the dispute shall be referred to an independent internationally recognised firm of chartered accountants (acting as experts and not as an arbitrator) agreed upon by the parties or, failing agreement, to be selected by the president for the time being of the Institute of Chartered Accountants in England and Wales. Its determination shall be binding on the parties. The expenses of the independent firm shall be borne between the parties in such proportion as the firm shall in its discretion determine.]

Liability

6.1 ABC shall use all reasonable care and skill in providing the Services. [If ABC shall fail to use such reasonable care and skill or shall otherwise be in breach of its obligations in respect of the supply of the Services, the sole remedy of the JVC shall be to require ABC to carry out as promptly as practicable such repeat or remedial services as shall be appropriate to ensure that the relevant Services are carried out (save only as to the time of their performance) as originally planned.]

6.2 Without prejudice to any other limitation or exclusion of liability under this Agreement:

(a) in no event shall ABC be liable to the JVC for loss of profits or other indirect or consequential loss of any kind whether arising from negligence, breach of contract or otherwise;

(b) the total liability of ABC to the JVC (whether in contract, tort or otherwise) arising [in any year of this Agreement] in respect of the provision of any [category of] Services, shall not exceed [the total charges payable by the JVC to ABC for [that category of] Services for that year].

6.3 Subject to clause 6.2, ABC shall indemnify the JVC against any claim or action (including reasonable legal costs and expenses incurred in relation to any claim) brought by any third party against the JVC arising from any negligence on the part of ABC or any of its personnel.

6.4 Nothing in this Agreement shall exclude either party's liability for death or personal injury.

6.5 For the avoidance of doubt, ABC shall have no liability to the JVC in respect of or arising out of the performance, or non-performance, of the Services save as expressly set out in this Agreement.

Confidential information

7.1 [Information disclosed under this Agreement shall be "Confidential Information" for the purpose of the obligations of the parties under clause _____ of the Shareholders' Agreement.]

or

7.1 Each party shall keep confidential all information (whether in writing or any other form) which has been disclosed to it pursuant to this Agreement by or on behalf of the other party in confidence or which by its nature ought to be regarded as confidential. Each party shall use all reasonable efforts to ensure that its officers, employees and representatives, and those of its Affiliates, keep the information confidential.

7.2 Clause 7.1 does not apply to information:

(a) which after the Effective Date is published or becomes otherwise generally available to the public (except as a result of a breach of any provision of this Agreement by the other party);

(b) made available to the recipient party by a third party who is entitled to divulge the information without any obligation of confidentiality;

(c) which has been independently developed by the recipient party;

(d) which the recipient party can prove was already known to it before its receipt from the disclosing party;

(e) to the extent required to be disclosed by any applicable law or by any recognised stock exchange or governmental or other regulatory or supervisory body or authority of competent jurisdiction.

Intellectual property rights

8.1 Nothing in this Agreement shall affect the ownership by ABC or its licensors of its Intellectual Property Rights (including rights in Proprietary Software and Third Party Software) existing at the Effective Date.

8.2 The Intellectual Property Rights in any software or other materials (including rights in Third Party Software and Proprietary Software) supplied, created or developed by or on behalf of ABC after the Effective Date are, and shall remain, the exclusive property of ABC or its licensors.

8.3 ABC grants to the JVC a non-exclusive, non-transferable licence to use the Proprietary Software, in object code form only, during the [period of this Agreement] [the relevant Service Term] to the extent reasonably necessary for the JVC to receive the full benefit of the Services.

Data protection

9.1 [Each party shall comply with the notification requirements under the Data Protection Act 1998 and the Data Protection Principles specified in that Act.

9.2 ABC shall from time to time comply with any reasonable request made by the JVC to ABC to ensure compliance with the Data Protection Principles and that appropriate technical and organisational measures are taken against unauthorised or unlawful processing of the personal data and against accidental loss or destruction of, or damage to, the personal data.]

Force majeure

10.1 Neither party shall be deemed to be in breach of this Agreement for any delay in performance or other non-performance of its obligations to the extent due to any Force Majeure which it has notified to the other party. If either party is affected by Force Majeure, it shall promptly notify the other party of the nature and extent of the circumstances in question.

10.2 If at any time ABC claims Force Majeure in respect of its obligations under this Agreement with regard to the provision of the Services or any of them, the JVC shall be entitled to obtain from any other person the provision of such Services as ABC is unable to provide.

10.3 ABC shall not be liable for any interruption, disruption or downtime in the Services caused by the acts or omissions of a third party outside ABC's Group.

Duration and termination

11.1 This Agreement shall come into force on the Effective Date and shall continue unless and until terminated in accordance with the following provisions of this clause 11.

11.2 [Each category of] the Services, subject to earlier termination under clause 11.5, shall terminate automatically at the close of the last Business Day of the relevant Service Term specified in the Schedule. [If specified in the Schedule, the JVC may terminate by notice a category of the Services before the end of a Service Term.]

11.3 Either party may terminate this Agreement with immediate effect by giving notice to the other if:

(a) the other party commits a material breach of this Agreement relevant to those Services and fails to remedy that breach within 45 days of a written notice giving reasonable particulars of the breach and requiring it to be remedied (and such notice specifies that, if the breach is not remedied, that party intends to exercise its rights under this clause); or

(b) if the other party goes into liquidation (whether compulsory or voluntary) except for the purposes of a bona fide reconstruction with the consent of the other party (such consent not to be unreasonably withheld) or if a petition is presented or an order is made for the appointment of an administrator, receiver, manager or similar officer over any substantial part of its assets or undertaking (and such petition or order is not discharged within 30 days).

11.4 [If a Controlling Interest in ABC is acquired by a third party, the JVC shall be entitled at any time following such event to terminate this Agreement by 30 days written notice to ABC. For this purpose, "**Controlling Interest**" means (i) the ownership or control (directly or indirectly) of more than 50 per cent of the voting share capital of ABC or (ii) the ability to direct the casting of more than 50 per cent of the votes exercisable at general meetings of ABC on all, or substantially all, matters or (iii) the right to appoint or remove a majority of the directors of the JVC.]

11.5 [Subject to clause 12.2 below, the JVC may give ABC at least 3 months' notice in writing to terminate all or any category of the Services.]

11.6 [ABC may terminate this Agreement on 3 months' notice ending on or after the sale of any interest in the JVC (whether by way of flotation or trade sale or otherwise) as a result of which ABC ceases to have a direct or indirect interest in at least _____ per cent of the voting rights attaching to the ordinary shares of the JVC.]

11.7 This Agreement may terminate at any time with the written agreement of both parties.

11.8 The rights to terminate this Agreement given by this clause 11 shall not prejudice any other right or remedy of either party in respect of the breach concerned (if any) or any other breach.

Consequences of termination

12.1 On termination of this Agreement [or a particular category of the Services]:

(a) (except as provided in clause 12.2 and subject to any rights or obligations which have accrued prior to termination) neither party shall have any further obligation to the other party in respect of the part or parts of this Agreement which have been terminated;

(b) the specific consequences (if any) set out in the Schedule in relation to the category of the Services terminated shall apply;

(c) [the licence granted to the JVC under clause 8.3 shall immediately cease in relation to the terminated Services and the JVC shall stop using the relevant Proprietary Software and the Third Party Software;]

(d) each party shall return or deliver to the other party all records and documents relating to the [relevant] Services (including, in the case of the JVC, all copies of the Proprietary Software and Third Party Software) and shall take all reasonable steps to expunge all data from any computer system, word processor or other device in the possession or under control of that party which relate to or contain the confidential information of the other party or, at the other party's direction, destroy it and certify that the destruction has taken place;

(e) the JVC shall promptly pay all amounts accrued for the [relevant] Services and work performed prior to termination which have not already been paid.

12.2 [If [any category of] the Services are terminated by the JVC under clause 11.5, the JVC shall continue to pay to ABC amounts in respect of the actual costs incurred by ABC [for a period of _____] following such termination as a result of having made available, inter alia, facilities and personnel in order to have been able to provide the Services so terminated. ABC shall use all reasonable efforts to reduce such costs.]

12.3 The following clauses shall survive termination of this Agreement or a [particular category of the Services]: [clauses 6, 7, 8, 16 and 17].

General

13.1 [Subject to the JVC's prior written consent (which shall not be unreasonably withheld), ABC shall be entitled to carry out its obligations under this Agreement through any agents or sub-contractors appointed by it in its absolute discretion for that purpose.]

13.2 Except as provided in clause 13.1, this Agreement is personal to the parties and neither of them may (without the written consent of the other) assign, mortgage, charge or dispose of any of its rights or sub-contract or otherwise delegate any of its obligations under this Agreement.

13.3 Nothing in this Agreement shall create, or be deemed to create, a partnership between the parties or constitute one party as the agent of any other party.

13.4 No variation of this Agreement shall be valid unless it is in writing and signed by or on behalf of both parties.

13.5 If and to the extent that any provision of this Agreement is held to be illegal, void or unenforceable, this shall not affect the validity of the other provisions of this Agreement.

13.6 No failure or delay by either party in exercising any right or remedy provided by law under or pursuant to this Agreement shall be construed as a waiver or variation of it or preclude its exercise at any subsequent time.

13.7 Each party shall pay its own costs, charges and expenses incurred in connection with the negotiation, preparation and completion of this Agreement.

Notices

14.1 Any notice to be given under this Agreement shall be in writing and signed by or on behalf of the party giving it. It shall be served by sending it by fax, delivering it by hand, or sending it by pre-paid recorded delivery, special delivery or registered post, in each case to the address set out in clause 15.2 and in each case marked for the attention of the relevant party (or as otherwise notified from time to time in accordance with the provisions of this clause 15).

14.2 The addresses and fax numbers of the parties for the purpose of clause 15.1 are as follows:

[ABC]	[JVC]
Address:	Address:
Fax:	Fax:
For the attention of:	For the attention of:
	Copied to:
	[XYZ]
	Address:
	Fax:
	For the attention of:

Entire agreement

15. This Agreement (taken with the Shareholders' Agreement) sets out the entire agreement and understanding between the parties in respect of the subject matter of this Agreement and supersedes any previous arrangements or agreements between the parties. Each party acknowledges that, in entering into this Agreement, it does not do so on the basis of or relying upon any representation, warranty or other provision except as expressly provided in this Agreement and, accordingly, all conditions, warranties or other terms implied by statute or common law are hereby excluded to the fullest extent permitted by law.

Disputes and arbitration

16.1 In the event of any dispute between ABC and the JVC arising in connection with this Agreement, the parties shall use all reasonable efforts to resolve the matter on an amicable basis. If one party serves formal written notice on the other that a material dispute has arisen and the parties are unable to resolve the dispute within a period of 30 days from the service of such notice, then the dispute shall be referred to the respective chairmen or chief executives of ABC, **[XYZ]** and the JVC with a view to the dispute being resolved as early as possible.

16.2 If any dispute is unresolved by the chairmen or chief executives within a period of 30 days from the date of such referral of such dispute to them, the dispute [(other than a dispute to be resolved in accordance with clause 5.8)] may be referred by either party to and finally settled by arbitration under the Rules of the London Court of International Arbitration by one or more arbitrators appointed in accordance with those Rules. The place of arbitration shall be London. The language of arbitration proceedings shall be English.

Governing law

17. This Agreement shall be governed by English law.

AS WITNESS this Agreement has been signed by the duly authorised representatives of the parties.

SCHEDULE

Service:	
Service Term: *(or period of notice)*	
Charge:	
Any special terms:	

[*repeat for each category of the Services*]

SIGNED by ─────────   }   SIGNED by ─────────   }
for **ABC**   }   for the **JVC**   }

....

Precedent 19

Technology Licence Agreement

> *This precedent establishes an arm's length basis for the disclosure of technology by one party to the JVC. It provides for royalties to be paid by the JVC on sales although the Agreement could also form the basis of a party's contribution of a licence and technical assistance in exchange for shares in the JVC (subject to local law limitations and requirements). This Agreement contemplates that royalties will be payable for a specified period although the licence for use by the JVC will continue thereafter.*
>
> *One important point for negotiation is whether the licensor (ABC) should provide an indemnity to the JVC if the use of the technology infringes third party rights (see clause 10.6) or whether any such liability is to be excluded.*
>
> *Given the dual interest of ABC (being, at least initially, a shareholder in the JVC), it will usually be sensible for the JVC to nominate a separate representative to deal with issues under the Agreement, particularly during the initial disclosure stage.*
>
> *Care needs to be taken in relation to the termination provisions (e.g. should the Agreement terminate if ABC ceases to be a shareholder in the JVC?). Any process of termination for breach will be a serious step and should sensibly involve the other joint venture party(ies).*

THIS AGREEMENT is made on _____ 200__

BETWEEN:

(1) _____, whose [registered] office is at _____ ("**ABC**")

(2) _____, whose [registered] office is at _____ ("**JVC**")

WHEREAS:

(A) ABC is, with XYZ, a party to a Shareholders' Agreement establishing the JVC whose business will be _____.

(B) ABC has developed a process for the manufacture of _____, together with a body of associated technical information, which the parties wish to be used in the business of the JVC.

(C) ABC has agreed to grant to the JVC a licence under its technology, and to provide the JVC with certain related services, on the terms of this Agreement.

NOW IT IS AGREED AS FOLLOWS:

Interpretation

1.1 In this Agreement:

"**Group**" means, in relation to any company, that company and any other company which, at the relevant time, is that company's holding company or subsidiary or the subsidiary of any such holding company, and a "**member**" of a Group has a corresponding meaning;

"**Improvement**" means any development or enhancement of the Technology;

"**Intellectual Property**" means any patent, copyright, registered design, unregistered design right or any other form of analogous protection, any application for such protection and any rights in relation to any confidential information;

"**Know-How**" means any methods, techniques, processes, discoveries or inventions (whether patentable or not), specifications, formulae, designs, plans, drawings, data or other technical information;

"**Man Hour**" means an hour or part of an hour during which an employee of ABC is engaged in the provision of any services for the JVC (including meal-breaks and rest periods);

"**Man Day**" means a day or part of a day during which an employee of ABC is absent from ABC's premises for the purposes of clause 4.3 (including time spent in travelling for those purposes and rest days);

"**Net Sales Value**" means, in relation to any of the Products:

(a) where the Products are sold on arm's length terms, the price charged to the customer less (i) any value added tax or other sales tax and (ii) any packaging, packing, freight, warehousing, carriage and insurance charges, to the extent that any of those items are included in the price, and after deducting any allowances for lost or damaged merchandise or returns but without deducting (or, to the extent that they have been deducted from the price, after adding back) any quantity or other discounts or rebates granted to the customer;

(b) where the Products are not sold on arm's length terms but are otherwise disposed of by the JVC, the price that would have been charged on an arm's length sale to an independent customer, calculated in accordance with sub-paragraph (a);

"**Patents**" means the patents and patent applications listed in Schedule 2 or any patent applications made by ABC in any part of the Territory in respect of any part of the Technology;

"**Plant**" means the machinery and equipment referred to in clause 5.1;

"**Process**" means the process of manufacture of the Products including any modification to that process in accordance with any Improvement;

"**Products**" means [_____ and any other] products of the description and specification given in Schedule 3 [(or otherwise agreed in writing between the parties from time to time)] which are manufactured in accordance with the Technology;

"**Quarter**" means the period of three months beginning on _____ and each successive period of three months during the term of this Agreement, and "**Quarterly**" has a corresponding meaning;

["**Retail Prices Index**" means the index of retail prices which is published by the Office for National Statistics or any other index (or table) substantially replacing that index (or table);]

"**Technology**" means any Know-How relating to the Process which has been made, developed or otherwise acquired by ABC (or any other member of its Group) on or before the date of this Agreement, including but not limited to (i) methods of manufacture of the Products in accordance with the Process; (ii) specifications, formulae and designs of the Products; (iii) methods of quality control for the

Products; [and (iv) designs, plans and drawings for the recommended configuration of the Plant;]

"**Royalty Term**" means a period commencing [on the date of Commissioning under clause 5] and ending _____ Years after that date;

"**Territory**" means _____;

"**Year**" means each period of 365 (or, in case of a leap year, 366) days ending on _____ and any anniversary of that date.

1.2 Any reference in this Agreement to:

(a) a statute or a provision of a statute is a reference to that statute or provision as amended or re-enacted at the relevant time;

(b) "**writing**" includes a reference to any communication effected by email, fax or similar means.

1.3 The headings in this Agreement are for convenience only and shall not affect its interpretation.

Grant of licence

2.1 ABC hereby grants to the JVC, subject to the provisions of this Agreement, a [non-exclusive] licence under its Intellectual Property and the Technology to manufacture, use and sell the Products in the Territory.

[**2.2** ABC shall not itself (except as otherwise provided in this Agreement) (i) manufacture, use, sell or otherwise deal in any of the Products or otherwise exploit the Technology within the Territory or (ii) grant any other person a licence to do so.]

Sub-licensing

3.1 The JVC shall not be entitled to grant sub-licences of its rights under this Agreement to any person [provided that the JVC may sub-contract some (but not all) of the manufacture of the Products if (i) the JVC has obtained the prior written consent of ABC (which shall not be unreasonably withheld) and (ii) the sub-contract contains undertakings by the sub-contractor to comply with provisions substantially similar to those contained in this Agreement with regard to confidentiality, non-assignability and termination.

3.2 The JVC shall at all times ensure the compliance by each sub-contractor with the provisions of the sub-contract and indemnify ABC against any loss, damages, costs, claims or expenses which are awarded against or incurred by ABC, as a result of any breach by any sub-contractor of the sub-licence, as if the breach had been that of the JVC.]

Disclosure of technology and technical assistance

4.1 ABC shall, as soon as practicable after the date of this Agreement, disclose to the JVC the Technology in sufficient detail to enable the JVC to manufacture the Products on a commercial basis. [Except as agreed between the parties, nothing in this Agreement shall be construed as requiring ABC specially to prepare any of the Technology or to engage in any special technical studies or research or development on the JVC's behalf.]

4.2 From time to time during the Royalty Term ABC shall, at the reasonable request of the JVC, consult with the JVC in relation to the use of the Technology in the manufacture of the Products, by telephone or in writing or by such other means as, in its reasonable opinion, ABC considers is appropriate for the particular circumstances.

4.3 During the period of [12] months from the date of this Agreement:

(a) the JVC shall be entitled to send to ABC's premises where the Products are manufactured suitably qualified employees of the JVC for training in the manufacture of the Products and the use of the Technology;

(b) ABC shall at the request of the JVC make available to the JVC the services of suitably qualified employees of ABC to visit the JVC's premises and to provide technical assistance in relation to the Commissioning of the Plant, the manufacture of the Products and the use of the Technology.

4.4 The numbers of the JVC's employees who are to visit ABC's premises and the numbers of ABC's employees who are to visit the JVC's premises pursuant to clause 4.3, and the times and duration of any such visits, shall be as may be agreed in advance between ABC and the JVC. ABC shall not be obliged to provide the services of its employees under clause 4.3 for periods exceeding _____ Man Days in any Quarter.

4.5 The JVC shall:

(a) give ABC all necessary assistance to obtain any visas, work permits, residence permits or other approvals which are required by any of the employees of ABC who are to be made available by ABC pursuant to clause 4.3 for entering into and working in any part of the Territory;

(b) bear the entire cost of all salaries, fringe benefits, travelling (including air travel), accommodation and other expenses of any employees of the JVC who are sent to ABC's premises pursuant to clause 4.3;

(c) reimburse ABC for any expenses incurred by ABC in respect of any employees of the JVC who are sent to ABC's premises pursuant to clause 4.3;

(d) pay ABC a fee at the rate of:

(i) _____ per Man Hour for any time spent by ABC's employees in providing consultation pursuant to clause 4.2 or technical assistance pursuant to clause 4.3;

(ii) _____ per Man Day for each visit made by ABC's employees for the purposes of providing technical assistance pursuant to clause 4.3.

4.6 Any fees or other sums payable pursuant to clause 4.5 shall be paid by the JVC within _____ days after receipt of an invoice.

4.7 Any employees of either ABC or the JVC who are sent to visit the premises of the other party under this Agreement shall remain employed by the party sending them. The employer party shall (i) ensure that each of its employees complies with all security, health and safety and other regulations in force at those premises and (ii) indemnify the other party against any damage to the property of the other party or any personal injury to any individual which is caused by the negligence of any such employee at the other party's premises.

4.8 Each of ABC and the JVC shall nominate a senior representative as [project leader] with responsibility for ensuring that the practical arrangements for disclosure, consultation and technical assistance contemplated by this clause 4 are established and carried out constructively and efficiently.

Installation and commissioning of the Plant

5.1 The JVC shall, in accordance with the Technology disclosed by ABC and a timetable to be agreed between the JVC and ABC, and at the JVC's own cost:

(a) purchase the machinery and equipment required for the installation of a _____ plant at the JVC's premises in the Territory for the manufacture of the Products;

(b) ensure that all necessary site preparation and modification is carried out for the purposes of the installation and operation of the Plant;

(c) install the Plant and procure its Commissioning.

5.2 For this purpose, "**Commissioning**" of the Plant for the manufacture of the Products shall be regarded as having been achieved when, in a trial on the Plant for a continuous period of [24] hours (commencing at a time after the Plant has started up and established stable operation), the Products are produced to commercially acceptable standards according to the relevant specification contained in Schedule [3], at an average rate of not less than _____ per hour.

Improvements

6.1 If at any time during the Royalty Term ABC makes or otherwise acquires any Improvement which ABC intends to incorporate in its own manufacture of the Products, it shall disclose the Improvement to the JVC unless (i) ABC is precluded from doing so by law or any obligation owed to a third party or (ii) the disclosure of the Improvement or its use by the JVC would (in the reasonable opinion of ABC) prejudice ABC's ability to obtain patent or other Intellectual Property protection in respect of the Improvement. The JVC shall be entitled to the same rights in respect of any Improvement disclosed pursuant to this clause, and any related Intellectual Property held or obtained by ABC, as the JVC has in respect of the Technology. Any such Improvement shall for the purposes of this Agreement be deemed to be included in the definition of the Technology.

6.2 If at any time during the Royalty Term the JVC makes or otherwise acquires any Improvement, the JVC shall disclose the Improvement to ABC, except to the extent that (i) the JVC is precluded from doing so by law or any obligation owed to a third party or (ii) the disclosure of the Improvement or its use by ABC would (in the reasonable opinion of the JVC) prejudice the JVC's ability to obtain patent or other Intellectual Property protection in respect of the application or Improvement. Subject to that exception, the disclosure of any such Improvement shall be made as soon as is reasonably practicable.

6.3 In relation to any Improvement referred to in clause 6.2:

(a) ABC shall be entitled to manufacture, use, sell or otherwise deal in any products manufactured through its use, and otherwise to use the Improvement by way of a non-exclusive, royalty-free licence under any Intellectual Property held or obtained by the JVC in relation to the Improvement, exercisable (to the extent that the JVC is entitled to grant such a licence) in any country in the world;

(b) subject to sub-paragraph (a), any such Improvement shall belong to the JVC which shall be entitled to use it for the purposes of the manufacture, use and sale of or any other dealings in the Products or for any other purpose.

Methods of manufacture and sale

7.1 The JVC shall:

(a) ensure that all Products manufactured by the JVC comply with the methods of manufacture, specifications, formulae, designs, standards of quality and quality control procedures laid down by ABC and forming part of the Technology and with all applicable standards and legal requirements;

(b) [ensure that all packaging and labelling for the Products contain and, wherever practicable, the Products themselves are marked with an indication (including, where applicable, the number) of any patent, registered design or other Intellectual Property relating to them and a notice to the effect that they are manufactured by the JVC under licence from ABC;]

(c) permit any duly authorised representative of ABC, at any time during normal working hours and on reasonable notice, to enter any premises of the JVC or any third party where any of the Products or any labelling or packaging for them are manufactured or stored by the JVC, in order to inspect them and take samples;

(d) provide ABC with a Quarterly report as to the manufacture and sale of and any other dealings in the Products, in such form as ABC may reasonably require.

.2 The JVC shall use reasonable efforts at all times to promote and expand the sale of the Products in the Territory in accordance with business plans from time to time approved by the JVC Board under the Shareholders' Agreement.

7.3 Except as otherwise provided in this Agreement, the JVC shall promote and market the Products in the Territory in such manner as the JVC may think fit (and in particular the JVC shall be entitled to use such trade marks in respect of the Products and to sell the Products to its customers at such prices as it may determine).

Financial terms

8.1 In consideration of the rights granted under this Agreement, the JVC shall pay to ABC:

(a) [the sum of £_____ on the date of this Agreement;]

(b) the sum of £_____ on the date of Commissioning;

(c) royalties in respect of all Products manufactured by the JVC (or any other member of its Group) which are sold or otherwise disposed of by the JVC (or any other member of its Group) at any time during the Royalty Term at the rate of _____ per cent of the Net Sales Value of those Products;

(d) royalties at the rate of _____ per cent of all royalties or other sums payable at any time during the Royalty Term by any third party in consideration of the grant to it of a sub-licence under all or any part of the JVC's rights under this Agreement;

[provided that no royalties shall be payable under sub-paragraph (c) in respect of any sales of the JVC made within [12] months after Commissioning.]

8.2 Within 30 days after each [Quarter], the JVC shall send to ABC a written statement showing (i) the quantity of the Products sold or otherwise disposed of on a commercial basis by the JVC (or any other member of its Group) otherwise than to another member of the JVC's Group during that [Quarter]; (ii) the Net Sales

Value in respect of that quantity of Products; (iii) the amount of the royalties payable under clause 8.1 in respect of that quantity. Payment of royalties or other sums due to ABC shall be paid by the JVC within [60] days after each [Quarter].

8.3 All royalties or other sums payable under this Agreement shall be paid in pounds sterling. Where any royalties are calculated in a currency other than sterling, they shall be converted into sterling by reference to the average of the relevant buying and selling rates of _____ Bank plc ruling in London on the last day of the [Quarter] to which they relate.

8.4 All royalties or other sums payable under this Agreement are exclusive of value added tax or other applicable taxes or duties, for which the JVC shall be additionally liable, and shall be paid in cleared funds to such bank account (or in such other manner as ABC may specify from time to time) without any set off, deduction or withholding except any tax which the JVC is required by law to deduct or withhold.

8.5 If the JVC fails to pay in full any of the royalties or other sums payable under this Agreement on the date or within the period specified for payment, the outstanding amount due shall bear interest, both before and after any judgment, at the rate of _____ per cent per annum [above the base rate of _____ Bank plc from time to time] from that date or the last day of that period until that amount is paid in full to ABC.

Accounts

9.1 The JVC shall:

(a) keep true and accurate accounts and records in sufficient detail to enable the amount of all royalties or other sums payable under this Agreement to be determined;

(b) at the reasonable request of ABC from time to time, allow ABC or its agents to inspect those records and books of account and, to the extent that they relate to the calculation of those royalties and other sums, to take copies of them;

(c) at its own expense, obtain and submit to ABC, within _____ days after the end of each Year in respect of which royalties are payable under this Agreement, a certificate by the JVC's auditors that the statement submitted to ABC pursuant to clause 8.2 in respect of [each Quarter in] that Year is true and accurate.

9.2 If, following any inspection pursuant to clause 9.1, ABC's auditors certify to ABC and the JVC that the amount of the royalties paid in respect of any [Quarter] pursuant to clause 8.1 falls short of the amount of the royalties which were properly payable in respect of that [Quarter], the JVC shall within [7] days of the date of the certificate pay the shortfall to ABC, together with the reasonable costs and expenses of ABC in making the inspection.

9.3 The provisions of this clause 9 shall remain in full force and effect, notwithstanding the termination of this Agreement for any reason, until the settlement of all outstanding claims of ABC under this Agreement.

Intellectual property protection and proceedings

10.1 ABC shall have full discretion to make any applications for patent or other forms of Intellectual Property protection in respect of the Technology. Any

Intellectual Property obtained pursuant to any such application shall be the absolute property of ABC.

10.2 ABC shall make all necessary filings and pay all requisite renewal fees to maintain the Patents in the Territory. ABC shall be entitled to give written notice to the JVC at any time that it does not wish to be responsible for any further renewal cost in respect of one or more of the Patents in any part of the Territory. The JVC may then give notice to ABC that it wishes to maintain the Patents. If the JVC gives such a notice, it shall at its own discretion be entitled to maintain the Patent in question itself [(in which event the JVC shall cease to be liable to pay any further royalties in respect of that part of the Territory)] or to allow the Patent in question to lapse.

10.3 The parties shall, at the request of either of them (and at the expense of the JVC but for no further consideration), enter into such formal licences relating to any Intellectual Property in respect of the Technology as may be reasonably necessary in accordance with the relevant law and practice in each part of the Territory for the protection of any such Intellectual Property.

10.4 The JVC shall at its own expense take all such steps as ABC may reasonably require to assist ABC in maintaining the enforceability of any Intellectual Property in respect of the Technology.

10.5 Each party shall notify the other as soon as practicable if it becomes aware of (i) any actual, threatened or suspected infringement of any Intellectual Property in respect of the Technology or (ii) any proceedings in which the validity of any such Intellectual Property is challenged or it is alleged that the use of the Technology infringes the Intellectual Property of any third party. As soon as practicable after any such notification, the parties shall meet to decide the appropriate course of action. Any decision shall (if the parties are not agreed) be taken finally by ABC. ABC shall have full regard to the interests of the JVC's business in making any decision in respect of such Intellectual Property.

[**10.6** The JVC shall notify ABC as soon as practicable if it becomes aware of any claim against the JVC by any third party that the exercise by the JVC of any rights granted under this Agreement by ABC infringes any Intellectual Property or other rights of any other person. ABC shall (subject to clause 10.7) indemnify the JVC against any loss, damages, costs or expenses which are awarded against or incurred by the JVC as a result of the claim, provided that:

(a) ABC shall be given control of the conduct of any proceedings in connection with the claim and exclusively entitled to appoint and instruct legal counsel in connection with any such proceedings;

(b) the JVC shall at its own cost give ABC all reasonable assistance for the purpose of any such proceedings;

(c) except pursuant to a final award, the JVC shall not pay or accept any such claim, or settle any such proceedings, without the consent of ABC (which shall not be unreasonably withheld);

(d) the JVC shall do nothing which might vitiate any policy of insurance which the JVC may have in relation to any such claim (and this indemnity shall not apply to the extent that the JVC recovers any sums under any such policy);

(e) ABC shall be entitled to any damages and costs which are awarded against, or which with the consent of the JVC (which shall not be unreasonably withheld) are agreed to be paid by, any other party in respect of any such claim;

(f) ABC shall be entitled to require the JVC to take such steps as ABC may reasonably require to mitigate or reduce any loss of the JVC.]

or

[**10.6** ABC shall have no liability to the JVC in respect of any claim for infringement of any Intellectual Property or other rights of any person which is based on the manufacture, use or sale of or any other dealing in any of the Products by the JVC. Nothing in this Agreement shall constitute any warranty or representation that the Products or the use of the Technology does not fall within the scope of any third party Intellectual Property rights (including patents).]

10.7 If either party becomes aware of any activities carried on by any third party which could constitute unauthorised disclosure or misuse of any of ABC's Intellectual Property or the Technology, it shall promptly notify the other and the JVC shall join ABC in taking all steps as may be reasonably necessary for the protection of ABC's rights in respect of the Technology. The costs incurred in taking such steps, and any profits or damages which may be obtained, shall (in the absence of agreement to the contrary) be for the account of ABC.

Warranties and indemnities

[**11.1** ABC warrants to the JVC that:

(a) it has the authority to enter into this Agreement and to grant the rights granted under this Agreement;

(b) it has not granted to any third party any rights which are inconsistent with the rights granted under this Agreement;

(c) it is not aware of any claim that any Intellectual Property in respect of the Technology is invalid or unenforceable or (in the case of an application) will not proceed to grant;

(d) it is not aware of any third party rights which would prevent the exercise by the JVC of any of the rights granted under this Agreement;

(e) the Technology to be disclosed to the JVC pursuant to this Agreement will in all material respects be that used at the date of this Agreement in ABC's own manufacturing premises for the manufacture of the Products;

(f) any employees of ABC through whom any technical assistance is to be provided for the JVC pursuant to this Agreement shall be competent and appropriately trained.]

11.2 Each party acknowledges that, in entering into this Agreement, it does not do so in reliance on any representation, warranty or other provision except as expressly provided in this Agreement, and any conditions, warranties or other terms implied by statute or common law are excluded from this Agreement to the fullest extent permitted by law.

11.3 Without limiting the scope of clause 10.6, ABC does not give any warranty, representation or undertaking (i) as to the efficacy or usefulness of the Technology; (ii) as to the volumes or quality of the Products which may be manufactured through the use of the Technology; (iii) that any Intellectual Property in respect of the Technology is or will be valid or subsisting or (in the case of an application) will proceed to grant; [or (iv) that the exercise of any of the rights granted hereunder will not infringe the Intellectual Property or other rights of any other person].

11.4 Without prejudice to any other limitation or exclusion of liability under this Agreement:

(a) in no event shall ABC be liable to the JVC for loss of profits or other indirect or consequential loss of any kind whether arising from negligence, breach of contract or otherwise;

(b) [the total amount of any claims for which ABC would otherwise be liable under this Agreement shall not exceed in any event [the total amounts paid by the JVC under clause 8 up to the date of the claim].]

11.5 The JVC shall indemnify ABC against any loss, damages, costs or expenses which are awarded against or incurred by ABC as a result of any product liability claim by any person relating to Products supplied or put into use by the JVC (or any member of its Group).

Confidentiality

12.1 The JVC shall not disclose to any other person, or use for any purpose except as contemplated by this Agreement, any of the Know-How or any other information which has been disclosed to the JVC under or pursuant to this Agreement, and the JVC shall use all reasonable efforts to keep all such Know-How or other information confidential (whether it is marked as such or not), except as provided by clause 12.2.

12.2 Any Know-How or other information which is disclosed to the JVC under or pursuant to this Agreement may be:

(a) disclosed by the JVC to any governmental or other authority or regulatory body or any other person to the extent required by law; or

(b) disclosed by the JVC to any customer, supplier or permitted sub-licensee of the JVC, or any person carrying out research or development on its behalf, to the extent necessary for the manufacture and sale of the Products (subject in each case to the JVC first obtaining a written undertaking from the person in question, as nearly as practicable in the terms of this clause 12, to keep the Technology or other information confidential and to use the same only for the purposes for which the disclosure is made);

(c) used or disclosed by the JVC for any purpose to the extent that it is or becomes (through no fault of the JVC) public knowledge.

12.3 Neither party shall make any press or other public announcement concerning the subject matter of this Agreement without first obtaining the prior consent of the other party to the text of that announcement.

Force majeure

13. If either party is affected by Force Majeure, it shall promptly notify the other party of its nature and extent. Neither party shall be deemed to be in breach of this Agreement by reason of any delay in the performance, or the non-performance, of any of its obligations under this Agreement to the extent that the delay or non-performance is due to Force Majeure. For this purpose, "**Force Majeure**" means any circumstances beyond the reasonable control of either party (including any strike, lock-out or other form of industrial action).

Duration and termination

14.1 This Agreement shall, unless terminated under clause 14.2 or by agreement between the parties, continue in force indefinitely.

14.2 Either party may terminate this Agreement with immediate effect by giving written notice to the other if:

(a) the other party commits a material breach of this Agreement and fails to remedy it within 45 days after being given a written notice containing reasonable particulars of the breach and requiring it to be remedied (and such notice specifies that, if the breach is not remedied, that party intends to exercise its rights under this clause); or

(b) if the other party goes into liquidation (whether compulsory or voluntary) except for the purposes of a bona fide reconstruction with the consent of the other party (such consent not to be unreasonably withheld) or if a petition is presented or an order is made for the appointment of an administrator, receiver, manager or similar officer over any substantial part of its assets or undertaking (and such petition or order is not discharged within 30 days).

14.3 The rights given by this clause 14 to terminate this Agreement for any breach shall not prejudice any other right or remedy of either party in respect of the breach concerned or any other breach prior to termination.

14.4 If ABC ceases to be a shareholder in the JVC at any time (whether as a result of a sale of its interest or otherwise):

(a) the parties shall in good faith discuss whether any changes to this Agreement are appropriate to reflect the new circumstances;

(b) (subject to any different arrangements agreed pursuant to (a)) the terms of this Agreement shall continue [except that the rate of royalties payable under clause 8.1(c) shall thereafter become _____ per cent of the relevant Net Sales Value and the rate payable under clause 8.1(d) shall thereafter be _____ per cent].

Effects of termination

15.1 Upon the termination of this Agreement:

[(a) the JVC shall be entitled, for a period not exceeding _____ months, to [(i) manufacture any of the Products to the extent necessary to satisfy orders accepted before termination and (ii)] sell, use or otherwise dispose of (subject to payment of royalties under clause 8.1) any unsold or unused stocks of the Products;]

(b) (subject to sub-paragraph (a) above) the JVC shall cease to use or otherwise exploit any of the Technology (except to the extent that the relevant Know-How or other information ceases or has ceased to be confidential through no fault of the JVC);

(c) the JVC shall return to ABC any documents or materials in its possession or control which contain or record any part of the Technology to the extent that it remains confidential;

(d) the JVC shall consent to the cancellation of any licence granted to it, or of any registration of it in any register, in relation to any of the Patents or other Intellectual Property in respect of the Technology;

(e) ABC's rights under clause 6.2 in respect of any Improvement made, devised or otherwise acquired by the JVC shall continue in force without limit of time.

15.2 The provisions of [clauses 10.6 (Indemnity) and] 12 (Confidentiality) shall continue in force in accordance with their terms, notwithstanding termination of this Agreement for any reason.

General

16.1 This Agreement is personal to the parties and neither party may assign or (except as provided in this Agreement) sub-license any of its rights, or sub-contract or otherwise delegate any of its obligations under this Agreement, except with the prior written consent of the other party.

16.2 Nothing in this Agreement shall create, or be deemed to create, a partnership, or the relationship of principal and agent, between the parties.

16.3 This Agreement may not be modified except by an instrument in writing signed by the duly authorised representatives of the parties.

16.4 No failure or delay by either party in exercising any of its rights under this Agreement shall be deemed to be a waiver of that right, and no waiver by either party of a breach of any provision of this Agreement shall be deemed to be a waiver of any subsequent breach of the same or any other provision.

16.5 If any provision of this Agreement is held by any court or other competent authority to be invalid or unenforceable, the other provisions of this Agreement shall continue to be valid.

16.6 Except as otherwise provided in this Agreement, the parties shall bear their own costs of relating to the preparation, execution and implementation of this Agreement.

Notices

17.1 Any notice or other information required or authorised by this Agreement to be given by either party to the other shall be given by (i) delivering it by hand or (ii) sending it by pre-paid registered [air-mail] post or (iii) sending it by fax or similar means of communication to the other party at the address given in clause 17.2.

17.2 The details for notices are:

ABC:

JVC:

copy to

[**XYZ** *(other joint venture party)*]

Governing law

18. This Agreement shall be governed by the laws of England.

Disputes and arbitration

19.1 If a dispute shall arise in relation to this Agreement while ABC is a shareholder in the JVC, the parties shall use all reasonable efforts to resolve the dispute on an amicable basis in the context of the overall joint venture arrangements between ABC, XYZ *(other joint venture party)* and the JVC. The dispute resolution provisions in clause _____ of the Shareholders' Agreement shall apply. No notice of termination for a material breach under clause 14.2 of this Agreement shall be given unless prior notice of the problem has been given in writing to the other party and also to XYZ.

19.2 Without prejudice to clause 19.1, if one party serves formal written notice that a material dispute has arisen and the parties are unable to resolve the dispute within 30 days of such notice, then the dispute shall be referred to the respective Chairmen or Chief Executives of ABC and the JVC with a view to the dispute being resolved as early as possible.

19.3 If any dispute is unresolved within a period of 30 days after referral to the Chairmen/Chief Executives under clause 19.2, such dispute may be referred by either party for final determination by arbitration under the Rules of the [LCIA] by [three] arbitrators appointed in accordance with those Rules. The arbitration shall be held in London and the language of the proceedings shall be English.

AS WITNESS this Agreement has been executed by duly authorised representatives of the parties.

SCHEDULE 1

PART A: THE PROCESS

PART B: THE KNOW-HOW

SCHEDULE 2

Part A: Patents

| Title | Country | Number | Date |

Part B: Patent Applications

| Title | Country | Number | Date |

SCHEDULE 3

The Products

SCHEDULE 4

Royalties

| **(1)** | **(2)** |
| Quantity | per cent |

Signed   Signed

....
for and on behalf of **ABC**   for and on behalf of **JVC**

Precedent 20

Trade Mark Licence Agreement

> *This Licence Agreement is in fairly standard form for a licensor. Clause 4.1 contemplates that the Marks will have been used in a business which has been contributed to the JVC. In the situation of a JVC, the practicalities and the importance of the use of the Marks to the JVC will usually mean that termination (e.g. for breach) is a serious event for the joint venture relationship. This Agreement provides for a termination procedure "tailored" to the venture.*

THIS AGREEMENT is made on _____ 200__

BETWEEN:

(1)_____ whose registered office is at _____ (the "**Licensor**")

(2)_____ whose registered office is at _____ (the "**JVC**")

WHEREAS:

(A) The Licensor is the owner of the trade mark(s) as more particularly described in the Schedule to this Agreement (such mark(s) including any corresponding registration from time to time in any part of the world being the "**Marks**").

(B) The Licensor has agreed to grant to the JVC certain rights in respect of the Marks on the terms and conditions of this Agreement.

IT IS AGREED AS FOLLOWS:

Interpretation

1.1 In this Agreement, the following terms shall (unless the context requires otherwise) have the following meanings:

"**Business**" means the business of the JVC and of any Subsidiary of the JVC;

"**Business Day**" means a day (other than a Saturday) on which banks generally are open in [London] for a full range of business;

"**Joint Venture Agreement**" means the Agreement dated _____ relating to the establishment of the JVC;

"**JVC Marks**" means the trade marks and/or logo(s) owned or developed independently by the JVC from time to time;

"**Subsidiary**" means, in relation to a company (the "**holding company**"), any other company in which the holding company for the time being directly or indirectly holds or controls either (i) a majority of the voting rights exercisable at general meetings of the members of that company on all, or substantially all, matters or (ii) the right to appoint or remove directors having a majority of the voting rights exercisable at meetings of the board of directors of that company on all, or substantially all, matters; and any company which is a Subsidiary of another company shall also be a Subsidiary of any further company of which that other is a Subsidiary.

1.2 For the purposes of this Agreement:

(a) statutory provisions shall be construed as references to those provisions as respectively amended or re-enacted from time to time; and

(b) headings are inserted for convenience only and shall not affect the construction of this Agreement or its Schedules.

Grant of licence

2.1 The Licensor hereby grants to the JVC during the term of this Agreement a non-exclusive, royalty free, world-wide right to use the Marks on or in relation to the goods and services of the Business and to use the Mark "_____" as part of its corporate or trade name ("Corporate Name"), subject to the terms of this Agreement. This licence is personal to the JVC and may not be assigned.

2.2 The JVC shall, at the Licensor's request, execute and at its own expense take all steps reasonably necessary for the registration or recordal with any appropriate authority in any jurisdiction of the licence(s) granted under this Agreement.

Conditions of use

3. The JVC hereby undertakes that:

(a) it will use the Marks and its Corporate Name (in so far as this includes any of the Marks) only on or in relation to goods and services which conform to such quality standards as the Licensor may from time to time reasonably require;

(b) it will use the Marks (including the presentation of the Marks on advertisements and other promotional material and the like) as respects shaping, printing style, colour, quality of materials and otherwise in such form and manner as may from time to time be approved or directed by the Licensor under clause 4;

(c) it will not use or seek to register any other trade or service mark in any jurisdiction which is similar to or substantially similar to or so nearly resembles any of the Marks as to be likely to cause deception or confusion;

(d) it will not use any of the Marks in a manner which is likely to cause material harm to the goodwill attached to the Marks; and

(e) it will, at the Licensor's request and cost, assist with any application for registration of the Marks in any country of the world and do all acts and execute all documents necessary to enable registration of the Marks and (if application is in the name of the JVC) the JVC shall assign forthwith any such registration to the Licensor.

Approved Standards and Directions

4.1 The standards, specifications and instructions required in relation to the goods and services on or in relation to which the Marks are used shall, so as to achieve the level of quality referred to in clause 3, be the level of quality generally achieved by the Licensor and/or its Subsidiaries in the course of its business in relation to those (or substantially similar) goods or services in the year preceding the date of this Agreement. These shall be deemed to be the standards, specifications and instructions approved by the Licensor for the purposes of clause 3 (the "**Approved Standards**").

4.2 The JVC shall accept the Licensor's reasonable directions ("Directions") concerning the form and manner in which the Marks and its Corporate Name (in so far as it includes the Marks) is to be used in order to comply with the other requirements of clause 3 *provided always* that the JVC shall have a period of 30 days (unless such period is extended in writing by agreement of the parties) following receipt of any Directions to take such steps as may be required to implement those Directions.

Approvals, inspection and quality control

5.1 The Licensor and its representatives or agents shall have the right, at all reasonable times and in all reasonable circumstances, to inspect the goods and services on or in relation to which any of the Marks is used (as well as the methods of manufacturing such goods or providing such services) on the premises of their manufacture or provision and elsewhere as the Licensor considers reasonably necessary as part of appropriate quality control and to ensure that the Directions are complied with.

5.2 If the goods and services on or in relation to which any of the Marks is used do not comply with the Approved Standards or if the Directions given by the Licensor to the JVC are not complied with, the Licensor may give written notice to the JVC giving full details of any alleged shortcomings and specifying its requirements. A copy of the notice shall also be sent to the Chairman of [*name of other shareholder in JVC*] whose representative shall also be entitled to attend the meeting specified in clause 5.3.

5.3 If the Licensor sends such a notice, then a meeting shall take place between the parties to discuss alleged shortcomings and the Licensor's requirements within 30 days of service of the notice, unless such period is extended as agreed in writing by the parties. If the JVC does not comply with the Licensor's requirements as discussed at the meeting within 30 days of such meeting being held, the Licensor may give the JVC notice (a "**Final Notice**") that the goods or services do not comply with its requirements. No such Final Notice shall be given unless the Licensor has referred the matter to the Chairman of [*name of other shareholder in JVC*] and the notice states that the Chairman or Chief Executive of [the Licensor] has agreed to the despatch of the notice.

Acknowledgement

6.1 The JVC acknowledges and agrees that:

(a) all intellectual property and other rights in the Marks are the exclusive property of the Licensor;

(b) it shall not acquire nor claim any right, title or interest in or to any of the Marks or the goodwill attaching to them by virtue of this Agreement or its use of the Marks, other than the rights specifically granted to it under clause 2.1;

(c) all goodwill arising from use of the Marks by the JVC before, during or after the term shall accrue and belong to the Licensor, and the JVC shall, at the

Licensor's request and cost, promptly execute all documents required by the Licensor to confirm this; and

(d) all use of the Marks by the JVC shall be deemed to be use by the Licensor.

Infringements

7.1 The JVC shall promptly give written notice to the Licensor of any of the following matters which may come to its knowledge at any time during the term of this Agreement:

(a) any infringement or suspected or threatened infringement by any third party of any of the Marks;

(b) any allegation or complaint made by any third party that the use by the JVC of any of the Mark(s) in accordance with this Agreement may be liable to cause deception or confusion to the public;

(c) any other form of attack, charge or claim to which any of the Marks may be subject.

The JVC shall not make any admission in respect of such matters other than to the Licensor and the JVC shall in every case furnish the Licensor with all information in its possession relating to such matters which may be reasonably required by the Licensor.

7.2 The Licensor shall have the right to assume the conduct of all actions and proceedings (whether in its own name or that of the JVC) relating to the Marks and shall bear the costs and expenses of any such actions and proceedings. Any costs or damages recovered in connection with any such actions or proceedings shall be for the account of the Licensor.

7.3 The JVC shall not be entitled to bring any action for infringement under section 28(3) of the Trade Marks Act 1938 and the Licensor shall not be obliged to bring or extend any proceedings relating to the Marks if it decides in its sole discretion not to do so.

7.4 The parties shall at all times during the term of this Agreement have due regard to the legitimate commercial and legal interests of each other and shall consult with each other where reasonably practicable in deciding any matters concerning any such actions, proceedings or settlement negotiations, including whether or not to bring, defend or assume the conduct of any such actions, proceedings or settlement negotiations.

Indemnity

8. The JVC undertakes and agrees that it will indemnify and hold the Licensor harmless from and against all costs and expenses (including legal costs, fees and expenses) actions, proceedings, claims, demands and damages arising from any third party claim which is attributable to an act or omission of the JVC which is a breach of this Agreement by the JVC or the JVC's use of any of the Marks on defective products.

Term and termination

9.1 This Agreement shall commence at the date hereof and shall, subject to the provisions of this clause 9, continue in force indefinitely.

9.2 The Licensor shall be entitled to terminate this Agreement upon written notice if the JVC:

(a) fails to comply with the Licensor's Directions and the Licensor serves a Final Notice under clause 5.3; or

(b) is in material breach of any other provisions of this Agreement and has failed to remedy that breach within 30 days of a notice specifying the breach and requiring it to be remedied

and such non-compliance or breach continues for a further period of 30 days after the matter has been referred by the Licensor to the Chairman of [*name of other shareholder of JVC*].

9.3 The Licensor shall be entitled to terminate this Agreement with immediate effect by notice if the Licensor ceases to hold not less than [50%] of the issued ordinary share capital of the JVC.

9.4 The termination of this Agreement shall not (i) relieve the JVC from any liability or obligation in respect of any matters, undertakings or conditions which have not been done, observed or performed by the JVC prior to such termination or (ii) affect the continuing obligations of the JVC under clause 8 (*Infringements*) and clause 10 (*Effects of termination*) and the corresponding rights of the Licensor to enforce the same following termination of this Agreement.

Effects of termination

10.1 Upon termination of this Agreement for any reason, the rights and licence(s) granted hereunder to the JVC shall cease and the JVC shall forthwith discontinue any and all use of the Marks (except that, with the Licensor's prior written consent which shall not be unreasonably withheld, the JVC may dispose of stocks of goods, literature or other material bearing or otherwise utilising the Marks (whether as a trade mark or as a part of its Corporate Name) existing at the date of termination, for a period of [60 days] from such termination, provided that the JVC shall comply with the terms and conditions of this Agreement during such period).

10.2 Upon termination, or expiration of the period referred to in clause 10.1, whichever is the later, the Licensor may direct that the JVC delete or remove the Marks from or (where such deletion or removal is not reasonably practicable) destroy or, if the Licensor shall so elect, deliver to the Licensor or any other company, firm or person designated by the Licensor, all goods and all price lists, marketing literature and the like and all other materials or documents in the possession or under the control of the JVC to which any of the Marks is then affixed.

10.3 Within [60 days] of termination, the JVC shall change its name to a Corporate Name that does not include the name "_____" or any similar name which is likely to cause deception or confusion.

10.4 Upon termination, the JVC (i) shall do all things reasonably necessary on its part to enable the Licensor to cancel any registration, recordal or published indication of any licence granted under this Agreement and (ii) agrees that the Licensor shall have the right to request cancellations of any registration, recordal or published indication of any such licence.

10.5 The JVC hereby appoints and authorises the Licensor and the Licensor's appointed representatives or agents to take all the necessary steps (including filing documents in the name of the JVC) to cancel any registration, recordal or published indication of such licence granted hereunder. The JVC agrees that the Licensor may do so without the necessity of the JVC appearing before any appropriate authority to give its consent to such cancellation.

Notices

11.1 Any notice under this Agreement shall either be delivered by hand or sent by facsimile transmission [or pre-paid delivery post] as follows:

(a) **Licensor**:

    Address:

    Fax No:

    Addressed for the personal attention of:

(b) **JVC**:	with a copy to:
Address:	Address:
Fax No:	Fax No:
Addressed for the personal attention of:	Addressed for the personal attention of:

The Licensor or the JVC may change the address, fax number or the name of the person for whose attention notices are to be addressed by serving a notice on the other in accordance with this clause 11.

11.2 All notices given in accordance with clause 11.1 shall be deemed to have been served as follows: (i) if delivered by hand, at the time of delivery; and (ii) if communicated by fax, at the time of transmission, PROVIDED THAT where delivery by hand or transmission by fax occurs after 6 pm on a Business Day or on a day which is not a Business Day, service shall be deemed to occur at 9 am on the next following Business Day. References to time in this clause are to local time in the country of the addressee.

Non-assignability

12. The rights and obligations of the JVC under this Agreement are personal to the JVC and shall not be assigned, mortgaged, delegated or sub-licensed or otherwise disposed of without the prior written consent of the Licensor.

Law

13. This Agreement shall be governed by and construed in accordance with English law.

AS WITNESS this Agreement has been signed by the duly authorised representatives of the Parties.

SCHEDULE

TRADE MARKS

1. REGISTERED TRADE MARKS

Mark	No	Class	Date of Regn.	Renewal Date	Goods/Services

2. APPLICATIONS

Mark   No.   Class   Date of Application   Goods/Services

3. UNREGISTERED TRADE MARKS

Mark

EXECUTED as a **DEED** by: }
EXECUTED as a **DEED** by: }

Precedent 21

Deadlock Resolution Clauses

1. RUSSIAN ROULETTE

This clause provides the framework for a "Russian roulette" type of deadlock resolution. See generally the discussion in chapter 10. The definition of a deadlock or other trigger point will depend on the circumstances. This could for instance be the failure to agree on a "reserved matter"—perhaps after at least two board/shareholder meetings; or a failure to agree a budget for the JVC within a stated period; or in some ventures it may be agreed that the deadlock resolution procedure can be triggered at any time by notice. An important issue is whether the recipient should have the right (see sub-clause 4(c) below) to call for liquidation of the JVC or whether it should be solely a buy/sell option. These types of clauses should be used with extreme care. This version includes provision for a "warning notice" and fairly lengthy time periods for commercial settlement.

1. For the purpose of this clause, "**Deadlock**" shall be deemed to occur if:

(a) [any of the Reserved Matters] [or any other matter relating to the JVC] has been raised at and/or considered by a board or general meeting of the JVC and no resolution has been passed on at least two successive occasions by such meeting as a result of an equality of votes cast for and against any resolution proposed in respect of that matter; or

(b) a quorum is not present at two successive duly convened board or general meetings by reason of the absence from that meeting of the same shareholder or, in the case of a board meeting, a person nominated as a director by that same shareholder; [or]

[(c) a party gives notice that, by reason of a fundamental difference relating to the strategy for the JVC or other circumstances seriously affecting the relationship of the parties as shareholders in the JVC, it is the wish of that party to terminate the joint venture relationship.]

2. In the event of a Deadlock, the matter shall be referred to the respective [chairmen/chief executives] of the parties pursuant to clause _____. If the Deadlock cannot be resolved within [30] days after such reference, either party may serve notice (a "**Warning Notice**") that it intends to implement the deadlock procedure contemplated by this clause.

3. If the Deadlock cannot be resolved within a further period of [30] days after service of a Warning Notice, either party may within a period of [30] days thereafter serve notice in writing on the other party (a "**Deadlock Option Notice**") specifying a single price at which the party giving notice (the "**Terminating Party**") offers either:

(a) to sell to the other party all (but not some only) of the Shares collectively held by the Terminating Party and/or members of its Group; or

(b) to purchase all (but not some only) of the Shares collectively held by the other party and/or members of its Group.

A Deadlock Option Notice shall be irrevocable.

4. The other party shall, within a period of [30] days after receipt of a Deadlock Option Notice, at its sole option elect either:

(a) to purchase, or to procure the purchase of, all of the Shares collectively held by the Terminating Party and/or members of its Group at the price stated in the Deadlock Option Notice; or

(b) to require the Terminating Party to purchase, or to procure the purchase of, all of the Shares collectively held by that other party and/or members of its Group at the price stated in the Deadlock Option Notice; [or]

[(c) to concur in taking all steps required promptly to place the JVC into liquidation.]

If no election is made in writing by that other party within the period of [30] days after receipt of a Deadlock Option Notice, then it shall be deemed to have elected for option [(a)] [(c) and the parties shall thereupon take all steps required promptly to place the JVC into liquidation]. If an election under option (a) or (b) is duly made, the parties shall be bound [(subject only to any Regulatory Approvals)] to complete the sale and purchase of the relevant Shares at the relevant price within [30 days] after such election [or, if later, the obtaining of all Regulatory Approvals].]

5. The provisions of clause _____ shall apply in respect of the completion of the sale and purchase of the relevant Shares.

2. TEXAS SHOOT-OUT

> *This clause builds on a framework similar to that applicable to Russian Roulette. Again the "trigger event" should be carefully considered along with the warnings discussed in chapter 10. In some circumstances, it may be appropriate to have a series or "rounds" of bids until, for example, the bid of one party exceeds that of the other party by a minimum margin. The bidding process, in such a case, may often be administered by the auditors.*

1. [*As per para. 1 of Russian Roulette.*]

2. [*As per para. 2 of Russian Roulette.*]

3. If the Deadlock cannot be resolved within a further period of [30] days after service of a Warning Notice, then the following provisions shall apply:

(a) Either party (the "**Terminating Party**") may within a period of [30] days thereafter serve notice in writing on the other party (a "**Deadlock Resolution Notice**") (i) stating that it is willing to purchase all of the other party's Shares in the JVC and (ii) specifying the proposed price per Share. A Deadlock Resolution Notice shall be irrevocable. No other party shall thereafter be entitled to serve a Deadlock Resolution Notice.

(b) The other party shall, within a period of [30] days after receipt of a Deadlock Resolution Notice, elect either:

(i) to sell all of its Shares in the JVC to the Terminating Party at the price stated in the Deadlock Resolution Notice; or
(ii) to purchase all of the Terminating Party's Shares in the JVC at a price per Share higher than that specified in the Terminating Party's notice.

(c) If an election under option (i) of sub-paragraph (b) is made, the sale and purchase of the other party's Shares shall proceed accordingly. If an election under option (ii) is made, the procedure set out in the remaining provisions

DEADLOCK RESOLUTION CLAUSES

of this clause shall apply (subject to such other terms or procedures as the parties may agree).

(d) Each party shall, within a period of [30] days after service of a notice under option (ii) of sub-paragraph (b) above, deposit at the registered office of the JVC (addressed to the [secretary] of the JVC) a sealed bid in writing under which that party shall unconditionally offer to purchase all (but not some only) of the Shares in the JVC of the other party and state the cash price per Share, payable on completion of the purchase, applicable to that bid.

(e) The respective bids shall be opened upon the expiry of such [30] day period by the [secretary] [auditors] of the JVC.

(f) The party who deposits the bid which states the higher price per Share shall be entitled and bound to purchase, and the other party shall become bound to sell, all the Shares of the other party in the JVC at the price stated in such bid.

4. The provisions of clause _____ shall apply in respect of the completion of the sale and purchase of the relevant Shares.

3. MULTI-CHOICE PROCEDURE

> *This clause again requires careful consideration of the appropriate "trigger event". It contemplates review of a number of methods of achieving the sale of the relevant party's shares. A crucial issue is whether or not to include a residual right for the party initiating the process (if a solution cannot be found) to require liquidation of the JVC.*

1. [*As per para. 1 of Russian Roulette.*]

2. [*As per para. 2 of Russian Roulette.*]

3. If the Deadlock cannot be resolved within a further [30] day period after service of a Warning Notice, then either party (the "**Terminating Party**") may thereafter serve notice in writing on the other party that it wishes to terminate the joint venture and to sell its Shares in the JVC whereupon the parties shall negotiate with each other in good faith and co-operate with a view to achieving the sale of that party's Shares by one of the following methods (or a combination of them) or resolving the Deadlock in another manner acceptable to the parties. The methods are:

(a) the purchase by the JVC of the Terminating Party's Shares on terms acceptable to all the parties (provided that such purchase by the JVC can lawfully be made and is financially practicable); or

(b) the purchase by one or more of the other parties of the Terminating Party's Shares; or

(c) the purchase by one or more third parties of the Terminating Party's Shares; or

(d) the sale of the whole issued share capital of the JVC to a third party.

4. If no such method has been agreed [or completed] by _____, the Terminating Party shall be entitled to serve a further notice requiring the JVC to be placed in liquidation and the parties shall be bound to join in all steps necessary for that purpose.

4. COOLING-OFF/MEDIATION

> *This clause encourages a period of specific negotiation between the parties followed by reference to a mediation procedure. It can be structured to apply to both legal and management disputes. In this case, it envisages the appointment of one mediator; in some cases, three may be more appropriate. See also Precedent 20 for other variants of mediation clauses.*

1. If any dispute arises between the parties in connection with this Agreement (including any deadlock arising out of a failure to agree on any of the Reserved Matters), the parties shall use all reasonable efforts to resolve the matter on an amicable basis in the best interests of the JVC.

2. If a party considers that a major deadlock or dispute has occurred in relation to any matters governed by this Agreement (including the inability of the parties or the Board of Directors to reach a decision on any Reserved Matter) and, as a result, the business and prospects of the JVC are materially and adversely affected, a party may deliver to the other parties a dispute notice ("**Dispute Notice**"). The Dispute Notice shall contain: (i) a summary of the dispute; (ii) alternative solutions for resolving the dispute, if any; and (iii) three alternative dates for a meeting of senior executives of the parties within the following 30 days for the purpose of resolving the dispute. Each party shall endeavour to agree a date for such a meeting or meetings and shall negotiate in good faith and attempt to resolve the dispute amicably.

3. If the parties fail to resolve the dispute within [60] days after the service of the Dispute Notice, they shall [consider] [adopt] a mediation procedure whereby they shall co-operate to select and appoint an appropriate person as mediator (the "**Mediator**"). [The Mediator shall be an independent person knowledgeable of the industry and geographic region in which the JVC principally operates.] The role of the Mediator shall be to mediate the difference of opinion and suggest solutions to the dispute which may be acceptable to the parties. The Mediator shall give the parties the opportunity to make written submissions in advance of the mediation. The parties shall provide the Mediator with such records and other information as the Mediator may reasonably request. The language of the mediation shall be English. The parties and the Mediator shall (if appropriate) enter into an agreement based on the [Centre for Dispute Resolution Model Mediation Agreement] in relation to the conduct of the mediation. The Mediator shall (but only if requested) issue a written decision recommending a solution to resolve the dispute, taking into account the written submissions and other information presented to them during the mediation. The parties shall give due consideration to the decision or recommendation of the Mediator, but the decision or recommendation shall not be binding on the parties unless all the parties agree to accept it.

4. All disputes or claims of a legal nature arising out of or in connection with this Agreement, which cannot be resolved despite the foregoing procedure, shall be referred to and finally settled under [the Rules of Arbitration of the International Chamber of Commerce by three arbitrators appointed in accordance with the those Rules]. The seat of the arbitration shall be _____. The language of the arbitration shall be English.

5. DETERRENT APPROACH

> *This clause provides an exit route following deadlock but acts as a "deterrent" to exercising this right unless the circumstances are so extreme that the relevant party is determined to terminate the venture. It provides for the determination of a Fair Price and a financial disincentive to the party who initiates a buy-out by this procedure.*

1. [*As per para. 1 of Russian Roulette.*]

2. [*As per para. 2 of Russian Roulette.*]

3. If the Deadlock cannot be resolved within a further [30] day period after service of a Warning Notice, then:

(a) either party (the "**Initiating Party**") may serve a written notice (a "**Trigger Notice**") on the other party requiring the Fair Price per Share to be determined, as at the date of the Trigger Notice, [in accordance with the procedure set out in _____];

(b) within [30] days after the Fair Price has been determined and notified to each party, the other party shall be obliged to elect either:

   (i) to require the Initiating Party to purchase, or to procure the purchase of, all that other party's Shares in the JVC at a price per Share which is equal to [120] per cent of the Fair Price as so determined; or

   (ii) to require the Initiating Party to sell all its Shares in the JVC to that other party at a price per Share which is equal to [80] per cent of the Fair Price so determined

   And, if no express election is made in accordance with this sub-paragraph (b) by the end of such period, the other party shall be deemed to have made an election under (i) above.

4. The provisions of clause _____ shall apply in respect of the completion of the sale and purchase of the relevant Shares pursuant to an election made under sub-clause 3.

Precedent 22

Arbitration and Mediation Clauses

A. INSTITUTIONAL ARBITRATION CLAUSES[1]

The following model clauses are recommended by the institution concerned:

1. International Chamber of Commerce

Model clause (1998 Rules)

> "All disputes arising out of or in connection with the present contract shall be finally settled under the Rules of Arbitration of the International Chamber of Commerce by one or more arbitrators appointed in accordance with the said Rules."

Comment

The ICC reminds parties that it may be desirable for them to stipulate in the arbitration clause itself the law governing the contract, the number of arbitrators and the place and language of the arbitration. The parties' free choice of the law governing the contract and of the place and language of the arbitration is not limited by the ICC Rules of Arbitration. Attention is also called to the fact that the laws of certain countries require that parties to contracts expressly accept arbitration clauses, sometimes in a precise and particular manner.

In order to ensure that the clause is as widely drawn as possible, the words "controversies or claims" (used in the UNCITRAL model clause) may be added after "disputes" so as to neutralise any argument as to arbitral jurisdiction, for example over undisputed claims.

2. LCIA (London Court of International Arbitration)

Model clause (1998 Rules)

> "Any dispute arising out of or in connection with this contract, including any question regarding its existence, validity or termination, shall be referred to and finally resolved by arbitration under the Rules of the LCIA, which Rules are deemed to be incorporated by reference into this clause."

Comment

The LCIA (formerly the London Court of International Arbitration) reminds parties that difficulties and expense may be avoided if they expressly specify the law

---

[1] The various clauses in this section reflect model provisions published by the relevant institutions and other material contained in *The Freshfields Guide to Arbitration and ADR* (Kluwer Law International, 1999).

governing their contract. The parties may, if they wish, also specify the number of arbitrators, and the place and language of the arbitration The LCIA suggest that the following provisions may be suitable:

> "The number of arbitrators shall be [one/three].
> The place of arbitration shall be [City and/or Country].
> The language to be used in the arbitral proceedings shall be _____.
> The governing law of this contract shall be the substantive law of _____."

As with the ICC clause, the phrase "controversy or claim" may be added after "dispute".

3. UNCITRAL

Model clause (1976 Rules)

> "Any dispute, controversy or claim arising out of or relating to this contract, or the breach, termination or invalidity thereof, shall be settled by arbitration in accordance with the UNCITRAL Arbitration Rules as at present in force."

Comment

UNCITRAL suggests that parties may wish to consider adding:

> "(a) The appointing authority shall be [name of institution or person];
> (b) The number of arbitrators shall be [one or three];
> (c) The place of arbitration shall be [town or country];
> (d) The language(s) to be used in the arbitral proceedings shall be _____."

If the parties opt for arbitration under the UNCITRAL Rules, it will be important to specify an appointing authority (i.e. to appoint an arbitrator in default of appointment by the parties) and, if required, to exclude any right of appeal expressly.

If the parties wish the appointing authority to be the ICC, the appropriate wording (which is recommended by the ICC to deal with the special features of the ICC's internal structure) should, instead of sub-clause (a) above, be as follows:

> "The appointing authority shall be the ICC acting in accordance with the rules adopted by the ICC for this purpose."

Consideration may be given to varying the UNCITRAL Rules (which always require majority awards) by providing as follows:

> "When three arbitrators have been appointed, the award is given by a majority decision. If there be no majority, the award shall be made by the Chairman of the arbitral tribunal alone."

It should be noted that parties who like the UNCITRAL Arbitration Rules but are uncomfortable with the notion of ad hoc arbitration may refer to an institution as an administering rather than merely as an appointing authority. The ICC does not act in such a role, but other institutions will do so. The LCIA has made it clear that it is willing to administer arbitrations under the UNCITRAL Rules, and has published explanations of how it acts in such circumstances. The LCIA suggests that for those purposes the following is used:

> "Any dispute arising out of or in connection with this contract, including any question regarding its existence, validity or termination, shall be referred to

and finally resolved by arbitration under the UNCITRAL Arbitration Rules, which are deemed to be incorporated by reference into this clause.

Any arbitration commenced pursuant to this clause shall be administered by the LCIA.

The appointing authority shall be the LCIA.

The LCIA schedule of fees and costs shall apply.

The number of arbitrators shall be [one/three].

The seat or legal place of arbitration shall be [City and/or Country].

The language to be used in the arbitral proceedings shall be [_____].

The governing law of the contract shall be the substantive law of [_____]."

Given the absence of any express language in the UNCITRAL Rules, it is advisable to add a specific waiver of rights to appeal, etc. along the following lines (modelled on the equivalent LCIA provision):

"By agreeing to arbitration pursuant to this clause, the parties waive irrevocably their right to any form of appeal, review or recourse to any state court or other judicial authority, insofar as such waiver may be validly made."

4. Dubai International Arbitration Centre

Model clause (2007 Rules)

> "Any dispute arising out of the formation, performance, interpretation, interpretation, nullification, termination or invalidation of this contract or arising therefrom or related thereto in any manner whatsoever, shall be settled by arbitration in accordance with the provisions set forth under the Rules of Commercial Conciliation and Arbitration ("the Rules") of the Dubai Chamber of Commerce and Industry, by one or more arbitrators appointed in compliance with the Rules."

Comment

Parties are also advised to include the following in their agreements:

1. the number of arbitrators (one or a panel of three) or an authorisation for the Dubai International Arbitration Centre (DIAC) to determine the number of arbitrators and their identities;
2. the place of arbitration (e.g. "Dubai") and venue to hold arbitration proceedings (e.g. "premises of the Dubai International Arbitration Centre"); and
3. the language of arbitration (e.g. "Arabic").

5. Stockholm Chamber of Commerce

Model clause (2007 Rules)

> "Any dispute, controversy or claim arising out of or in connection with this contract, or the breach, termination or invalidity thereof, shall be finally settled by arbitration in accordance with the Rules of the Arbitration Institute of the Stockholm Chamber of Commerce."

Comment

The parties are advised to make the following additions to the clause, as required:

> "The arbitral tribunal shall be composed of _____ arbitrators (a sole arbitrator).
>
> The place of arbitration shall be _____
>
> The language to be used in the arbitral proceedings shall be _____ "

It would be rare for an arbitration under these Rules to take place outside Sweden; indeed the reason for choosing the Stockholm Institute has generally been thought to be the geopolitical situation of Sweden in the arbitration context. As with other model clauses, we recommend a provision identifying the applicable substantive law.

The Stockholm Chamber of Commerce also provides specific rules for fast track arbitration to which reference can be made ("the Rules for Expedited Arbitrations of the Arbitration Institute of the Stockholm Chamber of Commerce"). There is a sole arbitrator appointed by the Stockholm Chamber of Commerce alone and time limits are considerably shortened.

6. American Arbitration Association—International Centre for Dispute Resolution

Model clause (2003 Rules)

> "Any controversy or claim arising out of or relating to this contract, or the breach thereof, shall be determined by arbitration administered by the International Centre for Dispute Resolution in accordance with its International Arbitration Rules."
>
> OR
>
> "Any controversy or claim arising out of or relating to this contract, or the breach thereof, shall be determined by arbitration administered by the American Arbitration Association in accordance with its International Arbitration Rules."

Comment

The International Centre for Dispute Resolution (ICDR) is the international division of the American Arbitration Association (AAA) charged with exclusive administration of all the AAA's international matters and is based in Dublin and New York. Because the ICDR is a division of the AAA, the two alternative versions of the model clause set out above lead to the same result. Further advice on ICDR model clauses can be found at: http://www.adr.org/si.asp?id=4945.

The ICDR suggests that the parties may wish to consider adding:

> "The number of the arbitrators shall be _____ [one *or* three]
>
> "The place of arbitration shall be _____ [*city and/or country*]
>
> "The language[s] of the arbitration shall be _____ ."

7. Singapore International Arbitration Centre (SIAC)

Model clause (2007 Rules)

"Any dispute arising out of or in connection with this contract, including any question regarding its existence, validity or termination, shall be referred to and finally resolved by arbitration in Singapore in accordance with the Arbitration Rules of the Singapore International Arbitration Centre ("SIAC Rules") for the time being in force, which rules are deemed to be incorporated by reference in this clause.

The Tribunal shall consist of _____ [*odd number, either one, or three*] arbitrator[s] to be appointed by the Chairman of the SIAC.

The language of the arbitration shall be _____."

Comment

SIAC was established in 1991 and is becoming an increasingly important institution for arbitrations in the Asia-Pacific region.

B. AD HOC ARBITRATION

The following is a framework for a possible clause. The warnings in chapter 14 should be considered before use.

"1. Any dispute, difference, controversy or claim arising out of or in connection with this Agreement shall be referred to and determined by arbitration in [*place*].

2. The arbitral tribunal (hereinafter referred to as 'the tribunal') shall be composed of three arbitrators appointed as follows:

   (i) each party shall appoint an arbitrator, and the two arbitrators so appointed shall appoint a third arbitrator who shall act as president of the tribunal,

   (ii) if either party fails to appoint an arbitrator within 30 days of receiving notice of the appointment of an arbitrator by the other party, such arbitrator shall at the request of that party be appointed by the [*appointing authority*];

   (iii) if the two arbitrators to be appointed by the parties fail to agree upon a third arbitrator within 30 days of the appointment of the second arbitrator, the third arbitrator shall be appointed by the [*appointing authority*] at the written request of either party;

   (iv) should a vacancy arise because any arbitrator dies, resigns, refuses to act, or becomes incapable of performing his functions, the vacancy shall be filled by the method by which that arbitrator was originally appointed. When a vacancy is filled the newly established tribunal shall exercise its discretion to determine whether any hearings shall be repeated.

3. As soon as practicable after the appointment of the arbitrator to be appointed by him, and in any event no later than 30 days after the tribunal has been constituted, the claimant shall deliver to the respondent (with copies to each arbitrator) a statement of case, containing particulars of his claims and written submissions in support thereof, together with any documents relied on.

4. Within 30 days of the receipt of the claimant's statement of case, the respondent shall deliver to the claimant (with copies to each arbitrator) a statement of case in answer, together with any counterclaim and any documents relied upon.

5. Within 30 days of the receipt by the claimant of any statement of counterclaim by the respondent, the claimant may deliver to the respondent (with copies to each arbitrator) a reply to counterclaim together with any additional documents relied upon.

6. As soon as practicable after its constitution, the tribunal shall convene a meeting with the parties or their representatives to determine the procedure to be followed in the arbitration.

7. The procedure shall be as agreed by the parties or, in default of agreement, as determined by the tribunal. However, the following procedural matters shall in any event be taken as agreed:

   (i) the language of the arbitration shall be [*language*]:
   (ii) the tribunal may in its discretion hold a hearing and make an award in relation to any preliminary issue at the request of either party and shall do so at the joint request of both parties;
   (iii) the tribunal shall hold a hearing, or hearings, relating to substantive issues unless the parties agree otherwise in writing;
   (iv) the tribunal shall issue its final award within 60 days of the last hearing of the substantive issues in dispute between the parties.

8. In the event of default by either party in respect of any procedural order made by the tribunal, the tribunal shall have power to proceed with the arbitration and to make its award.

9. If an arbitrator appointed by one of the parties fails or refuses to participate in the arbitration at any time after the hearings on the substance of the dispute have started, the remaining two arbitrators may continue the arbitration and make an award without a vacancy being deemed to arise if, in their discretion, they determine that the failure or refusal of the other arbitrator to participate is without reasonable excuse.

10. Any award or procedural decision of the tribunal shall if necessary be made by a majority and, in the event that no majority may be formed, the presiding arbitrator shall proceed as if he were a sole arbitrator."

C. INSTITUTIONAL MEDIATION CLAUSES

1. Centre for Effective Dispute Resolution (CEDR)

Model clause (2007 Procedure)

"If any dispute arises out of this Agreement, directors or other senior representatives of the parties with authority to settle the dispute will, within [_____] days of a written request from one party to the other, meet in a good faith effort to resolve the dispute.

If the dispute is not resolved at that meeting, the parties will attempt to settle it by mediation in accordance with the CEDR Model Mediation Procedure. Unless otherwise agreed between the parties, the mediator will be nominated by CEDR. To initiate the mediation a party [by its Managing Director/_____] must give notice in writing (ADR notice) to the other party(ies) to the dispute [addressed to its/their respective Managing Director/_____] requesting a mediation. [A copy of the request should be sent to CEDR Solve. The mediation will start no later than [_____] days after the date of the ADR notice.]"

Comment

In its Guidance Note on its Model ADR Contract Clauses, CEDR proposes certain optional/additional wording. Most importantly, the mediation clause should specify that if the parties have not settled the dispute within a given period of time from commencement of the mediation, the dispute shall be referred to arbitration or some other binding procedure.

> "If the dispute is not settled by mediation within [ ] days of commencement of the mediation or within such further period as the parties may agree in writing, the dispute shall be referred to and finally resolved by arbitration under [the arbitration provision]."

2. CPR Institute for Dispute Resolution (CPR)

Model clause (US) (2005 Procedure)

"(A) The parties shall attempt [in good faith] to resolve any dispute arising out of or relating to this [Agreement/Contract] promptly by negotiation between executives who have authority to settle the controversy and who are at a higher level of management than the persons with direct responsibility for administration of this contract. Any person may give the other party written notice of any dispute not resolved in the normal course of business. Within [15] days after delivery of the notice, the receiving party shall submit to the other a written response. The notice and the response shall include (a) a statement of that party's position and a summary of arguments supporting that position, and (b) the name and title of the executive who will represent that party and of any other person who will accompany the executive. Within [30] days after delivery of the initial notice, the executives of both parties shall meet at a mutually acceptable time and place, and thereafter as often as they reasonably deem necessary, to attempt to resolve the dispute. [All reasonable requests for information made by one party to the other will be honoured.]

All negotiations pursuant to this clause are confidential and shall be treated as compromise and settlement negotiations for purposes of applicable rules of evidence.

(B) If the dispute has not been resolve by negotiation as provided herein within [45] days after delivery of the initial notice of negotiation, [or if the parties failed to meet within [30] days after delivery,] the parties shall endeavour to settle the dispute by mediation under the CPR Mediation Procedure [then currently in effect OR in effect on the date of this Agreement], [provided, however, that if one party fails to participate in the negotiation as provided herein, the other party can initiate mediation prior to the expiration of the [45] days.] Unless otherwise agreed, the parties will select a mediator from the CPR Panels of Distinguished Neutrals."

Model clause (Europe) (2005 Procedure)

"The parties shall endeavour to resolve any dispute arising out of or relating to this agreement by mediation under the CPR European Mediation Procedure. Unless the parties agree otherwise, the mediator will be selected from the CPR Panels of Distinguished Neutrals and, if they require it, the parties shall notify CPR to initiate a selection process. Any controversy or claim arising out of or relating to this contract or the breach, termination or validity thereof, which

> remains unresolved 45 days after appointment of a mediator, shall be settled by arbitration by [here insert appropriate arbitration provision, including specified venue, appointing authority, administering body (if any), governing procedural rules (if any) and governing procedural law]. Judgment upon the award rendered by the arbitrator(s) may be entered by any court having jurisdiction thereof."

CPR also publishes variations of this dispute resolution clause involving face-to-face negotiation prior to mediation.

CPR is willing to serve as an appointing authority under the UNCITRAL Arbitration Rules. If they so choose, parties may also use the CPR Rules for Non-Administered Arbitration of International Disputes. When incorporating the CPR arbitration rules into a pre-dispute clause, please note that the choices indicated by parentheses must be made.

> "Any dispute arising out of or relating to this contract, including the breach, termination or validity thereof, shall be settled by arbitration in accordance with the CPR Rules for Non-Administered Arbitration of International Disputes, by (a sole arbitrator) (three arbitrators, of whom each party shall appoint one) (three arbitrators, none of whom shall be appointed by either party). Judgment upon the award rendered by the Arbitrator(s) may be entered by any court having jurisdiction thereof. The seat of the arbitration shall be the (city, country). The arbitration shall be conducted in (language). The Neutral Organisation designated to perform the functions specified in Rule 5, 6 and 7 shall be (name of CPR or other organisation)."

D. GENERAL PURPOSE ADR CLAUSES

1. Short form

> "If any dispute or difference arises out of or in connection with this Agreement the parties shall [with the assistance of the Centre for Dispute Resolution] seek to resolve the dispute or difference amicably by using an alternative dispute resolution (ADR) procedure acceptable to both parties [before pursuing any other remedies available to them].
>
> If either party fails or refuses to agree to or participate in the ADR procedure or if in any event the dispute or difference is not resolved to the satisfaction of both parties within [90] days after it has arisen, the dispute or difference shall be referred to arbitration . . . [add arbitration clause]."

2. Long form

> "If any dispute or difference arises out of or in connection with this Agreement [which the parties are unable to resolve by negotiation] (the 'dispute'), the parties shall seek to resolve the dispute amicably by using the following procedure [before pursuing any other remedies available to them]:
>
> 1. The parties shall submit the dispute to a neutral adviser appointed by agreement between the parties to assist them in resolving the dispute. Either party may give written notice to the other describing the nature of the dispute, requiring the dispute to be submitted to such a neutral adviser and proposing the names of up to three suitable persons to be appointed. If no such person is appointed by agreement between the parties within [14] days after such notice is given (or, if no such notice is given, within 28 days after the dispute has arisen), either party may request [the Centre for Dispute Resolution] to appoint a neutral adviser.

2. The parties shall, with the assistance of the neutral adviser appointed in accordance with paragraph 1 above, seek in good faith to resolve the dispute by using an alternative dispute resolution (ADR) procedure agreed between the parties or, in default of such agreement, established by the neutral adviser.

3. If the parties accept any recommendations made by the neutral adviser or otherwise reach agreement as to the resolution of the dispute, such agreement shall be recorded in writing and signed by the parties (and, if applicable, the neutral adviser), whereupon it shall become binding upon the parties.

4. If:

   (a) the dispute has not been resolved to the satisfaction of both parties within [60] days after the appointment of the neutral adviser; or
   (b) either party fails or refuses to agree to or participate in the ADR procedure; or
   (c) in any event the dispute is not resolved within [90] days after it has arisen,

   then the dispute shall be referred to arbitration . . . *[add arbitration clause]*.

5. In the event that the dispute is referred to arbitration [in accordance with paragraph 4 above]:

   (a) any neutral adviser involved in the ADR procedure shall not, unless the parties jointly agree otherwise, take any part in the arbitration or any other related proceedings, whether as an arbitrator, witness or otherwise, and no aspect of the ADR procedure, including any recommendations made by him in connection with the ADR procedure, shall be relied upon by either party without the consent of the other party and the neutral adviser;
   (b) neither party shall make use of nor rely upon information supplied, or arguments raised, by the other party in the ADR procedure.

6. The costs and fees of the neutral adviser the ADR service provider and any neutral venue shall be borne equally by the parties. [The parties shall bear equally by the parties.] The parties shall bear their own costs of all other aspects of the ADR procedure."

PART F

JOINT VENTURE AND ALLIANCE CHECKLISTS

1   Preparing for the Joint Venture: Initial Issues

2   Drafting the Joint Venture Agreement

The accompanying disc also contains the following checklists set out in prior chapters of this book:

Checklist	Para.
R&D/Technology Collaborations: Checklist of Key Issues	4–12
Works Project Consortia: Checklist of Key Issues	4–17
Risk and Revenue Sharing: Key Topics	4–23
Partnerships: Key Issues for Joint Ventures	5–24
Shareholders' Agreement: Key Issues	5–49
UK Articles of Association: Key Issues	5–58
Transfer of Assets to JVC: Key Issues	6–24
Property Agreements: Issues	6–31
Management Agreement: Key Issues	6–33
Supply Agreements: Key Issues	6–35
Offtake/Purchase Contracts: Additional Issues	6–37
Marketing Agreements: Key Issues	6–38
Strategic Minority Investment: Some Key Issues	9–39

1. PREPARING FOR THE JOINT VENTURE: INITIAL ISSUES

The following are legal and transactional issues to be considered at the outset of discussions regarding a proposed joint venture—in addition to issues relating to the terms of the joint venture itself (see checklist 2 below).

1. Initial steps

Basic initial steps or questions to consider include:

☐ Has a feasibility study or business plan been prepared?

☐ Will confidential information be disclosed during negotiations? Has a confidentiality agreement or information exchange agreement been put in place?

☐ Is each party still free, pending its signature, to negotiate with third parties regarding arrangements which may be alternatives to the joint venture? Should there be exclusivity obligations, preventing such negotiations, for a specified period?

☐ Is a letter of intent or memorandum of understanding appropriate to establish points of principle?

☐ Is any of the parties a publicly quoted company with announcement obligations or stock exchange requirements for shareholder approval relating to the venture?

☐ What material authorisations, consents, licences or other conditions precedent will be required for the joint venture to commence?

☐ If an international joint venture, consider the effect of local laws of the country in which the venture is to be established (see 3 below).

☐ What governing law should apply?

2. Structure of the joint venture

Consider the appropriate structure for the joint venture (n.b. tax considerations):

☐ Unincorporated collaboration or association?

☐ Corporate joint venture?

☐ Limited or unlimited liability company?

☐ Partnership? Limited partnership?

☐ Limited liability partnership (LLP)?

☐ Profit pooling or revenue sharing arrangement?

☐ European Economic Interest Grouping (EEIG)?

☐ European Company?

☐ Jurisdiction of joint venture entity?

☐ Series of joint venture vehicles in different jurisdictions?

☐ Existing entity—or new entity to be formed?

3. Local law issues

Consider issues raised by local laws of the jurisdiction in which the joint venture will be principally located or undertake business:

- ☐ Registration requirements? Inward foreign investment review by governmental authority?
- ☐ Requirement for local ownership/control?
- ☐ Local governmental consents/licences required?
- ☐ Effect of local employment laws?
- ☐ Taxes: duties on share capital or loan capital? withholding tax on dividends? availability of capital allowances? corporate tax rates? any tax holidays or incentives? import duties on raw materials/goods?
- ☐ Requirement to prepare and file publicly any corporate returns and/or accounts?
- ☐ Non-cash contributions: requirement for independent valuation?
- ☐ Currency of payments; convertibility; exchange controls?
- ☐ Any restrictions on repatriation of profits and/or payment of dividends?
- ☐ What rights in land will the joint venture parties obtain?
- ☐ Do local laws recognise intellectual property rights? Any special laws relating to transfer of technology?
- ☐ Any specific laws relating to joint ventures?
- ☐ Lawyers?
- ☐ Governing language for texts?

4. Contribution of existing assets

Where existing assets or businesses are being vested in the joint venture by any of the parties, consider the following acquisition-type issues:

- ☐ Due diligence investigation to be undertaken into assets/business to be contributed by the other?
- ☐ Tax/transfer duty considerations affecting method and timing of contributions?
- ☐ Method of valuation of contributed assets? Accounting policies?
- ☐ Any equalisation payment required as between the parties? Method of calculation and payment?
- ☐ Any minimum net worth obligation on either party in respect of assets to be contributed? Any subsequent completion account adjustment as between the parties?
- ☐ Warranties and/or indemnities to be given by either party to the JVC/other party regarding business or assets contributed? Limits as to time and/or amount?
- ☐ Any material contracts/assets/properties which require third party approval prior to vesting in the joint venture?

- [ ] Need to provide for partial, delayed or conditional completion of asset contributions?
- [ ] Need for separate contribution agreement under relevant local laws?

5. Regulatory matters

Identification of regulatory issues and filings/consents required will be an important part of the initial analysis:

- [ ] Will the joint venture result in a significant market share in any particular market or jurisdiction?
- [ ] Is it a full-function joint venture for purposes of the EC Merger Regulation?
- [ ] Are turnover thresholds of the EC Merger Regulation exceeded?
- [ ] Co-operative joint venture? Does it appreciably affect inter-Member State trade under Article 81(1)? Does it qualify for exemption under Article 81(3)?
- [ ] Does the joint venture constitute a qualifying merger under Enterprise Act 2002?
- [ ] Does the Competition Act 1998 apply? Does it qualify for s.9 exemption?
- [ ] Are any industry-specific regulatory approvals required?
- [ ] Make provision for co-operation between parties in the event of subsequent regulatory action?
- [ ] Are regulatory approvals required in any foreign jurisdictions? Competition laws? Foreign investment approvals?
- [ ] Specific approvals of regulatory authorities be made conditions precedent of establishment of the JVC?

6. Tax

Tax considerations may play a major part in structuring the joint venture and, if so, will require detailed attention and planning. Possible issues among many include:

- [ ] Capital gains on contribution of assets/shares to the joint venture?
- [ ] Capital allowances/balancing charge on transfer of assets?
- [ ] Need to transfer tax losses?
- [ ] Stamp duty cost?
- [ ] Is ongoing consortium or group relief required?
- [ ] Do tax considerations lead to a preference for a "tax transparent" structure?
- [ ] In the case of an international joint venture, will the structure be affected by:
    - [ ] need for efficient repatriation of profits?
    - [ ] thin capitalisation?
    - [ ] transfer pricing rules?
- [ ] Identify tax clearances to be obtained. Will any be conditions precedent of establishment of the joint venture?

7. Accounting

It may be important to establish early how the joint venture will be treated in the accounts of the joint venture parents:

- ☐ Will it be a subsidiary undertaking (i.e. requiring full consolidation)?
- ☐ Will there be "severe long-term restrictions" affecting a parent's rights (which may lead to gross equity accounting)?
- ☐ Will it be an associated undertaking (i.e. gross equity accounting)?
- ☐ If it is an unincorporated joint venture, is proportionate consolidation desired?
- ☐ Will International Accounting Standards (IAS) apply?

8. Employee issues

Employment issues should be considered early. They include:

- ☐ Is there a transfer of a business? Will the Acquired Rights Directive/Transfer of Undertakings Regulations apply?
- ☐ Does the Employee Consultation and Information Directive apply?
- ☐ Will employees be seconded to the JVC, or employed by the JVC?
- ☐ Are there existing share option or other incentive arrangements? How will they be affected?
- ☐ Are employees members of an existing pension scheme? Will there be a need for a new JVC scheme?
- ☐ Will service contracts be required for key employees?
- ☐ Will there be a need to harmonise employment terms and conditions within the JVC?

9. Intellectual property

The principal IPR issues need to be identified early:

- ☐ Will material technology be provided by the parties to the JVC? Is it protected by IPR?
- ☐ Is technology predominantly in the field of the JVC, or is it used (mainly/partly) in the separate operations of the parties (or one of the parties)?
- ☐ Is it preferable to vest ownership in the JVC, or to license?
- ☐ Will parties need ongoing access to IPR generated by the JVC?
- ☐ Will competition laws apply to the terms relating to IPR? Consider possible application of Technology Transfer Block Exemption?
- ☐ Will trade marks (including "house marks") of the parents be licensed to the JVC for its use-including in its name/logo?
- ☐ What should be the rights to IPR in the event of termination?

10. Property and related services

Property and related issues to be considered at the outset include:

☐ Will property be transferred/leased to the JVC?

☐ Will "site-splitting" be necessary?

☐ Will transitional arrangements be necessary to support the JVC in respect of services: e.g. property-related facilities, IT/communication systems, accounting and other professional support?

☐ Need for environmental audits? Allocation/indemnities regarding potential environmental liabilities attributable to pre-completion circumstances?

2. DRAFTING THE JOINT VENTURE AGREEMENT

This checklist addresses specific issues to be considered when drafting the joint venture or shareholders' agreement. It assumes that a limited liability company will be used as the joint venture vehicle. Many of the items listed below nevertheless apply, on a similar basis, to other joint venture structures.

---

1. Identity of parties

It is important to identify the most appropriate parties to the Agreement:

☐ Parent companies to be parties—or shareholding subsidiaries?

☐ Parent company guarantee to be provided to support obligations by any contracting party?

☐ JVC itself to be a party?

---

2. Conditions precedent

Identify matters which are so fundamental that they should be pre-conditions of completing the joint venture:

☐ Governmental or regulatory approvals required for transfer of assets and/or establishing the joint venture?

☐ Licence required for the JVC to commence business?

☐ Third party consents required to enable key contracts, intellectual property licences etc. to be vested in the JVC?

☐ Tax clearances?

☐ Approval required from trustees of debenture stocks or other lender consents?

☐ Completion of due diligence by either party?

☐ Approval of shareholders of either party under rules of any stock exchange?

☐ Long-stop date to be set for satisfaction of conditions precedent?

---

3. Business of the JVC

It is generally desirable to establish clearly the intended scope of the JVC's activities:

☐ Objectives? Agreed business plan?

☐ A specific project or a continuing business?

☐ Any geographical limits to JVC's business? Need to regulate exports?

☐ Any fundamental authorisations, consents, licences or other conditions precedent required for the JVC to commence business?

4. Capital and funding

A variety of important issues relate to capital and funding of the JVC:

- ☐ Number of initial shares to be issued? Fully or partly paid?
- ☐ Proportions of equity to be held respectively by the parties?
- ☐ Amount of initial investment (equity and loans) by each party?
- ☐ Payment in cash or kind (e.g. equipment, goods or know-how)?
- ☐ Non-cash consideration to be valued? Method of valuation? Approval by any regulatory or other third party? Any legal requirement for independent valuation (e.g. does s.593 Companies Act 2006 apply)?
- ☐ Timing of payment? Committed instalments?
- ☐ Shares or loans? If shareholder loans, are they to be secured? or subordinated?
- ☐ Different classes of shares to be established to reflect different interests or contributions of the parties?
- ☐ Any right of a party to preferential dividends?
- ☐ Future finance: any obligations on shareholders to make additional finance available to the JVC? any limit (time/amount) to that obligation? Authority and procedure for making cash calls?
- ☐ New shares to be offered to shareholders in proportion to existing shareholdings?
- ☐ Any default or dilution provisions to apply if finance commitments are not met?
- ☐ Obligation to give parent company guarantees to support JVC borrowings?
- ☐ Provision for ensuring that any liability under such guarantees is borne in agreed equity proportions as between the parties?
- ☐ Availability to the JVC of grants or subsidies (e.g. regional development/ EU grants)?
- ☐ Tax considerations which affect form of financing? Are any "thin capitalisation" rules applicable?
- ☐ Any authorisations or consents required by a party for financial investment in the JVC?

5. Constitution of JVC

The main constitutional documents of the JVC should be identified and agreed:

- ☐ Memorandum and Articles of Association, by-laws or equivalent documents?
- ☐ Table A (in the UK) to be adopted with specific amendments—or long-form Articles of Association?
- ☐ Special rights to attach to separate classes of shares?
  - ☐ right to appoint directors?

- ☐ presence in quorum?
- ☐ voting rights?
- ☐ Pre-emption provisions on share transfers to be included in articles?
- ☐ Registration/prior clearance with any governmental registry?

6. Board of directors

The principles relating to board and management structure should be clearly established:

- ☐ Number of directors?
- ☐ Number of directors to be appointed by each party?
- ☐ Can the board itself appoint additional directors?
- ☐ Is a two-tier board structure desirable (e.g. board of directors/management committee comparable to supervisory board/management board in some EU countries)?
- ☐ Voting: one man one vote, or weighted voting rights?
- ☐ Simple majority for decisions—or special majorities?
- ☐ Chairman to have casting vote?
- ☐ Appointment of chairman? Rotation of right to appoint chairman between the parties?
- ☐ Names of first directors?
- ☐ Frequency of meetings? Location?
- ☐ Quorum? Length of notice of meetings? Alternates?
- ☐ Authority of board representatives to bind the parent companies?
- ☐ Any mechanisms for resolution of deadlock? (See also 17 below.)
- ☐ Appointment of chief executive, executive directors or officers? Any rights of appointment of particular executives or management positions to attach to particular shareholders?
- ☐ Autonomy of board—or are specific matters to be reserved for shareholders?
- ☐ Any restrictions on voting by directors on contracts or matters in which they are "interested"?
- ☐ Terms of reference required for chief executive/other executives?

7. Shareholder meetings

Although as a matter of law procedural details can generally be left to the Articles of Association, it is often easier (certainly in the case of an international joint venture) to include basic principles regarding shareholder meetings:

- ☐ Quorum to require a representative of each party?
- ☐ Notice of meeting? Provision for short notice? Written resolutions?

- ☐ Location of meetings?
- ☐ Weighted voting rights on any particular issues?
- ☐ Chairman's casting vote?
- ☐ Separate class rights?
- ☐ Proxies?

8. Matters requiring unanimity or special majority

It is generally of crucial importance to set out matters which require unanimity (or a "super" majority vote) before they can be undertaken by the JVC:

- ☐ Are specified matters to require unanimity (or "super" majority) at board level?
- ☐ Are specified matters to be reserved for unanimous (or "super" majority) decision by the parties at shareholder level?
- ☐ What matters are to be covered?
    - ☐ alteration of constitutional documents?
    - ☐ change of JVC name?
    - ☐ issue of new shares?
    - ☐ admission of new shareholder?
    - ☐ strategic business plan?
    - ☐ approval of annual budgets?
    - ☐ capital expenditure commitments by the JVC above specified level?
    - ☐ declaration of dividends?
    - ☐ new types of business/geographical expansion?
    - ☐ any merger, joint venture or material co-operation arrangement with third parties?
    - ☐ acquisition/disposal of material assets or securities?
    - ☐ formation of subsidiaries?
    - ☐ loans/borrowings/mortgages/guarantees in excess of specified limits?
    - ☐ entry into or termination of other material contracts?
    - ☐ pricing/trading terms?
    - ☐ employment/removal of chief executive or other senior management?
    - ☐ appointment/removal of auditors?
    - ☐ alteration of accounting policies?
    - ☐ commencing/settling substantial litigation?
    - ☐ establishment of JVC pension scheme?
    - ☐ licensing of intellectual property rights by the JVC?
    - ☐ liquidation of the JVC? Dissolution of any subsidiaries?
    - ☐ dealings between the JVC and any shareholder (other than trading on arm's length terms in the ordinary course of the JVC's business)?
- ☐ Is provision necessary or desirable to deal with deadlock—see 17 below?

9. Administrative or corporate matters

The Agreement should generally deal with a number of basic administrative or corporate matters:

- ☐ Registered office?
- ☐ Secretary?
- ☐ Form and timing of management information or other financial reporting from JVC to shareholders?
- ☐ Obligation to maintain proper accounting records?
- ☐ Each party's rights of inspection of the JVC's accounts and records?
- ☐ Insurance?

10. Profit distribution

The parties should establish clearly the principles to apply in respect of profit distribution:

- ☐ Dividend policy? Minimum level of profits to be distributed (or retained) each year?
- ☐ How can profit distribution policy be changed?
- ☐ Provision for interim dividends?
- ☐ Any authorisations or consents required from regulatory authorities for payment of dividends?
- ☐ Any withholding tax?
- ☐ Any need to consider establishment of a special structure (e.g. income access shares) to enable shareholder(s) to receive dividends directly from a country of an operating subsidiary of the JVC rather than from jurisdiction of the JVC?

11. Intellectual property

Rights and obligations of the parties regarding technology and intellectual property will often be vitally important. These may be addressed in separate ancillary agreements (to which the JVC may be a party) with the principles set out in the main Agreement. Basic issues include:

- ☐ Transfer to the JVC of intellectual property/technology by each party? Timing and procedure for technology transfer?
- ☐ Territorial scope? Exclusive licence to the JVC? Availability of improvements?
- ☐ Licence by the JVC to shareholders of intellectual property (and improvements) developed by the JVC?
- ☐ Arrangements for training and technical assistance?
- ☐ Rights of parties on termination to intellectual property developed or owned by the JVC?
- ☐ Licence of a party's trade names/product marks to the JVC?

12. Restrictions on shareholders/parents

Clarify the extent of any non-compete or other restrictions on the independent business freedom of the parties:

☐ Restriction not to compete with the JVC's business? Territorial scope?

☐ Any exceptions for any existing activities of either party not contributed to the JVC?

☐ Obligation on parties to refer to the JVC orders/business within field of the JVC?

☐ Confidentiality undertaking by parties in respect of affairs and technology relating to the JVC? Similarly, in respect of affairs of other shareholders?

☐ Are restrictions to apply—for a limited period?—after a party ceases to be a shareholder in the JVC and/or the termination of the joint venture agreement?

☐ Restriction on a party poaching employees of the JVC?

☐ Parent company guarantees of performance (if not a party) and of compliance by affiliates.

13. Change of control of shareholder

A sensitive issue is whether any rights are to be triggered by a "change of control" of a party. If so, this needs to be clearly stated:

☐ Define change of control?

☐ Obligation to be imposed on a party, affected by a change of control, to offer to sell its shareholding interest to other party? If so, establish valuation procedure and criteria?

☐ Change of JVC name?

14. Transfer of shares

The Agreement should set out clearly the rules to apply if a party wishes to "exit" by transferring its shares in the JVC:

☐ Pre-emption provisions in favour of other part(ies) to be included? Right of first offer—or right of first refusal (i.e. is third party purchaser required to be identified by seller?).

☐ Can a party sell some (or only all) of its shares?

☐ Any minimum period during which no sales to third parties are permitted?

☐ Valuation procedure and formula if a party wishes to exercise pre-emption right? Guidelines as to price? (Pro-rata market value? fair value? discount/premium for size of shareholding?)

☐ Is a party free to sell shares in the JVC to a third party if pre-emption right is not taken up? Alternatively, should a party have a right to call for liquidation of the JVC if the pre-emption right is not exercised?

- [ ] Should the continuing joint venture party have a second right to pre-empt the sale if and when a third party purchaser is identified?
- [ ] Is it appropriate to include a "shoot out" provision (e.g. party receiving notice must elect either to purchase shares of other party or to sell its shares to that party)?
- [ ] Should a "tag-along" provision be included (e.g. transferor must require third party purchaser to offer to buy also the other party's interest at the same price per share)? Or a "drag-along" provision (e.g. selling party can oblige other party also to transfer its shares to the same purchaser)?
- [ ] Is a party free at any time to make intra-group transfers?
- [ ] Any specific put/call options to be included at the outset? If so, what price formula and at what times can option be exercised?
- [ ] Should there be a requirement for change of JVC name if existing participant sells shares?

15. Ancillary contracts

Although detailed terms may be set out in separate agreements, consider whether it is desirable to refer to arrangements dealing with any of the following potential arrangements between a party and the JVC:

- [ ] Secondment of staff?
- [ ] Management agreement?
- [ ] Provision of accommodation/support services/facilities?
- [ ] Transitional arrangements for sharing computer or other IT facilities, including software?
- [ ] Transfer (sale or contribution) of business assets?
- [ ] Provision of technical assistance/know-how/training?
- [ ] Distributorship agreements?
- [ ] Supply of goods/raw materials?
- [ ] Trademark, tradename or other intellectual property agreements?

16. Termination

Exit strategies and options should always be considered:

- [ ] Fixed or indefinite term for the JVC?
- [ ] Any circumstances in which termination will automatically occur (e.g. loss of licence)?
- [ ] Right of an "innocent" party to call for transfer of shares upon material breach by a "defaulting" party? Or insolvency of another party (or its parent company)?
- [ ] Right of a party to give notice of termination (leading to liquidation unless otherwise agreed) after minimum period? Or is exit solely by transfer of shares?

- ☐ Arrangements upon termination/liquidation: distribution of assets; return of confidential material; disposal of outstanding orders and inventory; payment of outstanding loans; non-compete obligations; and performance of outstanding contracts at termination?
- ☐ Rights of each party to use the JVC's intellectual property/know-how after termination?
- ☐ Division of any other assets and liabilities of the joint venture? Any auction process as between the shareholders? Any pre-agreed right of a party to particular assets/business—at valuation?

17. Deadlock

Consider whether it is necessary or desirable to develop procedures for resolving any major deadlock or breakdown:

- ☐ Need to define deadlock or breakdown?
- ☐ Reference to chairmen/chief executives of parties for "agreed" resolution?
- ☐ Chairman's casting vote?
- ☐ Independent third party (or director) to be given a "swing" vote?
- ☐ Reference to expert or panel of arbitrators?
- ☐ Any mediation or other alternative dispute resolution (ADR) procedure to be developed?
- ☐ Exit by transfer of shares to new joint venturer?
- ☐ Specific right to serve notice to trigger "shoot out" formula (e.g. other party must either buy first party's shares or sell its own)?
- ☐ Specific right (after minimum period?) for either party to call for liquidation of the JVC?

18. Standard provisions

A number of "standard" provisions should be considered if not already covered:

- ☐ Confidentiality?
- ☐ Costs of preparation to be borne equally? Stamp duty?
- ☐ Force majeure?
- ☐ Notices?
- ☐ Amendments?
- ☐ Assignment of rights/obligations?
- ☐ Exclusion of Third Party Rights (Contracts) Act?
- ☐ Conflict between joint venture agreement and the JVC's constitutional documents (i.e. supremacy of joint venture agreement as between the parties)?
- ☐ No partnership?
- ☐ Interpretation?

☐	Severability?
☐	Entire agreement?
☐	Provisions relating to public announcements?
☐	Governing law?
☐	Dispute resolution: submission to arbitration? choice of arbitral institution?

INDEX

Note: References prefixed by D, E or F refer to Part D (International Joint Ventures and Selected Jurisdictions), Part E (Precedents) and Part F (Joint Venture and Alliance Checklists) respectively.

Accounting
  associates
    IAS 28, 19–24—19–25
    nature of undertaking, 19–12—19–13
    transactions with reporting entity, 19–16
    UK rules, 19–12
    US GAAP, 19–31
  disclosure, 19–18
  EC law
    Seventh Company Law Directive, 19–06
  issues, 19–01
  International Accounting Standards (IAS)
    associates, 19–24—19–25
    EU listed companies, 19–22
    joint ventures, 19–26—19–29
    subsidiaries, 19–11, 19–23
    UK non-listed companies, 19–22
  joint arrangements which are not entities ("JANES")
    meaning, 19–20
    requirements, 19–20
  joint venture entities
    additional disclosure, 19–18
    categories under IAS, 19–26
    consolidated balance sheet, 19–16
    exceptional items, 19–16
    financial statements, 19–16
    FRS 9, 19–14—19–16, 19–19
    future developments, 19–29
    individual company accounts, 19–27
    transactions with parties, 19–28
    transactions with reporting entity, 19–16
    turnover, 19–16
  joint venture parents
    consolidation, 19–04
    equity method, 19–04
    investment, 19–04
    proportionate consolidation, 19–04
    relevant treatment, 19–05—19–06
  joint venture's own accounts
    corporate vehicles, 19–02
    partnerships, 19–02
    unincorporated ventures, 19–02
  profit and loss accounting presentation, 19–16
  proportionate consolidation, 19–30
  subsidiaries
    control rules, 19–23
    exclusion from consolidation, 19–09—19–11
    IAS 27, 19–23
    nature of undertaking, 19–08
    UK rules, 19–08
    US GAAP, 19–31—19–32
  UK GAAP
    corporate vehicles, 19–02
    difference from IAS, 19–22
    distinctions drawn, 19–07
    summary of accounting treatment, 19–07
  US GAAP
    associates, 19–31
    subsidiaries, 19–31—19–32

Acquisitions
  mergers and
    advantages, 1–04
    disadvantages, 1–04

Agreements
  see also **Shareholders' agreements**
  asset transfer agreements, 6–24
  competition
    agreements outside Article 81, 16–21
    Minor Agreements Notice, 16–21
  co-operative agreements, 16–39, 16–40—16–43
  confidentiality agreements, 2–06—2–09
  e-commerce ventures, 6–09
  employee secondment agreements, 6–32
  foreign production joint ventures
    asset transfer agreements, 6–06
    component supply agreements, 6–06

distribution agreements, 6–06
technology licence agreements, 6–06
framework agreements, 2–38—2–39
funding agreements, 6–25—6–29
intellectual property agreements, 6–30
joint operating agreements, 7–05—7–06
joint venture agreements, 2–37, F(2)
management agreements, 6–33
power station joint ventures, 6–11
property agreements, 6–31
sale and purchase agreements, 2–40—2–41, 6–24
shareholders' agreements, 5–47—5–56
specialisation agreements, 4–13
subscription agreements, 2–41
supply agreements, 6–35
technology agreements, 4–11
technology licence agreements, 6–05, 6–30, E(19)
works project joint ventures agreements, 4–18—4–19

Alliance charter
contractual alliances, 4–08—4–09
duties between joint venture parties, 11–14

Alliances
see also **Contractual alliances**
advantages, 1–03
best practice, 1–29—1–30
business risks, 1–23
business strategy, 1–06—1–07
commercial drivers, 1–31
commercial transaction types, range, 1–11
corporate venturing, 1–05
criteria for success, 1–24—1–31
disadvantages, 1–14—1–22
equity, 1–13
failure causes of, 1–21
formation, 1–30
non-equity, 1–13
range, 1–11—1–12
trend towards, 1–01—1–07

Alternative dispute resolution
advantages, 14–06
application to joint ventures, 14–08—14–11
expert determination
 binding nature, 14–13
 use, 14–12
international joint ventures, 14–10
mediation, 14–04—14–07, 14–11, E(22)

project joint ventures, 14–09
purpose, 14–05

Ancillary contracts
asset transfer agreements, 6–24
B2B e-commerce joint ventures
 membership agreements, 6–09
 software supply/services agreements, 6–09
 structure, 6–08
common issues, 6–12—6–22
competition law, 6–22
conflicts of interest, 6–13
dispute resolution, 6–21
distributorship, 6–38
employee secondment agreements, 6–32
enforcement by JVC, 6–14
establishment of joint venture, and, 6–23
examples of overall structures, 6–04—6–11
foreign production joint ventures, 6–09
funding agreements
 documentation, 6–25
 shareholder loans, 6–27
 third-party borrowing, 6–26
 venture capital, 6–28—6–29
governing law, 6–20
importance, 6–01—6–02
intellectual property agreements, 6–30
management agreements, 6–33
marketing contracts, 6–38
offtake/purchase contracts
 offtake/purchase contracts, 6–37
ongoing business contracts, 6–34—6–40
power station joint ventures, 6–11
property agreements, 6–31
sale and purchase agreements, 6–24
separation of contracts from joint venture agreement, 6–17
services contracts, 6–39—6–40, E(18)
supply agreements, 6–35
technology joint ventures, 6–30
termination, 6–15—6–16
timing, 6–18—6–19
trade mark licences, E(20)
transfer of assets, 6–24

Arbitral awards
enforcement, 14–20, 14–22—14–23, 14–27
New York Convention, 14–22—14–23

Arbitration
ad hoc arbitration, 14–25

advantages
  choice of place of arbitration, 14–20
  confidentiality, 14–20
  enforcement of awards, 14–20
  finality of awards, 14–20
  identity of arbitrators, 14–20
  neutrality, 14–20
  procedural flexibility, 14–20
  speed and cost, 14–20
arbitral tribunal
  establishment, 14–28—14–31
arbitration clauses
  ad hoc arbitration, 14–36
  drafting, 14–34—14–37
  institutional arbitration, 14–35
  model clauses, 14–35, E(22)
  UNCITRAL Rules, 14–37, E(22)
arbitrators
  appointment by independent authority, 14–30
  identity, 14–20
  nomination, 14–29
  number, 14–29
  presiding arbitrator, 14–31
  sole arbitrator, 14–29
  three-member tribunal, 14–29
awards
  enforcement, 14–20, 14–22—14–23, 14–27
  New York Convention, 14–22—14–23
commercial issues, 14–38
disadvantages
  limited powers of arbitrators, 14–21
  multi-contract disputes, 14–21
institutional arbitration
  American Arbitration Association, 14–26
  Arbitration Institute of the Stockholm Chamber of Commerce, 14–26
  China International Economic and Trade Arbitration Commission, 14–26
  choice of, 14–24, 14–26
  Dubai International Arbitration Centre, 14–26
  Hong Kong International Arbitration Centre, 14–26
  International Chamber of Commerce, 14–26
  International Commercial Arbitration Court at the Chamber of Commerce and Industry of the Russian Federation, 14–26
  LCIA, 14–26
  Singapore International Arbitration Centre, 14–26
interim measures, 14–32—14–33
litigation, and, 14–19—14–21
place of arbitration
  enforceability of award, 14–27
  geographical convenience, 14–27
  London, 14–27
  supportive legal system, 14–27

Arbitrators
appointment by independent authority, 14–30
identity, 14–20
nomination, 14–29
number, 14–29
presiding arbitrator, 14–31
sole arbitrator, 14–29
three-member tribunal, 14–29

Articles of association
joint venture provisions, 5–58
key issues, 5–58
local law, and, 5–57
minority shareholders
  share rights, 9–32
  variation of class rights, 9–36
  veto rights, 9–32, 9–33
  weighted voting rights, 9–37
  whether use preferable to shareholders' agreement, 9–32—9–35
nature of contract, 5–59
precedent, E(11)
relationship with shareholders' agreement
  conflicting provisions, 5–63
  drafting, 5–60
  legal differences, 5–61
  pre-emption rights, 5–62
  veto rights, 5–62

Association of Strategic Alliance Professionals (ASAP)
best practice guidelines, 1–29—1–30
memorandum of understanding, 2–12

Best practice
ASAP guidelines, 1–29—1–30

Board of directors
alternates, 8–21
appointment, 8–14, 8–16, 8–18—8–19
chairman, 8–20
composition, 8–02, 8–16—8–24
independent directors, 8–22
nomination, 8–16—8–17
two-tier structures
  advisory board, 8–24
  European and UK models, 8–23
  executive committee, 8–24

912 INDEX

two-company structure, 8–24
Brazil
international joint ventures, D(1)
Capital
choice of structure, 7–02
initial contributions, 7–01
joint operating agreements,
7–05—7–06
structures
contractual alliances, 7–03—7–06
corporate joint ventures, 7–09
partnerships, 7–07—7–08
Capital gains
contributions to partnership, 15–19
transfer of companies by both
parties, 15–18
transfer of subsidiary
advantages, 15–15
de-grouping charge, 15–17
share for share rollover relief,
15–16
UK substantial shareholding
exemption, 15–16
transfer of trading assets, 15–14
UK corporation tax on chargeable
gains, 15–13
China
international joint ventures, D(2)
Competition law
Art.81 EC Treaty
actual or potential competitors,
16–22
agreements outside Article 81,
16–21
ancillary restrictions,
16–16—16–17
appreciable effect on competition,
16–21
appreciable effect on trade, 16–21
assessing application of Article 81,
16–22
block exemptions, 16–24
enforcement, 16–28—16–30
exemptions under Article 81(3),
16–23—16–26
foreclosure of opportunities, 16–22
hard-core restrictions, 16–22
individual exemption,
16–25—16–26
intra-group joint ventures, 16–21
Minor Agreements Notice, 16–21
minor sales/purchasing joint
ventures, 16–21
network of joint ventures, 16–22
self-assessment, 16–27—16–28
spill-over effects, 16–22
unnecessary restraints, 16–22

Competition Act 1998
Chapter 1 prohibition,
16–40—16–43
consequences of infringement,
16–42
effect on joint ventures, 16–43
non-application, 16–41
co-operative agreements
EC and UK law, 16–39
UK Competition Act 1998,
16–40—16–43
co-operative ventures, 16–04
EC Merger Regulation
ancillary restrictions,
16–16—16–17
application to joint venture,
16–05—16–09
clearance test, 16–12—16–15
Commission's powers, 16–19
commitments, 16–19
Community dimension, 16–06
co-operative aspects of
full-function joint ventures,
16–14—16–15
co-ordination between parties,
16–15
fines, 16–19
full-function joint venture,
16–08—16–09, 16–14—16–15
joint control, 16–07
notification, 16–18
one-stop-shop principle,
16–10—16–11
procedure, 16–18
substantive assessments, 16–13
thresholds, 16–06
generally, 16–02—16–03
merger-type ventures, 16–04
UK merger control
Enterprise Act 2002,
16–32—16–35
joint ventures caught by
Enterprise Act, 16–34
joint ventures not caught by
Enterprise Act, 16–35
jurisdictional thresholds, 16–36
non-application of EC law, 16–31
notification, 16–38
procedure and timetable, 16–38
substantive test for clearance,
16–37
Confidentiality
agreements, 2–06—2–09
Contracts
ancillary contracts, 2–43, 6–01—6–41
importance of negotiations,
2–44—2–46

language, 2–45
negotiating team, 2–45
Contractual alliances
  advantages
    flexibility, 3–06
    lack of formality, 3–06
    resource management, 3–06
    tax efficiency, 3–06
    termination, 3–06
  alliance charter, 4–08—4–09
  anti-trust, 4–06
  basic issues, 4–06—4–07
  capital, 7–03—7–06
  confidential information, 4–06
  contributions, 4–06
  co-operative agreements, 3–08
  corporate governance, 8–03
  cost, 4–06
  disadvantages
    competition law, 3–07
    drafting, 3–07
    identity, 3–07
    organisational structure, 3–07
    partnership risk, 3–07
    transfer, 3–07
  dispute resolution, 4–06
  drafting, 4–06
  examples, 4–10—4–33
  governance, 4–06
  indemnity, 4–06
  information flows, 4–06
  intellectual property rights, 4–06
  inter-party transactions, 4–06
  joint operating agreements, 7–05—7–06
  liability, 4–06
  management committee
    appointments, 8–07
    meetings, 8–07
    precedent, E(5)
    terms of reference, 8–06
  memorandum of understanding, 4–07
  non-compete clauses, 4–06
  objectives, 4–06
  operational management, 4–06
  profit-sharing, 4–06
  property development joint ventures
    advantages, 4–25
    structures, 4–26—4–27
  R&D collaborations
    agreement, E(5)
    checklist of key issues, 4–12
    types of agreement, 4–10
  range of non-equity alliances, 4–01—4–05
  risk and revenue sharing arrangements
    drafting, 4–24
    example, 4–22
    key issues, 4–23
    Specialisation Block Exemption, and, 4–24
  specialisation agreements
    examples, 4–14
    main features, 4–13
  supplier/procurement partnerships
    binding partnering arrangements, 4–31—4–33
    non-binding charters, 4–29—4–30
    partnering, 4–28
  technology collaborations
    checklist of key issues, 4–12
    examples of agreements, 4–11
  termination, 4–06
  terminology, 3–05
  umbrella legal form, as, 4–34
  works project joint ventures
    agreements, 4–18—4–19
    checklist of key issues, 4–17
    formation of jointly-owned company, 4–16
    integrated joint ventures, 4–15
    non-integrated joint ventures, 4–15
Co-operative ventures
see **Limited function ventures**
Corporate governance
  alliance governing body
    contractual alliances, 8–04—8–07
    equity joint ventures, 8–08—8–11
    responsibilities, 8–04
    role, 8–02, 8–04—8–11
  board of directors
    alternates, 8–21
    appointment, 8–14, 8–16, 8–18—8–19
    chairman, 8–20
    composition, 8–02, 8–16—8–24
    independent directors, 8–22
    nomination, 8–16—8–17
    two-tier structures, 8–23—8–24
  contractual alliance, 8–03, 8–05—8–07
  control
    appointment of managers, 8–15
    contractual arrangements, 8–15
    HR structures, 8–15
    informal mechanisms, 8–15
    management models, 8–12
    relationship with parents, 8–15
    voting rights, 8–13, 8–14
    whether shared, 8–02
  directors' duties, 8–42—8–66
  dispute resolution, 8–02
  equity joint ventures, 8–03, 8–08—8–11

joint venture parents
  decision-making by board, 8–26—8–29
  reporting relationship, 8–30
  reserved matters, 8–27—8–29
  supervision by, 8–25
management deadlock, 8–41
minority protection, 8–02, 8–40
operational management, 8–02, 8–31—8–39
parent companies, 8–02
Corporate joint ventures
see also **Equity joint ventures**
advantages
  accounting, 3–16
  corporate laws, 3–16
  financing, 3–16
  identity, 3–16
  limited liability, 3–16
  share rights, 3–16
  transfer of interests, 3–16
appropriateness, 3–15
capital structure
  accounting treatment, 7–09
  anti-dilution, 7–09
  class rights, 7–09
  debt/equity ratio, 7–09
  default, 7–09
  equity proportions, 7–09
  exit, 7–09
  loan finance, 7–09
  management, 7–09
corporate governance, 8–11
default, 7–46—7–48
disadvantages
  compliance requirements, 3–17
  formality, 3–17
  loss of flexibility, 3–17
  publicity, 3–17
  winding-up procedure, 3–17
European models, 3–18
location, 3–19—3–20
shareholders' agreements, *see* **Shareholders' agreements**
Corporate venturing
as business opportunity, 1–05
Czech Republic
international joint ventures, D(3)
Deadlock
see **Management deadlock**
Directors' duties
articles of association
  modification of disclosure requirement, 8–55
  precedent, E(11)
breach of duty, 8–46
care, skill and diligence, 8–47—8–48

Companies Act 2006, 8–43—8–45, 8–51, 8–56, 8–60, 8–62, 8–65
enforcement
  duties to joint venture company, 11–28—11–30
  statutory derivative actions, 11–31—11–33
fiduciary duties
  Australian case law, 8–52
  confidential information, 8–58
  conflicts of interest, 8–56—8–57
  disclosure of interest, 8–54—8–55
  enforcement, 11–28—11–30
  independent judgment, 8–49—8–53
  New Zealand company law, 8–52
  promoting company's success, 8–49—8–53
  US rules, 8–52
indemnities
  company indemnifying own directors, 8–60
  groups of companies, 8–62
  third-party proceedings, 8–61
insolvency, 8–59
insurance, 8–63
introduction, 8–42
liability for acts of co-directors, 8–48
shadow directors, 8–65—8–66
shareholders
  liability for director's breach of duty, 8–48
Dispute resolution
see also **Alternative dispute resolution; Mediation**
executive level dispute resolution, 14–02—14–03
importance of provisions, 14–01
Distribution of profits
tax costs
  form of costs, 15–29
  income access structures, 15–32
  income from operating subsidiaries, 15–30
  payment to joint venture parents, 15–31
Documentation
ancillary contracts, 2–43
business plans, 2–42
checklist, F(2)
confidentiality agreements, 2–06—2–09
drafting, 2–36
framework agreements, 2–38—2–39
importance, 2–44—2–46
joint venture agreement, 2–37
sale and purchase agreement, 2–40—2–41

shareholders' agreements, *see* **Shareholders' agreements**
subscription agreement, 2–41
transaction "road map", 2–04—2–05
Due diligence
  planning joint ventures
    circumstances of venture, 2–20
    importance, 2–18
    investigations, 2–19
    timing, 2–21
  questionnaire, E(3)
Duties between joint venture parties
  see also **Directors' duties; Unfairly prejudicial conduct**
  confidential information
    after termination or transfer, 11–06
    during joint venture operations, 11–06
    during negotiations, 11–06
    misuse, 11–06
  contractual remedies
    alliance charter, 11–14
    default remedies, 11–10, 11–12—11–13
    right of termination by notice, 11–10, 11–11
  contractual terms
    incentives, 11–05
    responsibilities, 11–04
  directors' duties
    enforcement, 11–28—11–33
  fiduciary duties
    contractual alliance, 11–16, 11–18—11–20
    corporate joint ventures, 11–16, 11–22—11–24
    good faith, 11–15—11–27
    implied duties, 11–17
    limited liability partnerships, 11–25
    partnerships, 11–16, 11–21
    United States, 11–19
  non-compete clauses, 11–07—11–09
  opportunistic behaviour, 11–01—11–03, 11–44—11–45
  remedies
    fraud on a minority, 11–35
    just and equitable winding-up, 11–42—11–43
    oppressive behaviour, 11–34
    unfairly prejudicial conduct, 11–36—11–41
E-commerce ventures
  capital structure, 5–11
  competition law, 5–11
  corporate governance, 5–11
  equity incentives, 5–11
  examples, 5–10
  exits, 5–11
  membership agreements, 6–09
  new participants, 5–11
  objective, 6–09
  public offering, 5–11
  software supply/services agreements, 6–09
  structure, 6–08
  trade sale, 5–11
EC law
  Art.81 EC Treaty
    actual or potential competitors, 16–22
    agreements outside Article 81, 16–21
    ancillary restrictions, 16–16—16–17
    appreciable effect on competition, 16–21
    appreciable effect on trade, 16–21
    assessing application of Article 81, 16–22
    block exemptions, 16–24
    enforcement, 16–28—16–30
    exemptions under Article 81(3), 16–23—16–26
    foreclosure of opportunities, 16–22
    hard-core restrictions, 16–22
    individual exemption, 16–25—16–26
    intra-group joint ventures, 16–21
    Minor Agreements Notice, 16–21
    minor sales/purchasing joint ventures, 16–21
    network of joint ventures, 16–22
    self-assessment, 16–27—16–28
    spill-over effects, 16–22
    unnecessary restraints, 16–22
  co-operative agreements
    EC and UK law, 16–39
  EC Merger Regulation
    ancillary restrictions, 16–16—16–17
    application to joint venture, 16–05—16–09
    clearance test, 16–12—16–15
    Commission's powers, 16–19
    commitments, 16–19
    Community dimension, 16–06
    co-operative aspects of full-function joint ventures, 16–14—16–15
    co-ordination between parties, 16–15
    fines, 16–19

full-function joint venture,
16–08—16–09, 16–14—16–15
joint control, 16–07
notification, 16–18
one-stop-shop principle,
16–10—16–11
procedure, 16–18
substantive assessments, 16–13
thresholds, 16–06
Emerging markets
alternatives, 20–06
areas of key importance, 20–07
conflicting priorities, 20–04
documentation, 20–18
evolution of alliances, 20–05
key issues, 20–16—20–17
process, 20–19—20–21
Employees
see also **Pensions**
benefits, 18–02
consultation
Consultation of Employees
Regulation 2004, 18–05
European Works Councils,
18–06—18–07, 18–11
Information and Consultation
Directive, 18–04
obligations, 18–02
employee share schemes
company share option plans,
18–37
enterprise management incentive
options, 18–39
future incentives, 18–36
impact of transfer, 18–36
JVC's own share incentive
arrangements, 18–40
participation in existing schemes,
18–37—18–38
SAYE schemes, 18–37
share incentive plans, 18–37
unapproved share options, 18–37
identification, 18–02
pensions
joint venture employees,
18–25—18–34
joint venture party liability, 18–35
nature of benefits, 18–02
secondments, 18–23
restrictive covenants
enforcement, 18–18—18–19
key individuals, 18–17
terms, 18–20
secondments
advantages, 18–22
authority of employees to bind
JVC, 18–23

consent, 18–23
control, 18–23
indemnities, 18–23
intellectual property, 18–23
liability to employee, 18–23
payment, 18–23
pensions, 18–23
structure, 18–21
VAT, 18–23
share incentives, 18–02
terms and conditions
consent to change of terms,
18–14—18–15
decision-making process, 18–16
harmonisation, 18–13—18–16
transfer
business transfers in UK,
18–09—18–11
existing business transferred to
JVC, 18–08
non-TUPE transfers, 18–12
TUPE transfers, 18–09—18–11
work permits, 18–02, 18–24
Employment
see also **Employees**
control procedures, 18–02
key issues, 18–01—18–03
legal implications, 18–41
terms, 18–02
Equity joint ventures
business form, as, 5–01—5–02
categories, 5–01—5–14
co-operative ventures
see limited function ventures
corporate governance, 8–03,
8–08—8–11
full-function joint ventures
creation by merger, 5–04
intellectual property, 5–05
management, 5–05
meaning, 5–03
termination, 5–05
transferability of interests, 5–05
hybrid structures
dual-headed structures, 5–46
limited liability companies, 5–46
limited liability partnerships, 5–46
tax planning, 5–46
joint venture companies
advantages, 5–34
constitutional documents,
5–57—5–63
European companies, 5–38—5–45
limited companies, 5–35—5–37
shareholders' agreements,
5–47—5–56
legal relationship, 5–64

limited function ventures
  acquisition vehicle, 5–12
  ancillary contracts, 5–06
  e-commerce platforms,
    5–10—5–11
  governance, 5–06
  meaning, 5–06
  outsourcing joint ventures, 5–09
  production joint ventures, 5–08
  specific provisions, 5–06
  transferability of interests, 5–06
minority equity investments
  examples, 5–13
  legal issues, 5–14
  meaning, 5–13
partners' meetings, 8–09
partnership board, E(6)
partnerships
  advantages, 5–16
  agreements, 5–20
  existence of partnership,
    5–18—5–20
  general partnerships, 5–21—5–26
  legal form, 5–15—5–33
  limited partnerships, 5–27—5–32
  Partnership Act 1890, 5–19
  types, 5–17
  UK limited liability partnerships,
    5–33
European companies
European private company
  advantages, 5–44
  Commission's proposals,
    5–44—5–45
  management, 5–45
Societas Europaea (SE)
  advantages, 5–41
  creation, 5–40
  development of single market,
    5–39
  disadvantages, 5–42
  employee participation, 5–40
  EU operations, 5–40
  management, 5–40
  national legislation, 5–40
  new rules, 5–43
  registration, 5–40
  share capital, 5–40
  subsidiaries, 5–40
  transfer to other Member States,
    5–40
European Economic Interest Grouping (EEIG)
  agreement, E(7)
  characteristics, 3–28
  EU Port EEIG, 3–29
  European Engine Alliance EEIG,
    3–29

  formation, 3–30
  uses, 3–29
Exit
  see also **Management deadlock;
    Pre-emption rights;
    Termination; Transfers of
    shares**
  ancillary contracts, 13–46
  change
    hardship, E(13)
    market conditions, 13–45
    reference to arbitration, 13–45
    review, 13–45
    terms of venture, 13–45
  completion mechanics, 13–46
  confidentiality, 13–46
  consequences, 13–46
  deadlock, 13–03, 13–44
  deed of adherence, 13–46
  fixed-term venture or alliance, 13–03,
    13–06—13–08
  good leaver/bad leaver, 13–46
  guarantees, 13–46
  intellectual property, 13–46
  joint renewal of alliance, 13–03,
    13–06—13–08
  loans, 13–46
  name, 13–46
  non-compete clauses, 13–46
  provisions
    change or transformation, 13–03
    complexity, 13–50
    deadlock, 13–03
    design, 13–03—13–05
    importance, 13–01—13–02
    put options, 13–03
    sale or public offering, 13–03
    transfer of interest, 13–03
  put and call options
    agreement, E(15)
    disadvantages, 13–34
    key issues, 13–38
    meaning, 13–33
    price formulae, 13–35—13–37
  realisation of assets, 13–46
  sale or public offering
    precedent, E(10)
    provisions, 13–39—13–40
    third party offer, 13–41—13–42
  tax, 13–46
  transfer of interest, 13–03, 13–43
  warranties, 13–46
  winding-up, 13–47—13–49
Financing joint ventures
  default
    corporate joint ventures,
      7–46—7–48

rights of non-defaulting party, 7–44
unincorporated joint ventures, 7–45
funding plan, 7–49
future financing
  agreed funding plan, 7–34
  emergency funding, 7–42
  equity funding, 7–38—7–40, E(10)
  long-term commitments, 7–37
  shareholder commitments, 7–35—7–37
  subscription obligations, 7–41
initial funding
  charges, 7–25—7–26
  guarantees, 7–24
  non-cash contributions, 7–17—7–18
  outside finance, 7–21—7–23
  preference shares, 7–12—7–16
  share capital, 7–10—7–11
  shareholder loans, 7–19—7–20
  sole risk, 7–43
  tax issues, 7–29—7–33
  venture capital finance, 7–27—7–28
shareholders
  funding agreement, E(16)

France
international joint ventures, D(4)

Full-function joint ventures
creation by merger, 5–04
intellectual property, 5–05
management, 5–05
meaning, 5–03
termination, 5–05
transferability of interests, 5–05

Germany
international joint ventures, D(5)

Good faith
duties between joint venture parties, 11–15—11–25
express obligations, 11–26—11–27
international joint ventures, 20–15

Governance
see **Corporate governance**

Guarantees
cross-indemnities, 7–24
joint and several basis, 7–24
joint venture agreement, 7–24

India
international joint ventures, D(6)

Institutional arbitration
American Arbitration Association, 14–26
Arbitration Institute of the Stockholm Chamber of Commerce, 14–26
China International Economic and Trade Arbitration Commission, 14–26
choice of, 14–24, 14–26
Dubai International Arbitration Centre, 14–26
Hong Kong International Arbitration Centre, 14–26
International Chamber of Commerce, 14–26
International Commercial Arbitration Court at the Chamber of Commerce and Industry of the Russian Federation, 14–26
LCIA, 14–26
Singapore International Arbitration Centre, 14–26

Intellectual property rights
competition law, 17–08
identification
  background technology, 17–06
  foreground technology, 17–06
  national rights, 17–05
  rights held by proprietor or licensee, 17–04
  technology, 17–03—17–06
importance, 17–01—17–02, 17–30
key issues in different phases
  establishment of joint venture, 17–07
  information exchange agreement, E(1)
  operation of joint venture, 17–07
  pre-contract, 17–07
  termination, 17–07
research and development collaborations
  access to results, 17–12
  collaboration agreement, E(5)
  competition law, 17–15—17–17
  contractual alliances, 17–09
  ownership of results, 17–13—17–14
  R&D Block Exemption, 17–17
  scope of rights licensed by each party, 17–10—17–11
technology transfer
  agreement checklist, 17–23
  block exemption, 17–26
  export controls, 17–24—17–25
  local party, 17–22—17–26
  technology licence, 17–23, E(19)
technology-based joint venture
  formation, 17–18
  key issues, 17–21
  licensing, 17–19—17–20

ownership, 17–19—17–20
Technology licence agreements, E(19)
trade marks
  key issues, 17–29
  licences, 17–27—17–29
  precedent, E(20)

International joint ventures
activities, 20–03
Brazil, D(1)
China, D(2)
civil law systems, 20–15
cross-border mergers, 20–01
Czech Republic. D(3)
dispute resolution
  arbitration, 20–25
emerging markets
  alternatives, 20–06
  areas of key importance, 20–07
  conflicting priorities, 20–04
  documentation, 20–18
  evolution of alliances, 20–05
  key issues, 20–16—20–17
  process, 20–19—20–21
France, D(4)
Germany, D(5)
governing law
  amiable compositeurs, 20–22
  choice of law, 20–22
  ex aequo et bono, 20–22
  local law, 20–22, 20–24
  state agencies as parties, 20–23
  trade-off with place of arbitration, 20–22
growth, 20–01—20–07
India, D(6)
instability of alliances, 20–04
Italy, D(7)
ITC model agreement, E(13)
Japan, D(8)
jurisdictions, 20–26, D(1)—D(14)
local law regime, understanding, 20–13
local partners, 20–01, 20–02
multi-national strategic alliances, 20–01
Netherlands, D(9)
Poland, D(10)
preparation
  commercial due diligence, 20–11—20–12
  convergence of approach, 20–08—20–10
  culture of local party, 20–12
  currency risks, 20–12
  financial information, 20–12
  local law regime, 20–13

  local party's existing business, 20–12
  political environment, 20–12
Russia, D(11)
South Africa, D(12)
Spain, D(13)
United States, D(14)

Italy
international joint ventures, D(7)

JANES
see **Joint arrangements which are not entities**

Japan
international joint ventures, D(8)

Joint arrangements which are not entities ("JANES")
meaning, 19–20
requirements, 19–20

Joint operating agreements
default, 7–45
oil and gas operations, in, 4–20
provisions, 4–21

Joint venture agreements
drafting
  checklist, F(2)

Joint venture companies
see also **Articles of association; Directors' duties**
advantages, 5–34
constitutional documents
  importance, 5–57
  shareholders' agreement and articles of association, 5–60—5–63
  UK articles of association, 5–58—5–59
corporate governance
  decision-making authority of board, 8–26—8–29
  reserved matters, 8–27—8–29
directors' duties, 8–42—8–66
European companies
  new legal forms, 5–38
  Societas Europaea, 5–39—5–43
limited companies
  European entities, 5–36
  UK private limited company, 5–35
  UK public limited company, 5–35
  UK unlimited company, 5–35
  United States, 5–37
shareholders' agreements
  checklist, 5–48,
  enforceability, 5–50—5–52
  joint venture company as party, 5–55—5–56
  key issues, 5–49
  meaning, 5–47—5–48

parties, 5–53—5–54
precedents, E(9), E(10), E(11)
Joint ventures
access to technology, 1–08
advantages, 1–03
best practice, 1–29—1–30
business risks, 1–23
catalyst for change, 1–08
commercial drivers, 1–31
communications, 1–20
contracts, 1–20
cost savings, 1–08
creeping sale or acquisition, 1–08
criteria for success, 1–24—1–31
culture, 1–20
customer base expansion, 1–08
disadvantages, 1–14—1–22
dispute resolution, 1–20
emerging economies, and, 1–08
equity, 1–13, 2–29
failure, 1–21
financing, 1–20
global competition, 1–08
increased collaboration, 1–09
legal form, 3–01—3–36
legal planning, 2–01—2–46
leveraged, 1–08
life-cycle, 1–16—1–19
management, 1–20, 1–22
negotiations, 1–20
non-equity, 1–13, 2–29
objectives, 1–10, 1–20
range, 1–11—1–12
reasons for, 1–08—1–10
risk sharing, 1–08
setting up, 1–26
technology, 1–08, 1–20
termination, 1–20
trend towards, 1–01—1–07
Legal forms
basic categories, 3–01
choice of forms, 3–35, 3–36
contractual alliances
advantages, 3–06
co-operative agreements, 3–08
disadvantages, 3–07
terminology, 3–05
corporate joint ventures
advantages, 3–16
appropriateness, 3–15
disadvantages, 3–17
European models, 3–18
location, 3–19—3–20
dual-headed structures
accounting, 3–33
distributions, 3–33
establishment, 3–31—3–32
management, 3–33
profit-sharing, 3–33
repayment of capital, 3–33
tax, 3–34
European Economic Interest Groupings
agreement, E(7)
characteristics, 3–28
formation, 3–30
uses, 3–29
hybrid structures, 3–21—3–34
issues in deciding form
accounting, 3–02
administration, 3–02
competition law, 3–02
customised drafting, 3–03
effect on business relationship, 3–04
financing, 3–02
liability exposure, 3–02
management structure, 3–02
national considerations, 3–02
reporting, 3–02
tax cost, 3–02
termination, 3–02
transferability, 3–02
limited liability partnerships
advantages, 3–24
agreement, E(8)
disadvantages, 3–25
key features, 3–23
legislation, 3–22
United Kingdom, in, 3–26
partnerships
advantages, 3–11, 3–13
disadvantages, 3–12
meaning, 3–09
model for equity joint ventures, 3–10, 3–14
US limited liability company, 3–27
Limited function ventures
acquisition vehicle, 5–12
ancillary contracts, 5–06
e-commerce platforms, 5–10—5–11
governance, 5–06
meaning, 5–06
outsourcing joint ventures, 5–09
production joint ventures, 5–08
specific provisions, 5–06
transferability of interests, 5–06
Limited liability partnerships
advantages, 3–24
agreement, E(8)
disadvantages, 3–25
key features, 3–23
legislation, 3–22
United Kingdom, in, 3–26, 5–33

Litigation
  arbitration, and, 14–14,
    14–19—14–21
  national courts
    generally, 14–15
    jurisdiction clauses, 14–17—14–18
    use of neutral country, 14–16
Management
see also **Management deadlock**
  management committees
    contractual alliances, 8–05—8–07
  management deadlock, 8–41,
    10–01—10–33
  operational management
    appointment of executives, 8–32
    board responsibilities, 8–31
    chief executive, 8–33
    decision-making, 8–34, 8–37
    delegation of authority,
      8–34—8–37
    management boards, 8–35
    tax, 8–38—8–39
    terms of reference, 8–36
  problems, 1–20, 1–22
  skills, 8–01
Management committees
  contractual alliances
    appointments, 8–07
    meetings, 8–07
    precedent, E(5)
    terms of reference, 8–06
Management deadlock
  avoidance measures
    constitutional documents, 10–06
    management structures,
      10–04—10–05
    section 306 Companies Act 2006,
      10–06
  board level, 10–01
  boycott of meetings, 10–01, 10–06
  "divorce" measures
    commercial consequences, 10–33
    multi-choice procedure, 10–16,
      10–30—10–32
    put/call options, 10–16,
      10–20—10–21
    sale of company, 10–16, 10–19
    "shoot out" procedures, 10–16,
      10–22—10–29
    termination provisions in
      agreement, 10–15
    voluntary winding-up, 10–16,
      10–17—10–18, 10–34
  provisions, 10–01—10–03
  resolution
    additional vote, 10–09—10–10
    dispute resolution, 10–12
    dispute review panel, 10–13
    "divorce" measures, 10–15—10–33
    enabling venture to continue,
      10–08—10–14
    independent director's swing vote,
      10–11
    precedent, E(21)
    reference to chair or chief
      executive of parent
      shareholders, 10–14
  shareholder level, 10–01
  shoot-out procedures
    deterrent approach, 10–29
    fairest sealed bid, 10–27
    highest sealed bid, 10–26
    Russian roulette, 10–22—10–24
    sale shoot-out, 10–28
    Texas shoot-out, 10–26
    trigger event, 10–25
Mediation
see also **Alternative dispute**
    resolution
Memorandum of understanding
  content, 2–12
  exclusivity agreements, 2–16
  heads of terms, 2–13—2–14
  precedent, E(2)
  purpose, 2–11—2–14
  usefulness, 2–10, 2–11
  whether legally binding, 2–15—2–17
Mergers and acquisitions
  advantages, 1–04
  disadvantages, 1–04
Minority investment
see **Minority shareholders**
Minority protection
see **Minority shareholders**
Minority shareholders
  access to information
    express rights, 9–21
  articles of association
    share rights, 9–32
    variation of class rights, 9–36
    veto rights, 9–32, 9–33
    weighted voting rights, 9–37
    whether use preferable to
      sharcholders' agreement,
      9–32—9–35
  background factors, 9–01—9–03
  balance of interests, 9–41
  claims against majority party, 9–24
  consent to major decisions
    decisions by board or
      shareholders, 9–12
    limitation of consent rights, 9–14
    "put"options, 9–11
    reserved matters, 9–09

super-majority vote, 9–13
veto rights, 9–10— 9–11
contractual protection
board representation, 9–06—9–08
consent rights, 9–09—9–14
dilution, 9–15— 9–18
key aims, 9–05
dilution
catch up option, 9–17
new issues of shares, 9–16
price protection, 9–18
safeguarding equity stake, 9–15
dividends
distribution policy, 9–19
leakage of profits to majority
shareholder, 9–20
exit
buy-back by JVC, 9–29
lack of exit route, 9–25
piggy backing on share placement,
9–31
put option, 9–27
redeemable shares, 9–28
"tag-along" right, 9–30
transfer, 9–26
protective undertakings
accounts, 9–23
contracts, 9–23
insurance, 9–23
legality, 9–23
tax planning, 9–22
shareholders' agreement
positive obligations, 9–32
precedent, E(10)
veto rights, 9–32—9–34
whether preferable to use of
articles of association,
9–32—9–35
statutory protection
Companies Act 2006, 9–04
strategic minority investment
commercial issues, 9–39
procedural issues, 9–39
regulatory issues, 9–39
share rights, 9–39
strategic alliance agreement, E(4)
strategic equity investment,
9–38—9–40
subscription agreement, 9–40
Netherlands
international joint ventures, D(9)
Non-equity alliances
agreement, E(4)
range, 4–01—4–05
Partnerships
see also **Limited liability
partnerships**

advantages
flexibility, 3–11, 5–16
public filings, 3–11
simplicity, 3–11
tax, 3–11, 3–13, 5–16
agreements, 5–20
capital, 7–07—7–08
disadvantages
external finance, 3–12
liability, 3–12
loss of corporate identity, 3–12
existence of partnership, 5–18—5–20
general partnerships
documentation, 5–26
European jurisdictions,
5–22—5–23
key issues, 5–24
legislative reform, 5–25
United Kingdom, 5–21
legal form, 5–15—5–33
limited partnerships
English law, 5–28—5–30
European national legislation,
5–31
meaning, 5–27
UK limited liability partnerships,
5–33
United States, 5–32
meaning, 3–09
model for equity joint ventures, 3–10,
3–14
Partnership Act 1890, 5–19
types, 5–17
UK limited liability partnerships,
5–33
Pensions
EC Pensions Directive, 18–26
existing scheme of joint venture
party, 18–29—18–31
joint venture company's own scheme,
18–32—18–34
joint venture employees,
18–25—18–34
joint venture party liability, 18–35
nature of benefits, 18–02
Pensions Act 2004, 18–27
secondments, 18–23
UK Pensions Regulator, 18–35
Planning joint ventures
see also **Documentation**
checklists, F(1), F(2)
confidentiality agreements,
2–06—2–09
contracts
ancillary contracts, 2–43
importance of negotiations,
2–44—2–46

due diligence
  circumstances of venture, 2–20
  importance, 2–18
  investigations, 2–19
  questionnaire, E(3)
  timing, 2–21
foreign jurisdictions, 2–21—2–22
importance of contract negotiations, 2–44—2–46
key issues, 2–03
lawyers, role of, 2–01—2–02
legal documents, 2–36—2–43
legal form, 2–27—2–29
memorandum of understanding
  content, 2–12
  EC law, 2–17
  exclusivity agreements, 2–16
  heads of terms, 2–13—2–14
  purpose, 2–11—2–14
  usefulness, 2–10, 2–11
  whether legally binding, 2–15—2–17
status report, 2–05
third party consents, 2–24—2–26
transaction "road map", 2–04—2–05
valuation
  different contributions, 2–34
  equalisation measures, 2–35
  legal rules, 2–33
  methodology, 2–30—2–34
  negotiations, 2–31
  net assets, 2–32

Poland
international joint ventures, D(10)

Pre-emption rights
change of control, 12–46
charges, 12–24
consent of continuing party, 12–31—12–32
drag-along, 12–35
entire holding, 12–25
guarantees, 12–37
hard and soft rights, 12–06
intra-group transfers, 12–38—12–39
loans, 12–36
multi-party joint ventures, 12–27—12–29, E(10)
partial transfers, 12–25—12–26
pre-emption provisions
  articles of association, 12–47
  shareholders' agreement, 12–47
procedure, 12–05, E(10), 12–22—12–23
price
  fair price determination, 12–18—12–21
  fair value, 12–18
  form of pre-emption right, and, 12–13
  market value on pro rata basis, 12–18
  set by seller, 12–14
  third-party purchaser, 12–15—12–17
regulatory approval, 12–40—12–42
revocation, 12–30
right of first offer, 12–07—12–10
right of first refusal, 12–11—12–12
share sale agreement, E(17)
shareholder approval, 12–40—12–42
tag-along, 12–33—12–34
valuation
  "baseball" determination, 12–20
  discounted cash flow, 12–18
  dividend yield, 12–18
  earnings basis, 12–18
  fair price determination, 12–18—12–21
  fair value, 12–18
  guidance, 12–19
  independent valuers, 12–21
  market value on pro rata basis, 12–18
  net asset value, 12–18
  start-up cost, 12–18
wrongful transfer, 12–49—12–50

Preference shares
convertible, 7–14
cumulative, 7–14
loan stock, 7–15
meaning, 7–12
outside UK, 7–16
participating, 7–14
precedent, E(12)
redeemable, 7–14
rights attached to shares, 7–13
UK types, 7–14

Preparation
international joint ventures, 20–11—20–12
joint ventures
  initial issues checklist, F(1)

Property development joint ventures
advantages, 4–25
forward funding arrangements, 4–26
joint ventures between developer and others, 4–26
joint ventures between developers, 4–26
profit-sharing lease, 4–26
structures, 4–26—4–27

Regulation
see also **Competition law**
competition law

Art.81 EC Treaty, 16–20—16–30
co-operative agreements,
16–39—16–43
co-operative ventures, 16–04,
16–20—16–30
EC Merger Regulation,
16–05—16–19
generally, 16–02—16–03
merger-type ventures, 16–04
UK merger control, 16–31—16–38
foreign investment review, 16–02
industry-specific regulation, 16–02,
16–44
international trade regulation
anti-dumping, 16–47
behavioural laws, 16–52
countervailing duties, 16–48
export/import controls,
16–49—16–51
generally, 16–02, 16–45
intellectual property, 16–53
subsidies, 16–48
trade remedy laws, 16–46—16–48
joint venture planning, and, 16–54
restriction of competition, 16–01
Research and development collaborations
agreement, E(5)
checklist of key issues, 4–12
types of agreement, 4–10
Risk and revenue sharing arrangements
drafting, 4–24
example, 4–22
key issues, 4–23
Specialisation Block Exemption, and, 4–24
Russia
international joint ventures, D(11)
Share capital
voting rights, 7–10—7–11
Shareholder loans
assignability, 7–19
debt/equity ratio, 7–19
default, 7–19
forfeiture, 7–19
interest, 7–19
precedent, E(16)
repayments, 7–19
security, 7–19
share transfers, 7–20
subordination, 7–19
tax, 7–19
termination, 7–19
timing, 7–19
tranches, 7–19
Shareholders' agreements

checklist, 5–48,
enforceability, 5–50—5–52
joint venture company as party
addition of JVC as party, 5–56
advantages, 5–55
disadvantages, 5–55
"no fetter" doctrine, 5–55
key issues, 5–49
meaning, 5–47—5–48
parties, 5–53—5–54
precedents, E(9), E(10), E(11)
relationship with articles of association
conflicting provisions, 5–63
drafting, 5–60
legal differences, 5–61
pre-emption rights, 5–62
veto rights, 5–62
Societas Europaea (SE)
advantages, 5–41
disadvantages, 5–42
main features, 5–40
South Africa
international joint ventures, D(12)
Spain
international joint ventures, D(13)
Specialisation agreements
examples, 4–14
main features, 4–13
Supplier/procurement partnerships
binding partnering arrangements,
4–31—4–33
non-binding charters, 4–29—4–30
partnering, 4–28
Tax
distribution of profits, 15–29—15–32
exit, 13–46
financing joint ventures
capital duties, 7–29
interest, 7–29
place of borrowing, 7–29
tax loss, 7–29
thin capitalisation, 7–30—7–33
international joint ventures, 20–13
operational management,
8–38—8–39
partnerships, 3–11, 3–13, 5–16
shareholder loans, 7–19
UK corporation tax on chargeable gains, 15–13
Tax planning
see also **Capital gains**
choice of joint venture vehicle
contractual alliances, 15–04
corporate entities, 15–07
fiscally transparent vehicles, 15–06
generally, 15–03

partnerships, 15–05
distribution of profits
  income access structures, 15–32
  income from operating
    subsidiaries, 15–30
  payment to joint venture parents,
    15–31
  tax costs, 15–29—15–32
establishment costs
  capital gains, 15–13—15–20
  tax costs of contributions, 15–12
financing costs, 15–28
income tax, 15–21
key issues, 15–01—15–02
location of JVC
  international JVC, 15–08
  third-country jurisdiction,
    15–10—15–11
  United Kingdom, 15–09
ongoing activities, effect on
  consortium relief, 15–35—15–38
  group relief, 15–34, 15–38
  objectives of planning, 15–33
recapture of alliances, 15–22—15–23
tax specialists, 15–46
termination
  capital gains tax, 15–41—15–43
  contractual alliances, 15–45
  general tax issues, 15–40
  partnerships, 15–44
transfer of losses, 15–24
transfer pricing, 15–39
transfer taxes
  stamp duty, 15–25—15–26
  VAT, 15–27

Technology collaborations
checklist of key issues, 4–12
examples of agreements, 4–11

Technology joint ventures
construction contracts, 6–05
structure, 6–04
supply/purchase contracts, 6–05
technology licence agreements, 6–05

Termination
ancillary contracts, 13–46
buy/sell options
  call options, 13–13
  effect on ancillary contracts, 13–14
  liquidation, 13–13, E(9)
  notices, 13–11
  shoot-outs, 13–13
buy-back of shares, 13–11,
  13–15—13–16
cause, for
  change of control, 13–21,
    13–28—13–31
  default, 13–21, 13–22—13–24
  end of purpose, 13–21, 13–32
  generally, 13–03, 13–20—13–21
  insolvency, 13–21, 13–26—13–27
  performance target, 13–21
  persistent use of veto, 13–21,
    13–25
completion mechanics, 13–46
confidentiality, 13–46
consequences, 13–46
convenience, for, 13–03,
  13–09—13–19
deed of adherence, 13–46
good leaver/bad leaver, 13–46
guarantees, 13–46
intellectual property, 13–46
liquidation, 13–11, 13–12
loans, 13–46
multi-choice approach, 13–11,
  13–18—13–19
name, 13–46
non-compete clauses, 13–46
notices
  buy/sell options, 13–11
  buy-back, 13–11
  contractual alliances, 13–11
  corporate joint ventures, 13–11
  multi-choice approach, 13–11
  partnerships, 13–11
  sale or public offering, 13–11
provisions, 13–50
realisation of assets, 13–46
sale or public offering, 13–11, 13–17
tax, 13–46
tax planning
  capital gains tax, 15–41—15–43
  contractual alliances, 15–45
  general tax issues, 15–40
  partnerships, 15–44
warranties, 13–46
winding-up, 13–11, 13–12,
  13–47—13–49

Third party consents
checklist, 2–25
competition, 2–25
contracts, 2–25
employees, 2–25
export controls, 2–25
financing, 2–25
identification of consents and
  clearances, 2–24
industry-specific approvals, 2–25
shareholders, 2–25
stock exchanges, 2–25
tax, 2–25
timetable, 2–26

Transfers of shares
see also **Pre-emption rights**

change of control, 12–46
deed of adherence, 12–45, E(14)
directors' discretion to refuse,
    12–43—12–44
intra-group, 12–38
legal form and transferability, 12–01
pre-emption provisions
    articles of association, 12–47
    relevance, 12–51—12–52
    shareholders' agreement, 12–47
transfer restrictions
    agreed sales between parties,
        12–04
    free transferability, 12–03
    precedent, E(9)
    pre-emption, 12–03, 12–05—12–48
    prohibition on transfers, 12–03
    range of potential restrictions,
        12–02—12–03
wrongful transfer
    consequences, 12–49—12–50

Unfairly prejudicial conduct
Companies Act 2006, 11–36
examples of UK cases, 11–39
meaning, 11–37
price, 11–41
remedies, 11–40
unfairness test, 11–38

United States
export controls, 16–49—16–50
international joint ventures, D(14)
joint venture companies, 5–37
limited liability companies, 3–27,
    5–46
limited partnerships, 5–32

Valuation
equalisation measures, 2–35
methodology
    choice of methods, 2–30
    different contributions, 2–34
    legal rules, 2–33
    negotiations, 2–31
    net assets, 2–32
    non-cash contributions,
        7–17—7–18

Venture capital finance
anti-dilution, 7–28
capital structure issues, 7–27
exit, 7–28
incentives, 7–28
income return before exit, 7–28
management rights, 7–28

Winding-up
compulsory, 13–49
exit or termination, on,
    13–47—13–49
voluntary, 13–48

Works project joint ventures
agreements, 4–18—4–19
checklist of key issues, 4–17
formation of jointly-owned company,
    4–16
integrated joint ventures, 4–15
non-integrated joint ventures, 4–15

Instruction for use of the companion disc

Introduction

These notes are provided for guidance only. They should be read and interpreted in the context of your own computer system and operational procedures. It is assumed that you have a basic knowledge of WINDOWS. However, if there is any problem please contact our help line on 0845 850 9355 who will be happy to help you.

CD Format and Contents

To run this CD you need at least:

IBM compatible PC
CD-ROM drive
Microsoft Word 6.0/95

The CD contains data files of the clauses in this book. It does not contain software or commentary.

Installation

The following instructions make the assumption that you will copy the data files to a single directory on your hard disk (e.g. C:\Joint Ventures).

Open your **CD Rom drive**, select and double click on **setup.exe** and follow the instructions. The files will be unzipped to your **C drive** and you will be able to open them from the new **C:\Joint Ventures** folder there.

LICENCE AGREEMENT

Definitions
1. The following terms will have the following meanings: "The PUBLISHERS" means Sweet & Maxwell of 100 Avenue Road, London NW3 3PF (which expression shall, where the context admits, include the PUBLISHERS' assigns or successors in business as the case may be) of the other part on behalf of Thomson Books Limited of Cheriton House, North Way, Andover SPI0 5BE.
"The LICENSEE" means the purchaser of the title containing the Licensed Material.
"Licensed Material" means the data included on the disk;
"Licence" means a single user licence;
"Computer" means an IBM-PC compatible computer.

Grant of Licence; Back up copies
2. (1) The PUBLISHERS hereby grant to the LICENSEE. a non-exclusive, non-transferable licence to use the Licensed Material in accordance with these terms and conditions.

(2) The LICENSEE may install the Licensed Material for use on one computer only at any one time.

(3) The LICENSEE may make one back-up copy of the Licensed Material only, to be kept in the LICENSEE's control and possession.

Proprietary Rights
3. (1) All rights not expressly granted herein are reserved.

(2) The Licensed Material is not sold to the LICENSEE who shall not acquire any right, title or interest in the Licensed Material or in the media upon which the Licensed Material is supplied.

(3) The LICENSEE shall not erase, remove, deface or cover any trademark, copyright notice, guarantee or other statement on any media containing the Licensed Material.

(4) The LICENSEE shall only use the Licensed Material in the normal course of its business and shall not use the Licensed Material for the purpose of operating a bureau or similar service or any online service whatsoever.

(5) Permission is hereby granted to LICENSEES who are members of the legal profession (which expression does not include individuals or organisations engaged in the supply of services to the legal profession) to reproduce, transmit and store small quantities of text for the purpose of enabling them to provide legal advice to or to draft documents or conduct proceedings on behalf of their clients.

(6) The LICENSEE shall not sublicense the Licensed Material to others and this Licence Agreement may not be transferred, sublicensed, assigned or otherwise disposed of in whole or in part.

(7) The LICENSEE shall inform the PUBLISHERS on becoming aware of any unauthorised use of the Licensed Material.

Warranties
4. (1) The PUBLISHERS warrant that they have obtained all necessary rights to grant this licence.

(2) Whilst reasonable care is taken to ensure the accuracy and completeness of the Licensed Material supplied, the PUBLISHERS make no representations or warranties, express or implied, that the Licensed Material is free from errors or omissions.

(3) The Licensed Material is supplied to the LICENSEE on an "as is" basis and has not been supplied to meet the LICENSEE's individual requirements. It is the sole responsibility of the LICENSEE to satisfy itself prior to entering this Licence Agreement that the Licensed Material will meet the LICENSEE's requirements and be compatible with the LICENSEE's hardware/software configuration. No failure of any part of the Licensed Material to be suitable for the LICENSEE's requirements will give rise to any claim against the PUBLISHERS.

(4) In the event of any material inherent defects in the physical media on which the licensed material may be supplied. other than caused by accident abuse or misuse by the LICENSEE, the PUBLISHERS will replace the defective original media free of charge provided it is returned to the place of purchase within 90 days of the purchase date.

The PUBLISHERS' enure liability and the LICENSEE's exclusive remedy shall be the replacement of such detective media.

(5) Whilst all reasonable care has been taken to exclude computer viruses, no warranty is made that the Licensed Material is virus free. The LICENSEE shall be responsible to ensure that no virus is introduced to any computer or network and shall not hold the PUBLISHERS responsible.

(6) The warranties set out herein are exclusive of and in lieu of all other conditions and warranties, either express or implied, statutory or otherwise.

(7) All other conditions and warranties, either express or implied, statutory or otherwise, which relate in the condition and fitness for any purpose of the Licensed Material are hereby excluded and the PUBLISHERS shall not be liable in contract or in tort for any loss of any kind suffered by reason of any defect in the Licensed Material (whether or not caused by the negligence of the PUBLISHERS).

Limitation of Liability and Indemnity
5. (1) The LICENSEE shall accept sole responsibility for and the PUBLISHERS shall not be liable for the use of the Licensed Material by the LICENSEE, its agents and employees and the LICENSEE shall hold the PUBLISHERS harmless and fully indemnified against any claims, costs, damages, loss and liabilities arising out of any such use.

(2) The PUBLISHERS shall not be liable for any indirect or consequential loss suffered by the LICENSEE (including without limitation loss of profits, goodwill or data) in connection with the Licensed Material howsoever arising.

(3) The PUBLISHERS will have no liability whatsoever for any liability of the LICENSEE or any third party which might arise.

(4) The LICENSEE hereby agrees that
(a) the LICENSEE is best placed to foresee and evaluate any loss that might be suffered in connection with this Licence Agreement;
(b) that the cost of supply of the Licensed Material has been calculated on the basis of the limitations and exclusions contained herein; and
(c) the LICENSEE will effect such insurance as is suitable having regard to the LICENSEE's circumstances.

(5) The aggregate maximum liability of the PUBLISHERS in respect of any direct loss or any other loss (to the extent that such loss is not excluded by this Licence Agreement or otherwise) whether such a claim arises in contract or tort shall not exceed a sum equal to that paid as the price for the title containing the Licensed Material.

Termination
6. (1) In the event of any breach of this Agreement including any violation of any copyright in the Licensed Material, whether held by the PUBLISHERS or others in the Licensed Material, the Licence Agreement shall automatically terminate immediately, without notice and without prejudice to any claim which the PUBLISHERS may have either for moneys due and/or damages and/or otherwise.

(2) Clauses 3 to 5 shall survive the termination for whatsoever reason of this Licence Agreement.

(3) In the event of termination of this Licence Agreement the LICENSEE will remove the Licensed Material.

Miscellaneous
7. (1) Any delay or forbearance by the PUBLISHERS in enforcing any provisions of this Licence Agicnient shall not be construed as a waiver of such provision or an agreement thereafter not to enforce the said provision.

(2) This Licence Agreement shall be governed by the laws of England and Wales, If any difference shall arise between the Parties touching the meaning of this Licence Agreement or the rights and liabilities of the parties thereto, the same shall be referred to arbitration in accordance with the provisions of the Arbitration Act 1996, or any amending or substituting statute for the time being in force.

Disclaimer

Precedents in this publication may be used as a guide for the drafting of legal documents specifically for particular clients but not for republication. Such legal documents may be provided to clients in print or electronic form, but distribution to third parties otherwise is prohibited. Precedents are provided 'as is' without warranty of any kind, express or implied, including but not limited to fitness for a particular purpose. The publishers and the author cannot accept any responsibility for any loss of whatsoever kind including loss of revenue business, anticipated savings or profits, loss of goodwill or data or for any direct or consequential loss whatsoever to any person using the precedents, or acting or refraining from actions as a result of the material in this publication.